The Libertine Reader

Zone Readers are edited by
Michel Feher and Ramona Naddaff

The

EROTICISM AND ENLIGHTENMENT

Libertine

IN EIGHTEENTH-CENTURY FRANCE

Reader

EDITED BY MICHEL FEHER

ZONE BOOKS   NEW YORK   1997

The publisher would like to thank the French Ministry of Culture for its assistance with this translation.

© 1997 Urzone, Inc.
611 Broadway, Suite 608
New York, NY 10012

The Supplement to Bougainville's Voyage © 1956 Jacques Barzun and Ralph Bowen. Reprinted from *Rameau's Nephew and Other Works* by Denis Diderot. Used by permission of Doubleday, a division of Bantam Doubleday Dell Publishing Group, Inc.

Chantal Thomas's introduction to *The Education of Women* was originally published in France © 1991 Editions Jérome Millon.

Jean Sgard's introduction to *The Sofa* was originally published in France © 1984 Editions Desjonquères.

The Sofa was originally published by Routledge & Kegan Paul Ltd., New York, 1927.

The Indiscreet Jewels © Marsilio Publishers and Sophie Hawkes. Reprinted by permission of Marsilio Publishers, New York.

The Wayward Head and Heart © 1963 Oxford University Press. Reprinted from *The Wayward Head and Heart* by Crébillon fils, translated by Barbara Bray (Oxford Library of French Classics, 1963).

Dangerous Liaisons © 1961 P.W.K. Stone. Published by agreement with Penguin Books Limited. The moral rights of the translator have been asserted.

Printed in the United States of America.

Distributed by The MIT Press, Cambridge, Massachusetts, and London, England

Library of Congress Cataloging-in-Publication Data

The libertine reader : eroticism and enlightenment in eighteenth-century France / edited by Michel Feher.
    p. cm.
Includes bibliographical references.
ISBN 0-942299-42-6 (cloth).
— ISBN 0-942299-41-8 (pbk.)
    1. Erotic stories, French. 2. French fiction — 18th century. 3. Erotic stories, French — History and criticism. 4. French fiction — 18th century — History and criticism. I. Feher, Michel.
PQ1276.E75L53   1997
843'.50803538—dc21   96-49079
                                        CIP

Contents

Acknowledgments

The series editors owe thanks to Meighan Gale, the managing editor of Zone Books, for her careful attention to the many, separate parts of this book. Her questions multiplied our pleasures. Peter Sahlins's knowledge of eighteenth-century French history and language was greatly appreciated and put to the best use we could imagine. Finally, we are grateful to the following individuals for their editorial advice and assistance: Eric Banks, Ted Byfield, Heather Caldwell, Eric Chinski, Ed Cohen, Amy Griffin, Leigh Hafrey, Sophie Hawkes, Jeanine Herman, Suzanne Jackson, Don McMahon, Georges May, Victoria Velsor, and Lara Young.

Libertinisms

by Michel Feher

What do lovers really want? Is it the carnal pleasures they take in their beloved's arms? Is it the vain satisfaction they get from being worshiped? Or is it the joy of bringing happiness to the person with whom they are in love? Moreover, do male and female lovers want the same thing? These questions inform the debates about love and desire that make up both the plots and the dialogues of most eighteenth-century French novels, and especially of those books associated with the "libertinism" of the declining aristocracy. The main participants in these debates are, respectively, the advocates of nature's way, the cynical analysts of society's wiles, and the believers in the power of the human heart to transcend natural appetites and social ambitions.

The members of the first group include the minor libertine types known as the *petits-maîtres* (fops) but also the spokespeople of naturalist and materialist philosophers, such as Diderot, La Mettrie, and Helvétius. According to these characters, lust is the sole natural motive of erotic attraction, for men as well as for women. Hence sexual pleasure is the only goal worthy of being pursued. As far as vainglory and generous love are concerned, both the *petits-maîtres* and the more philosophical naturalists see them as artificial and dangerous aberrations of sensual desire: the former incites men and women to seek dubious triumphs rather than innocent pleasure, while the latter leads them to overestimate their emotional capacities, thereby paving the way for bitter disappointments. For the members of the second group, however, which includes pessimistic moralists in the vein of La Rochefoucault as well as the more vindictive libertine characters known as the "dangerous men," society's denatured mores have made vanity the primary motivation of lovers. In their cynical view, women mainly revel in both the quantity and the pain of their frustrated suitors, while men's chief purpose is to overcome their mistresses' resistance and brag about their successes. Lastly, eighteenth-century debates about lovers' motives also include the so-called "sensitive women." Contrary to their libertine opponents, these successors of the seventeenth-century *précieuses* argue that true love exists, that it is a matter of the heart, and that heartfelt inclinations seek nothing else than the happiness of the beloved. Indeed, the "sensitive women" claim that the lovers who listen to their heart will go so far as to renounce sexual gratification and foresake their pride if the felicity of their beloved so requires. Yet these upholders of the heart also believe that, in their own society, only women are capable of selfless love. While the aristocratic code of ethics encourages men to indulge in their sensual desires and to treat seduction as a glorious feat, the members of the female sex are brought up to resist the calls of their flesh and to take pride in their own modesty. Therefore, the new *précieuses* claim that only through the overwhelming urge to make her lover happy can a woman overcome both the principles she has been taught and the fear of damaging her reputation.

Through their characters' deeds as well as through their relentless reflections on lovers' motives and purposes, the works gathered in this reader revolve around these debates. Despite the strikingly contrasted sensibilities of their authors – Diderot's earnestness, Sade's irony, Crébillon fils's bitterness, Denon's lightheartedness, Laclos and Prévost's inscrutable ambiguity – all of them speculate on the possibility of overcoming the inconstancy of natural appetites and the hypocrisy of social conventions, in order to experience a feeling of love that would be constant without being artificial.

This introduction is divided into two sections: the first one attempts to trace the evolution of the meaning of libertinism, from the early occurrences of the word itself to its radical redefinition by Sade, as well as to sketch the portraits both of the various male libertine types – the *petit-maître*, the dangerous man, the Sadian libertine – and of their female counterparts or antagonists – the *petite-maîtresse*, the prude, the coquette, and the "sensitive woman." The second section introduces the various works gathered in this reader and justifies the three headings under which they appear: Diderot and Laclos's "natural utopias," Crébillon fils, Diderot, and Prévost's "Oriental dreams," and the "ways of the world" according to Crébillon fils, Denon, Laclos, and Sade.

Libertine Ethos: From Audacity to Hypocrisy

Libertinism, as developed in this reader, refers first and foremost to the licentious ways of the declining French aristocracy. However, before the eighteenth century, the word "libertine" did not refer exclusively to sexual mores. The term appeared as early as the middle of the sixteenth century within a theological context: Calvin used it to denounce a sect of dissident Anabaptists whom he accused of abusing their freedom by "transforming Scripture into allegory." Others used

it more generally as a synonym for an "atheist."[1] By the beginning of
the seventeenth century, the words "libertine" and "libertinism"
became associated with an actual school of thought.[2] The "scholarly
libertines" (*les libertins érudits*), an assortment of scholars, poets, and
dilettantes, formed a small group of freethinkers who shared an aversion to dogma; seeking to demystify superstition and to dismantle
baseless belief and preconceived ideas, they contested both political
and religious authority. Every watchword imposed by the powers that
be, or accepted without question by the public, inevitably raised the
libertines' hackles. Conversely, any thinker persecuted for his opinions
was counted, by definition, as a member of their circle.[3]

The first "libertines" were not concerned with substituting new
truths for old certainties. Following Montaigne, whom they held up as
a guide, they mistrusted anything that appeared to be immutable. They
believed in a generalized *inconstancy*, inherent both in the nature of
things and in the heart of man. The freedom of the libertine, then,
consists in espousing this universal inconstancy: he presents himself as
emancipated and, as such, scornfully rejects the prejudices that aim to
pin him down, whether in regard to an idea, a god, or a lover. The
exemplary libertine of this first generation, the hero and soon-to-be
martyr of their cause, is Théophile de Viau. Poet, dramatist, and novelist, Théophile was the emancipated man par excellence: jealously
protective of his independence and freedom of movement, he objects
to preconceived ideas[4] as well as emotional attachments.[5]

As a radical and flamboyant rejection of dogma, libertinism was a
relatively short-lived phenomenon. Under the direction of Cardinal
Richelieu, the French monarchy took rapid steps toward absolutism,
and a violent repression soon swept down upon those who contested
the authority of king or religion. Théophile was arrested in 1623,
condemned to make full apology and to be burned alive. In fact, he
was burned only in effigy; shattered and living in exile, he died three
years later. The trial of Théophile de Viau, and especially the effect of
his retractions on his companions, marked the end of this first libertinism: it had lasted only for the first quarter of the seventeenth century. Then, from Théophile's trial until the death of Louis XIV in
1715, an increasingly implacable political and religious censorship made
life particularly difficult for overt libertines; in fact, their spirit survived only by sacrificing its bravura and espousing one of two forms of
caution – compromise or retreat.

The practice of compromise was adopted by a number of coteries
that formed in Paris during the second half of the seventeenth century.

They brought together such "moderate" libertines as the abbot of Chaulieu, the Marquis de La Fare, and, more peripherally, La Fontaine.[6] These were salons in which epicureanism took on forms acceptable from the perspective of Christian faith and morality. While religious bigots and courtiers remained the favorite targets of such coteries, it was no longer because they practiced blind piety and affected a fearful respect for royal power but, rather, because they were hypocritical and corrupt. Thus, this tamer epicurean libertinism prudently gave true faith and just monarchs their due, while taking issue only with unworthy ministers and false piety – a shrewd balance between the requirements of public morals and freethinking.

The strategy of retreat functioned differently: rather than compromising freedom by sugar-coating its audaciousness, it invited its adepts to simulate the strictest conformism in order to keep their inner autonomy intact.[7] This doctrine of strategic retreat is perfectly summarized by the heroine of the *Dialogues de Luisa Sigea*, an erotic tale published anonymously by Nicholas Chorier,[8] himself a prominent Latinist and stern magistrate in the eyes of the world, but an unrepentant libertine in his heart: "When in public," Tullie explains to her young cousin, "live for other people; in secret and alone, live for yourself, covering yourself with a veil of decency.... Cover yourself with decency, the kind you can easily be rid of as needed...."[9]

The regency of Philippe d'Orléans, an unbridled interregnum following the somber years of Louis XIV's old age, gave birth to the form of libertinism illustrated in this reader. Following Philippe d'Orléans and those close to him, the aristocracy, wittingly controlled by Louis XIV,[10] left Versailles to continue its decline in Paris – this time in a carefree and openly libertine fashion. "The spirit of incredulity and libertinism together made the rounds of society," writes the cardinal of Bernis. "The irreligion of the Regent and his debauched friends easily found imitators.... Corruption became almost the general rule."[11]

In the last years of Louis XIV's reign, the religious zeal that Mme de Maintenon communicated to the aging Sun King had plunged the Court into an atmosphere heavy with suspicion. The nobles who gathered at Versailles were required to feign a piety and moral austerity for which they were hardly cut out. No doubt, hypocrisy and dissimulation often sufficed to keep the courtiers in the king's good graces; all the same, the death of the old despot, crowned by the audacious decision of the regent to annul his will, produced both a sudden relaxing of spirits and a considerable slackening of morals among the aristocracy.[12]

At first, the word "libertine" was used only to qualify the licentious ways of the regent's entourage, whom Philippe himself called his rakes (*roués*). Soon, though, libertinism became associated with the mores of the aristocratic class as a whole; as such, it stigmatized the French nobility under the reigns of Louis XV and Louis XVI, and it remained a major theme in French literature until the Revolution. However, it should be noted that the authors who best express the libertine mood of the era – Crébillon fils, Duclos, Prévost, Dorat, Denon, Laclos – adamantly denied that they themselves were libertines or that they condoned the licentious ways of their works' characters. Thus, eighteenth-century libertinism designates not so much a school of thought as an aristocratic way of life that many writers described and analyzed tirelessly, but were also expected to condemn.

This lifestyle, as depicted, primarily centers on a type of decadent aristocrat called the *petit-maître*, who combines, to the point of carica-ture, all the worldly practices and all the affectations of his class. Less concerned than seventeenth-century libertines with the precious freedom reputed to live beneath his masks, he devotes his energies to making his efforts of social conformity pay off; indeed, he devotes himself entirely to the "small" pleasures and "small" gains that the world never refuses the well-born, so long as they bend to its rules.

The *petit-maître*, though, is not the only libertine type represented in eighteenth-century French literature. Writers also depict a unique, more somber character, often called the "dangerous man" or ironi-cally the "man of principles." Not satisfied with merely living the flaky life of a *petit-maître* and looking beyond the small pleasures and gains sought by his peers, this more ambitious libertine endeavors to take revenge on his milieu. There is no better example of this "grand" liber-tinism than the redoubtable Versac, whose principles Crébillon fils exposes in *The Wayward Head and Heart* (1738) (included in this reader). A high-flying libertine, and remarkable teacher as well, Versac takes charge of educating the young Meilcour, the novel's still-naive hero. He proposes to inculcate his student with what he calls the "science of society," an indispensable science without which "the advantages we have received from nature, instead of contributing to our enlighten-ment, may often hinder it."[13]

The first goal set by this dubious science, for a well-born young man such as Meilcour, consists of "making a name for himself" in soci-ety – that is, in the jargon of the century, the *public*, which includes only the high society of Paris and Versailles. This public, whose sole preoccupation is to create and recreate trends and reputations, is sub-divided into a constellation of variously influential circles, assuring the circulation of intrigues and conversations. Furthermore, at the heart of each circle, and thus at the heart of the public as a whole, women are empowered to establish reputations. To triumph in society thus amounts to having oneself crowned by the "chorus of women," the repository of public sanction; it must therefore "appear that all your actions are undertaken with only women in mind, that you believe in no other charm but that which attracts them, and think the kind of wit that pleases them is the only kind that ought to please at all. It is only by seeming to defer to all their wishes that one succeeds in dominating them."[14]

Unlike the regular *petits-maîtres*, a "grand" libertine such as Versac is not content with society's mediocre pleasures. While he too sacrifices the straightforwardness of his heart and the wealth of his mind to the contemptible approbation of social circles, it is revenge rather than "social benefits" that seem to him a worthy compensation for his lost innocence. Such a revenge clearly takes the public as its target – aiming particularly at the chorus of women – but it must also be carried out in a systematic fashion. By feigning to bend himself to his world's order, the man of principles endeavors to penetrate its lesser workings, then to turn its absurd rules and fallacious principles against the people who abide by them.

Libertine Eros: Pleasure and Vengeance

An Inconclusive Debate

Although the budding Enlightenment benefited from the regency, the fact remains that, after 1715, libertinism pertained almost exclusively to erotic matters. The reputation of libertinism associated with Philippe d'Orléans's brief interregnum refers only to a licentious climate promoted by the regent himself. As of that moment, the term "libertine" suggested only a way of conducting one's love life – even as the latter came to be the almost exclusive concern of the declining aristocracy.

Neither moralistic nor strictly amoral, libertine fiction is nevertheless primarily about morals. Its main purpose is to examine critically the ethos of the *petits-maîtres* and of the dangerous men, as well as of the women who are the target of the libertines' maneuvers. In this respect, the writers in question paid special attention to their characters' views on love, desire, and pleasure: first, because the libertines they describe spend most of their time devising and executing campaigns of seduction, and second, because they use their philosophical positions on love, nature, and society as a justification for their reckless ways.

Although libertine fiction is largely devoted to describing the schemes and the prowess of the *petits-maîtres* and the dangerous men, it also endeavors to underline the problems, the impasses, and even the tragedies to which the libertine life can lead. Yet while authors such as Crébillon fils or Laclos manage to be persuasive in their critique of libertinism, they nevertheless convey an equal dissatisfaction with alternative approaches to love and pleasure. In their works, the fickleness of the *petit-maître* and the cynicism of the man of principles are thus matched by the hypocrisy and the bitterness attributed to the champions of virtue. Moreover, libertine authors seem to be at least skeptical about the existence of a feeling of love at once generous, mutual, and lasting. Hence the tragic fate that usually awaits their female characters – the "tender" or "sensitive" women – who actually believe that a lover's sole desire is to bring happiness to his beloved. Are libertine authors wary because they ultimately agree with their reckless heroes, who are convinced that pleasure and vanity are the only motives of human pursuits? Or, rather, is it because they consider a constant and reciprocal devotion to be too tall an order for the aristocratic society they describe? In any case, the fact remains that libertine writings fall short of turning their condemnation of libertinism into a celebration of true love. Despite its wit and lightness, libertine fiction is thus informed by a painfully inconclusive debate about eros: all the characters who engage in this debate, no matter how articulate, are destined to sound either insincere, too cynical, or too naive.

Civilization and Its Discontents

Libertine erotics are based on a naturalistic theory of desire, according to which the desire that a woman inspires in a man – the primary concern of a male seducer – is a purely physical phenomenon. It begins as a sensual excitation, and it has no other satisfying outcome than carnal pleasure, with the woman who inspires it. However, humans, unlike other animals, this theory purports, are not governed by instinct: before being consummated, a man's desire travels from his senses to his imagination, whereupon it creates a *fantasy*. The function of this fantasy is to "interpret" desire, to cause the subject to imagine what it is that he desires. Yet as a fantasy translates a physical arousal into a series of mental images, it also turns a sensual excitation into an attraction to a specific person. While a man fantasizes about the woman he desires, he comes to realize that she too is a desiring subject, and that his own pleasure depends on his ability to communicate his fantasy to her. In other words, fantasies give rise to the specifically human art of seduction.

From the viewpoint of nature, however, fantasies are only about enticing humans to accomplish "freely" what the other animals do instinctively. Undoubtedly, desire's detour through the imagination demonstrates the superiority of humans over animals, since the former are the only natural beings endowed with the privilege of governing their own appetites. However, this special freedom also involves a major risk, because it allows men and women to depart from nature's wishes. Indeed, lovers can let their fantasies stray: for instance, their unbridled imagination can lead them to believe that their desires need no carnal outlet, or that the pleasures of the flesh are sinful unless consummated within marriage. Now, according to the libertines, such deviations from the natural course of desire are far from exceptional – in fact, they have become society's norm. Hence the discontents that the libertines, in agreement with many philosophers of their century, associate with civilization.

The danger inherent in what is known as the "social state" (*l'état de société*) resides in the delays imposed on lovers – that is, in the unreasonable extension of the interval between the emergence of a fantasy and the sexual act that both fulfills and dissipates it. As time goes by, libertines and naturalists argue, an unfulfilled fantasy ferments in the imagination and takes on a life of its own. Withdrawn into his own reverie, a man begins to idealize his mistress beyond all measure, and may even sublimate his desire to the point of directing it toward such inappropriate objects as intelligible beauty or divine providence. In short, a frustrated lover tends to lose sight of the natural purpose of his own fantasy: forgetting sexual pleasure, he lets his desire pursue dead ends, which engender nothing but melancholy.

For the libertine, a lover need not renounce sexual gratification in order for his healthy fantasy to become a dangerous aberration. It is enough that the moment of pleasure arrives too late. As time passes, the frustrated lover obsesses about his mistress, and thus believes that her long-awaited favors will bring him nothing less than eternal bliss. Thus, when his desire is finally satisfied, his disappointment is on a par with his wait: his fantasy, swollen with chimeras, suddenly deflates, while his pleasure, spoiled by his mind's wanderings and ridiculously high hopes, is soon transformed into repugnance.

According to the naturalist philosophy informing eighteenth-century libertinism, these excessive delays between desire and pleasure are attributes of the civilizing process itself. Because sexual relations between men and women can lead to procreation, and because societies seem to require stable family structures, governments tend to subject the sexual encounters of their subjects to very restrictive conditions. Central to this channeling of desire is the institution of marriage, which often implies a severe condemnation of all other sexual relations. Legislators and priests further justify the enforcement of repressive laws by developing and promoting a moral system that champions deeply unnatural values such as modesty, constancy, and fidelity. Thus, while the fear of punishment is the primary cause of lovers' restraint, tales of sin, honor, and devotion continually reinforce it. Taking hold of people's imagination, these stories succeed in impressing upon them a totally artificial notion of virtue.

In every culture, as Diderot and Laclos point out, women are the prime targets of this propaganda. They are taught to be modest and faithful, and to take pride in resisting their own desires. Imposed on women as an essential feature of womanhood, modesty is anything but a natural "virtue": it not only causes women to fear the approach of men but even teaches them to feel shame at the call of their own senses. While a "respectable" woman is expected to remain modest at all times, once married, she has to embrace a second and no less artificial virtue called "constancy." Indeed, her honor, as well as her husband's, requires that she no longer wish to make love to anyone but him. In many societies, the combination of modesty and constancy leads to even more excessive demands on women, such as the virginity of the maiden before marriage, and the faithfulness of the wife for the rest of her days. According to naturalistic wisdom, these impositions injure the human temperament, which is as sensual and as inconstant in the female as in the male. Yet religious and political authorities are so committed to these unnatural values that they are usually more inclined to extend the obligation of conjugal fidelity to men, than to loosen the bonds stifling women.

Yet the promoters of public morals make sure to provide their deserving victims with some symbolic compensation. Women, beyond being encouraged to take pride in their modesty and their constancy, even enjoy a glorious reputation as compensation for the pleasures they renounce. For each "victory" over their own natural appetites, virtuous women are entitled to the admiration of the public, and are thus expected to feel self-righteous joy. Moreover, priests do not hesitate to promise eternal bliss to those women who spend their whole lives mortifying their flesh in order to remain virgins. Those wives who are considered the most venerable assert their disgust with fleshly commerce while they submit faithfully and steadfastly to their conjugal duty.

Although the moral principles inculcated in women cannot eradicate natural impulses, they at least have the effect of slowing the process that leads from desire to pleasure. While women both resist the call of their own senses and take pride in their unnatural behavior, fantasies tend to ferment for a dangerously long time in their lovers' imaginations. Deprived of their natural outlet by the fearful combination of virtue and pride, these inflated fantasies give rise to yet another perversion of desire called "passionate love," a malady of the imagination stemming from frustration and consisting of an irrational overestimation of the desired person. Far from treating it lightly, the libertines consider amorous passion to be at best debilitating and at worst deadly.

Above all, the *petits-maîtres* and the "men of principles" stigmatize passionate love as a humiliating experience, since the victims of this emotional disorder become deaf to the calls of reason and submit blindly to their beloved's will. But libertines also dread love's power because they know it to be a strangely addictive and often contagious disease. Indeed, passionate lovers seem to worship their own subjection, while people around them can become fascinated and even envious of their sorry state. In short, if we are to believe the reasoning behind libertinism, the natural process of desire faces three major obstacles in the "social state." First, it confronts an artificial moral system that promotes modesty and constancy; second, it is subjected to the shrewdly stimulated vanity of women, who have been raised to feel admirable when they uphold these unnatural virtues; and third, it is threatened by the infectious aberration called passionate love. Having come to this diagnosis, the libertines vow not to let their own fantasies go astray: they thus endeavor to overcome women's virtue and circumvent their pride while avoiding the traps of passionate love. In the eyes of its practitioners, then, libertinism appears as the revenge of nature's course against society's aberrations.

Yet despite the libertines' harsh criticism of the "social state," the rakes never cease to belong to their own world. Accustomed to the privileges as well as the sophistication of aristocratic culture, they long neither for a lost golden age nor for a future revolution: the *petits-maîtres* and the "dangerous men" have no intention of returning to some kind of "natural state" or of advocating social reforms that would reduce the discrepancies between the laws of nature and the demands of society. Regarding public morals and private desires as an established fact, their sole purpose is to turn the tensions between moral principles and natural appetites to their own advantage.

Double Entendre and Misunderstandings

Beyond their common distaste for all the obstacles hindering their desires, the *petit-maître* and the "man of principles" embody two very different projects. The former, also known as the "man of good fortune" seeks to accumulate moments of pleasure. His modest brand of libertinism consists primarily in warding off boredom, which he sees as a permanent threat, while resisting love's sway, which he sees as a source of grief and humiliation. More than charm or elaborate strategies, the key to the *petit-maître*'s success is his sense of timing.

His first task is to pay close attention to the tone of voice and the body language of the women he covets, for the pleasure he seeks depends on his ability to seize what libertine authors call "the moment." In Crébillon fils's words, such a moment can be defined as a "certain disposition of the senses, as unexpected as it is involuntary, which a woman can conceal but which, should it be perceived or sensed by someone who might profit from it, puts her in the greatest danger of being a little more willing than she thought she ever should or could be."[15] The *petit-maître* is convinced that every woman, whatever her guiding principles, is sooner or later subject to such moments; yet he also knows that these opportunities are fleeting. According to libertine wisdom, a "moment" appears when a woman reveals a hint of desire that her virtue has not yet acknowledged, and it disappears as soon as her pride leads her to sacrifice carnal pleasures for the dubious glory of "invincibility." Determined to take advantage of this relatively short moment of weakness, a *petit-maître* sees his timely move as a matter of his own safety. Indeed, he knows that if he does not seize the moment, virtue and vanity will soon take hold of his mistress's imagination and henceforth enhance her resistance. In turn, his own fantasy, deprived of sexual outlet, will ferment unduly, thereby exposing the frustrated libertine to the dangers of passionate love.

Timeliness, an essential feature of the art of seduction, is just as crucial when it comes to ending a liaison. True to the fundamental principle of seventeenth-century libertinism, the men of good fortune still contend that human desires are naturally inconstant. Thus, even if a liaison begins exactly at the right moment, lovers cannot expect it to fend off boredom for very long. In short, to maximize his pleasure, a *petit-maître* must also know when to end an affair. A pleasurable liaison involves a prompt consummation and a quick separation: "Our fancies are touched: we are lovers forthwith," says Clitandre, the *petit-maître* in Crébillon fils's *The Opportunities of a Night* (1755). "Does the relation become tedious? Then we part with as little ceremony as we came together."[16]

At the same time, a single day without fantasy is considered to be unbearably boring. Therefore, since their potential female partners are limited to the women of their world, the *petits-maîtres* realize that their happiness demands a collective commitment to an active amorous *commerce*. Indeed, public satisfaction rests on the incessant succession of adventures, which are all the more intense when they are new. Hence, politeness requires that lovers abstain both from making each other languish excessively and from staying together for too long. "A faithful man is as guilty as a miser who stops the flow of commerce," we read in an apocryphal letter – published during the regency – from Ninon de Lenclos to the Marquis de Sévigné.

Similarly, in *The Confessions of the Count of* ——— (1740), Duclos recounts the following anecdote: the count, who is still an aspiring *petit-maître*, has been Mme Derval's lover for two months. Satisfied with their affair, he has no intention of leaving her when he receives a "note written in the following terms":

> When you took up with Mme Derval, monsieur, I had the same idea; but you got there first, and your fantasy seemed quite simple to me; so I opted to wait until it had passed to satisfy my own. Your pleasure, however, must have been spent during these two months; so long a time smacks of love, even of constancy. I was still hoping that you would leave Mme Derval; I was awaiting my turn, and, in this hope, I broke off with a mistress that otherwise I would have kept. You are too gallant a man to trouble society's order: give it back a woman who belongs to it; surely you must appreciate the correctness of my demand.[17]

Disconcerted by such a call to order, the count immediately informs his mistress. To his great surprise, she agrees that the remonstrances addressed to him are well founded. Suddenly aware of his responsibilities, the count apologizes and immediately "returns Mme Derval to society."

As this anecdote demonstrates, the lifestyle of a *petit-maître* is far from "free"; on the contrary, it is burdened by responsibilities, both to himself and to his peers. For his own sake, he must carefully pace his pleasures, which are constantly threatened either by a lack or by an excess of emotion. But his sense of timing is crucial not only to his personal well being – it is just as important for the other *petits-maîtres* and their mistresses, who depend on him for sustaining the flow.

In order to make good on his responsibilities, a man of good fortune can never let his pride take the best of him. This means that he must accept being left by a mistress who has grown tired of him – indeed, he must do so with the same equanimity he would have expected of her, had he been first to lose interest. Yet he must also be modest enough to realize that he cannot undertake anything too complicated or too risky. Since his own pleasure and his peers' satisfaction call for an accumulation of short liaisons, he must renounce all women whose seduction seems hazardous: these include women who take pride in their virtue as well as women who hold passionate love as an ideal rather than a disease. Cautiously avoiding difficult conquests, a *petit-maître* devotes his attentions exclusively to the *petites-maîtresses*, that is, to the women of his class who share his views regarding the conditions of a happy erotic life.

He knows full well, though, that even when an aristocratic woman has not been tainted by unnatural values or sentimental delusions, she should not flaunt her acceptance of the laws of nature. The public demands that women pay at least lip service to received ideas about vice and virtue: they are thus expected to lament the licentious ways of their contemporaries and to long for a world where women would be appreciated for their modesty and constancy. Relentlessly exposed to these clichés, the *petits-maîtres* have no stake either in openly challenging public morals or in enticing the women of their class to rebel against their oppressed condition. Their only purpose is to make sure that the actions of their female partners do not reflect the words they are required to utter. To this end, the men of good fortune seek to establish their relationships with their mistresses on the basis of tacit but systematic double entendre.

According to the public, a woman who follows the natural course of her desires is inexcusable and ruins her reputation, while a woman who succumbs to love's sway is worthy of compassion and even of respect – especially if she surrenders to her lover's sincere and passionate love for her. *Petits-maîtres*, though they find these judgments deeply objectionable, see no point in overtly denouncing them; it makes more sense to turn these received ideas into a coded language. Thus, instead of expressing their intentions literally, these men of good fortune convey their modest fantasies to the women they desire by pretending that they are madly in love with them; in turn, and provided that they are interested in their suitors' "real" propositions, the *petites-maîtresses* respond in similarly conventional ways.

These dialogues tend to be somewhat formulaic, of necessity. At first, when a *petit-maître* declares his love, his *petite-maîtresse* is expected to take offense: her virtuous ears are not even supposed to listen to such a bold confession. Then the *petit-maître* protests that his love is as respectful as it is passionate, which leads the *petite-maîtresse* to question his sincerity. To convince her, the man of good fortune pretends that his love will never die, even if it remains unrequited. Finally, the *petite-maîtresse* affects to believe her suitor's pledge to her but vows to resist the call of love at all cost; this last phase, which can be reached after a few days or even a few hours, signals to the attentive *petit-maître* that the "moment" has come for him to make his move. In short, both the *petit-maître*'s declarations and the *petite-maîtresse*'s protestations are carefully coded performances. While they speak only of virtue and love, the man of good fortune and his mistress are merely preparing themselves and each other for a brief moment of immodest and loveless pleasure.

A *petit-maître* sees his practice of double entendre as the most "polite" way to maximize his pleasure. On the one hand, he claims to be polite vis-à-vis the women he seduces, because he enables them both to deny and satisfy their desires: thanks to his timely moves, they can indulge in the pleasures of the flesh without ceasing to sing the praises of virtue, and blame the irrepressible power of passionate love for their moments of weakness. On the other hand, he is also convinced that fostering libertinism without openly challenging society's morals is a supreme form of politeness vis-à-vis the public, which is divided between the moral values it is supposed to uphold and the steady flow of affairs and gossip that is its unique preoccupation.

The libertinism of the *petits-maîtres* seeks to harmonize social rules and natural appetites. While they are convinced that male and female sexuality are "naturally" identical – in terms of the dynamic leading from sensual desire to fantasy, and from fantasy to carnal pleasure – they understand that "culture" has endowed men and women with very different sexual roles, in order to channel lust into a stable familial order. Rather than seeking to challenge or reform this social "gendering" of sexual mores, their use of double entendre endeavors to make the social constraints inherent in male seduction and female resistance as painless as possible.

This modest brand of libertinism is nevertheless very fragile, since it requires a silent complicity between the *petits-maîtres*, the *petites-maîtresses*, and even the public at large. Such complicity is indeed indispensable if one is to prevent a dialogue based on double entendre from degenerating into misunderstanding. The participants in this dialogue are never supposed to say what they mean, so they can never be sure that the other does not really mean what he or she says. For instance, how can a *petite-maîtresse* ever be certain that her suitor is not experiencing the sincere and passionate feelings in whose grip he claims to be? And how is a man of good fortune to know whether the woman he covets does not really believe in the virtues she professes? Words, both know, can be extremely infectious for the people who pronounce them, and the imagination does not take long to stray. And yet, the polite libertinism of the *petits-maîtres* also runs the opposite risk – to wit, that a double entendre will be too transparent. If the signals sent out by a man of good fortune and a *petite-maîtresse* cease to present any ambiguity, if each knows exactly where the other stands at every point in the seduction, then their respective fantasies will be insufficiently nourished, making their eventual liaison more boring than pleasurable.

Thus, libertine double entendre seems to be constantly tossed between too much and too little uncertainty. While a lack of connivance between *petits-maîtres* and *petites-maîtresses* slows the progress of desire, thereby exposing the libertine couples to wayward fantasies, a completely transparent code also ruins their pleasure by depriving their relationships of any form of seduction whatsoever. Therefore, if we are to believe libertine authors, a *petit-maître* is rarely able to find the golden mean that he is looking for: despite his good intentions, he most often fails to sustain the happy mixture of pleasure and freedom that keeps him from being bored while carefully avoiding love.

Revenge and Bitterness

Although the "dangerous men" are informed by the same theory of desire and by the same views on nature and society, they have nothing but contempt for their more modest libertine brethren. This higher breed of libertine rejects both society's moral values and the type of politeness ostensibly upheld by the *petits-maîtres*. The dangerous men too are attached to their privileges, both as males and as aristocrats, and thus uninterested in reforming the mores of their world. Rather than bringing about the triumph of the Enlightenment, they seek only to avenge themselves on their hypocritical milieu. The thirst for vengeance driving these men shields them from any complicity with a society they wish to punish for its duplicity. Their intention is to lead the public to betray itself by prompting its most eminent female members to depart from the principles they profess and exposing these failings to public reproach. Like the men of good fortune, the dangerous men are quite convinced that all women have their "moments" of weakness, and that libertine savoir faire consists in knowing how to take advantage of them. However, where the *petit-maître* seeks to protect the reputation of his mistresses, the dangerous man wants to make their "fall" humiliating and exemplary.

Women, then, are the sole object of libertine vengeance. Clearly, from the viewpoint of the dangerous man, the responsibility for the unnatural morals characteristic of the "social state" lies with religious and political institutions: women seem to be the first victims of a social order that has always made their bodies and minds the favorite targets of its most cruel laws and most false principles. All the same, these men's mission is not to "liberate" women, or even to appeal to them to throw off their yoke. On the contrary, they openly contend that women are merely the first to have let themselves be locked up in the shackles of the laws against nature. Furthermore, it is women who have also succumbed in great numbers to the bitter lies of the priests, to their promises of heavenly bliss, and to their criteria of respectability on earth. In time, women have become the most faithful guardians of worldly hypocrisy and the most adamant propagandists for the artificial manners that society demands of its members. Such is the chorus of women, which presents itself at once as the stock market of social values and the arbiter of reputations – and, thus, finds its public enemy in the figure of the dangerous man.

The vengeful erotics of the man of principles takes the form of a rigorous demonstration. He seeks to demonstrate to the public that all society women, despite their pretensions, end up submitting to the power of the moment, provided that they are approached in the appropriate manner. While a man of good fortune limits his field to the *petites-maîtresses* who share his modest concerns, a dangerous man chooses his victims among women who most flaunt their denatured condition: his favored prey are *prudes* with a reputation for moral austerity, who pretend to despise sensual pleasure; *coquettes* who seek to exacerbate men's fantasies and take pleasure only in their lovers' desperate passion; and so-called sensitive women, heiresses to the seventeenth-century *précieuses*, who claim to cherish an ardent yet purified form of love.

The dangerous man's desire takes the form of a challenge he must meet. Like the gallant knight of the Middle Ages, he measures his own ardor against the obstacles raised by the woman he covets. Rejecting the caution of the *petits-maîtres*, he revives the original meaning of aristocratic distinction: he returns to a spirit of chivalric conquest that becomes enflamed only in the face of supposedly impregnable fortresses. However, where the chivalric lover felt respect and devotion for the lady who put him to the test, the dangerous man seeks only to humiliate the women who resist him. In order to fulfill this desire for vengeance, he resorts to the methodical elaboration of a plan of seduction: "I am going to tell you, the confidante of all my inmost secrets, the most ambitious plan I have yet conceived," writes Valmont, the hero of Laclos's *Dangerous Liaisons* (1782), to the Marquise de Merteuil, when announcing his new infatuation with Mme de Tourvel.[18] In fact, the attraction that a dangerous man finds in a woman is directly proportional to the complexity of the plan that her conquest would represent, and his ultimate satisfaction resides in the shock experienced by the public when it learns of the downfall of a woman thought immune to weakness.

The thirst for vengeance stems from the lost innocence of the man of principles – that is, from the initiation of a naive young man who loses his illusions shortly after losing his virginity. This formative wound is inflicted upon him by a worldly woman who endeavors to "introduce him into society,"[19] that is, to erotic war games; she takes advantage of the young man's inexperience to enflame his imagination, then uses his bewilderment to betray his confidence.[20] On discovering his mistress's hypocrisy – which he is quick to impute to all women – and the illusions that have inflated his own fantasy, the young man, suddenly wise to the ways of the world, turns his disgust into cold resolve: he henceforth devotes his entire existence to "plans" of avenging his outraged innocence.[21]

Thus, taking up the challenges presented to him by society becomes a matter of principle. The grand libertine considers the accumulated pretensions of artificial virtue, female vanity, and amorous passion to be the three components of a challenge to his freedom. Virtue, represented by the devout and the prude, challenges his autonomy by interfering with the natural course of his desires. Vanity, embodied in the figure of the coquette, threatens to make him subject to the whims of a mistress who takes pleasure in her power over her ensnared lovers. Lastly, tender love, the ideal of the sensitive women, constitutes the most fearsome threat for the man of principles: not only is it a sickness of the imagination which ends up enslaving a lover to his mistress, but also, and more serious still, the victim of passionate love ends up worshiping his own enslavement.

The ideal of a sensitive woman involves one of the great enigmas of eighteenth-century psychology, namely, the "heart."[22] Indeed, physicians, philosophers, and novelists never cease wondering about the existence of the heart – not as an organ, of course, but as the more or less metaphorical seat of a sentiment, called "sensitivity" (*sensibilité*) or "tenderness," independent of sexual attraction and rational judgment. Should the heart be recognized as harboring feelings all the more profound because they often oppose natural appetites and rational motivations? Or must one, on the contrary, treat it as the imaginary site of all fantasies gone astray? The dangerous men resolutely stake their honor on the demystification of the heart and the illusions with which it is adorned.

On this point, they go against the tradition of the *précieuses*, whose eighteenth-century defenders — notably, Thérèse de Lambert and Mme Riccoboni — defined true love as an impulse of the heart, manifested in the desire to bring happiness to the beloved.[23] Heartfelt love thus consists of a sentiment of pure solicitude which the "new *précieuses*" uphold against two counterfeits — one that passes off a vulgar sensual appetite as true love, and the other that confuses the joy of loving with the vain satisfaction of being worshiped. In other words, the love that comes from the heart is a thirst for giving, or at least for making the person one loves happy, whereas its two counterfeits belong to the covetous passions — respectively, lust and vanity.

The fact that heartfelt love is distinct from lust and vanity does not mean that it must remain chaste or unrequited. All the same both the pleasures that sensitive women agree to share and the attentions of which they are the object matter to them only insofar as the men they love find their own happiness in giving them pleasure and tender care. Conversely, the new *précieuses* claim that a sensitive woman will willingly renounce the pleasures of the flesh if the happiness of her beloved demands this sacrifice, and her solicitude protects her from any fits of vanity.

Such ideas can only vex the men of principles. For them, this generous love hardly figures among the natural inclinations of the human species. Convinced that men and women are motivated only by their appetites for pleasure and power, the dangerous men endeavor to demonstrate that the claims of the heart are little more than an alibi of desire and a stratagem of vanity. They denounce the hypocrisy that hides behind the notion of tenderness — women, they say, invoke their "sensitivity" only to excuse their pleasures, passing off their enjoyment as a sacrifice of their virtue to their beloved's happiness — and they accuse these promoters of "precious" love of spreading their cult for the sole purpose of being loved, of becoming the idols of the men they hope to convert. For if the sensitive women begin by vaunting the merits of their own sensitivity, they soon make it understood to their suitors that only a tender man is capable of moving them: thus, the love they worship is not so much the generous ardor they invoke but, rather, the devotion they demand from their lovers. Far from being the source of an innate sentiment distinct from the senses as well as the mind, the heart appears to its libertine critics to be the most subtle artifice inspired in women by their denatured state. In the name of a heartfelt love that aspires only to give, these women not only enjoy the pleasures of the flesh while pretending to scorn them but even lead men into servitude while preaching solicitude and self-effacement.

In revolting against the insincerity they attribute to the followers of the "heart," the dangerous men do not hesitate to stand on moral ground. Their primary concern, however, is less to condemn the morals of the new *précieuses* than to protect themselves from the captious illusions contained in the notion of tenderness. Indeed, such a notion is the worst threat to the libertine's freedom, for where prudes and coquettes make no mystery of the frustrations they intend to inflict on their suitors, the tender woman subjugates her victim by inviting him to share her pure "joy of loving." Thus, one can say that the struggle against tender love is the dangerous man's main challenge.

In all his undertakings, the man of principles seeks resounding success. Not content to conquer within the confines of a boudoir, he craves for the public to learn about his triumphs. However difficult the challenges he takes on, he knows that the greatness of his victories ultimately depends on the shock they create among the public. One might even say that the astonishment of his contemporaries is his real objective, and the women whose weaknesses he exploits serve merely as the tools for his glory. At the same time, the women he seeks to victimize collectively form the milieu in which he wishes to "make a name for himself." Within his limited social sphere, his reputation issues from the fear experienced by the female guardians of the social order when they learn of the downfall of an eminent member of their guild; beyond his mistresses' "defeats," it is the humiliation he inflicts on the chorus of women as a whole that ensures his prestige. In the feeling of powerless and fascinated indignation that his feats inspire in women, he finds at once a confirmation of his rigor, a reward for his efforts, and a recognition of his talent.

Since the mere seduction of the most difficult women is not enough to establish his glory, the dangerous man must also be a skillful propagandist. Indeed, he must publicize the beginning as well as the end of his adventures: that is, he must give as much luster to the announcements of his breakups as to the revelation of his conquests. By revealing the names of his victims to a public greedy for intrigues, the man of principles makes the women of the chorus realize that none of them is safe from weakness. Moreover, his systematic indiscretion clearly announces to those haughty women who pride themselves on being able to resist him that all their failings will be pitilessly exposed: the dishonor that awaits them in defeat will be proportional to the arrogance they display in combat. Finally, through the noisy and cruel publicity he gives to his breakups, he hopes to prove that the pleasures of the flesh and the joys of fame will never make him a hostage to love. Anxious to show that the heart plays no part in his liaisons, he is ever keen to abandon his mistresses in very noisy fashion, once the consummation and publicizing of his successes leave him with nothing more to desire.

Seducing, publicizing, and finally breaking up with a din: such are the three steps of the libertine master plan. However, libertine literature seeks to demonstrate that the dangerous man's victories eventually turn against him – for while he may devote his life to humiliating the world to which he belongs, he nevertheless remains dependent upon the reputation his caste reserves for him. Indeed, how much value could the admiration of the chorus of women have when it is made up exclusively of former and future victims of libertine vengeance? How could women who have already been conquered or who are fated for imminent downfall be in any position to appreciate in full the talent of an exceptional conqueror? As noted, the dangerous man's triumph depends on the consternation that his feats create among the female guardians of the social order; but while the accumulation of his victories may justify the dangerous man's claims to glory, it also tends to deprive him of a public that is qualified to praise him.

If the chorus of women proves less and less suited to honor their tormentor, society men are no more able to appreciate the feats of an elite conqueror: whether they are submissive to social convention, victims to the maneuvers of coquettes, or slaves to their own passions, most of them cannot even conceive of the uncompromising freedom of a man of principles. As for the *petits-maîtres*, they escape subjection to virtue and love only by bending their desires to the pusillanimity of their characters – that is, by limiting their ambitions to trifling endeavors and to affairs without risk. Finally, those rare individuals whose competition the dangerous man may actually fear are too important a threat for him to embrace them as witnesses to his own achievements. Disturbed by the shadow that a glorious rival might cast on his own work, the main fear of a man of principles is that in giving himself over

to a feeling of esteem, even toward just one person, he might compromise the power of his desire for vengeance, the driving force of his
existence. Thus, he considers the respect another man might inspire
in him to be a new challenge, one he takes up by vowing to find some
"weakness" in his competitor – in other words, by tracking down
the fault that will bring this "dangerous" rival back to the common
horde of men.

Because the public who helped the dangerous man to establish his
reputation consists of the expiatory victims of his vindictive eroticism,
he seems to arrive at an impasse: having set out to show the social
world that the values and sentiments it cherishes cannot resist his assaults, he ends up, through the very success of his undertaking, faced
with the futility of his efforts. In conquest after conquest, he has
proven that his invincible freedom could breach the wall of virtue,
crush the ambitions of vanity, and thwart the trap of love – but once
he has given proof of all this, what lessons can he draw from his satisfied vengeance? Victim of the harsh light he himself has brought to
society, he faces a difficult end to his career, for if he can no longer
believe in the virtues and sentiments he has put on trial, even less can
he content himself with the mediocre pleasures of a *petit-maître*.
Moreover, he has no accomplices with whom he might share his contempt for the public. Embittered by his own system, the aging libertine thus falls prey to regrets. More precisely, he comes to experience
a strange nostalgia for the time of his own innocence, that former
time when he believed he was in love with the woman who so brutally
introduced him into society. "I would even admit, I dare say," writes
Crébillon fils's libertine Lord Chester, at the moment of his retirement, "that far from recalling with pain that time of ignorance when I
was so gullible, I cannot think back on it without a kind of voluptuous pleasure."[24] The charm he attributes to his lost illusions actually
takes so strong a hold of him that the dangerous man now does not
hesitate to condemn the path his life took thereafter.

Yet, for the disillusioned conqueror, there is no question of turning
back: the years devoted to cruelty and cynicism have irremediably
spoiled him, and, in spite of his nostalgia, he still believes in his original diagnosis of amorous intoxication. Try as he might to assert that
the pleasure of his first emotions is the only one that retains any value
in his eyes, he nevertheless remains convinced that his naive passion
was nothing but a fantasy, too long fermented, which a coquette
exploited in order to subjugate and humiliate him. Beyond his own
experience, he continues to think that passionate love issues from an

aberration of the imagination and leads inevitably to servitude. In short, at the end of his career the dangerous man may deplore his loss of innocence, but he never questions his "science of society." Despite his nostalgia for his long-lost naïveté, he remains convinced that pleasure and power are the sole motivating forces of humanity. He thus maintains that love is a manipulation of a lover's desire by his vain mistress, rather than a pure impulse of tenderness which the former feels toward the latter. In other words, even the man of principles most critical of his own lifestyle still refuses to recognize the existence of the heart, such as it is conceived by the sensitive women.

The very success of the dangerous man's efforts to assert his freedom leads him to the most bitter of disappointments: first, because he eventually ceases to enjoy a glory that he receives from the very public he humiliates; and second, because the only pleasure of which he retains a fond memory is that of the lovesickness of his youth – that is, the freedom-killing trap he has spent his whole life fighting. Consequently, if he wishes to arm himself against the bitterness that haunts him without giving up his principles, he has but two choices: either find a way to ward off passionate love without falling prey to boredom, or else conceive a way of taking pleasure in love without becoming its slave. At the end of the eighteenth century, these two alternatives will inform the work of the two most important libertine authors. As I try to show in my introduction to *Dangerous Liaisons*, Laclos has explored the second one, the association of love and freedom, while the radical libertinism developed by Sade may be understood as an embracing of the first.

Beyond the Preservation Principle

Confronted by the bitterness eating away at the men of principles, Sade denounces what he believes to be the two mistakes causing it: the disproportionate importance which libertines attach to society's judgment, and their misconceptions about the designs of nature. The first effort of the "divine Marquis" consists in emancipating the dangerous men from the public they humiliate but to which their fate remains tied. For Sade, the true libertine must be absolutely independent and thus must consider other men and women as mere instruments of his own pleasure. The Sadian libertine's refusal to acknowledge the existence of a "fellow man" forces him to overcome the fear of solitude and the need for security; but it also means that he must remain vigilant with regard to the pitfalls of vanity. Without doubt, the satisfactions of pride contribute to the spice of sensual delight; yet vanity threatens to derail the pleasures it supposedly embellishes. Since vanity makes a man's happiness conditional on the admiration or fear he inspires, it subjects him to sentiments of which he is not master: thus, the libertine who is too complacent about his own vanity ceases to be independent.

That Sade's heroes mistrust the charms of notoriety certainly does not prevent them from nurturing great ambitions: indeed, a number of them aspire to commit crimes that would change the course of history, even disrupt the order of the universe. Yet the fact remains that the greatness of which they dream resides in the "physical" upheaval their actions should bring about (as much on the world as on their own nerves). The goal of their projects lies neither in the way the crowd greets their exploits nor in the sincere admiration of their accomplices. Consequently, these libertines escape from the quest for vainglory, which exposes dangerous men to a disillusioned maturity.

Emancipated from the public and its suffrage, Sade's eroticism is devoted to enhancing the faith of its followers in the pleasures of nature. Sade's heroes justify their offenses on morality and religion by claiming a scrupulous respect for natural wisdom. From Sade's point of view, one can even say that if the men of principles waste their time seeking the admiration of the public, it is first and foremost because they lack confidence in the vigor of their own natural appetites – and this because they do not understand the true nature of naturalism.

Libertine or not, the naturalists who precede Sade had endowed the universe with an imperious instinct of preservation. According to them, nature orchestrates a renewal of the human population – as well as other species – in order to ensure its own perpetuation, and it is only in order to incite men and women to procreate that it endows them with carnal appetites. Sade, by contrast, refuses to consider procreation as the only natural motivation for desire, nor is he any more willing to accept that the propagation of the species is the principal preoccupation of nature. For him, nature intends to preserve nothing beyond the impermanence of all beings to which it gives birth, and therefore it knows no other law than the perpetual movement of matter. As for natural beings, they are both the transitory products and the instruments of this perpetual movement. To respond to the desires of such a nature, men and women thus have no other task than to participate in the universal effervescence – something they do by leading a life as active as it is passionate. The existence of an individual finds its worth only in the quantity of *energy* – a key Sadian term – that he or she succeeds in setting in motion. From this perspective, sterile sexual acts are certainly no less "natural" than fecund copulation, as long as they are sufficiently "energetic."

More profoundly, Sade's heroes maintain that nature's perpetual movement – that is, the energy it constantly sets in motion – corresponds to a process of recycling of its materials: thus, each of its new creatures proceeds from the decomposition of older examples in such a way that destruction is no more dispensable than creation. Because creation and destruction are but two sides of one same perpetual and periodic movement, there can be no difference between the procreative sexual act and sterile pleasures: one can even assign equal usefulness to the birth and death of an individual, and thus lend the same value to childbirth and murder. In support of his thesis, Sade never ceases to remind us that some men and women harbor *only* desires that are incompatible with the reproduction of the species, and that certain individuals even experience an irrepressible attraction to the cruelest crimes. In other words, if it pleases nature to inspire them with such penchants, it is certainly because nature profits from their lechery and misdeeds. The consistent naturalist must therefore consider it his duty to satisfy all the passions he experiences: for in letting himself be guided by his whims and impulses, he acts as a missionary of a design superior to his own existence.

Up until this point, Sade's reasoning tends to show that, with regard to nature, all desires are useful and worthy of satisfaction. This, however, is not where his demonstration ends. Sadian naturalism cannot be satisfied with a perfect equivalence between the penchants his contemporaries deem virtuous and those they regard as infamous vices. Once the equal dignity of all inclinations dictated by nature has been clearly established, Sade's spokespeople push their reasonings further, proclaiming not merely that the maintenance of perpetual movement suffices for the natural order, but, further, that those lusts condemned by the Christian world (and also by most naturalist philosophers) are in reality the closest to the desires of nature.

To support this audacious propostition, Sade presents two types of argument. The first, invoking historical reasons, endeavors to advance libertinism as the antidote to the ravages of the dominant "nativism" – that is, as a compensation made necessary by the counternatural laws to which man has learned to submit. Ever since humanity allowed itself to be overwhelmed by the fear of perpetual movement, Sade asserts, the partisans of a strict channeling of desires succeeded in imposing their principles on others, and, consequently, cast shame on those who heed only their own temperaments. Moreover, the alliance of priests and legislators did not just lead to the condemnation of murderous outbursts and other passions capable of inflicting some damage on their objects – it even achieved the criminalization of *all* erotic pleasures that deviate from procreation.

Thus, Sadian libertines argue, even though nature sets about restoring equilibrium with the scourges it spreads across the earth – epidemics, catastrophes, and other bloody tyrannies – the fact remains that certain individuals' practice of vice also contributes to reestablish nature's energetic potential. Indeed, it is the energy of individuals, and their aptitude to serve nature, which suffers from the penalization of sterile or destructive pleasures, and even more from the excess of population caused by this coercive politics. In short, if Sadian libertinism promotes reprobate pleasures – sodomy, tribadism, cruel passions, murderous orgies, and so on – this is first and foremost to fight the "ecological" disequilibrium produced by a repressive civilization and unnatural morality.

The second argument for the superiority of vice invokes not historical circumstances but, rather, the system of nature itself.[25] In the long dissertation that Pope Pius VI offers Juliette, the eponymous heroine of Sade's last novel, the pontiff distinguishes between a primary nature, which he associates with a permanent process of mutation animating matter, and a secondary nature, which corresponds to the world of creatures – that is, to the universe of realms, species, and individuals, which must be understood as so many fortuitous and temporary lapses in the perpetual movement impelled by primary nature. Now, once primary nature has "launched" natural beings into the world, they emancipate themselves from the effervescence that gave rise to them in order to submit to the instinct of self-preservation, which is the law of secondary nature. In other words, secondary nature corresponds to the motivations dear to the naturalists prior to Sade – namely the genetic appetite that ensures the propagation of the species and the will for survival which informs the morality of human individuals. However, the Pope also points out that the laws of secondary nature are opposed to those of primary nature. Thus the friend of primordial effervescence behaves like the bitter enemy of all forms of preservation and reproduction. An individual endowed with inclinations incompatible with the propagation of the human species seems at once like a "chosen one" of primary nature and like an ascetic who does violence to his own self-preservation instinct in order to maintain perpetual movement.

Sade often repeats that consistent naturalists have no other task than to obey all their impulses submissively, without concern for the pleasure or the pain their whims cause. Yet among these free men and women, Sade favors those whose passions stimulate nature's creative faculties, those adepts of practices opposed to the proliferation – or better yet, to the continued existence – of already-constituted species and realms. The rejection of procreation and the destruction of organized beings are thus the forms of human conduct most worthy of nature. However, in order for nature to be fully satisfied, Sade's heroes concede, as one put it, that "much more complete destructions would be necesssary... much more than those we are able to effect; it is atrocity, it is scale [that nature] wants in our crimes; the more our destructions are of this sort, the more they will please her."[26] Quite frequently, those libertines most given over to theorizing their acts end up lamenting the mediocrity of their misdeeds; and since nature inspires them with ambitions they are incapable of realizing, they sometimes even turn their shame into a hatred of nature. Yet much as the Sadian libertines might blush at the distance between their utopian aspirations and the actual ravages they manage to achieve, their dissatisfaction attests to their energy. They are thus the living proof of Sade's credo that the man who listens to the voice of nature is immune to boredom.

The Savage, the Barbaric, and the Civilized

This reader is divided into three parts. The first, entitled "Natural Utopias," offers two different visions of the so-called natural state on which libertine authors base their theories of desire as well as their critiques of the social state. Most eighteenth-century writers who addressed the issue of libertinism saw the strategies of their reckless characters as a reaction against the moral values and the social conventions of an overly sophisticated civilization. To emphasize this diagnosis, some sought to contrast the lifestyle of their contemporaries with that of the "savages," whose mores remain in harmony with nature's wishes – hence Diderot's depiction of Tahitian life in his *Supplement to Bougainville's Voyage* (1772) and Laclos's portrayal of the "natural woman" in his essay *On the Education of Women* (1783).

Diderot is a harsh critic of libertinism, which he treats as the defect of a declining aristocracy. Nevertheless, some of the positions he presents in the *Supplement* – about the function of fantasy, the innocence of sexual pleasure, and the social and emotional damage wrought by modesty and constancy – have much in common with the opinions defended by Crébillon fils's *petits-maîtres*. In agreement with the founding principles of libertinism, Diderot's naturalism defines carnal delight as a gift of nature. Thus he insists on the fact that humans, because they are free to dispose of such a gift, also have the means to pervert it. On the one hand, they can subject their natural appetites to a corset of strict laws and take pride in the misery they inflict on themselves and their communities; on the other, they can decide to wallow in debauchery, with no concern either for their own health or for the happiness of those around them. This asceticism and this licentiousness, both opposed in equal measure to the designs of nature, tend to provoke each other. They thus become entangled in a vicious circle where deliberate depravity and cruelly repressive laws constantly use the other to justify their own escalation.

For Diderot, as for the *petits-maîtres*, sexual pleasure is the only natural outcome of erotic attraction. Diderot even endows the mutually gratifying sexual union of man and woman with the status of a solemn and mysterious ceremony honoring nature. Moreover, sharing the libertine belief in the natural inconstancy of desire, he vehemently criticizes society's celebration of faithfulness. However, unlike the libertines, Diderot is concerned with reforming mores, not with bending rules. Since the reforms he champions aim at reconciling social conventions and natural laws, he searches for inspiration in the wisdom of the "natural man," represented in the *Supplement* by Orou and his Tahitian compatriots.

"Tahitian wisdom" distributes the roles among men and women according to their respective "metabolisms": the male, who is excited more rapidly, must try to stimulate his mistress's desire, while the female, whose passion rises more slowly but lasts longer, must exert a reasonable resistance in order to fan and then maintain her lover's ardor. In other words, even though shared pleasure responds to nature's wish, it nevertheless demands differentiation according to sex in the exercise of the art of gallantry. In the absence of differentiated sexual roles, the clumsy haste of the young man and the initial timidity of the girl will leave them both ashamed and frustrated. Yet the happiness of men and women requires that their gallantry never ceases to serve the goals of nature. In this respect, Diderot attempts to establish a difference between gallantry and deceitful *coquetry*, "for it consists of simulating a passion one doesn't feel at all and promising favors that one has no intention of conferring. The coy male is making sport of the female, and the female of the male. It's a perfidious game that often ends in the most deplorable catastrophes imaginable; a ridiculous sort of merry-go-round in the course of which both deceiver and deceived are equally punished by the waste of the most precious parts of their lives."[27]

According to Diderot, fostering gallantry while averting coquetry is not simply a matter of guaranteeing the happiness of individuals – it is also about making them face their responsibilities to the order of nature, because nature relies on the pleasures of men and women to assure its own perpetuation. Thus, the erotic regime advanced by Diderot integrates love and procreation, whereas for a *petit-maître* these domains are utterly separate. The naturalist perspective presiding over the *Supplement* even sees the conception of a child as nature's ultimate goal; the happy combination of pleasure and progeniture thus gives to marriage its only natural function.[28] Therein lies the superiority of the Tahitian marriage, which bothers with neither faithfulness nor constancy, yet celebrates the birth of a child, no matter who fathered it.

The origin of the malaise that Diderot exposes in the amorous relations of "civilized" men and women, as opposed to the happiness of Tahitians, undoubtedly is the most audacious part of the *Supplement to Bougainville's Voyage*. Unhappiness, he contends, occurs once a man decides to convert the physical possession of a woman, inherent in the anatomy of the sexual relationship, into a right of exclusive ownership. This tyrannical act, through which a man allows himself to consider a free human being as *his* wife, constitutes the prototypical act of all the forms of slavery to come. Furthermore, this abuse of power leads the despotic husband to demand that "his" wife remain absolutely faithful to him. Such a demand, which in no way conforms to his victim's temperament, only bears witness to his own privilege as an owner. Indeed, not content with this state of affairs, the possessive "civilized" man even makes his law of possession retroactive, by requiring that his future wife never "belonged" to anyone before him, and that the parents of the young girl ensure her virginity until marriage. As for these women who are unable to reclaim their lost freedom, they can only seek revenge in demanding the same fidelity of their abusive spouses.

Once Diderot has established the ills of the social state, the question remains whether he thinks the situation is reversible. It is here that his indictment of society's ways turns to a mixture of pragmatism and prudence. Undoubtedly, the chastity of young girls, the faithfulness of spouses, the constancy of husbands, and the legitimacy of children

are artificial values to Diderot, the consequences of which the naturalist reformers are right to denounce; yet he does not believe that his
European contemporaries can ever return to Tahitian bliss. Therefore,
rather than calling for a moral revolution, he argues only against the
indissolubility of marriage and asks for more tolerance with regard
to the fleeting infidelities of spouses. In short, when it comes to practical matters, his radical naturalism gives way to an "enlightened"
bourgeois morality: pleading for the legalization of divorce and against
marital jealousy, he attempts first and foremost to make libertine excess
less attractive by bestowing some "pleasure" on marriage.

Laclos's *On the Education of Women* offers an even more radical contrast between the "natural" and the social state. Although his essay
purports to be about the proper way to educate women, the author of
Dangerous Liaisons quickly drops this first topic: according to him,
education is useful only for people who are free. Women, who were
free while nature reigned, have been enslaved since the beginning
of the social state; thus, the issue of their education cannot be properly
addressed until they recover their independence. Rather than speculate on the possibility of a women's revolution, though, Laclos devotes
the rest of his essay to the description of the "natural woman" and to
the story of her enslavement by men.

For Laclos, the words "civilization" and "subjection" are almost
synonymous. In chapter 10, "On the First Effects of Society," he claims
that "nature creates only free beings," while "society makes only
tyrants and slaves."[29] To justify this second assertion, Laclos contends
that the social state is based on a social contract, and that such a contract necessarily creates obligations for the people who agree to it.
Thus, in spite of the security and the material advantages of "social"
life, individuals nevertheless experience their entry into society as a
painful hindrance to their natural freedom: the "social man does not
cease to strain against his bonds, he is inclined to escape them, he seeks
to throw off their weight onto his fellow men...."[30] One could even
claim that the barely socialized man immediately encounters the conditions that will inspire the harshest form of libertinism, since he
already dreams of *avenging* himself on his partners for the restrictions
to which he has consented. While the resentment that accompanies
the emergence of civilization is widespread, those individuals who are
privileged by nature will compensate for their lost autonomy by turning the social contract to their advantage. More precisely, Laclos contends, "every agreement made between two subjects unequal in strength
produces, can only produce, a tyrant and a slave; it follows as well

that, in the social union of the two sexes, the women, generally weaker, have necessarily been generally oppressed...."[31]

According to Laclos, the most primitive societies are those in which women are under the heaviest yoke:

> It is here that one sees the women alone burdened with the basest and most arduous work, always worn out, often ill treated, sometimes killed by their idle and capricious masters who reward in this way the care the women take of them, the substances they furnish them, and the pleasure they procure them....[32]
>
> Oppression and scorn, thus were and must have been generally the share of women in emerging societies; this state lasted in all its force until centuries of experience taught them to substitute skill for force. Women at last sensed that, since they were weaker, their only resource was to seduce; they understood that if they were dependent on men through force, men could become dependent on them through pleasure. More unhappy than men, they must have thought and reflected earlier than did men; they were the first to know that pleasure was always beneath the idea that one formed of it, and that the imagination went farther than nature. Once these basic truths were known, they learned first to veil their charms in order to awaken curiosity [...] from that moment on, they knew how to set men's imaginations afire, they knew how to arouse and direct desires as they pleased: thus did beauty and love come into being....[33]

Unlike other naturalist thinkers, Laclos does not see the birth of amorous sentiment as the fortuitous consequence of the delays society imposes on human desires; rather, he clearly defines love as a trap deliberately conceived by women – a trap made all the more formidable by the fact that its victims worship both their yoke and their tyrant. However, despite their invention of love, women have not recovered their natural state of freedom: their newfound trap is merely the revenge of slaves, forced by their weakness to prove themselves clever. Instead of regaining their independence, women have carved out a domain for themselves in which the relations of power between the sexes have been reversed. Still subjugated outside of the erotic sphere, they can only avenge themselves of the humiliations they suffer elsewhere by becoming their lovers' "mistresses": that is, by exerting their own tyranny over love relations. Even here, though, their ascendency proves fragile, for while they may initially be captivated by their enflamed imaginations, men soon learn how to turn against their mistresses "these weapons [the women] had forged to combat them."[34] And women will let themselves be caught in their own trap: fascinated by the very passion that their skillful manipulations inspire in their lovers, many mistresses will succumb to the temptation to taste the poison they themselves have concocted for their victims. As a result, they soon join men in their aberrations. Laclos even claims that, in the final account, the invention of love has perhaps made women's lot even more intolerable.

The second part of this reader, "Oriental Dreams," includes three so-called Oriental novels. While eighteenth-century writers like to portray the "savages" living in harmony with nature as a model of wisdom and simplicity, the "barbaric" Orient stands for all the ills and errors of an overly sophisticated society. Whether Turkish, Persian, or Indian, all "Oriental" societies are treated by French writers – in the wake of Montesquieu – as the ultimate perversion of the social state. Politically, they are associated with the rule of ruthless despots whose tyrannical power reduces their subjects to humiliated yet conniving and resentful slaves. And the mores attributed to these societies seem to gather the most contradictory forms of excess: at once too refined and strikingly brutal, oppressive to the point of extreme cruelty – especially regarding the condition of women – and licentious to the point of extreme debauchery. In short, "Oriental despotism" mainly serves as the perfect antithesis of what a just society should be.

All the same, when eighteenth-century authors situate their novels in such an "Oriental" setting, their purpose is not to contrast the barbaric ways of the sultans and their entourage with the "civilized" mores of the French monarchy but, rather, to convey a disturbing similarity between French high society, under the reigns of Louis XV and Louis XVI, and its Oriental counterparts. In other words, while Diderot's or Laclos's savages belong to an age of innocence forever lost, Diderot's or Crébillon fils's Oriental palaces and seraglios are meant to be fitting caricatures of the French court society in its current state: the former are thus supposed to represent what eighteenth-century men and women have ceased to be, whereas the latter point to what French aristocrats have become. Indeed, some of these "Oriental" novels are very precise romans à clef; but even when they are not, they provide their authors with a roundabout and thus relatively safe way of criticizing the mores of the French upper class.

Both Crébillon fils's The Sofa (1742) and Diderot's The Indiscreet Jewels (1748) try to emulate the Thousand and One Nights, which had been translated into French by Antoine Galland at the beginning of the eighteenth century. Like their Arabic model, the two French nov-

els revolve around a sultan who must be kept amused; yet unlike
Schahriar in the *Thousand and One Nights*, Diderot's and Crébillon fils's
sultans are not haunted by murderous jealousy. Their only problem,
familiar to every French *petit-maître*, is boredom. In order to fend it
off, the sultan in *The Indiscreet Jewels* seeks the help of a genie, who
offers him a magic ring: if turned toward a woman, this ring has the
amazing power of making the woman's vagina – her "jewel" – speak out
loud. As for the sultan of *The Sofa*, he is the grandson of Shah Riar
and Scheherezade, and thus has inherited a weakness for good storytelling. His entertainment will be provided by a young courtier named
Amanzei. The latter does indeed have interesting stories to tell, for
he remembers that in his previous life his soul was locked up in a sofa:
a victim of the god Brahma, who wanted to punish him for his dissolute ways, his soul was in fact condemned to travel from sofa to sofa in
search of true love. More precisely, Brahma told Amanzei that he would
not be reincarnated into a human body until a man and a woman,
sincerely in love with each other, had consummated their passion on
"his" sofa.

Amanzei's memories and the stories told by the "jewels" enable
Crébillon fils and Diderot to expose the disingenuous ways of their contemporaries. Amanzei has of course a very good personal reason to
seek heartfelt love; yet from the various sofas he inhabits, he sees for
the most part the ploys of coquettes and of cynical libertines, the
hypocrisy of prudish women, and the fickleness of men of good fortune. Similarly, the Sultan Mangogul's ring mainly serves to reveal the
discrepancies between the raw but truthful speeches delivered by
the "jewels" and the sophisticated but deceitful words coming from
women's mouths: it thus uncovers men's deficiencies while exposing
women's duplicity. However, through the various tableaux of their
respective novels, both Crébillon fils and Diderot are actually looking
for true love. On that score, the latter shows that even when he writes
licentious books, he remains first and foremost a bourgeois reformer:
indeed, in *The Indiscreet Jewels* the most rewarding relationship appears
to be the stable, friendly, enduring but tepid bond between Mangogul
himself and his tolerant mistress Mirzoza, the only woman whose
jewel and mouth say exactly the same things. Crébillon fils, on the other
hand, proves that he is the ultimate libertine writer, for he can neither
fully believe in mutual, passionate, and lasting love, nor completely
discard it as a dangerous illusion. In *The Sofa*, Amanzei eventually
encounters a couple that puts an end to his curse – yet he finds no joy
in recovering his human condition, because he has fallen in love with

the woman who saved him. In other words, he is enamored with the woman who sets him free by making love to another man.

Prévost's *The Story of a Modern Greek Woman* (1740) also involves "Oriental dreams," but from a different perspective: it tells the story of a French ambassador to Turkey who becomes obsessed with a young Greek courtesan. When he meets Théophé, the young woman belongs to the seraglio of his good friend Chériber, a Turkish pasha who shows his affection for the French diplomat by letting him visit his harem. Immediately attracted to the young Greek, the diplomat eventually manages to take her away from Chériber's seraglio and to bring her back to France; yet in order to lure her into coming along with him, he has told Théophé that in France, "men will go to any length for women's happiness, treating them as queens rather than slaves, surrendering themselves completely, asking in return only gentleness, tenderness, and virtue."[35] Hence, the diplomat finds himself trapped by his own discourse when Théophé, freed from the harem, declares that she wants to express her gratitude to her savior by loving him as though he were her father and by devoting the rest of her life to virtue. Is the Greek courtesan's conversion sincere? Is she, on the contrary, a brilliantly devious manipulator? In any case, *The Story of a Modern Greek Woman* both demonstrates the danger inherent in double entendre – for uncertainty will drive the diplomat to madness and physical decay – and offers a strikingly ironic perspective on the alleged moral superiority of Western civilization.

The third and last part of this reader, entitled "Ways of the World," gathers four works of fiction that take place in eighteenth-century France and, thus directly address the libertine ways of its declining aristocracy. Included are two novels, *The Wayward Head and Heart* by Crébillon fils and *Dangerous Liaisons* by Laclos, as well as two tales, *No Tomorrow* (1777) by Denon and *Florville and Courval* (1800) by Sade.

Crébillon fils's *The Wayward Head and Heart* is the ultimate libertine bildungsroman. It recounts the progress of young Meilcour's education under the competing guidance of Versac, a dangerous libertine, and Mme de Lursay, a woman who professes tender love in the tradition of the seventeenth-century *précieuses*. In keeping with the moral concerns of libertine literature, Crébillon fils clearly shows that the lifestyle proposed by Versac, aside from being reprehensible, necessarily leads the young man who embraces it to a bitter maturity; yet Crébillon fils also exposes the affectations and the hypocrisy of Mme de Lursay, who wants to seduce the young Meilcour while teaching him that true love has little to do with carnal pleasures. Is there a golden

mean between the cruel cynicism of a man of principles and the disingenuous idealism of a *précieuse*? True to the skepticism permeating
libertine novels (especially his own), Crébillon fils cannot bring himself to answer such a question. On the one hand, he introduces the innocent and sincere Hortense de Tréville, with whom Meilcour instantly
falls in love, and who seems to secretly share the young man's feelings;
but on the other hand, and despite promising a happy ending in his
preface, Crébillon fils interrupts his novel long before the hypothetical reunion of the young couple, thereby revealing his doubts about
the credibility of such a conclusion.

Where *The Story of a Modern Greek Woman* emphasized the disastrous consequences of double entendre gone astray, and *The Wayward
Head and Heart* exposed the mixture of pain and rancor at the core of
high libertinism, *No Tomorrow* gives a rare example of duplicity's
joyful triumph – indeed, Denon's only work of fiction can be seen as
a unique manifesto in favor of libertine politeness. *No Tomorrow* shows
how Mme de T——, thanks to her artful mastery of double entendre,
manages at once to seduce and dazzle the young narrator, deceive her
other lover, confuse her husband, and last but not least damage the
reputation of the Comtesse de ——, who is the narrator's beloved
and her own best friend. Yet, at the same time, one can argue that
Mme de T——'s mischievous ways contribute to the happiness of her
entire entourage: she has offered the narrator a wonderful and memorable night; she has convinced her "official" lover that she went out of
her way just to protect their secret affair; she has successfully defused
Monsieur de T——'s jealousy; and she returns a less naive and thus
more interesting lover to the Comtesse de ——. In short, *No Tomorrow* appears to be the most persuasive argument against the critics of
libertinism, who claim that there is no pleasurable middle ground
between boredom and passionate love.

Dangerous Liaisons is both the masterpiece and the swan song of
libertine literature. As I argue in my introduction to the novel, Laclos
acknowledges the critical state of aristocratic libertinism on the eve of
the French Revolution, and thus departs from the original quest of the
libertines – namely, the search for a golden mean between love and
boredom. Instead, he wonders about the possibility of a relationship
that would reconcile the joys of passionate love with the exigencies of
libertine freedom. While the tragic ending of *Dangerous Liaisons* seems
to suggest that there is no way to combine devotion and autonomy,
one can nevertheless argue that this failure in no way necessarily reflects
any intrinsic flaw of the project. Rather than underlining the absolute

incompatibility of love and freedom, the novel shows that the main obstacle to their conciliation lies in the social condition of women; indeed, the respective fates of Mme de Merteuil and Mme de Tourvel, the two heroines of *Dangerous Liaisons*, clearly incriminate the society in which they live. More precisely, Laclos's novel accuses this society of turning the notion of "free love" into an oxymoron by reducing a woman's freedom to her capacity of resisting her own desires, and of sublimating her passionate feelings. In his essay *On the Education of Women* – published a few years after *Dangerous Liaisons* – Laclos claims that the education of women is irrelevant until women recover their independence. Likewise, his novel seems to say that love will remain a pernicious form of enslavement until women successfully challenge their condition.

The last piece included in this reader, *Florville and Courval*, is one of the "heroic and tragic tales" gathered in the collection entitled *The Crimes of Love* (1800). Because it is one of the very few books that Sade did not publish anonymously, *The Crimes of Love* presents him with a new challenge. On the one hand, writing under his own name, Sade seeks to escape censorship, and even to avert the public's indignation. On the other hand, he neither wants to conceal his views about nature and morals nor spare his readers from the usual Sadian mix of sex and violence. On both accounts, *Florville and Courval* is remarkably successful. Borrowing its structure from a famous Greek tragedy and espousing the tone of English gothic novels, it reveals the unmistakable mark of its author only in its particularly dramatic finale (we *strongly* advise our readers to read Marcel Hénaff's introduction *after* reading Sade's tale). Without revealing too much, one can say that *Florville and Courval* is Sade's idea of a moral tale. As such, it delivers the same message, albeit more succinctly, as *Justine* (1791) and *The Story of Juliette* (1797) – namely, that true naturalists are rewarded with a charmed life, while nature shows no mercy for those so-called virtuous people who systematically oppose its designs. Hence the fate of poor Florville, the impeccable and therefore deserving victim of nature's revenge.

NOTES

1. See Raymond Trousson, "Préface" to *Romans Libertins du XVIIIème siècle* (Paris: Laffont, 1993), pp. ii–iii.

2. See René Pintard, *Le Libertinage érudit dans la première moitié du XVIIème siècle*

(Boivin, 1943); Frédéric Lachèvre, *Le Libertinage au XVIIème siècle* (Champion, 1924); Antoine Adam, *Les Libertins au XVIIème siècle* (Buchet-Chastel, 1964); and Joan DeJean, *Libertine Strategies: Freedom and the Novel in Seventeenth-Century France* (Columbus: Ohio State University Press, 1980).

3. Such would be the case notably with Campanella, who was pursued by the Inquisition. As René Pintard writes, the libertines "cared little to approve or disapprove of the theories of the Calabrian monk.... What difference did it make? He was persecuted, and that was enough for them" (*Le Libertinage érudit*, p. 97).

4. "Besotted antiquity left us fables / which to a sensible man are not believable, / And never will my mind find sane / Anyone who likes a phantom so vain..." (Théophile de Viau, *Oeuvres poétiques* [Paris: Droz, 1967], vol. 1, p. 80).

5. "I wish to seize an object where my free desire / distinguishes pain from pleasure, / Where in full my senses, without fraud or constraint, / Are troubled no more by hope or fear's restraint..." (*ibid.*, vol, 2, p. 27).

6. Wendy Perkins, "Le Libertinage de quelques poètes épicuriens à la fin du XVIIème siècle," in *Laclos et le libertinage* (Paris: Presses Universitaires de France, 1983), pp. 21–46.

7. See Claude Reichler, *L'Age libertin* (Paris: Minuit, 1987), pp. 19–42.

8. One of the many variants of a work written in Latin in the middle of the seventeenth century entitled *Aloisiae sigaeae toletanae* (1660), and of which the best-known version appeared in 1680 under the title *L'Académie des Dames*. See Pascal Pia, *Les Livres de l'enfer, du XVIème siècle à nos jours* (Paris: Coulet and Faure, 1978).

9. Cited by Claude Reichler, *L'Age libertin*, p. 22.

10. See Norbert Elias's famous analysis in *La Société de cour* (Paris: Flammarion, 1985), esp. ch. 5. Elias demonstrates that Louis XIV is both the "oppressor" and the "preserver" of the French nobility. In drawing them to Versailles, he succeeds in taking the levers of economic, judicial, and even military power away from them; at the same time, he preserves the privileges of the aristocratic caste, and notably that of creating the chosen public "for whom" the king still distinguishes himself as a *primus inter pares*, that is, as a king-knight. In other words, the grandees of the kingdom, reduced to powerlessness, nonetheless remain the privileged recipients of the monarchic spark, as opposed to the soaring bourgeoisie, "from whom" the king and his *public* are together distinguished.

11. Cited by Ernest Sturm, *Crébillon fils et le libertinage au XVIIIème siècle* (Paris: Nizet, 1970), p. 52.

12. "The king became devout as he grew old, and immediately the court became devout, or appeared to be. After his death, the tables turned completely, and under the Regency they dispensed with the hypocrisy" (Duclos, *Les confessions du comte de* ———, in *Romanciers du XVIIIème siècle* [Paris: La Pléiade, 1965], vol. 2, p. 222).

13. Crébillon fils, *The Wayward Head and Heart*, p. 879.

14. *Ibid.*, p. 881.

15. Crébillon fils, *Le Hasard au coin du feu* (Paris: Desjonquères, 1983), pp. 195–96.

16. Crébillon fils, *The Opportunities of a Night*, trans. Eric Sutton (New York: Benjamin Blom, Inc., 1971), p. 23.

17. Duclos, *Les Confessions du comte de* ———, p. 267.

18. "You know the Présidente de Tourvel," Valmont adds, "her piety, her conjugal devotion, her austere principles. That is where I have launched my attack. There is an enemy worthy of me. That is the goal I aspire to attain" (Laclos, *Dangerous Liaisons*, letter 4, p. 946).

19. The *Lettres de Ninon de Lenclos au Marquis de Sévigné*, in *Mémoires sur la vie de Mademoiselle de Lenclos*, by M. B ——— (Amsterdam, 1763) use this expression, emphasizing it as a kind of second birth. On libertine initiation, see Claude Reichler, *L'Age libertin*, pp. 45–55.

20. "I was desperately in love with the Comtesse de ———," declares the hero of *No Tomorrow* at the start of his story. "I was twenty years old and I was naive. She deceived me, I got angry, she left me. I was naive, I missed her. I was twenty years old, she forgave me, and, because I was twenty years old, because I was naive – still deceived, but no longer abandoned – I thought myself to be the best-loved lover, and therefore the happiest of men" (Denon, *No Tomorrow*, p. 732).

21. "I have yet to meet a man," asserts Alcibiade, "who does not remember with bitterness the constraint he was put through, or the humiliation to which he was subjected; and of all those who have had reason to complain of one or to blush about the other, there is scarcely one who remembers it with so much desire for vengence as I still retain" (Crébillon fils, *Lettres athéniennes* [London, 1777], VI, vol. 12, pp. 60–61).

22. On this threefold division – the head, the senses, and the heart – see Laurent Versini, *Laclos et la tradition: essai sur les sources et la technique des Liaisons dangereuses* (Paris: Klincksieck, 1968), pp. 443–79.

23. "Tender and delicate souls," writes Mme de Lambert, "are concerned with one sentiment alone: they live only for what they love.... Can all one's hours ever be too much to give to the object of one's love?" (Anne Thérèse de Lambert, *Réflexions nouvelles sur les femmes* [Côté-femmes éditions, 1989], pp. 65–66.) This neo-precious argument is also found in Laclos, in the declarations the author puts in the mouth of Mme de Rosemonde. When she warns Mme de Tourvel against the perils of love, the old lady further specifies that the tenderness of the heart, and hence the need to give oneself to one's beloved, are affections reserved for women. Incapable of having her lover share her sensibility, a woman thus encounters only "misfortune in the very feeling that promised her so much happiness!" As for men, "they feel, of course, the same delight; often they are more carried away by it. But they are ignorant of that anxious eagerness, that careful solicitude, which provokes us to the constant and tender attentions whose sole object is always the man we love. A man enjoys the happiness he feels, a woman the happiness she gives" (Laclos, *Dangerous Liaisons*, letter 130, pp. 1183–84).

24. Crébillon fils, *Les Heureux Orphelins*, in *Oeuvres complètes* (London, 1777), vol. 8, pp. 145–46.

25. On this point, see Pierre Klossowski, *Sade mon prochain* (Paris: Seuil, 1967), pp. 117–28.

26. Sade, *Histoire de Juliette, ou les Prospérités du vice*, in *Oeuvres complètes* (Paris: Pauvert, 1987), vol. 9, pp. 172–73.

27. Diderot, *Supplement to Bougainville's Voyage*, p. 105.

28. *Ibid.*

29. Laclos, *On the Education of Women*, p. 154.

30. *Ibid.*

31. *Ibid.*

32. *Ibid.*, p. 155.

33. *Ibid.*, p. 156.

34. *Ibid.*

35. Prévost, *The Story of a Modern Greek Woman*, p. 557.

Translated by Michel Feher and Sophie Hawkes.

Natural Utopias

Supplement to Bougainville's Voyage

by Denis Diderot

Translated by Jacques Barzun and Ralph Bowen

Introduction

by Marcel Hénaff

Supplement to Diderot's Dream

by Marcel Hénaff

> *Nothing that exists can be against nature or outside nature,*
> *and I don't even exclude chastity and voluntary continence*
> *which, if it were possible to sin against nature, would be*
> *the greatest of crimes against her as well as being the most*
> *serious offences against the social laws of any country in*
> *which acts were weighed in scales other than those of*
> *fanaticism and prejudice.*
> – Diderot, "D'Alembert's Dream" [1]

Arrival at New Cythera

In 1771 the Parisian booksellers Saillant and Nyon published Louis-Antoine de Bougainville's *A Voyage around the World*. This highly descriptive, serious, and often rather technical work immediately enjoyed a remarkable success. Educated circles in the French capital had already gained some familiarity with its author in the two preceding years: Bougainville had returned in March 1769 from a trip around the world, whose purpose was to complete maritime maps while claiming new lands as the property of the French crown.

This voyage had been marked by something very special, though, something that had profoundly shaken Bougainville and his crew – a stop of barely a week on the island of Tahiti. Tahiti was all that was spoken of in the other expedition members' accounts, such as those of the naturalist Commerson and the writer Michau. The curiosity of the Parisians was sparked even more by the fact that Bougainville paraded along with him, from salons to dinner parties, a native Tahitian by the name of Aotourou, who, though he had not realized that the trip would be so long, nonetheless came of his own will – this is strongly emphasized – to discover the country of those who had visited his.

What had happened in Tahiti that would capture the interest not only of high society but of even the most serious philosophers, such as Diderot (1713–84)? The answer is to be found in chapters 8, 9, and 10 of Bougainville's account, wherein the natives' welcome, the island's landscapes, and the crew's stay are described:

As we came nearer the shore, the number of islanders surrounding our ships encreased. The periaguas were so numerous all about the ships, that we had much to do to warp in amidst the crowd of boats and the noise. All these people came crying out *tayo*, which means friend, and gave a thousand signs of friendship; they all asked nails and ear-rings of us. The periaguas were full of females; who, for agreeable features, are not inferior to most European women; and who in point of beauty of the body might, with much reason, vie with them all. Most of these fair females were naked; for the men and the old women that accompanied them had stripped them of the garments which they generally dress themselves in. The glances which they gave us from their periaguas, seemed to discover some degree of uneasiness, notwithstanding the innocent manner in which they were given; perhaps, because nature has every where embellished their sex with a natural timidity; or because even in those countries, where the ease of the golden age is still in use, women seem least to desire what they most wish for. The men, who were more plain, or rather more free, soon explained their meaning very clearly. They pressed us to choose a woman, and to come on shore with her; and their gestures, which were nothing less than equivocal, denoted in what matter we should form an acquaintance with her. It was very difficult, amidst such a fight, to keep at their work four hundred young French sailors, who had seen no women for six months. In spite of all our precautions, a young girl came on board, and placed herself upon the quarter-deck, near one of the hatch-ways, which was open, in order to give air to those who were heaving at the capstern below it. The girl carelessly dropt a cloth, which covered her, and appeared to the eyes of all beholders, such as Venus shewed herself to the Phrygian sheperd, having, indeed the celestial form of that goddess.[2]

To the captain and his men this welcome seemed so astounding (as it does even today) that they felt they had come upon an island paradise and rediscovered "the golden age," as if the most outrageous dreams of free love and social tolerance had been realized in Tahiti. They decided, moreover, to name the country New Cythera, in tribute to the island dedicated to Venus, the goddess whose name appears more than once in the narrator's account. Despite its measured tone, the text of the skeptical Bougainville reveals what was obviously considerable emotion:

Our people were daily walking in the isle without arms, either quite alone, or in little companies. They were invited to enter the houses, where the people gave them to eat; nor did the civility of their landlords stop at a slight collation, they offered them young girls; the hut was immediately filled with a curious crowd of men and women, who made a circle around the guest, and the young victim of hospitality. The ground was spread with leaves and flowers, and their musicians sung an hymeneal song to the tune of their flutes. Here Venus is the goddess of hospitality, her worship does not admit of any mysteries, and every tribute paid to her is a feast for the whole nation. They were surprised at the confusion which our people appeared to be in, as our customs do not admit of these public proceedings. However, I would not answer for it, that every one of our men had found it impossible to conquer his repugnance, and conform to the customs of the country.[3]

Added to this felicity in love (still expressed in the language of ancient mythology) were the ease of life, the generous climate, and social tranquillity:

I have often, in company with only one or two of our people, been out walking in the interior parts of the isle. I thought I was transported into the garden of Eden; we crossed a turf, covered with fine fruit-trees, and intersected by little rivulets, which keep up a pleasant coolness in the air, without any of those inconveniences which humidity occasions. A numerous people there enjoy the blessings which nature showers liberally down upon them. We found companies of men and women sitting under the shade of their fruit-trees: they all greeted us with signs of friendship: those who met us upon the road stood aside to let us pass by; every where we found hospitality, ease, innocent joy and every appearance of the happiness amongst them.[4]

Such is the description that intrigued Diderot. It came from a man who was, in his eyes, totally reliable: Bougainville was both a scholar (he was an excellent mathematician, the author of a treatise on integral calculus) and a man of action (he had fought in the French and Indian War in Canada and in the conquest of the Falkland Islands). Thus, he was considered well qualified to make a fair and impartial evaluation of the natives.[5] Diderot, like all the thinkers of his time, believed in the universality of human nature: diverse peoples, depending on climate and physical conditions, elaborated variations on this common nature, thereby accounting for the differences in culture to be found here and there. Evaluating them seemed a simple task for a traveler enlightened by reason. Bougainville remained in Tahiti for barely a week, but the brevity of his stay did not strike his readers as an obstacle to the validity of the judgment he formed about this island and its population. Diderot, from all evidence, was undeterred, particularly since it suited his purposes: Bougainville seemed to him to be endowed with the honesty of a philosopher and the rigor of a scholar. He was a firsthand witness of top quality.

It was only much later, after his voyage, in talking with Aotourou, that Bougainville was to come to a more lucid view of the sociopolitical system of New Cythera: "I have mentioned above, that the inhabitants of Taiti seemed to live in an enviable happiness. We took them to be almost equal in rank amongst themselves; or at least enjoying a liberty, which was only subject to the laws established for their common happiness. I was mistaken; the distinction of ranks is very great at Taiti, and the disproportion very tyrannical."[6]

Diderot apparently did not notice this passage, or perhaps he preferred to ignore it. Yet he was no doubt extremely interested in this one:

> Polygamy seems established amongst them; at least it is amongst the chief people. As love is their only passion, the great number of women is the only luxury of the opulent.... Jealousy is so unknown a passion here, that the husband is commonly the first who persuades his wife to yield to another. An unmarried woman suffers no constraint on that account; everything invites her to follow the inclination of heart, or the instinct of her sensuality; and public applause honors her defeat; nor does it appear, that how great so ever the number of her previous lovers may have been, it should prove an obstacle to her meeting with a husband afterwards.[7]

It is not difficult to imagine the effect such a description would have had on the minds of an era impatient to strip off the constraints of Christian morality. For Diderot this book coincided with an intense examination of the notion of natural law and the arbitrary nature of institutions. He who had been so circumspect with regard to Rousseau and his defense of primitive man had indisputably changed his mind. And it was precisely the question of sexual mores – the sexual freedom of the inhabitants of Tahiti – that triggered his critique of an orderly society that until then he had celebrated with unswayable conviction.

But we must return to the circumstances in which this text was written: more than a supplement to Bougainville's voyage, it is undoubtedly a supplement to Diderot's dream.

The Manuscript Found in a Garden

> A. Do you mean to go and spin that fable about how wonderful life is in Tahiti?
> B. It isn't a fable at all. And you would have no doubt about Bougainville's sincerity if you had read the supplement to his account of his voyage.
> A. And where can one find this supplement?
> B. It's right over there, on that table (p. 81).

It must be said right off that Diderot never had the pleasure of learning his contemporaries' reaction to this text, which, like so many of his other writings, was published only posthumously (the first edition dates from 1796, twelve years after the author's death, and the second, Naigeon's, came out in 1798). In 1771 Diderot proposed to his friend Friedrich Melchior Grimm, organizer of the *Correspondance littéraire*, a revision of Bougainville's work (which was never published); a year later Diderot returned to this outline to write his *Supplement to Bougainville's Voyage*, with which he was very satisfied, as he commented in a letter to Grimm. In the same period he contributed to Abbé Raynal's *Philosophical History of the Settlements and Trade of the Europeans in the East and West Indies* (1770), which immediately became a surprise success, and which could be considered the first truly critical account of European colonization since Columbus. Diderot wrote some of its most important pages.[8] This appears to have been a very rich period for Diderot's political and philosophical reflection: he wrote "Galiani's Apology" (1770), "Conversation of a Father with His Children" (1771), and *Jacques the Fatalist* (1771). It was also a troubled period of the author's life, for he was caught in an unhappy love affair and was being criticized by his brother, a man of the Church, over his daughter's marriage. It is clear that both his personal problems and his research have precise echoes in the text of the *Supplement*, in those sections dealing with sexual relations as well as social and political organization.

Bougainville's work brought a sort of confirmation of his theories, unexpected proof from a faraway, as yet completely unknown island that humanity was not necessarily doomed to a destiny of moral rigidity and political tyranny. However, the scholar and sailor had limited himself, despite his obvious enthusiasm, to rather strict reportage. Diderot would have liked to know more or to read, in the navigator's own words, about his thoughts and hopes; he therefore extended the text, added on a "supplement," while claiming no other rights than those accorded to a work of fiction.

To this end he imagined a scene in which two characters, referred to simply as A and B, who have just read *A Voyage around the World*, discuss its contents and author in terms both social and philosophical. One of them ("B," who obviously represents Diderot himself) informs the other of the existence of another text by Bougainville, a manuscript unknown to the public, which has mysteriously appeared on a table in the garden in which the two friends are strolling. The manuscript contains a speech by an old Tahitian who is hostile to the newcomers, as well as a dialogue between the expedition's chaplain and a young inhabitant named Orou. (It should be noted that Bougainville's chaplain never set eyes on Tahiti, for he died in a dramatic stopover in Uruguay.) One may well ask what exactly the *Supplement* is — a supposed manuscript by Bougainville or the entire narrative, the dialogue of A and B which incorporates that text? The answer is certainly that it is both — and, further, Diderot's own text is without doubt his most compelling philosophical fable.

At this point, of course, we encounter the issue of versimilitude, a problem formulated for the reader by one of the characters: "The [old man's] oration strikes me as forceful enough, but underneath a somewhat abrupt and savage tone I detect what seem to be a few European ideas and turns of phrase" (p. 86). To which the other replies: "You must remember that it is a translation from Tahitian into Spanish and from Spanish into French. . . . Orou wrote down the old man's harangue in Spanish, and Bougainville had a copy of it in his hand while the old man was speaking" (p. 86). Aside from the fact that this last detail hardly adds the desired credibility, the Tahitians' knowledge of Spanish makes no sense if one does not also realize that Diderot had learned from Bougainville himself that Fernandez de Queiro had undoubtedly discovered the island late in the sixteenth century. However, that navigator was Portuguese, not Spanish; even if one chooses to overlook this error, one might be surprised by the expediency of the approach. It is clear that Diderot was trying to prove something, and that the search for historical confirmation is a sign of this desire. In short, even if the author realized that his cultivated readers would not be fooled by this tactic, he was seeking above all the authoritativeness of firsthand testimony, which would appear to guarantee the validity of his reasoning, whose emotional power he was well aware of. This shows us, at the same time, how important this essay was for Diderot, as evidenced in this remark by B: "Bougainville's account of his voyage is the only book that has ever given me the taste for a country other than my own. Until reading it, I had always thought that one is never so well off as when one is home" (p. 80).

There are two central points to his argument. The first concerns the relationship between European civilization (whose received ideas Diderot vigorously questions) and the inevitability of change in societies; the second has to do with the relativity of customs and above all the great freedom in Tahitian practices of love. The second point is without doubt the main one in Diderot's view. However, this relativistic and libertarian conception of traditions and cultures can only be viewed as part of an entire philosophy of nature and a reflection on the goals of political institutions. All this is subtly interwoven in this philosophical dialogue, where the conversation between the two Parisians is a constant counterpoint to the utterances of the two Tahitian characters.

Meteorology, Philosophy

> A. When we returned home yesterday evening the sky was
> like a splendid vault studded with stars. But evidently it
> has broken its promise of good weather (p. 76).

The text begins, surprisingly, with a discussion of the weather. From the opening lines, it is not at all clear that the weather in question is that of the day before – unless one realizes that in Diderot's eyes the *Supplement* was the continuation of a tale entitled "Madame de la Carlière." The chatting pair, A and B, had already appeared there, and their conversations were indeed interspersed with observations on the movements of the clouds, the twinkling of the stars, and the rising of the mist. Was this simply an attempt to provide a backdrop against which to situate the characters? If so, it was rather unsuccessful. Something else is being shown, the intrusion by nature itself into human discourse, its powerful presence, its calm, immemorial indifference. The philosophers are no more than anonymous ciphers designated by the first two letters of the alphabet, two human voices lost in the concert of the physical world. We are thus shown, from the very beginning, the relative proportions that Diderot proposes to establish among social institutions, cultural and moral facts, and metaphysical theories, on one hand, and the natural universe in its incomparable naked richness, on the other. Clearly, for Diderot there is an arrogance in man that must be brought down; he invites us to recognize our modest place in the grand scheme and to acknowledge that we are but a moment, a tiny parcel in the cosmos. He seems to be trying to tell us that we think too much, or rather that it is our capacity for thought that produces explanations like the religions and the metaphysical systems that are the single cause of our misfortunes. For it is in the name of their beliefs that men have always killed one another, enslaved their brothers, and made the history of civilizations one long series of horrors. Not that we must give up that which constitutes our greatness in relation to other species; but our talents should be used only for spreading useful knowledge and establishing institutions and ideas that will simply enable us to occupy our rightful place in the republic of natural beings. Restoring mankind's modesty before that which is Other is, in Diderot's view, the first step to wisdom.

Thus, by attending to meteorology he reminds us of the vanity of ideology (a term, it should be noted, that will not appear until later in the century): it is a way of saying that the only legitimate philosophy is one that accepts and understands the world in its material truth. Furthermore, much as we are directly defined as natural beings by our bodies, it may well be that our philosophy is simply an emanation of our physical constitution; we must therefore not doubt, writes Diderot, that "the condition of our organs and our senses greatly influences our metaphysics and our morals, and that our most purely intellectual ideas, if I may say so, are largely derived from the shape of our bodies."[9]

The Code of Nature

Starting in the late fifteenth century, Europe's discovery of multiple cultures brought about a tendency toward skepticism among philosophers. Montaigne opened the debate stunningly with his essay "Of Cannibals," along with many other pages of his *Essays*, such as those having to do with this custom.[10] When civilizations were compared, the purely local character of many taboos and constraints on behavior became clear, thus questioning the two major sources of untouchable spiritual dogma, the Bible and the body of texts handed down from classical antiquity. People then had the audacity to proclaim that the mores of the Hebrews, the Greeks, and the Romans were not very different from those of the Iroquois, Tupinambas, or other peoples; consequently, the former could not be considered models of morality by virtue of their link to the religious, philosophical, and literary texts that formed the basis of traditional thought in the West.

Against this background of doubt, an intellectual crisis regarding the historical and cultural foundations of our judgments arose, and with it the need for a new, stable, and incontestable referent – nature – and for a reliable instrument with which to decipher its message. The

Renaissance and the classical age had clearly defined this instrument: reason. Thus, it came to be understood that knowledge could no longer be based on written revelation or on the meditation on a body of canonical texts but, rather, must be furnished by reading another text written in a language even more primal, the physical world itself. Whence the metaphor of the book, particularly pervasive among the Italian neo-Platonists, which has been applied to it from this time on. For Descartes this world is even the "Great Book" that he chose to study, turning his back on libraries.

All the philosophers staked a claim on nature; not all found in it the same text, nor did all speak the same language. But for all of them it clearly formed the basis of all cultural and political institutions, the foundation of all the fruits of human activity or conventions. How was its message to be deciphered? How could one be sure, on a question of such grave importance – the criteria of truth – to speak in a way guaranteed to be universal? Diderot answered that our guide, in this quest, must be science, which questioned nature in its materiality and the objectivity of its laws. The thinker should be motivated by the spirit of science, and it was by the privileged path of science that he might understand the ways by which nature expressed itself in human activity and institutions.

One might say, then, that Diderot was a materialist – but his was a happy, even "enchanted" materialism, to borrow Elisabeth de Fontenay's expression.[11] There is in him a kind of joy in recognizing our finiteness and the ability to admit that man is indeed but one living being among others, a being composed of many particles, but an amazing one, like nature itself, ceaselessly producing other beings – those born of sexual reproduction as well as those born of his intelligence and his art. Taken in the totality of the universe and the movement of matter, man should be able to live, like all beings, according to the internal law of his nature. This is the call of happiness itself: "My wish to be happy is the first article of a Code which precedes all legislation, and of every religious system."[12] Such is the essential intuition that dominated Diderot's thought during this period, the "mature" period that followed his melancholy years of 1760–62.[13] He then saw, with a kind of exaltation, the relationship that existed between an understanding of the physical world and the need for a moral norm corresponding to the spontaneous activity of living beings. This intuition underlies the theories of the "Supplement," especially the critique of European familial and conjugal institutions.

But what is materialism? At the very least, simply this: for Diderot,

the universe of physical phenomena and that of human phenomena
are one and the same, or, rather, the latter is the expression of the former.
This is what constitutes the unity of what he calls "nature." The consequences of such a position are obvious: history, culture, and customs
can neither be considered separately nor granted a privileged status,
for human history is a moment in natural history. Here Diderot becomes
a student of Georges-Louis Buffon. This approach defines his method
concerning politics and morality as much as it does his most general
philosophical positions. Regarding institutions, traditions, mores, rituals, taboos, responsibilities, and customs, he says, we must always ask
what nature tells us. Does its voice speak through these practices,
or is it completely stifled and unrecognizable? If other laws are added
to those it dictates, how can man discern his duty and live in harmony
with his equals? Diderot starts with this affirmation:

> We live under three Codes, the Code of nature, the civil Code, the religious
> Code. It is obvious that as long as these three kinds of laws contradict
> each other it is impossible to be virtuous. It will sometimes be necessary
> to trample on nature to obey social institutions; and sometimes we will have
> to go against social institutions to follow the precepts of religion. What
> will be the result? It is that, by turns contravening these different authori-
> ties, we shall respect none; and that we shall be neither men, nor citizens,
> nor devout. [14]

This passage from the *Histoire des deux Indes* (1783) repeats almost
word for word a passage in the *Supplement*; it is one of Diderot's central
hypotheses. For him, the only true code is the natural code; the civil
code is its translation into restrictive societies, whereas the religious
code can be only a distortion of it, if not its negation. In a letter to
Grimm he confirms this clearly: "What makes men unhappy is not the
law of nature. It is our opinions and the prejudices that we have dared
set up against it ... the code of the Republic should be the interpretation of nature's code." [15]
    For Diderot – and this is what makes his materialism so original –
institutions as well as techniques are defined as an extension of nature.
Indeed, for him every good law is necessarily inspired by nature's
code; why, then, are not laws the same everywhere? Here Diderot follows Montesquieu: the differences come from climates and the other
natural determinants (fertility of soil, altitude, temperature, the proximity and kind of water, and so on). The need for adaptation produces differing traditions but the moral sense remains essentially the

same: "Everywhere justice and injustice are recognized, but these ideas are not universally applied to the same actions."[16] This remarkable observation evokes the subtitle of the *Supplement*: *On the Difficulties of Attaching Moral Ideas to Certain Physical Acts That Carry No Such Implications*.

Here we find Diderot's constant intuition that ideas – everything concerning judgments, values, moral determinations – are not themselves related to certain objects, contrary to popular opinion. Our sense of fairness and unfairness, good and evil, is certainly innate, but each society attaches it to this or that object, links it to this or that circumstance in virtue of local determinations that may depend on chance or caprice. Thus, what is a sin for some is a virtue for others and what is monstrous for us is the norm among others – or vice versa. Thus, very lucidly, Diderot has Orou say to the chaplain: "But you cannot condemn the ways of Europe for not being those of Tahiti, nor our ways for not being those of Europe. You need a more dependable rule of judgment than that. And what shall it be? Do you know a better one than general welfare and individual utility?" (p. 98).

Pleasure and Sociability: The Right to Happiness

The desire and the freedom to seek pleasure are the only two sources of action, the only two principles of sociability among men.[17]

Unlike Rousseau, who viewed passion as something that could obstruct knowledge of the general will and therefore preclude the formation of the social ties on which political society is built, Diderot saw a profound continuity between natural energy and social existence. Desire naturally drives us toward each other, and the shared nature of this desire keeps us together. This principle of sensual pleasure is, in a way, the nonutilitarian version of the "invisible hand," and is the transcending principle of this naturalistic philosophy: "If man is made only to work, harvest, eat, and sell, all is well. But it seems to me that a creature who feels is made to be happy in all his thoughts.... I want society to be happy but I also want the citizen to be happy, and there are as many ways of being happy as there are individuals. Our own happiness is the foundation of all our true duties."[18]

Everyone produces the happiness of others by seeking his own, for the result is the harmony of passions and thus social peace. This optimism startlingly foreshadows what was to become Sade's position (very clearly expressed in "Yet Another effort, Frenchman"); one might say, moreover, that Diderot views the social tie as an effect of "generalized pleasure."[19] Very obviously, this is contrary to Rousseau's idea of morality, as well as to Kant's. Just as obvious, however, is the fact that to maintain this position Diderot must grant Rousseau his hypothesis of original goodness: "Nature did not make us evil; bad education, bad examples, bad laws corrupt us."[20] At the same time, he borrows from Hobbes the idea of the "artificial man," except that for Hobbes this expression refers to the kind of society that brings an end to the state of war, whereas for Diderot it means the moral posturing that brings an end to peace. This, indeed, is what the *Supplement* says: "Shall I outline for you the brief history of nearly all our unhappiness? It is simply this: Once there was a natural man; then an artificial man was built up inside him. Since then a civil war has been raging continuously within him. Sometimes the natural man proves stronger; at other times he is laid low by the artificial, moral man" (p. 109).

Here Diderot seems to be touching on a sort of contradiction, for if it is true that social nature is born of sensual pleasure, how may we explain the birth of this artificial man? What process permitted his emergence? Diderot does not say. However, since elsewhere he praises industry, commerce, the production of wealth – in rigorous opposition to Rousseau this time – how can he consider *artifice* to be the root of all our ills? Is Diderot contradicting himself? One might think so unless one understands that the artifice he denounces is uniquely moral: it is neither conventions (necessary for all communal life) nor the possessions and splendors of civilization (sources of well-being) nor the sciences and technologies (sources of freedom and progress) that corrupt men, nor, indeed, the passions, which remain good as long as they express natural energy. It is only prejudices that do so – and these, according to Diderot, are essentially religious. In sum, what is artificial is not society but morality, and not just any morality, but the morality of taboos and arbitrary rules. Rousseau declares that man is good, but it is society that perverts him; Diderot replies that society too is good, but it is religion that perverts it. Thus, he writes to Mme d'Epinay about the cruelty of the Iroquois, "Who has corrupted these Iroquois? The gods, my friend, the gods.... There is not a single country, a single people among whom God's orders have not consecrated some crime."[21] Civil law should serve to make concrete and apply natural law, but religion, which has no legitimacy, brings unhappiness for no reason, steps in and disturbs both. Its sole use is to guarantee the power of those who hold sway over the masses of believers.

Thus, it is clear that, for Diderot, the critique of religion conditions and precedes all other critiques. This is why it is not the scholar or the philosopher but the *priest* that he chooses to embody, in all its aspects, the absurd character of the taboos of European society. When political institutions are bad, it is because they have been shaped by the arbitrariness of religious beliefs. Hence, the conversation in the *Supplement* between Orou and the chaplain, immediately after addressing the notion of a single God, creator of the universe, passes directly to a debate on conjugal morality. Orou's naive questions demonstrate the existential contradictions of the Christian God, eternal but ageless, the armless worker, fatherly and kind, but the maker of arbitrary decisions about good and evil. They also show how strange it is to hold, as the chaplain does, that the two sexes, which were made in order to come together, cannot do so without being condemned, without appropriating one another, without vowing an unreasonable faithfulness. To Orou this is surprising, to the chaplain embarrassing – for he is forced to recognize that all these rules of which he speaks are very little respected. The chaplain's admission allows Diderot to speak his mind through Orou:

> OROU: And are your legislators severe in handing out punishment to such disobedient people or not? If they are, then they are wild animals who war against nature; if they are not severe, they are fools who risk bringing contempt upon their authority by issuing futile prohibitions.
> THE CHAPLAIN: The guilty ones, if they escape the rigor of the laws, are punished by public opinion.
> OROU: That's like saying that justice is done by means of the whole nation's lack of common sense, and that public folly is the substitute for law (pp. 92–93).

This "public folly" is what we have already met as the power of prejudice; in Diderot's view, it is the inevitable outcome of imposing interpretations on physical phenomena (such as the actions of living beings), which are simply the result of a natural law. And if there is an area where the relationship between an action and a moral idea is completely without basis, it is surely in that of sexual relations. These activities are not "susceptible to any morality" according to the *Supplement*, whence the subtitle – *On the Difficulties of Attaching Moral Ideas to Certain Physical Acts That Carry No Such Implications*. Yet social, moral, and religious rules have proliferated around these activities. Here Diderot clearly displays his naturalism: sexuality is within the realm of reproduction and, through individuals, it is the species that decides and enforces its laws. These matters can thus be left to nature, which in this area can make its own laws directly – and, indeed, it does so. Nature repays with pleasure, health, and serenity those who use it in a natural way, and it punishes with suffering, illness, and worry the excesses of those who violate its laws. This is why human conventions are completely useless and even dangerous in matters relating to love relationships; at best they can merely hamper natural and spontaneous movement, and at worst they heap sin and punishment onto something that nature intended for our happiness. This, for Diderot, is one of the most disgraceful aspects of our civilized world.

Such is the lesson that the decidedly Diderotian Orou gives the chaplain: for him the Europeans described by the priest must be hypocrites and extremely unhappy creatures. But the unhappiness from which we suffer is the sign that the voice of nature has not yet been silenced, that its law survives beneath our posturing – and we need only follow it, giving up our wild ideas and dangerous conventions. The priest yields to this argument. The debate had begun when, faced with the amorous advances of Orou's wife and daughters, he had protested, crying out, "But my religion, my holy orders!" He winds up spending a night with each of them and admitting that he regrets mightily having to leave the island.

Savage Calculation, or the Economy of Seduction

Should we conclude that Diderot is calling for a sort of generalized libertinage? This would be an overly hasty and incorrect reading of the *Supplement*. If the Tahitians' mores appear to be quite free (to the point, in Diderot's naive view, of according no significance to incest) this is because individuals are left to follow the law of nature, hence their rights to the joys of sexual attraction are recognized. But at this point – judiciously, this time – Diderot invokes an argument involving cultural differences: what Europeans consider seductive behavior is not necessarily so for Tahitians, for their sexuality is not the same as ours. One of the two philosophers (B, to be precise) points this out to the other, contrasting Europe and Tahiti in this regard: "To be considered beautiful there [in Europe] a woman must have a high color, a wide forehead, a small mouth, large eyes, finely modeled features, a narrow waist, and small hands and feet.... Here [in Tahiti], scarcely one of these things is of any importance. The woman who attracts the most admirers and the most lovers is the one who seems most likely to bear many children [...] and whose children seem likely to be active, intelligent, brave, healthy, and strong" (p. 96).

This brings to mind the dialogue between Orou and the priest on this point (which takes up a very large part of their debate):

> THE CHAPLAIN: You spoke about the children that a wife brings to her husband as dowry.
>
> OROU: Certainly. [...] The more children our girls have, the more desirable they are. The stronger and lustier our young men are, the richer they become. Therefore, careful as we are to protect our young girls from male advances and our young boys from intercourse with women before they reach sexual maturity, once they have passed the age of puberty [...] (pp. 94–95).

Thus, the sexual freedom that Bougainville and his men had found was not without its own rules; rather, it was part of a precise system of organization of sexual relations between men and women, which, as Orou explains, are prohibited before the ceremonies that distribute the rights of each. Moreover, this freedom is granted only for the purpose of procreation. In sum, Diderot reassures us that his fable of freedom is not an apology for amorality but, rather, it speaks to us of the implementation of the laws of nature, meaning the search for balance, prosperity, and well-being. In this way nature itself reestablishes a morality that has been weakened above all by its artificial forms. This new conception of morality is not a set of arbitrary taboos but instead the will of the species as inscribed in individuals. Diderot accepts nature's wisdom exactly in the manner that a good father wisely manages the prosperity of his inheritance: as conceived by Diderot, nature speaks the language of an upstanding burgher of the day –it looks ahead, invests, limits risks, and expects dividends from its investments.

Orou then admits the truth about the Tahitians' welcome:

> Shall I tell you a secret? But be careful not to let it out. When you came, we let you do what you liked with our women and girls. You were astonished and your gratitude made us laugh. You thanked us, even though we were levying the heaviest of all taxes on you and your companions. We asked no money of you; we didn't loot your ship; we didn't give a hang for any of your stores of food – but our women and girls came to draw the blood out of your veins. When you go away, you will leave us with a brood of children. Do you think we could have extracted a more valuable tribute from you than this tax collected from your own bodies and from your own substance? (p. 101).

So what looked to some like libertinage was, for the others, a very reasonable calculation. The priest should have heeded Orou's earlier words, in which this very economic conception of procreation appeared: "A child is a precious thing because it will grow up to be a man or a woman. [...] The birth of a child is the occasion for public celebration and a source of joy for its entire family. For the hut it means an increase in wealth, while for the nation it signifies additional strength. It means another pair of hands and arms for Tahiti" (p. 94).

Diderot, the Physiocrats, and Rousseau (in harmony, for once, with their time) held to one well-established principle: the human race has the obligation to propagate. Procreation is even, according to some, the first duty of every citizen.[22] Rousseau constantly stresses the need for increasing the population, for example, asserting in the *Social Contract* that this par excellence is "the sign of a good government."[23] As he writes in his "Constitutional Project for Corsica," it is a matter of supplying bodies for agriculture. Diderot consistently returns to the same argument: "Living and breeding being the goal of all species, it seems that sociability, if it is one of the major facilities of man that leads him to the social state, should necessarily guide all the moral and political laws toward the outcome of a longer and happier existence for the majority of men."[24]

Nature, then, is wise: as it rules the natural species and assigns precise goals to them, it also seeks an equilibrium for mankind's behaviors that is profitable for all. It is as if Diderot found in the name of utility a morality that he had previously excluded in the name of lust – "...since a child is an object of both interest and value, you can understand that it is rare to find libertine women among us and that our young men keep away from them" (p. 97). As if having said, "Don't go against nature, get rid of absurd taboos," Diderot were concluding that sensuality is not some egotistical and wild pleasure, this liberty is not libertinage, nature does not want to be restrained, but nor is it trying to destroy society. Nature is prudent, wise, in short, *economical.* This is why the savage is not wild; he is as calculating and management-minded as the European. In fact, he is more so: his skillful economy starts at the very point where the European's leaves off, or at best where it admits a modicum. Nature begins with the domain of pleasure, reins it in, supervises it, and finally guides it to the goal that is useful to society. The economy of pleasure manages pleasure itself, and it is the first sign of a wisdom that confounds our reason. Thus, Wilda Anderson justifiably declares, "The *Supplément* is, therefore, an antiutopian text. It is not a negative utopia, but a text constructed against the

very utopian impulse itself defined as a nostalgia for fixity and universality, whether natural or cultural. Necessarily belied by the dynamic
of the material world, a utopia is not a model to aim for, therefore, but
a philosophical trap to be avoided. It leads to alienation from the dy-
namically material world and hence to cultural atrophy and oblivion."[25]

Thus, one kind of nature may conceal another: beneath the one that
seemed to speak only the language of pleasure lay another that spoke
the language of interest. The second does not contradict the first,
it simply assigns it a goal – equilibrium, prosperity, and harmony. By
way of economics, Diderot has returned pleasure to morality without
having to depart from the code of nature. However, such an achievement may well rest on one of the major shortcomings of Enlightenment thought.

Naturalism, Functionalism

Diderot, indeed, viewed his Tahitians as Physiocrats to a certain extent,
and he assumed that the dowry system, which existed in European
societies, must have been more or less the same among other peoples.
It is surprising that so many commentators, succumbing to Diderot-
Orou's reasoning, have not been more suspicious of the ethnographic
contents of this rationalist fable. One would assume, reading these
commentaries, that the *Supplement* was a primary source on the Tahitian
matrimonial system. These authors should have known (as we all
should) that in traditional societies, whether we call them "primitive"
or not, the dowry system does not exist; what exists everywhere, on
the contrary, is exogamous marriage, wherein the acquirers of brides are
in debt to the group from which the bride comes. Thus, it is the
man who offers gifts to the appropriate members of the other group. If
one insists on speaking about a dowry, one must realize that it is the
duty of the husband. Such was the case in Tahiti as everywhere else. In
works ranging from Lewis Morgan to Claude Lévi-Strauss, this is one
of the best-documented points of modern anthropology. We cannot, of
course, blame Diderot for not knowing this, but it is nevertheless
important to stress one of the major faults of Enlightenment thinkers,
which was to impute a universal nature to their own society's practices and ways of thinking. In this way their critical rigor was obviously more limited than they realized. The curious result in the
Supplement is that Diderot, believing that he is giving voice to nature
in its earliest origins, turned his savage into a perfect representative
of the species of Homo oeconomicus that was then taking hold in Western civilization. The error, then, is twofold: one in the ethnographic

domain (the dowry), the other in the philosophical domain (the economic interpretation of procreation).

Although it would be unfair to fault the philosopher for a lack of knowledge that was widespread, we must not forget that the primary objective of the *Supplement* was to capture the attention of its readers, and that, considering the system of thought prevalent at that time, it was a striking attempt to view things from the perspective of the Other. But investing that perspective with one's own ideas, no matter how generous, runs the risk of turning the Other into a ventriloquist mouthing one's own thought (as is obviously the case with the character of Orou). Diderot's stance is polemical. The concept of nature serves, above all, as a way to challenge the religious and moral prejudices of his time, the only stable referent henceforth available – whence the temptation among Enlightenment thinkers to connect everything to this nature whose universality was seen as the opposite of our errors, and therefore to adopt naturalism, the tendency to explain facts of culture solely in terms of material conditions and limits. Several significant examples appear in Diderot, such as the explanation of cannibalism by the scarcity of food in the islands:

> A: What will become of them if they continue multiplying on a little spit of land that is less than three miles across?
>
> B: Probably they will kill themselves off by eating each other. Perhaps, in the very condition of island life are the origins of a very ancient and very natural cannibalism (p. 79).

Diderot foreshadows the type of explanation characteristic of the English-speaking functionalist school, from Lewis Henry Morgan through Bronislaw Malinowski to G.P. Murdock, which postulates that every social institution corresponds to a physical need.[26] Indeed, the image of a rough and rustic savage, even viewed in a positive light, reinforces all the more the type of humanity still tightly linked to elementary needs – one that, furthermore, is gratuitously doomed to a difficult material existence, marked by the laborious quest for food.[27] Whence his "savagery" – that is, his crudeness or even cruelty – the extreme consequence of his naturalness, as evidenced in the "Supplement" by this remark: "Apparently they acquire their harsh character from the daily necessity of defending themselves against wild animals – at least this may explain what many travelers have observed. Whenever his peace and safety are not disturbed, the savage is innocent and gentle" (p. 80).

Another problem, again an instance of the philosopher's naïveté, concerns the critique of conventions, hence the image of the savage as a man without laws or, rather, man governed only by the law of nature. He is assumed to be very close to his original state, for it is only later, it is said, that man "policed" himself and thereby acquired social organization and public institutions. This prejudice is a constant from the jurisconsults to Rousseau, and it even survives in the Freudian theory of the primitive horde. Ethnographic studies in this century have in fact shown that every society appears thoroughly organized according to a kinship system.

Diderot's naturalism, which was shared by all his contemporaries, reveals to us both the greatness and the limits of Enlightenment anthropology. Its greatness lies in having challenged its own tradition and attempted to relativize its own viewpoint by acquiring a solid basis for implementing this critique; yet this basis, the concept of nature, was also a source of confusion, provoking as it did perhaps as many prejudices as it eliminated. For the philosopher, believing that he has captured nature in its purest state, sure that he is hearing its voice from the bottom of his soul, does not realize that his own inner being, far from the font of origins, is heaped with the sediment of his culture. The main problem of Enlightenment thought, then, is the blind spot created by the very source of its light.

The critical point is the following: when all civilizations are traced to one common natural origin, they are treated as so many expressions of the same entity, varying from each other merely accoding to their climate and geography. By the same token, religion, viewed by d'Holbach as a result of fear and the personalization of the natural elements, becomes nothing more than a manifestation of superstition, while customs are judged as neither legitimate nor illegitimate. They exist everywhere, apparently, but can just as well be shaken off; only those that can be justified before the court of reason are worthy of being kept. It is precisely on this point that the Enlightenment's universalist and functionalist thought falls short. Moreover, it would become the inspiration for all the gratuitous general theories that sprouted during the nineteenth century, concerning the ages of humanity, the differences between the races, the origins of matriarchy, the reasons for totemism, the incest taboo, cannibalism, and so on. Only the patient and laborious fieldwork undertaken in this century by ethnographers has allowed us to understand that the same needs do not necessarily produce the same institutions if, indeed, they produce any at all. We should even say, with Marshall Sahlins, that it is rather the forms of civilizations that define needs, which is to say, confer on them both content and specific functions.[28]

Nor can the problem of religion be reduced to the two principles outlined by d'Holbach. We now understand better how beliefs, myths, and rituals form part of a vast arrangement of symbolic systems, the ordering, classifying, and poetic forms of thought. Religious representations organize the world on the basis of perceived experience, environmental conditions, technical developments, contact with other groups, even as they imbue this experience with an intense emotional value that constitutes the particularity of symbolic phenomena. Yet this is an entirely different question from that of the institutional organization of beliefs linked to the emergence of a clerical caste exercising power over a given society. That phenomenon (to which the phenomenon of religion must not be reduced) totally obscured the other one from the eyes of Enlightenment thinkers.

Love, Freedom, Property

Nevertheless, Diderot did not struggle in vain. The fact that the rationalism of his era – and his own – propagated as many illusions as it denounced did not prevent it from posing new, urgent questions in the face of injustice. It is to his and a few other thinkers' great credit to have admitted them – to have had the intellectual courage not only to formulate them but also to have defended the answers at the cost of their personal tranquillity. In the *Supplement* Diderot sees the relation between the freedom of mores and colonization in a completely new light. He gives an exemplary demonstration of the ways in which men's domination of women is analogous to Western domination over the savage. In both cases we are faced with comparable claims of appropriation, and this idea is clearly stated: no human may enslave another or make him his property. This is why Orou criticizes the chaplain and considers his precepts:

> contrary to nature because they assume that a thinking being, one with feelings and freedom, can be the property of another being like himself. On what could such a right of ownership be founded? Do you not see that in your country you have confused things that have no feelings, thoughts, desires or will – things one takes or leaves, keeps or sells, without them suffering or complaining – with the thing that can neither be bought nor sold, which has freedom, volition, and desires of its own, which has the ability to give or to withhold itself for a moment or forever, which suffers

and complains? This latter thing can never be treated like a trader's stock
of goods unless one forgets what its true character is and does violence
to nature (pp. 90–91).

At the same time, Diderot defines the limits to the naturalism he
constantly defended: all beings are not at the same level, for there
is a difference, marked by the idea of freedom. In this, Diderot is no
doubt closer to Rousseau than he thinks, and he foreshadows what was
to become Kant's major theory: the order of freedom is incommen-
surable with the order of nature, even if it is always in relation to nature
(which we may take to mean the universe of objective laws) that this
freedom is exercised.

The paradox and the difficulty of Diderot's thought is that, for
him, this message of freedom is expressed through the voice of nature,
which cries out against institutional oppression. This becomes clear
when he has B say: "Yet nature's sovereignty cannot be destroyed; it
will persist in spite of all obstacles" (p. 108). So it is nature, seen as
original truth, that is in favor of man's liberty, which is more than natural. We have here the strange conflicting strands that make Diderot's
position so complex: because man is free, he is capable of perversion.
In this way he is the cause of the nefarious institutions that restrict
him. He must therefore return to nature and hear its voice again, in
order to regain this more-than-natural freedom. Nature provides a criterion of truth that becomes necessary for the evaluation of human
institutions, which are generated by a liberty that oversteps and obscures
the original equilibrium.

Nature and the Inner Savage

This is Diderot's solution, and his way of combining the philosophical
question with the encounter of exotic civilizations. But where to find
natural man? Is he the savage that was then being discovered around
the world? Yes and no, replies Diderot, for this natural man is entirely
present in each of us and is indestructible – and because of this, he can
constitute the absolute reference point for any moral system and any
institution. We must, then, find him in his pure state in order to gain
access to the standard by which we may reform society. Each man
must find him in himself, even though it is not easy to discern him
under the layers of "artificial man." Thus, the encounter with the
savage man was so valuable, because this man embodies humanity's
childhood: in him, the truth of natural man still shines forth. The
savage is not more natural than we are; his naturalness is simply more

transparent. He is the intact evidence of what we are beneath our trappings. He tells us what we have been, and that we can always bring it back. As B notes, European civilization is old, and like everything that is old, it is more molded by its acquisitions than by its own natural dispositions. In this Diderot shared with the other philosophers a historicist conception of the relations between cultures; his originality, though, consists in seeing more advantages in the beginnings than in what follows. But because his vision is strictly a naturalistic one, he does not doubt that every civilization must age and that savages, even without meeting Westerners, would necessarily have evolved in the direction of what we are. We think we are discovering the savage; in reality he comes toward us, just as the river flows into the ocean, just as the current flows in the direction of its slope. Our present is his future; our destiny has been promised to him. For Diderot, though, this incontrovertible fact about civilizations contains its inverse: the savage survives in each of us and bears witness to the time when nature spoke out loud. His past remains our present in the scattered but still vital signs of our origins: "I have sometimes thought of all the trees planted around our kings' palaces —the sight of a bodice that both reveals and conceals a woman's breasts suggests the same idea — and in both instances I seem to detect a secret wish to escape into the forest, a suppressed impulse to recapture the freedom of our old habitat" (pp. 106–107).

NOTES

1. Denis Diderot, "D'Alembert's Dream" (1769), in *Rameau's Nephew/D'Alembert's Dream* (New York: Penguin, 1966), pp. 230-31. Publication of Diderot's works remains unfinished. The most recent edition, begun in 1975 and still in progress, is that of Hebert Dikermann, Jacques Proust, and Jean Varlot (Paris: Editions Hermann). Azézat and Touneux's edition, 1875-1877 in twenty volumes, despite its gaps, remains the authoritative one; it is cited as "AT," followed by the volume and page numbers. The quotations from Diderot's correspondence refer to the edition by G. Roth and J. Varlot (Paris: Editions de Minuit, 1955-), under the title *Correspondance*. The quotations from *L'Histoire des deux Indes* refer to Raynal's work (in which Diderot's contributions are clearly identified) *Histoire philosophique et politique des établissements et du commerce des Européens dans les deux Indes* (Neuchâtel and Geneva: Libraires associés, 1783).

Among the excellent works on Diderot, not mentioned below, are: Yvon Belaval,

L'Esthétique sans paradoxe de Diderot (Paris: Maspéro, 1971), ch. 5; and Jacques Proust, *Diderot et l'Encyclopédie* (Paris: A. Colin, 1967).

2. Louis-Antoine de Bougainville, *A Voyage around the World*, trans. John Reinhold Forster (London: J. Nourse, 1772), pp. 217–19.

3. *Ibid.*, pp. 227–28.

4. *Ibid.*, p. 228.

5. "Bougainville possessed the necessary scientific preparation and the requisite personal qualities – a philosophical attitude, courage, and veracity; he had a quick eye for comprehending things without wasting time in observations; he had caution, patience, and a real desire to see, to educate himself; he knew the sciences of mathematics, mechanics, geometry, astronomy; and he was sufficiently acquainted with natural history" (*Supplement*, p. 77).

6. Bougainville, *A Voyage around the World*, p. 269.

7. *Ibid.*, pp. 256, 257.

8. Diderot, "AT," vol. 1, p. 228.

9. See Michèle Duchet, *Diderot et L'Histoire des deux Indes ou l'écriture fragmentaire* (Paris: A.G. Nizet, 1978).

10. Michel de Montaigne, *Essays* (New York: Knopf, 1934), vol. 1, chs. 23, 31.

11. Elisabeth de Fontenay, *Diderot: Reason and Resonance* (New York: G. Braziller, 1982).

12. Diderot, *Observations sur le Nakaz*, in *Political Writings*, trans. and eds. John Hope Mason and Robert Walker (Cambridge: Cambridge University Press, 1992), p. 101.

13. Georges May, *Quatre visages de Diderot* (Paris: Bovin, 1951), ch. 2.

14. Diderot, *L'Histoire des deux Indes*, in Raynal, *Histoire philosophique*, vol. 9, pp. 297–98.

15. Diderot, letter to Grimm, in Michèle Duchet, *Anthropologie et histoire au siècle des lumières* (Paris: Maspéro, 1971), p. 440.

16. Diderot, *L'Histoire des deux Indes*, in Raynal, *Histoire philosophique*, vol. 9, p. 296.

17. *Ibid.*, vol. 3, p. 98.

18. Diderot, *Observations sur le Nakaz*, p. 125.

19. This felicitous expression was used by Pierre Saint-Amand in *Les Lois de l'hostilité* (Paris: Seuil, 1992), ch. 5.

20. Diderot, letter of Nov. 1760, in *Correspondance*, vol. 3, p. 224.

21. Diderot, letter to Mme d'Epinay, Nov. 1760, in *Correspondance*, vol. 3, p. 227.

22. The populationist theory was upheld particularly by the Physiocrats, above all by Mirabeau in *L'Ami des hommes, ou Traité de la Population* (Paris and Hamburg, 1758).

23. Jean-Jacques Rousseau, *The Social Contract* (Harmondsworth, UK: Penguin, 1968), bk. 3, ch. 9.

24. Diderot, *L'Histoire des deux Indes*, in Raynal, *Histoire philosophique*, vol. 9, p. 40.

25. Wilda Anderson, *Diderot's Dream* (Baltimore: Johns Hopkins University Press, 1990), p. 152.

26. "The road from the wilderness to the savage's belly and consequently to his mind is very short, and for him is an indiscriminate background against which there stand out the useful, primarily the edible, species of animals or plants" (Bronislaw Malinowski, *Magic, Science and Religion* [Garden City, NY: Anchor, 1954], p. 44). This statement by Malinowski is vigorously contested by Lévi-Strauss in *Totemism* (Boston: Beacon Press, 1963), p. 57.

27. The ridiculousness of this stereotype is revealed by Marshall Sahlins in *Stone Age Economics* (Chicago: Adline-Atherton, 1972).

28. Marshall Sahlins, *Culture and Practical Reason* (Chicago: Chicago University Press, 1976).

Translated by Shelley Temchin.

SUPPLEMENT TO BOUGAINVILLE'S VOYAGE

Or, a Dialogue between A and B

On the Difficulties of Attaching Moral Ideas to Certain Physical Acts That Carry No Such Implications

by Denis Diderot

At quanto meliora monet, pugnantiaque istis,
Dives opis Naturae suae: tu si modo recte
Dispensare velis, ac non fugienda petendis
Immiscere! Tuo vitio rerumne labores,
Nil referre putas?[1]
— Horace, *Satires*

The Critical Account of Bougainville's Voyage

A. WHEN WE RETURNED home yesterday evening the sky was like a splendid vault studded with stars. But evidently it has broken its promise of good weather.

B. How can you be so sure?

A. The fog is so thick that you can't see the tops of the neighboring trees.

B. True enough. But if the fog only hangs low because the atmosphere near the ground is already heavy with moisture, it may condense and its moisture fall to the ground.

A. But, conversely, what if it rises higher, past this layer of moist air, into the upper levels where the air is less dense? Up there it may not be saturated, as the chemists say.

B. Nothing to do but wait and see.

A. And what will you do while you wait?

B. I'll read.

A. Still Bougainville's account of his voyage?

B. Yes.

A. I can't make heads or tails of that man. When he was young, he studied mathematics, which supposes a sedentary life. And now, suddenly, he abandons his retreat and his meditations and takes up the active, difficult, wandering, dissipated career of an explorer.

B. Not totally. A ship, after all, is only a floating house, and the sailor traversing enormous distances is shut up in a narrow little space in which he can barely move about. Look at it this way, and you will see how he can go around the globe on a plank, just as you and I can make a tour of the universe on your floor.

A. And another thing that's very odd – the disparity between the man's character and his undertaking. Bougainville has a taste for the amusements of society; he loves women, the theater, fine meals. He takes as easily to the social whirl as to the inconstancy of the elements that have knocked him about so much. He is cheerful and genial; he is a real Frenchman, ballasted on the port side with a treatise on integral and differential calculus, and to starboard with a voyage around the world.

B. He's only doing what everybody does – after a period of strenuous labor he looks for distraction, and after a period of distraction he looks for labor.

A. What's your opinion of his "Voyage"?

B. Well, so far as I can judge after a rather superficial reading, I would say that there are three chief merits: it gives us better knowledge of our old abode and its inhabitants, greater safety on the seas, which he sailed with a sounding line in hand, and better information for our cartographers. When he undertook his voyage, Bougainville possessed the necessary scientific preparation and the requisite personal qualities – a philosophical attitude, courage, and veracity; he had a quick eye for comprehending things without wasting time in observations; he had caution, patience, and a real desire to see, to educate himself; he knew the sciences of mathematics, mechanics, geometry, astronomy; and he was sufficiently acquainted with natural history.

A. What about his style?

B. Without affectation; just right for the subject, direct and clear, especially when one is familiar with the language of sailors.

A. Was it a long voyage?

B. I've marked his course on this globe. Do you see that line of red dots?

A. Which starts at Nantes?

B. Yes, and runs down to the Straits of Magellan, enters the Pacific Ocean, twists among the islands of the great archipelago extending from the Philippines to New Holland, touches Madagascar, the Cape of Good Hope, continues into the Atlantic, follows the coast of Africa, and finally concludes where the navigator embarked.

A. Did he have a very difficult time?

B. All navigators take risks, and accept the need to expose themselves to the perils of air, fire, earth, and water. But the worst hardship is that when he finally makes port somewhere after wandering for months between sea and sky, between life and death, after being battered by storms, risking death from shipwreck, disease, hunger, and thirst, having his ship all but torn apart under his feet — when he falls exhausted and destitute at the feet of a brazen monster and he is either refused the most urgent relief or made to wait interminably for it — it is very hard!

A. It's a crime that ought to be punished.

B. It's one of the disasters our explorer didn't reckon on.

A. And he shouldn't have had to. I had thought that the European powers were careful to send out to their possessions overseas only upright men of character and benevolent disposition, humane and sensitive to other people's distress...

B. Oh, yes, you may be sure they worry a lot about that!

A. Have you come across any oddities in this book of Bougainville's?

B. A great many.

A. Doesn't he report that wild animals often come right up to a human being, and that birds even fly down and perch on a man's shoulder, since they have not yet learned the danger of such familiarity?

B. He does, but others have said the same thing before.

A. How does he explain the presence of certain animals on islands that are separated from any continent by stretches of impassable sea? Who could have brought wolves, foxes, dogs, deer, or snakes to such places?

B. He doesn't explain it; he only confirms the fact.

A. Well, how do you explain it?

B. Who knows anything about the early history of our planet? How many pieces of land, now isolated, were once continents? The general direction of the mass of water between them is the only clue on which to base some theory of what might have happened.

A. What do you mean?

B. You would have to reason from the shape of the pieces that are missing. Some day we can have a good time working this problem out, if the idea suits you. But for the moment, do you see this island called Lancer's Island? Looking at the position it occupies on the globe, who wouldn't wonder how men ended up there? What means of communication were there between them and the rest of their species? What will become of them if they continue multiplying on a little spit of land that is less than three miles across?

A. Probably they will kill themselves off by eating each other. Perhaps, in the very condition of island life are the origins of a very ancient and very natural form of cannibalism.

B. Or population growth may be limited by some superstitious law – perhaps babies are crushed under the feet of a priestess while still in their mothers' wombs.

A. Or perhaps they slit the throat with the edge of a priest's knife. Or they take recourse to castration. . . .

B. Or some women undergo infibulation, and there would be the origin of many, many strange customs as cruel as they are necessary, the reasons for which have been lost in the darkness of the past and still torment philosophers. One rule that seems fairly universal is that supernatural and divine institutions seem to grow stronger the longer they remain in effect and are eventually transformed into national constitutions or civil laws. Similarly, national or civil institutions become sanctioned and degenerate into supernatural or divine precepts.

A. The worst sort of palingenesis.

B. It is just one more thread of the rope with which we are bound.

A. Wasn't Bougainville in Paraguay around the time the Jesuits were expelled from there?

B. Yes, he was.

A. What does he say about it?

B. Less than he might have said. But he does say enough to make it clear that those cruel sons of Sparta in black robes treated their Indian slaves as badly as the ancient Lacedemonians treated their helots. They forced them to work incessantly, grew rich on their sweat, deprived them of all property rights, kept them under the brutal influence of superstition, exacted the most extreme veneration, and strode among them whip in hand, beating them whether young or old, man or woman. In another century, it would have been impossible to get rid of them, or else the attempt would have touched off a long war between the monks and the sovereign, whose authority they had been undermining little by little.

A. And what about those Patagonian giants about whom Dr. Maty and La Condamine, the academician, made such a fuss?

B. They are good fellows who come running up to you and shout "Chaoua!" as they embrace you. They are strong and energetic, but the tallest of them stands no more than five feet five or six inches – there is nothing gigantic about them except their fatness, the largeness of their heads, and the thickness of their limbs.

Man is born with a taste for the marvelous, with a tendency to exaggerate everything he sees, so how should he be able to maintain a just proportion among the things he has seen, especially when he must, as it were, justify the long trip he has made and the trouble he has taken to go to some remote place to look at them?

A. And what does Bougainville think about the savages?

B. Apparently they acquire their harsh character from the daily necessity of defending themselves against wild animals – at least this may explain what many travelers have observed. Whenever his peace and safety are not disturbed, the savage is innocent and gentle. All warfare begins in conflicting claims over the same property. The civilized man has a claim which conflicts with that of another over the possession of a field of which they respectively occupy the two ends, and thus the field becomes the object of a dispute between them.

A. And the tiger has a conflicting claim with that of the savage over the possession of a forest. This must be the first case of conflicting claims as well as the most ancient cause of war.... Did you happen to see the Tahitian that Bougainville took aboard his vessel and brought back to this country?

B. Yes, I saw him. His name was Aotourou. When they first sighted land after leaving Tahiti, he mistook it for the voyagers' native country, whether because they had misrepresented the length of the voyage to him or because, being naturally misled by the smallness of the apparent distance from the seashore where he lived to the point at which the sky seemed to touch the horizon, he had no idea of the true size of the earth. The Tahitian custom of sharing all women was so firmly ingrained in his mind that he threw himself upon the first European woman who came near him, and he was preparing, in all seriousness, to render her one of the courtesies of Tahiti. He soon grew bored among us, though. Because the Tahitian alphabet has no *b, c, d, f, g, q, x, y*, or *z*, he could never learn to speak our language, which demanded too many strange articulations and new sounds from his inflexible mouth. He never ceased longing after his own country, and this doesn't surprise me. Bougainville's account of his voyage is the only book that has ever given me the taste for a country other than my own. Until reading it, I had always thought that one is never so well off as when one is home.

Consequently, I thought that everyone in the world must feel the same. All this is a natural result of the attraction of the soil, and this attraction is bound up with all the comforts one enjoys at home and is not certain of finding elsewhere.

A. What? Don't you find that the Parisian is just as certain that grain grows in the fields of the Roman countryside as in the fields of Beauce?

B. Honestly, no. Bougainville finally sent Aotourou back, after having provided for his expenses and made certain that he would arrive safely.

A. O Aotourou! Weren't you pleased to see your father and mother, your brothers and sisters, your mistresses, your fellow countrymen – and what did you have to say about us!

B. Very little, you may be sure, and they didn't believe any of it.

A. Why do you say he had only a few things to tell them?

B. Because he couldn't have taken in very much, and because he wouldn't have been able to find the words in his language to talk about those things he had gotten some idea of.

A. And why shouldn't they have believed him?

B. Because when they came to compare their customs with ours they would prefer to think that Aotourou was a liar rather than that we are so crazy.

A. Are you serious?

B. I do not doubt it. The life of savages is so simple, and our societies are such complicated machines! The Tahitian is like the origin of the world, while the European is like its old age. The interval that separates us is greater than the difference between a newborn baby and a broken-down old man. They understand absolutely nothing about our customs or our laws, and they are bound to see in them nothing but shackles disguised in a hundred different ways. These shackles could only provoke the indignation and scorn of creatures in whom the most profound feeling is love of liberty.

A. Do you mean to go and spin that fable about how wonderful life is in Tahiti?

B. It isn't a fable at all. And you would have no doubt about Bougainville's sincerity if you had read the supplement to his account of his voyage.

A. And where can one find this supplement?

B. It's right over there, on that table.

A. Would you entrust it to me to read at home?

B. No. But if you would like, we can read it over together.

A. Of course I would like to. Look over there – the fog is starting to retreat, and the blue sky is beginning to reappear bit by bit. It seems that it's my fate to be on the wrong end of any argument with you, even a trifling one. I must have a very good disposition to be able to forgive you for being so consistently superior!

B. Here, take it and read aloud! Skip over the preamble, which doesn't amount to anything, and begin directly with the farewell speech made by one of the island's chiefs to the explorers. That will give you some idea of how eloquent those people can be.

A. But how was Bougainville able to understand the farewell speech if it was spoken in a language he didn't know?

B. You'll find out. It's an old man who speaks.

The Old Man's Farewell

He was the father of a large family. When the Europeans arrived, he looked upon them scornfully, though he revealed neither surprise, alarm, nor curiosity. They approached him; he turned his back on them and retired into his hut. His thoughts were only too well revealed by his silence and his concern, for inwardly he groaned over the now-gone happy days of his people. At the moment of Bougainville's departure, when all the natives ran swarming onto the beach, tugging at his clothing and clasping their arms around his companions and weeping, the old man stepped forward solemnly and spoke:

"Weep, wretched Tahitians, weep — but rather for the arrival than for the departure of these wicked and desperate men! The day will come when you will know them for what they are. Someday they will return, bearing in one hand that piece of wood you see suspended from this one's belt and in the other hand the piece of steel that hangs at the side of his companion. They will load you with chains, slit your throats, and enslave you to their follies and vices. Someday you will be their slaves, as corrupt, as vile, and as wretched as they are. But I offer this consolation — my life is nearly over, and I will not live to see the calamity I foretell. O Tahitians, my friends! You have the means to escape a terrible fate, but I would rather die than advise you to make use of it. Let them leave, and let them live."

Then, turning to Bougainville, he went on: "And you, leader of these brigands who obey you, take your vessel swiftly from our shores. We are innocent and happy, and you can only spoil our happiness. We follow the pure instinct of nature, and you have tried to efface its imprint from our hearts. Here everything belongs to everyone, but you have preached to us I know not what distinction between 'yours' and 'mine.' Our women and our girls are communal property; you have shared this privilege with us, and your coming has awakened in them a frenzy they have not known before. They have become mad in your arms; you have become ferocious in theirs. They have begun to hate one another; you have cut each other's throats over them, and they have come home to us stained with your blood.

"We are free – but see how you have driven into our earth the symbol of our future servitude. You are neither a god nor a devil – who are you, then, to enslave our people? Orou! You who understand these men's speech, tell us, as you have told me, what they have written on that strip of metal – 'This land belongs to us.' This land belongs to you! And why? Because you set foot on it? If some day a Tahitian should land on your shores and engrave on one of your stones or on the bark of one of your trees: 'This land belongs to the people of Tahiti,' what would you think? You are stronger than we are! And what does that mean? When one of our boys carried off some of the miserable trinkets with which your ship is loaded, what an uproar you made, and what revenge you took! And at that very moment you were plotting, deep down in your hearts, to steal a whole country! You are not enslaved; you would rather suffer death than be enslaved, yet you would make slaves of us! Do you believe, then, that the Tahitian does not know how to die in defense of his liberty? This Tahitian, whom you want to possess like chattel – this Tahitian is your brother. You are both children of nature – what right do you have over him that he does not have over you?

"You came; did we attack you? Did we plunder your vessel? Did we seize you and expose you to our enemies' arrows? Did we force you to work in the fields alongside our animals? We respected our own image in you. Leave us with our own customs; they are wiser and more decent than yours. We have no wish to trade what you call our ignorance for your useless enlightenment. We already possess all that is good or necessary for our existence. Do we merit your scorn because we have not been able to create excessive needs? When we are hungry, we have something to eat; when we are cold, we have clothing. You have been in our huts – what is lacking there, in your opinion? You are welcome to drive yourselves as hard as you please in pursuit of what you call the comforts of life, but allow sensible people to stop when they see they have nothing to gain but imaginary benefits from continuing their painful labors. If you persuade us to exceed strict necessity, when will we reach the end of our labor? When will we have time for enjoyment? We have reduced our daily and yearly work to the least possible amount, because to us nothing seemed more desirable than leisure. Go and make yourselves restless in your own country; torment yourselves there as much as you want;

but leave us in peace, and do not fill our heads with a hankering after your false needs and imaginary virtues. Look at these men – see how healthy, straight, and strong they are. See these women – how straight, healthy, fresh, and lovely they are. Take this bow in your hands – it is my own – and call one, two, three, four of your comrades to help you try to bend it. I can bend it myself. I work the earth, I climb mountains, I open up a pathway through the dense forest, and I can run four leagues on the plain in less than an hour. Your young comrades have been hard-pressed to keep up with me, and yet I have passed my ninetieth year.

"Woe to this island! Woe to all the Tahitians now living, and to all those yet to be born, woe from the day of your arrival! We used to know but one disease – the one to which all men, all animals, and all plants are subject – old age. But you have brought us a new one: you have infected our blood. We will perhaps be compelled to exterminate with our own hands our own daughters, our wives, our children, those who have lain with your women, those who have lain with your men. Our fields will be spattered with the impure blood that has passed from your veins into ours. Or else our children, condemned to die, will nourish and perpetuate the evil that you have given their fathers and mothers, transmitting it forever to their descendants. Wretched men! You will bear the guilt either of the ravages that will follow your baneful caresses or of the murders we must commit to arrest the progress of the poison! You speak of crime! Can you conceive of a greater crime than yours? In your country, how do they punish the man who has killed his neighbor? Death by the ax! How do you punish the man who has poisoned his neighbor? Death at the stake! Compare the second crime with your own, and then tell us, you poisoner of whole nations, what tortures you deserve!

"Just a little while back, the young Tahitian girl blissfully abandoned herself to the embraces of a Tahitian youth and awaited impatiently, by virtue of reaching puberty, the day when her mother would remove her veil and uncover her breasts. She was proud of her ability to excite desire, to attract the amorous glances of strangers, of her own relatives, of her own brothers. In our presence, without dread or shame, in the center of a throng of innocent Tahitians who danced and played the flute, she accepted the caresses of the young man whom her young heart and the secret voice of her senses had designated for her. The notion of crime and the fear of disease have appeared among us only with your arrival. Now our enjoyments, once so sweet, bring remorse and terror. That man dressed in black, who stands near you and who listens to me, has spoken to our young boys, and I don't know what he has said to our young girls, but they are hesitant and our girls blush. Creep away into the dark forest, if you wish, with the perverse companion of your pleasures, but allow the good, simple Tahitians to reproduce without shame under the open sky and in broad daylight.

"What more honorable or nobler feelings could you put in place of those we have nurtured in them and by which they live? When they think the time has come to enrich the nation and the family with a new citizen, they glorify the occasion. They eat in order to live and grow; they grow in order that they may multiply, and in that they see neither vice nor shame. Listen to the consequences of your crimes. Scarcely had you appeared before our people than they had become thieves. Scarcely had you set foot on our soil than it began to reek of blood. You killed the Tahitian who ran to greet you, crying 'Taïo – friend!' And why did you kill him? Because he was tempted by the glitter of your little serpent's eggs. He gave you his fruit; he offered you his wife and daughter; he gave you his hut to live in – yet you killed him for taking a handful of those little glass beads without asking your permission. And the others? At the sound of your murderous weapons they fled to the hills. But you should know that had it not been for me they would have soon returned to destroy you. Oh, why did I appease them? Why did I calm them? Why do I still restrain them, even now? I do not know, for you surely have no claim to pity. Your heart is hard and will never feel any.

"You and your men have gone wherever you pleased, wandered over the whole island; you have been respected; you have enjoyed everything: no barrier or refusal has been placed in your path. You have been invited into our homes; you have sat at our tables; our people have spread before you the abundance of our land. If you wanted one of our young girls, her mother presented her to you naked, unless she was not yet old enough to have the privilege of showing her face and breasts. Thus you have enjoyed possession of these tender victims sacrificed in the name of hospitality. For the girl and for you we have strewn the ground with leaves and flowers; the musicians tuned their instruments; nothing has troubled the sweetness or disturbed the freedom of your caresses or hers. We chanted the hymn, the one that urges you to be a man, that urges our child to be a woman, an obliging and voluptuous woman. We danced around your couch. Yet you had hardly left this woman's embrace, having experienced in her arms the sweetest intoxication, than you killed her brother, her friend, or perhaps even her father.

"And you have done worse still – look there at that enclosure, bristling with arrows, with weapons that up to now have threatened only our foes – see them now turned against our own children. Look now on the unhappy companions of your pleasures! See their sorrow! See their fathers' distress and their mothers' despair! That is where they are condemned to die at our hands or from the disease you have given them. So leave this place, unless your cruel eyes delight in the spectacle of death! Go! And may the guilty sea that spared you when you came here now absolve itself and avenge our wrongs by swallowing you up on your way home! And you, Tahitians, go back to your huts, go inside, all of you, so that as these unworthy strangers depart they may hear nothing but the growling of the waves and may see nothing but the foam whose fury whitens a deserted shore!"

He finished speaking, and in an instant the throng of natives disappeared. A vast silence reigned over the whole stretch of the island, and nothing was to be heard but the shrill whistling of the wind and the dull pounding of the waves along the whole length of the coast. It was as though the winds and waters, sensing the old man's voice, obeyed him.

B. Well, what do you think of that?

A. The oration strikes me as forceful enough, but underneath a somewhat abrupt and savage tone I detect what seem to be a few European ideas and turns of phrase.

B. You must remember that it is a translation from Tahitian into Spanish and from Spanish into French. The previous night, the old man made a visit to Orou, the one to whom he appealed while speaking, in whose family the knowledge of Spanish had been preserved from time immemorial. Orou wrote down the old man's harangue in Spanish, and Bougainville had a copy of it in his hand while the old man was speaking.

A. Now I understand only too well why Bougainville suppressed this fragment. But I see there is more, and I am more than mildly curious to know what's in the rest.

B. Perhaps what follows will interest you less.

A. Never mind.

B. It is a conversation between the ship's chaplain and a native.

A. Orou?

B. The very same. When Bougainville's ship approached Tahiti, a great swarm of hollowed-out tree trunks were cast out from the shore. In an instant his vessel was surrounded by them. In whatever direction he looked he saw demonstrations of surprise and goodwill. The natives threw food to the sailors, welcomed them with outstretched arms, clambered up the ship's ropes, and clung to its sides. They filled the captain's gig, shouting back and forth between ship and shore. More natives came running down to the beach. As soon as the Europeans had set foot on land, dozens of pairs of friendly arms were thrown around the members of the expedition, who were passed about from group to group and finally led off, each to the hut of a different family. The men kept on embracing their guests around the waist, while the women stroked and patted their hands and cheeks. Imagine what it might have been like to have been there! As a witness to this hospitable scene, at least in thought, tell me what you think of the human race.

A. It's very fine.

B. But I almost forgot to tell you about a most peculiar thing. The friendly display of generosity I have described was suddenly marred by cries for help. It was the servant of one of Bougainville's officers. Several Tahitian lads had taken hold of him, stretched him out on the ground, removed his clothes, and were getting ready to render him the customary politeness of the country.

A. What! Do you mean that those simple people, those good decent savages...?

B. You're jumping to false conclusions. The servant was a woman disguised as a man. Her sex had been kept secret from the crew during the whole voyage, but the Tahitians recognized it at once. She was born in Burgundy; her family name was Barré; she was neither beautiful nor ugly, and she was twenty-six years old. She had never left her hammock before. She had suddenly gotten the urge to travel, and her first idea was to circumnavigate the globe. She showed courage and good sense at all times.

A. Those frail constitutions sometimes conceal the strongest characters.

Conversation Between the Chaplain and Orou

B. When the members of Bougainville's expedition were distributed among the native families, the ship's chaplain fell to the lot of Orou. The Tahitian and the chaplain were men of about the same age, that is, about thirty-five or thirty-six years old. At that time, Orou's family consisted of his wife and three daughters, who were called Asto, Palli, and Thia. The women undressed their guest, washed his face, hands, and feet, and fed him a wholesome although frugal meal. When he was about to go to bed, Orou, who had stepped outside with his family, reappeared and introduced him to his wife and three girls — all nude — and said to him: "You are young and healthy and you have just had a good supper. He who sleeps alone, sleeps badly; at night a man needs a woman at his side. Here is my wife and here are my daughters. Choose whichever one pleases you, but if you would like to do me a favor, choose my youngest girl, who has not yet had any children."

The mother said: "Poor girl! I don't hold it against her. It's not her fault."

The chaplain replied that his religion, his holy orders, his moral standards, and his sense of decency all prevented him from accepting Orou's invitation.

Orou answered: "I don't know what this thing is that you call 'religion,' but I can only have a low opinion of it because it forbids you to partake of an innocent pleasure to which nature, the sovereign mistress of all, invites everybody. It seems to prevent you from bringing one of your fellow creatures into the world, from doing a favor asked of you by a father, a mother, and their children, from repaying the kindness of a host, and from enriching a nation by giving it another citizen. I don't know what it is that you call 'holy orders,' but your chief duty is to be a man and to show gratitude. I am not asking you to take my mores back with you to your own country; but Orou, your host and your friend, begs you merely to lend yourself to the customs of Tahiti. Is our moral code better or worse than yours? This is an easy question to answer. Does the country in which you were born have more people than it can support? If it does, then your morals are neither better nor worse than ours. Or can it feed more people than it now has? Then our morals are better than yours. As for the sense of propriety that leads you to object to my proposal, this I understand, and I freely admit that I am in the wrong. I ask your pardon. I cannot ask you to do anything that might harm your health; if you are too tired, you should by all means go to sleep at once. But I hope you won't persist in disappointing us. Look at the distress you have brought to the faces of these four women – they are afraid you have noticed some defect in them that arouses your distaste. But even if that were so, would it not be possible for you to do a good deed and have the pleasure of honoring one of my daughters in the sight of her sisters and friends? Come, be generous!"

THE CHAPLAIN: "You don't understand – it's not that. All four of them are equally beautiful. But my religion! My holy orders!"

OROU: "They are mine and I offer them to you; they belong to themselves, are all of age, and they give themselves to you. However clear a conscience may be demanded of you by this thing, 'religion,' or by those 'holy orders' of yours, you need not have any scruples about accepting these women. I am not abusing my authority, and you can be sure that I recognize and respect the personal rights to their own persons."

At this point in his account, the honest chaplain had to admit that until then Providence had never exposed him to such strong temptation. He was young, he was agitated, he was tormented. He turned his eyes away from the four lovely suppliants, then let his gaze wander back to them again. He lifted his hands and his eyes to Heaven. Thia, the youngest of the girls, threw her arms around his knees and said to him: "Stranger, do not disappoint my father and mother. Do not disappoint me! Honor me in this hut and among my own family! Raise me to my sisters' level, for they make fun of me. Asto, my eldest sister, already has three children; Palli, the second oldest of us, has two; and Thia has none! Stranger, good stranger, do not reject me! Make me a mother! Give me a child whom I can some day lead by the hand as he walks at my side, to be seen by all Tahiti – a little one to nurse at my breast nine months from now, a child of whom I can be proud, and who will be part of my dowry when I go from my father's hut into that of another. Perhaps I will be more fortunate with you than I have been with our Tahitian young men. If you will only grant me this favor, I will never forget you; I will bless you all my life; I will write your name on my arm and on that of my child; we will always pronounce it with joy; and when you leave this shore, my prayers will go with you across the seas all the way to your own country."

The poor chaplain records that she pressed his hands, that her eyes met his with the most expressive and touching gaze, that she wept, that her father, mother, and sisters went out, leaving him alone with her, and that despite his repetition of, "But my religion, my holy orders!" the next morning he found himself lying next to the young girl. She overwhelmed him with caresses, and when her father, mother, and sisters came in, she called on them to add their gratitude.

Asto and Palli, who had left the room briefly, soon returned bearing native food, drink, and fruits. They embraced their sister and wished her good fortune. They all ate breakfast together; then, when Orou was left alone with the chaplain, he said to him:

"I see that my daughter is pleased with you, and I thank you. But would you be good enough to tell me the meaning of this word, 'religion,' which you have spoken so frequently and so mournfully?"

After thinking for a moment, the chaplain replied:

"Who made your hut and all the furnishings in it?"

OROU: I did.

THE CHAPLAIN: Well, we believe that this world and everything in it is the work of a maker.

OROU: Then he must have hands and feet and a head.

THE CHAPLAIN: No.

OROU: Where is his dwelling place?

THE CHAPLAIN: Everywhere.

OROU: Even here!

THE CHAPLAIN: Here too.

OROU: But we have never seen him.

THE CHAPLAIN: He cannot be seen.

OROU: He sounds like a rather indifferent father. He must be old, for he must be at least as old as his works.

THE CHAPLAIN: No, he never grows old. He spoke to our ancestors and gave them laws; he prescribed to them the way he wishes to be honored; he ordained that certain actions are good and others he forbade as being evil.

OROU: I see. And one of these evil actions he has forbidden is that of a man going to bed with a woman or girl. But in that case, why did he make two sexes?

THE CHAPLAIN: In order that they might unite – but only when certain conditions are satisfied and only after certain initial ceremonies have been performed. By virtue of these ceremonies one man belongs to one woman and only to her; one woman belongs to one man and only to him.

OROU: For their whole lives?

THE CHAPLAIN: For their whole lives.

OROU: So that if it should happen that a woman should go to bed with some man who was not her husband, or some man should go to bed with a woman who was not his wife...but that could never happen because the maker would know what was going on, and since he doesn't like that sort of thing, he wouldn't let it occur.

THE CHAPLAIN: No. He lets them do as they will, and they sin against the law of God (for that is the name by which we call the great maker) and against the law of the country; they commit a crime.

OROU: I don't want to offend by anything I might say, but if you don't mind, I'll tell you what I think.

THE CHAPLAIN: Go ahead.

OROU: I find these strange precepts contrary to nature and contrary to reason. I think they are admirably calculated to increase the number of crimes and endlessly to annoy the old maker – who made everything without hands, head, or tools, who is everywhere but can be seen nowhere, who exists today and tomorrow but grows not a day older, who gives commands and is not obeyed, who is able to prevent what he dislikes but fails to do so. His commands are contrary to nature because they assume that a thinking being, one with feelings and freedom, can be the property of another being like himself. On what could such a right of ownership be founded? Do you not see that in your country you have confused things that have no feelings, thoughts, desires or will – things one takes or leaves, keeps or sells, without them suffering or complaining – with the thing that can neither be bought nor sold, which has freedom, volition, and desires of its own, which has the ability to give or to withhold itself for a moment or forever, which suffers and complains? This latter thing can never be treated like a trader's stock of goods unless one forgets what its true character is and does violence to nature. Furthermore, your laws seem to me to be contrary to the general order of beings. For in truth, is there anything so senseless as a precept that forbids us to heed the changing impulses that are inherent in our being, or commands that require a degree of constancy that is not possible, that violate the liberty of both male and female by chaining them perpetually to one another? Is there anything more unreasonable than this perfect fidelity that would restrict us, for the enjoyment of pleasures so capricious, to a single partner – than an oath of immutability taken by two individuals made of flesh and blood under a sky that is not the same for a moment, in a cavern that threatens to collapse upon them, at the foot of a cliff that is crumbling into dust, under a tree that is withering, on a bench of stone that is being worn away? Take my word for it, you have reduced human beings to a condition worse than that of the animals. I don't know what your great maker is, but I am very happy that he never spoke to our forefathers, and I hope that he never speaks to our children, for if he does he may tell them the same foolishness, and they may be foolish enough to believe it. Yesterday, as we were having supper, you told us all about your magistrates and priests. I do not know who these characters are whom you call "magistrates" and "priests" and who have the authority to govern your conduct – but tell me, are they really masters of good and evil? Can they transform justice into injustice and vice versa? Is it within their power to call harmful actions "good" or harmless or useful deeds "evil"? One can hardly think so, because in that case there would no longer be any difference between true and false, good and bad, beautiful and ugly – only such differences as it pleased your great maker, your magistrates, or your priests to define as such. You would then have to change your ideas and behavior from one moment to the next. One day you would be told, on behalf of one of your three masters, "kill," and in all good conscience you would be obliged to kill. Another day they might say, "steal," and you would be bound to steal. Or, "do not eat this fruit," and you would not dare to eat it; "I forbid you to eat this vegetable or this meat," and you would be careful never to touch them. There is not a single good thing they could not forbid you to enjoy, and no wickedness they could not order you to commit. And where would you be if your three masters, disagreeing among themselves, took it in their heads to permit, enjoin, and forbid you to do the same thing, as I am sure must occasionally happen? Then, to please your priest, you would have to get yourself into hot water with the magistrate; to satisfy the magistrate, you would have to risk displeasing the great maker; and to make yourself agreeable to the great maker, you would have to fly in the face of your own nature. And do you know what will finally happen? You will come to despise all three, and you will be neither man, nor citizen, nor pious believer – you will be nothing at all. You will be at odds with all the authorities, at odds with yourself, malicious, tormented by your own conscience, persecuted by your witless masters, and miserable, as you were yesterday evening when I offered you my wife and daughters and you could only wail: "But my religion. My holy orders!" Would you like to know what is good and what is bad in all times and places? Pay close attention to the nature of things and actions, to your relations with your fellow creatures, to the effect of your behavior on your own well-being and on the general welfare. You are mad if you believe that there is anything in the universe, either on high or below, that can add or subtract from the laws of nature. The universe's eternal will is that good be chosen rather than evil, and the general welfare rather than the individual's well-being. You may decree the opposite, but you will not be obeyed. By threats, punishment, and guilt, you create more wretches and rascals, more depraved consciences and more corrupted characters. People will no longer know what they ought or ought not do. They will feel guilty when they are doing nothing wrong and proud of themselves in the midst of crime; they will have lost the North Star that should guide their course. Answer me honestly – in spite of the express commands of your three legislators, do the young men in your country never go to bed with a young woman without having received permission?

THE CHAPLAIN: I would be lying if I said they never do.

OROU: And the women, once they have sworn an oath to belong to only one husband, do they never give themselves to another man?

THE CHAPLAIN: Nothing happens more often.

OROU: And are your legislators severe in handing out punishment to such disobedient people or not? If they are, then they are wild animals who war against nature; if they are not severe, they are fools who risk bringing contempt upon their authority by issuing futile prohibitions.

THE CHAPLAIN: The guilty ones, if they escape the rigor of the laws, are punished by public opinion.

OROU: That's like saying that justice is done by means of the whole nation's lack of common sense, and that public folly is the substitute for law.

THE CHAPLAIN: A girl who has lost her honor can no longer find a husband.

OROU: Lost her honor! And for what cause?

THE CHAPLAIN: An unfaithful woman is more or less despised.

OROU: Despised! Why should that be?

THE CHAPLAIN: And the young man is called a cowardly seducer.

OROU: Coward? Seducer? Why that?

THE CHAPLAIN: The father, mother, and child are desolate. An erring husband is a libertine; a husband who has been betrayed shares his wife's shame.

OROU: What monstrous foolishness you're talking! And still you must be holding something back, because when people take it upon themselves to rearrange all ideas of justice and propriety to suit their own whims, to apply or remove the names of things in a completely arbitrary manner, to associate the ideas of good and evil with certain actions or to dissociate them for no apparent reason – then of course people will blame each other, accuse each other, suspect each other, tyrannize, become jealous and envious, deceive and wound one another, conceal, dissimulate, and spy on one another, catch each other out, quarrel, and tell lies. Girls will deceive their parents, husbands their wives, and wives their husbands. Unmarried girls – yes, I am sure of it – unmarried girls will suffocate their babies; suspicious fathers will neglect or despise children that are rightfully their own; mothers will abandon their infants and leave them to the mercy of fate. Crime and debauchery will appear in every imaginable shape and form. I see all that as clearly as if I had lived among you. These things are so because they must be so, and your society, whose well-ordered ways your chief boasts to you about, can't be anything but a swarm of hypocrites who secretly trample the laws under foot, or a multitude of wretched beings who serve as instruments for inflicting willing torture upon themselves; or imbeciles in whom prejudice has utterly silenced the voice of nature, or ill-fashioned creatures in whom nature cannot claim her rights.

THE CHAPLAIN: That is a close likeness. But do you never marry?

OROU: Oh yes, we marry.

THE CHAPLAIN: Well, what does marriage mean to you?

OROU: It consists of an agreement to live in the same hut and to sleep in the same bed for as long as we both find this good.

THE CHAPLAIN: And when you find it bad?

OROU: Then we separate.

THE CHAPLAIN: But what becomes of the children?

OROU: O stranger! That last question of yours reveals to me the final depths of your country's wretchedness. Let me tell you, my friend, that the birth of a child is always a happy event, and its death is an occasion for weeping and sorrow. A child is a precious thing because it will grow up to be a man or a woman. Therefore we take infinitely better care of our children than of our plants and animals. The birth of a child is the occasion for public celebration and a source of joy for its entire family. For the hut it means an increase in wealth, while for the nation it signifies additional strength. It means another pair of hands and arms for Tahiti — we see in the newborn baby a future farmer, fisherman, hunter, soldier, husband, or father. When a woman goes from her husband's hut back to that of her family, she takes with her all the children she had brought with her as her dowry; those born during the marriage are divided equally between the two spouses, and care is taken to give each an equal number of boys and girls whenever possible.

THE CHAPLAIN: But children are a burden for many years before they are old enough to make themselves useful.

OROU: We set aside for them and for the support of the elderly one-sixth of our harvests; wherever the child goes, this support follows him. And so, you see, the larger the family a Tahitian has, the richer he is.

THE CHAPLAIN: One-sixth!

OROU: Yes. It's a dependable method for encouraging population growth, for promoting respect for our old people, and for safeguarding the welfare of our children.

THE CHAPLAIN: And does it ever happen that a couple who have separated decide to live together again?

OROU: Oh, yes. It happens fairly often. However, the shortest time any marriage can last is from one moon to the next.

THE CHAPLAIN: Assuming, of course, that the wife is not pregnant, for in that case, wouldn't the marriage have to last at least nine months?

OROU: Not at all. The child keeps the name of its mother's husband at the time it was conceived, and its paternity, like its means of support, follows it wherever it goes.

THE CHAPLAIN: You spoke about the children that a wife brings to her husband as dowry.

OROU: Certainly. Take my eldest daughter, who has three children. They are able to walk, they are healthy and attractive, and they promise to be strong when they are grown up. If she should take it into her head to get married, she would take them along, for they are hers, and her husband would be extremely happy to have them in his hut. He would think all the better of his wife if she were still carrying a fourth child at the time of her wedding.

THE CHAPLAIN: From him?

OROU: His or another's. The more children our girls have, the more desirable they are. The stronger and lustier our young men are, the richer they become. Therefore, careful as we are to protect our young girls from male advances and our young boys from intercourse with women before they reach sexual maturity, once they have passed the age of puberty we exhort them all the more strongly to have as many children as possible. You probably haven't fully realized what an important service you will have rendered my daughter Thia if you have succeeded in making her a child. Her mother will no longer plague her every month by saying, "But Thia, what is the matter with you? You never get pregnant, and here you are nineteen years old. You should have had at least two babies by now, and you have none. Who is going to look after you in your old age if you throw away your youth in this way? Thia, I begin to think there is something wrong with you, some defect that keeps men away from you. Find out what it is, my child, and correct it if you can. At your age, I was already a mother three times!"

THE CHAPLAIN: What precautions do you take to safeguard your boys and girls before they reach maturity?

OROU: That's the main object of our children's education within the family circle, and it's the most important point in our code of public morality. Our boys, until the age of twenty-two, that is, for two to three years after they reach maturity, must wear a long tunic that covers their bodies completely and a little chain around their loins. Before our girls reach nubile age, they would not dare to go out without white veils. The two misdeeds of taking off one's chain or of raising one's veil are rarely encountered, because we teach our children at a very early age what harmful results will ensue. But when the proper time comes — when the male has attained his full strength, when the principal symptoms of virility last for a sufficient time, and when we are confirmed in our judgment by the quality and by the frequent emission of the seminal fluid — and when the young girl seems wilted and bored, when she seems mature enough to feel passion, to inspire it, and to satisfy it — then the father unfastens his son's chain and cuts the nail on the middle finger of the boy's right hand. The mother removes her daughter's veil. The young man can now ask a woman for her favors or be asked by her to grant his. The girl may walk about freely in public with her face and breasts uncovered; she may accept or reject men's caresses. All we do is to point out in advance to the boy certain girls and to the girl certain boys whom they might do well to choose as partners. The day when a boy or girl is emancipated is a great day of celebration. In the case of a girl, the young men assemble around her hut the night before and the air is filled all night long with singing and the sound of musical instruments. When the sun has risen, she is led by her father and mother into an enclosure where dancing is going on and where games of wrestling, running, and jumping are in progress. A naked man is paraded in front of her, allowing her to examine his body from all aspects and in all sorts of positions. For a young man, the young girls do the honors of the occasion by letting him examine the nude female body unadorned and unconcealed. The remainder of the ceremony is enacted on a bed of leaves, just as you saw on your arrival here. At sunset the girl returns to her parents' hut or else moves to the hut of the young man she has chosen and remains there as long as she pleases.

THE CHAPLAIN: But is this celebration a marriage ceremony or is it not?

OROU: Well, as you have said ...

A. What do I see written there in the margin?

B. It is a note in which the good chaplain says that the parents' advice on how to choose girls and boys was full of common sense and contained many acute and useful observations but that he could not bring himself to quote the catechism itself because it would have seemed intolerably licentious to corrupt and superficial people like us. He adds, nevertheless, that he was sorry to have left out certain details that would have shown, in the first place, what vast progress a nation can make in some important areas without the assistance of physics and anatomy, if it works continually at it, and in the second place, the different ideals of beauty that prevail in a country where one judges forms in the light of momentary pleasures, as contrasted with a nation where they are appreciated for their usefulness over a longer period of time. To be considered beautiful there a woman must have a high color, a wide forehead, a small mouth, large eyes, finely modeled features, a narrow waist, and small hands and feet.... Here, scarcely one of these things is of any importance. The woman who attracts the most admirers and the most lovers is the one who seems most likely to bear many children (like the wife of Cardinal d'Ossat) and whose children seem likely to be active, intelligent, brave, healthy, and strong. The Athenian Venus has next to nothing in common with the Venus of Tahiti — the former is a coquettish Venus, the latter a fertile Venus. A woman of Tahiti said scornfully one day to another woman of her country: "You are beautiful enough, but you bear ugly children; I am ugly, but my children are beautiful, so the men prefer me."

Following this note by the chaplain, Orou continues:

OROU: What a happy moment it is for a young girl and her parents when it is discovered that she is pregnant! She jumps up and runs about, she throws her arms around her father's and mother's necks. She tells them the wonderful news amid outcries of mutual joy. "Mother! Father! Kiss me! I am pregnant!" "Is it really true?" "Really and truly!" "And who got you with child?" "Such-and-such a one."

THE CHAPLAIN: How can she know who the father of her child is?

OROU: How could she not know? With us the same rule that applies to marriage applies also to love affairs — each lasts at least from one moon to the next.

THE CHAPLAIN: And is the rule strictly observed?

OROU: You can judge for yourself. First, the interval between two moons isn't long, but when it appears that two men have well-founded claims to be the father of a child, it no longer belongs to the mother.

THE CHAPLAIN: To whom does it belong?

OROU: To whichever of the two men the mother chooses to give it. This is the only right she has, and since a child is an object of both interest and value, you can understand that it is rare to find libertine women among us and that our young men keep away from them.

THE CHAPLAIN: Then you do have a few libertine women? That makes me feel better.

OROU: Yes, we have some, and more than one kind — but that is another subject. When one of our girls gets pregnant, she is twice as happy if the child's father is a handsome, well-built, brave, intelligent, industrious boy, because she has reason to hope that the child will inherit its father's good qualities. The only thing a girl would be ashamed of would be a bad choice. You have no idea how much store we set by good health, beauty, strength, industry, and courage; you have no notion what a tendency there is, even without our having to pay any particular attention to it, for good physical inheritance to be passed on from generation to generation among us. You are a person who has traveled in all sorts of countries — tell me whether you have seen anywhere else so many handsome men and beautiful women as in Tahiti. Look at me. What do you think of me? Well, there are ten thousand men on this island who are taller than I am and just as strong; but there is none braver, and for that reason mothers very often point me out to their girls as a good father for their children.

THE CHAPLAIN: And of all these children you have sired outside your own hut, how many fall to your share?

OROU: Every fourth, be it a boy or a girl. You see, we have developed a kind of circulation of men, women, and children – that is, of able-bodied workers of all ages and occupation – which is much more important than trade in foodstuffs (which are only the products of human labor) in your country.

THE CHAPLAIN: I can easily believe it. What is the significance of those black veils that I have seen a few persons wearing?

OROU: They indicate barrenness, either from birth or that which comes with advanced age. Any woman who lays aside such a veil and mingles with men is considered libertine, and so is any man who raises such a veil and has commerce with a barren woman.

THE CHAPLAIN: And the gray veils?

OROU: That shows that the woman is having her monthly period. Failure to wear this veil when it should be worn also stigmatizes a woman as libertine if she has relations with men during that time, and likewise the man who has relations with her.

THE CHAPLAIN: Do you punish this libertinism?

OROU: Only with public disapproval.

THE CHAPLAIN: May a father sleep with his daughter, a mother with her son, a brother with his sister, a husband with someone else's wife?

OROU: Why not?

THE CHAPLAIN: Well! To say nothing of the fornication, what about the incest, the adultery?

OROU: What do you mean by those words, "fornication," "incest," and "adultery"?

THE CHAPLAIN: They are crimes, horrible crimes for which people are burned at the stake in my country.

OROU: Well, whether they burn or don't burn in your country means nothing to me. But you cannot condemn the ways of Europe for not being those of Tahiti, nor our ways for not being those of Europe. You need a more dependable rule of judgment than that. And what shall it be? Do you know a better one than general welfare and individual utility? Well, now, tell me in what way your crime of incest is contrary to the two aims of our conduct. My friend, you are mistaken if you think that everything is settled once and for all because a law has been promulgated, a derogatory word invented, and a punishment established. Why don't you tell me what you mean by "incest"?

THE CHAPLAIN: Why, incest ...

OROU: Yes, incest...? Has it been a long time since your great maker without hands, head, or tools made the world?

THE CHAPLAIN: No.

OROU: Did he make the whole human race at one time?

THE CHAPLAIN: No, he made only one man and one woman.

OROU: Did they have children?

THE CHAPLAIN: Of course.

OROU: Let's suppose that these two original parents had only daughters and that the mother was the first to die. Or that they had only sons and that the wife lost her husband.

THE CHAPLAIN: You embarrass me. But in spite of anything you may say, incest is a horrible crime, so let's talk about something else.

OROU: That's all very well for you to say. But as for me, I won't speak another word until you tell me why incest is such a horrible crime.

THE CHAPLAIN: All right, I'll grant you that perhaps incest does not offend nature, but isn't it objection enough that it threatens the political order? What would happen to the security of a leader and the tranquillity of a state, if a nation of millions should come under the thumbs of fifty or so fathers of families?

OROU: That would be the lesser of two evils: there would be no single great society but fifty or so little ones, more happiness, and one less crime.

THE CHAPLAIN: I should think, however, that even here it must not be very common for a son to sleep with his mother.

OROU: No, not unless he has a great deal of respect for her, or a degree of tenderness that makes him forget the disparity in their ages and prefer a woman of forty to a girl of nineteen.

THE CHAPLAIN: What about intercourse between fathers and daughters?

OROU: Hardly more frequently, unless the girl is ugly and little sought after. If her father has a great deal of affection for her, he helps her in getting ready her dowry of children.

THE CHAPLAIN: What you say suggests to me that in Tahiti the women on whom nature has not smiled have a rather difficult time.

OROU: What you say only shows that you don't have a high opinion of the generosity of our boys.

THE CHAPLAIN: As for unions between brothers and sisters, I imagine they are very common.

OROU: Yes, and very strongly approved of.

THE CHAPLAIN: According to you, the same passion that gives rise to so many evils and crimes in our countries is completely innocent here.

OROU: Stranger, you have poor judgment and a faulty memory. Poor judgment, because whenever something is forbidden, it is inevitable that people should be tempted to do it, and will do it. Faulty memory, because you have already forgotten what I told you. We do have old libertine women who sneak out at night without their black veils and offer themselves to men, even though nothing can come of it. If they are recognized or surprised, the punishment is either exile to the northern tip of the island or slavery. There are precocious girls who lift their white veils without their parents' knowledge — for them we have a locked room in the hut. There are young boys who take off their chain before the time established by nature and law — in that case the parents get a strong reprimand. There are women who find the nine months of pregnancy a long time; women and girls who are careless about wearing their gray veils — but as a matter of fact we attach little importance to all these lapses. You would find it hard to believe how much our morals have been improved on these points by the fact that we have come to identify in our minds the idea of public and private wealth with the idea of increasing the population.

THE CHAPLAIN: But doesn't disorder ever arise when two men have a passion for the same woman or when two girls desire the same man?

OROU: I haven't yet seen four instances. The choice of the woman or man settles the matter. If a man should commit any act of violence, that would be a serious misdemeanor, but even then no one would notice unless the injured party were to make a public complaint, and it is almost unheard of for a girl or woman to do so. The only thing I have noticed is that our women are a little less considerate of homely men than our young men are of unattractive women; but no one is worried about this state of affairs.

THE CHAPLAIN: So far as I can see, jealousy is practically unknown here in Tahiti. But tenderness between husband and wife, and maternal love, which are strong, beautiful emotions — if they exist here at all, they must be fairly lukewarm.

OROU: We have put in their place another impulse, which is more universal, powerful, and lasting — self-interest. Examine your conscience in all candor, put aside the hypocritical parade of virtue which is always on the lips of your companions, though not in their hearts, and tell me whether there is anywhere on the planet a man who, if he were not held back by shame, would not prefer to lose his child — a husband who would not prefer to lose his wife — rather than lose his fortune and all the amenities of life? You may be sure that if a man can ever be led to care as much about his fellow men as he does about his own bed, his own health, his leisure, his house, his harvests, or his fields, he can be depended on to do his utmost to look out for the well-being of other people. Then you will see him shedding tears over the bed of a sick child or taking care of mothers when they are ill. Then you will find fruitful women, nubile girls, and handsome boys highly regarded. Then you will find a great deal of attention paid to the education of the young, because the nation grows stronger with their growth and suffers a material loss if their well-being is impaired.

THE CHAPLAIN: I am afraid there is some reason in what this savage says. The poor European peasant wears out his wife in order to spare his horse, lets his child die without help, and calls the veterinarian to look after his ox.

OROU: I didn't quite hear what you were just saying. But when you get back to your own country where everything is so well managed, try to teach them how well our method works. Then they will begin to realize how precious a newborn baby is and how important it is to increase the population. Shall I tell you a secret? But be careful not to let it out. When you came, we let you do what you liked with our women and girls. You were astonished and your gratitude made us laugh. You thanked us, even though we were levying the heaviest of all taxes on you and your companions. We asked no money of you; we didn't loot your ship; we didn't give a hang for any of your stores of food – but our women and girls came to draw the blood out of your veins. When you go away, you will leave us with a brood of children. Do you think we could have extracted a more valuable tribute from you than this tax collected from your own bodies and from your own substance? If you would care to try and estimate its value, imagine that you have yet to sail along two hundred leagues of coastline, and that every twenty miles they collect the same tribute from you! We have vast areas of land yet to plow; we need workers, and we have tried to get you to give them to us. We have epidemics from time to time, and these losses must be made up; we have used you to fill up the gaps in our population. We have external enemies to deal with, and for this we need soldiers, so we have allowed you to give them to us. We have a surplus of women and girls over men, and we have enlisted your services to help us out. Among these women and girls there are some with whom our men have thus far been unable to beget any children, and these were the ones we first assigned to receive your embraces. A neighboring country holds us in vassalage, and we have to pay an annual tribute to them in men; you and your friends have helped us pay off this debt, and in five or six years we will send them your sons if they turn out to be inferior in some way to our own. Although we are stronger and healthier than you, we have observed that you have the edge on us when it comes to intelligence. So we immediately marked out some of our most beautiful women and girls to collect the seed of a race superior to ours. This is an experiment we have tried and that we hope will succeed. We have taken from you and your fellows the only thing we could get from you. Just because we are savages, don't think we are incapable of calculating where our best advantage lies. Go wherever you will, and you will always find a man as shrewd as you are. He will give you what he has no use for, and he will always ask for something he needs. If he offers to trade you a piece of gold for a scrap of iron, that is because he doesn't care one bit for gold and desires iron. By the way, why is it that you are not dressed like the others? What is the significance of the long robe that covers you from head to foot, and what is that pointed bag that you let hang over your shoulders and sometimes draw up around your ears?

THE CHAPLAIN: The reason I dress as I do is that I am a member of a society of men who are called monks in my country. The most sacred of their vows is never to have intercourse with any woman and never to beget any children.

OROU: Then what kind of work do you do?

THE CHAPLAIN: None.

OROU: And your magistrates allow that sort of idleness – the worst of all?

THE CHAPLAIN: They more than allow it: they honor it and make others do the same.

OROU: My first thought was that nature, or some accident, or some cruel art, had deprived you of the ability to reproduce your kind and that out of pity they had let you go on living instead of killing you. But my daughter tells me that you are a man as robust as any Tahitian and that she has high hopes of getting good results from your repeated caresses. Well, at last I know why you kept mumbling yesterday evening, "But my religion, my holy orders!" Could you explain to me why it is that your magistrates show you such favor and treat you with so much respect?

THE CHAPLAIN: I don't know.

OROU: Still, you must know why it was that, although you are a man, you have condemned yourself of your own free will to be one no longer?

THE CHAPLAIN: That's hard to explain, and it would take too long.

OROU: Are monks faithful to their vows of sterility?

THE CHAPLAIN: No.

OROU: I was sure of it. Do you also have female monks?

THE CHAPLAIN: Yes.

OROU: As well behaved as the male monks?

THE CHAPLAIN: They are kept more strictly in seclusion, they dry up from unhappiness and die of boredom.

OROU: So nature is avenged for the injury done to it! Ugh! What a country! If everything is managed the way you say, you are more barbarous than we are.

The good chaplain tells us that he spent the rest of the day wandering about the island, visiting a number of huts, and that in the evening, after supper, the father and mother begged him to go to bed with Palli, the second oldest daughter. She offered herself in the same way as Thia, and he tells us that several times during the night he cried out, "My religion! My holy orders!" The third night he suffered the same guilty torture in the arms of Asto, the eldest, and the fourth night, not to be unfair, he devoted to his hostess.

Continuation of the Dialogue

A. I like this courteous chaplain.

B. And I have formed a high opinion of the manners and customs of Tahiti, and of Orou's speeches.

A. Yes, even though they are cast in a somewhat European mold.

B. I suppose they are. But now, to continue, the good chaplain complains that his visit to Tahiti was too short. He says that it is very difficult to form a just estimate of the customs of a people wise enough to stop when it has attained a golden mean, happy enough to inhabit a part of the world where the fertility of the soil guarantees a long and languid life, industrious enough to provide for the most pressing needs, and indolent enough so that their innocence, repose, and felicity are not endangered by too rapid an advance of knowledge. They have no laws and hold no opinions that would stigmatize as evil something that is not of its own nature evil. Their plowing and their harvesting are done in common. Their sense of property is very limited. The passion of love, reduced to a simple physical appetite, produces none of the disorders we connect with it. The whole island lives like one large family, in which each hut is like a single apartment in one of our big houses. The chaplain ends by assuring us that he will never forget the Tahitians and confesses that he was tempted to throw his vestments into the ship and spend the rest of his days with them. And he fears that he will on more than one occasion be sorry he didn't.

A. But despite this eulogy, what practical conclusions can you draw from the strange morals and picturesque customs of an uncivilized people?

B. As I see it, human shrewdness began when certain physical causes – for example, the necessity of winning a livelihood from stony soil – brought man's cunning into play. This first push was enough to carry him forward beyond his original goal. Once the aim of satisfying his elementary needs was achieved, he was swept into the boundless ocean of imagination, with no means of returning. May the happy Tahitians stop where they are now! I see that, except in that remote corner of the earth, there has never been any morality and that perhaps in no other part of the world will there ever be any.

A. What do you mean by morality?

B. I mean a general obedience to and a conduct arising from the laws, whether they be good or bad. If the laws are good, morals are good; if the laws are bad, morals are bad. If the laws, good or bad, are not observed – the worst possible condition for a society – there are no morals. Now, what chance is there of getting people to observe laws when they are contradictory? Read the history of centuries and nations, ancient and modern, and you will find that there are three codes of law under which men have lived – the code of nature, the civil code, and the laws of religion. They have been obliged to violate each of these codes in turn because the codes have never been in harmony. The result has been that nowhere do we find anyone (as Orou suspected in speaking of our own country) who can be called at once a man, a citizen, and a believer.

A. From which you conclude that if morality were to be based on the eternal relations of men with one another, the religious law would perhaps become superfluous, and the civil law should become nothing more than an explicit statement of the laws of nature.

B. Exactly; otherwise the penalty will be that we will increase the numbers of the wicked instead of multiplying the good.

A. Or else, if it is considered necessary to preserve all three sets of laws, civil and religious law should be strictly traced from the law of nature, which we carry with us, impressed on our hearts, wherever we go, and which will always be the strongest.

B. What you say is not wholly true. When we are born we bring nothing in the world with us except a constitution similar to that of other human beings – the same needs, an attraction toward the same pleasures, a common aversion to the same pains: that is what makes man what he is, and a code of morality appropriate to men should rest on no other foundations than these.

A. Yes, but it's not easy to work out.

B. Nothing could be more difficult. Indeed, I believe that the most primitive people in the world, the Tahitians, who have simply held fast to the law of nature, are nearer than any civilized nation to having a good code of law.

A. For the reason that it would be easier for them to get rid of some of their rustic ways than for us to turn back the clock and reform our excesses.

B. Especially those connected with the relations between men and women.

A. You may be right. But let's start at the beginning. Let us put nature resolutely to the question and see, without prejudice, what answers it will give to this question.

B. A good idea.

A. Is marriage in the realm of nature?

B. If, by marriage, you mean the preference the female has for one male over all others, or that a male has for one female over other females — in other words, a mutual preference, leading to the formation of a more or less durable union that perpetuates the species by reproducing individuals — if you mean no more than that, then yes, marriage is part of the order of nature.

A. I think so, and for the same reason, because the preference you speak of can be observed not only among human beings but also in various other animal species. You only have to think of the large number of stallions that go chasing after the same mare in our pastures every spring. Only one of them is finally selected as her mate. But how about courtship?

B. If, by courtship, you mean the variety of expedients, both subtle and forceful, that passion inspires in both male and female when one of them is trying to obtain that preference which leads to the sweetest, most important, and most universal of enjoyments — then yes, courtship is part of the order of nature.

A. I think so too. Witness the whole variety of small attentions the male renders the female in order to please her, and the countless ways females of all species have of stirring up the passion and attracting the preference of the male. But what about coquetry?

B. That is nothing but deception, for it consists of simulating a passion that one doesn't feel at all and promising favors that one has no intention of conferring. The coy male is making sport of the female, and the female of the male. It's a perfidious game that often ends in the most deplorable catastrophes imaginable; a ridiculous sort of merry-go-round in the course of which both deceiver and deceived are equally punished by the waste of the most precious part of their lives.

A. So you would say that coquettishness is not in nature?

B. I wouldn't say that.

A. What about constancy?

B. Nothing I could say on that subject would equal what Orou told the chaplain; it is the vain delusion of two children who know nothing about themselves or who are blinded by a moment of ecstasy to the transitory character of everything in nature.

A. And that rare phenomenon, fidelity?

B. In our part of the world it is the punishment for stubbornness which an honest man and woman must suffer. In Tahiti it is a chimera.

A. And jealousy?

B. It's the passion of a starved, miserly creature who is afraid of being deprived. In man it is an unjust sentiment produced by our false moral standards and the extension of property rights to a free, conscious, thinking being with a will of its own.

A. Then, according to you, jealousy has no place in nature?

B. I didn't say that. Nature includes both vices and virtues.

A. A jealous man is gloomy.

B. For the same reason that tyrants are gloomy – they know what they are up to.

A. And modesty?

B. Now you're asking me to give a course on the moral principles of lovemaking. A man does not want to be disturbed or distracted while he is involved in his pleasures. The delights of love are followed by a weakness that would abandon a man to the mercy of his enemy if the latter attacked him at that moment. Apart from this there is nothing natural about modesty – all the rest is social convention. The chaplain himself, in a third fragment that I haven't yet read to you, notes that a Tahitian is not embarrassed by certain involuntary movements of excitement that seize him when he is next to his wife and among his daughters; and the women and girls are never flustered – though they are sometimes moved – by the sight of such things. As soon as a woman became the property of a man, and as soon as the furtive enjoyment of a girl's favors came to be considered robbery, then the words "modesty," "demureness," and "propriety" were born, along with a whole set of imaginary vices. In a word, people tried to build a barrier between the sexes that would hinder them from tempting one another to violate the laws imposed on them – but these barriers often produce the opposite effect, since they serve to heat up the imagination and provoke desires. I have sometimes thought of all the trees planted around our kings' palaces – the sight of a bodice that both reveals and conceals a woman's breasts suggests the same idea – and in both instances I seem to detect a secret wish to escape into the forest, a suppressed impulse to recapture the freedom of our old habitat. The Tahitians would say, "Why do you hide your body? What are you ashamed of? Is it wrong to yield to the noblest urges of one's nature? Man, show yourself frankly if you are well liked. Woman, if this man is attractive to you, welcome his advances with the same frankness."

A. Don't get angry. Although we may begin by acting like civilized people, rarely do we not end up acting like the Tahitians.

B. Yes, but the preliminaries required by convention waste half the life of a man of genius.

A. True enough, but what's the harm in it? It merely slows down by that much the pernicious impetuosity of the human spirit against which you were inveighing not so long ago. Someone once asked one of our most eminent living philosophers why men court women and not the other way around, to which he replied that it is natural, when you want something, to ask someone who is always in a position to give it.

B. That explanation has always struck me as more ingenious than correct. Nature – indecently, if you like – forces both sexes toward each other equally, and in the dreary wild state of nature, which one may imagine, although it probably doesn't exist anywhere...

A. Not even in Tahiti?

B. No...the gap that divides a man from a woman would be crossed first by the more amorously inclined of the two. If they wait for each other or run away from one another, if they pursue or avoid each other, if they attack or defend themselves, the reason is simply that passion, which flares up more abruptly in the one than in the other, does not act on them with equal force. Hence it happens that sexual desire is aroused, consummated, and extinguished on one side while it is scarcely developed on the other, and both remain sad and dejected. This is a realistic account of what might happen between two young people who were perfectly free and innocent. But after women have learned through experience and education what more or less painful consequences can follow a blissful moment, their hearts tremble at a man's approach. The man's heart is far from trembling; he is urged on by his senses and he obeys. The woman's senses cry out for gratification, but she is afraid to listen to them. It's up to the man to find ways of putting her fears to rest, to sweep her off her feet and seduce her. Men have retained all of their natural desire for women, whereas, as a geometrician might say, the natural attraction that women feel toward men is directly proportional to the passion they feel and inversely proportional to their fears.

This ratio is complicated by a number of elements in our society that work together to augment the timidity of one sex and the length of time the other sex spends in pursuit. It is a kind of tactical exercise in which the plan of defense and the power of the offense have kept exactly in pace. We have consecrated the woman's resistance, we attach blame to the man's violence – violence that would be only a slight injury in Tahiti but becomes a crime in our cities.

A. But how did it come about that an act so solemn in purpose, an act to which nature so powerfully invites us – how did it come about that this act, the greatest, sweetest, and most innocent of pleasures, has become the chief source of our depravity and ills?

B. Orou explained it ten times over to the chaplain. Listen once more to what he said, and try to remember it:

It is due to the tyranny of men, who have converted the physical possession of a woman into a right of property.

It is due to the development of moral codes and customs, which have burdened marriage with too many conditions.

It is due to our civil laws, which have subjected the institution of marriage to endless formalities.

It is due to our form of society, in which the disparity of rank and of wealth has given rise to notions of propriety and impropriety.

It is due to a strange contradiction that is found in all existing societies – the birth of a child, although it is always considered an increase in the national wealth, usually means a greater certainty of even more abject poverty for the family into which it is born.

It is due to our rulers' political philosophy, which teaches them to subordinate everything to their own interests and security.

It is due to religious institutions, because their teachings have attached the labels "vice" and "virtue" to actions that are completely independent of morality.

How far we have departed from nature and happiness! Yet nature's sovereignty cannot be destroyed; it will persist in spite of all obstacles. Men may write as much as they like on tablets of bronze – to borrow the saying of Marcus Aurelius – that it is criminal to rub two intestines together voluptuously – the human heart will only be torn between the threats contained in the inscription and the violence of its own impulses. But the untamed heart will not cease to cry out against its oppressors, and in the course of a lifetime the terrible inscription will be ignored a hundred times by the average person. You may engrave on marble: Thou shalt not eat of the ixion nor of the wild vulture; thou shalt have carnal knowledge of no woman other than thy own wife; thou shalt not take thy sister in marriage – but you must not forget to increase the severity of the penalties in proportion to the arbitrariness of your prohibitions. Indeed, you may make them as ferocious as you please; still you will never be able to root out natural impulses.

A. How concise the legal codes of nations would be if they only conformed strictly to the law of nature! How many errors and vices would be spared!

B. Shall I outline for you the brief history of nearly all our unhappiness? It is simply this: Once there was a natural man; then an artificial man was built up inside him. Since then a civil war has been raging continuously within him. Sometimes the natural man proves stronger; at other times he is laid low by the artificial, moral man. But whichever gains the upper hand, the poor freak is racked and torn, tortured, stretched on the wheel, continually suffering, continually wretched, whether because he is out of his senses with some misplaced passion for glory or because imaginary shame curbs and brings him down. But despite all this, there are occasions when man recovers his original simplicity under the pressure of extreme necessity.

A. Poverty and sickness are two great exorcists.

B. Yes, you've put your finger on it. What, in fact, becomes of all our conventional virtues under such circumstances? A man in dire need is without scruples, and grave illness makes a woman forget her modesty.

A. So I have noticed.

B. And there's another thing that has probably not escaped you – the gradual reappearance of the moral, artificial man follows step by step during one's progress from illness to convalescence and from convalescence to full recovery. The internal warfare breaks out again as soon as the illness is cured, although the invader is almost always at a temporary disadvantage.

A. That's very true. I have learned from my own experience that during a period of convalescence the natural man seems to manifest a vigor that is downright damaging to the artificial, moral man. But tell me, in a word, is it better to civilize man or allow him to follow his instincts?

B. Must I be frank?

A. Certainly.

B. If you want to become his tyrant, civilize him; poison him as best you can with a system of morality that is contrary to nature. Devise all sorts of hobbies for him, contrive a thousand obstacles for him to trip over, saddle him with phantoms that terrify him, stir up an eternal conflict inside him, and arrange things so that the natural man will always have the artificial, moral man's foot on his neck. Do you want men to be happy and free? Then keep your nose out of his affairs – then he will be drawn toward enlightenment and depravity, depending on all sorts of unforeseeable circumstances. But as for our celebrated lawgivers, who have cast us in our present awkward mold, you may be sure that they have acted to serve their interests and not ours. Witness all our political, civil, and religious institutions – examine them thoroughly: unless I am very much mistaken, you will see how, through the ages, the human race has been broken to the halter that a handful of rascals were itching to impose. Watch out for the fellow who talks about putting things in order! Putting things in order always means getting other people under your control. The Calabrians are just about the only ones who have refused to be taken in by the flattery of lawgivers.

A. You are an admirer of the state of anarchy in Calabria?

B. I am only appealing to experience, and I'll wager that their barbarous society is less vicious than our "polite society." You hear a great deal about their grand crimes, but how many of our everyday little scandals do you suppose it would take to even up the score? I look on uncivilized people as a number of separate, isolated springs. Naturally these springs occasionally come loose and snap against each other, and then one or two of them may get broken. In order to prevent this, some sublime genius endowed with profound wisdom fitted all the little springs together into a complicated machine called society. All the springs are wound up in such a way that they are always pushing against each other, and more get broken in a single day in the state of civilization than would have in a whole year had they been left in their natural anarchy. What a mess! What wreckage! And what wholesale destruction of little springs when two, three, or four of these gigantic machines happen to run smack into each other!

A. So you would prefer to live in the raw, wild state of nature?

B. In truth, it's a difficult choice to make. Still, I have heard that on more than one occasion city people have set to plundering each other and then taken to the woods to live, and I've never heard that any forest dwellers ever put on proper clothes and went to live in the city.

A. I have often thought that for every individual the sum total of good and bad was different, but that for any species of animals there was a definite aggregate of happiness and unhappiness that was not subject to change. So perhaps, for all our striving, we do ourselves as much harm as good. Perhaps we have only tormented ourselves in order to make both sides of the equation a little larger without disturbing at all the eternally necessary balance between its two sides. On the other hand, it can't be doubted that the average lifespan of a civilized man is longer than the average lifespan of the uncivilized savage.

B. Well, but what conclusion can you draw from that, seeing that the length of time a machine lasts is not a true measure of the stresses and strains that are put on it?

A. I see that you are inclined, on the whole, to believe that men become more wicked and unhappy the more civilized they become.

B. Without going through the list of all the countries in the world, I can only assure you that you won't find the human condition perfectly happy anywhere but in Tahiti. And in only one little spot on the map of Europe will you find it even tolerable — there a set of haughty rulers, anxious over their own safety, have found ways to reduce man to what you would have to call a state of bestiality.

A. Are you talking about Venice?

B. Possibly. At least you won't deny that there's no place where enlightenment has made so little headway, where there is less artificial morality, or where there are fewer imaginary vices and virtues.

A. I didn't expect you to sing the praises of the Venetian government.

B. No, I'm not singing its praises. I am only pointing out to you one of the ways slavery can be compensated for, a way that all visitors to Venice have noticed and commented on.

A. A poor compensation!

B. Perhaps so. The Greeks proscribed the man who added one string to Mercury's lyre.

A. And that prohibition in itself is the most biting satire on their early lawgivers. They should have cut the first string instead of adding a new one.

B. You see what I'm driving at. Wherever there is a lyre you may be sure it has strings. Wherever natural appetites will be raised to a level of sophistication you can be sure there will be wicked women.

A. Just like the Reymer woman.

B. And abominable men.

A. Just like Gardeil.

B. And people who get into trouble through no fault of their own.

A. Like Tanié, Mademoiselle de la Chaux, the Chevalier Desroches, and Madame de La Carlière. No doubt in Tahiti you would search in vain for a parallel to the depravity of the first two or to the misfortunes of the last three. So what should we do — go back to the state of nature or obey the laws?

B. We should speak out against foolish laws until they are reformed, and meanwhile we should obey them as they are. Anyone who takes it upon himself, on his private authority, to break a bad law thereby authorizes everyone else to break the good ones. There is less harm to be suffered in being mad among madmen than in being sane all by one-self. We should say to ourselves — and shout incessantly too — that shame, dishonor, and penalties have been attached to actions that are in themselves perfectly harmless. But let us not do those things, because shame, dishonor, and penalties are the greatest evils of all. Let us follow the good chaplain's example — be monks in France and savages in Tahiti.

A. Put on the costume of the country you visit, but keep the suit of clothes you will need to go home in.

B. But especially, be scrupulously honorable and truthful in our deal-ings with those frail creatures who can only gratify our desires by jeop-ardizing the most precious advantages of society.... Well, what has become of that thick fog?

A. It seems to have settled.

B. So when we've had our dinner, we'll have a choice between staying inside and going for a stroll?

A. I suppose that will depend more on the ladies' inclination than ours.

B. The women again! You can't take a step in any direction without running into them.

A. What do you say, shall we read them the chaplain's account of his talk with Orou?

B. What do you suppose they would say if we did?

A. I haven't the foggiest idea.

B. Well, what would they think of it?

A. Probably the opposite of what they would say.

NOTE

1. How much better it is, and how contrary to certain other precepts, that you, a rich man, should be willing to allot your resources correctly according to their own nature, so as not to mingle desirable things with those that should be avoided! Do you count it as a matter of indifference that you must toil because of your own shortcom-ings and those of your subject matter?

Originally published as *Supplément au Voyage de Bougainville* (1796).

On the Education
of Women

by Choderlos de Laclos

Translated by Lydia Davis

Introduction by Chantal Thomas

On the Education of Women,
or: Portrait of the Natural Woman[1]

by Chantal Thomas

> *Her adornment is her flowing hair, her perfumes*
> *are a bath of clear water.*
> – Choderlos de Laclos, *On the Education of Women*

In March 1783 Laclos (1741–1803) tried to answer a question posed by
the Academy of Châlons-sur-Marne: "What would be the best means
of perfecting the education of women?" He broke off his answer after
a few pages, though certainly not out of indifference to the problem,
for he returned to it shortly thereafter in the form of an essay that was
likewise to remain unfinished – *On the Education of Women* (*1783*).
These two undeniably strange texts demonstrate Laclos's enduring interest in this question.

Captain Choderlos de Laclos, forty-two years old in 1783, had returned
the year before to La Rochelle, where he had first been assigned as a
young lieutenant in 1762, after a series of postings in Toul, Strasbourg,
Grenoble, and Besançon. He had just met Marie-Soulange Duperré,
a woman of twenty-three, whom he soon married. She would remain
until his death the object of his unflagging love, a "darling mistress,
excellent woman, and loving mother," whose praises he sang constantly
in his letters. This mutual conjugal love was, he attested, his true
reason for living: "Ah! Thanks to you, happiness is no stranger to me....
A solitary existence would be painful and withered, but I exist now
only in you, I live by your life...."[2]

By the time Laclos fell in love with Marie-Soulange, he was known
first and foremost as the author of *Dangerous Liaisons*, as is still the
case today. Indeed, while Laclos's peacetime career won him no military
glory, his writing brought him instant fame. The immediate success
of *Dangerous Liaisons* upon its publication in 1782 was not particularly
well received by the captain's superiors. The rhetorical disclaimers
Laclos had inserted at the beginning had done nothing to diminish the
book's notoriety. Readers of both sexes were more titillated by the
diabolical complicity of the Vicomte de Valmont and the Marquise de
Merteuil, in the throes of their criminal transports, than chastened

by the moralistic advice enjoining mothers to allow their daughters to read *Dangerous Liaisons* only at the appropriate time and place, only when they were no longer at risk of succumbing to seduction:

> Far from recommending this book to young people, it seems to me very important to keep it away from them. The time at which it may cease to be dangerous and become useful has been very well determined, for her own sex, by a good mother who is not only intelligent but sensible as well: "Having read this correspondence in manuscript," she told me, "I should consider it a true service to my daughter to give her the book on her wedding day." If mothers in every family were to think like this, I should never cease to congratulate myself for having published it.[3]

Dangerous Liaisons as a wedding gift! All these protestations of good intentions notwithstanding, it was not the pedagogical value of the book that caught the eye of the critics or the public. Was Laclos himself being serious? Or was this just a virtuous façade, as credible as Sade's declarations about *Justine* (1791) (blaming the immorality of his novel on economic factors): "I needed money, my publisher requested that I spice it up, and so I did, enough to arouse the devil."[4] In his biography of Laclos, Georges Poisson opts for the first hypothesis:

> Laclos the moralist, the satirist, must have been profoundly shocked by the way his novel had been interpreted, by the label of scandal seeker that had been attached to him, comparing him to a vulgar Andréa de Nercia. With this discourse for the academy of Châlons, he would attempt to regain his reputation, stubbornly clinging to moral concerns, but this time in a positive sense....[5]

On the Education of Women was to provide, in the words of Rémy de Gourmont, "the moral of *Dangerous Liaisons*, its dynamic and positive conclusion, which would reassure La Rochelle society."[6] However, this essay was never published in its author's lifetime, so the good people of La Rochelle and elsewhere were condemned never to be completely reassured about Laclos. And it is not clear that even after its publication all doubts were erased.

The inverse of a reading that stresses the "moralistic, satiric" aims of *Dangerous Liaisons* is one that posits a Laclos with profoundly immoral and subversive tendencies, despite his disclaimers. Of Goya's disapproving comments on his own *Caprichos*, André Malraux writes, "His notes to the *Caprichos* assert that the scenes depicted are the result of superstition and poor education. It is wrong to believe in ghosts. Why, then, paint them so convincingly? We are reminded of Laclos proclaiming about the same time the moral nature of *Dangerous Liaisons*."[7] Malraux is not imputing any duplicity to these two artists, who were equally influenced by the Enlightenment; rather, in a more complex and perhaps undefinable way, he posits, at the very heart of their inspiration and style, a deep identification with the evil they denounce. In the "Editor's Preface" that introduces *Dangerous Liaisons* and is an integral part of the fiction it precedes, Laclos writes that, "I, at any rate, think that it's a service to public morals to reveal the methods employed by those who are wicked in corrupting those who are good..." (p. 940). The novel is indeed a brilliant exploration of the "ways of evil" and their extraordinary richness, in contrast to which the "ways of goodness" seem practically nonexistent and very unattractive. The desire to prove a point, if it exists, does not take the form of some uncertain battle between vice and virtue. In a more radical, darker way the work depicts the total impotence of virtuous resolve in the face of libertine whims. One may then doubt its ability to awaken in the reader the desire to take up the cause of a good so ineffectual, so hopelessly victimized – a cause that, through the voice of Mme de Tourvel, articulates ideals more likely to encourage resignation or arbitrary willfulness than to spur exaltation, such as this admission: "I was happy, I had to be happy...."

Whichever perspective on the ideas about women and their education in *Dangerous Liaisons* one opts for, it is clear that the two texts complement one another. Indeed, *On the Education of Women*, far from negating the universe of *Dangerous Liaisons*, is necessary for a more complete understanding of Laclos and the complexity and power of his intellect and imagination. The question of the education of women lies at the heart of the novel, for it is against the backdrop of a mother's negligence that Mme de Merteuil spins her intrigues. And the novel's denouement attests that any mother who allows anyone other than herself to gain the confidence of her daughter is at the very least imprudent.

"At the very least imprudent" Mme de Volanges certainly is. Having removed her daughter from the convent to marry her off, the mother is so negligent about her instruction that the girl takes all the men she meets for potential suitors – even mistaking the kneeling position of a shoemaker putting on her shoe for the solicitousness of a lover! The innocent Cécile de Volanges, whose years in a convent have in no way prepared her for life in the world, is the blank slate on which Mme de Merteuil will project her darkest intrigues. Cécile, whose mother fails not only to help her but even to talk to her, has as her confidant, guide and, on occasion, lover, the perfidious marquise. "It is most extraordinary" writes Cécile to her friend Sophie, "that a woman who is scarcely a relation takes more care of me than my own mother! How lucky I am to know her!" she exults, with her usual perceptiveness (p. 983). Her seductress, for her part, uses all the resources of her fertile brain to get Cécile back to her convent after a quick foray onto the world's stage. The young woman, her youthful illusions dashed forever, has gained no new knowledge: destroyed by a string of affairs, each disastrous in its own way, she has learned nothing. The marquise, moreover, has quickly realized that Cécile is unable to move beyond victimization to libertinage. Unlike Eugénie in Sade's *Philosophy in the Bedroom* (1795), who proves from the start to be a creature of pleasure *and* principle, Cécile takes no joy in transgression. Lacking any philosophical bent, she can emerge from her exploits only as a "fallen woman."

Mme de Merteuil does not educate Cécile; rather, abetted by the withdrawal of the girl's mother, she uses her. It is not that the marquise is indifferent to questions of education; on this point, she considers her knowledge too precious to be shared with a "little snippet" whose only virtue is her submissiveness.

Madame de Merteuil's Lesson

Already in *Dangerous Liaisons* Laclos issues a negative verdict on the education society offers to women. Packed off to the convent as children, girls are given no knowledge, either theoretical or practical. When they return, their mothers, separated too long from their children and strangers to them, have no idea of how to educate them; there is no transmission of wisdom or experience. In place of trust and friendship there is only the cold affirmation of authority. To whom can those rare women turn who despite this experience seek to be educated? In the character of Mme de Merteuil, Laclos offers a radical alternative. Given the current state of affairs, a woman can expect nothing from anyone: it is up to her to understand that she must educate herself. She is alone; and not only does she lack institutional and parental support but she also exists in tacit opposition to society in general and to the opposite sex in particular. The Marquise de Merteuil is the successful, exceptional example of such a heroic undertaking. Whence the condescending tone of the famous autobiographical letter (number 81) to the Viscount de Valmont. Exasperated by the boastfulness of his latest missive, she relates to him how she became what she is or, rather, how she created herself. What is the principle of the marquise's

self-education? Distrust. Dissimulation is the cardinal rule of the long
and rigorous training period to which she has subjected herself. Even as
an adolescent she does not deviate from the absolute rule of duplicity. We are reminded that she first felt a thrill of pleasure while confessing to a sin she had not committed: "the good priest made so
much of the crime that I concluded the pleasure of committing it must
be extreme, and my desire for knowledge gave way to a desire for
gratification" (p. 1075). Yet she hides from her husband the pleasure
his caresses give her: "faithful to my principles and aware, perhaps by
instinct, that no one should lie further from my confidence than my
husband, I decided, for the very reason that I had become susceptible
to pleasure, to appear in his eyes as impassive" (p. 1076). Later she
takes advantage of her recent widowhood to remove herself for a time
from society. The young woman develops herself intellectually; she
reads prodigiously and she works methodically. "I studied our manners in the novelists, our opinions in the philosophers; I went to the
strictest moralists to find out what they demanded of us, so as to
know for certain what it was possible to do, what it was best to think,
and what it was necessary to seem to be" (p. 1076). She quickly concludes that appearances alone count, and that as long as one's true
thoughts remain hidden all misdeeds are possible. She thus refines her
theoretical reflections with an important practical corollary: maintaining absolute control of her expression. Her intellectual passion
and her taste for erotic experimentation are inseparable from a perfect
mastery of her acting talents.

Mme de Merteuil proclaims herself to be her own creation. To this
end she subjects herself to a strict training regimen – total control at
all times, both spiritual and muscular, which consists essentially of
fashioning a mask in place of a face. To say that Mme de Merteuil
never stops observing herself is an understatement: she goes further,
turning her expressions into so many signs designed to mislead others.
"When I felt annoyed I practiced looking serene, even cheerful; in my
enthusiasm I went so far as to seek pain voluntarily so as to achieve a
simultaneous expression of pleasure" (p. 1074). Whence the accuracy
of the commentary accompanying the final "fall" of Mme de Merteuil,
ruined and outcast, half-blind and horribly disfigured by smallpox:
"The Marquis de ———, who never loses an opportunity to be spiteful, said yesterday in speaking of her 'that the disease had turned her
inside out, and that her soul is now visible on her face'" (p. 1250).
There could be no more agonizing defeat for her than this failure of
her lifelong striving for self-mastery and absolute secrecy. And this

elevation of both the everyday social lie and worldly hypocrisy to the status of art, to an ascetic exigency, is one of the beauties of Mme de Merteuil as a character. If Rameau's nephew could say of himself, "I never tire," Mme de Merteuil could have said, "I never rest."

Mme de Merteuil is unequaled on the public scene for the refinement, virtuosity, and intelligence with which she exercises this talent, culled from social conventions, following rules of her own making. She is not the inventor of this game of dissimulation; rather, it is an integral part of the world she lives in, a part that has been strictly formalized through the centuries. One finds it set down as early as the sixteenth century in studies of physiognomy and the various codes of etiquette by which the individual tries at once to decipher the expressions of others and to attain self-mastery. Thus, in his book *La Fisionomia dell'Huomo* (1623), G.B. Della Porta developed a "kind of science" by which the subject, a skillful decoder of other's faces, learns to elude external scrutiny by others. As Jean-Jacques Courtine and Claudine Haroche write in their *Histoire du visage*:

> *Being one's own face-reader:* the forms of social control by facial expression must be extended to the internal being: the face thus appears as a personal discipline.... In this exercise of looking *at himself as another*, the internal man can, with effort, detach himself from his appearance: private space increases with the exercise of this discipline; and with it the possibility of belying one's appearance by reshaping one's soul, but also of masking corrupted morals behind pleasant appearances.[8]

The treatises which claim to offer objective knowledge in service of virtue, imply an important theatrical dimension of behavior, and along with it innumerable possibilities for duplicity, lies, and deceit. The seventeenth century, which witnessed the triumph of court society, furthered the perfection of the face as mask, the art of duplicity:

> The codification of linguistic exchange testifies to the strengthening of social controls, in a universe dominated by appearances.... Treatises on social conversation throughout the seventeenth century develop ways of being simultaneously present and absent in society, elaborating a theory and practice of *detachment from the self* that turn the actor's paradox, that distantiation that separates the actor from his character, into a way of being.[9]

The eighteenth-century character Mme de Merteuil simply pushes what society has established as an ideal of conviviality and worldly refinement to the point of excluding any form of authenticity, purely for the sake of artistic performance. And, sacrificing all to appearances, she overlooks the idea of a truthful compromise, some possible concordance of an individual's inner truth and its external manifestations. The theatrical mask she has created for herself certainly expresses her acting talents and the pleasure she takes in them, but it also has a defensive function; that is why it suffers no flaws. Society is an entertainment, but a dangerous one: its rules may be artificial, but the killings it decrees are real. Society's theater is a theater of cruelty. Any sincere confession is a weakness upon which others will immediately pounce.

The Model of the Natural Woman

To understand the rush of freedom, the liberation from all constraints which underlies the utopia of *On the Education of Women*, one must bear in mind this vision of society as a sinister theater, an implacable killing machine (whose chosen victims are women). When the natural woman springs forth, outside of any social context, before language and naming, one must remember that her innocence – which Laclos simply allows us to imagine – has meaning only within the framework of that evil genius so splendidly incarnated in Mme de Merteuil. For in the state of war that is the real world, the pitiless and solitary education that Mme de Merteuil gives herself must remain the only meaningful choice.

In this portrait of a world dominated by oppression and corruption the influence of Jean-Jacques Rousseau, Laclos's admired and uncontested master, is undeniable. As Laurent Versini observes, some of Laclos's sentences are slight variations on passages from the *Discourse on the Arts and Sciences* (1749) or *The Social Contract* (1762).[10]

Laclos, however, starting with Rousseauian precepts concerning the enslavement that life in society represents, adheres to a syllogistic rigor that prevents him from positing even the slightest possibility of improving the female condition. Only free individuals can be educated; consequently women, as slaves, are ineducable. "Thus, I must dare to say, there is no way to improve the education of women" (p. 129). Laclos's text can neither be developed programmatically nor literarily – he is committed to brevity (he could have been awarded the prize for succinctness which Saint-Just proposed instituting in this era of oratorical excess of the Revolution's speech makers) – but the natural woman thereby gains total freedom, the assurance of not having to tolerate the shadow of domination. Woman is ineducable? Fine. In that case she will make no attempt to learn and will not move forward in any way. But — and here is the simultaneously revolutionary and time-less dimension of the work — she will discover a new body; she will invent for herself a new sensuality. Woman is beyond rehabilitation? Perfect! Let us do away with the convents and go swimming. The natural woman, this miracle of spontaneity, this marvel of freshness, whose shining eyes need neither makeup nor tears, is rescued in one turn of phrase from cold hours of prayers, from the boredom of les-sons, from the whole weight of traditional schooling, as well as from reason and the dreariness of well-intended reforms — whether moti-vated by the spirit of more rigorous domination, as in Rousseau, or by the more practical middle ground, as in Diderot, who was fascinated by the question of the education of women, in particular as it con-cerned his own daughter, Angelique.

For Rousseau the choice is clear. Starting with the notion of sub-servience, he prescribes an educational program that is even more restrictive. Woman are slaves — but are they enslaved enough? Revolt is always possible. And, above all, from their very weakness they have devised the only weapons at their disposal: duplicitousness. All that women need to learn may be summarized in the word *obey.* "Girls ought to be vigilant and industrious. That is not all. They ought to be constrained very early.... Accustom them to being interrupted in the midst of their games and brought back to other cares without grumbling...."[11] The goal of this plan for the education of girls is not simply to break their physical impulses and their spirit of play, but also — and the one is inseparable from the other — to destroy their intelligence. In any case, states Rousseau, by their natural dispositions, women are more inclined toward coquetry than instruction: "In fact, almost all little girls learn to read and write with repugnance. But as for holding a needle, that they always learn gladly."[12] Rousseau's hatred for women of letters is well known. Without dabbling in writing, a woman could at least lay some claim to the pleasures of the intellect. No, protests Rousseau, that too is intolerable; besides, her ever-present desire to please could only distort her judgment. The ideal compan-ion that Rousseau envisions for his Emile will have none of these flaws: "Sophie has a mind that is agreeable without being brilliant, and solid without being profound — a mind about which people do not say anything, because they never find in it either more or less than what they find in their own minds."[13] Society makes woman the slave of man. The woman's reaction to this is to perfect the sole resource at her disposition, deceitfulness. Woman speaks only to deceive. "Why do you consult their mouth when it is not the mouth which ought to speak? Consult their eyes, their color, their breathing, their frightened manner, their soft resistance. This is the language nature gives them for answering us."[14] From the observation that the social state is a state of slavery Rousseau draws two opposite conclusions, depending upon the gender under consideration: for men, it is an unnatural state, for women, an extension of their "natural language," that reveals their weakness and dependence. Women are made to be imprisoned. Reversing the usual rule that makes the passage from the convent to the status of married woman an entrance into the world, Rousseau tries, on the contrary, to make the bride live in her house as she would in a convent. She should impose on herself, as her conjugal duty, a seclusion as strict as that of the nun hidden from the seductions of the outside world.

With this vengeful outlook Rousseau represents an extreme position in the domain of misogyny. It has nothing in common with the progressive ideas put forth by Diderot in *Rameau's Nephew* in a dialogue between the nephew and the philosopher ("He" and "I"). But while manifesting no hostility toward women, these ideas could hardly be greeted by them with any enthusiasm:

HE: And what will you teach her, then?

I: To reason correctly, if I can. An uncommon thing in men and even rarer in women.

[...]

HE: [...] What, no dancing lessons?

I: Only what is needed for curtseying, standing up properly, having a good presence and deportment.

HE: No singing?

I: No more than you need for good enunciation.

HE: No music?

I: If there were a good teacher of harmony I would willingly send her to him for two hours a day for a year or two, but not more.

HE: And in the place of the essential things you are cutting out ...

I: I put grammar, literature, history, geography, a bit of drawing and a great deal of ethics.

HE: How easy it would be for me to prove the uselessness of all those subjects in a world such as ours. Uselessness? I would even say danger, perhaps.[15]

Laclos, whose pessimism concerning the world that surrounded him was at least as great as that of Rousseau or Diderot, was not drawn to the former's coercive program. To make the chains weighing on women even heavier was, for him, an inconceivable option. As his letters reveal, he would lean rather toward the practical and common-sensical reforms promoted by Diderot. During his imprisonment under the Reign of Terror (briefly incarcerated in 1793 at the Abbey, he was released, only to be arrested and imprisoned again at La Force and then Picpus, where he remained from November 1793 to December 1, 1794), Laclos studied rural economy. Indeed, his never-realized hope was to "cultivate some small field, when [he was] freed." He also reflected on the education of his children: his goal was "to be able to explain this veritable science" to his children. "To my children," he clarifies, "for this includes my daughter, who is perhaps to have pref-erence for this subject. I see the time coming when war, agriculture, and commerce will require the attentions of all men and all the seden-tary occupations, other than legislation and government, will be left to women."[16] And a few days later, he specified, "I want my son to be trained in agriculture and one of the necessary arts; and my daughter in the work of her sex, rural economy and commercial transactions."[17] But in writing his essay on the education of women, unconcerned as yet with the concrete paternal issues of this program, he indulged in an unwavering theoretical radicalism. Rejecting Rousseau's punitive rigor and Diderot's progressive moderation, he abandoned any realistic compromises in favor of a surrealistic theory of total revolution. Thrust-ing aside the pedagogical problem, he set up a perfect apparition. Laclos used the state of nature as a conceptual model in a way that allowed him to create the character of the natural woman, a pure phys-ical presence whose fulfillment would transport us to a paradise of transparency and immediacy. In the same way his thoughts on the society of his time had inspired the character of Mme de Merteuil, the woman who epitomized sophistication and manipulative intelligence, and who carried to its ultimate consequences the war between the sexes and the reign of hypocrisy. *Dangerous Liaisons* and *On the Educa-tion of Women* are two texts dominated by extreme female characters, whose strength and beauty, though derived from opposing criteria, are viewed by their author with a similar glow of desire.

Laclos offers no answer to the question of what women should be taught. In a more basic way, and with incalculable social and moral consequences, he imagines a different sort of woman. He envisions for her a different concept of motherhood, and he fashions for her an entirely new body, unhindered by the constraints and the weaknesses of the old one.

Following Rousseau, Laclos argues here for a closer physical and emotional link between mother and infant. He makes motherhood more natural. He is for breastfeeding by the mother, over and against the use of the wetnurses and later governesses, to whom mothers turned over the care of the child. This phenomenon had become alarmingly widespread, raising the infant mortality rate. According to a study by Elisabeth Badinter,

> it was in the eighteenth century that the use of wet nurses expanded to all segments of urban society. From the poorest to the richest, in small and large cities, sending the child away to a wet nurse was the general rule.
>
> Paris, as was usually the case, led the way, sending its infants far beyond its walls, sometimes as far as 125 miles away, to Normandy or Burgundy.[18]

Laclos hoped mothers would have a more physical and more sensitive relationship with their children. In one of his letters to his wife from prison he wrote, "I suppose that when you are settled you will take your daughter with you. The greatest favor you can do for her, in my opinion, is to nourish her young soul with your tender care."[19] He further champions for women more generally a program of bodily awareness, one that was unusual for his time. He envisions a female body hitherto unknown, more rested and attentive to hygiene, more energetic, flexible, and hardy: a woman, full of life, enjoying all the pleasures of movement, whether it be walking or swimming, a creature whose beauty is an expression of health, and whose deep-seated equilibrium makes her even more responsive to desire. In his *Tableau de Paris* (1782) Louis-Sébastien Mercier criticizes the "posture of weakness" so typical of his female contemporaries who, squeezed into their tight corsets, had no form of exercise and, perpetual victims of vapors and other forms of dizziness, regularly succumbed to fainting fits:

> Weakness is becoming to a woman, as she knows: she knows she is more interesting if she appears to be delicate. This is why our women, although healthy, learn to walk uncertainly, to speak nasally, to act sickly, to complain about their nerves.[20]

Laclos, who never neglected to remind his wife of the advantages of walks, stresses the seductiveness of "the state of strength." Inseparable from the hygienic and even medical value of his commentary, Laclos outlines a new feminine ideal. The natural woman he describes is offered not merely for her descriptive value; endowed with the three essential properties "freedom, strength, and health," she is also the object of erotic dreams and fantasies.

On the [Impossible] *Education of Women* includes a vision of women's sexuality and its development, in which Laclos shows himself to be simultaneously traditional — he posits a total sensual unawareness before the "awakening" that is puberty — and daring. He gives the woman, once she has surpassed her initial numbness, a spontaneous sex life of irrepressible intensity. Laclos imagines the young girl tormented by desires she does not understand, racked by worry and sleeplessness. Discovering the beauty of nature around her, the songs of birds, and the greenness of the trees, she nevertheless remains devoured by an intolerable lack. "It is then," writes Laclos, as heedless of the rules of proper behavior as he is of those of realism,

> that at some distance she sees a man; a powerful instinct, an involuntary motion, causes her to run toward him; closer, she becomes shy, she stops. But, carried away once again, she joins him and clasps him in her arms. [...] Delicious joy, who will ever dare to describe you? (p. 139).

This study of the female body is part of a paean to the free expression of desire. Having elaborated on desire in all its mediated modes, in all its plays with mirrors in *Dangerous Liaisons*, Laclos highlights, in the brightness of a perfect morning, the very locus of immediate pleasure, the erogenous zone par excellence: the skin, offered in all its freshness and nudity. As much as a visual presence, the natural woman is understood as a tactile presence, a sensual gift.

The natural woman is not pale like those women who are shut up in their apartments, with that pallor vaguely considered to be a sign of class and beauty. Heedless of prevailing standards, she overturns all stereotypes. She is taller and heavier than the woman of the time.

> Her skin, colored by the sun, is a darker yet livelier hue; in truth, she is less delicate, but if for that reason her sensation of touch is reduced overall, it becomes stronger in the parts which are its seat and organ, and which have retained all their sensitivity. Her flesh, continually assaulted by a brisk breeze, is firmer and more alive (p. 140).

Laclos strays from the question of the education of women to that of their physical identity. Speculating on the natural woman he seeks to discover a body language as yet unknown, a face that is not a mask, a demeanor that expresses self-assured strength rather than weakness – a woman, in other words, as fearless of others as of her own desires.

NOTES

1. I have given this essay the title chosen by Laurent Versini in Laclos's *Oeuvres complètes* (Paris: Gallimard, La Pléiade, 1979). Versini uses the title of Laclos's second essay to cover Laclos's entire section on women.

2. Laclos, *Lettres inédites*, published by Louis de Chauvigny (Paris: Société du Mercure de France, 1904); letter of the nineteenth of prairial, year Sd of the one and undivided Republic, p. 61.

3. Laclos, *Dangerous Liaisons*, included in this volume, p. 940. Subsequent citations will be marked parenthetically.

4. Lawrence W. Lynch, *The Marquis de Sade* (Boston: Twayne, 1984), p. 41.

5. Georges Poisson, *Choderlos de Laclos ou l'obstination* (Paris: Editions Grasset, 1985), p. 153.

6. *Ibid.*, Poisson is paraphrasing Gourmont.

7. André Malraux, *Saturn: An Essay on Goya*, trans. C.W. Chilton (New York: Phaidon, 1957), pp. 78–79.

8. Jean-Jacques Courtine and Claudine Haroche, *Histoire du visage, XVIe- début XIXe siècle* (Paris: Editions Rivages, 1988), p. 78.

9. *Ibid.*, pp. 188–90.

10. For example, Laclos writes, "Come learn how, born the companions of man, you became his slave" (*Oeuvres complètes*, p. 390) is an explicit reference to Rousseau. Versini writes, "Laclos did no more than put the first sentence of chapter 1 of the *Social Contract* in the feminine" (*ibid.*, p. 1419).

11. Jean-Jacques Rousseau, *Emile, or on Education*, trans. Allan Bloom (New York: Basic, 1979), pp. 369, 370.

12. *Ibid.*, p. 368.

13. *Ibid.*, pp. 395–96.

14. *Ibid.*, p. 385.

15. Denis Diderot, *Rameau's Nephew/D'Alembert's Dream*, trans. Leonard Tancock (New York: Penguin, 1966), pp. 56–57. This work was written between 1761 and 1773, but not published until 1821.

16. *Lettres inédites*, letter of the twenty-first of prairial, year Sd of the one and undivided Republic, p. 63.

17. *Ibid.*, letter of the twenty-sixth of prairial, p. 74.

18. Elisabeth Badinter, *Mother Love: Myth and Reality* (New York: Macmillan, 1981), p. 42.

19. *Lettres inédites*, letter of the thirteenth of the floréal, year Sd of the one and undivided Republic, p. 32.

20. Louis-Sébastian Mercier, *Tableau de Paris* (Amsterdam, 1782), vol. 5, p. 90.

Translated by Shelly Temchin.

CONTENTS

ON THE EDUCATION OF WOMEN

by Choderlos de Laclos

PART I

DISCOURSE ON THE QUESTION PUT FORTH BY THE ACADEMY OF CHALONS-SUR-MARNE

How Can the Education of Women Best Be Improved

There is no cure for evil once vice becomes habit.
– Seneca, *Letter 39*.

MARCH 1, 1783

A COMPANY OF scholars and sages today is awarding a literary prize to the person who can best describe *how to improve the education of women*. The crowd of speakers is coming forward. Each of them shall present to the judges the fruit of his work, and all hope to obtain their prize. Other motives bring me here. I have come to this respectable assembly to devote to truth, more respectable still, a faint but steadfast voice which the fear of offending or the hope of succeeding will not alter. Such is the commitment that I enter into on this day. The first duty it imposes on me is to replace a seductive error with a strict truth. Thus, I must dare to say, there is no way to improve the education of women. This assertion will appear reckless, and already I hear around me complaints of paradox. But often a paradox is the beginning of a truth. This shall become one should I succeed in proving that the so-called education given to women until now does not in fact deserve the name education; that our laws and our customs are equally opposed to our ability to give women a better one; and that if, despite these obstacles, a few women were to succeed in procuring it for themselves, it would be yet another misfortune for them and for us. Here it becomes necessary to lay down some principles. And if this didactic progression is not one of eloquence, it suffices for my intentions that it be one of truth.

Either the word "education" has no meaning, or else one can take it to mean elevating the development of the individual's faculties and the direction of these faculties toward social utility. This education is more or less perfect in proportion as the development is more or less complete, the direction more or less constant; if, instead of stretching the faculties, one restrains them, well, then it is no longer education, it is deprivation; if, instead of directing them toward social utility, one turns them back on the individual, then it is merely instinct perfected. Yet the faculties are divided into the sensory and the intellectual. Hence, physical education and moral education, though separate in their object, come together again in their goal — the perfection of the individual for the advantage of the species. In the particular case with which we are concerned, woman is the individual; the species is society. The question, then, is to find out if the education given to women develops, or tends at least to develop, their faculties, to direct their use according to the interests of society; if our laws do not oppose this development and we ourselves this direction; and lastly, if in the present state of society a well-educated woman such as one may imagine her would not be very unhappy remaining in her place and very dangerous if she tried to leave it. These are the subjects I propose to examine.

Oh, women! Approach and come hear me!

Let your curiosity, once it is directed toward useful objects, contemplate the advantages which nature has given you and of which society has robbed you. Come and learn how, born man's companion, you have become his slave; how, fallen into this abject state, you have come to like it, to regard it as your natural state; how, lastly, degraded more and more by a long habit of slavery, you have come to prefer its debasing but convenient vices to the more difficult virtues of a free and respectable existence. If this faithfully drawn picture leaves you unmoved, if you can contemplate it without emotion, return to your futile occupations. *There is no cure for evil once vice becomes habit.* But if at the recital of your misfortunes and your losses you blush with shame and anger, if tears of indignation pour from your eyes, if you burn with the noble desire to recover possession of your advantages, to reenter the fullness of your being, do not continue to allow yourselves to be deluded by false promises, do not expect the help of the men who created your ills: they have neither the will nor the power to end them, and how could they wish to educate women before whom they would be forced to blush; learn that one does not emerge from slavery except through a great revolution. Is this revolution possible? That is for you alone to say, since it depends on your courage, in itself likely. I will say nothing about this question; but until it happens, and as long as men rule your fate, I shall be justified in saying, *and it will be easy for me to prove, that there is no means of improving the education of women.*

Wherever there is slavery, there can be no education: in every society, women are slaves; thus, the social woman is not amenable to education. If the principles of this syllogism are proven, one cannot deny the consequence. Now, that wherever there is slavery, there can be no education, follows naturally from the definition of the word; it is the nature of education to develop the faculties, the nature of slavery to stifle them; it is the nature of education to direct the developed faculties toward social usefulness, the nature of slavery to make the slave an enemy of society. If these unquestionable principles leave any doubts, they can be removed by applying these principles to freedom. It is apparent that one cannot deny freedom to be one of woman's faculties, and this implies that freedom can develop in slavery; it implies further that freedom can be directed toward social utility, since the freedom of a slave would be a blow against the social pact based on slavery. It would be useless to try to resort to differentiations or disagreements. One cannot depart from this general principle, that without freedom there is no morality, and without morality no education.

PART II

ON WOMEN AND THEIR EDUCATION

CHAPTER I

On Women and the Aim of This Work

An ancient defined man as a two-footed, featherless animal; woman is the female of that animal – not woman disfigured by our institutions but such as she emerged from the hands of nature. Destined like other animals to be born and to reproduce, she received, like them, an attraction to pleasure, a means of preserving the species; a fear of pain, a means of preserving the individual. Of these two means, the first, being less important, must be and is in fact subordinate to the second. After the age of reproduction, nature seems to abandon the individual, feelings become dulled, organs become blocked. Pleasure and pain seem to leave at the same time; insensibility increases, and we call it old age; total insensibility is death. Self-preservation and reproduction, then, are the laws to which nature has subjected women. Thus, to provide their own food, to receive the approaches of the male, to feed the child that issues from this and not to abandon it until it can do without her care – these are the natural impulses that women receive. Our institutions often distance them from this, and nature unfailingly punishes them for it. Have they gained or lost by these institutions? We do not claim to resolve this question so much as to put our readers in a position to do so, and for this we will follow women, from those of nature to those of our day. This journey is a vast one to make. Once we have arrived at this point, we shall try to recognize how far they have gone astray, and indicate the path they must take in order to find their way again. Perhaps that second journey will be as long as, and more difficult than, the first.

CHAPTER II

On the Natural Woman

The natural woman is, like the natural man, a free and strong creature; free, in that she has the entire exercise of her faculties; strong, in that her faculties are equal to her needs. Is such a creature happy? Yes, without doubt, and if, according to our ideas, her happiness seems paradoxical, a more thoughtful examination soon allows us to recognize the truth of this.* Men wanted to perfect everything, and they have corrupted everything; they burdened themselves with chains then complained of being overwhelmed by their weight; senseless and unjust, they abandoned the nature that made them happy, then they slandered it, accusing it of the ills that this abandonment caused them, which they themselves brought about.

---

*"The Researches which can be undertaken concerning this Subject must not be taken for historical truths, but only for hypothetical and conditional reasonings better suited to clarify the Nature of things than to show their genuine origin..." (Jean-Jacques Rousseau, *Discourse on the Origins of Inequality* [Hanover, NH: University Press of New England, 1992], p. 195).

CHAPTER III

On Childhood

Civilized man, at the moment of his birth, is tightly bound in swaddling clothes; it seems that his parents already wish to accustom him to the eternal slavery that has been prepared for him; in this state of discomfort and suffering, his mother pushes him away and distances him from her; she deprives him of the maternal warmth that alone is suited to his weakness; she refuses him the milk prepared for his nourishment. The natural child is not treated thus; when he is about to be born, a state of enfeeblement, uneasiness, and *displeasure* leads his mother to seek solitude. Her *painful* limbs demand a softer resting place, and, without understanding the cause, she is already preparing the place where the work of nature is to be accomplished. Stretched out peacefully, she awaits an event unfamiliar to her, without fear and without foresight. Yet a beneficial pain comes to restore some of her vital force, urges her on to the movement necessary to facilitate this process, even irresistibly induces her to assume the position most favorable to the emergence of the child. At last he is born, and the cessation of pain (a state so similar to pleasure) is the first feeling that attaches the mother to the child. Whoever wishes to know how delightful and strong is the feeling of maternal love should not enter the palaces of the great, where procreation is prompted by interest and vanity alone; he should avoid the huts of the poor, where destitution sometimes stifles it; he should shun the men of today, who are too depraved; rather, let him consult the animals. Is there one among them, however timid, that does not become courageous in the defense of its young, one, however cruel, that is not gentle and playful with them; one, however fickle, that does not settle in order to care for them?... Woman alone consents to be separated from her son.... But no; even in her, nature is still alive, and thus violated, rather than seduced. Answer me: Which of you has seen her newborn child taken away without shedding some tears? Natural woman is happier; nothing deprives her, nothing separates her from the object of her affection; all her care will be devoted to him; soon after giving birth she rises, she goes to bathe her child in a nearby stream; she bathes in it herself;* after drying herself on the grass, she dries him in turn, not with irritating rubbing, not by exposing him to a *desiccating* heat, but by placing him on her breast; it is there that he finds at once a ben-

---

*This practice still occurs among some of the people of India.

eficial warmth and a nourishment suitable to him. The milk is the natural bond that unites the mother and child; if it is necessary for the one
to receive it, it is at least dangerous for the other to deny it to him.
Happy is the society whose basis is reciprocal benefit. Thus, the mother
never wishes to leave her child; in her expeditions, which her need for
food requires, she carries him in her arms; in her moments of rest, she
plays with him and makes him exercise his budding strength; if a danger should appear, she hides her child, she exposes herself alone and
comes back to him as soon as possible. Likewise, the child cannot
remain far from his mother; if he no longer sees her near him, he cries,
he becomes agitated. And when she is returned to him? He is at peace,
his hands, still weak, try to reach out toward her, his infant smile reveals
his joy, and that joy echoes in the heart of his mother. We ask, now,
despite the ostentatious display of obstetricians, guards, nurses, governesses, which of the two is abandoned at birth, the son of a prince or
this primitive child?*

However, as the milk becomes more rare, the child becomes less useful to his mother, and the mother less necessary to her child; he has
already acquired some strength, the instinct to imitate has taught him,
by his mother's example, to seek, recognize, and take foreign food. He
knows how to walk like her; there is no more difference between them,
except in the degree of strength and common experience, which time
alone can make him acquire. Here is where the bonding contract between mother and child, along with the necessity that established it,
ends; the first random event that divides them will separate them forever; soon they will not even be able to recognize each other anymore,
and the child will live alone under the charge of nature. This is where
the second stage begins.

CHAPTER IV

Continuation of the Same Subject

Man's childhood has two distinct periods for which our language provides only a single word. The Latins, who distinguished between them,

---

*Should anyone wish to doubt that a woman who has recently given birth has the strength
necessary to perform easily the duties indispensable to motherhood, we would send him
to the negresses of our colonies who, soon after giving birth, themselves wash their children; to the provisioners of our armies, who give birth during a march, swaddle their
child in haste, and continue to drive before them the mule that carries their provisions,

expressed them by the words *infans* and *puer*. The meaning of the word *infans* (one who cannot speak) suggests that they were considering civilized man more than natural man. For our part, we shall establish that period as one in which the child can provide for his needs on his own, that is, walk and eat alone; without claiming to indicate this period exactly, we shall point out that, for children of the peasants, it is ordinarily from three to four years of age. We shall also observe that the natural child must be more advanced, and that comparison with certain animals leads us to believe that this time must be, more or less, the thirtieth part of an ordinary life. After this brief digression, we shall continue to use the word "child" to designate the second stage of man, which we shall consider.

This second stage comprises a fairly large span of time, which nature employs to improve the individual and to put him in a condition to reproduce himself. Nature's means to accomplish this are movement, appetite, and sleep — means so felicitously united that one never fails to induce the other; indeed, movement arouses appetite, appetite in turn necessitates movement, and both, as soon as they are satisfied, provoke sleep. One need not have observed children a great deal to know that movement is their natural state. The hindrances one places on them, the threats one makes to them, the punishments one inflicts on them sometimes constrain them, and never change them. Should one lose them from sight for an instant? They run, they jump, they become excited, they must move. A peaceful child, unless he is tired, is a sick child; that symptom is certain. Our pupil, or, to be more exact, that of nature, is not constrained to this forced repose; this wise governess forces him, on the contrary, to exercise himself ceaselessly; he has too much to do to remain in one spot.

Of all the animals, man is undeniably the one that adapts best to different foods; vegetables, grains, fruits, fish, meat, everything is good for him. Despite this aptitude, one senses well enough that the attention to his food must be a long and laborious occupation for a child without strength and without experience. Vegetables contain little nourishing essences, in proportion to their volume; grains are scattered, and are gathered a little at a time; fruits, for the most part, are

---

and a few days later resume the arduous labors to which they are subjected; to the wives of poor peasants, who, much closer to our customs, do not cease, during the ceremony of the baptism, to tidy their bedrooms and prepare the collation, then return to their beds in order to play sick, in imitation of our ladies.

elevated and require that one learn to climb trees; fish, animals, present still more difficulties. Lacking strength, the child can attack only weak animals, but these are ordinarily timid and quick to flee; the hunting expedition is a very uncertain resource, if cunning does not play a part in it, and cunning is the fruit of experience. He will therefore be daily exercised, often even wearied, but never grieved or disheartened, and who could find tiresome a task undertaken out of desire, sustained by hope, and crowned by success? Yet it is not enough to eat, one must drink as well; another expedition to be made, but this one is made more slowly than the others, for, on the one hand, the child has already dissipated a part of his strength, on the other, he is walking toward a certain and fixed goal; he is driven neither by the uneasiness of finding his prey, nor by the fear of losing it. He therefore arrives more exhausted than excited.

Here he drinks and bathes; he even swims, for he has learned this art from his mother, an art unknown only to educated peoples; he finds in this pastime at once relaxation, pleasure, and the only tonic that is always effective and never dangerous. One would imagine, then, that eating and drinking occupy a great deal of our pupil's time. How will he employ the rest? In sleeping. A fine life, one might say. Let someone tell us, then, what most men do more than this, if not while away the time, if they are weak and oppressed. If they are powerful, are such pastimes worth the sleep they replace? Our pupil sleeps, we say, sometimes a deep sleep, during which nature labors silently; and sometimes a light sleep in which one can sense a sweet repose which the guilty do not know and of which the ambitious deprive themselves, one that relaxes the voluptuary, when his excesses have not deprived him of it, which the innocent and just taste sometimes, despite our institutions, and which, for the natural man, is a pleasure both sound and assured. Guided by his needs, then, our pupil gradually educates himself; soon he is able to pass through a thicket, clear a path through a dense wood, leap over a ditch, climb a steep mountain, scale a tree. Every day he receives a new lesson from nature; each prey he pursues is a subject of study for him, each of his meals is the reward for his dexterity or his reflections.

Thus passes the long interval that nature (if one can speak in this way) uses for preparing the human species, a time in which each individual, still taking shape, does not yet have any distinct character, in which sexual differences are still nonexistent, or at least without influence,* in which each one, as Evagrius put it, is man among men, and

---

*Analyse raisonnée (London, 1755–70), by Pierre Bayle, vol. 4.

woman among women. But at last nature separates and branches out, in some sense; she perfects her work and divides the sexes. We shall follow her in her progress; until now we have made our remarks general, because what we said was equally appropriate to the male and the female child. The state of puberty separates them, and so we abandon the male and confine ourselves to the subject we have proposed to cover.

CHAPTER V

On Puberty

The choice of more or less nourishing foods, a sedentary or an active life, are physical causes that contribute, almost as much as the climate, to accelerating or delaying the moment of puberty. The fires of the imagination — in society they are almost always ignited either by the sight of actions or of related pictures or by unchaste speeches or readings, and the solitary reflections that result — are a moral cause, no less powerful, for hastening nature. The imagination appears, then, to yield to a foreign power, and the signs of puberty manifest themselves well before the individual is perfected. But this disruption of the natural laws never takes place without its attendant penalty; the subject that exists too early never exists fully. If, especially, he is in too great a hurry to revel in pleasure, if he abandons himself to it too unsparingly, he soon has no more than a languishing and weak life; in vain he seeks help in aphrodisiacs, often illusory and always dangerous, and he only worsens his condition. Real pleasure obstinately eludes him, and even if he should encounter it sometimes, this pleasure seems imperfect to him, he no longer has the strength to savor it; similar to those precocious fruits which art wrests from nature, he has neither quality nor taste, he is only a vain appearance: thus does nature avenge itself on the imprudent creature who dares violate her laws. Still, he would be fortunate if he alone bore the penalty for his temerity; but his posterity shares it — hence those vaporous generations, scrawny and phlegmatic, so common today in our big cities, hence those degenerate men who cause us to regard the monuments to the strength of our fathers as unlikely fictions. The natural girl is sheltered from this danger; never has a delicately laid table provoked her satisfied appetite; never has a flabby idleness allowed too many essences to circulate in her blood; never, above all, have lascivious ideas inflamed her imagination. Twenty times, a hundred times, she has seen the act of procreation performed in front of her; she does not blush, she does not run away – she merely continues on her way indifferently, and does not glance furtively behind her. She sees with the eyes of the body and not those of the soul; her senses are still dormant: they are waiting for the cry of nature to rouse them. We can therefore affirm that, in all likelihood, the puberty of the natural girl will not manifest itself (at least in a climate similar to ours) until the body is almost grown, and we can affirm with certainty that, in all climates, nature left to itself will not grant a girl the ability to become a mother until after it has given her the strength to fulfill her duties; we need not be afraid of seeing nature in the forest, as in our towns, sometimes betray the tenderness of a mother by refusing her the milk that she intended for her child. At last the time comes when the child will cease to be a child, when her existence, concentrated until now, will divide and spread outward. Already her shape is rounding out, her breasts are growing perceptibly, her genitals are tightening and covered with down. Often, until this day, in a hunting society, or in some other situation, our young girl has found herself among men without inspiring, nor experiencing, any sensation;* some new chance brings her among them, but scarcely has she touched the hand of one of them than a sweet shiver spreads through the whole of her body; her hand withdraws; she blushes involuntarily, not from modesty, but from disturbance; she desires, but still she is afraid to draw near; this unknown feeling will occupy her entirely. Already she seeks solitude; here she withdraws in a sense, for the first time she will be absorbed in her thoughts; a bleak tedium and a vague uneasiness will torment her in turn; a slight numbness in her groin, an almost painful sensitivity in her joints, make her condition still more distressing; she tires easily on her walks and remains in one place without finding rest; soon she experiences heaviness in her head, and all the signs of fullness, as much in her breasts as in all the reproductive organs. She remains in this state until the first menstrual flow comes both to relieve her and to prepare nature's laboratory;† undoubt-

---

*Let us make this temporary analogy. This is not to fall into the error, so often committed, of transferring to the state of nature a fact that is appropriate only to the state of society. One can find many examples of this among animals that are hunters and yet solitary.

†We also know that there have been examples of women who have become mothers without having had any menstrual periods; there are even accounts of an entire people in which the women are not prone to this. But, setting aside the fact that these exceptions are rare, are we not justified in believing that in these cases the flow takes place internally, as several authors claim in the case of all women during pregnancy?

edly, during this time, the natural girl believes she is sick, not that she has any idea of illness such as we conceive of it, but she feels that she is suffering and that a change is occurring in her. In the meantime, these symptoms disappear, but they leave behind them the devouring fire which nature has lit and which pleasure alone can extinguish.

Victim of a need of which she is unaware, a secret ardor consumes her; uneasy days are followed by nights even more restless; the first light of dawn no longer finds her in the arms of sleep, she no longer tastes the refreshing repose of morning; everyone around her is asleep, she alone in nature is awake; the faint light scarcely allows her to distinguish objects, and already she is wandering about uneasily; she runs to the nearest stream, she wants to extinguish in its waters the fire that is tormenting her, the first rays of sunlight illuminate her in her bath. Useless remedy! She emerges and burns anew. She casts her ardent and uneasy glances about her; they settle, enchanted by the spectacle of morning. She has felt the first flames of love; nature comes to life for her; the sweet perfume of the flowers prepares her for sensual pleasure; the warbling of the birds is no longer useless noise — it is a touching harmony that responds to her heart. Their repeated caresses affect her even more; her hands upraised, her lips parted, her eyes moist, she watches and is afraid of distracting them. Her short and hurried breathing, the precipitous motion of her breast, all are sufficient evidence of the disturbance in her heart. It is then that at some distance she sees a man; a powerful instinct, an involuntary motion, causes her to run toward him; closer, she becomes shy, she stops. But, carried away once again, she joins him and clasps him in her arms.... Delicious joy, who will ever dare to describe you?

CHAPTER VI

On Womanhood

With puberty occurring, according to our hypothesis, later in the state of nature than among civilized peoples,* the interval between puberty and womanhood is not as long. The latter begins when the body has grown completely and ends, for women, when they become barren.† This stage is specifically that of reproduction, and it is when the mother's attentions, as described above in the chapter on childhood, come into play.

---

*See the beginning of the preceding chapter.
†We are still leaving aside the exceptions. See note to p. 138.

We cannot see that it brings any other change in the uniform life of the natural woman; but she has reached her point of perfection – now she can only decline. Before she begins to experience the abandonment of nature, let us stop a moment to consider her. We will observe first that the natural woman enjoys three assets, the loss of which is the source of all our afflictions, namely, freedom, strength, and health. We shall leave to our readers the task of comparing her, on these points, with the civilized woman, and we shall not waste our time questioning these advantages. However, there are two assets without which women consider all the others nothing: beauty and love. Here we will need more reflection, in order to recognize the wealth of the natural woman: indeed, her beauty is not that of the woman we know. She has neither the delicate, white skin whose touch caresses us so voluptuously, nor the soft flexibility, the apparent weakness, that seems to provoke attack, in the hope of success, and to prepare defeat, through the facility of refusal; above all, she has none of the resources of ornamentation which women of all climates are so adept at turning to their advantage. Her skin, colored by the sun, is a darker yet livelier hue; in truth, she is less delicate, but if for that reason her sensation of touch is reduced overall, it becomes stronger in the parts which are its seat and organ, and which have retained all their sensitivity. Her flesh, continually assaulted by a brisk breeze, is firmer and more alive. We can only compare these two women to two fruits, the first of which has grown in the open countryside and the other in a hothouse. The features of her face are usually tranquil and serene; however, when she becomes animated, her face assumes character – not that one can say of her, as of so many other women, that her face is more spirited than she. She does not know how to simper, but she knows still less how to restrain herself; her soul is painted on her face, and if it expresses anger or terror forcefully, desire or pleasure are painted there with no less energy. Her figure is tall and strong, and her embraces, which the natural man no doubt finds still too weak, would smother our delicate fops.

Her adornment is her flowing hair, her perfumes are a bath of clear water.* This state, if we may be so bold as to declare, is the most favorable to pleasure.† But, one will say, what is pleasure without love? Sensitive souls, we think as you do. Love is the comforter of society.

---

*Should anyone doubt the rigorous cleanliness of the natural woman, he must never have observed wild animals.

†Coquettish and disdainful women, look around you. The ardent young man is seeking you out. This is not the difficult age; but the man who is beginning to lose his forces

Social man has paid for this asset with all those possessed by natural man, just as our earliest ancestors, according to tradition, experienced pleasure only after their expulsion from earthly paradise. And yet, is natural woman without love? We agree that sustained passion cannot exist between two creatures who come together without having ever seen each other before, and who will separate in a moment, never to acknowledge each other again. But this moment is not indivisible, and if we observe it closely, we can perceive in it all the nuances of sentiment. For them, the first caresses take the place of a declaration; by turns, the woman flees and provokes. This is how desires grow; soon at their peak, they give rise to intoxication; it is expressed not with elegant phrases but with moist eyes and burning sighs, which belong to all languages; they know how to conspire to have their pleasure in concert, and perhaps what differentiates them the most is that they take leave of each other without disgust. Why should we be afraid to say it? Sincere women, it is you we are questioning. Is there one among you who has had her pleasure constantly without fear, without jealousy, without remorse, or without the difficult tedium of duty or uniformity? You will not answer us; but have the courage to examine your hearts and judge for yourselves. In vain, then, would proud pity feel sorry for the natural woman; she has freedom, strength, health, beauty, and love. What more does she need to be happy?

CHAPTER VII

On Old Age and Death

It is sad to move from the spectacle of love to that of death, but such is the law of nature in the eternal succession of times and things: painstaking with the species, it seems to take few pains with individuals; in its hands, they are only instruments of general reproduction, abandoned after having been used; then begins old age, which death brings to a close. This stage is the age of infirmities; everything about it heralds decay – the hair turns white, the teeth fall out, the flesh softens,* the skin wrinkles, all the limbs falter, all the organs are dulled; to these natural and inevitable effects of old age, to these ills common to every-

---

has none left for you; he comes to life again at the sight of a young and innocent village girl. Such is the great charm of nature.

*We say that the flesh softens, whereas on the contrary it hardens – but one should understand what we mean.

one, are joined all too often gout, rheumatism, constant catarrhs, and so on and so forth — the bitter fruits of profligacies of all varieties, the near-inevitable torment of all old people — but which the natural man and woman will be spared. Even more fortunate, they shall neither miss the past nor fear the future; they shall neither torment nor be tormented because of their melancholy humor.* Listen to this old man: according to him, everything is deteriorating, everything around him collapsing; dishes are less succulent, women less beautiful, joy less pure, all pleasures less lively. Like the passenger who sails for the first time, he thinks, seduced by his perspective, that objects are moving into the distance, and he does not perceive that it is he who is moving away; like him, he seems to forget his destination and is concerned only with his departure; this earth, which he will not see again, still occupies all his affections; his attention, fixed on it, reveals the ideas that occupy him; soon he no longer distinguishes objects, but he gazes at the spot where he saw them. He seeks to delude himself, he wishes to believe that he still sees. While the natural man calmly follows the gentle and easy slope that must lead him to his eternal rest, the worldly old man obstinately disputes the place that nature has destined for his posterity. Placed on a narrow path between a steep rock and a bottomless precipice, he crawls along trembling; he clings to everything he encounters, he would like to climb up again, to reascend toward his youth. An impossible return — his time is over. The one eventually arrives, without noticing it, at the end of his journey; the last step of the other is a dreadful fall from the summit of life into the abyss of nothingness. The sad effect of a disordered imagination, which ceaselessly transports man from the place he occupies to the one he desires. All the weapons of philosophy are not strong enough to combat this tendency, the inevitable tragedy of weak minds, the eternal scourge of women who never find in their spirits the resources necessary to conquer their imaginations. And what a hideous spectacle the unbridled woman presents, whose age has not been able to moderate her desires, and who is still seeking a pleasure that she can no longer give! What afflictions await her, what humiliation is in store for her. Man, in the same situation, is no less ridiculous, but he may be less unhappy; he possesses some remnant of power, his base interest will allow him to find a willing girl who will help his vanity delude him; he will be the plaything of all that surrounds, but he will be able to remain ignorant of it; he will not be aware of his

---

*We do not fear to include ill humor among the other maladies and to assert that it is more distressing for the person who has it than for those who must endure it.

condition. The woman does not even have that dubious resource; in vain has she employed the same means to gain the affections of a man who, in her arms, loses the force he had promised; he remains dead, between her and her destiny. Happy are the women who, through hard work, succeed at least in putting off their ardent imaginations and are able to deflect them onto objects no less futile but which correspond to their age; happier is the natural woman, who need not fear any of these misfortunes. The social woman's imagination brings her senses to life and lives on after them; that of the natural woman is born and dies with them; once the age of pleasures is past, she is nothing more than a better-educated child; at peace, she has no need to wallow in illusions; she will be able to grow old without being a gambler, a slanderer, or a religious bigot. To these advantages, whose value it will be easy to perceive, the natural woman adds one more precious still, which social man sometimes boasts of without enjoying it, and which she enjoys without boasting of it: she is not afraid of death. That moment, so dreaded, does not exist for her; she has no idea of it, her last moment is as serene as all the others; she ends rather than dies, but she lets herself go without defending herself; if she suffers agony of the body, she does not suffer that of the spirit; she is free of terrors of all sorts which, among us, relentlessly beleaguer the dying. We shall point out, on this subject, that it is one of the greater advantages of the natural man and woman to be freed from the fear of foresight; certainly, they will be frightened at times, but at least they will only have to fight or to flee the present danger and not the phantoms of their imaginations. This advantage is perhaps inestimable, especially for women, whom we see tormented every day by a thousand fears which, childish though they may be, are no less distressing to them for all that; similarly, in their maladies, they will suffer only their pain; they will be neither impatient nor uneasy; it is in them that we must seek perfect resignation; beyond that, they will perhaps have accidents, but their illnesses will be rare, and who would cause them? They have neither passions, nor cooks, nor doctors.

CHAPTER VIII

Reflections on the Preceding

We have followed the natural woman through the different periods of her life, we have seen her at birth, the object of her mother's most tender care, receiving from her the assistance necessitated by her weakness. Still a child but already stronger, we have seen her free from the constraints to which her fellows are reduced, growing freely and developing her strengths under the eyes of nature. We have observed the changes brought about in her by puberty; we have seen her first desires come to life, followed by pleasure, pleasure as pure as it is lively, unpoisoned by the ills that our institutions ceaselessly mingle with it. Having reached womanhood, while her days went by divided between the sweet cares of love and those of maternity, we have sought to know all her advantages, and we have found that she lacked none that one could reasonably desire; in her old age, we have seen her subjected only to the infirmities that are inseparable from it, avoiding both the pains of the body and the afflictions of the spirit; we saw, lastly, a peaceful death ending a happy life. What woman will now dare to present herself and argue about happiness with her? If it will be that powerful queen, proud of ruling over vast states, where will she seek her felicity? No doubt in that of her subjects: she will therefore hasten to make herself fearful to enemies from outside and to quell domestic disturbances; at once thrifty and liberal, she will bestow nothing on the courtiers' scheming greed and will always be rich enough to reward those who render service. Her wars, just and favored, will be followed by victory, and the multiplied taxes will not devour the substance of the poor; the weak will not implore her unsuccessfully against the oppression of the powerful; her vigilant justice will save the credulous from the plots of bad faith; cherished by the good, her name will be the terror of the wicked, they will flee from her, they will seek out those places, not so very uncommon, where they will prosper easily. And so she shall no doubt be blessed, but let her not hope for a moment of rest. Does she not have to watch over everyone? Does she wish to spend a moment on her pleasures? She will have to wait for a moment that none of her subjects will claim, or else her life will be continuous action and she will *die on her feet*, a victim devoted to the happiness of her people. Or, discouraged by the sight of so arduous a career, will she choose instead to be weak and voluptuous, will she forget her people in order to spend time only on her pleasures? Pleasures will surround her; the zeal of her courtiers will surpass her imagination; but for this very reason, her joys shall be imperfect. Unhappy, she will not have the time to desire. Yet, under a weak reign, intrigue deploys all its forces; the ambitious courtier, not content with oppressing the people, also wants to dominate his sovereign. Mistress of so many states, she is not mistress of her own will; driven by secret motives, she yields to a foreign and unknown impulse; out of weakness, she

orders the removal of those she cherishes and finds, to her surprise, that she is delivered over to those she fears. Then she loses the habit of loving; defiance and insensitivity wither and constrict her soul; soon she no longer opens herself to pleasure; she is now susceptible only to distractions, and even distractions have become difficult; her palace bores her, and yet she is afraid to leave it; does she pass through the towns? The dismal silence of her people saddens her heart. Does she travel through countryside? The sight of poverty afflicts her inopportune glances, and she resents the places where she lives because of the boredom she brings to them; she avoids herself, she wanders, without choice as without design, she seeks the vast solitude of the forests, let us allow her this sad recourse: the only moments in which she can tolerate herself are those in which she succeeds in forgetting herself. What other woman is there, whose brilliance can surpass even that of a queen? With her perfect beauty, her enchanting air, her magic power, she seems like a fairy; surrounded by a numerous court, whose fate she rules, she erects, she pulls down what she pleases, she lightheartedly turns the wheel of fortune; she has hurled an angry look at a powerful man, and his power has vanished; she has put out her hand to a man crushed and outlawed, and he has become powerful and honored. The greatest events of history are often no more than the result of one of her caprices; she seems to desire something, and everyone bustles around her; she speaks, and obstacles disappear. By these traits, who does not recognize a king's mistress? This is indeed the spectacle she presents to the crowd that contemplates and envies her; but the attentive observer is not seduced by these deceptive appearances: he sees this woman, he knows she is the idol and victim of fortune, with everything at her disposal except herself, obliged to appear gay when she is sad, tender when her heart is cold, sprightly and playful when overcome by ill humor, confident and calm when a thousand fears obsess her. He sees her among the malcontents and ingrates; he listens to her bitterly repeat that phrase so familiar – *I have admirers and not a single friend.**
He listens to her muffled sobs; he notices her tears, still wet on her

---

*The chosen mistress of a powerful monarch, afflicted by a disease of which she was dying, wanted to know her condition, which was stubbornly concealed from her; she employed a very simple means; every day she asked for a count of the persons coming to see her; for a long time, the entire court was named; one day, at last, only one person was mentioned. "What, he alone?" she said. "He alone," she was answered. "Well then," she went on immediately, "I must die, I am doomed." She was not mistaken and died, in fact, only a few hours later.

cheeks; he goes off at last and says with truth, this is not where happiness is. But, one might say, you claim to seek happiness and you are afraid to find it. We hear this reproach, and we leave the palaces of kings.

Perhaps someone will cite as an example of happiness that young, pretty, and sensitive woman who has wed the husband she adores and who cannot believe the happiness of a moment. But how great is the distance between a moment of happiness and a fortunate life! Do we know anything about this woman's childhood and youth, about her old age and her death, or who will protect her from accidents of all sorts? The fear that they alone will inspire in her will change her happiness, and, besides, after having enjoyed everything, will she not have to leave everything? The more delicious the pleasure, the more painful its loss, the more bitter the regrets. Let us seek in our imagination, at least, what society does not offer us. Let us create to our liking a perfectly happy woman, at least insofar as humanity allows; born of a tender mother, this will be a woman who will not have been handed over at birth to the care of a mercenary; older, she will have been raised under the eyes of an equally indulgent, wise, and enlightened teacher, who, without ever forcing her, or vexing her with her lessons, will have given her all useful knowledge and will have preserved her from all prejudice. Having reached the age of pleasure, she will have found a husband who is always new, loving without being jealous, attentive without being irksome; having become a mother in her turn, she will have tasted the sweetness of motherly love, without feeling its perpetual worries, which are often followed by a frightful despair; her sweet imagination will have watched without regret her happy youth flee. She will have been able, as she grew old, to avoid illness and ridicule; finally, she will be able to see death without fear, and to fall peacefully into her final sleep. Free of her own sorrows, she will not receive any alien to her; her fortune will be such that, abundantly provided with what is necessary, she will never be hampered by what she does not want; she will live without ambition as without fear. After having had the greatest sensitivity to pleasure, she will find in pain or in privation the most philosophical stoicism. But is this woman not an idle dream? No, this is, feature for feature, and merely in different words, the faithful story of a woman in the state of nature. However, some will persist in saying to us, this state never existed, it is impossible, it is unlikely. The question merits discussion.

Examination of the Reasons Brought Forward Against the State of Nature

Friend of truth, we shall not conceal the fact that many philosophers have argued against the existence, and even against the possibility, of the state of nature such as we have envisaged it – or that, should they admit its existence, they have denied its advantages. The fear of an overly long discussion, the uselessness of responding to objections that are always the same though made in diverse ways, will prevent us from answering everyone, but of the number, our choice will be such that we cannot be reproached for having sought weak opponents in order to fight with more advantage; those whom we shall try to answer are Monsieurs Buffon and Voltaire: "Can one say in good faith," asks M. Buffon, "that this primitive state merits being missed, that man the wild animal was worthier than man the civilized citizen? Yes, for all misfortunes come from society, and what does it matter whether there were virtues in the state of nature if there was happiness, if man, in this state, was less unhappy than he is? Are freedom, health, strength, not preferable to indolence, sensuality, pleasure itself? Accompanied by slavery, the lack of afflictions is quite equal to the enjoyment of pleasures, and in order to be happy, what is needed, if not to desire nothing?"*

Such is the objection that M. Buffon proposes.

We shall observe, first, that it does not seem to have been made sincerely. Why, for instance, grant pleasure exclusively to social man? Whatever meaning one wishes to give this word, one will find that the pleasure of the natural man, though in a form that is foreign to us, nevertheless exists in a real way for him. *The lack of afflictions is quite equal to the enjoyment of pleasures.* Well, now! Has the natural man only the lack of afflictions? Is he deprived of the enjoyment of pleasures? And, *in order to be happy, what is needed if not to desire nothing?* It is not in desiring nothing that happiness consists, but in obtaining what one desires. The question lies in knowing who, the natural man or the social man, has more facility for achieving it.

Let us now look at M. Buffon's answer.

"If this is so," he continues, "let us also say that it is sweeter to vegetate than to live, to crave nothing than to satisfy one's craving, to sleep

---

*Georges Buffon, "Les Animaux carnassiers," *Histoire naturelle* (Paris, 1749–1804), vol. 14, p. 35.

an apathetic sleep than to open one's eyes to see and to feel; let us consent to leave our soul in numbness, our mind in darkness, never to use
one or the other, to put ourselves below the animals, to be, in the end,
only masses of raw matter attached to the earth."

We could answer, in our turn, that *it is sweeter to vegetate than to live*
unhappily, *to crave nothing* than to be able *to satisfy one's craving, to sleep
an apathetic sleep than to open one's eyes to see* unpleasant objects and to
feel pain, that it is better *to leave our soul in numbness* than to draw it
out through suffering, to have *our mind in darkness* than in error, *never
to use one or the other* than to put either to a pernicious use – and that,
provided one is happy, it would matter little whether one was above
or *below the other animals.* But this pointless ranting would force us,
as well as him, outside the question. In fact, natural man does not vegetate; he lives, he craves, and satisfies his craving; he sleeps not an
apathetic sleep but a tranquil sleep; he is able to open his eyes to see
and to feel; his sensitive soul knows compassion and love; his mind is
enlightened about his needs; he uses of both the one and the other; he
is not at all below the animals – he is the first, the most fortunate of
them all.

"We are not supposing" – this is still M. Buffon speaking – "that
a greater distance exists between man in pure nature and the savage
than between the savage and us. . . . We see that one descends almost
imperceptibly from the most enlightened nations . . . most civilized,
to less industrious peoples; from these peoples to others cruder, but
still subject to kings and laws; from these crude men to the savages. . . .
That some form rather numerous nations subject to chieftains; that
others, in smaller societies, are subject only to customs; that, lastly,
the most solitary, the most independent, form families and are subject to their fathers. An empire, a monarch, a family, a father – here
are the two extremes of society: these extremes are also the boundaries of nature."

This last statement, which summarizes all that precedes it, seems
to us more brazen than philosophical; we would have thought that the
boundaries of nature could be situated only between two things that
are contradictory.

"If they extended beyond [these boundaries], would not one have
found, in traveling all the wildernesses of the globe, human animals
deprived of speech, deaf to the voice as to signs, males and females dispersed, young abandoned, and so on. . . ."

Traveling all the wildernesses of the globe! And who, may we ask, has
traveled *all* of them? Reading this, who would believe that, according

to M. Buffon himself, "what remains for us to know about the southern pole is so considerable, that one could conceivably estimate it at more than a quarter of the surface of the globe, so that in these climates a terrestrial continent could exist as great as Europe, Asia, and Africa put together."*

Would not one have found human animals.... Does it follow from the fact that one has not found any that there are none? Did America not exist before its discovery, in that very time when the assembled scholars of Portugal declared unanimously that Columbus's plan *was that of a mad visionary, of a man seeking territories in the orb of the moon?... Deprived of speech....* Doesn't the clucking of cave dwellers, though an already civilized people, more closely approximate a formed language than the emphatic cries of the natural man?

Deaf to the voice as to signs.... Why deaf to all that? *The males and females dispersed, the young abandoned.* Once again, who knows, who will dare to say that all this does not exist? But when this globe has been totally explored, and when no man in the state of pure nature has been found on it, how should one conclude from this that such a state never existed, since it is proven and generally agreed that the human species is capable of perfection?

"I would even say that unless one claims that the constitution of the human body was quite different from what it is today and that it grew much more quickly, it is not possible to maintain that man has ever existed without forming a family, since children would perish were they not protected and looked after for several years, whereas newborn animals need their mother only for a few months."

All newborn animals need their mother for a greater or lesser period of time, and we do not see that their association continues to exist after the need has passed. We think we can establish this period for men as being between two and three years,† and M. Buffon himself seems to establish it at four years for the child of a social man,‡ which agrees more or less with our calculations; the only difference, then, is between the greater and the lesser, and if a certain animal (the she-wolf, for example), which lives twenty years, cares for her young for one year,§ it seems to us that a woman who lives sixty or eighty years can certainly devote

---

Histoire naturelle, vol. 1. See, on the same subject, *L'Histoire des voyages aux terres australes* by M. le Président de Brosse.

†See chapter 3, above.

‡*Histoire naturelle*, vol. 14, p. 39.

§*Histoire naturelle du loup*, vol. 14.

three years to this care, and once that time is past, abandon her child.

"This physical necessity is enough in itself, therefore, to demonstrate that the human species could not have endured, and multiplied, except by means of society."

We have just seen whether this demonstration is sufficient.

"The union of fathers and mothers with children is natural, since it is necessary."

The union of father with children appears to us absolutely useless, even in M. Buffon's system, and as for mothers, could we not say that their union with children ceases to be natural as soon as it is no longer necessary?

"Now, this union cannot fail to produce a respective and lasting attachment between the parents and the child."

Here is what remains positively to be proven and which does not seem probable to us.

"Thus the state of pure nature is a known state; it is the savage living in the wilderness, but living in a family, knowing his children, known to them, using speech and making himself understood."

Are we not justified in saying that this is not the state of nature?

"The wild girl picked up in the woods of Champagne, the man found in the forests of Hanover do not prove the contrary."

They prove at least that the contrary is not impossible.

M. Buffon, after having gathered men into families, at the first moment of their existence, forms an empire at the fourth generation. We shall not follow him in his rapid progression; it is enough for us to have examined whether he is victorious in arguing against the advantages and the possibility of the state of nature, such as we have envisioned it, and to have put our readers in a situation to judge whether one can, according to his reasons, declare that state unhappy or impossible. We shall add not one word more. M. Buffon, who confuses savage man with natural man, asks himself if this man is happy, and decides that he is not. Here we shall counter M. Buffon with M. Buffon himself. Listen to him speak in his history of wild animals: "Nature has given them all freedom with consistent habits, all desires and love, always easy to satisfy.... Love and freedom, what benefits! These animals whom we call wild because they are not ruled by us – what more do they need to be happy? They also have equality, they are neither the slaves nor the tyrants of their fellows."*

What force, what energy in this picture! But why would the *human*

Histoire naturelle, vol. 2.

animals alone be deprived of these advantages? Does M. Buffon give us some reason for this unfortunate exclusion?

It appears to us that the reasonings of this philosopher are not enough to destroy the system that we have followed. Let us see if M. Voltaire, who opposes this same system with such scorn and ill humor, gives more convincing reasons.

M. Voltaire begins by saying that no one has ever seen a country in which the state of pure nature survived.*

We have already seen how this point of fact was not enough to settle the matter.

"Certain practical jokers," he continues, "have so deluded themselves as to venture the surprising paradox that man was originally made to live alone, like a lynx, and that it was society that depraved nature. One could as well say that, in the sea, herrings were originally made to swim in isolation, and that it is through an excess of corruption that they travel in schools from the glacial sea to our coasts; that in ancient times cranes each flew in the air separately, and that through a violation of the law of nature, they made the decision to travel in company."

Is it not a worse joke to try to establish an analogy between man, herrings, and cranes? The flaw in this reasoning is, above all, that it can be turned back on itself with as much advantage.

Certain practical jokers (one could say) have so deluded themselves as to venture the surprising paradox that man was originally made to live in society.... One might as well say that cattle and horses were originally made to live in herds, and that it was only through an excess of corruption, or through a violation of the law of nature, that they wandered isolated in the woods.

"Each animal has its instinct," continues M. Voltaire, "and man's instinct, strengthened by his reason, leads him to society, as to food and drink."

This is to state absolutely as fact what is in question.

"Whosoever would live absolutely alone would soon lose the faculty of thinking and expressing himself."

The isolated man would not acquire the faculty of speaking; but why would he not have that of thinking and expressing himself? The most savage animal has its thoughts and its expression.

"He would be a burden to himself."

We do not see why.

"He would only end up turning into an animal."

---

*Voltaire, *Question sur l'encyclopédie* (Geneva, 1770–72), art. "*homme*," p. 100ff.

For most, that transformation would not be difficult.

M. Rousseau had said, "It is not a matter of knowing why the man will remain attached to the woman after delivery, but why he will become attached to her after conception. His appetite satisfied, the man no longer needs a given woman, nor the woman a given man. The man has not the least concern nor perhaps the least idea of the consequences of his action. One goes off in one direction, the other in another, and there is no likelihood that at the end of nine months they have any memory of having known each other.... Why will he assist her after delivery? Why will he help her to raise a child he does not even know belongs to him?"*

"All of this is deplorable," cries M. Voltaire. But why? Are animals that treat one another this way deplorable? "But," he continues, "happily nothing could be more false." Let us see how he proves it.

"If this indifference were nature's true instinct, the human species would almost always have behaved this way. Since instinct is immutable, its inconsistencies are very rare, the father would always have abandoned the mother, the mother would have abandoned her child, and there would be far fewer men on the earth than there are carnivorous animals, for the savage beasts, better equipped, better armed, have a quicker instinct, surer means, and a more secure source of food than does the human species."

It is not necessary to observe domestic animals very much in order to see how training alters and varies instinct; but, above all, to what extent have men not opposed their own? What! Does the instinct of the hungry man not lead him to steal the bread being eaten before his eyes by a man weaker than he? Does the instinct of a vigorous man not lead him to enjoy a young and pretty girl he finds himself near? Does not she herself, urged by her desires, by those of her lover, feel induced by her instinct to yield herself? Does not the instinct of those hundred thousand men ranged in battle before a hundred thousand others, at the moment of a discharge of artillery and musketry, lead them to run away rather than to kill or let themselves be killed for a cause that is foreign to them? Yet all of them resist their instinct, and then we are told that its inconsistencies are very rare. Is not the natural instinct in all of these cases stifled under the weight of our institutions? If, in the social state, the mother remains tied to the child, and the child to the mother, after the need is past, if each of them remains tied to her husband or its father, who can declare that this bond is not rather the fruit of our insti-

---

*Rousseau, *Discourse on the Origins of Inequality*, p. 89.

tutions than the necessary impulse of natural instinct? The history of animals does not provide any example of this respective attachment of mothers and children that does not cease with the need of the latter. In a few species we find, in truth, a temporary union of male to female which always disappears with the need of the young; but, beside the fact that this union of man to woman does not appear necessary to their child, we dare to say that it is impossible; in fact, the animals among whom this union continues always have a designated time for the desires of love; once this time is past, the desires go away in one and the other sex; and, what is more, this time is always followed by fertility. It is not thus for man and woman; man will have new desires, and if he satisfies them with another woman, to which of the two shall he attach himself? Let us suppose that, against all species of reason, he fixes on one alone. Is it certain that this woman will be impregnated by him – or, if she is not, what will become of their union? How long will it last? An indissoluble marriage with a single woman would become, in this case, a necessary consequence of that natural and immutable instinct of which M. Voltaire speaks.

M. Voltaire proposes that *the instinct of carnivorous animals is quicker than that of man.*

We would agree even less with this, as regards natural man, in that we see it belied in primitive man, who must already have lost a part of that instinct. *They have,* he adds, *a more secure source of food than the human species.* We have already said above, that according to the most learned naturalists, the human species was that which adapted to different foods most easily. He derives from this the consequence that, in our supposition, *there would be fewer men on the earth than carnivorous animals.*

If this were so, it would not be a sufficient reason to destroy a system that would otherwise be true, but this supposition seems to us absolutely gratuitous.

"The most hardened men," M. Voltaire continues, "love, through dominant instinct, the child that is not yet born, the womb that carries it, and the mother, who redoubles her love for the man from whom she received in her belly the seed of a creature like her."

We agree that their children are one more bond for the husband and wife joined in the social state, and we shall have occasion later to give the reasons for this; but we have some difficulty understanding how men (hardened or not) *can love through dominant instinct the child they do not know is to be born, the womb they do not know is carrying it,* nor how *a mother can be all the more in love with a man, although she has no idea that, in her womb, she has received from him the seed of a creature like her.*

"The instinct of the Black Forest coal miner speaks to them as loudly, moves them as strongly, in favor of their children as the instinct of the pigeons and nightingales forces them to feed their young."

We agree with all this; but the pigeons and the nightingales abandon their young as soon as the latter can do without them.

Cannot we say, now, as does M. Voltaire, but with a different application, "Is not the great flaw of all these paradoxical books always to imagine nature differently from what it is?"

Let us summarize. We have seen that it is not proven that the state we call "the state of nature" does not exist; that it is impossible to prove that it has never existed; that, far from being unlikely, one cannot attack it except by gratuitous suppositions or rash assertions. We have therefore been justified in considering it as the point from which women started, we are going to examine at present which and how many changes the social institutions have caused them to undergo.

CHAPTER X

On the First Effects of Society

Nature creates only free beings; society makes only tyrants and slaves; every society implies a contract, every contract a respective obligation. Every obligation is a hindrance repugnant to natural freedom; thus, social man does not cease to strain against his bonds, he is inclined to escape them, he seeks to throw off their weight onto his fellow men, he wishes to hold only the end of the chain in order to direct them as he pleases; hence, it follows that, if the oppression of the weak by the strong is not a natural law, in the sense in which the moralists take these words, it is nonetheless a law of nature or, rather, the first vengeance that nature, abandoned, extracts from social man; hence, it follows that every agreement made between two subjects unequal in strength produces, can only produce, a tyrant and a slave; it follows as well that, in the social union of the two sexes, the women, generally weaker, have necessarily been generally oppressed; here the facts come to support the arguments. Travel through the known universe, and you will find the man strong and a tyrant, the woman weak and a slave; if sometimes she has the skill to bind the hands of her master and command in her turn, this case is extremely rare. When one surveys the history of the different peoples and examines the laws and the customs promulgated and established with regard to women, one is tempted to believe that they only yielded, but did not consent, to the social contract, that they were originally subjugated, and that man has a right of conquest over them, which he uses rigorously. Thus, far from thinking, as some do, that society began with the raising of families, we believe, rather, that the first association was made by men alone, who, considering themselves relatively equal in strength, must have feared each other less; but they soon felt the need for women; they therefore turned their attentions to forcing them, or persuading them, to join in. Whether it was force or persuasion, the first woman who yielded forged the chains of her entire sex. We are quite aware that in these early times there was no exclusive property, the fruits of a field cultivated in common were shared equally; the same was done with game killed in a general hunt; even the women came under this law; all of them belonged to everyone.* None of them had the idea of choice. Nevertheless, in this community of labors and fruits, it is easy to foresee that sharing could not be equal for long; that soon the law of the fittest would make itself felt: that women, though they were the weakest, were subjected to the most arduous work, and received from it the least fruit; men extended to women this same idea of property which had seduced the men and brought them together; from the sole fact that the women met the men's requirements and that the men were able to seize them, they concluded that the women belonged to them: this, in general, was the origin of the right. Lacking strength, women could not defend and preserve their civil existence: companions in name, they soon became slaves in fact, and unhappy slaves; their fate could hardly have been better than that of the blacks of our colonies. If one wishes to find tangible vestiges of this abuse of force, consider for a moment those still crude peoples whom we call savages, who, brought together only a short time ago, have already lost the advantages of the state of nature and have not yet been able to make up for the first vices of society. It is here that one sees the women alone burdened with the basest and most arduous work, always worn out, often ill treated, sometimes killed by their idle and capricious masters who reward in this way the care women take of them, the substances they furnish them, and the pleasure they procure them. It is thus that we see them even today, rowing like our galley slaves in the canoes of the Greenlanders, and subjected to such treatment; among the Kalmuks, in the end, at the age of forty, after being the companions of their husbands, they become the servants of the house and of the young women who succeed them; among the Koreans,

---

*We know of several small tribes that still live in this entirely communal manner.

treated as their slaves, and often driven away, along with their children, for slight faults; severely beaten among the peoples of the hills of Lebanon and enslaved there, not only by their husbands but even by their male children; burdened in the Congo with all the hard labor, they serve their husbands and dare neither eat with them nor sit down in their presence; it is thus that one still sees the Hottentots, though raised by their mothers, make it a point of honor to scorn them, even to strike them, when at the age of nineteen they are admitted among the men; that if, in these countries, the men appear to have reserved for themselves the hardships of hunting, it is because this occupation, far from appearing arduous to them, is in them a natural inclination, strengthened further by the desire for power and domination, the first fruit of the social spirit. They regard hunting as such a pleasure that among some peoples (the Lapps, for example) it is not even allowed to women. Oppression and scorn, thus, were and must have been generally the share of women in emerging societies; this state lasted in all its force until centuries of experience taught them to substitute skill for force. Women at last sensed that, since they were weaker, their only resource was to seduce; they understood that if they were dependent on men through force, men could become dependent on them through pleasure. More unhappy than men, they must have thought and reflected earlier than did men; they were the first to know that pleasure was always beneath the idea that one formed of it, and that the imagination went farther than nature. Once these basic truths were known, they learned first to veil their charms in order to awaken curiosity; they practiced the difficult art of refusing even as they wished to consent; from that moment on, they knew how to set men's imagination afire, they knew how to arouse and direct desires as they pleased: thus did beauty and love come into being;* now the lot of women became less harsh, not that they had managed to liberate themselves entirely from the state of oppression to which their weakness condemned them; but, in the state of perpetual war that continues to exist between women and men, one has seen them, with the help of the caresses they have been able to invent, combat ceaselessly, sometimes vanquish, and often more skillfully take advantage of the forces directed against them; sometimes, too, men have turned against women these weapons the women had forged to combat them, and their slavery has become all the harsher for it. From beauty

---

*So that the inattentive reader does not accuse us of saying here what we advanced earlier in speaking of the natural woman, we advise him that we are speaking about elective beauty and about exclusive love.

and love is born jealousy; these three illusions have totally changed the respective state of men and women; they have become the basis and the guarantee of every contract sealed between them. Infinitely varied in their form, they are no less so in their effects; they are finally today the only source of our passions; but before considering their effects, let us examine, and know, their causes.

CHAPTER XI

On Beauty

What is beauty? The question is always asked and never answered in a satisfying manner; proof of this can be found simply by moving from one place to another. If one questions the Frenchman, the American, the Chinese on this subject, if one travels thus around the world, one will find beauty to be inconstant, changing form at every step, leaving different ideas everywhere or at least different expressions; if one remains within the narrow circle of a single society, one will hardly be better satisfied. *This woman is beautiful, but she is not to my liking* is a phrase heard in all countries, the frequent use of which shows quite clearly that people do not agree on the idea of beauty – for what is beauty that does not please? Where do these numerous contradictions come from, if not from a lack of agreement? To make beauty vanish, it is enough to reduce its expression to its simplest terms. Beauty, according to us, is simply the appearance most favorable to pleasure, a way of being that makes one hope for the most delicious pleasure. It is in this sense that the natural woman is beautiful; it is in this sense that one can say that every woman who is young, tall, and strong is a beautiful woman. If this definition is accurate, it should, on the one hand, apply indiscriminately to all people, and on the other, naturally engender that host of ideas, always different and often contradictory, that each nation, or rather, each man forms of beauty.

From the moment that men were brought together, they lost their peace of mind. Natural man sleeps as soon as his needs are satisfied, yet it is not so for civil man: he must see to the execution of the social contract; he no longer gives himself up to sleep, he accords it only the time he cannot refuse it. Ceaselessly on his guard against the attacks of his associates, he keeps watch, not to act but to be prepared to act if necessary. In this state of inaction, man occupied himself with comparing his ideas; the past returned to his memory, the future was depicted in his imagination; memory and anticipation developed, and acted forcefully on him; one has since often seen them somehow stifle the sensation of the present moment. Man's needs provided him with his first ideas; those of pleasure immediately followed; as soon as his memory was practiced enough to retrace the effect of the sensations he had experienced, he compared his past joys, he made decisions about his joys to come. Until then, man had enjoyed beauty without concerning himself with it; then he concerned himself with it sometimes even without enjoying it. He felt that, in pleasure, his enjoyment was not always equally keen; a thousand reasons could contribute to that inequality; he was ignorant of those within him, those he could not even know; he therefore sought them in objects outside himself. The woman who had procured for him the keenest pleasure became most precious to him; he sought her out again; failing her, he chose the one who resembled her the most; he must have been mistaken sometimes; but at last, he studied, he knew or thought he knew, he came to prefer, he realized at last that a soft and delicate skin stretched over a firm and elastic flesh, the exclusive attribute of youth, and a normal consequence of it, procured him a more agreeable touch by causing him to rest more gently; he desired youth. He noticed that a large woman multiplied his sensations by touching him in more places; he desired a larger size. He noticed that it was not enough for him to clasp tightly the object of his pleasure, if he did not experience in his turn a delicious embrace; he desired strength. Thus, he sought the woman who possessed these different advantages: thus youth, size, and strength became incentives for preference; thus their combination constituted beauty: we can name it "natural beauty."* If today, men sometimes seem to contradict these principles, they are deceived by some illusion, or constrained by alien sentiments that will not be difficult to discover. One must recall that, in these early times, women were naked and compliant; that every glance cast on them was an entire examination; and that desire, as quickly satisfied as it was formed, always left men the cool sense necessary to form judgments; but when women began to clothe themselves,

---

*Ever since women, in order to multiply their pleasures, were clever enough to interest the vanity of men in considering themselves stronger than women, men have often preferred the appearance of weakness and have neglected size and strength. Sometimes, also, a libertine curiosity has caused some men to seek out women who have known many other men, either in the hope of learning through them new modes of pleasure, or out of the vanity of teaching them more, and, often, out of the supposition that a woman so sought-after must in fact deserve to be; and then they have neglected youth. Yet these examples, though fairly frequent in our customs, are nevertheless merely exceptions.

the imagination was obliged to compensate for what the eyes could no longer see; and the imagination is easily seduced and sometimes mistaken. Curiosity awakened desire, and desire always embellished its object. When women possessed the power to refuse or to grant as they pleased, the illusion grew further; sometimes desire was born from the hope of satisfying it easily, sometimes it died from that same idea of facility; sometimes it was irritated by the feeble resistance of a feigned refusal, sometimes it was smothered under the humiliation or sorrow of an absolute refusal: thus men came to desire before knowing; thus, the ease or difficulty of obtaining contributed, as much as the object itself, to giving more or less energy to this desire; thus illusion was born everywhere. Clothes hid the woman almost entirely from the eyes of the man. Now, it is not easy for the eye to pierce the folds of cloth and recognize the true forms it is hiding; one cannot judge all at once by sight the resistance that the sense of touch must feel; this art demands some experience, and the most practiced men still make mistakes sometimes. The multitude thus endeavored to consider the face that they saw and came to judge the rest according to it. So the face, which until then could not have been more than a small part of the beauty of women,* became their principal ornament everywhere; then man's mind formed its systems concerning beauty, and, unable to know the laws of nature, he tried to submit it to his own. But this new code was subject, like all the others, to the variations of places and times, and Venus, who won her judgment in Aulis, would most likely have lost it a thousand leagues from there. The reasons for these contradictions are not difficult to find; man knows objects only through the impression he receives of them; beauty acts on him only through memory; it does not exist for the man who has had no idea of sensual delight; this is why, let us say in passing, the man or woman who still wants to please after having faded, prefers to seek out persons young enough not to have been able yet to compare ideas of pleasure; they know that these persons cannot be familiar with beauty; they hope to profit from the first desires that nature arouses, before, through the effect of an unfortunate comparison, their looks suffice to destroy those desires. It is not thus for the man who has some experience. The features that nature only rarely produces, whatever form they may have, do not evoke any memory in him, give him no hope and consequently are not beautiful in his eyes. Even if they are too unfamiliar, or if they resemble too much those of old

---

*If one bothers to examine those populations in which the women still go naked or almost naked, one will be convinced of the truth of this assertion.

age or childhood, times when pleasure has ceased to exist or does not yet exist; if they remove him too much, finally, for whatever cause from the idea of pleasure that he never ceases to bring to that examination, then, far from captivating him, they disgust him; it is the combination of these features that he has named ugliness. Those, on the contrary, which he is accustomed to seeing, which remind him more readily of his ideas of pleasures, please him and captivate him: it is the combination of these features that he has named beauty. Indeed, if one examines the rules that artists prescribe for themselves regarding the proportions of features, one will find that each of these features, taken separately, are encountered most often in nature; their combination is rare, and, for the very reason that it is rare, it is ineffective; and when it is encountered, it is so rare that we are obliged to look for examples of it in the works of our artists; but they suffice for our purposes; one can observe, in considering them, that when the faces they have produced are strictly regular, we certainly say they are beautiful, and in this we comply with prevailing convention; but they are never to our liking; they are never the face we would desire; we find in them, for example, the character of Juno, because the queen of the gods presents a vague idea of perfection to our imaginations; never that of Venus, because the mother of love arouses in us the idea of a pleasure we know, of which this face we say is beautiful nevertheless does not remind us. At this point, the phrase cited above is easily explained: *that woman is beautiful but she is not to my liking*. We understand, then, either that the face of this woman is in accordance with prevailing conventions, or that one thinks her face will recall to many the idea of the pleasures they have tasted, even though it does not produce this effect in us. Should one wish to convince himself at once that beauty acts in fact only by recalling the idea of pleasure, and that the attractiveness of the face consists only in the combination of the features we are most accustomed to seeing, it suffices to change places. Transport a Frenchman, for example, to Guinea: he will at first be disgusted by the faces of the negresses, because their features, unfamiliar to him, will not recall to him any voluptuous memory. Yet as soon as he ceases, from habit, to be shocked, he will first rediscover and prefer youth, size, and strength, which constitute beauty everywhere. And, if he then pays some attention to the face, it will be to choose the one that is least remote from European faces. Soon after, habit grows; he prefers the combination of features he sees every day to that of which he no longer has more than a slight memory; he wants a flat nose and thick lips, and so on: Hence is born that host of opinions on beauty; hence, those obvious contradictions in men's tastes. We have found the reasons for this diversity by considering man and woman only in their physical relations; if we now consider them in their moral relations, we shall find still more reasons for this prodigious variety. We have just seen beauty change form by the mere impression of the objects that surround us; we are now going to see it lend itself again to the fickleness of our ideas. As soon as society, which ceaselessly alters the work of nature, changed the momentary union of the sexes into a permanent relationship, voluptuous sensations ceased to be the only bond that joined them. A value was placed on moral qualities, and from that moment on the external signs that revealed them became part of beauty in the eyes of those who sought them. As peoples became more consistent, customs, having become constant, formed for each a national character to which the idea of beauty was soon submitted. A few, like the Asiatics, having made women absolutely dependent, and feeling only sensations and not sentiments in regard to them, have distanced themselves less from the idea of natural beauty; they have added to it only the semblance of gentleness and tenderness, more flattering to the spirit of domination that drives them. There, the character of beauty that we call physiognomy must be and is, in fact, the expression of submission. Among the ancient Romans, on the other hand, the enthusiasm for freedom, greatness of the soul, rigorous virtue presents beauty in a nobler and more austere form. This country, whose artists have passed down to us monuments from every century, provides us with proof of the perpetual variations to which the idea of beauty was submitted; the depravity of the customs has remained painted on the faces; to be convinced of this, one need only examine the difference in the character of beauty among the women of the time of Brutus and those of the time of Augustus. It is thus that we see, in our time, the Swiss and the English, more austere in their ways, always attach to the idea of beauty the idea of gentleness and modesty, while in France we more readily seek out the expression of vivacity and pleasure. These are the general differences that, in the name of physiognomy, cause beauty to vary according to times and places; they are such, and so marked, that an attentive observer could judge by them the customs of a nation with more exactitude perhaps than most historians. Not only does the idea of beauty vary from nation to nation, but it also changes from one man to another; one, more sensitive to the number than to the choice of his conquests, is seduced by the expression of facility, another, on the contrary, is excited by the sight of the difficulties that a severe beauty seems to present to him; one is captivated by the charm of a sweet languidness, another is drawn by the intoxication of a vividly expressed pleasure;

quite often in the eyes of many, spirit, graces, and talents have compensated through a fortunate illusion for the lack of beauty, or rather they have become beauty, since they have been able, like beauty, to arouse the hope of pleasure. Beauty of all times, of all places, of all persons, then, is always, as we said above, the appearance most favorable to pleasure, and because of this very fact, it must vary according to the diversity of opinions about what gives the most or the least value to that pleasure. It follows from these reflections that natural man enjoys beauty without knowing what it is, that he has no idea of elective beauty, and that for him *Philip's skull is like those of the other Macedonians:* that, in the countries where men assemble together many women for the pleasure of only one man, and hold them in a complete dependence, the ease of comparing and of judging with cool sense must establish their choice in favor of natural beauty such as we have defined it; and that, in our customs, beauty, eternal plaything of our opinions, varies to such a degree that the woman we call ugly can easily and unanimously usurp from the one we call beautiful, the tributes and desires of the men who surround them.* But if that illusion is possible, it is not easy; nature, which never entirely loses its rights, sometimes tears away the veil with which art sought to cover it. Often the flame of truth eclipses in a moment the false gleams of a long succession of illusions; thus women always begin by seeking to give themselves *the appearance most favorable to pleasure* properly speaking; it was in order to succeed in this that they invented adornment.

CHAPTER XII

On Adornment

We know two sorts of adornments: one that consists in keeping the body in the state of perfection of which it is capable, and the other, in taking best advantage of the clothes or ornaments, the use of which has been established by need, whim, or reason. Although adornment is subjected to even more variations than beauty, of which it is the com-

---

*It is not uncommon, in the theater, to see the roles of the most interesting women played by ugly actresses, while their confidants are both young and pretty. What spectator, then, has not often caught himself desiring the ugliness of the one in preference to the beauty of the other? Here the point of the illusion is discovered: it is only a matter of prolonging its charm; several celebrated actresses have proven that this charm did not always end with the magic of the spectacle that aroused it.

pliment in a sense, it nevertheless has some general rules that may be suitable to all peoples and be adapted to all clothing. Adornment is not merely the art of taking advantage of the gifts of nature but also that of lending them the charms of the imagination. Seen in this light, it becomes a stimulus of sensual delight, and we do not consider it unworthy of engaging the attention even of philosophers, since it serves man's happiness by contributing to his senuousness. There was an arid, rocky field traversed by a stream whose green and stagnant water one could scarcely see beneath the rushes with which it was covered. The rushes were pulled out, the waters channeled; the stream was adorned by keeping it in the state of perfection of which it was capable. Afterward, woods were planted on its banks, and the field, where no one went, became a charming grove whose shade is cherished. It was adorned with the help of foreign ornaments, but the wood was arranged so that, though not very expansive, one seemed to be in an immense forest. The wood was adorned by lending it the charms of the imagination: what was done in that field, every woman or almost every one can perform on herself. If need invented the first clothes, adornment considerably augmented their use. With the exception of a belt, useful to all peoples to protect the parts of the body that, being the seat of touch, are naturally delicate and sensitive, and some animal skins, useful to many for protection against the abuses of the wind, adornment is responsible for the rest. More attention is paid to the quality of ideas than to the quantity of needs. If anyone denies this fact, let him tell us why the civilized people of Hindustan wear clothes under a burning sky, while the savage of Greenland, living amidst ice, removes his clothes upon entering his hut, not to put them on again until the excessive cold of the outdoors forces him to do so. The latter is prompted by the fear of pain, the other by the attraction of pleasure; the fortunate Moor, placed in a climate where nature eagerly anticipates his needs, abandons himself to sensuousness, for he wishes to preserve for his entire body a sensitivity only to pleasure: he remains clothed. The unfortunate Greenlander, living under a harsh sky, solely occupied with searching among the ice floes of the sea for subsistence it does not always grant, and one that the earth constantly refuses, has ideas only by way of his needs; he seeks to numb a sensitivity that is almost always painful to him; he remains naked as soon as he can go without clothing. The first effects, relative to adornment, that clothes produced were to preserve for our bodies more sensitivity and to give them a softer sense of touch; soon the skillful learned to put this to good use, either to veil a deformity or to present a more agreeable shape, or lastly to call attention to what

one wanted others to see; but just when we need these external ornaments most, when their illusion could be most necessary to us, we take
them off; then, on the contrary, the gifts of nature shine in all their
brilliance; they are ours more fully, they are more precious, they deserve
our foremost attention. Coquettish and wealthy women, you think you
adorn yourselves by overloading yourselves with precious ornaments;
you applaud yourselves for the stupid admiration of a multitude easily
seduced by the brilliance of wealth. In fact, you engage the attention
for but a moment, and soon recall the comment Apelles made to his
pupil: *Unable to make her beautiful, you make her rich.* Do you want to
be truly adorned? This is how: know first how to follow a gentle and
salutary diet. This will maintain your health; without it there is no
freshness, and without freshness there is no beauty; especially avoid
uselessly staying up all night; rest is more becoming than the illusory
glow of candles. Do not tire yourself through any excess; you will be
beautiful even in daylight; the nights you steal from your amusements
will render more precious those you devote to your pleasures. Beware
also the use of spirituous drinks: a smooth skin does not cover an inflamed blood. Leave to the women who lack resources that feeble
means of exciting; let them engage in this sort of debauch, in the hope
of profiting from the desires that result from them, which they would
not have been able to arouse otherwise. You are young and beautiful:
what need have you of strong liquors? It is love that must intoxicate you.
Avoid the rays of a burning sun that would dim the brilliance of your
complexion; neither should you let your delicate skin be roughened
by the effect of an excessive cold, but protect yourself even more from
too sedentary a life; the flesh softens and loses its elasticity in the stagnant and stuffy air of your apartments; the friction of the outside air,
on the contrary, makes it firm and lively. In the winter, take advantage
of the moment when the gentle influence of the sun tempers the harshness of the cold. In the summer, be as diligent as the dawn; like linen
whitened by the sun, you must whiten yourself with the dew. Not content with regulating your actions, master also the affections of your soul.
There are some that destroy beauty; if you do not repress overly frequent fits of anger, your muscles will acquire a dangerous mobility, and
soon every expression will become a grimace. The convulsive laughter
of noisy merriment produces, to a lesser degree, drawbacks of the same
nature. Never allow yourself to be dominated by ill humor: that state
of inner vexation manifests itself externally, and no one bothers to please
a woman unafraid of displeasing others. If envy or ambition consume
you, your sunken eyes, your leaden complexion, your excessive thinness

will soon tarnish your beauty; if you abandon yourself to the passion of games, the frequent contraction of your muscles will soon wear down their elasticity; the fatigue of a game is, without exception, that which wears one out the most and the most quickly; beware as well, though, the fatigue of pleasure in the state of exhaustion that follows it; the circles around your eyes, your faded lips, your colorless cheeks will not be able to arouse desires that it is rather clear you can no longer share. This is a sort of adornment too little known, perhaps, but especially too rarely practiced. After these initial attentions, which nothing can replace, there are easier ones that sensuousness demands. There is also no adornment without rigorous cleanliness; before seeking to adorn yourselves with clothes, strip yourselves and enter the bath; do not be afraid to make daily use of it; to eliminate the drawbacks that it can entail, accustom yourselves to endure them cold; then, far from destroying your elasticity, they will augment it. If their coolness damages your skin slightly, repair this effect with a gentle cosmetic;* afterward, efface with a mild perfume the stale or aromatic odor they leave behind them. Use it but do not abuse it; one readily suspects the woman who perfumes herself too much of being impelled to it by some secret reason. Without this, even too strong an odor, however agreeable, would destroy intoxication by diverting attention – for it is not with the rose or the carnation, it is with you that you want your lover to be concerned; he should therefore think that you yourself are exhaling the perfume that he breathes. In these solitary treatments, above all, do not imitate those women who are more vain than sensitive, who, satisfied with a temporary triumph, think only of the public, and forget their lover. Unjust women, you complain of being soon abandoned by them, you accuse them of fickleness; blame yourselves for this apparent perfidy – your fresh and merry face fooled them, your withered body disillusioned them. The face attracts, but it is the body that holds. The soul is the net and the other the cage; but the prudent fowler, before setting his traps, attends to the means of preserving the prey he may catch; imitate him in his precautions, then contemplate embellishing your face. This care requires a few more remarks. Art should help nature, not change it. Before attempting to compare yourselves, examine yourselves and try to know yourselves; so that your facial expression might

---

*There is a simple and wholesome one used too infrequently, it seems to us, that we will be happy to describe here: take some white poppy seed and crush it in a mortar, adding some water so that the milk resulting from it will be thicker than it is clear; strain the whole, and use it at least the whole week.

be agreeable, know how to choose the one that suits it. If your features are fine and delicate, if your figure is small, do not affect an air of dignity that would become ridiculous; if your features are noble, if you are tall, leave to others the childish graces; too much plumpness mars you and, though it may be overlooked so that attention can be paid to your freshness, this defect becomes strikingly noticeable if you want to appear slight. If your eyes are lively and full of fire, it will be useless for you to seek to make them tender; you will only dim their brilliance; if, on the contrary, they are gentle and caressing, you will destroy, with an assumed vivacity, the charm they would have inspired. Each of them has means suitable to them and suitable only to them; arrive at your goal by the path that nature has traced for you – it is at once the surest and the shortest. Let your lively glance act at intervals; redouble its blows, but distance them; like lightning, let it dazzle at once by the flame with which it shines and by the shadows that surround it. Yet the action of a tender gaze should be continuous; it should engage us in order to please us, and make its way into our hearts one step at a time, like a soft daylight into delicate eyes. Above all, do not believe you can obtain this expression from the advice of your mirror alone; it is the result of your inner qualities. Do you want to make your gaze more tender? Exercise the sensitivity of your soul. Do you want to make it more vivacious? Cultivate your mind, increase the number of your ideas; in vain will nature have bestowed beautiful eyes on you if your soul is cold; if your mind is empty, your gaze will be vacant and mute. Here we speak only of that expression of the eyes which is a result neither of a profound feeling nor of a lively sensation. We know that the great impulses of the soul or of the senses are portrayed in the eyes, surmounting even the obstacles one places in their way. Such is nature's right; art has sought to imitate it, and has succeeded: the use of this imitation is frequent in the theater, the abuse of it has slipped into society, and looks have become false and perfidious. It makes itself felt even in adornment; if one believes the reports of travelers, the dancing girls of Hindustan are able, with the help of a powder, to give their gaze the expression of pleasure, by keeping in their eyes those burning tears that sensual delight causes to well up; and without having recourse to such reports, we see around us European women who make their eyes shine with the ardor of desire, by the reflection of the rouge placed on their cheeks.

Originally published as *De l'éducation des femmes* (1783).

Oriental Dreams

The Sofa
A Moral Tale

by Crébillon fils

Translated by Bonamy Dobrée

Introduction

by Jean Sgard

Crébillon fils's *The Sofa*

by Jean Sgard

By virtue of its very title, *The Sofa* (1742), introduces itself as a libertine novel. The title does not lie; no novel of the eighteenth century takes us so close to the realities of the love, pleasure, secrets, confessions, and sorrows shared in bed; no other novel evokes, in so lively and convincing a manner, the thing confessors call the "vehemence" of the pleasures of love. The work is assuredly bold, fully erotic, and worthy of its bad reputation. It surpasses this reputation, however, in a paradoxical fashion. In subtitling his story "A Moral Tale," Crébillon fils (1701–77) fully expected to be taken seriously; when he invokes, in a letter to the police chief in 1742, the morality he "tried to distribute throughout," he is certainly speaking in good faith. But no one imagined that this morality was drawn from love itself, and people still consider it, as did Frédéric-César de La Harpe, "the ever so facile art of veiling obscenity." In France, modern readers have given *The Wayward Head and Heart* (1738) its due but have yet to discover the wisdom which at times guides the feat of love in *The Sofa*. A few have caught a glimpse of it, and they were not poor judges: Voltaire, who called Crébillon fils "the father of *The Sofa*," Diderot, Laclos, and Stendhal, who knew the best parts by heart. No doubt, they understood the gravity of this light work; it is our task to discover it anew.

The work is libertine in nature, in every sense of the word. A narrator, condemned by divine decree to be reincarnated into sucessive sofas, takes part in more than a dozen female conquests, by turns pleasant, happy, and catastrophic. Not only does Crébillon fils take advantage of this arrangement to expose the ruses of false virtue, worldly hypocrisy, and religious scruples, but he further demonstrates how instinct, vanity, and fantasy will prevail at the expense of avowed morality. Moreover, since the narrator's tale is intended for an unrefined and indiscreet monarch, and since the guilty parties are by preference scarcely disguised monks, confessors, and people from high society, the tale becomes satire. Erotic libertinage, flagrant immorality, and impertinence give the work its scandalous flavor; this was enough to condemn the author. Three months of exile was not a minor sentence for a well-known author, a man admitted at court, a man with powerful friends, the son of a famous dramatist, and Crébillon fils was not soon to forget it. For the next twelve years he published nothing in his own name; and in his later tales, one never again finds the same blithe audacity, verve, and happy imagination of *The Skimming Ladle* (1734), *The Wayward Head and Heart*, or *The Sofa*. With this ill success, a time of unhampered invention and creative improvisation ended for Crébillon fils, a time during which, particularly in *The Sofa*, he seems to have surrendered, to borrow an expression from *Rameau's Nephew* (1761–73), to "the full libertinage of his mind."

This total freedom of an inventive spirit is evident in the composition of the work, where order and disorder follow upon one another without clashing. The order is that of a social inquiry, a "survey" novel. It was not unusual in the 1740s for a fictive narrator to lead the reader through high society with a series of amorous intrigues, and the model of the genre, the *Confessions of the Count of ——* (1740) by Duclos, so enchanted Crébillon fils that he supposedly gave up the idea of finishing *The Wayward Head and Heart*. The oriental setting, overtly taken from the *Thousand and One Nights*, simply adds a touch of fantasy to this pattern. Following Amanzei, the narrator-sofa, we discover love in different kinds of company, some good, some bad. The decree that condemns Amanzei to life as a series of sofas will not be lifted until two lovers in good faith give each other their "first fruits" on this bed. Thus, the inquiry becomes a quest for true love, through Sodom and Gomorrah. Will this corrupt society be saved by the miraculous survival of the natural? This is, let us not forget, the central theme of *The Indiscreet Jewels* (1748), which owes a great deal to *The Sofa*; but it is certainly the common preoccupation of Crébillon fils, Diderot, and Rousseau at that time. Searching for nature beneath the masks of society, Crébillon fils is likewise in his own right a philosopher. This ordered investigation is not, however, his main passion; social realism matters little to him, and it is from a "moral" plane that he claims to observe the different ways of love. Seven couples successively help us to glimpse other depths: the hypocrite Fatima gives herself in secret to her slave; Amina, an intrepid prostitute, is humiliated by a steward no less abject; sweet Phenima, after eight years of virtue, gives in to the passion of the timid Zulma; Almaida, forty years old, allows herself to be seduced by her spiritual guide; Zephis yields, with sweetness and tenderness, to Mazulhim, a libertine threatened with impotence, who betrays her immediately with a depraved society woman, Zulica, who in turn betrays him with his best friend, Nasses, before being humiliated by them both. It falls to the young lovers Zeinis and Phileas to enact the perfect union in front of Amanzei, which both frees and dismays him, for the enchanted narrator is suddenly smitten with Zeinis and experiences in his own heart the thing he had most dreaded, a final twist that gives the tale an unexpected ending. In the end, Crébillon fils has described not the conventional forms of love but, rather, its paradoxes.

He ties them together with a perfect insouciance, twice running through the circle of intrigues he has set for himself. The first time around he stages the impostures of false virtue, affected religiosity, worldly snobbery, and depraved coquetry, before bringing us to a first, happy resolution with the love of Phenima and Zulma; the spell that binds Amanzei should now be lifted but, curiously, it is not, and the author says nothing about this. In the seven chapters that make up a third of the work, everything seems to have been said. What will keep it going from this point on is the deepening of conflict, and the play of hypocritical modes of language imprisoned in their own conventions. Men seek no more than to expose the desire and reveal the inconsistencies of feminine modesty, while women seek desperately to obtain the confessions of love which would justify their undoing. Whether we have two fundamentally honest souls such as Almaida and Mochles, or perverse ones such as Mazulhim, Zulica, and Nasses, the dialogue unfolds in infinitely dazzling spirals. Crébillon fils no longer seems to care about an outline, and the chapter titles seem to refer only to the whims of the author. When he undertakes the tale of Mazulhim, it seems nothing more can stop him; this comedy of rogues and dupes unfolds in ten connected chapters – more than half of the work. Using a theme sketched by Marivaux at the end of the *Paysan parvenu* (1735-36), Crébillon fils develops five or six variations that bring to light every angle of the conflict. The tale in dialogue has definitively found its form; Crébillon fils will take it no further.

The same question runs through all these intrigues: "What value do you really give to love?" Zulica and Nasses, who have just asked this question, are ready to hate each other all the same; and all of Crébillon fils's lovers come back to it in different guises. For Crébillon fils, love is certainly the greatest experience in life, and its only "value." It is impossible to find, in his work, anything that is not derived from love. Yet where does its truth lie? Crébillon fils describes aberrations, implicitly indicating a straight path, a referential axis which is that of wisdom; but this wisdom always comes from love itself, whose ways are always unexpected. "Love alone reigns here," he wrote in the preface to *The Wayward Head and Heart*; he could have said this, and even more deservedly, about *The Sofa*, where twice he refers to the ideal image of fulfilled love. The first time, speaking of the exemplary lovers Phenima and Zulma, he evokes the perfect union of desire and feeling, using such terms as "eagerness," "voluptuousness," "extreme tenderness," and "true ecstasy," confidence and loyalty. The vast wealth of human relations is summed up in such a union: "To all the delight and exuberance of the most ardent passion they added the intimacy and trust of the tenderest friendship…" (p. 220). On this note, Crébillon fils seems to bring his tale to its first conclusion. In the last chapter, we find again the same union of desire, tenderness, and passionate imagination, but here it is less analyzed, and as if enveloped in the illusions of youth. The conclusion nonetheless is introduced by the enigmatic title, "Soulful Delights": could this refer to the dubious diversions of a narrator who is prisoner to his sofa as the soul is prisoner to the body? Undoubtedly, and we might well imagine that here we see the diversions of the novelist himself. But one might also imagine that the "wanderings of the head and heart" are the opposite of these "diversions of the soul," the soul recovered by the grace of love.

It is not the least of the paradoxes of this libertine novel that the word best represented in its psychological and moral vocabulary is the word "soul." Amanzei is a soul in search of love, which will give him a body; but many of the sensitive women who haunt this tale (the "lady" in chapter 5, or Phenima, Zephis, and Zeinis) have souls. The libertines have none: totally socialized, they have lost their feelings, their dreams, their consciences. They are equally haunted by a sort of nostalgia which comes from boredom. The Sultan is obsessed with boredom from the very first pages of the tale, and boredom reappears as a leitmotif in the finest definitions of libertinage: "People say, without feeling it, that they find each other attractive; they unconsciously become involved; they see that they wait for love in vain, and they part for fear of becoming bored. Sometimes it happens that one is mistaken about one's feelings; one thought it was passion and finds it was mere fancy, an impulse, which does not last long and wears itself out in pleasure, instead of seeming to renew love" (p. 302). In the end, the most deceptive language always uses this vanished ideal, which justifies the most miserable defeats in the last resort, and thus pays homage to virtue. However, for Crébillon fils there is only one virtue, sincerity in love. Love is perhaps a passing fancy, an illusion, "the binding of sentiment," but it remains for him the only chance for a human being, the only possible fulfillment for what he calls "nature."

Thus, the libertine adventures presented to us seem like so many deviations or irremediable mistakes. Fatima sacrifices her life to her reputation and compensates herself with the brutal caresses of a slave; Amina has chosen money and boldly throws herself into abjection; Almaida and Mochles have refused the slightest temptation until the age of forty, and then approach each other awkwardly, remorsefully and in bad faith, crushed by shame, without finding happiness. The libertine Mazulhim, trapped in vanity and obsessed by his physical failings, ignores Zephis's tender indulgences and chooses imposture instead, while delegating the task of finishing up with Zulica to his friend and accomplice Nasses. The theme of "fiasco" as Stendhal conceived it in *On Love* (1822), reappears insistently in all of these aborted endeavors. Nevertheless, with Stendhal the fiasco is most often the result of romantic excess and imaginary anticipation, while with Crébillon fils it is due to bad faith alone. Almaida's first lover and the libertine Mazulhim fail inasmuch as their plan of seduction is based solely on will. Devoid of illusion and sentiment, and at times even desire, the libertine is as though stricken with sterility; far from giving himself over to nature's calling, as even the touching Zephis does, Mazulhim refuses it and condemns himself to impotence, to the point that his punishment seems again moral. It is true that Crébillon fils imagines, on several occasions, the triumph of libertinage, and in this way serves as a direct inspiration for *Dangerous Liaisons* (1782). Fatima for an instant recalls the Marquise de Merteuil: "Devoted to deceit from her tenderest years, she strove less to correct her heart's vicious propensities than to veil them under the guise of the most forbidding virtue" (p. 192). Mazulhim and Zulica are not far from making the perfect couple of damned lovers: "'You have been fickle,' he answered, 'and, I confess, I have been inconstant. But as incapable as we have hitherto been of a serious attachment, the more glorious will be our bond'" (p. 262). This is, however, but a passing suggestion; in the end, only Nasses combines — and in this way gives the tale a first pessimistic conclusion — the taste for erotic play, the relentless wickedness, and the concern for a libertine masterpiece, all of which prefigure *Dangerous Liaisons*'s Valmont. As Mazulhim and Nasses reduce their victim to the deepest state of humiliation with their refined cruelty, evil genius finally emerges. Yet in *The Sofa* this strange and unexpected couple is merely the last and ultimate incarnation of denatured mores.

Crébillon fils's great libertines and his "philosophical" women emerge from this seemingly frivolous book fully armed. Evil, however, is still but the expression of a social ill. Behind this adventurous and often unhappy libertinage, one discerns the society that produced it. The wicked libertine indeed seeks only vanity's pleasures and scarcely acts on his own behalf. Public opinion, to which he always refers, is ever present. It is public opinion that condemns weak and unfaithful women, at least those who betray their weakness or proclaim their unfaithfulness. It likewise denounces false virtues and praises bombastic seducers. All this functions according to an ever-changing code, similar to fashion and just as tyrannical. Glory, virtue, and piety are reduced to fashions, pure appearances with which one must clothe oneself. Language no longer expresses what one feels, but what befits the situations and assigned roles. Amorous attachments develop according to acknowledged contracts or according to the collective laws of supply and demand, with the slightest infractions being punished with ridicule and exclusion. Denouncing, humiliating, unmasking are but the mechanisms of a social machine created to subjugate, level, and oppress. Crébillon fils does not give a name to power, but he shows it as ever present in language. Love – the sole chance for the freedom of an individual – the sentiments and all the impulses of the lovers' bodies are free, unexpected and beyond words; prescribed relations will, by contrast, fit into the code of proprieties and a conventional vocabulary that people use and abuse. Crébillon fils's lovers speak well, often too well; facile speech is their curse – it alone transforms the lovers' exchange into a relationship of power. People know from the beginning, as soon they find themselves with someone else in a boudoir or on a sofa, exactly what will happen: that is what they came for. Nevertheless, it is necessary that consent become defeat; that love is reduced to desire; that all modesty be formally renounced. Obtaining favors is not enough for the libertine: the victim must admit dependency, renounce pride, and recount past adventures in detail. Valmont was content with letters; Mochles, Mazulhim, and Nasses want an ordered recital, both exhaustive and humiliating. In this way, confrontation between people is circumscribed in dialogue from beginning to end. In deadly fencing matches, the actors rival each other in virtuosity in the art of defining euphemism, preterition, dodging, or argumentation in order to extort a confession of love, or at times of hate, or at times of both, as happens when the libertine wants to prolong the torture of his victim. This cruel art of pushing each person to his limits rests entirely on dialogue, and Crébillon fils is perfectly aware of having endowed the tale with a property previously inseparable from theater – dialogued action. One of his characters remarks in passing, "this conversation, which you find tedious, is, so to speak, an act in itself. It is not a useless digression, leading nowhere, it is … an act. Is that not what we call dialogue?" (p. 280). Crébillon fils, in writing

The Sofa, discovers that everything can be done in dialogue: the secret trajectories of passion, bad faith, vanity, their conflicts, and their failures. From simple conversations are born conflicts, revelations, and resolutions. One cannot imagine a more lucid and more moral art — but one would be tempted to use the term as it is used today by the filmmaker Eric Rohmer, likewise the creator of "moral" tales in which all illumination comes from simple conversation. And one would be less surprised that the most libertine of tales is in its way also the most serious.

———————

Translated by Sophie Hawkes.

THE SOFA

A Moral Tale

CONTENTS

THE SOFA
by Crébillon fils

*"It is nice to translate authors... where there is hardly
anything but the matter to reproduce; but those who have
given much care to grace and elegance of language are
dangerous to undertake...."*
—Montaigne, *Apology for Raymond Sebond* [1]

PREFACE

NOT MANY CENTURIES ago, a certain prince named Shah Baham ruled
over India. He was a grandson of the magnanimous Shah Riar, whose
great doings have been recorded in the *Thousand and One Nights*, and
who, among other things, took so great a pleasure in strangling women
and in listening to tales; the very one, indeed, who reprieved that
incomparable lady Scheherezade, solely on account of the lovely tales
she could tell.

It was either because Shah Baham was not extremely nice in points of
honor, or because his women did not lie with their blacks, or (which is
quite as likely) because he was kept in the dark about it – in any event, he
was a kind and easy husband. From Shah Riar he had inherited nothing
but his virtues and his liking for stories. It is even stated that the collection of Scheherezade's tales, which his august grandfather had had written in letters of gold, was the only book he had ever vouchsafed to read.

Yet, even if it be true that tales adorn the understanding, and that
the knowledge or notions that we glean from them are both agreeable
and sublime, it is dangerous to read nothing but books of this sort.
Only those who are really enlightened, above prejudice, knowing the
hollowness of science, realize how useful to society such books really
are; and how much one ought to esteem, and even revere, those who
have genius enough to invent them, and sufficient firmness of mind to
devote their lives to making them, in spite of the stigma of frivolity
which pride and ignorance have attributed to this sort of writing. The
important lessons such fables contain, the fine flights of imagination

so often encountered in them, and the ludicrous notions in which they always abound, make no appeal to the vulgar — who commend most what they least understand, while flattering themselves that they do so perfectly.

Shah Baham provides a memorable instance of mankind's blindness in this matter. Although he was as familiar with the earliest days of faerie as if he had lived in them; although no one was more curiously acquainted than he with the notorious realm of Djinnistan, or had more knowledge of the famous dynasties of the first kings of Persia; and although, beyond question, he knew more than any man of his time about such events as have never taken place, he was said to be the most ignorant prince in the world.

It is true that he told stories with so little skill (which was all the more tiresome, as he was forever telling them) that he was unavoidably considered a bit tedious: especially since his only audience consisted of women and courtiers, who, commonly as refined as they are superficial, are likely to care more for an elegant turn of phrase than to be struck by the boldness or truth of an idea. It is no doubt from what his own court said about Shah Baham that an author of that prince's day, Sheikh Ibn Taher Abu Feraki has drawn him for us, such as we shall see him below, in his great history of India. In the place where he speaks of the stories he says:

Shah Baham, the first of that name, was an ignorant and completely spineless prince. No one could have less sense; and (which is usual enough in those who are like him in that respect) no one could credit himself with more. He was always astonished at every ordinary thing, and never really understood but what was absurd and unnatural. Although he might go a whole year without a thought, there was hardly a day in which he would for a minute hold his tongue. Nevertheless, he would modestly say of himself that he laid no claim to being witty: but that for profound contemplation he believed he had no fellow.

He did not care a jot for any of the pleasures which call for the use of the mind; any sort of exercise displeased him: and yet he was not idle. He had birds, which never ceased to amuse him enormously; parrots which, thanks to the pains he took over their education, were the stupidest parrots in all India, not to mention his monkeys, on which he spent no small part of his time; and his women, who, when all the animals in his menagerie palled, seemed to him very proper for his diversion.

In spite of such high avocations, and such varied pleasures, the Sultan still could not avoid boredom. Even his darling stories, which never failed to arouse his astonishment and veneration, and which it meant death to criticize, became insipid by dint of being repeated too often. He still admired them, but though he admired, he yawned. At last tedium pursued him into the very apartments of his women, where he spent a part of his life watching them embroider and make patchwork, arts of which he thought extremely highly, considering their invention as the masterpiece of human ingenuity, and to which, in the end, he required all his courtiers to apply themselves.

He rewarded those who excelled in them too well for any in his Empire to neglect them. To embroider or to patch was at that time the only means by which anyone in India could rise to a post of honor. The Sultan recognized no other kind of ability whatever, or at least took it for granted that a man who had such talents would naturally possess those requisite for being a good general or a consummate statesman. To show how far he was convinced of it, he raised an idle courtier to the post of Grand Vizier, one of that breed who, not knowing how to pass their time, employ it in pestering kings with their very existence, thereby boring themselves. This man, who had for a long time been lost among the crowd, luckily for himself was discovered to be one of the finest patchworkers in the kingdom, just at the period when it pleased Shah Baham to honor patchworking; and since he was not, like so many others, forced to corruption, he owed to the superiority of his genius alone the splendid honor of cutting patches next to his master, and in the highest post in the Empire.

Among all the Sultan's wives the Sultana Queen was especially looked up to, for by reason of her wit she was the delight of all who still had the spirit to think and to improve their minds in so frivolous a court. She alone discerned and encouraged merit, and the Sultan himself rarely dared to be of a mind different from hers, although she approved little of his tastes or of his pleasures: and when she rallied him upon his monkeys and his other pastimes, he would confine himself to saying she was caustic, which is the objection fools invariably make to persons of wit.

One day Shah Baham was in the women's apartments of his court, where, though he was watching patchworking with incredible earnestness, he could not combat the tedium that weighed him down, and said with a yawn: "My falling asleep is not to be wondered at. No one has a word to say. Oh I *would* like some conversation!"

"Well, and what do you wish us to talk to you about?" the Sultana asked.

"How can I tell?" he answered. "Am I supposed to know that into the bargain? Merely because I want you to speak to me about something, must I also indicate what is to be said to me? You know, you are not nearly so intelligent as you think you are: you dream more than you talk; and apart from the occasional clever sayings, three-quarters of which I do not understand at all, you seem to me as flat and dusty as anything. Do you suppose that if Queen Scheherezade were still alive and here, she would not tell us the most lovely stories in the world, without waiting to be begged by my aunt, Dinazarde, either? But there, speaking of her, I have an idea! However good her memory may have been, she could not possibly have retained all the stories she had heard, and someone must know just those she had forgotten; nor can I believe that nobody has made any up since her time, nor that somebody does not make them up nowadays."

"Spare your doubts, Sire, on that count," the Vizier cried, "for I can assure your Majesty that not only do I know some but I even have the gift of making up such fanciful ones, that your late grandmother's do not better them in that respect."

"O Vizier! Vizier!" said the Sultan, "that is saying a great deal! My grandmother was a person of rare genius."

"Truly," the Sultana cried, "genius is surely needed to tell stories! Would one not think, to listen to you, that a tale is the masterpiece of the human mind? And yet, what can be more puerile or absurd? What sort of work – if, indeed, a tale deserves the name – what sort of work is it, I ask, where nature is always flouted, and in which the common notions of things are continually upset? Which, based upon the sham-marvelous and trivial, relies only on the extraordinary, and on the omnipotence of faerie; which turns the order of things and the elements upside down, only to manufacture ridiculous playthings, strange to think of, I agree, but which often have nothing in them to compensate for the extravagance of the invention? We should be lucky, indeed, if these wretched fables only damaged the understanding without, as they do, inflaming the heart with pictures too lively drawn for modest minds."

"Mere chatter," the Sultan said gravely. "Big words which mean nothing. What you have just said sounds very fine at first, striking enough, I admit, but on reflecting a little one cannot help...After all, here we are concerned to know only whether you are in the right: for, as I meant to say, and as I have just proved, I do not believe you are. And I assure you that it was not merely for the sake of airing my wit; but since I have always liked a story, it is obvious that a story cannot be a silly thing. I am the last person whom you will persuade that a Sultan can be an ass. Besides, that is to say, by the way, it is equally clear that a marvelous thing, by which I mean a thing...as I could explain if I wished to...but let us be frank, what does it matter, after all? I maintain, personally, that I like stories, and besides, that I find them amusing only when they are a little risqué, as people of taste have it. That makes them so interesting, so affecting! In any event, I see, I take your meaning perfectly: it is as though you were to tell me that you know a few stories, and that you make them up as well. You are the very man for me. It occurred to me that, to make the days seem less long, we should each of us tell a story – and when I say story, I know what I am talking about. I want wonders, fairies, talismans, make no mistake on that point at least; for those are the only things that are really true. Well then? Are we all agreed to tell stories? Muhammad help me! But why do I ask for his help? For even without it I could make up stories better than anybody else, seeing that I come from a house well known for them and – I need not be accused of boasting – no bad ones, neither.

"Further, as there is nothing of favoritism about me, I rule that each one of us is to speak in turn; the order will be decided not by my wishes but by casting lots. I graciously permit everyone to tell me a tale, which shall be told every day for half an hour, more or less, according to my fancy."

Having uttered these words, he made all the court draw lots: and, to the mortification of the Vizier, the choice fell upon a young courtier, who, after receiving permission of the Sultan, began as follows:

CHAPTER I

The Least Tedious in the Book

"Sire, your Majesty is not unaware that, although I am his subject, I do not live under the same divine law as he does, and that I acknowledge no other god but Brahma."

"And if I *am* aware of it," the Sultan said, "what difference does that make to your story? In any case, it is your own affair. So much the worse for you if you believe in Brahma; you would do a hundred times better to believe in Muhammad! I speak as a friend; do not get it into your head that I am merely showing what a theologian I am, for I assure you it is all the same to me. Well?"

"We adherents of the Brahmin sect believe in metempsychosis," Amanzei (such was his name) proceeded. "That is to say, not to burden your Majesty's mind out of season, that when our soul leaves one body it enters into another, and so on successively, for as long as it shall please Brahma, or until our soul is become sufficiently purified to be ranked among those which he considers worthy of everlasting bliss.

"Although the doctrine of metempsychosis is generally received among us, we have not all the same reasons for believing in it, since there are very few persons to whom it has been granted to remember the different transmigrations of their souls. Ordinarily, when a soul leaves a body in which it has been confined and enters into another, it loses all recollection either of the knowledge it had acquired or of the events in which it had played a part.

"Thus, our errors are continually hidden from us, and we embark upon a new career with a soul as fresh, and as prone to error and vice, as when Brahma first drew it out of that vast flaming whirlpool of which it formed a part while awaiting its destination.

"Many among us bemoan this edict of Brahma, but I doubt if this be reasonable. Our souls, fated to pass from body to body throughout a long cycle of centuries, would nearly always be woeful if they remembered what they had been. A soul, for instance, that had once animated the body of a king, and now housed in a reptile or in the body of one of those obscure mortals whose great wretchedness makes them still more to be pitied than the vilest beast, could not bear its new condition without despair.

"I grant that a man who found himself in the lap of luxury or raised to the highest rank might, if he remembered having been an insect, less abuse the affluent or dazzling position that the goodness of Brahma had provided for him. Nevertheless, when I consider the pride, harshness, and insolence of those born in the rabble and raised high by fortune, and how promptly they forget their former state, I am led to believe that in passing from one body to another, their former humility would slip from their minds even more quickly, and would have no effect upon their conduct.

"Moreover, the soul would necessarily be overburdened by the vast number of its memories of earlier days, and, being perhaps more concerned for what it could have been than for what it would be, might neglect the duties proper to its present body, and so disturb the order of the universe instead of contributing to it."

"By Muhammad! my dear fellow," the Sultan said, "I believe you are moralizing at me."

"Sire," Amanzei answered, "these are mere preliminary reflections, which I think are not useless."

"They are entirely useless, I tell you," Shah Baham answered. "I have no taste for morals, and I shall be much obliged if you will drop them."

"I shall obey your commands," Amanzei answered. "Nevertheless, it remains for me to tell your Majesty that Brahma does sometimes allow us to remember what we have been, especially when he has inflicted some especially disagreeable thing upon us: and to prove that this is so, I remember perfectly well having been a sofa."

"A sofa!" the Sultan exclaimed. "That sort of thing does not happen. Do you take me for an ostrich, to expect me to digest stories like that? I have a good mind to have you toasted a little, to teach you to tell me such trumped-up stuff in such a barefaced way."

"Your benign Majesty is out of sorts today," the Sultana said. "It is part of your august nature to question nothing, and yet you refuse to believe that a man may have been a sofa. That is not like your usual self."

"Is that so?" the Sultan asked, graveled by the objection. "All the same, it does not seem to me that I am wrong. I cannot possibly be... No, egad! I am right. In all conscience, I cannot believe what Amanzei says. Am I a Muslim for nothing?"

"Bravo!" the Sultana replied. "Well then, since it is a question of conscience, listen to what Amanzei has to say, and do not believe him."

"True!" the Sultan continued. "Then it will not be because the thing is incredible that I shall not believe it, but because, even were it true, I ought not to believe it. I quite see that this makes a difference. Then you have really been a sofa, my dear Amanzei? What a terrible experience that must have been! And tell me, were you embroidered?"

"Yes, Sire," Amanzei answered. "The first sofa in which my soul dwelt was rose-colored, embroidered with silver."

"Well done!" the Sultan said. "You must have been a rather fine piece of furniture. And why did your Brahma make you a sofa of all things? What was the point of that farcical prank? A sofa! That is beyond me!"

"That," Amanzei answered, "Brahma did to punish my soul for its poor discipline. If he had put it into another human body, he would not have been able to approve its behavior, and no doubt he thought it would be more humiliating for me to be a sofa than to be a reptile.

"I remember that, on leaving the body of a woman, my soul entered that of a young man. And as he was an egregious fop, a busybody, a scandal monger, a vain butterfly, an authority in trifles, serious only about his dress, his complexion, and a hundred other vapid nothings, my soul hardly noticed that it had changed its abode."

"It would be extremely curious," the Sultan interrupted, "to know what you did while you were a woman: it would make a vastly diverting tale. I have always thought that women were mysterious creatures.

I do not know if I make myself clear – I mean that one finds it hard to tell what they are really at."

"Perhaps," Amanzei answered, "we should not be at such a loss on that subject if we believed them less artful. As far as I remember, when I was a woman I found a mine of mirth in persons who believed my thoughts were studied when they were the spontaneous flights of my unrestrained fancy, and who, because they imagined me to be deep, never saw through me an inch. I was thought to be double-dealing when I was candid, and when I was frank I was called a flirt; and whenever my heart was really touched I was made out to be callous. I was nearly always supposed to be what I was not, or, at any rate, no longer was. Those most concerned to know me well, with whom I was most open, to whom even, by reason of my natural indiscretion or the inclinations of my heart, I revealed my most secret actions and my truest feelings, were not those who believed in me most or understood me best. They only wanted to judge me according to their preconceived idea of me, and vowed they knew me well once they had portrayed me to their own satisfaction."

"I was sure of it," the Sultan said. "One never knows women properly, and, as you say, I have long given over trying, as far as I am concerned. But let us drop the subject: it sharpens the mind unduly, and has been your excuse for making a long preamble that I could have very well done without, and for not answering what I asked you. I thought I said I wanted to know what you *did* while you were a woman."

"I have only a very faint idea of that," Amanzei answered. "What I remember most clearly is that I was wanton in my youth, and could neither hate nor love; that, born without a strong character, I became what people would have me be, or what my interests or my pleasures demanded; that at the end of a lax life I turned hypocrite, and finally, in spite of a prudish mask, died thinking of all my favorite past delights.

"It was apparently owing to my addiction to couches that Brahma conceived the idea of confining my soul in such a piece of furniture. He decreed that it should retain all its faculties in that prison, no doubt not so much to mitigate the horrors of my lot as to make me feel them the more. He further decreed that my soul should begin a new life only when two persons, while seated upon me, should render each other the first fruits of mutual affection."

"There now!" the Sultan cried. "There's a deal of fiddle-faddle, simply to say that..."

"Surely you will not be so gracious as to give us an explanation!" the Sultana interjected.

"Why on earth not?" he replied. "I like to hear a spade called a spade. However, if you are not of my mind, by all means let Amanzei be as obscure as he pleases. Thanks be to the Prophet, I shall always understand him."

"I remembered enough both of what I had done and of what I had seen," Amanzei proceeded, "to realize that the conditions under which Brahma was granting me my new life would keep me no small length of time in the furniture he had chosen for my prison; but the permission he gave me to transfer myself at pleasure from sofa to sofa somewhat alleviated the hardship. This freedom brought a variety into my life which could not but make it less wearisome; and, moreover, my soul was as alive to the absurdities of other people as when it had animated a woman; and the pleasure of being able to ensconce myself in the most private corners, and of being a third party in matters supposed to be a dead secret, made amends for my sufferings.

"After Brahma had pronounced my doom, he himself bore my soul into a sofa, which the maker was about to deliver to a woman of quality, reputed to be superbly chaste; but just as it is said that few men are heroes to those who see them close up, so I may safely affirm that few women are virtuous to their sofas."

CHAPTER 11

Will Not Be to Everybody's Taste

"A sofa was never relegated to a hall, and, at the house of the lady to whom I was to belong, I was placed in a boudoir apart from the rest of her palace, where, she said, she often retired simply for pious meditation, and to devote herself more wholly to Brahma. When I entered this boudoir, I found it hard to believe, from the way it was arranged, that it served only for such solemn purposes. Not that it was at all sumptuous, or that anything in it seemed too elaborate; at first sight everything in it appeared distinguished rather than cozy; but, on considering it maturely, one could not but detect a hypocritical indulgence, furniture convenient for certain agreeable usages, things, in fact, which do not lend themselves to austerity, and which are not habitual with it. It struck me that I myself was a trifle gay in color for a woman who was supposed to be so unconcerned with flirtation.

"Soon after my arrival, my mistress came into the boudoir: she looked indifferently upon me, seemed satisfied, but did not praise me mightily, and with a cold, absentminded air, sent the maker away. As soon as she was alone, her gloomy and severe expression relaxed. I beheld another bearing and other eyes: she tested me with a care that showed me that she did not intend to keep me only for show. Yet this frolicsome trial of myself, and the gay and tender expression she had assumed the moment she was sure of being unobserved, did not make me modify the high opinion they had of her in Agra.

"I knew that souls, however perfect they may be considered, always have a pet vice, often resisted but usually victorious; that they seem to deny themselves certain pleasures only to taste of them later with greater relish – in short, that for them virtue resides in repentance rather than in self-denial. I drew the conclusion that Fatima was lazy, and I would have blamed myself had I at that stage allowed my conjectures to travel further afield.

"The first act she performed after the one I have described was to open a secret cupboard let into the wall, artfully hidden from all eyes, and take a book out of it. From this cupboard she went to another, where many volumes were ostentatiously displayed. From there likewise she took a book, which she tossed upon me with an impatient disdain, and returned, with the one she had first chosen, to relapse into the downiest part of the pile of cushions heaped upon me."

"Tell us now, Amanzei," the Sultan interrupted, "was this sensible woman of yours at all pretty?"

"Indeed she was, Sire," Amanzei answered. "She was beautiful, more so than one might suppose. I went so far as to think that with less prudishness, with fewer of those soulful looks – which arouse contempt, it is true, but also kindle desire – she might have held her own with anybody. Her features were beautiful, but without lure or liveliness, and they wore only that smug disdain without which women of her cast think themselves lost to virtue. At first sight, everything about her seemed to indicate neglect of her person, and contempt of how she might look. Although she had a good figure, she held herself poorly; and if her walk was distinguished, it was because she thought a slow, stately step became persons whose minds were bent on serious things. Her apparent hatred of self-adornment did not go to that extreme of negligence by which virtuous women nearly always make themselves repulsive: her clothes were simple and sober in hue; but even in their decorum one could detect a taste and deliberation: she even took care to lose nothing of the elegance of her figure, and one could easily see that under her austere trappings she luxuriated in extravagant cleanliness.

"The book she had taken last did not seem to be the one that pleased her most. Nevertheless, it was a ponderous volume of maxims, composed by a Brahmin. Whether she preferred the ones she made up her-self, or whether these did not bear upon the subjects she liked, in any event she did not choose to read so much as a couple of them, and soon dropped this book, to take up the one she had slipped out of the secret cupboard, and which was a romance full of tender situations and lively images. This literature seemed to me so little suited to Fatima that I could not recover from my surprise. 'No doubt,' I assured myself, 'she is making a trial of her strength, to see how far her soul is proof against those many suggestions so apt to unsettle the minds of others.'

"Far from guessing, at that time, the motives that made her act in a manner so opposed to the principles I believed to be hers, I ascribed only good ones to her. Nevertheless, this book appeared to enliven her; her eyes sparkled and she left off reading it, less to rid herself of the thoughts it awakened in her than to give herself over to them with greater zest. Recovering at last from the reverie she seemed buried in, she was about to take the book up again, when she heard a noise that made her hide it away. She armed herself, against all eventualities, with the Brahmin's work, which she evidently thought better suited for show than for reading.

"A man came in who bore himself so respectfully, that, in spite of the nobility of his features and the richness of his dress, I first of all took him for one of Fatima's slaves. But she greeted him with such ran-cor, seemed so put out at his presence, and so wearied with what he said, that I began to suspect that this ill-used man could be none other than her husband. I was not mistaken. For some considerable time she sourly repelled his earnest entreaty to be allowed to sit by her, and in the end she gave her consent, only to overwhelm him, in galling detail, with the faults she declared him daily guilty of. This husband, the unhappiest in all Agra, submitted to this petulant upbraiding with so great a gentle-ness as to make me indignant on his account. But his high opinion of Fatima's virtue was not the sole reason of his meekness: Fatima was beautiful, and though she appeared not to care a rap for being attrac-tive, she was so all the same. However little she wished to appear lov-able in her husband's eyes, she roused his flame. But the most bashful lover, even if he were declaring his love for the first time to the woman he was most afraid of, would be a thousand times less put to it than this husband was, to tell his wife what his feelings for her were. He implored her both tenderly and respectfully to respond to his ardors; she refused to do so for a great while, and ultimately yielded ungraciously.

"Although she most stubbornly refused to give him the least hint that she had not the utmost repugnance toward what he required of her, I believed I could detect that she was more susceptible than she wished to be thought. Her eyes glowed, she seemed more alert, she breathed a sigh or two, and, though still cool, she became less lethargic. Yet it was not her husband whom she loved. I do not know what impelled Fatima, whether gratitude made her more pleasant, or whether she wished her husband to renew his assiduousness, but she allowed some tender though sententious words to replace the harsh, scolding phrases she had hurled at him when he arrived. It was plain that he did not guess her object or was not much affected by it; and it was equally plain that his coldness and unresponsiveness were not to Fatima's liking. Little by little she worked up a quarrel, and in a trice endowed her husband with all the most odious vices. What horrible habits did he not indulge in! What debauchery! What dissipation! What a life! At length she showered so much abuse upon him that he was forced to leave her. Fatima was piqued at his departure; the disquiet in her eyes, which I was able to interpret more readily than her husband, told me that it was not by going away that he would soothe her; and indeed, some strange enough words that she gave vent to when she was once more by herself enlightened me as to the exact nature of her feelings.

"How this woman, the example and terror of her sex in Agra, whom they all hated, yet were proud to imitate; before whom the least reticent women, who never concealed their passions, though themselves obliged to be hypocritical – how many people this woman would have reassured had they, like me, been able to see her in the freedom and solitude of her boudoir!"

"Yes indeed!" the Sultan struck in. "Was she a woman who really...? And there are some who pretend...It happens anyway! You must not think that what I mean is so uncommon. You know what, eh?"

"Your Majesty's explanation is so lucid," Amanzei answered, "that it is not very difficult to guess what you mean; and, without wishing to boast of my perspicacity, I dare believe that I have grasped your thought."

"Really!" the Sultan said laughing. "Well then, out with it! What did I think?"

"That Fatima was nothing less than what she wished to seem," Amanzei answered.

"That's it, let me die!" the Sultan exclaimed. "Go on! Upon my honor, you have a deal of wit."

"To all appearances," Amanzei went on, "Fatima shunned all delights, only to indulge in them with greater safety. She was not one of those reckless women who – having devoted their youth to making a stir, to dissipation, to the young man whom whim has made the fashion –

when older abandons makeup and dress; and, after earning the scorn and shame of their generation, wish to become its example and ornament; only to be despised for pretending to a virtue they do not possess than considered brazen for the way in which they flaunted their sins. No! Fatima was better advised. Lucky enough to be born with that duplicity which incites women to disguise their natures, and yet long to be honored (not always their earliest longing), she had realized in good time that it is impossible to deny oneself pleasures without dragging out a cruelly dull existence, and that a woman cannot openly indulge in them without laying herself open to opprobrium and risks, so turning these joys sour. Devoted to deceit from her tenderest years, she strove less to correct her heart's vicious propensities than to veil them under the guise of the most forbidding virtue. Her soul by nature – shall I say voluptuous? no; that was not Fatima's temper; her soul was set upon pleasure. Not refined, but sensuous, she gave herself over to lust, but knew nothing of love. She was not yet twenty years old; it was five years since she had been married, and eight since she had forestalled marriage. The things that usually captivate women had no charms for her; an amiable face, much readiness of mind may perhaps have awakened her desires, but she did not succumb to them. The objects of her desire were chosen from those who would not be suspect, forced by their style of life to be silent as to their pleasures, or from those whose low circumstances shield them from public suspicion; who are won by money, silenced by fear, and who, apparently engaged in the most base employment, for all that sometimes turn out to be the most fit for the mysteries of love. Fatima, moreover, being spiteful, choleric, and haughty, gave rein to her impulse without incurring any danger: even a flaw would have been grist to the mill of her reputation. Superior, imperious, harsh, cruel, and unfeeling, untrustworthy and incapable of friendship, her zeal for Brahma, the distress she testified at the irregularities of others, and her desire to bring them back to their better selves, cloaked and gilded her vices. Whenever she did harm, she meant so well! She was so piously vindictive! Her soul was so pure! How could one suspect a heart so upright and so candid of harboring any selfish motive behind its righteous hatreds?"

CHAPTER III

Which Contains Some Things Hard to Believe

"After her husband had gone away, Fatima was about to resume her reading when an old Brahmin came in, followed by two old women whose spiritual adviser he said he was, though really he was their despot. Fatima rose to receive them in so demure and reserved a manner that anyone might have been hoodwinked. The old Brahmin had even to prevent her from prostrating herself before him, but he did it so complacently that I could at once see the value he set upon himself; he seemed so satisfied with her intentions with regard to him, so convinced even that he deserved still more, that I could not forbear laughing within myself at the holy vanity of this ridiculous person.

"Conversation between four people so unusually meritorious cannot but be at the expense of others. It is not, of course, rare for people given to dissipation to indulge in detraction; but being more concerned with foibles than with vices, detraction is only a pastime for them, and they are not virtuous enough to regard it as a duty. They sometimes do harm to others, but they do not always mean to, or at least their levity or their taste for frolic prevents them either from dwelling on it or from wanting to make capital out of it. They know nothing of this dour, pompous way of speaking ill of others, which would be unforgivable were it not so needful to general reform; they..."

"No more of that!" the Sultan broke in angrily. "A pox on these musty aphorisms you keep on dishing up to us!"

"But, Sire," Amanzei pleaded, "they are occasionally indispensable."

"I tell you they are not," the Sultan retorted. "And even if they were... In short, since these stories are being told for my sake, I expect them to be of the kind I like. Amuse me! And a truce, if you please, to all these endless moralizings, which make my head ache. You want to set up for an orator: but, good heavens, I will see to it, and I swear, on the word of a Sultan, that I will kill the first man who dares serve me up an aphorism. We will see, by and by, how you get along."

"I will steer clear of aphorisms," Amanzei answered, "since they have the poor luck to displease your Majesty."

"That's fine!" the Sultan said. "Now get on!"

"Those who take a pleasure in speaking ill of others are ever agreeable to speaking well of themselves. Fatima, and those with her, had too good cause to think highly of their own persons not to despise all who were unlike them. While waiting for games to be brought them, they entered upon a conversation that did not belie their characters. The old Brahmin, however, spoke well of a woman whom Fatima knew, and the homage displeased her. Of all the things against which she lifted up her voice, love was the one that seemed the most blameworthy to her. If a woman loved, she might have all the most estimable qualities in her favor, yet nothing could save her from Fatima's hatred: but if she was a sink of the most pestilential and odious vices, so long as she was known not to have a lover, she was acclaimed as a most respectable person whose virtue made her deserving of all homage.

"The lady whom the Brahmin praised, was, unhappily for her, in the class that aroused Fatima's indignation. 'Ah! that lost woman!' she said in a sour tone, 'how can you praise her?' The Brahmin excused himself on the grounds that he did not know her to be addicted to such a censurable manner of living, and Fatima was charitable enough to enlighten him on her reasons for despising her.

" 'Fatima,' then said one of the women who was visiting her, 'I am sure, knowing as I do your generous nature and your love of righteousness, that you will be greatly touched by what I am about to tell you. Nahami, that very Nahami whose fall we have both so much deplored, Nahami, out of love with her errors, has all of a sudden withdrawn from society: she no longer paints her face.' 'Alas!' Fatima cried, 'she is indeed to be praised if this return to the fold be sincere! But, Madam, you are of the pure, to whom all things are pure, and thus so easily gulled; I know, for I have found it so, that when one is born with such rectitude of heart as yours, one cannot conceive that others can be so unlucky as not to be the same as oneself. Still, it is a fault much on the right side to judge others leniently. But to come back to Nahami, I cannot help fearing that, at the bottom of her heart, being given over to the world as she is, she has not sincerely abjured her errors. It is easier to renounce face paint than one's vices, and people often assume a more reserved and modest air not so much as a first step toward virtue as to impose upon the world with regard to the disorders to which they are still in leash.' "

"My dear sir," Shah Baham said, yawning, "this conversation is deadly; if you love me, cut it short. These people fret me beyond words. Honestly now, are you not sick of them yourself? For Heaven's sake get them out of the way."

"With the best will in the world, Sire," Amanzei answered. "After having made the utmost of their conversation about Nahami, they flung wide their net of detraction, and in a twinkling I heard all the gossip of Agra. Afterward, they praised each other, sat down glumly to play, and continued to do so in a spiteful, miserly way until they took their leave."

"I was on tenterhooks," the Sultan said. "You have made me very much obliged to you. Do you give me your word that those people will not come back?"

"Yes, Sire," Amanzei replied.

"Well," the Sultan proceeded, "to show you how well I can reward men for their services, I create you an Emir; it is also because you embroider well, because you work hard, and because I believe you will make something of your story; in fact...I like doing that sort of thing; and besides, one ought to encourage merit."

The new Emir, after having thanked the Sultan, went on as follows:

"In spite of Fatima's affability, I thought I could perceive that the visit of these persons had just the same effect upon her as it has had upon your Majesty, and that, had she been her own mistress, she would have spent her time in amusements different from those they had provided for her.

"As soon as they were gone out, Fatima sank into a deep but not gloomy reverie: her eyes softened, they wandered languishingly around her boudoir; it seemed as though she desired something she had not, or was afraid to allow herself. At last she called someone.

"At the sound of her voice, a young slave whose face was fresh rather than attractive, made his way into the room. Fatima gazed at him with eyes full of love and longing, but she nevertheless seemed irresolute and fearful.

"'Shut the door, Dahis!' she said at last. 'Come, we are alone: you can, without the least danger, remember that I love you, and give me proofs of your affection for me.'

"On this command, Dahis, throwing off a slave's respectful mien, assumed that of a man made happy in his love. He seemed to me to have small delicacy or tenderness, but to be robust and full of fire, driven by his appetites, incapable of seeming to gratify them by degrees, and unversed in the arts of love, not wasting his time over delicious preludes, but applying himself at once to the main issue. He was no lover, but for Fatima, who was not in search of style, he was something more essential. Dahis flattered her crudely, but the want of refinement in his encomia did not offend Fatima, for while he continued to give her vigorous proofs of the power of her charms, she felt she had praises enough.

"With Dahis, Fatima made generous amends for the restraint she had inflicted upon herself with her husband. Less punctilious in observing the strict rules of decency, her eyes sparkled with a joyful fire: she was prodigal of the most endearing epithets as well as of the most eager caresses; and far from screening from him anything that she felt, she surrendered herself wholly to her ecstasy. When she was calmer she called his attention to all the beauties she indulged him with, and even compelled him to solicit her anew for proofs of her goodwill, which, in his heart of hearts, he did not pine for.

"Dahis, on the contrary, seemed quite unmoved. He gazed stupidly at everything that Fatima's kindness offered to his sight, but only mechanically did he take it all in. His boorish heart felt nothing; it was not formed to leap for rapture. Nevertheless, Fatima seemed satisfied. That he was tongue-tied and oafish did not wound her pride in the least, since she had too many good reasons for believing him conscious of her charms not to prefer his unresponsiveness to the most extravagant ravings and the most wordy transports of a finished seducer.

"In suffering herself to be the instrument of his pleasures, Fatima showed plainly enough that she had as little delicacy as virtue, and that she did not expect from Dahis either that alertness in delight or those tender nothings which sensibility and polite manners rank higher than gratification, or in which, to speak more properly, gratification itself consists.

"At last Dahis went out, not before yawning two or three times. He is to be counted among those unfortunate people who, since they never think of anything, never have anything to say, are more fit to employ than to listen to.

"Whatever opinion of her Fatima's amusements may have given me, I confess that I thought, now that Dahis had left her, that there was nothing more for her to muse upon in her boudoir, and that she would shortly go out. I was wrong. She was an indefatigable muser in this kind. She had not long been supplied with the thoughts for which Dahis had supplied such ample food, when something occurred to give her more.

"A Brahmin, serious but young and fresh-looking, with one of those faces that is sprightly in spite of their self-possessed expression, came into the boudoir. Though he was in a Brahmin's frock, which is not exactly graceful, it was easy to see that he was got up in such a way as to stir the imagination of not a few prudes: indeed, he was the most exclusive, most consolatory, most sought-after Brahmin in all Agra. He spoke so sweetly! they said. He made the taste for virtue steal so gently over erring souls! It was so easy to go astray if he was not there! So they spoke of him in public; you shall soon see to what in particular he owed these praises, and whether those which were the most loudly sounded were the ones he had most truly earned.

"This fortune-favored Brahmin came toward Fatima in a suave, milky manner, insipid rather than courtly. You could see that he aimed at something else but copied poorly those he chose for models, and the Brahmin peeped out beneath the borrowed mask.

" 'Queen of hearts,' he said fatuously, 'today you are more beauteous than the blissful Beings assigned to the service of Brahma! On seeing you my soul is wafted to a realm which has something celestial in it, and of which I would wish you to partake with me.'

"Fatima, in a languid voice, answered him in his own style; and since the Brahmin did not change it, they entered upon a conversation that was tender enough, but in which love spoke so very oddly, and in a way so little suited to it, that had it not been for what they did, I should hardly have understood what they were talking about.

"Fatima, who was naturally quite deaf to eloquence, and who, despite all that she said, did not think the Brahmin particularly eloquent, was the first to grow weary of phrases. The Brahmin, whom they pleased no more than they did her, soon followed her lead in dropping them, and this conversation, so insipid and sickly, finished in the same way as that with Dahis had begun. It must be observed, however, that Fatima, though she did the same things, was more particular about externals. She wished to appear delicate, and to make the Brahmin think that love alone had conquered her.

"The Brahmin, who, as far as character and face went, was not unlike Dahis, did not in any way fall behind him, and deserved all the compliments that Fatima in her good nature continually lavished upon him. After they had paid their tribute to the warmth of love, they set to ridiculing virtue, enjoyed together the delight of deceiving others, and took and gave mutual lessons in hypocrisy. At last these two odious beings separated, and Fatima went off to plague her husband and to make a great to-do about her fleshly mortifications.

"During my stay with her, I never discovered that she had any way of whiling away the time other than that which I have described to your august Majesty.

"Cautious as she was, Fatima was sometimes off her guard. One day when she was solacing with her Brahmin, chance brought her husband to the door of her boudoir, where he heard sighs and certain expressions that surprised him. Fatima's public conduct gave so little hint of her private amusements that I doubt whether her husband guessed at once whence came those sighs and strange words which reached his ears.

"Either because he thought he recognized Fatima's voice, or because simple curiosity made him wish to clear the matter up, he tried the door of the boudoir.

"Unluckily for Fatima, due care had not been taken of the door, and he burst it open at the first attempt.

"The sight that met his eyes surprised him so greatly that the tide of his fury was stemmed, and he seemed for a few moments to disbelieve his senses, and to be in doubt as to what to do.

" 'Traitors!' he cried at last, 'take the punishment your crimes and your hypocrisies have earned!'

"At these words, without heeding the supplications either of Fatima or of the Brahmin, who had flung themselves at his feet, he struck them dead.

"Frightful as the sight was, it did not distress me much. They had deserved death too well to call for pity, and I was delighted that so terrible a catastrophe should enlighten all Agra as to the real nature of two persons who had been looked upon as patterns of virtue."

CHAPTER IV

Wherein Some Things Will Be Seen Which Might Well Not Have Been Foreseen

"After Fatima's death, my soul took wing, and flew into a neighboring palace where life seemed to be lived much as it had been in the one I had left. Below the surface, however, it was all very different.

"It was not that the lady who lived there was on the threshold of that age when sensible women, even if they do not regard lovemaking as a vice, at least look upon it as ridiculous. She was young and beautiful, and one could not say that she trod in the paths of virtue merely because she was unfit for love. From her unaffected modesty, from the care she took to hide her charities, from the peace that seemed to prevail in her heart, one was bound to think that she was born to be what she seemed. Good without self-compulsion or vanity, she made neither a burden nor a virtue of doing her duty. I never saw her sad or peevish for a moment; she was sweetly and serenely good, and she did not consider that this gave her the right either to lord it over or to despise others. In this matter, she was much more reluctant than those women who, conscience-stricken in everything, will allow nobody to be free from reproach. Her temper was naturally gay, and she did not try to curb her spirits. You see, she did not believe, as many do, that one is most respectable when one is most disagreeable to others. She libeled nobody, but was no less amusing for that. Supposing that she had as many weak points as anyone else, she readily forgave the flaws she found in others. Nothing appeared to her vicious or criminal but what was really so. She was not like Fatima, who denied herself legitimate pleasures for the sake of enjoying illegitimate ones. Her house was not luxurious but nobly kept. All the decent society of Agra was proud to be invited there; everybody was ambitious to know so rare a lady, and everybody held her in honor; so that, in spite of my perversity, I was in the end compelled to fall in with their opinion.

"When I first went to this lady's house, I was still so full of Fatima's perfidy that I had no doubt she did the same things; and at the beginning I did not distinguish between the woman of virtue and the hypocrite. I never saw a slave or a Brahmin come in without thinking that I should be made party to their concerns, and for a long time I was astonished at being left out of them.

"At length, the inactivity to which I was condemned in this house gave me the spleen; and sure that I should wait in vain in the hopes of seeing anything advantageous, I forsook this lady's sofa, charmed to have been convinced that there was indeed such a thing as a chaste woman, but not much wishing to meet any more of them.

"To vary the scenes made available to it under the conditions of its life, my soul did not, on leaving this palace, go to reside in another; rather, it fluttered down into a horrid, dingy little dwelling, where I was doubtful even of finding a retreat. I crept into a dreary room, not even well furnished, where I was nevertheless lucky enough to find a sofa, which, sullied and rickety, bore clear enough witness that it was at its expense that the other furniture of the room had been acquired. That was the first idea that struck me, even before I knew where I was, and when I did know, I did not alter my opinion.

"This room, in fact, was the lair of a pretty enough wench, who, though by birth and nature is known as 'bad company,' nevertheless saw something of persons of what is called 'the best.' She was a young dancing girl who had just been admitted among the Emperor's, and who had not yet made either her name or her fortune, although she was intimately known by nearly all the young bucks of Agra, to whom she was infinitely obliging in return for their promises of protection. Yet I doubt whether her fortunes would have changed so suddenly had it not been for a steward of one of the Emperor's estates taking a fancy to her.

"Abdulatif was this steward's name, and neither his birth nor his character made him a brilliant conquest. He was by nature boorish and coarse, and since making his fortune had added insolence to his other defects. It was not that he did not aspire to be well mannered; but since he believed that a man such as he conferred an honor upon people by showing them respect, he aped the cold, dry politeness of some persons of rank, which in their case one is ready to call dignity, but which in Abdulatif merely marked him as a highly impertinent dolt. He was born in the gutter, and he had not only forgotten the fact but left no stone unturned to prove himself of illustrious descent; and he drew attention to this crowning absurdity by perpetually playing the lord. Inane and insolent, his familiarity jarred as much as his haughtiness; and, since he was vulgar and tasteless, his display only made him the more ridiculous. With little brain and less education still, he thought himself adept at everything, and was forever dictating to everybody. Such as he was, however, he was born with; for though he could do no harm, he could be of some use. The greatest men of Agra were assiduously agreeable and flattering to him, while their wives were either on the footing of forgiving him his impertinences, which he carried excessively far, or of refusing him nothing. But although he was extremely sought after in Agra, he was sometimes glad to escape from the importunities of women of quality, and to seek out pleasures that were no less keen for being less dazzling, nor often (he was insolent enough to say) much more dangerous.

"One evening, on leaving the Emperor, before whom Amina had danced, this new protector took her home. His arrogant, distracted glances wandered over her dismal, mean abode, and he said, barely deigning to look at her:

"'This place is not fit for you; we must get you out of it. It is as much for my sake as for yours that I want you to be better set up. I should be sneered at if a girl I patronized were not in a respectable situation.'

"After saying this, he sat down upon me, and roughly drawing her to him, unceremoniously took all the freedoms he wished with her: but as he was a libertine rather than desirous, he was not very excessive in this use of them.

"Amina, whom I had seen disdainful and wayward with the lords who visited her, far from offering to be familiar with Abdulatif, treated him with the greatest respect, and dared not look at him unless he seemed to wish her to.

"'You suit me very well,' he told her at last, 'but you must be good: no young men, right living, good behavior – otherwise we shall not be friends for long. Good-bye, my dear,' he added, rising. 'Tomorrow you shall hear from me. Your surroundings are not good enough for me to sup with you today; but I will see to it forthwith.'

"After saying this, he went away. Amina showed him out with all respect, and came back to fling herself upon me, and give way to her prodigious joy at her good luck. She reckoned up with her mother the diamonds and other rich ornaments she expected on the morrow from Abdulatif's generosity.

"This mother, who, although she was an honorable woman, was yet the most indulgent of mothers, exhorted her daughter to act wisely in the midst of the good fortune it pleased Brahma to send her; and, comparing their present lot with that to come, made a thousand reflections upon Divine providence, which never abandons those who deserve its gifts. After that, she enumerated at length all the lords who had been Amina's friends.

" 'How little their friendship has been worth to you!' she said to her. 'And it is entirely your own fault! I have told you thousands of times, you are too good-natured. Either you allow them through sheer indolence to take you, which is a horrid vice; or you give way to your fancies, which is no better, and has made you a laughingstock. I do not go so far as to say that you should never please yourself, God forbid! But one should never sacrifice business to pleasure. Above all, you must never let it be said that a girl like you ever lets herself be carried away by love, and, unfortunately, you have given them much to gossip about on that score. However, you are still very young, and I hope that all this may not have done you much harm. Nothing ruins people in your walk of life more than those madcap follies I have heard called free love. Once it gets about that a girl has contracted the unfortunate habit of occasionally giving her love for nothing, everyone thinks he can get it on the same terms, or at least very cheap. Look at Roxana, Elzira, Atalis: not a frailty to reproach themselves with, and Brahma has prospered their lives. They are not so pretty as you, but see how rich they are! Profit by their example; they are very sensible girls.'

" 'Oh, dear me, yes, Mother,' Amina answered growing impatient at this lecture, 'I will think of that. All the same, you cannot expect me to reserve myself entirely for my present monster! That is impossible, I warn you beforehand.'

" 'To be sure, no,' the mother answered. 'Where the heart is concerned one is not mistress of oneself; I merely say that you must give up these Court lords, unless you see them *incognito*, and they treat you better than they have so far. If you like, I will give them a talking to. You have Massoud, whom you love. I have nothing to say against your choice there: no one knows him; you can do anything you like with him. You pass him off as your cousin, and he is looked upon as such. You are safe there. This gentleman, who wants to be good to you, will be taken in like the others; if you are careful he will suspect nothing, and...'

" 'Do you think, Mother,' Amina interrupted, 'that he is going to give me diamonds? Yes, he will give me some. Not that I am vain,' she added, 'but when one belongs to a certain station in life, one likes to be like everybody else.'

"Thereupon she set to counting up all the wenches who would be wild at the diamonds and splendid dresses she would have: a vision that tickled her vanity more even than did her good luck.

"Early the next day a cart came for her, and my soul, being curious to see to what use Amina would put her mother's advice, followed her. She was taken to a pretty, well-furnished house, which belonged to Abdulatif, on a roundabout street. When we arrived there, I took up my abode in a superb sofa that had been put in a very decorated boudoir. I have never seen anyone so idiotically agape with admiration as Amina was at everything she saw. After she had carefully examined it all, she sat herself down at her dressing table. The array of precious pots which met her eye, a box full of diamonds, well-dressed slaves obsequious to serve her, the merchants and artificers who awaited her commands, all these heightened her amazement, and intoxicated her with grandeur.

"When she had somewhat recovered, she remembered the part it was suitable to play before such a large audience. She spoke haughtily to her slaves, impertinently to the merchants and artificers, chose what she wanted, ordered everything to be ready for her by the next day at latest, returned to her dressing table, where she remained for a while, and, as a makeshift until she should possess all her destined splendor, attired herself in a magnificent chamber gown, which had been made for a princess of Agra but which she thought hardly fine enough for her.

"She spent most of the day toying with everything she saw, and waiting for Abdulatif. At last, toward evening, he appeared.

"Amina flung herself at his feet, and, in the most abject terms, thanked him for what he was doing for her.

"I, who till then had always been in good society, was astounded at the words that reached my ears. Of course, I had often heard such foolishness, but it had at least been elegant, and uttered with that noble grace which almost makes it seem that it is not being said at all."

CHAPTER V

Better to Omit than to Read

"Before embarking on a longer conversation, Abdulatif drew from his pocket a long purse full of gold, which he threw carelessly onto the table.

" 'Take hold of this,' he said to her. 'You will not need it much. I will see to all your household and personal expenses. I have sent you a cook; he is the best cook in Agra next to mine. I mean to sup here often. We shall not always be alone. Some lords, friends of mine, and some choice wits to whom I lend money, will come now and again. We will add some of your fellow dancers, the prettiest, of course. In that way we shall have some merry suppers, which I like.'

"While saying this he brought her into the boudoir, where I was, and that respectable woman, Amina's mother, who till then had been present at the conversation, withdrew and shut the door.

"I will not," Amanzei interrupted his story to say, "give your Majesty an exact account of such a conversation, one in which Amina showed herself very tender, and animated almost to transports. Abdulatif had taken care to tell her beforehand that he hated women to be reserved in their speech, so that, seeing how much Amina wished to please him, and knowing what her education and habits of life were, your Majesty can easily imagine that certain things transpired which it would be difficult to repeat to you, and which, moreover, would not take your fancy."

"Why not?" the Sultan asked. "Perhaps I should like them very much. Try a few."

"Try by all means," the Sultana said rising; "but as I am sure they will not amuse me, you will allow me to retire."

"There now!" the Sultan cried. "There's fine modesty for you! You think perhaps you can take me in? Rid yourself of that idea! I know all about women now, and, besides, I remember that a man who knows as much about them as I do, or nearly as much, told me that women love nothing so mightily as doing what is forbidden them, and that the only talk they like is talk they think they ought not to hear: therefore, if you go out, it is not that you really have a mind to. But let it be; Amanzei will tell me when I go to bed all that you do not want him to tell me now. That will be just the way for me not to miss any. Is that not so?"

Amanzei took good care to agree with the Sultan, and, after making the most of his discreet conduct, continued thus:

"When Abdulatif and Amina had finished their interview, which was longer than it was interesting, supper was served. Since I was not in the dining room, Sire, I cannot tell you what they said to each other there. They returned, and although they had supped alone together, that did not appear to have contributed to their sobriety; after some very undistinguished conversation, Abdulatif fell asleep upon his lady's bosom.

"Amina, docile as she was, was at first not altogether pleased that Abdulatif should treat her so cavalierly. Her vanity was sore at the small account he made of her. The high praise he had bestowed upon her for the way in which she had carried on her interview with him had swelled her pride, and made her think that she was worthy of the trouble it would give him to continue to entertain her. In spite of the consideration she was bound to show for Abdulatif, she grew weary of the constraint he imposed upon her, and would impetuously have shown her irritation had not Abdulatif, opening his heavy eyes, rudely asked her what time it was. He got up without waiting for her answer.

" 'Good-bye,' he said, fondling her roughly, 'I will let you know tomorrow if I am to sup here.'

"Having said this, he would have gone out; but however much Amina may have wished to be left to her own devices, she thought she ought to try to keep him back, and carried her artfulness to the length of bursting into tears. He was inexorable, and freed himself from Amina's arms, telling her that, though he was glad to be loved, he by no means intended to be pestered.

"As soon as he had gone out she rang the bell, bestowing upon him, and only half under her breath, the names he deserved. While she was being undressed, her mother came to whisper something to her. The news she told Amina made her hurry her slaves, and finally she ordered them to leave her alone. A few moments after her mother and the slaves had withdrawn, the former returned. She ushered in an ill-shapen Negro, horrible to look at, whom, however, Amina no sooner saw than she ran to embrace him fervently."

"Amanzei," the Sultan said, "if you were to drop that Negro out of your story, I do not think it would be any the worse for it."

"I fail to see how he spoils it, Sire," Amanzei answered.

"Then I will tell you, I will," the Sultan replied, "since you have not the wit to see it for yourself. The first wife of my grandfather, Shah Riar, had slept with all the blacks in her palace. It was a rather notorious thing. In consequence of this, my said grandfather not only had that wife strangled, but all the others that he had afterward, up to my grandmother Scheherezade, who cured him of the habit. And so I consider it hardly respectful, after what has happened in my family, for people to come and tell me about blacks, as though they were no concern of mine. I will excuse you this one, since he has turned up, but I must ask you to bring no more in."

Amanzei, having begged the Sultan's pardon for his folly, went on thus:

" 'Ah, Massoud!' Amina said to her lover, 'how terrible to have been two days without seeing you! What a hideous thing it is to sacrifice oneself to a career!'

"Massoud did not say much to all this. However, he told her that, though he loved her with infinite delicacy, he was not sorry that she was the object of Abdulatif's attentions. Later he adjured her to do everything proper to ruin him; and when he had submitted to the tempest of Amina's caresses, they began a kind of conversation made livelier by the thought that they were deceiving Abdulatif. Before he left her boudoir, she rewarded Massoud bountifully for the very great love he had shown her.

"She spent the greater part of the night with him, sending him away only when she saw daylight appear; and Amina's mother, who had let him in by a door that opened from her room into her daughter's, let him out by the same way.

"Amina spent the morning trying on all the dresses she had ordered, and ordering some more. She amused herself thus until it was time for her to go and dance before the Emperor. She was brought back by Abdulatif: they were followed by some pretty colleagues of Amina's, by some young omrahs, and three of the most renowned wits in Agra. They outvied one another in their praises of Abdulatif's magnificence, his taste, his distinguished appearance, the subtlety of his mind, and the clarity of his wisdom. I could not conceive how persons, distinguished by birth or talent, could allow themselves the baseness and falsity of their praises. They did not even forgo praising Amina; but, to tell the truth, it was in such a way as to make her feel that she was only secondary, and that if they had not wished to show deference to Abdulatif, they would have treated her with as much familiarity as they were now studious to avoid. After flattering Abdulatif, they scattered about the chamber, each man with whomsoever pleased him best. The conversation, depending on the speaker, was at times lively, at times dull, and on the whole it seemed to me that they showed very little consideration for the ladies who were to sup in Amina's house, and that these were hardly offended by such behavior.

"At last they went down to supper. As there was no lair for my soul in the room where they ate, I could not overhear the remarks made there. To judge from those which preceded the supper, and from those which followed, one could bear the disappointment of not being within earshot.

"Abdulatif, sodden with wine, intoxicated with complements, which the excellence of his cook had made still more high-flown and plentiful, soon fell asleep. A young man who wanted him to leave so that Amina would be free to dispose of herself, actually dared to awaken him, to represent to him that such a man as he was, loaded with the weightiest business, and so necessary to the State, might allow himself pleasures as a diversion, but should not surrender to them. In the end, by proving to Abdulatif how much he was beloved by prince and people alike, he convinced him that he could not delay going to bed if the stoutest pillar of the State were not to be endangered.

"He left, and everybody left with him. Some looks that I had intercepted between Amina and the young man who had so successfully harangued Abdulatif made me suspect that I should soon see him again. She began to undress nonchalantly, as though nothing were in the wind, and, once rid of that superb raiment which impedes pleasure even more than it caters to vanity, gave orders that she was to be left alone.

"Amina's respectable mother, won over, apparently, by the tale of woe the young man had told her (for I shall never believe so pure a soul could have been moved by profit), introduced him discreetly into her daughter's room and retired only after he had given his word of honor that he would say nothing to Amina likely to shock the modesty of so innocent and well-brought-up a young girl.

" 'Truly,' Amina said to the young man once they were by themselves, 'I must love you very dearly to have brought myself to do this! For, when all is said, I am deceiving a worthy gentleman, whom, to be sure, I do not love, but to whom, all the same, I ought to be faithful. I am wrong, I feel it; but love is a dreadful thing, and what it is making me do today is very far from my nature.'

" 'I am all the more grateful to you,' the young man answered, trying to kiss her.

" 'Ah, that now!' she answered, pushing him away, 'that I cannot possibly allow you to do: sympathy, tenderness, the pleasure of seeing each other – I have promised you those, but if I were to go further I should be failing in my duty.'

" 'But, my dear child, are you mad?' the young man said; 'What is all this canting talk of yours? I am ready to believe that you possess every imaginable delicacy of feeling, but how do you think that can serve us? Do you suppose I came here for that?'

" 'You were mistaken,' she pursued, 'if you expected anything else of me. Although I do not love his lordship Abdulatif, I have sworn to be true to him, and nothing on earth will make me break faith with him.'

" 'Ah, my little queen,' the young man rallied her, 'since you have sworn, I have nothing more to say: that is highly respectable, and, merely for the rarity of the thing, I will allow you to remain true to your oath. Here! Tell me! Have you taken many of that sort in your life?'

" 'You may scoff as much as you please,' Amina replied, 'but all the same I am very scrupulous.'

" 'Oh? Well, I am hardly surprised,' he answered. 'Your sort of girls, the moment you begin to devote yourselves to the public good, pride yourselves on your scruples, and as a rule are much more scrupulous than honest women. But to come back to your oath, you might just as well have told me about it a little while ago, and saved me the trouble of coming to spend the night here.'

" 'That is true,' she replied awkwardly. 'But you made me such brilliant offers that I admit they dazzled me.'

" 'So,' he asked her, 'thinking about them has tarnished them? Here,' he proceeded, pulling out a purse, 'here is what I promised you; I am always as good as my word: here is something in that to ease your scruples with, and to release you from all the oaths you may ever have made. You will not deny that, at any rate.'

" 'What a tease you are,' she answered, seizing hold of the purse. 'You know me very little. I swear, that if it were not for the inclination I feel for you...'

" 'Let us finish all that,' he broke in. 'To prove to you how noble my soul is, I will dispense with your thanks, and even with that prodigious attraction you feel toward me – especially since it was not included in our bargain. I am even paying you as heavily as if I were the first string, and that, you know perfectly well, is not according to the rules.'

" 'It seems to me that it is,' Amina replied. 'I am doing an abominable thing for your sake, and...'

" 'If I paid you only what the doing of that cost you,' he interrupted, 'I guarantee I should have you for nothing. But, I repeat, let us be done with it; although you have as much wit as it is possible for anyone to have, this conversation is wearing thin.'

"Although he exhibited much impatience, he could not prevent Amina, who was prudence itself, from counting out the money he had just given her. It was not, she said, that she did not trust him, but that he might himself have made a mistake. In fact she complied with his desires only after she had made quite sure that he had not blundered in his arithmetic.

"When day was about to break, Amina's mother reappeared, and told the young man that it was time for him to be off; he was not entirely of her opinion. Although Amina begged him to take every care of her reputation, this consideration would not have budged him, and he would have stayed in spite of her entreaties had she not promised him in the future as many nights as she could filch from Abdulatif.

"Beyond Abdulatif, Massoud, and this young man to whom she some-times kept her word, Amina, who had realized the importance of her mother's sage counsels, received indifferently all those who found her beautiful enough to covet, provided, however, that they were rich enough to make their sighs persuasive. Bonzes, Brahmins, imams, sol-diers, cadis, men of every nationality, rank, and age – none were denied. It is true that, since she had principles and scruples, it cost foreigners, especially those whom she looked upon as infidels, more than it did her own countrymen and men of her own faith. It was only the argu-ment of money that could overcome her distaste, and, after she had given herself, override her remorse. On that point she even invented some very pretty rules. There were some cults that she held in greater abhorrence than others, and I shall always remember that, to win her kindness, it cost one infidel more than it would have cost ten Muslims.

"Either because Abdulatif was too convinced of her honesty to think that Amina could be unfaithful to him, or because, with equal foolish-ness, he counted on the vows she had sworn never to belong to any-body but him, he stayed with her for a long while in perfect confidence; and, had it not been for an unexpected occurrence – which, however, is not without its parallel – it is clear that he would have dwelt in it forever."

"I understand," the Sultan said. "Someone told him that she was unfaithful."

"No, Sire," Amanzei answered.

"Ah, yes!" the Sultan took up again. "Now I see that it was some-thing quite different; it is easy to guess: he saw her in the act."

"Not at all, Sire," Amanzei went on. "It would have been lucky for him if he had gotten off so cheaply."

"Then I do not know what it was at all," Shah Baham said. "In any event, those things are not my business, and I need not rack my brains to guess something that does not in the least concern me."

CHAPTER VI

No More Extraordinary than Entertaining

"The fated moment had come when all the grandeurs, the diamonds, and the riches that Amina possessed were to vanish from her sight. But at any rate, as a consolation for her loss, she could cherish the memory of a gorgeous dream; if Abdulatif, too, dreamed, he did not do so as pleasantly as she.

"For some days I had noticed that Amina was less gay than usual; her house was barred at night, and during the day she saw no one but Abdulatif. She had received many letters, and each one had deepened her melancholy. I lost myself in a maze of conjecture as to what could be the matter, and, not being able to discover anything, was witless enough to believe that a gnawing remorse was the sole cause of her evident sadness.

"Although what I knew of her character ought to have prevented that error, the difficulty of finding the cause of her disquiet made me form it. I was not long in discovering that I was astray in all that I had thought.

"One morning when Amina, weighed down with gloomy thoughts, was dressing, Abdulatif came in. She blushed at seeing him; she was not used to being visited by him of a morning, and this unexpected appearance was not to her taste. She was so nervous and disturbed she hardly dared look at him. From Abdulatif's horrid frown, from the terrible way in which he glared at her from time to time, it was not difficult to guess that he was much pained at some unpleasant notion, of which she was, apparently, the origin. Amina no doubt knew what it was, for she dared not so much as ask him. For some time he was dumb, but at last, full of raging irony, he burst out:

"'You are a pretty creature, indeed a pretty creature! Extremely faithful, also. Oh, of course, my Queen, of course! I will show you what goodness is; I will put you somewhere where you will have to behave yourself, for a while at any rate.'

"'What is this speech, sir, pray?' Amina answered him haughtily. 'Surely it is not addressed to a person of my quality? I beg of you to measure your words, please!'

"Such insolence from a person in Amina's situation seemed so monstrous to Abdulatif that at first it put him out of his stride; but at last, his rage getting the better of him, he heaped upon her all the contemptuous insults he considered she deserved. Amina began to justify herself, but Abdulatif, who doubtless had undeniable evidence to back his case, roughly bade her hold her tongue. Amina was then convinced that this was no idle fury on Abdulatif's part, but it seemed to her so impossible that she could be the cause that she could not leave well enough alone. She even saw fit to tax him in turn for his infidelities, and even to upbraid him upon his miserable taste in choosing his mistresses; and she added that she only mentioned these things because of her deep concern in anything that affected his person.

"Such barefaced impudence galled Abdulatif so cruelly that he feared he would lose all restraint. Amina, seeing that he was not at all imposed upon either by her haughtiness or revilings, and fearing from some words he had let drop before that this scene might end tragically for her, finally had recourse to tears and fawning. It was all useless: nothing soothed Abdulatif. I will spare you a description of him, but I have never seen a man so beside himself. Every minute wrought him to higher frenzies, in the course of which he would no doubt have smashed everything in the house, if everything in it had not belonged to him. This timely prudence held him back from making a grievous wreck of the place, which might have eased him; but the violence he did himself by his restraint only added fuel to his wrath against Amina. What incensed him most was that anyone could so cruelly fail in their duty toward a man of his standing. That alone was beyond his power to conceive.

"After giving vent to all the rude things that first anger and then vanity prompted, he laid hands wholesale on all he had given Amina. Realizing that he was throwing her over, she had now and again consoled herself by stealing a look at the diamonds and other moveables that she thought would still be hers; but when she found that Abdulatif was intent upon stripping her of everything, she set up the most ear-splitting howls and wails. At that her mother came in, cast herself at Abdulatif's feet again and again, and thought to soothe him greatly by swearing that the whole thing had been due to a cursed bonze. But all she said about the bonze seemed, on the contrary, only to make Abdulatif more than ever set upon severity, and did not mollify him in the least.

"'Alas!' Amina's mother concluded, 'we are fairly rewarded for having trusted in an infidel! My daughter knows what I thought. I always told her it could only bring bad luck.'

"While these lamentations were proceeding, Abdulatif, holding in his hand an inventory of all the things he had ever given Amina, had everything restored, article by article. That done, he said quietly to Amina:

"'As for the money I have given you, you may keep it: it has not been my fault, my dear, that you have not had better luck. No doubt, being victimized in this way will make you more careful; I sincerely hope so. Now go!' he added; 'I have no more use for you here. You may thank your stars that I do not carry my resentment any further.'

"Having said this, he ordered his slaves to turn them out of doors, as little disturbed by the gross invectives they then hurled at him as he had been by the tears he had seen them shed.

"Curiosity to see to what use Amina would put her humiliation made me resolve, in spite of the nausea her way of life induced in me, to follow her back to the dingy hovel whence Abdulatif had dragged her, and where she continued to hide her shame and sorrow at not having despoiled him utterly.

"It was in this disgusting hole that I witnessed the regret and heard the imprecations of her virtuous mother. But the salvage of the fortune, by no means inconsiderable, at least provided some consolation for what they had lost.

" 'Well, child,' Amina's mother said one day, 'is what has happened really so great a mischance? I agree that your late monster was the very soul of liberality, but is he the only man you can charm? Moreover, even if you never again find anybody so rich, are you in such a wretched plight as all that? No, child: quantity must make up for the lack of quality. If four men are not enough to replace him, you must take ten – more if necessary. You will argue, maybe, that that is a very dangerous plan, which is true enough; but if one never rises superior to anything, if one is afraid of everything, one will remain in poverty and in obscurity all one's days.'

"However ready Amina might have been to put these sage counsels into practice, the despondency into which she had sunk made it out of the question for her to do so as quickly as she might have wished. Her adventure with Abdulatif had given her such a name for unreliability in business, that except for the faithful Massoud, whose love would be daunted by nothing, I saw nobody at her house for a long time, except some of her colleagues, who no doubt, came to see her to rejoice in her sorrow rather than to console her.

"But at last, time, which obliterates all things, wiped Amina's reputation clean. They thought her changed, or believed that the leisure she had had to brood over her past would have cured her of her passion for fickleness. The lovers came back. A Persian grandee, who at that time came to Agra, and was not familiar with its gossip, saw Amina, found her pretty, and became all the more headstrong about her when one of those obliging persons whose sole business it is to work nobly for the pleasures of others assured him that if he was lucky enough to take Amina's fancy, his obligation would be the greater, since it would be the first frailty she would have to reproach herself with.

"Anyone else would have known this was impossible; the Persian merely thought it extraordinary. The novelty spurred him on, and, with the help of the irreproachable voucher for Amina's chastity, he bought at the highest rate favors that were beginning to be valued at their lowest, and were even then not so often flouted as they should have been.

"Thus, the dreary house Amina dwelt in was once more exchanged for a superb palace, glittering with all the riches of India. I do not know if Amina made wise use of her new fortune, for my soul, repelled by the study of hers, went in search of objects worthier of its attention, objects maybe as despicable at bottom, but which, more skillfully adorned, revolted me less and amused me more.

"I flitted into a house that by its magnificence and by the good taste that ruled in every part, I could see was one of those where I would like to reside, where pleasure and gallantry are always to be met with, and where vice itself, in the garb of love, embellished with every possible refinement and elegance, is never seen except in the most attractive guises.

"The mistress of this palace was charming, and by the tenderness in her eyes as much as by her beauty, I judged that my soul would find diversion there. I stayed in her sofa for some time without her even deigning to sit down upon it. Nevertheless, she was in love, and was beloved. Pursued by her admirer, persecuted by herself, it did not seem likely that I should always be so indifferent an object to her as she seemed to assume.

"When I came into her house she had already granted him permission to speak of his love; but, although he was agreeable and eager, and though he might have already persuaded her, he was far from conquering her.

"Phenima (such was her name) had a hard struggle to forgo her virtue, and Zulma, too respectful to be bold, waited for time and assiduity to bring her to love him as much as he did her. Knowing better than he did what Phenima's leanings were, I could not conceive how he could be so blind to his happiness. It is true that Phenima never told him that she loved him, but her eyes never ceased to do so. Even if she spoke to him about some trifle, without her wishing it, without her even noticing it, her voice would grow cooing and her turn of speech more glowing. The more tightly she kept a hold upon herself in his presence, the more she betrayed her love. Nothing in her suitor was indifferent to her; she was afraid of everything to do with him, and the people she least cared for were, to all appearance, more civilly treated than he. Sometimes she insisted he be silent, then immediately forgot, and pursued a conversation she had tried to end. Every time that he found her alone (and without designing it, perhaps, she gave him a thousand opportunities), the most tender and evident emotions took possession of her against her will. If, in the course of a long and animated conversation, he should happen to kiss her hand or fall on his knees, Phenima betrayed alarm, but no anger, and it was very gently indeed that she chided him for his temerity."

"And do you mean to say," the Sultan interrupted, "that he desisted?"

"Certainly, Sire," Amanzei answered. "The more he was in love..."

"The more he was an ass, that's plain," the Sultan said.

"Love," Amanzei answered, "is never so timid as when..."

"Timid!" the Sultan interrupted once more. "There's a pretty story! Did not he see that he was tantalizing the lady? If I had been she, I would have sent him packing, I can tell you that."

"No doubt," Amanzei went on, "that had he been dealing with a flirt, Zulma would not have been lost; but Phenima, who really wanted not to be conquered, accounted her lover's timidity for merit. Besides, the more he respected Phenima's scruples, the more certain he was of victory. Not to seize the opportunity offered by a passing whim is perhaps to lose it forever, but, where true love is concerned, the less it is clutched at, the more eager it is to be caught."

"All the same," the Sultan said, "I have heard it remarked that women do not like men who are slow at grasping opportunities."

"Sometimes, perhaps," Amanzei answered. "But Phenima was not of their mind, and always loved Zulma most when he was even more respectful than she might have wished."

"And," the Sultan asked again, "did he often miss the chance?"

"Yes, Sire," Amanzei replied. "And sometimes so egregiously as to make himself laughable. One day, for instance, he went in to see Phenima: for more than an hour she had been wholly given over to sweet thoughts of him, and, her imagination gradually growing more vivid, she reveled in her fond fancies, and was at the height of her disarray when Zulma reappeared. Her confusion increased, and she actually blushed at seeing him. Ah, if he had only guessed what it was that made Phenima blush! If he had only dared to plead! But he thought he was out of favor with her for some very innocent liberties he had taken with her on the previous evening; and he wasted an opportunity when nothing could have offended her by begging her pardon."

"Oh, the owl!" the Sultan cried. "How could anybody be such a dolt!"

"Still, that must not surprise you, Sire," Amanzei answered. "For during the time I was a sofa I saw more opportunities lost than seized. Women, trained from the cradle to hide their thoughts from us, are especially careful to hide their tender impulses; and many a one, perhaps, who boasts she has never succumbed, owes her advantage less to being chaste than to making others think her so.

"I remember that I was once for a long time with a lady renowned for her rare virtue, without seeing anything that belied her reputation in society. It is true that she was not lovely, and one must admit that no women find it easier to be chaste than those who have no charms. Besides her ugliness, this woman had a harsh, austere nature, at least as repulsive as her face. Although no one had been adventurous enough to try to soften her heart, it was nonetheless believed that it would be a waste of time to try. As luck would have it, a man more daring or more whimsical than usual, or perhaps he did not believe that women could be chaste, being alone with her one day, ventured to say that he thought her attractive; and although he said it so coldly as not to be in the least degree convincing, so unaccustomed a speech had its effect upon her. She answered modestly, but not calmly, that she was not made to inspire such feelings. He kissed her hand, she trembled; her confused look, her blushes, the fire that all of a sudden sparkled in her eyes, were undeniable signs of the tumult rising in her breast. Then he clasped her rapturously in his arms, vowing once more that she moved him most deeply. I do not know what he did to prove what he said was true (for she was still astonished), but her modesty began to give way under the evidence, and, whatever the nature of the proof he gave her, it ended in her defeat. Perhaps the very novelty of the situation disarmed her, or perhaps at that moment she was weary of the weight of her virtue, but in any case she hardly remembered that good manners called for at least a show of resistance, and she yielded even more quickly than women who are little given to resistance. This example, and a few others of the same kind, have led me to suppose that unassailably virtuous women are few indeed, and that none are more easily won than those most foreign to love; but I must return to the two lovers whose story I was telling your Majesty."

CHAPTER VII

In Which There Are Many Things to Find Fault With

"One night, as he was leaving Phenima, Zulma asked her when he might see her again. Although she was very afraid of being with him, she could not live without seeing him, and thus, after some hesitation, told him he might come the next day.

"Phenima, fully sensing the danger she ran in being alone with him, had meant to invite some other friends; nevertheless, when the time came she gave orders to deny all but Zulma. It seemed to her that when she had company, he made up for his inability to speak of his love by trying to show her, in a thousand different ways, that she occupied all his thoughts: and the world notices these things! She understood Zulma so well, and scandal might easily provide the world with that perspicacity she herself owed to love. Zulma was less dangerous for her when they were alone, because then he was respectful, whereas in front of others he was not careful enough; thus she believed she ought to see him in company as seldom as possible.

"Moreover, he was so melancholic when he could not speak to her. Would it not be too inhuman to deprive him of a pleasure that she had until then found so little risk in granting him?

"Thus Phenima had argued it out, or at least she thought she had; and thus she had convinced herself that the things she did, really out of pure love for Zulma, were based on custom, or something equally reasonable.

"That very day she had been extremely tempted to complete his happiness; she told herself everything that a woman can who wishes to give herself up to love: she had exaggerated the attentions and constancy Zulma displayed, his ever-eager desire to please her. She even remembered gladly that he had always said he would rather be cheated on than be unfaithful. Besides, Zulma was young, intelligent, and well-built, all things she thought did not count with her at all, but which in him, nonetheless, had most captivated her."

"Then what the devil held her back?" the Sultan asked. "This woman makes me cross."

"Eight years' chastity," Amanzei answered. "Eight years' glory of which a momentary weakness might rob her."

"A fine loss indeed!" the Sultan cried.

"For a thinking woman," Amanzei answered, "the loss is more considerable than your Majesty might think. Virtue always goes hand in hand with a deep tranquillity; it is not diverting, but it is satisfying: a woman happy enough to have it, being always pleased with herself, can always look upon her life with complacency: her self-esteem is always justified by that others have for her, and the pleasures she sacrifices are not as great as those the sacrifice procures her."

"Tell me just," the Sultan said, "do you think I would have been chaste if I had been a woman?"

"Really, Sire," Amanzei answered, boggling at the question, "I cannot say at all."

"Why cannot you say at all?" the Sultan asked.

"How can you ask such questions!" the Sultana put in.

"I am not speaking to you," the Sultan retorted. "I merely want Amanzei to say whether or not I should have been chaste."

"I believe you would, Sire," Amanzei declared.

"Then, my dear fellow, you are wrong," the Sultan replied. "I would have been exactly the opposite. What I am saying, by the way," he added, turning to the Sultana, "is not meant to make virtue repellent to you. What I think about this is entirely my own opinion, and very possibly, were I a woman, I might change my mind. On this sort of question everyone is entitled to his own ideas: I do not want to influence anybody."

"Your master is getting entangled," the Sultana said to Amanzei, smiling. "And I assure you he will be highly obliged to you for going on with your story."

"There now, I like that," the Sultan exclaimed. "One would think it was I who had interrupted."

"Zulma came in," Amanzei went on, "and, although he had come earlier than she expected, Phenima immediately told him that he was very late.

" 'Oh, how delighted I am that you should think so!' he said tenderly.

"It was only then that Phenima realized the force of her reproach; she tried to turn it off, and did not know what to say. Zulma smiled at her embarrassment, and the smile made her blush. He fell to his knees, and kissed her hand with extreme ardor: she moved to pull it away, but as he made no attempt to keep it, she gave it back.

"Meanwhile, Zulma was whispering the tenderest things: she made him no answer but listened with an attention and eagerness for which she would certainly have blamed herself if she could have unraveled her feelings. Her bosom was slightly exposed; she noticed that his glance wandered there, and tried to fasten up her dress.

" 'How cruel you are!' Zulma cried.

"That exclamation was enough to arrest her hand. To allow Zulma the delight of the very small favor she granted him without his being able to draw any favorable augury from it, she pretended one of her locks needed settling. Zulma's eyes could not without glowing rest for long upon the object Phenima had abandoned to them. For a while she surrendered to the pleasure of being admired by what she admired; her eyes, cast languidly at Zulma, grew large with emotion, and she appeared sunk in the tenderest dreams."

"Now to it, Zulma!" the Sultan then said. "But did he not see even that, the barbarous beast?"

"Phenima," Amanzei pursued, "in spite of the disorder that was gaining on her, noticed that of her lover; and fearing Zulma's emotion as much as her own, started up from her seat. He made some attempt to detain her, and, no longer able to speak, bathed her hand in his flowing tears, trying to bring her to see that he was cut to the quick by her cruel intent. So much regard brought Phenima's emotions to a pitch, but since love had not absolutely conquered her, she triumphed not only over her own desires but also over those of her lover, perhaps more dangerous for her than her own.

"As soon as she had freed herself from Zulma's clasp, she signaled to him to get up, which he did. For a while they gazed at one another speechless. At last Phenima said that she wanted to play some game. Although the motion seemed ill timed to Zulma, he could not thwart Phenima's lightest wish, and got everything ready with as much zeal as if it had been he who had wanted to play. This fresh proof of his enslavement touched Phenima deeply, and I saw that she was almost ready to beg his pardon for a whim that now seemed ridiculous to her.

"Phenima's repentance did not last as long as was needed to make Zulma happy, and the more she felt her strength was ebbing away, the more she thought she ought to hide her feelings from him. Thus, she set herself to the game but soon grew so weary of it that she saw the armor she had chosen against Zulma was a very poor protection. However, she would not at once admit that it was her tenderness for him that made her so languid, and, attributing it entirely to the game she had chosen, besought her lover to fetch another; he did so with a sigh, and she was no less tormented by it. The tumult of emotion which she thought to soothe, these dear fancies she tried to dispel, seemed to wax greater by the violence she did herself and to tighten their hold upon her. Lost in reverie, she believed she was paying attention to the game, while she was conscious only of Zulma.

"The agony she saw in his face, the deep sighs he fetched, the tears she saw ready to fall – which only his profound regard for her seemed able to withhold – finally melted Phenima's heart. A prey to the tender palpitations he caused in her, she could do nothing but look at him. At last, either her own confusion or her inability to face Zulma's look, proved too much for her; she leaned her head upon her hand. No sooner did Zulma see her thus than he threw himself at her feet, which Phenima was either too distraught to notice, or did not wish to prevent. He took advantage of this moment of weakness to kiss her disengaged hand, and he kissed it with more rapture than an ordinary lover feels when reveling in the completest happiness.

"Crowned with a favor that, as their relations stood, he had not dared to hope for, he sought to discover his fate in Phenima's eyes. She still rested her head upon her hand; he raised it gently, and as Phenima uncovered her face, he saw it was wet with tears. The sight called forth answering tears from Zulma.

"'Ah, Phenima!' he cried, heaving a profound sigh.

"'Ah, Zulma!' she answered tenderly.

"At these words they gazed at one another with that tenderness, that fire, that languishing, that wild ecstasy which love alone, and only the truest love, can provoke.

"At last Zulma, his voice broken by his sighs, said in a transport of joy, 'Ah, Phenima! If it be true that my love has at last awakened your passion, and that you are still fearful of telling me so, at least let those charmer's eyes, those eyes that I adore, divulge the happy tidings.'

"'No, Zulma,' she answered. 'I love you, and could not be so mean as to lessen a triumph you have so well deserved. I love you, Zulma, my lips, my eyes, my heart, all of me must tell you, and all of me does tell you. Zulma! My Zulma! I am happy now that at last I can express all my feelings for you.'

"Zulma thought he would die when he heard such soft and unhoped for words. But, though his rapture was excessive, he did not forget that Phenima could make him happier still. Though he understood that the foregoing declaration authorized a thousand things which, until that moment, he had hardly presumed to think of, his respect outweighing his desires, he chose to delay until she should be pleased to determine his fate.

"Phenima understood Zulma too well to mistake the motive that subdued his flame; she still gazed at him with extraordinary love, and yielding at last to the sweet impulses that mastered her, flung herself upon his breast with an impetuousness of fondness to which the strongest terms and the most flamboyant imagination could not do justice. What openness! What genuine passion! No, a more moving sight has never offered itself to my view. Both, intoxicated, seemed to have lost the use of their reason. Here was not the fleeting pulse of desire, but the true delirium, the soft fury of love, so often sought, so seldom felt.

"'O gods, gods!' Zulma breathed from time to time, unable to utter more. Phenima, for her part, devoured by her love, clasped Zulma tenderly in her arms, tore herself away the better to gaze upon him, again enfolded him, again looked rapt upon him.

"'Zulma!' she cried in ecstasy, 'ah, Zulma! How long happiness has tarried!'

"These words were followed by that delicious silence upon which the soul floats blissfully when words cannot express its exquisite feelings.

"Zulma, however, still felt that much was lacking; and Phenima, whose flame at this moment made her feel an almost equal want, far from wishing to deprive him of a single, lightest joy, met him freely. It seemed even that it was he, and not she, who was making the greater gift; having resisted much, she thought she ought to show him how difficult it had been to resist at all, and compensate him for the tortures she had made him undergo for so long a time. She would have been ashamed to arm herself with that prudery which often allays, and even spoils enjoyment, and which, seeming to pair love with remorse, leaves a greater delight to be wished for even in the midst of delight. Phenima, loving sincerely, would have felt guilty toward Zulma had she in the least degree cloaked anything of the fierce passion he inspired in her. She seemed to forestall his every caress, and, just as a few moments before she had prided herself on her resistance, so now her whole ambition was to convince him of her flame.

"In one of those pauses that, short as they are, contain a thousand tender protestations, Zulma said ardently, 'Phenima! You are too true to yourself in all your feelings for me not sometimes to have thought that you loved me. Why did you so long delay telling me so?'

"'My heart soon decided in your favor,' Phenima answered, 'but my reason long opposed my inclination. The more I felt myself capable of sincere love, the more I feared to embark upon it; never having loved, I felt that I would demand more affection than I could inspire. You alone have proved to me that there are still men who can love; you had shaken me, you had not yet conquered me. Shall I admit it, Zulma? The chastity that it has given me so much pleasure to sacrifice to you today was your enemy for a long time. I could not without affliction think that one frailty would rob me both of the sweet knowledge that I was estimable and of the joy of being esteemed. Ah Zulma!' she added, pressing him in her arms, 'how hateful you have made to me all the time I have not spent in telling you how much I loved you. Yes, Zulma, I was able to resist you! I made you shed tears – they were not always such as you have shed today! Forgive me, I was far unhappier than you! Yes, Zulma, I will always upbraid myself for having been able to imagine that my every happiness was not bound up in you, and that in possessing you I was not possessed of all. You loved me, and yet I was able to think of the good opinion of others! Ah! Do I still deserve yours?'

"Your Majesty," Amanzei continued, "will easily divine how such a conversation was bound to end. Great as was the delight that it gave me, it is impossible for me to recollect the discourse of two lovers, who, enraptured with each other, asked each other questions they never waited to hear answered, and whose disconnected ideas, descriptive only of the disorder of their souls, could not have for another person nearly the charm it had for them. I was as much surprised by the boundlessness of their passion as I was by the expedients they devised to express it. They did not part until very late, and Zulma had hardly left her than Phenima, who had vowed every moment to him, sat down to write to him.

"Zulma came back very early the next day, still more in love, still more beloved, to enjoy the most delicious moments, either in Phenima's lap, or in her arms.

"In spite of my propensity to frequent changes, I could not resist my curiosity to know whether Zulma and Phenima would love each other long, and so I stayed in her house for nearly a year. But realizing at length that their love, far from getting less, seemed to renew itself more strongly every day; and that to all the delight and exuberance of the most ardent passion they added the intimacy and trust of the tenderest friendship, I went elsewhere to seek my deliverance, or other pleasures."

CHAPTER VIII

"On leaving Phenima's palace, I retired to a house in which, seeing only things so ordinary as not to be worth either looking at or speaking about, I did not stay long. I was some days hunting about the different places where my restlessness and curiosity led me before I found anything either new or likely to amuse me. In one place some person or another yielded through vanity; in others, whimsy, advantage, habit, or even indolence were the sole motives of the frailties revealed to me. I met often enough with that lively, transient emotion, honored with the name of taste; but nowhere else did I see that love, that delicacy, that sweet abandonment which, at Phenima's, had so long been my admiration and my delight.

"Weary of the wandering life I led, convinced that the emotion everyone would like to seem filled with is in fact rarely felt, I began to grow impatient at my fate, and to wish ardently for the occasion that should put an end to the torture to which I was condemned.

"'What morals!' I sometimes cried. 'Oh, Brahma knew he was flattering my vain hope; he never thought that amid the frantic pursuit of pleasure all Agra joins in, and amid this widespread contempt for principles, I should ever find two persons such as are required to call me to another life.'

"A prey to these melancholic thoughts, I flitted to a house where everything looked peaceful. It was inhabited by a solitary maiden lady of about forty years of age. Although she was still pleasing enough to engage in an affair without appearing ridiculous, she was prudent, shunned bruited pleasures, saw few people, and even seemed to have tried not to gather an agreeable circle of acquaintances, so much as to live with persons who either by their age or callings seemed to shield her from all suspicion. Thus, there were few houses in Agra duller than hers.

"Among the men who visited her, the one who seemed most agreeable to her, and who was the most often with her, was a person already middle-aged, solemn, cold, reserved, more by temperament than by status, although he was at the head of a College of Brahmins. He was hardhearted, a hater of pleasures, and did not believe there was a single pleasure that would not taint the soul of a truly virtuous person. From his moroseness and somber exterior I first of all took him for one of those people who are more ferocious than virtuous, unrelenting toward others, indulgent toward themselves, inveighing bitterly in public against the vices they indulge in private; in fact, I thought of him as falsely devout. Fatima had distorted my mind horribly with regard to people who looked good and pure. Although I have seldom erred in thinking badly of them, I was mistaken in Mochles, and when I knew him, I found he deserved to be thought of better. At that time he was upright, and sincerely chaste. Everyone in Agra thought more highly of him even than he wished: no one doubted that his aversion from pleasure was real, and that, strict as his principles were, he had never strayed from them. Almaida, the name of the lady with whom I lodged, was equally well thought of. The close friendship between her and Mochles had given rise to no whispers against them; and spiteful as the world is with regard to friendships, there was no one who did not respect theirs, and believe it cemented by their common love of virtue.

"Mochles visited Almaida every evening, and, whether they were in company or alone, their actions were above reproach, their conversation blameless and temperate. Usually they argued some moral point, and in these discussions Mochles shone in learning and discretion. Only one thing displeased me: it was that two persons so superior to others, keeping all their passions within such strict bounds, should not have triumphed over pride enough to refrain from setting each other up as examples. Often, even, not satisfied with their mutual esteem, they would praise themselves with a complacency, a warmth, and a vanity, of which their virtue can surely not have approved.

"Although such a dull house became very tiresome to me, I resolved to stay there a little while. Not that I hoped ever to see anything amusing there, or to find my freedom. The more I thought Mochles and Almaida capable of giving it me, the less I dared hope for a slip on their part: but still, tired with my wanderings, in horror at the cynicism to which the world had brought me, I was not sorry to listen to a little moralizing, though I do not know whether it was merely the novelty of the thing which made it pleasing, or whether I thought that as I then was it might be beneficial to me."

"Ah, now I understand!" the Sultan cried. "I do not wonder at my growing drowsy all at once; I see what you are at. But so as not to tempt you to display either your eloquence or your powers of recollection ever again, I repeat the warning I was well advised to give you when you began to tell your story. If I were less merciful, I would let you go on, and, since you love the sound of your own voice so much, you would no doubt go on at length; but I hate trickery, and I will impress upon you once more that nothing is worse for the health than moralizing."

Amanzei went on: "In spite of the unusual virtue that dwelt in both Almaida and Mochles, they sometimes mingled with their moralizings some pictures of vice which were rather too detailed. No doubt their intentions were good; but that did not make it any the wiser for them to dwell upon thoughts that cannot be kept too far away if one wishes to avoid the troublesome feelings they usually engender.

"Almaida and Mochles, who did not realize their danger, or else thought themselves superior to it, were not cautious enough when they discussed pleasure; though it is true that after having vividly displayed its charms, they exaggerated its shame and its dangers. They were agreed, of course, that true felicity was to be found only at the breast of virtue, but they agreed to it without enthusiasm, as a truth too well known to need discussion. They were by no means so laconic in their researches upon love; they enlarged upon so interesting a subject, and stressed the most dangerous details with so much confidence, that at last I hoped they might someday be caught by it.

"For at least a month they entertained themselves with these lively descriptions I thought so little in tune with their character; and whatever subject they started off upon, they always fell back upon the one they should have avoided. Mochles, whose temper had insensibly been softened by these discussions, would come to visit Almaida earlier than usual, be more amused there, and go away later. Almaida, on her part, would await his coming more eagerly, take greater pleasure in seeing him, and listen to him more attentively. If, when Mochles came, he found company with her, he appeared constrained and embarrassed, and she herself did not seem less so. When at last they were left alone, I could read in their faces the joy two lovers feel, who, after long enduring an importunate visit, can at last give themselves over to their feelings. Almaida and Mochles drew eagerly together, complained of not being left more to themselves, and looked at one another with much satisfaction. They spoke in nearly the same way as they used to, but the tone was different. In short, they lived in a familiarity that could not fail to carry them further, inasmuch as they were intoxicated by what had given rise to their friendship, or by what (I am more inclined to think) they did not quite understand.

"One day Mochles launched into a panegyric upon Almaida's spotless character.

" 'As far as I am concerned,' she said, 'it is not to be wondered at that I have remained chaste: to a woman, popular prejudice is a great help, but to a man it is a snare. In you it is a kind of foolishness not to be flirtatious; in us it is a vice to be so. You, for instance, though you praise me, ought yourself to be praised still more for thinking as I do.'

" 'Without examining things with that exact reasoning which shows them for what they are,' he answered solemnly, 'one might indeed think that I am more praiseworthy than you – but this would be wrong. It is easy for a man to resist love: everything prompts a woman to yield to it. If it is not affection, it is the flesh. Even if these two springs are lacking – though every day they give rise to myriad irregularities – there is always their vanity, which, although it is the least excusable reason for their frailty, is not perhaps the least usual; and what is still more dreadful for them,' he added, sighing deeply, and rolling up his eyes to the heavens, 'is the perpetual want of employment in which they idle away their lives. This fatal indolence breeds the most dangerous notions; the imagination, by nature evil, seizes upon and expands them. Passion, already born, governs the heart more and more, or, if the heart is still free from disturbance, these voluptuous visions, so pleasant to consider, dispose it to weakness. When alone, and rapt on the wings of her imagination, a woman pursues a chimera her idleness has engendered; and, so as not to be made uneasy in her imaginary pleasure, she dismisses every pious thought that might make her blush at the creations of her fancy. The less real the seductive object is, the less she thinks she need resist it; it is in silence, and in her own company, that she is at her weakest: what has she to fear? But this heart in which she cherishes tender thoughts, these faculties she molds to the uses of love – will they always be satisfied with illusions? Supposing that she is not desirous even of exposing her virtue to damage, can she be sure that when (perhaps just at the time when she is inwardly straying) a tender, ardent, eager lover moans at her feet, dissolved in passionate tears, she will find in a heart she so often allowed to drift on amorous seas, those principles which alone enable her to triumph in so dangerous a moment?'

" 'Ah, Mochles!' Almaida cried blushing, 'how hard it is to practice virtue!'

" 'You of all the world,' he answered, 'have the least reason to say so; who, with every charm to please, born to dwell in the midst of delights, have sacrificed all to this very virtue, which is nowadays sacrificed to things that ought to count least with it.'

" 'I do not flatter myself,' she replied demurely, 'that I have reached perfection: but it is true to say that I have been on my guard against everything, especially against that indolence you have mentioned, and those books, and profane spectacles, which cannot but relax the soul.'

" 'Yes, I know,' he went on, 'and it is chiefly to your continual care to busy yourself that you owe your integrity, for (and I see it in men) nothing delivers one into the hands of passion more than idleness. And if it has such an effect upon our sex, which is much less fragile, think how much more it must have on yours.'

" 'It is true,' she said, 'that we have everything to struggle against.'

" 'Infinitely more than we think,' he replied, 'as I was just saying. And besides, you must consider that it is always the women who are attacked (excepting those few without shame or principles, who, even without being in love are the first to dare to say they are), so that, as a rule, in spite of modern licentiousness, we do not have to hold out against the kindnesses, tears, and determination that we daily employ so successfully against women. Moreover, if you add to the devotion shown them, the example...'

" 'As to that,' she interrupted, 'we have no advantage over you; example must tell with you, who are the aggressors, far more than with us.'

" 'That is not strictly true for all men,' he pursued, 'since there are many whose position is enough to forbid that frenzy of the soul called the joy of loving: that, for instance, is my case.'

" 'Even if it were not so,' she answered, 'born so lucky as to be impervious to passion, you would always...'

"Here Mochles lifted his eyes to the heavens and sighed.

" 'What!' Almaida continued. 'Can you have something to reproach yourself with? If you, Mochles, are not at peace with yourself, who else can presume to be? What! You have wanted to know love?'

" 'Yes,' he answered sadly. 'Such a confession humiliates me, but truth must have its due. It is true that I never yielded to this dire temptation. In admitting to you that I have sometimes been obliged to struggle, I no doubt reveal to you weaknesses of which, from your astonishment, I plainly see you thought me incapable. But in undeceiving you of an error that was to my advantage, I fear I will increase the good opinion you already have of me. It is less humiliating to be tempted than it is glorious to resist temptation. In avowing my weaknesses, I am obliged to tell you of my triumphs: what I lose on the one hand, I seem to wish to regain on the other. And I wonder whether I ought not to fear your attributing to pride a confession made only to avoid falsehood.'

"At the end of this modest speech, Mochles lowered his eyes.

" 'Oh, you have nothing to fear with me,' Almaida said promptly. 'I know you too well. So, you have sometimes been tempted to succumb? That does not surprise me. However much we may strive after perfection, we never attain it.'

" 'What you say is unhappily only too well proven,' he answered.

" 'Alas!' she cried dolorously, 'do you suppose I have so much to boast of, and that I am free of the weaknesses you accuse yourself of?'

" 'What!' he said to her. 'You, too, Almaida?'

" 'I have too much faith in you to hide anything from you,' she went on. 'And I will confess that I have had to struggle terribly. What has long amazed me, and which even today I cannot understand, is how this disorder that takes possession of our feelings and confuses them can be out of our control. A hundred times it has come upon me unawares in the midst of the most serious duties, and one would naturally think the soul would be less accessible at those times. Sometimes I resisted successfully enough; at others, less so – in spite of myself, it bent my will, inflamed my imagination, and enslaved all my faculties. That these shameful tendencies should master a soul that likes to harbor them and is only happy when it is under their yoke, that does not surprise me; but why is one left at their mercy when one is making the greatest, most continuous effort to smother them?'

" 'What one calls being good,' Mochles answered, 'consists less in not having been tempted than in being able to resist temptation; and there would be little virtue in piety if there were no obstacles to surmount. But since we are on the subject, tell me, pray, now that you have reached the age when the blood flowing less impetuously in the veins makes you less susceptible to desires, do you still have these outrageous impulses?'

" 'They are not so common,' she told him, 'but I am still liable to them.'

" 'That is also my case,' he said smiling.

" 'But we are mad to talk as we do,' Almaida said blushing. 'This is not at all the right sort of conversation for us.'

" 'I think, all things considered, we have not much to fear from it,' Mochles answered with a complacent smile. 'It is right to mistrust one-self, but it would also be to have too poor an opinion of our character to think ourselves so easily undermined. I grant that the subject we are on necessarily leads to certain thoughts, but it is one thing to discuss with a view to enlightenment, quite another to do so with intent to seduce. And I think we can, in all good faith, rely upon each other's motives, and be at rest about them. Besides, you must not think that such things, which are so dangerous to people who lead dissolute lives, can have the same effect upon us; by themselves they are innocuous. People of the greatest purity are sometimes forced to consider them, without even the most detailed discussion of such matters having any effect upon their blameless behavior. All is evil and corruption to cor-rupt hearts, just as the things that seem most contrary to chastity have no hold upon those who do not seek to indulge them.'

" 'There can be no doubt of that, if you think so,' she replied. 'And I should not dream of being scrupulous when you think I ought not to be.'

" 'You will never guess,' he said to her, 'what the curiosity is that burns me; I dare not reveal it, because that would be too indiscreet, and yet I cannot resist. I would so much like to know if anyone has ever made proposals of a certain kind to you, if ever, in fact (to give my curi-osity full rein) you have ever experienced the passionate outbursts of a man, either with, or against, your will?'

"Almaida was thunderstruck at this unexpected question; she blushed, and fell into a muse; at last, taking the plunge, she stammered out: 'Yes, indeed, and since you must know, I will admit without reserve, that one day a rash young fellow, who (for I am hiding nothing from you), in spite of my aversion from men seemed to me agreeable enough, catch-ing me alone, said an abundance of those fine things to me which men think it their duty to say to us before we have reached that happy age which calls forth only their respect, and while we are miserable enough to have faces that incite them to desire. We were alone; I answered him according to the maxims I had prescribed for myself. But my answer, far from making him desist, made him suppose not that I was seeking to avoid his embraces, but that I was making my surrender a more con-siderable triumph for him: he dared even assure me that I loved him. You may well imagine that I stoutly maintained the contrary. I do not know what women this young coxcomb usually frequented, but certainly they had not taught him to respect them. He came to me, and clasping me brutally in his arms, flung me upon a sofa. I beg of you please to spare me the rest of a story, which it would offend my modesty to tell, and which might still agitate my senses. Let it be enough for you to know –'

" 'No!' Mochles broke in, 'you shall tell me everything! It is, I see (and I do not see it without trembling for you), not so much the fear of stirring your passions, or of offending your modesty, which closes your mouth, as the shame of confessing how deeply tempted you were; and this motive, far from being praiseworthy, cannot be too harshly reprehended. I can, I even think I must, add to what I say: that if it be true that you fear the story I demand of you will move you too much, you cannot suppress it or palliate it without incurring guilt. Is it of no concern to you to be unaware of the power certain ideas have over you? Can you presume to be sure of yourself if you have never put yourself to the test? In this way, by continually flattering your soul, you will never know its weakness. Almaida, take my word for it, we are never fearful enough of the dangers to which we are strangers, and it is usually through overconfidence that we fall. Thus, you cannot be too particular over every detail of your story. It is only from the effect each passage has upon you now that you will be able to judge what progress you have made along the path of virtue; or (what is more essential still) what is still left in you to root out before you can reach that complete aversion from all joy which alone makes people virtuous.'

"In the mouth of Mochles this doctrine surprised me not a little. I knew how upright and enlightened he was, and I could not conceive what could now make him argue in a way so contrary to his principles. 'What!' I said to myself in amazement, 'this is Mochles, the virtuous Mochles, advising Almaida to dwell upon details that may wound her modest feelings and incline her to ill doing?' The curiosity I felt to discover his motives made me scrutinize him earnestly, and I found his eyes glowing so strangely that I began to think that I might well gain my freedom in the last place in the world I would have dared hope for it.

"Whilst I was enraptured by such sweet expectations, founded doubly, first upon the virtue of Almaida and Mochles, then upon the confusion beginning to gain upon both of them, Almaida continued her story."

In Which You Will Find an Important Point to Settle

" 'I will obey you blindly,' Almaida told Mochles. 'You have convinced me it was only vanity that made me silent, and I shall chastise myself for it by telling you, without veiling anything, the most mortifying details of my story. I told you, I think, that the young man in question flung me backward upon a sofa: and, before I could recover from my surprise, he flung himself upon me. Although my unbounded astonishment hindered me from expressing my anger, he read it plainly in my eyes, and wanting to guard against my crying out, he succeeded, in spite of my resistance, in stopping my mouth with the most insolent kiss. It is beyond my powers to describe how greatly I was revolted at first; nevertheless, I must confess I was not indignant for long. Nature, which was betraying me, soon bore the kiss to my innermost heart; and suddenly the kiss mingled with my anger and abated it. All my senses were stirred, an unknown fire rushed through my veins, some strange pleasure urged me on although I hated it, and flowed over my soul. My shrieks were changed into sighs; I was carried away by feelings that, for all my rage and my grief, I could no longer battle against; and even while I bemoaned my condition, I had no strength for self-defense.'

" 'Ah, what a horrible situation!' Mochles cried. 'Well – and then?' he continued, with eyes aflame.

" 'What shall I tell you?' she went on. 'Whenever I could I reproved him, but only by rote. I believe that I spoke to him and treated him with all the scorn he deserved – I say that I believe I did, for I dare not vouch for it. As my disorder increased, I felt my strength and my anger dwindle away; my mind was in a fearful chaos. I had not yet surrendered – but how feebly I resisted! Oh, Mochles, I cannot remember this without horror; and the shame it brings back to me makes it all as vivid as if I were still moaning in the arms of that audacious lover. What a critical moment for my chastity! Oh, Mochles, knowing the whole value of the innocence he sought to make me lose, and even in the midst of my confusion fearing nothing so much as the misery of losing it, how could the pleasure be such a pleasure? How is it that such lively terrors did not swamp the pleasure, or why did the pleasure yet have the upper hand over my virtue? I wished (but what effort it took, and how I suffered to wish it!) that someone would come and rescue me from my impending fate. And even while I formed the wish, a contrary wish surged violently through me, and yet displeased me less than the first, which was a hope that nothing should hinder my undoing. Blushing at what I felt, I burned to feel yet more. Without being able to imagine further delights, I longed for them, until my ardor began to torture me, and to wear me out. Though I was far gone in this delirious whirl, I had not yet been able to still the importunate voice that cried out from the depths of my heart, and which, not having been able to strengthen my weakness, continued to reproach me for it, when the young man, noticing no doubt the impression he was making on me pushed his insults to the farthest point. He...but how can I put into words what I blush to think of? Solely engaged, as much as my confusion would allow, in repelling the kisses he ceaselessly showered upon me, I was not prepared in other respects. In spite of the pitiful state I was in, this fresh insult reawakened my anger. Alas! not for long. I soon felt my disorder increase. The very efforts I made to break from the clutches of the audacious fellow only helped to bring about my fall. Finally, lost in ineffable bliss, in raptures of which I can give you no idea, I fell limply, devoid of strength, into the arms of the cruel man who offered me such gross indignity.'

" 'How terrible!' Mochles cried. 'And how I dread the sequel!'

" 'Yet it was not what you suppose,' Almaida answered. 'At the crisis of a situation that I needed to fear all the more since I no longer feared anything, I do not know why, but my enemy suddenly desisted from his attempts, and the tumult in him died down. By a miracle I have never been able to fathom, and which you may not perhaps believe, it is so extraordinary, at the very moment when I could no longer have refused him anything, and when he himself seemed at the utmost pitch of uncontrol, his eyes, glowing with a luster that affected me more than I could bear, changed. A kind of languid look drove the madness out of them; he relaxed, and folding me in his arms more tenderly, less violently than before, he became (just judgment for the wrong he had done me) as limp as I was myself. At that moment my own confusion began to abate, and I was happy in being able to enjoy the abjection of my foe. After having let my eyes dwell upon him with all the pleasure in the world, and having inwardly thanked Brahma for the protection he had manifestly thrown over me, I tore myself forcibly from him. The calmer I grew, the clearer my mind became, the more bitterly did I feel my shame. Twenty times I opened my mouth to upbraid the temerarious man as he deserved, but the inner confusion that still dominated shut it again every time; and, after having looked upon him with all the indignation his insolence demanded, I left him abruptly. To tell you the truth, I chose rather to be silent than to go into details that would have driven the blood into my cheeks, and which the frailty I had recognized in myself made me fear. That,' she concluded, 'is the only time I have been in the danger I had always dreaded before knowing what it was, and which after knowing I have taken more care than ever to avoid. I thought myself the more obliged to flee it, no longer doubting from the emotions I had felt, that I had a greater propensity to love than I thought.'

" 'You see,' Mochles then said, 'how important it is to put one's soul to the test. By the way, how is yours now? Has telling this story had any alarming effects upon you?'

" 'Well, really,' she answered blushing, 'it is not so calm as it was.'

" 'So that if some bold fellow were to appear now,' he took up, 'you might be a little shaken?'

" 'Ah, do not even suggest it!' she cried. 'That would be the worst misfortune that could happen to me.'

" 'Indeed,' he answered in agitation, 'I can well believe it.'

"Saying this, he became extremely pensive: from time to time he glanced furtively at Almaida, with his eyes full of desire and irresolution. Almaida's avowal of her perturbation encouraged him; but, not knowing in his inexperience how to take advantage of it, it came near to being wasted. How he ought to proceed to seduce Almaida was not the only thing that engrossed him. Restrained by his past integrity, lashed by his desires, now giving way, now resisting, I saw he was ready by turns either to flee or to risk everything.

"While he was involved in these struggles, Almaida was feeling no calmer. The story Mochles forced her to tell had released all the feelings she had feared. Her eyes were alight; she blushed in a way not born of shame; broken sighs, restlessness, languor, all these told me more than she knew herself how far she was straying. I waited impatiently to see the outcome of a situation in which two such discreet persons were entangled. I even feared for a while that they would see the pitfall toward which an excessive sense of security had led them, and that with hearts accustomed to virtue they would not fall into error so readily as my own state and Brahma's promise forced me to wish.

"At last I thought I could see by the looks in the eyes of Almaida and Mochles, which were becoming less timid and more laden with desire, that it was less their fear of succumbing which held them back than ignorance of how to bring about their fall. Both seemed equally tempted, both seemed to have the same wishes and the same need to satisfy their curiosity. Such a situation would have given no trouble to persons with a trifle of social skill; Almaida and Mochles, having no idea how to encourage each other, dared neither declare their condition nor, except by uneasy glances, reveal the flame that seared them. Even if they had known that each was having the same thoughts, would they have known to what point they had both been seduced? What shame would overwhelm the first to speak if he found any dregs of virtue still left in the other's heart! And how could they enlighten each other when both had such good reason to remain silent? Even supposing Almaida to be frailer than Mochles, she yet had to await his overtures. The modesty and propriety of her sex, added to the chastity she had always professed, did not allow her to make a declaration; and though the rule is not considered inviolable by all women, Almaida, being either new or ill-suited to flirtation, feared the scorn rightly attached to taking such a step. Besides, could she be sure how Mochles would take it? Perhaps if she had felt certain that Mochles needed to despise her before he could take her, she might have worked up to this rashness; but what if he stopped short at despising her?

"After they had debated within themselves, for some time, how they might speak without exposing themselves to the shame of failure, Mochles, whose pride and position would have received too cruel a bruise from an outright avowal, thought that sophistry would be the best way – provided, however, that the choice of means should still rest upon what his clearer reason might have to say to it, and that he should not bewilder himself by his own sophistry, nor use it to save his face in case of the failure of the attempt, but only to deceive Almaida with. How much better it would have been to use all this ingenuity not to seduce, nor to justify seduction, but to protect himself."

"Egad!" the Sultan remarked. "If he goes awkwardly about the business, one cannot say it is from lack of thinking about it."

"But," the Sultana said, "I cannot see why you are so surprised at his thinking it over so long. It seems to me that his situation called for a few reflections."

"A few, by all means," the Sultan retorted. "And it is precisely because only a few are wanted that he had no call to make so many. Those people must have been horribly tempted not to recover themselves in all the time they took about it."

"You have narrowly escaped making a judicious remark," the Sultana said.

"Narrowly escaped!" the Sultan cried. "May I venture to ask what you mean? You have some little habits of speech which lack respect as much as any I have heard, and which perhaps no other Sultan in the world would bear."

"I merely mean to say," the Sultana answered, "that it leads one astray. The dizzy ideas that engaged Almaida and Mochles ran through their minds with great rapidity; and if you would think of it for a moment, you would see that those things which Amanzei has taken a quarter of an hour to tell us would not delay their actions more than a couple of minutes."

"Well then," the Sultan replied, "the storyteller must be an ass who takes so long to say what his people thought so quickly."

"I should be glad," she answered, "to see you do as much for us."

"I have good reasons for thinking that I should acquit myself very well," he said. "But I should do even better; for what I found so hard to describe I should make no bones about leaving out."

"The thoughts in which Mochles was floundering, his desires, the efforts he made to smother them, the pleasure it gave him to indulge them, made him look so serious and distracted that at last Almaida judged it proper to ask him what ailed him to be silent so long.

" 'I fear,' she added, 'you are giving way to gloomy thoughts.'

" 'You are right,' he exclaimed. 'And they arise from the story you have just told me.'

"Almaida seemed astonished to hear this.

" 'Do not be surprised,' he continued. 'And do not be unduly shocked at what I am going to tell you, extraordinary as the words may seem in my mouth. I am deeply grieved that the rash coxcomb who had so little regard for you did not have time to consummate his outrage.'

" 'Ah, Mochles!' she cried out, 'Why? why?'

" 'Because,' he answered, 'you would then be in a position to calm the doubts that have tortured me for so long, and which you have stirred to the depths in me, and which our common inexperience will never alleviate, for you will not be able to answer my questions, and it would be too dangerous for me to put them to any person other than yourself. My curiosity wanders over things that are strange and unnatural to a man of my character and known convictions, and unless others knew me as well as you do, they would not fail to fasten discreditable motives upon me.'

" 'But surely,' she said, 'you can tell me everything without the slightest risk of that.'

" 'It is just that,' he went on, 'which nearly makes me wish that you were more informed; for having as much confidence in me as I have in you, you would certainly hide nothing from me. Even if I had doubted your friendship, and how far you trusted my discretion, I should have been convinced by the frankness with which you have confessed your most intimate feelings to me.'

" 'At least let me know what troubles you,' she answered. 'Perhaps by dint of reasoning we shall discover –'

" 'No, no!' he interrupted. 'It would only be guesswork; and the question that troubles me is of the kind that demands the utmost certainty. Without alarming you further, I will tell you what it is, and you will tell me whether, thinking as I do, I ought to be satisfied with such profound ignorance upon a capital point. Moreover, your interests and mine are the same in this, since, seeing how virtuous you are, you must be tormented by exactly the same doubts as I am.'

" 'You frighten me,' Almaida told him. 'I implore you to speak.'

" 'Well,' he said, 'I think it may be possible that we deserve very little credit for having never strayed from the path.'

" 'Can that be!' she cried, nettled that the conversation should take so serious a turn.

" 'No doubt of it,' he pursued. 'And I will convince you. You, yourself, have never known the pleasures of love (for, whatever you may think, there can be no doubt that what happened to you with that young man can have given you only a very poor idea of them); and as for me, I have always shunned them. Can we argue from that that we are so perfect? But, you say, we have had desires, and have vanquished them. Is that so glorious a victory? Did we know what it was that we desired? Can we be quite sure that we felt those desires? No! Our pride has imposed upon us: what we took for the most burning desires, were, no doubt, very trifling temptations. It may well be that sheer ignorance misguided us – Heaven be praised were it so! But if it be true (as I greatly fear) that the mere wish to magnify our victories, or even to think we had won any at all, has deceived us on this point, in what a culpable error have we not passed our lives! We have flattered ourselves with being virtuous, while we were perhaps more imperfect than those we dared censure, and thus our vanity may have given us one more vice than it gave them.'

" 'That,' Almaida said, 'is a very true and very distressing thought.'

" 'It is not merely from today that it tortures me,' he resumed sadly. 'All the more that, to cure me of my doubts, I see but one way, which, simple as it is, is no less dangerous for being so.'

" 'Yet tell me what it is,' she begged him. 'For as I am in exactly the same state as you, I am intensely anxious to hear what your idea is.'

" 'It is only because I know you as well as I do,' he replied, 'that I am not afraid to tell you. You and I think ourselves chaste; but, as I told you just now, we do not really know what this implies, and I will convince you of it. In what does virtue consist? In denying ourselves the things that most delight the senses. And who can tell which things most delight the senses? Why, he who has tried them all. If to enjoy pleasure is the only way of getting to know what it is, he who has not experienced it cannot know. What then can it be that he denies himself? Nothing – a chimera; for what other name can we give to desires for a vague, unknown something? And if, since we grant that the only value of self-denial lies in its difficulty, what virtue can there be in denying oneself an idea? But having abandoned oneself to pleasures and finding them delicious, then to renounce them, then to immolate oneself, there is the great, the only, the true virtue, which neither you nor I can boast of possessing.'

" 'I see it only too clearly,' Almaida said. 'It is manifest that we have nothing to boast of.'

" 'Yet we have done so,' Mochles went on rapidly, fearing that, if he gave Almaida time to consider, she would see through his false reasoning. 'We have presumed to think so, and at that moment we have been guilty of pride. I am very glad,' he continued, 'and I heartily congratulate you for seeing that so long as one is not in a position to compare virtue and vice, one can have no adequate notion of either. Besides (for this evil, great as it is, is not the only one), we are forever plagued by the desire to find out what we obstinately determine not to. The soul, absorbed in spite of itself by this curiosity, surely neglects its other duties on account of it; a prey to frequent distractions, it wastes time reasoning, illuminating, pursuing, analyzing, searching deeply into its conceptions – time that, without this tormenting, obsessive notion, it would spend solely in the practice of virtue. If the soul knew what to think of what it wishes to know, it would be more tranquil, nearer perfection: it follows, therefore, that we ought to know vice, both for the sake of more calmly pursuing virtue, and of being sure of our own.'

"Although Almaida was in such a state as hardly to be able to grasp the argument that, in proving the necessity for pleasure, delivered her from the terrors of remorse, this sophism made her shudder; for a few moments she remained dumbfounded, but the desire she had, either to be enlightened as to the mysteries of love, or to bathe in them once more, carried the day against her fears, and in the end she seemed to be more pleased than frightened at what she heard.

" 'You believe then,' she asked him, in a voice that trembled, 'that we should be the more perfect for it?'

" 'Upon my honor,' he declared, 'I have no doubt of it. For I pray you, consider the position we are in, and tell me if there is a more deplorable one.'

" 'I see it only too plainly,' she said. 'It is truly appalling.'

" 'In the first place,' he went on, 'we do not even know if we are virtuous; a sad state for people who think as we do. This doubt, bitter as it is, is not the only misfortune consequent upon our situation. It is only too certain that, satisfied with our self-imposed privation, there are a thousand things, even more essential perhaps, we have considered ourselves exempt from having to study; in consequence, sheltered by a virtue that may well be imaginary, we have committed real crimes or (and this, though not of the same importance, nevertheless has considerable drawbacks) we have omitted to perform good deeds. Finally, supposing even that we were what we have hitherto believed ourselves to be, I would still distrust a virtue that we have chosen, and would not believe there was much merit in possessing it. Let a man have his choice of burdens, and it is certain that he will shoulder the lighter of the two.'

" 'I see,' she said with a sigh. 'You mean that we have done the same thing. How many scruples you arouse in my breast!' she went on, casting down her eyes. 'And how can one not be tortured by them when the only means to rid oneself of them arouses as many more?'

" 'The means,' he took up rapidly, 'is really less to be feared than one thinks. Let me suppose (and would to Heaven that I had not to suppose it!) that, weary of uncertainty, feeling, in fact, that it is our duty to dispel it, we desired to experience pleasure and judge of its charms for ourselves: what danger would there be, in this trial, of our not being able to wrest ourselves from it once we have experienced it? For feeble souls, I grant, there might be a risk; but it seems to me that, without too great presumption, we can rely upon ourselves a little. If, to hide nothing from you, if, as I imagine, this pleasure is less entrancing than it is said to be, it will give us no pain to do without a thing that, rightly or wrongly, one gains so much glory in depriving oneself of. If, on the other hand, it is as profoundly disturbing to the soul as we are assured it is, how much greater joy shall we get from our privations in knowing how truly virtuous they are!'

"This reasoning, which would no doubt have revolted Almaida had she been more in possession of herself, had on a soul that only waited for the shadow of an excuse to succumb, all the effect the wretched Mochles had hoped. After she had gazed on him for a while with troubled and irresolute eyes, she said to him: 'I feel the necessity for this experiment as much as you do. But with whom could we safely carry it out?'

"As she said this, she leaned languidly over toward Mochles, who had little by little come so close to her that by now he held her in his arms.

" 'I believe,' he answered her, 'that if we wanted to try it, it would have to be between ourselves: we are sure of each other, and as we can have no doubt that it is only in the quest for chastity that we decide upon an action that seems to be injurious to it, we are sure that we shall not make a habit of an instinct of curiosity which springs from such laudable principles. Indeed, whichever way it may turn out, we shall gain from it, since at least the memory of our fall will save us from sinful pride.'

"Although Almaida did not answer, she still seemed to waver; Mochles, who wished at any price to bring her over, proposed to her, to conclude the conquest, to make this experiment only by degrees, so that then, he said, they could desist if in their first approaches they found enough rapture to determine their doubts. She consented. Soon they were in full stream, and, sharpening their desires by actions, which though gracelessly and awkwardly performed, inflamed their senses nonetheless for that, they soon forgot the bargain they had struck. Both of them, finding perhaps too much, perhaps too little account in what they felt, either thought it proper to proceed, or could not stop, and then..."

"And then you straightaway became something else?" the Sultan interrupted.

"No, Sire," Amanzei answered.

"Then I don't understand at all," Shah Baham went on. "And I know why: the thing is incomprehensible, for it is obvious that they were everything your Brahma required."

"I thought at first just as your incontrovertible Majesty does," Amanzei replied. "Yet of necessity one of them must have deluded the other."

"I imagine that you were terribly vexed," the Sultan answered. "And tell me, which of the two did you suspect most?"

"Almaida's story," Amanzei replied, "made me very doubtful of her; and the ignorance she affected when she gave herself to Mochles, though absolute, did not prevent me from thinking that in telling her story she had suppressed the circumstance that held me prisoner still."

"Indeed! Women!" the Sultan cried. "Oh yes, your notion is the right one. Well, I did not say anything, but I would have laid odds that she did not tell the whole story: if I had boasted about it, there are plenty of people here who would have accused me of trying to be a cynical wit. There there now, take my word: it was she who prevented your release."

"Very probable as it is," Amanzei answered, "there are certain difficulties. Mochles, for a man hitherto so irreproachable, did not seem to me to lack experience."

"That alters the case," the Sultan said; "for...Oh yes! Now it is quite plain: it was he."

"But do at least make up your minds," the Sultana said. "It was she! It was he! Why not, without all this pother, believe that both of them were liars?"

"You are right," the Sultan answered. "Strictly speaking, it might be so; all the same, I think it would be more amusing if it were one or the other. I cannot tell why, but I should prefer it that way. At any rate, let us hear what they said afterward: that is the most interesting point now."

"Mochles was the first to recover from his delirium; he seemed astonished at first to find himself in Almaida's arms, and, as his mind asserted itself by degrees, horror followed astonishment: he did not seem able to grasp what he saw; he tried to doubt his eyes, and to beguile himself into thinking that only a dream could show him so cruel a sight. At last, only too convinced of his misfortune, he sadly turned his glance within himself, and going back step by step over all he had done to seduce Almaida, remembering how his criminal passion had blinded her and with what art he had gradually corrupted her, he fell into the most woeful despondency.

"Almaida at last opened her eyes also, but, still under the sweet influence, did not see things so clearly as Mochles. At first she was bewildered rather than afflicted; at length, either the despair she saw written upon him made her aware of her fall or she realized of her own accord all that she had to reproach herself with; she burst into tears and wailed out:

"'Oh, Mochles! You have undone me!'

"Mochles admitted to it: he accused himself of having seduced her, lamented over her, tried to comfort her, and spoke to her, as a man really humiliated might do, of the danger of trusting oneself too far. At last, having said all that the deepest sorrow and the most sincere repentance can prompt, without daring to look at her, he took leave of her forever.

"Left to herself, Almaida was as much ashamed and upset as he: she spent the whole night weeping and blaming herself for everything, down to the last reproach she had uttered against Mochles, finding that there was too much of vanity in it. The next day, Mochles shut himself up in the most austere seclusion..."

"That settles it, to my mind," the Sultan interrupted. "It was not he."

"And Almaida," Amanzei continued, "as inconsolable as ever, followed his example a few days later."

"Well, that puts me out," the Sultan took up again. "Then it could not have been she. I never came across a more puzzling question in my life, and let him who can unravel it."

CHAPTER X

In Which, Among Other Things, You Will Find a Way of Killing Time

"Whatever taste for morality I may have acquired by living at Almaida's, I was beginning to be sick of it by the time Mochles seduced her. Another day of it, and I should have left, in the belief that there were in Agra at least two women not amenable to love. Luckily, my patience saved me from that error.

"After leaving Almaida, I wandered aimlessly for a long time; absurdities or vice of a kind already known to me holding small prospect of pleasure for me, I was careful to avoid all houses that seemed decent and regular. My ramblings led me into a suburb of Agra full of very ornate houses, and the one I fixed upon belonged to a young lord who did not live there, but sometimes came there *incognito*.

"The day after I had settled there, I saw a lady mysteriously arrive toward evening whom, from her splendor and still more from her aristocratic air, I took to be a woman of the highest rank. My eyes were dazzled by her charms; with still more radiance than Phenima, she had the same modesty and so sweet a face that I could not look at her without being keenly interested in her. From the way in which she entered the boudoir where I was, it seemed as though she were confounded at the step she was taking; she trembled as she spoke to the slave who showed her in, and, without daring to raise her eyes, she came to sit upon me in a pensive muse, but all so languorously that it was not difficult to guess what emotion it was that occupied her thoughts.

"Scarcely was she left alone with her cogitations, which were of the saddest, than she sighed two or three times, and tears welled in her lovely eyes. Nevertheless, her sorrow seemed tender rather than painful, and she seemed to weep less at misfortune than from the fear of it. She had hardly dried her tears when a handsome young man, superbly dressed, came dashing into the room with a song upon his lips. His appearance completed her confusion; she blushed and, turning her eyes from him and hiding her face, she tried to conceal her turmoil from him.

"As for him, he came toward her in the least sympathetic but most rakish manner, and, throwing himself on his knees, cried, 'Ah, Zephis! Do my eyes tell me true? Can it really be Zephis whom I see here? Is it you, you whom I adore, and whom I barely dared hope to see here? What? Is it you I at last hold in my arms?'

" 'Yes,' she answered sighing, 'it is I, who ought never to have come here. It is I, dying of shame at being here, but who yet was not afraid to come.'

" 'How dear you make this secluded spot to me!' he cried, kissing her hand.

" 'Ah!' she replied, 'and how much regret may it not cost me someday! The proofs of frailty which I hereby give you will become the bitterer to me as they fade from your mind, as fade they will, Mazulhim; or, if you sometimes remember them, it will only be to despise me for what I have done for your sake.'

" 'What nonsense!' he answered banteringly. 'How can a person so beautiful as you think such fantastic things? Do you know that I have really never loved anyone as tenderly as I love you? And yet you doubt my feelings!'

" 'No,' she sorrowfully replied, 'I have not even the pleasure of doubting: I know that you can love neither long nor faithfully. I doubt even if you know what love is. Nevertheless, I love you, I have told you so, and I have come to this place to tell you so again. I feel the whole extent of my weakness; I pity myself for it, I see all the consequences, and yet I yield to it. My reason makes me see all I have to fear: my love makes me defy all danger.'

" 'But truly,' he answered, 'do you know that you do me a mortal injury in not believing in my affection for you?'

" 'Ah, Mazulhim!' she cried. 'Is it thus that you feel all that I am sacrificing for you? Is it thus that you reassure my trembling heart? I love you, Mazulhim; if you knew me better you would be sure of it. This heart that adores you has never (and you cannot but know it) belonged to anyone but you. Tell me that you wish it always! If you knew how much I need to think you love me, you would not refuse to tell me you do, if only out of humanity. My happiness now depends upon you only; to see you and to love you always is my only felicity and my only wish. Can it be true that you are incapable of feeling for me what I feel for you?'

" 'Ah!' he cried, 'I protest . . .'

" 'Mazulhim,' she interrupted, 'leave your justifications to me: I shall manage them better than you, and I am more eager to believe you love me than you are to persuade me of it.'

"'I swear to you, Madam,' he said in a voice that was solemn rather than moved, 'I did not think that in the six months I have tried to mark my affection for you I had so little succeeded. I know, of course, that a great love such as I have been fortunate enough to inspire in you is never without a bit of mistrust: if that which you show for me hurt only me,' he added, folding her in his arms, 'I would complain much less of it, and my delight at discovering how delicate you are would make me forget how unjust you are; but it is your own serenity that is in question here, and, if you knew my feelings better, you would have no difficulty in believing that it is infinitely more precious to me than my own.'

"As he finished these remarks, he tried to take the tenderest liberties with Zephis, but she checked him so sincerely that he could not think that with her it was merely that formal coyness of which nobody takes any notice nowadays. He looked at her in astonishment.

"'What! Zephis, is that the way you show your affection for me?' he asked her. 'Was I to expect such coldness?'

"'Mazulhim,' she answered weeping, 'please listen to me! I did not come here without knowing what I was to expect, and you would see me shed fewer tears if I had not made up my mind to give myself to you. I love you, and were I to follow only the dictates of my heart, I should be in your arms now. But, Mazulhim, there is time enough, and we have not yet been committed to each other so long that you ought to have to hide your feelings from me. At any time I should be crushed to hear that you did not love me, but think how much I should have to reproach you with, think what a state I should be in, if I discovered it only after my frailty had left you nothing more to wish for! Urged on by the desire to please, accustomed to fickleness by the successes that no one denies you have had, you only want to conquer, not to love me. Perhaps you laid siege to me without having the least passion? Inquire well of your heart: you are the master of my fate, and I do not deserve your making it a miserable one. If anything less than the most heartfelt love draws you to me; if, in a word, you do not love me as I love you, do not be afraid to tell me so. I should not blush to be the prize of love, but I should die of sorrow and shame if I thought I was merely the object of a whim.'

"Although neither these words nor the tears that accompanied them had the least effect on Mazulhim's heart, they made him speak to her less indifferently than he had before.

"'How your fears move my heart!' he said. 'But how little I deserve to have been their cause! Can you possibly imagine that I see no difference between you and those despicable wretches who, until today, have alone seemed to engross me? I confess that my way of living may have given ground for your suspicions; but, Zephis, would you really have wished me to add to the absurdity of spending my idle hours with these women, the shame of loving them? It is true that I have dreaded love; well, how could I have laid better plans to escape it forever than by living with women without morals or principles, who, even while they seduced me by their attractions, saved me from love by their natures? I am, you say, accustomed to fickleness by success. Do you think so meanly of me as to suppose I was proud of any of my victories once I had seen you? There is not a single one of these victories of which you think me so vain that has not inwardly revolted me. There is not one, in fact, that I would not give my blood not to have won, since they make me less worthy of you.'

"At this, Zephis seemed a good deal comforted, and stretched out her hand to Mazulhim, gazing at him with her glorious eyes full of the tender and touching expression that love alone can give.

"'Indeed, Zephis,' Mazulhim went on, 'I love you; oh, how dearly! How glad I am to feel, seated at your knees, that even in the midst of the most ardent transports it was not really love that I experienced. How blessed it is for me to know this, and to know it through you. Without your charms, without your virtues, I may say, I would always, no doubt, have missed that feeling to which, until I met you, I refused to yield. It is to you alone that I owe it, it is for you alone that I want to be filled with it forever.'

"'Ah, Mazulhim!' she cried. 'How happy we should be if you really believed what you say! If you really love me now, you will always love me.'

"In saying this she bent over Mazulhim, and, taking him gently in her arms, brought her head near his. Her eyes swam in tender exaltation, and soon Mazulhim, by his passionate response, penetrated her very soul. Gods! What eyes she had when he had raised them to the zenith of confusion! I had never seen any like them, save Phenima's.

"Although fully prepared to make Mazulhim the happiest of lovers, she could not see him so near his bliss without remembering her fears, and perhaps her virtue also.

"'You have no doubts as to my love for you,' she said, offering but the slightest resistance to him, 'but can you not...'

"'Ah, Zephis!' he broke out, 'Zephis! Can you still be afraid of giving me a proof of your affection for me?'

"Zephis sighed, and answered nothing. Overcome rather by her love than persuaded of his, she yielded at last to his desires. Too happy Mazulhim! What charms revealed themselves to his eyes, and how much the shyness of Zephis added to their worth! Indeed, Mazulhim seemed to me to be very much struck; everything astonished him; all in Zephis was the object of praise and kisses. Although, far from blaming him for being overwhelmed with an admiration that I shared with him, this procedure seemed to me, for that stage in his affairs, to drag out too long, and even to suspend, if not to obliterate, his desires.

"It is perfectly true that the more refined one is, the more one delights in trifling. Sentiment alone enjoys those tender deviations it invents, and continually varies; but to tell the truth, one cannot be content with them forever, and if one lingers over them it is less to rein in one's desires than to find new fuel to feed one's flame. For some moments I thought highly enough of Mazulhim to attribute his inaction to an excess of love, and Zephis's charms justified this notion. Most likely, Zephis thought so as well, and for longer than I did. I could not conceive how the transports of a lover, so eager to be happy, could grow more tame as they found the more to excite them. He was brisk without fire, profuse in praises, constant in admiration; but has a lover no other way to express his desires than by praises?

"Although Mazulhim concealed his difficulties with great artfulness, Zephis noticed the poor success of her charms. She seemed neither surprised nor shaken, and, turning her beautiful eyes on her lover, she said, with the softest smile: 'Get up. I am luckier than I supposed.'

"On hearing this, which seemed to him nothing less than insulting, Mazulhim made every effort, but in vain, to prove to Zephis that he did not deserve the opinion she seemed to have of him. At last, forced to admit his humiliation, he said to her in a voice that made me laugh: 'Alas, Madam! You dampened my spirits.'

"'Your distress amuses me,' Zephis answered. 'But your grief would offend me. It would hurt me too much if you thought my heart was wounded...'

"'Ah, Zephis!' Mazulhim interrupted, 'how dreadful it is to be in the wrong with you, and how difficult to excuse oneself!'

"'Take it no more to heart,' Zephis answered tenderly. 'I believe you love me, indeed I came to believe it only a moment ago, and I cannot have a better proof of your affection for me than the very thing you blame yourself for.'"

"Oh, that, as the saying goes," the Sultan remarked, "is all very fine as claptrap; but at the bottom of her heart the lady was certainly nettled. In the first place, that sort of thing is in itself disappointing, and what apparently disappoints every woman cannot possibly amuse one; or, at least you will agree, in that case she must be very fanciful. Besides, when it comes to a case of this sort, sentiment is not so great a consolation as you might think. By the way, I remember that once (I was young, egad! very young) there was a woman. I will not tell you how it came about; all the same, we were both of us...Really, I would never have suspected it; but there, all of a sudden...I hardly know how to put it. Well, then! It was in vain that I said the most loverlike things to her; the more I said, the more she blubbered. I have never seen such a thing before or since, but it was certainly very moving. Nevertheless, I told her, among other things, that one must not give up hope, that I had not done it on purpose..."

"Come, finish your heartrending tale!" the Sultana broke in.

"There's a nice thing now!" Shah Baham retorted. "*I'm* not allowed to tell a story, and in my own house, too! From that, as I was telling you, I concluded, once and for all, that there are no women who do not get a certain degree of pleasure from it. Therefore, Mazulhim's lady, who was given to saying such fine things –"

"Would have been as well pleased had she not had to say them," the Sultana put in. "That is likely; but let me tell you that what you think so grievous for a woman embarrasses her more than it grieves her."

"Ah, yes!" the Sultan went on. "For instance, I would only have to...But do not be afraid! Go on, Emir."

"However confounded Mazulhim was by his misadventure, he was still more astounded by the way Zephis took it.

" 'If,' he said, 'anything could console me for this frightful disgrace, it is seeing that it has had no effect upon your heart. How many women would hate me if they had this against me!'

" 'I confess,' Zephis answered, 'that I would perhaps do the same if I could attribute this incident to your coldness; but if, as you have told me, and as I believe, it is love alone that brings your faculties to a standstill, this adventure is only something a thousand times more flattering for me than all your raptures. I love you too much not to believe that you love me. Perhaps,' she added with a smile, 'I am also too vain to think that it is in any way my fault. But whatever the cause of my indulgence may be, it is at least true that I forgive you. I warn you of one thing more, that I would be less calm at the least hint of your unfaithfulness than at what you call a crime. Yes, Mazulhim, be true to me, and I do not care if I always find you as you are at present. What I lose in the way of what you call pleasure, shall I not find again in the certitude of your faithfulness?'

"While Zephis was speaking, Mazulhim, who would have wished to be under a lesser obligation to her spared no pains to be free of his misfortune. Zephis lent herself to his desires with a good naturedness that he likely did not appreciate inwardly, since every minute it gave him less excuse. Her complaisance became ever more sympathetic: it increased little by little. Zephis protected herself less; she granted with a better grace; her eyes glowed with a fire I had not yet seen in them; it was as though she had not until then surrendered, but had only suffered Mazulhim's ardors. That repugnance which always accompanies the first moment, which so many women act but so few feel, had passed away. Zephis was unembarrassed by Mazulhim's praises, and seemed even to wish he could give her fresh ones: the blood rushed to her cheeks, but not from modesty; her eyes no longer avoided what had at first seemed to offend them; the compassion that Mazulhim at length made her feel was boundless. Nevertheless..."

"Oh, yes," the Sultan remarked. "Nevertheless...I understand perfectly. What a rascally man! I know of nothing that, in the long run, is so insufferable as Mazulhim's procedure with Zephis. I am quite sure that she got annoyed."

"And I," the Sultana said, "am quite sure that she did not: to be annoyed at such a misfortune is to deserve it."

"Splendid!" the Sultan retorted. "Would you think a woman would make such a comment? All I am sure of is this, that in a like case I should be annoyed, and I would not think the less of myself for it, not I. At any rate, let us hear what Zephis did say; for, as far as I can see, in this, as in everything else, everyone has his own taste."

"Indulgent as she was," Amanzei went on, "it seemed to me that her lover's continued difficulties began to vex her. Either, having done more for him than the first time, she thought she deserved it less; or being now more favorably inclined herself, she found fewer arguments for bearing with it.

"Mazulhim, not so sure of his defeat as Zephis was, or perhaps used to facing down such situations, had not such deference for Zephis as he should have had, and attempted what with more policy or more politeness he would not have done. It seemed to me that she was displeased at this ordeal, less from the presumption of it than from the indignity it dared foist upon her charms.

"In spite of her agitation she gave a malignant smile, as though to let Mazulhim know that she was not a person with whom this boldness was well placed or could succeed. Certain that he would soon bring his own punishment upon him, she lent herself to his ridiculous endeavors with a courage every woman is proud to have in such a case, but which is not always justified by success. Although Mazulhim was not now in quite so pitiable a condition, he was not yet in one to be congratulated, and great as his efforts were Zephis was right not to have been afraid of them.

"From Mazulhim's astonished expression I was forced to believe that, if he was accustomed to a part of what had happened, he was not so to women who, like Zephis, would provide no resources for him in his difficulties. May I be guiltless of wishing to offend any of them; and besides, how can one tell whether it is always they who are to blame?

"However it may have been, Mazulhim's surprise was so ludicrously portrayed, and, by throwing odium on other women, so flattering to Zephis, that she could not help laughing.

" 'If you had asked me about it,' she said, 'I could have told you how it would be – but perhaps you would not have believed me.'

" 'Evidently, I would have been wrong,' he answered, 'but I could not in the least expect it to turn out so. A continuously happy experience of ten years made me suppose that what I vainly attempted with you would always give good results. Ah! Zephis,' he added, 'must I find in what ought to crown my desires only fresh food for misery?'

" 'Indeed,' she answered laughing, 'I can understand how unhappy you feel, and you must also be quite sure how much I pity you.'

" 'Zephis!' he continued in a more sincerely passionate strain than I had yet heard in him, 'only your charms are equal to my affection. Every moment increases my love and my despair, and I feel –'

" 'Come, Mazulhim!' she interrupted. 'What after all would have been the delight you so much deplore missing? No: if it be true that you love me, you are not to be pitied. A single look from me ought to make you happier than the joys you seek, if you have ever found those with another person.'

" 'Your feelings charm me, and go straight to my heart,' he said. 'But in doubling my love, they increase my regrets and my grief.'

" 'Let us waive this topic,' Zephis said, getting up.

" 'What!' he cried. 'Do you wish to leave me already? Ah! Zephis, do not leave me alone in my terrible despair.'

" 'No, Mazulhim,' she answered, 'I have promised to spend today with you. Ah! May it not seem longer to you than it does to me! But let us leave this; let us go and enjoy the delicious coolness of the evening, dissipate your melancholy, and turn your mind from things that perhaps sadden you. Mazulhim, the more we are bent on pleasure, the less we enjoy it; let us try, by being less intent on it, to be better fit for it.'

"As she ceased speaking, generous Zephis left the room, and Mazulhim gave her his hand with the utmost respect.

"What is so curious is that Mazulhim, who turned his assignations to such poor purpose, was the most sought-after man in all Agra. There was not a woman who had not been, or who did not wish to be, his lover. Lively, amiable, flighty, ever a deceiver, but not for that finding fewer to deceive, all the women knew him for what he was — yet all sought to find favor in his eyes. In short, his reputation was astonishing. They believed he was... what did they not believe him to be? And yet, what was he? How much did he not owe to the discretion of women, for whom he was such a bad bargain, and whom he treated so ill?

"After strolling for an hour, Zephis and he came back from the garden. I at once tried to read in their eyes whether they were happier than when they had gone out. From Mazulhim's downcast appearance, I thought not; nor was I wrong. Zephis sat down carelessly upon me, and Mazulhim sank at her feet upon the tiled floor. Having little to say to her, and being able to think of no kind of amusement he was in a position to give her, he sank into a muse, looking at her very tenderly. A little later, ashamed of the figure he was cutting before the most beautiful woman in Agra but still in consternation at his misfortunes, afraid that in trying to make up for them he would sink deeper still, he did not know how to proceed. At length he was frightened that his silence and coldness would seem to Zephis to betray indifference rather than repentance. He snatched her in his arms, and, giving her the most passionate kisses, seemed to want to lift himself by some sudden bound from the profound sluggishness in which he was sunk. At first Zephis seemed to deliberate whether she would lend herself to Mazulhim's fresh enterprise. If her sympathy prompted her to grant him everything, this same sympathy made her realize with sorrow that she was never more cruel to Mazulhim than when she refused him nothing. Did he really want to succeed, or did he know her so little as to suppose that she would be hurt if he did not try to? Finally, was it love or vanity that urged him to this renewal?

"While she was thinking this over, Mazulhim (either because he was merely trying to extricate himself from a position that vexed him, or, being adept in the little fripperies of love, he wanted to save Zephis from tedium) thought he would resort to those nothings which are charming at the beginning or the end of a conversation, but which, on account of their frivolity, cannot be a substitute for it. At first, Zephis refused to be a party to them; but, believing in the extreme eagerness with which Mazulhim asked for her indulgence, she consented out of pure generosity, and with a shrug of her shoulders at what he thought so highly of, and from which, to do him justice, she expected far less result than he did.

"Her prolonged inattention, to use a mild word, far from annoying Mazulhim, spurred him to still greater exertions, and being most proficient in the trifling things of love, he forced her to take notice; from notice he brought her to interest. The unreality of what he offered her gradually effaced itself from her mind; she even furthered the illusion he fabricated for her, and in the end found out how much the pleasures depend on the imagination, and how trivial a thing nature would be without it.

"To crown their bliss, that which Mazulhim had looked on rather as a kind of compensation he owed Zephis than as a help for himself, had a stronger effect on him than he had hoped for. The charms of Zephis, more moving than ever, made him feel the emotion he had until then so fruitlessly sought, and, in the sweet confusion that began to suffuse his senses, having forgotten his woe or being incited rather than depressed by it, he at last overcame all those bitter obstacles which had hitherto so cruelly impeded him."

"I see. Well done," the Sultan cried. "Better late than never; that is to say..."

"Do not go and explain that to us," the Sultana interrupted. "You must realize that Amanzei has had the discretion, or the subtlety, to leave us something to guess at."

"I know nothing about it," the Sultan went on. "That sort of thing is not my business; but, you see, the fact is, and you know as well as I do, that this fellow Mazulhim was a little liable to accidents, and it seems to me quite natural to ask...because, maybe, perhaps...Anyhow, clear it up a little: Mazulhim...?"

"Sire, he was in luck's way; but he was better qualified to offend than to atone for offenses he had given, and I doubt whether his petty reparation would have won him forgiveness if he had had to do with anyone less generous than Zephis. Imbued with vanity rather than with love, he seemed to me to care less for the pleasure of possessing Zephis than for the relief it gave him to have less to blush for in her presence. They entered upon a tender conversation wherein Zephis displayed a deal of feeling, and Mazulhim uttered a great deal of flummery.

"A little later they were served a supper that was the epitome of refinement and taste. Zephis, made ever gayer by her lover's presence, said a thousand delicate and passionate things to him, which made me admire her mind as much as her heart. Although he was himself astonished at so much charm, it did not have so much effect upon him as it did upon me, and it seemed to me that his pride was more elated by his conquest of Zephis than his heart was touched by the ardent yet delicate passion she felt for him, and which, in spite of her fears of his fickleness, filled her completely.

"If the possession of Zephis had not inspired as much love in him as it ought to have done, at least it had made him more lively. His heart, incapable of real feeling, still repined: all Zephis's virtues, which the ungrateful brute praised without appreciating, and perhaps without believing in, far from attaching him to her, seemed to distance and constrict him. I could not see that he was ever in the least touched by the true and tender love she had for him, but she began to stir his desires. He looked at her rapturously; he sighed; he spoke to her passionately of the delight she had given him, and seemed to await the end of supper with much impatience. He even said as much; but perhaps she did not care as much as he did about the prospects following supper and was less impatient. Nevertheless, she loved him; soon he entreated her... Ah! Mazulhim, how happy you would have been if you had known how to love!

"A little later Zephis went away, and Mazulhim followed her, loud in protestations of love and gratitude, which I believed the less sincere as they were the more deserved. Zephis was too good for him to be faithfully attached to her: she was sincere without pretense or coquetry; Mazulhim was her first affair; but what would have constituted happiness for any other man was for that corrupt heart but a bond in which he found neither pleasure nor diversion. All he needed were those women who, born without feeling or shame, have a thousand adventures without having a single lover, and whose indecency would make one suppose that they seek dishonor rather than delight. It is not to be wondered at that Mazulhim, who was nothing more than a fatuous ass, appealed to women of this stamp, and that he, in his turn, sought them out."

"But, Amanzei," the Sultana asked, "how could such a worthless fellow have appealed to such an excellent creature as you have made Zephis out to be?"

"If your Majesty will please to remember the portrait I painted of Mazulhim," Amanzei answered, "you will be less astonished that Zephis should have found him attractive. He had some pleasing qualities, and could wear the garb of excellence. Besides, Zephis was not the first superior woman to be unlucky enough to fall in love with a coxcomb, and your Majesty is well aware that such things are seen every day."

"Not a doubt of it," the Sultan said. "I should think so indeed; he is quite right; one sees it every day. Now, don't go and ask me why, for I know nothing about it."

"In any case, I am not asking you," the Sultana continued. "There are some things which it seems to me quite simple that you should not know, in spite of your keen wits. For a sensible woman," she went on, "to return an equally tender and constant love, and sure of the feelings and honesty of a man who loves her (if we grant that anything can ever make her sure) should finally surrender to him, that does not surprise me. But that she should be capable of frailty for the sake of a Mazulhim, that I can by no means understand."

"Love," Amanzei answered, "would not be what it is, if..."

"If, if!" the Sultan broke in. "How much longer are you going on with your silly subtleties? And have you forgotten that I have put a ban on disquisitions? What does it matter to you, I ask, that this Zephis woman loved that Mazulhim fellow, or that the one was a ninny and the other a coxcomb? There it is. She loved him such as he was. You want to know why? Why did you not ask Amanzei while he was a woman? Do you imagine that he remembers that now? Not he! In any case, you, with all your discourses, are the reason why the stories I am told drag on so — and that infuriates me. Come, Emir, where were you? What became of this Zephis, who is so sensible that I am sick of her? How did all this end?"

"As it was bound to," Amanzei proceeded. "Mazulhim, not wanting at first to be entirely lacking in consideration for Zephis, deceived her as secretly as possible. But either he was not artful enough to deceive her for long, or his infidelties were too public and too frequent for him to hide them forever. Whichever it was, she complained; but, as she had all the blindness as well as all the delicacy of the most whole-hearted love, he soothed her easily. He continued to deceive her, and she reproached him again. At last he could bear it no longer, and, un-moved by either her love or her tears, he broke with her completely, and left her with the shame of having loved him, and the emptiness of having lost him."

"Upon my word," the Sultan said, "he was quite right to leave her; and the proof is that I should have done the same myself! I know that she was very lovely, that she had every merit; but it is just that merit which would have wearied me — I who want above all to be amused. It is not, of course, that I am a Mazulhim; no one, I think, can bring that against me. But in any event it is very agreeable to break with women, if only to hear what they have to say about it."

CHAPTER XI

Which Contains a Recipe Against Enchantments

"Three days after I had seen Zephis for the first time, Mazulhim arrived alone. He hardly had time to give a few orders before a little woman, whose bearing was lively, indecorous, giddy, and yet affected, came into the boudoir. At a distance she had a certain radiant beauty, but up close offered a very middling face, which without its quaintness, its poutings and pursings, and the prodigious vivacity that its owner put on, one simply would not have looked at twice. Indeed, this was the only thing that had made Mazulhim wish to have her.

"'Ah!' he cried as she appeared, 'it's you! Do you know, it is divine of you to come so soon?'

"This beauty, who, in spite of her childish mannerisms, came toward Mazulhim with that noble impropriety which was almost her only grace, and, without answering him, and hardly even looking at him, she said: 'You were right when you told me your little retreat was pretty; really now, it is charming, furnished so tastefully, with everything so luxuriously soft. It is delicious.'

"'Is it not true,' he answered, 'that it is the prettiest in the whole quarter?'

"'From that remark,' she replied, 'one would think that I was familiar with a great many. This boudoir is delightful,' she went on, 'just made for love.'

"'I am charmed to see you in it,' he said. 'And charmed that you should like it.'

"'Oh, as to that,' she answered, 'no doubt I did not make as much to-do about coming here as I should have done; naturally I know as well as anybody how to be difficult and decent in an affair; but...'

"'You do not exercise all your knowledge,' he struck in. 'Oh, everybody gives you credit for that.'

"'That at any rate is true, perfectly true,' she took up. 'I am above pretense. Yesterday, when you told me that you loved me, and suggested that I should come here... I was, I may tell you, very much inclined to say no, but my honesty would not let me: I am frank, natural, you attract me, so here I am. Perhaps you do not think any the worse of me for it?'

"'Who, I?' he answered, shrugging his shoulders. 'What an idea! I would think a thousand times better of you for it, if that were possible.'

"'Really, you are delightful,' she said. 'But tell me, have you been waiting long?'

" 'I had just this moment come,' he replied. 'And I blush for it: I am most upset. You must have thought you had arrived first.'

" 'That would have been a nice thing,' she said. 'And I would certainly not have failed to be duly grateful.'

" 'You know very well,' he answered, 'that people do not do that sort of thing on purpose, yet it can happen even to the best-intentioned people.'

" 'Yes, yes,' she replied, 'I can see that, but all the same I would not care for it. But listen, I have some news for you. Zobeida has this very minute left Areb Kham.'

" 'Is that all she has done to him?' he asked.

" 'And Sophia,' she pursued, 'has just taken Dara.'

" 'And no one besides?' he asked again.

"While she was speaking, Mazulhim, who knew the sort of person she was far too well to have any respect for her, took the greatest liberties. Far from her seeming more moved by this than he, her eyes wandered disinterestedly round the room, until, looking at her watch, she said to him, 'But how silly we are being, Mazulhim. Shall we be by ourselves all day?'

" 'What a question!' he answered. 'Of course we are to be by ourselves!'

" 'Really? I did not expect that,' she replied. 'Oh, do leave off!' she added, without in the least wishing him to, or, for that matter, minding whether he went on (and so he took no notice). 'You are really too silly for words; and what is the object of our being by ourselves, please?'

" 'It seems to me,' Mazulhim answered coldly, and not prevented from amusing himself by this conversation, 'that we were agreed upon that.'

" 'Agreed?' she said. 'What a story! Where did you get hold of that? I'll swear I did not say a word about it: in any case, it is all the same to me, and I shall be able to keep you in order. Oh! Leave off already! You have very queer ways...'

" 'Not so much as all that; it seems to me that I am no queerer than other folk. Besides, seeing that we are by ourselves, I do not think I am overstepping the bounds. Oh, Zulica,' he added, 'your taste is so good; tell me, what do you think of my ceiling?'

" 'I was just considering it,' she said. 'I would like less gilt on it. Still, as it is, I think it very fine,' she added, sitting on his knees, which, as far as I could see, did not at all disturb him. 'Now that I think of it,' she continued, 'I must be out of my senses to believe that you will be true to me, you who have never yet been so to anyone.'

" 'Ah, do not let us speak of that,' he answered, still busying himself, and (thanks to Zulica's kindness) very commodiously. 'You might,

I fancy, be not a little inconvenienced if I turned out to be a more constant man than you took me for.'

" 'Will you not let me be!' she said, without stirring a finger either
to escape from or to hinder him. 'As far as trustworthiness goes,' she
went on, as calmly as though he were not proceeding, 'that is a part of
my nature.'

" 'Nowadays constancy is no merit, it is so common,' he answered.
'And it is not even boasting to say one is capable of it. Nevertheless,
you have sometimes, however much you may pride yourself on it,
changed your...'

" 'Not often, do not think it!'

" 'But I know, and you know that I know, who your lovers have been,'
he answered.

" 'Very well,' she said, 'in that case you will admit that I might easily have had more if I had wanted to. But do be quiet! How you torment me!'

" 'Much less than I ought.'

" 'Anyhow,' she retorted, 'it is more than I like.'

" 'What?' he asked her. 'Do you not love me? Come, no shilly-
shallying! Did we not settle everything?'

" 'Well, but...ah, Mazulhim! I cannot abide you! This is a story!' she
replied. 'This is impossible!'

"Thereupon he placed her gently upon me.

" 'I assure you, Mazulhim,' she said as she settled herself down, 'that
I am furious with you; and I tell you I shall never forgive you.'

"In spite of Zulica's terrible threats, Mazulhim tried to complete her
displeasure. But as, among other things, he had the bad habit of never
waiting for himself, and she, apparently had that of waiting for nobody,
he did, as a matter of fact, displease her beyond description. However,
in spite of her anger, she waited, her vanity making her suspend her
judgment. In all her previous experience (which had certainly been large
and varied) she had never been failed, and this, to her, was incontrovertible proof of her value. Moreover, this Mazulhim, whom she found
so little deserving of praise, was, according to popular report, capable
of the most wonderful feats. If (as seemed to be sufficiently attested)
she had nothing to reproach herself with, by what freak of fortune was
Mazulhim, who had never been in the wrong with anyone, so strangely
in the wrong with her? She had heard everyone say that she was charming; and Mazulhim's reputation was too good for him not to deserve it
in one way or another; and so, this state of things, which was giving
her so much to think about, was unnatural, and could not last.

"With these consolatory notions, and going over in her mind from hearsay to hearsay, Zulica armed herself with patience, and dissembled her scorn as well as she could. Mazulhim, meanwhile, discoursed in a most loverlike manner on those beauties which seemed to affect him so little. For him to be as he was, he said, all the sorcerers of India must surely have been at work against him. 'But,' he continued, 'what strength have their charms against yours, Zulica? They have delayed the power, they cannot prevent it.'

"Zulica, more angry than Mazulhim was bothered, answered all this only by wicked little smiles, into which, however, for fear of depressing him altogether, she did not put all the expression she would have liked to.

" 'Have you,' she asked banteringly, 'been mixing yourself up with sorcerers? I should advise you to get on good terms with them again; people who can play such tricks are dangerous enemies to have.'

" 'They would be less formidable if you were more inclined to give them the lie,' he answered. 'And I believe also that, in spite of their ill will, if I loved you less ardently, I would have felt...'

" 'Oh, that argument you are dishing me up now,' she interrupted, 'is one in which I believe very little,' for having decided within herself how long a man might remain spellbound, she thought that by this time she had allowed him respite enough.

" 'I am very well aware,' he replied, 'that if you judge me strictly you cannot be pleased with me; but the less so you are, the more you ought to try to put an end to my misfortune.'

" 'I do not think,' she retorted, 'that that would be quite proper.'

" 'I thought you less of a slave to decorum,' he went on in a scoffing voice. 'And I dared hope...'

" 'Truly, your time for joking is happily chosen,' she interrupted. 'You are right; nothing can show you to greater advantage than this adventure!'

" 'But, Zulica,' he pursued, 'will you never realize that the tone you are adopting is just the very one to do me harm, and perpetuate my humiliation?'

" 'I assure you,' she said, 'that is the last thing I care about.'

" 'But,' he asked her, 'if you care about it so little, why are you so angry?'

" 'Allow me to tell you, sir, that that this is a very stupid question.' Thereupon she got up, in spite of all his attempts to retain her.

" 'Leave me alone,' she said acidly. 'I want neither to see nor to hear you.'

" 'Truly,' he cried, 'I have seen women as unhappy as this, but never so infuriated.'

"This exclamation of Mazulhim did not please Zulica: greatly irritated by the accident that had happened to her, vexed beyond measure at Mazulhim's frigid bearing, she vented her rage on a large china vase that she found to hand, and smashed it into atoms.

" 'Alas! Madam,' Mazulhim said smiling, 'you would have found nothing here to break if all the ladies who have been discontented with me had avenged themselves in the same way; however,' he added, seating himself upon me, 'I pray you not restrain yourself.' "

"There now," Shah Baham said, "that's a woman after my own heart: she has feelings, and is not like your Zephis, who took everything as it came, and who, besides, was the silliest piece of preciosity I have ever come across in my life! Now this one interests me very much, and I recommend her to you, Amanzei, do you see? Do not let her always be so vexatiously placed."

"Sire," Amanzei answered, "I will do all I can for her as far as my respect for truth will allow me.

"When he had finished speaking, Mazulhim fell into a dreamy and distracted state. Zulica, who had gone to sit down in a corner far from him, for some time bore well enough the scornful indifference with which he treated her, and, to pay him back, began to sing.

" 'I may be mistaken,' he said to her when she had finished, 'but I believe the song you have just sung me is such-and-such opera.'

"She did not answer.

" 'You have a pretty voice,' he went on. 'Not of a large compass, but with a lovely tone, which goes straight to the heart.'

" 'How lovely that it pleases you,' she answered, without looking at him.

" 'You may not believe it,' he went on, 'but you may really well be flattered, for few people know as much about music as I do. Another quality I find you to have – which I would enlarge upon were I at the moment so lucky that you felt me worthy to praise you – is a charming expression, which could not be bettered for its liveliness and truth, and which is so well supported by your eyes that it is impossible to hear you without being touched to the heart. You will, I suppose, say once more that it is lovely that it pleases me.'

" 'No,' she answered more gently, 'I am not angry that you should find nice things in me; and the more I know you to be a connoisseur, the more your praises are bound to please me.'

" 'That is exactly the reason that would make me wish to deserve yours,' he said.

" 'Oh, no doubt,' she remarked.

" 'Surely you are not going to say that you are not a judge of any-thing?' he went on. 'And do not be so outrageously unjust as to imagine that I am indifferent as to whether you think well or ill of me. Will you add this insult to all those you have already heaped upon me? Ah, Zulica! Can it be that what ought to increase your affection for me merely irritates you the more?'

" 'And can it also be,' she replied heatedly, 'that you think me fool enough to take as a proof of love the most hideous affront you could possibly offer me?'

" 'An affront!' he cried. 'My dearest Zulica! You know very little about love if you think that what has happened need make either of us blush. I shall make bold enough to go further: the people you have honored with your affection loved you very little if you did not find them as unfortunate as I am.'

" 'Really, sir,' she said, 'on that topic, I pray you give over – or I shall leave you. I can no longer endure the absurdity, the indecency of your remarks.'

" 'I am aware that they hurt you,' he answered. 'And I confess that I am surprised they should affect you in this way; but what I cannot reconcile myself with is that you should obstinately continue to find me guilty. I would think it quite natural for an ordinary woman, raw, and unused to good society, to be mortally offended by such an incident – but you! That you should be exactly the same as an ignoramus! Really, that is unforgivable.'

" 'Indeed!' she said. 'One must be the first of fools not to be flattered by it, and I am astonished that I should not yet have thanked you for the extraordinary impression I have made upon you.'

" 'Joking apart,' he said, beginning to rise, 'I will prove to you that I am not wrong.'

" 'No, no!' she cried. 'I forbid you to come near me.'

" 'I will obey your orders, unjust as they are, and I will prove it from a distance, since you see fit.'

" 'By all means,' she answered. 'That will certainly be more convenient for you. But let us do better: let us drop the subject, for I am not such an imbecile as ever to be persuaded that the more a man loves, the less he can show his mistress that he does.'

" 'That is to say,' he replied carelessly, 'that you believe exactly the opposite?'

" 'Yes,' she retorted, 'exactly. Nobody could be more convinced of anything than I am of this.'

"'Well then, Madam, you can boast of being the most indelicate person in the world, and, if I did not love you so much that nothing under heaven could tear me from you, I confess that your way of looking at things would separate me from you forever.'

"'It would certainly be very odd if it pleased you,' she said.

"'Oh, no,' he resumed coolly, 'I am not so interested to declare against it as you do me the honor to believe; but what has been proven since the beginning of time is that the more one loves, the less one is in possession of one's faculties, and that only to hearts of grosser mold, incapable of being pierced by the arrows of passion, does belong the ability to command them at such a moment as when you found me so unlike myself. If the hope of delight is enough to upset a lover, think what affect the approach of the happy instants he so keenly desired must produce upon him: think how his soul must have been exhausted in the raptures that precede them, and whether the disorder with which you reproach me is as disobliging to a woman of sense as that self-possession of which, no doubt thoughtlessly, you wish me to have been capable. Frankly,' he added, as if about to throw himself at her feet, 'this cannot be the first time that you –'

"'Oh, cease this fantastic jesting,' she interrupted him. 'Leave me alone. I wish to go out and never to see you again.'

"'But Zulica,' he said, leading her toward me, 'will you not realize that it seems, from the way you treat my misfortune, that you do not give yourself credit for enough charms to put a stop to it?'

"Whether Mazulhim's subtle dialectic had already disposed Zulica to mercy, or whether the great reputation he had gotten himself made his statements seem more likely, she allowed herself to be brought upon me, though she offered that slight resistance which commonly inflames rather than impedes. Little by little Mazulhim obtained more, and at last found himself placed as he had been when Zulica had got so angry.

"Soon agitated by Mazulhim's ardor, she began vehemently to wish that he would allow his faculties to be less paralyzed than at the first time; she was already hoping this was so when Mazulhim, more refined than ever, failed woefully in meeting her sweet hopes. She was all the more indignant since, vanity apart, it would then have been a pleasure to her if he had behaved otherwise."

"Oh, well!" the Sultan said, "then let him give up: this wearies me as much as it did her. Not that I have taken sides with Zulica, but I ask you if there is anyone in the whole world who would not become impatient, if even the long suffering of a dervish would stand it. Egad! He need not have taken all that trouble to make her stay. Amanzei, you promised me better than that. In the end you will make me think that you bear that woman a grudge; and I tell you outright, I should take that ill."

"Sire, I do not in the least," Amanzei answered. "If I were inventing a story for your Majesty's pleasure, it would be easy to arrange matters to your taste, but I am telling you what I saw, and I cannot, short of tampering with the truth, make Mazulhim behave otherwise than he did."

"Oh, what a dolt that Mazulhim was!" Shah Baham cried. "And how he provokes me!"

"But," the Sultana said, "I do not know why you should be so incensed against him; he did not do it on purpose any more than you did."

"Who? He?" he went on. "Faith! I'm not so sure. He was a dreadful fellow."

"Besides," the Sultana spoke once more, "this Zulica whom you like so much was one of the least –"

"I beg you, Madam," he checked her. "Think what you will of her to yourself, but tell me no ill against her. I know very well that it is enough for me to take a liking to someone for you to dislike them; and that offends me, I warn you."

"Your anger does not alarm me," the Sultana answered. "And what is more, I should not be in the least astonished if this Zulica, whom you love so much today, should give you a mortal spleen tomorrow."

"I doubt it," the Sultan retorted. "I don't tread on my own heels as you do – not I. And until that does happen, let us at any rate hear the rest of her story."

"Zulica grew red with fury at the fresh insult Mazulhim passed upon her charms.

" 'Really, sir,' she told him, pushing him violently away from her. 'If this is your way of making much of me, I suggest that it is very ill-timed.'

" 'I would be the first to say so,' he answered, 'if for a moment I could imagine that you believed you deserved my shortcomings; but I see no sign that you do, and I admit freely that I have no excuse.'

" 'Well then,' she said, 'when people know that they are made a certain way, they ought not to plague others.'

" 'I shall no doubt make up my mind thus if what has happened occurs again,' he answered. 'But you will allow me to flatter myself with contrary hopes.'

" 'Really,' she said, 'I should not advise you to do so.'

"Then she got up, took her fan, put on her gloves, and drawing forth a pot of rouge, placed herself in front of a looking glass. While she was trying with the greatest care to make herself as she had been when she first arrived, Mazulhim, coming behind her and interfering with her task, begged her tenderly not to take so much trouble over what she would certainly have to do again. At first Zulica only answered with a grimace, which should have told him what little faith she put in his prophecies; but, finding that he continued to tease her, she said:

" 'Well, sir, is this to go on forever? And do you not want me to be able to go out? You have only to say.'

" 'But as far as I can remember,' he answered, 'all has already been said on that subject. Are you not going to sup here?'

" 'Not that I know of,' she replied.

" 'You are sure,' he said with a smile, 'that you did not count on doing so?'

" 'To be brief,' she answered, 'I am engaged for supper, and it is getting late.'

" 'That's nonsense,' he remarked, throwing her upon me, and trying once more to see if he could not find the means of making the time seem shorter to her.

" 'Listen, Mazulhim!' she said to him gently. 'You may believe as you will, and I will second it ungrudgingly; but the part you are making me play is preposterous.'

" 'A little more kindness on your part would have made me less to be pitied; but you are so unbending.'

" 'Really!' she retorted. 'It would be inhuman to deprive you of the only excuse you have left.'

"He answered manfully that he would willingly take the risk.

"Then she entered upon his style of reasoning, so as to have the pleasure of putting him entirely in the wrong. The more he deserved her pity, the more indignant she felt, for she was not of a generous nature. Hurt that he should have been so unaffected by her charms, she seemed to be more so still that he responded so ill to her last favors; her vanity alone made her bear what wounded her so deeply. No sooner did she begin to congratulate herself upon success, than she saw him wilt. Twenty times she was forced to renounce a hope that seemed to offer itself only the more cruelly to disappoint her. But there! after all she had done for Mazulhim, could she leave him to his fate? Perhaps another minute would conquer his ingratitude. It would have been sweeter for her to owe everything to Mazulhim's tenderness, but it was more to her glory to snatch a stubborn victory.

"Maybe this argument which Zulica advanced was somewhat lacking in logic; but under the circumstances, it was something to have any logic at all.

"Mazulhim, who was aware from the way she looked at him that she needed support to bear the stubborn frigidity which, in spite of himself, he showed toward her, lavished encomia upon her compassionate nature.

" 'Assuredly,' she cried out in her turn, at a moment when, impatience perhaps gaining the upper hand, she was led to regard as more than ever meritorious the kindness she showed him, 'assuredly it must be admitted that I have a noble soul.'

"At this so extremely just observation Mazulhim could not help bursting out laughing, and Zulica, who knew how dangerous it sometimes is to laugh, grew very angry at him for it.

"Mazulhim's gaiety, however, was not so fatal as she had feared. The sorcerers, who until then had persecuted him so ruthlessly, began even to withdraw their malign spells from him. Although much was still needed to make the victory he was gaining over them complete, she did not refrain from congratulating herself aloud. It was not that, with her enlightenment, she was deceiving herself; rather, she wanted to fortify Mazulhim with a show of confidence in him: she knew him very ill to suppose he needed it.

"Mazulhim, who was the best man in the world for taking advantage of anything, no sooner felt himself less prostrated than he carried temerity to the point of believing himself capable of the boldest undertakings. Whatever Zulica, who was in a position to judge in a more balanced way, might say, she could not dissuade him. Whether he imagined he could not delay without being lost, or whether (which is more likely) he thought he need explain nothing more to her, he began to try what had only once failed him, and that by the merest accident. Zulica, who was not easily carried away, and who, moreover, was not the last woman in Agra to think well of herself, was astounded at Mazulhim's presumption, and made some quite unequivocal remarks upon his audacity. They had no effect, and since Mazulhim was as obstinate as ever, she refused, no more than Zephis had, both as a necessary corollary to her faith in her charms and to humble him, to lend herself to methods she thought inconceivably ridiculous.

" 'Oh, well then!' she said disdainfully.

"Suddenly her expression changed, and I judged from her color and contempt, as well as from Mazulhim's mocking and insulting air, that what she had stated to be impracticable was really as easy as anything."

"D'you see that now!" the Sultan cried. "So the women either complain, or else make themselves out to be fine ladies! It's as well to know that."

"Why?" the Sultana asked. "What startling discovery have you made now?"

"Oh, now I know where I am," the Sultan answered. "And if anyone should take it into her head to reproach me, I shall know what to answer. All the same, I am very sorry that Zulica should have been mortified like this; she certainly deserved it less than anybody. But go on, Emir! There are some very good things in what you have just told us, and this gives me high hopes for the rest."

CHAPTER XII

Not Much Different from the Foregoing

"Though the unpleasantness Zulica experienced humiliated her very much, it did not rob her of the presence of mind needful at so vexatious a juncture. She congratulated Mazulhim, and complained of anything rather than of the thing that filled her with resentment; and, to try to save her fame, did not hesitate to do him the honors he certainly did not deserve.

"I do not know whether it was to mortify Zulica, or whether, contrary to his custom, he wanted to give himself some due, but, in any event, whatever he did, he would on no account believe he was what she said. There were, he stubbornly maintained, such things as unlucky days, days one would die rather than live through, if one could foresee them.

"Zulica agreed that there were no doubt days that did not begin brilliantly, but which in the end afforded more cause for congratulation than for complaint.

" 'I protest to you,' she added, with a tenderness she was at that moment very far from feeling, 'that I have had grounds for supposing that the things you have told me over and over about my beauty were not sincere, or that the things you seemed to admire in me were effaced by defects that shocked you all the more as you did not expect them; but you have set my mind at rest.'

" 'Ah, Zulica!' the pitiless Mazulhim cried out. 'How ill your fears were founded! I feel how much I owe your goodness; but it does not blind me, and the more generous you are, the more remorse you heap upon my head.'

" 'How absurd!' she replied. 'At least do not be seized by such a false idea; nothing can be more unjust.'

"At the end of this interchange they set to walking up and down the room, each made uneasy by the other, both without love or desire, and reduced, by their mutual imprudence and the exigencies of a rendezvous in a little retreat, to spending together the rest of a day they seemed not disposed to put to any pleasurable use. Zulica had some fine maxims to ponder on the hollowness of reputations. What inwardly drove her to distraction (for I could easily read into her soul) was the impossibility of taking her revenge upon Mazulhim. 'If I tell, who will believe me?' she asked herself. 'Or if they believe me, would their prejudice in his favor let them believe that he could have been so much in the wrong with me, had I the wherewithal to prevent his being in the wrong? Whatever I may do about it, I shall never be able to undeceive everybody.'

"These notions kept her dismally occupied. As for Mazulhim, he did not seem to take the least interest in such questions. For some minutes they walked up and down without saying anything; at the same time they occasionally smiled at one another in a cold and constrained way.

" 'You are pensive,' he said at last.

" 'Does that surprise you?' she answered prudishly. 'Do you suppose that to be on terms such as I am with you is nothing extraordinary for a right-thinking woman?'

" 'Indeed,' he replied, 'I believe right-thinking women to be quite used to it.'

" 'It is clear,' she retorted, 'that you do not know how such a thing perturbs them, and what terrible struggles they have to go through before surrendering.'

" 'What you say there is very probable,' he answered, 'for, to judge from the way these inward struggles are cut short, they must be distressingly fatiguing.'

" 'That,' she cried, 'is one of the most unmannerly things you could say. Did you think you were being very witty when you said it? Do you know that that is exactly the sort of thing professional seducers say?'

" 'I would not think the worse of it for that,' he declared.

" 'At least you would think it very unfair,' she went on, 'if you knew how much it had cost me to accept you.'

" 'Why,' he cried, 'you dreamed of it! I am outraged; I flattered myself to the contrary, and I bear you a grudge for disabusing me of false impression under which I was happier without your losing anything of my consideration. Well, tell me, I pray you, did Zadig cost you as much thinking?'

" 'What do you mean?' she asked coolly. 'Who is this Zadig person?'

" 'I beg your pardon,' he answered mockingly. 'I would have sworn you knew him.'

" 'Know him, yes,' she answered, 'as one knows anyone else.'

" 'I believe that, little as he is known to you, he would be very annoyed if he knew you were here,' he continued. 'And unless I am much mistaken, your kindnesses to me would grieve him terribly. Be honest!' he said, seeing her shrug her shoulders. 'Zadig pleased you before I had the honor of pleasing you, and I would even bet that at the present time you are on terms with each other.'

" 'That jest,' she answered, 'is in very bad taste.'

" 'After all,' he continued, 'even if you were unfaithful to him, he would still be tóo fortunate: a man like Zadig is little made to be loved, and I have always wondered how a gay, sparkling creature like you could take such a cold, taciturn lover.'

" 'There you wrong him, Mazulhim,' she replied. 'He is all tenderness. I have sacrificed him for you – it would be fruitless for me to deny it. But I am afraid you will very soon make me repent of having done so.'

" 'You have been fickle,' he answered, 'and, I confess, I have been inconstant. But as incapable as we have hitherto been of a serious attachment, the more glorious will be our bond.'

"As he said this he led her toward me, but in a way that plainly showed that propriety alone directed this step.

" 'Truly, you are charming,' he told her. 'And without a certain nicety, which you do not quite discard even with me, I know of no one better suited to make a lover happy.'

" 'I confess,' she agreed, 'that I am naturally reserved; nevertheless, you have no cause to complain of that.'

" 'No doubt,' he replied, 'you make me happy. But, born without desires, you do not sufficiently meet those you arouse. I feel a certain constraint in all that you do for me; you are always afraid of giving yourself too freely, and, between ourselves, I suspect you of having very little sensibility.'

"While Mazulhim was speaking thus to Zulica, he squeezed her hands most passionately.

" 'Though your too great charms have already done me damage,' he pursued, 'I cannot deny myself the pleasure of admiring them again. Even if I should die of it, such a number of treasures shall no longer be hidden from me. Gods!' he cried in a transport, 'ah, if it may be, render me worthy of my good fortune!'

"Whatever Zulica may have said of his want of sensibility, the admiration that seemed to overwhelm Mazulhim, the liveliness of his rapture, and the pains he took to make her share it moved and troubled her.

"'Must you still complain?' she asked, tenderly.

"He answered only by wanting to prove all his gratitude; but Zulica still had in mind how little he was to be depended upon, and, altogether mistrustful of his tumultuous condition, said in a voice that betrayed all her fears:

"'Ah, Mazulhim! Are you not about to love me too much?'

"Although Mazulhim could not help laughing at her terrors, she found she was less loved than she feared.

"Their mutual happiness relieved them of the constrained and wearied looks that had for some time existed between them. Their conversation grew livelier; Zulica, who thought she had delivered Mazulhim out of the hands of sorcerers, gave herself great credit for her charms; and Mazulhim, better pleased with himself, gave himself up to his pleasure as well.

"While they were in this happy frame of mind, supper was brought in, and their meal was a gay one. Zulica and Mazulhim, who were perhaps the two most malicious people in the whole of Agra, spared no one at all.

"'Can you tell me,' Mazulhim asked, 'why Altun Khan has for the last few days taken on that puffed-up air?'

"'Heavens, of course!' she answered. 'Surely you know he is on the best of terms with Ayesha?'

"'But that, as far as I can see,' he said, 'would only be one more reason for being modest.'

"'Oh, yes, for anyone else,' she retorted, 'but don't you think it very lucky for him?'

"'I must confess not,' he replied. 'However absurd Altun Khan may be, I cannot help pitying him: a man whom Ayesha has got hold of is, without question, the unluckiest of men.'

"'What is so curious about it,' she said, 'is that she is keeping it quiet.'

"'Oh, come now!' he answered. 'You are trying to make out that there is some hitch. Ayesha has never concealed a lover, and I can swear that at her age, and with her enormous face, she will be less inclined than ever to —'

"'All the same, it is perfectly true.'

"'Well, if so,' he maintained, 'it is because Altun Khan asked her to keep it secret. And tell me about little Messim; you seem never to see her now.'

"'Because it is impossible to see her now,' she answered, assuming prudery. 'Her behavior is shocking.'

" 'You are right,' he replied seriously. 'Nothing is more important for a self-respecting woman than to see only good company. I think her looks are improving,' he went on.

" 'On the contrary,' she answered. 'She is growing hideous.'

" 'I do not agree with you,' he replied. 'Her skin is taking on an undertone of yellow, which, with her air of fatigue, suits her admirably; if she goes on looking unhealthy, she will be charming.'

"I should never come to an end, Sire," Amanzei broke off to say, "if I were to tell your Majesty all the idle things they remarked upon."

"Ah, yes, I can well believe it," the Sultan answered. "And I give you leave to cut them short; all the same, now that I think of it, you will please to repeat them all to me."

"I dare suggest to your Majesty," Amanzei went on, "that there would be many that would not be interesting enough to –"

"Yes, quite so," the Sultan interrupted. "Those would not interest me; but why – I have often thought of this point – why isn't everything in a story, or a tale, or whatever you call it, interesting?"

"For many reasons," the Sultana said. "What leads up to an event could obviously not be so interesting as the event itself. Besides, if things were all at the same level of interest, they would fatigue one by their sameness: the mind cannot always be alert, the heart cannot always be moved, and both must have a little rest from time to time."

"I see," the Sultan said. "It's like being bored sometimes on purpose to enjoy amusements more. When one has judgment, and thinks in a certain way, whatever one does one clears everything up. Well, then, Amanzei?"

"After supper, Mazulhim, less stirred by Zulica's charms than he had been earlier in the day, proposed a thousand amusements to her but never hit upon the only one that would have suited her, and Zulica got ready to go away in a fashion that made me suspect I should never see her again.

"Nevertheless, in spite of Zulica's ill humor, and the way in which Mazulhim had treated her, he boldly asked before parting from her that they see each other again, and added eagerly that it must be in two days' time. Although I believe that at that moment she had little desire to grant him what he seemed to want so ardently, she answered that she would like to, but so coolly that I did not think she meant to keep her word.

"I then reflected that after Mazulhim had gone I should be bored in his little retreat; that it would be time enough for me to come back when he came back himself, and that I could not do better, both for amusement and instruction, than to follow Zulica to her home. I acted upon this idea, and got into her palanquin with her. As soon as I was in her palace, I went, by the gravitational quality Brahma had put into me, to hide myself in the first sofa I saw.

"The next day Zulica had just begun to dress when Zadig was announced. She bade them have him wait, either not wishing to appear before him without all the beauty with which she was usually prepared for visitors, or thinking that it would be indecent for him to see her in her disarray. Given Zulica's falseness, this last reason was not perhaps so flimsy as it might appear.

"At last Zadig came in. Even if he had not been announced by name, I should have known him from the description I had heard Mazulhim give of him the evening before. He was serious, chilly, constrained, and looked exactly as though he would treat love with that dignity of feeling, and that scrupulous delicacy, which we think so ridiculous nowadays, and which, perhaps, has always been more wearisome than worthy.

"Zadig came toward Zulica as shyly as if he had never declared his love to her; on her side she received him with a studied and ceremonious politeness, and in a manner just as prudish as was necessary to beguile him.

"While Zulica's maids were in the room, they spoke indifferently of news or other frivolous things. Zadig, who thought he was the only person Zulica had ever loved, and who did not consider the greatest attentions equal to what she deserved, did not permit himself the smallest glance at her; and Zulica, who, contrary to all likelihood, had found a man fool enough to esteem her, imitated his reserve, or only looked at him with those hypocritical and veiled glances to be seen in most prudes on all and every occasion.

"However carefully Zadig might put his guard up, Zulica thought she could read in his eyes a sadness different from that which he usually displayed; she asked him in vain what ailed him. To all the questions she put to him so gently, he answered only with profound bows and sighs still more profound.

"Her maids went out when they had done her hair.

"'Now, Zadig,' she said with authority, 'will you please tell me what is the matter with you? Do you imagine that I, taking to heart as I do everything that concerns you, can fail to be hurt at your silence? In short, answer me! I wish it: I will not forgive you if you persist in being mum.'

"'Perhaps you will forgive me still less if I do speak,' he answered at length. 'And think that what upsets me ought on no account be told you.'

"Zulica insisted, and so earnestly, that he thought he could no longer hold his tongue without offending her.

" 'Will you believe it, Madam,' he said, growing red at the absurdity he found in what he was going to tell her, 'I am jealous!'

" 'You, Zadig?' she cried in astonishment. 'You love me, I love you, and yet you are jealous! Can you be in earnest?'

" 'Ah, Madam!' he answered, deeply moved. 'Do not crush me with your anger! I feel to the full how absurd my notion is – indeed it makes me blush. My mind rejects the whispers of my heart, and denies their truth; yet they carry me away, and all the respect I have for you, all the honor you deserve, do not prevent me being horribly tormented. In fact, the shame I heap upon myself for my suspicions does not banish them.'

" 'Listen to me, Zadig,' she answered him grandly, 'and remember forever what I am telling you. I love you, I am not afraid of saying so again, and I will give you a proof of my feelings which you will find incontrovertible: it is to forgive you your suspicions. Perhaps I could say to you that the difficulty you had in making a conquest of me, and my manner of life, ought to give you no excuse for doubting me, and that a person of my character should inspire confidence. I ought even to despise your fears, or be angry at them. But it is sweeter for me to reassure you, and my love can even descend to an explanation.'

" 'Oh, Madam!' Zadig cried, flinging himself by her knees. 'I believe you love me, and I would die of grief if I could think that the suspicions, which I did not even entertain for long, would give you a reason for doubting my respect for you.'

" 'No, Zadig,' she answered, smiling. 'I do not doubt it; but let me hear something of what caused you this disquiet.'

" 'What matter, Madam, since I no longer feel it,' he replied.

" 'I want to know,' she insisted.

" 'Well then,' he said, 'the attentions Mazulhim has seemed to pay you...'

" 'What!' she interrupted. 'It is of him you were jealous? Ah, Zadig! Is it for you to be afraid of Mazulhim, and did you despise me enough to think that he could ever please me? Ah, Zadig, ought I to, can I, ever forgive you for that?' "

CHAPTER XIII

The End of One Adventure and
Beginning of Another

"As she finished speaking, her eyes grew moist with tears, and Zadig, believing them sincere, could not help mingling his own with them.

"'Oh, I am at fault,' he told her tenderly. 'And I feel that even the violence of my passion for you is no excuse.'

"'Ah, cruel man!' she answered with a sob. 'Be jealous if you will; give loose to all your frenzy – I give you leave. But if you know me so little as to mistrust my affection, at least do not think me capable of loving Mazulhim!'

"'I believe you dislike him,' he answered, 'and I never thought you could be taken by him; yet I could not help trembling at seeing him come here.'

"'Yet,' she replied, 'of all the people you know, he is the least dangerous as far as I am concerned. Even if my heart were not preoccupied with a deep passion, even if Mazulhim adored me and if his charms outnumbered his vices, if that were possible, he would still be the least of men in my eyes. How do you suppose any woman (I do not say a self-respecting one, but one who has not lost all sense of shame) could take Mazulhim, a man who has never loved, who declares outright that he is incapable of a passion, and for whom even the feeblest sentiment is an idle dream; a man, in short, who knows no pleasure but that of bringing dishonor upon the women he has? I will speak of his absurdities no more, not because I have not the wherewithal to enlarge upon them, but that, in truth, I would blush to speak to you about him longer. Finally, I am very glad, although I think your suspicions as insulting as they are misplaced, that you should have told me what they were, and I promise you that you shall see Mazulhim here only for so long as will be necessary for me to break with him completely.'

"Zadig, kissing her hand rapturously, thanked her a thousand times for doing for him what she did.

"'But, for what are you thanking me?' she asked him. 'I am making no sacrifice for you.'

"'But, Madam,' he said to her, 'is it possible that Mazulhim has never told you that you seemed charming to him?'

"'What an idea!' she cried smiling. 'Oh, no! I assure you that Mazulhim knows me better than you do, and, giddy as he wishes to seem, he is not giddy enough to pay his addresses to women of a certain distinction.

Notwithstanding this, though, I should not be surprised if, without ever having wanted me and without ever having in his life approached me, he should say publicly one of these days, either that he has been, or that he is, on the best of terms with me. Really now,' she added laughing, 'could anyone but a jealous lover believe it?'

" 'No,' he replied. 'I may be ridiculous enough to fear it sometimes, but I swear I will never believe it.'

" 'I declare I would not depend upon it,' she answered. 'With your temperament it must be a delicious thing to hear your mistress spoken ill of, and to come and raise the most dreadful quarrel with her on account of the words of the first coxcomb who, knowing your character, wishes to make you uneasy.'

" 'For pity's sake, spare me!' he cried. 'And remember that the jealousy you are pardoning me –'

" 'Will perhaps not be the last for today,' she continued. 'Mazulhim's arrival would be enough to make you relapse into your woes.'

" 'Let us say no more about it,' he begged. 'And since you have forgiven me, and since everything, even my injustice, proves that I love you, do not let us waste precious moments, but seal your forgiveness of me!'

"At these words, which Zulica understood very well, she assumed an embarrassed air, and said to him: 'How importunate you are with your desires! Will you never restrain them for my sake? If you knew how much I should love you if you were more reasonable . . . It is true,' she added, seeing him smile, 'I would love you much better; I should think so, at least, and having nothing to fear from you on that side I so greatly detest, you would see me give myself with much more warmth to the things which please me.'

"Yet while she was uttering these august words, she languorously allowed herself to be led toward me.

" 'I swear to you,' she told Zadig, once she was seated upon me, 'that I shall never quarrel with you as long as I live.'

" 'That is how I would like it,' he replied. 'But I do not hope it.'

" 'As for me,' she answered, 'from the trouble I am taking to make up with you, I am beginning to think it true.'

"In spite of her repugnance, Zulica at length yielded to Zadig's eager attentions, but with a decorum, majesty, and modesty unparalleled anywhere else. Anyone but Zadig would no doubt have complained: for him, attached to the most minute punctilio, Zulica's misplaced virtue exalted him with pleasure, and he imitated as best he could the airs of dignity and grandeur she put on; and the less she seemed to love him, the better he was pleased.

"Although I do not know what Zulica made of it all, in any case she proposed Zadig should spend the day with her. So that no one should know that they were together, she gave orders to say that she was not at home. Zadig, whom jealousy had only made more loving than ever, as is usual, responded very satisfactorily to Zulica's kindness; and, in spite of his taciturnity, he did not weary her for a moment. At last, toward midnight, he went away, convinced, as far as a man can be, that she was the most affectionate and right-thinking woman in all Agra.

"I have said that from the way Zulica had bidden farewell to Mazulhim, and much more from the way she looked at things, I did not believe that she would wish to continue an acquaintance so barely agreeable to a woman of her character, in a place where neither love nor pleasure had anything to give her. Nevertheless, curiosity carried the day against all other considerations. As Zadig was leaving her, she told him that some very important piece of business would prevent her from seeing him the next day; and the time for her evening appointment had hardly come, when she got into her palanquin, and with my soul, which followed her, took the road for the little retreat where we found a slave waiting for her, and for Mazulhim.

" 'How now!' she asked the servant peremptorily. 'He is not yet here? It is charming of him to keep me waiting! How admirable for me to get here first!'

"The slave answered her that Mazulhim would arrive soon.

" 'Indeed,' she replied, 'these are very peculiar airs and graces he is putting on.'

"The slave went out, and Zulica sat down angrily upon me. As she was naturally impulsive, she could not stay quiet, and, while upbraiding herself with being unusually accommodating, swore a thousand times over that she would never come to see Mazulhim again. At last she heard a carriage stop outside. She was primed to tell Mazulhim everything that rage could suggest; and, rising briskly, she flung open the door, crying out, 'Indeed, sir, your manners are vastly singular and unusual! Ah, Heavens!' she added, seeing the man who came in.

"I was almost as astounded as she was at seeing a man I did not know."

"What?" the Sultan asked, "it was not Mazulhim?"

"No, Sire," Amanzei answered.

"It was not he!" the Sultan repeated. "That's very odd now. And why was it not he?"

"Your Majesty," Amanzei answered, "is about to hear."

"You know," the Sultan went on, "this is one of the funniest things in the world. That man was apparently mistaken. Oh, no doubt of it, he was mistaken, that is obvious. But tell me, Amanzei, what is a 'little retreat'? Whenever you have mentioned it I have pretended to know, but now I can hold no longer."

"Sire," Amanzei answered, "a little retreat is a secluded house, where, without attendants or onlookers, people go..."

"Ah, yes!" the Sultan interrupted, "I can imagine that must be very convenient. Go on!"

"Filled with anger and amazement at the sight of the man who had just come in, Zulica could not utter a word.

"'I know, Madam,' this Indian said to her respectfully, 'how astonished you must be at seeing me. Moreover, I am not ignorant of the reasons you have for wishing to see here anyone rather than myself. If my presence confounds you, yours causes me as deep an emotion. I did not suspect that the person to whom Mazulhim begged me to bring his apologies would be the very last person whom (were I lucky enough to be in his place) I would wish to fail. It is not in any way Mazulhim's fault; no, Madam, he knows what he owes to your kindness; he was burning to fling himself before you to speak of his gratitude: cruel orders, which he even thought of disobeying, sacred as they ought to be to him, have torn him away from such sweet pleasures. He thought it better to count upon my discretion than upon that of a slave, and never for a moment thought of hazarding a secret in which such a person as you, especially, is involved.'

"Zulica was so astonished at what was happening to her that the Indian might have gone on speaking without her finding the strength to interrupt him. Her embarrassment even made her wish that he had still more to say to her. In consternation, almost rigid, she lowered her eyes, did not dare to look at him, flushed red with shame and anger, and at last began to weep. The Indian, taking her civilly by the hand, brought her to sit upon me, upon whom she sank without saying a word.

"'I see, Madam,' he continued, 'that you persist in thinking Mazulhim in fault, and all that I can say to excuse him seems only to incense you further against him. How lucky he is! Friend of mine though he be, I envy him those precious tears. So much love...'

"'Who says that I love him?' Zulica, who had had time to recover herself, answered proudly. 'May I not have come here for reasons having nothing whatever to do with love? Is it impossible to see Mazulhim without being overcome by those feelings you attribute to me? On what grounds, in fact, do you dare suppose that he is wounding my heart?'

"'I dare believe,' the Indian answered, with a smile, 'that, if my conjectures are not true, they are at any rate likely. The tears you shed, your anger, the time of day at which I find you in a spot ever dedicated to love, all make me believe that love alone had the power to bring you here. Do not deny it, Madam,' he added. 'You are in love. If you will, decry the object of your passion, but not the passion itself.'

"'What!' Zulica cried, for nothing could make her depart from falsehood, 'Mazulhim dared tell you that I loved him?'

"'Yes, Madam.'

"'And you believe him?' she asked, in amazement.

"'You will allow me to suggest,' he answered, 'that the fact is so probable that it would be ridiculous to doubt it.'

"'Well, yes,' she admitted. 'Yes, I loved him. I have told him so; I came here to prove it him; the ungrateful wretch has brought me to that point. I do not blush to confess it to you, but the perfidious man will never have further proofs of my frailty than my avowal to him. A day later, Heavens! what would have become of me?'

"'Now, Madam,' the Indian said coolly. 'Do you suppose that Mazulhim had so poor an opinion of me as to tell me only half the truth?'

"'What can he have told you?' she asked acidly. 'Has he added slander to insult? Has he been unworthy enough to . . . ?'

"'Mazulhim may be indiscreet,' he answered. 'But you will find it hard to persuade me that he is a liar.'

"'Ah, the villain!' she cried. 'This is the first time I have ever been here.'

"'Very well, if you will have it so,' he replied. 'And I would rather believe Mazulhim has gulled me than doubt what you tell me. But, Madam, before whom are you defending yourself? If you want to give me my due, I dare flatter myself that you might be less afraid of trusting me with your secrets. You are in tears? Ah! That is doing the ungrateful man too much honor. Is it fitting, with your beauty, to believe that you could not have your revenge? Yes, Madam, yes; Mazulhim told me everything. I know that you crowned his wishes; I even know certain details of his felicity that would surprise you. Do not be offended at it,' he pursued. 'His happiness was too great to be stifled: had he been less happy, less enraptured, he would no doubt have been more discreet. It is not his vanity, but his joy, that cannot hold its tongue.'

"'Mazulhim!' she put in furiously. 'Ah! Traitor! Mazulhim is sacrificing me! Mazulhim has told you all? Yet it is as well,' she added in a calmer tone. 'I did not yet know what men were; and, thanks to his attentions, I shall have paid but one frailty for the knowledge.'

"'Well, Madam,' the Indian answered frigidly, pretending to believe her, 'that is to punish, not avenge, yourself.'

" 'No,' she replied; 'no. All men are treacherous, and I have had too cruel an experience to be able to doubt it. No, they are all like Mazulhim.'

" 'Ah, do not think it!' he cried. 'I dare swear to you that, if you had allowed me his place, you would never have seen him in mine.'

" 'But then,' she continued, 'the orders that detain him are only an empty excuse, and he is simply abandoning me? Ah! Do not be afraid of telling me so.'

" 'Well, Madam, yes,' the Indian answered. 'It would be useless to disguise it from you. Mazulhim no longer loves you.'

" 'He no longer loves me!' she cried dolorously. 'Ah! The blow will kill me. Ungrateful man! Is that the way he rewards my affection?'

"After saying this she made a few more exclamations, and feigned tears, rage, and despair by turns. The Indian, who knew the sort of person she was, let her be, and all the time pretended to be full of admiration for her.

" 'I feel that I am dying, sir,' she told him, after much weeping. 'A heart as sensitive and delicate as mine cannot be dealt such staggering blows and be immune. But what would he have done if I had deceived him?'

" 'He would have adored you,' the Indian answered.

" 'I cannot understand such proceedings at all,' she went on. 'I am all in the dark. If the ungrateful man no longer loved me, and was afraid to tell me so himself, could not he write to me? Could one break more shabbily with the most contemptible wench? And, again, why should he choose you to tell me?'

" 'I see only too clearly,' the Indian replied, 'that the choice of the messenger displeases you more than the message itself, and I can swear to you, knowing as I do your unjust aversion for me, that you would not have seen me here had Mazulhim named the lady to whom he begged me carry his excuses. I even doubt – since my feelings for you are so different from the feelings I am unfortunate enough to recognize you have for me – whether I should have believed him, had he spoken the name Zulica; I should never have been able to think that anyone existed who would not have found all his happiness in being loved by her. It is thus in all innocence,' he added, 'that I have a part in giving you the most dreadful pain you can feel, and that I find myself involved in secrets that you would rather have in anyone's hands but mine.'

" 'I do not know what makes you think that,' she answered, in an embarrassed manner. 'Secrets of the kind you have come to possess today are ordinarily confided to no one; but I have no special reasons for –'

" 'Excuse me, Madam,' he interrupted quickly. 'You hate me; I am aware that at every opportunity you have ridiculed, or most severely criticized, my wit, my appearance, and my way of life. I will even confess that, had I any virtues, they are due to the wish I have always had to be worthy of your praise, or at least to oblige you to spare me those bitter strokes with which you have always assailed me since we have been in society.'

" 'I, sir?' she said flushing. 'I have never said anything at which you could be angry. Besides, we hardly know one another; you have never given me any cause for complaint, and I do not look upon myself as absurd enough to –'

" 'Pray, let us drop the subject, Madam!' he broke in. 'You would find a longer explanation difficult. But since we are at this question, allow me to tell you that, for the feelings I have always harbored toward you – feelings that your injustice has never been able to dampen – I have been more deserving of your pity than any other man, and least deserving of your hatred. Yes, Madam,' he added, 'nothing has been able to quench the unhappy love I have felt for you; your contempt, your hatred, your vindictiveness against me have made me groan but have not cured me. I know your heart too well to delude myself into thinking that it could ever hold the feelings for me I could wish, but I hope that my discretion as to what concerns you will make you abandon your prejudice, and if your heart is so made that you can never give me your friendship, do not at least deny me your esteem.'

"Zulica, won over by so respectful a speech, admitted that she had indeed, by a whim she had never been able to account for, openly declared herself his enemy; but that it was a wrong she expected to be able to repair, so that this would no longer be an issue between them; and she promised him her esteem, her friendship, and her gratitude.

"After having begged him to keep her secret inviolate, she rose with the intention of going out.

" 'Where are you going, Madam?' the Indian asked, holding her back. 'None of your people are here; I have sent away mine, and they are not to come back for a long time yet.'

" 'No matter,' she replied. 'I cannot stay in a place where everything upbraids my weakness.'

" 'Forget Mazulhim!' he went on. 'Today this house is not his; he has ceded it to me: allow the man who of all the world is most truly interested in you to beg you to command everything here. At least think of what you are about to do. You cannot go out at such an hour without the risk of being met. Do not let your anger make you forget your duty to yourself! Think of the dreadful scandal you would bring upon your-self, think that you would tomorrow be the gossip of all Agra, and that with a chastity and with feelings that ought to be respected, you will be believed the sort of person given to this kind of adventure.'

"Zulica for a long time resisted the arguments that Nasses (such was the Indian's name) brought up to make her stay. And he added, 'Every-thing here was made ready to receive you: allow me to spend the eve-ning here with you. What you are, what I am myself, should be enough to answer for my behavior. I will not lay stress upon my feelings: if I dare to refer to them again, it is merely to make you realize how much I am concerned for you, and to try to drive away those sinister thoughts which Mazulhim's indiscretion seems to have awakened in you.'

"At last, after some resistance, Zulica was persuaded by what Nasses said, and she consented to stay.

" 'With your principles, Madam,' he said to her, 'you must be very astonished to find that you are so susceptible —' "

"Aha!" the Sultan interrupted. "He doesn't know what he is talking about; for, as far as I can make out, this is the same lady who was so vexed that Mazulhim had not behaved well to her?"

"Of course it is the same one," the Sultana said.

"One moment, please," the Sultan went on. "Let us get this straight. If it is the same one, why does he say... you know, what he said? You see, he must be making a mistake. That lady is used to having lovers, and therefore it is ridiculous for him to say that she must be very astonished."

"Do you not see that he is making a fool of her?" the Sultana queried.

"Ah, that's another matter!" the Sultan replied. "But why was I not warned? How can one be expected to guess that? That's what I should like to know."

"No doubt, that is what Amanzei will tell you, if you will let him go on."

"Very well," the Sultan said. "What I say, you know quite well, is not said because I care a fig one way or the other; one speaks for speaking's sake, it amuses one — and for my part, I am no enemy to conversation."

CHAPTER XIV

Which Contains More Words than Deeds

The next day Amanzei continued thus: " 'With your principles, Madam,' Nasses was saying to Zulica, 'you must be very astonished to find that you are so susceptible.'

" 'That is indeed true,' she answered. 'And I assure you that such a thing has never happened to me before.'

" 'That you should have loved,' he went on, 'is not what astonishes me: there are few women who have escaped love. Rather, that it should be Mazulhim who triumphed over your heart, that heart which seemed so little amenable to love, that, I confess, is what I cannot understand.'

" 'I do not understand it myself,' she answered. 'And really, when I look into my heart, I cannot conceive how he should have been able to please and seduce me.'

" 'Ah, Madam!' he cried, as though stricken to the heart. 'What a cruel fate is ours! You love one who no longer loves you, and I love one who will never love me. Why was I always prevented from telling you how much I was hurt by the unjust aversion I knew you felt for me! Perhaps, alas, my assiduity, my constancy, my respect, would have disarmed you!'

" 'And perhaps also,' she said, 'you would have treated me as Mazulhim is treating me!'

" 'No, no!' he answered, taking her hand. 'No! Zulica would have seen herself adored as religiously as she deserves.'

" 'But,' she answered, 'Mazulhim said exactly the same things to me as you do. Why should I not believe that you would do the same things as he?'

" 'Everything ought to make you suspect the sincerity of his feelings,' he answered. 'Mazulhim, fickle and debauched as he is, has never felt what it is to be in love. You must have known that he was more indiscreet and deceiving than any man could possibly be. All the same, it is nonetheless true that, however unfaithful he may be, you could, without being accused of overweening pride, flatter yourself you might bind him. The difficulty of being pleasing to you, the sweet, rare joy of being sovereign in a heart no one has yet made subject, entitled you to expect an abiding love. What in anyone else would have been ridiculous vanity can have been for Zulica only a simple idea she could not help conceiving.'

" 'At least it goes without saying,' she answered modestly, 'that with my principles I could expect a certain consideration.'

" 'Consideration!' he cried. 'You! Ah, is consideration all that you deserve? Thus, in return for your kindness you demand only what would be given the least respected woman?'

" 'Nevertheless,' she replied, 'you see that even that demand was too heavy.'

" 'If it were permitted to me to say something to you –' Nasses began again.

" 'It is permitted,' she interrupted. 'You cannot doubt but that what is taking place between us today must bind us in the tenderest friendship.'

" 'Yes, Madam,' he said with the most loving eagerness, 'but is it to me, to Nasses, whom she has hated so long, that Zulica deigns promise the tenderest friendship?'

" 'Yes, Nasses,' she answered. 'Zulica recognizes her unfairness, and it wrings her heart; thus she swears to repair the injury by a heartfelt confidence nothing can shake.'

"Thereupon, she looked at him gratefully; he had a very pleasant face, and, although less in fashion than Mazulhim, was in nothing his inferior.

" 'What!' he cried again. 'You! *you* promise to love me?'

" 'Yes,' she replied. 'My heart will be an open book to you: you shall read in it as in your own. My slightest feelings, my thoughts, all shall be known to you.'

" 'Ah, Zulica!' he said, casting himself on his knees, and ardently kissing her hand. 'How cheerfully my love will find ways to repay your kindness to me! What a pleasure it will be to unfold all my thoughts to you! Sovereign mistress of my being, your commands alone shall order my life.'

" 'Enough!' she said with a smile. 'Get up! I do not like seeing you at my feet; come back to what you wanted to say to me.'

"He rose and seated himself beside her, still holding her hand, and continued thus: 'I will ask you some questions, since you allow me. By what arts did Mazulhim succeed in pleasing you? By what enchantment did he make the most right-thinking and right-living woman, to wit Zulica, think him lovable? How could such a vain, feckless man commend himself to a woman as pure as you? That he should please women of his own kind, frivolous, giddy, dissipated women, who can bring themselves to love no one and yet are seduced by everyone they see, that he should please them, I say, does not surprise me – but you!'

" 'To begin the interchange of confidences which I promised you,' Zulica replied, 'I must naturally tell you that I had no fear that Mazulhim could ever be dear to me. It was not that I thought myself safe from frailty. Without having ever passed through that bitter experience, as I have since done, I knew that a moment might be enough to plunge the most virtuous woman into the most hopeless depths; but, reassured by my feelings, and also by the time I had been in society without straying in the slightest from the prescribed path, I dared flatter myself that this calmness would endure forever.'

" 'No doubt,' Nasses remarked very gravely. 'Nothing entraps women more readily than the security of which you speak.'

" 'That is true,' she agreed. 'A woman is never in worse danger of succumbing than when she feels herself invincible. I was in this deceptive calm when Mazulhim brought himself to my notice. I will not tell you how he managed to seduce me. All I know is that, having resisted him for a long time, my heart was moved, and my mind disturbed. I felt emotions gaining upon me, all the more so as I was unused to feeling them. Mazulhim, who knew the nature of my agitation better than I did myself, took advantage of it to lead me to the consequences which I did not foresee; and at last he wrought me to the point of coming here. I thought, as he promised, that he only wished to converse with me with more freedom than we could hope for in the hurly-burly of society. I came; his presence moved me more than I had thought; alone with him I found myself less armed against his desires. Without knowing what I granted, I was able to deny him nothing. Love at length seduced me to the end.'

"As she finished speaking, her eyes were damp with tears she forced herself to shed. Nasses, who seemed to partake most sincerely of her affliction by pretending to console her, said the very things most calculated to bring her to despair. Above all, he laid stress on the short time Mazulhim had kept her.

" 'Surely,' he told her, 'it is not that you lack anything which can contribute to a man's happiness, at least so one has every right to suppose. Nevertheless, if it were anyone but you, such prompt inconstancy on Mazulhim's part would certainly make people think the most unflattering things.'

"To this suggestion Zulica answered with a grimace that told Nasses plainly enough that she did not think she had any need to reproach herself on that score.

" 'It is well known,' Nasses went on to say, 'that men are so unfortunate as not to be able to enjoy even the most lovable creature without their desires ebbing; but at least they love for three months, six weeks, even a fortnight, more or less: no one has ever dreamed of leaving a woman so suddenly as Mazulhim left you. It is ridiculous, horrible even. Who could have imagined such a thing? Ah, Zulica!' he added, 'I dare repeat it, you would have found me more constant.'

"Zulica answered that she was quite prepared to believe it, but that since she no longer wished ever to love, it was henceforth all the same to her whether men were constant or not; that she would even wish, out of her sincere friendship for him, that the love he protested for her were not real, and that she would be vastly upset if he were to retain for her feelings that she could never reward.

" 'Yes,' Nasses answered sadly, 'I feel the force of all you say. I find in your character all that firmness I always feared in you, which I could not prevent myself admiring, to my own misery. If you were to be esteemed less, I should be less to be pitied; for, in short, it would be permissible for me to imagine that, since you had loved Mazulhim, it would not be impossible for you to love me also. It is a hope one could cherish with regard to any woman of society without insulting her; but, unluckily, you are unlike anybody else, and your having lapsed once is no augury for the future.'

"Zulica, who was no doubt laughing inwardly at the false idea Nasses seemed to have of her, assured him he was describing her truly, and enlarged widely upon the happy turn of mind with which nature had endowed her, her reluctance to allow herself to be touched, and the coldness in which things that gave other women the keenest pleasure had left her, in spite of the violent passion Mazulhim had been able to arouse in her.

" 'So much the worse for you, Madam,' Nasses told her. 'The more you are to be esteemed, the more you are to be pitied. Your lack of susceptibility will be the great sorrow of your life. The vision of Mazulhim will always be before you. The memory of the humiliating way in which he jilted you will not leave you for a moment: it is a torture that will overwhelm you in your solitude, which dissipation and the pleasures of society will never be able to chase away entirely.'

" 'But what am I to do,' she asked him, 'to wipe so bitter a remembrance from my mind? I agree with you that a new love could blot out the memory of Mazulhim; but, without taking into account the fresh sorrows it might bring, can I believe that my heart could surrender enough to ensure my being cured? No, Nasses, believe me; self-respecting women can never love twice.'

" 'You are wrong there,' he cried. 'I know some who have loved more than a half-dozen times and think no less of themselves for it. Besides, you have come to such a wretched pass that you are above the rules; and if your adventure were public, even if you were known to have ten lovers at once, it would be said that even so you were not being compensated.'

" 'Those who said so would certainly be very tolerant,' she said with a smile.

" 'Not at all,' he insisted. 'It would be accepted much more simply than you think. In any event, you must not suppose that I am in favor of your taking them, since only one would be enough to kill me with grief.'

" 'Ah!' Zulica mused. 'You see, we are blameworthy when we love only once, with a single-hearted and constant passion, and even then we hardly escape contempt: and such is our hard lot that what, in you, is looked upon as a virtue is, in us, accounted a vice.'

" 'Yes, people were used to think that,' he answered. 'But morals having changed, our notions have changed with them. Oh, were it only the fear of being blamed that restrained you, you would abandon yourself to love.'

" 'At bottom,' she said, 'you are right. For why should one's heart not be occupied? In the last analysis, I do not see the least harm in it.'

" 'And yet,' he replied, 'with a keen mind that enables you to distinguish admirably between right and wrong, you bow to prejudice just like a person who cannot reason. There you are, determined to spend your life lamenting your weakness with Mazulhim instead of wisely thinking of consoling yourself, because you think that a self-respecting woman should love only once. You inwardly feel the principle upon which you are modeling your behavior to be false; but you are resisting your powers of reason so as to enjoy the noble pleasures of affliction, and also, apparently, that people may always say that you are still lamenting the loss of Mazulhim. What fine things to have said about one!'

" 'About me!' she retorted. 'I flatter myself that no one will say anything about me.'

" 'You may well do so,' he answered. 'I know that you, Madam, will divulge nothing of all this; it is equally certain that I shall say nothing about it, and it does Mazulhim so little honor that his silence is ensured. Yet if you do not change your point of view, everyone is sure to know about it.'

" 'But why?' she asked.

" 'Egad!' he answered. 'Do you think that people will see you looking mournful without trying to find out why you are so; and that if people try doggedly enough they will not succeed? Do you suppose that Mazulhim himself, whose vanity your sorrow will flatter, will be able to resist the pleasure of telling everybody that his jilting you is the cause of it?'

" 'That is true,' she said. 'But, Nasses, does it depend upon me whether I am sad or not?'

" 'Of course it depends upon you,' he replied. 'In reality, what do you regret now? Mazulhim? If he were to come back to you, would you receive him?'

" 'I?' she cried. 'Ah! I would rather give myself to the most despicable of men than be his.'

" 'Thus, if nothing he could do would reinstate him in your heart,' he went on, 'it is very ridiculous of you to weep for him.' "

"Tell me," the Sultan said, "is there much more of this sort of thing?"

"Yes, Sire," Amanzei answered.

"By Muhammad! I'm sorry to hear it," Shah Baham replied. "It is just conversations like these which give me the most dreadful spleen, I warn you frankly. If you could leave them out, or at least shorten them, it would be a great relief to me, and I should not be ungrateful."

"You are wrong to complain," the Sultana told him. "This conversation, which you find tedious, is, so to speak, an act in itself. It is not a useless digression, leading nowhere, it is...an act. Is that not what we call dialogue?" she asked Amanzei, with a smile.

"Yes, Madam," he answered.

"It is a very pleasing way of treating things," she went on. "It better and more broadly describes the characters in play, but it has certain drawbacks. In trying to make everything profound, or to catch every subtlety, one risks straying into minor details, in themselves agreeable enough, but not important enough to linger over; and those who listen are wearied with details long drawn out. To know exactly where to stop short is perhaps harder than to invent. The Sultan is wrong to wish you to go faster at this particular point, but I should think you wrong, and so would every person of taste, if an unruly verbosity were to carry you away, and if you were not now and again to sacrifice even what seem to you the most delightful bits when you could tell them only to the detriment of what we want to hear."

"The Sultan is wrong!" Shah Baham remarked. "That's easy to say. As for me, I maintain that this fellow Amanzei is nothing but a babbler, who mirrors himself in all he says, and who, if I know anything at all about it, is addicted to the vice of liking long tirades and playing the clever wit. That may offend you," he added, turning toward Amanzei, "yet I am only being plain with you, and if you were to be so with me, I bet you would admit I am right."

"Yes, Sire," Amanzei answered. "And, apart from a courtier's complaisance, I am all the more inclined to agree, since I have long been found fault with for the very defect your Majesty upbraids me with."

"Then cure yourself of it!" Shah Baham said.

"Were it as easy to cure myself of it as to admit it," Amanzeï replied, "your Majesty would not have had to take me to task for it." And he continued:

"The force of Nasses's argument had a great effect upon Zulica.

" 'At bottom you are right,' she said to him. 'And thus it is not Mazulhim I weep for, it is for my own frailty, it is for having given myself to a man so unworthy of me.'

" 'I admit,' Nasses answered ingenuously, 'that the trick he is playing on you cannot make him seem agreeable to you; nevertheless, if you were to judge him without bias, I believe you would see certain good qualities in him, for I assure you he has some.'

" 'I will judge him, if you like,' she replied disdainfully. 'To begin with, he is not well built.'

" 'Perhaps not,' he answered. 'Yet nobody is more graceful than he; he has a fine face, and the finest legs in the world, an easy, noble carriage, and a lively, bright, and entertaining mind.'

" 'Oh, yes,' she conceded, 'I do not deny that he is a pretty enough bauble; but, after all, he is only that; and, besides, I assure you that he is far from being as amusing as they make out. Between ourselves, he is a conceited, presumptuous, self-important –'

" 'I can forgive a man fortunate enough to have appealed to you,' Nasses interrupted. 'People puff themselves up for less every day.'

" 'But, Nasses,' she complained, 'for a man who says he loves me, and apparently wants me to believe him, your remarks strike me as most singular.'

" 'Odious as Mazulhim may seem to you,' Nasses answered, 'he is, all the same, less so than I am; and I believe I should be more a fool to speak to you of a lover whom you will never love than of one whom you have loved so tenderly. He still occupies your mind so painfully that I never utter his name without your eyes filling with tears; at this very moment they are welling over, and you vainly try to hide it from me. Ah! Crush back your tears, charming Zulica!' he cried. 'They stab me to the heart! I cannot, without an emotion that is undoing me, see them flow from your eyes.'

"Zulica, who had felt not the least inclination to cry for some time, could not help thinking, on hearing these words, that she ought to shed some tears. Nasses, who was very diverted at all the antics he was making her go through, left her a while in this factitious woe. Nevertheless, so as not to waste his time while he was with her, he occupied himself in bestowing kisses upon her breast, which was generously exposed. For some time she did not vouchsafe to notice what he was doing, and it was only after she had left him completely free for a while that she found it proper to object.

"'How unthinking you are, Nasses,' she said, still holding her handkerchief to her eyes. 'Truly, I am pained by these liberties.'

"'Naturally,' he answered, 'I could not expect you to welcome them. Look at me,' he added, 'so that I can see your eyes.'

"'No!' she replied. 'They have wept too much to be beautiful.'

"'Without your tears,' he declared, 'you would seem less lovely to me. Listen to me,' he continued. 'Your present state wrings my heart: I want you above all things to rise superior to it. I have proved to you how essential it is for you to love again, and I will, as far as I can, now prove to you that it is me whom you ought to love.'

"'I much doubt of your success,' she answered.

"'That we shall see,' he went on. 'In the first place, you admit that you hated me for no reason at all; that wrong you can only right by loving me madly.' She smiled. 'Moreover,' he continued, 'I love you. And although it would be easy for you to make anybody fall in love with you, even more than you might wish, you will never find anybody so ready as I am to love you with all the affection you deserve. Rightly or wrongly, we generally think ill of women: we are convinced that they are neither faithful nor devoted, and arguing from that, we believe that we have no call to be faithful or devoted to them. Thus, we hardly ever see real passion; to make us determine to have one, we must be sure that a woman is worthy of feelings less light than those we usually bestow upon her. We must scrutinize her character and her way of living and thinking, and regulate by them the amount of esteem we can lay at her feet –'

"'Well,' she interrupted, 'what is stopping you?'

"'That is jest, Madam,' he replied. 'Such a study takes time; while we are about it a woman will forestall us by her inconstancy; and that is so heartrending an event for us that, to avoid it, we often leave her without knowing whether she might deserve a longer attachment.'

"'But,' she asked, 'what can all of this amount to for you?'

"'This,' he answered. 'But must you keep your handkerchief to your eyes forever?'

"'Have I not looked at you?' she said.

"'Not enough,' he contended. 'I do not want to see that handkerchief anymore: it will make me hate you, if possible, as much as you used to hate me.'

"Thereupon she smiled at him, affectionately enough.

"'Go on then,' she said, leaning against him.

"'Yes,' he replied, clasping her in his arms, 'I will go on; do not be afraid. What I have seen of you here,' he pursued, 'is equivalent to the study of which I spoke; it has captivated all my esteem, and thus has doubled my love for you. No one else can love you as much as I do; another would be conscious only of your charms, and the beauty of your soul would be a thing he never could be sure of, because nothing could have shown him how exquisitely delicate your feelings are. He will find that out, you will say, by seeing how you behave. Ah! Madam, I must speak ill of my sex – do you think that a flighty, dissipated man, without morals, especially where women are concerned, can find a better way of assuring his constant scorn for them than by always refusing them the honor of scrutiny? Do you think, I say, that he notices the things that ought to win his esteem, or that he will not accuse you of gilding your character and clothing yourself before him in virtues you do not possess?'

"'Yes, I can well believe it,' she agreed. 'Nothing could be more sensible than the things you have said.'

"Nasses, to thank her for her commendation, was first of all about to kiss her hand; but Zulica's mouth being closer, he thought it just as well to testify his gratitude thereon.

"'Ah, Nasses,' she said, 'slow down, we shall have a falling out.'

"'You must see,' he went on, without taking any notice of this, 'that, since I esteem you more than anyone else in the whole world, having the most reason for doing so, I am the only man you can possibly love.'

"'No,' she replied. 'Love is too dangerous.'

"'That,' he retorted, 'is an operatic platitude, so stale and flat that nowadays no one would even use it in a book of verse, and which, moreover, would not in the least prevent your loving me, I can tell you that.'

"'If that would not prevent me...' she answered. 'But why do you ask for love? Have I not promised you friendship?'

"'Of course,' he replied, 'that would mean a noble-minded struggle for you. Naturally, did I not love you, I would demand nothing further from you, perhaps less; but my feelings for you can be met only by the warmest reciprocation, and I swear that I shall omit nothing to make you feel all the ardor I ask of you.'

"'I, for my part,' she retorted, 'protest that I will omit nothing to protect myself from it.'

"'Aha!' he said, 'you are going to take precautions against me; I am delighted, for that is a proof that I am dangerous to you. You are right. Loving you as I do, I should be more so for you than anyone else is.

With a woman less estimable than you, I would not be so sure of my victory.'

" 'Yet,' she replied, 'the more estimable I am, the more I shall resist.'

" 'Quite the contrary,' he answered. 'Only flirts are difficult: they are easily persuaded that they are made to be loved, but they are not so easily caught, and the easiest conquests are those over moderate, thinking women.'

" 'I should never have thought so,' she said.

" 'Nothing, however, is more true,' he continued. 'You cannot, I know, doubt that I love you. Answer me! Do you doubt it? Be honest!'

" 'I have just been so foolishly credulous,' she answered, 'that I think it will be a very long time before I can be persuaded of anybody's love.'

" 'But leaving Mazulhim aside,' he insisted, 'what do you think?'

"She answered that she believed he did not altogether dislike her; he persisted, and at last brought her to admit that she was sure he loved her.

" 'And you,' he pressed her on, 'you do not find me odious any longer?'

" 'Odious!' she exclaimed. 'Oh no, not odious. I may be inclined to indifference, but I do not wish to be unfair.'

" 'You believe that I love you?' he cried. 'And you do not loathe me — and yet you imagine that you can resist me for long, you, with your sincere nature? You deceive yourself with thinking that you could make me miserable, when your own desires will speak in my favor? That you will fix a date for yielding, and only when the time has come will you give yourself without impropriety? No, Zulica, no! I have a better opinion of you than you have of yourself. You could not be so insincere as to drive a man you love to despair: you are innocent of the horrible act of leading me on from favor to favor, to the one that must forever crown and revive my desires; the moment I melt you will be the moment I shall die with pleasure in your arms, and that charming mouth...' he added rapturously –"

"Good! Good!" the Sultan broke in. "You relieve me of terrible tortures. Upon my life, I began to think it was never going to happen. Oh, what a stupid creature that Zulica was, with all her bother and nonsense!"

"Indeed," the Sultana said, "one must admit that favors cannot be withheld longer than that. Think of it! To resist for a whole hour! That has no parallel."

"The truth of the matter is," the Sultan answered, "I found the business as tedious as if it had lasted a fortnight; and, if Amanzei had drawn it out a moment longer, I should have died of spleen and vapors – but not before it would have cost him his life. I would have taught him to make a crowned head die of tedium."

CHAPTER XV

Which Will Not Amuse Those Who Have Found the Previous One Wearisome

"In the silence of the moment which so much gratified your Majesty yesterday, I gathered that Nasses was preventing Zulica from speaking, and that she was preventing him from going on talking.

" 'Ah, Nasses!' she cried as soon as she could. 'Think what you are doing! If you loved me...'

"The more Nasses feared Zulica's reproaches, the less chance he gave her of making any. I have never understood, so well as I did at that moment, how useful it is to be headstrong with women.

" 'But listen to me,' Zulica was saying. 'Do listen to me! Do you want me to hate you?'

"These words, being intermittently and feebly spoken, had little force, and no effect. Zulica clearly saw that it would be useless for her to speak further to a man lost in rapture, one to whom the finest things in the world would have been said fruitlessly. What was she to do? Why, just what she did. After taking due precautions against the attempts that Nasses, disordered by his emotions, was hazarding with the greatest temerity, and having made everything safe in this respect, she waited patiently for him to be in a fit state to listen to what she had to say to him regarding his impertinent behavior. Nasses, meanwhile, either to make her grant an easier pardon or because Zulica had really stirred him, freed her, only to fall upon her breast in a state of collapse, conscious only of his own condition. This made it all the more difficult for Zulica; for what is the good of speaking to someone who cannot hear? The only thing that could have made less painful the silence enforced upon her at this juncture was that Nasses did not seem to be enough in command of his wits to be able to use it for his own comments. Nevertheless, she tried to withdraw herself altogether from his arms, but failed. And when he had recovered from his stupor he looked so affectionate! His first glances strayed so touchingly over Zulica! He closed his eyes so languorously, let out such profound sighs, that far from being able to show as much anger at him as she had promised herself she would, she began, in spite of her natural insusceptibility, to feel moved and to share his transports. Our virtuous lady would have been undone had Nasses been able to notice the feelings that wrought her. At last, brought back to himself, he seized Zulica's hand.

" 'Nasses!' she said angrily, 'do you think that that is the way to make me love you?'

"Nasses sought to excuse the violence of his ardor by saying that it had not allowed him to be punctilious. Zulica argued that love, when it is sincere, is always accompanied by respect, and that people only had such ill-regulated manners as he had been guilty of with those whom they despise. He, on his side, maintained that one showed lack of respect only to those people for whom one felt passion, and that his being carried away, which Zulica was determined to blame him for, was the very thing that ought to prove to her how much he loved her.

" 'If I esteemed you less,' he pursued, 'I would have asked you for what I seized; but, trifling as are the favors I stole from you, I was aware that you would refuse them. If I had been sure of being granted them, I would not have thought it necessary to rely on myself alone for them. The better one thinks of a woman, the more one is compelled to make oneself guilty of too much boldness in her eyes – and that is the truth.'

" 'I do not believe a word of all that,' Zulica answered. 'But even if there were any truth in what you have just said, still, it is an invariable rule that one does not begin declaring one's feelings in such very odd ways as you have.'

" 'Even had I pushed matters so briskly as you say I have,' he replied, 'it would still be a compliment for which you ought to thank me.'

" 'No,' she resumed impatiently, 'your head is full of the most unheard-of, fantastic notions.'

" 'It is entertaining to think,' he retorted, 'that those very opinions you dub "fantastic" are all based on reason. The one with which you are upbraiding me now is extremely sound, as I shall make you see, for not only have you a ready wit but a balanced one as well, a virtue so rare in women that I must congratulate you upon it.'

" 'That compliment does not make me relent,' she said sternly. 'And I warn you that I shall treat it as it deserves.'

" 'It really makes me very uneasy,' he answered, 'to see you so little affected by the graceful things I am saying to you.'

" 'In short, sir,' she stopped him, 'allow me to tell you that before you undertake certain things, you must first of all persuade.'

" 'I follow you, Madam,' he took up. 'You want me to ruin your reputation. Very well then, I shall. I wanted to make it possible for you to love me without anyone in the world suspecting it, but since my delicacy in the matter displeases you, I shall be of use to you in another way, Madam. It will be public that I am in love with you, and I will

spare you none of those tender indiscretions which will inform the
world what my feelings for you are.'

"'Why, what do you mean?' she asked. 'You are indeed a strange man!
You are guilty of an impertinence toward me I ought never to forgive,
and you say it is out of respect for me; you tumble me as though I were
a woman who is beneath contempt, and you declare that it is because
you are infinitely solicitous of all that concerns me! You do a thousand
unpardonable things, and then you say it is I who am in the wrong! For
Heaven's sake, explain yourself to me!'

"'If you were more experienced in love,' he answered, 'you would
spare me all these explanations. Nevertheless, however bothersome they
may be for me, I would, I assure you, much rather give you lessons on
this subject than find you so schooled as not to need them. Have you
still to learn that it is far less the kindnesses a woman shows her lover
that bring her down than the time she takes over granting them? Do
you think that I could love you and be unhappy without my attentions
to you, without the efforts I would make to touch your heart, attracting
notice? I should grow melancholy; and, even if I were extremely discreet, it would be known that it was your severity that made me woebegone. Finally, for we must always come back to this, you would make
me happy. Do you suppose that whatever guard I might put upon myself,
that your eyes, my eyes, that sweet intimacy which, in spite of all our
efforts, would grow up between us, would not reveal our secret?'

"By her astonished silence, Zulica seemed to agree with what Nasses
said.

"'You see clearly,' he went on, 'that when I beg you to make me
promptly happy, it is for your sake rather than for mine. If you follow
my advice, if you spare me tortures, you also save yourself from the buzz
that always accompanies the beginnings of an affair. Moreover, having
been together in this situation, I could not, without letting the cat out
of the bag, begin to show that I loved you. But, if we were agreed, we
could deceive the public as to our relations as much as we thought fit;
believing that you hate me, no one would never imagine that you could
so rapidly have passed to love from a feeling so contrary to it. And then
it will be easy for you to bring about our reconciliation naturally. At
Court, or at the first Princess's where we meet, you will seize upon
some opportunity or other of showing me some civility. Do not fear
that it will not arise: I shall manage it. I shall eagerly respond to your
advance and loudly declare my wish that you should no longer hate me.
I will even get some common friend to suggest that you should see
me; you will be quite agreeable; I shall be brought to your house, and

I shall come to see you again, and proclaim how pleasant it is to know you, and how unfortunate I was to have been outcast so long. Nothing more will be needed to account for my attentions; they will seem quite simple and natural, and we shall get all the more delight from our love in hiding it from everybody.'

" 'No,' she answered thoughtfully. 'Were I to make you happy so promptly, I should fear your inconstancy. I confess I should not be averse to your entering into a friendship with me which was based on more confidence and real affection than is ordinarily to be encountered in society. I shall go further: I would not be an enemy to love if a lover asked nothing more of a woman than to be told she loved him.'

" 'What you ask,' he said tenderly, 'is more difficult with you than with any other woman imaginable. I also confess that a little love from you would be more flattering than complete devotion from anybody else. But believe me, Zulica, I adore you, you love me – so make happy the man who feels the greatest passion for you.'

" 'If you could limit your desires,' she said, as though very moved, 'and if what one granted you did not seem to give you the right to demand more, I might try to make you less unhappy; but –'

" 'Oh, Zulica!' he broke in hastily. 'My obedience will satisfy you.'

"Upon this promise, which Zulica clearly felt to be a precarious one, as indeed it was, she leaned carelessly against Nasses, who, casting himself upon her, inconsiderately took advantage of all the favors he had just been granted.

" 'Ah, Zulica!' he murmured a minute later, 'must I owe such sweet moments to your complaisance only, and do you not wish them to be as sweet for you as they are for me?'

"Zulica did not answer, but Nasses complained no more. Soon he communicated all his flame to Zulica's soul. He shortly forgot the promise he had made her, and she did not remember what she had demanded of him. It is true that she objected, but so gently, that the objection which escaped from her lips was more like a tender sigh than a reproof. Nasses, sensible of how rapt she was becoming, thought he ought not waste such a precious opportunity.

" 'Ah, Nasses!' she said in a smothered voice. 'If you do not love me, how pitiable you will have made me!'

"Even were Zulica's fears as to Nasses's love as keen and real as they seemed to be, it looked as though Nasses's transports had dissolved them. Thus, almost convinced that she could not much longer doubt his ardor, he did not see fit to waste time answering her when he could reassure her, and much more forcibly than the most touching speeches could ever have done. Zulica was not offended by his silence: soon – for often the merest trifles are enough to make us forget the most important things – she seemed to take no more account of a fear that it seemed to her she could no longer retain without giving Nasses mortal offense. Other notions, no doubt sweeter ones, supervened. She tried to speak, but could only utter some disconnected words, which seemed but to express the discomposure of her soul.

"When he was finished, Nasses threw himself on his knees beside her.

" 'Ah, let me be!' she said, repelling him feebly.

" 'What!' he answered in astonishment, 'can I have been so unlucky as to displease you, and can it be possible that you can complain of me in any way?'

" 'If I do not complain,' she replied, 'it is not that I have no cause.'

" 'And of what would you complain?' he pursued. 'Should you not be tired of such cruel resistance?'

" 'I admit,' she said, 'that many women would have yielded sooner; but nonetheless, I think that I should have resisted you longer.'

"Then she looked at him with that cloudy, languorous look in the eyes which both betrays and excites desire.

" 'Do you love me?' Nasses asked her, as tenderly as if he had loved her himself.

" 'Ah, Nasses!' she cried. 'What pleasure would you get from an avowal your furious actions have already wrested from me? Have you left me anything to say?'

" 'Yes, Zulica,' he answered. 'Without that charming confession I crave from you, I cannot be happy; without it I can never regard myself as anything but a ravisher. Ah! Will you leave me with such a cruel reproach to gnaw my breast?'

" 'Yes, Nasses,' she said sighing, 'I love you.'

"Nasses was about to thank Zulica, when Mazulhim's slave came in with supper; he sighed –"

"Egad! I should think so," the Sultan interrupted. "That is so typical of servants. One never sees them except when one least wants them. There was no fear of his coming in when Nasses and Zulica were wearying me so dreadfully. He must come and interrupt just when I should have liked to hear what they had to say."

"Indeed," the Sultana said, "I was surprised at your saying nothing."

"Zounds!" he retorted. "I took care not to disturb them; I was far too anxious to know how it would all end. I am highly satisfied," he added, turning to Amanzei, "that is what may be called a touching situation; my eyes are still full of tears."

"What?" the Sultana asked him. "Is this making you cry?"

"Why not?" he answered. "It is very affecting, unless I am gravely mistaken. It seems as good as a tragedy to me, and if it doesn't make you cry, that is because you are not kindhearted."

After delivering what he considered a biting epigram at the Sultana's expense, he very complacently gave Amanzei orders to go on, which he did as follows: "Nasses sighed at being interrupted; not that he was in love, but he was possessed by that impatience, that ardor, which, without being love, produces in us emotions that resemble it, which women invariably look upon as signs of a true passion, either because they know how necessary it is for them to seem convinced by us, or because they really know no better. Zulica, who gave her charms all the credit for the impatience she observed in Nasses, was extremely grateful for it; but to maintain the part of 'reserved woman' she had undertaken to play, she informed him by a pressure of the hand that they were to be circumspect in front of Mazulhim's slave. They sat down to supper.

"After supper was over –"

"Slow down, if you please!" Shah Baham broke in. "If it's all the same to you, I would like to see them at supper. I like table talk above all things."

"What a singularly inconsequent mind you have!" the Sultana said to him. "You have girded a dozen times at necessary conversations, and now you insist upon hearing one that has no connection with the story, and can only draw it out."

"Well," the Sultan answered, "if I want to be inconsequent, is there anyone who can stop me? See here; I wish it to be known that a Sultan can use his mind as he pleases; that all my ancestors had the very privilege that is now being called in question; that a bluestocking has never been allowed to prevent them speaking as they wished, and that even my grandmother, with whom I do not think you will have the audacity to compare yourself, was never allowed to contradict Shah Riar, my ancestor, son of Shah Mahmoun, who begat Shah Tekni, who...all of which I am telling you, by the way," he continued more moderately, "merely to let you see that I know my family tree, rather than to annoy anyone. You may go on, Amanzei."

" 'It is,' Zulica said, as soon as she sat down to supper, 'very curious how the most important events of our lives are brought about. Whosoever would tell a woman, "Tonight you will madly love a man whom not only have you never thought of as a lover, but whom you even hate," would not be believed. And yet, the case is not without parallel.'

" 'I can answer for that,' Nasses took up. 'And I should be very vexed if it did not happen. Moreover, nothing is more common than to see women fall violently in love with somebody they have never seen before, or whom they have loathed. That is even how the deepest passions are born.'

" 'And yet,' she continued, 'you will meet people, many people, who say there is no such thing as love at first sight.'

" 'Do you know,' Nasses answered, 'who the people are who say that? They are either youngsters who know nothing of life, or women who are prudish and cold: those indolent women who never start a love affair without taking every precaution, who warm up only by degrees and make you pay heavily for a heart that always contains more remorse than affection, one that one never enjoys completely.'

" 'Well!' she replied. 'Those women, with all their absurdity, are much approved of; and I myself, till quite lately, was of their mind.'

" 'You!' he protested. 'But do you know, you have every conceivable prejudice?'

" 'That may well be,' she answered. 'But now I have one less, for I believe in sudden love.'

" 'As for me,' he said, 'I know that it is very common. I even know a woman who is so subject to it that she experiences it three or four times a day.'

" 'Ah, Nasses! That is impossible!' she cried.

" 'If you were to say merely that it is unusual,' he went on, 'do you know you would still be wrong, and that a woman who is unfortunate enough to be born very tenderhearted – if it be a misfortune – cannot answer for herself from one minute to another? Now, supposing you felt an absolute necessity to love me, what would you do?'

" 'I would love you,' she answered.

" 'Well then, now imagine a woman who feels an absolute necessity for loving three or four men every day.'

" 'She would be much to be pitied,' she said.

" 'Very well, I agree, but what would you have her do? Run away, you will tell me? But you cannot run far in a room; when you have walked up and down it a few times you are tired, and must sit down again. The person who has struck you is ever present to your eyes. Your desires are exacerbated by your resistance, and the need for being loved, far from being diminished, has only become more acute.'

" 'But,' she answered, as though in a dream, 'to love four!'

" 'Since the number shocks you,' he replied, 'I will deduct two.'

" 'Ah!' she said, 'that seems more likely, even possible.'

" 'Yet,' he cried, 'what a to-do you have made about loving only one!'

" 'Be quiet,' she said, smiling at him. 'I cannot imagine where you get all your arguments from, nor where I get my answers.'

" 'From nature,' he answered her. 'You are frank and artless, you love me enough not to wish to hide your thoughts from me, and I love you all the more for it, seeing that there are so few women who care for truth as you do.'

"With these remarks, and a few others no more interesting, Nasses succeeded in tiding over the time until dessert. No sooner was it put before them, and they were left alone, than he got up impulsively, and throwing himself at Zulica's feet, asked her, 'You do love me?'

" 'Have I not told you so often enough?' she answered languorously.

" 'Heavens!' he cried, rising and taking her in his arms, 'can I hear you say it often enough, and can you prove it to me too thoroughly?'

" 'Ah, Nasses!' she replied, allowing herself to relapse into his arms. 'How you abuse my weakness!' "

"And what the devil did she want him to do with it?" the Sultan said. "This is really too much! I think she would have been very nettled if he had left her alone. No, women are too queer...very queer indeed! They never know what they want. One never knows where one is with them, and –"

"What anger!" the Sultana interrupted. "What a torrent of epigrams! What have we done to you, I should like to know?"

"No," the Sultan answered, "I am saying all this quite coolly. Need one be angry with women to think them absurd?"

"You are caustic beyond parallel," the Sultana told him, "and I fear that you, who hates wits so much, are about to become an incorrigible one yourself."

"It's that Zulica who has vexed me!" the Sultan retorted. "I don't like ill-placed affectations."

"May your Majesty be pleased to be less incensed against her," Amanzei said. "She is not going to keep them up for long."

CHAPTER XVI

Which Contains a Dissertation Which Will Not Appeal to Everyone

"After she had said those few words which displeased your Majesty, Zulica said no more.

" 'Do you think,' Nasses asked her at last, 'that Mazulhim loved you better than I do?'

" 'He praised me more,' she answered. 'But it seems to me that you love me better.'

" 'I will give you no excuse for doubting my affection,' he replied. 'Yes, Zulica, you will soon know how short of mine Mazulhim's feelings fell.'

" 'What?' she said. 'What –'

"Nasses did not give her time to conclude, and she did not complain at having been interrupted.

" 'Ah, Nasses!' she cried dotingly, 'how tenderly you deserve to be loved!'

"Nasses answered this eulogy only as a man does who thinks he would be less praised for his present performance were it not to encourage him to greater prowess. He had softened Zulica; he ended by astonishing her – thus she conceived a great regard for him, almost a respect, which, given the motive to which he owed them, became very agreeable, for they must always flatter a man, especially as with women they are not the result of frustration, as the emotions are. Nasses, well satisfied with himself, thought he might allow Zulica's admiration to relax. It was nothing to him that he had overcome her, he knew her too well to be flattered by that, and the kindness she had shown him, far from diminishing his hatred for her, only increased it. He felt for her that deep scorn which it is impossible for us to hide from the people for whom we feel it, or to varnish over; and in this condition of mind he did not think he could too soon show her the contempt her conduct had aroused in him.

" 'So you find,' he asked her, 'that I do not praise you as much as Mazulhim did?'

" 'Yes,' she answered. 'But at the same time I find you know more about love than he does.'

" 'That is a subtlety I cannot understand,' he went on. 'What meaning do you at the moment give to the word love?'

" 'The one it has,' she retorted. 'It only has one that I know of, and that is the only one I claim to speak about. But why do you, who seem to love so well, ask me what love is?'

" 'If I ask,' he replied, 'it is not that I do not know; but, as everybody defines the emotion differently according to his nature, I want to know what especially you meant when you said I loved you better than Mazulhim. I cannot understand what the difference is that you make between him and me if you do not tell me what his way of loving was.'

" 'Why,' she answered, pretending to blush, 'his heart is worn out.'

" 'His heart is worn out!' he repeated. 'That is an expression which, to my thinking, means nothing in particular. No doubt the heart gets tired when an affair goes on too long; but Mazulhim could not have been like that with you, since you were new both to his eye and to his mind. Therefore, what you are telling me about him is not what I want to know.'

" 'Nevertheless,' she retorted, 'that is all I shall tell. What I know about him is that there are few men less made for loving than he is, or so I suppose; and do not ply me with any more questions about him, for on that point I have nothing more to say.'

" 'Ah, now I understand you,' he answered. 'All the same, I do not recognize Mazulhim in the picture you give me of him.'

" 'But,' she protested, 'it seems to me that I am not telling you anything about him.'

" 'I beg your pardon!' he took up. 'One can easily guess what you are accusing a man of when you say his heart is worn out; it is a decorous and polite expression but quite well understood. Yet I am surprised that you have had to complain of him.'

" 'I am not complaining, Nasses,' she replied. 'But since you want to know what I think of him, I must tell you that as a matter of fact I also was very surprised.'

" 'Ho, ho!' he said. 'What now? He was...?'

" 'It is astonishing,' she agreed. 'At least I believe he is.'

" 'Oh, I am quite prepared to take your word for it.'

" 'No doubt,' she answered ironically. 'Experience has given me vast knowledge on the subject!'

" 'Experience or not,' he replied, 'everyone knows what a lover ought to be like when one has been good enough to leave him no more to ask for; on that matter tradition is clear. But I must confess once more that you surprise me, for Mazulhim –'

" 'And really, Nasses,' she interrupted, 'to such a degree that you can hardly imagine it.'

" 'I cannot get over my astonishment,' he answered. 'I know he has done some incredible things, wonders, really.'

" 'No doubt, he himself told you about them,' she said.

" 'Were it only out of self-love,' he declared, 'I should suspect such a tale. No, he has told me nothing of the sort, and, what is more, he is really modest on that score.'

" 'Modest,' she replied, 'he cannot be; perhaps, however, he is sometimes truthful about it.'

" 'Madam! Madam!' he said, 'such a brilliant reputation as Mazulhim's must have some foundation, and you will never induce me to believe that a man of whom all the women in Agra think so highly can be so despicable a fellow.'

" 'But,' she argued, 'do you suppose that any woman who was dissatisfied with Mazulhim – if indeed there can be any who are affected by what we are talking about – would breathe a word to anyone as to why she was so dissatisfied with him?'

" 'Precisely yes,' he replied. 'She would not tell everyone, but she would tell someone, and the proof of this is: here are you telling me. I am aware that I owe this confidence only to our peculiar relations. But Mazulhim has attracted others besides you. After loving him, they have loved others, to whom, no doubt, they confided their adventures. In Agra there are perhaps a thousand women who have found Mazulhim irresistible: thus, there must be forty thousand men, or thereabouts, who know, with great accuracy, what he is, and you expect a secret of this sort to be buried away among these piqued ladies and envious gentlemen? That is hardly likely. No, Madam – once more, no; a man such as Mazulhim seemed to you to be could not have impressed everybody for so long. Shall I tell you another thing? You know Telmissa? She is certainly no longer either young or beautiful. It is only three days ago at most that Mazulhim proved his esteem for her to the full, and deserved and acquired hers. That, at any rate, is a fact. Telmissa declares it to whomsoever wants to listen, and she is not given to saying good of a man without due cause, and we men know of no woman whose praises do us greater credit, or which are harder to come by. Can you think ill of Mazulhim after that?'

" 'No,' she answered drily. 'I believe he is incomparable. It is doubtless my fault,' she added, with a disdainful smile, 'that I have not found him so.'

" 'I am not prepared to take that view,' he continued. 'Yet you must admit that it seems inconceivable. And, besides, though you may not believe it, if I were a woman, people of the kind you took Mazulhim for would please me much more than the others.'

" 'I do not see,' she replied, 'that this would be a reason for not wanting them, or for leaving them; but I must confess that I do not see upon what ground they are to be preferred.'

" 'They love better,' he said. 'They alone understand delicacy, consideration. The more they feel they are being handsomely treated by being loved, the more eagerly they try to deserve it. Necessarily subservient, they are slaves rather than lovers. Sensual and refined, they are forever inventing compensations, and perhaps to them are due love's most recondite delights. If they are transported, it is not to the vehemence of a blind passion, which is not flattering to a woman, that they owe the ardor which fills his heart; it is she alone, her charms alone, that conquer nature. Can she ever know a sweeter, a more real triumph?'

" 'Your opinions are all so perverse that what you say does not surprise me,' Zulica said.

" 'You think too correctly to think this one perverse,' he answered. 'And I know more than one woman who –'

" 'Let us quit this conversation,' she interrupted. 'I have never cared to argue about things that do not concern me. In any case, as far as I can see, it is for Mazulhim rather than for you to gain consent to this opinion.'"

"Quite right," the Sultan said. "When is she going away?"

"How impatient you are!" the Sultana remarked.

"Not that I find this tedious," the Sultan went on. "Far from it. But, though I am very amused, it occurs to me that I would just as soon listen to something else. That's just how I am!"

"What do you mean?" the Sultana asked him.

"Isn't it plain?" he answered. "I think I'm very clear. When I say that's how I am, I mean that I think one pleasure doesn't always prevent a man wanting another. I will explain myself better still."

"A great many things lose in the explanation," the Sultana broke in. "We understand you. Can you want anything else?"

"Yes," the Sultan said. "I want Amanzei to polish off his tale."

"To do that he must go on with it," the Sultana stated.

"On the contrary," Shah Baham retorted. "It seems to me that if he left off now he would finish it much sooner; but, as I am complaisance itself, I allow him to go on – on condition, however, that this does not commit me to anything."

" 'And besides,' Zulica continued, 'I shall be obliged if you will talk to me no more of Mazulhim.'

" 'Very willingly,' he answered. 'It was this worn-out heart of which you spoke that drew us into a conversation, an idle one to boot, and one for which I would blame myself, since it has vexed you, did I not remember that my affection for you, and my wishfulness to know why you thought I loved you more than Mazulhim, was the only thing that brought it about. The more I value your feelings for me, the less I think you ought to blame me for a curiosity I feel only because I love you.'

" 'Yet,' she answered sadly, 'it seems to me that for the last few minutes you have not loved me as much as you did. I do not know why I think it, but I do, and the notion hurts me.'

" 'I am enchanted to find that it does,' Nasses replied. 'That sort of uneasiness, which is no less acute though it is baseless, can only be felt by a heart as tender as it is delicate; you do me an injustice, but that very injustice proves to me how much you love me, and makes you all the dearer to me. Reassure yourself, my charming Zulica,' he pursued. 'Heavens! How delicious it is to banish your fears! Sweet Zulica! Ah, for your happiness and mine, may these fears return again and again!'

"As he said this he took Zulica in his arms and covered her with the tenderest caresses.

" 'What raptures you give me!' she cried. 'I feel yours enter my heart: they fill it, disturb it, penetrate it. Ah, Nasses! What a pleasure it is for me to feel such sweet raptures! I have never felt like this before. You only! Yes, you only!...But, Nasses! Cruel!'

"Although Zulica did not stop talking, it was impossible for me to hear what she said."

"I suppose because she spoke too softly?" the Sultan suggested.

"Most likely," Amanzei answered.

"In any case," the Sultan went on, "you certainly did not lose much by not hearing her, for, if I am not mistaken, there was not much sense in what she said – at least, as far as I am concerned, I haven't understood a word."

"I am of your opinion, Sire," Amanzei agreed. "Nothing could have been less lucid. However, either Nasses understood her, or he had not at that moment any more sense than she had, for he said nearly the same things."

"Didn't I tell you so?" the Sultan chimed in. "These folk had no sense at all."

"When Nasses and Zulica had become more reasonable," Amanzei continued, "Zulica said to him, with the tenderest glances, 'How delightful you are, Nasses. Ah! Why did I not love you sooner!'

" 'You have less to complain of than I,' he answered. 'I, I say, whom every minute teaches that I have begun to live only since you have loved me. When I consider to what beauties Mazulhim has closed his eyes, how I pity him! In this very spot, which your kindness to me makes as dear as your kindness to him at first made odious to me – how, Zulica, how can the ungrateful man not have blushed to have loved others nor renounced his inconstancy forever! What djinn, what god even, was watching over my welfare, who, after having made him insensible to so many charms, inspired him with the notion of choosing me to tell you of his perfidy? Ah! Zulica, how miserable I should have been if he had been faithful to you, or if someone else –'

" 'Enough!' Zulica interrupted majestically. 'Had he been faithful to me I should never have loved another, but it needed none less than Nasses to oust him from my heart.'

" 'Since you have chosen me,' he replied, 'I believe I am indeed the only man who could have pleased you; but when I think of the position you were in here, of what some giddy rascal Mazulhim might have sent here could have demanded of you, of what price he might perhaps have put upon his silence, I cannot help shuddering.'

" 'I do not quite see why,' she answered. 'Since I should not have wished to gratify him, it would have been all the same to me what he asked.'

" 'You cannot answer for yourself,' he said. 'Some situations are dreadful for a woman, and the one I found you in was perhaps one of the most dreadful –'

" 'As dreadful as you care to make it,' she interrupted him. 'But I beg you to believe that it is less bitter for a woman of feeling to be abandoned by a man who loves her than to give herself to someone she does not love.'

" 'That is beyond doubt,' he answered. 'But it is a terrible thing to be caught in a little retreat. I do not know what I should do if I were a woman and that happened to me; but it seems to me that I should be very glad for the man who discovered me there to say nothing about it.'

" 'You would be very glad,' she caught him up. 'Apparently you think that a very natural thing to say; and I also should have been very glad for the man who discovered me here to say nothing about it. What a remark! You must be going out of your wits to say such things. Do you think that a gentleman needs to be bribed to silence in the way you seem to imagine; and, moreover, do you think certain proposals are made to a certain type of woman?'

" 'Yes, certainly,' he answered. 'Every woman discovered in a little retreat betrays her susceptibility; from that terrible deductions are drawn; and, as a rule, the more agreeable a woman is, the less generous a man is.'

" 'Oh, that is a fairy tale,' Zulica retorted. 'Only attraction, I say only the strongest attraction, can excuse a woman's giving herself; and I do not believe, whatever people may say about it, that a single one of them would buy so dear as you think the discretion she would stand in need of; and honor –'

" 'Right!' he interrupted. 'Do you think a woman ever hesitates to sacrifice her honor to her reputation?'

"'In any case,' she replied, '*I* would not, and I do not know of any situation, however horrible, in which I should be induced to grant a man what my heart persisted in refusing him.'

"'How delicate one must be,' he went on, 'to make that distinction and go no further: while waiting to win her heart, one tries to engage a woman, so that the best thing she can do is to give one her heart; and often she is only too happy to be able to do so in the end.'

"'I begin to see your meaning, sir,' she said to him. 'You are trying to make me feel that you think you owe me only to the situation in which you found me here, and you would rather deprive yourself of any charm than not think ill of me. There,' she added in tears, 'is the happiness I was congratulating myself upon. Ah, Nasses! Was I to expect such cruel treatment from you?'

"'But, Zulica,' he protested, 'do you think I have forgotten the resistance you offered me, and the pains it cost me to win my happiness from you?'

"'And do you think,' she answered sobbing, 'that I do not understand that you are blaming me for not resisting longer still? Alas! Drawn by my inclination for you, even more than by that you showed for me, I yielded without dreading that someday you would make a crime of my not having held out long enough.'

"'What foolishness have you got in your head now, Zulica?' he asked, drawing closer to her. 'That I, I am upbraiding you for having made me happy? Can you think that? I adore you,' he added, forgetful of nothing that might convince her he was telling the truth.

"'Let me be!' she said, repulsing him feebly. 'Let me be! If you can, forget how much I have loved you!'

"Zulica's resistance was so gentle that, even had Nasses's advances been less vigorous, they would have prevailed.

"'You? Cease loving me?' he said tenderly to her, reinforcing his remarks with everything that could make them more persuasive. 'You, who are to make me eternally happy! No, your heart has no hatred for me in it, while mine has nothing but the tenderest feelings for you.'

"'No,' Zulica answered in a voice no longer able to express anger. 'No, traitor! You will deceive me no more. Heavens,' she added even more gently, 'are you not the most unjust and cruel of men? Ah! Let me be...No! You shall not persuade me...I must not forgive you... How I hate you!'

"In spite of all the protestations of hatred Zulica heaped upon Nasses, he would not believe for a moment that he could be hated; and, indeed, Zulica did not seem particularly eager for him to believe it.

" 'I do not know if I am too vain,' he said to her at last, 'but I would almost swear that you hate me less than you say you do.'

" 'You are welcome to that vanity,' she answered, shrugging her shoulders. 'Do you suppose I hate you the less for it? Is it my fault that... But it is true, I hate you tremendously. Do not laugh,' she added, 'nothing can be more definite.'

" 'I have too high an opinion of you to believe it,' he replied. 'So much so that I might catch you in inconstancy and still not believe it. I am, and will be, convinced that you love me as much as you can love anything.'

" 'In that case,' she retorted, 'I love you as much as it is possible to love. I am not one for mild emotions.'

" 'That I believe,' he answered. 'And that is what I wished to convey. The more refined one is, the more passionate one is; and, now I come to think of it, a woman of your turn of mind is very unfortunate. In all truth, I dare to say it: we are so depraved nowadays that the more estimable a woman is, the more she is laughed at. I do not say that it is women alone who do her this wrong – that would be simple enough; but what is inconceivable is that men do so also! Men, who are always demanding fine feelings!'

" 'That is only too true,' she agreed.

" 'I see it in society,' he continued. 'What do we look for there? Love? No, certainly not! We want to gratify our vanity, to have our names on everybody's lips, to go from woman to woman. So as not to miss one, we rush after the most despicable victories, prouder of having won so many women than of possessing one worthy of pleasing; to pursue them all the time, and never to love them.'

" 'Ah, how right you are!' she cried. 'But it is also the women's fault. You would despise them less if they all had a certain standard, if they all had feelings that call for respect.'

" 'I admit it with regret,' he declared. 'But one certainly cannot deny that feelings have depreciated a little.'

" 'A little!' she said in astonishment. 'Ah! Say a great deal. Of course, there are still some right-thinking women, but they are not in the majority. I speak not of those who love, for I believe that even you consider them more to be pitied than blamed; but for one whom love alone guides, how many are there who, far from being able to make that an excuse, do all they can to prevent themselves from ever being suspected of knowing love!'

" 'There are,' he took up, 'very few women fair-minded enough to speak as you do.'

" 'What is the good of trying to conceal such obvious things?' she asked. 'I tell you, for my part, that just as much as I wish right-thinking women to be considerately treated, so much would I like contemptible, disreputable women to be overwhelmed with scorn. Every weakness has its excuse; but, really, vice cannot be too roughly reviled.'

" 'It is reviled,' he said, 'but it is tolerated. Vice only wears its true colors in the eyes of those not fashioned to arouse desires; and perhaps the greatest attraction among women today is that indecent air which proclaims them to be won easily.'

" 'I am aware,' she replied, 'that those are the ones you seek out most; it is never the heart you ask for. Since you do not love, you do not care about being loved; and, provided that you have your way with the person, any other kind of conquest seems useless to you.' "

"One moment, Amanzei," the Sultan said. "When exactly does he despise her?"

"What a superb question!" the Sultana cried.

"What I say is not from disagreeableness," the Sultan responded. "A question is simply a question – and, as far as I can see, there was nothing wrong in asking that one. I am being bored, and I am taken to task for saying so. There's a nice thing now! Yes, instead of a story, I am fobbed off with a conversation where there is nothing to laugh at except when they stop speaking, and then I am told that I am in the wrong! One word to the wise is as good as a thousand, Amanzei, and if Nasses does not despise Zulica by tomorrow... I say no more; and it's me you'll have to deal with."

CHAPTER XVII

Which Will Teach Inexperienced Ladies, If Such There Be, How to Evade Embarrassing Questions

"Your Majesty," Amanzei said the next day, "no doubt remembers –"

"Yes," the Sultan interrupted abruptly, "I remember that yesterday I nearly died of tedium. Is that what you mean?"

"If the story wearies you," the Sultana remarked, "it has only to be stopped."

"Not at all, if you please!" the Sultan answered. "I want it to go on, and that it not bore me – if possible, of course, for I don't ask for impossible things."

Amanzei took up the thread thus: " 'I fear that you seem,' Zulica went on, 'to have very little delicacy.'

"'There you wrong me,' he replied calmly. 'I am by nature very prone to love. Nevertheless, I confess that I have had more women than I have loved.'

"'But that is disgraceful!' she answered. 'I cannot conceive how you can boast of it!'

"'I boast not,' he denied. 'I merely state a fact.'

"'I think you have deceived many women,' she said.

"'I have left some, and deceived none,' he replied. 'They had not implored me to be faithful, and so I did not promise them I would be; and you must admit that, if people take up with each other without making conditions, neither can accuse the other of violating them.'

"'I am terribly curious to hear all your adventures,' Zulica said.

"'Do you want a very detailed story of my life?' Nasses asked. 'It would be long, and I fear you would find it very tedious. However, I can obey you without taking that risk, by suppressing a few trifles. I have been ten years in society, I am twenty-five, and you are the thirty-third beauty with whom I have had a regular affair.'

"'Thirty-three!' she cried.

"'Yes, on my honor, only thirty-three,' he answered. 'But that is nothing to be surprised at: I have never been the fashion.'

"'Ah, Nasses,' she said, 'how much I am to be pitied for loving you! And how little I shall be able to depend upon your constancy!'

"'I do not see why,' he replied. 'Do you think that my having had thirty-three women will make me love you the less?'

"'Yes,' she maintained. 'The less you had loved, the more you would have had left to love me with, and, in fact, your emotions would not be so absolutely blunted.'

"'I believe,' he answered, 'that I have proved to you that my heart is not worn out: besides, to tell you frankly, there are very few affairs where the emotions come into play at all. Opportunity, politeness, idleness cause nearly all of them. People say, without feeling it, that they find each other attractive; they unconsciously become involved; they see that they wait for love in vain; and they part for fear of becoming bored. Sometimes it happens that one is mistaken about one's feelings; one thought it was passion and finds it was mere fancy, an impulse, which does not last long and wears itself out in pleasure, instead of seeming to renew love. All that, as you see, makes it come about that, though one may have had several affairs, one may never have been in love.'

"'So you have never been in love?' she enquired.

"'Pardon me,' he replied. 'I have twice been madly in love, and I feel, from the way I am beginning with you, that if since that time my heart has not been moved, it was not because I was never to love again, as I thought, but that I had not yet met the person who could once more give it more than it had lost. But, since you have asked me, might I be allowed to ask in my turn, how often you have been set afire?'

" 'Yes,' she assented. 'And I would allow you all the more willingly, had I not already told you: you must know that you and Mazulhim are the only people who have stirred me.'

" 'If we were less intimate,' he said, 'it would be quite natural for you to say such things. I have not even objected, though it was quite impossible to hide Mazulhim from me, to your having tried to do so; but now that confidence ought to be established, and that I have hidden nothing from you, I confess it would seem strange were you not to make me the repository of your secrets.'

" 'You would certainly be such,' she answered, 'had I kept any back, but I swear to you that I have nothing to reproach myself with on that score, and even that it seems amazing to me, seeing how short a time I have loved you, that I should have such great confidence in you, and finally that I should be as sure of you as I am of myself.'

" 'I am charmed to hear it, Madam,' he replied, in a nettled tone. 'Nevertheless, I am bold enough to say that, considering the way I gave myself into your hands, I had a right to expect better of you.'

"As he said this he made as if to separate from her, but she held him back and asked tenderly: 'What is this fancy of yours, Nasses? How can it be that a moment ago you upbraided yourself for doubting what I said, and that now, as it seems, you would blame yourself for believing me?'

" 'If I must tell you, Madam,' he said, 'just now I did not believe you; but, being then engaged in something more important to me, I thought it more worthwhile to work you to persuasion than to enter into details that could, at that moment, only have displeased you, and which, indeed, I had no right to exact from you.'

" 'But, Nasses,' she insisted, 'I swear that I have nothing to tell you beyond what I have told you.'

" 'Impossible, Madam!' he interrupted bluntly. 'It is unbelievable that during the fifteen years you have been in society nobody should have made advances to you, and that you should not have succumbed, at least once or twice. You would be the first who, in such a long time, would have had only two lovers, or else you will be forced to agree that the taste for dalliance came upon you very late in life.'

" 'That would not be so new as to be unbelievable, sir,' she answered. 'And I am very much mistaken if many others besides myself have not long remained indifferent from not having early on met the man who was destined to make them feel. I have, I assure you, nothing to tell you; but, even had I anything of the sort to confide to you, the fear of losing you would still prevent me from doing so. In my experience, contempt has always resulted from such confidences; and, though having previously loved does not make us guilty toward the man who engrosses us, it is, nevertheless, very rarely that his vanity forgives us for his not having been the first man to arouse feelings in us.'

" 'What an idea!' he said. 'That I of all people would despise you because you were to give me, by confessing all you have done, renewed proofs of your affection, and perhaps the most convincing of all, seeing how difficult it usually is to get it! Well now! You have loved Mazulhim – did that shock me? Why should a few more lovers be disagreeable to me? Have I any bone to pick with my predecessors? Is it your fault if fate did not place me before your eyes the first of all of them? No, Zulica, no! I am not even among those who think that a woman who has loved often is incapable of loving again. Far from thinking that the heart exhausts itself in loving, I am, on the contrary, convinced that the more often one loves, the more ready one is to feel deeply, and the more delicacy one develops.'

" 'According to that principle, then,' she answered, 'you would not be flattered at being a woman's first lover?'

" 'I am bold enough to say no,' he replied. 'And this is my basis for holding an opinion that may seem absurd to you. At that tender age when a woman has not yet loved, if she wishes to be conquered, it is less that she is urged by her feelings than that she wishes to have them: in short, she would rather please than love. She is dazzled rather than moved. How can you believe her when she says she loves? Has she anything with which to compare the nature and strength of her feelings? In a heart where the newness of the most feeble emotions makes them important, the most trivial sentiment appears to be passion, and mere desire, rapture. In short, it is not at a stage at which one is so ignorant of love that one can flatter oneself that one feels it, or ought to be convinced that one does.'

" 'Perhaps one does exaggerate one's emotions,' Zulica agreed. 'But at least one says only what one thinks one feels; and is the lover any less happy whether the disorder arises from the heart or from the imagination? No, Nasses, whatever the disadvantages of first love, I would love you a thousand times more than I do, if that were possible, if I were the first girl to whom you rendered homage.'

" 'You would lose more than you think,' he pursued. 'I am at the present moment a thousand times better able to recognize your value than

I should have been at the period when you would have liked me to love you. At that time I appreciated nothing of wit, delicacy, or true feeling. Always tempted, never in love, my heart was never stirred, even at those moments when, carried away by my transports, I was no longer my own master. Nevertheless, I was believed to be in love, and I believed it myself. They congratulated themselves on being able to make me feel so much, and on my side I was delighted at being capable of such delicate voluptuousness; it seemed to me that no one else in the world was lucky enough to be able to feel the charms of love as keenly as I did. Ceaselessly at the feet of the person I loved, sometimes languid, never extinguished, I found in my soul a hundred possibilities I was astonished to be able to use to such little purpose. A single glance would make my being tremble and catch fire, and since my imagination always outdistanced my pleasure –'

" 'Ah, Nasses, Nasses!' she cried rapturously. 'How delicious you must have been! No, you no longer love as you did then.'

" 'A thousand times more,' he replied. 'At the time of which I am telling you, I did not love at all. Carried away by the fire of my youth, it was to that, and not to my heart, that I owed all those feelings I believed to be love, and since then I have come thoroughly to know –'

" 'Ah!' she interrupted. 'You must have lost much by being disillusioned. Jealousy, suspicion, a thousand monsters that then you would have been ashamed to think of poison your pleasures now. Knowing more, you have loved less, and so have been less happy. Your mind has been enlightened at the cost of your heart; now you argue better about love, but you no longer love so well.'

" 'That argument,' he went on, 'would tell as heavily against you as against me, and I must believe, still supposing that Mazulhim was your first lover, that you cannot love me as much as you loved him.'

" 'I am not at all surprised at your making that point,' she answered. 'You like to pursue only those arguments in which I am bound to figure badly; but let us drop the subject.'

" 'Drop the subject!' he said. 'By no means.'

" 'In any case,' she continued sourly, 'seeing how you have lived, it is not at all surprising that you should think ill of women.'

" 'And supposing,' he interrupted, 'it was because of how women behave that I do not think well of them? You will say that that is impossible.'

" 'No, I assure you,' she said disdainfully, 'I would not take the trouble.'

" 'Ah, I understand!' he retorted. 'You are afraid it would be useless. So you absolutely refuse to tell me that you have loved before?'

" 'What!' she cried. 'Are you still harping on that string? If you loved me, could you doubt what I tell you?'

" 'Truly, Zulica,' he declared, 'believe that if you like, but this is becoming monstrously ridiculous.'

"Zulica, as your Majesty has seen," Amanzei said, "had for a long time been trying to turn the conversation –"

"She was quite right to," the Sultan interrupted. "And, as for you, you would have done much better to shorten it a little, and to spare me all those dissertations which you have dragged in without any earthly excuse. Admit that you are nothing but a babbler and do it from sheer itch of telling! How can one take the least interest in these liars? In a word, get on with your story!"

"Zulica," Amanzei went on, "for a long time clumsily parried Nasses's questions. At last she apparently surrendered; and, after making him give his word that he would think no less of her, said: 'I ought all the more to forbid myself to satisfy your curiosity, seeing how long I have held out. Perhaps your grudge at my refusing you so long will outweigh your gratitude at receiving the confession you are at last wresting from me. You must know that it is easier to arouse new feelings in a woman than to make her admit to those she has had. I do not know whether it is from falsity that some think this way; but, as far as I am concerned, I can swear that my reticence was not based on so unworthy a motive. I believe that it is impossible to recall with pleasure a frailty, which, far from presenting itself to your mind with the charms it once had for you, never comes back but hand in hand with the remorse consequent upon it, or the unhappy memory of the bad behavior of a lover.'

" 'That is perfectly true,' Nasses remarked. 'A sensitive woman is much to be pitied.'

"Very good!" the Sultan said. "But for the sake of the pleasure your story gives me, I wish you to postpone until tomorrow the continuation – for I dare not yet say the end – of this preposterous conversation."

CHAPTER XVIII

Full of Allusions Very Difficult to Trace

" 'You must know then,' Zulica continued, 'that, when I came into society, I did not fail, without being more beautiful than any other girl, to find more lovers than I wished for, being as I then was so foolish about what is called the empire of beauty. When I say lovers, I mean that crowd of idle people who say they are in love more from habit than from feeling, to whom one listens because one must, and who are more successful in making us think that we are attractive than in being so themselves. For a long time they tickled my vanity without touching my heart. Born sensitive, I feared love: I felt that it would be hard to find a heart as tender as mine, and that the greatest misfortune that can befall a woman is to have a passion, however happy she may be in it. While I was indifferent, these considerations governed me; but at last I found out that they had ruled my heart only because no one had succeeded in reaching it, and that the calm we congratulate ourselves upon is a matter of luck rather than of thought. One moment, one single moment was enough to disturb my heart. To see, to love, even to adore; to experience, at the same time, with extreme violence all the sweetest and bitterest feelings; to be swung up on the most extravagant hopes, and to plunge from the height into the most tortuous uncertainties – all that was the work of one minute and one look. Astounded, even embarrassed by a state so new to my soul; devoured by desires that until then had been unknown to me; feeling the necessity of untangling the cause, and fearing to do so; sunk in the sweet emotion, that divine languidness which had overtaken all my senses, I dared not apply my mind to destroying the impulses that, confusing and inexplicable as they were for me, already let me enjoy that happiness for which no name can be found, either when one feels it or has ceased to feel it. Loving, I began to live. I tried to struggle against whatever hold these emotions had over me. The claims of duty, the fear of losing my position in society, sighs, tears, remorse, all were useless; rather, all increased the cruel emotion that made me its slave. Ah, Nasses! How immeasurable was my delight when, by the eager yet respectful attentions of the man I adored, I knew that I was loved! What turmoil! What rapture! With what delicacy, with what tact, did he not reveal his love! What anguish it was to hold my own in leash! How lucky you men are, Nasses, to be able to tell the person you love that you love her as soon as you feel the first tremors! Not to have to practice that dissimulation so necessary for us if we are to keep your good opinion, but so agonizing for a tender heart! How often, hearing him sigh beside me, did I not sigh with sorrow at not being able to do so for him! When his eyes gazed tenderly into mine, how clear I found that sweet, languorous expression, how plainly at last I read love itself! Ah! At those moments, which took me so far from myself, how had I the strength to elude that voluptuousness which enticed me? At last he spoke. Nasses! You cannot know the pleasure which that charming, tender confession gives. You are told you are loved only after you have begged to be told it, and sometimes begged too long, after having been made to repeat your declaration a thousand times. But to see a bashful lover, an adored lover, who does not guess his good fortune, possessed by affection, by fear, by respect, come to your feet to utter his feelings for you; even to be unable to find words to tell you them; trembling as much from sheer love as from the fear of being refused; to anticipate his words, to mutter them to yourself, to engrave them upon your heart while you answer that you do not believe him, and inwardly to deplore your lie; even to exaggerate to yourself what he says, to add to all the love he shows for you all that you feel for him – Nasses! Believe me, no sight or pleasure can be nearly so sweet as those.'

" 'If vanity alone is enough to make you enjoy the sight you depict to me so vividly,' Nasses answered, 'I suppose that, when love infuses the heart's desires, nothing in the world can be more satisfactory to you. But this man you loved so tenderly spoke at last; did you answer?'

" 'Imagine my confusion!' she replied. 'Torn between love and virtue, if the latter did not win, it at least enabled me to mask the former, but not so much as I wished for. Too long enthralled by his words, my emotion revealed the secret of my heart; and while I believed that I was answering him coldly, my mouth and my eyes told him a thousand times over that my flame burned as strongly as his.'

" 'That is a misfortune that has happened to others,' Nasses remarked coolly. 'Well, and who was this dangerous man, whom, in spite of your pride, to see was to love?'

" 'What is his name to you?' she asked. 'Am I not telling you what you want to know?'

" 'Not yet,' he averred. 'And you yourself feel that the confession is not complete.'

" 'Well,' she replied, 'it was the Rajah Amagi.'

" 'Amagi!' he cried. 'When on earth did you have an affair with him? He is my friend, he hides nothing from me, and I know that since he has been in society he has never been in love with anyone but Canzada. Amagi!' he repeated. 'Are you sure that you are not making some mistake?'

" 'Certainly not!' she cried in her turn. 'What an extraordinary question! Absolutely unheard of!'

" 'Not at all,' he pursued. 'You will see that it is quite natural. Amagi has told me that, in spite of his unbounded affection for Canzada and his desire not to fail her, he has sometimes amused himself elsewhere because some women make such unequivocal advances; and men are so conceited that their contempt for women does not prevent their being grateful, at least momentarily, for what women do for them. In telling me of his lapses from Canzada, he confessed that he blamed himself for them all the more since, among the women who had sometimes seduced him from her, he had never found one who deserved his good opinion or his friendship, and who had not done for him merely from light-headedness what he had sometimes been absurd enough to think due to feelings so strong as to make them forget all propriety. Surely you cannot be among those? In consequence, I am bound to believe that he has not had an affair with you.'

" 'Now you know that he does not tell you everything,' she answered. 'For he was in love with me for over three years, and most passionately.'

" 'If he did not tell me about it,' he retorted, 'it was not because he wanted to make a secret of it; but, apparently, because he simply forgot all about it. Was it you who were unfaithful to him?'

" 'How much longer are you going to ask me such questions?' she demanded.

" 'I beg your pardon for asking it,' he replied, 'but you are not at all the sort of person who is jilted, and so it must not surprise you. He left you then? And who engaged your attention after him?'

" 'Nobody,' she answered with a candid expression. 'Given over for a long time to the sorrow of having lost him, I hoped I could never be susceptible again; but Mazulhim appeared, and I did not keep my promise.'

" 'Egad!' he cried. 'Women are most unlucky, and quite cruelly exposed to slander.'

" 'That is only too true,' she said. 'But what should bring that into your mind just now?'

" 'Your case,' he replied, 'to which, since I must tell you, a few more adventures have been ascribed than I see you can have had.'

" 'Oh,' she answered, 'that neither vexes nor astonishes me. A woman need merely be something less than frightful, and everybody at once imagines that she is more amenable to love than she ought to be. And often it is the men to whom she has least lent her ear whom the public associates her the most firmly with. But it does not matter to me, whatever they may say. Would it not be possible to get you to speak of something else?'

" 'Then it is not true that you have had all the lovers they say you have?' he persisted.

"Zulica replied to this fresh impertinence with a mere shrug of her shoulders.

" 'Do not be annoyed with me for saying this,' he pursued. 'Were you less lovable, I should find it easier to believe that you are not condensing your history.'

" 'I beg your pardon,' she said acidly. 'I have had the whole world.'

" 'That is exactly what I was told,' he remarked. 'Your beginnings are not certain, but it is known that in your earliest youth, desiring eagerly to be talented and believing that the best way to become highly so was to be keenly interested in those who were, you did not disdain your teachers, which is the reason why you sing so tastefully and dance with so much grace.'

" 'Good God! What horrors!' Zulica gasped.

" 'You are right to cry out about it, Madam,' he commented coldly, 'for, in fact, it is horrible. But, for my part, I do not condemn you, and I cannot even honor you enough for having – at an age when women who someday will be the least reserved have every imaginable prejudice – had the strength of mind to uproot all those which your birth and your education must have implanted in you. When you entered society, convinced that one could not be too hypocritical, you hid your inclination to pleasure under a cold, prudish manner. Born without much feeling but full of curiosity, all the men you saw pricked this curiosity; and, as far as you could, you probed them all to the bottom. When one has as much wit and insight as you, it is not very difficult to decipher a man, and I have heard say that the man who cost you most pains took you no more than a week to analyze. These philosophic amusements became known; people gave your motives an ill turn; without sacrificing your curiosity, you curbed it. Not for long, however. Your particular occupations not being approved by those who observed them, you thought you would remove yourself from their sight, and, renouncing solitude, you brought into society your natural bent to know everything. At that time, the Princess Sahab had Iskander for a lover; you wanted to judge for yourself if her taste was to be trusted, so filched him from her. She has never forgiven you, and even now laments it daily.'

" 'Ah, just Heavens!' Zulica cried, beside herself with rage. 'Can there be more atrocious calumnies than this?'

" 'I have been assured,' he went on as coolly as before, 'that you soon left Iskander to take Akbar Mirza, with whom – since you found him tiresome, though he was a prince – you associated the Vizier Atamulk and the Emir Noureddin. The prince's conversation with you being entirely about his ailments (which you knew to be even worse than he admitted), the Vizier being too much occupied with state affairs to be as occupied with your charms as he ought to have been, and his sole entertainment of you being the details of his profound political schemes, while the Emir's were of his great feats of arms, you were disgusted with three men who were more important than agreeable. People dare add that, knowing how dangerous it is to have enemies when one is at Court, you kept them in ignorance of the roles you made them play; and that, forced to humor them, you threw yourself with the greatest secrecy into the arms of young Velid, who, less great, less profound, less of a warrior, but more charming than his rivals, was for some time your only compensation for the spleen they gave you. It is also said that, finding Velid cooling in his affection, and wishing to revive his flame by giving him some uneasiness, you took Jemla; that Velid, annoyed at seeing a rival and carefully spying upon you, ended by discovering the other three, and that the whole affair, until then so judiciously organized, finished in a scandal most damaging as far as you were concerned, for which you suffered the most bitter and public mortification.'

" 'Ah, this is too much!' Zulica interposed, rising. 'And I am going to –'

" 'One moment more, if you please, Madam,' Nasses said, holding her back. 'People have even been so outrageously impudent as to say that, seeing you were unsuccessful in fixed affairs, hating love but still loving pleasure, you allowed yourself only fleeting amusements, agreeable enough to fill your idle hours but never keen enough to stir your heart. A kind of philosophy, one may mention, which has not failed to take some hold in this century, and whose wisdom and usefulness I could easily demonstrate, were this a fitting occasion to do so.'

"At the conclusion of this statement Zulica burst into tears; Nasses, pretending not to notice, continued thus: 'You realize, of course, that I am far too fair, and know you far too well to believe implicitly everything I have been told about you.'

" 'You are too tolerant,' she answered.

" 'No,' he replied modestly. 'The attitude I adopt toward you is perfectly simple, and to test it I have only to appeal to the way you yielded to my desires; but though I do not believe the whole story, it would be impossible for me not to believe any of it.'

" 'But why?' she asked. 'Everything you have been told is so likely that I cannot conceive why you should have such a misplaced consideration for me.'

" 'Then,' he said, 'I believe only –'

" 'Ah, believe it all!' she interrupted. 'Believe it all, and let us never meet again!'

" 'Even if I ought to,' he answered, 'the effort would be too great for me. Think whether, believing you innocent, I could so burden myself or be so barbarous as to do what you apparently advise me to.'

" 'No, no,' she replied, 'you believe everything you have been told, you believe it, and you are not worth my bothering to disabuse you.'

" 'So then we are falling out!' he pursued. 'The same evening will have seen the birth and death of your flame – for I am not speaking of mine,' he added with a sigh – 'since I fear only too strongly that it will last forever!'

" 'Yes,' Zulica answered, 'we are falling out, and forever.'

" 'Forever!' he cried. 'That is to say you will leave me as readily as you accepted me? That, upon my honor, is a thing I did not think possible. But how can this prodigious constancy on which you so plume yourself, this sensitive soul of yours, lend itself to such a proceeding? What violence will you not do yourself in keeping your word? How I pity you! For, after all, since you must change, what can be better for me than your changing so quickly? Longer dealings with you would have made your breaking with me too painful. Nevertheless, I like to suppose that you will think it over, and that – if it be true that your inclination for me has indeed faded away – you will at least fear that I might say that, though I was crowned with your most special favors, and that you had every reason for giving me the highest praise, you were unable to discipline yourself to constancy for twenty-four hours. I warn you that after the liberties you have allowed me, the world will not view your behavior good-naturedly. No,' he continued, drawing closer to her, and taking her tenderly in his arms, 'no, you will not be so unkind to the most ardent of lovers.'

" 'What is this?' she cried, struggling violently in his arms. 'You expect me to give myself to you again?'

"Thereupon she unburdened on Nasses all the words she could think of to show how very indignant with him she was. He tried in vain to overcome her resistance, for her scorn served her better than that severe chastity of which she had made so out-of-place a display, and he was forced to put forth his most valiant efforts to gain favors so small that he had not even asked her for them hitherto. She was still protecting herself against him, when the sound of an approaching carriage put an end to attack and defense alike.

" 'No doubt, these are my people, sir,' she said. 'And I am going away. I shall not urge you to reflect upon what has happened between us, for that would be useless for you: the more capable one is of behaving badly, the less capable one is of realizing it.'

"She got up as she concluded this speech, and was about to go out when something I shall tell your Majesty about tomorrow compelled her to stay."

"Why tomorrow?" the Sultan asked. "Do you suppose that you

wouldn't tell me today if I had a fancy for it? Luckily for you, I haven't the least curiosity about all this; so tomorrow, or any other day – it's all the same to me."

CHAPTER XIX

Ah! So Much the Better!

"After what had happened between Zulica and Mazulhim, she must have little expected to see him again, yet it was he who came in. She drew back in surprise when she saw who it was; and, tears succeeding her astonishment, she let herself sink upon me. He pretended not to notice the state his arrival had thrown her into and went boldly toward her, saying:

" 'I have come, Queen of my heart, to beg your pardon. A network of troublesome, vexatious, maddening business prevented me from complying with your commands. What is this? You are crying? Oh, Nasses, this is not well done; you have abused my easiness, my friendship, my trust in you!... But really, upon my word, I do not understand anything of all this. Are you angry? I am furious that you should be; sorry beyond words; I shall never get over it. This is a unique occurrence, astonishing, most extraordinary!... Come, may I not know what it is all about? Tell me, you two! You are as dumb as stones. Ah! I see what it is; I am the innocent cause. You think I am unfaithful, yes you do! How little you know me! I come back to you a thousand times, I say a thousand times more tender, more in love, more enchanted than before.'

"The more Mazulhim pretended affection, the more obstinately Zulica, disconcerted and shattered, held her tongue. Nasses, spitefully enjoying her confusion, feared that if he answered Mazulhim she would seize the opportunity to recover, and impatiently expected her answer, in vain. For some time all three remained without speaking.

" 'For Heaven's sake, clear up this mystery,' Mazulhim at last begged Nasses. 'Is it of you or of me that her ladyship has to complain? Does she not love me anymore? Does she love you?'

" 'By no means,' Nasses answered. 'Since I must tell you, it is me this unfaithful creature no longer loves; we have had a falling out.'

" 'Oh, perfidious lady!' Mazulhim said. 'After all the oaths you made me to be faithful forever!... How horrible!'

" 'It was only with extreme difficulty that I succeeded in consoling her for the loss of you,' Nasses went on. 'It is only fair to say that; and to do my duty to the last, I will, at whatever cost to myself, leave you to try if you can console her for the loss of me any more easily. Farewell, Madam,' he proceeded, addressing Zulica. 'My happiness did not last long; but I know the kindness of your heart too well to despair of your someday making up to me what your circumspection causes me to lose now. In case you should be pleased ever to remember me, be sure that I shall always be at your beck and call.'

"Once Nasses had gone, Zulica got up abruptly, and tried to go out also.

" 'No, Madam,' Mazulhim said respectfully, 'I cannot bring myself to let you go without justifying my behavior; perhaps you also might have some little excuses to offer me, and, however that may be, I should think it improper for us to separate without some little explanation on both sides. Are you never going to say anything? Have you already forgotten that you promised me everlasting faith?'

" 'Ah, sir!' she answered weeping, 'do not add to your other delinquencies that of speaking to me again of a love you never felt!'

" 'Well now!' he answered. 'That is what women are like! One misses an appointment through no fault of one's own, one groans, wilts, dies of pain, and when one deserves nothing but pity, when one comes back full of the most tender passion to throw oneself at the feet of one's beloved, one finds oneself held in abhorrence. Still, you would be less unjust only were you less sensitive. With refined minds, one can never err lightly. Thus, I am grateful for your anger, since without it I should never all my life have known how much you loved me, and would therefore have loved you less myself. But tell me though,' he added, going up to her in a familiar way, 'are you really very cross?'

"A savagely scornful look was Zulica's sole answer to this question.

" 'Because really,' he said, 'it would be very easy for me to acquit myself. Yes, indeed,' he added, seeing her shrug her shoulders, 'too easy – I am not exaggerating. For come now, how have I wronged you?'

" 'Upon my soul!' she cried. 'I admire your impudence! To make me come here, and not come yourself! As spiteful, impertinent, and despicable as that behavior is, it is in keeping with your character and did not astonish me. But to add the vilest trick, to send here a stranger whom you had told of my frailty, when you ought to have kept it hidden from everyone –'

" 'Oh, hidden!' he interrupted. 'A fine secret that would be, and of marvelous use! Do you imagine that an affair between people like us can ever be kept secret? But even supposing that, despite all your experience, you were blind enough to think your name would never come up; how, permit me to inquire, have I exposed you? Is not our secret safer in the hands of a gentleman than in those of a slave? And had I even with me the one who acts for me in these matters, who was waiting for us here? Time was short. I chose for my messenger the man who among all my friends I knew to be the best behaved, Nasses, in fact, who besides being well behaved is intelligent, and deserved more than anyone else to be pleasantly received; and who, I am bold enough to say, ought to be considered highly and well treated. And, finally, I shall take the liberty of saying that I do not quite see why, after the thanks you have so generously put him in a position to give you, you need complain of the man I sent you. Between ourselves, this point might be worth clearing up; however, you will do this only if it pleases you to do so: for – and I hope my saying this will not vex you – I am neither so inquisitive nor so difficult as you are.'

" 'What impertinence and fatuity!' Zulica cried.

" 'Gently please, Madam, in expressions of that kind,' Mazulhim said severely. 'Whatever I may be, there are a thousand things I could take you to task about as well, and I beg you not to force me to work my revenge. If you will do me the honor of taking my advice, we will discuss this in a friendly way; perhaps you will gain as much by it as I shall. Let us see now! First of all, I have no doubt, Nasses's presence annoyed you; and I have as little doubt that to put yourself at your ease with him, you showered upon him all those favors you were so kind as to design for me.'

" 'And if that were the case?' Zulica answered proudly.

" 'I understand,' he declared. 'It was.'

" 'Well then, yes,' she maintained bravely. 'I did love him.'

" 'Do not let us misuse words at this point,' he answered. 'You did not love him, but it came to the same thing. Admit, now that you know him rather better, that he is an exceptional fellow.'

" 'All I know,' she retorted coldly, 'is that if he is an insolent and inconsiderate coxcomb, he has at least something with which to make up for it, and that others who are bold enough to adopt his manner might well, for many reasons, be less presumptuous.'

" 'Obscure as your epigram is,' he replied, 'I realize perfectly well that it is aimed at me, and I am quite ready, for what it is worth, to allow you the small consolation of hearing me admit it. I will even carry my deference further, and deny myself a refutation that might perhaps outrage politeness.'

" 'What wretched things you say!' she cried, looking at him with pity. 'And how ill this light, bantering tone befits a *thing* like you!'

" 'Say what you will, Madam,' he answered, 'I shall neither falter in my respect for you nor swerve from the plan I am determined to follow with you. I shall not be sorry to offer you, in myself, the picture of moderation. Perhaps merely seeing me be true to my principles will tempt you to imitate me.'

" 'You will exercise this boasted moderation by yourself then,' she retorted rising, 'for I am going to –'

" 'Not so, Madam, if you please,' he said, holding her back. 'You shall not leave me! It is not in this manner that people like ourselves should conclude; for your honor's sake as for mine, we must lend ourselves to a mutual enlightenment, and avoid a scandal that would be much more dreadful for you than for me. In short, Zulica, you will hear me out!'

"Whether Zulica appreciated the damage this adventure might do her were it widespread, and thought, all things considered, that she ought to omit nothing to quiet Mazulhim on the subject; or whether, too despicable to be angry for long at being despised, her anger began to abate, I do not know. In any case, she fell back upon the sofa, but without looking at Mazulhim, who, unmoved by this mark of her scorn, continued thus: 'You admit that you took Nasses; anyone else might tell you that ordinarily a woman enters upon a new affair only when the old one is completely broken off, and thereupon would crush you with all the contempt such behavior seems to call for. But, for myself, being enough a man of the world to understand how it happened, far from bearing you a grudge for it, I love you all the more for it.'

" 'That, however, is not the effect I wanted it to have on your heart,' she answered.

" 'You cannot really know,' he replied. 'Could you in your disordered state unravel the threads of your motives? You thought I was fickle, you were urged to take your revenge. If you had loved me less you would not have done so, and Nasses would have tried in vain to take you as far as he did. Believe me, only the strongest passions arouse those emotions which give one's mind no time for thought or freedom of action. I am utterly astonished that Nasses should have been so thoughtless as to wish to take advantage of your state, or so blind not to see that even in his arms you were wholly another's; and that, without your love for me, you would never have made him a happy man.'

" 'Not at all,' she said. 'I liked him; and I have, without any doubt, been formally unfaithful to you according to the rules.'

" 'Sheer vanity on your part,' he retorted. 'Do not go and believe that – it is not in the least true.'

" 'What!' she demanded. 'Not in the least true? I find it very peculiar that you should know more about it than I do.'

" 'Yet I know so much about it that I could tell you word for word how he set about seducing you,' he answered. 'Nasses thought you lovely, and preferred telling you of the desires you aroused in him to proffering my excuses; and I would even bet that, far from speaking in my favor, he –'

" 'There is not doubt of that,' she interrupted.

" 'Am I not telling you?' he continued. 'What a wretched victory he won, and how inglorious. After all, some people have to be forgiven these little stratagems: without them they could never make themselves attractive.'

" 'What?' she asked in amazement. 'You dare maintain that you were not being unfaithful to me?'

" 'Of course I was not,' he declared. 'And that is what makes me relish your adventure so highly.'

" 'You were not guilty?' she repeated. 'Then what had become of you?'

" 'I only got away from the Emperor's the moment before I came here, and Zadig himself – who, by the way, was being rallied tremendously for being lost to view all yesterday – was with me all the time. He will be able to confirm my statement.'

"Zulica trembled on hearing Zadig's name, and reddened as she looked at Mazulhim, who, without seeming to notice her agitation, continued thus: 'Although I still like you very much, you realize that we shall no longer live in that intimacy you permitted me. It is not that I do not forgive you everything; but a settled relationship is no longer fitting for you. And, after all, we took each other from whim rather than from love; we were not joined by affection. What is taking place now need neither mortify you nor displease me, nor prevent us from yielding to a fancy, if, without wishing to come together again, we should at intervals feel attracted to each other.'

" 'I hope,' she answered disdainfully, 'that you feel how absurd this arrangement is even as you suggest it, and that you have no illusions about making me agree to it.'

" 'Pardon me,' he replied. 'You are too sensible not to feel that one owes a certain tact and consideration to one's old friends; besides, you must be well aware that it is an established custom nowadays to form as many ties as possible, and to grant everything to one's new acquaintances without, for that reason, lessening one's gifts to the old. I am sure you will approve the arrangement I have had the honor to put before you, and I regard it as absolutely settled between us.'

"Zulica, though very well adapted to such a shameful traffic, was nevertheless highly offended that Mazulhim should think her capable of doing something she did every day, and tried to put on an air of dignity with him, which, since it made her appear only more wretched, made him only the more inclined to treat her without any delicacy whatsoever.

" 'If it were not so late,' he told her, 'I would prove to you that, far from having any cause for complaint against me, you owe me unlimited thanks. I know quite well that Zadig spent yesterday with you, alone with you, and not only the day, but a great part of the night. Curious rather than jealous, and sure that you would break the promise you gave me never to see him again, I had you both watched –'

" 'There was no need for you to take that trouble,' she interrupted. 'I made no attempt to hide the fact, and the reasons that made me receive Zadig yesterday can only redound to my honor.'

" 'Aha!' he said, as though surprised. 'This is something very subtle!'

" 'Your mockery does not prevent its being the truth,' she answered. 'I had not yet finally broken with him, and it was to tell him that I would never see him again, that I –'

" 'Spent the whole day and the whole night with him,' he broke in. 'I do not dispute your motive, extraordinary as it is. You will not deny that it is unusual for a woman to shut herself up with a man for twenty-four hours merely to break with him. But a thing being unprecedented may, for all that, be very reasonable; and I, who strive only to make a case for you, suppose that Zadig, receiving his unhappy dismissal from you, almost died of despair at your feet; and that, moved by the despondency into which your unfaithfulness had cast him, you consoled him with the whole wealth of your humanity, without your care for him at all affecting the faith you swore to me. A desperate man is most unreasonable; one can hardly bring him to act with any common sense; and one must tell him the same thing over and over again in different ways, submit to lamentations, reproaches, tears, rage – it all takes a very long time. In any event, I may tell you that you have no cause to repent of the time you spent in trying to soothe Zadig: today he was charmingly gay. Zadig gay! Can you imagine it? If your story is true – and I shall take care not to doubt it – either your arguments made a great impression upon him, or, to bear his regret so easily, he must have loved you very mildly. If the one does honor to your mind, the other does little enough to your charms; but I have no desire to wound you – you will know which it is. In any case, you ought to have advised him to look sad, at least for so long as you wished to deceive me.'

"Here, Zulica wanted to make some plea, but Mazulhim, interposing, said, 'Anything you might say to me, Madam, would be useless. Spare me excuses, which I neither ask for nor wish to receive, and which would give you trouble without satisfying me. Farewell,' he added rising. 'It is getting late, and we ought to have separated long ago. Oh, by the way, what are you going to do about Nasses?'

"This question appeared to astound Zulica.

" 'Surely my question is a sensible one,' he persisted. 'You parted on bad terms, and I think that was imprudent of you. You would do well to see him again. Take my advice – avoid a scandal. It cannot be more difficult for you to keep him while hating him than it was to take him without loving him. If you insist on not seeing him, he will probably talk; and though what you did was the most natural thing, there are sure to be some low-minded people unjust enough to think ill of you and to turn this ordinary thing into the most fantastic and ridiculous story. Not, of course, that what people might say can upset you at all; when one has a certain reputation, one affair more or less calls for no particular notice. But one should avoid making enemies. I shall formally introduce him to you tomorrow.'

" 'What?' she cried. 'Am I to see you again?'

" 'Why, of course,' he answered, offering her his hand to lead her out. 'You must submit to that. If by any chance Zadig should be so absurd as to object, you may rely upon me: either he will be forced to give you up, or else, in the end, he will become used to seeing us court you assiduously.'

"Having said this, he again offered her his hand; and, seeing that she persisted in refusing it, said, taking it by force, 'How paltry! Your childishness is unbearable.'

"Then they went out."

"They went out!" the Sultan cried. "Ah! What a relief! In my opinion, that's the best part of your story. And they didn't come back again?"

"I never saw Zulica again," Amanzei replied, "but I saw Mazulhim for some time."

"And was he always..." the Sultan said. "You know?...Gad! He was an odd customer! And whom did he have after Zulica?"

"Many women worth about as much as she was, and some who deserved better than to get him, and whom I pitied."

"By the way," Shah Baham asked the Sultana, "didn't you think Mazulhim treated Zulica very badly?"

"I find her so contemptible," the Sultana answered, "that I wish he had punished her more severely still, if possible."

"It seemed to me," the Sultan declared, "that she was too meek with him; it was not natural."

"And I think the contrary," the Sultana said. "A woman like Zulica has no resources against contempt; since the ignominy of her behavior exposes her to the cruellest insults, the foulness of her character, and the inward shame – which, in spite of herself, weighs upon her – leave her no strength to parry. Besides, even if Amanzei had a little exaggerated Zulica's humiliation, far from upbraiding him with it, I should be grateful to him. To paint vice as happy and triumphant would be in some measure to recommend it."

"Yes, yes, of course," the Sultan said. "All that is very necessary. But let us quit that point; such a discussion sours me, and I shall no doubt lose my temper if we go on with it. Where did you go after you left Mazulhim, Amanzei?"

CHAPTER XX

Soulful Delights

"Whatever pleasures I found in Mazulhim's little retreat, the interests of my soul forced me to tear myself away; and convinced that I would never find my release there, I went to look for a house where I would be happier than I had been in my previous dwellings. After several attempts – during which I saw only things I had already seen or hardly worth telling your Majesty about – I went into an enormous palace that belonged to one of the greatest lords in Agra. I wandered about in it for some time, and at last made my lair in a boudoir, decorated with a great deal of magnificence and good taste, though the one usually excludes the other. Everything there exuded voluptuousness: the ornaments, the furniture, the smell of the exquisite perfumes that were always kept burning – everything brought them to the eye, everything conveyed them to the soul. In fact, this room might have been taken for the temple of languour, the true abode of pleasures.

"No sooner had I settled myself there than the goddess to whom I was to belong came in. She was the daughter of the omrah in whose house I was. In her face dwelt youth, and grace, and beauty, and that indefinable something which alone can give them value: she was the embodiment of charm and pleasure. My soul could not look upon her and remain calm: the sight of her gave birth to a thousand delicious sensations I thought beyond its scope. Destined sometimes to support so lovely a creature, not only did I cease to grieve over my fate but I feared to be compelled to enter upon a new existence.

" 'Ah, Brahma!' I murmured, 'what can be the state of felicity you reserve for those who have been your good servants, if those whose soul has deserved your righteous anger are allowed joyfully to behold such marvelous beauties? Come!' I pursued enraptured. 'Come, charming image of the goddess, come to soothe an unquiet soul, which would instantly mingle with yours if cruel commands did not hold it fast in its prison!'

"And it seemed as though at that moment Brahma was granting my wishes. The sun was then at its height, and the heat was tremendous: Zeinis soon got ready to enjoy the sweets of slumber, and, drawing the curtains herself, let in the room that half light so conducive to sleep and to delight, which conceals nothing from the eyes and adds to their passion, which emboldens bashfulness, and allows it to yield itself more freely to love.

"A simple shift of gauze, almost completely open, was soon Zeinis's sole garment. She cast herself carelessly upon me. Gods! With what rapture I received her! And as Brahma, in confining my soul to a sofa had given it the choice of being in whatever part it wished, with what pleasure did I not at once take advantage of this liberty!

"I carefully chose the spot whence I could best feast my eyes upon Zeinis's charms, and set myself to contemplate them with the ardor of the most tender lover; and the admiration of the coldest man could not have refused them. Gods! What beauties offered themselves to my gaze! At last, slumber came to close those eyes which filled me with so much love.

"I then occupied myself in going over all the charms I had still to examine, and in returning to those I had already feasted my eyes upon. Although Zeinis slept quietly enough, every now and again she turned over, and each movement she made, in altering the drape of her shift, revealed new beauties to my hungry eyes. Such attractions finally conquered my soul. Prostrated by the number and the violence of my soul's desires, all its faculties remained for some time in abeyance. I vainly strove to gather my wits. I could feel only that I loved, and, without foreseeing or fearing the consequences of such a fatal passion, I gave myself over to it wholly.

"'Delicious creature!' I cried at last. 'No, you cannot be a mortal. It is not their lot to have so many charms. Even supra-aerial beings, there is not one of them you do not eclipse. Ah! Deign to accept the homage of a soul that adores you! Refrain from preferring some vile mortal to him! Zeinis, divine Zeinis! No, no one is worthy of you; no, Zeinis, since not one of them can equal you in glory!'

"While I was so ardently engaged with Zeinis, she became restless and turned over. The position she now assumed was favorable to me, and in spite of my discomposure, I had enough wits left to take advantage of it. Zeinis was lying on her side, her head just above the sofa cushion, which her lips almost touched. Thus, I could, in spite of Brahma's strict commands, somewhat gratify my violent desires: my soul transferred itself to the cushion, so close to Zeinis's mouth that at length it succeeded in adhering wholly to it.

"The soul, I am convinced, experiences delights that the term *pleasure* does not express, and for which even the word *rapture* is inadequate. This sweet, impulsive intoxication into which my soul swooned, which occupied all its faculties so deliciously, defies description.

"No doubt a soul, hampered by its bodily organs, forced to measure its transports by their weakness, cannot, when imprisoned in a body, give itself over to them so strongly as when it is rid of it. Sometimes we even feel it, during a keen pang of pleasure, trying to force the barriers of the body, diffusing itself throughout its prison, filling the whole with its devouring fire and turmoil, vainly seeking for outlet, till at last, spent by its efforts, it sinks into that lethargy which seems for a time to blot it out. That, it seems to me, is the cause of the exhaustion excessive delight brings upon us.

"Such is our fate that our soul, fretting even in the midst of the greatest pleasures, is ever bound to seek more than it can find. My soul, clinging to Zeinis's mouth, drowned in its own felicity, sought to win a still greater one. It tried, but in vain, to glide entirely into Zeinis; but, held back in its prison by Brahma's cruel commands, not all my soul's struggles could set it free. Its violent efforts, its ardor, its furious desires, apparently warmed Zeinis's. No sooner did my soul perceive the effect it was having on hers than it redoubled its attempts. It fluttered more rapidly over Zeinis's lips, dashed over them with greater speed, clung to them with hotter fire. The disorder that began to suffuse Zeinis's soul increased the pain and the pleasure of mine. Zeinis sighed, I sighed; her lips formed some broken words, and a ravishing pink flushed her cheeks. At last, the most seductive dream led her senses astray. The sweetest emotions came to disturb the calm on which she floated.

"'Yes! You love me!' she cried tenderly. These words were followed by a few more, hindered by the most heartfelt sighs.

"'Do you doubt my love for you?' she continued.

"Still less free than Zeinis, I listened to her with rapture, and had not the power to respond. Soon her soul, as much disturbed as mine, yielded itself altogether to its consuming fires, and a sweet shudder... Heavens! How beautiful Zeinis became!

"My delight and hers vanished with her awakening. Of that sweet illusion which had enthralled her senses nothing remained but a soft languor, which made her seem only the more worthy of the pleasures she had just experienced. Her looks, wherein love itself ruled, were still effulgent with the fire that coursed through her veins. When she was able to open her eyes, they had already lost the look of dreamy rapture with which my love and the turmoil of her senses had impregnated them, but they were still entrancing! What mortal, knowing himself to be the cause of their splendor, would not have died in the excess of his yearning and his bliss?

"'Zeinis!' I cried in ecstasy. 'Beloved Zeinis! It is I who have just made you happy; it is to the union of your soul with mine that your delights are due. Ah! May it be always so, and may you respond to my ardor alone! No, Zeinis, the world does not contain a heart more tender or more faithful than mine! Ah! If it could escape the toils of Brahma, or if he could forget it, bound to yours forever it would be, by you alone, such that its immortality could be a joy for it, and that it would hope to perpetuate its being. Oh! If I were ever to lose you, soul that I adore! Oh, how in the vastness of the universe, or shackled by the cruel bonds with which Brahma might load me, how could I ever find you again? Ah, Brahma! If your supreme power wrests me from Zeinis, at least, however bitter the pain of it, let me never lose the memory of her.'

"While my soul was so tenderly adoring Zeinis, this charming girl seemed given over to the sweetest reverie, and I began to be alarmed at the tranquillity the dream had induced in her, and on which I had a few seconds earlier congratulated myself.

"'Zeinis,' I told myself, 'is no doubt used to the delights she has just tasted. Whatever grip they may have had on her senses, they have not startled her thoughts. She is in a muse, but she does not seem to be inquiring as to the cause of the feelings that possessed her. Familiar with the sweetest and tenderest raptures love can give, I have done no more than recall them to her. A luckier mortal has already developed in her heart that germ of love which nature embedded there. It was his image, not my flame, that made her burn; she seemed in the midst of her tumult to be engaged in reassuring a lover, who is perhaps in the habit of pouring out his fears and his troubles within her arms. Ah, Zeinis! If it be true that you love, then in the position Brahma's anger has placed me my lot is going to be terrible!'

"My soul was wandering in the maze of these notions when I heard someone knock softly at the door. Zeinis's blushes at this unexpected noise increased my fears. She hastily adjusted the disorder into which

the restlessness of her sleep had thrown her dress, and, more presentable, bade the person come in.

"'Ah!' I said to myself, stricken with a piercing grief. 'Perhaps I shall
see a rival. If he is a happy one, what tortures for me! If he becomes so,
and Zeinis is what I sometimes think her to be, and it is to her I am to
owe my deliverance, what a terrible blow it will be to me to have to
leave her after she has inspired such feelings in me!'

"Although, with my knowledge of the morals of Agra, I should have
been protected against this fear of leaving Zeinis, and knowing it was
likely enough that, at fifteen years old or thereabouts, as she appeared
to be, she would not have all that Brahma required to deliver me back
into human life, it was possible that I might have everything to fear on
that score; and, however painful it might be for me to witness her kindness to my rival, I preferred that torment to the one of losing her.

"At Zeinis's summons, a young Indian, with the most radiant face,
came into the room. The more worthy to please he seemed to me, the
more my hatred against him was aroused; it was multiplied by the way
in which Zeinis greeted him. Confusion, love, and fear were by turns
depicted upon her face, and she gazed at him for some time before she
spoke. He seemed to be as agitated as she was, but from his timid and
respectful manner I guessed that, even were he loved, he was not yet
favored. But in spite of his shyness and his extreme youth – I took him
to be hardly older than Zeinis – this did not seem to be his first love
affair, and I began to hope that out of this adventure I would reap only
the sorrow I could bear.

"'Ah, Phileas!' Zeinis said to him with emotion. 'What are you
doing here?'

"'What I hoped to do – see you,' he answered, throwing himself on
his knees. 'You without whom I cannot live, and who were good enough
yesterday to say that you would see me alone.'

"'Ah,' she said promptly, 'do not expect me to keep my word! Let
us go out; I do not want to stay in this room any longer.'

"'Zeinis,' he pleaded, 'do you grudge me the joy of being alone with
you for a while. And can it be that you so soon repent of the first favor
you have ever granted me?'

"'But,' she answered with embarrassment, 'can I not speak to you
somewhere else, and, if you love me, can you insist on asking me for
something I am reluctant to give?'

"Phileas, without answering, seized one of her hands and kissed it
with as much passion as I could have. Zeinis looked at him languidly;
she sighed, still affected by the dream that had depicted her lover to

be so eager and herself so frail. More disposed to love by the impression the dream had left, each time her eyes turned toward Phileas they became softer and, gradually, they took on once more that voluptuousness which my love had put there a short time before.

"In spite of Phileas's lack of experience, his affection, which caused him to react to all Zeinis's impulses, made him observe them well enough not to doubt that she was pleased to see him. Zeinis, moreover, frank and artless, hiding from modesty alone the state into which his presence threw her, thought she was concealing much of her tumultuous condition, whereas she was revealing it all. Phileas did not know enough to make a conquest of a flirt whose false virtue and parade of decorum would have frightened him away, but he was only too dangerous for Zeinis, who, urged onward by her love, did not know, even though she feared to yield, in what manner she could have protected herself.

"Although she saw Phileas at her knees with great pleasure, she bade him rise. Far from obeying her, he clasped them with so tender an expression and such lively delight that Zeinis sighed at it.

" 'Ah, Phileas!' she said, much moved. 'Let us go out of here, I beg of you!'

" 'Will you always fear me, Zeinis?' he asked softly. 'Ah, Zeinis, how little my love affects you! What can you fear from a lover who adores you, who has almost from birth been subject to your charms, and who, since then, moved by them alone, has wanted to live for you only? Zeinis,' he added, shedding tears, 'look what you reduce me to!'

"As he said his last words, he raised his tear-laden eyes to hers. For a time she gazed at him with a softened look; yielding at length to the deep feelings that love and the sorrows of Phileas aroused in her, she said in a voice choked by the tears she tried to crush back: 'Oh, cruel one! Have I deserved your reproaches? And what proofs can I give you of my love, if, after all those you have had, you still doubt me?'

" 'If you loved me,' he replied, 'would not you forget yourself with me in this solitude, and, far from wishing to leave it, what other fear would you have than that of being disturbed?'

" 'Alas!' she answered naively, 'who says I have any other?'

"Thereupon, Phileas, leaping up from her knees, ran to the door and latched it; on his way back he met Zeinis, who, guessing what he was going to do, had risen to prevent him. He took her in his arms, and, in spite of the resistance she offered, placed her back upon me, and sat down close beside her."

XXI

The Final Chapter

"I do not know whether Zeinis imagined that once a door is latched it is useless to put up any defense, or whether, now that she no longer needed to fear detection, she feared herself even more; but no sooner was Phileas beside her than, blushing rather for what she feared he might try to do than for what he did, she asked him in a trembling, halting voice not to ask anything of her, even before he did so. But Zeinis's voice was tender rather than imposing, and it neither vexed nor hindered Phileas. Stretched beside her, he folded her so fiercely in his arms that Zeinis, even while she began to know how much she had to fear from him, partook of his transports in spite of herself.

"Though very moved, she tried to escape from Phileas's arms, but she did this so much against the grain, that Phileas did not have to make any great efforts to overcome hers. They gazed at one another for some time without saying anything; but Zeinis, feeling her inward tumult increase and afraid at last that she would not be able to master it, begged Phileas – but oh so gently! – please to let her be.

" 'Then are you never going to make me happy?' he asked her.

" 'Ah!' she answered, with a thoughtlessness I have never forgiven her, 'you are only too much so, and before you arrived you were still more so.'

"The more baffling these words seemed to Phileas, the more imperative it seemed to him to know what Zeinis meant by them. For a long time he urged her to explain them to him, and, though she was very reluctant to say any more, he urged her so tenderly, with such passionate looks, that at last he ended by shaking her resolve.

" 'But if I tell you,' she said in a trembling voice, 'you will take advantage of it.'

"He swore he would not, but so mildly that, far from soothing her fears, she must have known that he would break his word. Too far carried away to be able to see this clearly, or too innocent to be aware of the full force of the confidence with which she was going to entrust him, after some feeble resistance to his solicitations, she confessed to him that just before he had come in, having fallen asleep, she had seen him in a dream, and with a rapture she had never had a notion of before.

" 'Was I in your arms?' he asked, clasping her in his.

" 'Yes,' she answered, turning on him eyes full of trouble.

" 'Ah!' he continued, in the extreme of emotion. 'So you loved me then more than you do now!'

" 'I could not love you more,' she replied. 'But I was less afraid of saying so.'

" 'And then?' he urged.

" 'Ah, Phileas!' she cried blushing. 'What are you asking me? You were happier than I wish you ever should be, and were not the less exacting for it.'

"On hearing this, Phileas, no longer able to control his ardor, and, emboldened by Zeinis's confidences, raising himself a little and bending over her, did all he could to press his lips to hers. Bold as this attempt was, Zeinis would not perhaps have minded, had not Phileas, intent only on achieving his own happiness, carried his audacity to such lengths as she thought herself unable to forgive.

" 'Ah, Phileas!' she cried. 'Where are your promises, and are you so little afraid of vexing me?'

"Violent as Phileas's impulses were, Zeinis protected herself so earnestly, and he saw so much anger in her eyes, that he thought it better no longer to insist upon a conquest that he could not achieve without offending his beloved, and in which even, owing to Zeinis's resistance, he was not sure of succeeding. At last, either from respect or timidity, he desisted, and, not daring to look at Zeinis, said to her sadly, 'No, however cruel you may be, I shall no longer lay myself open to your displeasure. Were I more dear to you, you would no doubt be less afraid of making me happy; but although I may no longer hope to make you feel delight, I shall love you no less tenderly.'

"Thereupon, he rose from beside her, and rushed from the room. Grievously hurt that Phileas should leave her, and yet not daring to call him back, she remained, weeping on the sofa, leaning her head in her hands. Yet, made uneasy by her lover's departure, she was getting up to find out what had become of him, when, brought back by his affection, he returned to the room. The blood swept over her face on seeing him again, and she fell back upon me, fetching a profound sigh. He ran to cast himself at her knees, gently took her hand, and not daring to kiss it, bathed it with his tears.

" 'Ah, get up!' Zeinis bade him, without looking at him.

" 'No, Zeinis,' he said, 'I shall hear my sentence at your feet! One single word ... But you are crying! Ah, Zeinis! Have I made these tears flow?'

"At this, Zeinis, cruel maid, squeezed his hand, and, turning toward him eyes made only more lovely by their tears, sighed without answering him. The emotion writ in her eyes was as plain for Phileas to read as it was for me.

" 'Heavens!' he cried, embracing her fiercely. 'Do you really forgive me?'

"Still Zeinis said nothing, but – alas! – Phileas missed nothing of what she seemed to say, and without questioning her further, sought at her very mouth the admission she still seemed to withhold from him.

"In that moment I heard only the sound of stifled sighs. Phileas had taken possession of that charming mouth where my soul, so short a time before him, had . . . But why do I recall a memory so bitter for me still? Zeinis had thrown herself into her lover's arms: love, and the relics of modesty that made her all the more beautiful, shone in her face and her eyes. This first ecstasy lasted a long while. Phileas and Zeinis, perfectly still, breathing each other's souls, seemed sunk in a lethargy of delight."

"All of which," the Sultan then remarked, "cannot have been very pleasant for you, eh? So why on earth did you go and fall in love when you didn't have a body? That was inconceivably silly of you; for, come now, to what end could this fancy have led you? You see now, one must use one's common sense sometimes."

"Sire," Amanzei answered, "it was only after my passion had taken a strong hold on me that I realized how much it was to torture me, and, as usually happens, reflection comes too late."

"I am really very upset at your misadventure," the Sultan went on, "for I liked you very well clinging to the lips of the girl you are telling us of. It is really a pity you were disturbed."

"So long as Zeinis resisted Phileas," Amanzei said, "I was in hope that nothing could conquer her; and, when I found she was more susceptible, I thought that, checked by the prejudice proper to her years, she would not carry frailty so far as to cause my unhappiness. However, I must admit that when I heard her tell her dream, which I thought had been due to me, and learned from her own lips that the vision of Phileas was the only one she had seen, and that it was to the influence he had over her senses and not to my raptures that she had owed her delights, I had little hope left of escaping the fate I dreaded so much. Yet, less delicately perceptive than I should have been, I consoled myself for Phileas's good fortune by being certain I would share it with him. Whatever he might have told Zeinis about his passion and the faith he had always kept toward her, it did not seem to me possible that he should have reached the age of fifteen or sixteen without having gratified some curiosity or other, which would prevent him from freeing my soul from the bondage that had so long seemed a harsh one to me, but which at that moment I preferred to the most glorious position a soul could occupy. Miserable as Zeinis's frailty made me, I awaited the consequences with less pain once I had persuaded myself that, whatever might happen, I should not be compelled to leave her.

"Dreadful as the deep lethargy into which they had sunk was for me, and which each sigh they fetched seemed only to increase, it delayed Phileas's bolder attempts, and, though it showed me how deeply they felt their love; I earnestly prayed Brahma not to let it cease. Useless prayers! I was too guilty for two innocent souls, worthy of their bliss, to be sacrificed for me.

"Phileas, after languishing for some time upon Zeinis's bosom, urged by fresh desires that the frailty of his lover made more ardent, gazed at her with eyes full of the delicious drunkenness of his soul. Zeinis perturbed by Phileas's glances, turned her own away and sighed.

"'What, you avoid my looks!' he said to her. 'Ah! Turn your lovely eyes toward me rather, and read in mine all the flame you arouse in me!'

"Then he took her in his arms. Zeinis still tried to evade his transports, but either she did not try to resist long, or, deceiving herself, she thought she was still resisting, and Phileas was soon gazed upon as lovingly as he could wish.

"Although Zeinis's uttermost kindness would have thrown her into a soft languor not very different from the one my own ardor had induced in her, and although she looked at Phileas with all the passion he had required of her, she seemed to repent of having delivered herself too far to her feelings, and tried to withdraw from Phileas's arms.

"'Ah, Zeinis!' he murmured. 'In the dream you told me of, you were not afraid to make me happy!'

"'Alas,' she replied, 'however much I may love you, without it, without the pulses it set beating in my veins, you would not have obtained so much!'

"Imagine, Sire, how great my distress when I learned that my rival's happiness was due to me alone!

"'You should be satisfied with your victory,' she continued. 'And you will offend me if you try to carry it further. I have done more than I should have to convince you of my love, but –'

"'Ah, Zeinis!' Phileas interrupted impetuously. 'If it were true that you loved me you would not be afraid of telling me so, or at least you would tell me so more completely. Instead of yielding only timidly to my love, you would abandon yourself to all my raptures, and even then think you had not done enough for me. Come!' he continued, flinging himself beside her with an eagerness which would have killed my soul if a soul could die. 'Come, consummate my happiness!'

"'Ah, Phileas!' timorous Zeinis cried in a faltering voice. 'Do you realize that you are undoing me? Alas, you swore to be so respectful! Phileas, is this how you show your respect for those whom you love?'

"Not all Zeinis's tears and prayers, commands and threats had the smallest effect on Phileas. Although the gauze shift between them already enabled him to enjoy only too many of her charms, and which his impulsive movements had even now disarranged as much as her sleep had, less contented with the beauties she offered to his gaze than carried away by his desire to see those she still kept concealed from him, he at length removed the veil to which Zeinis's modesty still clung, and throwing himself upon the beauties that his temerity gave to his gaze, he overwhelmed her with such eager and urgent caresses, that he had no strength left to do more than sigh.

"But modesty and love still struggled for mastery in Zeinis's heart and eyes. The first refused the lover everything, the latter left him nearly nothing to wish for. She dared not let her eyes linger upon Phileas, for she reciprocated all the transports she aroused in him. She guarded one thing, only to leave a still more essential one unguarded; she wanted, and no longer wanted; she hid one of her beauties to reveal another; she repelled him with horror, and drew him toward her with joy. Sometimes modesty subdued love, and the next moment was sacrificed to it, but with reserve and precaution that, though it had seemed to be overcome, still left it master. Zeinis felt by turns shame at her easiness, and shame at her reluctance. The fear of displeasing Phileas, the emotions aroused by his raptures, the exhaustion consequent on so long a struggle, at last compelled her to surrender. Herself a prey to all the desires she had aroused in him, only impatiently bearing with pleasures that agitated her without satisfying her, she sought for the deep delight they pointed to from afar but did not give her.

"At this moment, beyond myself with agony at what I saw, and beginning to fear from certain notions of Phileas, which proved to me his lack of experience, that he would expel my soul from a place where, in spite of the grief caused it there, it liked to dwell, I tried to leave Zeinis's sofa for a moment, to elude the decrees of Brahma. But in vain: the same power that had chosen the place of my exile frustrated my efforts and made me await in despair the issue of my destiny.

"Phileas...Oh, terrible memory! Bitter moment, the image of which will never fade from my mind! Phileas, intoxicated by his love, and made master, by the tender kindnesses of Zeinis, of all the charms that I adored, made ready to complete his happiness. Zeinis surrendered herself swooningly to Phileas's raptures, and, if the fresh impediments that still trammeled their love delayed it, they did not lessen it. Zeinis's lovely eyes shed tears, her mouth wanted to moan, and at that moment her love alone prevented her from heaving a sigh. Phileas, the author of so many ills, incurred, however, no hatred for them: Zeinis, of whom Phileas complained, was only the more tenderly loved. At last, a louder cry she uttered, a more lively joy I saw sparkle in Phileas's eyes, declared my unhappiness and my freedom; and my soul, filled with its love and its sorrow, went repining on its way to receive from Brahma fresh orders and new shackles."

"What! Is that all?" the Sultan asked. "You were a sofa for a very short time, or else you saw very little while you were one."

"It would have been tiresome for your Majesty had I told you all I had seen while I dwelt in sofas," Amanzei answered. "And I have attempted to bring before you only such things as might amuse you rather than tell you all."

"Even supposing the things you have told us," the Sultana said, "are more amusing than those you have omitted, which I am prepared to believe – I have no means of comparing them – you must yet be blamed for having brought only a few characters into play while all were at your disposal, and for having of your own accord limited a subject that is by nature so extensive."

"No doubt, Madam," Amanzei replied, "I should have been in the wrong had all the characters been equally interesting or remarkable; had I been able to consider them all without falling into the sorry state of showing you mean or commonplace people; or had I been able to be prolific on a subject that, however much I might have varied the characters, must have become tiresome by endless repetition of its essential fabric."

"Indeed," the Sultan said, "I believe that if all these things were to be weighed, he might very well be right; but I would rather have him wrong than bother about it all. Ah, Grandmother!" he concluded with a sigh, "this was not the way you told *your* stories!"

NOTE

1. [Michel de] Montaigne, trans. Donald M. Frame, *The Complete Essays of Montaigne* (Stanford, CA: Stanford University Press, 1958), p. 521.

Originally published as *Le Sopha* (1742).

The Indiscreet Jewels

by Denis Diderot

Translated by Sophie Hawkes

Introduction

by Chantal Thomas

The Indiscreet Jewels:
A Dangerous Pastime

by Chantal Thomas

> *The symbol of women in general is that of the Apocalypse,*
> *on whose front was written* MYSTERY.
> — Diderot, *On Women*[1]

Preexisting Models

It is customary to consider *The Indiscreet Jewels* a minor work that
Diderot (1713–84) himself repudiated. Diderot's first novel — and the
only one published during his lifetime — is indeed a product of circumstance. Written in less than six months, it appeared in 1748, when
Diderot was thirty-five, and was an instant success. Introduced as the
outcome of a bet with his then-mistress, Mme de Puissieux, and a cynical expedient to make money, the book may appear to lack originality
and seriousness. Diderot does indeed fall back on preexisting models without attempting any innovations. "From the point of view of
literary history," writes Aram Vartanian, "*The Indiscreet Jewels* should be
situated at one of those active crossroads where several tendencies
and influences intersected. The generic precursors of Diderot's novel
derive, of course, from an entire body of literature that goes back to
the Middle Ages, if not before, whose best-known examples are perhaps the *fabliaux*, *The Decameron*, *Les Cent Nouvelles Nouvelles*, Brantôme's
Les Dames galantes, La Fontaine's *Contes*, and so forth. What this traditional collection has in common with *The Jewels* is above all the
demystifying attitude that runs throughout it, which makes women's
modesty and virtue the most detachable of masks."[2] Vartanian refers
also to Rabelais and, above all, to *Nocrion, Conte Allobroge* (1747), a
brief tale attributed to Caylus. Caylus's story of a young man, the knight
Amador, to whom a fairy has given the power to make women's sexual
organs speak, directly inspired *The Indiscreet Jewels*. The tale is told by
a young girl, Nocrion, to "melt away the prince's ill humor." *Nocrion* is
written in medieval style — "Begin your tale, then, and speak boldly.
The bawdier it is, the better I'll like it," says the king. *Nocrion* is based,
in turn, on a thirteenth-century text by Garin, *Le Chevalier qui faisait
parler les C——— et C——— ls.*

The "erotico-oriental" fantasy of *The Indiscreet Jewels* was thus a variation on a theme. It could also be read as a roman à clef. The public saw the characters of the Sultan and his beloved as images of Louis xv and his mistress, Mme de Pompadour. Marie Leczinska, the king's devout wife, became the Manimonbanda of the novel. These associations, however piquant they may have been for a contemporary audience, hold little fascination for us. It is nevertheless interesting to point out a biographical quirk of Louis xv, who had reports of the morals police read to him regularly. Sade speaks of these reports being made "to rouse the sovereign from his sluggishness." And a pamphlet of the time raged: "it is with this that our worthy police lieutenants courted and tried to titillate the bored indolence of Louis xv and the licencious curiosity of his mistress." We must recall, however, as Erica-Marie Benabou points out, that the *Journal des inspecteurs* was very dry, containing such entries as the following: "The Marquis of Olaville dined on the 27th at the Brissault's small house with four strangers. Their companions were the young ladies Denesle, Saint-Gerand, and Dubuisson, etc."[3]

This novel, in which Diderot's sole aim was to amuse himself and to entertain his readers, was for him an arena of total freedom, or a last moment of freedom before undertaking the hard work and the continual crushing worry that the *Encyclopédie* (1751–72) was to become. *The Indiscreet Jewels* was a work of youth, a way of remaining young, of prolonging this playful, irresponsible interlude. As Pierre Lepape observes, "Diderot had to choose between the promises of youth, the dreams of a permanent student life, and the burdens of adulthood. *The Indiscreet Jewels* was a way to roll back the deadline at the same time that it was an unconscious declaration of irresponsibility."[4]

One can read *The Indiscreet Jewels* as trivial entertainment and view the idea of an accommodating genie who gives his master, Sultan Mangogul, a magic ring to keep him from boredom as a stock element of the fantastic with which Diderot played. At the same time, to the extent that this ring is presumed, according to the Freudian analytic scheme, to give voice to the forbidden, the fable of the jewels cannot be reduced to a literary game, a mere exercise in variations on a theme. Perhaps this text, protected by the obvious innocence of its conception and the exoticism of its decor and characters, even reveals naively, and thus more directly, Diderot's relation to the "mystery" of women. Diderot certainly does not take this tale seriously, but for this reason he reveals himself here with surprising candor, perhaps *unwittingly*, just as the jewels do.

The Rage to Speak

In Diderot's *Jacques the Fatalist and His Master* (1771), the origin of
Jacques's irrepressible chattering is explained as a result of his grandparents' unfortunate pedagogical practices. Peddlers of secondhand
wares, they had poor verbal skills: "During her entire life, which was
long, [the servant tells his master] the only thing my grandmother ever
said was 'Hats for sale,' and my grandfather, who would always be
amongst his ledgers, upright, his hands under his frock-coat, had only ever
said 'One sou.' "[5] To maintain silence in their home, the grandparents
were forced to put a gag on the child. In the evening, in the room
where the family said nothing, the child ran around, furious, his mouth
bound. Of course, as soon as they took it off, he did not stop blabbing:
"it's because of that damned gag that I've got a mania for talking."[6]

This excess is typical of Diderot's characters: they "never stop talking" and never tire of the "delicious pleasure of orating." Diderot's
writing captures the unstoppable flow of words, recreating the vibrant
disorder of conversation. "Conversation," observes Jean-Claude Bonnet in his analysis of Diderot's *Rameau's Nephew* (1761–73), "is neither
plagarism, nor idle dissipation, nor time wasted for the deepening of the
self," but rather "a materialist choice of exteriority."[7] With *The Indiscreet Jewels*, Diderot brings the sexual organs themselves into this exte-
riorizing dynamic of conversation. This libertine novel does not spring
from a libertine vision of desire; rather, it is Diderot's penchant for
conversational "libertinage" that leads him to write a libertine novel.

The guiding idea of *The Indiscreet Jewels* – a ring possessing the magic
power to unveil the secrets of female sexuality – is, superficially, a
convenient device for stringing along a series of licentious episodes that
allow for all sorts of digressions. On a deeper level, this idea, borrowed from earlier texts, meshed with Diderot's peculiar genius, with
his reason, desire, and need to write: the rage to tear off the gags, to
ward off silence, to liberate forbidden voices, to confront the scandal
of their enunciation. For Diderot, pure silence does not exist. Silence
is only a word made inaudible, the deceptive quiet of a hushed voice.

When the Sultan Mangogul turns his ring on a woman, he introduces "a new speaker." Through its delivery and peculiarity, the voice
of the jewel skews normal speech and disturbs the natural flow of the
conversation. The Sultan opens the conversational arena to new vocal
forces that are socially uncontrolled and morally inadmissible. The
jewels thus summoned proclaim a raw truth, indifferent to the rules of
proper behavior and the game of human relations: "a jewel speaks dispassionately and adds nothing to the truth" (p. 361). The jewels often

speak "tonelessly," Diderot specifies; they are also deaf to each other and the desperate entreaties with which the mouth attempts to bring an end to their revelations. Furthermore, adding to the scandal, once a jewel gets started, it is impossible to stop it. Panic is sown in the Sultan's feminine entourage, due as much to what they say as to the fact that they can speak at all. And one sees in these women – repeatedly referred to as "crazy" by the Sultan and his courtesans in a tone of superior amusement – an anguish opposed to the one suffered by the young Jacques, with his gag: it is the anguish of this voice, half-mechanical, half-animal, that they carry within them unknowingly and that is set off by the magic ring.

The Jewels' Chatter

Summoned to speak out loud at the Sultan's whim, the female sexual organ distorts or contradicts the voice from above. It produces, at first, a bizarre syncopated conversation, until the woman quickly gives up and stops speaking, yielding to the disruptive force of what Diderot calls the "chatter of the jewels." According to Littré's dictionary, a chatter, the cry of the magpie, denotes figuratively a "loud and noisy babble," or "conceited prattle." This caricature is derived from well-known stereotypes of women gossiping. But also, in relegating this voice emanating from the genitals to the subhuman level, to the noises of the barnyard, Diderot precludes any possible sympathy with the jewels. There is no getting along with the voice of the jewels. The woman from whom it emanates submits, dazed and frightened. She never acknowledges it as her own voice. (One can read in the panicky dispossession suffered by the women who come under the power of the magic ring an extreme expression of the strange sensation felt by anyone confronted by a recording of his or her own voice.) To silence this nether voice the women attempt to stifle it the way adults do a child. The activities of the ring produce a new kind of commerce, the sale of "muzzles" that supposedly keep the genitals from speaking. This idea of the "muzzled jewel" is already present in *Nocrion*, where it is developed with less restraint. The knight vainly addresses the sexual organ of a woman, which "does not unseal its lips." He then attempts to question the nearest orifice: "Pray thee, kind neighbor, my dear, tell me why the *Fotz* does not want to speak to me."[8] "And how the devil could it speak," replies the neighbor, in a clear and strong voice. "Its mouth is full of cotton or wool, for that place is so dark that I cannot see clearly in there. In a word, Madame has stuck so much into its mouth that it is about to choke."[9] But, like Jacques, whose family tried vainly to stifle his prattle, the muzzled sex organ always triumphs over all obstacles, irrepressible in its rage to speak.

The panicked woman,[10] ready to do anything to restore silence beneath her skirt, is met with laughter from the Sultan and his courtesans. The "chatter of the jewels," also referred to as "gibberish," a "plaintive noise," and "shrill," is presented as comical. Its triumph is a grandiose cacophony during an evening at the opera. Mangogul then experiments with turning the powers of his ring on the singers on stage: "Thirty girls were suddenly struck dumb; they opened their mouths wide and froze in the theatrical gestures of the moment before. Their jewels, however, sang their hearts out.... All, in fact, expressed themselves in such a high-pitched, baroque, and mad tone that they formed the most extraordinary, boisterous, and ridiculous chorus" (p. 375).

The Sultan invokes the genie Cucufa as a way to relieve his boredom. This impromptu concert that he can unleash at any time, in all its comical discordance, never fails to make him laugh. But the jewels, bizarre "haranguers" that they are, come out with confessions that are at once reassuring and troubling.

They are reassuring in the sense that the clear and plainly audible voice of the jewels, despite the author's insistence on the raucous anarchy of its manifestations, neither upsets nor even shakes the Sultan's beliefs about women's sexuality. He has created a representation, localized precisely in the vagina, and the jewel called on to express itself (Diderot also uses the expression "give throat") teaches him nothing else. It is only as a receptacle, a mere location, that a jewel speaks of itself. From the conjugal bed to wayside hotels, with all possible degrees of satisfaction and company, the jewels speak only of visits. The *I* of the female sex organ when it speaks is no different from the *I* of Crébillon fils's *The Sofa* (1742) (included in this reader). When the sofa finally finds itself free to speak, it reveals the secret life of an object. The sofa, having been moved several times, is installed "in a boudoir, decorated with a great deal of magnificence and good taste." Happy in its new decor, it soon sees Zeinis, the "goddess" of the place, appear. "A simple shift of gauze, almost completely open, was soon Zeinis's sole garment. She cast herself carelessly upon me. Gods! With what rapture I received her!"[11] Women's jewels likewise do no more than record comings and goings, but with a point of view that is even more limited. The deafening, low, heaving, strident chatter of the "freed" female organs does not block out the constant presence of another voice, the grammatical one, which can only be passive: " 'So, you have altars, do you? Pray, how are they honored?'... each jewel responded in turn, in different tones, 'I am visited, battered, neglected, perfumed, fatigued, ill-attended, bored....' Their jargon, now muffled, now shrill, accompanied by the laughter of Mangogul and his courtiers, created a new kind of din" (p. 361).

There is power in the resounding strangeness of the jewels, the shock of their emergence from silence. But all this noise, this baroque cacophony, carries a message of neither deviance nor delirium, a message that in no way departs from a nearly mechanical, if not geometric conception of sexual relations. "From time immemorial these jewels have been destined to join one to the other. A nut-shaped female jewel is predestined for a screw-shaped male jewel" (p. 390). An ironic statement that nonetheless corresponds to one of Diderot's deepest convictions: this belief in a kind of anatomical fatalism that leads him to describe sexual relations, with such metaphors as anvil and hammer, sheath and knife. This simple vision underlies the utopia of a kind of sexual harmony that can be mathematically calculated and empirically verified that Diderot places at the center of his novel. It is found again in the dream, totally stripped of erotic elements, that Diderot recounts to his friend and lover Sophie Volland (whose reaction we do not know, although it is hard to see how she might have found it of interest other than as a mark of frankness): "What a night last night was! It's been such a long time since I have felt that pleasure and that pain. But is it not strange that this dream almost never offered my imagination anything other than the narrow, necessary space for voluptuousness, nothing around it, an envelope of flesh and that is all."[12]

The phantasmagoria of *The Indiscret Jewels* goes no further than this "narrow, necessary space." This is why the jewels, far from saying what they like, what gives them pleasure, how they have orgasms, are essentially bookkeepers. They tally the register of visitors and *their* orgasms. They count attacks and are not fooled by false goods. " 'I can still remember, as if I were there,' said Thelis's jewel immodestly. 'Nine proofs of love in four hours. Oh, what a time! What a divine man, that Zermounzaid! Far different from the old and icy Sambuco. Dear Zermounzaid, before you I did not know true pleasure, true well-being. It was you who showed me what it is' " (p. 410). Diderot may well have a lewd side, but he is no libertine. That implies a taste for transgression, a philosophically reflexive pursuit of pleasure. In the world of *The Indiscreet Jewels* the voice of the sex organs may contradict social proprieties but it is perfectly in accord with the laws of nature. It grants no truth to sexual deviance. Unlike the script indications of Sade's *The 120 Days of Sodom* (1785), or the intrigues of seduction in

Laclos's *Dangerous Liaisons* (1782), the idea of mental sensual pleasure does not exist for Diderot. The jewel exhibits desire within a kind of animal, organic autonomy that is separate from the imaginative and intellectual capacities of the person. And it wants to be visited, to receive its complement. The "chatter of the jewels" reveals no fantasy. It is not by chance that the only perversion revealed here is bestiality. Even then, Haria fornicates with dogs only when she is no longer attractive to men. It is true that once she has tried dogs she does not return to men, but this perversion is exceptional. The jewels show no indiscretions toward those tastes that specifically reject vaginal penetration. The silence of a jewel that has been asked a question may thus signify two things: that it is either virtuous or takes pleasure in another way. It is thus during his investigation into "the dark continent of female sexuality" that the Sultan ends up coming upon a jewel (that of the beautiful Fricamona) that has nothing to say. Surprised, he does not know what to think: " 'I questioned her jewel, but received no answer. I redoubled the powers of my ring by rubbing and rubbing. Nothing happened. It must be, I told myself, that this jewel is deaf' " (p. 474). Deaf or dutiful – that is to say, without clandestine affairs to confess. The Sultan was about to give up and conclude that perhaps, exceptionally, the young woman was virtuous, when she started to speak – *with her mouth*: " 'Dear Acaris,' she cried, 'how happy am I in these moments I snatch from my obligations to devote myself to you!... I command my imagination; it calls you forth and I see you' " (p. 474). The invocations, and the sighs... Acaris, like men, expresses herself with her mouth, and her jewel does not betray her. This failure of the Sultan's power and curiosity corresponds to the "aberration" of a jewel that is uninhabited and happy to remain so and the enigma of a sexual organ divorced from all nature's arrangements for the reproduction of the species.

The Women's Conspiracy

Fricamona's obstinately silent jewel is the first manifestation in Diderot's work of a theme that would not cease to trouble and fascinate him: that of lesbian love, to which he devoted his novel *The Nun* (1796). In this startling text, written in the first person, Suzanne, who has become a nun against her will, provokes a desperate passion in the mother superior of the convent of Arpajon. [She writes, afraid and uncomprehending,] "The result of my reflections was that it was probably an affliction to which she was subject, then another thought came, that perhaps the malady was catching, and that Saint-Thérèse had caught it and I should too."[13] The nun, like Mirzoza, the favorite in *The Indiscreet Jewels*, is a reasonable character. She is astounded by women's folly.

The "lesbian disease" brings Diderot back to the double horror of its physiological abstraction and the sequestration that promotes it. In his eyes the convent is thus the most hated (and the most obsessively fascinating) of institutions. Women shut up together, cut off from normal heterosexual relations, abandon themselves to all kinds of delirium. Whether they lose their minds over the image of God or another woman, this is, in any case, a dangerous love, for it is essentially deviant, corrupt, and corrupting, a love that turns them away from the human community, from happiness in society. Two nuns cannot truly love one another. They wander through the corridors of the convent shouting the name of the one who has contaminated them.

The love affairs between women that appear in the narration of *The Indiscreet Jewels* only as blank spaces, mysterious gaps in the irrepressible babble of the jewels, constitute the main theme of *The Nun*. In Diderot's hallucinatory fantasies they are a daily obsession born of proximity. Numerous passages of his correspondence with Sophie Volland reveal his jealously over what he considers an incestuous link between Sophie and her sister: "While I waste my time talking to you of I know not what, Uranie is gaining possession of your soul."[14] Or, "I congratulate you both, dear sisters, for possessing each other."[15] Becoming more and more agitated, he writes, "So you have seen her, your dear sister, and embraced her! How happy you must have been! How your two hearts must have beaten!"[16]

This is a far cry from a libertine view of feminine homosexuality, which only adds more sensual stimulation to the scenes of pleasure in which the libertine delights. For Diderot, on the contrary, women's desire for each other, the sisterly tie, torrid, incomprehensible, and unimaginable, which snatches them from male domination, is the aggravated form of their distinctive reserve of mystery and dissimulation. For embedded in the text of the lighthearted entertainment provided by the jewels' indiscretions is the constant presence of a female nature that is frightening because it is inscrutable. "Women are undefinable," declares the old courtier Selim, who is supposedly a connoisseur of women. This admission is repeated and magnified by the voice of Diderot himself in his brief and fiery essay entitled *On Women*.[17] They are undefinable and essentially duplicitous: "They will simulate the intoxication of passion if they are greatly anxious to deceive you: they will experience an intoxication without forgetting themselves."[18]

Questioning that inner voice that comes from within an "organ subject to terrible spasms,"[19] Mangogul and his friend Selim pay dearly for their lighthearted search for diversion. What they discover, constantly repeated through the amusing babble of the jewels, through these disparate unknown voices, is a power of dissimulation as irrepressible as it is undecipherable, a capacity for secretiveness whose enormity is eloquently revealed by some inadvertent evidence. We deceive you and continue to deceive you, say the genitals shamelessly when pressed to speak the truth. And it is no accident that the majority of lovers admitted by the voice of the jewels are priests: "Impenetrable in dissimulation, cruel in their vengeance, persevering in their schemes, unscrupulous in the methods they employ, animated by a profound and secret hatred of male despotism, they seem linked by a loose plot for domination, in a sort of league such as that which subsists between the priests of every country; they know the articles of their bond without its having to be first communicated to them."[20] The jewels speak, but what they confess reveals to the Sultan the unfathomable nature of women. This is what drives the Sultan from the simple desire for an unusual erotic diversion to the anguish of the question, "Am I loved?"

The tales of *The Indiscreet Jewels* lead to the praise of the loving woman embodied in the wise Mirzoza, of whom he comments, in a telling detail, that she has little temperament. Mirzoza is never carried away or overcome by sexual drive. Her love is at once reasonable, sensible, and enduring, an ideal that constitutes for Diderot an oasis of transparency. Her jewel has no secrets to reveal. Does this mean that it remains silent? No, the loving woman does not confront men with the enigmatic silence they perceive as threatening. Her sex organ speaks, but it says only what the heart's voice says. The fable of *The Indiscreet Jewels* skirts the obsession with strangeness to return to the reassuring dream of a faithful woman.

NOTES

1. Denis Diderot, *Dialogues* (London: Routledge, 1927), p. 195.

2. Aram Vartanian, *Préface, Les Bijoux indiscrets (Fiction I), Diderot* in *Oeuvres complètes* (Paris: Hermann, 1978), vol. 3, p. 11.

3. Cited by Erica-Marie Benabou in *La Prostitution et la police des moeurs au XVIIIème siècle* (Paris: Librairie Académique Perrin, 1987), p. 162.

4. Pierre Lepape, *Diderot* (Paris: Flammarion, 1991), p. 81.

5. Denis Diderot, *Jacques the Fatalist and His Master* (New York: Penguin, 1974), p. 115.

6. *Ibid.*

7. Jean-Claude Bonnet, *Diderot, Textes et débats* (Paris: Librarie Générale Française, Le Livre de Poche, 1984), p. 222.

8. The word *Fotz* was chosen as the one least likely to shock, because it was in German, a language that, according to the author, no one understands. The use of this masculine word to designate the female sex organ further widens the gap between the two voices, the one that speaks with the mouth and the other, radically different one. "Sire, *Fotz*, object of my dearest desires, tell me what your so beautiful mistress just did in her cabinet," implores the Knight. Diderot makes similar use of the masculine term *bijou* (jewel) to point out the impossible cohabitation of the mores that a woman displays and the truth of her sexuality.

9. Caylus, *Nocrion, Conte Allobroge* (Brussels: Gay et Doucé, 1881 [1747]), pp. 36–37.

10. The story of *Nocrion* describes in these terms the reaction of a young girl to the first words of her sex organs: "The poor maidservant, dumbfounded at hearing herself speak so without opening her mouth, was so frightened that, rising abruptly from her bed, she fled in her nightgown to the room of her mistress, the lady of the manor" (*Nocrion*, p. 31).

11. Crébillon fils, *The Sofa*, pp. 320, 321 in this volume.

12. Diderot, *Correspondance, Lettres à Sophie Volland* (Paris: Gallimard, 1930), vol. 2, p. 114.

13. Denis Diderot, *The Nun* (New York: Penguin, 1986), p. 140.

14. Diderot, *Correspondance, Lettres à Sophie Volland*, p. 89.

15. *Ibid.*, p. 128.

16. Denis Diderot, *Diderot's Letters to Sophie Volland*, trans. Peter France (London: Oxford University Press, 1972), p. 111.

17. This text, published in 1772, echoes Thomas's *Dissertation sur les Femmes*. Casanova's pamphlet entitled *Lana Caprina, Epistola di un Licantrope* (1772) was a response to Thomas's text. Unlike Thomas and Diderot, Casanova rejects the explanation of the nature of women by the existence in them of "an internal animal, known by the name *Uterus,* which, not satisfied with a certain number of whims of a physical nature, seeks in addition to take over their heads." He offers this elegant proof: "It is usual for a pretty girl to be the ruin of a miser, but it is absolutely exceptional for a woman to ruin herself for a handsome man. Here there is no apparent influence of the uterus."

18. Denis Diderot, "On Women," in *Dialogues of Diderot* (London: Routledge, 1927), p. 188.

19. *Ibid.*, p. 190.

20. *Ibid.*, p. 187.

Translated by Shelley Temchin.

THE INDISCREET JEWELS
by Denis Diderot

CONTENTS

THE INDISCREET JEWELS
by Denis Diderot

To Zima

SEIZE THE MOMENT, Zima. The aga Narkis is entertaining your mother, and your governess is on the balcony, watching for your father's return. Come and read, there is nothing to fear. Should someone discover *The Indiscreet Jewels* behind your dressing table, do you think it would come as any surprise? No, Zima, no; it is hardly a secret that *The Sofa*, *The Tanzai*, and *The Confessions* have all spent time under your pillow. Still you hesitate? You should know, then, that Aglae herself has not disdained to set her hand to the work you blush to accept. "Aglae!" you say, "the prudent Aglae!" None other. While Zima was bored, or perhaps distracted by the young bonze Alleluia, Aglae innocently amused herself by telling me of the adventures of Zaida, Alphana, Fanni, and others, and provided me with the few moments in Mangogul's story which I like, reviewing it and pointing out to me ways to improve it. For if Aglae is one of the most virtuous and least moralizing women in the Congo, she is likewise the least impressed with wit and the most witty. Does Zima still think it becomes her to feign scruples? Once again, Zima – take up the book, read it, read it all, even the story of "The Roving Jewel," which may be interpreted for you without cost to your virtue, provided that the interpreter is neither your confessor nor your lover.

CHAPTER I

Birth of Mangogul

Yaouf Zeles Tanzai had long reigned in greater Chechianea, and this luxurious prince still continued to be the delight of his subjects. Acajou, King of Minutia, had suffered the fate foretold by his father. Zulmis was no more. The Count de ————[1] was living still. Splendidus, Angola, Misapouf, and a few other potentates of the Indies and Asia had died suddenly. The people, weary of obeying idiot sovereigns, had thrown off the yoke of their posterity, and the descendants of those unfortunate monarchs now wandered unrecognized and almost unknown in the provinces of their empires. The grandson of the illustrious Scheherazade was the only one who had maintained his throne, and he ruled in Hindustan under the name of Shah Baham[2] at the time Mangogul was born in the Congo. Obviously, the dark period of Mangogul's birth saw the passing of numerous sovereigns.

His father, Erguebzed, did not summon the fairies around the cradle of his son, for he had observed that most of the princes of his time, whom these female intelligences had educated, were no better than fools. He merely requested that his son's horoscope be charted by a certain Codindo, a man better read about than known.

Codindo was the head of the Haruspex College of Banza, the former capital of the empire. Erguebzed had granted him a large pension and had favored him and his descendants with a magnificent château on the frontiers of the Congo to reward the merits of their great uncle, who was an excellent cook. Codindo was in charge of observing the flights of birds and the state of the heavens, and was required to report thereof in Court, a duty he carried out rather poorly. If it was true that Banza had the best plays and the worst theaters and concert halls in all Africa, it could also be said that they had the most beautiful college in the world – and the worst predictions.

Codindo, informed of what was wanted of him at Erguebzed's palace, set out with great embarrassment, for the poor man could no more read the stars than you or I. He was awaited with great impatience. The most powerful lords of the Court had gathered in the great Sultana's chamber. The women, magnificently attired, surrounded the infant's cradle. The courtiers made haste to congratulate Erguebzed on the great things he was surely soon to learn about his son. Erguebzed, being a father, found it quite natural that one should see in an infant's unformed features the man he would one day become. At last Codindo arrived. "Come close," Erguebzed said to him. "As soon as the heavens granted me the prince you see before you, I ordered the instant of his birth to be registered exactly and had this fact communicated to you. Speak openly to your master, and tell him boldly of the destiny that the heavens hold in store for his son."

"Most magnanimous Sultan," answered Codindo, "the Prince, born of parents as illustrious as they are fortunate, could have no other destiny than one that was both prosperous and grand. I would be imposing on Your Highness were I to pretend to a science that I lack. The stars rise and set for me just as they do for other men. They enlighten me about the future no more than they do the most ignorant of your subjects."

"But," replied the Sultan, "are you not an astrologer?"

"Magnanimous Prince," answered Codindo, "that honor is not mine."

"What! What the devil are you, then?" said the old but impetuous Erguebzed.

"A haruspex!"

"By the heavens! I had no idea that you so much as thought of it. Take my advice, Sir Codindo: let your chickens feed in peace, and pronounce on the fate of my son, as you recently did on the catarrh of my wife's parakeet."

Codindo immediately pulled a magnifying glass from his pocket, took hold of the infant's left ear, rubbed his eyes, turned his spectacles again and again, peered at the ear, did the same to the right ear, and pronounced that the reign of the young prince would be as happy as it proved long.

"I see," replied Erguebzed. "My son will accomplish the finest things in the world, if he has the time. But, by God, what I want to be told is whether he will have the time. What do I care, once he is dead, if he would have been the greatest prince upon earth had he lived? I called you here to give me my son's horoscope and you give me his funeral oration!"

Codindo assured the Prince that he was sorry not to know more, but he begged His Highness to appreciate that his knowledge was perfectly commensurate with the short time he had been a soothsayer. Indeed, the moment before, what had Codindo been?

CHAPTER II

Mangogul's Education

I shall pass lightly over Mangogul's first years. The childhood of princes is the same as that of other men, except that princes have the gift of saying a thousand charming things before they know how to speak. Thus before Erguebzed's son was fully four years of age he had supplied the material for a volume of *Mangoguliana*. Erguebzed, a sensible man who was resolved that his son's education should not be as neglected as his own had been, decided early on to assemble and retain at his Court, with pensions of considerable size, every sort of great man in the Congo:

painters, philosophers, poets, musicians, architects, masters of dance, mathematics, history, fencing, and so on. Thanks to Mangogul's natural gifts and the constant lessons of his masters, he lacked nothing that a young prince might usually learn in the first fifteen years of life, and he knew, by the age of twenty, how to drink, eat, and sleep as well as any other potentate of his years.

Weary of holding the reins of the empire, alarmed by the troubles that threatened it, full of confidence in Mangogul's superior qualities, and urged on by religious sentiments, sure signs of approaching death, or of the imbecility of great men, Erguebzed, the weight of whose years began to make him feel the weight of his crown, stepped down from the throne to seat his son thereon. And this good prince believed that in his retirement he must expiate the crimes of what was the fairest administration recorded in the annals of the Congo.

Thus it was that in the year 1,500,000,003,200,001 of the world, year 390,000,070,003 of the empire of the Congo, began the reign of Mangogul, the 1,234,500th of his race in a direct line. The frequent conferences with his ministers, the wars to be waged, and the management of affairs instructed him rapidly in what there was left for him to learn once he was out of the hands of his pedagogues – and that was considerable.

Nevertheless, in less than ten years Mangogul acquired the reputation of a great man. He won battles, captured towns, enlarged his empire, quieted his provinces, repaired the disorder of his finances, caused the arts and sciences to flourish, erected monuments, immortalized himself by creating useful institutions, reinforced and corrected the legislative power, and even founded academies; and he accomplished all of this without knowing a single word of Latin, which his university never could understand.

Mangogul was no less amiable in his seraglio than on the throne. It never occurred to him to regulate his conduct according to the ridiculous customs of his country. He broke down the gates of the palace inhabited by his women. He banished those guards who slandered their virtue. Prudently he entrusted each with her own fidelity. One entered their apartments as freely as one might any convent of Flemish canonesses, and they were undoubtedly just as well behaved. What a good sultan was he! His equal was nowhere to be found, except in certain French novels. He was mild, gracious, cheerful, and gallant, comely of aspect, and a great lover of pleasures; indeed he was made for them, and he was more of a wit than all of his predecessors combined.

One can well imagine that with such uncommon merit as his, many women aspired to make his conquest; and a few succeeded. Those who failed to win his heart endeavored to console themselves with other lords of the Court. The young Mirzoza was among the former. But I shall not amuse myself with detailing Mirzoza's charms and qualities; the task would be without end, and I am resolved that this history shall have one.

CHAPTER III

Which May Be Regarded As the First Chapter of This History

Mirzoza had already engaged Mangogul's attentions for some years. The two had professed and repeated a thousand times all the things that a violent passion might suggest to the most spirited lovers. They had become confidants; and they would have considered it a crime to conceal the smallest detail of their lives from each other. Such unusual conjectures as, "If the heavens that placed me on the throne had seen me born in a condition of abject obscurity, would you have deigned stoop as low as me, would Mirzoza have crowned me?"...and, "Should Mirzoza lose the few charms she is thought to have, would Mangogul love her still?" – such conjectures, I say, which exercise the fancy of clever lovers, which sometimes cause misunderstandings between delicate lovers and frequently cause the most sincere lovers to tell untruths – had been quite worn out by the pair.

The favorite, who possessed in the highest degree the necessary and uncommon talent of telling a good tale, had exhausted the scandalous history of Banza. Since she had little inclination for such things, she was not always disposed to receive the Sultan's caresses, nor was the Sultan always in the mood to offer them. In short, there were days when Mangogul and Mirzoza had little to say, almost nothing to do, and during which, though loving each other no less, they had very little fun together. Such days were rare indeed, but there were some, and this was one of them.

The Sultan was idly stretched out on a sofa, across from his favorite, who was knotting in silence. The weather did not permit them to take a stroll. Mangogul did not dare propose a hand of piquet. This sullen situation had already lasted nearly a quarter of an hour, when the Sultan, yawning several times, said,

"It must be admitted that Geliote sang like an angel..."

"And that Your Highness is dying of boredom," added the favorite.

"No, Madame," answered Mangogul, half yawning. "When I see you there are never times of boredom."

"It is up to you to make them gallant," replied Mirzoza. "But you are dreaming, distracted, yawning. Prince, what ails you?"

"I know not," said the Sultan.

"But I can guess," continued the favorite. "I was eighteen when I had the good fortune to win your fancy. You have loved me a full four years now. Eighteen plus four makes twenty-two. I am very old now."

Mangogul smiled at this arithmetic.

"Yet if I am no longer worth anything for pleasure," added Mirzoza, "I will at least show you that I am still very good for advice. The variety of amusements at your disposal have not shielded you from boredom. You are bored. That, Prince, is what ails you."

"I don't allow that you are correct," said Mangogul, "but supposing you are — do you know of a remedy?"

After a moment's pause, Mirzoza replied that as His Highness seemed to her to have taken such pleasure in the account she had given of the gallant adventures of the town, she was sorry that she had no more such tales to tell him, and that she was not better informed of those of the Court; but that she would try this device until she thought of something better.

"I think it is a good idea," says Mangogul. "Anyway, who knows the stories of all those foolish women? And were they known to any, who would recount them to me as you do?"

"Let us learn of them all the same," replied Mirzoza. "Whoever tells them, I am certain that Your Highness will gain more from the content than he will lose on account of the form."

"We may both imagine, if you will, the adventures of the women of my court, and find them very entertaining," said Mangogul. "But even if they were one hundred times more so, what difference would that make if it is impossible to know them?"

"It might be difficult," answered Mirzoza, "but no more than that, in my opinion. The genie Cucufa, your relative and friend, has done more difficult things. Why do you not consult him?"

"Ah! Joy of my heart!" cried the Sultan. "You are admirable! I have no doubt the genie will employ all his power in my favor. I shall close myself in my study this moment and invoke him."

Mangogul then rose, kissed his favorite on the left eye, according to the customs of the Congo, and departed.

CHAPTER IV

The Evocation of the Genie

The genie Cucufa was an old hypochondriac who, fearing lest the concerns of the world and dealings with other genies might prove an obstacle to his salvation, took refuge in the void, in order to immerse himself quite at leisure in the infinite perfections of the Great Pagod, pinching himself, scratching himself, playing tricks on himself, getting bored, getting angry, dying of hunger. He sleeps on a mat there, his body tucked into a sack, his flanks tied with rope, his arms crossed on his breast, his head buried in a cowl, from which only the tip of his beard protrudes. He sleeps, but one would think that he is meditating. For company he has only an owl that nods at his feet, a few rats that gnaw his mat, and bats that fly about his head. One summons him by reciting, to the sound of a bell, the first verse of the nocturnal office of the Brahmins. He then raises his cowl, rubs his eyes, puts on his sandals, and sets out, the image of an old Camaldolite,[1] borne through the air by two fat wood owls, which he holds by the legs. It was in this fashion that Cucufa appeared before the Sultan.

"May the blessing of Brahma be with you," he said, swooping down.

"Amen," replied the Prince.

"What is your wish, my son?"

"A simple thing," said Mangogul. "To procure some pleasure at the expense of the ladies at my court."

"My son," answered Cucufa, "you alone have more appetite than an entire monastery of Brahmins. What do you wish from this flock of silly women?"

"For them to tell me of their amorous adventures past and present, no more."

"But it is impossible," said the genie, "to expect women to confess their adventures. That has never been and shall never be."

"Yet it must be," added the Sultan.

At these words the genie began to think, scratching his ear and combing his beard with his fingers in distraction. His meditation was brief.

"My son," he said to Mangogul, "I am so very fond of you. Your wish shall be satisfied."

He then plunged his right hand into a deep pocket made under his arm on the left side of his robe, and along with images, holy beads, small leaden pagodas, and mildewy candy, he drew out a silver ring, which Mangogul at first mistook for a Saint Hubert's ring.[2]

"You see this ring?" he said to the Sultan. "Put it on your finger, my son. Every woman toward whom you turn the stone will recount her intrigues in a loud, clear, and intelligible voice. But do not imagine that they shall speak through their mouths."

"Whence," cried Mongogul, "shall they then speak?"

"From the most honest part of them, and the best instructed in the things you desire to know," said Cucufa. "From their jewels."

"From their jewels!" repeated the Sultan, bursting into laughter. "This is something new. Talking jewels! How preposterous!"

"My son," said the genie, "I have performed many greater prodigies as a favor to your grandfather; you can count on my word. Go, and may Brahma bless you. Put your secret to good use, and remember that curiosity can be misdirected."

This said, shaking his head, the genie donned his cowl once more, took up his wood owls by the legs, and disappeared into the air.

CHAPTER V

Mangogul's Dangerous Temptation

No sooner was Mangogul in possession of Cucufa's mysterious ring than he was tempted to put it to its first test on the favorite. I have forgotten to mention that in addition to having the power to make women's jewels speak when the stone was turned toward them, the ring could also make the person who wore it on his little finger invisible. Thus in the twinkling of an eye Mangogul could transport himself to a hundred places where he was not expected, and see with his own eyes many things that usually occur without witnesses; he had only to put on the ring and say, "I will be there," and instantly he was there. And so, there he was, in Mirzoza's chambers.

Mirzoza, who was not expecting the Sultan, had had herself put to bed. Mangogul approached her pillow softly, and by the light of the taper saw that she was asleep. "Good," said he, "she is asleep, let us quickly shift the ring to another finger, resume our own shape, turn the stone toward this fair dreamer, and awake her jewel a bit... But what stops me?... I tremble... could it be that Mirzoza...? No, that is impossible. Mirzoza is faithful to me. Be gone, slanderous suspicions, I will not, I must not, listen to you." This said, he brought his fingers to the ring, but he let go as quickly as if it were on fire, and cried to himself: "What am I doing, wretch that I am! I am ignoring Cucufa's advice. To satisfy a silly curiosity I risk losing my mistress and my life... If her jewel took it upon itself to talk extravagantly, I should see her no more and die of sorrow. And who knows what a jewel may have in its soul?" In his agitation Mangogul forgot himself; he spoke these last words a bit loudly, and the favorite awoke.

"Ah, Prince," she said to him, less surprised than charmed by his presence, "you are here! Why were you not announced? Were you waiting for me to awake?"

Mangogul answered the favorite by telling her of the success of the meeting with Cucufa. He showed her the ring he had received, concealing none of its properties from her.

"Ah, what diabolical secret has he given you there?" cried Mirzoza. "But, Prince, do you intend to use it?"

"Mercy, what is that?" exclaimed the Sultan. "Do I intend to use it? I shall begin with you if you try to argue with me."

At these terrible words the favorite paled, trembled, pulled herself together, and besought the Sultan in the name of Brahma and all the pagods of the Indies and the Congo not to test on her a secret power that showed so little faith in her fidelity.

"If I have always been good," she continued, "my jewel will not say a word, and you will have done me such a wrong as I shall never forgive. If it does speak, I shall lose your esteem and your heart, and you will be in despair. Until now you have been, it seems to me, rather content with our love. Why risk destroying it? Prince, do as I say and heed the genie's advice. He has had great experience, and the counsels of genies are always worth heeding."

"I was saying the same to myself," Mangogul answered her, "when you awoke. And yet if you had slept two minutes longer, I cannot answer for what might have happened."

"What would have happened," said Mirzoza, "is that my jewel would have told you nothing, and you would have lost me forever."

"That may be," replied Mangogul, "but now that I see the risk I was taking, I solemnly swear to you by the eternal Pagod that you shall be excepted from those toward whom I shall turn my ring."

At these words Mirzoza brightened, and began to make jokes at the expense of the jewels that the Prince would hereafter put to the test.

"Cydalisa's jewel," she began "has many a story to tell. And if it is as indiscreet as its mistress, it will not have to be asked twice. Haria's jewel retired years ago, and from it Your Highness will hear only tales from my grandmother's time. As for Glaucia's jewel, I think it is a good one to consult, for she is flirtatious and pretty."

"And for that very reason," replied the Sultan, "I expect it will be mute."

"Ask Phedima's then," returned the Sultana. "She is ugly and loves gallantry."

"Yes," continued the Sultan, "and so ugly that only one as cruel as you would accuse her of gallantry. Phedima is chaste, I tell you. I know about these things."

"As chaste as you please," answered the favorite, "but her gray eyes speak to the contrary."

"Those eyes fooled you," the Sultan said sharply. "You try my patience with your Phedima. One might imagine that there was only this one jewel to question."

"But is it possible, without offending Your Highness," added Mirzoza, "to ask which one he will honor with his choice?"

"We shall soon see what we shall find," said Mangogul, "in the Manimonbanda's circle (such was the name of the Congolese Grand Sultana). We shall soon have no lack of subjects, and when we happen to tire of the jewels at my court, we can travel around Banza. Perhaps we shall find those of the bourgeoises more reasonable than those of our duchesses."

"Prince," said Mirzoza, "I have some acquaintance with the former, and I can assure you that they are simply more circumspect."

"We shall soon hear from them; but I cannot help laughing," continued Mangogul, "when I think of the confusion of those women and their surprise at hearing their jewel's first words. Ha! ha! My heart's delight, that I shall expect you at the Grand Sultana's, and I shall not use my ring until you have come."

"Prince," said Mirzoza, "I shall count on the promise you have made."

Mangogul smiled at her fears, repeated his vows, sealed them with kisses, added a few caresses, and retired.

CHAPTER VI

First Trial of the Ring
Alcina

Mangogul arrived before Mirzoza at the Grand Sultana's and found all the women playing cavagnole.[1] He looked over those who enjoyed good reputations, resolved to try his ring out on one of them. His only difficulty was in the choice. He was uncertain with whom to begin, until he saw in a window a young lady from the Manimonbanda's palace. She was making sport with her husband, which seemed unusual to the Sultan, for they had been married for more than eight days. They had appeared in the same box at the Opera, had ridden in the same coach at the Bois de Boulogne, had completed their visits, and now custom dispensed them from loving or even seeing each other. "If this jewel," said Mangogul to himself, "is as silly as its mistress, we shall have a delightful monologue." At this point the favorite appeared.

"Welcome," the Sultan whispered in her ear, "I have cast my line while waiting for you."

"On whom?" asked Mirzoza.

"On the couple you see frolicking in that window," answered Mangogul with a wink.

"A good beginning," replied the favorite.

Alcina, for such was this young lady's name, was vivacious and pretty. The Sultan's court had few women more comely than she, and not a one more gallant. An emir of the Sultan had lost his head over her. He was not left long in ignorance of what the papers had published about Alcina. He was alarmed but followed the custom and consulted his mistress about it. Alcina swore to him that the slander was the gossip of wretches who would have kept silent had they any reason to speak; furthermore, she added, no harm had been done, and he was free to believe whatever he deemed fit. This confident answer convinced the enamored emir of the innocence of his mistress. He reached his own conclusions, and took the title of Alcina's husband, with all its prerogatives.

The Sultan turned his ring toward her. A loud burst of laughter, which had seized Alcina at some quip from her husband, was suddenly syncopated by the workings of the ring. Immediately a murmuring noise was heard from beneath her petticoats: "Well, now I have a title. I am truly glad of it. There is nothing like having a station. Of course, if she had listened to my first advice, she could have found me something better than an emir. But still, an emir is better than nothing."

At these words, all the women left off the game to search from whence came the voice. This agitation created a great deal of noise.

"Silence," said Mangogul, "this merits our attention."

Silence fell, and the jewel continued: "A husband must be an important guest, judging from the precautions taken to receive him. So many preparations! So much myrtle water! Two more weeks of this regimen would have been the end of me. I would have disappeared, and my lord the Emir would have had to find lodgings elsewhere, or ship me off to the Island of Jonquille."[2] Here my author says that all the ladies paled, looked at each other without a word, and preserved their gravity; this he ascribes to their fear lest the conversation should get out of control or become too general.

"Nonetheless," continued Alcina's jewel, "in my opinion, the Emir did not require such a fuss, although I understand my mistress's prudence. She was preparing for the worst, and I was readied for Monsieur and his squire alike."

The jewel was about to continue its effusions when the Sultan, observing that this strange scene shocked the modest Manimonbanda, interrupted the speaker by turning around his ring. The Emir had disappeared at the first words from his wife's jewel. Alcina, unabashed, feigned a fainting spell, while the women whispered that she had the vapors. "Of course!" said a fop. "The vapors! Cicogne[3] calls them hysterics, which means things that come from the lower region. He has a divine elixir for it; it is a principle, principiating, principiated, which revives...which...I recommend to the lady." People smiled at this banter, and our cynic continued:

"Nothing could be truer, ladies. I myself have used it for a dwindling of substance."

"A dwindling of substance, Monsieur le Marquis?" asked one young woman. "What is that?"

"Madame," answered the Marquis, "it is one of those fortuitous accidents that can happen...But everyone knows about that."

Meanwhile, the simulated fainting spell ended. Alcina sat down to play as brazenly as if her jewel had said nothing, or as if it had said the nicest things in the world. She was the only one able to play without distraction. This round won her a considerable sum. The others did not know what they were doing, could not recognize their squares, forgot their numbers, neglected their advantages, wagered wrong, and committed one hundred other blunders from which Alcina profited. At last the game ended and everyone retired.

This adventure caused a great stir not only at Court and in town, but all over the Congo. Poems circulated about it. The discourse of Alcina's jewel was published, revised, corrected, enlarged, and commented on by the darlings of the Court. The Emir was lampooned, and his wife immortalized. They pointed her out at the theater; they followed her on public walks; they flocked around her, and she heard them buzzing, "Yes, there she is; that is her; her jewel spoke for two whole hours."

Alcina bore her new reputation with remarkable composure. She listened to all these remarks, and many others, with a calmness that other women lacked. They anticipated at every moment some indiscretion on the part of their own jewels, and the adventure in the following chapter would make their confusion complete.

When the company had dispersed, Mangogul offered his arm to the favorite, and led her back to her quarters. Gone was the playful and lively spirit that was her wont. She had lost a considerable amount at the game, and the effect of the terrible ring had cast her into a pensive state. She was familiar with the Sultan's curiosity and did not have sufficient faith in the promises of a man less amorous than despotic to be entirely at her ease.

"What ails you, my soul's delight?" Mangogul asked her. "You seem lost in thought."

"I played with incomparable bad luck," she answered him. "I lost everything. I had twelve numbers, and I don't think I scored three times."

"That is a shame," replied Mangogul, "but what do you think of my secret?"

"Prince," the favorite said to him, "I still consider it diabolical. Doubtless it will amuse you, but that amusement will have dire consequences. You will spread discord in every household, undeceive every husband, drive every lover to despair, ruin wives, dishonor maidens, and cause countless other disturbances. Ah! Prince, I beseech you..."

"Mercy!" said Mangogul, "you moralize like Nicole![4] I would very much like to know why the fate of others touches you so deeply today? No, Madame, no, I will keep my ring. What do I care for these undeceived husbands, despairing lovers, ruined wives, and dishonored maidens as long as I am amused? Am I Sultan for nothing? Until tomorrow, Madame. Let us hope that the scenes to come will be more comical than the first, and that you will gradually acquire a taste for them."

"I doubt it, my lord," answered Mirzoza.

"And I promise you: you will find some jewels amusing; so amusing that you will not be able to refuse them an audience. What would you do if I sent them to you as ambassadors? If you like, I will spare you the boredom of listening to them. But you shall hear of their adventures nonetheless, if not from their mouths then from mine. It has been decided; I cannot recant. Resolve to familiarize yourself with these new tellers of tales."

With these words, he kissed her and then went to his study, reflecting upon the trial he had just made, and devoutly thanking the genie Cucufa.

CHAPTER VII

Second Trial of the Ring
The Altars

The next evening a small supper was held at Mirzoza's. The guests assembled early in her chambers. Before the wonders of the preceding day, people came by choice; this evening they came only out of a sense of duty. All the ladies had an air of constraint and spoke only in monosyllables. They were wary, expecting that at any moment a jewel might join in the conversation. In spite of their longing to further explore Alcina's misadventures, none dared take it upon herself to proceed with this resolution. Not that they were restrained by her presence; although she was included in the supper list, she did not put in an appearance. They assumed she had a headache. Nonetheless, either because they feared danger the less for having heard only mouths speak that day, or in a pretense of courage, the conversation, which had been dragging, gradually picked up. The most suspect women composed themselves, feigning confidence. Mirzoza asked the courtier Zegris if he had any entertaining news.

"Madame," answered Zegris, "you have been informed of the upcoming marriage of the aga Chazour to the young Siberina. I inform you now that it has been canceled."

"Why?" demanded the favorite.

"Because of a strange voice," continued Zegris, "which Chazour claims to have heard in the Princess's boudoir. Since yesterday the Sultan's court is full of people who go about with ears cocked in the hopes of overhearing, I cannot imagine how, confessions that assuredly no one would wish to make."

"But that is mad," replied the favorite. "Alcina's misfortune, if it be such, is far from established. It still has not been looked into –"

"Madame," interrupted Zelmaida, "I heard her most distinctly. She spoke without opening her mouth; the facts were well articulated, and it was not very difficult to guess whence this extraordinary sound issued. I confess that I would have died in her situation."

"Died!" retorted Zegris. "People survive worse accidents."

"What," cried Zelmaida, "could be worse than an indiscreet jewel? After that, there is no middle course; one must either renounce gallantry or be resolved to pass for a woman of pleasure."

"Indeed," said Mirzoza, "the choice is a bitter one."

"No, Madame, no," another joined in. "You will see that women will make the best of it. They will allow their jewels to prate as much as they please, and will go about their business without troubling themselves about what people say. For what difference does it make, after all, whether it be a woman's jewel or her lover that proves indiscreet? Is one any the less exposed?"

"All things considered," continued a third, "if a woman's adventures must be divulged, better by her jewel than by her lover."

"A most curious idea," said the favorite.

"And true," answered she who had suggested it. "For observe: a lover is generally dissatisfied before he becomes indiscreet, and is therefore tempted to take revenge by exaggerating things. Conversely, a jewel speaks dispassionately, and adds nothing to the truth."

"For my part," Zelmaida added, "I do not agree. It is not so much the relevance of the testimony as its source that convicts the guilty party. A lover who through talk dishonors the altar upon which he has sacrificed is impious and thus undeserving of credence; but if the altar itself raises its voice, what can one say?"

"That the altar does not know what it is saying," replied another.

Monima broke the silence she had kept up to this point to say in a lethargic, careless tone, "Oh, let my altar, since you call it so, speak or hold its peace; I fear nothing it can say."

At this moment Mangogul entered, and Monima's last words did not escape him. He turned his ring toward her and her jewel was heard to cry out, "Do not believe her, she lies." The women next to her looked at each other, asking themselves to whom belonged the jewel that just answered.

"It was not mine," said Zelmaida.

"Nor mine," said another.

"Nor mine," said Monima.

"Nor mine," said the Sultan.

Each, including the favorite, responded in the negative.

The Sultan, taking advantage of this doubt, and addressing the women, said, "So you have altars, do you? Pray, how are they honored?" As he spoke, he nimbly turned his ring toward each woman in quick succession, with the exception of Mirzoza; each jewel responded in turn, in different tones, "I am visited, battered, neglected, perfumed, fatigued, ill-attended, bored..." and so on. Each had its say, but so abruptly that it was not possible to distinguish which said what. Their jargon, now muffled, now shrill, accompanied by the laughter of Mangogul and his courtiers, created a new kind of din. The women agreed, in all seriousness, that it was very amusing. "What have we here?" asked the Sultan.

"We are delighted that jewels deign to speak our language and contribute to the conversation. Society can only benefit tremendously from this duplication of faculties. Possibly we men, in turn, shall one day speak from somewhere other than the mouth. Who can tell? That which accords so perfectly well with jewels might be destined to question and to answer them. Nonetheless, my anatomist thinks otherwise."

CHAPTER VIII

Third Trial of the Ring
The Supper

Supper was served. People ate. At first they amused themselves at Monima's expense. All the women agreed her jewel had spoken first, and she would have succumbed to this consensus had not the Sultan come to her defense.

"I make no claim," said the Sultan, "that Monima is less gallant than Zelmaida, but I think her jewel is more discreet. Besides, when a woman's mouth and her jewel contradict each other, which should be believed?"

"My lord," answered a courtier, "I cannot guess what the jewels will say in the future; but till now they have spoken on matters with which they are most familiar. As long as they have the good sense to speak only of what they know, I shall believe them as if they were oracles."

"More reliable ones," said Mirzoza, "might be consulted."

"Madame," responded Mangogul, "what interest could these have in disguising the truth? Their motive could only be an illusion of honor. But a jewel has no illusions; it is surely not the seat of prejudice."

"Illusions of honor!" exclaimed Mirzoza. "Prejudices! If Your Highness were exposed to the same inconveniences as we, he would understand that whatever relates to matters of virtue is far from illusory."

All the ladies, encouraged by the Sultana's response, maintained that it was unnecessary to put them through certain tests; Mangogul conceded at least that these tests were almost always dangerous.

This conversation led to champagne, and the ladies gave themselves over to it. It went to their heads, and to their jewels as well. At this moment Mangogul decided to resume his mischievousness. He turned his ring on a very gay young lady seated quite close to him and across the table from her husband. From beneath the table the plaintive sounds of a feeble and languishing voice were heard to say: "Ah, how harassed I am! I cannot go on; I am all worn out."

"By the Pagod Pongo Sabiam!" cried Husseim. "My wife's jewel speaks! What can it have to say?"

"We shall see," answered the Sultan.

"Prince, please permit me to excuse myself from among its auditors," replied Husseim, "for should it say anything ridiculous, does Your Highness think…"

"I think that you are a fool," answered the Sultan, "to be alarmed at the babbling of a jewel. Do we not already know a great deal of what it might say, and can we not guess the rest? Sit down, then, and try to enjoy yourself."

Husseim sat down, and his wife's jewel began to chatter like a magpie.

"Shall I always have this big oaf Valanto?" it cried. "Some take their time, but this one…"

At these words, Husseim lept up in a fury, seized a knife, hurled himself across the table, and would have stabbed his wife in the breast had he not been restrained by her neighbors.

"Husseim," the Sultan said to him, "you make too much of a fuss. We cannot hear a thing. Do you think that your wife's jewel is the only one to lack common sense? And what would happen to these women if all husbands had a temper like yours? You fall into despair over a miserable little adventure with a certain tireless Valanto! Return to your seat; act like a gentleman. Control yourself and take care never again to disappoint a prince who lets you partake in his pleasures."

While Husseim, concealing his rage, leaned on the back of a chair, eyes closed and hand on forehead, the Sultan suddenly turned his ring and the jewel continued: "Valanto's young page would suit me rather well, but I do not know when he will ever begin. So, while waiting for the one to begin and the other to end, I console myself with the Brahmin Egon. He is hideous, I admit, but he has a talent for ending and beginning again. Oh! What a great man a Brahmin is!"

By the time the jewel made this exclamation, Husseim was blushing to have suffered for a woman so unworthy, and began to laugh like the rest of the company. He did, nevertheless, hold it against his wife. When the meal was over, everyone went home except Husseim, who took his wife to a house for veiled women and shut her up in it. Mangogul, informed of her disgrace, went to visit her. He found the whole community busy consoling her, and still busier drawing from her the reasons for her exile.

"It is for a trifle," she told them, "that I am here. Yesterday, dining at the Sultan's, we had swilled champagne and toasted with tokay. People hardly knew what they were saying, when suddenly my jewel decided to babble. I do not remember what it said, but my husband lost his temper."

The young nuns replied: "Certainly, Madame, he was wrong: people ought not get angry over trifles..."

"What? Your jewel spoke! Can it speak still? Oh, how delighted we should be to hear it! It must express itself with wit and charm..."

They were immediately satisfied, for the Sultan turned his ring on the unfortunate exile and her jewel thanked them for their civilities, protesting to them at the same time that however pleased it was with their company, that of a young Brahmin would suit it much better.

The Sultan took advantage of the occasion to learn a few details of the lives of these maidens. His ring questioned the jewel of a young nun named Cleanthis, and the supposedly virginal jewel confessed to two gardeners, a Brahmin, and three cavaliers. It recounted that, with the assistance of a purging draught and two bloodlettings, she had avoided creating a scandal. Zepherina confessed, through the organ of her jewel, that she was indebted to the errand boy for the honorable title of mother. One thing that shocked the Sultan was that although the sequestered jewels expressed themselves in very indecent terms, the virgins to whom they belonged heard them without blushing, which made him conjecture that what they lacked in practice in these retreats they made up for in speculation.

To clear up this matter, he turned his ring on a young novice of fifteen or sixteen years of age. "Flora," her jewel explained, "has more than once cast glances at a young officer through the gate. I am certain he is to her taste; her little finger told me so." This was unfortunate for Flora. The elders condemned her to two months of prayer and penance; they also ordered prayers that the jewels of the community might remain silent.

CHAPTER IX

The State of the Academy of Sciences of Banza

Mangogul had scarcely quitted the recluses among whom I had left him, when a rumor spread throughout Banza that all the maidens in the Congregation of the Brahma's Coccyx were speaking from their jewels. This rumor, to which Husseim's rash act lent credence, pricked the curiosity of the learned. The phenomenon was examined thoroughly, and the great minds began to seek in the properties of matter for the explanation of a thing they had at first deemed impossible. The chatter of jewels produced a great number of excellent works, and this important subject swelled the collection of the academies with several treatises that may be considered among the most advanced efforts of the human mind.

To shape and perpetuate the Academy of Sciences in Banza, invitations and encouragements had been and continued still to be given to the brightest minds in the Congo, Monoemugi, the Beleguanza, and the neighboring kingdoms. The academy comprised, under different titles, all the distinguished figures in natural history, physics, mathematics, and the greater part of those who showed promise of future distinction in these fields. This swarm of busy bees worked without respite in search of truth. Each year the public collected the fruits of their labors in a volume full of discoveries.

The academy was currently divided into two factions, the one composed of Vorticists, and the other of Attractionists. Olibrio, a skillful geometer and great physicist, founded the sect of the Vorticists. Circino, an able physicist and great geometer, was the first Attractionist. Both Olibrio and Circino took it upon themselves to explain nature. Olibrio's principles have, at first glance, a seductive simplicity. They satisfy the principal phenomena on the whole, but they contradict themselves in the details. As for Circino, he appears to base his ideas on an absurdity; but it is only this first step that works against him. The minute details that ruin Olibrio's system serve to establish Circino's. He follows a path that is obscure at the beginning, but which becomes more and more clear as one advances. Olibrio's, on the contrary, clear at the beginning, heads ever toward obscurity. Olibrio's philosophy demands less study than understanding, whereas one cannot be a disciple of the other without much understanding and study. No preparation is necessary to enter into Olibrio's school. Anyone can hold its key. Circino's is accessible only to the finest geometers. Olibrio's vortices are within the reach of all minds. Circino's central arguments are for first-rate algebraists alone. There will therefore always be one hundred Vorticists for every Attractionist; and one Attractionist will always be worth one hundred Vorticists. Such was the state of the Academy of Sciences in Banza when it debated the issue of the talking jewels.

This phenomenon was slippery; it eluded attraction; subtle matter was not drawn to it. In vain did the director call upon those with ideas to communicate them; a deep silence reigned in the assembly. At last the Vorticist Persiflo, who had published treatises on an infinite number of subjects that he had not understood, rose up and said, "This occurrence, gentlemen, could very well stem from the global system.

I suspect, on the whole, it has the same cause as the tides. In fact, note that today we are in the middle of the full moon of the equinox; but, before we can count on my conjecture we must wait and see what the jewels will say next month."

People shrugged. No one dared inform him that he reasoned like a jewel, but he was shrewd enough to realize that they thought as much.

The Attractionist Reciproco took the floor, and added, "Gentlemen, I have some tables deduced from a theory on the height of the tides in every port of the kingdom. It is true that observation contradicts my calculations somewhat; but I hope that this inconvenience will be countered by the usefulness it will provide if the chatter of jewels continues to conform to the phenomena of ebb and flow."

A third stood up, walked over to the blackboard, traced a figure and said, "Let AB be a jewel..." and so on.

Here the ignorance of the translators has deprived us of a demonstration that, without doubt, the African author had preserved for us. Following a blank of about two pages or so, we read, "Reciproco's reasonings seemed conclusive, and it was agreed, based on the tests to which his dialectics had been subjected, that he would one day succeed in deducing that women should today speak through their jewels about what they have always heard through their ears."

Doctor Orcotomus, from the Anatomist camp, then said, "Gentlemen, I think it is more proper to disregard a phenomenon than to search for its cause in empty hypotheses. For my part, I would have kept silent had I but futile conjectures to offer you; but I have scrutinized, studied, and reflected. I have seen jewels in the state of paroxysm; and, with the help of experiment and my knowledge of anatomy, I have come to be convinced that that which in Greek is called the *delphus* has all the properties of the trachea, and that there are some subjects who can speak just as well with the jewel as with the mouth. Yes, gentlemen, the *delphus* is a string and wind instrument, but much more string than wind. The outer air that bears upon it actually serves as bow on the tendinous fibers of the wings, which I call ribbons or vocal chords. It is the gentle collision of this air and the vocal chords that causes them to tremble. Through quicker or slower vibrations they create different sounds. The person modifies these sounds at will, speaks, and can even sing.

"As there are but two ribbons or vocal chords, and as they are approximately the same length, you will no doubt ask me how they can suffice to create the multitude of high and low notes, loud and soft, of which the human voice is capable. My answer, to continue the comparison of this organ to musical instruments, is that their lengthenings and shortenings are sufficient to produce these effects.

"That these parts are capable of distension and contraction need not be demonstrated to an assembly of scholars of your caliber; but the consequences of this distension and contraction, the fact that the *delphus* can render sounds of varying pitch – in short, all the inflections of a voice and all the modulations of song – is something I pride myself on being able to prove to you beyond doubt. I now appeal to experiments. Yes, gentlemen, I shall undertake to make *delphus* and jewel alike reason, speak, and even sing before you."

Thus argued Orcotomus, promising no less than to raise jewels to the level of the trachea of one of his colleagues, whose success had been immune to attacks of envy.

CHAPTER X

Less Scholarly and Less Tedious than the Previous One
Continuation of the Academic Session

Given the objections raised against Orcotomus while the assembly awaited his experiments, his ideas seemed to be considered more ingenious than well founded. "If jewels possess a natural ability to speak," he was asked, "why have they waited until now to use it? If it is by the grace of Brahma, whom it pleased to inspire in women so violent a desire to speak, to double their organs of speech, it is strange indeed that they were unaware or neglectful of so precious a natural gift for so long a time. Why has each jewel spoken but once? Why do they all speak about the same things? What mechanism causes one mouth perforce to shut while the other speaks? Furthermore," they added, "judging from the circumstances under which most of the jewels spoke, and from the things that they said, there is every reason to believe that it is involuntary and that these parts would have remained mute had it been within the power of their owners to silence them."

Orcotomus set about attempting to satisfy these objections, maintaining that jewels have always spoken, but so softly that what they said was at times barely audible, even to those to whom they belonged. He added that it was not surprising that they had raised their voices today, since conversation had become so free that the most intimate things were discussed without impudence or indiscretion; that if they spoke out loud once, it did not mean that they would not speak out loud again; that there is quite a difference between being mute and keeping silent; that if they all spoke only of the same things, it would appear that this is the only topic on which they have an opinion; that those which have not yet spoken would speak; that if they keep quiet, it is because they have nothing to say, or they are misshapen, or they lack ideas or terms.

"In a word," he continued, "to claim that it was Brahma in his goodness who granted women the means to satisfy their violent desire to speak by multiplying in them the organs of speech, is to grant that if this blessing carried in its wake certain inconveniences, Brahma in his wisdom ought to have anticipated them; and this he did, in constraining one mouth to fall silent while the other spoke. Already it is distressing for us that women change their minds from one minute to the next. How would it have been had Brahma given them the ability to voice two contradictory opinions at once? Furthermore, the gift of speech is granted in order to make oneself understood. How could women, who have so much trouble making themselves understood with one voice, have made themselves understood speaking with two?"

Orcotomus had just answered many questions; but if he imagined he had satisfied everyone, he was mistaken. They pressed him hard with more questions, and he was about to succumb when the physicist Cimonazes came to his assistance. Then the dispute became unruly. They went off on tangents, got lost, came back, got lost again, got angry, shouted, went from shouts to insults, and the academic session came to an end.

CHAPTER XI

Fourth Trial of the Ring
The Echo

While the chatter of jewels occupied the academy, it became the news of the day in various circles and the talk of the morrow, and of many days after that: it was a subject of inexhaustible interest. To real events fictitious ones were added; anything was possible: the miracle had made everything believable. More than six months passed with people immersed in these conversations.

The Sultan had tried his ring but three times; nonetheless, in the circle of women who enjoyed the privilege of the tabouret at the Manimonbanda's, people told stories of the jewels of a judge's wife and a marquise. Next they disclosed the pious secrets of a woman of the veil, then those of many women who were not even there, and God only knows what remarks were attributed to their jewels. Indecencies were not spared and after the facts they turned to reflection.

"One must admit," said one of the women, "that this spell – for that is what has been cast over the jewels – keeps us in a pitiful state. Always in dread of hearing an impertinent voice issuing from below!"

"But, Madame," answered another, "this fear of yours surprises us. When a jewel has nothing ridiculous to say, what does it matter if it keeps quiet or speaks?"

"It matters so much," answered the first, "that I would willingly give half of my gemstones to be assured that mine will keep silent."

"Verily," replied the second, "to buy discretion so dearly, one must have good reasons."

"My reasons are no different from those of others," retorted Cephisa. "Still, I do not retract what I said. Twenty thousand crowns to set my mind at ease; it is not too much, for I shall tell you frankly that I am not any surer of my jewel than I am of my mouth, and I've said many silly things in my life. Every day I hear so many outrageous adventures disclosed, confirmed, and detailed by jewels, that even if three-quarters of them were refuted, the rest would suffice to destroy a reputation. If mine should prove half as great a liar as the others, still I would be ruined. Is it not enough that our conduct is dictated by our jewels, without our reputations depending on them as well?"

"For my part," Ismene replied briskly, "without entering into endless arguments, I let things take their natural course. If it is Brahma who causes jewels to talk, as my Brahmin has proved to me, he would not suffer them to lie. It would be impious to assert the contrary. My jewel may then speak when and as much as it likes: and what could it say, after all?"

A muffled voice that seemed to come from below ground was heard to answer, as if by echo, "Many things." Ismene, having no idea whence the answer issued, flew into a rage, upbraided her neighbors, and thus prolonged the amusement of the group. The Sultan, delighted that she had taken the bait, left his minister, with whom he was in conference in the corner, approached her, and said, "Beware, Madame, you may have once confided in some of these women, and their jewels might have the malice to remember the stories that your own has forgotten."

At the same time, by turning his ring round and round with dexterity, Mangogul established a rather unusual dialogue between the woman and her jewel. Ismene, who had always handled her affairs rather well, and who had never confided in anyone, answered the Sultan that all the slanderers' wiles would be quite useless with her.

"Perhaps," answered an unknown voice.

"What is that! *Perhaps?*" retorted Ismene, stung by this insulting doubt. "What have I to fear from them?"

"Everything, if they know as much as I."

"And what do you know?"

"Many things, I tell you."

"Many things! That boasts much but means nothing. Can you give a few examples?"

"Without a doubt."

"What kind? Have I been in love?"

"No."

"Have I had intrigues, affairs?"

"Certainly."

"And with whom, if you please? With fops, military men, senators?"

"No."

"Actors?"

"No."

"Would it be with my pages, my footmen, my confessor, my husband's chaplain?"

"No."

"Impostor, have you not yet finished?"

"Not quite."

"And yet I can think of no one else with whom one might have an affair. Was it before or after my marriage? Answer me, rascal."

"Ah, Madame, no insults, please. Do not compel your best friend to do something rash."

"Speak, my dear; tell everything, tell it all. I hold your services in as little regard as I fear your indiscretion. Explain yourself, I give you permission. I command you."

"What are you making me do, Ismene?" asked the jewel, heaving a deep sigh.

"Render justice to virtue."

"Very well, virtuous Ismene, do you no longer remember the young Osmin, the sanjak[1] Zegris, your dancing master Alaziel, your music master Almoura?"

"Horrors!" cried Ismene. "My mother was too watchful to expose me to such licentiousness; and my husband, were he here, would attest that he found me exactly as he desired me."

"Oh yes," replied the jewel, "thanks to the secret of your friend Alcina."

"That is so extravagantly and grossly absurd," retorted Ismene, "that it deserves no refutation. I do not know," she continued, "which of these ladies' jewel pretends to so great a knowledge of my affairs, but it has just recounted matters about which my own does not know the first thing."

"Madame," replied Cephisa, "I can assure you that mine has been content to listen."

The other women said the same, and returned to the game without being quite sure as to the identity of the interlocutor in the conversation I have just recounted.

CHAPTER XII

Fifth Trial of the Ring
The Game

Most of the ladies in the Manimonbanda's party played tenaciously, and one hardly needed Mangogul's wisdom to notice this. The passion for gaming is one of the hardest to conceal; it manifests itself, both for winners and losers, in striking symptoms. "But where do they get this mania?" he asked himself. "How can they decide to spend the night around a faro[1] table, trembling in the hopes of an ace or a seven? This frenzy affects their health and their beauty, when they have any, not to mention the disorders that I am certain it brings on."

"I have a great desire," he said softly to Mirzoza, "to do something impulsive."

"And what might that be?" the favorite asked him.

"To turn my ring," Mangogul answered, "on the most unbridled of these gamblers, to question her jewel, to convey through this organ some advice to all those weak husbands who allow their wives to stake the honor and fortune of their houses on a card or a die."

"I rather like that idea," Mirzoza answered him. "But you should know, Prince, that the Manimonbanda has just sworn by her pagods that there will no longer be any gatherings at her place if she finds herself exposed to the impudence of the engastrimyths[2] again."

"What did you say, joy of my soul?" Mangogul interrupted.

"I was using," replied the favorite, "the name that the modest Manimonbanda has given to those whose jewels know how to talk."

"It is the invention of her foolish Brahmin, who prides himself on knowing Greek but not Congolese," replied the Sultan. "Nonetheless, with all due respect for the Manimonbanda and her chaplain, I want to interrogate Manilla's jewel; and it is appropriate that the interrogation should take place here, for the edification of others."

"Prince, please take my advice," said Mirzoza, "and spare the Grand Sultana this unpleasantness: you can do it with no loss to either your curiosity or mine. Why not go to Manilla's place?"

"Since it is your wish, go I shall," said Mangogul.

"But at what time?" the Sultana asked him.

"At midnight," the Sultan answered her.

"At midnight she is gaming," said the favorite.

"Then I shall wait until two," answered Mangogul.

"Prince, you would not think it true," replied Mirzoza, "but that is the most beautiful time of day for card players. If Your Highness takes my advice, he will catch Manilla in her first sleep, between seven and eight."

Mangogul followed Mirzoza's counsel and visited Manilla at seven. Her women were about to put her to bed. He judged by the sadness that governed her features that she had played with bad luck. She came, went, stopped, raised her eyes to the heavens, stamped her foot, rubbed her eyes with both fists, and muttered something between her teeth that the Sultan could not hear. Her women, who were undressing her, trembled as they followed her every movement, and if they succeeded in getting her to bed, it was not without enduring harsh language and worse. In bed at last, Manilla's only evening prayer was a few curses called down upon an ace that had come to ruin her seven times in succession. Scarcely had she shut her eyes when Mangogul turned his ring toward her. Immediately her jewel cried out sorrowfully, "This time I am tricked and trumped." It made the Sultan smile that everything about Manilla spoke gaming, even her jewel. "No," continued the jewel, "I will never play against Abidul; he always cheats. And do not speak to me of Dares; all he brings is bad luck. Ismal plays rather well, but he does not have what it takes. Mazulhim was a treasure, before he passed into Crissa's hands. I know of no player more capricious than Zulmis. Rica is less so, but the poor boy is washed up. And what to do with Lazuli? The prettiest woman in Banza could not make him play high. And what a piddler Mollius is! In truth, despair has spread among all the players, and soon it will be hard to know with whom to go a round."

After this lamentation, the jewel set about relating the unusual moves it had been witness to, and then expatiated on the tenacity and resourcefulness of its mistress during setbacks. "Without me," it said, "Manilla would be twenty times ruined; all the Sultan's treasures could not discharge such debts as I have paid. In one game of brelan,[3] she lost more than ten thousand ducats to a financier and an abbot. Only her gems were left, but her husband had so lately redeemed them that she dared not wager them. Nonetheless she took cards and was dealt one of those seductive hands that fortune sends when she is about to cut your throat. Manilla was pressed to speak. She looked at her cards, put her hand into her purse, where she was certain to find nothing, went back to her hand, examined it again, and decided nothing.

"'Will Madame bid?' the financier asked her.

"'Yes, I...' she said. 'I...bid my jewel.'

"'At what value?' replied Turcares.

"'One hundred ducats,' said Manilla.

"The abbot withdrew; the jewel seemed too expensive to him. Turcares accepted. Manilla lost and paid.

"The foolish vanity of possessing a titled jewel got the better of Turcares. He offered to finance Madame's gaming, on the condition that I serve his pleasures. Soon it was a deal. But since Manilla played high and the financier's resources were not endless, we soon came to the bottom of his coffers.

"My mistress had planned a most brilliant party of faro: all of her acquaintances were invited. They were to punt with nothing less than ducats. We were counting on Turcares's purses, but on the morning of the big day the cad sent us word that he had not a penny, and left us in a fine predicament. We had to get out of it, and there was not a moment to lose. We fell back upon an old head Brahmin, to whom we sold some very costly kindnesses, which he had been soliciting for ages. This meeting cost him twice his ecclesiastical preferment.

"Turcares nevertheless returned after a few days. He was desperately sorry, he said, that Madame had caught him short of money; he was still counting on her favors.

"'Well, you count rather poorly, my dear,' Manilla responded. 'In all decency, I can no longer receive you. When you were in a lending position, all the world knew why I admitted you; but now that you are good for nothing, you would compromise my honor.'

"Turcares was stung by this – and so was I, for he was perhaps the best man in all Banza. He dispensed with his customary politeness and gave Manilla to understand that she had cost him more than three Opera girls, who would have amused him better.

"'Alas!' he cried sadly, 'why did I leave my little milliner! She loved me madly and was so thrilled with a taffeta!'

"Manilla, who did not appreciate comparisons, interrupted him in a tone that made him tremble, and ordered him to leave at once. Turcares knew her; he preferred to leave peacefully by the stairs than to exit through the window.

"Next, Manilla borrowed from another Brahmin who came, she said, to console her in her sorrow. The saintly man succeeded the financier, and we reimbursed him for his consolations in the same coin. She lost me still other times, and everyone knows that gambling debts are the only ones ever repaid in this world.

"When Manilla happens to win, she is the most well-behaved woman in the Congo. With her game under control, she reforms her ways surprisingly; she stops swearing, is such a dear, pays her tradesmen, is liberal to her servants, gets her things out of hock, and caresses her great dane and her husband. But thirty times a month she risks these happy dispositions and her fortune on an ace of spades. Such is the life she has led, and will continue to lead, and God knows how many times I shall be wagered."

At this point the jewel fell silent and Mangogul went off to rest. He was awakened at five in the afternoon, and he left for the Opera, where he had promised to meet the favorite.

CHAPTER XIII

Sixth Trial of the Ring
The Banza Opera

Of all the forms of spectacle in Banza, none but the Opera maintained its standing. Utmiutsol and Uremifasolasiututut, famous composers, the one beginning to age and the other just emerging, alternately dominated the lyric stage. Each of these original artists had his followers. The ignorant and the graybeards were all for Utmiutsol. The young fellows and the virtuosi were for Uremifasolasiututut, and people of taste, young as well as old, held them both in high esteem.

Uremifasolasiututut, said the latter, is excellent when he is good, but he nods from time to time, and to whom does this not happen? Utmiutsol is steadier, more sustained; the beauties of his work are myriad. Nonetheless there is not one of which even more striking examples could not be found in his rival, who has melodic passages that are his alone and to be found only in his works. Old Utmiutsol is simple, natural, smooth, at times too smooth, and that is his flaw. The young Uremifasolasiututut is unusual, brilliant, composed, learned, too learned at times, but this is perhaps a flaw of his listeners. The one has but one overture, beautiful indeed, but repeated at the opening of all his pieces;

the other has as many overtures as pieces, and they all pass for master-works. Nature led Utmiutsol down the paths of melody, whereas study and experience led Uremifasolasiututut to discover the sources of harmony. Who could ever, or will ever, give us a recitativo like the old man? And who could ever write light ariettas, voluptuous melodies, and spirited symphonies like the young one? Utmiutsol alone understood dialogue. Before Uremifasolasiututut, no one had ever distinguished the delicate nuances that separate the tender from the voluptuous, the voluptuous from the passionate, the passionate from the lascivious. A few of the latter's followers go so far as to claim that if Utmiutsol's dialogue is superior, this is due less to the inequality of their talents than to the differences between the poets they have made use of.... "Read," they cry, "read the libretto of *Dardanus*,[1] and you will be convinced that if good lines were given to Uremifasolasiututut then Utmiutsol's charming scenes would come to life again." Be that as it may, in my day, the whole town raced to the latter's tragedies, and suffocated at the former's ballets.

An excellent piece by Uremifasolasiututut was being performed in Banza at that time, yet it would not have drawn much attention had not the favorite sultana been curious to see it. Moreover, the periodic indisposition of jewels not only aroused the jealousy of the "little violins"[2] but also caused the leading actress to be absent. Her replacement had a less beautiful voice, but she made up for it with her acting, and there was no reason for the Sultan and the favorite not to honor this performance with their presence.

Mirzoza has already arrived, and here is Mongogul; the curtain is raised, and the show begins. Everything was going perfectly. La Chevalier had effaced the memory of Le Maure.[3] They were in the fourth act when the Sultan decided, in the middle of a chorus that had lasted too long for his taste and which had already caused the favorite twice to yawn, to turn his ring on the chorus girls. A more odd and comical sight had never before been seen on the stage. Thirty girls were suddenly struck dumb; they opened their mouths wide and froze in the theatrical gestures of the moment before. Their jewels, however, sang their hearts out; one sang a *pont-neuf*,[4] another a bawdy vaudeville tune, another an indecent parody, all of them follies in keeping with their natures. To one side was heard, *Oh! It's true! It's true!*; to the other, *What? Twelve times?*; here, *Who will do me? Come on, Louis!*; and there, *Shoo, old man! There's nothing for you here!* All, in fact, expressed themselves in such a high-pitched, baroque, and mad tone that they formed the most extraordinary, boisterous, and ridiculous chorus ever heard before or after that of...no...d...on...[The manuscript is damaged here.]

All the while the orchestra went along as usual, and the laughter from the parterre, the balcony, and the boxes joined with the noise of the instruments and the jewels' songs to heighten the cacophony.

Some of the actresses, fearing that their jewels might tire of humming idiocies and begin to give real voice to them, ran behind the scenes; but in the end they escaped with only a fright. Mangogul, convinced that the public would learn nothing new from it all, turned back his ring. Instantly the jewels fell silent, the laughter ceased, the house calmed down, and the performance resumed and ended peacefully. The curtain fell, the Sultan and Sultana disappeared, and our actresses' jewels went off to their various engagements, where they would amuse themselves with something other than singing.

This affair created a considerable stir. The men laughed. The women were alarmed. The bonzes were scandalized, and the academics racked their brains. But what did Orcotomus have to say? Orcotomus was triumphant. He had predicted in one of his papers that jewels would inevitably sing. They had just sung, and this phenomenon, which baffled his colleagues, was for him a new ray of light and succeeded in confirming his system.

CHAPTER XIV

Orcotomus's Experiments

It was on the fifteenth day of the moon of ———— that Orcotomus presented his treatise to the academy and expounded his ideas on the chatter of jewels. Since he had given great assurances of his ability to produce experiments – which he had already repeated many times, always with the same success – the majority of people was dazzled. The public persisted in the favorable impression it had formed, and for a full six weeks it was believed that Orcotomus had made considerable discoveries.

To complete his triumph, it was only a matter of repeating, in the presence of the academy, the famous experiments he had so extolled. A most illustrious assembly gathered on this occasion. The ministers of state came, and even the Sultan himself did not disdain to appear, though he kept himself invisible.

As Mangogul was a great monologuist, the futility of conversation in his time having instilled in him the habit of soliloquy, he said to himself: "Either Orcotomus is a hopeless charlatan, or the genie, my protector, a hopeless fool. If the academician, who is decidedly not a conjurer, is able to make dead jewels speak, the genie who protects me was wrong to sell his soul to the devil for the power to grant the power of speech to jewels full of life."

Mangogul was puzzling over these reflections when he found himself in the middle of his academy. As we saw, Orcotomus had, for his audience, all that Banza possessed of people knowledgeable on the topic of jewels. To be happy with his audience, he needed only to make them happy. But the success of his experiments was sorry indeed. Orcotomus took a jewel, applied his lips to it, blew on it until out of breath, left it, came back to it, then tried another, for he had brought samples of every age, size, condition, and color. But no matter how much he blew, the only audible sounds were inarticulate and very different from those he had promised.

A murmur rose through the company, which disconcerted him for a moment, but he collected himself and declared that such experiments were not easily carried out before so many people; and he was right.

Indignant, Mangogul rose, left, and reappeared in the wink of an eye before the favorite sultana.

"Well, Prince," she said when she noticed him, "who won, you or Orcotomus? His jewels worked wonders, without a doubt."

The Sultan paced up and down, without responding.

"I say," replied the favorite, "Your Highness seems dissatisfied."

"Ah, Madame," answered the Sultan, "the impudence of this Orcotomus is unrivaled. I do not want to hear another word about him... What will you say, O future generations, when you learn that the great Mangogul allowed a hundred thousand crowns in yearly pensions to such fellows, while the brave officers who watered with their blood the laurels that gird his brow, were reduced to four hundred francs a year?... By Jupiter, I am enraged! I have enough ill humor to last a whole month."

At this point Mangogul fell silent, and continued to pace across the favorite's chambers. His head hung low, he came and went, stopped, and stamped his foot from time to time. He sat down tentatively, got up at once, took leave of Mirzoza, forgetting to kiss her, and shut himself in his quarters.

The African author who immortalized himself with the history of the great and marvelous deeds of Erguebzed and Mangogul, continues in the following terms:

Judging by Mangogul's ill humor, it was thought he would banish all scholars from his realm. Not at all. The next day he awoke in fine spirits, tested out the ring in the morning, supped in the evening with his favorites and Mirzoza in a magnificent tent set up in the seraglio gardens, and never seemed less concerned with affairs of state.

The dissatisfied and disaffected of the Congo, and the newsmongers of Banza, did not fail to criticize this conduct. Is there anything with which these people will not find fault? "Is that," they asked on the promenades and in coffeehouses, "any way for a head of state to act! Lance in the hand all day, and all night at table!"

"Ah, if only I were Sultan!" cried a little senator ruined by gambling, separated from his wife, and whose children had the worst upbringing in the world. "If I were Sultan, I would rule the Congo in a very different way. I would be the terror of my enemies and the darling of my subjects. In less than six months I'd restore the police, the laws, the army, and the navy to their full force. I would have one hundred tall ships. Our wilderness would soon be cleared, our highways repaired. I would abolish, or at least halve, taxes. As for pensions, my fine high-minded gentlemen, you would not touch them, by faith, but with the tips of your fingers. Good officers – Pongo Sabiam! – good officers, old soldiers, magistrates like us, who work day and night to bring justice to the people, these are the men on whom I would bestow my favors."

"Gentlemen," added a toothless old politician with flat hair, shredded cuffs, and a doublet worn at the elbows, speaking in a serious tone, "have you forgotten our great emperor Abdelmalek, of the Abyssinian dynasty, who ruled two thousand three hundred and eighty-five years ago? Have you forgotten how he had two astronomers impaled for being three minutes off in their prediction of an eclipse, and how he had his surgeon and his chief physician dissected alive for having prescribed a dose of manna[1] at the wrong time?"

"Moreover, I ask you," continued another, "what good are these idle Brahmins, these good-for-nothings fattened with our blood? Would not the immense riches they glut themselves with be better suited to honest people like ourselves?"

From another quarter was heard, "Forty years ago, did anyone know of the new cooking and liqueurs of Lorraine? Our rulers are indulging in a luxury that threatens the imminent demise of the empire, a necessary consequence of the contempt for the pagods and the dissolution of morals. At the time when only rich meats were eaten, and only sherbet drunk at great Kanoglou's table, what regard was there for cut-paper ornaments, Martin's varnishes, or the music of Rameau? The Opera girls were no less cruel than today, but they were had for a fraction of what they cost now. The Prince, you see, is spoiling things. Ah, if only I were Sultan!"

"If you were Sultan," an old military man hotly retorted who had survived the battle of Fontenoy, and who lost an arm beside his prince at Lawfeld,[2] "you would do even more stupid things than you say. My friend, you cannot govern your tongue and yet you wish to rule an empire! You haven't the wherewithal to manage your family and yet you want to meddle with affairs of state! Quiet, wretch. Show some respect for the powers on earth, and thank the gods for having given you birth in the empire and under the reign of a prince whose prudence enlightens his ministers, whose soldiers admire his valor, who is feared by his enemies and beloved of his people, and in whom one can reproach only the moderation with which his government treats people like you."

CHAPTER XV

The Brahmins

Once the scholars had worn themselves out with the jewels, the Brahmins took over. Religion insisted that the chatter fell within its jurisdiction, and its ministers claimed that the hand of Brahma was here at work.

There was a general assembly of pontiffs, who decided that the best pens would be called upon to give formal proof that the event was supernatural and that, while waiting for the publication of their works, this view would be maintained in treatises, in private conversations, in the direction of consciences, and public speeches.

But if they agreed unanimously that the event was supernatural, they were still divided, since two principles were acknowledged in the Congo, and there existed a sort of Manicheanism between them on the question of which of the two principles the chatter of jewels should be attributed to.

Those who seldom or never left their cells, and who had never read anything but religious books, ascribed the prodigy to Brahma. "There is only one," they said, "who can so disturb the natural order, and time will reveal his profound reasons for all this."

Those who, on the contrary, frequented the ladies and were more often found on the streets than in their cells, and thus feared lest some indiscreet jewels might disclose their hypocrisy, attributed their chatter to Cadabra, a mischievous deity, enemy of Brahma and his followers.

The latter theory encountered great objections and did not lead so directly to moral reforms. Even its defenders did not impose any on themselves. But it was necessary to screen themselves, and there was not a single minister of the religion who had not sacrificed the pagods and their altars one hundred times over to accomplish this.

Mangogul and Mirzoza regularly attended the religious services of Brahma, and the whole empire was informed of this by the gazette. They had gone to the great mosque on the day of one of the principal solemn ceremonies. The Brahmin in charge of explaining the laws mounted the speaker's rostrum, poured forth a volley of stock phrases and tedious compliments to the Sultan and his favorite, and spoke very eloquently on the correct, orthodox way to sit in public. He had already cited countless authorities to demonstrate the necessity thereof when, suddenly seized by a divine enthusiasm, he uttered the following tirade, the effect of which was all the greater for its having been unexpected:

"What do I hear in all the social circles? A confused murmur, a noise unheard of reaches my ears. All is perverted, and the power of speech, which by the grace of Brahma has hitherto been assigned to the tongue alone, has been transferred to other organs as a result of his vengeance. And what organs! You know, gentlemen. Ungrateful people, was it necessary for a new miracle to rouse you from your torpor! Had not your crimes enough witnesses, without their principal instruments raising their voices! Undoubtedly their time is come, since heaven's wrath has wrought new punishments. In vain did you hide yourselves in darkness. In vain did you choose mute accomplices. Do you not hear them now? They have testified against you from every quarter, and revealed your turpitude to the universe. O you who govern them with your wisdom! O Brahma! Your judgments are just. Your law condemns theft, perjury, lying, and adultery. It proscribes the heinousness of calumny and the corruption of ambition, the fury of hatred and the wiles of bad faith. Your faithful ministers have not ceased to utter these truths to your children, and to threaten them with the punishments that you in your rightful anger reserve for the unjust. But in vain. The fools have given themselves over to the tide of their passions. They have followed those torrents; they have scorned our admonitions; they have laughed at our threats; they have taken our curses lightly. Their vices have increased, grown stronger, multiplied; the voice of their impiety has risen up to you, and we have not been able to prevent the deadly scourge with which you have smote them. Having long implored your mercy, let us now praise your justice. Overwhelmed by your blows, no doubt they will return to you and recognize the hand that has fallen hard upon them. But, O prodigy of callousness! O crowning blindness! They have imputed the effect of your power to the blind workings of nature. In their hearts they have said: Brahma does not exist. All the properties of matter are not known to us; and this latest proof of his existence is but a proof of the ignorance and the gullibility of those who contest it. On this foundation they have built systems, imagined hypotheses, carried out experiments. But from the heights of his eternal abode, Brahma has laughed at their vain attempts. He has confounded impudent knowledge, and, like glass, the jewels have broken the useless restraints that were set against their loquacity. May these vainglorious worms therefore confess the weakness of their reason and the futility of their efforts. May they cease to deny the existence of Brahma, or determine the limits to his power. Brahma is! He is almighty, and he shows himself to us no less clearly in these terrible scourges than in his ineffable favors.

"But who has brought these scourges down upon this unfortunate land? Is it not your injustice, greedy and faithless man! Your gallantries and foolish loves, worldly and unchaste woman! Your excesses and shameful debaucheries, infamous man of pleasure! Your callousness toward our monasteries, miser! Your injustices, corrupt magistrate! Your usuries, insatiable merchant! Your effeminacy and lack of religion, impious and self-indulgent courtier!

"And you in whom this affliction is most widespread, you women and maidens given to licentiousness: whereas we, renouncing the duties of our state, would maintain a deep silence with regard to your disorderly life, you carry within you a voice more importunate than ours. It follows you, and will everywhere reproach you your impure desires, your dubious attachments, your criminal liaisons, all that excessive desire to please, that artifice in enticement, that cunning in snaring, the impetuosity of your transports, and the fury of your jealousy. What is keeping you from throwing off the yoke of Cadabra, and reverting to the sweet laws of Brahma? But let us return to our subject. I was telling you, then, that the worldly ones sit down heretically for nine reasons. The first..." and so on.

This discourse made widely diverse impressions. Mangogul and the Sultana, who alone possessed the secret of the ring, were convinced that the Brahmin had explained the chatter of the jewels with the help of religion just as well as Orcotomus had done by the light of reason. The court ladies and fops declared the sermon seditious and the preacher a fanatic. The rest of the audience took him for a prophet; they shed tears, began to pray, even to flagellate themselves, and did not change their lives.

It caused a stir even in the coffeehouses. A wit pronounced that the Brahmin had but grazed the issue and that his speech was but a cold and insipid harangue. The pious women and the illuminati, however, judged it the most solid piece of eloquence to be uttered in the temples in a hundred years. In my opinion, the wit and the pious women were both right.

CHAPTER XVI

Mangogul's Vision

Amidst the chatter of the jewels, another problem arose in the empire. It concerned the custom of the penum, the small scrap of cloth applied to the dead. Ancient rite prescribed that it be placed on the mouth. Reformers now claimed that it should be placed below. Tempers flared. People almost came to blows when the Sultan, whom both parties had petitioned, permitted a colloquium of the wisest of their leaders. They cited tradition, the sacred books, and the commentaries. Strong arguments and powerful authorities abounded on both sides. Mangogul, perplexed, postponed the decision for a week. When that time was up, the sectarians and their antagonists reappeared before him.

THE SULTAN: Pontiffs, and you priests, be seated, he said to them. Filled with the importance of the dispute that divides you, we have not ceased, since the conference held at the foot of our throne, to pray for illumination from on high. Last night at the hour when it pleases Brahma to communicate with the men he loves, we had a vision. We seemed to hear an exchange between two solemn personages, one of whom believed he had two noses in the middle of his face, the other two holes in his arse. Here is what they said to each other. The personage with two noses was the first to speak.

"Touching your behind all the time, now there's a ridiculous tic..."

"True enough..."

"Can you not get rid of it?..."

"No more than you can get rid of your two noses..."

"But my noses are real. I see them. I touch them. And the more I see them and touch them the more I am convinced that they are mine. Instead of touching yourself for ten years and finding that you have an arse like anyone else, you should have cured yourself of your madness..."

"My madness! Go on, man with two noses – it is you who are mad."

"Let us not quarrel. Desist. I have told you how I got my two noses. Now, tell me the story of your two holes, if you can remember it."

"If I can remember! It is not the kind of thing one forgets. It was the thirty-first of the month, between one and two in the morning."

"Yes?...And?..."

"Allow me, if you please. I fear — no, if my calculations are correct, that was the exact time."

"How very strange! On that night, then?..."

"On that night I heard a voice that was not familiar to me, crying out, 'Help! Help!' I look and I see a young, frightened, disheveled creature racing toward me. She was pursued by a violent, churlish old man. Judging this person by his dress and by the tool with which he was armed, he was a carpenter. He was in knee-breeches and a shirt. His sleeves were rolled up to his elbows; he had sinewy arms, swarthy skin, wrinkled brow, bearded chin, puffy cheeks, sparkling eye, hairy chest, and a head covered with a pointed hat."

"I see him."

"The woman he was about to overtake continued to cry out, 'Help! Help!' and the carpenter said as he pursued her, 'You flee in vain. I will get you. May it never be said that you are the only one who does not have one yet. By devil, you shall have one like everybody else.' Suddenly the wretched woman stumbled and fell flat on her belly, calling out more vigorously, 'Help! Help!' while the carpenter added, 'Cry, cry as much as you like. But, big or small, you shall have one, I assure you.' Then he lifted up her petticoats and exposed her behind. This behind, white as snow, plump, firm, rounded, chubby, and dimpled, resembled that of the Chief Pontiff's wife — as two peas in a pod."

THE PONTIFF: My wife!

THE SULTAN: Why not?

The character with two holes added: "It was she, for I remember her well. The old carpenter placed one of his feet on her loins, bent over, ran his two hands under her buttocks to the back of her thighs, pushed her knees under her belly and raised up her arse, so that I could recognize it at my leisure, a recognition that in no way displeased me, even though from beneath the petticoats came a faint voice that cried, 'Help me! Help me!' You will think me ruthless and hard-hearted, but a man should never make himself out to be better than he is, and I admit, to my shame, that at that moment I felt more curiosity than compassion, and I thought less to help than to look."

At this point the high pontiff interrupted the Sultan again, and said to him, "My lord, might I, perhaps, be one of the two speakers in this conversation?..."

"Why not?"

"The man with two noses?"

"Why not?"

"And I," added the leader of the innovators, "the man with two holes?"

"Why not?"

"The wicked carpenter took up the tool that he had left on the ground. It was a drill. He put the bit in his mouth to moisten it. Then he steadied the handle roughly in the pit of his stomach, and leaned over the unlucky woman, who still cried, 'Help me! Help me!' Then he prepared to pierce a hole for her where there should have been two and where there was none."

THE PONTIFF: Not my wife.

THE SULTAN: "Suddenly the carpenter interrupted this operation, changing his mind, and said, 'What a fine mess I almost made of it! But it would have been her fault as well. Why not give in graciously? Madame, show a little patience.' He places his drill back on the ground. From his pocket he draws a pale pink ribbon. With the thumb of his left hand he affixes one end at her coccyx, twisting the rest into the crack. Pressing it between the two buttocks with the edge of his other hand he wraps it round the base of her lower abdomen, and the woman, all the while crying, 'Help! Help!' wriggled, struggled, threw herself left and right, and disarranged the ribbon and the measurings of the carpenter, who said, 'Madame, this is not yet time to cry. I have not hurt you yet. I could not proceed with more care. If you are not careful, the thing will go askew, and you will have only yourself to blame. One must give each thing its due. There are certain proportions to respect. This is of greater importance than you can imagine. In a moment there will be no turning back, and you will be in despair.' "

THE PONTIFF: You heard all this, my lord?

THE SULTAN: Just as I hear you now.

THE PONTIFF: And the woman?

THE SULTAN: "It seemed to me," added the speaker, "that she was half persuaded, and I presumed, by the distance between her heels, that she had begun to resign herself. I am not sure what she said to the carpenter, but the carpenter answered her: 'Ah yes, how true! Women are so difficult!' Having then taken his measurements a bit more calmly, master Anofore stretched his pale pink ribbon across a little folding ruler, and picking up a pencil, said to the woman, 'How do you want it?'

" 'I do not understand.'

" 'Do you want the classic proportion, or the modern one?...' "

THE PONTIFF: Oh, the profundity of decrees from on high! How mad this would be were it not a revelation! Let us suspend our disbelief and pray.

THE SULTAN: "I do not recall the woman's answer, but the carpenter replied, 'Verily, she talks nonsense. That will not look like anything. People will ask, who is the ass that pierced that hole?' "

THE LADY: Enough talk, master Anofore, make it the way I tell you...

ANOFORE: Make it the way I tell you! Madame, each man has his honor to protect...

THE LADY: That is how I want it, there, I tell you. I want it, I want it...

"The carpenter roared with laughter, and as for me, do you think that I kept a straight face? Meanwhile Anofore traces the lines on the ribbon and sets it back in place and cries, 'Madame, this will not do; this lacks common sense. Whoever sees this arse, if he is anything of a connoisseur, will laugh at us both. Everyone knows that from here to here must be a space, but it has never been extended to such length. Too much is too much. You want it like that?...' "

THE LADY: Yes, that is how I want it, let us be done with it...

"The next moment master Anofore took up his pencil, marked the woman's buttocks with lines that corresponded to those he took from the ribbon. He drew his mark, shrugging his shoulders and muttering softly, 'How odd it will look! But that is her fancy.' He seized his drill and said, 'Madame wants it here?'

" 'Yes, there. Go on, then...'

" 'But, Madame.'

" 'What now?'

" 'What now? It is not possible.'

" 'And why not, if you please?'

" 'Why not? Because you are trembling, and you are squeezing your buttocks together, and I've lost sight of my mark, and I shall pierce too high or too low. Come now, Madame, a little courage.'

" 'Easy for you to say. Let me see your bit. *Mercy!*'

" 'I swear to you that it is the smallest one in my shop. While we have been talking I could have pierced half a dozen. Come now, Madame, relax. Very good. A little more. Perfect. More. More.' Meanwhile I saw the sly carpenter slowly bring his tool closer. He was about to... when a mixture of rage and pity took hold of me. I struggled. I wanted to run to the assistance of the patient, but I felt myself garroted about the arms and unable to move. I shout at the carpenter, 'Stop, you scoundrel.' I shout with such force that the ties binding me break. I hurl myself at the carpenter. I seize him by the throat. The carpenter says to me, 'Who are you? With whom are you angry? Do you not see that she does not have a hole in her arse? I will have you know that I am the great Anofore, I am the one who makes arseholes for those who have none. And I must give her one. It is the wish of him who sends me. After me, another, stronger than I, will come. He will not have a drill, he will have a gouge, and he will succeed with his gouge in restoring to her that which she lacks. Be gone, profane one, or with my drill, or with the gouge of my successor, I shall give you...'

" 'Me?'

" 'You, yes, you...' At that moment, with his left hand he sawed the air with his tool.

"And the man with the two holes, whom you have heard up until now, said to the man with two noses, 'What is wrong, why you are backing away?'

" 'I am afraid that in your gesticulating you will break one of my noses. But, continue.'

" 'Now, where was I?'

" 'You were at the tool with which the carpenter was sawing the air.'

" 'He dealt a backhanded blow to my shoulder with his right arm, a blow so violent that I fell over on my stomach. And so my shirt was thrust up – another bottom in the air. The redoubtable Anofore, threatening me with the tip of his tool, then says to me, "Beg for mercy, rascal, beg for mercy, or I will give you two..." Then I felt the cold bit of his drill. Horror seized me. I woke up, and since then I think that I have two arseholes.' "

"These two speakers," added the Sultan, "then began to poke fun at each other, 'Ha, ha, ha, he has two holes in his arse!'

" 'Ha, ha, ha, they're cases for your two noses.' "

Then turning solemly toward the assembly, he said, "And you, Pontiffs, and you servants of god, you laugh too! What is more common for a man than to imagine he has two noses, and to mock him who believes he has two holes in his arse?"

Then, after a moment of silence, resuming an air of serenity and addressing the leaders of the sect, he asked them what they thought of his vision.

"By Brahma," they answered, "it is one of the most profound that the heavens have ever granted to any prophet."

"And do you understand anything about it?"

"No, my lord."

"What do you think of the two speakers?"

"That they are mad."

"And if they took the fancy to make themselves leaders of a group, and if the sect of the two holes in the arse began to persecute the sect of two noses?..."

The pontiffs and the priests lowered their eyes, and Mangogul said, "I want my subjects to live and die as they see fit. I want the penum to be applied either on the mouth or on the behind, as it pleases each of them. Let me not be further bothered by these impertinences."

The priests withdrew; and in the synod held a few months later it was declared that Mangogul's vision would be entered into the canonical books, and it was a worthy addition indeed.

CHAPTER XVII

The Muzzles

While the Brahmins were inducing Brahma to speak, parading the pagods about, and exhorting the populace to penitence, others dreamt of making a profit from the chatter of the jewels.

Big cities teem with people whom poverty makes industrious. They do not steal or swindle; but they are to swindlers what swindlers are to thieves. They know everything, they do everything, they have ways around everything. They come and go, insinuate themselves at Court, in the city, the palace, the church, at the theater, with courtesans, at coffeehouses, the ball, the Opera, in the academies. They are everything you want them to be. If you solicit a pension, they have the minister's ear. If you have a lawsuit, they will solicit for you. If you like gambling, they are croupiers; as for eating, they keep a good kitchen; and as for women, they will introduce you to Amina or Acaris. From which of the two would you prefer to buy disease? Make your choice; and once you are infected, they will see to your cure. Their chief concern is to discover people's foibles, and to take advantage of the stupidity of the general public. It is on their behalf that on street corners, at temple doors, theater entrances, and park exits people distribute leaflets informing you, free of charge, that so and so, who resides at the Louvre, at Saint-Jean, at the Temple or the Abbaye, at such-and-such address, such-and-such floor, swindles at home from nine in the morning until noon, and the rest of the time in town.

Hardly had the jewels begun to speak when one of these schemers filled the houses of Banza with a leaflet of the following form and tenor. The title, in capital letters, read as follows:

Advice to the Ladies

And underneath, in italics:

By Courtesy of His Eminence the grand Senechal, and by approval
of the gentlemen of the Royal Academy of Sciences.

And below, it read:

Sir Eolipila, of the Royal Academy of Banza, member of the Royal Society
of Monoemugi, the Imperial Academy of Biafara, the Academy of the Curious of Loango, the Society of Camur of Monomotapa, the Institute of Erecco,
and the Royal Academies of Beleguanza and Angola, who for many years
has given lessons in baubles to the delight of the Court, the town, and the
province, has, for the benefit of the fair sex, invented muzzles or portable
gags that deprive jewels of the use of speech without obstructing their natural function. They are neat and convenient, they come in all sizes, for all
ages, and at every price. He has had the honor to serve persons of the highest
distinction with them.

There is nothing like being human. As ridiculous as a work may be,
if it is praised it will succeed. Thus did Eolipila's invention make a
fortune. People flocked to his house. Gallant ladies went there in carriages, prudent ladies in hackney coaches; pious women sent their confessors or footmen, and even nuns were seen there. All wanted a muzzle;
and from the duchess to the bourgeoise, there was not a woman who
did not have her own, for the sake of fashion, or for a reason.

The Brahmins, who had proclaimed the chatter of jewels a divine
punishment, and who had promised reforms in customs and other advantages, trembled at the sight of a device that cheated the vengeance
of heaven, and their own hopes. They had barely stepped down from
their pulpits when they climbed back up again, thundered, exploded,
induced the oracles to speak, and pronounced that the muzzle was a
diabolical machine, and that there could be no salvation for those who
used it. "Worldly women, discard your muzzles!" they shouted. "Submit to the will of Brahma. Allow the voice of your jewel to awakenen
the voice of your conscience, and do not blush at confessing the crimes
you had no shame to commit."

But they shouted in vain. Muzzles came into vogue just as sleeveless
dresses and quilted, fur-lined coats had done. This time the preachers
were left to catch cold in their temples. The women acquired the gags
and did not give them up until they discovered they didn't work, or
when they grew tired of them.

CHAPTER XVIII

The Travelers

It was in these circumstances that, after a long absence, considerable expense, and unprecedented efforts, there reappeared at Court the travelers Mangogul had sent to the most distant lands to gather knowledge. Mangogul held their log book in his hands and burst out laughing at each line.

"What are you reading that you find so humorous?" Mirzoza asked him.

"Even if these fellows lie like all the others," Mangogul answered her, "at least they are more amusing. Sit down on this sofa; I will entertain you with a use of thermometers that you would never imagine."

"'Yesterday I promised you,' Cyclophilus said to me, 'an amusing spectacle...'"

MIRZOZA: And who is this Cyclophilus?

MANGOGUL: An islander...

MIRZOZA: And from which island?...

MANGOGUL: What difference does it make?...

MIRZOZA: And whom is he talking to?...

MANGOGUL: To one of my travelers...

MIRZOZA: Your travelers have returned?...

MANGOGUL: Of course. You did not know?

MIRZOZA: I did not know...

MANGOGUL: Ah, yes, one thing, my queen. You can be a bit prudish at times. I give you permission to leave should you find my story shocking.

MIRZOZA: And if I should leave right away?

MANGOGUL: As you wish.

I do not know if Mirzoza stayed or left, but Mangogul took up Cyclophilus's story again, and read the following:

"This amusing spectacle involves the practices that take place in our temples. Here the propagation of the species is a subject to which both politics and religion devote their attentions; and the manner in which they attend to it is not unworthy of your own. We have cuckolds here. Is that not what in your language you call those men whose women allow themselves to be loved by other men? Anyway, we do have cuckolds here, as many or more than anywhere else, even though we have taken infinite measures to assure that marriages are well matched."

"Then you possess," I answered him, "the secret, unknown or forgotten among us, of matching couples well?"

"Not quite," replied Cyclophilus. "Our islanders are shaped in such a way that all marriages are happy, provided that the written laws are followed to the letter."

"I do not quite understand you," I continued, "for in our world nothing is ordered according to law more than a marriage, yet nothing is more often contrary to happiness and reason."

"Very well," said Cyclophilus, "I shall explain. But I am amazed. Do you mean to say you have lived among us for two weeks and are still unaware that male and female jewels are of different shapes here? How, then, have you been spending your time? From time immemorial these jewels have been destined to join one to the other. A nut-shaped female jewel is predestined for a screw-shaped male jewel. Do you understand?"

"Yes," I said to him, "this agreement of shape must be useful up to a point. But I do not find it sufficient to insure conjugal fidelity."

"What more could you want?"

"In a country where all is ordered by geometric laws, I want some consideration to be shown for the warmth of the affections between the two parties. What! Do you expect for an eighteen-year-old brunette, a lively little devil, to keep herself for an icy sexagenarian alone! That could never be, even if this old man had a jewel shaped like an endless screw…"

"You are very insightful," Cyclophilus said to me. "We have provided for that."

"And how is that?…"

"By a long series of observations on well-verified cuckolds…"

"And where have these observations led you?"

"To the determination of the degree of warmth necessary between the two spouses…"

"And once this degree was known?"

"Once it was known, thermometers, applicable to both men and women, were calibrated. The shapes are not the same. The base of the female thermometer resembles a male jewel about eight inches long and one and a half inches thick. The male thermometer has a concavity of the same dimensions. And here they are," he said, taking me into the temple, "those ingenious devices whose effect you shall soon see, since the gathering people and the presence of the priests indicate that the sacred rituals are about to begin."

We penetrated the crowd with difficulty and arrived at a sanctuary where the altars were but two damask beds without curtains. The priests

and priestesses were standing around them, in silence, holding the thermometers entrusted to their keeping like the sacred fire of the vestal
virgins. At the sound of oboes and bagpipes, two pairs of lovers, led by
their parents, approached. They were naked, and I saw that the girl had
a circular jewel and her lover a cylindrical one.

"That is not so unusual," I said to Cyclophilus.

"Look at the other two," he answered me.

I turned my eyes toward them. The young man had a parallelepipedal
jewel, and the girl a square one.

"Pay attention to the holy office," added Cyclophilus.

Then two priests lay one of the two girls on the altar. A third applied
the sacred thermometer to her, and the high pontiff attentively observed
the degree to which the mercury rose in six minutes. At the same time,
the young man was laid down on the other bed by two priestesses, while
a third adapted the thermometer to him. The high priest, having observed the rising of the mercury in the same given time, pronounced
the marriage valid, and sent the couple to be united at the paternal
home. The square female jewel and the parallelepipedal male jewel were
then examined with the same rigor and tested with the same precision;
but the high priest, examining the progression of the solutions, noticed
an increase of a few degrees less in the boy than in the girl according
to the ratio established by the ritual (for there were limits), and then
climbed into the pulpit and declared the two parties unfit to unite. It
was forbidden for them to be joined under pain of the provisions established by ecclesiastical and civic laws against incest. Incest, on this
island, was therefore not something completely devoid of meaning.
And likewise, the coupling of two jewels of the opposite sex whose
shapes could neither be inscribed within nor circumscribed without
each other was also considered a veritable sin against nature.

A new marriage was at hand. It was a girl with a jewel that termi-
nated in a regular shape with an odd number of sides, and a young man
with a pyramidal jewel, such that the base of the pyramid could inscribe
itself within the girl's polygon. They were tested with the thermometers, and the excess or lack in the ratio of the heights of the mercury
being negligible, the Pontiff pronounced that an exception could be
made, and granted it. The same was done for a female jewel with an
odd number of sides sought by a prism-shaped male jewel, when the
rising of the mercury was more or less equal.

As little geometry as one may know, it is easy to understand that on
this island the measuring of surfaces and solids had been advanced to a
high degree of perfection, and that all that had been written on isoperi-

metric shapes was indispensable there, whereas for us these discoveries are still waiting to be put to use. The girls and boys with circular and cylindrical jewels were considered the luckiest, for of all shapes the circle is the one that encloses the most space of the same contour.

Meanwhile the priests waited for suppliants. The head priest singled me out in the crowd, and motioned to me to approach. I obeyed. "O stranger!" he said to me. "You have witnessed our august mysteries, and you have seen that among us religion is intimately tied to the well-being of society. Were your stay longer, more unusual and rare cases would present themselves. But perhaps pressing concerns draw you back to your native land. If so, go, and teach our wisdom to your fellow men."

I bowed deeply, while he continued as follows:

"If it happens that the sacred thermometer is of a dimension that cannot be applied to a young girl – an extraordinary occurrence, although I have seen five cases in twelve years – then one of my acolytes administers the sacrament to her, while all the people pray. From what you have seen, you need no explanation from me to form an idea of the qualities essential for entrance to the priesthood, and the reasons for the ordinations.

"More often the thermometer cannot be applied to the boy, because his indolent jewel does not lend itself to the operation. In this case, the older girls of the island are allowed to approach him and see to the resurrection of the dead. This is called making devotions. A girl who shows zeal in this exercise is called pious: she uplifts. Yes, stranger, how true it is," he said to me, looking me squarely in the eye, "that all is opinion and prejudice! An act considered a crime among you is regarded as pleasing to the godhead here. It would bode ill among us for a girl to reach her thirteenth year without having yet approached the altar, and her parents would justly and severely reprimand her for this.

"If a late-blooming or misshapen girl offers herself to the thermometer without making the mercury rise, she is allowed to enter a convent. But it happens on our island as much as anywhere else that she sometimes repents, and if the thermometer were applied to her later, she would make the mercury rise as high as any worldly woman, which led to endless abuses and scandals I will not mention. And some, for this reason, have even died of despair. To do honor to my pontificate, I have published a decree that establishes when and how often a girl should be thermometered before taking her vows, notably on the day before and the day itself designated for her profession. I have encountered numerous women who have thanked me for the wisdom of my laws, and whose jewels have been devoted to me as a consequence; but these are small privileges that I leave to my clergy.

"A girl who causes the mercury to rise to a height and with a speed such as no man can match is declared a courtesan, a very respectable and very honored role on our island. You should know that every great lord on our island has his courtesan, just as every woman of quality has her geometer. These are two equally respectable positions, although the latter is beginning to fall out of use.

"If a worn-out, low-born, or unfortunate young man fails to move the mercury in the thermometer, he is condemned to celibacy. Another, on the other hand, who causes the mercury to rise to a level such as no woman could match is obliged to become a monk, just as one becomes a Carmelite or Franciscan. He becomes a resource for a few pious, wealthy women for whom secular assistance is no longer available.

"Alas," said he, raising his eyes and his hands toward the heavens, "how the church has fallen from its past splendor!"

He was about to continue when his chaplain interrupted him to say, "His Eminence the High Priest has not noticed that the service has ended and that the supper awaiting him will soon grow cold because of his eloquence." The prelate stopped, allowed me to kiss his ring, and we left the temple with the rest of the people. Then Cyclophilus resumed the train of his narration.

"The high pontiff did not tell you everything," he said to me. "He neglected to mention either the accidents that have taken place on the island or the occupations of our wisewomen. These subjects are nonetheless worthy of your curiosity."

"And apparently you can satisfy it," I responded. "Very well! What of these accidents and these occupations? Do they concern marriages and jewels as well?"

"Exactly," he replied. "About thirty-five years ago a dearth of cylindrical masculine jewels was noticed on the island. All the circular female jewels complained, and presented themselves to the State Council of Reports and Requests, petitioning that provisions be made for their needs. The council, still preoccupied by higher considerations, gave no answer for a month. The cries of the jewels began to resemble those of the famished crying out for bread. The senators then appointed deputies to establish the facts and report them to the council. This took another month and more. The cries redoubled, and things came close to a revolt, when a certain jeweler, an industrious fellow, presented himself to the academy. Successful tests were conducted, and by warrant of the commissioners, and with the permission of the police lieutenant, he was granted a patent by the council providing him with exclusive privileges to service the needs of circular jewels for twenty consecutive years.

"The second accident was a total dearth of polygonal female jewels. All artisans were invited to apply their skills to this calamity. A prize was offered. A multitude of machines were invented, and in the end they shared the prize.

"You have seen," added Cyclophilus, "the different shapes of our female jewels. They always retain the shape they have at birth. Is it the same among you people?"

"No," I said to him, "A European, Asian, or African female jewel has an infinitely variable shape, *cujuslibet figura capax, nullius tenax.*"

"Then we have not been misled," he continued, "by the explanations furnished us by our physicians concerning a phenomenon of this nature. About twenty years ago a very comely young brunette appeared on the island. No one knew her language, but as soon as she learned ours she never wanted to say which was her native land. Nonetheless, her attractive figure and charming temperament enchanted most of the young lords of the island. A few of the richest ones proposed to her, and she decided in favor of the senator Colibrius. On the appointed day she was led to the temple, according to custom. The beautiful stranger, stretched out on the altar, presented a jewel of indeterminate shape to the eyes of the surprised spectators; once the thermometer was applied, the mercury rose at once to one hundred and ninety degrees. The high priest immediately pronounced that this jewel relegated its owner to the class of courtesans, and the amorous Colibrius was prohibited from marrying her. As it was impossible to possess her as a wife, Colibrius made her his mistress. One day when she was especially satisfied with him, she confessed to him that she was born in the capital of your empire, which contributed not a little to the high opinion we have of your women."

The Sultan was at this point of the story when Mirzoza returned.

"Your always ill-timed modesty," he said to her, "has deprived you of a most delightful story. I would like for you to tell me the good of this hypocrisy you share with all other women, whether chaste or libertine. Is it that these things shock you? No, for you know about them. Is it the words? Indeed, it is not worth the trouble. If it is ridiculous to blush at the act, is it not infinitely more so to blush at its expression? I am madly in love with these islanders who are the subject of this precious journal. They don't mince words; their language is simpler, and their sense of honest and shameful things much better defined..."

MIRZOZA: Do the women wear clothes there?...

MANGOGUL: Certainly, but it is not for the sake of decency but for that of coquetry. They cover themselves to arouse desire and curiosity.

MIRZOZA: And you find this completely in keeping with morality?

MANGOGUL: Certainly...

MIRZOZA: I suspected as much.

MANGOGUL: Oh, you and your suspicions!

As they chatted thus, he casually flipped through the journal and said, "There are some extraordinary customs in this. Look, here is a chapter on the appearance of the inhabitants. There is nothing that your excellent modesty could not hear. This one is on the women's dress, which would be of interest to you, and from which you might get some ideas. You don't answer! You are still wary of me."

"Am I so wrong?"

"I must put you in Cyclophilus's hands, so that he can take you among his islanders. I swear to you that you would return infinitely perfect."

"It seems to me that I am already so."

"It seems to you! And yet I can barely say one word without upsetting you. Indeed you would be much better off, and I much more at ease, if I could always speak and if you could always listen to me."

"And why does it matter if I listen to you?"

"Well, you are right, after all. Agreed. The chapter on the appearance of our islanders and their women's dress will have to wait until tonight, or tomorrow, or another day."

CHAPTER XIX

The Appearance of the Islanders and Their Women's Dress

It was after dinner. Mirzoza was knotting and Mangogul, stretched out on a sofa, eyes half closed, was gently allowing his digestion to proceed. He had spent a good hour in silence and repose when he said to the favorite, "Does Madame feel inclined to listen to me?"

"That depends."

"Yes, of course, as you said with as much good sense as good grace, what difference does it make whether you listen to me or not?" Mirzoza smiled, and Mangogul commanded, "Somebody bring me the journal of my travelers, and let no one misplace the markers I have put in it, or, by my beard...."

The journal was brought to him. He opened it and read: "The islanders were not at all like other people. At birth each bore signs of his vocation, and usually people were what they were supposed to be. Those whom nature destined for geometry had elongated compass-fingers, my host among them. A fellow destined for astronomy had snail-eyes; for geography, a globe-head; for music or acoustics, trumpet-ears; for surveying, staff-legs; for hydraulics..." The Sultan had stopped; Mirzoza queried, "For hydraulics?" Mangogul answered her: "Since you ask...a nozzle-jewel that pisses in jets; for chemistry, an alembic-nose; for anatomy, a scalpel-forefinger; for mechanics, file-arms or saw-arms, and so on."

Mirzoza added, "The lives of those people are very different from ours. Here people who have received nervous arms from Brahma, and thus seem destined for plowing, take up the helm of your state, sit at your tribunals, or preside over your academy; the man who sees no better than a mole spends his life making observations, a profession requiring the eyes of a lynx."

The Sultan continued to read: "Then among the inhabitants one noticed individuals who had, all together in one person, fingers like compasses, heads like globes, eyes like telescopes, and ears like trumpets. 'These,' I said to my host, 'must be your virtuosi, the sort of universal men who bear the mark of all talents.'"

Mirzoza interrupted the Sultan, saying, "I'll bet I know how the host replied."

MANGOGUL: And how might that have been?

MIRZOZA: That these people, whom nature seems to have destined for everything, are in fact good for nothing.

MANGOGUL: By Brahma, you are correct. Indeed, Sultana, you are most clever. My traveler adds that these attributes made the islanders look somewhat like automatons. When they walked they appeared to survey. When they gestured they appeared to draw circles. When they sang, they mouthed the words emphatically.

MIRZOZA: In that case, their music must have been bad.

MANGOGUL: Pray, why is that?

MIRZOZA: Because it ought not be overdone.

MANGOGUL: "Barely had I completed a few turns in the public garden when I became the subject of conversation and the object of curiosity. 'He fell from the moon,' said one. 'You are mistaken,' said another, 'he comes from Saturn.' 'I think that he lives on Mercury,' said a third. A fourth came up to me and said, 'Stranger, may I ask where you are from?'

"'I am from the Congo,' I answered him."

" 'And where is the Congo?'

"I was about to satisfy his curiosity when the sound of a thousand male and female voices rose up around me, repeating, '*He's a Congo, he's a Congo, he's a Congo.*' Deafened by this din, I covered my ears with my hands and hastened to leave the garden. Meanwhile they had stopped my host, to learn from him whether a Congo was a man or beast. The following days his door was beset by a crowd of people who demanded to see the Congo. I showed myself; I spoke; and they went away disdainfully, hooting and shouting out, '*For shame, he is a man.*' "

Here Mirzoza burst into laughter. Then she added, "And the women's dress?"

Mangogul said to her, "Does Madame remember a certain black Brahmin who was very odd, half mad, half sane?"

"Yes, I remember him. He was a good man who put spirit into all he did, and whom the other black Brahmins, his confreres, caused to die of sorrow."

"Very good. You must have heard of, or perhaps yourself seen, a certain harpsichord on which he had tuned all the colors according to the musical scale, and upon which he claimed to perform a sonata, an allegro, a presto, an adagio, or a cantabile for the eyes, which were just as pleasing as well-executed pieces for the ears."

"Even better: one day I asked him to translate a minuet of sounds into a minuet of colors, and he did this quite well."

"And did this amuse you a great deal?"

"Very much, for I was still a child then."

"Well! My travelers found the same device among the islanders, but put to its true use."

"Yes, of course, to women's dress."

"True enough – but how?"

"How? I will tell you that too. For any given article of dress, one had only to strike a certain number of chords on the harpsichord to discover the harmonics of the article, and to determine the different colors for the rest."

"You are unbearable! You can be taught nothing; you guess everything."

"And I would imagine that in this type of music there are certain dissonances to cultivate and preserve."

"Right you are."

"Consequently I think that the talent of a lady-in-waiting presupposes as much genius, experience, intuition, and study as that of a choirmaster."

"What is next?...Do you know?"

"No."

"Next I close my journal and have a sherbet. Sultana, your cleverness puts me in a bad mood indeed."

"In other words, you would prefer me a trifle stupid."

"Why not? It would bring us closer, and we would have more fun. A man must have quite a passion to withstand never-ending humiliations. Be careful."

"My lord, please do me the kindness of taking up your journal again, and continuing to read."

"Willingly. It's my traveler who is speaking here."

"One day, leaving the table, my host threw himself on a sofa and immediately fell asleep, while I accompanied the ladies to their chambers. Having passed through several rooms, we entered a large and well-lit study with a harpsichord standing at the center. Madame sat down, ran her fingers across the keys, eyes fixed inside the instrument's body, and said with an air of satisfaction:

" 'I think it is in tune.'

"I said to myself softly, 'I think she is dreaming, for I did not hear a sound.'

" 'Madame is a musician, and plays accompaniments, no doubt?'

" 'No.'

" 'What, then, is that instrument?'

" 'You shall see.' Then, turning to her eldest daughter, she said, 'Ring for my ladies-in-waiting.'

"Three came, to whom she addressed more or less the following words: 'Ladies, I am very disappointed with you. For more than six months now, neither my daughters nor I have been tastefully dressed. You are very costly, and I have given you the best instructors, yet it seems to me that you still lack the basic principles of harmony. Today I want to wear my green and gold fontange.[1] Find the rest for me.'

"The youngest touched the keys with one hand and caused white, yellow, crimson, and green beams to emerge. Blue and violet beams came out of the keys she touched with the other hand.

" 'That is not right,' said the mistress impatiently. 'Soften the tones.'

"The waiting maid touched the keys again: white, lemon, turquoise, poppy-red, rose, saffron, and black.

" 'Still worse!' said the mistress. 'You can do better than that. Use the top keys.'

"The maid obeyed, and the result was: white, orange, light blue, flesh, sulfur, and gray.

"The mistress cried out: 'I cannot bear it.'

" 'If Madame would note,' said one of the two other women, 'that with her big hoop and her little slippers...'

" 'Well, yes, that might do.'

"Next the woman went into a back chamber to dress herself in this modulation. Meanwhile the oldest of her daughters begged the waiting maid to play a fanciful gown for her, adding: 'I have been asked to a ball; I would like to be elegant, unusual, and striking. I am tired of bright colors.'

" 'Nothing could be easier,' said the waiting maid, and she touched a pearl gray and an otherworldly chiaroscuro, saying, 'Mademoiselle can see how well this would suit her Chinese headdress, her peacock-feather cape, her celadon and gold skirt, her cinnamon stockings, and her jet slippers, especially if she goes as a brunette, with her ruby aigrette.'

" 'You are priceless, my dear,' replied the young girl. 'Come, execute your ideas yourself.'

"The youngest's turn came; the remaining waiting maid said to her: 'Your older sister is going to the ball, but you, are you not going to temple?'

" 'Precisely, and it is for this reason that I want you to play something very coquettish for me.'

" 'Very well,' answered the waiting maid, 'get your flame-colored gauze dress, and I will search for accessories. Just a minute...here it is...no, not that...yes, I have it. You will be ravishing...See, Mademoiselle: yellow, black, flame, azure, white, and blue. This will be marvelous with your Bohemian topaz earrings, a touch of rouge, two assassins,[2] three crescent combs, and seven beauty marks.'

"Then they left, bowing deeply to me. Alone, I said to myself, 'They are just as mad here as at home. Nonetheless, this harpsichord saves a lot of trouble.' "

Mirzoza, interrupting the reading, said to the Sultan, "Your traveler should have brought us back at least one arietta of transcribed attire, with figured bass."

THE SULTAN: That is precisely what he did.

MIRZOZA: And who will be able to play it for us?

THE SULTAN: One of the disciples of the black Brahmin, the one in whose care the ocular instrument has remained. But have you heard enough?

MIRZOZA: Is there much more?

THE SULTAN: No, just a few pages, and you will have done with it.

MIRZOZA: Read them.

THE SULTAN: "I was thinking this," says my journal, "when the door of the chamber the mother had entered suddenly opened and revealed a figure so strangely disguised that I did not recognize her. Her pyramidal coiffure and stilt-slippers made her taller by a foot and a half. With this she had on a white fur tippet, an orange cape, a dress of light-blue, short-napped velvet, a flesh-colored petticoat, sulfur-colored stockings, and squirrel slippers. But what struck me most was a pentagonal hoop skirt, with corners jutting out a yard in all directions. She looked like a walking dungeon, flanked by five bulwarks. One of the daughters appeared next.

" 'Mercy!' cried the mother, 'who dressed you like this? Begone! You disgust me. Were not the hour of the ball so near I would undress you. I hope that you will wear a mask, at least.' Then, addressing the younger daughter, 'As for you,' said she, looking her up and down, 'you look both reasonable and respectable.'

"Meanwhile, Monsieur, who had also gotten dressed after his midnight meal, appeared in a hat the color of dead leaves, beneath which flowed the curls of a long wig; a jacket of brocaded cloth, patterned with large checks each a foot and a half long, with five buttons in front, four pockets, no pleats or paddings; chamois knee-breeches and stockings; and slippers of green Moroccan leather. It all held together, and formed an ensemble."

Here Mangogul stopped and said to Mirzoza, who was holding her sides, "These islanders seem quite ridiculous to you."

Mirzoza, stopping him short, added, "You may dispense with the rest. This time, Sultan, you are correct. Pray, let it be; do not draw any conclusions therefrom. If you advise me to be more reasonable, all is lost. Certainly we would appear just as bizarre to these islanders as they appear to us; and in matters of fashion, fools lead wise men, courtesans lead honest women, and others have nothing better to do than follow suit. We laugh when we see portraits of our ancestors, without thinking that our grandchildren will laugh in turn at ours."

MANGOGUL: So, for once in my life I have shown common sense!

MIRZOZA: I forgive you for it; but let us not discuss it any longer.

MANGOGUL: But, with all your wisdom, what of harmony, melody, and the ocular harpsichord?...

MIRZOZA: Stop, let me continue...they gave rise to a schism that divided men, women, and all the citizens. One school revolted against another, master against master; people argued, traded insults, hated one another.

"Very well, but that is not all."

"As a matter of fact, I have not finished."

"Finish, then."

"Just as was recently discovered in Banza with the argument over sounds — when the deaf showed themselves to be the most stubborn wranglers — in the country of your travelers, those who cried loudest and longest over the colors were the blind..."

Suddenly, the vexed sultan took up his travelers' notebooks and tore them to pieces.

"What are you doing?"

"I am getting rid of a useless work."

"Useless for me, perhaps, but for you?"

"Whatever adds nothing to your happiness is of no interest to me."

"Am I then so dear to you?"

"That is a question asked by all women. They feel nothing; they think that everything is their due. No matter what is done for them, it is never enough. One moment of irritation erases a year of indulgence. I am going."

"No, you are staying. Come, come closer and kiss me."

The Sultan kissed her and said, "We are merely puppets, are we not?"

"Yes, at times."

CHAPTER XX

Two Pious Women

The Sultan let the jewels alone for a few days. Important affairs with which he was engaged had suspended his trials of the ring. During this interval, two ladies from Banza became the laughingstock of the whole town.

These ladies were pious by profession. They had conducted their liaisons with all possible discretion, and enjoyed a reputation that even their spiteful peers respected. In the mosques people talked of nothing but their virtue. Mothers cited them as examples for their daughters, husbands as examples for their wives. Each one maintained, as her principal maxim, that scandal is the worst of sins. This conformity of sentiment, and, above all, the difficulty of finding a clear-sighted and crafty confidante at little expense, outweighed their differences in character, and they were the best of friends.

Zelida received Sophie's Brahmin; and it was at Sophie's place that Zelida conferred with her spiritual guide. With even a little observation of each other, the one could hardly be unaware of the business of the other's jewel. But all the bizarre indiscretion among the jewels of the kingdom now had them both in a state of cruel apprehension. They felt themselves on the brink of being unmasked and losing this reputation of virtue that had cost them fifteen years of dissimulation and guile, and which had suddenly become a great encumbrance.

There were moments when they, or at least Zelida, would have given their lives to be just as discredited as most of their acquaintances. "What will people say? What will my husband do?...What! A woman so reserved, so modest, so virtuous? That Zelida is not... like the others! Alas, that idea drives me to despair!...I wish I did not have to think of it; I wish I had never thought it at all!" Zelida cried out suddenly.

She was with her friend, who was entertaining the same type of thoughts, but was not so agitated. Zelida's last words made her smile.

"Laugh, Madame, do not restrain yourself. Go ahead," said Zelida, vexed. "To be sure, you have good cause."

"I know as well as you," Sophie answered coldly, "all the danger that threatens us; but how can we get out of it? You must agree that there is no indication that your wish will be granted."

"Think of something, then," returned Zelida.

"Oh!" continued Sophie, "I am tired of racking my brains. I can think of nothing...To bury oneself in the provinces is one way...But abandon the pleasures of Banza, and withdraw from life – that I would never do. I sense that my jewel would never get used to that."

"What, then, shall we do?"

"What shall we do? Leave everything to Providence, and laugh, as I do, at what people say. I have tried everything to reconcile reputation with pleasure, but since it is decreed that we must renounce our reputations, let us keep pleasure, at least. We were unique, but now, my dear, now we shall be like a hundred thousand others; does this seem to you so hard a fate?"

"Yes, without a doubt," replied Zelida, "it seems hard to me to resemble those for whom we affected such supreme disdain. To avoid this humiliation I would flee, I think, to the ends of the earth."

"Go ahead, my dear," continued Sophie. "As for me, I am staying... By the way, I advise you to provide some secret way of preventing your jewel from tattling along the way."

"Indeed," replied Zelida, "this is hardly the moment for pleasantry, and your boldness..."

"You are mistaken, Zelida, my position is hardly bold. To let things take a course that cannot be changed is resignation. I see I must be dishonored; very well! As a dishonored woman, I shall at least spare myself as much worry as I can."

"Dishonored!" continued Zelida, bursting into tears. "Dishonored! What a blow! I cannot bear it...Alas, accursed bonze! It is you who have ruined me. I loved my husband; I was born virtuous; I should have loved him still, had you not betrayed your ministry and my confidence. Dishonored! Dear Sophie..."

She could not continue. Her sobs cut her off; she fell upon a sofa, nearly at wit's end. As soon as Zelida recovered the power of speech, she cried out unhappily, "Alas, my dear Sophie, I shall die from it...I must die. No, I shall never survive my reputation."

"But, Zelida, my dear Zelida, do not be in such a hurry to die," Sophie said to her. "Perhaps..."

"There is no perhaps in this. I must die."

"But perhaps one might..."

"One might nothing, I tell you...But speak, my dear, what might one do?"

"Perhaps one might hinder a jewel from speaking."

"Ah, Sophie, you seek to comfort me with false hopes; you deceive me."

"No, no, I do not deceive you; just listen to me instead of raving like a madwoman. I have heard talk of Frenicole, of Eolipilus, of gags and muzzles."

"Pray, what do Frenicole, Eolipilus, and muzzles have to do with the dangers that threaten us? How does my jeweler enter into this? And just what is a muzzle?"

"I will tell you, my dear. A muzzle is a device invented by Frenicole, approved by the academy, and perfected by Eolipilus, who now takes credit for the invention."

"And what of this device conceived by Frenicole, approved by the academy, and perfected by Eolipilus?"

"Oh, you are petulant beyond belief! Very well...This device is applied to a jewel and renders it discreet, in spite of..."

"Can this be true, my dear?"

"That is what people say."

"We must find out about this at once," said Zelida.

She rang; one of her maids appeared; she sent for Frenicole.

"Why not Eolipilus?" asked Sophie.

"Frenicole will be less conspicuous," answered Zelida.

The jeweler did not keep them waiting.

"Ah, Frenicole, here you are," Zelida said to him. "Welcome. Please make haste, my dear, and help two women in a cruel predicament."

"What is the matter, ladies? Do you need some rare jewels?"

"No, we have two already and we would like..."

"To get rid of them, right? Very well, ladies! Let me see them. I will take them or offer you an exchange..."

"You are mistaken, my dear Frenicole; we have nothing to barter..."

"Ah! I understand; you have a few earrings that you would like to lose, in such a way that your husbands should find them in my shop..."

"Not at all. Come now, Sophie, tell him what we want!"

"Frenicole," continued Sophie, "we need two... What! Do you not understand?..."

"No, Madame, how can I understand? You tell me nothing..."

"That is because when a woman is modest it is difficult to speak openly of certain things..."

"And yet," Frenicole replied, "speak openly she must. A jeweler cannot read minds."

"And yet you must try..."

"Upon my word, ladies, the more I look at you the less I understand you. When one is as young, rich, and pretty as you she need not resort to artifice: in any case, I will tell you sincerely that I sell trinkets no longer. I have left that commerce to my colleagues who are just starting out."

Our pious friends found the jeweler's mistake so amusing that they burst out laughing at the same time, which disconcerted him.

"Allow me, ladies," he said to them, "to pay my respects to you and leave. You might have spared yourselves the trouble of calling me here to laugh at my expense."

"Wait, my dear, wait," Zelida said to him, still laughing. "That was not our intention. But as you failed to understand us, you came up with such comical notions..."

"Only you, Mesdames, can give me a more correct one. What is it you want?"

"Oh, dear Frenicole, allow me to laugh freely before I answer you."

Zelida laughed till she gasped for breath. The jeweler thought to himself that she had the vapors or that she was mad, and patiently waited. At last Zelida stopped.

"Very well!" she said to him. "The business relates to our jewels, our own jewels. Do you understand, my dear Frenicole? You must know that for some time now there have been a number of jewels that have begun to chatter like magpies. Now, we would not like for our own to follow this bad example."

"Aha! Now I understand," continued Frenicole. "You mean you want muzzles!"

"Very good, there you have it. Indeed I had been told that Frenicole was no fool..."

"Madame, you are very kind. As for your request, I have all kinds, and I shall get some for you."

Frenicole left. Meanwhile Zelida embraced her friend, thanking her for her idea. And as for me, says the African author, I went to rest while waiting for his return.

CHAPTER XXI

The Jeweler's Return

The jeweler returned and presented our ladies with two muzzles of the finest sort.

"Ah, mercy!" cried Zelida. "What muzzles! What enormous muzzles! Who are the unfortunate women whom these will fit? This one is a yard long! Indeed, my friend, you must have taken your measurements on the Sultan's mare."

"Yes," Sophie said indolently, having looked them over and measured them with her fingers. "You are right; these would fit only the Sultan's mare, or old Rimosa."

"I protest, ladies," replied Frenicole, "that is the usual size, and Zelmaida, Zyrphila, Amiana, Zulica, and a hundred others have taken similar ones."

"That is impossible," retorted Zelida.

"But it is true," continued Frenicole, "and they all said the same thing as you. Like them, if you wish to undeceive yourselves, you have only to try them on..."

"Frenicole may say what he will, but he will never persuade me that this will fit me," said Zelida.

"Nor me," said Sophie. "Let him show us others, if he has any."

Frenicole, who had found out many times that a woman's mind cannot be changed on this subject, showed them muzzles for thirteen-year-olds.

"Yes, that is what we want," both cried out at the same time.

"I wish it were so," Frenicole whispered under his breath.

"How much are you selling them for?" asked Zelida.

"Only ten ducats apiece, Madame..."

"Ten ducats! You don't mean it, Frenicole..."

"Madame, in good conscience..."

"You make us pay for the novelty..."

"I promise you, ladies, it is money well spent..."

"It is true that they are very nicely crafted; but ten ducats is quite a sum..."

"I will take nothing less."

"We will go to Eolipilus."

"You may indeed, ladies, but there is workmanship and workmanship; there are muzzles and muzzles."

Frenicole held his ground, and Zelida gave way. She paid for the two muzzles, and the jeweler departed, quite sure that they would be too small for them and that they would not be long in returning them to him for one quarter of the price they had paid. He was mistaken. As Mangogul did not happen to be inclined to turn his ring on these two ladies, their jewels were not moved to speak any more loudly than usual, which was lucky for them, for Zelida, having tried her muzzle, had found it too small by half. Nonetheless she did not get rid of it, imagining almost as much inconvenience in exchanging it as in being unable to use it at all.

Everyone learned of this from one of her serving women, who told it in confidence to her lover, who told it again in confidence to others, who spread it in secret to all of Banza. Frenicole talked; the adventure of our two pious ladies became public and occupied the scandal-mongers of the Congo for some time.

Zelida was inconsolable. This woman, more deserving of pity than blame, developed an aversion for her Brahmin, left her husband, and shut herself up in a convent. As for Sophie, she threw off the mask, braved the talk, put on rouge and beauty marks, went out into society, and had affairs.

CHAPTER XXII

Seventh Trial of the Ring
The Stifled Jewel

Although the bourgeois ladies of Banza doubted that jewels of their kind would have the honor to speak, nonetheless they all equipped themselves with muzzles. In Banza, muzzles became as common as national mourning here.

Here the African author remarks with surprise that neither the reasonableness of price nor their widespread use diminished their popularity in the seraglio. "This once," he said, "practicality triumphed over prejudice." Such a trite observation was not worth repeating; but it seems to me that this was a defect of all the ancient authors of the Congo, that of falling into useless repetition, whether because they thereby hoped to lend an air of verisimilitude and facility to their work or because they were not by any means as prolific as their admirers imagined them to be.

Be that as it may, one day Mangogul, walking in his gardens accompanied by his whole court, took it into his head to turn his ring on Zelais. She was pretty and suspected of many intrigues. Nonetheless her jewel stammered and uttered but a few broken words that meant nothing, and which the wits interpreted as they saw fit. "Here," said the Sultan, "is a jewel that speaks with great difficulty. There must be something impeding its efforts." He applied his ring more forcefully. The jewel made a second attempt to express itself. In some measure overcoming the obstacle that sealed its lips, it was heard to say, very distinctly, "Oh...oh...I am...I am suff...I am suffocating...I cannot take it any longer...Oh...oh...I cannot breathe."

Zelais herself felt as if she were suffocating: she turned pale, her throat swelled, and she collapsed, eyes closed and mouth half open, into the arms of those around her.

Anywhere else she would have been promptly relieved. One had only to remove the muzzle from her and allow her jewel to breathe; but how could one lend her a helping hand in the presence of Mangogul? "Physicians, quick, quick," cried the Sultan. "Zelais is dying."

Pages ran to the palace and returned, the physicians marching solemnly behind them. Orcotomus was at the lead. Some were in favor of bloodletting, others favored the kermes mineral,[1] but the discerning Orcotomus had Zelais carried into an adjoining room, examined her, and cut the braces of her harness. This muzzled jewel was one of those he boasted to have seen in the state of paroxysm.

Nonetheless the swelling was great, and Zelais would have continued to suffer had not the Sultan taken pity on her condition. He turned his ring; her humors settled back into equilibrium. Zelais came to, and Orcotomus took credit for this miraculous cure.

Zelais's accident and the physician's indiscretion greatly discredited the muzzles. Orcotomus, with no regard for Eolipilus's interests, proposed to raise his fortunes on the ruins of the other's. He advertised himself as the appointed physician of congested jewels, and one can still see his notices posted along some side streets. He began by making money, and ended up despised. The Sultan took pleasure in putting the quack in his place. If Orcotomus boasted of silencing a jewel that had never breathed a word, Mangogul had the cruelty to make it speak. People eventually noticed that any jewel that was tired of remaining mute had only to receive Orcotomus two or three times. Soon he was relegated, along with Eolipilus, to the class of charlatans, and there both of them will remain until it pleases Brahma to remove them.

People preferred shame to apoplexy. "One kills you," they said, "the other does not." Thus they renounced muzzles; jewels were allowed to speak, and no one died from it.

CHAPTER XXIII

Eighth Trial of the Ring
The Vapors

There was a time, as we have seen, when women suffocated and nearly died for fear that their jewels might talk. But there came a day when they rose above this fright, rid themselves of the muzzles, and had nothing more than the vapors.

Among her attendants, the favorite had a very unusual girl. Her disposition was charming, though uneven. She changed expressions ten times a day, yet whatever expression she assumed was pleasing. As unique in her melancholy as in mirth, she uttered the most exquisite and extravagant remarks, even when sad.

Mirzoza was so completely accustomed to Callirhoa, for such was the name of this mad young girl, that she could hardly be without her. Once the Sultan was complaining to the favorite of some sort of restless and remote quality he observed in her.

"Prince," she said to him, surprised by his reproach, "without my three companions – my canary, my Persian cat, and Callirhoa – I am good for nothing; and you can see that I am missing the latter."

"And why is she not here?" Mangogul asked her.

"I do not know," answered Mirzoza, "but a few months ago she announced to me that if Mazul joined the campaign, she would not be able to avoid having the vapors, and Mazul set out yesterday..."

"That is to her credit," replied the Sultan. "That is what I call having the vapors for a good reason. But why do a hundred others take it into their heads to have them when their husbands are still young and they have no want of lovers?"

"Prince," answered a courtier, "it is a very fashionable illness. It is genteel for a woman to have the vapors. If she hasn't a lover or the vapors, she has no breeding; there is not a bourgeoise in Banza who does not affect to have them."

Mangogul smiled and decided on the spot to visit one of these vaporish women. He went straight to Salica's house. He found her in bed, breasts bared, eyes aflame, hair disheveled, and at her bedside the little stammering, hunchbacked physician, Farfadi, who was telling her stories. Meanwhile she stretched out one arm, then the other, yawned, sighed, brought her hand to her forehead, and cried out bitterly, "Oh... I cannot go on... Open the windows... Give me air... I cannot go on; I am dying..."

Mangogul took advantage of a moment when her worried women were helping Farfadi lighten her bedclothes to turn his ring on her; immediately the following words were heard: "Oh, how bored I am of these goings-on! Madame has taken it into her head to have the vapors! This farce will last a week, and I'll be damned if I know the reason. After all the remedies Farfadi has applied, I should think it would be gone by now."

"Very good," said the Sultan, turning his ring, "I understand. This one has the vapors for her doctor's sake. Let us try elsewhere."

He went from Salica's place to Arsinoa's, which was not far. From the entrance to her chambers he heard great bursts of laughter; as he approached he expected to find that she had company. Yet she was alone, and Mangogul was not too surprised. "When a woman gives herself the vapors," he said, "she feels melancholy or cheerful, depending on what is most convenient."

He turned his ring on her, and immediately her jewel began to laugh a full-throated laugh. Then it went suddenly from this uncontrolled laughter to ridiculous lamentations over the absence of Narcis, whom it advised as a friend to return with all speed, and continued anew to sob, weep, moan, sigh, and fall into despair, as if it had just buried its entire family.

The Sultan, who could hardly keep from laughing aloud at so strange an affliction, turned his ring back and departed, leaving Arsinoa and her jewel to lament at leisure, and thinking to himself that the proverb was false.

CHAPTER XXIV

Ninth Trial of the Ring
Of Things Lost and Found

To serve as a supplement to the learned treatise on Pancirollus and to the Acts of the Academy of Inscriptions

Mangogul, preoccupied with the ridiculous airs women give themselves, returned to his palace. Due perhaps to distraction on his part, perhaps to some blunder of the ring, he found himself beneath the portico of the sumptuous building that Thelis decorated with the rich spoils of her lovers. He profited from this occasion to interrogate her jewel.

Thelis was the wife of the emir Sambuco, whose ancestors had ruled Guinea. Sambuco had gained renown in the Congo through five or six famous victories he won against the enemies of Erguebzed. A clever negotiator as well as a great captain, he had been awarded diplomatic assignments of the highest distinction and executed his offices with superior talent. On his return from Loango, he discovered Thelis and was smitten. He was then in his fiftieth year and Thelis had not yet reached twenty-five. She had more charm than beauty; women said she was good company, but men found her adorable. Powerful matches had been proposed to her, but whether she already held her own opinions, or whether there was too great a disproportion between the fortunes of her admirers and her own, they had all been refused. Sambuco saw her, placed at her feet his immense riches, a name, glories, and titles surpassed only by those of sovereigns, and won her.

Thelis was, or appeared, virtuous for a full six weeks after her marriage; but a jewel born voluptuous rarely overcomes itself, and a quinquagenarian husband, however heroic he might be elsewhere, is mad if he thinks he can conquer that enemy. Although Thelis behaved cautiously, her first adventures did not pass unnoticed. Thereafter people suspected her of secrets, and Mangogul, curious to know the truth, hurried from the vestibule of her palace into her chambers.

It was the middle of summer. It was extremely hot, and after dining, Thelis had thrown herself on a couch in a back room decorated with mirrors and paintings. She was sleeping, her hand still pressed against the collection of Persian tales that had made her drowsy.

Mangogul contemplated her awhile, agreed that she had charm, and turned his ring on her. "I can still remember, as if I were there," said Thelis's jewel immodestly. "Nine proofs of love in four hours. Oh, what a time! What a divine man, that Zermounzaid! Far different from the old and icy Sambuco. Dear Zermounzaid, before you I did not know true pleasure, true well-being. It was you who showed me what it is."

Mangogul, who wished to know the details of the commerce between Thelis and Zermounzaid, which the jewel hid from him by mentioning only those things that most impress a jewel, rubbed the stone of his ring a few times against his coat, and leveled it, all sparkling with light, at Thelis. The effect soon reached her jewel, which, better informed of what was asked of it, continued in a more historical strain.

"Sambuco commanded the army of Monoemugi, and I followed him into the field. Zermounzaid served under him in the capacity of colonel, and the general, who honored his colonel with his confidence, placed us under his escort. The zealous Zermounzaid never quit his post. It seemed too agreeable to him to cede it to another; and the danger of losing it was the only one he feared during the whole campaign.

"During winter quarters, I entertained a few guests, Cacil, Jekia, Almamaoum, Jasub, Selim, Manzora, and Nereskim, all military men commended by Zermounzaid, but who were inferior to him. For the credulous Sambuco entrusted his wife's virtue to the woman herself, and to the care of Zermounzaid. Preoccupied with the many details of war and the great operations he was planning for the glory of the Congo, he never had the slightest suspicion that Zermounzaid had betrayed him, and that Thelis had been unfaithful.

"The war continued; the armies took the field, and we took up our litters again. Since these moved very slowly, little by little the army corps overtook us, and we found ourselves in the rear guard, which Zermounzaid commanded. This good boy, whom the sight of great danger never deterred from the path of glory, was unable to resist the sight of pleasure. He entrusted a subaltern with the care of watching the movements of the enemy bearing down on us, and came into our litter. Barely had he come when we heard a confused sound of arms and outcries. Zermounzaid, leaving his business half done, attempted to leave. But he was struck down, and we fell into the hands of the conqueror.

"Thus I began by swallowing up the honor and the services of an officer who, given his bravura and merit, might have attained the highest military distinctions, had he never known his general's wife. More than three thousand men perished on that occasion, so many good subjects we robbed from the nation."

One can imagine Mangogul's surprise at this speech. He had heard Zermounzaid's funeral oration, and he did not recognize him in this portrait. Erguebzed, his father, had regretted the loss of this officer; the gazette, having lavished praise on his fine retreat, attributed his defeat and his death to the enemy's superior numbers, which, they reported, were six to one. All the Congo lamented this man who had performed his duty so well. His wife had obtained a pension; his regiment had been granted to his eldest son, and an ecclesiastical preferment promised to the younger.

"What horror!" cried Mangogul. "A husband dishonored, the state betrayed, subjects sacrificed, crimes not only concealed but rewarded as virtues, and all this for a jewel."

Thelis's jewel, which interrupted itself to catch its breath, continued: "And so was I abandoned to the mercy of the enemy. A regiment of dragoons was about to descend upon us. Thelis seemed to lament her predicament, yet would have liked nothing more. The charms of the prey, however, sowed discord among the predators. Scimitars were drawn and thirty to forty men fell in the twinkling of an eye. The sound of this confusion spread to the presiding officer. He came running, calmed the hotheads, and sequestered us in a tent. We barely had a moment to collect ourselves, when he came to request payment for his services. "Woe to the vanquished!" cried Thelis, throwing herself down upon a bed; and the whole night was spent tasting her misfortune.

"The next day we found ourselves on the banks of the Niger. A saic[1] was waiting for us and we set sail, my mistress and I, to be presented to the Emperor of Benin. During this twenty-four-hour voyage, the captain of the ship offered himself to Thelis, was accepted, and I experienced firsthand that service at sea is much more lively than service on land. Next we saw to the Emperor of Benin. He was young, passionate, voluptuous. Thelis made another conquest of him; but it was her husband's conquests that terrified him. He asked for peace and it cost him only three provinces and my ransom.

"Other times, other worries. Sambuco learned, I know not how, the reasons for the misfortunes of the preceding campaign and during this time he deposited me on the frontier with a chief Brahmin friend of his. The holy man never even tried to defend himself; he succumbed to Thelis's provocations, and in less than six months I devoured his immense revenues, three lakes, and two open forests."

"Mercy!" cried Mangogul, "three lakes and two open forests! What an appetite for a jewel!"

"It was a trifle," resumed the jewel. "Peace was made and Thelis followed her husband to his embassy at Monomotapa. She gamed and lost well nigh a hundred thousand sequins in one day, all of which I regained in one hour. A minister, whose master's affairs did not occupy all his time, fell into my grasp, and in three or four months I devoured his handsome estate, a furnished château, a park, and a coach with little piebald horses. A four-minute favor, well done, brought us feasts, presents, and jewelry, and the blind or politic Sambuco bothered us no longer.

"I say nothing," added the jewel, "of the marquisates, earldoms, titles, coats of arms, and so on, that have fallen before me. Ask my secretary yourself, who will tell you what became of them. I took a big corner off of Biafara, and I possess an entire province in Beleguanza. A little before his death, Erguebzed made overtures to me..." With these words Mangogul turned his ring back around, and silenced that abyss. He respected the memory of his father, and wanted to hear nothing that might tarnish the luster of the great qualities that he saw in him.

Returning to the seraglio, he entertained the favorite with the tales of the vaporish ladies and his ring's test of Thelis. "You admit this woman," he said to her, "into your company; but apparently you do not know her as well as I."

"I understand, my lord," replied the Sultana. "Her jewel probably foolishly recounted its adventures with the general Micokof, the emir Feridour, the senator Marsupha, and the grand Brahmin Ramadanutio. But pray! Who does not know that she keeps the young Alamir, and that the old Sambuco, who says nothing, is just as well informed of it as you!"

"Not quite," continued Mangogul. "I have just made her jewel spit out everything."

"Had it swallowed anything of yours?" asked Mirzoza.

"Not mine," said the Sultan, "but much belonging to my subjects, the men of power of my empire, my neighboring potentates: estates, provinces, châteaux, lakes, forest, diamonds, and carriages with pie-bald ponies."

"Not to mention, my lord," added Mirzoza, "reputations and virtues. I do not know what benefit you will reap from your ring; but the more you try it, the more odious my sex becomes to me: even those whom I thought merited some esteem are not exempted from this. They have put me in such an ill temper that I ask Your Highness to allow me to give myself over to it for a few moments."

Mangogul, who knew Mirzoza to be inimical to all constraints, kissed her three times on the right ear and retired.

CHAPTER XXV

A Sampling of Mangogul's Morals

Mangogul, impatient to see the favorite again, slept little, rose earlier than usual, and appeared before her at the crack of dawn. She had already rung for her serving women; they had just opened her curtains and were preparing to dress her. The Sultan took a long look around, and seeing no dog, asked her the reason for this oddity.

"You think me odd in this," she answered him, "yet that is not the case."

"I assure you," replied the Sultan, "that I see dogs with all the women of my court. You would greatly oblige me by telling me why they have them, or why you have none. Most of them have several, and not a one fails to lavish hers with caresses, which she seems to begrudge her lover. What do these beasts do to deserve such preference? What is their purpose?"

Mirzoza did not know how to answer these questions.

"But one has a dog," she said to him, "just as one has a parrot or a canary. Perhaps it is foolish to attach oneself to animals, but it is not strange to have them; sometimes they are amusing but never are they hurtful. And if they are caressed, these caresses are of no consequence. Besides, do you believe, Prince, that a lover is satisfied with such a kiss as a woman gives to her hound?"

"Without a doubt, I believe it," said the Sultan. "He would have to be very difficult indeed not to be satisfied with it."

One of Mirzoza's women, who had won the affection of the Sultan and the favorite through her sweetness, talents, and zeal, said, "These animals are troublesome and unclean; they stain clothes, ruin furniture, destroy lace, and in a quarter of an hour they do more mischief than would bring disgrace on the most faithful waiting maid. And yet people keep them."

"Although, according to Madame, they are good only for such things," added the Sultan.

"Prince," Mirzoza responded, "we all cling to our fancies; keeping a hound is one such fancy, like many others; and they would not be fancies if we could account for them. The reign of monkeys is past; the reign of parakeets is still in full swing. Dogs had fallen out of favor, but now they are coming back again. Squirrels had their day. With animals it is just as it has been, by turns, with Italian, English, geometry, farthingales, and flounces."

"Mirzoza," continued the Sultan, shaking his head, "is not as enlightened as she might be on this subject; and the jewels..."

"Your Highness cannot be going so far as to imagine," said the favorite, "that he will learn from Haria's jewel just why this woman, who saw her son, one of her daughters, and her husband die without shedding a tear, cried for two weeks over the loss of her puppy?"

"Why not?" returned Mangogul.

"Really," said Mirzoza, "if our jewels could explain all our fancies, they would be wiser than we."

"Pray, who would argue that with you?" continued Mangogul. "For my part, I believe that a jewel makes a woman do a hundred things of which she is unaware; and I have noticed on more than one occasion that a woman who thought she was following her head was actually obeying her jewel. A great philosopher placed the soul — ours, that is — in the pineal gland. If I granted woman a soul, I know very well where I would place it."

"I excuse you from telling me about it," Mirzoza rejoined forthwith.

"But you will permit me at least," said Mangogul, "to communicate a few ideas my ring suggested to me about women, assuming that they do have souls. The experiments I have made with my ring have turned me into a great moralist. I have neither the wit of La Bruyère, nor the logic of Port-Royal; neither the imagination of Montaigne, nor the wisdom of Charron; but I have gathered evidence that perhaps they never did."

"Speak, Prince," said Mirzoza ironically, "I am all ears for you. It will be curious indeed — discourses on morality from a sultan of your age!"

"Orcotomus's system is extravagant, with all due respect to his famous fellow academician Hiragu; yet I find some sense in the answers that he gave to his opponents. If I granted a soul to women, I would willingly assume, as does he, that jewels have spoken from all time, but softly, and that the effect of Cucufa's ring has been merely to raise their pitch. Assuming this, it follows that nothing is easier than to define the whole female sex:

"The chaste woman, for example, would be she whose jewel is mute, or ignored.

"The prude, she who pretends not to listen to her jewel.

"The gallant, she whose jewel is too demanding, and who gives in too much.

"The voluptuary, she who listens to her jewel indulgently.

"The courtesan, she whose jewel is ever demanding and never denied.

"The coquette, she whose jewel is mute, or not yet attended to, and who gives hope to all men who come near her, hope that one day her jewel will speak, and that she will not turn a deaf ear to it.

"Well, my soul's delight, what do you think of my taxonomy?"

"I think," replied the favorite, "that Your Highness has forgotten the affectionate woman."

"If I have not yet mentioned her," replied the Sultan, "it is because I do not yet know what the term means, and because clever people say that the word affection, having no relation whatsoever to jewels, is devoid of meaning."

"What! devoid of meaning?" cried Mirzoza. "So, is there no middle ground, and must a woman necessarily be a prude, a gallant, a coquette, a voluptuary, or a libertine?"

"My soul's delight," said the Sultan, "I am ready to admit the inexactitude of my list, and I would add the affectionate woman to the preceding characters, but only on the condition that you give me a definition thereof that does not fall under one of my categories."

"Most willingly," said Mirzoza. "I hope to accomplish this without going outside of your system."

"We shall see," added Mangogul.

"Very well!" continued the favorite. "The affectionate woman is she..."

"Courage, Mirzoza," said Mangogul.

"Pray, do not distract me. The affectionate woman is she... who has loved though her jewel has never spoken... save in favor of the man she loved."

It would not have been polite for Mangogul to tease the favorite, and ask her what she meant by love; so he said nothing. Mirzoza took his silence for consent, and added, proud to have extricated herself from a situation that seemed diffcult to her, "You men think that because we do not argue, we cannot reason. Learn once and for all, then, that we could discover the falsity of your paradoxes just as easily as you find those in our reasonings, if we wished to take the trouble. If Your Highness were less in a hurry to satisfy his curiosity about hounds, I in turn would give him a sampling of my philosophy. But nothing is lost; we will wait for another day, when he has more time to offer me."

Mangogul answered her that he had nothing better to do than to benefit from her philosophical ideas, and that the metaphysics of a twenty-two-year-old sultana should not be any less unusual than the morals of a sultan of his age.

But Mirzoza feared that Mangogul was merely humoring her, and asked him for some time to prepare herself, thus providing the Sultan with a pretext to fly whither his impatience beckoned him.

CHAPTER XXVI

Tenth Trial of the Ring
The Hounds

Mangogul immediately transported himself to Haria's place, and since he spoke quite readily to himself, he said, inaudibly, "This woman will not go to bed without her four hounds, and if jewels know anything about these animals, her jewel will tell me a thing or two, for, thanks be to God, everyone knows she loves her dogs to the point of adoration."

By the end of this monologue, he found himself in Haria's antechamber, and could tell from afar that Madame was resting in her usual company, a little spaniel, a Great Dane, and two boxers. The Sultan drew out his snuffbox, took two pinches of his Spanish snuff as a precaution, and approached Haria. She was sleeping, but the pack, who kept watch, heard some noise and began to bark and awakened her. "Hush, my children," she said to them in a voice so sweet that one would have never mistaken her for speaking to her daughters. "Sleep, sleep, do not disturb my rest or your own."

Haria was young and pretty once. She had had lovers of the same station as she, but they disappeared even sooner than her charms. To console herself for the abandonment, she gave herself over to a strange ostentation, and her lackeys were the best-looking in all of Banza. She continued to age; her years forced her to mend her ways, and she restricted herself to four dogs and two Brahmins and became a model of edification. In fact, the most venomous satires found nothing in her to sink their teeth into, and for more than ten years Haria had enjoyed in peace both a reputation of great virtue and these animals. People even knew of her marked tenderness for her hounds, and no longer suspected the Brahmins of receiving a share of her favors.

Haria repeated her request to her animals, and they were kind enough to obey. Mangogul then brought his hand to his ring, and the aged jewel began to relate its most recent adventures. So much time had passed since the first ones that it had almost forgotten them. "Go away, Medor," it said in a husky voice. "You tire me out. I prefer Lisette; I find her more gentle." Medor, to whom the voice of the jewel was unfamiliar, went looking for it; but Haria, waking up, continued, "Get off, naughty boy, you are preventing me from resting. Sometimes it is good, but enough is enough." Medor went away, Lisette took his place, and Haria went back to sleep.

Mangogul, who had suspended the effects of his ring, turned it back around, and the ancient jewel, heaving a sigh, began to ramble, saying: "Alas, I am so angry about the loss of my big greyhound! She was the best little woman, the most caressing creature; she never ceased to amuse me, always so sweet and gentle; you all are beasts by comparison. That wicked man killed her...poor Zinzolina; I never think of her without a tear in my eye...I thought my mistress would die, she spent two days without eating or drinking, and nearly lost her senses. You can imagine her sadness. Her confessor, her friends, even her hounds did not come near me. She ordered her women, under pain of dismissal, to refuse my master entrance to her chambers...'This monster has bereft me of my dear Zinzolina,' she cried. 'I never want to see him again as long as I live.'"

Mangogul, curious to learn the circumstances of Zinzolina's death, revived the electric current in his ring by rubbing it against the tail of his coat, pointed it at Haria, and the jewel continued: "Haria, Ramadec's widow, took a fancy to Sindor. This young man, though wellborn, had little fortune; but he did have a certain talent pleasing to women, which was, after the hounds, Haria's dominant preference. Sindor's indigence conquered his repugnance for Haria's age and her dogs. Twenty thousand crowns managed to conceal my mistress's wrinkles and the inconvenience of the dogs from his eyes, and he married her.

"He had flattered himself into thinking that, with his talents, he would win out over our animals and banish them at the beginning of his reign, but he was mistaken. At the end of a few months he believed he had quite merited us, and took it upon himself to inform Madame that in bed her dogs were not as good company for him as they were for her, that it was ridiculous to have more than three, that she was making the nuptial bed into a kennel, and that only one should be allowed at a time.

" 'I advise you,' answered Haria angrily, 'not to talk to me like that! Really, it ill becomes a miserable youth from Gascony, whom I rescued from a garret, to give himself such airs of nicety! I suppose they scented your sheets, my little man, when you lived in a furnished room? I'll have you know, then, once and for all, that my dogs laid claim to my bed long before you, and that you may leave it or resolve to share it with them.'

"This declaration was terse, and our dogs remained masters of their post; but one night when we were all resting, Sindor, in turning over, had the misfortune of kicking Zinzolina. The greyhound, not at all accustomed to such treatment, bit him in the thigh, and Madame was awakened by Sindor's cries.

" 'What is wrong, sir?' asked Haria. 'One would think you were being murdered. Are you dreaming?'

" 'Your dogs, Madame,' answered Sindor, 'are devouring me, and your greyhound has just taken a bite out of my leg.'

" 'Is that all?' asked Haria, turning over. 'You make quite a lot of noise over nothing.'

"Sindor, stung by these words, got out of bed, swearing not to return until the pack was banished. He appealed to some mutual friends to attempt to obtain the dogs' exile, but they all failed in these important negotiations. Haria told them that Sindor was a vain young man whom she had rescued from a garret he shared with mice and rats. She added that it was not becoming of him to be so hard to please; he slept all through the night; she loved her dogs; they amused her; from earliest childhood she had been fond of their caresses; and she was resolved not to be separated from them except in death. 'Tell him besides,' she said, addressing the mediators, 'that if he does not submit to my wishes, he shall regret it for the rest of his life, for I shall retract his share of the inheritance and add it to the amount I leave in my will for the care and maintenance of my dear children.'

"Between you and me," added the jewel, "Sindor must have been a great fool to hope that he would be granted what twenty lovers, a spiritual guide, a confessor, and a long string of Brahmins who had wasted their words, had failed to obtain. Meanwhile, every time Sindor encountered our animals, he became filled with a rage that he had difficulty containing. One day the unfortunate Zinzolina fell into his hands; he seized her by the collar and hurled her from the window. The poor beast died from her fall. This caused a great commotion. Haria, face ablaze, eyes bathed in tears..."

The jewel was about to repeat what it had already said, for jewels easily repeat themselves. But Mangogul cut it short, although its silence did not last long. When the prince thought he had sufficiently distracted the doddering jewel, he gave it liberty to speak again, and the chatterbox, bursting into laughter, resumed by way of recollection:

"By the way, I forgot to tell you what happened on Haria's wedding night. I have seen many ridiculous things in my time, but none so ridiculous as this. After a great feast, the newlyweds were led to their chambers. Everyone left except for Madame's women, who undressed her. Once undressed, she was put to bed, and Sindor was left alone with her. Noticing that the spaniel, the boxers, and the greyhound, more alert than he, were taking possession of the bride, he said, 'Permit me, Madame, to disperse these rivals.'

"'My dear, do what you can,' Haria said to him. 'As for me, I have not the heart to chase them away. The little animals are attached to me, and for a long time have been my only company.'

"'They might show me the courtesy,' replied Sindor, 'of ceding me the place that is rightfully mine today.'

"'We shall see,' said Madame.

"At first Sindor tried kindness, and begged Zinzolina to withdraw to a corner. But the intractable animal began to growl. Alarm spread throughout the pack, and the spaniel and the boxers barked as if their mistress were being murdered. Vexed by this racket, Sindor tossed one of the boxers away, shoved aside the spaniel, and seized Medor by the paw. Medor, faithful Medor, abandoned by his allies, tried to recover his losses with the advantages of his post. Glued to his mistress's flanks, eyes aflame, hair on end, and mouth agape, he puckered his snout and showed his enemy two rows of very sharp teeth. Sindor made several assaults on him. More than once Medor drove him back with nipped fingers and torn ruffles. The action had gone on for more than a quarter of an hour with a persistence that amused Haria alone, when Sindor, having no hope of conquering the enemy by force, resorted to trickery. He provoked Medor with his right hand. Medor was attentive to this movement and did not notice the left hand, which grabbed him by the collar. His struggles to free himself were in vain, and he was obliged to abandon the battlefield and surrender Haria. Sindor took possession of her, but not without bloodshed. In all likelihood, Haria had decided that the first night of her wedding should be bloody. Her animals put up a good defense and did not disappoint her expectations."

"Here is a jewel," thought Mangogul, "that could write my gazette better than my secretary." Knowing now what he wanted to know about the hounds, he returned to the favorite.

"Prepare yourself," he said from afar, as soon as he saw her, "to hear the most extraordinary things in the world. It is much worse than Palabria's dunces. Would you believe that Haria's four dogs were the rivals, the preferred rivals, of her husband, and that the death of a greyhound estranged these two forever after?"

"What are you saying about dogs and rivals?" answered the favorite. "I do not know what you are talking about. I know that Haria loves her dogs to distraction; but I know as well that Sindor is a hot-tempered man, who has perhaps shown fewer indulgences than might be expected toward the woman to whom he owes his fortune. Moreover, whatever his behavior, I cannot imagine that she could attract rivals. Haria is so venerable that I wish Your Highness would deign explain himself more clearly."

"Look here," said Mangogul, "you must admit that women have excessively whimsical tastes, to say the least."

Forthwith he recounted Haria's story, word for word as her jewel had told it. Mirzoza could not refrain from laughing at the battle on the wedding night. Collecting herself, she said to Mangogul in a more serious tone:

"I do not know why I feel such indignation. But from now on I shall dislike these animals and all those who have them, and declare to my women that I shall dismiss the first one suspected of keeping a hound."

"Pray," replied the Sultan, "why spread such hatred? There you go, you women, always acting in extremes! These animals are good for hunting, necessary in the country, and have I know not how many other uses, not to mention the one made by Haria."

"Indeed," said Mirzoza, "I am beginning to think that Your Highness will have trouble finding one virtuous woman."

"I told you so," said Mangogul, "but let us not be rash. You may one day reproach me for considering your impatience a confession of the sort I owe uniquely to the exploits of my ring. I have some in mind that will astonish you. All the secrets have not yet been revealed, and I expect to wrest more important discoveries from the jewels I have yet to consult.

Mirzoza still feared for her own. Mangogul's words threw her into such turmoil that she was not able to conceal it from him. But the Sultan, who was bound by oath, and who was religious to the depths of his soul, reassured her as best he could, gave her several tender kisses, and repaired to his council, where important matters awaited him.

CHAPTER XXVII

Eleventh Trial of the Ring
The Pensions

The Congo had been troubled by bloody wars during the reign of Kanoglou and Erguebzed, and these two monarchs immortalized themselves by their conquests of their neighbors. The Emperors of Abex and Angote regarded Mangogul's youth and the beginning of his reign as favorable indications that they might reappropriate the provinces that had been taken from them. Thus they declared war on the Congo, and attacked it from all sides. Mangogul's council was the best there was in Africa. The old Sambuco and the emir Mirzala, who had fought in the previous wars, were put in charge of the troops and won victory after victory. They also groomed generals capable of succeeding them, an accomplishment even more important than their immediate triumphs.

Thanks to the activity of the council and the excellent leadership of the generals, the enemy, who had thought themselves sure of success, did not get so far as our frontiers, badly defended their own, and saw their posts and their provinces ravaged. Nonetheless, in spite of such constant and glorious success, the Congo grew weaker as it grew larger. The frequent raising of troops had depopulated the towns and countryside, and the treasury was spent.

The sieges and fighting had cost a great number of lives. The grand vizier, hardly sparing of soldiers' blood, was accused of having waged battles that led to nothing. Every family was in mourning; there was nary a one that did not weep for a father, a brother, or a friend. The number of officers killed was prodigious, and could be compared to nothing save the number of their widows who now solicited pensions. They assailed the ministers, and overwhelmed the Sultan himself with petitions, in which the merit and service of the deceased, the grief of their widows, the suffering of their children, and other touching details were not omitted. Nothing seemed more justified than their demands – but how was one to fund pensions that added up to millions?

The ministers, having exhausted fine speeches and resorted to rough, peevish language at times, were forced to consider ways to bring this affair to an end; there was, however, one excellent reason for doing nothing at all: not a sou was left.

Mangogul, put out over the unsound arguments of his ministers and the lamentations of the widows, found the expedient that they had so long been seeking. "Gentlemen," he said to the council, "it seems to me that before granting the pensions it would only be right to examine the legitimacy of each claim."

"Such an examination," answered the Grand Seneschal, "will be vast and require endless debate. How shall we hold up against the cries and determinations of these women, by whom you, my lord, are driven to distraction?"

"It will not be as difficult as you imagine, Sir Seneschal," replied the Sultan, "and I promise you that by noon tomorrow all will be completed according to the most exacting laws of fairness. Simply grant them an audience with me at nine in the morning."

The council adjourned. The Grand Seneschal went back to his office, thought deeply, and drew up the following proclamation, which was printed three hours later and then announced to the sound of a trumpet and posted at every public place in Banza.

By Order of the Sultan and Monseigneur
The Grand Seneschal

We, Goosebeak, Grand Seneschal of the Congo, Vizier of the First Bench, Train-bearer to the Great Manimonbanda, Chief and Superintendent of the

Sweepers of the Divan, give notice that tomorrow, at nine o'clock in the morning, the magnanimous Sultan will give audience to the widows of the officers slain in his service to determine the legitimacy of the claims in light of their demands. Issued from our seneschalsy, the twelfth of the moon of Regeb, year 147,200,000,009.

None of the unfortunate women of the Congo, and there were many, failed to read the proclamation, or to send their footmen to read it, nor did they fail to appear at the appointed hour in the antechamber to the throne. "To avoid confusion," said the Sultan, "have these women enter six at a time. Once we have heard them, the door at the back that leads to my exterior courtyard will be opened for them. You, gentlemen, pay attention, and judge their demands."

This said, he signaled to the first usher, and the six who were closest to the door found themselves admitted. They entered in long mourning dresses, and solemnly greeted His Majesty. Mangogul addressed the youngest and prettiest. Her name was Isec. "Madame," he said, "has it been long since you lost your husband?"

"Three months, my lord," Isec answered, weeping. "He was a lieutenant general in Your Majesty's service. He was killed in the last battle, and six children are all that he has left me."

"That *he* left you?" interrupted a voice that, though issuing from Isec, was not exactly the same as hers. "Madame knows better than that. They were all begun and ended by a young Brahmin who came to comfort her when Monsieur was at war."

One may easily guess from whence issued the indiscreet voice that uttered this response. Poor Isec, mortified, grew pale, reeled about, and fainted.

"Madame is suffering from the vapors," Mangogul said calmly. "Someone carry her to an apartment in the seraglio and assist her." Then turning immediately to Phenica:

"Madame," he asked her, "was not your husband a pasha?"

"Yes, my lord," Phenica answered in a trembling voice.

"And how did you lose him?"

"My lord, he died in his bed, exhausted by the pressures of the last campaign."

"Exertions of the last campaign indeed!" retorted Phenica's jewel. "Really, Madame, your husband returned from the battlefield in sound and solid health; and he would have it still, if not for two or three mountebanks...you know what I mean; be careful what you say..."

"Write down," said the Sultan, "that Phenica requests a pension for the good services she rendered to the state and to her husband."

A third was asked the name and age of her husband, who was said to have died in the army, of smallpox.

"Smallpox!" said her jewel, "well, I never! Tell him, Madame, about the blows he received from the sanjak Cavaglio's scimitar when he became incensed that people were saying his oldest son was the spitting image of the Sanjak. Madame knows as well as I," added the jewel, "that never was a resemblance truer."

The fourth was about to speak, when her jewel was heard to cry out from the lower regions that during the ten years of the war she had made pretty good use of her time; that two pages and a great scamp of a footman had stood in for her husband; and that no doubt she intended the pension for the actor she kept from the Opéra-Comique.

A fifth advanced fearlessly and with an air of confidence asked to be compensated for the military services of her late husband, Aga of the janissaries, who had lost his life on the walls of Matatras. The Sultan turned his ring toward her, but to no effect. Her jewel was mute. "It must be noted," says the African author, who had seen her, "that she was so ugly that one would have been very surprised had her jewel had something to say."

Mangogul had come to the sixth, and here are the very words spoken by her jewel:

"Really, she is fortunate indeed," it said, referring to the woman whose jewel had obstinately kept silent, "to solicit pensions, when she lives the high life; she keeps a brelan table, which yields her more than three thousand sequins a year; she holds suppers at the players' expense, and she received six hundred sequins from Osman to lure me to one of those suppers, where that traitor Osman..."

"Due respects will be paid to your petitions, ladies," the Sultan said to them. "You may leave now."

Addressing his advisers, Mangogul asked them if they found it ridiculous to grant pensions to the little bastards of Brahmins and others, and to women who spent their time dishonoring the brave fellows who set out in search of glory in his services, at the cost of their lives.

The Senechal rose, replied, held forth, recapitulated, and spoke obscurely, as was his wont. While he was speaking, Isec, recovered from her fainting spell and furious about the experience, no longer expected a pension for herself but was distraught that another might receive one, which would in all likelihood have happened. She returned to the antechamber and whispered into the ears of two or three of her friends that they had been assembled merely so the chatter of their jewels might be listened to at leisure. She added that she herself had heard one, whom she would not name, tell shocking things in the audience chamber, and that a woman had to be mad to expose herself to such danger.

This word of warning passed from one to the next, dispersing the crowd of widows. When the usher opened the door a second time, none remained.

"Very well, Seneschal, will you believe me next time?" Mangogul asked this good man, slapping him on the back, when he heard of the desertion. "I promised to deliver you from these weepers, and now you are rid of them. They pursued you quite diligently, in spite of your ninety-five years. But whatever your expectations, for I know how easily you form such expectations with regard to these women, I hope you will be grateful to me for their disappearence. They caused you more worry than pleasure."

The African author tells us that the memory of this trial was preserved in the Congo, and that this is why the government is so sparing in granting pensions. But this was not the only beneficial effect of Cucufa's ring, as we shall see in the next chapter.

CHAPTER XXVIII

Twelfth Trial of the Ring
Questions of Law

Rape was severely punished in the Congo, and there occurred in Mangogul's reign a most notorious case. When he took the crown, this prince had sworn, like his predecessors, never to pardon this crime. Laws, severe as they might be, never deter those bent on breaking them. The guilty party was condemned to lose that part of himself with which he had sinned, a cruel operation from which he usually perished, since he who performed it used considerably less caution than Petit.[1]

Kersael, a young man of good family, had now languished for six months in jail while awaiting this punishment. Fatma, a young and pretty woman, was his Lucretia and his accuser. They had been very close at one time; everyone knew this, and, as Fatma's indulgent husband took no exception to it, it would have been tasteless for the public to meddle in their affairs.

After two years of tranquillity, through inconstancy or distaste, Kersael took a fancy to a dancer at the Banza Opera and neglected Fatma, though without openly breaking off with her. He resolved to make a decent retreat, which obliged him still to visit her. Fatma, furious about this neglect, contemplated revenge, and took advantage of what was left of his attentiveness to destroy her unfaithful lover.

One day when the accommodating husband had left them alone, Kersael, having unbuckled his scimitar, tried to soothe Fatma's suspicions with the sort of protestations that come effortlessly to lovers but never persuade a jealous woman. Fatma, wild-eyed, set her dress in disarray with five or six strokes of her hand, screamed dreadfully, and called her husband and servants to her assistance. They came running and became witnesses to the offense Fatma claimed to have received from Kersael. She showed the scimitar "that the wretch raised to my head ten times to make me submit to his desires."

The young man, dumbfounded by the heinousness of the accusation, had neither the strength to answer nor the strength to flee. He was seized, led to prison, and abandoned to the prosecution of the Cadilesker.[2]

The laws required that Fatma be examined, and this was done. The report of the matrons was very unfavorable to the accused. They had a protocol whereby they ascertained the state of a violated woman, and all the necessary conditions conspired against Kersael. The judges questioned him; Fatma confronted him; testimony was heard. Try as he might to protest his innocence, to deny the deed and show that because of the intimacy he had shared with his accuser for more than two years, she was hardly a woman he might ravish, the presence of the scimitar, the solitude of the tête-à-tête, Fatma's cries, and Kersael's confusion at the sight of husband and servants – all these things constituted, according to the judges, overwhelming circumstantial evidence. For her part, Fatma, far from admitting favors granted, did not acknowledge even having given him a shred of hope, and maintained that her strong sense of duty, which she had never relinquished, had no doubt pushed Kersael to wrest from her by force what he despaired of obtaining from her by seduction. The matrons' deposition was another terrible thing; one had only to glance through it and compare it to the provisions of the penal code to see therein the condemnation of the unfortunate Kersael. He could expect salvation neither from his defense nor from the influence of his family. The magistrates had set the date for the definitive sentence of his case for the thirteenth of the moon of Regeb. It had even been announced to the public, with a blast of a trumpet, according to custom.

This affair became the topic of many a conversation, and it divided public opinion for quite some time. Some prudish old women, such as never had cause to fear rape, went about crying "that Kersael's crime was serious indeed, and that unless a severe example were made of him, innocence would never be safe again, and an honest woman would risk outrage even at the foot of the altar." Then they cited examples in which impudent rogues had dared attack the virtue of respectable women, and the details left no doubt that the respectable women in question were themselves. And all these statements were made to Brahmins less innocent than Kersael, by pious women as virtuous as Fatma, in the form of edifying exchanges.

The fops, on the other hand, and even a few belles, maintained that rape did not exist, that women never surrendered except by capitulation and that, if a fort is defended, be it ever so little, it is absolutely impossible to take it by force. Examples followed to support these arguments; the women knew of cases firsthand; the fops made them up, and they ceaselessly cited instances in which women had not been ravished. "Poor Kersael," they said, "what the devil prompted him to take up with little Bimbreloqua (which was the dancer's name)? Why not stick with Fatma? He was better off with her; the husband let them alone; it was a blessing. The matrons, those witches, forgot to put on their glasses!" they added. "They did not see a thing! Besides, who sees very clearly down there? The Senators will deprive him of his joy for having broken down an open door. The poor lad will die from it, that is certain. And we shall see, after this, the sorts of things dissatisfied women will be allowed to do..."

"If this execution takes place," interrupted another, "I shall become a Freemason."

Mirzoza, a naturally compassionate woman, pointed out to Mangogul, who for his part was making light of Kersael's fate, that whereas the laws argued against Kersael, common sense testified against Fatma.

"It is unheard of in any case," she added, "that a good government should so adhere to the letter of the law that the simple allegation of an accuser suffices to place a citizen in peril of his life. The reality of rape is not so easily proven, and you will agree, my lord, that this falls at least as much within the jurisdiction of your ring as within that of your senators. It would be most unusual if the matrons knew more about this than the jewels themselves do. Until now, my lord, Your Highness's ring has done little more than satisfy your curiosity. Might not the genie from whom you acquired it have intended more important uses for it? If you use it to uncover truth and to make your subjects happy, do you think that Cucufa would take offense? Try. You have in your hand an infallible way to draw from Fatma a confession of her crime or proof of her innocence."

"You are right," answered Mangogul, "and you shall be satisfied."

The Sultan left at once; he had no time to lose, for it was the evening of the twelfth of the moon of Regeb, and the Senate was to make its pronouncement on the thirteenth. Fatma had just gone to bed. The curtains were partly opened. A candle cast a dim light on her face. The Sultan thought her beautiful, in spite of the violent agitation that contorted her features. Compassion and hatred, grief and revenge, audacity and shame were painted in her eyes, as they followed one upon the other in her heart. She sighed deeply, shed a few tears, dried them, shed them anew, remained a few moments with head bowed and eyes lowered, then raised her eyes abruptly and looked fiercely heavenward. What was Mangogul doing in the meantime? He was talking to himself, saying softly, "These are the symptoms of despair. Her old tenderness for Kersael is reawakened in all its fury. She has lost sight of the offense done her and thinks only of the tortures awaiting her lover." Having thus spoken, he turned the fatal ring toward Fatma and her jewel cried out excitedly:

"Twelve more hours and we shall be avenged. He will die, the traitor, the ungrateful wretch, and his blood will flow..." Fatma, terrified by the extraordinary emotions coursing through her, and struck by the muffled voice of her jewel, clapped both hands to it, trying thus to silence it. But the powerful ring continued to act upon it, and the indocile jewel, overcoming all obstacles, added, "Yes, we will be avenged. You shall die, unhappy Kersael, my betrayer; and you whom he preferred to me, you, Bimbreloqua, shall despair... Twelve more hours! How long this time will seem to me. Do hurry, sweet moment when I shall see the traitor, the ungrateful Kersael, beneath the executioner's knife, his blood flowing... Ah! Wretch, what have I said?... Would I not shudder to see the object I most loved perish? Would I see the fatal knife raised... Ah! Begone cruel thought... He hates me, it is true, he has left me for Bimbreloqua, but perhaps one day... What am I saying, perhaps! Love will no doubt bring him back under my sway. This little Bimbreloqua is but a passing fancy; sooner or later he will realize the unjustness of his preference and the ridiculousness of his new choice. Console yourself, Fatma, you shall see him yet. Get up at once, run, fly to prevent the terrible danger that threatens him. Do you not tremble to arrive too late? But whither shall I fly, fainthearted me? Did not Kersael's scorn tell me he had left for good? He belongs to Bimbreloqua; and it is for her I would save him! Ah! Let him die a thousand deaths! If he no longer lives for me, what do I care if he dies?... Yes, I feel it, my wrath is justified. The ungrateful Kersael deserves all my hatred. I shall regret nothing. Once I did everything in my power to keep him. Now

I shall do everything I can to destroy him. Nevertheless, one more day and my revenge would have missed its mark. But his ill luck delivered him to me, at the very moment he was escaping me. He fell right into the trap I set for him. I caught him. The rendezvous I contrived to bring you to was the last you planned to give me: but you shall not forget me so easily...How artfully you led him where you wanted him, Fatma! How well you effected your disarray! Your cries, your pain, your tears, your confusion, everything, even your silence, has ruined Kersael. Nothing can save him from the fate that awaits him. Kersael is dead...You cry, unhappy woman. He loved another, what do you care if he dies?"

Mangogul was filled with horror at this speech. He turned the ring around, and while Fatma came to herself again, he flew back to the Sultana.

"Well, my lord," she said to him, "what have you learned? Is Kersael still guilty and the chaste Fatma..."

"I beg you," answered the Sultan, "do not ask me to repeat the abominations I have just heard! How fearsome is an angry woman! Who would believe that a body shaped by the graces could at times contain a heart formed by the furies? But the sun shall not set on my dominions tomorrow before they are purged of a more dangerous monster than the ones born in my deserts."

The Sultan then called the Grand Seneschal, ordered him to seize Fatma, to transfer Kersael to one of the apartments in the seraglio, and to announce to the Senate that His Highness was himself assuming jurisdiction over the affair. His orders were carried out that same night.

The next day, at daybreak, the Sultan, accompanied by the Seneschal and an effendi, went to Mirzoza's chambers and had Fatma led in. This unhappy woman threw herself at Mangogul's feet, confessed her crime in full, and begged Mirzoza to intercede on her behalf. Meanwhile Kersael was brought in. He expected to die, yet he appeared with the self-assurance that innocence alone can grant. A few practical jokers quipped that he would have been more concerned had that which he risked losing been worth the trouble; the ladies pressed them to explain. Kersael bowed down respectfully before His Highness. Mangogul signaled him to rise, and said, holding out his hand to him:

"You are innocent, you may go free. Thank Brahma for your salvation. To compensate you for the injustice you have suffered, I grant you two thousand sequins from my treasury as a pension, and the first available commandery in the Order of the Crocodile."

The more favors bestowed on Kersael, the more Fatma feared her punishment. The Grand Seneschal held out for death, according to the law *si foemina ff. de vi C. calumniatrix*. The Sultan was in favor of life imprisonment. Mirzoza, finding one judgment too harsh and the other too lenient, condemned Fatma's jewel to lock and key. The Florentine instrument[3] was applied in public, upon the very scaffolding erected for Kersael's execution. From there she was conducted to a house of correction, along with the matrons who had decided this case so intelligently.

CHAPTER XXIX

Mirzoza's Metaphysics
The Souls

While Mangogul was questioning the jewels of Haria, the widows, and Fatma, Mirzoza had full time to prepare her philosophy lesson. One evening when the Manimonbanda was performing her devotions and there were no gaming tables or drawing rooms active at Court, and the favorite was almost sure of the Sultan's visit, she took two black petticoats, put one on the usual way and the other on her shoulders, pushing her arms through the slits; she donned a wig from Mangogul's seneschal, a square hat from his chaplain, and believed herself to be dressed in the manner of a philosopher, whereas she was, in fact, disguised as a bat.

Thus attired, she walked to and fro in her chambers like a professor at the Royal College waiting for his students. She affected even the somber and studied countenance of a scholar thinking. Not for long did Mirzoza retain this forced seriousness. The Sultan entered with a few of his courtiers and bowed deeply to the new philosopher. Her gravity disconcerted her audience, and she was in turn disconcerted by the bursts of laughter she provoked.

"Madame," Mangogul said to her, "have you not enough advantages as far as your wit and figure, without resorting to that of the robe as well? Without it, your words would yet have carried all the weight you might wish."

"It seems to me, my lord," answered Mirzoza, "that you hold little respect for this robe, and that a disciple ought to have more regard for the thing that creates at least half his master's merit."

"I perceive," replied the Sultan, "that you have already assumed the spirit and the tone of your new position. At present I have no doubts that your abilities are equal to the dignity of your attire, and I await the proof of this impatiently."

"You shall be satisfied directly," answered Mirzoa, sitting down in the middle of a large couch.

The Sultan and the courtiers seated themselves around her and she began, "Did the philosophers of Monoemugi, who presided over Your Highness's education, ever hold forth on the nature of the soul?"

"Oh yes, often," answered Mangogul, "but all their systems succeeded only in giving me vague notions of it; and without an inner feeling that might suggest to me that it is a substance different from matter, I would either have denied its existence or confused it with that of the body. Are you undertaking to clarify this mess?"

"Far from it," answered Mirzoza, "and I confess that I am hardly more advanced than your pedagogues on this issue. The only difference between them and me is that I presume the existence of a substance different from matter, whereas they take it as proven fact. But this substance, if it exists, must be nestled someplace. Have they not spouted many foolish things on this subject?"

"No," answered Mangogul. "All more or less agree that it resides in the head, and this opinion seems likely to me. The head thinks, imagines, reflects, judges, disposes, and commands, and, every day, people say of a man who does not think that he has no brain or lacks a head on his shoulders."

"So your long studies and all your philosophy," continued the Sultana, "are thus reduced to presuming a thing and applying it to popular expressions. Prince, what would you say to your top geographer if, presenting Your Highness with a map of his states, he put the east in the west or the north in the south?"

"That is too gross an error," answered Mangogul. "A geographer would never make such a mistake."

"Perhaps not," continued the favorite, "but in that case your philosophers were clumsier than the clumsiest geographer would ever be. They did not have a vast empire to survey; they were not asked to define the limits of the four corners of the earth; they had only to look into themselves and locate the true site of their souls. Nonetheless they put east west, or south north. They pronounced that the soul is in the head, whereas most men die without it ever having dwelt there, for its first place of residence is in the feet."

"In the feet?" interrupted the Sultan. "That is the most preposterous notion I have ever heard."

"Yes, in the feet," continued Mirzoza, "and this notion, which appears so mad to you, has only to be examined to become sensible, contrary to all those that you find true and which are recognized as false upon closer inspection. Your Highness agreed with me just now that the existence of the soul was founded on an inner testimony alone, which it gives itself; I shall now show him that all imaginable proofs of this idea contribute to situating the soul in the place I ascribe it."

"That is what we are waiting to hear," said Mangogul.

"I am not asking for any favors," she continued, "and I invite you to propose to me any objections that might occur to you.

"I said to you that the soul has its first abode in the feet; it is in the feet that it begins to exist, and through them it advances throughout the body. I shall call upon experience to support this fact, and shall perhaps lay the first foundations of an experimental metaphysics.

"We have all seen that in infancy the sleeping soul remains for whole months in a state of torpor. The eyes open without sight, the mouth without speech, the ears without hearing. Elsewhere the soul seeks to expand and awaken; only in other limbs does it exercise its first functions. A child's formation is first announced with his feet. His body, head, and arms are immobile in his mother's womb, but his feet stretch out, kick, and manifest his existence and needs. Come time to be born, what would become of the head, body, and arms – they could never leave their prison without the help of the feet: the feet play the principal role, and chase the rest of the body before them. Such is the natural order, and when any other limb tries to mix itself up in their command, when the head, for example, takes the place of the feet, everything turns askew, and God knows what sometimes befalls the mother and child.

"Once the child is born, again the feet make the first moves. People are obliged to restrain them, for they are never still. The head is a block with which one may do as one pleases, but the feet feel, shake off the yoke, and seem jealously to guard the freedom of which we would deprive them.

"Once the child can stand alone, the feet make a thousand attempts to move; they set everything into motion; they command the other limbs, and the dutiful hands lean up against walls, and fly in front to prevent falls and facilitate the action of the feet.

"Where do a child's thoughts turn, and what are his pleasures once he is confident on his legs and his feet acquire the habit of moving about? He thinks of nothing but using them – going, coming, running, jumping, capering. This turbulence pleases us, for it is a sign of spirit, and we predict that a child will be stupid if we see him indolent and sullen. If you want to make a four-year-old unhappy, sit him down for fifteen minutes, or hold him prisoner between four chairs: anger and vexation will seize hold of him, especially since it is not his legs alone that you thus deprive of exercise; it is his soul you hold captive.

"The soul remains in the feet until the age of two or three. At four it inhabits the legs, and reaches the knees and the thighs at fifteen. At that time, young people love dancing, fencing, racing, and other rigorous exercises of the body. These are the favorite pastimes of all young people, and the passions of some. Does not the soul reside in the places where it manifests itself almost uniquely, and where it experiences the most agreeable sensations? And if its residence varies from childhood to youth, would it not vary throughout the course of a lifetime?"

Mirzoza delivered this speech so rapidly, she was left breathless. Selim, one of the Sultan's favorites, took advantage of a moment in which she was catching her breath to say to her, "Madame, I shall make use of the liberty you granted us to raise objections. Your system is ingenious, and you have presented it with as much grace as clarity. However, I am not so seduced by it to believe it proven. It seems to me that one could argue that in childhood the head rules the feet, and that from the head issue the spirits. Spreading through the nerves into all the other limbs, these spirits stop or activate them according to the will of the soul, which resides in the pineal gland, just as His Highness's orders, which govern his subjects' actions, emanate from the Sublime Porte."

"Undoubtedly," replied Mirzoza, "but in so saying, one would be telling me something questionable, to which I would respond with a personal observation. In childhood there is no certainty that the head thinks, and you yourself, my lord, who have such a good head and who, in your most tender years, passed for a prodigy, do you remember thinking at that time? You may very well be assured that when you romped about like a little demon, driving your governesses to distraction, it was your feet that governed your head."

"That proves nothing," said the Sultan. "Selim was very spirited and so are hundreds of other children. They never reflect, but they do think; time goes by, the memory of things slips away, and they do not remember having thought."

"But where does this thought originate?" replied Mirzoza. "For that is the point of the question."

"From the head," answered Selim.

"Always this head, where one cannot see a thing," answered the Sultana. "Pray, drop this dark lantern in which you presume a light, seen by none save he who holds it. Now listen to my observations and grant the truth of my hypothesis. So certain is it that the soul begins in the feet, that there are men and women in whom it never rises any higher.

My lord, many a time you have admired Nini's agility and Saligo's speed; answer me sincerely, then – do you think that these creatures have the soul elsewhere than in their legs? And have you not noticed that in Volucer and Zelindor the head obeys the feet? The eternal temptation of a dancer is to contemplate his legs. At every step his attentive eyes follow his foot's lead, and his head bows respectfully before the feet, as invincible pashas bow down before His Highness."

"I acknowledge the observation," said Selim, "but I disagree that generalizations can be drawn from it."

"I am not claiming," replied Mirzoza, "that the soul resides in the feet alone; it moves along, travels, leaves one spot, comes back to it only to leave it again; but I maintain that the other limbs are always subordinated to the one in which the soul resides. This varies according to age, temperament, and circumstance. From there, differences of taste, diversities of inclinations and characters are born. Do you not admire the fruitfulness of my system? Do not the multitude of phenomena it covers prove its certainty?"

"Madame," Selim answered her, "if you give us a few examples, perhaps we shall attain a degree of conviction, which we still lack."

"Willingly," replied Mirzoza, who was beginning to feel her advantage. "You shall be satisfied, just follow the train of my thoughts. I do not pretend to formal argumentation; I speak from the heart. This is the philosophy of my sex, and you men understand it almost as well as we do. It is quite likely," she went on, "that the soul inhabits the feet and legs until the age of eight or ten, but then, or perhaps even later, it abandons this abode either of its own accord or by force. By force, that is, when a tutor uses strategies to chase it from its native land and to lead it to the brain, where it usually transforms itself into memory, and very occasionally, if ever, into judgment. Such is the fate of schoolboys. Similarly, if it happens that a foolish governess labors hard to form a young girl and crams her mind with facts, neglecting her heart and morals, the soul rapidly flees to the head, stops on the tongue, or sticks in the eyes; and this pupil is merely a tiresome prattler, or a flirt.

"Thus the voluptuous woman is she whose soul resides in her jewel, and never strays from there.

"The gallant woman is she whose soul is in her jewel one moment, in her eyes the next.

"The affectionate woman, she whose soul is usually in her heart, but sometimes also in her jewel.

"The virtuous woman, she whose soul is now in her head, now in her heart, but never elsewhere.

"If the soul stays in the heart, it forms a sensitive, compassionate, true and generous character. If, leaving the heart, never to return, it burrows into the head, then it forms those we call hard, ungrateful, sly, and cruel.

"Many are those in whom the soul visits the head as if it were a country house, where the stay is brief. These are the fops, flirts, musicians, poets, novelists, courtiers, and all those whom we call pretty women. Listen to these people argue, and you will immediately recognize vagabond souls that are influenced by the different climes they inhabit."

"If this be so," said Selim, "then nature has created many useless things. And yet our sages maintain as a constant maxim that nature has produced nothing in vain."

"Let us leave your sages and their lofty sayings out of this," said Mirzoza. "As for nature, if we look at her through the eyes of experience, we learn that she has placed the soul in man's body as if in a vast palace, in which it does not always occupy the finest chambers. The head and the heart are the principal destinations intended for it, as the center of virtue and the site of truth; but more often it stops along the way, preferring a hovel, a place of dubious character, or a miserable inn where it goes to sleep in perpetual torpor. Ah, if only for twenty-four hours I could arrange the world according to whim, I would amuse you with a strange sight indeed: in an instant I would deprive each soul of the superflous aspects of its abode, and you would see each person characterized by what remained to him. Dancers would be reduced to two feet, or two legs at the very most; singers, to a throat; most women, to a jewel; heroes and bullies, to an armed fist; certain scholars, to a skull without a brain. All that would remain of a cardplayer would be two hands ceaselessly shuffling cards; a glutton, two jaws in constant motion; a flirt, two eyes; a rake, the sole instrument of his passion; the ignorant and the lazy would be reduced to nothing."

"Just grant women hands," interrupted the Sultan, "and those men reduced to the sole instrument of their passions would be pursued. It would be a pleasant chase to see, and if women everywhere were as greedy for these birds as in the Congo, the species would soon die out."

"And what of tender, sensitive women, or faithful and constant lovers? Of what would they be made?" Selim asked the favorite.

"A heart," answered the favorite, "and I know well," she added, looking tenderly at Mangogul, "which heart mine would seek to join."

The Sultan could not resist this talk. He bolted from his armchair toward the favorite: his courtiers disappeared, and the new philosopher's chair became the theater of their pleasures. Several times he proved to her that he was no less delighted with her sentiments than with her discourse, and her philosophical trappings were put in disarray. Mirzoza returned the black petticoats to her women, sent the enormous wig back to the Seneschal and the square hat to the Abbot, with the assurance that he would be on the list for the next nomination. Yet what might have been his fate, had he been a bit more clever? A seat in the academy was the least he might have hoped for as compensation; but unfortunately he knew only two or three hundred words and had never succeeded in creating so much as a refrain or two with them.

CHAPTER XXX

Continuation of the Preceding Conversation

Mangogul was the only one who had listened to Mirzoza's philosophy lesson without interrupting her. Since he quite readily contradicted people, she was astonished by this.

"Could it be that the Sultan accepts my system in its entirety?" she asked herself. "No, that is not likely. Perhaps he found it too weak to deign contest it? That may be. My ideas are not, admittedly, the soundest ever had; but they are not the least sound either. I do believe that people have at times had worse ideas than mine."

To clarify this doubt, the favorite decided to question Mangogul.

"Well, Prince," she said to him, "what do you think of my system?"

"It is admirable," answered the Sultan. "I can find but one flaw in it."

"And what is that?" the favorite asked him.

"That it is as untrue," said Mangogul, "as it could possibly be. According to you we all have souls. This assumption lacks common sense, my heart's delight. Take the following argument: 'I have a soul; and here is an animal that most of the time acts as if it had none; perhaps it has none, even if it acts as if it did. It has a nose like mine. I feel that I have a soul and that I think: therefore this animal has a soul and also thinks.' People have been making this argument for a thousand years and the idea is as impertinent now as it was a thousand years ago."

"I admit" said the favorite, "that it is not always obvious that other people think."

"Add to that," continued Mangogul, "that hundreds of times it is obvious that they do not."

"But it seems to me that it would be going too far to conclude from this," said Mirzoza, "that they have never thought, nor ever will. One is not always a fool for having been so at times, and Your Highness —"

Mirzoza, fearing lest she offend the Sultan, stopped abruptly.

"Continue, Madame," Mangogul said to her. "I understand – has My Highness never acted the fool, you wanted to say, did you not? I answer you that I have now and then, and that I even forgive others for thinking of me as such, and you can be sure that they have done so, although they would never dare to tell me so..."

"Oh, Prince!" cried the favorite. "If men denied a soul to the greatest monarch on earth, to whom would they grant one?"

"Enough compliments," said Mangogul. "For a moment I have put aside my scepter and my crown. I have ceased to be a Sultan in order to be a philosopher, and I may hear and speak the truth. I have, I believe, given you proof of being the first; and you have felt free to insinuate, without offending me, that at times I have been a mere fool. Allow me to carry out the duties of my new role.

"Far from agreeing with you," he continued, "that every creature that has legs, arms, hands, eyes, and ears like me must also have a soul like me, I tell you that I am thoroughly persuaded that three-quarters of men and all women are no more than automatons."

"There may well be," replied the favorite, "as much truth as politeness in what you say."

"Oh, do not take offense, Madame," said the Sultan, "But why the devil did you think yourself a philosopher if you did not wish to hear the truth? Does one go to school looking for politeness? I have given you elbow room; leave some to me too, if you please. As I was saying, then, all women are animals."

"Yes, Prince, but you have yet to prove it," added Mirzoza.

"Nothing could be easier," answered the Sultan.

He then set about recounting all the insolent, oft-repeated charges, with the least amount of wit and delicacy possible, against the sex that possesses both of these qualities in the highest degree. Never had Mirzoza's patience been put to a greater test; and never would you be more bored in all your life were I to report Mangogul's arguments in their entirety. This prince, who did not lack common sense, was unimaginably absurd that day, as you shall see.

"It is so true, by Jupiter," he said, "that women are mere animals that I wager that in turning Cucufa's ring on my mare I will make it speak like a woman."

"That," said Mirzoza, "would be the strongest case that has ever been, or ever will be made against us."

Then she began to laugh like a madwoman. Mangogul, vexed by this unending laughter, left abruptly, resolved to try the bizarre experiment that had just seized his fancy.

CHAPTER XXXI

Thirteenth Trial of the Ring
The Little Mare

I am not a great portraitist. I have spared the reader the portrait of the favorite sultana, but I could never spare him that of the Sultan's mare. Her height was average; her bearing was good enough; people reproached her only for letting her head fall forward a bit. She was blonde, with blue eyes, a small foot, thin legs, firm hocks, and light haunches. Long ago she had been taught to dance, and she bowed like a master of ceremonies at a red mass.[1] On the whole she was quite a pretty animal, and sweet-tempered above all. She was easily mounted, but one had to be an excellent horseman to stay in the saddle. She had belonged to a senator named Aaron, but one fine evening the skittish creature bolted, raised four hooves in the air, threw her distinguished rider, and ran off at full speed to the Sultan's studs, carrying on her back saddle, bridle, harness, saddlecloth, and fancy caparison, all of which suited her so well that it was deemed unnecessary to return them.

Mangogul went down to his stables, accompanied by his first secretary, Zigzag.

"Listen carefully," he said to him, "and take notes."

Immediately he turned his ring on the mare, which began to hop, frisk, jib, bolt, and whinny under its tail.

"What are you waiting for?" the Prince asked his secretary. "Write!"

"Sultan," answered Zigzag, "I am waiting for Your Highness to begin..."

"My mare," said Mangogul, "will dictate to you this time."

Zigzag, humiliated by this command, took the liberty to tell the Sultan that he had always considered himself honored indeed to be his secretary, but not his mare's.

"Write, I tell you," repeated the Sultan.

"Prince, I cannot," replied Zigzag. "I do not know the spelling of this sort of words."

"Write, I say," the Sultan repeated.

"I am sorry to disobey Your Highness," added Zigzag, "but..."

"You are a rascal," interrupted Mangogul, irritated at such an impertinent refusal. "Leave my palace at once, and never come back."

The poor Zigzag disappeared, taught by this experience that a sensitive man should never enter into the service of most great men, or he should leave his feelings at the door. His assistant was called in. He was a true Provencal, honest, but above all disinterested. He flew whither he imagined his duty and fortune called him, bowed deeply to the Sultan, and more deeply still to his mare, and wrote down everything that it pleased the mare to dictate.

I refer all those who might be curious about this discourse to the Congo archives. The Prince immediately had copies of it distributed to his interpreters and professors of foreign languages, both ancient and modern. One said it was a scene from a Greek tragedy which seemed to him touching indeed; another succeeded, by sheer force of will, in discovering that it was an important fragment of Egyptian theology; another claimed it was the exordium of Hannibal's funeral oration in the Punic tongue; yet another claimed that it was from the Chinese, and that it was a very devout prayer to Confucius.

While these erudite men were trying the Sultan's patience with their learned conjectures, he remembered Gulliver's travels, and did not doubt that a man who had stayed as long as this Englishman had on an island where horses had a government, laws, kings, gods, priests, religion, temples, and altars, and who seemed so perfectly instructed in their manners and customs, would have a perfect knowledge of their language. In fact, Gulliver read and translated fluently the entire discourse of the mare in spite of the many spelling mistakes. Indeed it is the only good translation in the entire Congo. Mangogul learned, to his satisfaction and to the credit of his system, that it was an abridged history of the loves of an old three-tailed pasha[2] and a little mare, which had been mounted by a great number of jackasses before him; an unusual tale, the veracity of which was not unknown to the Sultan or any other at Court, in Banza or the rest of the empire.

CHAPTER XXXII

Perhaps the Best, and the Least Read, of this Story
Mangogul's Dream; or, A Journey to the Land of Hypotheses

"Ohhh," said Mangogul, yawning and rubbing his eyes, "I have a headache. Let no one speak to me of philosophy ever again; these conversations are unwholesome. Yesterday I went to bed with empty ideas, and instead of sleeping like a sultan, my brain worked harder than my ministers work in a year. You laugh, but to convince you that I do not exaggerate, and to avenge myself for the bad night your arguments gave me, you shall have to endure my dream in its entirety.

"I began to fall asleep and my imagination to soar when I saw a most unusual animal leap up beside me. It had an eagle's head, a griffin's feet, a horse's body, and a lion's tail. I seized it in spite of its caracoles, and, holding on to its mane, I leapt lightly onto its back. Immediately it spread two long wings that grew from its flanks and I found myself traveling through the air with incredible speed.

"We had covered a great distance when I noticed a castle suspended in the haze as if by magic. It was vast. And I could not say that its foundations were faulty merely because it was built on thin air. Its columns, which were not half a foot in diameter, rose up as far as the eye could see, and supported vaults that one could make out only by virtue of the apertures with which they were symmetrically pierced.

"At the entrance to this edifice my mount stopped. At first I hesitated to dismount, for it seemed less dangerous to stay on my hippogriff than to walk under this portico. Reassured, however, by the multitude of inhabitants and by the remarkable confidence that prevailed on every face, I dismounted, forged ahead, and threw myself into the crowd, scrutinizing the people in it.

"They were old men, either bloated or scrawny, neither plump nor strong, and almost all misshapen. One had a head too small, another arms too short. This one was deficient in body, that one in legs. Most of them had no feet and went about on crutches. A gust of wind was enough to make them fall, and they remained on the ground until some newcomer felt like picking them up. In spite of all these defects, the first impression they gave was pleasing. In their physiognomy they had something at once engaging and fearless. They were almost naked, for their only clothing consisted of little shreds of cloth that did not cover even one one-hundredth of their bodies.

"I continued to force my way through the crowd and I reached the foot of a rostrum upon which a large spiderweb served as a dais. Moreover, the boldness of its construction corresponded to that of the building; it looked to me as if balanced on the point of a needle, poised in equilibrium. Many a time I trembled for the person on it. He was an old man with a long beard, more shriveled and naked than any of his disciples. He dipped a reed into a cup filled with a thin liquid, which he then raised to his lips, and blew bubbles to a throng of spectators surrounding him, who tried to drive them up toward the clouds.

" 'Where am I?' I said to myself, confused by these childish antics. 'What is the meaning of this reed-blower with his bubbles and these decrepit children making them fly about? Who will explain these things to me?' The little scraps of cloth caught my attention again, and I noticed that the larger they were the less those that wore them were interested in the bubbles. This unusual observation encouraged me to approach the one who seemed to me the least undressed of the lot.

"There was one whose shoulders were half covered with scraps of cloth so well sewn together that the seams were not visible. He came and went in the crowd, troubling himself little with what was going on there. I found him pleasant looking, with a smiling face, a noble bearing, and a mild gaze, and I went right up to him.

"'Who are you? Where am I? And who are all these people?' I asked him without ceremony.

"'I am Plato,' he answered me. 'You are in the Land of Hypotheses, and these people are systematics.'

"'What brings the divine Plato to a place like this?' I asked him. 'And what is he doing among these fools?'

"'Finding recruits,' he said to me. 'Far from this portico I have a little sanctuary to which I bring those who abandon systems.'

"'And how do you keep them busy?'

"'With learning about man, practicing virtue, and sacrificing to the Graces.'

"'Those are fine occupations; but what are these shreds of cloth, which make you look more like beggars than philosophers?'

"'Ah, what a question.' he said, sighing. 'It stirs old memories in me. This was once the temple of philosophy. Alas! How it has changed. Socrates' chair was over there...'

"'What!' I interrupted him. 'Did Socrates have a reed and did he also blow bubbles?'

"'No, he did not,' Plato answered me. 'That was not how he earned the privilege of being called the wisest of men by the gods. He formed minds, he formed hearts – that is how he spent his life. The secret was lost when he died. Socrates died and the flowering of philosophy was past. These scraps of cloth that the systematics give themselves the honor of wearing are shreds of his cloak. His eyes were barely closed when those who aspired to the title of philosopher threw themselves on his cloak and tore it to shreds.'

"'I see,' I said. 'And these scraps served as labels both to them and their long posterity...'

"'Who will collect these pieces,' continued Plato, 'and restore Socrates' cloak to us?'

"He was making this pathetic exclamation when I saw in the distance a child who was walking toward us with slow but sure steps. He had a small head, a thin body, weak arms, and short legs, but his limbs grew larger and longer as he advanced. Throughout his successive spurts of growth, he appeared to me in many different guises; I saw him point a long telescope skyward, assess the rate of a falling body with the help of a pendulum, ascertain the weight of the air with a tube full of mercury, and break up light with a prism in his hand. He became a huge colossus; his head touched the skies, his feet were lost in the abyss, and his arms stretched from one pole to the other. With his right hand he shook a torch whose rays spread out in all directions lighting the depths of the waters and penetrating into the bowels of the earth.

" 'What,' I asked Plato, 'is this gigantic figure before us?'

" 'He is Experiment,' he answered.

"Hardly had he made this brief reply when I saw Experiment approach and the columns of the Portico of the Hypotheses tottered, its vault collapsed, its pavement cracked beneath our feet.

" 'Let us flee,' Plato said to me again, 'let us flee; this building will not stand a moment longer.'

"With these words, he left, and I followed. The colossus arrived, struck the portico, and it crumbled with a frightful racket, and I awoke."

"Ah, Prince," cried Mirzoza, "only you would have such dreams. I would have been happy had you had a good night's sleep. But now that I have heard your dream, I would have been sorry had you not had it."

"Madame," Mangogul said to her, "I know of nights better employed than in this dream, which you find so pleasing. Had I been master of my voyage, there is every reason to believe that, since there was no hope of finding you in the Land of Hypotheses, I would have turned my steps elsewhere. And I would not have this headache, or at least I would have occasion to be comforted for it."

"Prince," Mirzoza answered him, "let us hope that it is nothing, and that one or two trials of your ring will cure you."

"We shall see," said Mangogul.

The conversation between the Sultan and Mirzoza lasted a few minutes more; he did not leave her until eleven o'clock, to do what we shall see in the following chapter.

CHAPTER XXXIII

Fourteenth Trial of the Ring
The Mute Jewel

Of all the women who shone at the Sultan's court, none had more charm and wit than the young Eglea, wife of His Highness's first cupbearer. She was present at all Mangogul's gatherings, for he liked her cheerful conversation. And since it seemed there could be no pleasures or amusements without Eglea, she was present as well at all the gatherings of the important figures of his court. Eglea was invited everywhere: to balls, performances, salons, feasts, private suppers, hunts, and games. And one ran into her everywhere; indeed, it was as though the spirit of amusements multiplied her according to the wishes of those who desired her company. Thus it is not necessary for me to say that if there was no woman as much in demand as Eglea, neither was there one more well known.

She was always followed by a crowd of suitors, and observers were convinced they were not all mistreated. Either through inadvertance or an easygoing manner, her simple politeness often resembled favor, and thus those who sought to please her sometimes imagined a tenderness in her glances, though she claimed it was nothing more than graciousness. Neither caustic nor backbiting, she never opened her mouth except to say flattering things, and did so in so heartfelt and spirited a way that on many occasions her praise had given rise to the suspicion that she was justifying a liaison. In other words, the world in which Eglea served as both ornament and delight was not worthy of her.

People might well think that a woman whom one could only reproach for an excess of goodness would have no enemies. But in fact she had some, and they were cruel. The pious women of Banza thought her manner too free and found something too careless in her bearing; in her behavior they saw only a passion for worldly pleasures, and they concluded that her morals were, at the very least, doubtful, an opinion they happily imparted to any who would listen to them.

She was treated no better by the ladies at Court. They suspected Eglea of having affairs, assigned her lovers, and went so far as to honor her with a few great passions, as well as several lesser ones; details were provided, witnesses cited. "Well," they whispered in one another's ears, "she was surprised alone with Melraim in one of the groves in the great park. Eglea is not lacking in wit," they added, "but Melraim has too much of his own to be interested only in her words at ten o'clock at night, in a grove..."

"You are mistaken," answered a fop. "Many times I have walked with her after dark, and I was well pleased with her wit. But, by the way, have you noticed that Zulmar is forever about her boudoir?..."

"Of course we noticed, and we also noticed that she only dresses up when her husband is in waiting at Court..."

"Poor Celebi," continued another, "his wife indeed advertises it, with the aigrette and brooches she received from the pasha Ismael."

"Is that really true, Madame?"

"Utter truth – she told me herself. But, in the name of Brahma, do not repeat this; Eglea is my friend and I would be very sorry..."

"Alas," cried a third, sadly, "the poor little thing is ruining herself with pleasure. What a pity. But twenty lovers at once, that seems a bit much to me."

She did not fare much better with the fops. One told of a hunt in which they were lost together; another dissembled, out of respect for the ladies present, the consequences of a very lively conversation they had at a masked ball where he had latched on to her. Another praised her wit and charm, and ended by showing her portrait, which, if he is to be believed, she gave to him herself. "This portrait," he said, "is a better likeness than the one she gave to Jenaki."

This talk made its way back to her husband. Celebi loved his wife, but with such propriety, however, that no one had the least suspicion of it; he ignored the first tales, but new charges were made, and from all sides, so that he ended up thinking his friends were more discerning than he. The more freedom he granted Eglea, the more he suspected her of abusing it. Jealousy seized hold of him, and he began to constrain his wife. Eglea suffered all the more impatiently at this change in his behavior, as she felt herself to be innocent. Her vivaciousness and the advice of her dear friends drove her to commit thoughtless acts that turned all appearances against her and nearly cost her her life. The violent Celebi turned over hundreds of plans for revenge in his mind – swords, poison, fatal snares – deciding finally on slower and crueler punishment: seclusion in his country estate. This is death indeed for a court lady. In short, the orders were given, and one evening Eglea learned of her fate: her tears were in vain, her arguments ignored. She was banished to an old castle, eighty miles from Banza, where her only company was two serving women and four black eunuchs who kept watch over her.

As soon as she was gone she became innocent: the fops forgot their tales, the women forgave her her wit and charms, and everyone pitied her. From Celebi himself Mangogul learned the reasons for the terrible measure he had taken against his wife, and the Sultan appeared to be the only one to approve of it.

The unhappy Eglea had been grieving in her exile for nearly six months when the Kersael affair took place. Mirzoza hoped Eglea was innocent, but she did not dare count on this. Nonetheless, one day she said to the Sultan, "Could not your ring, which just saved Kersael's life, save Eglea from her exile? But I suppose there is little chance of it, since her jewel would have to be consulted and the poor recluse is dying of boredom eighty miles from here."

"Are you very concerned about Eglea's fate?" Mangogul asked her.

"Yes, Prince, especially if she is innocent," said Mirzoza.

"You shall have tidings of her within an hour's time," replied Mangogul. "Have you forgotten the properties of my ring?"

With these words he went into the garden, turned his ring, and in less than fifteen minutes found himself in the park of the castle where Eglea lived.

He found Eglea alone and overcome with sorrow. Her head hung in her hands, and tenderly she repeated her husband's name while weeping tears into the lawn, upon which she sat. Mangogul approached her as he turned his ring; Eglea's jewel said sadly, "I love Celebi." The sultan waited for more, but more did not follow; he grasped his ring and rubbed it two or three times against his hat, before pointing it again at Eglea; but his efforts were in vain. The jewel answered, "I love Celebi," and stopped there.

"Here," said the Sultan, "is a very discreet jewel. Let us try again and squeeze the stone tighter." At once he put all his energy into the ring and turned it sharply on Eglea; but her jewel was mute. It kept silent, and broke this silence only to repeat these plaintive words, "I love Celebi and have never loved another."

Mangogul left and returned to Mirzoza in fifteen minutes.

"What! Prince," she said, "are you back already? Well? What have you learned? Have you learned anything new?"

"Nothing," said the Sultan.

"What? Nothing?"

"Indeed, nothing. I have never heard a more taciturn jewel, and I could only draw these words from it: 'I love Celebi, I love Celebi and have never loved another.'"

"Ah, Prince," Mirzoza said with feeling, "what do you say about this? What happy news! Here at last is a virtuous woman. Will you suffer her to be unhappy any longer?"

"No," answered Mangogul, "her exile shall end. But do you not fear that it will be at the expense of her virtue? Eglea is chaste, but consider, my heart's delight, what you are asking me to do — to recall her to my court so that she may continue to be so. Nonetheless, you shall be satisfied."

The Sultan immediately sent for Celebi and told him that he had looked into the rumors spread about Eglea and had found them false and slanderous, and ordered him to bring his wife back to Court. Celebi obeyed and presented his wife to Mangogul: she was about to throw herself at His Highness's feet, but the Sultan stopped her.

"Madame," he said to her, "thank Mirzoza. Her friendship for you persuaded me to seek the truth about the actions of which you were accused. Please continue to grace my court, but remember that sometimes a pretty woman does as much harm to herself through imprudence as through infidelity itself."

The very next day Eglea reappeared at the Manimonbanda's, where the Grand Sultana received her with a smile. The fops redoubled their insipid attentions toward her; all the women ran to embrace her, congratulate her, and commenced tearing her apart once more.

CHAPTER XXXIV

Was Mangogul Right?

Ever since Mangogul had received Cucufa's fateful gift, the foolishness and vices of the opposite sex had become the eternal butt of his jokes. He went on and on, and often the favorite's patience was sorely tried. One cruel effect of Mangogul's teasing was that it put her, like so many others, out of sorts and in a terrible temper. Woe to anyone who approached her! And she did not discriminate; the Sultan himself was not spared.

"Prince," she said to him one day in one of these angry moments, "you who know so many things, perhaps you haven't heard the latest."

"And what might that be?" asked Mangogul.

"That each morning you learn three pages of Brantôme or Ouville by heart. People cannot determine which of these two profound writers you prefer."

"They are mistaken, Madame," replied Mangogul, "it is Crébillon whom —"

"Oh, you need not defend your choice of reading," interrupted the favorite. "The scandalous tales written about us today are so gloomy, it is better to revive the old ones. There are some very good things in this Brantôme. And if you supplemented his little tales with three or four chapters of Bayle, you would, all by yourself, be as consistently witty as the Marquis D'—— and the Chevalier de Mouhi. This would add spice to all of your conversations. As soon as you had finished with the ladies, you could take on the pagods. After the pagods, you could return to the ladies. In truth, all that you lack, to be entirely amusing, is a small collection of blasphemies."

"You are right, Madame," Mangogul answered her. "I shall provide myself with a good stock of them. He who fears being duped in this world and in the next cannot be too mistrustful of the power of the pagods, the integrity of men, and the virtue of women."

"In your opinion, then," answered Mirzoza, "this virtue is something rather dubious."

"More so than you can imagine," answered Mangogul.

"Prince," returned Mirzoza, "many a time you have pointed out your ministers to me as the most honest men in the Congo. I have so often endured the praises of your seneschal, the governors of your provinces, your secretaries, your treasurer, in a word, all of your officials, that I could repeat them word for word. It is strange that the object of your affection should be the only one exempted from the high opinion you hold of those granted the honor of serving you."

"And who told you that this is so?" the Sultan replied. "Do not imagine, Madame, that you are included in the remarks, true or false, that I make about women, unless you consider yourself representative of your entire sex."

"I should not advise this to Madame," added Selim, who was present at this conversation. "She would acquire nothing but defects from it."

"I do not appreciate compliments," replied Mirzoza, "addressed to me at the expense of my peers. When someone takes it into his head to praise me, I prefer no one else to suffer from it. Most of the pretty phrases offered us resemble the sumptuous feasts Your Highness receives from his pashas – they are always at the expense of the public."

"Enough," said Mangogul. "But, in good faith, are you not convinced that the virtue of the women of the Congo is but an illusion? Pray, consider, my soul's delight, the type of education in vogue today, the examples mothers set for their daughters, and how people fill the head of a pretty woman with the prejudice that to confine herself to her home, to manage her household and be faithful to her husband is to lead a dismal life, to die of boredom and be buried alive. And then again, we are such bold pursuers, we men, and a young girl without experience is overwhelmed to find herself pursued. I claimed that virtuous women were rare, excessively so; and far from changing my opinion, I might add that it is surprising that they are not more so. Ask Selim what he thinks of the matter."

"Prince," answered Mirzoza, "Selim owes too much to our sex to slander it pitilessly."

"Madame," said Selim, "His Highness, who has never had the opportunity to meet any cruel women, must naturally think of women as he does. And you who have the goodness to judge others through yourself, could hardly have any other sentiments than the ones you defend. I confess, however, that I am inclined to believe that there are women of good sense to whom the advantages of virtue are known firsthand, and whom serious reflection has convinced of the unfortunate consequences of a dissolute life, wellborn, well-bred women who have learned to know their duty and who love it and will never stray from it."

"And not to lose ourselves in abstractions," added the favorite, "is not the witty, lovely, charming Eglea a model of virtue as well? Prince, you can have no doubts about this. All of Banza knows it from your lips, and if there is one good woman, there may well be hundreds of them."

"Oh, I do not dispute the possibility," said Mangogul.

"But if you allow that it is possible," continued Mirzoza, "what makes you think that they do not actually exist?"

"Nothing but their jewels," answered the Sultan. "I admit that this evidence is not as strong as your argument. May I turn into a mole if you have not borrowed it from some Brahmin. Call in the Manimonbanda's chaplain, and he will tell you that you have proved the existence of virtuous women much as he demonstrates the existence of Brahma with Brahminology. Did you by any chance take a course in this sublime school before you entered the seraglio?"

"Enough bad jokes," replied Mirzoza. "I do not draw my conclusion from possibility alone. I am basing it on fact, on experience."

"Yes," continued Mangogul, "on a distorted fact and an isolated experience, whereas I have performed a multitude of trials, as you well know. But I will not contribute to your bad mood with further contradictions."

"It is fortunate," said Mirzoza, in a sad tone, "that after two hours you tire of persecuting me."

"If I am guilty of such a wrong," answered Mangogul, "I shall endeavor to make amends for it. I will relinquish all my past advantages, and if I find one truly and consistently virtuous woman in the trials still ahead of me –"

"What will you do?" Mirzoza interrupted briskly.

"I shall make public, if you like, that I am satisfied with your arguments on the existence of virtuous women. I shall authorize your logic with all my power, and give you my château at Amara, and all the Saxon porcelain with which it is decorated, including even the little enamel spider monkey and the other valuable knickknacks that I received from Madame de Vérue's cabinet."

"Prince," said Mirzoza, "I will settle for the porcelain, the château, and the little monkey."

"So be it," answered Mangogul. "Selim will be our judge. I ask only that we wait a little before interrogating Eglea's jewel. We must allow time for the atmosphere of the Court and her husband's jealousy to take their toll."

Mirzoza granted Mangogul one month – half again the amount of time he had asked for – and they each parted in high hopes. Had the Sultan's promise been revealed, all of Banza would have bet for and against. But Selim kept silent, and Mangogul prepared to win or to lose in secret.

As he left the favorite's apartment, he heard her call out from the depths of her chamber:

"And the little monkey, Prince?"

"And the little monkey," answered Mangogul as he left.

He went directly to the pleasure house of one of his senators, where we shall follow him.

CHAPTER XXXV

Fifteenth Trial of the Ring

Alphana

The Sultan was not unaware of the fact that the young lords at Court had pleasure houses; but he had recently learned that these retreats were likewise used by some senators. He was shocked. "What do they do there?" he asked himself (for in this volume he still has the habit of talking to himself that he acquired in the first volume). "It seems to me that a man to whom I have entrusted the tranquillity, fortune, liberty, and lives of my people ought not to keep a pleasure house. But perhaps a senator's pleasure house is something quite different from a fop's pleasure house. A magistrate before whom the most pressing interests of my subjects are discussed, and who holds in his hands the fateful urn from which he draws a widow's lot, might forget the dignity of his position and the importance of his task. While Cochin tires out his lungs in vain to bring the cries of orphans to his ears, he would be thinking to himself of matters of gallantry that should rather serve to decorate the spaces above the doorways of a place of secret debauchery...This cannot be...We shall see."

This said, he left for Alcanto, where the senator Hippomanes had his pleasure house. He enters, walks through the rooms, and examines the furnishings. To him everything seems suited to love. It was no different from the pleasure house of Agesilas, the most refined and most luxurious of his courtiers. He made up his mind to leave, not knowing what to think — for judging from all the beds, mirrored alcoves, plush sofas, and the cabinet with exquisite liquors, the rest was but mute testimony of what he had sought to find out — when he noticed a large figure stretched out on a sofa, deep in sleep. He turned his ring toward her, and drew the following anecdotes from her jewel:

"Alphana is a magistrate's daughter. Had her mother enjoyed life any less I should not be here. The vast family fortune slipped through the silly old woman's fingers, and she left almost nothing to her four children, three boys and a girl, whose jewel am I. Alas, for me and my sins! How many indignities have I suffered and how many more must be endured! People said that the convent suited my mistress's face and fortune. But I sensed that it was not for me. I preferred the military arts to the convent, and I had my first campaign under the emir Azalaph. I perfected myself under the great Nangazaki, but the ingratitude of the military made me leave, and I abandoned the sword for the gown. I am about to belong to a little scoundrel of a senator, all puffed up with his talents, his wit, his figure, his coach-and-four, and his ancestors. For two hours I have been waiting for him. Presumably he will come, for his steward warned me that when he comes, it is his fancy to keep people waiting for a long time."

Alphana's jewel was speaking thus, when Hippomanes arrived. Bestirred by the racket of his coach-and-four and the attention of his pet greyhound, Alphana awoke. "At last! There you are, my queen," the little senator said to her. "How very difficult it is to see you. Speak up; how do you like my little house? It is as good as any, is it not?"

Alphana, affecting a simple, shy, and distressed air — "as if we had never seen a pleasure retreat before," said her jewel, "and I never counted for anything in her adventures" — cried out unhappily, "My lord Senator, for your sake I have acted rashly. I must be carried away by a terrible passion indeed to be so blinded to the danger I risk. What would people say if they suspected my presence here?"

"Quite right," Hippomanes said to her. "Your actions are indeed questionable, but you may count on my discretion."

"But," replied Alphana, "I count as well on your good conduct."

"Oh, as far as that is concerned," Hippomanes said to her, sneering, "I shall be very good indeed. How can one fail to be good as an angel in a pleasure house? Really now, you have a most charming bosom..."

"Enough," Alphana said to him, "you are breaking your word already."

"Not at all," said the Senator. "But you have not answered me; what do you think of these furnishings?" Then, turning to the greyhound:

"Come here, Favorite, give me your paw, good girl. What a good girl Favorite is...Would Mademoiselle like to take a turn in the garden? Shall we walk on my terrace? It is most charming. I have a few neighbors, but perhaps they do not know you."

"My lord Senator, I am not curious," Alphana answered him in an irritated voice. "I think we are better off in here."

"As you like," said Hippomanes. "If you are tired, here is a bed. However little your inclination, I recommend you try it. Young Asteria, and little Phenica, who know about such things, assured me it was good."

While Hippomanes was making these impertinent suggestions to Alphana, he pulled off her gown by the sleeves, unlaced her corset, undid her petticoats, and disengaged her large feet from their little slippers.

When Alphana was almost naked, she began to notice that Hippomanes was undressing her...

"What are you doing?" she cried in surprise. "Senator, you cannot be serious. I shall become angry in earnest."

"Ah, my queen!" Hippomanes said to her. "To be angry with a man who loves you as I do would be a caprice of which you would be incapable. Dare I ask you to get into that bed?"

"Into that bed?" retorted Alphana. "Ah, Senator, you take advantage of my affections. Get into bed? Me? Into bed!"

"Ah, no, my queen," Hippomanes said to her. "Who said you must go by yourself? But you must, if you please, allow yourself to be led, for you will understand that at your size I cannot be eager to carry you." Meanwhile he put his arm around her waist, and made some attempts..."Oh, how heavy she is," he said, "My child, if you will not assist me, we shall never get there."

Alphana sensed he spoke the truth, assisted him, succeeded in helping herself up, and went toward the bed that had so frightened her, half on her own, half supported by Hippomanes, to whom she simpered and stammered, "Indeed, I must be a fool to have come here. I was counting on your goodness, and you are bold beyond measure."

"Not at all," the Senator said to her, "not at all. You see that what I do is very, very proper."

I think that they said many other nice things; but the Sultan did not see fit to follow their conversation any longer, so these words are lost to posterity. What a pity!

CHAPTER XXXVI

Sixteenth Trial of the Ring
The Fops

Twice a week, a drawing room was held in the favorite's apartments. The night before, she would name the women she wanted to see, and the Sultan would give a list of men. The company always came very well dressed. The conversation was mixed or divided by sex. When the love affairs at Court did not provide amusing tales, people made them up, or else they set about telling bad stories, and this was called "continuing the *Thousand and One Nights*." The men had the privilege of saying whatever extravagant things came into their heads, while the women knotted as they listened. The Sultan and the favorite would mingle with their subjects, and their presence inhibited nothing amusing that might emerge. Rarely was anyone bored. Early on, Mangogul had learned that pleasures are not to be found above the foot of the throne, and no man had ever stepped down from it more gracefully, or known better how to divest himself of his majesty.

While he was surveying the pleasure house of his senator, Mirzoza awaited him in the rose-colored salon with young Zaida, cheerful Leocris, lively Serica, Amina and Benzaira, the wives of two emirs, the prude Orphisa, and the Grand Seneschal's wife, Vetula, temporal mother of all the Brahmins. Mangogul was not long in arriving. He entered, accompanied by Count Hannetillon and the chevalier Fadaes. Alciphenor, an old libertine, and the young Marmolin, his disciple, also followed him, and two minutes later the pasha Grisgrif, the aga Fortimbek, and the selictar Velvet-Paws arrived. These were the most assiduous fops of the Court. Mangogul had brought them together by design. Having often heard tales of their gallant exploits, he had resolved to inform himself thereon, to dispel any further doubts. "Well, gentlemen," he said to them, "you all keep abreast of what is happening in the world of gallantry. What is new? What of the talking jewels?"

"My lord," answered Alciphenor, "their uproar increases daily. If this continues, very soon we shall be unable to hear ourselves. But nothing has been so amusing as the indiscretion of Zobeida's jewel, which has just given her husband a catalog of its adventures."

"And a prodigious one," continued Marmolin. "It mentioned five agas, twenty captains, almost an entire company of janissaries, and twelve Brahmins. They say it mentioned me as well, but that was only a joke."

"The best part of it," continued Grisgrif, "is that the terrified husband fled, stopping his ears."

"Horrible," said Mirzoza.

"Horrible indeed, Madame," interrupted Fortimbek, "horrible, shocking, deplorable!"

"Worse still," said the favorite, "is to dishonor a woman on hearsay."

"Madame, this is all exactly as she told it. Marmolin has not added one word to the truth," said Velvet-Paws.

"That is correct," said Grisgrif.

"Right," added Hannetillon, "an epigram is circulating about it already, and people do not make up epigrams for no reason. And why should Marmolin be safe from the chattering jewels? Cynara's jewel saw fit to speak when the time came, and to mix me up with people not at all to my liking. But it cannot be avoided."

"You had better get used to it," said Velvet-Paws.

"Quite right," said Hannetillon, and suddenly he began to sing:

So great was my good fortune
Scarce could I believe it.

"Count," said Mangogul to Hannetillon, "do you know Cynara well?"

"My lord," answered Velvet-Paws, "how could there be any doubt of it? She was on his arm for more than a moon. People made up little songs about them, and it would still be going on, had he not noticed that she is not very pretty and has a large mouth."

"True enough," said Hannetillon, "but this defect was offset by her unusual charm."

"Was this liaison long ago?" asked the prude Orphisa.

"Madame," answered Hannetillon, "I do not remember that period at present. One would have to look into the chronological tables of my good fortune for the date and time. It is a thick volume with which my servants amuse themselves in my antechamber."

"Wait," said Alciphenor, "I remember that it was exactly a year after Grisgrif broke off with Madame the seneschal's lady. She has the memory of an angel and can tell us exactly..."

"Nothing could be falser than your calculations," replied the Seneschal's lady solemnly. "Everyone knows that fools have never been to my liking."

"Nonetheless, Madame," continued Alciphenor, "you will never persuade us that Marmolin behaved himself when he entered your chambers by a hidden staircase each time His Highness called the lord Seneschal into council."

"I cannot think of anything more absurd," added Velvet-Paws, "than to enter a woman's chamber clandestinely, for no reason at all. People thought of these visits as nothing more than what they were, and Madame already enjoyed the reputation of virtue which she has since then so well maintained."

"But that was ages ago," said Fadaes. "It was more or less at the same time that Zulica gave the slip to the lord Selictar, who had served her so well, to amuse herself with Grisgrif, whom she left in the lurch six months later. Now she is with Fortimbek. I am not sorry for my friend's small stroke of luck. I see it, I admire it, but entirely without expectation for myself."

"Zulica," said the favorite, "is winning nonetheless. She has wit, taste, and something, I know not what, engaging in her countenance, which I prefer to charm."

"I grant that," said Fadaes, "but she is thin, flat-chested, and has thighs so emaciated that one feels sorry for her."

"Apparently you know this firsthand," added the Sultana.

"Oh, Madame," continued Hannetillon, "one can well imagine it. I have visited Zulica but seldom, and yet I know as much as Fadaes about her."

"I am inclined to believe that," said the favorite.

"By the way," said the Selictar, "could we not ask Grisgrif if he intends to possess Zirphila for long? Now there is a pretty woman indeed. What a fine figure she has."

"Ah, who would disagree?" added Marmolin.

"The selictar is fortunate indeed," continued Fadaes.

"I submit that Fadaes," interrupted the Selictar, "is the best-provided gallant in the Court. To my knowledge, he has the Vizier's wife, the two prettiest actresses of the Opera, and an adorable grisette whom he has set up in a pleasure house."

"And I would give," replied Fadaes, "the Vizier's wife, the two actresses, and the grisette for just one look from a certain woman whom the Selictar knows well, and who has no idea that everyone is wise to them." Approaching Leocris, he said, "In truth, Madame, your blushes are ravishing..."

"For I know not how long," said Marmolin, "Hannetillon could not decide between Melissa and Fatima, two charming women. One day he was for the blonde Melissa, the next day for the brunette Fatima."

"Now that was a fine predicament," said Fadaes. "Why not take both of them?"

"That is just what he did," said Alciphenor.

As one can see, our fops were too far along to leave it at that, when Zobeida, Cynara, Zulica, Melissa, Fatima, and Zirphila were announced. This distraction disconcerted the fops for a moment, but they were not long in collecting themselves and falling upon other women whom they had spared in their slander merely because they had not yet gotten around to tearing them to pieces.

Mirzoza, losing patience with their remarks, said to them, "Gentlemen, with all the merit, and especially the integrity, that one is obliged to grant you, there can be no doubt that you have enjoyed all the good fortune of which you boast. I must confess to you, however, that I would be eager to hear out the jewels of these women on this matter, and that I would thank Brahma with all my heart if it pleased him to do justice to truth through their mouths."

"In other words," said Hannetillon, "Madame would like to hear the same things all over again; very well, we shall repeat them."

Meanwhile, Mangogul directed his ring, following order of seniority. He began with the Seneschal's wife, whose jewel coughed three times and said in a trembling, broken voice, "I am indebted to the Grand Seneschal for the first fruits of my pleasures; but I had belonged to him scarcely six months when a young Brahmin gave my mistress to understand that a woman can do no injury to her husband as long as she is thinking of him. I learned much from this morality and believed I could next admit, in good conscience, a senator, a privy counselor, a pontiff, then one or two scribes, then a musician."

"And Marmolin?" asks Fadaes.

"Marmolin?" replies the jewel. "I know him not, unless he was the young fop my mistress had chased from her hotel for a few impertinences I cannot remember."

Cynara's jewel took the floor next, and said, "Alciphenor, Fadaes, and Grisgrif, you ask? I have been fairly well served, but this is the first time in my life I have heard these names. However, I may find out something about them through the emir Amalek, the financier Tenelar, or the vizier Abdiram, who oversee the entire land, and are my friends."

"Cynara's jewel is most discreet," said Hannetillon. "It has failed to mention Zarafis, Ahiram, the old Trebister, and the young Mahmoud, who is not to be forgotten, and has not accused even one little Brahmin, although it has been making the rounds of the monasteries for twelve years now."

"I have been paid a call or two in my life," said Melissa's jewel, "but never from Grisgrif or Fortimbek, and certainly not from Hannetillon."

"My dear jewel," Grisgrif answered, "you are mistaken. You can deny

Fortimbek and me as much as you like, but as for Hannetillon, he is a little closer to you than you wish to admit. He has told me a thing or two, and he is the most honest lad in the Congo, a better man than any you have known, one who can still make a jewel's reputation."

"His own reputation is that of an impostor, like his friend Fadaes," said Fatima's jewel, weeping. "What have I done to these monsters to deserve their dishonoring me? The son of the Emperor of the Abyssinians came to Erguebzed's court. I caught his fancy. He paid me court, but he would have failed, and I would have continued to be faithful to my husband, whom I loved, had not the traitor Velvet-Paws and his base accomplice Fadaes corrupted my women and introduced the young prince into my bath."

The jewels of Zirphila and Zulica, who had the same cause to defend, spoke at once, in such quick succession that it was difficult to differentiate between them: "Favors!" cried one..."To Velvet-Paws," said another..."Zinzim perhaps...Cerbelon...Benengel...Agarias... the French slave Riqueli...and the young Ethiopian Thezaca...But as for the insipid Velvet-Paws...the insolent Fadaes...I swear by Brahma ...as the Great Pagod and the genie Cucufa are my witnesses...I do not know them...I have never had a thing to do with them..."

Zirphila and Zulica would be talking still, had Mangogul not turned his ring. Indeed, as his mysterious ring ceased to act upon them, their jewels suddenly fell still, and a deep silence followed the noise they had made. Then the Sultan rose, and looked wrathfully at our young fops.

"You are bold indeed," he said to them, "to slander women whom you have not had the honor to approach, and whom you barely know by name. Who made you so impudent as to lie in my presence? Tremble, wretches!"

With these words he brought his hand to his scimitar, but the ladies' frightened screams stayed his hand.

"I was going to deal you the death you deserve," said Mangogul, "but these ladies, whom you have insulted, shall decide your fate. Vile insects, they shall decide whether you are to be crushed or allowed to live. Speak, ladies, what is your will?"

"Let them live," said Mirzoza, "and hold their tongues, if that is possible."

"Live, then," said the Sultan, "since these ladies wish it; but if you ever forget the conditions, I swear on my father's soul..."

Mangogul did not finish his oath. He was interrupted by one of his valets, who informed him that the actors were ready. This prince had made himself a rule never to delay a performance. "Let them begin," he said, and in an instant he gave his hand to the favorite, whom he accompanied to her box.

CHAPTER XXXVII

Seventeenth Trial of the Ring
The Performance

Had there been a taste for the art of recitation in the Congo, many actors could have been dispensed with. Among the thirty people who made up the troupe, there was but one good actor and two actresses who were tolerable. The talent of the authors was obliged to conform to the mediocrity of the whole, and there was little hope that a play would be performed with any measure of success unless the characters were tailored to the defects of the actors. In my time this is what we called the theater. Formerly, actors could play any role. Now the roles are written for the actors. If you present them with a work, they examine it without complaint if the subject is interesting, the plot well concocted, the characters sustained, and the diction pure and fluent; but if there is no role for Roscius and Amiane, they refuse it.

The kislar Agasi, superintendent of the Sultan's pleasures, had sent for the troupe such as it was, and that day they presented a tragedy, the first ever performed in the seraglio. It was by a modern author who had been well received for so long that his play could have been a mere string of impertinences and people would have continued their habit of commending him. But he did not belie his reputation. His play was well written, his scenes constructed artfully, and the action aptly handled. One's interest grew as the passions steadily developed. The acts were full and followed one another naturally and kept the audience in suspense about the future and satisfied with the past. They were watching the fourth act of this masterpiece, a lively scene that was leading up to another more interesting still, when, to spare himself the embarrassment of listening to the pathetic parts, Mangogul took out his opera glasses and, taking advantage of people's inattention, began to look over the boxes. In the amphitheater he noticed a woman who was deeply moved, but with an emotion that had very little to do with the play and seemed out of place. Immediately he directed his ring at her and in the middle of a moving recognition, a panting jewel was heard addressing the actor in these terms. "Oh!... oh...do finish, Orgogli...you move me too deeply...Oh, oh...I can bear it no longer."

People listened and looked to see whence the voice had issued. Word ran through the orchestra that a jewel had spoken. "Which one, and what did it say?" people asked each other. While waiting for further news thereof, the audience clapped and cried out, "Encore, encore!" Meanwhile, the playwright, seated in the wings, who had feared that this mishap might interrupt his play, fumed in rage and sent all jewels to the devil. The noise was loud and it lasted long. If not for the respect due to the Sultan, the play would have gone no further; but Mangogul gave a signal for silence. The actors resumed their parts and the play was completed.

The Sultan, curious of the consequences of so public an avowal, arranged for the jewel that had made it to be followed. He soon learned that the actor was on his way to see this Eriphila. He arrived there first, thanks to the power of his ring, and was in the lady's chambers just as Orgogli was announced.

Eriphila was in full battle array, which is to say that she was in a gallant state of undress and was wantonly stretched out on a couch. The actor entered with a stiff, conquering, presumptuous, and vain attitude. With his left hand he shook a plain hat with a white feather, and with his right hand he stroked his upper lip, a theatrical gesture much loved by the connoisseurs. His bow was dashing and his greeting familiar.

"My queen," he cried in an affected tone, bending toward Eriphila, "there you are! Do you know that in your negligee you are absolutely adorable?"

The cad's tone of voice shocked Mangogul. The Prince was still young, and may have been unaware of certain customs.

"Then I am to your liking, my dear..." Eriphila answered him.

"Absolutely ravishing..."

"I am so glad. I wish you would recite a bit from the part that so moved me. That part...there...yes, that's it...How seductive that rogue is!...But continue, it truly moves me."

As she spoke these words, the glances that Eriphila sent her hero said everything. She held out her hand, and the impertinent Orgogli kissed it for the sake of form. Prouder of his talent than of his conquest, he recited his lines emphatically, and the lady was so enraptured that she begged him one moment to continue, the next moment to stop. Mangogul, who judged by her expressions that her jewel would gladly assume a role in this play, preferred to guess the rest of the act than to be witness to it. He disappeared and went to the favorite, who was waiting for him.

As she heard the Prince narrate his adventure, she cried, "Prince, what are you saying? Have women thus fallen to the lowest depths of degradation? An actor! The public's slave! A buffoon! It would not be so bad if these people had only their station against them; but most of them lack morals and feelings, and compared to the rest this Orgogli is but a machine. He has never had a thought in his life, and if he never learned lines he would probably be unable to speak."

"My heart's delight," Mangogul replied, "you are not thinking things through with your complaints. Have you forgotten Haria's dog pack? By Jupiter, an actor is as good as a hound, it seems to me."

"You are right, Prince," the favorite answered him. "I am foolish to rack my brains over creatures who are not worth it. Let Palabria dote upon her dunces. Let Salica be treated for her vapors by Farfadi as she sees fit. Let Haria live and die among her beasts. Let Eriphila abandon herself to all the buffoons of the Congo. What does it matter to me? In all this I have only a château at stake. I feel I must detach myself from this, and I am now resolved..."

"To say farewell to the little monkey," said Mangogul.

"Farewell to the little monkey," replied Mirzoza, "and farewell to the high opinion I had of my sex; I fear I shall never get over it. Prince, will you permit me to refuse to admit ladies to my chambers for at least a fortnight?"

"You must, however, have company," added the Sultan.

"I shall take pleasure in your company, or enjoy waiting for it," replied the favorite. "And if any time remains on my hands, I shall devote it to Ricaric or Selim, who are fond of me, and whose company I love. When I tire of the erudition of my lecturer, your courtier will entertain me with stories of his youth."

CHAPTER XXXVIII

A Conversation About Literature

The favorite loved men of fine wit, without claiming to be a wit herself. On her dressing table, between the diamonds and the pompons, were many novels and pamphlets of the times, of which she was a marvelous judge. She passed with ease from a game of cavagnole or biribi[1] to the discourse of an academician or of learned men, and all admitted that the natural keenness of her judgment allowed her to see beauties or defects in these works that were at times hidden to their own eyes. Mirzoza surprised them with her insights, embarrassed them with her questions, but never took advantage of her own wit and beauty.

No one was ever displeased at being proven wrong by her.

Toward the end of an afternoon she had spent with Mangogul, Selim arrived and she sent for Ricaric. The African author has saved the description of Selim's character for another occasion. But he does tell us here that Ricaric was a member of the Academy of the Congo; that his erudition had not prevented him from being a man of wit; that his knowledge of centuries past was profound; that he was scrupulously attached to ancient laws, which he was forever citing; and that he was a creature of principle. Never was there a more zealous partisan of the first writers of the Congo, but above all of a certain Mioufla, who had, about three thousand and forty years ago, composed a sublime poem in the Cafric tongue, about the conquest of a great forest, whence the Caffres chased away the monkeys that had lived there from time immemorial. Ricaric had translated it into Congolese, and it had been printed in a very beautiful edition with notes, scholia, variants, and all the embellishments of a Benedictine edition. He also wrote two bad tragedies following all the rules, an homage to crocodiles, and a few operas.

"Madame, I have brought you," Ricaric said to her, bowing, "a novel attributed to the marquise Tamazi, but in which, unfortunately, one recognizes the hand of Mulhazen; the response of our president Lambadago to the discourse of the poet Tuxigraphus, which we heard yesterday; and the latter's *Tamerlane*.

"How admirable," said Mangogul, "that our presses never stop! If the husbands of the Congo performed their duties as well as the writers do, in less than ten years I could put one hundred thousand men on their feet and assure myself the conquest of Monoemugi. We shall read the novel at our leisure. Let us now look at the speech, especially at the parts that concern me."

Ricaric skimmed it and came upon the following passage:

"The ancestors of our august emperor without a doubt achieved much fame and glory. But Mangogul, greater still than they, has given future generations far more to admire. What am I saying, to admire? To gaze upon in disbelief, to speak more precisely. If our ancestors were right to assume that posterity would take the wonders of the reign of Kanoglou for fables, how much greater will be our grandchildren's disbelief at the prodigies of wisdom and valor to which we are witness!"

"My poor Monsieur Lambadago," said the Sultan, "you are full of hot air. I have good reason to believe that one day your successors will eclipse my glory with that of my son, just as you cause my father's glory to disappear before mine, and so on, as long as there are academics. What do you think, Monsieur Ricaric?"

"Prince, all I can say," rejoined Ricaric, "is that the part I just read to Your Highness was greatly to the public's liking."

"Too bad," replied Mangogul. "Does this mean that the true taste for eloquence has been lost in the Congo? That was not the way the sublime Homilogo praised the great Aben."

"Prince," continued Ricaric, "true eloquence is nothing more than the art of speaking in a noble manner, creating a whole that is pleasant and persuasive."

"Add sensible to that," said Mangogul, "and judge your friend Lambadago according to that principle. With all due respect to modern eloquence, his is a false elocution."

"But, Prince," answered Ricaric, "with all due respect to Your Highness, will you permit me..."

"What I permit you," Mangogul retorted hotly, "is to respect common sense more than My Highness and to tell me clearly if an eloquent man can ever be exempted from displaying it."

"No, Prince," said Ricaric.

He was about to run through a long list of authorities and cite all the rhetoricians of Africa, the Arabias, and China to prove the most indisputable thing in the world, when Selim interrupted him.

"All your authors," the courtier said to him, "will never prove that Lambadago is not an ungainly and most indecent haranguer. Forgive me my choice of words, Monsier Ricaric," he added. "I respect you a great deal, but in truth, setting aside your bias of confraternity, would you not agree with us that the reigning sultan is just, kind, beneficent, and a great warrior who does not need the stilts of your orators to be as grand as his ancestors; and that a son who is exalted by belittling his father and grandfather would be quite ludicrously vain if he did not feel that in being embellished with one hand he were disfigured with the other? In your opinion, to prove that Mangogul's stature is equal to that of his predecessors, is it necessary to knock the heads off the statues of Erguebzed and Kanaglou?"

"Monsieur Ricaric," continued Mirzoza, "Selim is right. Give to each his due, and let us not permit the public to suspect that our praises rob our fathers' memories: say that to the whole academy on my behalf when it is next in session."

"This practice has been too long the custom," said Selim, "for us to hope that this advice might bear fruit."

"I think, Monsieur, that you are mistaken," Ricaric replied to Selim. "The academy is still the sanctuary of good taste; and its golden age offers us neither philosophers nor poets whom we cannot match today.

Our theater can still claim itself as Africa's finest. What a fine work is Tuxigraphus's *Tamerlane*! It has all the pathos of Eurisopa and the loftiness of Azopha. It is pure antiquity."

"I saw," said the favorite, "the first performance of *Tamerlane*, and, like you, I found the work well staged, the dialogue elegant, and the conventions well respected."

"What a difference, Madame," interrupted Ricaric, "between an author such as Tuxigraphus, nurtured on the classics, and most of our authors today!"

"But these modern authors," said Selim, "whom you criticize so freely, are not so contemptible as you claim. Now, then, do you not find genius, inventiveness, passion, detail, character, and speeches in them? And what do rules matter to me if I like a work? Assuredly, it is not the observations of the wise Almudir or the learned Abaldok, or the poetics of the erudite Facardin, which I have never read, that make me admire the plays of Aboulcazem, Muzardar, or Albaboukre, or so many other Saracens! Is there any other rule than the imitation of nature? And are not our eyes as good as the eyes of those who have studied her?"

"Nature," answered Ricaric, "offers us a different face at every turn. All are true, but they are not equally beautiful. One must learn to choose among these works, on which you seem not to set any great value. These are collections of their own experiences and also of those which were made before them. Whatever strength of understanding a man may possess, things must be observed successively, and no single man can boast of being able to see, in the short course of his lifetime, all that has been discovered in the centuries before him. Otherwise we could say that any given science might owe its conception, its progress, and its perfection to a single mind, which is contrary to experience."

"Monsieur Ricaric," replied Selim, "the only consequence that follows from your argument is that the moderns, taking advantage of the treasures amassed before their time, must therefore be richer than the ancients, or that, if this comparison displeases you, as they are mounted on the shoulders of these colossi, they should be able to see farther still. Indeed, how can their natural philosophy, their astronomy, their navigation, their mechanics, and their calculus compare to ours? And why should not our eloquence and our poetry be superior as well?"

"Selim," answered the Sultana, "one day Ricaric will explain the reasons for this difference. He will tell you why our tragedies are inferior to those of the past. For my part, I shall willingly undertake to show you that this is so. I am not accusing you," she continued, "of not having read the classics. Your mind is too well adorned for their theater to be unknown to you. If we leave aside certain ideas relative to their customs, morals, and religion, which shock you because the contexts have changed, you will agree with me that their subjects are noble, well chosen, and interesting; that the action develops as if of its own accord; that their dialogue is simple and very close to natural speech; that the unraveling of the plot is never forced; and that one's interest is not divided nor the action overburdened with episodes. In your mind, take yourself to Alindala's island. Look at everything happening there. Listen to what is said, from the moment when the young Ibrahim and the crafty Forfanty land there. Approach the wretched Polipsile's cave, and miss not a word of his laments. Then tell me if anything strikes you as illusion. Tell me if you know of a modern play that can bear the same scrutiny and claim the same degree of perfection, and I shall admit defeat."

"By Brahma," cried the Sultan, yawning, "Madame has given an academic dissertation!"

"I do not know the rules," continued the favorite, "much less the learned words by which they are expressed; but I do know that truth alone can please and touch an audience. I also know that perfection in a play consists in an imitation of an action so exact that the spectator, continually deceived, imagines himself part of the action itself. Now, is there anything similar to this in the tragedies you have just praised to us?

"Do you admire their construction? Usually it is so complicated that if so many things ever truly happened in so short a time, it would be a miracle. The ruin or salvation of an empire, the marriage of a princess, the loss of a prince, all this happens in the twinkling of an eye. If the subject is a conspiracy, it is outlined in the first act, brought together in the second, and then all measures are taken, the obstacles overcome, and the conspirators ready for action in the third. Then there is always a revolt, a fight, perhaps an army in battle array, and you will call this structure, interest, warmth, verisimilitude! I cannot excuse this, especially in you who know how difficult it is at times to end a miserable plot and how much time the slightest political matter takes up in proceedings, negotiations, and deliberations."

"I grant, Madame," answered Selim, "that our plays are rather full of this, but it is a necessary evil; if not for the use of episodes, the audience would be lost."

"In other words, to breathe life into the representation of a fact, it should be rendered neither such as it is nor as it should be. That is the most ludicrous thing I have ever heard, unless it is more absurd still to play lively ariettas and jigs on violins while people's minds are occupied with a prince about to lose his mistress, his throne, or his life."

"Madame, you are right," said Mangogul. "Lugubrious airs are more in order then. I shall order some for you."

Mangogul rose and left, and the conversation continued among Selim, Ricaric, and the favorite.

"At least, Madame," replied Selim, "you will not deny that if the episodes distract us from the illusion, the dialogue brings us back to it. I do not know anyone who understands this better than our tragedians."

"Then nobody understands it," retorted Mirzoza. "Their bombast, glibness, and ostentation are a thousand miles from nature. The author may try to hide in vain, but my eyes are keen and I incessantly see him behind his characters. Cinna, Sertorius, Maximus, and Aemilius are Corneille's speaking trumpets on every page. That is not how people talk in our ancient Saracen texts. Monsieur Ricaric, if you like, will translate a few lines for you, and you will hear nature herself expressed through their mouths. I would gladly say to the moderns, 'Gentlemen, instead of making your characters witty in every circumstance, try to place them in situations that make them so.'"

"After the judgment Madame has just passed on the structure and the dialogue of our plays, it is unlikely," said Selim, "that she will spare their conclusions."

"Unlikely," said the favorite, "since there are a hundred bad plots for every good one. One is poorly executed, another is miraculous. If an author is encumbered by a character he has dragged through scene after scene for five acts, he will dispense with him by having him suddenly stabbed: everyone cries while I burst into laughter. Moreover, have people ever spoken the way we declaim? Do princes and kings walk any differently from a man who walks well? Do they ever gesticulate like madmen or lunatics? Do princesses speak in a shrill whistling tone? It is generally supposed that we have brought tragedy to a high level of perfection. I, on the other hand, consider it almost a proven fact that of all the literary genres to which the Africans have applied themselves in the last few hundred years, it is the least perfect."

The favorite was at this point in her attack on our plays when Mangogul returned.

"Madame," he said to her, "you will oblige me and continue. I have, as you can see, secret ways to abridge a poetic subject when I find it long-winded."

"Let us imagine," continued the favorite, "a newcomer from Angote, who has never heard of the theater, but who is not lacking in common sense or experience. He knows a little about princes, court intrigues, the jealousies of ministers, and the double-dealings of women. I say to him in confidence, 'My friend, terrible things are happening in the seraglio. The Prince, displeased with his son, in whom he suspects a passion for the Manimonbanda, is a man capable of taking the cruelest revenge on them both. In all probability this adventure will have terrible consequences. If you wish, I will make you a witness to everything that happens.' He accepts my proposition, and I lead him to a box screened by a blind whence he can see the stage, which he takes for the Sultan's palace. For all the seriousness I might feign, do you think the illusion would last more than an instant for this man? Do you not agree, on the contrary, that upon seeing the stiff carriage of the actors, the oddity of their dress, the extravagance of their gestures, the pomposity of their strange rhymed, cadenced language, and hundreds of other shocking dissonances, he would burst out at me in the very first scene and tell me that either I was mocking him or that the Prince and his whole court were raving mad?"

"I admit," said Selim, "that I find this hypothesis very impressive. But may I call your attention to the fact that people go to the theater knowing that it is an imitation of an event and not the event itself that will be seen?"

"And should this knowledge," replied Mirzoza, "prevent the representation of the event from being as natural as possible?"

"In other words, Madame," interrupted Mangogul, "you are now at the head of the fault-finders."

"And if what you say is true," continued Selim, "then the empire is menaced by the decay of good taste. Barbarism will revive, and we shall soon revert to the ignorance of the ages of Mamurrha and Orondalo."

"My lord, fear nothing of the kind. I despise doomsayers and do not wish to join their number. Furthermore, the glory of His Highness is so dear to me that I would never try to tarnish the splendor of his reign. But if people took our ideas to heart, is it not true, Monsieur Ricaric, that literature would perhaps shine with greater luster?"

"What is this?" asked Mangogul. "Do you perhaps have a treatise to present to my seneschal?"

"No, my lord," replied Ricaric. "But thanking Your Highness on behalf of all men of letters for the new inspector you have given them, I would point out to your seneschal, in all humility, that the choice of scholars in charge of the revision of manuscripts is a very delicate affair indeed. This task is assigned to people who seem to me far beneath it, and who, in many cases, produce bad results — such as mangling good works and stifling the best minds, who, lacking the freedom to write in their own manner, either do not write at all or allow their works to earn large sums abroad; and forbidding the discussion of certain subjects, and hundreds of other inconveniences that would take too long to enumerate to Your Highness. I would advise him to cut off the pensions of literary bloodsuckers, who demand them unreasonably and unceasingly — I speak of glossarists, antiquarians, commentators, and others of their kind, who would be useful indeed if they did their jobs, but who have the unfortunate habit of passing over obscure matters and dwelling on parts that are quite clear. I would be most happy if he would see to the suppression of almost all posthumous works, and not suffer that the memory of a great author be tarnished by the greed of a bookseller who gathers and publishes, long after his death, works that the author condemned to oblivion during his lifetime."

"And I," continued the favorite, "would point out to him a small number of distinguished men, such as Monsieur Ricaric, among whom he could redistribute his favors. Is it not surprising that the poor fellow hasn't a sou, whereas the Manimonbanda's precious palm reader collects one thousand sequins from your treasury each year?"

"Very well, Madame," answered Mangogul. "In consideration of the marvels you tell me about him, I assign as much to Ricaric from my coffers."

"Monsieur Ricaric," said the favorite, "I must do something for you as well. I relinquish my wounded pride, and in view of the compensation Mangogul has just granted you, I forgive the insult he made to me."

"Might one inquire what this insult may be, Madame?" asked Mangogul.

"Yes, my lord, I shall tell you. You yourself led us into this discussion of letters. You began with a piece on modern eloquence, which is not extraordinary; and when, to oblige you, we set about pursuing the disagreeable argument which you had raised, you became so bored you could not keep from yawning. You tortured yourself in your seat, changing positions one hundred times and finding none comfortable. Tired at last of pulling the longest face in the world, you left abruptly. You left, disappeared, and where did you go? Perhaps to listen to some jewel?"

"I own to the deed, Madame, but I see no offense in it. If it happens that a man grows bored with fine things and amuses himself in hearing bad things, so much the worse for him. This unjust preference takes nothing away from the merit of that which he chose not to hear; he is merely deemed poor judge. I might add to that, Madame, that while you were engaged in conversation with Selim, I was working almost as unfruitfully in trying to procure a château for you. And if I must be guilty, since you have pronounced me so, I can tell you that you were immediately vindicated."

"And how is that?" asked the favorite.

"This is how," said the sultan. "To refresh myself from the fatigue of the academic seance I had endured, I went to examine some jewels."

"Well, Prince?"

"Well, I have never heard such tedious jewels as the two upon which I stumbled."

"I am overjoyed to hear this," returned the favorite.

"They began to speak, both of them, in an unintelligible language. I remember well what they said, but may I die if I understood a word of it."

CHAPTER XXXIX

Eighteenth and Nineteenth Trials of the Ring
The Flattened Spheroid and Girgiro the Entangled

Catch who catch can

"How strange," continued the favorite. "Until now I have thought that if the jewels could be reproached for anything, it was for speaking too clearly."

"Mercy, Madame!" replied Mangogul. "These two were not clear at all; and I defy anyone to try to understand them.

"You know that little round woman, whose head is sunk into her shoulders, whose arms are barely visible, whose legs are so short and her belly so low that she could be mistaken for a hedgehog or an enormous misshapen embryo, the one nicknamed the Flattened Spheroid, who took it into her head that Brahma had called her to the study of geometry because she had been given a body like a globe, and who by the same logic could have joined the artillery, since to judge by her shape, she must have emerged from nature's womb like a ball shot from the mouth of a cannon?

"I wanted to hear news of her jewel, and so I questioned it. But this Vorticist explained itself in terms of such profound geometry that I did not understand it, nor perhaps did it understand itself. It talked of nothing but straight lines, concave surfaces, given quantities, length, width, depth, solids, living forces, dead forces, cones, cylinders, conic sections, curves, elastic curves, curves curving back onto themselves, with its conjugate point..."

"I pray, Your Highness, spare me the rest," implored the favorite. "You have a cruel memory. It is devastating. I'm afraid I shall have a headache for a week. Was the other one by any chance equally amusing?"

"You shall judge that for yourself," replied Mangogul. "By Brahma's big toe, I have performed a prodigious feat; I retained its gibberish word for word, although it is so lacking in sense and clarity that if you can give me a fine critical exposition of it, Madame, you will be giving me a gracious gift indeed."

"What did you say there, Prince?" cried Mirzoza. "May lightning strike me if you have not stolen that phrase from someone else."

"I cannot tell how this has happened," replied Mangogul, "for these two jewels are the only ones to whom I have given audience today. The second upon which I turned my ring, after a moment's silence, said, as if addressing an entire assembly:

" 'Gentlemen,

" 'I shall dispense with seeking, in defiance of my own reason, a model for thinking and expressing myself. If, nevertheless, I put forth something new, it will not be through pretense; I shall have drawn it from the subject itself. If I repeat something that has already been said, I shall have thought of it just as the others did.

" 'Let not irony turn this beginning to ridicule, and accuse me of having read nothing or having read for naught. A jewel such as I was not made to read or to make use of its reading, to raise objections or to answer them.

" 'I shall not deny myself reflections and embellishments proportionate to my subject, all the more so as my subject is, in this respect, an extremely modest one, which does not allow either for quantity or brilliance. But I shall avoid stooping to the tiny and insignificant details that are the share of a sterile orator; for it would grieve me deeply to be suspected of this defect.

" 'Having informed you, gentlemen, of what you can expect from my discoveries and my elocution, a few strokes should suffice to sketch my character to you.

" 'You know as well as I, gentlemen, that there are two types of jewels, proud jewels and modest jewels. The former want to excel and have the upper hand. The latter, on the contrary, affect docility and present themselves with an air of submission. These two intentions appear manifestly in the execution of their projects and determine both sorts to act according to their guiding spirits.

" 'I imagined, through an attachment to the prejudices of my earliest education, that I would embark upon a career that would be safer, easier, and far more gracious if I favored the role of humililty over that of pride. Thus I offered myself with a childish bashfulness and winning supplications to those whom I had the fortune to meet.

" 'But, oh, what miserable times these be! After ten times more *ifs*, *ands*, and *buts* than would drive the idlest jewel to exasperation, my services were accepted. Alas, it was not for long. My first possessor, surrendering himself to the flattering luster of a new conquest, forsook me, and I found myself idle again.

" 'My treasure was gone, and I bore no illusion that fortune would make amends for it. Indeed the vacant place was occupied, but to no good end, by a sexagenarian who possessed more goodwill than ability.

" 'He worked with all his might to rid me of the memories of my former state. With me he acted in all the ways considered polite and cooperative in the career that I pursued, but his zeal failed to overcome my regrets.

" 'If honest effort, which they say never falls short, helped him find in the treasures of natural ability some alleviation of my grief, this compensation seemed insufficient to me, in spite of my imagination, which tired itself out seeking new resemblances, and even making them up, though in vain.

" 'Such is the advantage of primacy: it seizes an idea and creates a barrier against all else that follows and would present itself in other guises; and such is, I must admit, to our shame, the ungrateful nature of jewels, for they never mistake goodwill for the deed.

" 'So natural does this remark seem to me, that, without being indebted to anybody for it, I do not think myself the only one to whom it has occurred. If anyone before me has been struck by it, at least, gentlemen, I am the first to undertake, by its demonstration, to assert its full value in the proper light.

" 'Far be it from me to hold it against those who have thus far raised their voices for having missed this point. My self-esteem is all too pleased, after so great a number of orators, to be able to present my observation as something new.' "

"Ah, Prince," cried Mirzoza emphatically, "I believe I hear the voice of the Manimonbanda's palm reader. Go to him: he alone can grant you the gracious gift of fine critical interpretation you would await in vain from any other."

The African author says that Mangogul smiled and continued, "But I have no intention to repeat the rest of its speech. If this beginning is not as amusing as the fairy Taupe's first pages, the rest would be more boring than the last pages of the fairy Moustache."

CHAPTER XL

Mirzoza's Dream

By the time Mangogul had finished the academic discourse of Girgiro the Entangled it was night, and they went to bed.

That night, the favorite might have expected to sleep soundly, but the evening's conversation returned to her in her sleep, and the ideas that had preoccupied her mingled with others and produced a disturbing dream, which she did not fail to recount to the Sultan.

"I was in my first moments of sleep," she said to him, "that I felt myself transported into a vast gallery full of books. I cannot tell you anything about their contents. They meant no more to me than they do to many others when they are awake. I did not look at a single title, for a more striking scene caught my attention.

"In the spaces between bookcases stood pedestals on which sat very beautiful marble and bronze busts. The ravages of time had spared them, and except for a few small imperfections they were whole and perfect. They were stamped with that nobility and elegance with which the ancients knew how to endow their works. Most had long beards, high foreheads like yours, and interesting countenances.

"I was anxious to learn their names and accomplishments when a woman came through a window frame and approached me. She was imposing in stature, majestic in gait, and noble in bearing: her glance was at once gentle and proud, and her voice had a pervasive but indefinable charm. A helmet, a breastplate, and a full skirt of white satin made up her attire. 'I understand your confusion,' she said to me, 'and I shall satisfy your curiosity. The men whose busts struck you were my favorites; they devoted their waking hours to perfecting the fine arts, whose invention is attributed to me. They lived in the most refined countries on earth, and their writings, which delighted their contemporaries, are admired in this century as well. Look closely and you will see, in bas-relief on the pedestals supporting the busts, some remarkable subjects that will at least suggest to you the nature of their writings.'

"The first bust I examined was of a majestic old man who seemed to me to be blind. Judging from appearances, he had sung of battles, for such were the subjects on the sides of his pedestal. A lone figure occupied the front of it: a young hero. His hand rested on the hilt of his scimitar, while a woman's arm held him back by his hair and seemed also to assuage his wrath.

"Opposite this bust was the bust of a young man. He was modesty itself: his gaze was directed at the old man with fixed attention. He too had sung of war and battles, but these were not his only concerns, for on the reliefs that surrounded him were laborers bent over their ploughs and cultivating their lands on one side, while on the other side shepherds lay on the grass, playing the flute among their sheep and dogs.

"The bust placed below the old man, and on the same side, had a wild look. His eye seemed to pursue some object that was eluding him, and beneath him were images of a lyre tossed carelessly aside, scattered laurels, broken chariots, and fiery horses escaping across a vast plain.

"Across from this one I saw a bust that so impressed me that I seem to see him still. He had a refined air, a pointed, aquiline nose, a steady gaze, and a wry smile. His pedestal was laden with such ornate reliefs that I would never finish were I to undertake describing them to you.

"After examining a few others, I began to question my guide.

" 'Who is this,' I asked her, 'who bears truth on his lips and probity on his countenance?'

" 'He was,' she said, 'friend and victim of both. He spent his life improving the knowledge and virtue of his fellow citizens, and these same ungrateful fellow citizens put him to death.'

" 'And the bust beneath him?'

" 'Which? The one that appears to be supported by the graces sculpted on the sides of the pedestal?'

" 'Exactly.'

" 'He is the disciple and heir of the spirit and principles of the virtuous and unfortunate man whom I just mentioned to you.'

" 'And this big, chubby-cheeked fellow, crowned with vine leaves and myrtle, who is he?'

" 'He is an amiable philosopher, whose sole endeavor was to sing and taste pleasure. He died in the arms of voluptuousness.'

" 'And this other blind man?'

" 'He is...' she said, 'but I did not wait for her answer. I felt at home there and hastily approached the bust opposite me. He was placed atop a trophy adorned with the different attributes of the arts and sciences. Cupids sported on one of the sides of the pedestal. On the other side, genii of politics, history, and philosophy had been grouped. On the third side were armies in battle formation: shock and horror reigned on every face, and traces of admiration and pity as well. These sentiments apparently were stirred by the scene before them. A young man was dying, and at his side was an older warrior turning his weapon against himself. Everything about these figures was exceedingly beautiful, the despair of the one, the mortal languor running through the limbs of the other. I drew near and read in letters of gold:

"'Alas! This was his son!'[1]

"Elsewhere, there was a relief of an enraged Soldan stabbing a young woman in the breast before a crowd of people. Some turned their heads, others broke into tears. These words were carved around the bas-relief:

"'Is it you, Nerestan?'

"I was about to go on to other busts, when a sudden noise caused me to turn my head. It was caused by a troop of men cloaked in long black robes, rushing en masse into the room. Some bore incense burners from which issued a thick smoke, others bore garlands of marigolds, and others flowers picked at random and arranged tastelessly. They flocked around the busts, burned incense to them, and chanted hymns in two languages unknown to me. The smoke from their incense stuck to the busts, and the flower-crowns upon their heads made a ridiculous sight. But soon the ancients returned to their former state. I saw the garlands wilt and fall to the floor, desiccated. A quarrel arose among these barbarians, because some had not bent their knees as deeply as others had wished. They were on the verge of blows when my guide scattered them with one look and reestablished calm in her abode.

"They had barely left when I saw a long train of pygmies enter through the opposite door in single file. These little men were not two cubits high, but in compensation they had very sharp teeth and very long nails. They divided into several bands and set upon the busts. Some tried to scratch the bas-reliefs, and the floor was sprinkled with the debris of their fingernails. Others, more insolent still, climbed on each other's shoulders to the height of the heads and tried to flick the noses with their fingers. I was pleased to see that these flicks, far from reaching the noses of the busts, turned back upon the pygmies themselves. When I looked at them up close, I found almost all of them to be snub-nosed.

"'You see,' said my guide, 'such is the audacity and the punishment of these midgets. This war has lasted a long time, much to their disadvantage. I am less severe with them than with the black robes: for whereas their incense might damage the busts, the efforts of these little creatures almost always end in increasing the busts' renown. But since you have only one or two more hours to spend here, I advise you to go on to other objects.'

"Suddenly a large curtain opened, and I saw a workshop filled with another kind of pygmy. These had neither teeth nor nails, but instead were armed with razors and scissors. In their hands they held heads that seemed alive, and they busied themselves in cutting the hair on one, cutting off the nose and ears of another, gouging out a right eye here, a left eye there, and dissecting almost all of them. After this fine operation, they looked at them attentively and smiled, as if they thought them the most beautiful things on earth. In vain did the poor heads cry out loudly; they barely deigned answer them. I heard one ask for his nose back, explaining that he was not presentable without this part.

"'Well, my friend,' the pygmy answered him, 'you are quite mad. This nose you miss so much disfigured you hideously. It was long, very long. You would never have made your fortune with it. But now that it has been shortened and trimmed for you, you are charming, and you will be much sought after.'

"I was pitying the fate of the heads when I noticed further off other, more charitable pygmies who crept along the floor with spectacles. They collected noses and ears, and fitted them onto old heads from which time had removed them.

"Among them were a very small number who succeeded at this pursuit; the others placed a nose where an ear should have been, an ear in place of a nose, and the heads became all the more disfigured.

"I was very eager to know what all these things meant, and I asked my guide. She opened her mouth to answer me when I awoke with a start."

"That was cruel," said Mangogul. "This woman would have explained many mysteries to you. But through default I suggest we ask my juggler, Bloculocus."

"Who?" asked the favorite. "That simpleton to whom you granted the sole privilege of showing a magic lantern in your court?"

"None other," answered the Sultan. "He will be able to interpret your dream for us, or no one will."

"Let Bloculocus be summoned," says Mangogul.

CHAPTER XLI

Twenty-First and Twenty-Second Trials of the Ring
Fricamona and Callipygia

The African author does not tell us what Mangogul did while waiting for Bloculocus. Most likely he went out to consult a jewel or two, and then, satisfied with what he learned, returned to the favorite, emitting the joyous cries that begin this chapter.

"Victory! Victory!" he cried. "You have triumphed, Madame, and the château, the porcelains, and the little monkey are yours."

"No doubt it is Eglea?" asked the favorite.

"No, Madame, no, it is not Eglea," interrupted the Sultan. "It is another."

"Ah, Prince," said the favorite, "do not withhold this paragon's name any longer."

"Very well! It is...who would ever have thought it?"

"It is...?" said the favorite.

"Fricamona," answered Mangogul.

"Fricamona!" returned Mirzoza. "I do not find that so difficult to believe. This woman has spent most of her youth in a convent, and since she got out she has led a most exemplary and secluded life. No man has ever set foot in her house; and she, in some measure, has made herself the abbess of a troop of devout young women who constantly fill her house, and whom she educates to perfection. You could hardly find fault with her," added the favorite, smiling and shaking her head.

"Madame, you are right," said Mangogul. "I questioned her jewel, but received no answer. I redoubled the powers of my ring by rubbing and rubbing. Nothing happened. It must be, I told myself, that this jewel is deaf. I prepared to leave Fricamona on the bed where I found her when she began to speak – through the mouth, that is."

" 'Dear Acaris,' she cried, 'how happy am I in these moments I snatch from my obligations to devote myself to you! After those I spend in your arms, these are the sweetest moments of my life...Nothing distracts me. Silence is all around me. My half-open curtains admit only as much light as I need to move me to tenderness and gaze at you. I command my imagination; it calls you forth and I see you...Dear Acaris! You look so beautiful to me!...Yes, those are your eyes, your smile, your lips... Do not hide those budding breasts from me. Allow me to kiss them...I have not seen enough of them...Let me kiss them again!...Alas, may I die upon them...What madness takes hold of me! Acaris! Dear Acaris, where are you? Come to me, dear Acaris...Ah! Dear and tender friend, I swear to you, unfamiliar sentiments are taking hold of my soul. It is full of them, overwhelmed, and cannot contain them...Flow, sweet tears, flow and ease the passion that devours me...No, dear Acaris, no, that Alizali whom you preferred to me will not love you as I do...But I hear a noise. Ah! It is no doubt Acaris!...Come, sweet soul, come...'

"Fricamona was not mistaken," continued Mangogul, "for it was Acaris herself. I left them twined together, strongly persuaded that Fricamona's jewel would continue to be discreet, and I ran to tell you that I have lost my wager."

"But," replied the Sultana, "I do not understand a thing about this Fricamona. She must be mad or suffer terrible vapors. No, Prince, no,

I have more conscience than you think. I have no objection to this trial. But I feel something that prevents me from taking advantage of it. And I will not take advantage of it. That is settled. I do not want your château, or your porcelains, or I will have them on better grounds than this."

"Madame," answered Mangogul, "I do not understand you. You are unsurpassably difficult. You must not have looked closely at the little monkey."

"Prince, I have looked at him well," replied Mirzoza, "and I know that he is charming. But I suspect that Fricamona is not the person I seek. If you wish him to be mine one day, you must look elsewhere."

"Well, well," said Mangogul, after having thought hard about it, "I see only Mirolo's mistress who may help you win the wager."

"Ah, Prince, you must be dreaming," answered the favorite. "I do not know Mirolo, but whoever he may be, the fact that he has a mistress must mean something."

"True," said Mangogul, "yet I would still wager that Callipygia's jewel knows nothing at all."

"Let us agree, then," continued the favorite, "on one of these two things: either Callipygia's jewel...But no, that argument is too ridiculous...Do whatever you please, Prince: consult Callipygia's jewel. If it is silent, too bad for Mirolo, and all the better for me."

Mangogul left and instantly found himself near a pale yellow sofa, embroidered in silver, upon which Callipygia was reclining. Scarcely had he turned his ring upon her when he heard a muffled voice murmuring the following discourse:

"What are you asking me? I do not understand your questions. No one pays any attention to me. It seems to me, however, that I am as good as any other. Mirolo often passes by my door, it is true, but..."

(At this point there is a considerable lacuna in the narration. The Republic of Letters would certainly be greatly beholden to anyone who recovered the speech of Callipygia's jewel, of which only the last two lines remain. We invite scholars to study them and consider whether this break might not be a voluntary omission on the part of the author, dissatisfied with what he had written and finding nothing better to say.)

"...People say that my rival has altars beyond the Alps. Alas, but for Mirolo, the whole world would erect them to me."

Mangogul returned to the seraglio and repeated the complaint of Callipygia's jewel word for word to the favorite, for he had a marvelous memory.

"Everything in it, Madame," he said to her, "makes you the winner. I surrender all to you, and you may thank Callipygia for it, when you find it proper to do so."

"My lord," Mirzoza answered him in all seriousness, "it is to the most certain virtue that I wish to owe my victory, and not..."

"But, Madame," said the Sultan, "I know of none more certain than that which has seen the enemy so near."

"As for me, Prince," replied the favorite, "I know whereof I speak. Here are Selim and Bloculocus; they shall be our judges."

Selim and Bloculocus entered. Mangogul stated the case and both decided in favor of Mirzoza.

CHAPTER XLII

Dreams

"My lord," said the favorite to Bloculocus, "I must ask another favor of you. Last night a host of mad images passed through my head. It was a dream, but what a dream! I have been assured that you are the best man in the Congo in dream interpretation. Tell me quickly what this one means." And she told him her dream forthwith.

"Madame," said Bloculocus, "I am but a mediocre oneirocritic..."

"Spare me, if you please, the technical jargon," cried the favorite. "Leave science aside and speak reason to me."

"Madame," Bloculocus said to her, "you shall be satisfied. I have some rather unusual ideas about dreams. It is perhaps to this alone that I owe the honor of conversing with you, as well as the epithet of The Dreamer. I shall explain matters to you as clearly as I can.

"You are not unaware, Madame," he continued, "what most philosophers and the rest of mankind have to say on the subject. Things, they say, that make a deep impression on us during the day occupy our souls during the night. The traces left imprinted in the fibers of the brain during waking hours live on; the animal spirits, accustomed to directing themselves to certain places, follow their familiar route, thus giving rise to the involuntary representations that afflict or delight us. According to this system, it would appear that a happy lover should always be well served by his dreams. It often happens, however, that a person who is not unkind to him in waking hours treats him like a slave in his sleep, or that instead of making love to a charming woman he finds instead a deformed little monster in his arms."

"That was precisely my experience last night," interrupted Mangogul, "for I dream almost every night. It is a disease that runs in my family, and we have all dreamed, from father to son, since the time of the sultan Togrul, who dreamed in the year 743,500,000,002 and began it all. As I was saying, last night I saw you, Madame," he said to Mirzoza. "I saw your skin, your arms, your breasts, your neck, your shoulders, your firm flesh, your lithe figure, your incomparable plumpness, you yourself; except that instead of that charming face, that adorable head that I expected to see, I found myself face-to-face with a hound's muzzle.

"I let out a terrible cry. Kotluk, my chamberlain, ran to me and asked me what was wrong. 'Mirzoza,' I answered him, half asleep, 'has just undergone the most hideous metamorphosis; she has become a Great Dane.' Kotluk did not find it necessary to wake me. He withdrew, and I fell back to sleep, but I can assure you that I recognized you perfectly, your body and the head of a dog. Could Bloculocus explain this phenomenon to me?"

"Do not worry," said Bloculocus. "As long as your majesty will agree with me on one very simple principle: that all beings have an infinite number of relations with each other through the qualities they share; and that it is a certain combination of qualities that characterizes and distinguishes them."

"That is clear," replied Mirzoza. "Ipsifila has the feet, hands, and the mouth of a spirited woman."

"And Pharasmane," added Mangogul, "wields his sword like a brave man."

"And if one is not sufficiently informed about the qualities that combine to characterize such and such a species, or if one judges hastily that this combination becomes or does not become such and such an individual, one risks mistaking copper for gold, baubles for diamonds, an accountant for a geometer, a prattler for a wit, Criton for an honest man, and Phedima for a pretty woman," added the Sultana.

"Well, Madame, and do you know what one might say," continued Bloculocus, "about the people who pass such judgments?"

"That they daydream?" asked Mirzoza.

"Very good, Madame," continued Bloculocus, "and nothing is more philosophical or more exact in a thousand circumstances than the familiar expression 'You must be dreaming,' for nothing is more common than men who imagine they are reasoning but who are dreaming with their eyes open."

"And they are the ones," interrupted the favorite, "for whom one might say, literally, that life is but a dream."

"I am astounded, Madame," said Bloculocus, "at the facility with which you grasp quite abstract ideas. Our dreams are but rash judgments that succeed each other with unbelievable rapidity, and which, by bringing together things whose connections lie only in the most diverse of qualities, compose a bizarre whole."

"Oh, how well I understand you," said Mirzoza, "and it is a work of inlay, in which the elements are more or less numerous, more or less regularly placed, according to the dreamer's quickness of wit, the rapidity of his imagination, and the faithfulness of his memory. Would this not also be the case in madness, when an inmate of the Petites-Maisons cries out that he sees lightening flashes, hears thunder rumbling, or feels abysses opening up beneath his feet? Or when Ariadne, sitting before her mirror, smiling to herself, finds her eyes bright, her complexion smooth, her teeth perfect, and her mouth small? Might not this be because these deranged minds, deluded by remote associations, regard imaginary things as both present and real?"

"Just so, Madame. Indeed, if madmen are examined closely," said Bloculocus, "one might be convinced that their state is but a perpetual dream."

"I," said Selim, addressing Bloculocus, "have had several dreams to which your ideas apply most excellently, which convinces me that I ought to adopt these ideas myself. Once I dreamed that I heard braying, and saw two parallel rows of strange animals coming out of the Great Mosque. They walked solemnly on their hind legs; the hoods with which their muzzles were equipped were pierced with two holes that allowed two long, mobile, and shaggy ears to protrude. Long sleeves enveloped their front legs. I racked my brains at the time to make sense of this vision; but today I remember that the night before I had been to Montmartre.

"Another time we were in the field, under the command of the great sultan Erguebzed himself. Exhausted by a long march, I fell asleep in my tent and it seemed to me that I had to petition the divan[1] for the conclusion of an important affair. I went to present myself to the regency council, but imagine how stunned I was to find the room full of racks, troughs, mangers, and chicken coops. In the Grand Seneschal's chair I saw a ruminating ox; a Barbary sheep in place of the seraskier;[2] an eagle with a hooked beak and long claws on the teftardar's[3] bench; two fat owls in the place of the kiara[4] and the cadilesker; and for viziers, there were only geese with peacock tails. I presented my request, and immediately heard a horrible racket that woke me up."

"That is not a difficult dream to decipher, is it?" asked Mangogul. "You had a matter for the divan, and before you went there you took a turn in the menagerie. But as for me, Sir Bloculocus, what do you say about my dog's head?"

"Prince," answered Bloculocus, "it is one hundred to one that Madame had a sable-fur tippet, or that you saw one on someone else, and that you thought of Great Danes the first time you saw one. We see here ten times more connections than were necessary to exercise your soul during the night – the similarity of color makes you substitute fur for a tippet, and immediately you plant a nasty dog's head in the place of the head of a very beautiful woman."

"Your ideas seem correct to me," answered Mangogul. "Why not make them public? They might contribute to the progress of divination through dreams, an important science that was much cultivated two thousand years ago, and which has been all too neglected since. Another advantage of your system is that it could not help but shed some light on many ancient as well as modern works, which are woven through with dreams, such as Plato's *Treatise on Ideas*, the *Fragments* of Hermes Trismegistus, the *Literary Paradoxes* of Father H——, the *Newton*, the *Optic of Colors*, and the *Universal Mathematics* of a certain Brahmin. For example, could you not guess, Sir Soothsayer, what Orcotomus had seen during the day when he dreamed up his hypothesis? Or what Father C—— had dreamed when he set about creating his color organ? And what Cleobulus had dreamed when he composed his tragedy?"

"With a little thought I could, sir," answered Bloculocus, "but I shall save these fine phenomena for the time when I shall present to the public my translation of Philoxenes, for which I beg Your Highness to grant me the privilege."

"Willingly," said Mangogul, "but who is this Philoxenes?"

"Prince," answered Bloculocus, "he is a Greek author who very well understood the matter of dreams."

"You know Greek?"

"Not a word."

"Did you not say that you were translating Philoxenes, and that he wrote in Greek?"

"Yes, my lord, but it is not necessary to know a language to translate it, for one translates only for people who do not know it either."

"This is marvelous, Sir Bloculocus!" said the Sultan. "Go ahead and translate Greek without knowing it! Upon my word, I shall not tell a soul, and I shall not respect you any the less for it."

CHAPTER XLIII

Twenty-Third Trial of the Ring
Fanni

There was enough daylight remaining at the end of this conversation to prompt Mangogul to conduct a trial of his ring before retiring to his chambers. In all probability this was so that he would fall asleep with more cheerful thoughts than those which had occupied his mind until this point. Thus he went to Fanni's place, but she was not in. He returned after supper, but she was still out, and so he postponed the trial until the next morning.

That morning, says the African author whose journal we are translating, Mangogul was at Fanni's at half past nine. She had just been put to bed. The Sultan drew close to her pillows, looked at her a moment, and could not understand how, with so few charms, she had had so many adventures.

Fanni was so blonde she was insipid. She was big, ungainly, and had an indecent gait; she had not one nice feature, few charms, and an air of fearlessness that is only acceptable at Court. As for wit, she was acknowledged to possess as much of it as gallantry can convey, for a woman would have to be a complete idiot not to know at least some jargon after twenty or so liaisons – which is the point at which Fanni found herself.

She belonged at this time to a man whose character matched her own. He was never troubled by her unfaithfulness, although he was never quite as well informed of its extent as the general public. He had taken up with Fanni on a lark and kept her, like a piece of furniture, by force of habit.

They had spent the night at a ball, gone to bed at nine o'clock, and fallen asleep unceremoniously. Alonzo's indifference would not have sat well with Fanni, if not for her easygoing nature. They were thus deep in sleep, back to back, when the Sultan turned his ring toward Fanni's jewel. Immediately it began to speak, its mistress to snore, and Alonzo to awaken.

After yawning several times, it said, "You are not Alonzo. What time is it? What do you want from me? It seems to me I've not been resting very long; leave me alone."

The good jewel was about to go back to sleep, but this was not what the Sultan had in mind. "What persecution," said the jewel. "Another knock. What do you want? Woe to those with illustrious ancestors! The pitiful plight of a titled jewel! If there were any consolation for the demands of my station, it would be the kindness of the man to whom I belong. Oh, on that account he is the best fellow in the world. He never pesters us at all. In return, we have made good use of the freedom he has granted us. Where would I be if, by the will of Brahma, I had fallen into the hands of one of those disagreeable men who spy about? What a fine life we would have led!"

Here the jewel added a few words that Mangogul did not understand, and then it set about sketching a host of heroic, comic, burlesque, and tragicomic events with surprising speed, and it was out of breath by the time it got to these words: "I have quite a memory, as you can see, but I am like all the others. I have retained but the smallest part of what has been confided to me. Therefore be thus content with what I have told you, for I can think of nothing more."

"That is honest," said Mangogul to himself, and yet he persisted.

"How impertinent you are!" retorted the jewel. "One might think I had nothing more than chattering to think about! All right. Let us chatter, since it is required of us; perhaps when I have said all, I shall be allowed to do something else.

"Fanni, my mistress," continued the jewel, "left the Court because of her unimaginably retiring spirit and shut herself up in her house in Banza. That was at the beginning of autumn, and there was not a soul in town. And what did she plan to do there, you ask? Mercy, I have no idea, but Fanni has never done but one thing, and if she is doing it, I know all about it. She was apparently idle; yes, I remember now, we spent a day and a half doing nothing, bored to death.

"I feared I should perish from this sort of life, when Amisadar took it upon himself to deliver us from it.

"'Ah! There you are, my poor Amisadar. Really, I am delighted. You have come to me just in time.'

"'Who would have guessed you to be in Banza?' Amisadar asked her.

"'Oh! Not a soul. Neither you nor the others would ever imagine it. Try to guess what brought me here.'

"'Really, I cannot. I have no idea.'

"'No idea?'

"'None at all.'

"'Very well, then. Listen up, my dear: I came to be converted.'

"'Converted?'

"'Well, yes.'

"'Look at me. But you are as charming as ever; I see nothing that would lead to a conversion. You must be joking.'

"'No, by faith, it is all quite in earnest. I have resolved to withdraw from the world. It bores me.'

"'Surely it is just a passing fancy. May I die if you ever become devout.'

"'I will, I tell you. Men are not sincere.'

"'Is it because you miss Mazul?'

"'No, I have not seen him in ages.'

"'Is it Zupholo, then?'

"'Still less. I stopped seeing him, I know not how, without so much as a thought.'

"'Ah! I have it! Is it the young Imola?'

"'No! Does anyone really keep trinkets like him?'

"'What, then?'

"'I don't quite know. I am angry at the whole world.'

"'Oh, Madame! You are mistaken, and the world with which you are angry can still provide you with things to compensate you for your losses.'

"'In truth, Amisadar, do you still think that there are any souls who have escaped the corruption of the age, who still know how to love?'

"'How to love! So that is the affliction you are suffering? You want to be loved – you?'

"'And why not?'

"'A man in love wants to be in love and only to be in love. You have too much sense to subject yourself to the jealousies and whims of a tender, faithful lover. Nothing is more tiring than that type of man. To see him alone, love him alone, dream only of him, to be witty, playful, and charming for him alone, that certainly would not suit you. What a sight you would make, mixing yourself with a fine passion. Before long you would be assuming all the airs of a little bourgeoise.'

"'I suppose, Amisadar, that I agree with you. In fact, I believe that it ill becomes us to live the dream of love. Let us change, then, for change we must. Likewise, I do not think that the loving women offered up to us as models are any happier than others.'

"'Who told you so, Madame?'

"'No one, but I sense it.'

"'Beware of such presentiment. A loving woman makes herself happy, and she makes her lover happy; but this role does not suit all women.'

"'Mercy, my dear, it does not suit anyone, and everyone is unhappy with it. What could possibly induce anyone to form such attachments?'

"'There are a great many reasons. A woman who forms an attachment saves her reputation and assures that she will always be respected by her lover. You have no idea how much love owes to respect.'

" 'I do not understand these things at all. You confuse everything: reputation, love, respect, and I know not what else. Do they not say that infidelity brings dishonor? What! I take a man; he is not to my liking. I take another who does not suit me. I exchange him for a third who does not suit me any better. And for having the misfortune of twenty or so such encounters, instead of feeling pity for me, you would...'

" 'I would, Madame, advise a woman who had made a mistake in her first choice not to make a second, lest she be mistaken again, and thus go from error to error.'

" 'Oh, a fine morality, that! It seems to me, my dear, that just now you were preaching quite another thing to me. Could one ask just how a woman to your taste would be?'

" 'Willingly, Madame, but it is late and this would lead us far...'

" 'So much the better; I am alone and you shall keep me company. So it is decided, is it not? Sit down on this sofa and continue. I shall listen to you in greater comfort.'

"Amisadar obeyed, and sat down next to Fanni.

" 'This mantelet, Madame,' he said, leaning toward her and uncovering her breasts, 'cloaks you most strangely.'

" 'I agree.'

" 'Ah! Why hide such nice things?' he added, kissing them.

" 'Enough. Do you know that you are mad? Your behavior has become unsurpassably bold. Sir Moralist, please continue the conversation you began.'

" 'In my mistress I would desire,' continued Amisadar, 'a good figure, wit, sensitivity, and above all, decency. I would wish for her to approve of my attentions and not to refuse me with sulks; for her to tell me in good faith that I please her, and to instruct me herself in ways to please her more; for her not to conceal the progress I make in her heart; for her to have ears, eyes, thoughts, dreams, and love for me alone; for her to be occupied with me alone and do nothing save try to convince me of this. Yielding one day to my raptures, I would wish to see clearly that I owe everything to my love, and to hers. What triumph, Madame! How happy a man would be to possess such a woman!'

" 'But, my poor Amisadar, you are raving. Nothing is further from reality. That was a portrait of a woman who does not exist.'

" 'I beg your pardon, Madame; such women exist. I admit that they are very rare. I have even had the honor of meeting one. Alas! If death had not taken her from me, for it is death alone that carries off such women, I might be in her arms still.'

" 'And how did you behave toward her?'

" 'I loved her madly, and I missed not one occasion to give her proof of my affections. I had the sweet satisfaction of seeing these well received. I was scrupulously faithful. She was the same for me. Our only quarrels concerned whose love was strongest. These little disagreements brought us closer. Never were we so affectionate as after examining our hearts. Our caresses were always more sincere after such explanations. How much love and truth shone in our eyes! I read in her gaze she read in mine that we burned with a passion both equal and shared.'

" 'And where did this lead you?'

" 'To pleasures unknown to all mortals less in love and less truthful than we.'

" 'And you tasted pleasure?'

" 'Yes, the pleasure of a boon that I made infinite. If respect does not intoxicate in itself, it adds a lot to intoxication. We revealed our hearts to each other, and you would not believe how much our passion gained from this. The more I examined her heart, the more good qualities I saw there and the more enraptured I became. Half my life was spent at her feet, the other half in regret. I was the source of her happiness, she the fulfillment of my own. It was always a pleasure to see her, always painful to leave her. This is how we lived. Judge for yourself, Madame, if loving women are so much to be pitied.'

" 'No, they are not, if you speak the truth. But I can hardly believe it. No one loves like that anymore. I can even imagine that a passion such as the one you experienced must pay for its pleasures in worries.'

" 'I had a few, Madame, but I cherished them. I felt the pangs of jealousy. The slightest alteration I noticed in my mistress's face brought alarm to the depths of my soul.'

" 'How foolish! When all is said and done, I conclude that it is better to love as people love today, taking a lover at one's leisure, keeping him as long as he is amusing, leaving him when boredom sets in, or when caprice demands another. Infidelity offers a variety of pleasures unknown to you bashful lovers.'

" 'I concede that your way is suitable enough for flirts and libertines, but a sensitive, loving man could never get used to it. At most such a woman could amuse him, if his heart were free and he wanted to make comparisons. In a word, gallant women are not at all to my liking.'

" 'You are right, my dear Amisadar, you argue wonderfully. But are you presently in love with someone?'

" 'No, Madame, if not with you; but I dare not tell you...'

" 'Oh, my dear; do tell me,' Fanni replied, looking him in the eyes.

"Amisadar understood this answer marvelously; he approached the couch and began to dally with a ribbon that hung over Fanni's bosom. She let him have his way. His hand, finding no resistance, slipped in. She continued to shower him with glances, which he did not misinterpret. I myself noticed," said the jewel, "that he was right. He kissed these breasts which he had so praised. He was asked to stop, but in a tone that would have taken insult if obeyed. So he took no notice of it. He kissed the hands, returned to the breasts, went on to the mouth, meeting no resistance. Gradually Fanni's leg found itself on Amisadar's thighs, he touched it, found it well turned and did not fail to comment on it. His praise encountered a distracted ear. Taking advantage of this inattention, Amisadar's hand continued to advance, and quickly came to her knees. As the lady's inattention persisted, Amisadar began to make ready, when Fanni came to herself. She accused the little philosopher of lacking respect, but he, in turn, was so distracted that he heard nothing, or rather, he answered the reproaches he received by consummating his joy.

"How charming he seemed to me! Of all those who preceded and followed him, none has been more to my liking. I cannot think of him without trembling. But allow me to catch my breath. It seems to me I have been talking a long time for one who is performing for the first time."

Alonzo had not missed a word of Fanni's jewel, and he was no less eager than Mangogul to hear the rest of the adventure. Neither one had time to grow impatient, for the tale-telling jewel began again with these words:

"From what I have gathered by dint of reflection, Amisadar left for the country a few days later. People asked him the reason for his stay in town, and he told the tale of his adventure with my mistress. Then a mutual friend, passing in front of our house, asked by chance, or by suspicion, if Madame was in. He was announced and up he came.

" 'Ah, Madame! Who would have thought you in Banza? How long have you been here?'

" 'For ages, my dear. For the two weeks since I renounced society.'

" 'Might one inquire, Madame, the reason?'

" 'Alas! I was tired of it. The women live in a world of libertinage so strange one can hardly grasp it. One must either join them or pass for a prude; and, frankly, both the one and the other seemed extreme to me.'

" 'But, Madame, how exalted your speech is. Could it be that the talk of the Brahmin Brelibibi has converted you?'

" 'No, it is a whiff of philosophy and a bit of devotion. It took me by surprise, quite suddenly; and it is thanks to that poor Amisadar that I am currently in retirement.'

" 'Madame has seen him recently, then?'

" 'Yes, once or twice...'

" 'And you saw him alone?'

" 'Oh, it is not what you think. He is the only thinking, reasonable, active person who has come here since the eternity of my retreat.'

" 'That is curious.'

" 'What is so curious about it?'

" 'Nothing except an adventure he recently had with a woman in Banza, alone like you, pious like you, in retreat like you. I shall tell you the story. Would that perhaps amuse you?'

" 'Undoubtedly,' said Fanni, and Amisadar's friend immediately set about telling the adventure word for word, just as I have done," said the jewel, "and just when he got to the part where I am now...

" 'Well, Madame,' he said to her, 'was not Amisadar fortunate?'

" 'But perhaps,' Fanni replied to him, 'Amisadar is lying. Do you believe that there really are women bold enough to yield so shamelessly?'

" 'But, Madame,' answered Marsupha, 'considering that Amisadar did not name names, it is not likely that he would have made it up.'

" 'I think I understand,' said Fanni. 'Amisadar is witty and nicely built; he probably filled this poor recluse with voluptuous ideas that swept her off her feet. Yes, that is it. That type of man is dangerous to people who listen to them, and Amisadar is unique among them...'

" 'How so, Madame?' interrupted Marsupha. 'Is Amisadar the only persuasive man around? Will you not do justice to others who deserve as much as he a little share of your esteem?'

" 'And of whom are you speaking, if I may ask?'

" 'Of myself, Madame, who finds you charming and...'

" 'You are joking, I am sure. Look at me, Marsupha. I have neither rouge nor beauty marks. I am frightful.'

" 'You are mistaken, Madame. Your negligee suits you ravishingly. It makes you look so winning, so tender!'

"Marsupha added more gallant phrases to these. I became involved in the conversation unwittingly, and when Marsupha had finished with me, he continued to my mistress:

" 'Seriously, did Amisadar try to convert you? He is admirably good at conversions! Could you give me an example of his moral code? I would bet that it is hardly different from my own.'

" 'We spoke in depth of certain qualities of gallantry. We analyzed the difference between a loving woman and a gallant one. He prefers the loving kind.'

"'And you too, I imagine?...'

"'Not at all, my dear, I tired myself out in showing him that all women are alike, and that we follow the same principles. He did not agree with this. He established an infinite number of distinctions that exist, I believe, in his imagination alone. He has created for himself I know not what type of ideal creature, a chimera of a woman, a creature dressed in words.'

"'Madame,' said Marsupha, 'I know Amisadar. He is a fellow of good sense who knows a lot about women. If he told you that there are —'

"'Oh! Whether there are or are not, I could never get used to their ways,' interrupted Fanni.

"'I believe you,' said Marsupha. 'You have taken a path more suitable to your birth and merit. You should leave those silly creatures to the philosophers; they would pass unnoticed at Court...'"

Fanni's jewel fell silent at this point. One of the main characteristics of these orators was that they stopped themselves at the right moment. They spoke as if they had never done anything else, and from this fact several authors concluded that they were merely machines. Their argument went as follows:... Here the African author repeats in its entirety the Cartesians' metaphysical argument against the souls of animals, which with all possible sagacity he applied to the jewels' chatter. In a word, his opinion was that jewels speak the way birds sing; that is, perfectly, without having learned how, being prompted undoubtedly from above.

And what did he do about his prince, you ask me? He sent him to dine with the favorite, or at least that is where we shall find him in the following chapter.

CHAPTER XLIV

Selim's Travels

Having questioned the most interesting jewels of his court, Mangogul, whose only thought was to vary his pleasures and multiply the trials of his ring, was curious to hear a few jewels from the town. But as he did not set great store by what he might learn from them, he wished to consult with them at leisure, and spare himself the trouble of seeking them out.

But how could he make them come to him? That was the question.

"You certainly do worry needlessly," said Mirzoza. "My lord, you have only to give a ball, and I promise you more chatterboxes that night than you would ever want to hear."

"Joy of my heart, you are right!" replied Mangogul. "Your idea is all the better because we shall be sure to have only the ones we need.

"Orders are given at once to the kislar Agasi and the master of revels to prepare the event, and to distribute only four thousand tickets. Presumably they knew here, better than elsewhere, the amount of space required for six thousand people."

While waiting for the ball, Selim, Mangogul, and the favorite took to discussing the latest news.

"Is Madame aware," Selim asked the favorite, "that poor Codindo is dead?"

"This is the first I have heard of it. What did he die of?" asked the favorite.

"Alas, Madame," Selim answered her, "he fell victim to gravitational attraction. He had become infatuated with this system in his youth, and it turned his brain in old age."

"How so?" asked the favorite.

"He had found," continued Selim, "according to the methods of Halley and Circino, two famous astronomers from Monoemugi, that a certain comet, which caused quite a fuss at the end of Kanoglou's reign, was supposed to reappear the day before yesterday. Fearing that it might come sooner, and that he might not have the joy of being the first to see it, he decided to spend the night on top of his observatory, and yesterday, at nine in the morning, he still had his eye glued to the telescope. His son, who feared he would take ill after so long a sitting, approached him at eight o'clock, pulled at his sleeve, and called several times:

"'Father, Father.' No answer. 'Father, Father,' repeated young Codindo.

"'It is coming,' answered Codindo, 'it is coming. Oh, mercy, I will see it, by Jove!'

"'But you do not realize, Father, there is a dreadful fog...'

"'I want to see it. I shall see it, I tell you...'

"Convinced by these answers that his unfortunate father had gone mad, the young man began to cry for help. People came running. Farfadi was called. I was at Farfadi's – for he is my physician – when Codindo's servant arrived.

"'Quick, quick, sir, hurry up. Old Codindo, my master...'

"'Well, what is it, Champagne? What has happened to your master?'

"'He has gone mad.'

"'Your master is mad?'

"'Yes, sir. He screams out that he must see the beasts, that he will see the beasts, that they will come. The apothecary is already there, and they are waiting for you. Come quickly.'

"'Mania!' cried Farfadi, putting on his robe and looking for his doctor's cap. Mania, a terrible bout of mania!' Then, addressing the servant, he asked, 'Champagne, does your master see butterflies? Is he tearing little tufts from his bedspread?'

"'Well, no, sir,' Champagne answered him. 'The poor man is atop his observatory, where his wife, daughters, and son are restraining him. Come quickly, you can find your doctor's cap tomorrow.'

"Codindo's illness seemed amusing to me. Farfadi climbed into my carriage and together we went to the observatory. At the foot of the stairs we heard Codindo screaming like a madman, 'I must to see the comet! I will see it! Get away, rogues.'

"Apparently his family, unable to convince him to return to his chambers, had had his bed brought to the top of the turret, for we found him reclining. The neighborhood apothecary had been called, as had the parish Brahmin, who shouted in his ears as we arrived:

"'My brother, your salvation is at stake. You may not, in good conscience, wait for a comet at this hour. You shall be damned...'

"'That is my business,' Codindo said to him.

"'What will you say to Brahma before whom you shall have to appear?' asked the Brahmin.

"'Sir Priest,' answered Codindo, without taking his eye from the telescope, 'I will tell him that it was your job to beg money from me, and Sir Apothecary's over there to praise his lukewarm water; that it was Sir Physician's job to feel my pulse, and to know nothing about it; and mine to wait for the comet.'

"Torment him as they might, they gained nothing more from him. He continued his lookout with heroic courage. He died in his rain gutter, left hand over the left eye, right hand on the shaft of the telescope, right eye glued to the eyepiece, in the company of his son, who cried out that he had calculated wrong; of his apothecary, who proposed a remedy; of his doctor, who, shaking his head, pronounced that nothing more could be done; and of his priest, who said to him, 'Brother, make an act of contrition and commend yourself to Brahma.'"

"Now that," said Mangogul, "is what I call dying on the bed of honor."

"Let us allow the poor Codindo to rest in peace," added the favorite, "and go on to more pleasant things."

Then, addressing Selim, she said, "My lord, at your age, gallant as you are, with your wit, talents, and handsome face, it is not surprising that, in a court ruled by pleasures, the jewels should praise you. I even suspect that they have not revealed all they know of your accomplishments. I am not asking you to supplement this, for you may have good reason to refuse me. But after all the adventures with which these good jewels have honored you, you must have an understanding of women, and this is one thing you might safely admit."

"This compliment, Madame," Selim answered her, "would have flattered my self-esteem at the age of twenty. But now that I have experience, one of my first observations is that the more one practices in this field, the less knowledge he obtains. Me, understand women! I am merely credited with having studied them a great deal."

"Well, and what do you think of them?" the favorite asked him.

"Madame," replied Selim, "regardless of what their jewels may have made public, I still hold them in great respect."

"In truth, my dear fellow," the Sultan said to him, "you should have been a jewel; you would not have needed a muzzle."

"Selim," added the Sultana, "drop the satiric tone and speak to us sincerely."

"Madame," the courtier answered her, "I could add some unpleasant touches to my tale, but do not require me to offend the sex that has always treated me so well, and which I revere –"

"What! Always veneration! I know none so caustic as mawkish people when they set their hearts to it," interrupted Mirzoza. Imagining that it was for her own sake that Selim held back, she added, "Do not let my presence inhibit your speech. We want to amuse ourselves, and I shall take it upon myself, word of honor, to apply to myself only the kind things you say about my sex, and to leave the rest to other women. So you say you have studied women a great deal, eh? Very well, then! Tell us the story of your observations. It must be one of the most brilliant, judging from your known successes, and one would assume that those as yet unknown will not persuade us to the contrary."

The old courtier gave in to her entreaties, and began as follows:

"The jewels have spoken about me a great deal, I agree, but they have not said everything. Those who could complete my story are no more, or do not live in this land; and those who began my story have but lightly skimmed its surface. Until now I have kept the inviolable secret I promised them, although I was more qualified to speak than they. But since they have broken their silence, it seems that they have excused me from keeping mine.

"Born with a fiery disposition, no sooner did I learn what a beautiful woman was than I was already loving them. I had governesses, whom I loathed; but, on the other hand, I took great delight in my mother's waiting women. They were for the most part young and pretty. They talked with each other, dressed and undressed in front of me unabashedly, and encouraged me to take liberties with them. My temper, already predisposed to gallantry, took advantage of all this. At the age of five or six I was put in the hands of men of the enlightened cast of mind, and God knows how this world opened up to me when the ancients were put under my nose, which my masters interpreted for me in certain parts, unaware perhaps themselves of the meaning. My father's valets taught me a few schoolboy pranks, and the reading of *Aloysia*,[1] which they lent me, filled me with the desire to perfect myself. I was fourteen years old at the time.

"I cast my eyes about me, seeking among the women who called at the house one to whom I might address myself. They all seemed equally suitable to deliver me from an innocence that weighed heavily upon me. A budding intimacy, and, above all, the courage I felt to attack someone of my own age, decided me in favor of one of my cousins. Emilie, for such was her name, was young, and so was I. I found her pretty, and she liked me as well. She was not difficult, and I was rather forward. I wanted to learn and she was no less curious to know. We asked each other very artless and bold questions, and one day she eluded her governesses' vigilance and we instructed each other. Oh, what a great teacher nature is! Soon she taught us pleasure, and we abandoned ourselves to her promptings, with no idea of the consequences. We did not know how to prevent them. Emilie became indisposed in ways that she hid all the less for being unaware of the cause. Her mother questioned her, drew from her a confession of our commerce, and my father was informed. He reprimanded me, not without an air of satisfaction, and it was decided on the spot that I should travel. I left with a tutor instructed to monitor my behavior strictly, but not to hinder it. Five months later I learned from the gazette that Emilie had died of smallpox, but a letter from my father informed me that her affection for me had cost her her life. The first fruit of my love serves with distinction in the Sultan's army. I have always given him the support of my influence, and to this day he knows me solely as his benefactor.

"We were in Tunis when I received news of his birth and of his mother's death. I was touched to the quick, and I would have been inconsolable about it, I think, were it not for the liaison I had entered into with a corsair's wife, which gave me no time for despair. The Tunisian woman was fearless, I was mad, and every day, with the help of a rope ladder she threw to me, I went from our hotel to her terrace, and from there into her study, where she perfected my skills, for Emilie had made but a beginning. Her husband returned from privateering precisely at the time when my tutor, who had his instructions, was making haste to take me to Europe. I took ship for Lisbon, but not without repeating tender farewells to Elvira, from whom I received the diamond you see here.

"The ship we boarded was loaded with cargo, but in my eyes the captain's wife was the most precious item aboard. She was barely twenty years old. Her husband was jealous as a tiger, and not entirely without cause. We were quick to understand one another: Doña Velina realized at once that I was taken with her; I realized that she was not indifferent to me; and her husband realized that he was in our way. The captain then resolved not to leave her side until we reached Lisbon. I read in the eyes of his dear spouse how enraged she was by her husband's diligence. Mine conveyed the same to her, and her husband understood us both perfectly. We spent two whole days in an inconceivable thirst for pleasure, and we would most assuredly have died of it had not the heavens, which always aid suffering souls, come to our assistance. We had barely cleared the Strait of Gibraltar when a furious storm arose. Were I not simply recounting history, I would not fail, Madame, to make the wind whistle in your ears, to crash thunder claps on your head, to enflame the sky with lightning bolts, to raise the waves to the very clouds, and to describe for you a tempest more terrifying than any you have ever seen in a novel. I shall tell you only that the captain was forced by the cries of the sailors to leave his room and thus expose himself to one danger for fear of another. He left together with my tutor, and I rushed without hesitation into the arms of my fair Portuguese lady. Quite forgetting sea, storms, tempests, and that we were borne by a frail ship, I abandoned myself unreservedly to perfidy. Our course was quick, and you may well judge, Madame, that with the weather such as it was, I saw land in a few hours. We put in at Cádiz, where I left the señora with a promise to meet up with her in Lisbon, if this suited my mentor, whose plan it was to go to Madrid.

"Spanish women are more closely confined, and more amorous, than our women. Love there is handled by ambassadresses who have orders to examine strangers, make propositions to them, and act as their guides, while the women take charge of making them happy. I did not go through this ritual, thanks to a combination of events. A great revolution had just placed a prince of French blood on the throne. His arrival and coronation gave rise to many festivities at Court, to which I was invited. I was accosted at a masked ball, and a meeting was proposed for the next day. I accepted, and went to a little house, where I found only a masked man, his nose wrapped in a cloak, who gave me a note from Doña Oropeza postponing the engagement until the same time the following day. When I returned, I was introduced into a sumptuously furnished apartment, lighted by candles. My goddess did not keep me waiting. She entered just after me, and threw herself into my arms without saying a word, and without removing her mask. Was she ugly? Was she comely? I had no idea. I only noticed, on the sofa where she led me, that she was young, well made, and pleasure loving. When she was satisfied with my homages, she removed her mask, and showed me the original of the portrait you see on this snuffbox."

Selim opened and presented to the favorite a gold box of exquisite workmanship and adorned with jewels.

"A gallant gift," said Mangogul.

"What I most admire," added the favorite, "is the portrait. What eyes! What a mouth! What a fine neck! But does this perhaps not flatter her?"

"So true to life is it," answered Selim, "that Oropeza might have kept me in Madrid, had not her husband, informed of our affair, disturbed it with his threats. For I loved Oropeza, but I loved life more. Nor did my tutor believe that I should expose myself to the danger of being stabbed by the husband, to enjoy a few more months of his wife. Thus I wrote the beautiful Spaniard a very touching farewell letter, which I took from a romance of that country, and I left for France.

"The king who ruled France at that time was the grandfather of the king of Spain, and his court was rightfully considered the most magnificent, the most cultured, and the most gallant in all of Europe, and I seemed rather exotic to them.

"'A young lord from the Congo,' said a beautiful marquise. 'Well, he must be entertaining indeed. Those men are better than ours. The Congo, I believe, is not far from Morocco.'

"Suppers were arranged at which my presence was required. As little sense as my talk made, people found it clever and admirable. They made a great fuss, especially since at first they did me the honor of suspecting I lacked common sense.

"'He is charming,' continued another court lady vivaciously. 'What a crime to let so fine a figure as he return to a nasty country where women are out of sight and guarded by men who are no longer men. Is it true, sir? People say they have nothing at all. That is quite unseemly in a man...'

" 'But,' added another lady, 'we must keep this big boy here. He is wellborn, though one would never make more than a knight of Malta of him. If he wants, I shall endeavor to find him employment. Duchess Victoria, my old friend, will speak to the King on his behalf if necessary.'

"Soon I had clear proof of their goodwill, and I put the Marquise in a position to judge the merits of the inhabitants of Morocco and the Congo. I found that the employment the Duchess and her friend promised me was difficult to fulfill, and I forsook it. It was during this time that I learned to form those great twenty-four-hour passions. For six months I moved about in a whirlwind, when the beginning of one adventure did not wait for the end of another. Pleasure was the only goal. If it was late in coming or came not at all, we flew into the arms of another."

"What are you saying there, Selim?" interrupted the favorite. "Is decency therefore unknown in those countries?"

"Pardon me, Madame," answered the old courtier. "People speak of nothing else these days, but the French are no more its slaves than their neighbors."

"What neighbors?" asked Mirzoza.

"The English women," continued Selim, "appear cold and disdainful, but are passionate, voluptuous, vindictive, less witty, and more rational than French women. The latter love sentimental phrases, the former prefer the language of pleasure. But in London, as in Paris, people love one another, leave one another, and get back together, only to leave again. From the daughter of a lord bishop (these are sorts of Brahmins who are not celibate), I went to the wife of a baronet. While he overheated himself in Parliament, supporting the interests of the nation over the concerns of the Court, his wife and I had many other debates in his house. When Parliament was adjourned, Madame was obliged to follow her knight to his country seat. I turned to the wife of a colonel whose regiment was quartered on the coast. Afterward I belonged to the Lord Mayor's lady. Ah, what a woman! I would never have seen the Congo again, if the prudence of my tutor, who saw me wasting away, had not dragged me from this galley. He pretended to have had letters from my family that requested my hasty return, and so we set out for Holland. Our plan was to cross Germany, and go to Italy, where we counted on finding frequent opportunities to return to Africa.

"We saw Holland only from the coach. Our stay in Germany was hardly any longer. All the women of rank resembled important citadels that must be besieged with due ceremony. Success was possible, but the advances required so many measures to be taken, so many *ifs* and *buts*, that when it came to settling the terms of surrender, these conquests soon bored me.

"I shall never forget the words of one wellborn German woman, at the point of granting me what she had not refused many others. 'Alas!' she cried sadly, 'what would the great Alziki my father have said if he knew that I was giving in to a little Congo man like you?'

" 'Nothing, Madame,' I answered her. 'Such grandeur frightens me and I shall withdraw.' This was prudent of me, for had I compromised her greatness with my mediocrity, I might have regretted it. Brahma, who protects the wholesome countries where we reside, undoubtedly inspired me in this critical moment.

"The Italian women, to whom we next applied ourselves, did not turn out to be so haughty. With them I learned the various modes of pleasure. In these refinements there is caprice and whimsy, but you will pardon me, ladies, if I say that at times there is no pleasing you without them. I came away from Florence, Venice, and Rome having acquired several recipes for pleasure unknown to our uncivilized country before me. I give all the glory to the Italian women who communicated them to me.

"I spent four years or so in Europe, and I returned by way of Egypt, formed, as you can see, and fortified by my rare discoveries in Italy, which I hastened to disclose."

Here the African author says that Selim noticed that the commonplaces he had just reported to the favorite about his adventures in Europe, and the character of the women in the countries through which he had traveled put Mangogul into a deep sleep. Fearing to wake him, Selim moved closer to the favorite and continued in a lower voice.

"Madame," he said to her, "if I were not afraid of having already wearied you with a tale that has been all too long, I would tell you of my first adventure in Paris, which I have somehow omitted."

"Tell me, my dear," said the favorite. "I shall redouble my attention to make up, as much as I can, for the sleeping Sultan."

"In Madrid," continued Selim, "we had been given recommendations for some lords in the Court of France, and we found ourselves, as soon as we disembarked, introduced everywhere. It was high season and my tutor and I went for a walk one evening at the Palais-Royal. We were accosted by a few fops who showed us the most celebrated beauties and told us their stories, true or false, never forgetting their own parts in all of it, as you can well imagine. The garden was already filled with a great number of women, but at eight o'clock a considerable reinforcement arrived. To judge from the quantity of their jewelry, the magnificence of their attire, and the crowd of their admirers, I took them to be duchesses at the very least. I communicated this thought to one of the young men in my company, and he told me that he could tell I was a connoisseur and that, if I so desired, I might have the pleasure of dining that very evening with some of the most charming of them. I accepted his offer, and immediately he whispered this to two or three friends, who went into the crowd and returned in less than a quarter of an hour and told us of their negotiation. 'Gentlemen,' they said to us, 'Duchess Asteria is expecting you for supper this evening.' Those who were not among our party proclaimed their amazement at our good fortune. We walked about the garden two or three more times. Then, after leaving the company, we got into our carriage to seek our pleasures.

"We got out at a little door at the foot of a very steep staircase, which we climbed to the second floor, where I found the apartments vaster and better furnished than they might seem to me today. I was introduced to the mistress of the house, to whom I made a deep bow, which I accompanied with compliments so respectful that she seemed almost disconcerted. Dinner was served, and I was seated next to a small charming woman, who began to play the duchess admirably. Indeed, I do not know how I dared fall in love with her, but so it was."

"Then you have loved once in your life?" interrupted the favorite.

"Yes, Madame," Selim answered her, "the way one falls in love at the age of eighteen, with an extreme impatience to consummate an affair just begun. I did not sleep that night, and at daybreak I set about composing the gallantest of letters to this beautiful, mysterious woman. I sent it, she responded, I obtained a rendezvous. Neither the tone of the lady's response nor her easy willingness undeceived me, and I flew to the appointed place, quite convinced that I was about to possess the wife or daughter of a prime minister! My goddess was waiting for me on a large sofa. I threw myself at her feet, took her hand, kissed it with great passion and congratulated myself on the favors she had deigned grant me. 'Could it be,' I asked her, 'that you permit Selim to love you and to tell you so, and that he may, without offending you, expect the sweetest of favors?'

"As I said these words, I kissed her breasts, and as she was lying on her back, I eagerly prepared to carry on the proceedings, when she stopped me, saying, 'Listen, my friend, you are a pretty boy. You are witty, and you talk like an angel, but I must have my four louis.'

" 'What did you say?' I interrupted...

" 'I am saying,' she continued, 'that you are out of luck if you do not have four louis...'

" 'What!' I answered her, shocked. 'Mademoiselle is worth no more than that? It was hardly worth coming here from the Congo for so little.'

"Immediately I collected myself, dashed to the stairway, and left.

"As you see, Madame, I began by mistaking actresses for princesses."

"I am quite astonished to hear this," said Mirzoza, "for the difference is great indeed!"

"I do not doubt," said Selim, "that their parts were poorly played, but what do you expect? A young man, and a foreigner too, does not look too closely. And in the Congo I had heard so many tales about the liberties granted by European women."

Selim was at this point in his story, when Mangogul awoke.

"It seems, damn me," he said yawning and rubbing his eyes, "that he is still in Paris. Might I ask you, handsome teller of tales, when you hope to return to Banza, and how long I am required to sleep? For you should know, my friend, that it is not possible to broach the subject of travel in my presence without sleep overtaking me. It is a bad habit I contracted reading Tavernier,[2] among others."

"Prince," answered Selim, "I have been back in Banza for more than an hour."

"Congratulations!" said the Sultan. Then, addressing the Sultana, he said, "Madame, it is time for the masked ball. Let us go, unless you are too weary from travel."

"I am ready, Prince," answered Mirzoza.

Mangogul and Selim were already wearing their dominoes, and the favorite likewise donned hers. The Sultan gave her his hand, and they went to the ballroom, where they separated, to mingle with the crowd. Selim followed them, as did I — says the African author — although I would have preferred to sleep than to watch dancing.

CHAPTER XLV

Twenty-Fourth and Twenty-Fifth Trials of the Ring
The Masked Ball and Afterward

The most extravagant jewels of Banza did not fail to rush where pleasures beckoned them. Some came in carriages, others in hired coaches, and some even came on foot. I would never finish, says the African author, whose *trainbearer* I have the honor to be, if I entered into the details of the tricks Mangogul played on them. On this night alone he exercised his ring more than he ever had since the genie had given it to him. He turned it now on one, now on another, and often upon twenty at once, creating a fine uproar indeed: one cried in a shrill voice, "Violins, the *Carillon de Dunkerque*, if you please"; another cried out in a hoarse voice, "I want the *Sautriots*"; a third, "I want the *Tricotets*"; and a multitude clamored in unison for old quadrilles such as *la Bourrée, les Quatre faces, la Calotine, la Chaîne, le Pistolet, la Mariée, le Pistolet, le Pistolet*. And all these cries were sprinkled with the most outrageous quips. From one side was heard, "A pox on the jerk! Send him back to school." From another: "You expect me to go home without getting any?" Here: "Who will pay for my carriage?" There: "He got away from me, but I shall hunt him down until I find him." Elsewhere: "Til tomorrow, but for at least twenty louis, or forget it." Everywhere the remarks told of desires or exploits.

Amidst this tumult, a young bourgeoise, young and pretty, singled out Mangogul. She pursued him, provoked him, and succeeded in prompting him to turn his ring on her. Immediately her jewel was heard to cry out, "Where are you running to? Stop, handsome mask, do not be so callous to the ardor of a jewel that burns for you." The Sultan, shocked by this rash declaration, resolved to punish the one who had dared utter it. He disappeared, and searched among his guards for one more or less his height, relinquished his mask and domino to him, and abandoned him to the pursuit of the little bourgeoise, who, deceived by appearances, continued to say many a foolish thing to the man she mistook for Mangogul.

The sham sultan was no fool. He was a man who knew how to speak the language of signs, and he made one that drew the beauty into a secluded spot, where she imagined herself the favorite sultana for more than an hour, and God only knows what projects she was spinning in her mind. But the enchantment did not last. After she had covered the supposed sultan with caresses, she begged him to take off his mask. He obliged, and showed a physiognomy equipped with a tremendous pair of whiskers which did not belong to Mangogul.

"Ah, for shame!" cried the little bourgeoise. "For shame..."

"Vell, mine little lady," said the Swiss, "vat ails you? Me tinks me done you goot zervices dat you no be ankry at knowing me."

But his goddess was not amused enough to answer, and brusquely quit his embrace and lost herself in the crowd.

Those among the jewels that did not aspire to such great honors did not fail to find pleasure, and all headed back to Banza well satisfied with their outing.

As people were leaving the ball, Mangogul heard two of his chief officers speaking heatedly to each other.

"She is my mistress," said one. "I have kept her for a year, and you are the first to take it into his head to try to poach on my preserves. Why do you bother me? Nasses, my friend, look elsewhere. You will find a hundred other lovely women who will be all too happy to have you."

"I love Amina," answered Nasses. "She is the only one I fancy. She has encouraged me, and you will permit me to pursue this."

"Encouraged you?" asked Alibeg.

"Yes, encouraged me..."

"Mercy, that is not so..."

"I tell you, that it is so, and you will give me satisfaction at once, sir, for your denial of the fact."

They hastened down the main staircase. They had already drawn their scimitars, and were about to end their disagreement tragically, when the Sultan stopped them, and forbade them to fight until after they had consulted their Helen.

They obeyed and went to Amina's place, with Mangogul following after them. "I am exhausted from the ball," she said to them. "I can hardly keep my eyes open. You are cruel indeed to come here just as I was going to bed. But you both look strange. May I ask why you have come?"

"A trifle," said Alibeg. "This man is boasting quite loudly." he added, pointing to his friend, "that you have encouraged him. Is there truth in this, Madame?"

Amina opened her mouth, but as the Sultan was turning his ring at the same time, she fell silent and her jewel answered for her: "It seems to me that Nasses is mistaken. No, he is not the one Madame wants. Does he not have a big footman much better than he? Really! How foolish these men are to think that their decorations, honors, titles, names — words devoid of substance — mean anything to jewels! Let each follow his own philosophy, and ours consists, above all, in distinguishing a man's merit, his true merit, from that which is merely imaginary. Not to take anything away from Monsieur de Claville,[1] but he knows less than we do on this subject, and you shall soon have proof of this.

"You are both acquainted with Marquisa Bibicosa," continued the jewel. "You know of her love affair with Cleandor, and her disgrace, and the deep devotion she professes today. Amina is a good friend of hers, and she has maintained contact with Bibicosa and still visits her at home, where one meets all kinds of Brahmins. One of them entreated my mistress to speak to Bibicosa on his behalf.

" 'Well! What do you want me to ask her?' asked Amina. 'She is a ruined and helpless woman. Really, she will be quite thankful to you for still treating her as a person of consequence. Believe me, my friend, Prince Cleandor and Mangogul will never do anything for her, and you may freeze in the antechambers...'

" 'Really, Madame,' said the Brahmin, 'it is but a trifle, but it depends on the Marquise herself. It is this: she had a little minaret built on her house, no doubt for the Sala,[2] which, truly, requires an imam; and this is the position I am seeking...'

" 'What are you saying?' asked Amina. 'An imam! You cannot be serious! Madame needs only the marabout[3] she calls in from time to time when it rains or when she chooses to have the Sala before going to bed. But to keep an imam, to clothe and feed and house him, and pay him a salary – this would not suit Bibicosa. I know her situation. The poor woman does not have six thousand sequins a year, and you expect her to give two thousand to an iman? Unlikely!...'

" 'By Brahma, I am sorry to hear this,' replied the holy man, 'for you see, had I been her imam, I would quickly have become indispensable to her, and when one is in that position, money and pensions rain down on you. Perhaps you are unaware, but I am from Monomotapa, and I perform my duties extremely well...'

" 'Well,' replied Amina in a faltering voice, 'this business may not be so impossible after all. What a pity that the merit you speak of is not more obvious...'

" 'One risks nothing in doing good deeds for the people of my country,' replied the man from Monomotapa. 'On the contrary...'

"He forthwith gave Amina complete proof of a merit so astonishing that from that moment on you two fell in Amina's esteem. Ah, long live the men of Monomotapa!"

Alibeg and Nasses pulled long faces and looked at each other in silence. Recovering from their shock, they embraced and, casting a scornful glance at Amina, ran to prostrate themselves at the feet of the Sultan, thanking him for having undeceived them about this woman, and for preserving their lives and mutual friendship. They arrived just as Mangogul, having returned to the favorite, was telling her the story of Amina. Mirzoza laughed about it, and the women of the Court and the Brahmins fell further in her esteem.

CHAPTER XLVI

Selim in Banza

Mangogul went to bed after the ball, but the favorite, feeling no inclination to sleep, called for Selim and entreated him to continue his amorous tales. Selim obeyed and resumed speaking as follows:

"Madame, gallantry did not take up all my time. From pleasure I stole a few moments which I gave over to serious endeavors; the intrigues I had embarked upon did not prevent me from learning about fortifications, horsemanship, fencing, music, and dance, from observing the arts and customs of the Europeans and studying their politics and military arts. When I returned to the Congo, I was presented to the Emperor, the Sultan's grandfather, who granted me an honorable post in his troops. I appeared at Court, and soon I was seen at all of Erguebzed's parties and was consequently involved in adventures with pretty women. I knew women of all nations, ages, and stations. Few I found cruel, either because my rank dazzled them, my banter pleased them, or my person predisposed them in my favor. I had at that time two qualities that go very far in love: audacity and presumption.

"At first I frequented women of rank. I would meet them in the evening at the salons or the games of the Manimonbanda. I would spend the night with them and we would barely recognize each other the next morning. One of the primary occupations of these women was to procure lovers for themselves, and to steal them from their best friends. Another occupation was to be rid of them. For fear of finding themselves wanting, while they actively pursued one intrigue they would flirt with two or three others. They possessed I know not how many subtle arts to lure the man they had in mind, and a thousand irritations for getting rid of their present beau. This has always been so, and will be so forever. I shall not name a soul, but I knew all the women of Erguebzed's court who had a reputation for youth and beauty, and all our engagements were formed, broken off, taken up again, and forgotten in the course of six months.

"Disgusted with this world, I headed in the opposite direction. There I saw bourgeois women and found them dissembling, conceited with their beauty, concerned with appearances of honor, and almost always beset with savage and brutal husbands or certain flat-footed cousins who irritated me enormously and spent whole days talking passionately to their pretty cousins. It was impossible to be alone with these women for more than a moment: those animals were perpetually on guard, and would disrupt a rendezvous and thrust themselves into the conversation on the slightest pretext. In spite of these obstacles, I brought five or six of these prudes to the point where I wanted them before jilting them. What I liked about their company was that they prided themselves on their sentiments, which I was likewise obliged to do, and they spoke so much about it that one nearly died of laughter. They also required certain attentions, little things, and one was always considered deficient in this respect. They preached a love so correct that it was necessary to renounce it. But the worst of it was that they had one's name forever on their lips, and sometimes one was embarrassed to be seen with them, and to incur the ridicule of a bourgeois love affair. One sunny day I simply delivered myself from their shops and their Rue Saint-Denis, never to return again.

"This was the time of the rage for pleasure houses. I rented one in the eastern suburbs and there I kept, in rapid succession, a number of those girls who are seen but not seen, to whom one speaks but says not a word, and with whom one dispenses with when tired of them. I gathered friends and actresses from the Opera there; we had little suppers, and sometimes Prince Erguebzed honored us with his presence. Ah, Madame, I had delicious wines, exquisite liqueurs, and the best cook in the Congo.

"But nothing amused me more than an adventure I had in a province far from the capital, where my troops were quartered. I set out from Banza to review my regiment, and as this was my only business, the trip would have been quite short if not for the extravagant project to which I devoted myself. In Baruthi there was a nunnery filled with rare beauties. I was young and beardless, and I thought to enter there as a widow seeking asylum from the dangers of the age. Indeed, I had women's clothes made for me, put them on, and presented myself at the recluses' gate. I was warmly received, and consoled for the loss of my husband. My room and board were agreed upon and I entered.

"The apartment given me adjoined the dormitory of the novices. There were a great number of them, young and for the most part surprisingly fresh. I won their sympathy with kindnesses, and soon I became their friend. In less than a week I was informed of the workings of this small republic. Characters were described to me, anecdotes told. I received all sorts of confidences and noticed that we, the profane, do not ply slander or calumny with any greater ease. I kept strictly to the rules, imitating the wheedling look and the mawkish tones, and soon the women were whispering to each other that the community would be fortunate indeed if I took the veil.

"As soon as I had established my reputation in the place, I latched on to a young virgin who had just taken her first veil. She was an adorable brunette. She called me her mama; I called her my angel. She kissed me innocently, and I returned her kisses very tenderly. Youth is strange. Zirziphila asked me everything about marriage and the pleasures of man and wife. As she asked me questions, I would artfully whet her curiosity, and from question to question I easily led her to practice the lessons I gave her. She was not the only novice I instructed, however, for several young nuns came to be edified in my cell. I managed the hours and meetings with utmost care, so that they did not interfere with one another. In short, Madame, what shall I say? The pious widow left a large progeny. But as soon as the scandal, which had caused many a private sigh, broke out, and a secret council assembled and the physician of the house was called in, I meditated my escape. One night, while the whole house slept, I scaled the garden walls and disappeared. I went to the baths at Piombino, where the physician had sent half the convent, and, there, dressed as a cavalier, I completed the task I had begun dressed as a nun. This, Madame, is a deed that the whole empire remembers but of which now you alone know the identity of the perpetrator.

"The rest of my youth," added Selim, "was spent in such diversions as this, always with women, of all kinds. Rarely was there mystery, often were there vows, and never was there sincerity."

"By the way," asked the favorite, "were you never in love?"

"Well!" answered Selim, "I certainly thought a great deal about love! I sought only pleasure, and only those women who promised this to me."

"But is there pleasure without love?" interrupted the favorite. "What can it be when the heart says nothing?"

"Well, Madame," replied Selim, "is it the heart that speaks at eighteen or twenty?"

"In the end, what is the result of all these experiences? What do you think of women?"

"That most of them lack character," said Selim, "and that they are influenced by three things: self-interest, pleasure, and vanity. Perhaps there is not a one of them who is not dominated by one of these passions; and those in whom all three traits combine are monstrous."

"As for pleasure," said Mangogul, who had just entered, "I will grant them that although one can never count on these women, it is not their fault. When the temper rises to a certain pitch, it becomes a spirited horse that carries its rider far afield; and most all women are mounted astride that beast."

"Perhaps that is the reason," said Selim, "that Duchess Menega calls the chevalier Kaidar her Master of the Horse."

"But is it possible," the Sultana asked Selim, "that you have never had the smallest affair of the heart? Could it be that your only sincerity is in dishonoring the sex that gave you pleasure when you were their darling. What! Among so many women, could it be that not one wanted to be loved, or deserved to be? That is difficult indeed to understand."

"Ah, Madame," answered Selim, "I feel, in the ease with which I obey you, that the years have not lessened the sway of a lovely woman over my heart. Yes, Madame, I have loved like all the rest. You wish to know everything. I will tell you, and you shall judge if I have fulfilled a lover's role in all its forms."

"Are there any travels in this part of your story?" asked the Sultan.

"No, Prince," answered Selim.

"So much the better," said Mangogul, "for I have no desire to sleep."

"As for me," said the favorite, "Selim will allow me to rest a moment, I am sure."

"Let him go to bed as well," said the Sultan, "and while you sleep I shall question Cypria's jewel."

"But, Prince," said Mirzoza, "Your Highness cannot be serious. This jewel will spin you tales of never-ending travels."

The African author tells us here that the Sultan, struck by Mirzoza's observation, took the precaution of the strongest antisleeping potion. He adds that Mangogul's physician, who was his friend, had told him the prescription, and that he had made it the preface of his book, but of this preface there remain only the last three lines, which I list here:

Take some . . .
   some . . .
   some . . .
   of *Marianne* and *Paysan* . . . four pages,
   of *Égarements du coeur*, one page,
   of *Les Confessions*, twenty-five and one-half lines.

CHAPTER XLVII

Twenty-Sixth Trial of the Ring
The Roving Jewel

While Selim and the favorite were resting from the exertions of the night before, Mangogul was viewing Cypria's magnificent apartments with astonishment. This woman's jewel had made her a fortune comparable to that of a financier. Having crossed a long series of rooms, one more richly decorated than the next, he arrived in the great salon, where, at the center of a populous circle, he recognized the mistress of the house by the huge quantity of gemstones that disfigured her, and her husband by the good nature painted across his face. Two abbots, a wit, and three academics from Banza sat beside Cypria's chair, and at the back of the room two fops fluttered about with a young magistrate who was putting on airs, blowing on his cuffs, incessantly readjusting his wig and touching his mouth, pleased to see in the mirror that his rouge suited him so well. Except for these three butterflies, the rest of the company was in deep veneration of the honorable mummy seated in an indecent pose, who yawned, spoke while she yawned, cast judgments on everything, found fault with everything, and not once was contradicted.

"How is it," Mangogul asked himself, not having talked to himself for quite some time and dying to do so, "that she has succeeded in dishonoring a man from a good family with her dull wit and a face like that?"

Cypria wanted to be considered fair, though her skin, with its yellowish tint streaked with rouge, looked like a striped tulip. She had big eyes that were shortsighted, a short stature, sharp nose, flat mouth, crowded features, hollow cheeks, narrow forehead, no neck, dry hands, and skinny arms. With these charms she had bewitched her husband. The Sultan turned his ring toward her, and a yelping sound was heard forthwith. The assembly was mistaken and thought that Cypria was speaking with her mouth, and that she was about to pass judgment. But her jewel began with the following words:

"The story of my travels:

"I was born in Morocco in 17,000,000,012, and I was a dancer on the operatic stage until Mehemet Tripathoud, who kept me, was named head of the embassy that our powerful emperor sent to the monarch of France. I followed him on this trip, and the charms of the French ladies soon deprived me of my lover; without delay I found revenge. The courtiers, eager for new pleasures, wanted to try *La Maroquine*, which is what they called my mistress. She was very sweet to them, and in less then six months' time her kindness earned her twenty thousand ecus in jewelry, as much in cash, and a small furnished house. But the French are fickle; soon I was no longer in fashion. I had no intention to roam the provinces; great talents need great stages and I left Tripathoud, destined for the capital of another kingdom.

"A wealthy lord, traveling through France, dragg'd me to London. Ay, that was a man indeed! He water'd me six times a day, and as often o'nights. His prick like a comet's tail shot flaming darts: I never felt such quick and thrilling thrusts. It was not possible for mortal prowess to hold out long, at this rate; so he drooped by degrees, and I received his soul distilled through his Tarse. He gave me fifty thousand guineas. This noble lord was succeeded by a couple of privateer-commanders lately return'd from cruising: being intimate friends, they fuck'd me, as they had sail'd, in company, endeavouring who should show most vigour and serve the readiest fire. Whilst one was riding at anchor, I towed the other by his Tarse and prepared him for a fresh tire. Upon a modest computation, I reckon'd in about eight days time I received a hundred and eighty shot. But I soon grew tired with keeping so strict an account, for there was no end of their broadsides. I got twelve thousand pounds from them for my share of the prizes they had taken. The winter quarter being over, they were forced to put to sea again, and would fain have engaged me as a tender, but I had made a prior contract with a German count.

"Duxit me Viennam in Austriâ patriam suam, ubi venereâ voluptate, quantâ maximâ poteram, ingurgitatus sum, per menses tres integros ejus splendide nimis epulatus hospes. Illi, rugosi et contracti Lotharingo more colei, et eo usque longa, crassaque mentula, ut dimidiam nondum acciperem, quamvis iterato coïtu fractus rictus mihi misere pateret. Immanem est usu frequenti vagina tandem admisit laxe gladium, novasque excogitavimus artes, quibus fututionum quotidianarum vinceremus fastidium. Modo me resupinum agitabat; modo ipsum, eques adhaerescens inguinibus, motu quasi tolutario versabam. Saepe turgentem spumantemque admovit ori priapum, simulque appressis ad labia labiis, fellatrice me linguâ perfricuit. Etsi Veneri nunquam indulgebat posticae, a tergo me tamen adorsus, cruribus altero sublato, altero depresso, inter femora subibat, voluptaria quaerens per impedimenta transire. Amatoria Sanchesii praecepta calluit ad unguem, et festivas Aretini tabulas sic expressit, ut nemo melius. His a me laudibus acceptis, multis florenorum millibus mea solvit obsequia, et Romam secessi.

"Quella città è il tempio di Venere, ed il soggiorno delle delizie. Tutta via mi dispiaceva, che le natiche leggiadre fossero là ancora più festeggiate delle più belle potte; quello che provai il terzo giorno del mio arrivo in quel paese. Una cortigiana illustre si offerisce à farmi guadagnare mila scudi, s'io voleva passar la sera con esso lei in una vigna. Accettai l'invito; salimmo in una carozza, e giungemmo in un luogo da lei ben conosciuto nel quale due cavalieri colle braghesse rosse si fecero incontro à noi, e ci condussero in un boschetto spesso e folto, dove cavatosi subito le vesti, vedemmo i più furiosi cazzi che risaltaro mai. Ognuno chiavo la sua. Il trastullo poi si prese a quadrille, dopo per farsi guattare in bocca, poscia nelle tette; alla perfine, uno de chiavatori *impadronissi del mio rivale, mentre l'altro mi lavorava. L'istesso fu fatto alla conduttrice mia; e ciò tutto dolcemente condito di bacci alla fiorentina. E quando i campione nostri ebbero posto fine alla battaglia, facemmo la fricarella per risvegliar il gusto à quei benedetti signori i quali ci pagarono con generosità. In più volte simili guadagnai con loro sessanta mila scudi; e due altre volte tanto, con coloro che mi procurava la cortigiana. Mi ricordo di uno che visitava mi spesso e che sborrava sempre due volte senza cavarlo; e d'un altro il quale usciva da me pian piano, per entrare soltanto nel mio vicino; e per questo bastava fare sù è giù le natiche. Ecco una uzanza curiosa che si pratica in Italia."*[1]

Cypria's jewel continued her story, half in Congolese, half in Spanish. Apparently it did not know enough of the latter to use it exclusively. One never learns a language, says the African author, who would hang himself rather than miss a cliché, without speaking it often; and Cypria's jewel had had little or no time to talk in Madrid.

"I left Italy," it said, "in spite of the secret desires that called me back, *influxo malo del clima! y tuve luego la resolucion di ir me a una tierra, donde pudiesse gozar mis fueros sin partir los con un usarpador.* I took a trip to Old Castile, where I was given back to my simple functions: but this did not suffice for my revenge. *Le impuse la tarea de batter el compas en los bayles che celebrava de dia y de noche;* and he performed so well that we were reconciled. We appeared at Court in Madrid on good terms. *Al entrar de la cuidad,* I hooked up *con un papo venerabile por sus canas:* luckily for me, for he had compassion for my youth and told me a secret, the fruit of sixty years of experience, *para guardar me del mal de que merecieron los Franceses ser padrinos, por haver sido sus primeros pregodes.* With this recipe, and a taste for cleanliness that I vainly tried to introduce into Spain, I saved myself from any accidents in Madrid, where my vanity alone was mortified. My mistress has, as you can see, a very small foot. *Esta prenda es el incentivo mas poderoso de una imaginacion castellana.* A small foot serves as a passport in Madrid for a girl *que tiene la mas dilatada sima entre las piernas.* I decided to leave a country where I owed most of my triumphs to foreign merit; *y me arrime a un definidor muy virtuoso que passava a las Indias.* Under the wings of his reverence I saw the promised land, that country where the happy Frayle carries gold in his purse, a dagger at his side, and his mistress behind him, without scandal. How delicious was the life I led there! What nights! ye gods, what nights! *Hay de me! al recordame de tantos gustos me meo... Algo mas... Ya, ya... Pierdo el sentido... Me muero...*

"After a yearlong stay in Madrid and the Indies, I set out for Constantinople. I did not at all relish the customs of a people among whom jewels are locked up, and I soon left that country where my liberty was in danger. I nevertheless frequented the Muslims enough to notice that they are much civilized by their commerce with Europeans. In them I found the levity of the French, the ardor of the English, the strength of the Germans, the forbearance of the Spanish, with strong tinctures of Italian refinement; in a word, a single aga is worth a cardinal, four dukes, a lord, three Spanish grandees, and two German princes.

"From Constantinople I came, as you well know, gentlemen, to the Court of the great Erguebzed, where I educated the most charming of our nobles. And when I was no longer good for anything, I threw myself on that person there," said the jewel, indicating Cypria's husband with a familiar gesture. "What a fall!"

The African author closes this chapter with a bit of advice to ladies who might be tempted to have the passages where Cypria's jewel expressed itself in foreign languages translated for them.

"I would have failed," he said, "not only in my duty as a historian were I to supress them, but also in my respect for the opposite sex were I to keep them in the work without informing virtuous ladies that Cypria's jewel had spoiled the quality of its speech during its travels, and that its stories are infinitely freer than any clandestine tales they have ever read."

CHAPTER XLVIII

Cydalisa

Mangogul returned to the favorite, where Selim had preceded him.

"Well, Prince," said Mirzoza, "did the tale of Cypria's voyages do you any good?"

"Neither good nor harm," answered the Sultan, "for I did not understand it."

"And why not?" asked the favorite.

"Because," said the Sultan, "her jewel speaks like a polyglot – every language except mine. It is a rather impertinent teller of tales, though it would make an excellent interpreter."

"What!" said Mirzoza, "you understood nothing of its tales?"

"Only one thing, Madame," answered Mangogul, "which is that travels are even worse for a woman's modesty than for a man's religion, and that there is little value in knowing many languages. One may know Latin, Greek, Italian, English, and Congolese to perfection and still have no more sense than a jewel. Do you agree, Madame? And does Selim?

Let him begin his story, but no mention of travels, please. They tire me to death."

Selim promised the Sultan that the scene would remain in one place, and said:

"I was about thirty years old when I lost my father. I married to keep up my name and lived with my wife in the appropriate manner – with consideration, attentiveness, politeness, decent behavior, but not much familiarity. Prince Erguebzed ascended to the throne. I had received kindnesses from him long before he was crowned, and he continued in this vein until his death. I tried to justify this mark of distinction by my zeal and faithfulness. The post of inspector general of his troops became vacant. I was awarded it, and this position obliged me to make frequent trips to the frontier."

"Frequent trips!" exclaimed the Sultan. "Only one will make me sleep until tomorrow. Think of that."

"Prince," continued Selim, "it was on one of these trips that I made the acquaintance of the wife of a colonel of the spahis,[1] named Ostaluk, who was a good man, and a fine officer, but a difficult husband, jealous as a tiger, and with a physiognomy to justify this rage, for he was hideously ugly.

"He had recently married the young, lively, pretty Cydalisa, one of those rare women for whom one feels, from the very first encounter, something more than politeness, from whom one parts with sorrow, and whom one revisits a hundred times in one's mind before seeing her again.

"Cydalisa had a very sharp mind and expressed herself gracefully. Her conversation was engaging, and, if one never tired of seeing her, one tired even less of listening to her. With these qualities, she was fated to make a great impression on many a heart, and I did not fail to suffer this effect. I admired her a great deal, and soon formed a more tender attachment; and from that point on, my behavior became colored by a strong passion. The ease that marked my first triumphs had spoiled me not a little, and when I set upon Cydalisa I imagined that she would offer little resistance, and that, honored by the attentions of an inspector general, she would put up but a conventional defense. One may well judge my surprise, then, at the answer she made to my declaration.

" 'My lord,' she said to me, 'were I presumptuous enough to believe you had been touched by the charms people find in me, I should be mad to take seriously the words with which you have deceived hundreds of others before addressing them to me. What is love without respect? Very little; and you do not know me well enough to respect me. However witty or insightful one may be, in two days' time one cannot delve deep enough into a woman's character to give her the attentions she deserves. Sir Inspector General seeks to amuse himself, and he is right; but so is Cydalisa, who does not wish to amuse anyone.'

"In vain I swore to her that my passion was sincere, that she held my happiness in her hands, and that her indifference would poison the rest of my life.

"'Nonsense,' she said to me, 'utter nonsense. Either cease to think of me, or do not believe me so giddy as to accept these trite protestations. What you have just said to me is said by all without a thought, and listened to by all without believing a word.'

"If I had not been smitten with Cydalisa, her severity would have mortified me. But I loved her, and it caused me pain. I left for the Court, and her image followed me. Absence, far from stifling the passion I had conceived for her, served only to augment it.

"Cydalisa had so taken possession of my thoughts that hundreds of times I considered sacrificing to her the employment and the rank that bound me to the Court; but the uncertainty of my success always prevented me.

"Unable to fly whither I had left her, I formulated a plan to bring her to where I was. I took advantage of the confidence with which Erguebzed honored me to praise the merit and the courage of Ostaluk. He was named lieutenant of the spahis of his guard, a past that fixed him at the Prince's side. Ostaluk appeared at Court, and with him Cydalisa, who instantly became the reigning beauty."

"You did well," said the Sultan, "to keep your employment and to bring your Cydalisa to the Court, for I swear to you, by Brahma, that I would have allowed you to set out alone for her province."

"She was ogled, scrutinized, and importuned, but all in vain," continued Selim. "I alone enjoyed the privilege of seeing her every day. The more I saw of her, the more merits and charms I discovered in her, and the more desperately I fell in love with her. I imagined that perhaps the recent memory of my many affairs lowered me in her esteem, and to erase this memory and convince her of the sincerity of my love, I banished myself from society, and the only women I saw were those whom chance brought to her place. It seemed to me that this behavior made an impression on her, and that she relaxed somewhat her former severity. I redoubled my efforts. I asked for love and was granted respect. Cydalisa began to treat me with consideration. She confided in me, consulting me on household matters, but never on those of her heart. If I spoke to her of feelings, she answered only in maxims, and I was distraught. This sorry state had lasted for a long time, when I resolved to get out of it, and to discover once and for all where I stood."

"And how did you go about this?" asked Mirzoza.

"Madame, you shall see," answered Mangogul. Selim continued:

"I have told you, Madame, that I saw Cydalisa every day. I proceeded now to see her less frequently. My visits became more and more rare, and at last I hardly saw her at all. If it happened that I found myself alone with her by chance, I spoke as little of love to her as if I had never felt the slightest spark. This change astonished her, and she suspected me of some secret engagement. One day I was telling her gallant tales of the Court.

" 'Selim,' she said to me in a distracted tone, 'you tell me nothing of yourself. You speak marvelously of the good fortunes of others, but you are all too discreet about your own.'

" 'Madame,' I answered her, 'this is because in all likelihood I have none, or that I think that it is appropriate to keep silent about them.'

" 'Oh, yes!' she interrupted me. 'How appropriate that you should hide from me today what everyone will know tomorrow.'

" 'Be that as it may, Madame,' I answered her, 'but no one shall know it from me.'

" 'In truth,' she replied, 'you are remarkably reserved. Yet who does not know that you have designs on the fair Misis, little Zibelina, and the dark Sephera?'

" 'And whom else, Madame?' I answered coldly.

" 'Really,' she replied, 'I would not be at all surprised if they are not the only ones. For the two months now that one can see you only by appointment, I am certain that you have not remained idle, and things go quickly with those kinds of women.'

" 'Me, remain idle!' I answered her. 'I should never forgive myself. My heart was made for love, and perhaps for being loved as well. I will admit that it is, but please, ask me no more. Perhaps I have already said too much.'

" 'Selim,' she said to me sternly, 'I hide nothing from you, please do not hide anything from me. Where are you in this affair?'

" 'Almost at its conclusion.'

" 'And with whom?' she asked eagerly.

" 'Do you know Marteza?'

" 'Yes, of course. She is a very comely woman.'

" 'Well! After having tried in vain to please you, I turned to her. She has desired me for more than six months. Two meetings have brought me closer to her, and a third will fulfill my happiness. This very evening, Marteza is expecting me for supper. She is delightful company, light and a bit caustic, but apart from that she is the finest creature in the world. It is better to have little affairs with these foolish women than with haughty women who –'

" 'But, my lord,' interrupted Cydalisa with downcast eyes, 'while I compliment you on your choice, might it be pointed out to you that Marteza is not young, and that she has had lovers before you?...'

" 'What does that matter to me, Madame?' I asked her. 'If Marteza loves me sincerely, I shall consider myself the first. But the time of my appointment draws near, allow me...'

" 'One more word, my lord. Is it true then that Marteza loves you?'

" 'I believe so.'

" 'And do you love her?' added Cydalisa.

" 'Madame,' I answered her, 'you yourself have driven me into Marteza's arms. I believe I have said enough.'

"I was about to leave, but Cydalisa pulled at my sleeve then turned abruptly.

" 'Does Madame wish something from me? Does she have orders for me?'

" 'No, sir. What, are you still here? I thought you would be far away by now.'

" 'No, Madame, but I shall hurry.'

" 'Selim...'

" 'Cydalisa...'

" 'You are leaving, then?'

" 'Yes, Madame.'

" 'Ah, Selim, for whom are you sacrificing me? Was not the esteem of a Cydalisa worth more than all the favors of a Marteza?'

" 'No doubt, Madame,' I answered her, 'if I had nothing more than esteem for you. But I loved you...'

" 'It was not so,' she cried out excitedly. 'If you loved me, you would have guessed my true feelings. You would have sensed them, and you would have convinced yourself that in the end your perseverance would win out over my pride. But you grew weary; you abandoned me, perhaps at the very moment...'

"With these words, Cydalisa stopped short, sighed, and her eyes filled with tears.

" 'Speak, Madame,' I said to her, 'finish your thought. If, in spite of your severity toward me, I was still attached to you, could you...'

" 'I could do nothing. You no longer love me, and Marteza is waiting for you.'

" 'And if Marteza meant nothing to me and if Cydalisa were dearer to me than ever, what would you do?'

" 'It would be foolish to explain myself on suppositions.'

" 'Cydalisa, I beg you, answer me as if I had supposed nothing. If Cydalisa were still the most desirable woman in the world in my eyes, and if I had never had the slightest designs on Marteza, once again, what would you do?'

" 'What I have always done, ungrateful man,' she finally answered me, 'I would love you…'

" 'And Selim adores you,' I said to her, throwing myself at her feet, kissing her hands and covering them with tears of joy.

"Cydalisa was confounded. This unexpected change troubled her. I profited from her confusion, and our reconciliation was sealed with signs of affection which she was not in any state to refuse."

"And what did the good Ostaluk say about this?" interrupted Mangogul. "No doubt he permitted his better half to be generous to the man to whom he owed the lieutenancy of the spahis."

"Prince," continued Selim, "Ostaluk was full of gratitude so long as I was ignored. But as soon as I was made happy he became unpleasant, sullen, and ill-tempered to me, and brutal toward his wife. Not content to trouble us in person, he had us watched. We were betrayed, and Ostaluk, certain of the supposed slight to his honor, had the audacity to challenge me to a duel. We fought in the grand seraglio park. I wounded him twice and obliged him to owe me his life. While he was healing from his wounds, I did not leave his wife's side. But the first use he made of his recovery was to separate us and to mistreat Cydalisa. She described all the unhappiness of her situation to me. I proposed to take her away. She consented, and upon his return from the hunt, wherein he had accompanied the Sultan, this jealous man was shocked to find himself wifeless. Without bothering to give vent to useless complaints against the perpetrator of the deed, Ostaluk immediately plotted revenge.

"I had hidden Cydalisa in a country house, two miles from Banza, and every other night I stole away from town to go to Cisare. Meanwhile, Ostaluk put a price on the head of his unfaithful wife, bribed my servants, and was let into my garden. One evening I was taking the night air with Cydalisa. We were at the end of a dark path, and I was about to lavish her with tender caresses when before my eyes an invisible hand pierced her breast. The dagger belonged to the cruel Ostaluk. The same fate threatened me, but I was quicker than Ostaluk. I drew my dagger and Cydalisa was avenged. I threw myself on this dear woman.

Her heart was still beating. I carried her into the house with all speed, but she expired before we arrived, her mouth pressed against mine.

"When I felt Cydalisa's limbs grow cold in my arms, I cried out bitterly. My servants came running, and tore me away from this place of horror. I went back to Banza, shut myself up in my palace, despaired over Cydalisa's death, and reproached myself cruelly. I loved Cydalisa sincerely, and she loved me deeply. I had all the time in the world to consider the magnitude of my loss, and to weep over it."

"But in the end," probed the favorite, "you found consolation?"

"Alas, Madame," answered Selim, "for a long time I thought that I would never get over it. Only later did I learn that no grief lasts forever."

"Speak no more to me of men," said Mirzoza. "You are all the same. In other words, Sir Selim, this poor Cydalisa, whose tale has so moved us, and whom you missed so much, was very foolish to depend on your word; and while Brahma punished her gullibility rather severely, you spend your time quite sweetly in the arms of another."

"Calm yourself, Madame," said the Sultan. "Selim is in love again. Cydalisa will be avenged."

"My lord," replied Selim, "Your Highness is perhaps misinformed. Hasn't the adventure with Cydalisa taught me, once and for all, that true love is detrimental to happiness."

"Undoubtedly," interrupted Mirzoza. "Yet in spite of your reflexions, I would wager that now you love another more passionately still..."

"More passionately," replied Selim, "I dare not say. For five years I have been devoted, in my heart, to a charming woman. It was not without great difficulty that I made her listen to me, for she had always been very virtuous..."

"Virtuous!" cried the Sultan. "Courage, my friend — and how enchanting to hear of the virtue of a woman in my court."

"Selim," said the favorite, "continue your story."

"And like a good Muslim, you must always believe in the faithfulness of your mistress," added the Sultan.

"Ah, Prince," replied Selim emphatically, "Fulvia is faithful to me."

"Faithful or not," replied Mangogul, "what difference does this make to your happiness? You believe it, and that is enough."

"So it is Fulvia you love now?" asked the favorite.

"Yes, Madame," replied Selim.

"Too bad, my friend," added Mangogul. "I have little faith in her. She is always beset by Brahmins, and Brahmins are the worst. Besides, she has little Oriental eyes, a turned up nose, and an air that suggests a thorough inclination toward pleasure. Between us, is this true?'

"Prince," answered Selim, "I believe she has no aversion to it."

"Well," replied the Sultan, "everything yields to that charm. You should know that better than I, or you are not..."

"You are mistaken," said the favorite. "A man may have all the sense in the world and not know that. I would wager —"

"All these wagers try my patience," interrupted Mangogul. "These women are incorrigible. Win your château first, Madame, and then you may lay more wagers."

"Madame," Selim said to the favorite, "might not Fulvia be of some use to you?"

"How so?" asked Mirzoza.

"I have observed," answered the courtier, "that the jewels have rarely or never spoken except in the presence of His Highness, and I have imagined that the genie Cucufa, who performed so many surprising things for Kanoglou, the Sultan's grandfather, might very well have granted his grandson the power to make them speak. But Fulvia's jewel has not opened its mouth, as far as I know. Might it not be possible to question it — as a means to procure you your château and to convince me that my mistress is faithful?"

"Without a doubt," said the Sultan. "What do you think of this, Madame?"

"Oh, I want no part in so delicate a matter. Selim is too much a friend to expose him to the risk of lifelong unhappiness for the sake of a château."

"But you fail to consider," said the Sultan, "that Fulvia is virtuous. Selim would put his hand in the fire to prove it. This was his suggestion, and he is not a man to go back on his word."

"No, Prince," replied Selim. "And if Your Highness will give me an appointment at Fulvia's house, I shall certainly be the first to arrive."

"Beware what you propose," continued the favorite. "Selim, my poor Selim, you go too fast; and, worthy of love as you may be..."

"Never fear, Madame. Since the die has been cast, I will hear Fulvia out. The worst that could befall me would be to lose an unfaithful woman."

"And die of sorrow for having lost her," added the Sultana.

"What an idea!" said Mangogul. "Do you really think that Selim has become so feebleminded? He lost the tender Cydalisa and still he stands before us full of life. If he finds Fulvia unfaithful, why should it kill him? I guarantee that he would never succumb to a blow of that sort. Until tomorrow, Selim, at Fulvia's house. It is agreed, then. You will be informed of the hour."

Selim bowed. Mangogul went out, and the favorite continued to warn the old courtier that he was overplaying his hand. Selim thanked her for these signs of her affection, and each retired in expectation of the great event.

CHAPTER XLIX

Twenty-Seventh Trial of the Ring
Fulvia

The African author, who had promised somewhere to describe Selim's character, decided to put it here, and I have too much esteem for works of antiquity to assert that it might have been better elsewhere. There are, he says, some men whose merit opens all doors, and who, by virtue of their physical charms and nimble wits, are the darlings of many women in their youth. In old age they are respected not only for having known how to reconcile duties with pleasures, but also for having distinguished their middle years with services to the state. In short, these men are always the delight of society. Such was Selim. Although he was already sixty years of age and had embarked young upon a life of pleasure, a healthy constitution and restraint had preserved him well. With his noble demeanor, easy manners, seductive speech, his great knowledge of the world based on long experience, and his habit of mingling with the opposite sex, he was the man all wished to emulate at Court; but without the natural endowment of talents and genius that so distinguished him, one could hardly imitate him successfully.

Now (continues the African author), I would like to know if this man was right to worry himself over his mistress and to spend the night like a madman? The fact is that a thousand thoughts coursed through his head, and the more he loved Fulvia, the more he feared to find her unfaithful. "Into what sort of labyrinth have I entered," he asked himself, "and why? How will it help me if the favorite wins a château? And what will be my fate if she loses?... But why would she lose? Am I not sure of Fulvia's affections?... Ah! I am her only concern, and if her jewel speaks, it will be of me alone... But if the traitor... No! No! I would have seen some prior indication of it. I would have noticed some irregularity in her manner. Some time or other these five years past she would have betrayed herself. Still, the test is dangerous... but it is too late to withdraw. I brought the cup to my lips and I must drink of it, though I should spill its contents... Perhaps the oracle will favor me... Alas! What can I expect? Why would others have failed in their attempts upon a virtue over which I triumphed?...Ah, dear Fulvia, I wrong you with my suspicions, and I forget how difficult it was for me to conquer you. A ray of hope shines on me, and I flatter myself that your jewel will remain stubbornly silent..."

Selim was in this state of agitation when the Sultan sent him a note that contained only the following words: "This evening, at exactly half past eleven, you shall be you-know-where." Selim took up a pen and wrote, trembling: "Prince, I will obey."

Selim spent the rest of the day as he had passed the preceding night, wavering between hope and fear. Nothing is truer than the belief that lovers are instinctive; if their mistresses are unfaithful, they are seized with a shudder quite like that which animals feel at the approach of bad weather. A suspicious lover is a cat whose ear itches when it rains. Animals and lovers have another thing in common: as domesticated animals lose this instinct, so is it dulled in lovers once they marry.

The hours passed slowly for Selim. He looked at the clock a hundred times. At last the fatal moment arrived and he ran to his mistress. It was late, but since he was admitted there at all hours, Fulvia's chambers were opened to him.

"I had given up expecting you," she said to him, "and went to bed with a headache, owing to the impatience you have caused me..."

"Madâme," Selim answered her, "duties, decorum, and even business, have as good as chained me to the Sultan's palace, and ever since we last separated, I have not had a moment free."

"And I," replied Fulvia, "have been in a terrible mood. What? Two whole days without a glimpse of you!"

"You know what my rank requires of me," answered Selim, "and that however certain the favors of the great may appear to be..."

"What?" interrupted Fulvia. "Has the Sultan been cool to you? Has he forgotten your services? Selim, you are distracted; you do not answer me...Alas! If you love me, why should the Prince's good or bad reception affect you? It is not in his eyes but in mine, and in my arms, that you should seek approval."

Selim listened attentively to these words, and examined his mistress's face and gestures in search of that mark of truth that is ever unmistakable and impossible to feign. When I say impossible, I mean to us men. For Fulvia behaved so naturally that Selim was beginning to reproach himself for having suspected her. When Mangogul arrived, Fulvia immediately fell silent, Selim shuddered, and the jewel spoke: "In vain does Madame make pilgrimages to all the pagodas of the Congo. She will bear no children for reasons well known to me, who am her jewel..."

At this beginning Selim became deathly pale. He wanted to rise, but his trembling knees buckled under him, and he fell back into his seat. The invisible sultan approached him and said in his ear:

"Have you had enough?"

"Alas! Prince," Selim cried out sorrowfully, "why did I not follow Mirzoza's advice, and the forebodings of my heart? My happiness has just vanished. I have lost everything. I shall die if her jewel does not speak and I shall die if it does. Let it speak, however. I expect horrible revelations, but I fear this less than I hate the confused state in which I find myself."

Meanwhile, Fulvia's first impulse was to bring her hand to her jewel and stop its mouth. What it had just said could be interpreted in a favorable light, but she dreaded the rest. Just as she was beginning to feel reassured by its silence, the Sultan, urged on by Selim, turned his ring. Fulvia was obliged to spread her fingers, and the jewel went on:

"I shall never hold up; I am too exhausted. Too many attentions from holy men thwart my purpose, so Madame will not have children. If I were entertained by Selim alone, perhaps I should become fertile, but I live the life of a galley slave. Now one, now another; I am always at the oar. The last man Fulvia sees is always the one whom she believes the heavens have destined to perpetuate her line. No one can escape this fancy. How tiring to be the jewel of a titled woman with no heir! For ten years I have been surrendered to people unworthy even to set eyes upon me."

Here Mangogul thought that Selim had heard enough to cure him of his confusion. He spared him the rest, turned his ring, and left, abandoning Fulvia to her lover's reproaches.

At first the unhappy Selim was petrified, but his fury gave him strength and speech. He cast a scornful glance at his unfaithful mistress, and said to her:

"False-hearted, ungrateful woman, if I still loved you I would take revenge. But you are unworthy of my affections, and likewise unworthy of my wrath. A man like me! Compromised with a pack of cads..."

"Indeed," Fulvia interrupted abruptly, with the tone of a courtesan unmasked, "it is quite like you to take offense at nothing; instead of being thankful to me for having spared you a knowledge of things that would have grieved you at the time, you fly into a rage and act as if you have been dishonored. For what reason, sir, would you prefer yourself to Seton, Rikel, Mollio, Tachmas, the handsomest cavaliers of the Court, to whom one need not bother disguising the passing fancies one has for them? A man like you, Selim, is spent, infirm, and long incapable of satisfying a pretty woman who is not a fool. You must agree that your presumption is misplaced, and your wrath impertinent. Besides, if you are unhappy, you may leave the field free to others who will make better use of it."

"So I shall, with all my heart," replied Selim, filled with indignation. He left, resolved never to see her again.

He went home, shut himself up for a few days, less grieved over the loss he had suffered than over his long error. His vanity was wounded more than his heart. Dreading the favorite's reproaches and the Sultan's teasings, he avoided them both.

He had nearly resolved to renounce the Court and to bury himself in solitude and end his days as a philosopher, having already wasted the greater part of his life in the role of a courtier, when Mirzoza, who guessed his thoughts, undertook to console him; she sent for him at the seraglio and addressed the following to him: "Well, my poor Selim, have you abandoned me, then? It is not Fulvia but me whom you punish for her unfaithfulness. We are all concerned about your adventure. We agree that it is a shame, but if you value the Sultan's protection and my esteem in the least, you will continue to enliven our company and forget this Fulvia, who was never worthy of a man like you."

"Madame," Selim said to her, "my age tells me that it is high time for me to retire. I have seen enough of the world; four days ago I would have boasted that I knew this world, but Fulvia's actions confound me. Women are unaccountable, and I would loathe them all were you not one of that sex whose charms you possess in full. May it please Brahma never to lead you astray! Adieu, Madame, I am going to devote myself to useful reflections in solitude. The memory of the kindness with which you and the Sultan have honored me will remain with me forever; and if my heart makes any vows hereinafter, they will be only for your happiness and his glory."

"Selim," replied the favorite, "your actions are dictated by spite. You fear a mockery that you shall avoid less by distancing yourself from the Court than by staying put. You may have as much philosophy as you like, but this is not the moment to put it to use. Your retreat would be interpreted as bitterness and sorrow. You were not made to confine yourself to a desert; and the Sultan..."

Mangogul's arrival interrupted the favorite. She told him of Selim's plans.

"Is he mad?" asked the Prince. "Has the treachery of this little Fulvia turned his head?"

Then, addressing Selim: "It shall not be so, my friend? You shall stay," he continued. "I need your advice and Madame needs your company. The wellbeing of my empire and Mirzoza's happiness depend on it, and so shall it be."

Selim, touched by Mangogul's and the favorites's sentiments, bowed respectfully, remained at Court, and was loved, cherished, sought after, and distinguished by the favors granted him by the Sultan and Mirzoza.

CHAPTER L

Marvelous Events of the Reign of Kanoglou, Mangogul's Grandfather

The favorite was very young. Born at the end of the reign of Erguebzed, she had scarcely a notion of the Court of Kanoglou. A word dropped inadvertently had pricked her curiosity about the marvels the genie Cucufa had worked on behalf of this good prince, and no one could acquaint her with this more faithfully than Selim. He was thoroughly versed in the history of his time, having been both its witness and participant. One day when she was alone with him, Mirzoza brought up this topic, and asked him if the reign of Kanoglou, about which such a fuss was made, had seen more astonishing marvels than those which commanded the Congo's attention today.

"I have no stake, Madame," he answered her, "in preferring the past to the present. Great things are taking place, but perhaps they are nothing more than preludes to more illustrious things that will further extend Mangogul's fame. My career is too well advanced for me to flatter myself that I shall live to see them."

"You are mistaken," Mirzoza answered him. "You have acquired, and shall retain, the epithet of eternal. But tell me what you have seen."

"Madame," continued Selim, "the reign of Kanoglou was long, and our poets have named it the Golden Age. This title suits it in many respects. It was marked by sucesses and victories, but its advances were nevertheless combined with setbacks, which is to say that this gold was at times mixed with bad alloy. The Court, which sets the tone for the rest of the empire, was very gallant. The Sultan had mistresses, the lords prided themselves on imitating him, and the people gradually assumed the same airs. The opulence of dress, furnishings, and equipages was excessive. Refinements in feasting were elevated to an art. People gambled heavily; they sank into debt, did not pay, yet continued to spend as long as they had money or credit. Fair laws were written to curb such luxury, but they were not enforced. Towns were captured, provinces conquered, palaces begun, and the empire drained of men and money. People sang of victory and died of hunger. The great had superb châteaus and fine gardens while their lands lay fallow. A hundred warships had made us the masters of the seas and the terror of our neighbors; but one clear mind calculated a rational estimate of just how much it was costing the state to maintain these carcasses, and in spite of the remonstrances of the other ministers, it was consigned to the bonfires. The royal treasury was a great empty coffer that this miserable economy could not fill, and gold and silver became so rare that the mints were one fine day converted to paper mills. To crown it all, Kanoglou allowed himself to be persuaded by fanatics that it was of the utmost importance that his subjects look like him, that they have blue eyes, snubbed noses, and red whiskers, and he chased from the Congo more than two million people who did not conform to these standards or who refused to counterfeit them.

"Such, Madame, was the Golden Age. Those were the good old days that you hear regretted every day. Let the dotards say what they will, but believe me, we have our own Turennes and Colberts,[1] and, all in all, the present is better than the past; if the people are happier under Mangogul than they were under Kanoglou, then the reign of His Highness is more illustrious than that of his grandfather, for the happiness of the subjects is the exact measure of the greatness of princes. But let us return to the particulars of the reign of Kanoglou.

"I shall begin with the origin of 'the puppets.' "

"Selim, I allow you to pass over this, I know this event by heart," the favorite said to him. "Let us go on to other things."

"Madame," the courtier returned, "might one ask from whom you have heard it?"

"Why," said Mirzoza, "it is published."

"True, Madame," replied Selim, "and by men who understand nothing about it. It puts me out of humor when I see these obscure little people, who have never been near princes except at entrances into the city, or public ceremonies, pretend to write their histories.

"Madame," continued Selim, "we had spent the night at a masked ball in one of the great salons of the seraglio, when the genie Cucufa, appointed protector of the ruling family, appeared before us and ordered us all to go to bed and sleep for twenty-four hours in succession. We obeyed, and when the time was up the seraglio was transformed into a vast and magnificent puppet gallery. At one end we saw Kanoglou on a throne, with a long, worn string hung down between his legs, which a decrepit old fairy jerked incessantly; with a turn of her wrist, she moved a great multitude of subordinate puppets, which responded to invisible strings attached to Kanoglou's fingers and toes. She pulled and immediately the Seneschal drew up and sealed ruinous edicts, or sang the praises of the fairy, words his secretary whispered in his ear; the minister of war sent matches to the army; the superintendent of finances built houses and let the soldiers die of hunger. And there were many other puppets as well.

"If some puppets moved clumsily, did not raise their arms high enough, or did not bow deeply enough, the fairy would break their strings with a blow of the back of her hand, and they would be paralyzed. I shall never forget two valiant emirs whom she found derelict in their duties and whose arms she crippled for the rest of their lives.

"The strings that were attached to every part of Kanoglou's body stretched out for great distances and caused armies of puppets, from deep within the Congo to the borders of Monoemugi, either to move or remain still. With a pull of a string a town was besieged, trenches were dug, walls were battered – and the enemy prepared to surrender. But with a second pull the artillery slowed its fire, the attacks slackened, relief appeared, disputes broke out among the generals, and we were attacked, surprised, and beaten soundly.

"These bad tidings never troubled Kanoglou. He learned of them only after they were long forgotten by his subjects, for the fairy would not allow for him to be informed of them except by puppets who had a string tied to the tips of their tongues, and who said only pleasant things that pleased her under pain of being struck dumb.

"Another time we were all charmed, we young fools, by an adventure that bitterly scandalized the pious. The women began to somersault, and to walk with heads upside down, feet in the air, and hands in their slippers.

"This changed everyone's point of view, and we were obliged to study physiognomy from a new angle. Many were slighted as soon as they showed themselves in this fashion, no longer considered attractive, while others, never noticed before at all, gained vastly in making themselves known. With petticoats and gowns falling in their eyes, women were in danger of losing their way or falling. This is why the former were shortened and the latter cut open. Such is the origin of short petticoats and slit gowns. When women went back to their feet, they kept this part of their dress as it had been; and if we consider our ladies' petticoats, we easily perceive that they were not made to be worn as they are worn today.

"All fashion that has but one function goes quickly out of style. In order to last, it must have at least two uses. In those days, a secret was discovered for supporting the breasts from above, just as today it is used for supporting them from below.

"The pious women, surprised to find their heads below and their legs in the air, at first covered themselves with their hands. But this made them lose balance and stumble about heavily. Upon the advice of the Brahmins, they then tied their petticoats to their legs with little black ribbons; though the more worldly women found this expedient ridiculous and announced that it hampered breathing and gave them the vapors. This marvel brought happy consequences with it. It produced many marriages, or what passed for them, and many conversions. All those who had ugly buttocks devoted themselves, body and soul, to religion, and adopted the little black ribbons. Four missions of Brahmins would not have converted so many.

"We had barely emerged from this trial when we were subjected to another, less universal but no less instructive. Young girls, from thirteen to nineteen years of age, twenty at the most, awoke one fine day with their middle fingers caught – guess where, Madame?" Selim asked the favorite. "Not in their mouths, not in their ears, not where the Turks put them. Their illness was quickly diagnosed, and a remedy found. From that time on, we have had the custom of marrying children at an age when we should be giving them dolls instead.

"Another blessing was that Kanoglou's court abounded in fops, and I had the honor to be one of them. One day as I was entertaining them with talk of young French lords, I noticed that our shoulders began to rise until they were higher than our heads. But this was not all, for we began at once to pirouette on our heels."

"And what is so rare about that?" asked the favorite.

"Nothing, Madame," Selim answered. "But note that the first of these two metamorphoses is the origin of high backs, so fashionable in your childhood, and the second is the origin of the scoffers, whose reign has yet to pass. As today, people used to begin a conversation with one person, then pirouette and continue it with another, and finish it with a third, for whom it was half unintelligible, half impertinent.

"Another time, we all found ourselves nearsighted, and were forced to consult Bion.[2] The knave made us pay ten sequins for glasses, which we continued to use even after we recovered our sight. That, Madame, is the origin of opera glasses.

"At about this same time, I do not know what the gallant women had done to Cucufa, but he took cruel revenge on them. At the end of a year in which they had spent their nights at balls, banquets, and gaming, and their days in their coaches or in the arms of their lovers, they were all shocked to find themselves turned ugly. One was as dark as a mole, another splotchy, another pale and thin, another yellow and wrinkled. As it was necessary to counter this fatal enchantment, our chemists discovered powder, rouge, pomades, waters, Venus's handkerchiefs, virginal milks, beauty marks, and a thousand other cosmetics that the ladies employed to cease being ugly and to become, instead, hideous. Cucufa kept them under this curse until Erguebzed, who loved beautiful women, interceded on their behalf. The genie did what he could, but the spell was so powerful that he could lift it only partially, and thus the women of the Court remain the way you see them today."

"And.was it the same for the men's enchantments?" asked Mirzoza.

"No, Madame," answered Selim, "some lasted a long time, others less so. The high backs subsided little by little; men stood up straight again, and for fear of being labeled humpbacked, they turned their noses to the wind and pranced as they walked. They continued however, to pirouette, and they pirouette still today. Begin a serious or sensible conversation in the presence of a nice-looking young noble, and presto, you will see him spin away from you like a windmill, muttering a parody to anyone who asks him news of the war or his health or whispering in his ear either that he supped the night before with Mademoiselle Rabon, an adorable girl, or that a new novel has come out, of which he has read a few pages and found it beautiful, very beautiful; and again, presto, he pirouettes toward a lady, whom he asks if she has seen the latest opera, and tells her that Mademoiselle Dangeville is ravishing."

Mirzoza found these ridiculous things so amusing that she asked Selim if he had had a part in them too.

"Well, Madame," replied the old courtier, "would it have been possible to ignore them without being taken for a man from another world? I arched my back, straightened up again, pranced about, looked through opera glasses, pirouetted, and scoffed like the others, and the only way I exercised my own judgment was in trying to be among the first to take things up, and avoid being among the last to shake them off."

Selim had gotten this far when Mangogul appeared.

The African author does not tell us what he had been doing, or how he had spent his time during the preceding chapter. Apparently the princes of the Congo are allowed to do insignificant things, to say silly things, and to resemble other men, who spend a great part of life involved in nothing, or at things that are not worth knowing.

CHAPTER LI

Twenty-Eighth Trial of the Ring
Olympia

"Madame, you will be delighted," Mangogul said upon entering the favorite's chambers. "I bring pleasant news. The jewels are little fools who know not what they say. Cucufa's ring may be able to make them speak, but it cannot make them tell the truth."

"Did Your Highness catch them in a lie?" asked the favorite.

"You shall hear," answered the Sultan. "Selim promised to tell you of all his adventures, and no doubt he has kept his word. Well! I have just consulted a jewel that accuses him of a naughty trick that he did not confess to you, and which assuredly did not take place, for it is not in his character. To tyrannize a pretty woman, to take advantage of her, under pain of military enforcement, do you recognize Selim in this?"

"And why not, my lord?" replied the favorite. "There is no malice of which Selim has not been capable. If he kept silent about the adventure you have discovered, it is perhaps because he is reconciled with this jewel and they are so happy together that he thought he could conceal this peccadillo from me without breaking his promise."

"The perpetual falsity of your conjectures," Mangogul replied, "should have cured you of the illness of ever making them. You imagine it all wrong. It was an extravagance of Selim's early youth. It concerns one of those women whom one gets to know in a minute and forgets shortly thereafter."

"Madame," Selim said to the favorite, "I have looked deep inside myself, and I can remember nothing more. At present I have an absolutely clear conscience."

"Olympia..." said Mangogul.

"Ah, Prince!" Selim interrupted. "I know her, but that story is so old I am not surprised that it escaped me."

"Olympia," continued Mangogul, "wife of the chief cashier of Hasna, was smitten with a young officer, a captain in Selim's regiment. One day her lover came in tearfully to announce to her that all soldiers had been commanded to depart and rejoin their respective regiments. My ancestor Kanoglou had resolved that year to begin his campaign early, an admirable project that failed only because he made his orders too public. Politicians censured it; women cursed it. Each had his or her reasons. I have told you Olympia's. This woman decided to see Selim, and to prevent, if possible, the departure of Gabalis, for such was the name of her lover. Selim was already considered a dangerous man. As Olympia thought it proper to have an escort, two of her friends, women just as pretty as she, offered to accompany her. Selim was at home when they arrived. He received Olympia, who entered alone, with the easy courtesy that you know so well, and asked to what he owed so agreeable a visit.

" 'Sir,' Olympia said to him, 'I speak on behalf of Gabalis; he has important business on his hands that requires his presence in Banza. I have come to request a six-month leave of absence for him.'

" 'A six-month leave, Madame? You fail to take into account,' Selim answered her, 'that the Sultan's orders are precise; I regret that I cannot win your favor by granting a leave that would destroy me.' Olympia continued to plead, and Selim to refuse her.

" 'The vizier promised me that I would be included in the next promotion. Could you be asking, Madame, that I ruin myself in order to oblige you?'

" 'Oh, no sir! You may oblige me without ruining yourself.'

" 'Madame, that is not possible; but perhaps if you went to the vizier.'

" 'Alas, sir, to whom do you send me? That man has never done a thing for the ladies.'

" 'I am stymied, Madame. I would like very much to be of service to you, and I can see but one way to do so.'

" 'And what might that be?' Olympia asked eagerly.

" 'Your intention is to make Gabalis happy for six months. Could you not spare a quarter of an hour from the pleasures you have in store for him?'

"Olympia understood perfectly, blushed, stammered, and at last complained of the severity of the proposition.

" 'Let us discuss it no longer,' the colonel replied coldly. 'Gabalis shall leave; the Prince's orders must be carried out. I could have taken some of the responsibility upon myself, but you are unwilling. Madame, if Gabalis departs, it is your wish.'

" 'My wish!' cried Olympia sharply. 'Oh, sir! Please make out his authorization at once, and allow him to stay.' The preliminaries of the pact were ratified on a sofa, and the lady thought she would obtain Gabalis for her troubles, when the traitor who stands here before you decided, as if by afterthought, to ask her who were the two ladies who had accompanied her, whom she had left in an adjoining room.

" 'They are two close friends of mine,' answered Olympia.

" 'Are they friends of Gabalis as well?' asked Selim. 'They must be. Given the circumstances, I do not believe they will refuse to discharge one third of the pact each. Yes, that seems fair to me. I leave it to you, Madame, to convince them of this.'

" 'Indeed, sir,' Olympia replied, 'you are a strange man. I swear to you that these women have nothing to do with Gabalis. To spare them and myself from embarrassment, if I am to your liking I shall endeavor to discharge the bill of exchange you would exact from them.' Selim accepted the offer. Olympia was as good as her word; and that, Madame, is what Selim should have told you."

"I forgive him," said the favorite. "Olympia was not worth knowing well enough for me to take him to task for forgetting her. I cannot imagine where you unearth these women. Indeed, Prince, you act like a man who cannot bear to lose a château."

"Madame, it seems to me that you have changed your mind entirely since the other day," answered Mangogul. "Allow me to remind you of how I first proposed to use the ring, and you will see that it is not my fault that I have not lost sooner."

"Yes," continued the Sultana, "I know that you swore not to include mine among the talking jewels, and that from then on you have approached only disreputable women, such as Aminta, Zobeida, Thelis, Zulica, whose reputations were well known beforehand."

"I grant," said Mangogul, "that it is ridiculous to rely on those jewels, but in the absence of any others, I had to confine myself to them. I have already said to you, and I repeat, that good society when it comes to jewels is far scarcer than you can imagine, and if you are not sufficiently determined to win on your own —"

"No!" Mirzoza interruped smartly. "Never in my life will I have a château if I must stoop so low to obtain one. A talking jewel! Fie! That is the most indecent...Prince, you know my reasons, and I repeat my threats to you in all seriousness."

"Then complain no more about my trials, or at least tell us to whom you think we might turn, for I despair of this matter ever coming to an end. We have seen naught but libertine jewels, more libertine jewels, always libertine jewels."

"I have great confidence," replied Mirzoza, "in Eglea's jewel, and I impatiently await the end of the fortnight you requested of me."

"Madame," replied Mangogul, "that ended yesterday, and while Selim was telling you tales of the old court, I learned from Eglea's jewel that, thanks to Celebi's bad temper and the attentions of Almanzor, its mistress is of no further use to you."

"Oh, Prince, can this be true?" cried the favorite.

"It is a fact," replied the Sultan. "I shall entertain you with the story another time, but in the meantime, find another string for your bow."

"Eglea, virtuous Eglea, succumbed at last!" said the favorite in surprise. "I shall not recover from this."

"You are at a loss, and you know not what to think," replied Mangogul.

"It is not that," answered the favorite. "But I must admit that I was counting very much on Eglea."

"Think no more of it," added Mangogul, "and simply tell us if she was the only virtuous woman you know of."

"No, Prince, there are a hundred others, comely women too, whom I will name for you," began Mirzoza, "and for whom I will answer, as if for myself..."

Mirzoza stopped suddenly, without having named a single name. Selim could not refrain from smiling, and the Sultan burst out laughing at the embarrassment of the favorite, who knew so many virtuous women, but could not remember one.

Mirzoza, piqued, turned to Selim and said, "Selim, help me, will you? You know about such things! Prince," she added, turning to him, "just try... Whom shall I name? Selim, help me."

"Try Mirzoza," responded Selim.

"You show me very little respect," said Mirzoza. "I do not fear the test, but I have an aversion to it. Name another quickly, if you would have me pardon you."

"You might see," said Selim, "if Zaida ever found the ideal lover she imagined, and to whom she used to compare all those who courted her."

"Zaida?" asked Mangogul. "I must admit, she could be just the woman to make me lose."

"She is perhaps the only one," added the favorite, "whose reputation has been spared by the prude Arsinoa and the fop Joneki."

"That carries some weight," said Mangogul, "but the test of my ring is better still. Let us proceed directly to her jewel: *That oracle is much more reliable than the oracles of Calchas*."[1]

"What!" said the favorite, laughing. "You remember your Racine like an actor."

CHAPTER LII

Twenty-Ninth Trial of the Ring
Zuleiman and Zaida

Mangogul did not respond to the favorite's joke. He left at once, and went to see Zaida. He found her alone in a study, next to a small table on which he noticed letters, a portrait, and some scattered trinkets from a cherished lover, as was easy to gather from the fondness she displayed for them. She was writing. Tears flowed from her eyes and soaked the paper. She kissed the portrait rapturously, opened the letters, wrote a few words, turned back to the portrait, snatched up the trinkets I mentioned just before, and pressed them to her breast.

The Sultan was shocked beyond belief. He had never seen a loving woman, except for the favorite and Zaida. He thought himself beloved of Mirzoza; but did Zaida not love Zuleiman perhaps more? And were not these two lovers the only true lovers in the Congo?

The tears that Zaida shed while writing were not tears of sorrow. It was love that made her weep. And at this moment a delicious sensation arising from the certainty of possessing Zuleiman's heart was the only emotion that touched her. "Dear Zuleiman," she cried, "how I love you! How dear you are to me! How pleasant are my thoughts of you! During those moments when Zaida has not the joy of seeing you, at least she may write to you of how she belongs to you: far from Zuleiman, her only pleasure is her commerce with his love."

Zaida was at this point in her amorous meditation when Mangogul pointed his ring at her. Immediately he heard her jewel sigh and repeat the first words of its mistress's monologue: "Dear Zuleiman, how I love you! How dear you are to me! How pleasant are my thoughts of you!" Zaida's heart and her jewel were too closely in harmony for them to be at variance in their speech. Zaida was surprised at first, but she was so sure that her jewel would say nothing that Zuleiman could not hear with pleasure that she wished he were present.

Mangogul tried his ring again, and Zaida's jewel repeated in a sweet and tender voice, "Zuleiman, dear Zuleiman, how I love you, how dear you are to me!"

"Zuleiman," cried the Sultan, "is the most fortunate mortal in my empire. Let us leave this place where the image of happiness I see is greater than my own and grieves me." He left abruptly, and went to see the favorite with a disturbed and preoccupied air.

"Prince, what is wrong?" she asked. "Have you nothing to tell of Zaida?"

"Zaida, Madame," answered Mangogul, "is an adorable woman! She loves as no one has ever loved before."

"Too bad for her," said Mirzoza.

"What do you mean?" returned the Sultan.

"I mean," replied the favorite, "that Kermades is one of the surliest men in the Congo. The self-interest and authority of the parents arranged that match, and never were two spouses more dissimilar than Kermades and Zaida."

"Ah, Madame," said Mangogul. "It is not her husband she loves..."

"Who is it, then?" asked Mirzoza.

"It is Zuleiman," answered Mangogul.

"So much for the porcelains and the little monkey..." said the Sultana.

"Alas," Mangogul said softly. "This Zaida made a great impression on me. Her image stays with me. It haunts me. I absolutely must see her again."

Mirzoza interrupted him with a few questions that he answered in monosyllables. He refused a game of piquet that she proposed, and, complaining of a headache he did not have, retired to his chambers, went to bed without supper – something he had never done before – and did not sleep a wink. Zaida's charms and affection, and Zuleiman's qualities and happiness, tormented him all night.

As one can well imagine, the next day he had nothing more pressing to do than to return to Zaida. He left his palace without inquiring after Mirzoza, which he had never neglected to do before. He found Zaida in the same place as the night before. Zuleiman was with her, holding his mistress's hands in his own and gazing deeply into her eyes. Zaida, kneeling, cast glances at Zuleiman that were burning with the keenest passion. They remained in this position for some time; yielding at the same moment to the force of their desires, they threw themselves into each other's arms and held each other tightly. The deep silence that, until then, had reigned between them was broken by their sighs, the sound of their kisses, and some inarticulate words that escaped them..."You love me!"..."I adore you!"..."Will you love me forever?...Ah! My last breath of life shall be for Zaida..."

Mangogul, overcome with sorrow, fell back in an armchair and covered his eyes with his hand. He feared seeing such things as are easily imagined, yet did not take place...After a silence of a few moments, he heard Zaida say, "Ah, dear and tender love, you have not always been as I find you now!" She added, "I shall not love you any the less for it, nor would I reproach myself...But you are crying, dear Zuleiman. Come to me, dear sweet love, come here, let me dry your tears...Zuleiman, you lower your eyes. What is wrong? Look at me...Come here, dear friend, come, let me console you: press your lips against mine, breathe your soul into me, receive my own, stop...Ah! No...no..." Zaida finished her sentence with a deep sigh, and fell silent.

The African author tells us that this scene made a deep impression on Mangogul, that the Prince based some hopes on Zuleiman's impotence, and that he had secret overtures delivered to Zaida. She rejected them, and did not so much as mention it to her lover.

CHAPTER LIII

Platonic Love

"But is Zaida unique? Mirzoza has no less charm than she. I have a thousand proofs of her affection. I want to be loved; indeed I am loved. Who says that Zuleiman is loved more than I? What a fool I was to envy another's happiness! No, there is no man under the stars happier than Mangogul."

So began the Sultan's reproach of himself. The author suppressed the rest, contenting himself with informing us that the Prince thought more about this than about the things brought to his attention by his ministers, and that Zaida did not enter his thoughts again.

One evening when he was quite satisfied with his mistress, or with himself, he decided to call for Selim, and to walk a bit in the groves of the seraglio garden. These were green chambers where many things could be said and done without witnesses. As they winded their way there, Mangogul turned the conversation to the reasons people have for loving. Mirzoza professed high principles, and was filled with ideas of virtue that certainly did not suit her rank, her figure, or her age. She maintained that often people love for the sake of loving, and that liaisons begun by bonds of character, sustained by respect, and cemented by confidence, could last very long and remain constant without a lover's demand for favors nor a woman being tempted to grant them.

"That, Madame," answered the Sultan, "shows how much you have been spoiled by romances. You have read of heroes respectable and princesses virtuous to the point of folly; and you have never considered that these beings have never existed save in the minds of their authors. If you asked Selim, who knows Cytherea's catechism better than anyone, what love is, I would wager that his answer would be that love is but —"

"Are you wagering," interrupted the Sultana, "that delicacy of sentiment is but an illusion and that without the promise of pleasure there would not be a grain of love in the world? If so, you must have a low opinion indeed of the human heart."

"So I do," replied Mangogul. "Our virtues are no more disinterested than our vices. The brave man pursues glory by exposing himself to danger. The lazy man loves rest and life itself. The lover loves pleasure."

Selim, siding with the Sultan, added that love would be banished from society, never to reappear, if two things took place.

"And what would those two things be?" asked the favorite.

"They are," answered Mangogul, "what would happen if you and I and everyone else lost what Tanzaï and Néadarné found in a dream."

"What! Do you believe," interrupted Mirzoza, "that without those paltry things there would be no esteem or confidence between people of different sexes? That a woman with talents, wit, and charm would turn no heads? That a man with a handsome face, a fine mind, and an excellent character would find no one to listen to him speak?"

"No, he would not, Madame," replied Mangogul. "For, pray, what would he have to say?"

"All the pretty things that have always, it seems to me, been agreeable to hear."

"But note, Madame," said Selim, "that these things are said every day without love. No, Madame, no; I have definite proof that love does not exist without a well-constituted body. Agenor, the most handsome boy in the Congo, with the most refined wit at Court, would, were I a woman, in vain show off his fine leg to me, turn his big blue eyes to me, offer me the finest praises, and present himself with his many other advantages. I would say but one word to him, and if he did not respond to this word immediately, I would have all the respect in the world for him, but I would not love him."

"That is certain," added the Sultan. "And you yourself will agree that this mysterious word is most appropriate and useful in love. Indeed, for your instruction, you ought to have Selim repeat for you the conversation between a wit from Banza and a schoolteacher. You would understand at once that the wit, who supported your thesis, agreed in the end that he had been wrong, although his adversary reasoned like a jewel. Selim can tell you all about this; it is he who told it to me."

The favorite imagined that a tale that Mangogul would not relate himself must be quite indecent. She went into an arbor without asking Selim about it, which was lucky for him, for even with all his wit, he would have ill satisfied the favorite's curiosity, or much alarmed her modesty. To amuse her, and to steer away from the story of the schoolmaster, he told her the following tale:

"Madame," the courtier said to her, "in a vast country near the source of the Nile, there lived a young boy, beautiful as love itself. He was not yet eighteen years old, but all the girls vied for his heart, and there was scarce a woman who would not accept him for a lover. Born with an amorous heart, he loved as soon as he was capable of loving.

"One day when he was attending the public worship of the Great Pagod, and, according to custom, was making his seventeen genuflections prescribed by law, the beauty with whom he was smitten passed by, glanced at him as she smiled, and threw him into such a state of distraction that he lost his balance, fell flat on his face, scandalized the congregation by his fall, lost count of his genuflections and performed only sixteen.

"The Great Pagod, irritated by the offense and scandal, punished him cruelly. Hilas, for such was his name, poor Hilas found himself suddenly enflamed with the most violent of desires, and deprived, as with the sweep of a hand, of the means to satisfy them. Surprised and saddened by so great a loss, he questioned the Pagod.

"'You shall not return to your former state,' it said to him, sneezing, 'until you are in the arms of a woman who, in full knowledge of your misfortune, loves you no less.'

"Presumption is often willing company to youth and beauty. Hilas imagined to himself that his wit and the charms of his person would soon win him a sensitive heart that, happy with what was left of him, would love him for what he was and hasten to restore to him that which he had lost.

"First he addressed himself to the one who had been the innocent cause of his misfortune. She was a vivacious young lady, voluptuous and flirtatious. Hilas adored her. He obtained a rendezvous, during which, through a series of provocations, the poor lad was led down a road he was incapable of following. Much as he fretted and sought in the arms of his mistress the fulfillment of the oracle, nothing came up. When she grew tired of waiting, she quickly set her clothes straight and left. The worst part of the affair was that the little fool spoke of it to one of her friends, who through discretion spoke of it to only three or four of hers, who spoke of it in secret to so many others that Hilas, the darling of all the women but two days before, was scorned, pointed out, and considered a monster.

"The unhappy Hilas, shamed in his own land, resolved to travel and seek the cure for his ailment abroad. He went alone and incognito to the Court of the Abyssinian emperor. At first the women were taken with the young stranger and they vied for his attentions, but the prudent Hilas avoided those engagements in which he feared that the disappointment of the women who pursued him would be proportionate to his own. But how prodigiously intuitive the fair sex is! A boy so young, so modest, and so handsome, they said, is quite a phenomenon. The combination of these qualities, and their apprehensions that he might not be a full-fledged man, almost led them to suspect his real defect and refuse him precisely what he needed most.

"After having studied the lay of the land for some time, Hilas took a fancy to a young woman who had passed, by I know not what caprice, from refined gallantry to the highest religious devotion. Little by little he gained her confidence, embraced her ideas, copied her practices, gave her his hand for the walks to and from temples and talked with her so often about the vanity of earthly pleasures that unwittingly he reawakened her taste as well as her memory of them. For more than a month they had gone to mosques, partaken of sermons, and visited the sick together, when he began to hope for his own cure – but in vain. Although his devout friend knew how things should be in the heavens, she knew no less how a man should be on earth, and thus in an instant the poor boy lost the fruits of his good deeds. If one thing consoled him, it was that his secret would not be revealed. One word would have rendered his ailment incurable, but this word was not uttered. Hilas frequented a few other pious women, whom he took, one after the other, for the one ordered by the oracle, but none broke his spell, for they loved him for the only thing he had not. Their inclination to spiritualize things did not help him in the least. They wanted to speak of sentiments, but only those born of pleasure.

" 'Then you do not love me?' Hilas asked them sadly.

" 'And do you not know, sir,' they answered him, 'that people must know one another to love? And do you not agree that, disgraced as you are, you are no longer lovable when one comes to know you?'

" 'Alas!' he said as he left. "This pure love people speak of so often is nowhere to be found. This delicacy of feeling, which all men and women imagine, is but an illusion. The oracle misled me, and I am doomed for life.'

"Along the way, he met some of those women who desire no other commerce with men than that of the heart, and who loathe forward men as much as toads. So seriously did they admonish him to let nothing earthly and coarse enter into his views, that he conceived great hopes for his cure. He went about it in good faith, and was shocked to find that after the amorous conversations they held with him, still he remained exactly as he was. 'It must be,' he said to himself, 'that I will have to cure myself by some other means than speech,' and he awaited an occasion to put himself in the position indicated by the oracle. Such a situation soon arose. A young Platonist who was excessively fond of walking took him into a secluded wood. They were far from any meddlers when she felt faint. Hilas rushed to her side, and spared no pains to rouse her, but all his efforts were in vain. The beautiful fainter noticed this as well as he.

" 'Ah, sir!' she said to him, disengaging herself from his arms. 'What kind of a man are you? I shall be more careful next time before I set out for these secluded places, where one may fall ill and die one hundred deaths before finding any assistance.'

"Others learned of his situation, took pity on him, swore that the tenderness they had come to feel for him should not be altered, yet never saw him again.

"The unfortunate Hilas, with the most charming face in the world and the most refined sentiments, left many women unsatisfied."

"But he was quite a fool," interrupted the Sultan. "Why did he not seek out some of the vestal virgins who fill our convents? They would have been charmed by him, and he would surely have been cured through the grate."

"My lord," replied Selim, "the chronicle assures us that he tried this route, and found that nowhere do women wish to love to no purpose."

"In that case," added the Sultan, "I think his illness was incurable."

"He felt the same as Your Highness," continued Selim, "and weary of making attempts that led to nothing, he buried himself in solitude, on the advice of a great many women who told him explicitly that he was useless to society.

"He had already been wandering in the desert for several days, when he heard some sighing from a lonely spot. He listened. The sighing began again. He approached and saw a young girl as beautiful as the stars, head in hands, eyes bathed in tears, and the rest of her body in a sad and pensive state.

" 'What are you looking for here, miss?' he asked her. "Should you be in a deserted place like this?'

" 'Yes,' she answered sadly, 'here one can at least suffer in peace.'

" 'And what is the cause of your suffering?'

" 'Alas! . . .'

" 'Speak, what is wrong?'

" 'Nothing.'

" 'What do you mean, nothing?'

" 'Nothing at all, and that is why I suffer. Two years ago I had the misfortune to offend a pagod, who deprived me of everything. That required so little that it was hardly a great indication of its power. From that time on, declared the pagod, all men will flee and continue to flee me until I meet a man who, knowing my misfortune, becomes attached to me and loves me such as I am.'

" 'What are you saying?' cried Hilas. 'This wretch at your feet has nothing either; it is his affliction too. He had, some time ago, the misfortune to insult a pagod who deprived him of everything, which, in all modesty, was quite something. From that time on, declared the pagod, all women will flee and continue to flee him until he meets a woman who, knowing his misfortune, becomes attatched to him and loves him such as he is.'

" 'Is it really possible?' asked the young girl.

" 'Is what you tell me true?' asked Hilas.

" 'Just look...' answered the young girl.

" 'Just look...' answered Hilas.

"They convinced each other that in no uncertain terms were they objects of divine wrath. The unhappiness they shared formed a bond between them. Iphis, for such was the name of the young girl, was made for Hilas; Hilas was made for her. They loved each other platonically, as you can well imagine, for they could know no other love. Instantly the spells were broken; they shouted for joy, and the platonic love disappeared.

"For several months they stayed together in the desert, having all the time in the world to assure themselves of the change. When they left, Iphis was perfectly cured; as for Hilas, the author says that he was threatened with a relapse."

CHAPTER LIV

Thirtieth and Last Trial of the Ring

Mirzoza

While Mangogul was entertaining himself in his gardens with the favorite and Selim, the death of Sulamek was announced. Sulamek had begun as the Sultan's dancing master, against Erguebzed's wishes. Several scheming ladies, whom he had taught to perform dangerous leaps, promoted him with all their might and machinated to the point that he was preferred over Marcel and others, to whom he was not even worthy to be an assistant. He possessed a mind for detail, knew the jargon of the Court, and had a gift for telling pleasant stories and for amusing children; but he knew nothing of fine dance. When the post of Grand Vizier became vacant, he succeeded, by dint of his obsequiousness, in supplanting the Grand Seneschal, who was a tireless dancer but a stiff man who bowed gracelessly. His ministry did not distinguish itself with deeds glorious to the nation. His enemies (and who does not have them?

even true merit has many) accused him of playing the violin badly and of having no flair for choreography; of allowing himself to be duped by the pantomimes of Prester John and terrified by a bear from Monoemugi that danced for him one day; of giving millions to the Emperor of Tombur to prevent him from dancing during a time when he himself had gout; and of spending yearly more than five hundred thousand sequins in resin, and more than that persecuting all the fiddlers who played minuets other than his own. In short, they accused him of having slept for fifteen years to the sound of a cymbal played by a clumsy native of Guinea who accompanied himself on his instrument while garbling some songs about the Congo.

It is true that he ushered in the fashion of Dutch lime trees, and so on...

Mangogul had a big heart. He missed Sulamek, and ordered a magnificent burial and a funeral oration for him, and Brrrouboubou the orator was charged with the latter.

On the appointed day of the ceremony, the chief Brahmins, the council of divans, and the Sultanas, led in by their eunuchs, gathered in the Great Mosque. For more than two hours, and with a surprising rapidity, Brrrouboubou demonstrated that Sulamek had succeeded through superior talents, he composed prefaces to prefaces, and had neglected neither Mangogul nor his exploits in the course of Sulamek's administration. He was exhausting himself with exclamations when Mirzoza, to whom lies gave the vapors, had an attack of lethargy.

Her officers and her women rushed to her assistance. She was put on her litter and immediately transported to the seraglio. Mangogul, informed of the danger, came running and the whole pharmacopoeia was summoned. The Garus,[1] General La Motte's drops, and English drops were tried, all with no success. The Sultan, distraught, alternated between crying for Mirzoza and cursing Orcotomus. At last he lost all hope, or at least he had hope only in his ring.

"If I have lost you, my soul's delight," he cried, "your jewel, like your mouth, will be eternally silent."

Immediately he ordered everyone to withdraw. They obeyed and he found himself alone with the favorite. He turned his ring toward her, but Mirzoza's jewel, which was bored during the service, as happens to so many others every day, and which was apparently feeling quite lethargic itself, at first but murmured a few confused and inarticulate words. The Sultan repeated the operation, and the jewel, expressing itself quite distinctly, said the following:

"Far from you, Mangogul, what would become of me?... Faithful even in the night of the tomb, I would have looked for you, and if love and constancy are rewarded in death, dear Prince, I would have found you... Alas, without you the delightful palace where Brahma lives, and which he has promised to his faithful believers, would have been a miserable abode for me."

Mangogul, transported by joy, did not notice that the favorite was gradually recovering from her lethargy, and that, if he waited any longer to turn his ring, she would hear the last words of her jewel, which in fact is what happened.

"Ah! Prince," she said to him, "what of your word? Have you dispelled your unfair suspicions? Did nothing restrain you, not the state I was in, nor the offense you were giving me, nor the promises you made to me?"

"Ah, Madame," the Sultan answered her, "do not attribute to shameful curiosity the impatience that only the despair of having lost you suggested to me. I did not test my ring on you; but I thought I might, without breaking my promises, make use of a resource by which to restore you to my vows and assure you of my heart forever."

"Prince," said the favorite, "I believe you, but pray give your ring back to the genie, and let not this fateful gift disturb your heart or your empire any longer."

Mangogul immediately began to pray, and Cucufa appeared.

"Almighty Genie," Mangogul said to him, "take back your ring, and continue to be my protector."

"Prince," answered the genie, "divide your days between love and glory. Mirzoza will assure you of the first of these blessings, and I promise you the second."

With these words the hooded specter seized his owls' tails and went off in a whirl, just as he had come.

NOTES

Chapter One: Birth of Mangogul

1. *The Count de* ——— : Character in the novel by Duclos.
2. *Shah Baham*: The hero of Crébillon fils's *The Sofa*.

Chapter Four: The Evocation of the Genie

1. *Camaldolite*: Member of a barefoot order of Benedictine hermits founded in 1012 by Saint Romuald at Camaldoli in central Italy.

2. *Saint Hubert's ring*: A ring that had touched the relics of Saint Hubert; it allegedly cured rabies.

Chapter Six: First Trial of the Ring

1. *cavagnole*: Popular game of chance, similar to a lottery.

2. *Island of Jonquille*: The unfortunate heroine in Crébillon fils's *Tanzaï et Néadarné* goes to this island to retrive the same organ Alcina fears she is losing.

3. *Cicogne*: Or Sigogne, a tanner boy turned apothecary turned physician thanks to the patronage of Chirac, Louis XV's head physician.

4. *Nicole*: Pierre Nicole (1625-95), Jansenist theologian and teacher at Port Royal.

Chapter Eleven: Fourth Trial of the Ring

1. *sanjak*: Governor of a Turkish province.

Chapter Twelve: Fifth Trial of the Ring

1. *faro*: A banking game in which players place bets, laid on a special layout, as to which cards will win or lose as they are drawn one at a time from a dealing box.

2. *engastrimyths*: Ventriloquists.

3. *brelan*: An old French gambling game.

Chapter Thirteen: Sixth Trial of the Ring

1. *Dardanus*: Opera by Rameau (1739) with a libretto by La Bruère. Lulli's librettist was Philippe Quinault.

2. *"little violins"*: François Francoeur (1698-1787) and François Rebel (1701-75); new to the Opera and hence called the "little violins," they collaborated on many operas and directed the theater from 1751 to 1767.

3. *Le Maure*: Catherine Nicole Le Maure (1704-83), considered one of the finest voices ever to sing at the Opera; she sang there until 1750.

4. *pont-neuf*: A popular and trivial song sung to a well-known tune; a vaudeville is a song of the same nature about a current event or person.

Chapter Fourteen: Orcotomus's Experiments

1. *manna*: A purgative, known more commonly as manitol.

2. *Fontenoy…Lawfeld*: The battle of Fontenoy was fought on May 11, 1745; Lawfeld, on July 2, 1747; both were glorious victories for the Maréchal de Saxe over the English and the Austrians.

Chapter Nineteen: The Appearance of the Islanders and Their Women's Dress

1. *fontange*: A knot of ribbon worn as a hair ornament; named for Mlle de Fontange, Louis XIV's mistress.

2. *assassins*: Small black dots women drew above their eyes.

Chapter Twenty-Two: Seventh Trial of the Ring

1. *the kermes mineral*: Used medicinally in the eighteenth century as a decongestant.

Chapter Twenty-Four

1. *saic*: A type of large-masted ship, Greek in origin, which the Turks used a great deal in their commerce with the Levant.

Chapter Twenty-Eight: Twelfth Trial of the Ring

1. *Petit*: Jean-Louis Petit (1674–1750), famous surgeon who invented a method to control hemorrhaging during an operation.

2. *Cadilesker*: A Turkish chief judge, in charge of both civic and religious law.

3. *The Florentine instrument*: The chastity belt, allegedly invented in Florence.

Chapter Thirty-One: Thirteenth Trial of the Ring

1. *red mass*: Mass celebrated by members of Parliament after their holidays, to which they wore red robes.

2. *three-tailed pasha*: The rank of a pasha was indicated by the number of horse tails on his standard.

Chapter Thirty-Eight: A Conversation About Literature

1. *cavagnole or biribi*: Two similar games.

Chapter Forty: Mirzoza's Dream

1. *"Alas! This was his son!"*: Verse from Voltaire's *Henriade*, song VIII, line 260.

Chapter Forty-Two: Dreams

1. *the divan*: The Turkish royal court.

2. *seraskier*: A general in the army of the Ottoman Empire; here, perhaps, the minister of war.

3. *teftardar*: A Turkish title, here designating the treasurer.

4. *kiara*: A deputy or lieutenant in the Turkish army.

Chapter Forty-Four: Selim's Travels

1. *Aloysia*: An erotic work, in dialogue form, by Nicolas Chorier (1612–92).

2. *Tavernier*: Jean-Baptiste Tavernier (1605–89) traveled to the Orient and wrote, in collaboration with Samuel Chappuzeau, several accounts of his findings.

Chapter Forty-Five: Twenty-Fourth and Twenty-Fifth Trials of the Ring

1. *Monsieur de Claville*: Author of *Traité du vrai mérite de l'homme* (*Treatise on Man's True Merit*).

2. *Sala*: A Muslim ritual.

3. *marabout*: A devout Muslim, a dervish.

Chapter Forty-Seven: Twenty-Seventh Trial of the Ring

1. The sections in italics are as they appeared in the original edition, in English, Latin, Italian, and a bit of Spanish. Diderot, at the end of this chapter, maintains that these sections were meant only for the polyglot reader and should not be translated, since they contain sexual references more explicit than any others in the book.

Chapter Forty-Eight: Cydalisa

1. *spahis*: Formerly, a unit of the Turkish cavalry.

Chapter Fifty: Marvelous Events of the Reign of Kanoglou

1. *our own Turennes and Colberts*: Henri de la Tour d'Auvergne (1611–75) was a victorious general who served in the Dutch War of Independence and the Thirty Years' War; Jean-Baptiste Colbert (1619–83) was a very influential secretary of state under Louis XIV.

2. *Bion*: French optician-inventor who died in 1733.

Chapter Fifty-One: Twenty-Eighth Trial of the Ring

1. *"That oracle…"*: From Racine's *Iphigenia*.

Chapter Fifty-Four: Thirtieth and Last Trial of the Ring

1. *Garus*: An elixir of the period used to settle irritations of the stomach.

Originally published as *Les Bijoux indiscrets* (1748).

The Story of a
Modern Greek Woman

by Abbé Prévost

———

Translated by Lydia Davis

Introduction

by Joan DeJean

Prévost's *The Story of a Modern Greek Woman*: Libertine Sensibilities

by Joan DeJean

When the eighteenth century dreamed of the Orient, the image most likely to be conjured up was that of a beautiful Oriental woman. Like her modern successor, the femme fatale, the Oriental woman was the object of ardent desire insofar as she remained obscure. Witness the founding example of her incarnation in eighteenth-century French literature: Roxane, favorite wife of Usbek, the wandering Persian hero of Montesquieu's *Persian Letters* (1721). Roxane's power over Usbek is dependent on her remaining, in his words, "inaccessible."[1] Before the revelations of the novel's explosive final letter, therefore, Roxane lets drop few veils indeed. Eighteenth-century French readers, like Montesquieu's petty Oriental despot, preferred to think of dangerously seductive women confined behind the seraglio's walls or contained within the boxes in which Usbek's wives are locked up whenever they venture outside the seraglio.

No eighteenth-century heroine better fulfills the conditions of this Oriental dream than Prévost's (1697–1763) "modern" Greek woman, Théophé. Throughout *The Story of a Modern Greek Woman* (1740), Théophé remains the obscure object of desire par excellence. Indeed, her obscurity, her "inaccessibility," may well be the closest approximation of a stable truth that Prévost allows readers of his novel.

Readers generally question the reliability of Prévost's better-known hero, Des Grieux, because they are instinctively made uneasy by his presentation of Manon Lescaut. Faced with what is more a portrayal of an obsession than of its object, they experience a sort of collective malaise. How can such excessive passion fail to distort? Both the question and the malaise seem more inevitable still apropos of *The Story of a Modern Greek Woman*, a novel that (mysteriously) has never approached *Manon Lescaut*'s (1732) canonical status, but one far more likely to appeal to twentieth-century readers.

The novel's opening lines thrust the reader abruptly into the heart of this interpretive dilemma: "Will I not incur suspicion by the confession that forms my exordium? I am the lover of the beautiful Greek woman whose story I am undertaking.... Will not a violent passion cause everything that passes before my eyes or through my hands to change its nature? In a word, what faithfulness will one expect from a pen guided by love?" (pp. 553–54). Indeed. From his "exordium" right to the end, the narrator's "suspicion" colors everything, especially the question of Théophé's "fidelity," so that readers are ultimately unable to decide between radically opposing visions of "the beautiful Greek woman." Some critics thus portray her as sexually depraved, a far more dissolute version of Manon Lescaut. Others see her as a paragon of a mode of female virtue new to the novel in Prévost's day – the independent woman who seeks above all to live her life outside of male control. Still other critics more astutely situate the novel's problem *beyond* virtue, beyond the issue of absolute choice: they present the central relationship in novelistic terms, that is, as a struggle between decidability (the narrator's desire to know and tell all) and inaccessibility or indeterminacy (Théophé's wish to remain outside of narrative).

On close inspection, the spiral of narrative indeterminacy appears more vertiginous still. Both the narrator and his Greek beauty conspire in the destabilization of the storytelling situation. For instance, the narrator's obsessive stress on his possible unreliability may simply be a ploy necessary to his desire to be believed, that is, to have the reader accept his conviction of Théophé's infidelity. However, it may betray instead a desire *not* to be believed, a desire to seem more like the obscure Greek beauty and therefore more complicated than he might otherwise appear. In short, is it fear or hope that still prompts the narrator to cry out "must I not fear that he will mistrust my testimony?" (p. 678), even as his "testimony" is nearing its end?

In addition, Théophé at the very least both seeks to become the object of male desire and understands the power of inaccessibility in the generation of that desire. In one of the rare moments of her story which the narrator allows her to tell in her own words, Théophé describes her decision to sell herself in the Constantinople slave market, in the hope of placing herself in as prestigious a seraglio as possible. The scene is extraordinary as much for the terms of her account as for its subject matter. Théophé alternately veils and unveils herself until she achieves her desired result, that of provoking intense curiosity about her origins, her availability, and her intentions: when a "stranger" is noticed in the lineup of slaves, a crowd gathers wondering aloud about "to whom [she] could belong" and what "plan could have brought [her] there" (p. 573). She thereby recreates for the narrator's obsessively curious gaze the "origin" of the nexus around which male anxiety and male desire converge throughout the novel.

In *The Story of a Modern Greek Woman*, Prévost thus stages a struggle for knowledge and power between two characters who constantly throw up smokescreens in their determination to remain undecidable. This elaborate avoidance ritual is an entirely appropriate center for a novel that ultimately calls into question virtually every conceivable marker of personal identity. Most notably, despite the fact that all the men in the novel conspire in a frantic effort to confirm or deny the status of each candidate proposed for the role of Théophé's biological father, the dilemma of her paternal origin is never resolved. In fact, we do not even know for certain that she is Greek. Théophé says only that "she believes she is Greek" because the man she took to be her father (a father figure whose authenticity is strongly denied by the narrator) gave her to think this was the case. In similar fashion, the narrator hints that his own origins are illustrious but, curiously, he fails to provide even the slightest bit of precise evidence about his past.

Prévost thus denies his readers access to his characters' origins. Instead, he has given us a work in which virtually all the major characters either have already re-created themselves according to received models that they explain to us, or learn to practice the art of self-recreation before our very eyes. Hence the novel's emphasis on maxims of national behavior (in France, men love in this way; in the Orient, women act like this; and so forth). By 1740, to stage the confrontation between Same (the French) and Other (the Oriental) in the form of comparative rules of cultural comportment was apparently to inscribe one's work in a familiar tradition, that incarnated most famously by Montesquieu's "how can one be Persian"?[2] However, it quickly becomes apparent that Prévost's inquiry is related only superficially to that important strain of Enlightenment thought.

For French *philosophes* such as Montesquieu, as Paul Hazard observed, travel was the beginning of doubt.[3] The doubt Hazard had in mind was philosophical and religious, the questioning of existential systems on which the great Enlightenment texts are founded. Hazard founds his observation on the authority of La Bruyère, who believed that those who came into contact with different religions inevitably began to doubt their own. Philosophical doubt was also the foundation of the particular brand of increasingly materialistic *libertinage* in which, by the end of the eighteenth century (most completely in Sade), a union was forged between the century's initial conception of *libertinage* as a commitment to uninhibited sensual indulgence and the libertine tradition's earliest definition in France, in the seventeenth century, when *libertinage* was synonymous with religious and philosophical freethinking. *The Story of a Modern Greek Woman* resists easy assimilation either to the tradition of Enlightenment travel literature or to the great tradition of eighteenth-century libertine speculation.

Prévost's anonymous narrator is generally referred to as "the diplomat." However, he seems in general totally unconcerned with diplomacy other than amorous; the only trade we see him negotiating is what he terms "the commerce of women" (p. 612). In similar fashion, in Prévost's novel, travel does not function as it does in Montesquieu's, as a prelude to a confrontation between rival religious or philosophical systems. Instead, Prévost stages the encounter between East and West as a clash between rival arts of love. In addition, he presents this amorous confrontation in curiously anachronistic terms, as a throwback to an earlier age rather than in a dialogue with contemporary discourses.

When the novel begins, the narrator has already completed the process that all the major characters in *The Story of a Modern Greek Woman* long to carry out, the replacement of one's native cultural identity with a self-selected personal identity. However, the diplomat's project should in no way be confused with eighteenth-century experiments in libertine self-fashioning, the most celebrated of which is recounted in the Marquise de Merteuil's autobiographical letter 81 in *Dangerous Liaisons* (included in this reader). The diplomat has made himself into "a Frenchman just as Turkish ... as that country's native inhabitants" (p. 554). In eighteenth-century terms, he has succeeded in forging an impossible union between what are always presented as irreconcilable cultural differences. In the project to which most of his narrative is devoted, he seeks to forge a second such union of irreconcilable cultural differences: he liberates the Greek beauty from the seraglio in the hope of making her into an Oriental as much a Frenchwoman as that country's native inhabitants. This time, his experiment goes wildly astray (as was so often the case when the Enlightenment's mania for scientific experimentation was unleashed on humans – witness the various attempts to educate so-called wild children). His failure may perhaps be explained by the fact that his vision of male-female relations is the product of still another strange union of irreconcilable constructions.

The self-made man is a self-described libertine: he refers repeatedly to his vast experience with woman and to the force of his penchant for sensuality. However, it is difficult to reconcile what he refers to as his "enlightened libertinism" (p. 609) with what he presents to Théophé as *the* system governing amorous commerce in France, a system that he holds up as an ideal that should be adopted by all nations – indeed, it is difficult to imagine why a self-avowed libertine would ever "preach" (the verb he uses to express the enthusiasm with which he endorses this code) such conduct to the woman he views as his next conquest. In France, according to the diplomat, "men will go to any length for women's happiness, treating them like queens rather than slaves, surrendering themselves completely, asking in return only gentleness, tenderness, and virtue" (p. 557).

Rather than a man of his age, the narrator sounds for all the world like a throwback to the golden age of *préciosité*, someone who still subscribes to an art of love most ardently "preached" in Parisian salons in the 1660s and subsequently enshrined in literary texts written by those who had frequented those salon gatherings. Witness a canonic example, from Pierre-Daniel Huet's *The History of Romances* (1670), published as a preface to *Zayde* (1670–71), the romance in which Lafayette formulated one of the last pure expressions of the salon ideal, according to which women ruled supreme by virtue of their superior knowledge of the language of sentiment. Like the narrator, Huet contrasts East and West; like the narrator, he pronounces the West superior because women there live in freedom and are free to frequent the opposite sex, rather than being locked away from the male gaze. Like the narrator, he claims that women dictate to men in France. And like the narrator, Huet contends that French women owe their tactical superiority to their virtue, which they have made into "a Fort more strong and secure than all the Keys, Grates...."[4]

The diplomat seduces Théophé out of the sociocultural code in which she had lived prior to their encounter, with promises of a world outside the seraglio in which the Oriental structure of female enslavement to male domination would be reversed: according to his portrayal of the West, to rule over men women need only remain virtuous. The narrator more than reinforces this view with the first volumes he selects for Théophé's instruction into Frenchness: Arnauld and Nicole's *The Logic of Port-Royal* (1662) and Nicole's *Moral Essays* (1671–95), two of the monuments of Jansenism, that most ascetic sectarian discourse of early modern Catholicism. When he suddenly realizes the obvious, that these works present as austere a moral code as is imaginable, he begins to blame her rejection of his amorous proposals on this reading. He then decides to substitute works of "less fierce principles," in particular *The Princess of Clèves* (1678) (p. 658).

The narrator rescinds this decision, but he might just as well have handed over to his protégée Lafayette's novel about a woman who concludes that the dictates of her "duty" and her inner "calm" are more important than passion, and who refuses on these grounds the hand of an ardent suitor in favor of life outside of the world of male desire. Prévost's modern Greek woman seems intuitively to understand the wisdom of her seventeenth-century French precursor. Théophé rejects the narrator's suit with explanations that echo uncannily those the princess offers the duc de Nemours: she contends that she is concerned only with "duty" and "repose" (p. 677).

Thus the narrator gets what he says he wants: he takes a Greek slave and teaches her to negotiate at least one cultural code just like a native-born French woman – albeit one living in a time warp, as though she had been born a century before. Yet he never gets an instant's pleasure from the success of his experiment in cultural refashioning. His newly Gallicized Greek protégée drives him instead to ever wilder fits of jealousy – perhaps the wildest of which culminates in a scene in which he measures and remeasures the sheets on her bed, trying frantically to determine if the rumpled area is large enough to contain more than one body. So consumed is he by his incessant jealousy that, in the course of the relatively brief span of their indeterminate love affair, the narrator undergoes an accelerated aging process: we meet him in what he repeatedly describes as "the prime of [his] life"; at the novel's end, he is a virtual invalid, "weakened" from his continuous physical "infirmities."

Prévost takes the confrontation between East and West to the stage beyond the scenario imagined by Montesquieu and his imitators. Usbek feels the attraction of foreign codes, but he never tries to reshape his cultural identity as the narrator does. In addition, with his exploration of the limits of cultural assimilation, Prévost gives that popular eighteenth-century genre, the Oriental novel, new psychological depth. Indeed, his new psychology is so recognizably modern that readers might well wonder whether Prévost – who rebaptized himself "Prévost d'Exil" or "Exiles" (according to his earliest biography in 1732, he was "inspired by his status as an exile and his desire to remain anonymous") and who repeatedly chose to exile himself from his homeland – was suggesting multiculturalism as the way of the future.

However, like Montesquieu's Usbek before him, the narrator possesses none of the wisdom and the mental suppleness necessary to survive life as a cultural exile. He never appreciates, in and of itself, the power of his wonderfully inventive, almost zany imagination, his gift of imagining endless permutations on the theme of the union of cultural opposites – the French Turk, the Jansenist libertine, the libertine *précieuse*, and so forth. The diplomat never realizes that those who try to imagine life outside of or beyond known categories can hardly hope to act out their fantasies literally, that they have to take their pleasure simply in living a life of contradiction. He is crushed by his failure to take reality to the place he can imagine for it in discourse.

Most seriously still, throughout the novel he resists with all his might the knowledge that he feels his most violent attraction of all for passionate love, the kind of "mad" passion that makes the Sicilian Maria Rezati and her chevalier forget all concerns of family and fatherland and decide to live only for each other (p. 681). The diplomat fights the lure of the Enlightenment's most impossible dream, the same dream that still torments Laclos's Valmont nearly a half century later. Like Valmont, the narrator is barely able to imagine the possibility of a libertine in love, a libertine with a heart.

The narrator's avoidance is of necessity as grandiose as this dream, which, if realized, would have signified nothing less than the union of the two most powerful discourses developed in eighteenth-century fiction, *libertinage* and *sensibilité*. The narrator's (impossible) dream was shared by some of the greatest eighteenth-century novelists — notably Samuel Richardson, with whom the French had a love affair negotiated by Prévost's translations of both *Pamela* (1740) and *Clarissa Harlowe* (1747–48), and Laclos. Prévost, Richardson, and Laclos all fantasized in various ways either the systematization of passion, affective *libertinage*, or a libertine sensibility. Their fantasy, of course, was the most impossible of all "Oriental" dreams: the union of decidability and inaccessibility, the state of being simultaneously in control and carried away. When Prévost dreamed of the Orient, he conjured up a vision at the extremes of Enlightenment thought.

NOTES

1. Montesquieu, *Persian Letters*, trans. Christopher Betts (New York: Penguin, 1973), letter 26.

2. *Ibid.*, p. 83.

3. Paul Hazard, *The European Mind: The Critical Years (1680–1715)*, trans. J. Lewis May (New Haven, CT: Yale University Press, 1953), pp. 11–12.

4. Pierre-Daniel Huet, *The History of Romances*, trans. Stephen Lewis (London: J. Hooke, 1715), p. 8.

CONTENTS

THE STORY OF A
MODERN GREEK WOMAN
by Abbé Prévost

Foreword

THIS STORY HAS no need of a preface, but custom requires one at the beginning of a book. This one will serve only to let the reader know that in this work we promise him neither a key to the names nor an explanation of the facts, nor the slightest counsel that might give him to understand or to divine what he cannot gather through his own intelligence. The manuscript was found among the papers of a man known to society. We have endeavored to clothe it in a tolerable style without changing anything of the simplicity of the tale or the force of the sentiments. Along with tenderness, everything in it radiates honor and virtue. Let it go forth under these good auspices, and let it owe its success only to itself.

We will not hide the fact, nonetheless, that its value may be twofold for those who have had some acquaintance with the principal characters. But take care not to confuse the heroine with a charming Circassian woman who was known and respected by an infinite number of good people, and whose story in no way resembled this one.

We have omitted a display of Turkish erudition that would have overburdened the narration, and we have rendered in French all foreign words that could be so changed. Thus, we have put *seraglio* instead of *harem*, even though everyone knows that *harem* is the word for private seraglios, *market* instead of *bazaar*, and so on. This is for the benefit of those who are not familiar with accounts of the East; for there are few such works in which one does not find an explanation of all these terms.

Book One

Will I not incur suspicion by the confession that forms my exordium? I am the lover of the beautiful Greek woman whose story I am undertaking. Who will think me sincere in the recital of my pleasures or my pains? Who will not mistrust my descriptions and my praise? Will not a violent passion cause everything that passes before my eyes or through my hands to change its nature? In a word, what faithfulness will one expect from a pen guided by love? These are the questions that must keep a reader on his guard. But if he is enlightened, he will judge right away that by declaring them with such frankness I am sure of soon effacing their impression by another confession. I loved for a long time, I confess it again, and perhaps I am not as free of that fatal poison as I have succeeded in persuading myself. But love has always brought me only hardship. I have known neither its pleasures nor even its illusions, which in my blindness would no doubt have sufficed to take the place of love itself. I am a lover rejected, even betrayed, if I must put my trust in appearances, the judgment of which I will leave to my readers; yet I have been esteemed by the one I loved, heeded like a father, respected like a teacher, consulted like a friend. But what price for feelings such as mine! And in the bitterness that still remains in me, should one expect overly flattering praises or exaggerations of feelings for an ingrate who was the continual torment of my life?

I was employed in the affairs of the king in a court whose customs and intrigues no one knew better than I. The advantage I had had when I arrived in Constantinople of knowing the Turkish language perfectly had allowed me a degree of familiarity and confidence at which most ministers arrive only after long trials. The peculiarity of seeing a Frenchman just as Turkish, if one will allow me this expression, as that country's native inhabitants, drew to me even in the first days ceaseless demonstrations of welcome and distinction. Even the taste that I affected to show for the manners and ways of the nation served to increase the attachment they acquired for me there. They went so far as to imagine that I could not have so many resemblances to the Turks without being well disposed toward their religion; and as this idea succeeded in bringing me closer to them in their esteem, I found myself as free and as familiar in a city I had lived in scarcely two months as in the place of my birth.

The occupations of my employment left me so much freedom to go out and about that I determined at first to derive from this ease all the fruits befitting my curiosity to instruct myself. I was, moreover, at an age when the taste for pleasure is still in harmony with that for serious affairs, and my plan, in making this voyage to Asia, had been to divide myself between these two inclinations. The amusements of the Turks did not appear so strange that I did not hope soon to be as sensitive to them as they were. My only fear was that I would find it less easy to satisfy the penchant I had for women. The constraint in which they were held, and the difficulty one found even in seeing them, had already caused me to plan to repress that part of my inclinations, and to prefer a tranquil life to such arduous pleasures.

However, I found myself in friendly relations with the Turkish lords who had the reputation of being the most refined in their choice of women and the most magnificent in their seraglios. They had welcomed and honored me many times in their palaces. I marveled at the fact that the objects of their gallantry never entered into the conversation and that their gayest speeches turned only on good food, hunting, and the little events of the court or the town which could serve as subject matter for pleasantries. I showed the same reserve, and I pitied them for denying themselves, through an excess of jealousy or through a defect of taste, the most agreeable subject that can fuel a conversation. But I did not understand their views very well. They were thinking only of putting my discretion to the test; or rather, because of the ideas they had of the French taste for the merit of women, they agreed as though in concert to allow me time to reveal my inclinations. This was at least the judgment they soon gave me reason to form.

An old pasha, who was calmly enjoying the riches he had accumulated in his long years of employment, had displayed feelings of esteem for me which I endeavored to respond to with continual demonstrations of gratitude and affection. His house had become as familiar to me as my own. I knew all of its apartments, with the exception of his women's quarters, toward which I took care not even to glance. He had noticed this affectation, and having no doubt that I knew at least where his seraglio was situated, he had induced me several times to walk with him around his garden, which a part of the building overlooked. At last, seeing that I preserved an obstinate silence, he said to me, smiling, that he marveled at my restraint. "You are not unaware," he added, "that I have beautiful women, and you are neither of an age nor a temperament that could inspire much indifference for this sex. I am surprised that your curiosity has not caused you to express the desire to see them." "I know your customs," I answered dryly, "and I will never propose you violate them for my benefit. A little experience of the world," I went on, looking at him with the same air, "has given me to understand, in arriving in this country, that since so many precautions are exercised in the keeping of women, curiosity and indiscretion must be the two vices least tolerated. Why would I run the risk of wounding my friends with questions that might displease them?" He praised my answer highly. And confessing that various instances of Frenchmen's boldness had ill disposed the Turks toward the gentlemen of that nation, he seemed all the more satisfied to find in me such reasonable sentiments. Immediately he offered to let me see his women. I accepted the favor calmly. We entered a place the description of which is not useful to my design. But I was too struck by the order that I saw reigning there not to recall all its details easily.

The pasha's women, who numbered twenty-two, were all together in a drawing room set aside for their activities. They were variously occupied, some painting flowers, others sewing or embroidering, according to their talents or inclinations, which they were free to follow. The material of their dresses appeared to me the same; they were at least the same color. But their hairstyles were different, and I gathered that they were coiffed to suit their faces. A great number of servants of both sexes – although I noticed that those who appeared to belong to my own were eunuchs – stood in the corners of the room to execute their every command. But this crowd of slaves withdrew as soon as we entered, and the twenty-two ladies, rising without leaving their places, appeared to await the orders of their lord or an explanation for a visit that apparently caused them much surprise. I considered them one by one, and their ages appeared unequal; but if I remarked none who appeared over thirty years of age, nor did I see any as young as I had imagined, for the youngest were not less than sixteen or seventeen.

Chériber – for that was the pasha's name – asked them politely to approach, and having briefly informed them who I was, proposed they undertake something for my amusement. They had various instruments brought to them, which several of them began to play, while the others danced with fair grace and lightness. This spectacle having lasted more than an hour, the pasha had refreshments brought in, which were distributed in each part of the room where the women had resumed their places. I had not yet had occasion to open my mouth. At last he asked me what I thought of this elegant assembly; and upon the praise I offered for such charms, he delivered several judicious remarks about the power of education and custom, which make the most beautiful women submissive and calm in Turkey, while he had heard, he told me, that all the other nations complain of the confusion and disorder women cause elsewhere by their beauty. I answered him with a few flattering reflections on Turkish ladies. "No," he went on, "it is not a characteristic that belongs more to our women than to those of any other country. Of the twenty-two whom you see here, there are not four who were born Turks. Most are slaves whom I bought without special regard." And asking me to cast my eyes on one of the youngest and most lovely, he said, "She is a Greek, whom I have had only six months now. I do not know from whose hands she came. The charm of her face and her mind alone caused me to take her by chance, and you see that she is as content with her fate as the rest of her companions. Yet, given the breadth and liveliness of character I know her to have, I sometimes marvel that she has been able to subject herself so quickly to our ways, and I can find no other reason for it than the power of example and habit. You may converse with her for a moment," he said, "and I am mistaken if you will not discover in her all the merit that among your people raises women to the highest fortune and makes them suited to the most important affairs."

I went up to her. Her taste was for painting; and seeming scarcely to notice what was going on in the room, she had left off dancing only to take up her brush again. After a few polite remarks about the liberty I took in interrupting her, nothing better occurred to my mind than what I had just learned from Chériber. I congratulated her on the natural qualities that endeared her to her master, and letting her know that I was not unaware of how long she had been his, I marveled that in so short a time she had trained herself so perfectly in the customs and activities of the Turkish ladies. Her answer was simple. Since a woman had no other happiness to hope for but that of pleasing her master, she said to me, she was very happy if Chériber had such a high opinion of her, and I would not be surprised that with this incentive she had conformed so easily to the laws he had established for his slaves. This sincere devotion to the wishes of an old man in a charming girl who was not more than sixteen appeared much more wonderful than all that I had heard from the pasha. I believed I could see from the young slave's appearance as much as from her remarks that she was imbued with the sentiment she had just expressed. The comparison that formed in my mind between the principles of our ladies and his led me to express candidly some regret at seeing her born for a different fate than that which she deserved by so much complaisance and goodness. I spoke to her remorsefully about the misfortune of Christian countries, where men will go to any length for women's happiness, treating them like queens rather than slaves, surrendering themselves completely, asking in return only gentleness, tenderness, and virtue, yet almost always find themselves deceived in their choice of a wife, with whom they share their name, their station in life, and their possessions. And seeing my laments listened to avidly, I continued to speak longingly of the French husband who might find in his life's companion virtues that were more or less wasted among Turkish ladies, due to their misfortune of never finding in men a reciprocity worthy of their sentiments.

This conversation, in which I confess I was carried away by the impulse of pity and left the young Greek woman little freedom to answer, was interrupted by Chériber. He may have noticed the warmth with which I was addressing his slave; but as the testimony of my heart reproached me with nothing that could wound his trust, I returned to him with a free manner. His questions, nevertheless, were not accompanied by any sign of jealousy. On the contrary, he promised to give me the same spectacle often, if I found it amusing.

Several days went by during which I deliberately refrained from seeing him, with the sole design of forestalling any mistrust he might have by affecting indifference toward the women. But during a visit which he paid me in order to reproach me for having neglected him, a slave from his retinue delivered a note to one of my servants. It was my valet, who brought it to me as mysteriously as he had received it. Having opened it, I found it written in Greek characters, which I did not yet understand, even though I had begun some time before to study the language. I immediately summoned my tutor, who was considered to be a very honest Christian, and I asked him to explain the document, as though it had fallen into my hands by chance. He wrote out the translation for me, and all of a sudden I realized that it came from the young Greek woman to whom I had spoken at the pasha's seraglio. But I was quite surprised by what it contained. After a few reflections on the misfortune of her condition, she entreated me in the name of the esteem I had shown for virtuous women, to use my influence to remove her from the hands of the pasha.

I had acquired for her only the feelings of admiration that were naturally due to her charms; and in the principles of conduct I had formed for myself, nothing was so contrary to my intentions as to involve myself in a situation in which I had more pain to fear than pleasure to anticipate. I had no doubt that the young slave, charmed by the image I had briefly drawn for her of the happiness of our women, had acquired a disgust for her life in the seraglio, and that the hope of finding in me all the dispositions I had vaunted to her in the men of my country had made her wish to enter into some love intrigue with me. As I reflected on the dangers of this undertaking, I was only confirmed in my first resolution. However, a natural desire to oblige a charming woman, whose condition I supposed would become a torment to her, caused me to wonder whether it was possible to gain her freedom by honest means. It occurred to me to simply try generosity, by offering to pay her ransom. A fear of shocking the pasha by this offer might have stopped me. But I formed a plan that satisfied all my delicacy. I was very close friends with the *selictar*, one of the most important figures in the empire. I resolved to unburden myself to him about my desire to buy a slave belonging to the pasha Chériber, and to induce him to take on this proposition as though he wished to make the transaction for himself. The selictar consented, without making too much of so slight a service. I left the price up to him. The consideration that Chériber had for his rank made it easier than I had dared to hope. The very same day I had the assurance of the selictar, who also advised me that it would cost me a thousand ecus.

I congratulated myself on such a fine use of that sum; but on the eve of obtaining what I desired, a thought occurred to me that had escaped me in the ardor of success. What would become of the young slave, and what were her intentions in leaving the seraglio? Did she propose to come to my home and settle permanently in my household? I found her charming enough to take an interest in her fate; but quite aside from the measures of propriety which I had to maintain with my servants, could I prevent the pasha from learning sooner or later where she had gone, and would I not fall once again despite myself into the very trap from which I had thought to protect myself? This thought cooled me so toward my enterprise that when I saw the selictar the next day, I expressed some regret at having employed him in an affair that I feared might irritate the pasha. And without any mention of handing over the thousand ecus, I left to pay my visit to Chériber. Torn at one and the same time between my desire to be of service to the slave, the difficulties I dreaded from it, and the fear of irritating my friend, I would have wished to find some pretext for disengaging myself completely from this situation. I deliberated as to whether the best decision was not to unburden myself enough to the pasha himself to find out at least if the sacrifice I had made into a sort of necessity was not causing him too much pain. It seemed to me that with an excuse as fair as that of regard for friendship, I could exempt myself without crudeness from satisfying the whims of a woman. My visit was so pleasing to Chériber that the signs of his joy delayed the disclosure for which I had prepared myself. He had the time to tell me without interruption that he had one less woman in his seraglio, and that the young Greek with whom I had spoken was sold to the selictar. He appeared so relaxed as he told me this, that, judging his feelings by his expressions, I did not believe him very afflicted by his loss. I even noticed afterward that he had no passion for his women. At his age, the needs of his sexual appetite caused him little worry, and the expenditure he made on his seraglio was less for the satisfaction of his heart than his vanity. This observation removed all my scruples, I even abandoned the thought of revealing them to him, and I believed I should leave him with the idea that he had earned the selictar's gratitude.

However, having proposed that we spend a few minutes in his seraglio, he appeared embarrassed over the pretext he had to make to his slave. "She does not know," he said to me, "that she is going to change masters. After all the tokens of my affection she has received, her pride will be wounded to see me consent so easily to putting her in another's power. You will be witness," he added, "to the manner in which she receives my farewells, for I am going to see her for the last time, and I have said to the selictar that he will be free to have her brought to him when he thinks fit." I foresaw that this scene would in fact hold some pleasure for me: but it was not for the reasons that might cause it to be embarrassing to the pasha. Not having dared risk a reply to the young Greek woman's note, I expected that she would be dismayed to learn that her slavery was to continue in the selictar's seraglio. What would it be to learn this in my presence and not dare to give vent to her resentment through complaints? Chériber's slave had come twice to ask me for my answer, and I had confined myself to telling him that I would respond to the opinion she had of me with all the zeal one might expect.

Instead of taking me to the drawing room, the pasha sent word that his slave was to join us in a small room where he gave orders that only she should be admitted after us. Her timidity, as she approached us, let me know of the agitation of her heart. She could not see me with her master without harboring the illusion that I had consented to her intentions and that I was perhaps bringing her the happy news of her freedom. The pasha's first remark must have confirmed this idea. With great gentleness and politeness he declared that, despite all the affection he had for her, he had not been able to prevent giving the rights he had over her heart to a powerful friend; but his consolation, he added, was to assure her as he lost her that she could not fall into the hands of a more gallant man; besides the fact that he was one of the most important lords of the empire and, because of his wealth and his fondness for love, the most capable of providing for the women who acquired some ascendancy over him. He named the selictar to her. The trembling look she cast on me and the sadness that suddenly spread over her face appeared to reproach me for having misunderstood her intentions. She imagined that it was I who was in fact removing her from Chériber's seraglio, but merely in order to make her exchange one form of slavery for another, and that I had misunderstood, consequently, or counted as nothing, the reasons she had given me for being of service to her.

Chériber had no doubt that the disturbance he saw in her came from her reluctance to leave him. She compounded his mistake by protesting that to live in the condition in which fortune had placed her, she wished for no other master than he; and her pain caused her to join to this protestation such tender and urgent entreaties that I saw that the pasha was on the verge of forgetting all his promises. But regarding his uncertainty as a transitory emotion, by which I was much less moved than by the tears of the beautiful Greek, I hastened to help them with a few words that were equally soothing to both. "You must be consoled," I said to the slave, "by the sorrow that your loss causes the pasha; and if you doubt the happiness that awaits you, I am close enough to the selictar to guarantee that he will make you mistress of your fate." She raised her eyes to me, and because of her astuteness she was able to read in my own eyes what I was thinking. Chériber saw in my remark only what related to his own ideas. The rest of our interview became more tranquil. He showered her with gifts, and he asked me to help her choose among them. Then, having begged me to allow him to be with her in private, he took her into another small room, where they remained together for more than a quarter of an hour; and I had no doubt that it was in order to give her the last manifestations of his affection. My heart was quite free, since I bore this idea without the slightest emotion.

However, as the affair was so advanced that there was no longer any question of deliberating, I thought only of returning home in order to fetch the thousand ecus, which I immediately carried to the selictar. He asked me pleasantly if I was going to keep my adventure secret from him; and as the only price for his favor, he asked me to tell him by what chance I found myself involved with one of Chériber's slaves. As nothing obliged me to lie, I gave him an account of the origin and nature of my intrigue. And when he showed some difficulty believing that it was my generosity alone that led me to be of service to a girl as charming as I had described this young Greek, I swore so sincerely that I had no passion for her and that, thinking only of setting her free, I was even somewhat perplexed as to the decision she would make when she emerged from her slavery, that there could not remain in him the least doubt about my feelings. He indicated the hour at which I could fetch her from him. I awaited it without impatience. We had agreed to choose a time during the night, in order to conceal this venture from the public. I sent my valet at about nine o'clock in the evening in an inconspicuous carriage, with orders to notify only the selictar that he had come on my behalf. They answered him that the selictar would see me the next day, and that he would defer until then giving me an account of what he had done on my behalf.

This delay did not cause me any concern. Whatever the reason for it, I had satisfied everything that honor and generosity had prescribed, and the joy that the success of my undertaking might bring derived its strength only from these two motives. I had thought seriously in this interval about the conduct I should adopt with the young slave. A thousand reasons seemed to forbid my receiving her in my home; and even dwelling only on the most flattering aspects of her decision to solicit my help, which was perhaps the hope that she would make an easy arrangement with me to enjoy her charms, my design was not openly to make her my mistress. I had addressed myself to my language tutor, whom I had at last taken into my confidence. He was married. His wife was to receive the slave from my valet, and I proposed to go find out the next day what she desired further from my zeal.

But the reasons that had delayed the selictar were stronger than I could have imagined. Reaching his house just when he thought, himself, to forestall me with a visit, my arrival and my first questions could not help but embarrass him. He paused a few minutes before answering. Then, embracing me with more tenderness than I had remarked in his character, he entreated me to recall what I had assured him the day before in terms that had not permitted him to suspect my good faith. He waited for me to confirm them with new assurances, and embracing me again more openly and gaily, he said that he was in that case the happiest of all men, since, having conceived a lively passion for Chériber's slave, he did not have to fear the rivalry or opposition of his friend. He concealed nothing from me. "I saw her yesterday," he told me. "I spent only an hour with her; not a word of love escaped me. But there remained with me an impression of her charms that will not allow me to live without her now. You do not see her in the same light," he continued, "and I have felt sure that for the sake of a friend you will have no difficulty abandoning a possession that touches you so little. Put on her whatever price you think she merits, and do not be so reserved as Chériber, who did not know what she was worth."

Although I had not in the least expected this proposal after the service he had done me, as I had nothing in my heart that could cause me to regard it as a betrayal, I did not complain that it wounded either honor or friendship; but the same motives that had led me to help the slave induced me to revolt against the thought of giving her a new master against her will. I made no other protest to the selictar. "If you were to tell me," I said to him, "that she responds to your tenderness, or that she at least consents to belong to you, I would forget all my plans, and as heaven is my witness you would not have to ask twice for the satisfaction I would hasten to grant you. But I know to the contrary that she would regard it as the worst misfortune to return to a seraglio, and this is the only reason that caused me to take an interest in her fate." He could not help returning here to the principles of his nation: "Must one consult," he asked me, "the inclinations of a slave?" I chose to remove this pretext from him immediately. "Do not call her by that name," I answered. "I bought her only in order to make her free: she became free the moment she left Chériber's hands."

He seemed extremely dismayed by this declaration. However, since I wanted to preserve his friendship, I added that it was not impossible that the tenderness and offers of a man of his rank might touch the heart of a girl of her age, and I gave my word to consent to anything that appeared to me voluntary. I proposed not to postpone this test further. He regained some hope. The young Greek was summoned. I was the one who served as interpreter of the selictar's feelings, but I wanted her to know all his advantages, so that nothing would be lacking in the freedom of her choice. "You belong to me," I said to her. "I bought you from Chériber through the mediation of the selictar. My intention is to make you happy, and the opportunity presents itself this very day. Here you may find, in the tenderness of a man who loves you and in an abundance of all sorts of possessions, what you would perhaps search for in vain throughout the rest of the world." The selictar, who found my language and conduct sincere, hastened to add a thousand flattering promises. He swore to his prophet that she would hold the highest rank in his seraglio. He described all the pleasures that awaited her and the number of slaves she would have to serve her. She listened to his speech, but she had caught the meaning of mine. "If you think to make me happy," she said to me, "you must put me in a condition to profit from your kindness." As this answer could not leave me any uncertainty, I thought only of providing her with all the weapons necessary to defend herself against violence, and although I might not fear any such from a man like the selictar, this precaution seemed useful for a thousand reasons. Just as the Turks have little consideration for their slaves, so do they respect free women. I wanted her to be shielded from all the dangers of her condition. "Follow your inclination," I said to her, "and entertain no fears, either from me or from another, for you are no longer a slave; I return to you all the rights I have over you and over your freedom."

She knew, having heard it a thousand times since she had been in

Turkey, how differently the Turks behaved with regard to free women. Whatever transport of joy she had been thrust into by my declaration, her first act was to assume the air and countenance she believed suitable to the change in her fate. I marveled at the modesty and decency that seemed of a sudden diffused over her face. She applied herself less to giving me proof of her gratitude than to letting the selictar understand where her obligation lay after the favor I had just granted her. He himself saw that he must acknowledge it, and, manifesting his sorrow only by his silence, he appeared disposed to allow her the freedom she wished to gain from this. I did not know where she proposed to be taken; but she herself, surprised that I had not explained my intentions to her, approached me to ask what they were. I did not judge it suitable to enter into a long explanation in the presence of the selictar, and, assuring her that she would continue to find in my services all the assistance she might need, I took her as far as the door of the apartment, where I put her into the hands of one of my men with orders to conduct her secretly to the language tutor's home. In Constantinople there are carriages specifically for the use of women.

What surprised me was that the selictar, far from opposing her decision to leave, gave orders that the door of his house be opened for her, and he received me with an exceedingly tranquil face when I returned. He entreated me with the same moderation to listen to what he had been thinking. "I praise," he said to me, "the generous sentiment that interests you in the happiness of this young Greek, and I find it so disinterested that it excites my admiration. But since you judge her worthy of it, your opinion of her serves to confirm the tenderness she inspires in me. She is free," he continued, "and I do not accuse you of having preferred her fortune to my satisfaction. But I ask one favor of you, which I promise you I will not abuse. That is not to allow her to leave Constantinople without my knowledge. And you will not be bound long by your promise," he added, "for I pledge you my own, that you will know in four days what my intentions are." I did not object to granting him so simple a favor. Having in fact feared he would harbor some vestige of resentment over my conduct, I was glad to preserve his esteem and friendship at this price.

Several matters that I had to finish the same day caused me to defer until evening the visit I owed my young Greek. I chanced to meet Chériber. He told me that he had seen the selictar and that he had found him extremely satisfied with his slave. This could only have been after I had left him. The discretion that had caused him to conceal our venture so carefully enhanced my opinion of his probity. Chériber pointed out the selictar's high opinion of my integrity, also, and from the way that lord had spoken of me, Chériber assured me that I did not have a more perfectly devoted friend. I received this compliment with the gratitude it deserved. As I had no very lively interest in finding out where this redoubling of friendship or the promise the selictar had demanded of me might lead, my imagination was as tranquil as my heart, and nothing had changed my disposition when I went to the language tutor's home that evening.

I was told that the young Greek, who had already changed her name from Zara, by which she had been known as a slave, to Théophé, was awaiting my arrival with every indication of a lively impatience. I presented myself to her. Her first reaction was to throw herself at my knees, which she embraced in a flood of tears. For a long time I made useless efforts to lift her up. Her sighs were at first the only language she gave me to understand; but as the tumult of her feelings diminished, she addressed me a thousand times as her liberator, her father, and her god. It was impossible for me to moderate this first transport, into which it seemed she was pouring her entire soul. And, touched myself to the point of tears by expressions of such a strong gratitude, I lost the power to reject her tender caresses, and I allowed her full freedom to satisfy herself. At last, when I thought I saw that she was recovering a little from her agitation, I raised her up in my arms and placed her in a more comfortable spot, where I sat down beside her.

After having spent a few moments catching her breath, she repeated more calmly what she had already begun to say in twenty interrupted speeches. She expressed affectionate thanks for the service I had rendered her, admiration for my goodness, ardent prayers to Heaven to return to me a profusion of favors which all her strength and all her blood would never enable her to repay. She had violently struggled to restrain her transports in the presence of the selictar. She had suffered no less from the delay of my visit, and if I was not convinced that she wanted to live and breathe only in order to make herself worthy of my kindnesses, I was going to make her more unhappy than she had been as a slave. I interrupted her to assure her that such lively and sincere sentiments were already a return equal to my services. And thinking only to deflect the imminent renewal of her transports, I asked her one favor only, which was to tell me how long ago and through what misfortune she had lost her freedom.

I must say that despite the charms of her face and the touching disarray in which I had seen her at my feet and in my arms, there had not yet arisen in my heart any sentiment other than compassion. My natural delicacy prevented me from feeling anything more tender for a young person who had come from the arms of a Turk and in whom, moreover, I presumed nothing more than the external merit that is not uncommon in the seraglios of the East. Thus I still had all the merit of my generosity, but it occurred to me more than once that had our Christians known of it, I would not have been able to avoid severe censure by those who would have considered it a crime that I had not used, for the good of religion or for the freedom of some miserable captives, a sum they would have thought squandered on my pleasures. One will judge whether what follows in this adventure makes me more excusable; but if I feared some reproach at its beginning, what one is about to read would not appear to justify me.

As the least of my desires appeared to be law for Théophé, she promised openly to acquaint me with what she knew about her birth and the events of her life. "I began," she told me, "in a town in Morea where my father was considered a foreigner, and it is only by his word that I believe myself to be Greek, although he always concealed my birthplace from me. He was poor, and having no talent for acquiring more wealth, he raised me in poverty. However, I cannot recall the circumstances of a destitution I never felt. I was scarcely six years old when I found myself transported to Patras; I remember this name because it is the first trace of my childhood preserved in my memory. The luxury in which I found myself there, after a very hard life, also made an impression on me that cannot be erased. I had my father with me; but it was only after having spent several years in that town that I became distinctly aware of my situation, learning of the fate for which I was destined. My father, without being a slave and without having sold me, had attached himself to the Turkish governor. Whatever charms found in my face had served to recommend him to the governor, who had promised to feed him during his whole life and to have me raised with care, with no other condition but that he deliver me to him when I reached the age that corresponds to men's desire. Along with a place to live and his food, my father obtained a small employment. I was brought up under his watch, but by one of the governor's slaves, who scarcely waited until I was ten years old before speaking to me about the good fortune I had had of pleasing her master and the expectation he fostered in looking after my education. What had been announced to me as the greatest good fortune no longer appeared to my imagination in any other form. The brilliance of several women who composed his seraglio, and whose happy condition was described to me, excited my impatience. However, the governor was so advanced in age that my father, despairing of enjoying the advantages that had attracted him to Patras for all his years, began to regret a promise whose fruits he would gather for such a brief time. He did not yet communicate these thoughts to me; but having no obstacle to fear in the principles with which I was being raised, he allied himself secretly with the governor's son, who was already manifesting a good deal of passion for women, and proposed to him that he share the rights of his father under the same conditions. I was shown to this young man. He was taken by a lively passion for me. More impatient than his father, he demanded of mine that the term of their agreement be abridged. I was delivered over to him at an age when I did not yet know the difference between the sexes.

"You see that a taste for pleasure had no part in my misfortune and that I did not fall into licentiousness but was born into it. Thus, I experienced neither shame nor remorse for it. My increase in years did not even bring me the understanding that could have served to rectify my principles. Neither did I experience, in those early times, the desires of which passions are formed. My situation was that of habit. It lasted until the time the governor had set for me to be brought to him. His son, my father, and the slave who was entrusted with my care, fell into an almost equal embarrassment; but far from sharing it with them, I was still persuaded that I was meant to belong to the governor. He was proud and cruel. My father, who had mistakenly counted on his death, saw himself so pressed by time that, abandoning himself to his fears, he resolved to take flight with me, without confiding either in the slave or the young Turk. But his attempt was so unsuccessful that we were stopped before reaching the port. As he was not a slave, his escape was not a crime that could expose him to torture. However, he was subjected to the governor's rage, who reproached him not only for his flight, regarding it as a betrayal, but for all the kindnesses he had received from him, regarding them as a theft. I was confined that same day in the seraglio. I was told the following night that I would have the honor of being counted among my master's women. I received this declaration as a favor, and not having understood the reasons that had obliged my father to take flight, I was astonished that he had wished suddenly to renounce his fortune and mine.

"Night came. They prepared me for the honor they had announced, and I was led to the apartment of the governor, where he received me with much affection and many caresses. At the same moment, someone came to advise him that his son was asking to speak to him with utmost insistence and that the matters which brought him there were so pressing they could not be put off to the next day. The governor had him brought in, and gave orders that he be left alone to listen to his son. I remained with them, nonetheless; but the father took his son into a small inner chamber, where they were together several minutes. In truth I heard some violent words, which made me judge that their discussion was not calm. This was followed by a noise that alarmed me, when the son, emerging with a distraught expression, came to me, took me by the hand, and exhorted me to flee with him. Then, no doubt worried about the servants, he went out alone, deceived them with feigned orders from his father, and left me in the state in which I was, that is, trembling from his agitation and not daring even to go as far as the small chamber to find out what had happened there. Meanwhile, the slaves, to whom the young Turk had declared that his father wanted to be alone for a quarter of an hour, reappeared after that interval and found me in the same situation, my disturbance arousing their suspicions. They questioned me. I showed them the small chamber, without having the strength to speak. There they found their master lying in his own blood, dead from two thrusts of a dagger. Their shouts immediately attracted all the women of the seraglio. I was required to tell the tale of this tragic event. I recounted not so much what I had seen as what I imagined I had heard; and not understanding any better than anyone else the motivation behind what had happened, my ignorance and my fear were equally evident from my tears.

"There could be no doubt that the governor had died by his son's hand. This opinion, which was confirmed by the flight of the young Turk, produced a very strange effect. The women and the slaves of the seraglio, believing they were henceforth without a master, thought only of seizing whatever seemed most precious in their eyes and profiting from the darkness to escape from their prison. Thus, the doors having been opened on all sides, I resolved to go out, with all the more reason since no one had thought either of comforting or of restraining me. My intention was to reach my father's lodging, which was in the neighborhood of the seraglio, and I thought I would easily find the way there. But scarcely had I gone twenty steps in the shadows than I believed I saw the governor's son. I did not recognize him, however, until after I ventured to ask him who he was. He told me that in the terror of the unfortunate act he had just committed, he was seeking to find out whether his father was dead, in order to save himself by running away. I gave him an account of all that I had seen. His grief seemed to me sincere. He informed me in a few words that he had gone with more fear than anger to explain the commerce he had had with me, and that his father, infuriated by this declaration, had tried to take his life with a dagger. The son had not been able to defend himself except by fore-stalling his father with his own. He proposed that I accompany him in his flight; but just as he was urging me with great insistence, we were surrounded by several persons who recognized him and who, as the news of his crime had already spread, were seeking to find and arrest him. I was left free. I went secretly to the house of my father, who received me with a transport of joy.

"As he was not involved in this dismal incident, he resolved imme-diately to gather all that he had amassed during his stay in Patras and to leave that town with me. He did not explain to me what his inten-tions were, and still less, in my simplicity, did I grasp them. We departed at once. But scarcely had we set out to sea when he spoke in a way that grieved me. 'You are young,' he said, 'and nature has given you all that may elevate a woman to the highest fortune. I am taking you to a place where you have much to gain from these advantages; but I want you to promise me on your oath to conduct yourself only according to my counsels.' He pressed me to make this promise in inviolable terms. I felt an extreme repugnance at binding myself in the way he demanded. Some reflections I had begun to make about the situations in which he had engaged me caused me to think that in becoming intimate with a man, I could derive more pleasure from my own choice. The gover-nor of Patras's son, with whom I had had that liaison, had never made an impression on my heart, whereas I had seen a thousand young men with whom I would not have minded having the same familiarity. How-ever, my father's authority was a yoke that I did not have the strength to resist, so I decided to submit. We reached Constantinople. The first months were employed in my acquiring the manners and attainments that make a woman attractive in the capital. I was not more than fif-teen. Without confiding his designs, my father flattered me ceaselessly with the hope of a fortune that would surpass my expectations. One day as he was returning from the city, he did not notice that he had been followed by two men, who did not stop until they had found out what house he was entering, and who caused several neighbors to accompany them as they entered after him. We occupied only a small part of it. They knocked so abruptly at our door that, in the uneasiness he felt at this noise, my father made me go into a second room, which adjoined the first. Having opened the door, he was surprised by a man he believed he recognized, since the sight of him caused him to lose his voice, and he said nothing to several insulting reproaches that I heard distinctly. They called him a traitor, a coward who would no longer escape justice and who would account for his treacheries and thefts despite himself. He did not seek to justify himself, and seeing no further likelihood of defending himself, he allowed himself to be led away without resistance to the cadi. Scarcely had I recovered from my first fright than, covering my head with a veil, I hastened to follow the route by which they had taken my father. Since the court hearing was open to the public, I arrived early enough to witness the complaints of his accusers and the sentence that immediately followed his confession. He was charged with having seduced the wife of a Greek nobleman, whose steward he was, with having abducted her along with the two-year-old girl she had had with her husband, and with having at the same time made off with his master's most precious possessions. Unable to deny these accusations, he sought only to excuse himself, swearing to Heaven as his witness that he had simply yielded to the lady's urgings, that she alone was guilty of the theft, and that he had derived not the least advantage from it, since he had had the misfortune of being so cruelly robbed himself and had fallen into the most dire poverty. When asked what had become of the mother and daughter whom he had abducted, he protested that he had lost both of them through death. The confessions he was forced to make appeared sufficient to the judge to condemn him to be tortured to death. I heard the pronouncement of this decision. All the shame I felt at being born of so guilty a father would not have stopped me from giving vent to my grief in cries and tears. But having asked the cadi for the grace to be heard a moment in secret, what my father said to this judge appeared to soften him and served at least to defer the execution of his punishment. He was taken away to prison. The delay, so contrary to custom, was believed to augur well. As for me, I had no other choice in my sad situation than to return to our lodging, to await the end of this cruel adventure there. But as I approached the house, I saw a crowd of people and signs of chaos which made me ask the cause of this commotion without having the boldness to advance further. Along with what I had already learned all too well, I was informed that the custom of the city was to seize the possessions of a criminal the moment his sentence was pronounced, and this harsh practice was already being put into effect on those of my father. My alarm increased so acutely that I had not the strength to disguise who I was, and tremblingly entreated a Turkish woman to whom I had addressed myself to take pity on the unfortunate daughter of the Greek who had just been condemned. She lifted my veil in order to observe my face, and, my grief appearing to touch her, she took me into her house with the consent of her husband. They both emphasized the service they were rendering me. The fear that gripped me caused me to exaggerate their power even further. I allowed them to decide my fate, and I believed I owed them my life when they promised to take me into their care. I did still foster, however, the hope that everyone had gleaned from the cadi's delay. But at the end of several days I learned from my hosts that my father's sentence had been carried out.

"In a city where I knew no one, at the age of about fifteen, with so little experience of the world and disturbed by such a humiliating disgrace, I believed myself at first condemned to misfortune and misery for the rest of my life. However, the extremity of my situation taught me to reflect on my earliest years, in order to seek some rule that could guide my conduct. In all the traces that remained of them, I found only two principles on which my education had been made to depend; one had caused me to consider men as the only source of women's fortunes and happiness; the other had taught me that using our desire to please, our submissiveness, and our caresses, we could acquire a sort of dominance over them, making them in turn dependent on us and giving us the opportunity to obtain from them everything needed to make us happy. However obscure I might have found my father's designs, I remembered that wealth and luxury had dictated all his thoughts. If he had taken such care to cultivate my natural qualities since our arrival in Constantinople, it was by ceaselessly placing before me the prospect that I might hope for a thousand more advantages than most other women. He therefore expected such advantages from me much more than he had the power to procure them for me; if his cunning opened the way for me, it was only through the means of success he knew me to possess that he guaranteed himself a share of the benefits to which he made me aspire. Had his death caused me to lose what he had told me a thousand times I had received from nature? This reasoning, which grew stronger in my mind during several days of solitude, caused me to conceive a thought that I believed might repay the debt that I owed my hosts. This was to tell them what my father had believed me to be suited for, and to ask them to do everything he would have done for me. I had no doubt that, knowing their country, they would understand immediately what I could do for them, and for myself. I was so satisfied with this idea that I resolved not to put off this opportunity another day.

"But what the simplicity of my mind had inspired in me had not failed to occur to people much more cunning than I. The sight of some charm in the face of a stranger who found herself alone and unprotected in Constantinople had been the sole motive to interest the Turkish woman in my fate. She and her husband had thought of a plan that she intended to try out on me; and the very day on which I intended to reveal mine to her was the one she had chosen for discussing this with me. She asked me several questions about my family and the place where I was born, and the information she obtained from my answers appeared to serve her plan. Finally, after flattering me about my charms, she offered to make me happy beyond my dreams if I would take her advice and trust in her guidance. She was acquainted, she told me, with a rich businessman who had a passion for women and who spared nothing to satisfy them. He had ten, of whom the most beautiful was quite inferior to me, and I should not doubt that with all his affection concentrating on me, he would do more for my happiness than for that of the ten others. She described at length the luxury that reigned in his house. I was to believe the testimony of her husband and herself, since they had been employed for a long time in his service and daily marveled at the blessings that the prophet had heaped on this very distinguished man.

"She painted this picture with enough skill to unsettle me; all the more so because, being full of the idea I was going to communicate to her, I was delighted that she had spared me the pain of so doing, by anticipating me. But I found in the lover she proposed only half of my pretensions. My father had always made me imagine an elevation of status along with wealth. The idea of a businessman was a shock to my pride. I made this objection to my hosts, who, far from yielding, further insisted on the advantages they were offering me and seemed hurt in the end by my resistance. I understood that what they pretended to allow me to decide had already been decided between them, perhaps with the businessman in whose name they were acting. I was all the more inspired to rebel against their urgings; but concealing my dissatisfaction, I asked them to give me until the next day to make up my mind. The reflections I made the rest of the day having increased my repugnance, I came to a decision during the course of the following night, which you would attribute to despair if I did not assure you that I came to it quite calmly. My father's great expectations, which I ceaselessly recalled, had the power to sustain my courage. As soon as I thought my hosts were asleep, I left their house in the same state in which I had come to it, and made my way alone through the streets of Constantinople, with the vague plan of addressing some person of distinction in order to entrust the care of my fate in him. So ill conceived an idea could not expect a happy outcome. I was not convinced of this until the next day, when, having spent the rest of the night in great confusion, I saw no more clearly by what means I could deliver myself from it. In the streets I found only common people, from whom I did not hope for more help than from the hosts I had left. Although it was easy for me to distinguish the houses of the great, I saw no likelihood of gaining access to them, and as the timidity against which I had struggled at last overcame my resolve, I believed myself more unhappy than in the first moments following my father's death. I would have returned to the house from which I had departed if I had had some hope of finding it again; but realizing my imprudence, I was so dismayed that my ruin seemed inevitable.

"However, I was just as little acquainted with the ills that threatened me as the benefits that I had wanted to procure for myself. My fears had no fixed object, and the hunger that began to beset me was still the most acute of my anxieties. Chance, which was my only guide, caused me to pass by the market where slaves were sold, and I inquired about the group of women I saw lined up under an archway. I was no sooner informed of their fate than I regarded this occasion as a resource. I approached them, and placing myself at the end of the line, I flattered myself that if I had the qualities that had been so often praised to me, it would not be long before I was singled out. Since all my companions had their faces covered, I did not yield at once to the desire to unveil my own. However, the hour of the market having arrived, I could not watch various persons being shown women who were not worth as much as I without feeling a lively impatience to lift my veil. No one had noticed that I was a stranger in the group, or rather no one had been able to divine the plan that had brought me there. But scarcely had they noticed that my face was uncovered than all the spectators, surprised by my youth and my appearance, gathered around me. I heard it asked on all sides to whom could I belong, and the slave merchants asked it themselves with awe. As no one could settle this question, they decided to address themselves to me. While agreeing that I was for sale, I asked in turn who they were and who was thinking of buying me. So extraordinary an event caused the crowd around me to swell. The merchants, as eager as the spectators, made offers that I disdained. A few people answered the question I had asked, stating their names and their stations; but as I heard nothing high enough to satisfy my ambition, I continued to reject their offers. The surprise of those who marveled at me appeared to redouble when, as I noticed at some distance from me a woman who was carrying some food, the hunger that was beginning to consume me caused me to approach her rapidly. I entreated her not to refuse me the assistance I urgently needed. She granted my request. I took advantage of this with an eagerness that captivated everyone's attention. They understood nothing. I saw in some compassion for my fate, in others curiosity, and in almost all the men the gazes and yearnings of love. Those impressions that I believed I could discern sustained my opinion of myself and persuaded me that this scene would turn to my advantage.

"After I endured a thousand questions that I refused to answer, the crowd opened at last to make way for a man who had inquired in passing as to what was attracting the curious multitude he saw in the marketplace. He had been told what was exciting everyone's surprise, and was approaching to satisfy his own. Although the respect being shown him disposed me to receive him more indulgently, I did not consent to answer him until he himself told me that he was the steward of the pasha Chériber. I wanted to know more about his master's character. He told me that he had been the pasha of Egypt and possessed immense wealth. Then, approaching his ear, I said that if he found me capable of pleasing the pasha, he would much oblige me by presenting me to him. He did not ask me to repeat this request, and, taking me by the hand, led me to his carriage, which he had left in order to come to me. I heard the regrets of those who saw me escape and their conjectures about an event that was now more obscure to them than ever.

"As we went along, the pasha's steward asked me to explain my designs and by what happenstance a young Greek, such as one could recognize me to be by my dress, found herself alone and her own mistress. I composed a story for him that was not without probability, but in which my naïveté betrayed itself enough to make him conclude that he could draw some profit from the service he was going to render his master. The joy I felt at falling into such fortunate circumstances made me lose all sight of my own interest, and I did not attend to it otherwise than to ready myself to show my gratitude to my hosts. I in no way opposed the entreaty made to me by the steward to acknowledge that he had bought me from a slave merchant. He promised me on this condition to perform such good offices for me with the pasha that I would soon hold first place in his esteem, and he explained in advance the means I ought to use to please him. As he had in fact warned the pasha of my arrival, he arranged a welcome that fulfilled almost immediately the idea I had had of my fate. I was settled in an apartment, the magnificence of which you know. A great number of slaves were appointed to serve me. I spent some time alone, receiving instructions that were to prepare me for my situation; and in the first days I tasted all the sweetness of being served at my least gesture, obtaining all that flattered my desires and being respected even in my whims, I was as happy as one can be in an illusory happiness. My contentment even increased when, after two weeks of preparation, the pasha came to tell me that he found me more pleasing than any of his women and that, in addition to all that I had already obtained from his generosity, he gave orders that a thousand new gifts should be offered, the abundance of which sometimes sated my desires. His age made him quite moderate in his own. But he saw me regularly several times a day. My liveliness and the joy displayed in all my movements appeared to amuse him. This situation, which lasted two months, was no doubt the happiest time of my life. But slowly I grew accustomed to what had had the greatest charm and had aroused my interest. The idea of my happiness no longer touched me, because I no longer saw anything in it that awakened my senses. Not only was I no longer flattered by the promptness with which I was obeyed, but I no longer had anything to command. The riches of my apartment, the multitude and beauty of my jewels, the sumptuousness of my clothes, nothing appeared to me in the guise I had at first found it. A thousand times when I felt burdened, I spoke to everything that surrounded me: Make me happy, I said to the gold and the diamonds. They were all mute and cold. I thought I was afflicted by some unknown malady. I told this to the pasha, who had already noticed the change in my mood. He judged that the solitude in which I spent a portion of every day had brought on this melancholy, even though he had provided me with a painting teacher, since I had shown an inclination for this art. He proposed that I move into the shared apartment of the other women, from whom he had separated me until then as a sign of distinction. The novelty of the spectacle served somewhat to revive my spirits. I took pleasure in their festivities and their dances, and I deluded myself into thinking because we shared the same lot, we would find we resembled one another in character and tastes. But while they manifested an eagerness to become intimate with me, I was disgusted almost immediately by their company. I found among them only petty concerns that corresponded neither to what confusedly occupied me nor to a thousand things that I desired without knowing what they were. I lived in this society for nearly four months, without taking any part in what went on there, faithful to my duties, avoiding giving offense to anyone, and better liked by my companions than I sought to be. The pasha, although his attentions to his seraglio did not abate, seemed to lose the taste that had attached him to me in particular. I would have been mortally sensitive to this in the early days; but as though my ideas had changed along with my mood, I viewed this cooling with indifference. I sometimes caught myself in a reverie, of which nothing remained in my mind when I emerged from it. It seemed to me that my feelings had greater reach than my knowledge and that what occupied my soul was the desire for some unknown thing. I asked myself again, as I had done in my solitude, why I was not happy with all that I had desired in order to be so. I sometimes asked myself if, in a place where I imagined all fortune and all goods to have been gathered, there was not some pleasure I had not yet tasted, some change that could dissipate the continual uneasiness I was experiencing. You saw me occupied with painting; it is the one pleasure to which I had been reduced after having hoped for so much from my condition. And even so, it was interrupted by long distractions that I could never account for.

"This was my situation when the pasha allowed you to enter his seraglio. This favor, which he granted to no one, made me impatiently expectant. He ordered us to dance. I did this with unusually increased reveries and distractions. My uneasiness caused me to return to my place immediately. I do not know what I was busy with when you approached me. If you asked me any questions, my answers must have expressed my disquiet. But the ordered, sensible speech that I heard you pronounce made me extremely attentive right away. Had I heard an agreeable instrument for the first time, it would have made the same impression. I did not remember anything that had ever harmonized so well with the order of my own ideas. This feeling intensified when, learning of the happiness of the women of your nation, you explained to me what it often depends on and what the men do to contribute to it. The words *virtue*, *honor*, and *conduct*, for which I needed no explanation, became fixed in my mind and they were instantly elaborated, as though they had always been familiar to me. I listened with extreme eagerness to everything the occasion caused you to add. I did not interrupt you with my questions, because there was nothing you uttered for which I did not immediately find proof deep in my heart. Chériber came to put an end to this sweet conversation; but I had not lost a single word of it, and no sooner had you left than I began recalling even its slightest detail. All of it was precious to me. From this moment I made it my continual study. Day and night afforded me no other object. There is a country, then, I said, where one finds a happiness other than that of fortune and riches! There are men who esteem in a woman other assets than those of beauty! There are for women other merits to be valued and other possessions to obtain! But how is it that I never knew what delights me with such sweetness and seems to conform to my inclinations? Although I would have wished for details, which I had not had the time to ask of you, finding myself agitated by such lively desires was enough for me to form a lofty idea of what was causing me so much emotion. I would not have hesitated to leave the seraglio if it had been possible for me to get out. I would have searched for you throughout the whole city merely to receive the explanation of a thousand things that I wanted to know, to have you repeat what I had heard, to hear you again and satiate myself on a pleasure I had only just tasted. I recalled at least one hope that I had always preserved and without which I would have taken more precautions with the pasha's steward. Since I had not been born a slave, and since nothing had forced me to become one, I had persuaded myself that, supposing I grew tired of my lot, I could not be kept there against my will. I imagined that it was simply a question of explaining myself to the pasha. But since I had occasion from time to time to see the steward, who was charged with the maintenance of the seraglio, I wished first to confide in him. He had kept his word. I was satisfied with his attentions and his services, and I did not doubt that he was equally disposed to oblige me. Yet scarcely had he understood where my remarks were leading, than, assuming a cold and serious air, he affected to be ignorant of the basis for my claims; and when I recalled my history to him, he appeared astonished that I myself had forgotten that he had bought me from a slave merchant. I realized clearly that I had been betrayed. The force of my grief did not prevent me, even so, from seeing that insults and laments were useless. I entreated him with tears in my eyes to do me the justice he owed me. He treated me with a harshness that he had never had for me; and informing me pitilessly that I was a slave for the rest of my life, he advised me never to speak such words again if I did not want him to notify his master.

"The illusion that had concealed my fate from me for so long dissipated at last. I do not know how my reason came to develop more after the brief interview I had with you than in all the use I had made of it until then. I no longer saw my past adventures as anything more than a subject of shame, on which I dared not cast my eyes; and without other principles than those whose seeds you had sown in my heart, I found myself as though transported into a new light by an infinity of reflections that caused me to look at everything with a different eye. I even felt a resolve in myself that surprised me in a situation so cruel; and more resolved than ever to open the doors of my prison, I thought that, before taking the path of despair, I should try a thousand ways that I could still hope for from my own skill and prudence. That of confiding in the pasha appeared to me the most dangerous. Exposing myself to his indignation could only serve to bring on me the hatred of his steward, and that would make all the other ways much more difficult for me. But it occurred to me to address myself to you. The change I was experiencing was not only your doing but would have to be completed by you. I hoped that, with a little of the predisposition you had shown in my favor, you would not refuse your assistance.

"The only difficulty was in letting you know my need. I took the risk of testing this idea out on a slave whose attachment to me was evident the moment I entered the seraglio. I found in her all the zeal to serve me I desired; but she was just as confined as I within our walls, and being unable to go out without committing a crime, she was able to offer me only the intermediary of her brother, who was in the service of the pasha. I resolved to take that chance. I entrusted to my slave's hands a letter that you no doubt received, since you could not have had any other motive for exerting yourself on behalf of my freedom, but which cast me into fresh uncertainty for several days. One of my companions, attentive to my behavior and judging from my distressed air that I was spinning some extraordinary plan in my mind, observed me as I was writing my letter and discovered no less cunningly that I had given it to the slave. She believed she was mistress of my secret. That very same day she found a way to take me aside, and having revealed the advantage she had over me, she confided in turn a very dangerous intrigue in which she had been engaged for several weeks. She was receiving a young Turk, who boldly risked his life in order to see her. He passed along the rooftops to a point just above her window, where he found a means of descending with the help of a rope ladder. The communication that I had with all the pasha's women did not mean that I had not kept my own apartment, and its situation seemed more convenient to my shrewd companion. The service she expected from me was to hide her lover there for a few days, since she could not see him as freely in her own room.

"This proposal dismayed me. But my hands were tied because of my fear of some betrayal. Even what I had learned could not serve to constrain this bold woman, because I had no proof of the confession she had made to me and because if I refused she could destroy all traces of her commerce by ceasing to receive her lover, whereas my letter and the two slaves who were in my confidence could always bear witness against me. I submitted to all the conditions she wanted to impose on me. Her lover was brought in the following night. I was obliged, in order to deceive the slaves that served me, to leave my bed while they slept and to lead the Turk into a small room to which I alone had the key. This was the place where my companion intended to receive him during the day. Some skill was required to hide this from a great number of women and slaves. But in a tightly cloistered seraglio, no one is alarmed at seeing us disappear sometimes, and the multitude of apartments favored these brief absences.

"However, the Turk, who had only seen me for an instant in the candlelight, had acquired for me the same feelings that he had for my companion. As early as the first visit she paid him with my key, which I had handed over to her, she remarked a coldness in him that she could not long attribute to his fear. He offered her reasons for wishing that I might be witness to a part of their conversations. These were so frivolous that, immediately suspecting him of infidelity, she resolved to prove it by satisfying his desires. I did not resist the request she made for me to accompany her. Her lover behaved with so little discretion that, shocked myself to see him so inattentive to her, I did not condemn her angry decision to send him away the following night. The sorrow he exhibited at this merely inflamed her jealousy, and his glances told me all too clearly that I was the cause of his regrets. But the punishment was far worse than the crime. In helping him to regain the roof through the window, she thrust him out so cruelly that he was killed in the fall. She herself told me of this barbarous revenge the next day.

"However, it had not occurred to her that he had fallen with his rope ladder and that this evidence, together with his sad state, would not fail to expose the nature of his undertaking. In truth, it might appear uncertain which window he had fallen from, because there were several that looked out on the same courtyard. But the alarm was no less acute in Chériber's house, and the effects of it were communicated right away to the seraglio. Chériber himself questioned all his women. He had all the places inspected that aroused his suspicions. Nothing was discovered; and I marveled at the tranquility with which my companion endured the activity around her. At last the steward's suspicions fell on me; but he did not communicate them to his master. He told me that after the fantasies I had entertained, he could not doubt that it was I who had disturbed the peace of the seraglio and who had perhaps thought to gain my freedom through a crime. The threats with which he attempted to wrest a confession from me caused me little dismay, but I thought I was lost when he told me he would arrest the slaves who were most attached to me. He observed my fear, and as he was preparing to execute his threat, I was obliged to inform him of what I could not allow him to discover himself without exposing my unfortunate slaves to the risk of dying a cruel death. Thus, the investigation into the profligacy of another served to wrest from me my own secret. I confessed to the steward that I was seeking to gain my freedom by a route that even the pasha could not condemn, and without emphasizing my rights any longer, I assured him that I did not think of obtaining it in any other way than as a slave, and at whatever price it might depend on. He wanted to know to whom I had addressed myself. I could not hide from him that it was to you. My frankness was useful to my companion, whose intrigue remained hidden; and the steward, apparently delighted by what he had learned, assured me that he would willingly assist my satisfaction by this route.

"His readiness surprised me as much as his harshness had dismayed me. I am still ignorant of his motives. But too content to see myself delivered from such a terrible obstacle, I sent to ask you several times if my request had made some impression on your heart. Your answer was doubtful. However, my experience has since taught me all too happily that you were attending to an unfortunate slave and that I owe my freedom to the most generous of all men."

If anyone, in reading this tale, has entertained even a fraction of the thoughts it inspired in me, he must expect those that will follow. Putting aside the differences in language, I found in the young Greek woman all the intelligence of which Chériber had boasted to me. I marveled, even, that with nature as her only teacher, she had arranged her adventures with such order and that, in explaining her reveries or her meditations to me, she had given a philosophical turn to most of her ideas. Their development had been perceptible, and I could not suspect her of having borrowed them from someone else, in a country where the mind does not commonly turn to this sort of exercise. I believed, therefore, that in her I had discovered a rich character, which, accompanied by an extremely moving appearance, made her without doubt an extraordinary woman. I found nothing shocking in her adventures, because, for the few months I had been in Constantinople, not a day had passed that I did not hear of the strangest events in relation to the slaves of her sex, and the continuation of this narrative will furnish many other examples. Nor was I surprised by the tale she had told me of her upbringing. All the provinces of Turkey are filled with these infamous fathers, who train their daughters for debauchery, having no other occupation for sustaining their lives or for advancing their fortunes.

But as I examined the impression she claimed to have formed from a moment's conversation, and the motives she had had for hoping to be obliged to me for her freedom, I could not surrender myself so credulously to the air of naïveté and innocence she had been able to assume in her bearing and her eyes. The more I acknowledged her wit, the more I suspected her of cunning; and the care she had taken to draw my attention several times to her simplicity was precisely what rendered it suspect to me. Today, as in the days of the ancients, the good faith of the Greeks is an ironic maxim. The most favorable light I could cast on her motives, therefore, was that, being tired of the seraglio and encouraged perhaps by the hope of a freer life, she had thought of leaving Chériber in order to change her condition, and that, hoping to inspire feelings of tenderness, she had used the remarks I had made to approach me in the manner to which I appeared most susceptible. If I assumed there was some truth to the description she had given me of her agitated feelings and mind, it was easy to find the cause of this in the situation of a young person who could not have tasted much pleasure with an old man. She had also praised the pasha's moderation. And, so as to hide nothing, I was in my prime; if others did not flatter me on my appearance, it was nevertheless capable of making an impression on a young girl in a seraglio whom I assumed to have as ardent a nature as lively a mind. I will add further that in her expressions of joy, I thought I noticed a zealousness that was not in proportion with the way she had always thought of the events of her life. These great transports were not summoned from so far away, nor did they have so perceptible a cause. For unless the power of Heaven had effected a change in her principles, what reason did she have to be so excessively touched by the service I had rendered her, and how could she suddenly regard with such horror a place of which she had scarcely any complaints other than the disgust born of plenty? From all these reflections, some of which I had entertained while she spoke, the conclusion I drew was that I had performed for a pretty woman a service of which I ought not to regret, but to which all the beautiful slaves would have had the same right; and although, contemplating her form with admiration, I was no doubt flattered by the desire I assumed in her to please me, the mere thought that she had come from Chériber's arms, after having been in those of another Turk and perhaps of a multitude of lovers whom she had concealed from me, served as a preservative against the temptations to which the ardor of my age might have exposed me.

However, I was curious to know clearly what her intentions were. She must have understood that, having given her her freedom, I had no right to demand anything from her, and that, on the contrary, I was waiting for her to explain her plans to me. I asked her no questions, and she was in no hurry to enlighten me. Returning to the subject of European women and to the principles in which I had told her they were raised, she had me answer a hundred queries which I took pleasure in satisfying. The night was well advanced when I noticed it was time for me to retire. As she had not told me of any plans, and as her remarks had always come around again to her happiness, her gratitude, and the satisfaction she felt at hearing me, I renewed, as I left her, my offers of assistance, and I assured her that as long as she was pleased with the house and the care of her host, she would lack for nothing there. The farewell she gave me seemed extremely passionate. She called me her master, her king, her father, and all the tender names that are familiar to the women of the East.

After having dealt with several important matters, I could not go to bed without recalling all the details of my visit. They returned even in my dreams. I found myself full of this idea when I awakened, and my first concern was to send to ask the language tutor how Théophé had spent the night. I did not yet feel drawn to her by a fondness that caused me any uneasiness; but as my imagination was full of her charms, and as I did not doubt that they were available to me, I confess that I reexamined my scruples concerning my initial reluctance to enter into a relationship of pleasure with her. I considered just how far I could take this whim without offending reason. Had the caresses of her two lovers, after all, left some stain on her, and should I turn into an object of disgust something I would not have noticed had I not known of it? Could this sort of stigma not be healed by a few days' repose and attention, especially at an age when nature renews itself incessantly on its own? Besides, what I had found most likely in her story was that she was still ignorant of love. She was scarcely sixteen years old. Chériber had not been capable of inspiring tenderness in her heart, and the fact that she was only a child in Patras – as much as the tale she had told of her feelings of disgust – must have protected her from it with the governor's son. I imagined that there would be sweetness in giving her this experience, and I hoped, as I thought about it more and more, to have been fortunate enough to cause her to feel something of it already. This thought, more than my reasoning, served to diminish my fastidious scruples. I arose quite different from what I had been the evening before, and if I did not rush into the adventure, I resolved at least to lay the basis for it before the end of the day.

I had been invited to dine at the home of the selictar. He questioned me closely as to the state in which I had left my slave. I reminded him that she was called by a different name now, and assuring him that my intentions were to allow her to enjoy all the rights I had given back to her, I confirmed him absolutely in the opinion I had given him of my indifference. Because of this, he thought himself all the more justified to ask me where she was lodged. This question embarrassed me. I could not defend myself against it except by bantering pleasantly about the repose she needed after coming out of Chériber's seraglio and the bad turn I would be doing her by revealing her place of retreat. But the selictar swore to me so seriously that she had nothing to fear from his importunities and that he thought neither of disturbing her nor of constraining her that, after the trust he had placed in my vows, I could not decently refuse to trust in his own. I informed him of the language tutor's home. He repeated his promise to me, with an air of sincerity that calmed me. Our conversation continued on Théophé's extraordinary merit. It was not without an effort that he had resisted his inclination. He confessed to me that he had never felt more touched by a woman's appearance. "I hastened to give her over to you," he said to me, "for fear that my weakness for her would increase as I came to know her better and that love would become more powerful than justice." This speech seemed to me that of a man of honor, and I owe it to the Turks to say in their favor that there are few nations where a natural fairness is better respected.

As he was explaining his feelings to me with such nobility, the pasha Chériber was announced and appeared at the same moment with signs of heat and agitation of which we impatiently asked him the cause. He was as intimate with the selictar as with me, and it was on the recommendation of the one that I found myself in the same familiarity with the other. His answer was to throw at our feet a bag of gold sequins, which contained my thousand ecus. "How pitiful it is," he said to us, "to be the plaything of one's slaves! Here is the sack of gold which my steward stole from you," he added, addressing the selictar. "And this is not his only theft. By dint of torture I have just wrested a horrible confession from him. I have preserved his life only in order to make him repeat the confession of his crime before your eyes. I would die of shame if that infamous slave did not do me justice." He asked the selictar to allow the slave to be brought in. But we begged him, both of us, to prepare us for the scene with a few words of explanation. He told us that another of his servants, jealous, in truth, of the power that the steward had usurped in his house, but interested for this reason in observing him, had noticed that the selictar's eunuch, who had come to take the young slave, had counted out a great deal of gold to the steward before receiving her from his hands. Being still without suspicions, he mentioned what he had seen, solely out of curiosity to know how great the sum had been. But the steward, abashed at having been found out, immediately begged him to keep silent and made him a large gift to bind him to it. This, on the contrary, merely sharpened the other's desire to ruin him. Having no doubt that the steward was guilty of some disloyalty for which he feared being punished, the servant immediately revealed his conjectures to the pasha, who had no difficulty in finding out the truth. The steward, pressed by his master's threats, confessed that when the selictar had come to ask the pasha to sell him the young Greek, he had heard these two noblemen arguing civilly over the price of the ransom and his master protesting that, as he was only too happy to be able to oblige his illustrious friend, he was resolved to give him his slave free of charge. Having seen that they had separated without having finished this courteous contest, he had followed the selictar and said to him, as though he had been sent by the pasha, that since he persisted in refusing to accept the slave as a present, he would sell her for a thousand ecus. He had added that he was charged with receiving them and with handing over the slave to those who would come to take her by his orders. Chériber, who had on the contrary ordered him to conduct her to his friend's home, had relied on him for this task and had not had the least mistrust of the account that he had given him of it. But learning that he had been no less deceived than the selictar, his rage had been boundless. And in a man to whom he had blindly entrusted the conduct of his affairs, he judged that this deception was not the first. Thus, in order to extract the confession of his other crimes as much as to punish him for this one, he had had him tortured so cruelly in his presence that he had forced him to reveal all the abuse he had made of his confidence. The story of Théophé had seemed to Chériber one of his blackest pieces of knavery. He could not pardon the injustices that the steward had caused him to commit against a free person. "Far from treating her as a slave," he told us, "I would have received her as my daughter, I would have respected her misfortunes, I would have looked after her fate, and what surprises me most is that she never made the truth known to me through her complaints."

This tale caused me far less astonishment than it did the selictar. However, I continued to hide what was useless to tell them, and the way in which I spoke to Chériber gave the selictar to understand that I still wished not to be implicated in this affair. The steward having been brought in, his master forced him to recount to us in what circumstances he had found the young Greek and through what perfidy he had abused her innocence in order to lure her into slavery. We had but little interest in the fate of this wretch, who was sent then and there to be put to death, as he deserved.

The selictar raised no objection, after this explanation, in taking back my sequins, which he had sent to my home the following day. But as soon as Chériber had left us, he returned more passionately than ever to the subject of Théophé, asking me what I thought of such an unusual adventure. "If she was not born for slavery," he said to me, "she must be of a condition far superior to appearances." His reasoning was based on the fact that, except for states of servitude in which young people are trained for some particular talent so that they can make a business of it, good education, in Turkey as elsewhere, is the mark of a birth above the common; just as one is not surprised in France to find graceful manners and elegant airs in a dance teacher, one would take the same characteristics, in a stranger, as evidence suggesting a man of quality. I left the selictar to his conjectures. I did not communicate to him even what might have cast some light on them. But I was struck by his idea all the same, and recalling that part of Théophé's story regarding the death of her father, I was astonished to have paid so little attention to the fact that he had been accused of abducting a Greek lady and her daughter. It did not seem impossible that Théophé was this two-year-old child who had disappeared with her mother. Yet how could I obtain any information about this? And would she not have had some suspicion herself had she seen in this story the least relation to her own? I proposed, nevertheless, to question her further in order to satisfy my curiosity, and I did not postpone this plan any longer than my visit.

My valet being the only one of my servants who knew of my relations with Théophé, I was resolved to keep this intrigue secret and to use only the night hours to go to the language tutor's home. I went there at nightfall. He told me that one hour before, a very fine-looking Turk had come there and urgently demanded to speak to the young Greek, but calling her by the name of Zara, which she had borne at the seraglio. She had refused to see him. After a show of his irritation at this refusal, the Turk had left the language tutor a box which he entrusted for her, along with a note in the manner of the Turks, which he had earnestly begged the tutor to have her read. Théophé refused to accept the note and the box. The language tutor handed them over to me. I took them with me when I entered the apartment, and more curious than she to find out what lay behind this incident, I persuaded her to open the note in my presence. It was easier for me than for her to recognize it as a love note from the selictar. Its expressions were measured, but they appeared no less to have come from a heart imbued with her charms. She was entreated to fear nothing from fate as long as she would deign to accept the help of a man who had nothing that was not at her disposal. In sending her a sum of money, along with other presents of worth, he was merely extending that generosity in a small way, and she would always find him prepared to increase it. Naturally I explained to Théophé who I thought had written the letter, and I added, in order to give her the opportunity to reveal her feelings, that the selictar had as much respect for her as love ever since he ceased to consider her a slave. But she appeared so indifferent to what he thought of her that, soberly going along with her ideas, I gave the box back to the language tutor to return it to the selictar's messenger when he should reappear. She had some regret that she had read his letter and that consequently she could not pretend not to know what it contained; but on further reflection for which she alone was responsible, she decided to answer him. I waited curiously to see what terms she would employ, for she had no thought of hiding her design from me. A lady of Paris, with as much experience of the world as wit and virtue, would not have adopted a different tone in order to extinguish love and hope in the heart of a lover. She calmly responded to the language tutor, by begging him to spare her henceforth anything that might resemble this incident.

I will not hide the fact that my vanity led me to interpret this sacrifice in my favor, and as I had not abandoned the plan that had intoxicated me that morning, I cut short everything that pertained to the selictar in order to begin gradually occupying myself with my own interests. But I was interrupted by an infinite number of reflections that emerged quite spontaneously from Théophé's lips, and whose source I recognized in a few superficial references that had escaped me the night before. Her mind, naturally inclined to meditate, grasped nothing without immediately enlarging upon it in order to consider it in all its aspects, and I noticed that she had had no other occupation since I had left her. She asked me a thousand new questions, as though she had thought only of preparing subjects of meditation for herself for the following night. If she was struck by some custom of my nation or by some principle she was hearing for the first time, I saw her become thoughtful for a moment in order to engrave it in her memory; and sometimes she begged me to repeat it, for fear of not having grasped the whole meaning of my expressions or for fear of forgetting it. In the midst of this serious conversation, she always found the means to interject expressions of the gratitude she owed me; but she had thrown me so far from my intentions by the remarks that had preceded these tender gestures that I could not collect myself quickly enough to take advantage of them in the way I would have wished. Besides, the interval was so brief that, by making me pass on immediately to other thoughts with another question, she compelled me continually to appear graver and more serious than I had wanted to be.

In the passion that kept bringing her back to this kind of philosophy, she scarcely left me the time to communicate the suspicions the selictar had aroused in me concerning her origin. However, as I needed no introduction to talk about her father, I begged her to suspend for a moment her curiosity and her thoughts. "A question has occurred to me," I said to her, "and you will recognize right away that it is inspired by my admiration for you. But before I explain it to you, I need to know if you ever knew your mother." She replied that not the slightest trace remained of her. I continued: "What? You do not know at what age you lost her? You do not know, for instance, if it was before that abduction assumed to be your father's crime; and you do not even know if she was different from that Greek lady whom he had persuaded to leave her husband and who was accompanied, if I recall your story correctly, by a two-year-old girl?"

My speech made her blush, though I could not yet distinguish the source of her emotion. Her eyes were fixed on me. At last, breaking the silence that she had kept for a moment, she asked: "Did the same thought occur to you as occurred to me, or did chance offer you some clarification of a question that I had not dared to confide in anyone?" "I do not know what you are thinking," I went on, "but as I admire the thousand natural qualities that distinguish you from most women, I cannot convince myself that you were born of a father as infamous as you have described; and the more I see that you know nothing about the earliest days of your life, the more I am inclined to believe you are the daughter of that same Greek nobleman whose wife was abducted by the wretch who falsely gave you his name." This statement had a surprising effect on her. She stood up in a sort of ecstasy. "Oh! That is what I have thought for a long time," she said to me, "without being so bold as to believe it altogether. Do you, then, see some likelihood in it?" Her eyes filled with tears as she asked me this question. "Alas!" she went on immediately, "why fill me with an idea that can only serve to increase my shame and my misfortune!"

Without understanding what meaning she attached to the words *misfortune* and *shame*, I dismissed those worrisome images by suggesting to her that, on the contrary, she had nothing more fortunate to hope for than to find herself born of a different father than the scoundrel who had usurped that title. And as the very fact that she was in doubt about this seemed to confirm my own doubt, I urged her not only to recall anything that might lead us to some enlightenment about the time of her childhood, but to tell me whether she had heard in the cadi's court the name of the Greek lady whose daughter I thought she was, or at least that of the accusers who had dragged the unhappy author of all her sufferings to his death. She recalled nothing. But even as I mentioned the cadi, it seemed that I might hope for some answers from this magistrate, and I promised Théophé to seek information the next day. And so, the evening I had intended to devote to some form of gallantry passed in discussions of fate and interests.

I reproached myself, as I withdrew, for having showed such moderation with a woman who had just emerged from a seraglio, especially after the tale she had told me of the other circumstances of her life. I asked myself if, in assuming she had for me all the inclination that I still believed she did, I was prepared to make an arrangement with her, what in France is called "keeping a woman"; and finding I was less reluctant than I had been at first to form this sort of relationship with her, it seemed to me that without employing so many detours, I had only to make the proposal quite openly. If she received it with as much satisfaction as I thought I could expect, the selictar's passion would not cause me any difficulty, since he had said himself that he did not intend to obtain anything through violence; and since the information that I intended to obtain would allow me to discover her birth, which would raise her a little in my eyes without changing the fact that she had once endured the disgrace she had described to me, I saw in all the discoveries I might make a reason for increasing my taste for her without making her less suited to the commerce in which I hoped to engage her. I settled absolutely on this plan. One can see how far I still was from any feelings of love.

The next day, I went to the cadi and reminded him of the case of a Greek whom he had condemned to death. He had not forgotten it and immediately went into detail about it, giving me the pleasure of hearing him repeat several times the names that I was trying to find out about. The Greek nobleman whose wife had been abducted was named Paniota Condoidi. It was he himself who had recognized the abductor in a street of the city and who had had him arrested. But he had derived from this meeting, added the cadi, only the satisfaction of being avenged; for neither his wife, nor his daughter, nor his jewels had been recovered. I marveled at this idea, when it seemed to me that all the efforts by which one might have succeeded in actually recovering them had been neglected. I even showed some surprise at this to the cadi. "What more could I do?" he said to me. "The criminal declared that the lady and her daughter were dead. This declaration had to be sincere, since the only means that remained to him to preserve his life was to produce them, if they had been alive: thus, no sooner had he heard his sentence pronounced, than he hoped to confuse me with fairy tales; but I soon realized that he was only trying to elude my justice."

As I recalled that in fact the execution of the sentence had been suspended, I begged the cadi to tell me the cause of that occurrence. He told me that the criminal, having requested to speak to him alone, had offered, in order to preserve his life, not only to produce the daughter of the nobleman Condoidi for him, but to deliver her to him secretly for his seraglio; and that because of the detail he had given him about several circumstances, he had been able to lead the cadi to find some air of truth in this promise. But all the exertions they had made to discover her had been useless; and judging at last that this had been the artifice of a wretch who was lying to delay his death, the indignation that the cadi had felt at his boldness and his infamy served only to make him hasten the criminal's death.

I could not help communicating to this foremost judge among the Turks a few reflections on his conduct. "What prevented you," I asked him, "from keeping your prisoner a few days more, and from taking the time to gather information in the places he had lived since his crime? Could you not have forced him to reveal where the Greek lady died and by what accident he had lost her? In fact, was it not easy to go back over his trail and follow it even in its minutest details? This is our method in Europe," I added, "and though we are no more zealous than you with regard to fairness, we are more skilled in the investigation of crime." He found my counsels so correct that he thanked me for them, and some remarks he added about the exercise of his profession convinced me that the Turks have more gravity than enlightenment in their courts of justice.

I extracted from the cadi both the name of the Greek nobleman and the location of his home; it was a small town in Morea which the Turks called Acade. It did not seem easy to establish communication there right away, and I thought first of addressing myself to the pasha of that province. But having learned that a number of slave merchants from the same country were in Constantinople, I was fortunate enough that the first person to whom I spoke assured me that the nobleman Condoidi had not left the city for more than a year, and that he was known here by all the persons of his nation. The only difficulty left was to find his house. The slave merchant did me this service immediately. I did not delay going there, and, as my initial successes had increased my ardor, I thought I was nearing the clarification I so desired. The house and the appearance of the Greek nobleman did not give me an impression of great wealth. He was from one of those old families that preserve less splendor than pride from their nobility, and who, in the abasement in which they are kept by the Turks, would not even dare to display their possessions had they enough to live with more distinction. Condoidi, who appeared, in a word, to be a good country gentleman, received me civilly, without having learned who I was, for I had sent my retinue away when I left the cadi; and patiently awaiting my explanations, he gave me ample time to make the speech I had prepared. After having explained that I was not unaware of his earlier misfortunes, I begged him to pardon the interest that, for various reasons, piqued my curiosity, a curiosity he could easily satisfy: finding out how long ago he had lost his wife and daughter. He replied that it had been fourteen or fifteen years ago. This period of time corresponded so exactly with Théophé's age (since she had been two at the time of the abduction) that I believed my doubts were half banished. "Do you think," I continued, "that despite the abductor's statement, it is possible that one of the two is still alive; and if it were your daughter, would you not feel some gratitude toward those who might help you find her again?" I expected this question to elicit an outburst of joy. But remaining sober, he told me that time, which had healed the pain of his loss, also prevented him from hoping for miracles to repair it; that he had several sons, to whom the inheritance that he was to leave them would scarcely suffice to sustain the honor of their birth, and that even supposing his daughter lived, it was so unlikely that she would have preserved any goodness in the hands of a scoundrel, and in a country such as Turkey, that he would never be convinced that she was worthy of reappearing in his family.

This last objection seemed to me the strongest. However, as the first moment seemed decisive for natural feelings, I decided to summon everything in my power to awaken them. "I will not examine," I said vehemently, "the strength of your scruples or of your reasons, because it can change nothing about the certainty of a fact. Your daughter lives. Let us pass over her virtue, for which I cannot answer; but I venture to guarantee that her intelligence and her charms lack nothing. It is up to you to see her again now, and I will write down the place where she is staying." And having asked for a pen, I indeed wrote down the language tutor's name, and I withdrew immediately thereafter.

I was convinced that if he were not entirely insensitive, he would not be able to resist nature's prompting for an instant, and I left so full of hope that in order to treat myself to an agreeable spectacle, I went directly to the language tutor's home, where I imagined Condoidi would perhaps arrive as soon as I. I did not go in to Théophé, because I wanted to enjoy her surprise. But after several hours passed without his appearing, I began to fear I had deluded myself, and I finally revealed to the woman whom nothing could prevent me any longer from regarding as his daughter what I had done to fulfill my promise. The testimony of the wretch who had abused her childhood made more of an impression on her than all the rest. "It will not grieve me," she said, "to remain uncertain about my birth; and if I were sure I owed it to your Greek nobleman, I would not complain that he was ill-inclined to acknowledge me. But I thank heaven for the right he gives me henceforth to refuse the name of father to the one man in all the world to whom I owed the most hatred and scorn." She appeared so moved by this thought that, as her eyes filled with tears, she repeated to me twenty times that it was to me that she believed she owed her birth, since I had given her a second one by delivering her from the infamy of the first.

But I did not think my work was finished, and in the heat of things, I proposed that she accompany me to Condoidi's home. Nature has rights against which neither vulgarity nor interest ever completely harden the heart. It seemed impossible that, on seeing his daughter, on hearing her, on receiving her embraces and her glances, he would not be brought back to the sentiments he owed her despite himself. He had made no objection to the possibility of finding her again. I hoped that nature would triumph over all the other objections. Théophé betrayed some fear. "Will I not do better," she asked, "to remain unknown and even hidden from all the world?" I did not examine the cause of these emotions, but forced her almost against her will to accompany me.

It was quite late. I had spent a part of the day alone in the language tutor's home, and, already accustomed to this atmosphere of furtive intrigue, I had had my dinner brought to me there by my valet. After I had convinced the young Greek to go out with me, night had begun to draw near, so that the darkness was already thick when we arrived at Condoidi's home. He had not come back from the city, where his affairs had summoned him in the afternoon; but one of his servants, who had seen me that morning, told me that while I waited for him I could speak with his three sons. Far from rejecting this proposal, I regarded it as the most felicitous thing I could wish for. I allowed myself to be ushered in with Théophé, whose head was covered with a veil. As soon as I informed the three young men that I had paid a visit to their father the same day, and that the same subject had caused me to return, they seemed to know what brought me; and the one I took by his appearance for the oldest replied coldly that there was little likelihood that I would convince his father to favor a vague and improbable story. I merely answered him with the detailed reasons that caused me to regard it differently, and when I had strengthened them with my arguments, I asked Théophé to lift her veil in order to give her brothers time to distinguish some family traits in her face. The two oldest considered her with a good deal of coldness; but the youngest, who seemed no older than eighteen, and who had struck me in the beginning by the resemblance I had seen in him to his sister, did not glance at her twice before advancing with open arms and giving her a thousand tender kisses. Théophé, not daring yet to yield to his caresses, attempted modestly to fend them off. But the two others did not leave her long in this difficulty. They approached brusquely in order to take her from their brother's arms, threatening him with the indignation of Condoidi, who would be strongly offended that he had acted in contradiction to his father's wishes. I was indignant at their harshness and reproached them in sharp terms, which did not prevent me from asking Théophé to sit down to wait for Condoidi. Besides my valet, I had the language tutor with me, and two men were enough to protect me from any attack.

At last the father arrived; but – and this I had not foreseen – scarcely had he learned that I was awaiting him and that I was accompanied by a young girl, than, going out with as much haste as if he had been threatened by some danger, he sent word by the servant who had admitted me that after the discussion he had had with me he was astonished that I should presume to force him to receive a girl he did not acknowledge. Shocked as I was by this boorishness, I took Théophé by the hand and told her that as her birth did not depend on her father's whim, it mattered little whether she was acknowledged by Condoidi, since it was obvious that she was his daughter. "The cadi's testimony and my own," I added, "will have as much force as your family's recognition, and I see nothing to regret, moreover, in the friendship that they refuse you here." I left with her, without anyone offering the least civility in showing me to the door. Having nothing to expect from three young men to whom I was not known, I forgave them their rudeness more easily than the harshness with which they had treated their sister.

The unfortunate girl appeared more afflicted by this disgrace than I would have thought she could be, given the reluctance she had shown at coming with me. I continued to share my ideas with her at the language tutor's home, and what had just happened supported them. But the air of sadness she preserved the whole evening made me think later that the moment had been ill-chosen. I confined myself to repeating several times that she ought to feel at ease in the certainty that she would lack nothing. She said that what touched her most in my offers was the assurance that she found in them of the continuation of my feelings for her; but although this compliment had an affectionate air to it, it seemed accompanied by so much bitterness of heart that I wanted to allow her sorrow the interval of the night in order to dissipate.

I spent the night more tranquilly, since, having at last decided what I intended to do, Théophé's birth, which seemed certain in my eyes, had succeeded in banishing the importunate ideas that had continually offended my delicacy. She had endured shocking trials; but with so many fine qualities, and given the nobility of her origins, would I have wanted to make her my mistress had she had nothing with which to reproach herself where honor was concerned? Her perfections and her faults compensated for one another in a manner that seemed to make her suited to the condition in which I hoped to engage her. I fell asleep with this idea, which I must certainly have already considered more pleasurable than I had imagined, since I was so upset by the news that came to trouble my awakening. It was the language tutor, who sent word at nine o'clock to say that he earnestly requested to speak to me. "Théophé," he told me, "has just left in a carriage that was brought to her by a stranger. She needed no prompting to go with him. I would have opposed this," he added, "had you not given me precise orders to leave her free in all her wishes." I interrupted this cruel speech with a sudden exclamation. "Oh, so you did not oppose it," I cried, "and shouldn't you have better understood what my orders meant?" He hastened to add that as she left he had insisted that I would be surprised by so precipitous a decision and that she owed me at least some explanation of her conduct. She had answered that she herself did not know what perils lay in store for her, and that whatever misfortune threatened her, she would take care to inform me of her fate.

One may think whatever one likes about the motives that caused my blood to boil. I myself am ignorant of their nature. But I arose with emotions I had never before experienced, and bitterly renewing my complaints to the language tutor, I declared with the same ardor that my friendship or my indignation would depend on the efforts he might make to discover Théophé's whereabouts. As he was not ignorant of what had taken place since she had been living in his house, he told me that if nothing more was concealed in her adventures than what he knew of them already, the stranger who had come to take her could only be a messenger from either Condoidi or the selictar. The alternative appeared as certain to me as it did to him. But I found it equally distressing, and without considering the reasons for my acute distress, I ordered the language tutor to go first to the home of the selictar and then to that of Condoidi. I gave him no other commission with respect to the former than to gather information at the door concerning the persons who had been seen there since nine o'clock. With respect to the latter, I charged him formally to find out from the man himself if it had been he who had sent to fetch his daughter.

I awaited his return with an impatience that cannot be expressed. His trip was so fruitless that in the fury into which I was thrown by this redoubling of uncertainty, my suspicions turned on him. "If I dared to trust," I said to him with a terrible look, "the doubts that are entering my mind, I would at once treat you in so cruel a manner that I would force the truth from you." He was frightened by my threats, and throwing himself at my feet, promised me the confession of something he had only allowed himself to be urged to do, he told me, with the greatest reluctance and without other motive than that of compassion. I waited impatiently to hear him out. He informed me that the evening before, only moments after I had left Théophé, she had had him called into her room, and after a very touching speech about her situation, had asked his help in carrying out a resolution on which she was absolutely decided. Unable to bear any longer, she had told him, the looks of those who knew of her shame and her misfortunes, she had made up her mind to leave Constantinople secretly and go to some European city where she could find a refuge in the generosity of a Christian family. She confessed that after the favors she had received from me, it was a poor acknowledgement to steal away without informing me, and to lack confidence in her benefactor. But just as I was the man to whom she was the most obliged in the world, I was also the one for whom she had the most esteem, and consequently the one whose presence, remarks, and friendship most acutely rekindled the shame of her adventures. At last, her entreaties rather than her reasons had persuaded the language tutor to take her at daybreak to the port, where she had found a Messinese vessel that she had been resolved to use to travel to Sicily.

"Where is she?" I interrupted with an even livelier impatience. "That is what I am asking you and what you should have told me right away." "I have no doubt," he told me, "that she is either on the Messinese vessel, which is not to set sail before two days from now, or in a Greek inn on the harbor where I took her." "Make haste to return there," I resumed vehemently. "Persuade her immediately to come back to your house. Take care you do not reappear without her," I added a threat to this command: "I will not tell you all that you have to fear from my anger if I do not see her before midday." He was about to go out without replying. But in the emotion that was agitating me, disturbed by a thousand fears that I did not stop to disentangle, I thought that everything I did not do myself would be either too slow or too uncertain. I called him back. With the knowledge that I had of the language, it appeared to me easy to go to the harbor and mingle in the crowd without being recognized. "I intend to go with you," I said to him. "After you have betrayed me so cruelly, you no longer deserve my trust."

My plan was to go out on foot, dressed simply, and without other retinue than my valet. The language tutor endeavored, while I dressed, to restore himself in my opinion through all sorts of excuses and apologies. I had no doubt that some motive of self-interest had entered into his intentions. But paying little attention to his remarks, I occupied myself solely with what I was about to do. Despite my strong desire to keep Théophé in Constantinople, it seemed to me that if I could have assured myself of her intentions and persuaded myself that she wanted seriously to consider the choice of a prudent life of retirement, I would have thought less of opposing her plan than of assisting it. But assuming she was sincere, what likelihood was there that at her age she would be able to resist all the occasions she would have to stray into new adventures? The Messinese captain, the first passenger who would find himself with her on the vessel – I suspected them all. And if she did not appear destined by fate for a more restrained conduct than that of the first years of her life, why allow another man to deprive me of the delights that I had intended to taste with her? Such were still the boundaries within which I believed I was confining my sentiments. I arrived at the inn where the language tutor had left her. She had not gone out. But we were informed that she was in her room with a young man whom she had had summoned when she saw him pass on the harbor. I asked with curiosity for the circumstances of this visit. Théophé, whom the young man had recognized immediately and whom he had embraced with the liveliest tenderness, had appeared to respond very freely to his caresses. They had shut themselves up together, and no one had interrupted them for more than an hour.

I thought all my predictions were already fulfilled, and in the vexation against which I could not defend myself, I nearly gave up all thought of an intimate relationship with Théophé and returned home without seeing her. But as the motive impelling me to act was still concealed from me, I decided to attribute to curiosity my interest in what I believed I no longer wanted for any other reason. I sent the language tutor up to inform her that I wished to speak to her. The disturbance into which she was thrown by my name deprived her for a long time of the power of responding. At last the language tutor, returning to me, told me that the young man he had found with her was the youngest of Condoidi's three sons. I went in immediately. She made a motion to throw herself at my feet; I restrained her despite herself, and, calmer at recognizing her brother than I should have been after so much agitation (had my feelings not been of a nature other than what I still believed them to be), I thought much less of reproaching her than of expressing the joy I felt on finding her again.

In fact, as if my eyes had somehow changed since the day before, I continued to look at her for some time with a pleasure, or rather with an avidity, that I had never before felt. Her whole appearance, for which, until then, I had thought I had had only a moderate admiration, so touched me that, in a sort of ecstasy, I moved my chair so as to place myself closer to her; the fear I had had of losing her seemed to increase upon finding her. I wished that she had already returned to the language tutor's home, and the sight of several vessels, among which I imagined must be that of the Messinese, caused me an uneasiness that heated my blood. "So you were leaving me, Théophé," I said sadly, "and when you made the decision to abandon a man who is so devoted to you, you thought nothing of the pain that your departure would cause me. But why leave me without advising me of your plan? Have you found that I responded poorly to your trust?" She kept her eyes lowered, and I saw a few tears flow down from them. However, lifting these eyes to me with an air of confusion, she assured me that she had nothing for which to reproach herself as far as gratitude was concerned; and if the language tutor had given me an account of the feelings she bore for me, she said, I ought not to suspect her of thanklessness. She continued to justify herself with the same reasons he had conveyed to me, and coming to the young Condoidi, whom I might be surprised to find in her room, she confessed that, when she had by chance seen him passing, the memory of the affection he had shown the day before had prompted her to have him called. What she had just learned from him became a new reason for hastening her departure. Condoidi had declared to his three sons that he no longer had the slightest doubt that she was their sister; but being none the more inclined for this reason to receive her in his family, he had, on the contrary, forbidden his sons to form even the slightest relationship with her, and without explaining the basis for his ideas, he appeared to be secretly turning over some dark plan in his mind. The young man, charmed at meeting his sister, for whom he felt his affection redouble, had urged her not to trust his father's humor; and finding her determined to leave Constantinople, he had offered to join her in order to accompany her on her voyage. "What advice would you give to an unfortunate girl," added Théophé, "and what other choice remains to me but to flee?"

I could have answered that, as the strongest reason she had for fleeing was the fear that her father inspired in her, the subject of my complaints remained the same, since this new misfortune had come only after her decision. But allowing everything else to yield to my desire to keep her here, and excepting not even her brother from my suspicions, I suggested that if her departure was just and necessary, it should be accompanied by a few measures that she could not prudently dispense with. And accusing her again of not having relied enough on my services, I urged her to postpone her plan in order to give me the time to seek out some opportunity less dangerous than that of an unknown captain. With respect to the young Condoidi, whose natural goodness I praised, I offered to take him into my own house, where she should easily persuade herself that, as far as life's comforts and the attention to his education were concerned, he would have no reason to miss his father's house. I do not know if it was her timidity alone that caused her to yield without resistance to my entreaties; but judging by her silence that she consented to go with me, I had a carriage brought in order to conduct her to the language tutor's home myself. He whispered a few words to her that I could not distinguish. Young Condoidi, who had learned from her who I was, displayed such joy at my offers that I acquired a worse opinion than ever of a father whose son was so content to be delivered of him; and one of my motives was the desire to be informed in depth of everything respecting that family.

As I returned to the language tutor's home, I firmly proposed not to defer my intention of confiding to Théophé the thoughts I had about her. But having been unable to separate myself with propriety from the young Condoidi, who seemed to fear that I would forget my promise if I lost sight of him for a moment, I was forced to reduce myself to vague expressions whose meaning, I was not surprised to see, she did not appear to understand. This language was nevertheless so different from that which I had always used with her that, with such astuteness as she naturally had, she must have noticed that it came from some other source. The only change I made in the language tutor's home was to leave my valet there, with the pretext that Théophé did not yet have anyone to serve her; but in truth it was to keep myself informed of all her movements, until I should have found for her some slave whose loyalty would put me at ease. I intended to procure two slaves, that is, one of each sex, and to take them to her that same evening. Condoidi went home with me. I immediately had him leave off his Greek dress in order to clothe him more suitably in the French manner. This change was so much to his advantage that I had seen few young men of so agreeable an appearance. He had the same features and the same eyes as Théophé, with a marvelous build, the charm of which his Greek dress had concealed. He lacked, nonetheless, a thousand things he might have received from his education, which continued to cause me to think very ill of the customs and sentiments of the Greek nobility. But it was enough, in my opinion, that he was so close to Théophé by blood to make me do my utmost to perfect his natural qualities. I gave orders that he should be waited on by my servants with as much attention as they waited on me, and that same day I engaged different teachers to train him in all sorts of disciplines. Nor did I further postpone asking him for some enlightenment about his family. I knew how old its nobility was, but I wanted information I could make useful to Théophé.

Repeating what I already knew about the ancient nobility of his father, he informed me that he was descended from a Condoidi who was a general under the last Greek emperor and who had made Muhammad II quake only a few days before the taking of Constantinople. He had been holding the country with considerable troops; but as the situation of the Turkish army did not allow him to approach the city, he resolved, upon hearing the latest news of the wretched state of Constantinople, to sacrifice his life to save the Eastern empire. Choosing a hundred of his bravest officers, he proposed that they accompany him down paths where there was no hope of introducing an army, and leading them along these paths in the greatest darkness of the night, he reached the camp of Muhammad, whom he had sworn to kill in his tent. The Turks indeed believed themselves so well covered on that side that the guard there was weak and negligent. Condoidi made his way, if not to Muhammad's tent, at least to the surrounding tents belonging to his retinue. He did not stop to destroy enemies whom he found wrapped in sleep, thinking only of approaching the sultan; and his initial advances were lucky. But a Turkish woman, who was apparently stealing from one tent to another, heard the muffled sound of a step, which alarmed her. She turned in her tracks with a dismay that she communicated immediately to all who surrounded her. Condoidi, as prudent as he was

valiant, immediately despaired of success, and judging his life necessary to its master, when it was no longer of use in defeating his enemy,
he used his courage and prudence to open a passage by which he and
his companions in this undertaking could escape. In the Turks' initial
confusion, he escaped, fortunate in losing only two men. But he had
preserved his life only to lose it even more gloriously in the frightful
revolution that took place two days after. His children, who were very
small, remained subjects of the Turks, and one of them established himself in Morea, where his descendants suffered countless further misfortunes. At last, the house of Condoidi was reduced to those who were
now in Constantinople and to a Greek bishop of the same name, whose
seat was in a town somewhere in Armenia. Their possessions still consisted of two villages (which brought them in about a thousand ecus in
our currency), the ownership of which would pass to the oldest through
a privilege that was rather rare in the estates of great lords and which
formed their family's sole distinction.

But other hopes had brought the father and his children to Constantinople, and these were apparently the reason for their harshness
toward Théophé. A rich Greek, their close relative, had left a will when
he died, in which he bequeathed them all his possessions on the sole
condition that the Church should have no cause to reproach them with
respect to religion or freedom; two sorts of merit to which the entire
Greek nation is extremely attached. And the Church, namely, the patriarch and the suffragans who were appointed the judges of this provision, had all the more interest in being very strict since they would be
substituted for the legatees in case the latter were excluded from the
succession. Condoidi's wife had been abducted in these circumstances,
and the Greek prelates had not failed to put forward the uncertainty of
her fate and that of her daughter as an obstacle to the execution of the
will. Whence the fact that Condoidi, after recognizing his steward, had
thought less of seeking information about what had happened to his
wife and his daughter than of having their abductor punished once he
had acknowledged himself guilty of the abduction and had declared that
they were dead. Condoidi had hoped that, whatever their situation, any
knowledge of them would be buried along with their abductor. Not
unaware that the wretch had confided in the cadi, Condoidi had been
the most eager to have it passed off as an imposture, and he did not
rest until he saw the steward led away to his execution. In truth, the
patriarch did not appear any more disposed, after this, to grant him the
inheritance; and not content with a testimony of death, he wanted
proofs that Condoidi believed could be dispensed with. His daughter,

presented to him as though she had fallen from Heaven, had thrown him into a mortal alarm. Far from being prompted to examine the basis of her claims, or how she had happened to find herself in Constantinople, he feared all the explanations that could blight his hopes. At last, having persuaded himself that after the steward's death she would have a good deal of trouble proving the truth of her birth, he had made the decision that not only would he not acknowledge her, but he would even accuse her of imposture and demand her punishment if she undertook to claim her legal rights.

"And I am mistaken," added the young man, "if he has not formed some more terrible plan; for we have seen him, since your visit, agitated such as he never is without some extraordinary effect, and I dare not tell you of what things hatred and anger have sometimes rendered him capable."

This account persuaded me that Théophé would have great difficulty in resuming the rights that were naturally hers; but I was scarcely alarmed by the intentions of her father, and in whatever way he might seek to harm her, I flattered myself that I could easily defend her from his endeavors. This thought even caused me to abandon the plan I had had of keeping him in the dark as to who I was, or at least as to the interest I took in his daughter. On the contrary, I urged his son to see him that same day, as much to tell him that I was taking Théophé under my protection as to inform him of the friendship I was showing to this young man by receiving him in my home. Forthwith, I sent for two slaves such as I judged necessary for the new arrangements that came to mind, and, awaiting only the evening to implement them, I went to the language tutor's home at nightfall.

My valet was awaiting me impatiently. He had been sorely tempted during the day to leave the post I had assigned him in order to come give me an account of certain observations that had seemed important to him. The selictar's messenger had come with sumptuous gifts, and the language tutor had conversed with him for a very long time in a very mysterious way. My valet, who did not understand the Turkish language, had affected all the more easily not to notice anything, since, not hoping to overhear their talk, he had confined himself to observing them from a distance. What had appeared strangest to him was seeing the selictar's gifts graciously accepted by the language tutor. These were precious fabrics and a quantity of women's jewels. He had endeavored to discover in what light they would be received by Théophé; but he assured me that having continually had his eyes on the door of her apartment and, as often as he could, on the girl herself, he had not seen these marks of favor taken into her room.

I had so little need for circumspection with the language tutor that, wishing for no other explanation than his own, I had him summoned immediately to give me an account of this behavior. He understood at the first word that he had not managed to conceal himself very well. And as he expected to gain nothing from guile, he chose to admit openly that he had represented his needs to Théophé and, with her knowledge, had put the selictar's gifts to his own use. The sum of money had had the same fate as the cloth. "I am poor," he told me. "I gave Théophé to understand that the gifts are certainly hers, since they were sent to her unconditionally; and the gratitude she believed she owed for some small services I had done for her made her consent to turn them over to me." It was easy, after this admission, to understand his motives for so readily assisting her in her flight. I immediately lost all confidence in a man capable of such baseness, and although I could not accuse him of having failed in his integrity, I declared to him that he had nothing more to hope for from my friendship. This heatedness was imprudent. The sway that I had over a man of his sort prevented me from considering this, and the resolution I had made, moreover, to move Théophé to another dwelling freed me from the need I had had of his services.

The two slaves I brought came to me from so reliable a source that I could trust them with perfect confidence. I had explained my intentions to them, and had promised them their freedom in return for their loyalty and zeal. The woman had served in several seraglios. She was Greek, like Théophé. The man was Egyptian, and although I had paid no attention to what their looks might be, they were both of an appearance superior to their condition. I presented them to Théophé. She readily accepted them, but asked me what use they could be to her during the short time she had left in Constantinople.

I was alone with her. I took the moment to confide my plan to her. But although I had thought about it and still flattered myself that my proposal would be listened to willingly, I had difficulty finding the facility I ordinarily had in expressing myself. Every glance I cast on Théophé caused me to feel emotions that would have been more pleasant to explain to her instead of brusquely proposing the sort of relationship that I wanted to form with her. However, as such a confused agitation made me incapable of suddenly changing a resolution on which I had settled, I told her rather timidly that since the interest I took in her happiness had made me regard her departure as a rash act that could never have a happy outcome, I had decided to offer her a much more pleasant choice, and one in which I could guarantee her both the repose she appeared to desire and all sorts of assurances against Condoidi's schemes. "I have, not far from the city," I continued, "a house that is very agreeable both in its location and in the extraordinary beauty of its garden. I offer it to you as a place to live. You will be free and respected there. Banish all the images of the seraglio, namely, those of solitude and perpetual constraint. I will be with you there as often as my affairs permit me. I will not bring you any other company than that of some French friends, with whom you will be able to try out the customs of my nation. If my caresses, my attentions, and my kindnesses can serve to make your life sweet, you will never see me shirk from them even for a moment. In short, you will see what a considerable difference there is, for a woman's happiness, between sharing the heart of an old man in a seraglio and living with a man of my age, whose every desire will be to please you and who will take great pains to make you happy."

I had kept my eyes lowered as I addressed this speech to her, as though I had overestimated the power I had over her and was afraid of having abused it. Preoccupied more with my feelings than with the plan I had formed with so much joy, I was much more impatient for her to express her desire for me than to discuss the repose and safety I was asking her to imagine. Her slowness in answering already caused me some uneasiness. At last, appearing to emerge from a doubt she had had trouble overcoming, she said that without changing her mind about the necessity of leaving Turkey, she agreed that, while awaiting the occasion I had promised her I would seek, she would be more comfortable in the country than in the city; and relapsing into her gratitude, she added that as my kindnesses were unbounded, she would no longer attempt to discover their price, since in helping an unfortunate woman who was not capable of doing me any sort of service, I no doubt intended only to satisfy my own generosity. It would have been natural, with the emotions that were pressing on my heart, for me to unburden myself in a more open declaration; but too happy to see her inclined to allow herself to be taken to my country house, I did not examine whether she had understood my intentions or whether her answer was a consent or a refusal, and I urged her to leave with me at once.

She made no objection to my insistence. I gave orders to my valet to have a calash brought around promptly. It was just nine o'clock in the evening. I planned to have supper with her in the country, and what did I not promise myself from this happy night after that? But as I began to express my joy to her, the language tutor entered with an air of consternation, and taking me aside he informed me that the selictar, accompanied only by two slaves, was asking to see Théophé. The agitation with which he informed me of this news did not allow me to understand at first that the lord was himself at the door. "Oh! Did you not answer," I said, "that Théophé cannot receive a visit from him?" He confessed, with the same confusion, that as he had not been able to divine that it was the selictar, and as he had taken him for one of his servants, he had thought he could get rid of him by answering that I was with Théophé; but at this the lord had seemed all the more anxious to come in, and he had even ordered that I be advised it was he. It appeared to me impossible to avoid this annoying inconvenience; and if I marveled at the things of which love rendered a man of his rank capable, it was not so much to apply to myself a reflection that suited me no less than him than to abandon myself to the distress of seeing him upset my plans. I had no doubt that this was a fresh betrayal on the part of the language tutor; but not deigning to turn my reproaches on the traitor, I hastened to urge Théophé not to grant any favors to a man whose intentions she knew. This uneasiness on my part must have succeeded in making her understand my own. She assured me that only the obedience she owed me could make her consent to receive a visit from him.

I went out to him. He embraced me with affection and, bantering agreeably over such an odd encounter, told me that it would be ungracious of the beautiful Greek to complain about friendship or love. Then, repeating everything he had already told me about his fondness for her, he added that, with the trust he still had in my word, it would not bother him if I were witness to the proposals he was about to make to her. I confess that this speech and the scene that it heralded caused me an equal consternation. How different I now felt from the way I had truly felt when I had declared to him that generosity alone caused me to take an interest in Théophé's fate! And in a state of mind about which I could no longer be uncertain, how could I assure myself enough moderation to be a tranquil witness to the offers or gallantries of my rival? However, I had to force myself, with a dissimulation all the more cruel because I myself had made it an indispensable law. Théophé was visibly embarrassed at seeing him appear with me. This increased even more when, having gone up to her, he spoke to her openly of his passion and burdened her with all the seemingly studied avowals of tenderness typical of the Turk. I tried several times to interrupt a farce that could not have been as intolerable to Théophé as it was to me, and I went so far as to answer for her that, as she proposed to make use of her freedom to leave Constantinople, she would have to feel some regret at not being able to lend an ear to sentiments so tender and so agreeably expressed. But that which I thought likely to cool his ardor, or to make him moderate his expressions at least, caused him, on the contrary, to hasten the offers he had prepared. He reproached her for a plan that she had formed, he said, only to make him miserable; but as he still flattered himself that he might touch her heart by letting her know what he wanted to do for her, he described to her a superb house he had on the Bosporus, the enjoyment of which he was resolved to surrender to her for her whole life, with a revenue that would correspond to the magnificence of such a beautiful dwelling. There, not only would she be free and independent, but she would have an absolute authority over all that belonged to him. He would give her thirty slaves of both sexes, all his diamonds, the number and the beauty of which would make her marvel, and the continual choice of all that might please her taste. He was in high enough favor at the Sublime Porte to fear the jealousy of no one. Nothing had a more secure foundation than a fortune he would make his own special concern. And so as to leave her in no doubt about his good faith, he took me as witness to all his promises.

These offers, spoken with a pomposity that is natural to the Turks, made enough of an impression on me to make me fear they had made too much of one on Théophé. It seemed so astonishing that they should so closely resemble my own, outshining them, moreover, in their brilliance, that I trembled all of a sudden for a plan I had so happily devised, in which I despaired at least of ever obtaining that which would be refused to the selictar. But how much more did I feel my alarms increase when Théophé, pressed to reveal her thoughts, displayed more sensitivity to his kindnesses than he himself had expected? The air of satisfaction that spread over her face revealed more charms than I had seen in it since I had met her. I had always seen her sad or uneasy. The stirrings of a cruel jealousy caused me to see all the flames of love afire in her eyes. And jealousy became rage, as I heard her add that she asked only twenty-four hours to make up her mind. She ended this scene with entreaties addressed only to him, to induce him to withdraw; and then, reflecting that he might find it shocking that she excepted me from this request, or that she was ill-disposed to suffer him for long in a place where he had found me, she added very cleverly that with a benefactor to whom she owed her freedom, she was less wary than with a stranger she had scarcely seen three times.

I would perhaps have found in the end of this speech something to diminish or suspend the resentment that was devouring me, if my ambitions had left my mind free enough to discover in it what was flattering and consoling for me. But struck by the term she had requested for her response, in despair at the selictar's joy, and almost smothered by the violence I was doing myself in order to hide my agitation, I thought only of going out into the street, in the hope of relieving myself at least with a few sighs. However, as I had not the strength to go out without the selictar, it was another torment for me to see myself obliged, in leaving with him, to endure his conversation for more than an hour and to hear with what satisfaction he already congratulated himself for his fortune. I could not persuade myself that the ease with which he had made himself heard was a momentary happiness, and, knowing his good faith, I asked him for some explanation of this surprise visit. He needed no prompting to reveal to me that, having sent Théophé various gifts that day, which she had received, he told me, without answering his letter, he had had the language tutor approached concerning his plan to go to his home secretly, and that the hope of being recompensed had induced that mercenary soul to open his house to him. In truth, the tutor had warned him that I was there regularly in the evening. "But as I have for her," continued the selictar, "only the feelings that you know me to have, and as I do not know the nature of your own, I did not find that your presence was disturbing to me, and I am delighted, on the contrary, to have had you as witness to the truth of my promises." He repeated to me that he was resolved to execute them faithfully and that he wanted to try out a happiness unknown to the Muslims.

Despite myself, I praised the nobility of the undertaking. Coupling the distress I had just suffered with the memory of the good terms I was on with him and a thousand honorable scruples to which I could not prevent myself from being sensitive, I resolved to combat the feelings I had allowed to hold too much sway over me, and I left the selictar with this thought. But scarcely was he a few paces away than I heard someone call out by name to my valet, who was the only servant I had with me. I recognized Jazir, the slave I had left with Théophé. The thought with which I had left the selictar was still affecting me so strongly that I opened my mouth to give Jazir orders that would have appeared harsh to his mistress. But he forestalled me with those he was bringing to me. Théophé had sent him after me to entreat me to return to her house and had instructed him to wait at some distance until I had left the selictar. There arose some struggle in my heart between my legitimate resentment, which had been intensified by the conversation I had just had, and the inclination that still drove me to regret the hopes that had been dashed. But I thought I could avoid the embarrassment of this discussion by adopting a pretext to retrace my steps that had nothing to do with the emotions troubling me. I had forgotten my watch, which I particularly liked for the excellence of its works. Thus, without examining whether it was not more suitable for my valet to go fetch it, I returned with the slave, rather satisfied to have this pretext for disguising my weakness from myself. What would the faithless woman say to me? With what excuse would the ingrate justify her fickleness? These complaints sprang to my lips as I walked, and far from reflecting that the names I was calling her assumed rights over her that she had not granted me, my imagination only grew more heated as I approached her house. I would inevitably have launched into the harshest reproaches if upon arriving I had found her fearful or confused. But my own confusion was extreme when, on the contrary, I saw her calm, smiling, and as though prepared to congratulate herself on the happiness she had just been assured. She did not allow my doubts to last very long. "Agree," she said to me, "that I had no other recourse in order to free myself of the selictar's obtrusiveness. But if your carriage is ready, we should leave the city before the night is past. And I would be vexed," she added, "if you have let the language tutor know of our secret, for I now see clearly that he is deceiving us." As I was still more perplexed by my joy than I had been by my grief, she had the time to tell me that, after she had confided her plan to leave to him, she had had the satisfaction of finding him very much disposed to serve her, but that through his zeal she saw that his only motive was self-interest. He had asked her permission to keep the selictar's gifts, pointing out to her that she should be quite indifferent to what anyone might think of her after her departure. The two words he had said to her secretly at the harbor were an entreaty to hide this agreement from me. And although it appeared, because of the care he had taken to act with the authority of her consent, that there remained enough honesty in him for him not to make himself guilty of a theft, she did not doubt that he had some part in the visit and the propositions of the selictar. In short, all sorts of reasons obliged her to accept the offer of my country house, and if I had enough goodness to satisfy her impatience, I would not put off this trip to the next day.

I was so charmed to hear her, and so resolved not to put off one minute longer the thing I desired much more than she, that without taking the time to answer her I gave orders again to hasten the return of my chaise. It had come while I was talking with the selictar, and I had ordered my valet to send it away. The difficulty was not how to hide Théophé's departure from the language tutor; but as all my joy could not drive away the idea of the selictar, I had some uneasiness about the manner in which he would take this turn of events. As far as I could tell from a quick examination of my scruples, I believed I was quite safe from his reproaches. The declaration I had made to him about my feelings was sincere at the time. I had not told him that they could not change, and since I had not even taken away from him the power of winning Théophé by means of his offers, I was not the one he should complain of, if she preferred mine to his. However, she had deluded him with some hope, and the term she had taken for making up her mind was a sort of promise that obliged her at least to see him again and explain her intentions to him clearly. I was afraid of embarrassing her by recalling this to her. But she had foreseen everything. As I returned to her room after giving my orders, I found her with a pen in her hand. "I am writing to the selictar," she said to me, "to destroy absolutely any ideas he might have formed about my answer. I will leave my letter with the language tutor, who will be quite content, no doubt, to have a new service to render him." She continued to write, and I answered her only in a few words to praise her resolution. I was still forcing myself to lock all my joy in my heart, as though the fear of seeing myself impeded by some new difficulty had caused me to suspend my ecstasy. The language tutor, to whom I scarcely gave a thought and whose own remorse perhaps drove him to seek some means of reconciling himself with me, sent for my permission to come in. "Of course," Théophé answered for me; and seeing him appear, she told him that as she had resolved to leave Constantinople, and as the reasons she had given me had forced me to approve of her resolution, she was quite pleased to show the selictar the gratitude she felt for his acts of kindness. She gave him her letter, which she had just finished. "You will perform this errand all the more willingly," she added slyly, "since you have already been recompensed for it and since the selictar will think no more than I of asking you to account for his gifts." I could not help taking the opportunity of this speech to make some reproaches against my cowardly confidant. He swore to me, to justify himself, that he had not thought he was offending the loyalty he owed me; and, reminding me how frankly he had confessed the part he had played in Théophé's absence when he saw that I was acutely afflicted by it, he begged me to judge the depths of his feelings by that good proof of their sincerity. But I could see all too well how much of this I should attribute to his fear of my revenge, and, dismissing his services, I charged him only with telling the selictar that I expected to see him soon.

In fact, I was already devising several strategies that I thought infallible for preserving that lord's friendship despite our opposing interests. But as my chaise could already be heard at that same moment, I thought of nothing more but to take Théophé's hand in order to lead her to it. I squeezed it with a stirring of passion that I no longer had the strength to disguise; and although it occurred to me to let her go off alone under the supervision of my valet, in order to leave the language tutor more uncertain as to her route, I could not resist the pleasure I was to have at finding myself with her in the same carriage, master of her fate and of her person through the voluntary consent she had given to our departure; master of her heart – for why should I hide the happiness with which I flattered myself? And what other explanation could I give to the decision she had made to throw herself into my arms with such confidence?

No sooner was I next to her than, drawing a passionate kiss from her lips, I had the pleasure of finding her sensitive to this tender caress. A sigh, which escaped her despite herself, caused me to judge still more favorably the emotions in her heart. During the whole of the journey I held her hand tightly in both of mine, and I thought I could tell that she experienced as much sweetness as I did in this. I did not say a word to her that was not mingled with some mark of tenderness, and even my conversation, though as measured as my actions by a preference for propriety which has always been natural to me, continually showed the effects of the fire that was growing ever stronger in my heart.

If Théophé sometimes defended herself against the ardor of my expressions, it was not out of scorn or severity. She merely begged me not to misuse such tender and sweet language on a woman who was accustomed only to the tyrannical customs of the seraglio; and when this manner of defending herself caused me to redouble my caresses, she added that it was not surprising that the lot of women in my country was happy, if all men treated them with such excessive kindness there.

It was close to midnight when we arrived at my country house, which was situated close to a village called Oru. Although I had not ordered any special preparations to be made, there was always something with which to entertain my friends decently, as I sometimes brought them there at hours when I could least be expected. I mentioned supper as we arrived. Théophé told me that she had more need of rest than of food. But I insisted on the need to refresh ourselves, at least, with a light and delicate meal. We spent little time at the table, and I employed it less to eat than to satisfy in advance a part of my tender desires through the banter of my conversation and the ardor of my glances. I had chosen the apartment in which I proposed to spend the night, and one of the reasons that had made me urge Théophé to take some refreshments had been to give my servants time to embellish it with the utmost elegance. At last, as she reiterated her need of rest, I took this remark as a modest declaration of her impatience to be alone with me. I even congratulated myself on finding in a charming mistress both the vivacity to look forward impatiently to the hour of pleasure and enough restraint to disguise her desires becomingly.

My servants, who had seen me form more than one liaison in my house in Oru and who had also been ordered to prepare only one bed, had arranged in the same apartment everything necessary for Théophé's comfort and my own. I led her there with a redoubling of joy and amorous attentions. Her slave and my valet, who were waiting for us there, each approached to render the services required of their station. In jest, I urged Bema (the name of the slave) not to incur my wrath by being too slow. It had seemed to me until then that Théophé had joined quite naturally in all my plans, and I believed her to be so well disposed to the conclusion of this scene that I had never thought of masking my expectations with the slightest veil. I hardly felt obliged, with a woman who had told me so openly about her adventures in Patras and those in the seraglio, to take the circuitous paths that sometimes soothe the modesty of an inexperienced girl; and if I may be permitted another reflection, neither would I have expected, from a woman over whom I had acquired so many privileges and who had, moreover, yielded herself to me so willingly, to find an excess of reserve and propriety. Furthermore, all the most intense and most passionate feelings I had had for her until then seemed to me only the ecstasy of an enlightened libertinism, which made me prefer her to any other woman because, with a face so striking, she seemed to promise all the more pleasure.

However, no sooner had she noticed my valet beginning to undress me, than, pushing away her slave, who was busy performing the same service for her, she remained contemplative for several minutes, as though uncertain, without lifting her eyes to me. At first I attributed this change of countenance only to the darkness of the night, which from one end of the room to the other might have caused me to imagine some change of her expression. But continuing to see her motionless and Bema idle beside her, I hazarded, with uneasiness, a few jesting remarks about my fear that I would become very weary waiting for her. This language, which became clearer to her apparently because of the circumstances, succeeded in disconcerting her completely. She left the mirror before which she had been standing, and, throwing herself listlessly on a sofa, she remained bowed over, forehead resting on her hand, as though she were trying to conceal the sight of her face from me. My first fear was still that she had been seized by some indisposition. We had made the trip during the night. Our meal had consisted simply of fruits and ices. I ran over to her with the greatest urgency and asked her if she was beginning to feel ill. She did not answer me. My uneasiness increased, I grasped one of her hands, the same one on which her head was resting, and I made some attempts to draw it to me. She resisted for a few minutes. At last, passing her hand over her eyes to wipe away a few tears whose traces I perceived, she asked me to be so kind as to send the two servants away and grant her a moment's conversation.

Scarcely was I alone with her than, lowering her eyes and her voice, she told me with an air of consternation that she could not contest anything I might demand of her, but that she would never have expected this. She was silent after these few words, as though pain and fear had suddenly deprived her of speech, and I noticed by her breathing that her heart was seized by the most violent emotion. My surprise, which immediately rose to its greatest height, and perhaps a feeling of shame that was impossible for me to conquer at once, threw me, for my own part, into the same state, so that it was the strangest spectacle in the world to see the two of us as dejected as though we had been struck suddenly by some malady.

However, I roused myself to shake off this heaviness, and attempting anew to take control of Théophé's hand, I succeeded at last in keeping it between both my own. "One minute," I said to her during this tender struggle. "Let me hold your hand for one minute in order to talk to you and listen to you." She seemed to surrender out of fear of offending me rather than a desire to satisfy me. "Alas! Have I the right to refuse you?" she repeated with the same listlessness. "Have I anything in my power that is not yours more than it is mine? But no, no, I never would have expected this." Her tears began to flow more freely. In the perplexity into which this scene threw me, I felt some doubt as to her sincerity. I remembered having heard a thousand times that most Turkish girls take pride in disputing the favors of love at length, and I was prepared, with this in mind, not to take her resistance and tears too seriously. However, the ingenuousness I saw in her grief, and the shame I would have felt at not living up to the opinion she had of me if she was sincere, caused me suddenly to restrain all my passion. "Do not be afraid of raising your eyes to me," I said, seeing that she continued to keep them lowered, "and recognize me as the man least capable, of all men in the world, of distressing you or doing violence to your inclinations. My desires are the natural effect of your charms, and I had thought that you would not refuse me what you granted willingly to the son of the governor of Patras and to the pasha Chériber." "But the movements of the heart are not free..." She interrupted me with an exclamation that seemed to come from a heart filled with bitterness; and whereas I flattered myself that I was speaking in a manner likely to soothe her, she let me know that I was instead causing her grief. No longer understanding anything about this bizarre situation, and not daring to add even a single word for fear of not comprehending her intentions any better, I begged her to inform me, in that case, what I ought to do, what I ought to say, in order to dispel the sadness I had caused her and not to hold against me as a crime what she could only regard, after all, as an offense. It seemed that my tone as I made this entreaty caused her, in turn, to fear that she had distressed me with her complaints. She squeezed my hand, with an anxious gesture. "Oh, best of all men," she said, using an expression common among the Turks, "think better of the feelings of your unfortunate slave and do not believe that anything that passes from you to me could bear the name of offense. But you have pierced my heart with a mortal distress. What I ask of you," she added, "since you give me the freedom to explain my desires, is to allow me to spend the night in my sad reflections and to permit me to communicate them to you tomorrow. If you find an excess of boldness in your slave's request, wait at least until you know my feelings before condemning them." She tried to fall down at my feet. I held her up against her will, and, rising from the sofa where I had sat down in order to listen to her, I adopted an air as free and as disinterested as though I had never thought of making the least proposal of love to her. "Abandon," I said, "terms that are no longer appropriate to your situation. Far from being my slave, you could have assumed a dominance over me that I have felt only too much inclination to grant you. But I would rather not owe your heart to my authority, when I would be right to use restraint. You will spend this night, and all the rest of your life, if that is your design, with the tranquillity that you seem to desire." I immediately called her slave, whom I calmly ordered to render her her services; and retiring with the same appearance of composure, I had myself taken to another apartment, where I immediately went to bed. There remained in me a depth of agitation which all the efforts I had made to control myself had not been able to calm entirely; but I deluded myself that the repose of sleep would soon restore peace in my mind and in my heart.

However, scarcely had the darkness and the silence of the night begun to collect my senses than all the circumstances that had just occurred before my eyes portrayed themselves almost as vividly in my imagination. As I had not forgotten even one of Théophé's words, the first feeling I had in rediscovering them in my memory was probably an emotion of resentment and confusion. It was even easy for me to fathom that the facility with which I had made the decision to let her alone, and all the disinterest that I had shown on leaving her, came from the same cause. I confirmed this disposition in myself for a few minutes by reproaching my weakness. Ought I not to have blushed at having yielded so imprudently these past few days to the inclination I had felt for a girl of this sort, and should the desire that I had for her have interested me to the point of causing me such uneasiness and disquiet? Was Turkey not full of slaves from whom I might expect the same pleasures? The only thing lacking, I added, mocking my own folly, was for me to acquire a serious passion for a girl of sixteen whom I had taken from a seraglio in Constantinople and who had perhaps entered Chériber's only after having tried out all the others. Progressing, then, to the refusal she had made me of her favors after having lavished them on any number of Turks, I congratulated myself on my delicacy, which caused me to attach such a high price to what old Chériber had left behind. But I found it even more marvelous that Théophé had learned in so short a time to know the value of her charms and that the first man to whom she solicited those charms, at such cost, was a Frenchman as versed as I in the commerce of women. She had imagined, I said, from the air of goodness evident in my face and my manners, that she would make me her first dupe; and the young coquette, in whom I had assumed there to be such naïveté and candor, was perhaps intending to lead me quite far with her wiles.

But after having in some sense satisfied my resentment with these insulting thoughts, I returned little by little to consider with less emotion what lay behind this situation. I recalled all of Théophé's conduct toward me since I had first seen her in Chériber's seraglio. Had she ever indulged in the slightest action or speech that could compare with the intentions I had attributed to her? Had I not been surprised, on the contrary, to see her time and time again interpret all the insights I had offered on her reflections as the most serious questions of morality; and had I not in fact marveled at the depth and the fairness that shone forth in all her reasonings? It is true that she had at times repeated them to me in an excessively tiresome way, and it was perhaps this sort of affectation that had prevented me from believing they were sincere. I had regarded them at the very most as an intellectual exercise, or as the effect of an infinite number of new impressions that the explanation of our rules of conduct and customs continually made on a lively and restless imagination. But why do her this injustice and not believe that, having a good character and a great deal of reason, she had, in fact, been deeply struck by a thousand principles that she found germinating deep in her heart? Had she not clearly rejected the selictar's offers? Had she not thought of leaving me as well, to seek in Europe a situation that corresponded to her ideas? And if she had later consented to give herself over to my care, was it not natural that she should trust a man to whom she owed the images of virtue she was beginning to entertain? Supposing this were so, was she not becoming respectable; and for whom was she respectable for more than for myself, who had begun to serve her without selfish interest and who, far from disturbing her modest plans with mad and licentious proposals, ought instead to honor a conversion that was really my own doing?

The more I thought about it, the more I felt that this way of looking at the situation suited me; having always prided myself on my lofty principles, it cost me almost nothing to sacrifice the pleasures I had deemed necessary to make Théophé a woman as distinguished by her virtue as by her charms. I never thought of inspiring her with discretion; and the discernment I attribute to her is only the happy effect of her character, sparked by some remarks I had uttered accidentally. How far might she progress were I to make a serious study of cultivating these rich gifts of nature? I imagined her complacently in the state to which I believed I could lead her. But, struck in advance by this portrait, what would she then lack, I added, to become the foremost woman in the world? What? Théophé could become as attractive for her qualities of mind and heart as for the exterior charms of her appearance? Ah! What man of honor and taste would not believe himself fortunate to be with this woman for his whole life...I stopped halfway through this reflection, as though frightened by the avidity with which my heart seemed to embrace it. It returned to me a thousand times until the moment when my senses grew drowsy; and far from experiencing the agitation I had dreaded, I spent the rest of the night in a delicious sleep.

In the morning, the first traces I found in my memory were those so pleasantly engraved there as I fell asleep. They had amplified so forcefully, more or less obliterating those of my first plan, that not the least desire resembling those with which I had sustained myself for the past few days returned to me. I burned with impatience to be with Théophé again, but it was in the hope of finding her such as I had had so much pleasure imagining her, or at least of seeing in her the disposition I had attributed to her. This ardor went so far as to provoke the fear that I had been mistaken in my suppositions. Scarcely had I learned it was light in her apartment than I sent for permission to see her. Her slave came to beg me on her behalf to allow her a moment to get out of bed. But I hastened to surprise her there, with the sole aim of letting her know through my restraint the change that the night had effected in my ideas. She seemed agitated at seeing me arrive so soon, and in her confusion she made excuses about the slowness of her slave. I reassured her with some simple words that she had nothing to fear from my intentions. How beautiful she was in that state, nonetheless, and how suited were her many charms to make me forget my resolutions!

"You promised me explanations," I said to her in a serious tone, "that I am burning to hear; but allow them to be preceded by my own. Whatever the desires I may have yielded to yesterday, you must have judged, from my respect for yours, that I do not desire from a woman what she is not disposed to grant me voluntarily. Today, I add to this proof of my feelings a declaration that will confirm them. Whatever your intentions were in agreeing to accompany me here, you will always have the freedom to pursue them as you have at present the freedom to explain them." I imposed silence on myself as I finished this speech, and I resolved not to break it until she had finished her own. But after looking at me for a moment, I was surprised to see her shed a few tears; and when the uneasiness I felt at this made me forget my resolution and ask her what was causing them, my astonishment increased further at her answer. She told me that no one was to be more pitied than she, and that the speech I had just made to her was precisely the misfortune she had been expecting. I urged her to speak more clearly. "Alas!" she went on, "by making that declaration of your feelings, how little justice you do to mine! After what happened here yesterday, you cannot take that tone with me except as a consequence of the same ideas; and I should die of sorrow for, while I have been trying to make you understand something deep within my heart, I have so ill succeeded in acquainting you with what is occurring there."

As this lament only increased my bewilderment, I confessed to her with as much frankness in my words as in my expressions that since our very first meeting she had been a complete enigma to me, and her last words served only to perpetuate this. "Come, speak openly," I said again. "Why do you hesitate? In whom could you ever confide with more trust?"

"It is your questions themselves," she answered me at last. "It is the necessity with which you ask me to speak openly that causes my sorrow. What? You need an explanation to understand that I am the most unhappy person of my sex? You, who opened my eyes to my shame, are surprised that I should find myself intolerable and that I think of hiding myself from the eyes of others? Oh, what is my lot henceforth? Is it to respond to your desires or to those of the selictar, when I find in the knowledge you have instilled in me a judge that condemns them? Is it to go off to those countries whose practices and principles you have praised in order to find, through the example of the virtues of which I was ignorant, a perpetual reproach for my infamies? Yet I attempted to leave this corrupt nation. I wanted to flee both those who had ruined my innocent youth and you, who taught me to know my ruin. But where was I allowing myself to be taken in my confusion and my remorse? I know only too well that without protection and guidance I would have taken a step into some new abyss. Your entreaties stopped me. Although I was more afraid of you than any other man – because you knew so well the extent of my misfortune – although each of your glances seemed to carry a sentence of my condemnation, I returned to Constantinople with you. Would an ill person, I said to reassure myself, blush to see his most shameful sores? Besides, after realizing that a voyage undertaken blindly was imprudent, I deluded myself, due to your promises, into thinking that you would provide a more secure way to leave. However, it is you who push me again, today, toward the precipice from which you pulled me back. I regarded you as my teacher in virtue, and now you want to drag me back toward vice; with all the more danger for my weakness because, if vice could offer me any charm, it would come from your hands! Alas! Did I explain myself badly or do you feign not to understand me? The limits of my mind, the disorder of my ideas and my remarks, may have made you ill judge of my feelings; but if you begin to know them through the efforts I make to explain them, do not take offense at the effect that your own lessons have produced in my heart. If you have changed your principles, I know too well that it is to the first that I owe my obedience, and I beg you to suffer me to remain attached to them." This speech, of which I report only what is still clearest in my memory, was long enough to give me time to understand all its power and to prepare my response. Filled, as I was, with the reflections that had occupied me during the entire night, I had been much less offended by Théophé's reproaches, much less afflicted by her feelings and her resolutions, than I was instead charmed to find them in conformance with the opinion I had already formed of them myself. Thus, the image that I had begun to form of her, and the virtuous satisfaction I had felt over it, only augmented as I listened raptly to her; and if she was paying any attention at all to my reactions, she would have noticed that I heard every word that came from her mouth with some sign of joy and congratulation. I nonetheless tempered the expressions of my response, in order not to give an air of superficiality or passion to the conclusion of such a serious discussion. "Dear Théophé!" I said to her in the abundance of my feelings, "you have humiliated me with your laments, and I will not deny that yesterday I was very far from anticipating them; but I have brought some foreknowledge of them to this visit, and I have come prepared to acknowledge myself guilty. If you ask me how I chanced to become so, it is because it would have been too difficult to persuade myself of what I have just heard with great admiration, and what would still seem incredible to me had I not such clear proof. I reproach myself for having had until now more admiration than esteem for you. Oh, when one knows how rare the love of virtue is in the countries most favored by Heaven, when one experiences how difficult its practice is, can one readily believe that in the heart of Turkey, having just come out of a seraglio, a person of your age should have grasped at once not only the idea but even the preference for the highest chastity? What did I say, what did I do that was sufficient to inspire you? Could a few random reflections on our customs have caused this happy inclination to be born in your heart? No, no, you owe it only to yourself; and your upbringing, which until now kept this inclination in some way bound by the force of habit, is a piece of bad luck for which no reproach can be made against you.

"What I want first to conclude," I continued with the same moderation, "is that you would be equally unjust either to take offense at the ideas I have had about you, since it was not natural that I should understand yours right away, or to believe that one can presume, based on the past, to refuse you the esteem you will merit by a conduct worthy of your feelings. Give up your plans to travel; young and lacking experience of the world, you could expect nothing good from them. Virtue, of which they have such specific ideas in Europe, is practiced scarcely any better there than in Turkey. You will find passions and vices in every country inhabited by men. But if my promises inspire you with any confidence, trust in feelings that have already changed their nature and will no longer inspire me with ardor except to perfect your own. My house will be a sanctuary; my example will predispose all my servants to respect you. Here you will find a constant resource in my friendship; and if my principles have appealed to you, perhaps there remains some enlightenment to be gained from my counsels."

She looked at me with such a dreamy air that I searched uselessly in her eyes to see if she was satisfied with my answer. I was even apprehensive, as she remained silent, that she might still have some doubt as to my sincerity, and that, given the experience she had had of my weakness, she did not dare trust in my protestations. But all her uneasiness was for herself. "Will I ever imagine," she went on after having allowed her silence to last a great deal longer, "that, with the ideas that you have of virtue, you could look without scorn on a woman whose every deviation is known to you? I have confessed them to you, and I cannot repent. I owed that confidence to the eagerness you had to learn of my misfortunes. But does this mean that I must flee from you, and will I ever be that far from those who may reproach me with my shame?" I could not control my delight at this speech. I interrupted her, and all the restraint that I had affected abandoned me. My laments must have been quite touching and my reasoning quite persuasive, since I confessed to Théophé that the better I knew the price of virtue, the more I admired the sentiments that filled her. I told her that, in the ideas of true modesty, scorn is due only to voluntary faults and what she called her deviations should not be called by that name, since it would suppose that she had already known what she only later learned on the occasion of talking to me at the seraglio. Finally, I promised her, along with a constant esteem, all the attentions necessary to complete the work that I had so happily begun, and I engaged myself with formidable oaths to leave her free not only to flee me, but to hate and scorn me should I fail to meet the conditions she imposed on me. And in order to remove all appearance of equivocation from my promises, I immediately made a plan and submitted all its articles to her decision. "This house," I said, "will be your home, and you will establish in it the order that best suits you. I will see you here only as often as you will permit me. You will see here only those it pleases you to receive. I will take care that nothing is lacking to occupy you in a useful way or to amuse you. And given the penchant you show for everything that may serve to form your mind and heart, I am thinking of having you learn the language of my nation, which will become useful to you by immediately familiarizing you with myriad excellent books. You will put aside some of my proposals, or you will add to them any you find inspiring, and you will always see executed whatever pleases you."

I did not examine where the warmth that animated these offers came from, and Théophé did not linger over this discussion either. She believed she saw in my frankness strong reasons for surrendering to my entreaties. She told me that as she owed everything to my generosity, her obstinacy could only make her fearful of becoming unworthy of it and that she would accept my all-too-felicitous offers should I be faithful in executing them. I do not know how I found enough strength to check the impulse to throw myself to my knees before her bed and to thank her for this consent as for a favor. "We will begin immediately," I said with more joy than I wished to reveal, "and you will realize some day that I am worthy of your confidence."

This sentiment was sincere. I left her without even venturing to kiss her hand, although, as she had the most beautiful hands in the world, she had inspired in me a hundred times the desire to do that in the motions she had made during our conversation. My plan was to return forthwith to Constantinople, not only to obtain what I believed was most suited to amuse her in her solitude, but also to give her the time to establish her authority and order in my house. I declared my intentions to the small number of servants I left there to serve her. Bema, whom I had summoned to witness this order, requested the liberty of speaking to me alone. I was extremely surprised by her remarks. She told me that the very freedom and authority I was granting her mistress proved to her quite clearly that I was ignorant of the nature of the women of her nation; that the experience she had acquired in several seraglios put her in a position to help a foreigner with her advice; that the loyalty to which she was obliged by her condition did not permit her to conceal what I had to fear from a mistress as young and as beautiful as Théophé; in a word, that I should have little trust in Bema's wisdom if, instead of leaving Théophé in absolute authority in my house, I did not subject her to the guidance of some loyal slave; that it was the custom of every sort of lord in Turkey; and that if I thought she was suited to this employment, she promised me so much vigilance and zeal that I would never repent of my confidence.

Although I had not seen enough intelligence in this slave to hope for extraordinary assistance from her, and although in the opinion I had of Théophé I did not need an Argus next to her, I chose a middle path between the counsel I was receiving and what I believed I could grant to prudence. "I do not conduct myself," I said to Bema, "by the principles of your country, and, moreover, I say to you that I have no rights over Théophé that authorize me to impose laws on her. But if you are capable of some discretion, I would be happy to charge you with observing her conduct. The recompense will be proportionate to your services and above all to your discretion," I added, "for I require absolutely that Théophé never notice the commission I am giving you." Bema appeared extremely satisfied with my answer. Her joy would perhaps have seemed suspect if the people from whom I acquired this slave had not boasted to me almost equally of her prudence and her loyalty. But I also saw that so simple a commission would demand little more than mediocrity in the two qualities that had been recommended to me.

What occupied me the most upon returning to the city was the difficulty of satisfying the selictar, who could not for long remain ignorant either of the fact that Théophé had left the language tutor or that I had granted her a retreat in my house. I had suddenly become quite calm about everything concerning her, ever since I had made sure of having her under my protection; and without examining what my heart dared to hope for from this, it seemed to me that whatever sentiments might fill it, the future offered me only promising opportunities. But though I could not dispense with giving the selictar some explanation, the reasons I had prepared the day before and that had then seemed enough to appease him lost their force even for me as the moment approached for trying them out on him. The one I had hoped to be most effective was the fear of her father, who would have had more rights than ever, not only to exclude her from his family but to call for her punishment if she yielded willingly to the love of a Turk. My protection, in her present situation, shielded her better than that of the selictar. However, quite apart from the idea he had of his prestige, I could not confess to him that, in my house, she would not be obliged to receive him as often as he pleased to present himself. To do this would cause as much distress to Théophé as to me. In this difficult position, I made a very different decision, the only one, perhaps, that could succeed with a man as generous as the selictar; I went to him directly. I did not wait for him to make my task more difficult with his complaints, and even forestalling all his questions, I informed him that the motive that had caused her to reject his offers was the young Greek's declared penchant for virtues that are little known to the women of Turkey. I did not hide from him that I had been surprised myself and had not trusted her yearnings for virtue until I had put them to the test; but that having found only objects of admiration in the sentiments of a person of that age, I had resolved to grant her all the assistance that could bring such noble inclinations to their perfection, and that, knowing him as I did, I did not doubt that he would be inclined to support my plan. Only the last words did I regret having allowed to escape from this speech, which I had shaped quite tactfully. The selictar answered by protesting that he respected sentiments such as I represented them in Théophé and that he had never claimed to exclude them from the commerce he had intended with her; but he took the opportunity to assure me that, as his tenderness increased with his esteem, he wished more than ever to declare to her the great importance he attached to her. I could not defend myself against the proposal he made to accompany me sometimes to Oru except by offering him all the freedom in my house that I granted to my friends, but with whatever restrictions Théophé herself might place on it, as my oaths had given her the right to see only those persons she wished to admit into her solitude.

Although I rightfully reproached myself for having given the selictar an opening from which I saw he was resolved to profit, I was satisfied at having saved myself so delicately from the uncertainty that had troubled me that I thought nothing of the difficulty of seeing him at Oru. He would have been offended had I hesitated in promising him that satisfaction, and the suspicions from which his own rectitude, as much as the opinion he held of mine, which had been strong enough to defend him until then would perhaps have begun to arise and immediately cause the ruin of our friendship. As I left him, I thought only of fulfilling the promises I had made to Théophé. Knowing the pleasure she took in painting, which she had not yet undertaken except to depict flowers, in accordance with the law that forbids Turks to depict any living creature, I sought a painter who could introduce her to drawing and portraiture. As I selected for her other teachers of the arts and disciplines of Europe, a thought occurred to me that I struggled against for a long time, but that Providence, whose secrets one cannot begin to fathom, finally caused to prevail over all my objections. Convinced as I was that the young Condoidi was her brother, it appeared to me all the more natural to bring them together for their education, since most of the teachers I was to provide each of them were the same. This plan assumed that Condoidi would also make his home at Oru; and far from finding in this the least cause for objection, I was delighted, on the contrary, to be able to give Théophé regular company, which would allow her to avoid the weariness of solitude. If I must confess it, the main objection I struggled against was not very clear in my mind, and perhaps the obligation I believed I was under to dismiss this objection prevented me from forming others that might have given me more reason to stop myself. I thought confusedly, and without daring to own it to myself, that the constant presence of this young man would deny me the freedom to be alone with Théophé; but having determined at heart to abide religiously by all my promises, I toyed with the idea for some time only to reject it.

Synèse (this was young Condoidi's name) was quite happy to learn what my esteem and inclination had prompted me to undertake for his sister. He was equally pleased with the resolution I had made to have him live with her and to have them receive the same instruction. I sent him off that very day to Oru, along with everything that I intended for Théophé's amusement. Their father, who now knew that I had taken his son under my wing and had already come to thank me for it, reappeared at my house upon learning from Synèse that I had arrived. He seemed surprised to see me, and I was convinced by his confusion that Synèse had had the faithfulness, following my orders, to hide the crux of this adventure from him. I had wanted both to amuse myself with his surprise and to profit from his first impressions to renew my entreaties in Théophé's favor. But I abandoned the second of these two hopes when the stubborn old man stated clearly that his religion and his honor forbade him to acknowledge a daughter who had been brought up in a seraglio. Even the offer I made him, to remove all difficulties by taking his place in performing the duties of a father, did not appear to change his mind. He remained so intransigent that, in the resentment I felt, I declared that he need not come to my home again and that I would not gladly receive his visits.

I did not return to Oru until the next day. My impatience to see Théophé again was a feeling I did not hide from myself, but having absolutely renounced all the claims I had had on her, I did not intend to deprive myself of an honest fondness, which might well agree with her ideas of chastity and with all my commitments. The sort of freedom I granted my heart prevented me from sensing all that it would have cost me had I undertaken to constrain it. I found Synèse with her, both of them in the first ardor of their studies and almost equally sensitive to the care I had taken in having them live together. I marveled at an air of tranquillity in Théophé which seemed to have increased her natural freshness and evidenced the satisfaction of her heart. I wanted to know from Bema what use Théophée had made of the authority I had granted her in my house. This slave, who was deeply offended at having so little herself, did not yet dare tell me that her mistress had abused it; but she repeated all the reasons she had already put forward in order to make me fear it. The cause of her zeal was so visible that I begged her, smiling, to be less uneasy. She had expected, based on what those who had bought her to me had told her, that I would give her a sort of authority over Théophé, and this sign of trust, which she had received in a seraglio, was the highest degree of distinction for a slave. I told her that the customs of the Turks were not the rule for a Frenchman and that we had our own customs, from which I advised her to profit, herself, for the enjoyment of her life. If she was not bold enough to complain, she acquired, perhaps starting at that very moment, a distaste for Théophé and for me, the effects of which she all too easily found occasion to make us feel.

The affairs of my employment leaving me more freedom than I had had for a long time, I took the fine season as a pretext to stay in the country for several weeks. I had at first feared that Théophé would too rigorously accept the offer I had made her to bar me from seeing her. But believing, on the contrary, that she took pleasure in my conversation, I forgot myself with her during entire days, and in this familiarity I began to know more and more all the perfections with which nature had adorned her character. It was from me, in fact, that she received her first lessons in our language. She made surprising progress. I had extolled to her the fruits she might derive from it in reading, and she was impatient to see in her hand a French book that she could understand. No less impatient than she, I satisfied her as best I could by tracing imperfect images of what she would find with more method and scope in our better writers. I said nothing that related to my feelings. The sweetness of seeing and hearing her were innocent pleasures with which I was intoxicated. I might have feared that I would diminish the trust she had placed in me by some return of weakness; and what surprised me was how little tormented I was by the hot-bloodedness that sometimes makes the deprivation of certain pleasures quite difficult at my age. I forewent them without difficulty, and even without giving it much thought, although until then I had not imposed very strict laws on myself concerning women, especially in a country where the needs of nature seem to increase with the freedom to satisfy them. Reflecting, since then, on the cause of this change, I have come to think that the natural faculties at the source of desires perhaps take a different course in a man who loves than in a man whose only incentive is the heat of his age. The impression that beauty makes on all the senses divides the force of nature. And what I call the natural faculties, in order to distance myself from ideas that might appear unclean, thus rises again by the same paths that have brought it into the ordinary reservoirs, mingles with the mass of blood, causes in it that sort of fermentation or fire of which love properly consists, and does not resume the route that serves the act of pleasure except when it is recalled to it through exercise.

The selictar sometimes came to disturb this delicious life. I had prepared my pupil for his visits, and wishing to accustom her to regard the society of men in a different light from Turkish women, who do not imagine that there may be interaction without love, I had recommended that she politely receive a man whose esteem did her honor and whose tenderness ought no longer to cause her any uneasiness. He had responded to the opinion I had of him with a conduct so modest that I now admired his sentiments. It became quite difficult for me to understand their nature; for, as the only path that could give him any hope of satisfaction was henceforth closed by his own agreements as much as by Théophé's refusal, he had nothing to expect from the future, and the present offered him only the simple pleasure of a serious conversation, which was not even as long as he would have wished. Théophé, who was obliging enough to receive him as often as he came to Oru, was not always obliging enough to weary herself with him when he stayed too long. She would leave us to resume her studies with her brother, and I would endure the recital of all the selictar's tender sentiments in her absence. As he no longer had any definite plan, and as he was reduced to vague declarations of his admiration and his love, I persuaded myself at last that, having heard me speak often of that delicate manner of loving which consists in the sentiments of the heart and which is so little known in his nation, he had acquired a sufficient liking for it to try it out. But how could I also believe that he would limit himself to the pleasure of warming his heart with tender sentiments, without showing more chagrin and impatience at not being able to obtain the least return?

These doubts did not prevent me from seeing him all the more readily, since the comparison I made between his fate and mine flattered certain sentiments that I secretly sustained. But I was less tranquil after another discovery, which I did not owe to any diligence of my own and which precipitated the unveiling of several intrigues that cast a good deal of bitterness over the rest of my life. I had been living at Oru for about six weeks, and being a constant witness to what happened in my house, I was charmed by the peace and contentment that I saw reigning there. Synèse was always with Théophé, but I left her no more than he. I had noticed nothing in their relationship that contradicted the opinion I had that they were of the same blood; or, rather, having not the least doubt that they were children of the same father, no mistrust of their familiarity could have entered my thoughts. Synèse, whom I treated with the tenderness one has for a son, and who indeed made himself worthy of it by the sweetness of his character, came one day to find me alone in my apartment. After talking to me unaffectedly about several things, he turned guilelessly to his father's objections to acknowledging Théophé; and using a language that seemed to me foreign to his tongue, he told me that, despite the pleasure he found in believing he had such a captivating sister, he had not been able to persuade himself sincerely that he was her brother. My attention being aroused by a declaration I had so little expected, I allowed him all the time he needed to continue. The confession of the wretch who had been executed by the cadi's sentence was enough, he said, to justify his father's refusal. What interest would a man have, who saw himself threatened with execution, in concealing whose daughter Théophé was? And was it not clear that, after protesting that Condoidi's own daughter had died with her mother, he had changed his speech only in order to win over the judge with an infamous offer or to obtain a delay in his punishment? It was no more likely, Synèse added, that a person as accomplished as Théophé should be the daughter of that scoundrel; but she could not be Paniota Condoidi's either, and a thousand circumstances he remembered having heard recounted in his family had never permitted him seriously to delude himself about it.

Although it seemed perfectly sincere, Synèse's speech, which he himself had introduced but which seemed so contrary to his penchant for Théophé, aroused extraordinary suspicions in me. I knew he was clever enough to be capable of some disguise, and I had not forgotten the selictar's proverb about the good faith of the Greeks. I concluded at once that some change I was unaware of had taken place in Synèse's heart, and whether it was hatred or love, he no longer saw Théophé in the same light. I did not think I should fear, after this confession, being duped by a man of his age. And opting, instead, to urge him to reveal his sentiments without his noticing, I feigned to agree, more easily perhaps than he was expecting, with the arguments he had just made to me. "I am no more certain than you," I said, "about Théophé's birth, and I think that if there is some information lacking on this subject, it is that of your family. Thus, once you are all agreed not to acknowledge her, it would not be appropriate for her to insist on her claims a moment longer." It was easy to see that this answer satisfied him. But as he was preparing to confirm what he had said to me with some new proof, I added: "If you are as persuaded as you appear to be that she is not your sister, not only do I wish you to cease to call her by that name, but I would be vexed if you felt you needed to continue living with her any longer. You will return to Constantinople this evening." This speech threw him into a confusion that I understood even more quickly than I had his joy. I did not give him time to recover: "As you must have known," I added, "that it was my consideration for her that convinced me to receive you in my home, you must understand that I cannot keep you here when I no longer have this reason for so doing. Thus, I will give orders that you are to be taken back to your father's house this evening."

I had said everything I believed might cast some light on Synèse's heart. I finished, without appearing overly worried by his obvious constraint; and for good measure, I advised him to say his farewells properly to Théophé, since there was little likelihood that he would ever see her again. After having changed color twenty times and become so discomposed as to make me feel sorry for him, he timidly resumed speaking in order to protest to me that his doubts about the birth of his sister would not diminish either the esteem or the tenderness he felt for her; that he regarded her, on the contrary, as the most charming person of her sex and that he believed himself very fortunate in the freedom he had had to live with her; that he would never lose these feelings; that he wished to take great pains to express them to her all his life; and that if he could join the satisfaction of pleasing her with the honor he felt at belonging to me, there was no condition for which he would wish to change his present one. I interrupted him. Not only did I believe I could read his innermost heart, but this heatedness, which did not permit me to mistake his feelings, caused another suspicion to arise in me that greatly disturbed all my own feelings. Brother or not, I said to myself, if this young man is in love with Théophé, if he has deceived me until now, how will I know that Théophé has not conceived the same passion for him and that she has not used as much cunning in disguising it? Who knows, in fact, if they are not trying in concert to rid themselves of an inconvenient bond, which prevents them perhaps from yielding to their inclination? This notion, which all the circumstances were likely to strengthen, threw me into a despondent and sorrowful state whose outward signs I was no better at disguising than Synèse. "Begone," I said to him. "I need to be alone, and I will see you again soon." He went out. But in the midst of the emotion that was so agitating me, I took care to observe whether he made his way directly to Théophé, as though I might have concluded something from the urgency I assumed him to feel to go and give her an account of our conversation. I watched as he sadly entered the garden, where I had no doubt he would surrender himself to his grief at having managed his undertaking so badly; but his disturbance had to be extreme if it surpassed my own.

My first concern was to summon Bema, whose observations, I did not doubt, would enlighten me. She affected to understand nothing of my questions, and I persuaded myself at last that as she had always been of the opinion that Synèse was Théophé's brother, she had not been aware of their relationship because her suspicions had not been turned in that direction. I resolved to discuss it with Théophé, and to go about it as cunningly as I had with Synèse. As I was sure that he had not been able to see her since he had left me, I informed her first of my plan to return him to his family. She showed a good deal of surprise at this; but when I had added that the only reason for the aversion I was feeling for him was his reluctance to acknowledge her as his sister any longer, she could not help expressing her great distress. "How little trust," she said, "one may place in men's appearances! Never has he shown me such esteem and such friendship as these past few days." This lament appeared so natural, and the reflections she added to it about her fate smelled so little of guile, that, recovering all at once from my doubts, I immediately passed to the most extreme confidence. "I am inclined to believe," I said, "that you have inspired him with love. He is burdened by a title that does not tally with his feelings." Théophé interrupted me with such lively exclamations that I needed no other proof to confirm my favorable opinion of her. "What are you telling me? What?" she said. "You believe he has feelings for me other than those of brotherly friendship? What have you exposed me to?" And telling me with a surprising naïveté all that had passed between them, she gave me a detailed recital, every word of which made me tremble. As her brother, Synèse had received caresses and favors that must have made his situation as a lover delightful. He had had the cunning to persuade her that it was customary practice between brothers and sisters to give each other a thousand testimonies of an innocent tenderness, and in accordance with this principle he had accustomed her not only to live with him in the closest intimacy, but to endure the continual satisfaction of his passion through his exploitation of her charms. Her hands, her mouth, even her breast had been in effect the domain of the love-smitten Synèse. I extracted all these confessions from Théophé one after another, and I was reassured as to other fears only by the very sincerity with which I heard her confess all that she regretted having allowed. All my prudent intentions could not defend me from the bitterest feeling I had yet experienced. "Ah, Théophé!" I said, "you have no pity for the pain you cause me. I struggle violently to leave you mistress of your heart; but if you bestow it on another, your hard heart will cause my death."

I had never before spoken to her with such openness. She herself was so struck by it as to blush. And lowering her eyes, she said, "You will

not make me guilty of a fault that can only be attributed to my ignorance; and if you have the opinion of me that I wish to deserve, you
will never suspect me of doing for another what I have not done for
you." I did not answer her. The painful feeling that I still felt made me
thoughtful and taciturn. What was more, I saw nothing in Théophé's
answer that sufficiently satisfied my desires to congratulate myself on
having at last declared them. What had I to hope for if she remained
firm in her ideas of virtue, and what should I presume if she had forgotten them in Synèse's favor? As this reflection, or rather the indifference I believed I saw in her response, renewed all my uneasiness, I
left her, with an air less tender than melancholy, in order to go and rid
myself of Synèse.

He had come in from the garden; and when I gave orders for him to
be summoned, I learned that he was in my apartment. But I received
at the same time news from Constantinople that caused me much more
serious alarm for several of my closest friends. I was informed by an
express letter that the aga of the janissaries had been arrested the day
before, on some suspicions regarding nothing less than the life of the
Great Lord, and that the same fate was feared for the selictar and the
bostangi pashi, who were considered his best friends. My secretary,
from whom I received this news, added conjectures of his own. Given
the degree of power and authority which the bostangi pashi enjoyed in
the seraglio of the Great Lord, he doubted, he wrote to me, that anyone would risk undertaking anything against his person; but he was
all the more persuaded because of this that his friends would not be
spared, foremost among whom were the selictar, Chériber, Dély Azet,
Mahmouth Prelga, Montel Olizun, and several other lords with whom
I was, like him, on friendly terms. He then asked me if I would not
undertake something on their behalf, or at least offer them some assistance against the danger that threatened them. The only venture I
could undertake for them consisted in the appeals I could make to the
grand vizier; but if it were a question of state interest, I foresaw that
they would not be listened to very closely. There was more I could do
to give them immediate help. Beyond procuring them the means to
escape, which I could easily do, it was not difficult for me to perform
for some of them the same service that my predecessor had performed
for Muhammad Ostun, namely, to receive them secretly in my home
until the storm abated; and in a country where resentments dissipated
after their first heat, the danger is never great for those who are able
to avoid it in the beginning. However, as the duties of my employment did not always leave me the freedom to yield incautiously to the

impulses of friendship, I made the decision to return promptly to Constantinople to assure myself of the events with my own eyes.

But as I was reading my letters, I noticed Synèse, who was in fact waiting for me and whose timid countenance seemed to herald another confrontation. He anticipated the reproaches with which I was about to condemn him. Scarcely had he seen me finish my reading, than, throwing himself at my knees, with an air of humiliation that is common among the Greeks, he begged me to forget everything he had said about Théophé's birth and to permit him to live at Oru, more disposed than ever to recognize her as his sister. He did not understand, he added, what caprice had caused him to doubt for a moment a truth whose evidence he felt deep in his heart, and despite his father's injustice he was resolved to maintain publicly that Théophé was his sister. I had no difficulty seeing through the young Greek's cunning. Having derived no profit from his artifice, he wished to preserve at least the pleasures of which he was in possession. They did not cause him much remorse since he had enjoyed them for so long with the same tranquillity, and it was apparently in order to take them further that he had thought to rid himself of the inconvenient role of brother. But he saw all his hopes dashed by my answer. Without blaming him for his love, I told him that, as the truth was independent of his consent or his disavowal, it was not what he had said to me, nor the agility with which I saw him change his story, that would determine my ideas about the birth of his sister; but that I would draw from this a more infallible conclusion concerning the certainty of his own feelings; that in vain might the mouth retract when the heart had explained itself; and that to inform him in a word of what I thought of him, I regarded him as a coward, who had acknowledged himself as Théophé's brother, who had disavowed that title, and who thought to take it back for even more contemptible reasons than those of his father. I confess that I owed this sort of insult to my resentment. Then, forbidding him to reply, I called one of my servants, to whom I gave orders to take Synèse back to Constantinople forthwith. I left him, ignoring his distress; and remembering the permission I had given him to say his farewells to his sister, I retracted it, strictly prohibiting him from speaking to her before his departure.

Relying on my servants to carry out my orders, I immediately got back into my carriage, which I had had prepared after reading my letters, and I went to gather new information at home before undertaking anything on behalf of my friends. The crime of the head of the janissaries was that he had gone to see Ahmet, one of the brothers of the sultan Mustapha in his prison. The bostangi pashi was suspected of having facilitated this visit for him, and they were trying to extract the secret from the aga. As he had been on bad terms for some time with the grand vizier, no one doubted that this minister, interested in his demise, would attack him mercilessly; and what caused me the most distress was learning that Chériber had just been arrested with Dély Azet, for the sole reason that they had spent a part of the day preceding his crime in the aga's home. Had I considered only my friendship with Chériber, I would have gone to the grand vizier immediately. But as I did not hope for much effect from a vague solicitation, I thought I could serve my friend better by first seeing the selictar, with whom I could take more judicious measures. I went to his house. He had gone out, and the sadness that I saw there persuaded me that they were very alarmed by his absence. A slave in whom I knew he had confidence came and told me secretly that his master had left in great haste at the first news of Chériber's arrest, and he did not doubt that the selictar's friend's misfortune had convinced him to flee for his own protection. My response was that the selictar should not wait a moment to take this precaution if he still could, and I had no trouble instructing the slave to offer him, on my behalf, a refuge in my house at Oru, on the sole condition that he go there at night and without retinue. Besides the example of my predecessor, I had that of the pasha Rejanto, who had sealed his fate by giving refuge to Prince Demetrius Cantemir. Furthermore, it was not a question of hiding a criminal from punishment, but of safeguarding a gentleman from unjust suspicions.

However, since I had not completed the arrangements I wished to make for my friends, I decided to see several Turkish noblemen from whom I could at least hope for more information. The rumor was beginning to spread that the aga of the janissaries, after making his confession under torture, had lost his life to the hangman's noose. The fact that there had been a delay in arresting the selictar augured well for him, and I heard no other crime attributed to him besides his friendship with the aga. But Chériber and Dély Azet appeared to me so threatened by public opinion that, in the uneasiness that overwhelmed me for two of my best friends, I could hesitate no longer. I went to the grand vizier's house. It was not with hidden motives that I sought to have my recommendation heard as an affair of state. I emphasized only the tenderness of my friendship, and taking care to exclude the case in which my two friends might be charged with some fault of which I did not believe them capable, I entreated the vizier to grant some favor to my pleading. He listened to me with a serious air. "You must be persuaded," he said, "that the Great Lord's justice is not blind, and that it can distinguish between crime and innocence. Fear nothing for your friends if they have nothing with which to reproach themselves." He added that my recommendation would nevertheless not be without weight in the Porte, and he promised me that the two pashas would be made aware of it. But suddenly bursting into laughter, he told me that the selictar must believe it to be very powerful, since his fear had caused him to seek refuge in my house. I did not understand the meaning of this joke. He continued in the same tone, affecting even to praise my confusion and my silence, which he regarded as the effect of my discretion. But when I protested to him in the clearest terms that I did not know where the selictar had retired, he informed me that as he had set spies on his trail, he knew that the selictar had gone to my house at Oru the preceding night, with so little retinue that there seemed no doubt that it was in order to protect himself. "I do not believe he is guilty of anything," he added, "and I do not see his former relations with the aga of the janissaries as a crime. But I had judged it suitable to have him watched, and I am not sorry that he was frightened enough to become a little more circumspect in the choice of his friends." He gave me his word, after this speech, that he would not cause the selictar any distress in my house; but he made me promise to hide from him what he had told me, in order to let his uneasiness continue.

I still did not understand how the selictar could be at my house. I had left it in the middle of the day. How likely was it that he was there without my knowledge and that he had convinced my servants to hide his arrival from me? His passion for Théophé was the first idea that occurred to me. Would he think less of the safety of his life than the success of his love? And if it were true, I said to myself, that he had been hidden in my house since the previous night, was it likely that he was there without Théophé's collusion? One may form whatever idea one likes about the feelings I had for her. If I do not deserve to be described as her lover, let me be regarded as her keeper or her critic; but the least of these titles was enough to inspire me with a lively alarm. I thought only of returning to Oru. Upon arriving, I asked the first servant who appeared where the selictar was and how he happened to be in my house. It was the one whom I had charged with taking Synèse back. Although I was surprised to find him returned so soon, I thought this might have been possible, with a good deal of haste; and it was only after he assured me that the selictar was not in my house that I asked him how he had carried out my orders. It is hard to believe he did not display some sign of confusion in his response; but as I had no reason to mistrust him, I scarcely stopped to notice the manner in which he answered that he had returned Synèse to his father's house. However, I was equally mistaken on both questions; the only difference was that he was in good faith about the first and that in answering the second he had lied to hide from me a betrayal in which he was an accomplice. In a word, whereas I remained persuaded that the selictar had not come to my house and that Synèse had left it, they were both there, though I did not know it for several days.

Synèse had regarded the order to leave as his death sentence. Having only his own cleverness to avoid obeying, he had realized that my servants were not informed of my motives and that he could perhaps convince them to let him stay at Oru at least until my return. Then, fearing, as indeed happened, that I would return at the moment when I was least expected, he had been reduced to bribing handsomely the lackey I had ordered to take him away. I do not know with what excuse he had clothed his proposition; but after persuading my slave to fall in with his interests, he had pretended to leave with him, and they had both come back a few minutes afterward. Synèse had shut himself up in his room, and the lackey had reappeared in the house at the end of several hours, as though he had arrived from the city after performing his errand.

The selictar's venture was more complex. One will not have forgotten that Bema was little pleased with her condition and that, whether because she was irritated that I seemed to lack confidence in her or whether vanity alone made her feel deprived of the rank she deserved in my house, she regarded me as a foreigner who did not set enough store by her talents and whom she could serve only with reluctance. As the selictar's visits had been frequent, she could not help but perceive the feelings that brought him there. Her character, formed for intrigue by long experience of seraglios, was agreeable to a plan that might serve her revenge. She had taken an opportunity to speak to the selictar, and having offered him her services with Théophé, she persuaded him that his happiness depended on her. The hopes she had given him far surpassed the idea she had of them herself; for being quite aware of the terms I was on with Théophé, she could not think that it would be easy to obtain for the selictar what she knew had not been granted to me. But she relied on this very knowledge to nourish the weakness of a lover. After having confirmed his suspicion that I did not have an amorous relationship with my pupil, she claimed to know the inclinations and temperament of a girl of that age well enough to guarantee that she would not resist the taste of pleasure forever, and the promise she had made was based primarily on the hope of finding no resistance.

It is true that, given her continuous association with Théophé and her cleverness, moreover, in governing her sex, she was more formidable in this enterprise than the very passion on which all the selictar's hopes were based. However, despite her skill, her plan must not have been very advanced when the aga of the janissaries' disgrace filled the selictar's mind with distress. As all his fears could not diminish his passion, he had pressed Bema all the more, because, in the uncertainties to which he had at first abandoned himself, he had wondered whether he should not flee to the Christians with all that he could collect of his fortune, and he would willingly have sacrificed it in its entirety to be accompanied by Théophé in his flight. But Bema, the schemer, who had not dared to promise him so prompt a success, ventured to propose a refuge close to her mistress. My house was ordered in accordance with our customs; that is, not submitting to the Turks' customs for lodging women, they were distributed randomly in the bedrooms that my head steward had assigned to them. Bema's adjoined Théophé's apartment. It was this poor little room that she offered the selictar for his asylum. She stressed its security all the more because, as I myself did not know the service that was being given him in my house, he did not have to fear that my friendship would yield to politics or that I might fail, on the other hand, to be highly satisfied, after the danger passed, to have been of some use to my friend. It is far less strange that this thought should have come to the mind of a woman practiced in intrigue than it is strange that a man of the the selictar's rank should have approved of it. Thus, I found this event so extraordinary, after I discovered all its circumstances, that I would offer it as an example of the greatest follies of love if this motive had not been seconded in the selictar by the fear he felt for his life.

But I may add that the pride of the Turks is the first thing to disappear in adversity. As all their greatness is borrowed from that of their master, whose slaves they profess to be, there remains nothing of it in them at the slightest disgrace; and in most of them the motives of pride are quite weak when they are reduced to their own merit. However, I knew there were enough good qualities in the selictar to believe he was quite formidable in love, especially with a woman raised in the same country, whose taste, consequently, could not be offended by what we would find displeasing in a Turk. I did not mention to Théophé the reasons that had brought me back from Constantinople. On the contrary, being all the more free with her because I found myself in fact relieved of the burden that had weighed on my heart, I displayed such contentment during our conversation that she asked me the cause of my joy. This was an opportunity to playfully repeat what I had declared to her that morning in too sad and languorous a tone. But certain though it was that she reigned over my heart, it was just as uncertain what course I ought to allow my feelings to take; and finding my mind free again after being delivered of my fears, I had enough strength to repress the impulse to talk to her about my affection. Today, as I think about the past, I can perhaps judge my dispositions better than I could at the time; it seems what I secretly desired was that Théophé should acquire for me some part of the inclination that I had for her, or at least that she should let me see some signs of it; for I still deluded myself that I had a greater share of her affection than anyone else, but restrained by my principles of honor as much as by my promises, I would not have wished to owe the conquest of her heart to my seductions; and what I desired from her would only have brought me happiness had she appeared to wish it as I did.

Book Two

It was the most beautiful season of the year. As my garden held everything agreeable that one may imagine in a country estate, I proposed to Théophé to take the air there after supper. We walked around several times on the most beautiful paths. It was not so dark that I did not think I had noticed the figure of a man in various recesses. I supposed that it was my shadow, or one of my servants. In another place, I heard some foliage move, and as my mind was not inclined to mistrust, I imagined that it was the wind. It suddenly grew colder. The movement I had heard appeared to me the sign of a storm, and I urged Théophé to go on toward an arbor where we could take shelter. Bema followed us with another female slave. We sat down for a few minutes, and I thought I heard the sound of a slow step at a short distance from the arbor. I called out to Bema, of whom I asked a casual question merely to ascertain how far away she was. She was not on the same side where I had heard someone walking. I then began to suspect that we were being listened to, and not wishing to cause Théophé any fear, I stood up under some pretext in order to discover who was capable of this indiscretion. It did not yet occur to me that it could be anyone other than one of my servants. But as I did not see anyone, I calmly rejoined Théophé. Night was beginning to advance. We returned to her apartment without meeting anyone.

However, since I could not rid my imagination of the idea that I had heard someone near us, and as it was important to punish such boldness in my servants, I resolved, as I left Théophé, to linger for some time at the garden gate, which was not far from her apartment. My thought was to surprise the curious person who had followed us, when he retired. The gate was an iron grille, through which one had to pass. I was not there long before I distinguished a man coming toward me in the shadows; but he saw me as well, though it was impossible for him to recognize me, and turning back the way he had come, he thought only of regaining the woods from which he had emerged. My impatience caused me to follow in his tracks. I even raised my voice, to make him hear who I was, and I ordered him to stop. My order was not heeded. The resentment I felt at this was so keen that, adopting another course to enlighten myself forthwith, I returned to my house and gave orders that all my servants at Oru should be summoned. There were not many. I had seven, who appeared at the same moment. I became so confused I had to hide my motive for assembling them, and remembering the selictar again with all the suspicions that could accompany that idea, I was indignant at a betrayal that I could no longer doubt. It seemed clear to me that he had found lodgings in some house in the vicinity, whence he flattered himself he would come into my house during the night. But was it with Théophé's consent? This doubt, which immediately came to mind, plunged me into a mortal bitterness. I would have given orders to all my servants to go down to the garden had I not been restrained by another thought, which caused me to make a completely different decision. It was much more important to find out the selictar's intentions than to stop him. I reserved this task for myself. I sent away all my servants, including my valet, and, returning to the garden gate, I hid there more carefully than I had done the first time, in the hope of seeing the selictar come back before the end of the night. But, unfortunately, I only tired myself quite uselessly.

He had come back in while I was assembling my servants. Bema, who had taken him into the garden herself, had guessed my suspicions, and, leaving her mistress under some pretext, had brought him back promptly enough to conceal him from my searches. I spent all the following day in a distress I could not hide. I did not see even Théophé, and her uneasiness that evening over my health appeared to me a perfidy for which I was already seeking the means of revenge. To add to my disturbance, I received word at the end of the day that the pasha Chériber's life was in the utmost danger and that his friends, who already knew of the steps I had taken in his favor, were entreating me to see the grand vizier again to renew my solicitations. What an inconvenience at the start of a night when I was resolved to keep watch again at my garden gate and when I was already reveling in the confusion into which I intended to throw the selictar! However, there can be no wavering between the demands of passion and those of duty. The only compromise was to make the trip to Constantinople promptly enough to be back before the night was very far advanced. But as I estimated every minute of my trip, my utmost haste could not return me to my home before midnight; and who would guarantee that no one would take advantage of my absence?

Thus I came by degrees to reproach myself for having rejected Bema's advice; and in the urgent plight in which I found myself, I saw no other recourse but to appeal to her at least on this occasion. I sent for her. "Bema," I said, "I have been called to Constantinople for unavoidable business. I cannot leave Théophé to herself, and I feel the necessity of leaving her with a governess as loyal as you. Take upon yourself, if not my title, at least my authority, until I return. I entrust you with the care of her health and her conduct." Never has anyone surrendered himself so foolishly to treachery. However, that wretch confessed to me later, when circumstances forced her to be sincere, that had I not limited her commission and, instead of indicating that it would end when I returned, had given her the hope of preserving the same influence in my house all her life, she would have broken all her promises to the selictar and served me faithfully.

I went off extremely relieved; but my trip was useless to my two friends. I learned when I arrived at my house that the grand vizier had twice sent one of his principal officers, who had expressed much regret at not meeting me, and some rumors that had begun to spread quietly made me fear for the fate of the two pashas. This news, together with what I was told about the grand vizier, did not permit me to rest even for a moment. I went to the house of that minister, although it was at least ten o'clock, and taking as pretext my impatience to know what he desired of me, I sent to urge him, even though he was at the seraglio, to grant me a moment's talk. He did not make me wait long, but he cut short my visit and my laments by anticipating my speech. "I did not want," he said, "you to accuse me of having lacked regard for your recommendation; and if my officer had found you at your house, he was charged with informing you that the Grand Lord could not avoid exercising his justice on the two pashas. They were guilty."

Whatever interest I might have in justifying them, there remained nothing I could oppose to such a formal declaration. But, admitting that crimes of state do not deserve indulgence, I asked the grand vizier if those of Chériber and Azet were a mystery I ought not to know. He replied that their crime and their execution would be made public the next day and that it was a small enough favor to grant me to inform me of this a few hours earlier. Aurisan Muley, aga of the janissaries, angry for some time with the court, which had undertaken to diminish his authority, had proposed to put Prince Ahmet on the throne, the sultan's second brother, whom he had raised as a child and who had been locked up for the past few months in a dungeon, for some malicious remarks he had unwisely let slip against his brother. It had been necessary to find out what the inclinations of this prince were and to be in secret communication with him in his prison. The aga had succeeded in this with a shrewdness whose secret methods were not yet known, and this remained the only embarrassment to the minister. While yielding to the torture that had forced the confession of his crime, he had maintained an inviolable loyalty to his friends, and the vizier himself admitted that he could not refuse him his admiration; but his close ties with Chériber and Dély Azet, who had been successively the last two pashas of Egypt, had caused the council to decide on their arrest. Both of them possessed immense riches, and their reputations were still so powerful in Egypt that no one had doubted they were the principal foundations of the aga's undertaking. In fact, the fear of a cruel torture, which they could not have endured at their age, had forced them to admit that they had joined in the conspiracy and that the plan formed among the conspirators was to go to Egypt with Ahmet if they did not succeed in setting him on the throne at the first attempt. This admission did not prevent them from being made to suffer various torments, in order to extract from them the names of all their accomplices and to find out in particular if the bostangi pashi and the selictar were guilty. But whether they actually did not know or whether they prided themselves on the same constancy as the aga, they had persisted until their deaths in not charging them with any treason. "Four hours ago," the grand vizier told me, "you would have found them lying in my antechamber, for it was with me that they had their last talk, and the Grand Lord ordered that they be executed as they left me."

Whatever shock I felt at this recent catastrophe, a vestige of friendship for the selictar made me ask the minister if he was sufficiently vindicated to show himself without fear. "Listen," he said, "I like him and I am not at all inclined to distress him unnecessarily; but as his flight caused unfortunate prejudices in the council, I hope he will not reappear without first spreading some rumor to explain the mystery of his absence. And since he has chosen to retire to your home, keep him," he added, "until I send you notice." The vizier's confidence appeared to me a new favor, for which I thanked him; but as I did not in fact know that the selictar was in my house, I thought it in my own interests to disabuse him of his opinion, and I protested so naturally that, as I had just arrived from Oru, where I had spent the preceding night and all the day, I was sure no one had seen the selictar there, that he preferred to believe his spies had deceived him than to doubt my good faith even for a moment.

As my trip was cut quite short by this unfortunate outcome, I felt a perceptible joy in being able to return to Oru before the end of the night, and I expected to be there early enough to surprise the selictar in my garden. I was already planning the means by which I should not miss him. But when I returned to my house in Constantinople, I found my valet there, waiting for me with the utmost impatience; he begged me to hear him in private right away. "I come," he told me, "with news that will cause you as much astonishment as distress. Synèse is dying of a wound that he received from the selictar. Théophé is reduced to the same state by fright. Bema is a wretch, whom I believe to be the source of all the trouble and whom I have had locked up as a precaution until your arrival. I believe your presence is necessary at Oru," he continued, "if only to forestall the designs of the selictar, who cannot be far from your house and who may return there with enough forces to take control of it. The regret he expressed for his violence appeared quite suspicious to me. Alone as he was, I would have had him arrested had I not feared displeasing you. However," my valet added, "the care I took to put the rest of your servants in a state of defense ought to reassure you against his enterprises."

As so unforeseen an event hardly allowed me to be reassured, I left forthwith, bringing four well-armed servants with me. The disturbance in which I still found the people of Oru proved that nothing had been exaggerated. They were standing guard at my door, with a dozen rifles that I used for hunting. I asked for news of Théophé and Synèse, since I did not yet understand what had happened to them. My servants were as unaware as I that he had not left my house, and as no one knew how the selictar had gotten in, this scene became amusing because of the precautions they were taking to keep him from coming back into the house, whereas he had never left it. However, as the circumstances were explained to me more carefully, I learned from them all that they had been able to discover. Synèse's cries had attracted them to Théophé's apartment, where they had found the young man struggling with the selictar and already wounded from a dagger thrust that threatened his life. Bema seemed to be siding against him and was urging the selictar to punish him. The two men had been separated. The selictar had slipped away with great dexterity, and Synèse had remained bathed in his own blood, while Théophé, trembling and almost fainting, begged my servants not to lose a minute in notifying me.

The care she had taken to think of me touched me to the point of spurring me to go immediately to her apartment. I was even more reassured by the signs of joy she showed when she saw me appear. I went to her bed. She seized my hand, which she pressed between her own. "Heavens!" she said to me, with the emotion of a heart that appeared relieved, "what horrors have I witnessed during your absence! You would have found me dead of fear if you had been much later." The tone in which she uttered these few words seemed so natural and so tender that, feeling not only all my suspicions but also the attention that I owed to the situation vanish, I was tempted to surrender to the first sweetness that had yet encouraged my tenderness. However, I locked all my joy in my heart and contented myself with kissing Théophé's hands. "Tell me, then," I said to her with a rapture I could not prevent from affecting my words, "what to think of the horrors you are lamenting. Tell me how you can complain of them, when they took place in your room. What was the selictar doing here? What was Synèse doing? None of my servants knows. Will you give me an honest account of this?"

"These are the very fears," she told me, "that have most dismayed me. I foresaw that as you would find only obscurity in what you learned here, you would have difficulty exempting me from suspicion; but I swear to Heaven that I do not understand any better than you what has just happened. Scarcely had you left," she continued, "when, as I was thinking only of retiring, Bema came to say many things to me to which I paid little attention. She mocked me for the pleasure I take in reading and in the other exercises that fill my days. She talked to me about tenderness and the sweetness people find in the pleasures of love at my age. The hundred love stories she told me seemed like so many reproaches against me for not following such pleasurable examples. She tested my feelings with various questions; and as this eagerness, which I had never before seen in her, was beginning to become tiresome, I suffered all the more from the necessity of listening to her because she had let me know that you had given her some control over me and claimed to want it only to make me happy. When at last she left me, after having put me to bed, scarcely an instant had passed when I heard my door open softly...I recognized Synèse by the light of my candle. The sight of him caused me more surprise than fright, yet as I remembered everything you had told me, I would have shown some uneasiness had it not occurred to me that you might have pardoned him when you arrived in Constantinople and that you had perhaps sent him back to me with some orders with which you had entrusted him. I allowed him to approach. He began a speech which contained only laments over his fate and which I interrupted when it appeared certain that he had not been sent by you. In the midst of a thousand testimonies of his grief, he threw himself on his knees before my bed with much agitation. It was at this moment that Bema came in with the selictar. Do not ask me for details that I was too disturbed to notice clearly. I heard Bema's cries reproaching Synèse for his boldness and inciting the selictar to punish him for it. Both were armed. Synèse, threatened, prepared to defend himself. But having been wounded, he grabbed the selictar, and I saw the two daggers shining in the air in the efforts they both made to strike each other and fend each other off. The noise of their struggle, rather than my cries, as my fright had made them too feeble to be heard, alerted your servants; and the only thing I have been able to recollect since that moment, is that they went off at my pleading to hasten your return."

Her innocence was so clear in this tale that, regretting having suspected her, I endeavored on the contrary to deliver her from the vestige of fright that still appeared in her eyes. And perhaps in the midst of my lively declarations of affection, at which I believed I could see her softening, I would by slow degrees have obtained what I had given up asking of her, had not my own resolutions sustained me against my emotions. But my plan was formed; and I believe that, given my renewed sentiments, I would have been vexed to find her compliant, an attitude that would have lessened my esteem.

However, overlooking nothing that might flatter my heart, I derived enough satisfaction from this meeting to regard the obscurities that still remained as events which affected me less and which I would examine with a freer spirit. "Please remember," I said to Théophé in order to let her know some of my hopes, "that you have allowed me to glimpse today what I flatter myself I will some day discover more completely." She appeared uncertain of the meaning of this speech. "I have explained myself sufficiently," I went on, and I was in fact persuaded, as I left her, that she had feigned not to understand me. I immediately had Bema brought to me. This guileful slave hoped for some minutes to deceive me with falsehoods. She tried to persuade me that it was chance that had brought the selictar to my house at nightfall and that, having noticed at the moment she met him that Synèse was in Théophé's apartment, her zeal for the honor of my house had driven her to beg the lord to punish the bold young man whose actions were an insult to me. Having seen the selictar disappear before she had been seized, she deluded herself further that if she had not left my house altogether, he would secretly have returned to his place of refuge and that in either case she would have time to warn him of what she had invented for his defense. But I had been in Turkey long enough to know the rights a master has over his slaves, and as I saw no likelihood that the selictar would have left secretly if he had come into my house with innocent intentions, I resolved to employ the harshest means to shed light on the truth. The reasons that prompted my valet to lock Bema up had to make at least as much of an impression on me as they had on him. In a word, I mentioned torture to my slave, and as the tone she saw me take made her believe the threat was in earnest, she confessed to me, trembling, the whole of her intrigue.

When I had succeeded in finding out that the selictar had only seen Théophé under the circumstances of that night, I found in his adventure more reason to mock him for his bad luck than to take offense at his stay in my house. Bema dissipated even the slightest traces of my resentment by informing me of the main reasons that had induced her to make a mystery of it. But the circumstances that allowed me to excuse my friend were insufficient to exonerate her, and I told her I would soon determine the punishment she deserved for having betrayed my confidence. It was then that she took the Prophet as her witness that I would never have had any reproach to make against her had I trusted her fully. This frankness lessened my anger a great deal. I still needed to learn from her what had become of the selictar. She did not hesitate, telling me that she believed he had returned to his room; and to find this out, it would suffice to see if that door was closed. When it was clear that he was there from that sign, the only revenge I decided upon was to leave him there until hunger forced him to come out, and to have my valet guard at the door to receive him the moment he showed himself. Bema, whom I left in her prison, could not disrupt the satisfaction I promised myself from this scene.

Bema had had no information to give me concerning Synèse, since no one had been more shocked than she in surprising him in Théophé's apartment. But he caused me so little worry that, learning that his wound was in fact very dangerous, I ordered it to be looked after, and resumed seeing him when he began to recover. That he had not left my house, or that he had returned there after leaving, was due to the infidelity of one of my servants, which was not important enough to hasten me to punish it. And as soon as I was sure of Théophé's chastity, it mattered so little to me whether she was loved by that young Greek that I foresaw on the contrary that she could derive some advantage from this with respect to her father. This thought had not occurred to me at first; but as I considered it, in light of the last conversation I had had with him, I believed that if his passion remained as ardent as ever, it would give me an opportunity to test his father by feigning to wish to marry Synèse to Théophé. If Lord Condoidi had not lost all feeling of honor and religion along with that of nature, he would be forced to oppose this incestuous marriage; and in a country where the rights of fathers are not very extensive, I could compel him to make that objection alone in order to prevent it.

Thus, the incidents that had caused me such acute alarm had no consequences more vexatious than Synèse's wound and the punishment of a few servants. I rid myself of Bema a few days later, under humiliating circumstances for her, by selling her for only half of what she had cost me. This is a sort of punishment suited only to rich persons who are also good enough not to treat a guilty slave too harshly; but insofar as these wretches have any feelings, they are all the more affected because, as they lose a certain price that they have in their own eyes, they believe themselves debased even further, if one can say that this is possible, below their sad condition. I knew, nevertheless, that, having recommended herself afterward to the selictar, Bema had obtained some gratitude from this lord, who bought her for his seraglio.

As for him, I did not have the pleasure I had hoped in seeing him yield to thirst or hunger. That same night, understanding from the long delay on the part of his confidante that she had been detained despite herself and that he was going to find himself cruelly embarrassed without her help, he chose not to wait for daylight to leave his refuge, and, knowing my house, he flattered himself that he could easily escape under cover of darkness. He fell into the arms of my valet, who was already at his post. I was exposing that faithful boy to the risk of dying of a dagger wound; but as he had suspected this himself, he took care to adopt a tone gentle enough to make the selictar understand at once that he need fear no violence and could expect to receive my sympathy and assistance. He allowed himself to be led away, with some signs of mistrust. I was in bed. I got up eagerly, and feigning much surprise I cried, "What? It's the selictar! Well! How do you chance to..." He interrupted me with a confused air. "Spare me," he said, "the mockery

I deserve. Even your reproaches will be just if you direct them only at the nocturnal visit I tried to pay to Théophé; but in the use I made of my dagger, I thought only of serving you, although the care with which your servants rescued the young man I wounded made me think that my zeal was mistaken; and in the liberty I took to take refuge in your house without your knowledge, we must see only the embarrassment of a friend, who, in considering your house as a haven, did not wish to expose you to the displeasure of the Porte." I interrupted him in turn to assure him that I would spare him even his justifications and that with respect to Théophé I found nothing to condemn in his conduct except what could hurt him, namely, a behavior that did not seem to be in accord with the delicacy of feeling he had heretofore shown. He admitted he was wrong with regard to this reproach. "The opportunity," he said, "was stronger than my virtue." The rest of this conversation turned into banter. I assured him that the most vexatious effect of his adventure would be to be lodged more comfortably and treated with more care than what he had found in Bema's room, without being thereby exposed to the dangers that had forced him to hide. And telling him what I had learned from the grand vizier made him feel as much relief for himself as compassion for the fate of the aga of the janissaries and the two pashas. However, he protested that he pitied them less if they were guilty and that, far from having joined in their plot, he would have broken absolutely with them had he suspected them of it. He wanted to leave immediately, and he spoke to me of alerting two slaves who awaited his orders in the neighboring village. But I explained the precautions with which the grand vizier wished him to approach Constantinople. Among several choices he could make, he heeded my advice to go to his country house the following day, as though he were returning from a visit to the storehouses and arsenals on the Black Sea. I did not even refuse to accompany him, and in order to let him know not only that I harbored no resentment over what had happened and still had the same opinion of his character which had made me seek out his friendship, I proposed to include Théophé in our excursion.

He scarcely dared believe this offer was sincere; but I was in such good spirits that, having spent the rest of the night with him, I led him to Théophé's apartment myself to make her agree to our proposal. The impression that remained with me from the last conversation I had had with her made me in some sense superior to all the weaknesses of jealousy, and I was so sure that the selictar would never succeed in touching her heart that I considered the efforts he would uselessly repeat in trying to affect her as a sort of triumph. Besides, whatever success might be reserved for my sentiments, I did not want him ever to reproach me for having put the least obstacle in his way. I owed him this kindness after having perhaps contributed to the arousal of his feelings through the openness with which I had at first approved of them; and if it ever happened that Théophé acquired those feelings for me that I so desired, I would be very glad for my friend to lose hope completely before perceiving that I was more fortunate than he.

If Théophé showed some surprise at our plan, she made no objection to it when she was assured that I would be with her constantly and that it was only a matter of accompanying me. I provided her with a retinue that would give her a distinguished appearance at the selictar's home. He had told me that his house was the center of his power and his pleasures; namely, that along with all the ornaments that are to the taste of the Turks, it also had a seraglio and a prodigious number of slaves. I had heard him praise it, moreover, as the most beautiful spot in the environs of Constantinople. It was eight miles from my house. We did not reach it until evening, and I was deprived that day of the pleasure of the views, to which there is perhaps nothing comparable in any other spot in the world. But as the selictar immediately lavished all the richness and elegance of the buildings' interiors on us, I was obliged to agree from the first moment that I had seen nothing in France nor in Italy that surpassed this beautiful sight. I will not offer a description of it; those details are always dull in a book. But if I feared for a moment that I would soon regret involving Théophé in this trip, it was when the selictar, after having made her admire such magnificence, offered her absolute control over it, with all the privileges he had already proposed to her. I had difficulty hiding the blush that spread over my face despite myself. I cast my eyes on Théophé and awaited her answer with a disturbance she later confessed to have noticed. Protesting to the selictar that she was aware of the value of his offers and that she was as grateful for them as he might rightly expect, she told him that her feelings were the most curious assemblage in the world, and would not let her enjoy the advantages that ordinarily flatter a woman's vanity. Although the tone that accompanied her response seemed quite playful, she said things about wisdom and happiness to us that were so just and so sensible that I marveled at a speech I so little expected and asked myself with astonishment from what source she had drawn it. She might have concluded that the rest of her life was destined for the practice of the principles for which she confessed to be indebted to my instruction and for which she believed she owed me much more gratitude than for her freedom. During this speech, the embarrassment from which I had not been able to defend myself passed over the selictar's face. He bitterly lamented his fate; and turning to me, he entreated me to convey some part of that power which Théophé attributed to my remarks to him. I answered him, jesting, that his wish was not in keeping with his own intentions, since, assuming what he appeared to desire, he himself would be serving to confirm Théophé in her principles. Deep within me, my heart was brimming with joy, and no longer disguising my happiness from myself, I believed it to be more firmly established by this declaration than by all the reasons I already had to trust it. I stole a moment to congratulate Théophé on the nobility of her sentiments, and I took her response as further confirmation of my hopes.

The selictar, as afflicted as I was happy, ceaselessly offered us all that could do honor to his politeness and to the beauty of his house as attentively as before. He opened his seraglio to us that same evening, and his design was perhaps to tempt Théophé again by the sight of a charming place where she could hold sway. But if she was struck by anything there, it was neither the riches nor the charms that were offered on all sides. The recollection of the condition from which she had come was so vividly renewed in her memory that I saw her fall into a profound melancholy, which did not lift for several days. The very next day, she took advantage of the selictar's offer to allow us to return there without him as often as we might wish, to spend a part of the day there, conversing with the women whose appearance had touched her the most in the seraglio. The pleasure she appeared to take in such a long visit charmed the selictar, while I perhaps felt some alarm at it. But discretion having stopped me from going in with her, I watched for her to come out, in order to rejoin her. The air of sadness she brought away with her made me suppress my reproaches. I asked her, instead, what had caused this change in her mood. She proposed a walk around the garden, without having answered my question. Her continued silence was beginning to surprise me, when at last she answered with a deep sigh. "How varied are life's events!" she said with the moral turn that she gave naturally to all her reflections. "What links between things that do not resemble one another and that do not seem made to follow one another! I have just made a discovery that you see has impressed me and inspired ideas that I want to convey to you. But I must soften you beforehand by my tale.

"A strong interest," she continued, "which I could not prevent myself from taking in the lot of so many unfortunate women, and which you will find pardonable after my own misfortunes, caused me to question some of the selictar's slaves about the adventures that had brought them to the seraglio. Most of them are girls from Circassia or neighboring countries, who were raised for their condition and who do not feel the humiliation of their lot. But the one I have just this minute left is a foreigner, whose gentleness and modesty struck me even more than the brilliance of her appearance. I took her aside, praising her beauty and youth. She received the compliments sadly, and nothing appeared so surprising to me as her answer: 'Alas!' she said, 'far from extolling these wretched advantages, if you are capable of some pity, regard them as a tragic gift of Heaven, which makes me detest life's every moment.' I promised her more than pity, and offering her consolation, I pressed her to explain the cause of such a strange despair. She told me, after shedding some tears, that she was born in Sicily, of a father whose superstition cost her her freedom and honor. He was the son of a mother extremely defamed for her licentiousness, and the same star caused him to marry a woman who, after deceiving him for a long time with appearances of virtue, dishonored herself in the end through her overt debauchery. Having one daughter by her, who was the selictar's slave, he had promised Heaven to train her in the ways of chastity through an education so severe that she could restore his family's honor. He had shut her away in a manor he owned in the country when she was very young, in the charge of two old and virtuous women to whom he had advised, in communicating his intentions, not to let his daughter know that she was distinguished by any natural advantages, and never to speak to her about the beauty of women as something deserving of attention. With this charge, and an upbringing in which she continually practiced all of the virtues, she led, until the age of seventeen years, such an innocent life that nothing ever entered her mind or her heart contrary to the views of her father. She had sufficiently noticed, on the few occasions she had had to appear in public with her two governesses, that certain people's glances had fixed on her and that they had been taken hold of by some extraordinary sentiment upon seeing her. But never having made use of a mirror, and the two old women's continual removal of everything that could cause her to turn her reflections on herself, she had never entertained the least suspicion of her appearance. She was living in this simplicity when – her governess having brought in a merchant who traveled around the countryside selling jewels – chance alone caused her to gain possession of a little box that enclosed a mirror. Her innocence had been such that she imagined her face, which she saw represented there, was a portrait attached to the box, and not having been able to consider it without some pleasure, she had given the two old women time to notice this. The cry they had uttered and the reproaches they had hastened to make against her would have sufficed to blot out this idea if the merchant, who had understood the cause of their laments, had not taken a moment to approach the young Sicilian and had not secretly given her one of his mirrors, informing her of the wrong they were doing her in depriving her of it. She had accepted it out of a feeling of shyness rather than a desire to put it to a use she was still unaware of; but scarcely had she found herself alone than she needed no more than a moment to discover what it was. Even had she not been capable of sensing what nature had bestowed on her by herself, the comparison with the two old women whom she had ceaselessly before her eyes would have sufficed to make her notice to what degree the difference favored her. Soon she found so much enjoyment in contemplating herself ceaselessly, in arranging her hair and tidying her clothes, that, without knowing what these charms made her suitable for, she had begun to think that what caused her so much pleasure must inevitably please others.

During this time, the merchant, who had been quite delighted by his adventure, took pleasure in recounting it in all the places he passed. The description he added of the young Sicilian's charms excited the curiosity and desires of a Knight of Malta who had just taken the last oaths of his order with little disposition to observe them. Having made his way into the vicinity of the manor, he found the means to secretly send this young woman a mirror in a box, which was larger than the merchant's, containing the portrait of a very agreeable man opposite the mirror. He also sent a tender letter calculated to reveal everything that had been hidden from her with such care. The portrait, which was that of the knight, produced the intended effect, and the information in the letter was so useful that it served quite felicitously in removing many obstacles. The young woman, to whom her governesses had never spoken of men except as the instruments Heaven chose to render women suitable to the propagation of humankind, and who had accustomed her to respect the sanctity of marriage in advance, took care not to heed the knight's tender remarks without asking him if he thought of becoming her husband. He spared no promises once he understood how they could serve him, and putting forth some reasons of self-interest for keeping his commitments hidden, he succeeded within but a few days in deceiving the father's expectations and the governesses' vigilance. This commerce lasted a long time without any interference. But remorse, and her fear for the future, made the Sicilian girl more pressing about the execution of the promises she had exacted from him. It became impossible for the knight to conceal any longer that he was sworn to an order that forbade him to marry. They cried and lamented for several days. However, they sincerely loved each other. The most terrible fate would have been to leave one another. They allowed all other fears to yield to this one, and in order to forestall vexing consequences that could not be far off, they decided to leave Sicily and retire to some country under the domination of the Turks. The two lovers had nothing with which to reproach each other, for, both born to great fortunes, they made the same sacrifice to love.

Their intention to withdraw voluntarily among the Turks would have guaranteed them slavery had they been able to carry it out. But having embarked on a Venetian vessel with the aim of getting off in Dalmatia, whence they believed they would easily penetrate further, they had the misfortune to be captured at the entrance to the gulf by some Turkish vessels that were seeking to provoke the state of Venice. The explanation of their plan was interpreted as guile. They were sold separately in a Morean port, whence the unhappy Sicilian woman was removed to Constantinople. If it was the height of misfortune to see her lover taken away, by what name ought she to call the situation into which she soon passed! Her continual tears having somewhat disfigured her, the merchants of Constantinople did not at once notice her beauty. An old woman, whose discernment was surer, used part of her property to buy her and promised herself to double it when she sold her again. But this was the worst disaster that could have befallen the Sicilian. Given the principles of modesty and decency in which she had been raised, the duties that this odious mistress performed in order to increase her charms and make her more suited to the taste of the Turks were so many forms of torture that she would have found death less cruel. Finally, she was sold for a large sum to the selictar, who had at first shown her a good deal of affection but who neglected her after having satisfied his desires, as he became disgusted by her profound sadness and continual tears.

The adventures of this sad stranger had caused Théophé only surprise. What filled her with compassion was to see her suffering a fate, the infamy of which she felt, and to have discovered in her so much shame and grief that she had not been able to distinguish which afflicted her more, the loss of her honor or that of her lover. I was so accustomed to these sorts of things from the tales I heard every day that I had not listened to Théophé's story with all the signs of pity she had expected. "You do not seem sensitive," she said to me, "to what I thought capable of touching you as much as me. You do not find, then, that this girl deserves the interest that I take in her unhappiness?" "I find she is to be pitied," I answered, "but much less than if she had not brought her misfortunes down upon herself by a voluntary fault. And that is the difference," I added, "that one must point out between your story and hers. Perhaps you are the only example of an innocent unhappiness of the same kind and the only person of your sex who, after having been dragged down into the abyss without knowing it, has changed her inclination in the name of and at the first notion of virtue. And that," I continued with passion, "is what makes you so admirable in my eyes that I think you are superior to all other women in the world." Théophé shook her head, smiling with great gentleness; and without responding to that which concerned her, she insisted on the feelings of the Sicilian, whose freedom she felt merited some action on our part. "It suffices that you desire it," I told her, "to make it a law for me, and I do not even wish you to be under this obligation to the selictar." He came to join us just as I was promising to talk to him about it that same day. I did not postpone my request further. And drawing him aside, as though I wanted to keep it a secret from Théophé, I asked him frankly if he was attached enough to the Sicilian girl to find some difficulty in sacrificing her to me. "She is yours as of this moment," he said; and when I talked about price with him, he rejected my entreaties as so many insults. I even judged from his joy that, aside from the satisfaction of obliging me, he imagined that this would be another inducement for me to serve him with respect to Théophé, besides the fact that my example might have some influence in causing her to think about pleasure. But in granting me the freedom to open the door of the seraglio to his slave, he informed me of a circumstance that she had hidden from Théophé. "I believed her at first," he told me, "to be solely afflicted by the loss of her freedom, and I took great pains to make her find consolation in her lot; but by chance I discovered that she was enamored of a young slave of her nation, who had had the cunning to introduce a letter into my seraglio and whom I chose not to punish out of consideration for his master, who is one of my friends. I do not know the origin of this liaison, and I confined myself to redoubling the diligence of my servants to safeguard my house from this licentiousness. But I took the opportunity to temper my feelings for my Sicilian, in whom I had seen, moreover, many charms." This warning, which the selictar believed he owed to our friendship, would have been quite a just precaution had I been filled with the feelings he attributed to me. But as I took no other interest in this than that of pleasing Théophé, I happily imagined, on the contrary, that the young slave of whom the selictar was complaining could only be the Sicilian knight, and I foresaw that I would soon find myself obliged to deliver him, too, from his chains. I nevertheless waited until I was alone with Théophé to inform her that the Sicilian girl belonged to us. She was so charmed to hear me add that I believed the knight was not far off, and that I proposed to return him to his lover, that she thanked me for it on their behalf with an extraordinary ardor. As I related everything to my own intentions, I did not doubt that the interest she was taking in the lovers' happiness was yet another sign that her heart had become sensitive, and from it I drew good omens for myself, which I thought better founded than those of the selictar.

The Sicilian was called Maria Rezati, and the name she had taken or that she had been given in slavery was Molene. I did not judge it fitting that she be informed of what I had done for her before the day of our departure. I only advised Théophé to tell her in a general way to expect a happiness she had not dared hoped for. As the news the selictar received from Constantinople had succeeded in reassuring him, I found myself recalled to the city by my own affairs, and I proposed to Théophé that we return to Oru. But quite apart from the vexation I had at not being able to prevent the selictar from accompanying us on our return, I had to endure an embarrassing scene as we left his house with him. The Sicilian knight, who was in fact a slave in the vicinity, had enough freedom during the day to steal a few hours from the exercises of his condition, which he employed in observing the selictar's gates. The danger he had been exposed to by another slave's betrayal had so little cooled his ardor that he had attempted a thousand times to make more overtures with the same danger. We left toward the middle of the day in a large calesh that I used for the country. He was twenty paces from the gate, from which he saw several of my servants emerge on horseback, assembling in order to await me. The French attire having struck him, he asked them in our language, which he spoke with fair facility, to whom they belonged.

I do not know what plan he might have formed upon their answer; but scarcely had he received it than, seeing my carriage advance, containing myself, the selictar, and the two ladies, he easily recognized his mistress. Nothing could have tempered his ecstasy. He threw himself at my door, where he remained hanging despite the lively pace of six powerful horses, calling me by my name and entreating me to grant him a moment to explain himself. His agitation had caused him to lose his breath, and in the efforts he made to hold himself up and to make himself heard, one would have taken him for a madman devolving some fatal design. We did not notice that Maria Rezati, or Molene, had fainted at our side. But the selictar's servants, who were following with his teams, seeing a slave who appeared to lack respect for their master and for me, came rushing up imperiously and violently forced him to leave my carriage door. Suspecting the truth, I shouted to the postilion to stop. At last he reined in his horses. I restrained the selictar's servants, who were mistreating the young slave, and I ordered them to let him approach. The selictar understood nothing of this scene, nor of the attention I was giving to it. But the knight's explanations soon gave him the information that I had already. This unhappy young man forced himself to regain his breath, and unaffectedly adopting the air that suited his birth, he addressed a speech to me that I would endeavor in vain to make as touching as it seemed when he uttered it. After having told me his story and that of his mistress in a few words, he noticed as he gestured to her that she was motionless beside me. "Ah! You see her," he cried, interrupting himself with new agitation, "she is dying. Take care of her. Alas! She is dying," he went on, "and you are not helping her!"

It was not difficult to revive her. Joy serves only to restore strength when it has not entirely smothered it in the first moment. She turned to Théophé: "It is he," she cried, "Ah! It is the knight, the very same." I had no need of this confirmation to know what to think. After consoling the young slave, I asked the selictar if he was on good enough terms with the knight's master to guarantee that his absence would have no ill consequences. He assured me that he was one of his best friends; and out of a politeness that I admired in Turkey, when I declared the desire I had to take the knight to Oru, he dispatched one of his servants to entreat his friend, who was a general officer, to allow him to use his slave for a few days. "I foresee," he said to me after having given this order, "that you will have further use for me; but in anticipating you by offering my services, I assure you that what is refused me by Nady Emir will not be granted to anyone." We had some horses on lead ropes and I ordered one to be given to the knight, who could hardly contain his joy. However, he was able to control its outward signs, and aware of what his attire and his situation still obliged him to, he also abstained both from approaching his mistress and from using a tone other than that which was appropriate to his unfortunate station.

During the rest of the journey, I could not avoid confessing to the selictar that it was the desire to do service to these unfortunate lovers that had prompted me to ask him for Molene's freedom, and I accepted his offer to act as intermediary in obtaining the young knight's from

Nady Emir as well. Théophé further excited his zeal by showing a lively interest in it. We arrived at Oru. The knight slipped away while we were descending from our carriage; but a moment later he sent to request a private interview, and the favor he asked me on his knees, as he called me his father and his savior, was to permit him immediately to change his clothing. Although the slightest change in attire was a crime for a slave, I did not believe it dangerous for him under the circumstances. He appeared several minutes later in a state that altered his manners as much as his appearance; and knowing already that his mistress was free, or that she no longer had any other master than me, he asked me for permission to embrace her. This scene moved us even more. I renewed the request I had made in his favor to the selictar, and although I had no particular relationship with Nady Emir, I counted on the consideration in which the Turks held me to believe I would succeed with him.

The obstinacy that the selictar had had in wishing to accompany us forced me to contain my sentiments, which, I confess at last, would have been impossible to augment. Along with the certainty of a constant chastity in the lovable Théophé, I believed I could also be certain that I had won her heart, and I had resolved to explain myself so openly to her that she would no longer have to struggle against her shyness, which I now regarded as the only obstacle between us. But I wanted to be free for such a great undertaking. The selictar had counted on our returning together to Constantinople. I exaggerated the importance of the affairs that called me back there, in order to make him consent to an immediate departure. The knight was coming with us. Aside from the reasons pertaining to his freedom, I had another reason for not leaving him at Oru in my absence; or at least I had to make up my mind about a perplexing problem. As there was little likelihood that he would think of returning to Sicily with his mistress, and as it was still less likely that he could be with her again without falling back into all the intimacies of love, I considered whether it was suitable to allow such a free commerce in my house. My principles were not more severe than those governing any ordinary courtship, and I did not claim to regard it as a crime if the two lovers made themselves as happy as I would have liked to be with Théophé; but if the passion of the age sometimes causes one to forget the laws of religion, one preserves moral decency as a check, and I was no less tied by propriety, which imposed a thousand duties on me in my employment. This scruple would have caused me to make distressing decisions for the knight had he not relieved me of this as we arrived in Constantinople. He told me that after the service I was going to render him, he planned to go to Sicily, not only to put himself in a position to repay me the cost of his freedom, but to find out if there was any hope of being relieved of his vows. His unhappiness had caused his feelings to mature. He considered Maria Rezati an only child whose conduct and fortune he had ruined. Along with a thousand qualities he had not ceased to love, which even the seraglio had not made distasteful to him, she had enough property to satisfy his ambition. All these reflections, which he communicated to me with a good deal of tranquillity and wisdom, determined him to spare nothing to procure the freedom to marry her.

I praised his intentions, although I foresaw difficulties that did not seem to dismay him. The selictar immediately saw Nady Emir, who had returned to the city. He obtained the knight from him as easily as he had flattered himself he would. But although his generosity still led him to give him to me unconditionally, I was so certain I would be reimbursed that I made him accept a thousand sequins, which he had paid to Nady. After what the young Sicilian had told me of his feelings, I did not hesitate to send him back to his mistress. He proposed only to bid her farewell, and in his ardor to undertake a voyage that promised him such happiness, I could scarcely persuade him to take a few days rest at Oru. However, I found him there two days later, and my astonishment at learning that he had changed his mind was extreme. I did not immediately understand this mystery, and I merely asked him what intentions he was substituting for those he had abandoned. He told me that after many new reflections on the difficulty of succeeding in his first plan, and the risks he would run of being grieved either by his order or by the Rezati family, he had returned to his original idea of establishing himself in Turkey; that he had some good opportunities in the area of Morea; that he would still marry his mistress, because in giving up the profession of Knight of Malta, he did not believe himself obliged to fulfill the duties of a state whose advantages he was abandoning; and, lastly, that, as he had not touched a considerable sum that he had taken in bills of exchange for Ragusa and had left in kind with a banker in Messina, he counted on finding himself rich enough to give me back the sum I had paid to the selictar and to lead a simple life in the country where he wanted to establish himself. He added that his mistress was the daughter of a very rich father, who would not live forever, and that as she could not lose her natural rights to this inheritance, she would sooner or later derive from it more than they both desired to make their lives very easy and to leave something to their children, if Heaven chose to grant them any.

A plan so quickly conceived appeared to me too well arranged for me not to suspect that it resulted from some extraordinary incident. I nonetheless would never have suspected that it came from Synèse. The knight had not been able to spend two days in Oru without learning that the young Greek was there with a dangerous wound. He had visited him out of politeness and, having found him agreeable, had formed a friendship with him right away, even telling him about his adventures. The difficulty his marriage plans were presenting had inspired this wonderful plan in Synèse, which he imagined would also have advantages for himself. He had offered the knight a refuge on his father's land, and revealing in turn the torments of his own heart, they had come, in an exchange of confidences, to the conclusion that Théophé, out of tenderness or out of selfish interest, would agree to go with them. They were quite far from having obtained her consent, and Synèse had warned his friend about the delicacy of that negotiation; they flattered themselves that with the help of Maria Rezati, who had joined ardently in this glorious plan, they would make her understand that, whether she was the daughter of Paniota Condoidi or whether she fell in love with Synèse, she could hope for no happier future for a girl of the same country.

Although the knight had left me with feelings of mistrust, they were so little directed toward Synèse and toward my own interests that, not wishing to penetrate further than he wished into his own, I made no objection to his design. "The price of your freedom," I told him, "is not such that it should cause you any distress, and I would not regret a larger sum if it could contribute to your happiness." However, I imagined that what was behind this new intrigue would not have escaped Théophé. I burned, moreover, with the desire to see her again. My impatience was so lively that the three days that I was obliged to spend in the city seemed mortally long; and after serious consideration of the state of my heart, I felt some confusion at having allowed it to take such ascendancy over me. But having abandoned myself to a passion from which I hoped for all the sweetness of my life, I disregarded everything that might diminish the force of this delicious feeling.

I went into Théophé's apartment with the resolution not to leave it without having made a firm agreement with her. There I found Maria Rezati. What a dreadful constraint! They had become attached to each other by a strong affection, and the Sicilian, unable to imagine that Théophé had any other bond with me than that of love, had already ventured several remarks about the happiness of a commerce as tranquil as she thought ours must be. This language had displeased Théophé. Scarcely had she received my first polite gestures than she addressed her companion. "Given the mistake you have made," she said to her, "you will be surprised to learn from Monsieur that I owe nothing to his love, and that, having showered me with kindnesses, I am indebted to his generosity alone." They both appeared to be awaiting my answer. I misunderstood the subject of their conversation; and following only the truth of my sentiments, I answered that indeed beauty had never inspired me with love and I had consulted only the impulses of my admiration in the first services that I had performed for her. "But so little time is needed to come to know you," I went on, casting a passionate look at her, "and once one has discovered what you are worth, it is so necessary to devote all of one's tenderness to you." Théophé, aware of the direction in which my speech was taking me, interrupted it adroitly. "In truth, I am flattered," she said, "that your favors have allowed you to acquire some feelings of friendship for me; and this is a possession I find so precious that it will stand forever in the stead of fortune and pleasure." She immediately changed the subject of the conversation. I was left in an uncertainty that caused a much stranger alteration in my mood. But as I could not endure the pain of the situation for long, I made a decision that will appear childish to anyone but a lover.

I went alone into Théophé's small room, and feeling only too well how my hopes had ebbed, I made use of a pen in order not to postpone further what I knew my tongue could not express in circumstances that had just filled me with such fear and bitterness. I wrote in a few lines all that a heart brimming with esteem and love can employ that is most acute and most touching to convince another of its tenderness; and although there was nothing obscure in my words, I repeated, in closing, in order to be perfectly clear, that I was not speaking of friendship, which was a feeling too cold for the transports of my heart, and that I would devote myself to love for my entire life. I added nevertheless that, having been able to regulate my love until now with a moderation to which anyone could readily testify, I wanted it to continue to depend on the desire of the one I loved; and that, aspiring only to the return of hers, I left to her the choice of signs.

I returned with a calmer air after having relieved myself by this confidence, and I coolly asked Théophé to go alone into her room. She remained there a few moments. Reappearing with a very serious countenance, she entreated me to return to the place from which she had just emerged. Below my note, I found one in her hand. It was so short, and of such an extraordinary nature, that I have not been able to forget it. A wretched creature, she said to me, who had learned the name of honor and virtue from me and who had not yet succeeded in finding out that of her father, the slave of the governor of Patras and of Chériber, did not feel she was suited to inspire in me anything but pity; thus, she could not recognize herself as the object of my other feelings. A very lively exclamation escaped me as I read this strange answer. The fear that some accident had happened caused her to run to the door of the room. I put out my arms to her, to invite her to receive my explanations; but although she saw this impassioned gesture, she returned to her companion, after having assured herself that she had nothing to fear for my health. I remained prey to the most violent agitations. However, unable to abandon my hopes, I took up the pen again to efface the horrible portrait that she had drawn of herself, and I drew another that represented her instead with all the perfections with which nature had embellished her. "This is what I love," I added, "and its features are so deeply engraved in my heart that it is not capable of mistaking them." I stood up, returned to her side, and proposed again that she return to the small room. She smiled, and she asked me to give her more time to examine what I had left there.

This answer consoled me. I withdrew, nevertheless, to allow my remaining agitation to dissipate. It seemed so surprising to me that I needed to take such precautions to explain my feelings to a girl whom I had taken from the arms of a Turk, and who in the first days of her freedom would perhaps have thought herself all too happy to have come suddenly into mine. In the very midst of the affection with which I was pleasantly intoxicated, I reproached myself for a timidity that suited neither my age nor my experience. But beyond some secret remorse, against which I could not defend myself, remembering the principles of chastity I had explained to Théophé a thousand times and the fear of making myself despicable in her eyes by a passion whose fulfillment could only mean, after all, the ruin of the virtuous sentiments I had helped inspire in her, I would have to give a fair idea of her person in order to make it clear that her appearance, designed only to inflame a heart, became for that very reason most capable of imposing fear and respect. Instead of finding in it the ease that so many charms made one desire and so many graces seemed to promise, one was not only stopped by the fear of displeasing, which is an ordinary feeling in love, but indeed deterred by the decency, the honesty, by the air and the language of all the virtues, which one did not expect to find behind such seductive appearances. Time and time again, given the principles of uprightness and honor that were natural to me, I had to force myself to give free rein to Théophé's virtuous inclinations; but carried away by a

passion that my silence and my moderation had continually strengthened, I went back to promising Heaven to contain myself within the
confines I had imposed on myself, and I believed I was wise to continue
in my resolution to ask of Théophé only what she would be readily disposed to grant me. I spent the remainder of the day calmly enough, in
the expectation of the new response that she had wished to be given
the time to contemplate, and I did not seek the opportunity to speak
to her in private. She appeared to avoid this as well. I even noticed in
her eyes an embarrassment that I had never seen there before.

The next day, as I was arising, one of the slaves who served her brought
me a carefully sealed letter. How eager I was to read it! But into what
despondency I immediately fell, on finding in it an absolute condemnation that seemed to wrest from me even the slightest hope! This terrible letter, which Théophé had spent all night composing, would have
been reported here in its entirety if, for reasons which will follow later
and which I cannot recall without grief and shame, I had not torn it
up in frightful vexation. But the first sentiments it caused in me were
only sadness and consternation. In it, Théophé retraced all the circumstances of her history, that is, her misfortunes, her faults, and my kindnesses. And arguing with more force and precision than I had ever seen
in our best books, she concluded that it was not fitting for her, who
had to repair as many mistakes as misfortunes, to engage in a passion that
was likely only to renew them; nor for me, who had been her teacher
in virtue, to abuse the just influence I had over her and the very inclination she felt to love me, in order to destroy sentiments that she owed
as much to my counsels as to her own efforts. If, nevertheless, she were
ever able to forget these obligations, the extent of which she was only
beginning to realize, she protested that I was the only one who could
make her succumb to this weakness. But for the sake of that confession itself, which she attributed to the inclination of her heart, she
entreated me not to renew declarations and attentions whose danger
she sensed; or if her presence was as disturbing to my repose as she
believed it to be, she requested I grant her the freedom to carry out
her earlier plan, which had been to withdraw to some quiet place in
one of the Christian countries, so as not to have to reproach herself for
ruining the happiness of a teacher and a father to whom she owed the
sacrifice of her own contentment at the very least.

I am abridging the ideas that have remained with me from this letter, because I would despair of giving them all the grace and force they
had in their natural expression. At the age I am as I write these memoirs, I must confess with some embarrassment that I did not at first see

these sensible reflections in the favorable light of virtue. Seeing in them, on the contrary, only the ruin of all my desires, I abandoned myself to regret at having given a girl of seventeen such powerful weapons to use against me. "Was it up to me," I said to myself bitterly, "to play the preacher and catechist? How ridiculous for a man of my station and my age! I should have been sure of finding the remedy I needed for myself in my maxims. I should have been convinced of all that I preached, in order to make it my own rule. Is it not wretched that, given as I am to the pleasures of the senses, I have undertaken to make a girl chaste and virtuous? Oh, I am well punished for it!" And yet even beyond the disorder of my ideas, I recalled all my conduct in order to justify in some way the folly of which I accused myself. "But is it my fault?" I added. "What did I actually teach her that was so likely to inspire her with this rigorous virtue? I showed her the infamy of love as it is practiced in Turkey; this ease with which women yield to the desires of men, the coarseness of pleasures, the ignorance of all that may be called taste and feeling; but did I ever think to give her an aversion to honest love, to an orderly commerce, which is the sweetest of all possessions and the greatest advantage that a woman can draw from her beauty? It is she who is mistaken and who has misunderstood me. I wished to warn her of this; my honor obliged me to do so. It would be too ridiculous for a man of the world to have urged upon a girl of this merit principles that are fit only for the cloister.

Far from easily renouncing these first ideas, it occurred to me that my main fault was to have given Théophé several works on morality whose principles, as happens in most books, were extremely strict and could have been taken too literally by a girl contemplating them for the first time. As soon as she began to know enough of our language to read our authors, I had given her Nicole's *Essais*, for the sole reason that, seeing her naturally given to thinking and reflecting, I had wanted to introduce her to a man who reasoned constantly. She had read him assiduously. *La Logique de Port-Royal* was another book that I had thought suitable to forming her judgment. She had read it with the same application and the same pleasure. I imagined that works of this nature had possibly caused more harm than good in a lively imagination and that, in a word, they had done nothing but spoil her mind. This thought made my own mind a little calmer, since I could easily procure other books for her whose effect I hoped would soon be quite the opposite. My library was furnished with books of all sorts. I did not intend for her to read dissolute books, but our good novels, our poetry, our dramatic works, even a few books of morality, whose authors were on good terms with the desires of the heart and the ways of the world, appeared capable of bringing Théophé back to less fierce principles; and I derived so much consolation from my plan that I had the strength to compose my face and my sentiments as I rejoined her. The occasion presented itself to talk to her alone. I could not help showing her some distress at her letter, but it was moderate; and, displaying more admiration for her virtue than regret at seeing myself rebuffed, I spoke of her resistance to my attentions only as a motive to induce me to struggle against my passion.

I immediately directed my remarks to the progress of her studies, and extolling some new books I had received from France, I promised to send them to her in the afternoon. Less temperate than I affected to be, she expressed her joy in transports of emotion. She took my hand, which she pressed against her lips. "So, I have found my father again!" she said to me. "I have regained my fortune, my happiness, and all that I hoped for in surrendering myself to his generous friendship. Ah! What fate could be happier than mine?" This effusion of feelings touched me to the bottom of my heart. I could not resist it; and leaving her without adding a single word, I withdrew to my room, where I abandoned myself for a long time to the disturbance that dominated all my reflections.

"How sincere she is! How naive she is! O gods, how lovable she is!" A thousand other exclamations escaped me before I was able to order my thoughts. However, it was virtue itself that had appeared to express itself through her mouth. My scruples were the first emotions that arose in my heart. "Would I, then, sacrifice such virtue to an immoderate passion!" My books were facing me. I cast my eyes on those I had proposed to give to Théophé. They were *Cléopâtre*, *The Princess of Clèves*, and so on. "Will I fill her imagination with a thousand chimeras from which her reason can gather no fruit? Supposing she takes some tender sentiments from them, will I be well satisfied to owe them to fictions, which can awaken the sentiments of nature in a heart naturally disposed to tenderness, but which will not make the happiness of mine, if I owe them only to my artifice? I know her. She will go back to her Nicole, to her *Art de penser*, and I will have the grief of seeing the illusion dissipated no sooner than I am able to inspire it; or, if she is constant, I will find only an imperfect happiness in a love that I will ceaselessly attribute to motives in which I do not play the least part."

Through thoughts of this nature I succeeded somewhat in calming the emotions that had agitated me. "Let me see," I resumed more tranquilly, "how far reason can take me. I have two difficulties to overcome, and I must choose one or the other to combat. I must either master my passion or triumph over Théophé's resistance. In which direction will I turn my efforts? Is it not more just that I turn them against myself and seek to procure for myself a peace of mind that assures Théophé's at the same time? Her inclination disposes her to love me, she says; but she has repressed it. What can I expect from her love? And if I seek her best interest and mine, will we not both do better to confine ourselves to simple friendship?

This truly was the wisest thing I could think; but I deluded myself that I was as much master of my heart as of my conduct. If I forthwith renounced the desire to employ other means than my attentions to touch Théophé's heart, and if I imposed stricter laws than ever upon myself in the unavoidable familiarity in which I lived with her, I still preserved, for all that, the arrow that I carried in the depths of my heart. Thus, the most interesting part of my life, namely the domestic details of my house, was to become a perpetual struggle for me. I sensed it from the first moment, and I blindly surrendered myself to this sort of torture. How far was I, nevertheless, from foreseeing the torments I was preparing for myself!

Synèse, whom I had not yet seen since he was wounded, and who was beginning to recover, now sent one of my servants, who came to interrupt my sad meditations to offer me his apologies. I had neglected him since his adventure, and finding that I was not strongly offended by the enterprises of a lover, I had contented myself with giving orders that he be cared for and sent back to his father's home after his recovery. But the submissiveness he showed me disposed me so well toward him that, informing myself more particularly as to his health, I had myself taken to his room, which I was told he could not yet leave. He would have entered the bowels of the earth had it opened, to hide himself from my gaze. I reassured him with my first words, and I asked him only to tell me of his intentions, of which, I added, I already knew the better part. This request was ambiguous, although my thoughts went no further than the visit he had paid Théophé. I saw him tremble with shock, and, as his embarrassment gave rise to suspicions that had not occurred to me earlier, I increased it by redoubling my entreaties. He made an effort to get up, and when I forced him to remain where he was, he begged me to take pity on an unfortunate young man who had never meant to offend me. I listened with a severe demeanor. He told me that he was still prepared to recognize Théophé as his sister and that he would be more ardent than his brothers in giving her this title should his father decide to explain himself; but that in truth, as he did not see enough certainty in her birth to pay much heed to this idea, he had yielded to other feelings, which could become as advantageous to Théophé as the revelation of her birth and some slight part of Condoidi's inheritance. In a word, he was offering to marry her. He said that, despite the law of his family, which guaranteed all his father's lands to his eldest brother, he was not without property from his mother's side; and with this in mind he had not thought he lacked respect for me in postponing his return to Constantinople by several days, in order to find the opportunity to declare his feelings to Théophé. He dared hope, on the contrary, that I would deign to approve them; with respect to the offers he had made to the knight, he had always supposed that they would not be executed without my consent. And explaining the plan for settling in Morea to me, he commendably and sincerely declared all that he feared I would learn another way.

As I coolly examined his remarks and his intentions, I found him less guilty than thoughtless and imprudent not to see that, because of the opinion he had of Théophé's birth, his proposal of marriage absolutely demanded that such an important problem be perfectly elucidated. Nor could I consider it a crime that he had tried to steal a heart from me when he did not know my claims to it. Thus, far from frightening him with reproaches, I limited myself to making him aware of the childishness of his plan. But what he undoubtedly did not hope for after this reflection was my promise to make a new attempt with his father to shed light on Théophé's birth, and I urged him to recover promptly so that he would be able to take me to Lord Condoidi, to whom I did not want to explain myself except in Synèse's presence. This promise and the air of goodness with which I took care to accompany it had more effect on his recovery than any other cure.

I did not promise anything that I was not resolved to do, but it was not Synèse whom I thought to serve. All my intentions served Théophé's advantage. The occasion could not be more favorable for testing Condoidi with the fear of his son's marriage. I had already formed this plan, and I still dare not confess what my heart dared hope from this. After a few days, which Synèse in his impatience found too long, he came to tell me that he believed he had recovered enough to return to the city. "Bring your father to me, then," I said, "but take care that he does not suspect the reasons that make me wish to see him." They came to Oru that evening. I gave a suitable welcome to Lord Condoidi, and immediately referring to the motive I had had in sending his son to fetch him, I said, "What risk have you exposed us to, and, if by chance I had not discovered Synèse's intentions, what misdeed would you have made us guilty of? He is resolved to marry Théophé. See if you are willing to suffer this marriage." The old man appeared a little disconcerted at first. But recovering right away, he thanked me for having put a halt to his son's bold inclinations. "I intend a match for him," he added, "that will suit his fortune better than a girl whose one advantage is the honor you bestow on her by your protection." I was insistent, pointing out that he would perhaps not always be able to oppose a young man's ardent passion. He replied coldly that he had infallible means for doing so, and sending our conversation in another direction, the clever Greek eluded all my efforts to bring him back to it for more than an hour. Taking leave of me with much politeness, at last he ordered his son to go with him, and the two of them started back on the road to Constantinople.

Several days later, as I was surprised not to have heard mention of Synèse, I sent one of my servants to Constantinople with orders to discover the state of Synèse's injury. His father, who knew that the servant came on my behalf, thanked me for my attention and maliciously added to this courtesy that henceforth I need not be worried as to his son's marriage, because, having sent him into Morea under close watch, he was sure that Synèse would not easily escape from the place where he had ordered his son locked up. I had enough goodness to sympathize with Synèse in his mistreatment. Théophé showed the same compassion. And as I did not hide this news from anyone, the knight, more touched that I would have thought by his friend's misfortune, formed a resolution that he carefully concealed from us. Under the pretext of going to Ragusa to collect his bills of exchange, he undertook to free Synèse from his prison, and the dangers he suffered for this friendship testify to the nobility of his character.

I did not hide from Théophé my renewed efforts to sway her father. She was grieved at the poor success of my endeavors, but not to excess, and I was charmed to hear her say that with the kindnesses I had shown her, one would never notice that she lacked a father. What would I not have answered this tender sign of gratitude, had my heart been free to express itself? But, faithful to my resolutions, I limited myself to the language of fatherly affection, and I assured her that she would always take the place of a daughter for me. An incident that, at the time, troubled Constantinople and all the neighboring countryside let me know further how dear I was to the precious Théophé. A contagious fever was spreading, for which a remedy had yet to be found. I was stricken with it. My first care was to have myself transported to the pavilion in my garden, where I wished to have only my doctor and my valet with me. This precaution, which I owed to charity, was also an act of prudence, because I would not have been able to free my house from this horrible malady once it had infected my servants. But this order, which regarded Théophé in particular, had no more power to stop her from coming with me than did fear. She entered the lodge despite my servants, and nothing could cool her in her attentions for a moment. She fell ill herself. My entreaties, my supplications, my complaints could not make her consent to withdraw. They set up a bed for her in my antechamber, whence all the force of her illness did not stop her from being continually attentive to my own.

With what feelings was my heart not imbued after we recovered our health? The selictar, who had been informed of my illness, paid me a friendly visit as soon as he believed he could without indiscretion. His heart was not easy. The time he had spent without coming to Oru had been employed in overcoming the passion that he had begun to see was fruitless. But when I told him of the tender care Théophé had given me, his discomfort and his flushed face revealed a jealousy that he had not felt before. He fidgeted impatiently during the remainder of our conversation. And when the time came to withdraw, he did not consider that my weak health obliged me to keep to my apartment; he asked me to accompany him to the garden. I did not wait to be urged. After remaining silent for a few steps, he said in an irate tone, "My eyes are open, and I blush that they were closed for so long. How easy it is," he added ironically, "for a Frenchman to dupe a Turk."

I confess that, as I had expected nothing like this abrupt invective, and as I had thought, in the complaisance with which I had praised Théophé's attentions, only of pointing out the natural goodness of her character, I searched, for a few minutes, for words with which to defend myself. However, whether a little natural moderation enabled me to keep myself from being blinded by my resentment, or whether the abatement of my illness was propitious to my reason, I gave the proud selictar an answer that was less offensive than firm and modest. "The French (for I put the interest of my nation before my own) know little of artifice," I told him, "and seek better ways for making a success of what they favor. As for myself, I have never thought of closing your eyes, and I am not sorry they are open. I warn you only that they delude you if they cause you to judge ill of my friendship and my good faith." This speech lessened the selictar's anger, but it did not cool all his ardor. "What?" he said to me. "Did you not tell me you were merely on terms of friendship with Théophé and that generosity was the only feeling that had interested you in her?" I interrupted him without emotion: "I did not deceive you if I said that to you; that was my first feeling," I told him, "and I would not be as content with my heart if it had begun with another. But since you press me to inform you of what is happening to it, I confess that I love Théophé and that I have not been able to defend myself against her charms any better than you. However, I add to this confession two circumstances that ought to ease your mind: I did not have these feelings for her when I took her from Chériber's seraglio, and it is no more use to me than to you to have conceived them since. This," I went on with less pride than courtesy, "is what I believe capable of satisfying a man whom I esteem and love."

The selictar abandoned himself to the blackest reflections, and recalling all that he had noticed in our commerce since I had received Théophé from his hands, he would not have failed to cast the poison of his heart over the least observation that appeared suspicious to him. But as he had nothing with which to reproach me but the innocent testimony I had received of that lovely girl's zeal, he concluded at last that I would not have boasted so imprudently of it had I believed it was due to love. This thought did not restore his repose and joy; but calming at least his black fits of passion, it disposed him to leave me without hatred and without rage. "You will not have forgotten," he said in parting, "that I sacrificed my passion when I believed that friendship made it my duty. We shall see if I have well understood your principles and the differences you vaunted to me between your customs and ours." He did not leave me time to answer.

This incident caused me to examine once again the reproaches I might make against myself where love and friendship were concerned. I would only have deserved the selictar's reproaches had my love been a happy one, which would have made him fear that my rivalry had diminished something of the tenderness he might have obtained. But ever since I had begun to love Théophé, it had not even occurred to me to put myself forward at the expense of my rival. I was assured by the girl herself that she had no liking for him, and the obstacle that he accused me of not respecting was precisely the only one that I did not have to overcome. Moreover, I myself had so many complaints about my lot that, finding myself perhaps less sympathetic to that of another, I chose to laugh at his distress in order to relieve my own. I returned to Théophé in this disposition and asked her, jesting, what she thought of the selictar, who accused me of being loved by her and who held against me as a crime a happiness from which I was so remote. Maria Rezati, whose attachment to her friend was growing every day, had acquired too much understanding from her own adventures not to recognize immediately the feelings that filled me. Not leaving Théophé for a moment, Maria had the cunning to share confidences that soon gave her a good deal of influence over all Théophé's reflections. Maria pointed out to her that she was not sufficiently aware of the benefits she was overlooking and that a woman of her merit could derive great advantages from a passion as strong as mine. Finally, endeavoring to raise her hopes, she made her consider the fact that I was not married and that nothing was so ordinary in Christian countries as to see a woman raised to fortune through a happy marriage. In the favorable predisposition that caused me to regard her earliest adventures as the faults and injustices of chance, she added, I would be likely only to pay heed to the manner in which she had conducted herself since gaining her freedom and, given my distance from my native country, I would take counsel only from my own heart. She repeated the same speech to her a thousand times, with some impatience at seeing it too coldly received; and as she had been able to draw from her only modest responses, which marked a soul without ambition, she protested that, independent of her and motivated only by the zeal of friendship, she was going to convince me gradually to assure her friend's fortune and happiness. In vain did Théophé oppose this with her strongest arguments; her resistance was considered fear and weakness.

Her embarrassment was without equal. Quite apart from her manner of thinking, which far removed her from all intentions of making her fortune or raising herself, she trembled at the opinion I would form of her vanity and her boldness. After having uselessly renewed her efforts to make her friend change her resolution, she decided to warn me about a negotiation that appeared to her to risk the loss of my esteem and my affection at the very least. But after having fought her timidity for a long time, she allowed herself to be overcome by it, and the only expedient that remained to her was to employ a *caloyer*, the head of a Greek church that lay two miles from Oru, with whom she had formed some connection. This good man readily undertook his commission. He explained it to me in a jesting tone; and redoubling the admiration he already had for so extraordinary a girl, he asked me if I saw a great deal of difference between her virtuous fear and that which induced a modest caloyer to hide himself in order to flee the higher ecclesiastical ranks. I laughed at his comparison. With a little more experience of the vanity and cunning of women than he, I would have suspected any woman other than Théophé, and I might have regarded this appearance of modesty as a very well devised trick to make me acquainted with her claims. But I would have been committing the ultimate outrage against my lovely student. "She had no need of such precaution," I said to the caloyer, "to give me a fair judgment of the sentiments of her heart, and tell her more than once that, were I free to follow my own sentiments, I would hardly delay demonstrating all the consideration that I have for her." This was the only answer befitting my situation. Might I dare confess that it was far more restrained than my true desires?

I did not fail to use the same language with Théophé, and I was indeed forced to pursue her in order to find an occasion to talk to her alone. I had stopped visiting her alone in her apartment. I no longer proposed that we walk in the garden. She had become so formidable to me that I no longer approached her without trembling. The sweetest moments of my life, nevertheless, were those I spent near her. I carried her image with me everywhere, and I was ashamed that sometimes, in the midst of my more serious occupations, I could not push away the memories that beleaguered me continually. Her acquaintance with the caloyer committed me to several walks that were perhaps rather ill suited to the propriety of my employment; but it was enough that I should accompany Théophé in order to be aware only of the pleasure of being with her. However, I could not forget the circumstances of the first visit we paid to the caloyer. He was, properly speaking, only a priest, respectable because of his age and the veneration he had earned from all the Greeks. His revenue had been multiplied by his thrift, and the presents he continued to receive from his congregation sufficed to provide him with a sweet and comfortable life. The ignorance in which he had persevered to the age of seventy did not prevent his having a library, which he regarded as the principal ornament of his house. It was here that he brought me, because of the high esteem that the Greeks have for French erudition. While I expected to see him display his literary wealth, I was surprised to hear him make his first observation about an old chair that he pointed out in a corner. "How many years," he said to me, "do you think that piece of furniture has spent in that same spot? Thirty-five years. For it has been thirty-five years that I have held my position, and I have had the pleasure of noticing that no one has ever used it." It even seemed that the very dust with which it was covered was respected. But at the same time, glancing at the books near it, I perceived that they were no less dusty. This observation inspired me with an amusing idea, which was to measure the thickness of the dust that was on the books and on the chair; in finding it more or less equal, I offered to wager the caloyer that for thirty-five years the chair had been no more immobile than the books. It was not easy for him to grasp my thought, although he had paid profound attention to what I was doing; and he believed, admiring my learning, that I had an extraordinary talent for discovering the truth.

He had been married three times, although the laws of the Greek Church forbade second marriages to clergymen. The reason he had put forward for obtaining this dispensation was that he had not had children from the first two beds and that, one of the goals of marriage being to contribute to the propagation of society, he ought to take as many new wives as he might lose, in order to fulfill more perfectly the aim of a legitimate vocation. The Greek council had allowed itself to be persuaded by so strange an argument, and the caloyer, who had no more fecundity with his third wife than with the first two, was grieved at not having known that he was so unsuited to marriage or that he had not better performed its functions. Such is the vulgarity of the leaders of a rather large church, although it is much smaller than they tell themselves. I have noticed so much diversity in their principles that they are scarcely united by more than the fact of being Christians and by the facility they all have in upholding their errors.

Maria Rezati, meanwhile, had not forgotten the promise she had made to Théophé; and the care that had been taken to warn me caused me to find much pleasure in noticing all the degrees of cunning by which a woman moves toward her goal. But at last I tired of a stratagem whose artifice I discovered too easily, and taking the opportunity of her enterprise to let Théophé know what I no longer had the boldness to say to her myself, I entreated her to be as convinced as her friend that my heart would never change its inclination. This is a promise I have kept faithfully. My reason again made me aware that I ought to limit myself to this. But I did not know all that I had to fear from my weakness.

About six weeks had passed since the departure of the Sicilian knight when Maria Rezati received a letter from him in which he let her know that his friendship with Synèse Condoidi had caused him to triumph over a thousand difficulties and that the young Greek, who no longer feared anything from his father's violence since he was free enough to hope to defend himself from it, was still disposed to grant them a retreat on a portion of the lands he had inherited from his mother. He added that they were counting on her to invite Théophé to share their establishment and that, if Maria had not yet induced her to feel so disposed, Synèse was resolved to return to Constantinople to solicit her himself to accept his offers. They did not seem uneasy about my consent, and I had the satisfaction of thinking that they held a very advantageous opinion of my commerce with Théophé, since they thought me capable of seeing her leave with such indifference. But they had taken good care not to reveal all their intentions in their letter. Supposing they found some obstacle on Théophé's part or on mine, they were resolved to spare neither courage nor cunning in order to take her away from me.

The experience they had just undergone no doubt inspired them to new enterprises. They were left in peace in Acade only through the indulgence of the governor, who had closed his eyes to an audacity for which he might rightly have punished them. Synèse, locked up under orders from his father in an old tower that made up the better part of their country house, did not know how long his imprisonment was meant to last and saw no likelihood of leaving it through his own efforts. He had only a small number of servants as his guards, who would not have been difficult to bribe had the knight been richer; but having gone off with only the modest sum I had lent him for his trip, he had had no other resource for freeing his friend than cunning or force. He did not speak Greek or Turkish very well, and I have never understood how he surmounted this obstacle, especially when he faced so many others. He might have been less bold had he been aware of all the difficulties of his undertaking; for half of all those who are reckless succeed only because they are ignorant of their danger. He arrived alone in Acade. He found lodgings in the vicinity of Condoidi's house, which was not far away. His occupation for several days was to find out where Synèse had been locked up and to study its layout. Far from being able to force its door, he found he could not even approach it easily. But with the use of an iron that he heated red-hot on a stove, he managed, in the space of one night, to burn the outer end of a thick beam that traversed the tower; and whether because he began with certain knowledge or merely allowed himself to be led by chance, he found that the spot at which he had been working corresponded to Synèse's room. Once he had made this opening, nothing was so easy as to separate the adjacent stones and penetrate the entire thickness of the wall. He only hoped that his friend would hear him, for one night could not suffice to open a passage and the light of day would have betrayed him if the disorder caused by his excavations had been too great. But having succeeded in making Synèse hear him, he told him his plan and what he had done so far toward freeing him. Conferring together, they agreed that they would meet every night, and Synèse, repeating to the servants who waited on him all that he had learned during these conversations, acquired the reputation of having a genie who kept him informed of all that happened in the empire. Indeed, this mad fancy soon spread, not only through

Acade, but through all the neighboring towns, and the two young men delighted for some time in the credulity of the public.

They had imagined, with reason, that so extraordinary a novelty would excite a good deal of curiosity in Synèse's circumstances and that the favor of the Turks, who are extremely superstitious, would serve to free him. But although the governor of Acade himself displayed some wonder at what was told to him, he did not appear any more disposed to offend paternal authority by restoring a son's freedom against the wishes of his father. Thus, having obtained no benefits from artifice, the knight resorted to violence. He found the means to get a sword to Synèse, and having formed an alliance with some of Condoidi's servants since staying in the area, he took advantage of a visit to Synèse in his prison to assist him with such vigor that Condoidi's entire household, attracted by the tumult, could not prevent their flight. They had the imprudence to publicize what they had done without considering the twofold risk of being punished, both for having passed off Synèse's intelligence as being religious in nature and for having used weapons in their escape, two rash acts rarely pardoned among the Turks. But the governor of Acade, informed of the reasons for the young Greek's arrest, found his father's harshness excessive and was easily inclined to forget an undertaking that he saw as a credit to friendship.

The moment of their victory, the knight had written to Maria Rezati. He told her they were leaving together for Ragusa, where Synèse had wished to accompany his friend, and that they would make other arrangements upon hearing Théophé's answer, which they expected to find on their return. All the terms of this letter were so restrained that Maria had no objection to communicating them to us. This frankness persuaded me at least that I could not reproach her for bad intentions. She had not waited long to confide in Théophé; or, rather, she had foreseen her inclinations from the very beginning of the plan, and as she had noted her preference for the Christian countries, she herself had somewhat given up her hopes after learning of Synèse's captivity. But as she saw paths that she had thought closed open for her again, and as she judged by my conduct, which she witnessed constantly, that I would allow Théophé to be mistress of herself, she did not wish to displease me; but she failed to foresee the anxiety she would cause by communicating the knight's letter to me.

However, my heart's excitation, which suddenly overcame my natural moderation, caused me to receive this confidence with more resentment than I ought to have shown to a woman. I called the settlement plan a licentious party, which corresponded quite well to the misguided steps Maria Rezati had taken by fleeing her father's house, but which could not be proposed without shame to a girl as reasonable as Théophé. I went so far as to call the plan, which had been formed in my own house, one of betrayal and ingratitude. I forgave it in Synèse, I told her, whose views then appeared to me as mad as those for which his father had justly punished him, and I did not wish to increase the unhappiness he had already brought down upon himself in my house with my reproaches. But I could not easily forgive it in a woman from whom I ought to expect some thankfulness and loyalty.

While these complaints were too harsh, their effect was also quite horrible. They inspired in Maria Rezati a hatred against me that was not in keeping with the services I had done her. I know that to reproach a person for a kindness is considered an offense. But there had been nothing too humiliating in my expressions, and I dare to add that excesses of delicacy did not befit a woman who had come out of a seraglio after having left her native country with a Knight of Malta, and whom, to be perfectly honest, I should not have suffered so long in my house in Constantinople as in my country house. Théophé did not hesitate to answer her in the manner most likely to calm my agitation. There was so little likelihood, she told her, in the idea of the settlement with which they were deluding themselves, that she was surprised that it could seriously be proposed. Aside from the fact that the flightiness of two young men did not promise much constancy in their enterprises, there could be no doubt that Lord Condoidi would soon disrupt a plan formed without his consent. As for her, whom they were so kind as to wish to involve, she did not understand what her role would be, and she felt as much aversion to that which Synèse appeared to offer her as indifference for that which her father persisted in refusing her. This speech calmed me down. However, as the same feeling caused me to fear that Maria Rezati's counsels would make more impression in my absence, I resolved to have her rejoin her lover. I was told that in a few days a vessel was leaving for Lepanto. I sent word to ask the captain to take a lady whose affairs summoned her to Morea on board, and I gave her one of my servants to take her there. Our separation took place in so constrained an atmosphere that I thought I could not rely much on the friendship of Maria Rezati henceforth. Théophé herself, who had cooled toward her after various signs of her indiscretion, saw her leave with little regret. But for all that neither one of us expected transports of hatred.

I enjoyed more repose after her departure than I had for a long time; and without changing the conduct that I had resolved to maintain all my life with Théophé, the very sweetness of being more at ease with her replaced all the pleasures I no longer dared to hope for from love. The selictar seemed to have given up all his ambitions. In the end it had cost me his friendship, for he had not appeared at Oru since my illness, and when I saw him on the frequent trips I made to Constantinople, I no longer found in him any vestige of that tender warmth with which he had always been eager to greet me and shower me with all sorts of courtesies. Nevertheless, I did not change my feelings for him. But after having treated me with this coldness for several weeks, he appeared irritated at seeing me so insensitive to it, and I learned that he had complained quite bitterly of my behavior. I then felt obliged to ask him for some explanation of his complaints. This conversation was at first so heated that I was afraid it would have regrettable consequences. I found myself offended by his remarks, which I felt to be scarcely considerate of me, and I did not know to what extent moderation and silence were compatible with honor. He nevertheless disavowed the tale that I had been told. He even promised me he would force the one who had done him this bad turn to openly retract what he had said. But being no more tractable where Théophé was concerned, he reproached me as sharply as he had in Oru for having sacrificed his affection to my own. I was satisfied as to my own complaints. Thus, resuming all the inclination that I had to love him, I hoped he would also resume the earlier opinion he had had of my good faith. After making him another avowal of my feelings for Théophé, I protested, in the terms that make the most impression on a Turk, not only that I was no happier than he, but that I did not seek to be. His answer could not have been quicker had it been planned. "You at least desire her happiness?" he said, regarding me steadily. "Yes," I answered without hesitating. "Well, then," he went on, "if she is the same as you received her from me, when she came out of Chériber's seraglio, I am resolved to marry her. I know her father," he continued. "I have gotten him to agree to acknowledge her on this condition; he allowed himself to be won over by several promises of fortune which I will faithfully keep. But at the moment I thought myself determined to carry out a plan that cost me a thousand pains, I found myself opposed by cruel reflections that I could not overcome. You have inspired me with too much delicacy. Your conversations and your principles have transformed me into a Frenchman. I could not bring myself to force a woman whose heart I believed belonged to another. What have I not suffered? However, if your honor guarantees me what I have just heard, all my resolutions are reborn. You know our customs. I will make Théophé my wife, with all the rights and all the distinctions that station assures her."

Few surprises could have been as terrible to me. My honor, which I had just pledged, my unfortunate passion, which still endured, a thousand ideas that immediately changed into cruel barbs to torment my mind and tear open my heart, caused me to feel in a moment more bitterness than I had ever felt in my whole life. The selictar noticed my discomposure. "Ah!" he cried, "you allow me to see what I would hate to imagine." He was letting me know that he suspected my honesty. "No," I said to him, "you should not offend me with your mistrust. But if I am not mistaken in your laws and your customs, should I not remind you or inform you that Théophé is a Christian? How can her father have forgotten it? I admit she was brought up in your ways, and since she has lived in my house, I have shown little curiosity to know what she thinks as far as religion is concerned; but she is friends with a caloyer whom she receives often, and although I have not seen her thus far exercise in any way your principles or ours, I think she has the inclination toward Christianity that she must derive from her blood, or at least from the knowledge she has always had of her native land." The selictar, struck by this reflection, answered that even Condoidi thought she was a Muslim. He added other reasons for hoping that whatever her religion, she would not be more difficult than most other women, who in Turkey are quite prepared to adopt the religion of their masters or their husbands. I had time to recover during this discussion, and, understanding that the objections should not come from me, I said to him at last that it was useless to create difficulties for himself over a fact that he could clear up during the first visit he paid to Théophé. I had two intentions in giving this answer: one was to avoid being burdened with his proposals; the other was to bring to a prompt end a new pain that slowness and doubt would have made much keener.

It certainly had not yet distinctly occurred to me that Théophé could ever have any relationship with me other than that of love; and supposing she were to allow herself to be blinded by the honor of becoming one of the foremost women of the Ottoman Empire, I felt I was capable of sacrificing all my affection to her fortune. I would have regarded the selictar's happiness with a jealous eye; but I would not have troubled it, even if it cost me a thousand times more violence; and perhaps I would have contributed my own efforts to elevating the only woman I loved. However, after leaving the selictar, who promised to rejoin me that evening at Oru, nothing was so pressing as to return there. I took no roundabout ways to discover gradually the impression I would make on Théophé. My heart demanded immediate relief. "I want you to know,"

I said to her, "the nature of my feelings. The selictar is thinking of marrying you, and far from opposing his plan, I approve of everything that may assure your fortune and your happiness." She received this speech with so little emotion that I understood right away what her answer was going to be. "Far from contributing to making me happy, you are preparing more sorrows," she told me, "with offers against which I know I will not be able to defend myself without greatly offending the selictar. How could I," she added, "have expected such an odious proposal from you? You do not have all the friendship for me that I imagined, or else I have not succeeded at all in convincing you of my feelings."

All too charmed by this obliging reproach, all too aware of what it seemed to contain that was favorable to my affection, I insisted on the selictar's plan for the sole pleasure of hearing her repeat what had filled my heart with such joy and admiration. "But do you realize," I said, "that the selictar is one of the foremost lords of the empire, that his wealth is immense, that the offer you listen to so coldly would be avidly received by all the women in the world, and that it is on the likes of him that sisters and daughters of the Great Lord are bestowed every day; lastly, do you realize that this is a man who has loved you for a long time, who adds a great deal of esteem to his love, and who proposes to treat you quite otherwise than the Turks treat their women?" She interrupted me. "I realize nothing," she said, "because nothing touches me but the hope of living at peace under the protection that you grant me, and because I desire no other happiness." After the many promises with which I had committed myself to silence, I could no longer permit myself any outward expression of my joy; but what was occurring secretly in the depths of my heart exceeded all that I have reported up to now of my feelings.

The selictar did not fail to come to Oru that evening. He asked me eagerly if I had confided his plan to Théophé. I could not disguise from him that I had hazarded some explanations that had not been received as favorably as he might wish. "But perhaps you will have better luck," I added, "and I am of the opinion that you should not postpone explaining what you have in mind yourself." There was some malicious joy in this advice. I was impatient not only to see his importunities end with a refusal that would completely deny him any further hope, but even more to take a perfect delight in my triumph by seeing my rival humiliated before my eyes. This was the only pleasure I could still derive from my passion, and I had never yielded to it with such enjoyment. I took the selictar to Théophé's apartment. He told her why he had come. Having had the time to think out her answer, she took care not to say anything that might mortify him; but her refusal seemed to me so decisive, and the reasons she brought to it were explained so forcefully, that I had no doubt that he would immediately form the same opinion I had. He did not ask to have them repeated. He rose without answering a single word and, seeming less afflicted than irritated, said to me several times as we went out, "Would you have believed it? Should I have expected this?" And when he was ready to leave, not wanting to spend the night in my house, he added, embracing me: "Let us remain friends. I was determined to do something foolish; but you will agree that the folly you have just witnessed is far greater than mine." His vexation was obvious even as he got into his chaise; as he left me I saw him raise his hands and join them with a motion that I imagined expressed as much shame as grief and surprise. Despite the feelings I have confessed, I liked him enough to feel sorry for him, or at least to wish that such a disappointing outcome might serve to cure him.

But perhaps I would not have directed my compassion toward him had I foreseen what new tribulations I was about to experience and what his disgrace itself would cause me in the way of vexation and humiliation. Scarcely had he left when I returned to Théophé's apartment and found her quite satisfied with his departure, of which she had just learned. Her quick and lively nature inspired many pleasant reflections on the fortune she had refused. No longer understanding anything about the principles of a woman capable of treating all that most men esteem with such scorn, I entreated her, after listening to her for a few minutes, to tell me what it was she sought through her conduct and feelings, which daily filled me with wonder. "One sets a goal for oneself," I said, looking at her with an expression made pensive by the very feelings agitating me, "and the more extraordinary the paths by which one wishes to walk, the nobler and loftier the end to which one aspires must be. I have the highest idea of yours, without being able, nevertheless, to discover what it is. You do not lack confidence in me," I added. "Why have you hidden your views up to now, and why not for friendship's sake grant what I no longer dare ask of you from any other motive?" I had spoken in a tone serious enough to persuade her that it was not curiosity alone that interested me in this question, and however faithful I might be in observing all my promises, she had too much insight not to have noticed that my heart was no more tranquil for all that. However, without changing the gay and light-hearted tone with which she had commended the selictar's departure, she protested that her only goal was the same one she had stated to me a thousand times and which she was surprised to see me forget. "Your friendship and your generous protection," she told me, "have made up from the very first moment for all the unhappinesses of my fate; but the regrets, the application, the efforts of my whole life will never repair the licentiousness of my conduct. I am indifferent to everything that cannot serve to make me wiser, because I no longer know of any greater good than wisdom and because every day I discover more and more that it is the thing I lack."

Responses of this sort would have made me fear once more that her reading and her thoughts had spoiled her mind had I not also noticed a wonderful equanimity deep within her character, a constant moderation in all her desires and always the same charm in her remarks and manners. It is here that I would begin to blush at my weakness had I not prepared my readers to pardon it for so fine a cause. I could not reflect on so many wonderful circumstances without feeling myself overcome by all the emotions I had kept more or less in check for the past several months, through the force of my promises. The offers of such a man as the selictar and the refusal I had witnessed had so changed Théophé in my eyes that she seemed to me clothed in all the titles she had rejected. She was no longer a slave I had bought back, an unknown girl who could not make her father acknowledge her, a girl unfortunately abandoned to the debauchery of a seraglio; I no longer saw in her, along with all the qualities that I had adored for so long, anything but a person ennobled by the very grandeur she had scorned and worthy of more elevation than fortune could ever offer her. In this disposition, which only increased on several days' reflection, I proceeded without distaste to formulate a plan to marry her; and what should have been surprising to me, after having spent nearly two years without daring to linger for a moment over this thought, was the fact that I became immediately accustomed to my plan, to the point where the only thing that occupied me was the means to make it succeed.

My imagination did not present me with obstacles to overcome, since I no longer found anything there that did not favor my inclination; nor did my family, who did not have the power to oppose it, and who, since I was so far away from my native country, would not learn of my resolution until long after it had been executed. Moreover, in yielding to the inclination of my heart, I was not forgetting what I owed to decorum; and if only to avoid the expense and the publicity, I was already resolved to confine the celebration of my marriage within the enclosed space of my walls. But in the midst of the delight I found in satisfying my dearest inclinations, I wished that Théophé had yielded to my affection for reasons other than those I had proposed to her, and I felt some regret at having needed this path to obtain a little love from her. Although I had flattered myself more than once that I had made an impression on her heart, it was sad never to have wrested from it the least recognition. Without hoping to lead her more openly to make such a declaration, I promised myself at least that by making her see somewhat vaguely what I was determined to do for her, it would be impossible that, in the secret stirrings of the strong gratitude she had so often expressed, there would not escape some words my heart could be content with and which would present the opportunity to declare to her immediately what love would make me capable of doing for her happiness and mine. In all these reflections, it did not even occur to me that the refusal she had made to the selictar was a reason to fear the same fate; and I took pleasure in persuading myself that if she had not rejected one of the greatest fortunes in the empire solely in order to pre-serve herself for me, at least a predisposition so favorable to our nation would make her more inclined to accept the same offers from me.

At last, several days having passed in this sort of preparation, I chose, for deciding my happiness, an afternoon on which nothing could dis-turb the conversation I wanted to have with her. I was entering her apartment when a thought that had not occurred to me suddenly chilled my blood and made me retrace my steps with great agitation and dis-may. I remembered that the selictar had taken at least some measures with respect to Condoidi to clarify Théophé's birth, and I trembled at the force of a passion that was blinding me to the point of making me fail to observe certain proprieties that a Turk found indispensable. But this was not the only thing that threw my ideas into confusion. I con-sidered that, as much as it was necessary to confide in Condoidi and to engage him to do for me what he had offered to the selictar, it would be just that difficult and humiliating to make my resolutions depend on the whims of a man I had treated so ungently. What if he decided to avenge himself both for the solicitations I had pressed for on his daughter's behalf and for the vexations he suspected me of causing him with respect to his son? Nevertheless, I saw no other choice, and I was surprised that such a necessary condition had escaped me. But is it believable that, after justly reproaching myself for this and unhurriedly deliberating on the path I ought to take to rectify my imprudence, my conclusion was to return to Théophé and carry out what I had thought myself obliged to suspend for such strong reasons? I will not put for-ward at too great length the arguments that recalled me to this resolu-tion. I would not persuade anyone that love did not have more part in it than prudence. However, it seemed to me that obstacles I did not despair of overcoming should not delay a declaration that would at last let Théophé know all the ardor of my passion and that would no doubt dispose her to favor my enterprise, at least with her desires. In informing her that my hand was meant for her, I did not intend to conceal the fact that in becoming her husband I expected to give her back a father. Must I say it? Whatever success I might obtain from Condoidi and from her, I flattered myself that she would be touched enough by the resolution I had taken in her favor to account for it with her feelings and sooner or later to bestow on me unconditionally what she could clearly see I wished to have at any price. My reflections were more numerous and perhaps not as distinct when I went back into her apartment. I did not allow her time to become uneasy over my agitation. I hastened to explain my designs, and having entreated her to listen to me without interrupting, I finished my speech only after describing in great detail even the slightest of my feelings.

The fervor that had compelled me to take such strange steps not only continued, but in some way increased during this explanation; and the presence of so dear an object having an effect even more acute than all my reflections, I was in a state in which nothing was perhaps comparable to the force of my love and my desires. But a glance I cast at Théophé plunged me into a state of fear a thousand times more acute than that which had stopped me at her door an hour before. Instead of the testimonies of gratitude and joy which I expected to see written on her face, I perceived only the signs of the most profound sadness and mortal dejection there. She appeared deeply impressed by all that she had just heard; but I saw only too well that what rendered her speechless was a rush of surprise and fear rather than a transport of admiration and love. At last, when, despite my own confusion, I was about to express some concern over her situation, she threw herself to her knees before me, and unable to hold back her tears, she shed such an abundance of them that for several minutes she was unable to speak. I was so acutely agitated by my own emotions that I found myself too weak to lift her up. She remained in that posture despite my efforts, and I was constrained to listen to a speech that pierced my heart a thousand times. I will not report her insulting and scornful remarks about herself which the ever-present memory of her offenses made her utter; but after painting herself in the most odious colors, she begged me to open my eyes to this picture and not to suffer an unworthy passion any longer. She recalled what I owed to my birth, to my rank, to honor itself, and to reason, her first notions of which I myself had given her and whose principles I had so happily taught her. She accused fortune of crowning the evils of her life by causing her not only to ruin the repose of her father and benefactor, but to corrupt the principles of a heart whose virtues, she claimed, had been her only model. Finally abandoning this tone of grief and lament for one that was firmly threatening, she protested that if I did not give up desires that equally offended my duty and hers, if I did not confine myself to the roles of her protector and her friend – those dear and precious roles to which she begged Heaven I would still join my feelings – she was resolved to leave my house without saying good-bye to me, and to use the freedom, the life, all the possessions, in a word, that she confessed she owed to me, to flee from me forever.

After this cruel protestation, she arose. Entreating me in a moderate tone to forgive the scarcely respectful words that the force of her grief had torn from her, she begged me to allow her to go hide her pain and recover from her shame in the small room next to this one, whence she was determined not to emerge except either to take leave of me altogether or to yield herself to the pleasure of finding me once again such as we ought both to hope for, for my happiness and her own.

She did indeed go into the small room, and I had not the boldness to make even the least effort to hold her back. My voice, my movement, my reflection, all my natural faculties were in some sense suspended by the excess of my surprise and my confusion. I would have hurled myself into an abyss had one opened before me, and the very idea of my situation seemed an intolerable torment. I remained there nevertheless for a very long time without regaining sufficient strength to leave. But this state must in fact have been very violent, since the first servant I met was alarmed by the alteration in my face, and, immediately spreading the alarm through my house, he gathered all my servants around me, who were zealous in offering me the help they thought necessary to my health. Théophé herself, alerted by the tumult, forgot the resolution she had formed not to come out of her room. I saw her run up with concern. But as the sight of her redoubled all my pains, I feigned not to have noticed her. I assured my servants that they had become alarmed without reason, and I made haste to shut myself up in my apartment.

There I stayed more than two hours, which were for me but an instant. What bitter reflections and violent agitations! But they ended at last in making me resume the decision from which I had strayed. I remained convinced that Théophé's heart was proof against all the efforts of men, and whether it was her natural character or virtue acquired through her studies and her meditations, I regarded her as a unique woman, whose conduct and principles ought to be proposed as models for her sex and for ours. The confusion arising from her refusal became easy for me to dissipate once I abided invariably by my resolution. I even wished to appear worthy in her eyes for having agreed so promptly with her views. I rejoined her in her room, and, declaring to her that I yielded to the force of her warnings, I promised to confine myself as long as she should wish to the role of the most tender and most ardent of her friends. How the movements of my heart nevertheless fought against this promise, and how her presence was enough to make me retract what I had recognized as fair and indispensable in a moment of solitude! If the idea I give of her in the rest of these memoirs does not correspond to that which the reader must have acquired so far from such glorious proofs of her virtue, must I not fear that he will mistrust my testimony and prefer to suspect me of some black sentiment of jealousy capable of altering my own dispositions, rather than to imagine that a girl so confirmed in virtue could have lost something of that wisdom I have delighted up to now in revealing? Whatever opinion he may form of it, I ask this question only in order to have the opportunity to reply that he will find me as sincere in my doubts and my suspicions as I have been in my praises, and that after having ingenuously reported facts that have thrown me into the utmost uncertainty, I wish to allow the reader to judge for himself.

But the new pact I had made with Théophé was followed by a rather long calm, during which I again had the pleasure of seeing her exercise all her virtues. I had learned from the guide I had given to Maria Rezati that this restless Sicilian had failed to respond to our expectations and no doubt to her lover's as well. The captain of the vessel on which I had had her embark for Morea, having been taken with a lively passion for her, had urged her to disclose her experiences and her plans. He had made use of this knowledge to depict so vividly the harm she would do herself for the rest of her life by rejoining her knight that he made her consent at last to be taken to Sicily, where he had not doubted that she would easily be reconciled with her family. He had certainly set his hopes on gathering the principal fruit of it, through a marriage to which it was easy to foresee he would find little opposition; and if I was to believe the testimony of a servant, he had not waited until disembarking in Messina to assure himself of the rights that went with it. Having at last introduced himself to the father of the woman he loved, who seemed very happy to find his daughter and heir again, he had obtained permission, by presenting himself as a well-born Italian, to marry Maria Rezati before the rumor of her return had spread; and this was indeed the only way for her to reenter her native land honorably.

She had wanted the guide I had given her to accompany her all the way to her father's house, apparently to make sure of winning over the kindly old man by giving him this proof of the interest I had taken in her fortune. The guide had left Messina only after the celebration of the marriage, and he brought me a letter from Lord Rezati that contained lively expressions of his gratitude.

Théophé had also received a letter from Maria, and we both thought we were done with this adventure. About six weeks had passed since the return of my valet when, as I was in Constantinople, I learned from another of my servants, who was returning from Oru, that the knight had arrived there the day before and that the news Théophé had communicated to him had thrown him into a despair whose consequences they feared. He nevertheless sent his apologies for the liberty he had taken in coming to my house, and begged me to allow him to stay there a few days. I sent him an assurance forthwith that I would be happy to see him, and no sooner was I free than my impatience to learn his feelings and plans made me leave the city. I found him in all the consternation that had been described to me. He even reproached me for having caused his unhappiness by giving his mistress the freedom to leave my house without informing him of it, and I forgave his reproaches as expressions of a lover's grief. But in a few days my consolations and my advice brought him back to sounder ideas. I made him recognize that the decision his mistress had made was the happiest thing that could have happened both to her and to him, and I urged him to profit from the help that I offered him to make his peace with his family and his order.

Having become calmer, he told us about his and Synèse's adventure, of which we had learned only the principal circumstances from his letter. They had made the trip to Ragusa together, and having found no obstacles to the payment of the bills of exchange, they had readied themselves to carry out with sufficient order and success the plan of establishing a settlement. But what he had difficulty confessing at first was that Synèse had come with him to Constantinople. Learning from Maria Rezati's reply, which they had found upon their return from Ragusa, that Théophé would not willingly join them, they had come in the hope of making a greater impression on her with their own pleadings; and the knight, aware of the courteous treatment he had received in my house, did not conceal the fact that Synèse's plan was to employ violence in place of the other means that had not succeeded for him. "I am betraying my friend," he said to me, "but I am sure that you will not use my confidence to harm him; whereas by hiding his plan from you, I would betray you all the more cruelly because it would be impossible for you to anticipate the threat to your house." He added that had he promised to assist Synèse, it was because, since he expected to find his mistress in my house and to return to Morea with her, he had wished her to have as agreeable a companion as Théophé, who, moreover, he was sure, would find that in the charm of their society there was more pleasure in Acade than she had expected to find there. Aware, moreover, of the efforts I had made to induce Condoidi to acknowledge her, he had persuaded himself that I would not be offended if they caused her to enter a family to which I wished to see her returned more or less against her will. But as the plan of the settlement was thoroughly destroyed, he was warning me of Synèse's intentions, in which he no longer saw the same security for Théophé nor the same advantages.

She was not present to hear this, and I entreated the knight not to tell her anything. The warning was all I needed in order to foil Synèse's plan, and I was quite sure, too, that without the knight's help, he would be left with as little facility as boldness. I nevertheless wanted to know the means they had proposed to employ. They were to choose a day when I would be in the city. I left few people at Oru. As they both knew my house, they thought they would easily gain entrance to it and there find all the less resistance since Maria Rezati would leave voluntarily; they could then persuade my servants that if Théophé seemed to accompany her against her will, it was nevertheless with my knowledge. I do not know if this rashness would have succeeded. But I relieved myself of all sorts of fears by sending word to Synèse that I knew of his plan, and I promised him that, if he continued to harbor it even for a minute, he would be punished with more severity than he had been by his father. The knight, who had not ceased to love him, also contributed to making him abandon the plans they had formed in concert. However, he could not rid his heart of a passion that had plunged him into more than one senseless undertaking.

How much should one rely on even the best characters at that age! I thought that this same knight had at last returned to reason, and in fact his conduct, until his departure, was such that I maintained a high regard for him. But on returning to Sicily he fell back into a licentiousness much less excusable than that from which he had emerged. I employed my strongest recommendations with the Grand Master of Malta and the Viceroy of Naples to procure him a gentler welcome than he dared hope for. He reappeared freely in his native land, and his flight passed for an error of youth. But he could not avoid seeing his mistress there, or rather he was weak enough, probably, to seek out the opportunity for it. Their passion was rekindled. Scarcely four months had passed since his departure when Théophé showed me a letter written from Constantinople, in which he indicated to her in a roundabout and timid way that he had returned to Turkey with his mistress and that, as they could not live without each other, they had renounced their home-land forever. He admitted the excess of his folly; but although he set forth the violence of a passion he had not been able to overcome as his excuse, he felt, he said, that in all decency he could not appear before me without anticipating my goodwill, and he entreated Théophé to awaken it in his favor.

I did not deliberate a moment over my answer. The case was so dif-ferent from the first, and I found myself so little disposed to receive a man who was violating a thousand duties at once in this new abduc-tion, that, dictating Théophé's letter myself, I told the knight and his mistress that they should not expect either favors or protection from me. They had taken enough measures to be able to do without them, and their aim in coming straight to Constantinople was much less to see me than to rejoin Synèse, with whom they wished to revive their ear-lier plan. However, as they had also resumed the plan of having Théophé take part in it, and as the close relationship they had had with her made them expect to be warmly received by her, they distinguished quite clearly that her answer had been dictated; and far from becoming dis-heartened at a refusal they attributed only to me, scarcely were they certain that I was in the city than they both went to Oru. Théophé, in the first embarrassment of this visit, told them honestly that, knowing my intentions, she was not at liberty to consent to see them, and she begged them not to expose her to the danger of displeasing me. They pressed her so insistently to listen to them, and the interval they asked of her was so short, that, unable to use violence to rid herself of them, she was forced to oblige them.

Their plan was set, and the letter by which the knight had attempted to regain some access to my house had merely been the effect of a feel-ing of remorse, on the eve of a new enterprise over which his honor gave him pause. Although I had never explained to him what I thought about his earlier ideas of settling in Morea, and although I had been even less open about the interest I had taken in it upon discovering that they wanted to involve Théophé, he was quite aware that she would not have been treated in my house with such attention and distinction had I not been happy to have her there, and that he could not lure her away or secretly abduct her without offending me. He would there-fore have wished to have me approve his plan, for the pleasure of his mistress as much as for the interest of his friend; and although I had refused to see him, he still hoped I would favor him after he had obtained Théophé's consent. Thus, he spared nothing to make her see as much usefulness as pleasure in joining his society. But she needed no help in resisting such foolish entreaties.

At the time, I was occupied with preparations for a celebration that was the talk of Europe. The difficulties I had encountered several times in the functions of my ministry had not prevented me from continuing to be on very good terms with the Grand Vizier Calaïlé, and I dare say the vigor with which I had maintained the privileges of my employment and the honor of my nation had served only to win me respect among the Turks. As the king's fête was approaching, I intended to celebrate it with more brilliance than it had been celebrated up to then. The fireworks were to be magnificent, and my house in Constantinople, which was in the district of Galata, was already filled with all the artillery that I had found on the vessels of our nation. As these brilliant rejoicings could not be executed without express permission, I had requested it of the Grand Vizier, who had granted it to me with much politeness. But on the very eve of the day I had chosen, when, satisfied with my efforts, I had returned to Oru to seek some rest that night and to take Théophé back with me the next day, since I wished to have her at my celebration, I learned, there, two pieces of news that clouded my joy. The first, as I arrived: this was the detail of the knight's visit and the efforts he had made to persuade Théophé to follow him. Learning at the same time that he was closer than ever to Synèse, I felt far more mistrustful than she did, and was almost sure that at her refusal and mine they would revive all the schemes the knight had confessed to me. However, I was not very alarmed by this because I was taking her to Constantinople the next day and had all the time I needed to take measures in the future to make my house in Oru a secure haven for her.

But as I was talking to her that evening about everything she had recounted to me, I was notified by my secretary that the Grand Vizier Calaïlé had just been deposed, and that they had named as his successor Chorluli, a man of haughty character with whom I had never had any relations. I suddenly realized what trouble I was going to have. This new minister could stop my celebration, if only out of the caprice that usually induces his like to change the order that they find already established and to revoke all permissions granted by their predecessors. My first thought was to feign that I did not know of this change and to follow the arrangements I had already made by virtue of Calaïlé's *ferman*.[1]

However, because the disputes from which I had emerged with honor obliged me to maintain greater circumspection, I at last decided to ask for another permission from the new vizier, and I dispatched a man expressly to obtain it. He found him so occupied with the new responsibilities of his promotion that it was impossible for my secretary to get an audience with him. I learned only the next day that he had not been able to talk to him. My impatience increasing, I determined to present myself at his door in person. He was in the *galibe divan*,[2] whence he was not to emerge except for the solemn procession that is customary with such changes. I abandoned hope of seeing him. All my preparations were complete. I returned to the idea that I had had first, that Calaïlé's permission could suffice for me, and I began the fireworks at nightfall.

Inevitably, the vizier was notified of it. He resented the display and immediately sent one of his officers to ask me what I meant by it and by what right I had formed an enterprise of that nature without his consent. I answered civilly that as I had obtained Calaïlé's approval two days before, I had not thought I needed a new *ferman*, and that moreover I had not only sent word several times, but had myself gone to his house to have it renewed. The officer, who apparently had his orders, declared to me that the vizier insisted that I break off the celebration immediately, otherwise he would take violent measures to force me to do so. This threat heated my blood. My answer was no less lively, and when the officer, irritated in turn, added that if I made any resistance, his orders were already given to advance a detachment of janissaries to humble my presumptuousness, I did not spare my words: "Report to your master," I told him, "that a step such as he is taking is worthy of the utmost scorn and that I do not know what fear is when my king's honor is at question. If he goes to the extreme with which you threaten me, I will not defend myself against such overwhelming numbers; but I will have all the powder that I have here in abundance brought into this room, and I will light the fire myself, exploding my house along with myself and all my guests. It is to my master, after that, that I will yield the duty of avenging me."

The officer withdrew, but the rumor of this incident immediately spread confusion among all the Frenchmen assembled for my celebration. I myself was in a fit of rage that certainly would have made me capable of carrying out the ideas that had come into my mind. And above all not wanting to show the least semblance of fear in my conduct, I gave orders that all my artillery, which was composed of more than fifty cannons, be discharged forthwith. My servants trembled as they obeyed me. My secretary, more alarmed than any of the others, thought to do me a good service by extinguishing some of the torches and Chinese lanterns, that is, taking care to extinguish some at different distances, in order to be able to say that they were executing the vizier's order.

I did not notice this right away; but the flight of some of my guests, who were no doubt afraid that I would go to the extreme with which I had threatened the minister's messenger, redoubled my agitation. I called those whom my efforts could not stop cowards and traitors; and soon noticing that the brilliance of my display was diminishing, I flew into a new fury on learning of my secretary's timid precaution. I was in this sort of rage when I heard the cries of a woman who was calling to me for help. I did not doubt that this was already the detachment of janissaries confronting my servants, and not wishing to undertake anything without being certain, I ran toward the cries, accompanied by some faithful friends. But what did I see? Synèse and the knight, aided by two Greeks, were carrying off Théophé, whom they had had the cunning to draw aside, and were endeavoring to cover her mouth with a handkerchief to stifle her cries. All the heat already animating me was not required to make my fury rise to its height. "Lay hands on those traitors," I said to my companions. I was immediately obeyed. They threw themselves on the four abductors, who nevertheless moved to defend themselves. The two Greeks, having less skill or resolution, fell under the first blows. The knight was wounded, and Synèse, hopeless, gave us his sword. I would perhaps have had him arrested, and in the first moment he would not have been treated with indulgence, if someone had not come to advise me that the vizier, appeased by the appearances of submission that were owed to my secretary, had called off his troops and declared himself satisfied. Pity easily found room in my heart once anger had left it. Some precautions were even required to hide the death of the two Greeks. I sent Synèse away, vehemently stressing my goodness, and I gave orders that the knight should be carefully bandaged. Fortunately, having only Christians in my house, everyone there believed he had an interest in keeping this incident secret.

Yet, my own adventure was followed by a few other events related to this work only in that they were the cause of my returning to my native land. Scarcely had I received the orders from the king than I thought of the conduct that I should show toward Théophé. I loved her too well not to ask her to go with me, but I dared not hope that she would consent. Thus, as my difficulty depended only on her inclinations, I took long roundabout ways to find out what they were. She spared me some of these detours by the doubt she herself expressed as to whether I would permit her to accompany me. I rose in a fit of ecstasy, and giving her my word that she would always find my feelings for her the same as before, I left her the choice of the conditions she might please to impose on me. She explained them to me frankly: my friendship, to which all good things, she told me kindly, seemed to be attached, and the freedom to live as she had lived in my house until then. I swore to her to be faithful in observing them. But I asked her to agree that before our departure I could make a new attempt to sway the insensitive Condoidi. She foresaw that it would be useless. And, in fact, although I was persuaded that he would become more tractable as he saw her leaving Turkey forever, I could obtain nothing from that hardened old man, who imagined, on the contrary, that the pretext of my departure was a trick I was using to deceive him. Synèse, whom I had not seen, nor the knight, since their rash enterprise, had no sooner learned that she was going with me to France than, overcoming all his fears, he came to beg me to allow him to say his farewells to his sister. This title, which the clever Greek affected to give her, and the air of tenderness he imparted to his pleading, made me decide not only to let him visit her right away, but to grant the same favor to him several times before our departure. The measures I had taken in the country and in the city left me nothing to fear for the security of my house, and I knew Théophé too well to mistrust her. This complaisance nevertheless inspired new hopes in Synèse. He had not paid her four visits when, requesting the liberty to speak to me, he threw himself at my feet and entreated me to resume my former feelings of kindness for him. Taking Heaven as his witness that he would regard Théophé as his sister throughout his life, he asked me to take him with me and to serve as his father as I did hers. The nature of his prayer, his tears, and the good opinion I still had of his character, would inevitably have induced me to agree to all this if I could have persuaded myself that it was not love that was disguised under deceptive appearances. I gave him no positive answer. I wanted to consult Théophé, whom I suspected of being in collusion with him and of having allowed herself to be touched by the power of blood or by his tears. But she answered me, without hesitating, that just as she would have asked me for this favor if she were certain she was his sister, so too did she beg me not to expose her to the perpetual embarrassment of not knowing how to conduct herself with a young man whose feelings for her were too passionate if he was not her brother. Thus, the sad Synèse was reduced to the consolations he no doubt found in the friendship of the knight, and I do not know what became of them after our separation.

Théophé employed the few weeks that remained between the king's order and my departure in occupations that would furnish me the material for another volume if I sought to enlarge these memoirs. Her reflections as much as her experience had made her feel that the most horrible of all misfortunes for a person of her sex was slavery; and since she had come to Oru, she had not lost a single occasion to learn which seraglios were the best filled and which noblemen most desired this sort of wealth. With the help of some slave merchants, who are as well known in Constantinople as our most celebrated horse traders are here, she had discovered several unfortunate girls, Greeks or foreigners, who found themselves bound against their wills in this sad condition, and her hope had always been to leave no stone unturned to free them. She had well understood that I could not ask these sorts of favors from all the Turkish noblemen one after another, and her discretion had also prevented her from suggesting too often that I employ my income for this. But seeing that she was about to leave, she was less timid. She began by selling all the jewels she had received from Chériber, and several considerable gifts I had made her accept. After confessing to me that she had converted them into money, she told me of the use she wished to make of this sum and urged me, out of the tenderest motives of charity, to add to it some part of my wealth. I divested myself of ten thousand francs, which I had intended to use to buy various curios of the Levant. Curiosity never induced me to find out what Théophé had put into this of her own, but I soon saw several extremely delightful girls in my house, whose chains she could not have broken for modest sums; and if one adds to this the expense that she incurred sending them back to their native lands, one will not doubt that her generosity went far beyond mine. I found it a highly agreeable entertainment, during several days, to listen to the adventures of this charming company, and I took care to write them down almost immediately, so as to fear nothing from the faithlessness of my memory.

At last we left the port of Constantinople on a vessel out of Marseilles. The captain had forewarned me that he needed to put into harbor for several weeks at Livorno, and I was not sorry to have the opportunity to see this famous port. Théophé showed perceptible signs of joy as we touched the shores of Italy. As the incognito I was obliged to maintain for a thousand reasons made me leave all my retinue on board, I lodged at an inn, where I did not refuse to eat in the company of some decent people who happened to be there. Théophé was assumed to be my daughter, and I an ordinary man coming back from

Constantinople with his family. At the very first meal we took with the other travelers, I saw that a young Frenchman, about twenty-five years old, was quite taken with Théophé's charms, his attentions continually aimed at making her notice him through his flattering remarks or his courtesies. His appearance, as prepossessing as his manners and his conversation, caused me to take him for a man of quality who traveled without wishing to be recognized, although the name of Count de M. Q. which he adopted, did not suggest to me the idea of a known house. He showered me with compliments, because he thought I was Théophé's father. At first I regarded his eagerness as the gallantry common to Frenchmen, and during the walks I took in the city during the following days, it did not occur to me that there was any risk in leaving Théophé alone, with only a woman of her nation to wait on her.

However, in less than a week I noticed that there had been some change in her mood. As the fatigue of the voyage alone could have caused some alteration in her, this observation caused me little uneasiness; I asked her, nonetheless, if she had any reason for feeling sad or any complaint to make. She answered that she knew of nothing that could grieve her; but she answered with an air of embarrassment that would have opened my eyes immediately had I been capable of any mistrust. Moreover, I did not know that the Count de M—— was spending all the time that I employed visiting the city's sights in conversation with her. We were in Livorno a fortnight without the least incident causing me to watch more closely over what was happening around me. If I returned before mealtime, I found Théophé alone, because of the care the count took to withdraw upon my arrival. I continued to find her air more somber and more constrained, but seeing no mark of the change I had feared for her health, I thought it sufficient to combat this melancholy by promising her that she would find more charm in France than in an Italian inn.

It is certain that at the table I remarked more familiarity between the count and her than a temporary acquaintance ought to have given her. They seemed to understand each other with glances or smiles. Their eyes often met, and the count's courtesies were received differently than they had been the first days. However, as it would have taken miracles to turn my mind toward mistrust after such long proofs of Théophé's chastity and even her coldness, I found a thousand reasons for excusing her. She had enough natural discrimination to have recognized in the count's noble manners the difference between our civility and that of the Turks. She was studying the count as a model. These excuses, which I naturally attributed to her, were all the more likely since I had noticed a thousand times that she had studied me and that, without finding in me as much elegance and refinement as in the count, she had derived an evident usefulness for imitating our manners. Another week or more went by before I allowed the least suspicion to arise, and I do not know how this secret commerce would have ended if chance had not brought me back one day at a time when I was so little expected that, entering Théophé's room suddenly, I surprised the count on his knees. The sight of a snake spitting its poison at me would not have shaken my senses more. I withdrew successfully enough so as not to be seen. But detained against my will at the door by my fears, by my suspicions, by my transports of gloom, I sought to redouble the despair that was gnawing at my heart by observing everything that could prove Théophé still more guilty. In truth, I discovered nothing to offend modesty. However, I remained at my post until the dinner hour, as agitated, as impatient, as though I had wanted to see or hear what I dreaded most mortally.

What reason did I have to be jealous? What commitment did Théophé have to me? What had she given me to hope for? What had she promised me? On the contrary, had I not renounced all claims to her heart, and was not the freedom to follow her inclinations one of the two articles I had granted her? I agreed with myself on all counts; but it seemed cruel that this heart that I had not been able to touch should have been so easily touched by another. Supposing she could become capable of a weakness, I would have wished that this would not have been as though by chance, and at the first glance of a stranger. Or, to reveal the very depth of my feelings, I was offended that those appearances of discretion that I had respected should be so soon abandoned. I blushed, in fact, at having been the dupe of those fine principles that had been repeated to me so many times so eagerly, and I reproached myself less for my goodness than for my credulity and weakness.

Along with confusion and resentment, there was so much malicious- ness in these reflections that, far from favorably interpreting the count's restraint, I believed that it was the repose of a satisfied lover, who was perhaps less eager only because he had already obtained all that could excite his desires. What new transports this thought caused me to expe- rience! But I had enough control over my composure not to do any- thing rash. In planning to surprise the cruel Théophé in the midst of her pleasures, I arranged to talk to her servant, less in order to confide in her, which I did not want to risk lightly, as to draw confidences from her that her simplicity might allow to escape; she was a Greek, whom I had substituted for Bema and who had readily engaged herself in my service. But whether she was more attached to her mistress than to me, or was as deceived as I by the cunning of the count and Théophé, I learned from her only that they were often together, and it did not even seem that she was trying to hide this from me.

I took good care not to leave our lodging, and feigning an inconvenience that kept me there against my will, I did not leave Théophé for the rest of the day. In the afternoon, the count asked for permission to keep us company. Far from opposing this, I was delighted that he would present himself to my observations, and for over four hours all his remarks and his gestures were their sole object. He did not betray himself by any indiscretion; but I noticed how skillfully he introduced into our conversation anything that could increase the inclination that I supposed Théophé had for him. He told us some of his amorous adventures, in which he was always distinguished by the virtues of tenderness and constancy. Whether this was truth or fiction, he had loved only one Roman lady, who at first had made him pay quite dearly for the conquest of her heart, but who had no sooner become acquainted with his character in depth than, yielding herself to him without reservation, she had no longer placed any limits on her tenderness. It was this adventure that had kept him in Italy for two years and that would have caused him to forget his own country forever had not the most horrible misfortune broken this beautiful bond. After delighting in his love for a long time in perfect tranquillity, his mistress's husband had discovered their commerce. He had given them the same poison during a meal. The young lady had died from it; as for him, his strong constitution had saved him; but having recovered only to learn of the death of his beloved, his grief had immediately thrown him back into a state more dangerous than the one from which he had just emerged. Despairing that it would have no more effect than the poison, he had sought death by a means less criminal than had he taken his life by his own hand, but that he had thought almost as certain. He had appeared before the husband whose hatred he had merited, and having reproached him a thousand times for his barbarity, he had bared his stomach and offered him the victim who had escaped him. He swore to Heaven that he had thought his death inevitable and that he would readily have endured it. But this cruel husband, mocking him for his passion, had answered him coldly that far from thinking further of killing him, he happily saw that he could not be better avenged than by allowing him to live, and that he sincerely rejoiced that the count was saved from a poison that would too soon have ended his woes. Since that time, the count had led a deplorable life, wandering through all the towns of Italy in order to efface the images that made his situation a perpetual torment, and seeking to redress the losses of his heart in commerce with any agreeable woman he could find. But he had arrived in Livorno without having felt the least change in a heart that sadness had always defended against love.

This implied clearly enough that the miracle was reserved for Théophé. I, however, had not perceived this profound melancholy, which should still have been noticeable when we arrived if he had only been cured of it so recently. But the attention with which I saw Théophé listen to all these fairytales did not allow me to doubt that they were making the desired impression on her. Night fell. I was awaiting it impatiently in order to clear up suspicions that were much more terrible. Théophé's room was next to mine. I got up as soon as my valet had put me to bed, and I sought a place where I could see anyone who might approach our apartment.

However, I felt a cruel remorse at the outrage I was committing against the good Théophé; and amid the agitation of a thousand feelings that were fighting in her favor, I wondered if my dark mistrust had enough basis to justify such insulting observations. The entire night went by without anything appearing that could offend my eyes. I even approached the door several times. I curiously bent my ear to it. The least noise aroused my suspicions, and I was tempted, at a slight movement that I thought I heard, to knock suddenly in order to have the door opened for me. At last, I was about to withdraw at dawn, when Théophé's door opened. A mortal shiver froze my blood; it was Théophé herself coming out with her servant. At first this haste to rise disturbed me; but I remembered she had told me several times that, in the excessive heat of the region, she would go take the air in the garden, which looked out over the sea. I followed her with my eyes, and I was reassured only after seeing her go in that direction.

It will seem that I ought to have been satisfied with the use I had made of the night, and that after a test of this nature there remained for me only to abandon myself to sleep, of which I felt a dire need. However, my heart was only half relieved. The movement I had heard in the room still left me some doubts. The key had remained in the door. I entered, in the hope of finding some vestige of what had alarmed me. It was perhaps a chair or a curtain that Théophé had moved herself. But as I looked curiously in all parts of the room, I saw a small door that I had not noticed before; it opened on a hidden stairway. All my feelings of agitation revived at this sight. "There is the count's passageway!" I cried sorrowfully. "There is the source of my shame — and that of your crime, wretched Théophé!" I can give only a feeble idea of the ardor with which I examined all the passages in order to find out where the stairway might lead. It led to a separate courtyard, and the door at the foot of it seemed securely locked. But could it not have been opened during the night? It occurred to me that if I had any certain knowledge to hope for, it would be in Théophé's very bed, which was still unmade. I seized on this thought avidly. I approached with a redoubling of fear, as though I were about to discover information that would carry the utmost conviction. I observed even the smallest details, the appearance of the bed, the condition of the sheets and covers. I went so far as to measure how much room Théophé required, and to discover whether anything seemed rumpled beyond those limits. I could not have been mistaken about this; and although I realized that in the heat she could have been restless during her sleep, it seemed that I could not possibly misjudge her traces. This examination, which lasted a long time, had an effect I could hardly have foreseen. Finding nothing that should not have served gradually to calm me, the sight of the place where my dear Théophé had just rested, her form which I saw imprinted there, a vestige of warmth which I found there still, the spirits exuded by her in gentle perspiration, so moved me that I kissed a thousand times all the places she had touched. Tired as I was from having stayed awake all night, I forgot myself so completely in this pleasant occupation that sleep took possession of my senses and I remained in a deep slumber in the very spot she had occupied.

During this time she was in the garden, where it was not surprising that she should find the count, because it was a more or less established practice in the house to take the sea air before the heat of the day. Various people from the neighborhood, in fact, also went there, which gave it the feeling of a public promenade. It so happened that, on the same day, the captain of a French vessel that had come into the port the day before chanced to be there with some passengers he was bringing back from Naples. The sight of Théophé, whom it was difficult to look at without admiration, attracted these strangers around her, and the count, who recognized the captain for a Frenchman, addressed him politely, which facilitated their meeting. The count learned from him not only what regarded his own affairs, but a part of mine, namely, that the captain, who had seen our vessel as he arrived in port, had found out from some sailors who had been on the decks, where they had come from and whom they had brought with them; and these vulgar men from whom I had not taken care to request silence as I left their boat, identified me by the post I had just occupied. The count, hearing my name and title, was extremely surprised not to have known that I was in Livorno, although it appeared from what the captain said that I must have been there for several days. Recalling everything he knew, he did not doubt that I was the one they were talking about and that I had wished for some reason to remain unknown. But, unable to moderate the first emotion that caused him to turn his thoughts upon Théophé, he apologized for not having been more careful to give her what he believed my daughter was owed. But, without having known him better, what has always persuaded me that he was not of common birth is that, on the basis of the information he had just received, he formed a plan that had not before entered his mind, resolving to offer his hand to Théophé, in the supposition that I was her father. This plan, which he sought the occasion to try out on her before leaving the garden, made their walk much longer, so that the morning was well advanced when, having given her his hand to lead her, he delivered her back to her apartment.

She had received his proposal with all the embarrassment one can imagine, and understanding immediately that she owed it only to the false idea he had of her birth, she had defended herself against it with vague excuses whose meaning he had not understood. However, as this did not shake his resolve, he told her as they entered her apartment that he would not let the day go by without revealing his feelings to me; and if anything could make me judge their commerce favorably, it was as much the facility with which he broke it off after the scene that I am about to describe as the desire he had to form a serious tie with her by the bond of marriage. I was still in the position in which sleep had seized me, that is, covered, it is true, by a robe, but lying in Théophé's bed; and the noise they had made in opening the door having suddenly awakened me, I had heard the count's last words. I would have taken good care not to be seen, and despite the vexation I felt at being surprised, I would have profited from my situation to hear the rest of their conversation. But as the curtains of the bed were open, the count was the first to cast his eyes on me. He had no trouble distinguishing that I was a man. "What do I see?" he said with the utmost astonishment. Théophé, who saw me almost immediately, uttered a cry in which there was as much dismay as confusion. It would have been useless to try to conceal myself. The only recourse that occurred to me was to make an effort to compose my face and look amused, and to turn into a joke an incident to which I could not give a better appearance. "I found your door open," I said to Théophé, "and as I had not been able to enjoy a moment's rest last night, I imagined that your bed would favor sleep better than mine." She had at first uttered a cry of shame and embarrassment, but finding nothing in her thoughts that could serve to explain an incident so inappropriate to the terms on which I lived with her, her silence expressed her uncertainty and her disturbance. The count, on the other hand, who thought he suddenly understood what before he had not even suspected, apologized to me for a lack of discretion with which he reproached himself as a crime; and assuring me that he respected me too much to interfere with my pleasures, he took leave of me in terms by which I easily saw that I was no longer unknown to him.

I remained alone with Théophé. Despite the effort I had made to affect a cheerful composure, it was difficult for me not to fall back into an embarrassment that was greatly increased by her own. I saw no other way to free myself of this constraint than to openly confess the mistrust I had felt concerning her behavior, especially since the promises that I had heard uttered by the count were a new object of worry about which I burned to receive explanations. Her face became as pale in listening to my first reproaches as it had become red when she saw me on her bed. She interrupted me nonetheless with a trembling air to protest that I insulted her with my suspicions and that nothing had occurred between her and the count which offended the principles that I knew her to have. A denial so absolute turned my resentment to indignation. "What? Traitor!" I said to her, as though I had had some right to reproach her for her betrayal. "Did I not see the count at your knees? Have you not treated him since our stay at Livorno with a desire to please which you have never had for me? Did he not promise you just now to spare nothing, today, to assure himself the happiness of belonging to you? What did he mean by that promise? Speak — I want to hear it from you. I will not spend my life as the plaything of an ingrate in whom my affection and my kind deeds have never inspired anything but hardness and hatred."

My anger had to be at its height to make me use such harsh words. She had never received anything but protestations of esteem and love from me, or complaints so tender that she must have believed she was respected even in the reproaches that my suffering prompted. Thus, she was so dismayed at hearing me that, shedding a stream of tears, she begged me to listen to what she had to say in her defense. I forced her to sit down; but as the bitterness of my heart was still more powerful than the pity that her sadness inspired, I changed nothing of the severity of my voice and expression.

After having repeated, with new protestations, that she had granted the count nothing with which she had to reproach herself, she confessed not only that he loved her, but that through a change she herself had difficulty understanding, she felt predisposed toward him by a violent inclination. "It is true," she continued, "that I fought against this penchant less than I should have, in accordance with my own principles; and if I dare tell you the reason for it, it is that, as I did not believe he had any knowledge of the wretched events of my life, I deluded myself that I could enter into the ordinary rights of a woman who has taken honor and virtue as her lot with him. He told me that his usual home was a house in the country. That was another reason to persuade myself that he would never learn of my misfortunes; and since he took you for a businessman, I did not believe that I was deceiving him in a disadvantageous manner by letting him think I was your daughter. However, I must admit," she added, "that since he learned of your rank, and since this knowledge has caused him to make the decision to ask you for my hand this very day, a sense of scruples arose that I would not have delayed communicating to you. These are my innermost feelings," she added, "and when you saw him at my knees, I was neither pleased by his assumption of this position nor did I authorize him to take it through criminal indulgence."

She seemed reassured after this confidence, and, expecting me to approve of her intentions, she looked at me with a calmer eye. But the opinion she had of her innocence was precisely what caused my despair. I was extremely upset that she paid so little attention to my feelings, or that she was so little touched by them that she did not even seem concerned by the fear of grieving me, and that she had nothing to overcome in order to yield to a new inclination. However, shame made me lock this cruel vexation in the depths of my heart, and, interpreting matters as good sense would dictate, I said, "I would like to believe your protestations, and I ought not to be easily persuaded that you have deceived me with false appearances of virtue; but if the count knows me, what hope have you that he may take you for my daughter, when he knows, or will soon know, that I have never been married? If he knows it already, you have too much intelligence not to see that his intentions cannot be sincere and that he thinks only of amusing himself with you. If he does not know it and his mistake makes him think today of marrying you as my daughter, will this plan not fade away when he learns that I am not your father? But you have realized it all too well," I went on, yielding to the jealousy that was tearing me apart. "You are not so simple as to have flattered yourself that a man of condition would marry you on a whim. You liked him. You followed only the impulse of your heart, and perhaps it carried you much farther than you dare confess. Why do you imagine I am in your room?" I added with new bitterness. "It is because I discovered your affair despite you. I read your passion in your eyes, in your remarks, in all the details of your conduct. I wanted to surprise you and cover you in shame. I would have done it last night if the force of my earlier affection had not led me to maintain some consideration. But be assured that I saw everything, heard everything, and one must be as weak as I still am to show you so little scorn and resentment."

One will easily fathom what the aim of this speech was. I wanted to free myself absolutely of the doubts that were still tormenting me, and I pretended to be well informed of all the objects of my fears. Théophé's denials were so clear, and the signs of her grief so open, that had there been any reason to rely on the justifications of a woman who had as much intelligence as love, there would perhaps have remained not the least mistrust of her sincerity in me. But I am not going to leave this to my readers to decide just yet. My ingrate's case has only been half examined.

Théophé and I employed all the time that remained until dinner in discussions from which I obtained no more information. We were at last told that the meal was served. I was impatient to see how the two lovers were going to act in my presence, and I was especially curious as to the first compliment I would receive from the count. Théophé no doubt felt as awkward as I impatient. But I did not see the count at table; it was only in the conversation I had with the other diners that I learned he had left in a post chaise after having said good-bye to the whole house. Whatever cause for surprise I found in this news, I affected not to think about his departure, and, merely casting a glance at Théophé, I observed that she was violently struggling to show no sign of change. She retired to her room after dinner. I would have followed her immediately had I not been detained by the French captain of whom I have spoken and who, having had until then the discretion not to show that he knew me, approached to pay me the civilities he thought he owed me. I did not yet know how he had discovered my name. As I talked with him, I learned not only what had happened in the garden, but the reasons for the count's flight. The captain made his excuses to me, as though he feared my reproaches. "As I was not forewarned," he told me, "about the notion you had given people here about the young person who is with you, I naturally answered the count's questions. He talked to me about your daughter. I had the imprudence to tell him that you had none; without knowing you personally, I knew along with all of France that you were not married. He had me repeat that answer several times, and I realized, from several details, that my indiscretion might have disturbed your intentions."

I assured the captain that he had given me no subject for complaint and that, had I concealed my name or taken any other disguise at Livorno, it was solely in order to avoid the embarrassment of ceremony. I gave him no other reason for choosing to remain in obscurity. But it was easy for me to see that once the count ceased to take Théophé for my daughter, he had imagined that she was my mistress. The state in which he had surprised me in her room must have made this thought occur to him; and in the confusion of having committed himself to her, he had found no other expedient but that of leaving right away without seeing her. I hastened to return to Théophé's room. I was only able to glimpse her dejection; for scarcely had she noticed me than, rousing herself to assume a calm demeanor, she asked me, smiling, if I was not quite surprised at the count's sudden decision. "You see," she added, "that his feelings were never very strong, since he was able in a moment to abandon them so completely as to leave without saying good-bye to me." I feigned to see no farther than this counterfeit amusement. "He loved you without rapture," I told her in a serious tone, "and if the expression of it was no more ardent than the effects, this passion must not have made him forget his Roman lady." Our conversation, which lasted all afternoon, was thus only a continual disguise, Théophé affecting still to seem indifferent to her loss, while with a malicious satisfaction, which came no doubt from the hope I felt reborn deep within my heart, I continued to disparage the count's passion and to speak of his departure as a vulgarity and an outrage. She endured this scene with great strength. As the captain of the vessel that had brought me seemed disposed that same evening to set sail again as soon as I would consent to it, I asked him to give me a day to prepare myself. It was not so much the requirements of my affairs that made me wish for a day's delay, but rather consideration for Théophé's health. I had too distinctly seen the efforts she was continually making to hide her sadness, and I wanted to be sure her health would not suffer from it.

She endured until our embarkation; but as soon as she thought she had lost all hope of seeing the count again, she stopped resisting the tumult of her heart and had herself put to bed, whence she did not emerge until Marseilles. I gave her all the care that duty would have had me give my daughter, or which love would have had me give a cherished mistress. However, I could not see her in this languorous state over another man without feeling that the liveliest affection is ultimately cooled by harsh ingratitude. Almost imperceptibly I noticed that my heart was becoming freer and that, without abandoning my aim of helping Théophé, I was no longer agitated by those uneasy emotions that for several years had been my habitual companions. I had the leisure to recognize this change during a calm of more than eight days which stopped us near the entrance to the Sea of Genoa. Such a perfect tranquillity in the air and sea was unparalleled. We were not six leagues from the coast, and as the water's surface was so motionless that we found ourselves as though fixed in the same spot, I thought more than once of getting into the longboat with Théophé and some of my servants in order to reach land by rowing. I would have spared myself an acute alarm caused by certain scoundrels who, yielding to their imaginations in their idleness, schemed to make themselves masters of the vessel by murdering the captain and the other officers. This conspiracy was perhaps planned before our departure, but the opportunity for executing it had never been so fine. We had on board five Italians and three Provençals, who were there with me only because they were passengers – people who, because of their dress and their manners, would not have tempted the captain or me to form the least association with them. Their only associations had been with some sailors from their countries, with whom they were continually drinking; and it was at these pleasant parties that they had arranged together to stab the captain and his lieutenant, fairly sure of finding little resistance from the rest of the crew, which numbered very few. Their plan with regard to me and my servants was to throw us out onto some remote shore of the island of Corsica and to seize all my belongings. Through an extraordinary stroke of Providence, my valet fell asleep on deck in the dark of night. There he was awakened by the talk of these wretched murderers, who, having gathered to arrange the execution of their undertaking, were distributing among themselves the main roles and were sharing out the authority and the loot in advance. As it was the captain's custom to appear on deck at the end of the day, they decided that he would be dispatched at that moment, while two of the accomplices would knock at the lieutenant's cabin, in order to cut his throat as soon as he opened the door. The others were to be spread throughout the vessel and to hold everyone in check with their threats and their weapons. While they agreed to treat me with a modicum of respect and to leave me on the island of Corsica with my servants, someone proposed to keep Théophé, as the most precious part of my possessions. But after a few minutes' deliberation, they recognized that such a beautiful woman would only serve to sow discord in the group, and they concluded to put her ashore with me.

Although trembling from so horrible a discovery, my valet had enough presence of mind to realize that we could only hope to save ourselves through diligence and secrecy. It was close to midnight. Heaven, which favored us, allowed him to slip along the deck and reach the captain's room, which, fortunately, communicated with mine. He awakened us with the same discretion, and, first exhorting us to silence, gave us a frightful account of the evil threatening us. The darkness had prevented him not only from recognizing the conspirators, but from discovering their number. However, having distinguished the most mutinous by their voices, he named some of them for us, and as far as he could judge, they might be twelve in number. I will not attribute false glory to myself if I boast of my boldness, which was quite well known. The eight servants in my retinue, the captain, his lieutenant, and I made eleven persons who were capable of some defense. Additionally, there were several sailors whose loyalty was not suspect and several other passengers as interested as we were in protecting themselves from the brigands. The only difficulty was to gather us together; I took this duty upon myself, and, after lighting several torches, I went out well armed and accompanied by all my servants, whom I also asked to bear arms. I quickly assembled all our allies and led them into my room, where we made enough preparations to fear nothing until dawn. However, our enemies, who noticed this movement, soon felt more fear than they had inspired in us. They were neither as well armed as we nor as great in number, not to speak of the terror that always accompanies crime. Imagining correctly that when day came it would be difficult for them to resist us, they made the only choice that could save them from punishment, and hastened to execute it. With the help of the sailors who were their accomplices, they threw the longboat into the sea and rowed to the nearest coast. We were not unaware of what they were doing; but although it would have been easy for us to cut them to pieces while they were making their preparations, or to kill them in the longboat by shooting them with our rifles and pistols, I was of the opinion that we should let them get away.

We had not been able to hide this adventure from Théophé. The noise of the weapons and the tumult she saw around her caused her a dismay from which she did not easily recover, or perhaps she gave this name to the increasing sorrow that had been secretly consuming her since Livorno. Her languidness resulted in a high fever, which was accompanied by several very dangerous episodes. She was not any better when we arrived in Marseilles. Whatever reasons I had for hastening my return to Paris, her delicate state did not permit me either to expose her to the agitations of a carriage nor to abandon her to the care of my servants in a city so far from the capital. I returned to her side, with the same willingness to please and the same zeal that I had not slackened during the course of our voyage. Each moment taught me that it was no longer love that continued to make her dear to me. It was the pleasure I took in seeing her and hearing her. It was the esteem for her character with which I was filled. It was my own acts of kindness, which seemed to attach me to her as though to my own creation. Not another word of passion escaped me, nor a single complaint over the torments I saw her suffer for my rival.

She gradually recovered, after having been so ill that the doctors had despaired more than once of curing her. But her beauty was affected by so long a prostration; and if she could not lose the regularity of her features nor the delicacy of her physiognomy, I found the beauty of her complexion and the sparkle of her eyes greatly diminished, although these vestiges nevertheless still composed a very attractive appearance. Several persons of distinction with whom I had formed some connection during her illness came often to my house, solely out of the desire to see her. M. de S——, a young man destined to inherit a large fortune, did not conceal the tenderness that she had inspired in him. After having spoken of it for a long time as though in jest, his feelings became so serious that he sought the opportunity to make them known to her. He found her as indifferent as she had been toward me, as though her heart could open only for the fortunate count, who had discovered the secret of moving her. She even begged me to deliver her from the importunities of this new suitor. I promised her this service without thereby assuming the right to remind her of my own desires. And to speak frankly about them, they had faded until they were no longer distinguishable from a simple penchant for friendship.

The discussion I had with M. de S—— did not at all produce what Théophé had expected from it, for he thought himself, on the contrary, all the more authorized to press her with continual displays of his affection. He had been restrained by the fear of finding himself in some rivalry with me. But learning that I confined myself to friendship with Théophé, and that the only reason that made me oppose the inclination he had for her was her own entreaty that I do so, he declared to me that, with the strong passion he had in his heart, he could scarcely be discouraged by the indifference of a beautiful woman and that he preserved at least the hope that suitors often have of winning through the constancy of his attentions what he had not been able to obtain through his merit and his mistress's penchant. I told him that after

Théophé's declarations, all his efforts would be useless. He was not discouraged in the least by this; especially when I had protested to him on my honor that I had obtained nothing from her that should cause him to doubt her chastity. Scarcely was she in a condition to enjoy some pleasure than he undertook to dissipate her melancholy with parties and concerts. She surrendered herself to this, less out of inclination than a willingness to please, especially when, far from finding that I was opposed, she saw that I would happily join in these amusements with her. M. de S—— was only the son of a merchant; and if it was a taste for merit that attached him to so amiable a girl, I saw nothing shocking in the desire I assumed he had to marry her. All Condoidi's obstinacy in refusing to give her the title of his daughter would not have prevented me from testifying that she was, and the proofs I had of it were sufficient to give me a kind of certainty about it. However, M. de S——, who discussed his passion with me sometimes, never associated with it the word marriage. In vain did I venture to inspire the idea in him through various reflections that could at least lead him to understand that I approved of his feelings only on that presumption. As I did not see all the ardor I would have wished at this proposal, I resolved, in order to justify my indulgence of his amorous attentions, to tell him quite frankly what I was thinking. Thus, through a peculiar change, it was I who assumed the task of assuring Théophé's conquest and I who thought of separating myself from her forever by making her the wife of another man. Quite aside from her own interest, which was my primary motive, I reflected that in Paris it would be difficult for me to avoid the suspicions that would arise over my relationship with her; and although I was not yet of an age when love is indecent, the notion I had of my own fortune did not accord with engagements of this nature.

If I explained myself freely to M. de S——, he replied in kind that he loved Théophé enough to wish to make her his wife; but as he had a thousand considerations with regard to his family, he did not dare engage himself recklessly in an enterprise that would expose him to his father's disfavor. However, as he was no longer of an age to be dependent, he would willingly marry her secretly; and he would leave it up to me to arrange the means and conditions. I thought twice about this offer. Although it assured me of all I had desired, it seemed wrong to facilitate a secret marriage, which I saw promised little pleasure for Théophé, since she would be condemned for a long time to keeping her condition secret, and which could jeopardize M. de S——'s fortune by sooner or later putting him on bad terms with his family. I replied flatly that a clandestine marriage was not suitable for Théophé, and I left him vexed by the thought that I was offended by his proposal.

However, since I did not yet know what Théophé's own inclinations were, and since, having once been mistaken about her feelings, I might have erred again in supposing that she had not reconsidered, I wanted to consult her and tell her what love was offering her. It did not seem surprising to hear her reject the affection and the hand of M. de S——; but when I stressed, in her own terms, the chance she would have to assume the rights of virtue and honor through an institution that could erase all memories of the past from her own imagination, she replied that she felt an aversion to the state of marriage. I could not help feeling a trace of resentment that caused me to reproach her with having, in that case, misled me when she had protested with such apparent sincerity that it was only this sort of advantage that had disposed her to endure the count's attentions. She was disturbed by this objection; but seeking to extricate herself from her difficulty by assuming the attitude of goodness and candor that had always succeeded with me, she entreated me not to misinterpret her feelings, or, if I preferred, not to judge her weaknesses too severely. And reminding me of my promises, she swore to Heaven that whatever disparities I might notice in her conduct, she had never ceased to regard the hope that I had given her of living close to me as the greatest good she could desire.

I thanked her for this feeling, and I renewed all the commitments I had made to her. As her health improved from day to day, our departure was not long deferred. In vain did M. de S—— endeavor to stop us, pleading often to the point of tears. He received from Théophé's own mouth the decree that condemned him to repress his passion – which did not prevent him from offering some pretext concerning his father's affairs to accompany us as far as Lyons in a post chaise that followed immediately behind my carriage. And when he was forced to leave us, he whispered in my ear that he planned to travel to Paris shortly, where he intended to play his hand more freely away from his father's gaze. I have always been convinced that he had secretly tried to obtain his family's consent and that only after his father's refusal had he proposed a clandestine marriage.

The unrelenting affairs that occupied me so constantly no longer permitted me to keep Théophé company in all her activities. I lodged her in my house, with all the consideration that I had always had for her, and I granted her all the rights that I had given her at Oru. My friends thought differently as they saw me arrive in Paris with this beautiful Greek woman. They were not satisfied with the tales I told them openly of some of her adventures; and as I always took care to hide those that did not do honor to her earlier years, they took the praises I sang of her principles and conduct for the exaggerations of a man in love. Others, coming to know her better, found she did indeed have all the merit that I attributed to her, and because of this were all the more inclined to believe me attached by love to a young person whom they did not imagine I could have brought from Turkey for any other reason. Thus, they believed, as I had foreseen, that I was on better terms with her than I actually was, and even the distractions of my affairs, which sometimes caused me to go three days without seeing her, could not change this opinion. But there was much more diversity and peculiarity in the judgments of the public. First they made her out to be a slave whom I had bought in Turkey and had grown to love enough to devote all my efforts to educating her. This was not entirely far from the truth. But they added – and in the Tuileries various persons whom I did not even know told me this – that the Great Lord, having fallen in love with my slave from the tale he had been told of her charms, had sent to ask me for her and that this was the cause of all the controversies I had gotten caught up in in Constantinople. And as Théophé's face, despite all the charm it still had, no longer corresponded to the idea of a woman who had attracted such admiration, they claimed that, in order to free myself from the torments of jealousy, I had disfigured a part of her charms with a potion I had had concocted. Others claimed that I had abducted her from a seraglio and that this boldness had cost me my employment.

I remained above all these fairytales by listening to them calmly, and I was always the first to turn them into a joke. As Théophé had become favorably known to all my associates, I soon saw that she had a great number of admirers. I did not see how she could continue to defend herself against the eager attentions of such brilliant young men, and I thought I owed her some counsels on the precautions necessary to her sex. The example of the Count de M—— had taught me that she was sensitive to the graces of appearance and manners. The danger was constant in Paris, and if love no longer caused me to take the same interest in it, I was at least obliged by my honor to keep all that could lead her into licentiousness from my house. She received my counsels with her usual docility. Her taste for reading had not diminished, and I even saw in her a new passion for learning. Perhaps vanity was beginning to do what until then I had attributed solely to her desire to embellish her heart and mind. However, whether my observations were no longer accurate enough to fathom her behavior, or whether she was more skillful than I thought in disguising it, I perceived nothing that offended my eyes until the arrival of M. de S——, who eventually filled me with suspicions I never would have come to on my own.

He was not so fortunate as to have them turned upon himself. But after spending some weeks in Paris and having appeared quite often in my house, where I showered him with courtesies, he took me aside one day to make the bitterest complaints. His aim in coming to Paris was, he told me, the same as the one he had explained in Lyons; but his fortune had changed a great deal. Instead of his beloved's coldness, which he thought was all he had to combat, he found several declared suitors ahead of him, whose attentions he had a thousand reasons to believe she would not similarly reject. He despaired particularly over the regard she showed for M. de R—— and for the young Count de ——, who seemed the most ardent. She did not allow them to visit her in my house; but this very exception was the most painful vexation of the young Marseillais, who had not been able to persuade himself that she differentiated between them and so many others whose visits she received indifferently, feeling little inclination toward them in her heart. How was it possible to imagine, nonetheless, that she loved two at once? He was still trying to understand this mystery. But having followed her to church, on walks, to shows, he had constantly seen these two troublesome rivals on her tracks, and the very air of satisfaction that appeared on her face always betrayed her when she saw them. He added nothing that could carry my suspicions further, and the request he joined to this complaint was likely, on the contrary, to stifle them. He entreated me to enlighten him further as to his hopes, and at least not to allow sentiments as honest as his to be scornfully rejected.

I promised him not only to take up his interests ardently, but to find out more about an intrigue of which I was utterly unaware. I had given Théophé an old widow as a companion, whose age, it would seem, would defend her against the follies of youth; and while I relied less on the behavior of the young Greek, I would have trusted in the warnings and lessons of so experienced a governess. They were never separated, and I saw with pleasure that they were bound as much by friendship as by my intentions. I informed this woman of the accusations that were being formed against her, for M. de S—— had confessed that he had never seen Théophé alone, and one could not have deserved reproaches that the other should not share. The old widow heard this with such an innocent air that it immediately caused me to attribute M. de S——'s torments to his jealousy. She even named the author of my worries. "He is not satisfied," she said to me, "to see that Théophé does not return his affection. He troubles her constantly with his speeches and letters. We have made a game for ourselves out of this annoying passion, and his frustration has no doubt moved him to complain to you. With respect to the crimes that he attributes to us, you know them," she added, "since I have only been following your orders in seeking some amusements for Théophé." She told me openly what their pleasures consisted of: they were the ordinary entertainments of decent people in Paris; and if the two rivals who were causing M. de S——'s alarms were sometimes included in their walks or other equally innocent outings, it was without any distinction they could take advantage of.

This answer calmed me, and I consoled M. de S—— only by exhorting him to deserve Théophé's heart, whose modesty and innocence I guaranteed. Nonetheless, his imaginings were not without foundation. My old widow, without being capable of indulging in licentiousness or approving of it, had still enough conceit and vanity to become the plaything of two young men, one of whom had undertaken to serve his friend by feigning love for a woman not less than sixty years old. Her eyes, being open only to the attentions that were being affected for her, did not notice what was happening with respect to her companion, and her blindness went so far as to make her believe that Théophé was very happy to share the gallantries of which she regarded herself as the only object. The testimony of M. de S——, who in the end discovered this comedy, and all the evidence that might have contradicted what my own eyes told me, would never have had the force to persuade me of it.

One day, especially aptly chosen because my affairs and my infirmities gave me some relief, M. de S—— asked me to take a coach with him so that I could witness a scene that would ultimately make me give more credence to his complaints. He had discovered, by his efforts, that Théophé and the old widow had agreed to join in a walking party, which was to end with a light meal in the gardens of Saint-Cloud. He was aware of both the place and the details of the party, and his imagination was heated to the point of making him introduce threats into his tale by the fact that he knew that M. de R—— and the young count were the two ladies' only company. Whatever color the widow might give to this party, I found so much indiscretion in it that I did not hesitate to condemn it. I allowed myself to be taken to Saint-Cloud, resolved not only to observe what would happen in so free a place, but reproach the two ladies whose modest intentions ought not to exempt them. They were already there with their lovers. They walked several times around a place so open that it was useless to follow them. M. de S—— carefully chose a position where nothing could escape us during their meal. He wanted not only to see them, but to hear them. Having known that the place where the preparations were being made was a circle of greenery in the upper part of the garden, we went there by long detours, and we were fortunately able to position ourselves behind a hedgerow only ten paces away.

They arrived a short time after us. Their behavior was decent. But as soon as they were seated on the grass, the prelude to their festivity was a long bantering conversation. It began with the widow, and I saw suddenly that the flatteries and caresses of the two young men were so much mockery that they had planned beforehand. After a hundred stale compliments on her graces, after having compared her to the nymphs, they bedecked her with leaves and flowers, and their admiration seemed to redouble as they saw her in this comical adornment. She was sensitive to her least praises, and as her modesty caused her to take a roundabout way of expressing the satisfaction that she felt, she praised the wit and charm she found in each word. What reflections did I make on the absurdity of a woman who forgets her age and ugliness! I found the old governess so justly punished that had I not been pressed by another interest than hers, I would have found the spectacle entertaining. But I saw the count dispensing with the intermediaries, and, turning more seriously to Théophé, intermittently addressing words to her that did not reach us. The fire that was consuming M. de S——shone in his eyes. He moved about so restlessly I was afraid the noise of his movements would betray us; and had I not held him back several times, he would have stood up suddenly to interrupt a spectacle that pierced his heart. How difficult it was to restrain him when he saw the count lower his head all the way to the grass in order to give a secret kiss to one of Théophé's hands, which she did not hasten to withdraw!

The meal was delicate and lasted a long time. Their joy was animated by a quantity of stories and pleasant witticisms. While they did not drink to excess, they tasted several different wines, and they did not need much prompting with the liqueurs. Finally, without anything absolutely condemnable having occurred, all I had seen had left me with a deep vexation, the signs of which I did not intend to conceal for very long. However, I would have borne it until Paris – and believing the ladies were ready to get into their carriage, my only difficulty was to avoid being seen returning to our own – when M. de R——, offering his arm to the governess, entered a covered alley that led to nothing less than the gate of the park. The count took Théophé in the same way, and, as I imagined that he was going to walk in the tracks of his friend, my design was only to follow them with my eye. But I saw them go in another direction. Trouble now seemed imminent. I did not want to wait for other signs, and I did not need to be aroused by M. de S——— to run to avert it. Having made him promise only that he would maintain his moderation, I followed him after the four lovers, and I feigned that, a taste for walking having brought me to Saint-Cloud, I had just been informed of their party and the path I should take to meet them. They were so disconcerted that, despite the air of amusement and freedom I affected in my manners, they did not recover right away; and it was only after a rather long silence that they mustered the civility to offer us what was left of their meal.

I was so little tempted to accept this that, thinking of interrupting forthwith a dangerous intrigue, I told the ladies that I needed to speak to them privately and asked them for a place in their carriage. "These gentlemen did not come without their team," I added, turning toward them, "and mine would be at their disposal in any case." M. de R——— had had his own follow after him. We promptly took the paths that led to the gate, and the two lovers had the mortification of seeing M. de S——— occupy one of the places they had filled.

It would have been too harsh to point out, in front of a stranger, the ladies' indiscretion. I postponed my lecture on morality until we reached Paris; but as I contemplated the governess from close up, as she was sitting across from me, I could not help laughing at the image I still retained of her adornment, nor could I help paying her some compliments on her charms, of the same sort as those she had been listening to. I quite believe that her imagination was already so spoiled as to think them sincere. Théophé smiled maliciously, but I was preparing a compliment for her that I thought capable of making her serious. She had the time nonetheless to pay one to M. de S——— which succeeded in dashing all his hopes. Whether she had some suspicion of the purpose that had led us to Saint-Cloud and she accused him of having inspired it in me, or whether she was in fact disgusted by his attentions, which, as I had noticed myself, were sometimes importune, she took advantage of the moment when he gave her his hand as she descended from the carriage. Having begged him not to trouble her peace further with visits and attentions that she had never enjoyed and no longer wished to receive, she told him that she regarded this leave-taking as the last. He was left so dismayed that, seeing her turn her back to go away, he did not have the courage to follow. Instead, he addressed his complaints to me. They touched me especially since I found in Théophé's conduct something extremely opposed to her natural sweetness and could not imagine that she would act in so extreme a fashion without having been provoked by a violent passion. I urged M. de S—— to console himself, like all lovers who are no happier, and I assured him the small compensation of my friendship. I held his good faith in high esteem much more than his possessions and his appearance. "Come to my house," I told him, "as often as you like. I will not force Théophé's inclinations; but I will make her aware of what she is missing by rejecting your offers, and I will no doubt make her ashamed of her feelings if she is abandoning herself to some licentious passion."

My infirmities obliged me to take my meals in my apartment, which deprived me of the pleasure of mingling with my household. But the same matter that had taken me to Saint-Cloud did not permit me to let night come without opening my heart to Théophé. I found out at what hour she had decided to retire; and having gone to her room with that familiarity which long habit had more or less established, I confessed that I was brought by extremely serious reasons. I do not know if she suspected the motive for my visit, but I saw a change in her face. She was nonetheless profoundly attentive to me. That was one of her good qualities, to want to understand what was said to her before responding to it.

I did not take my remarks too far. "You have shown," I said, "eagerness to live with me, and you know the reason, which you have repeated to me a thousand times: the preference for a virtuous and tranquil life. Do you not find that in my house? Why, then, do you go to Saint-Cloud after pleasures so far from your principles, and what dealings do you have with M. de R—— and the Count de ————, you who profess to a modesty so opposed to their rules of conduct? You do not yet understand our customs," I added. "This is the excuse that my affection lends you; and I gave you for a guide a foolish woman who forgets them. But as to this outing at Saint-Cloud, this intimate familiarity with two young men in whom I see nothing in common with your way of thinking, what can I say? This neglect of common decency fills me with worry, which I cannot conceal any longer."

I lowered my eyes as I finished, and I wished to leave her every freedom to prepare her answer. She did not make me wait for long. "I realize," she said, "the extent of your suspicions, and my weakness at Livorno is all too likely to justify them. However, you are doing me an extreme injustice if you believe that, either at Saint-Cloud or in any other place where you have observed me, I have for a moment strayed from the principles that I carry deep in my heart. You have repeated to me a thou-

sand times yourself," she continued, "and I learn every day in the books
that you put in my hands, that one must accommodate another's weaknesses, make oneself fit for society, pass with indulgence over the
defects and the passions of one's friends; I put into practice your ideas
and the rules of conduct that I derive continually from my books. I
know you," she added, looking at me with a steadier eye. "I know that
a secret is safe with you; but you have given me a companion whose
weaknesses I must treat with consideration. She is your friend, she is
my guide; what other choice have I but to obey her and please her?"

It would have required much less to make me lock away all my
reproaches and indeed make me repent having expressed them too
freely. I thought I understood all at once the heart of the mystery. The
count loved Théophé. M. de R—— pretended to love the old widow
in order to help his friend. And Théophé listened to the count in order
to oblige her governess, to whom she thought she was doing a service
by contributing to the facility of her courtship. What delusions! But
what renewal of esteem I felt for Théophé, whose past perfections all
seemed to reemerge. My infirmities made me credulous. I embraced
the lovely Théophé. "Yes," I said, "it is of me you ought to complain. I
have given you a foolish woman as a guide, whose ridiculous imaginings must, I realize, bother you constantly. I am speaking of what I saw.
I am a witness to it. I needed only to understand your dispositions better in order to do you all the justice that you deserve. But let us not go
further. I will set you free from this disagreeable slavery tomorrow, and
I already have in mind a companion who will be much better suited to
your inclinations.

It was night. I was in my dressing gown. Théophé had still, in my
eyes, the all-powerful charms that had made such an impression on my
heart. The underlying modesty that declared itself so openly in this honest willingness to please revived vestiges of feeling in me that I had
thought more completely effaced. Even my weakened condition was
not an obstacle, and I still cannot understand how feelings of honesty
and virtue produced the same effects as the image of vice. I granted no
more freedom to my senses for all that, but carried away a new fire from
this visit, from which I had thought myself henceforth shielded by my
continual infirmities as much as by the maturity of my reason. A feeling of shame at my weakness seized me as I made my way back to my
room – that is, after I had surrendered to it completely – because I did
not resist it any more than I had in Constantinople; and if I was much
less able to form desires because of the state of my health, I thought
myself only the more justified in giving in to sentiments whose effects

had to be locked up in my heart. But that very same night, they produced one effect I had not foreseen. They revived that passionate jealousy that had possessed me for so long and was perhaps, of all the weaknesses of love, the one least suited to my situation. Scarcely was I in bed when, not being able to understand how I could have cooled toward so charming an object, I abandoned myself to regret at not having taken better advantage of the occasions I had had to please her, and regret at having brought her to France perhaps only to see some adventurer gather the fruits that I would sooner or later have obtained with a little more ardor and constancy. Finally, while the delicacy of my health did not permit my passion to resume its old violence, it became proportionate to my strength, that is, capable of occupying me entirely.

In this state, it did not require much effort for Théophé to satisfy me. The only kindness I proposed to ask of her was that she be often in my room, where my pain kept me in bed sometimes for entire weeks. The new companion I intended to give her was gentle enough and sensible enough to submit to this habit and to find nothing distasteful in the company of an invalid. The mere idea of this new plan held enough charm to procure me a tranquil sleep. But the very next morning Théophé sent for permission to enter my room, and all my plans came to be disrupted by the proposal she was coming to make. From whatever source her grief came, she had been so moved by my reproaches, or so offended by what had happened at Saint-Cloud, that, finding all her pleasures and the kind of life she was leading an affliction, she came to ask my permission to retire to a convent. "The pleasure of seeing you," she said to me kindly, "which has made me wish only to live near you, is a benefit of which I am continually deprived by your illness. What am I doing in the tumult of a city such as Paris? The flatteries of men importune me. The dissipation of pleasures amuses me less than it wearies me. I am thinking," she added, "of making for myself a kind of life such as I observed at Oru; and of all the places with which I have become acquainted here, I see none that is more in keeping with my inclinations than a convent."

Who would not have thought that proposing my own plan was the best response I could make to this request? Thus, I hastened to say to Théophé that, far from opposing her desires, I wanted to have her find in my house all the advantages that she hoped for in a convent; and explaining to her those that I myself would find in seeing her near me constantly, occupied with reading, painting, and conversing or playing with a new companion, in short, making for herself a pleasant occupation of all the exercises she loved, I expected in the simplicity of my heart that she would avidly embrace a choice that included all that she had seemed to wish. But insisting on the resolution she had formed to retire to a convent, she urged me with new entreaties to consent to it. I was surprised that she did not mention losing the constant pleasure of seeing me. In fact, this should have been the first consideration to strike her, as she had just told me that being deprived of my company because of my illness had greatly afflicted her. I could not prevent myself from turning my reflections in that direction. But always coming back to her ideas, believing herself rid of me at the cost of a few polite remarks, she continued to speak to me of the convent as the only place, henceforth, for which she had any desire. I felt so mortified by her indifference that, heeding only my resentment, I declared to her in a fairly morose tone that I did not approve of her plan and that, as long as there remained in her any consideration for me, I asked her to dismiss the idea absolutely. I gave orders to send for the person I had chosen as her companion and whom I had already warned the day before with a note. She was the widow of a lawyer whose husband had left her little property; thus she had received my proposal, from which she could derive several advantages, with much joy. She lived in my neighborhood, so that she arrived almost at once, and I explained to her at greater length the service she could render me by forming a close friendship with Théophé. They acquired all the liking for each other that I had wished for, and Théophé submitted to my intentions without a murmur.

Such pleasant company became the charm of all my torments. I took nothing but the hand of my dear Greek. I talked only to her. I had attention only for her replies. In the cruellest attacks of an illness to which I was condemned for the rest of my life, even the smallest tasks she did for me brought me relief, and the feelings of pain I was experiencing at the time did not prevent me from feeling, sometimes, the most delicious emotions of pleasure. She seemed to take an interest in my situation, and it did not seem that even her longest attentions were a burden to her. What was more, not a day went by that I did not persuade her to take several hours of pleasure in walking or attending the theater with her companion. She sometimes had to be forced to comply. Her absences were brief, and I never noticed that her return seemed to her a painful duty. However, in the midst of a situation so charming, her first governess, who had not allowed herself to be dismissed without some resentment, came to disturb my rest once again with suspicions that I was never able to clear up. It is here that I yield absolutely the judgment of my difficulties to the reader, and I leave it to him to form whatever opinion he must of all that may have appeared to him obscure or uncertain in Théophé's character and conduct.

This woman's accusations were not very tactful. After having complained to me of an unfortunate situation that prevented me from keeping my eyes open to what was going on in my house, she informed me plainly that the Count de ——— was regularly seeing Théophé and that he had now succeeded, as he never had while the young Greek woman was under her guidance, in inspiring her with love. And not waiting until I had recovered from my initial surprise, she added that the two lovers saw each other at night in Théophé's own apartment, Théophé apparently leaving me in the evening only to receive her suitor in her arms.

The time she had chosen to do me such an ill turn was fortunately one when Théophé was absent. I would not have been able to hide the devastating impression her speech made on me, and in an affair of this nature the important thing was not to make a scandal of a disturbance that could only be penetrated with much secrecy and precaution. My first thoughts were still favorable to Théophé. I recalled all her behavior since she had decided to be with me almost constantly in my solitude. With the exception of the time I made her spend walking, she was never out of my apartment a quarter of an hour. Did she thus accord her passion only such brief moments; and is love capable of such constant moderation? Night was always well advanced when she left me. In the morning I saw her customary vivacity and freshness. Does one bring back much of that from the company of a passionate lover? And then, did I not always see in her the same air of chastity and modesty? And was not what I found most charming in her this perpetual harmony of prudence and playfulness, which seemed to manifest as much restraint in her desires as order in her ideas? Lastly, I was aware of the flightiness and imprudence of her accuser; and although I did not think her capable of a calumny, I had not doubted that she was sensitive enough to the displeasure I had shown over her conduct to seek to wreak some vengeance either on me or on Théophé, or on the person whom I had substituted for her duties.

However, as she still made her home in my house, and as I would not have wanted the secret that she had confided in me to issue from her mouth or from mine, I told her that with such serious accusations it was necessary, first, to keep them secret, as much for the honor of my house as for that of the young Greek woman; and second, not to regard them as certain truths before they had been confirmed by clear evidence. "Discretion," I said, "is a duty which I recommend to you so urgently that you could not fail in it without making me your mortal enemy; and as for the certainty I wish to obtain, you must understand how necessary it is since you will have exposed yourself to strange suspicions if you do not find the means to verify your discoveries." We parted company very ill satisfied with one another; for if she had not found in me all the trust that she would have wished for her tale, I had perceived in her zeal more bitterness and heat than I should have expected from the mere wish to oblige me.

Two days went by, which for me were centuries of unease and torment because of the constraint in which I was obliged to live with Théophé. Much as I wished not to find her guilty, I would have been just as annoyed, supposing she was, not to know all the licentiousness of her conduct. At last, on the evening of the third day, half an hour at most after she had left me, her enemy entered my apartment with an air of urgency and warned me in a whisper that I could surprise Théophé with her lover. I had her repeat more than once an announcement so cruel and so humiliating for me. She confirmed it with a circumstantial detail that overcame all my doubts.

I was in bed, prostrated by my usual pains, and I needed considerable effort to put myself in a condition to go with her. How many precautions were necessary, moreover, to give my servants the slip? It is true that a good deal of time passed in these preparations. My feelings of repugnance and dread made me even slower. I found myself disposed, nonetheless, to go to Théophé's apartment. Our only light was a candle, and Mme de ——— carried it herself. It went out two steps from the door. It took several more minutes to light it again. "It is to be feared," my guide told me as she rejoined me, "that the lover has profited from this moment to escape! However," she added, "the door would not have opened and closed without noise." We knocked on it. I was trembling, and I was not so carefree in my mind that I could distinguish details. After having made us wait for a few minutes, Théophé's companion opened the door, and showed much astonishment at seeing me so late at her mistress's door.

"Is she alone? Is she in bed?" I asked her several questions of this sort with a lively agitation. Her accuser wanted to go abruptly in. I restrained her. "It is impossible," I said, "for anyone to escape now without being seen. This is the only door. And I would be in despair at the outrage we would do to Théophé if she were not guilty." The companion assured me meanwhile that her mistress was in bed and that she was already sleeping tranquilly. But the very noise we were making was enough to awaken her; we heard some movements that appeared to increase her enemy's impatience. It was necessary to follow after her and cross the antechamber. Théophé, after having called in vain for her chambermaid, who slept in an adjoining room, had apparently followed the movement of her fear, to the noise that she heard at her door. She had gotten up, and in the background I was oddly surprised to find her coming forward to open the door for us.

It had not taken her very long to dress. She was covered only in a very thin robe; and I was not surprised, either, to find lights on in her bedroom, because I was quite aware that this was her custom. But I saw her awake, whereas I had just been assured that she was asleep. I saw her looking afraid and confused, which I could not attribute merely to her surprise at seeing me. Lastly, as my imagination was full of all the imputations of her accuser, the slightest disorders that I thought I noticed in her room seemed to me so many traces of her lover and proofs of the licentiousness with which she was being reproached. She asked me, trembling, what brought me here so late. "Nothing," I told her in a tone more brusque than I was accustomed to use with her; and casting my eyes in all directions, I continued to take in all that could serve to clarify my suspicions. The room was so open that nothing in it could be concealed from my gaze. I opened a cabinet, though it would not have been easy for anyone to hide there either. I stooped down to look under the bed. Finally, having left no spot uninspected, I withdrew without having uttered a single word and without having thought, even, of answering the various questions that Théophé had asked in astonishment at this scene. If shame and indignation had disturbed me as I came thither, I was no less disturbed in going out, by the fear of having committed an injustice. The accuser had remained as a sort of guard in the antechamber. "Come," I said to her in an altered tone. "I truly fear that you have engaged me in an infamous proceeding." She seemed as agitated as I, and it was only after we left that she protested that the count must have escaped, since she swore to me that she had seen him with her own eyes climb the staircase and go into the apartment.

I had so little objection to make either to the testimony of a woman whom I dared not suspect of imposture or to that of my own eyes, which had not discovered anything in Théophé's room, that, seeing only causes of horror and confusion in this adventure, I chose to go promptly back to my bed in order to recover from the cruel agitation from which I was suffering. However, the present memory of the agitation in which I had just left Théophé, and a thousand sentiments that fought for her in my heart, led me to send one of my servants to ask her not to worry. I reproached myself for the silence I had so stubbornly maintained. She might have drawn frightful conclusions from it; and what impression must they not have made on her mind and her heart if she were innocent? It was reported to me that she had been found dissolved in tears and that, to the compliment which had been conveyed to her from me, she had responded only with sighs and laments over her fate. I was so touched by this that had I heeded only the voice of my compassion, I would have returned to her room to console her. But the doubts that clouded my mind, or rather the almost invincible reasons that seemed to ruin any hope of finding her innocent, kept me there against my will in a prostration that endured the entire night.

My resolve was to anticipate her the next day with a visit, as much in order to relieve her confusion as to draw from her the confession of the licentiousness with which she was accused. A long habit of living with her and knowing her dispositions caused me to hope that I would soon discover the truth; and if I was forced to withdraw my respect for her, I thought at least to save her from the mockery of her enemy, by hiding from the latter what I might discover by my own private efforts. Something of this plan had been part of the silence I had kept during my searches the night before. I did not want anyone to be able to reproach me with having blinded myself voluntarily, and I would not have spared Théophé had I had the ill fortune of surprising her with the count; but as a vestige of hope still counterbalanced my fears, I was resolved to seize the least pretexts to make the governess abandon her imaginings; and nothing had confounded me so much as to hear her insist on the evidence of her own eyes at the moment when I was going to accuse her of having given in to her prejudices too thoughtlessly.

I was preparing, therefore, to go up to Théophé's room, when I was told that she had entered my apartment. I was grateful to her for making the first move. The care she had taken to compose her face did not prevent me from noticing the traces of her tears. She had her eyes lowered, and for several minutes she did not dare lift them to me. "Well now, Théophé," I said, forestalling her, "so it seems you have managed to forget all your principles? You are no longer the wise and modest girl whose virtue has always been more dear to me than her beauty? Oh, God! Lovers in the middle of the night! I did not have the mortal grief of surprising you with the Count de ————; but he was seen entering your room, and this horrible occurrence is not the first." I watched her with sharp attention, in order to distinguish even the least of her emotions. She cried for a long time, she sobbed, her voice was as though stifled by it; and perceiving nothing more that could assist my judgment, I was as moved by my impatience as she appeared to be by the feeling that was agitating her. At last regaining the power to speak, she cried, "He was seen entering my room! Who saw him? Who dares to charge me with so cruel an accusation? It is no doubt Madame de ———," she added, naming her former governess, "but if you believe her hatred, it is useless to try to defend myself."

These words caused me some surprise. I concentrated all my attention on them. They made me think not only that Théophé was informed about the subject of my complaints, but that she knew this woman had a firm resolution to do her harm. "Listen," I answered, interrupting her, "I will not hide from you that it was Madame de ——— who saw the count. Should I have mistrusted her evidence? But if you know something that may weaken it, I will not refuse to hear you." This encouragement seemed to give her more audacity. She told me that ever since the day that this lady had ceased to be her companion, M. de R———, who was no longer inclined to encumber himself with seeing Mme de ———, had responded rather harshly to some note by which she had indicated to him that he could continue to come to her despite some changes that did not concern her. He had declared to her that the comedy was over and that the reasons he had had for performing it had ended with the change she had advised him of. This declaration having opened her eyes to the humiliating role she had been playing, she had persuaded herself that Théophé must be on even better terms with *her* lover than she herself had thought she had been with hers, and the desire to avenge herself had made her resort to all sorts of means to discover proofs of it. "I was not unaware of her artifices," Théophé told me. "She had me followed every time I went out, and imagining finally that I was receiving the count during the night, she took her maliciousness so far as to have my bed carefully examined. What offers did she not make to my maid? It was not two days ago that she seized at the door a letter that the count had written to me. She brought it to me right away completely open; and, piqued at finding in it only respectful expressions, she gave it all the meaning that maliciousness may invent, threatening me that she would tell you of it.

"I did not doubt," Théophé added, "when I saw you yesterday in my room with her, that it was her accusations that had brought you there. But your presence, or rather the despair which I felt at seeing you pay heed to my enemy, caused me the consternation you may have noticed. Today I come to entreat you to deliver me from so cruel a persecution." Here, redoubling her tears suddenly and reducing herself to certain Greek humiliations the habit of which she ought to have lost in France, she threw herself to her knees against my bed and begged me to grant her what I had refused her before. "A convent," she said in a voice muffled by her tears, "a convent is the only lot remaining to me, and the only one that I desire."

I do not know what my answer would have been; for, moved though I was by her tears, and even persuaded by her justification, I was to the same extent loath to regard her accuser as the wickedest and blackest of all women. For several minutes I remained uncertain, and all my reflections brought me no more understanding. My door opened. I saw Mme de ———, that is, Théophé's enemy, and perhaps mine, and the source of all our woes. Was I to expect enlightenment or more darkness from her visit? I did not have time to form this doubt. She could not have been unaware that Théophé was in my apartment, and it was apparently the fear of seeing her gain some ascendancy over my confidence that brought her here in order to attack Théophé or to defend herself. Thus did she begin by treating Théophé without consideration. She made such harsh reproaches against her that innocent or guilty, the sad Théophé could not resist this torrent of insults. She fell into a profound faint, from which the assistance of my servants was long in reviving her. As the governess's accusations began again with renewed ardor, I saw nothing more clearly in this frightful contention than her obstinacy in claiming that she had seen the Count de ——— enter the place where we had searched for him, and Théophé's constancy in asserting that this was a horrible lie.

I suffered more than she at so violent a spectacle. At last, torn by a thousand feelings that were too much for me to understand, unable to abandon the opinion I had of Mme de ———'s honor nor to resolve to hate and scorn Théophé, I decided with more than one sigh to impose silence on them and told them both to efface the memory of an incident the very idea of which must cause them as much horror as it did me. "You will not leave me," I told Théophé, "and you will maintain a conduct that is above suspicion. You," I said to Mme de ———, "will continue to live in my house, and if you should happen to renew accusations that are not better proven, you will immediately go seek another refuge." I had a right to make this threat to her, because it was by my generosity alone that she subsisted.

I continued after this strange incident to enjoy the sight and the company of Théophé, without claiming to take other satisfaction from it than that of seeing her and listening to her. The force of my illness, and perhaps the lasting impression of so unfortunate a scene, gradually healed me of all the wounds of love. If she yielded herself to other weaknesses, it is from her lovers that the public must expect an account of them. They did not find their way into the place to which I was confined by my infirmities. I did not even learn of her death until several months after the dismal accident, because of the care that my family and all the friends who saw me in my solitude took to keep it from me. It was immediately after the first news I was given of it that I formed the plan to gather in writing all that I shared with this lovely foreigner, and to let the public judge if I had misplaced my esteem and my tenderness.

———————

NOTES

1. An order given by the sultan or in his name.
2. The sultan's council.

Originally published as *Histoire d'une Grecque moderne* (Amsterdam, 1741).

PART THREE

Ways of the World

No Tomorrow

by Vivant Denon

Translated by Lydia Davis

Introduction

by Catherine Cusset

A Lesson of Decency
Pleasure and Reality in Vivant Denon's
No Tomorrow

by Catherine Cusset

Point de lendemain, or *No Tomorrow* – the title seems to announce clearly the stakes of the story: an affair without sequel and without consequences. This brief story of a one-night seduction – which was published anonymously in 1777 and published again with a few changes and the author's name, Vivant Denon (1747-1825), in 1812[1] – has recently attracted much critical attention because it seems to capture the essence of the art and spirit of the eighteenth century.[2] *No Tomorrow* becomes the pretext for a contemporary debate about pleasure.

The general, contemporary critical attitude toward Denon's story can be summarized as follows: it is a wonderful, but perfectly utopian, dream of pleasure. For example, in *Slowness*, Milan Kundera asks a series of questions about *No Tomorrow*'s hero: "But how did he really feel? And how will he feel as he leaves the château? What will he be thinking about? The pleasure he experienced, or his reputation as a ludicrous whelp? Will he feel like the victor or the vanquished? Happy or unhappy? In other words: is it possible to live in pleasure and for pleasure and be happy? Can the ideal of hedonism be realized?"[3] Kundera concludes that the story's "hedonism" is "hopelessly utopian." This is also the judgment Thomas Kavanagh passes in his chapter on Denon, "Writing of No Consequence," in *Enlightenment and the Shadow of Chance*. There Kavanagh writes, "As the story of a moment defined as inconsequential, this text describes a utopia – the impossible dream of a moment cut off from past and future, of a now with no tomorrow to extend its implications beyond the present of the event's occurrence."[4]

Both Kundera and Kavanagh see *No Tomorrow* as an episode of a longer narrative (such as, for instance, *Dangerous Liaisons* [1782]): if the sequel to the one-night affair were written, it would lead necessarily to the characters' unhappiness. It is in the name of the tomorrow after that the critics condemn *No Tomorrow* as a utopia. Tomorrow becomes synonymous with reality. Pleasure, obviously, is also a reality.

But "reality" here means our social, moral, and psychological existence, which implies duration, continuity, and consequences, whereas pleasure is experienced only in the moment.

This judgment that pleasure and reality are incompatible is the starting point for my analysis of the story. This is an old idea in Western metaphysics and literature: the reality principle and the pleasure principle have always been said to be contradictory. The eighteenth century, with its tradition of libertinism, is probably the only period that attempted to reconcile these two dimensions. Is such a reconciliation possible?

First, it is wrong to think that *No Tomorrow* is not concerned with the tomorrow. The first proof is the title: a title that contains the word "tomorrow," even if only to deny this word, is obviously not ignorant of tomorrow. We also see the day after dawn at the end of the first paragraph, when the narrator writes: "Mme de T—— seemed to have some designs on me yet did not wish to compromise her dignity. As we shall see, Mme de T—— possessed certain principles of decency to which she was scrupulously attached (p. 732)."

We learn two things about Mme de T——: that she has designs on the narrator but also "principles of decency." The word *projet* belongs to the French libertine vocabulary and designates the manifest intention to seduce. Decency, on the contrary, consists in not showing, in not allowing to see. The word "decency" comes from the Latin *decet*, meaning "it is proper" or "advisable." The *Encyclopédie* (1751–72) of Diderot and d'Alembert defines decency as "the conformity of exterior actions with the laws, customs, usage, spirit, mores, religion, point of honor, and prejudices of the society of which one is a member."[5] In eighteenth-century society, a woman must not draw attention to herself: decency is the primary condition of her existence. Decency is obviously a critical notion in *No Tomorrow*, since the narrator mentions it a second time at the beginning of the second paragraph when, upon Mme de T——'s introduction into the story, he ironically calls her "that decent Mme de T——." The stakes are clearly posed: How can the seduction be decent? Or, how will Mme de T—— be able to appear still decent the day after?

How can a seduction be decent? By not being visible. Indeed, after abducting her young companion, Mme de T—— never looks like she is trying to seduce him. If any contact occurs between the protagonists, it is attributed to chance. Chance plays a large role in the first part of the story. The first physical contact is the effect of chance: "The lurching of the carriage caused Mme de T——'s face to touch mine.

At an unexpected jolt, she grasped my hand; and I, by the purest chance, caught hold of her in my arms" (p. 733).

Even kisses happen by chance. When Mme de T—— and the narrator exchange their first kiss, there is nothing erotic about it. It is a symbolic kiss the young man asks of Mme de T——, to be sure that she forgave him for the scene in the carriage. She gives him the kiss to show that she is not scared of him – that is, not scared of being seduced by him. But something happens that was not planned, as the narrator explains: "Kisses are like confidences: they attract each other, they accelerate each other, they excite each other. In fact, I had barely received the first kiss when a second followed on its heels, and then another: their pace quickened, interrupting and then replacing the conversation. Soon they scarcely left us time to sigh" (p. 735).

It is beyond their will. The only thing Mme de T—— can do is to stop the kisses as soon as she realizes what is happening. Finally, it is also by chance that the seduction comes to its conclusion. While the two characters are lost in a conversation about the charms of confidence and sentiment, Mme de T—— sees a pavilion at the end of the garden and regrets not having the key to it, because she would have liked to show the beautiful furniture to her companion. "Still chatting, we approached the pavilion. It had been left open" (p. 738). Not only is the pavilion open – by chance – but it acts according to its own law: "This was love's sanctuary. It took possession of us: our knees buckled, our weakening arms intertwined, and, unable to hold each other up, we sank down onto a sofa that occupied a corner of the temple" (p. 738).

The scenario is repeated each time: whenever an erotic contact occurs between the two protagonists, it is attributed to chance. Mme de T——'s decency leads her to react to this chance and to resist the slippage toward seduction. But then, another chance event occurs and makes her slip further. This insistence on chance is too strong for the narrator's irony to be mistaken. We understand that "chance" is Mme de T——'s method. Chance allows the seduction to progress while decency is preserved. The pavilion found open by chance, for instance, is encountered at the precise moment when the hero can no longer have any suspicion of indecency, because carnal possession, as it is prepared by Mme de T——, has value only through the exaltation of sentiment, spoken in terms of the "soul," not the body. Before showing the pavilion to her companion, Mme de T—— has presented herself as a sincere and sensitive woman, unlike the narrator's mistress, whom she criticizes for being perfidious, hypocritical, and insensitive:

sentiment, like chance, hides the physical reality of pleasure behind a decent veil, by giving a moral meaning to the physical act. The narrator, however, does not allow us to forget the reality that is hidden behind this veil of decency, when he punctuates the description of the sublime amorous moment with these words: "I beg the reader to remember that I was twenty years old" (p. 740) – the virile age at which one can prove his love four times over. This ironic aside to the reader recalls that the whole seduction is a matter of physical pleasure and not of sentiment.

The hero, of course, ignores that he is being manipulated by Mme de T——. But the narrator does not let us be duped by her stratagems: "It was a masterful maneuver.... My lover appeared to be the falsest of all women, and I believed to have found a sensitive soul" (p. 737). The irony of the text is deployed in the gap between the naïveté of the hero, persuaded that he holds the most sensitive of beings, and the intelligence of the narrator, now restored from his illusions. As an epigraph to the second edition, Denon borrowed a sentence from one of Saint Paul's letters to the Corinthians: "The letter kills, the spirit vivifies." This epigraph, Denon's warning to his readers, is the key to reading *No Tomorrow*. To read the text at face value is to kill it. The letter of the story is chance, the autonomy of things and of bodies, and sentiment: these are the masks that protect decency by erasing the visibility of the *projet*. The spirit of the story is the irony that acknowledges this chance to be a pure and necessary sacrifice to the conventions of society. The narrator's irony serves to reveal that the insistence on chance and the vocabulary of sentiment are but masks hiding the only truth: pleasure.

The ironical denunciation of the hypocrisy of the social code is even stronger in the second episode, as it is made by Mme de T—— herself, who radically changes both her tone and her discourse. In the first half, she had been so concerned for her dignity, but now that her plan has been realized she unmasks her true colors: " 'What a delicious night we've just spent,' she said, 'all because of the attraction of pleasure, our guide and our excuse!' " (p. 740). She teaches the narrator that there is no reality other than physical pleasure: as long as the public knows nothing about it, their night of pleasure need not create any sentimental bond nor moral engagement between them. She analyzes the pleasures of love, "reducing them to their simplest forms" (p. 740). This reduction enchants the narrator. Inspired by Mme de T——, he feels "a strong disposition for the love of freedom," and he excuses himself for it to the reader:

We are such *machines* (and I blush at the idea) that, instead of all the delicacy that tormented me before the scene which just took place, I found myself at least half to blame for the boldness of her principles" (p. 740).

Decency – that is, the hypocrisy of the social code – is done away with once and for all in the episode that follows. Mme de T——
awakens the hero's curiosity about a chamber that her husband had had built before their marriage "as evidence of the artificial resources Monsieur de T—— needed to strengthen his affections" and "of how little [she] was able to stimulate his soul" (p. 741). Although he is exhausted, the young man is dying to discover this place and comments, "it was no longer Mme de T—— whom I desired, it was the little room" (p. 741).

The story seems to show that decency and sentiment are but masks concealing desire, and that desire itself is but a mechanical artifice acting independently of people. Just as the doctor-philosopher La Mettrie argued in his 1748 treatise *Machine Man*, *No Tomorrow* would ultimately show that man is nothing but a machine.

M. de T——'s little room is an indecent place. Before actually taking the narrator to the chamber, Mme de T—— tells him about it. Reflective glass covers the interior walls of the chamber and transforms it into "a vast cage of mirrors" (p. 742). What had been hidden under the veils of romance, chance, and a moonless night is now revealed, exposed, and reflected. Pleasure is now born of this exposition: "Desires are reproduced through their images" (p. 743). One could also call "indecent" (in a moral rather than social sense of the word) Mme de T——'s words to her lover after their last sacrifice to love: "Well then! Will you ever love the Countess as much as you love me?" (p. 743). This last question prevents the hero from forming any illusions about the nature of his sentiment: the excitement produced by the artificial room (and not even by Mme de T——) suddenly becomes stronger than all love and all links with the past.

If the story stopped here, one could conclude that it is only a utopia. It would say little about the relationship between reality and pleasure. It would make us laugh at the expense of decency, shown to be only a hypocritical semblance, and reveal that the truth is played out elsewhere: the truth is that of the body, of the mechanical being of human nature. But finally, in spite of all its irony, the story would end up recognizing that decency (that is, the social appearance) still must be respected: the style remains "decent" and the narrator, after his intense night of pleasure, must slip out of the chamber at dawn so that Mme de T——'s reputation will not be compromised.

But the story does not end here. *No Tomorrow* does indeed describe the tomorrow, in two steps. As the young hero, alone in the garden, asks himself whether or not he is Mme de T——'s lover, the Marquis, the official lover of Mme de T——, arrives impromptu, and reveals that the marvelous night is but a comedy directed by Mme de T—— and the Marquis in order to fool the husband by directing his suspicions to the wrong lover. The suspected young man will leave and the Marquis will stay and be happy with Mme de T—— in her husband's castle. Decency is safe. But the comedy gets even more complicated when the Marquis declares that the only fault he sees in Mme de T—— is her physical insensibility: "She inspires everything, causing all sorts of feelings, and yet she herself feels nothing. She's made of stone" (p. 745). What are we to believe? Does Mme de T—— feign her frigidity to preserve the space of her pleasures? Or does she discover pleasure by chance, during that unexpected night? Or, finally, has she faked pleasure in order to better fool the narrator? The text provides no response to these questions; it simply poses them and leaves the choice of a response to us. Again, if the story ended here, the relation between pleasure and reality would not be clear, and one would not know which reality triumphs over the other: that of physical pleasure, or that of the social code?

The scene which brings together Mme de T—— and her two lovers is the true conclusion of the story, and the true "tomorrow," since this scene takes place after Mme de T—— slept and woke up. The narrator introduces it with these words: "Nevertheless, I wanted to see Mme de T—— again; it was a pleasure I couldn't refuse myself" (p. 746). We expect a final scene of confrontation in which the young man will expose the manipulative Mme de T——, express his anger at being fooled, or, at the very least, take pleasure in her confusion. Paradoxically, the only feeling the narrator expresses in this final scene is that of admiration: "We found ourselves all together. M. de T—— had ridiculed and then dismissed me; my friend the Marquis was duping the husband and mocking me; I was paying him back in kind, all the while admiring Mme de T——, who was making fools of us all, without losing her dignity" (p. 747).

What the narrator admires in Mme de T—— is not her intelligence, her mastery of the game, or her talent as an actress. He admires the fact that she wages everything "without losing her dignity." What is important here is the link between the notions of the game and of dignity. The narrator admires the dignity of Mme de T—— in the game, this dignity that, as we learned in the first paragraph of the novel, is tied to decency. But this decency, which the narrator never ceased to deride, from the moment of the encounter at the opera until the episode in the chamber, is it not definitively compromised by the elapsed night and by the revelation of the game?

The notion of decency reappears just before the revelation: "She spoke tenderly to him, and honestly and decently to me" (p. 747). The two lovers, both deceived by Mme de T——, find themselves at the head of her bed when she awakens. She addresses tender words to the Marquis: there could be no more natural reaction when a lover has just arrived. In contrast, she addresses honest and decent words to the narrator. Here the word "honest" must be understood in its seventeenth-century sense, as in the expression *honnête homme*, which designates the *gentilhomme* and not the man of good values, good mores. Thus, "honest" does not have a moral implication, but signifies, rather, "conforming to the norms of high society." This is exactly the meaning of the word "decent," as we saw before. So why would Denon use two adjectives to say the same thing? Should we understand a more modern sense of "decent," as the contrary of indecent? It is obvious, however, that, in the presence of her lover the Marquis, Mme de T—— could not address the narrator with indecent allusions to the pleasures of the elapsed night. Why then does the narrator specify that her words are "decent"?

To fully understand the meaning of the word "decent" here, we must read it in its context. Just before its appearance, the narrator had written: "She laughed about [the game] with me as much as was necessary to console me, and without lowering herself in my esteem" (p. 747). Mme de T—— makes her laughter proportionate to the situation, that is, to the states of mind of the two men at the head of her bed. She laughs with the Marquis out of politeness; but she moderates her laughter and puts a stop to the Marquis's laughter out of respect for the man she deceived: "Come, Monsieur," said Mme de T——, "let's speak no more of it" (p. 747). In the course of this brief scene, decency is redefined: it is no longer only the mundane code derided by the narrator; it now comes to designate a sense of the measure that allows one to accomplish exactly the gestures adequate to the situation at hand.

It is thanks to her decency that Mme de T—— avoids the two pitfalls of the tomorrow: the contempt that results from pleasure too easily given, which she avoids by respecting the appearances of chance and of sentiment, and the love that prolongs the moment of pleasure, which she avoids thanks to the episode in the chamber. She gave the hero everything so that he no longer has anything to desire and hence leaves of his own accord. The episode in the chamber, which one could have taken as an act of indecency, is thus a "decent" act in the etymological sense of the word: it is an act that is proper in the present situation. This suitability is not simply the respect for social graces but the skillful adaptation to a delicate situation. If the narrator admires Mme de T—— at the end of the story, if *No Tomorrow*'s characters do not go to "war" as the protagonists of *Dangerous Liaisons* do, if this is a complete story and not simply an episode that should be integrated into a longer narrative, it is because of Mme de T——'s decency and the narrator's admiration for her, which proves that he appreciates all the subtlety of her behavior.

The focus of the narrator's irony has shifted by the end of the story: it is now directed at the reader's expectation of a moral to the story: "I stepped into the coach awaiting me. I looked hard for the moral of this whole adventure...and found none" (p. 747). It is obvious that the absence of a moral, and, even more so, the announced rejection of morals, does indeed represent a moral: so what is meant by this ironic allusion to the absence of moral at the story's end?

It signifies that the very utterance of the moral (or of the "meaning" of the story) would itself be indecent. To draw the conclusion of the story would be to lack subtlety and levity. In the desire for meaning and interpretation, there is a heaviness that would be indecent, unbefitting in a story about pleasure. It is this heaviness that the narrator shows when he first finds himself alone in the garden at dawn and wonders whether he is the lover of the woman he just left. It is this heaviness, too, that the official lover also shows when he proclaims proudly to have had some difficulty in capturing the heart of Mme de T—— and declares her only flaw to be her frigidity. In comparison to Mme de T——, the two lovers of the story are equally ridiculous, the one who laughs secretly just as much as the one who wants to force the other to laugh: "Oh! What a fine adventure! But I fear you're not laughing about it enough for my taste. Don't you see just how comical your role is?" (p. 745).

This phrase by the Marquis is a direct echo of the famous scene in Molière's *The School for Wives* (1661) in which Horace, the young lover, informs Arnolphe, the old fogy, of the trick the ingenue Agnès just played on him. Having discovered his pupil's deception and the failure of all his precautions, Arnolphe is not able to laugh as Horace encourages him to ("You haven't laughed about as much as I thought you would").[6] Thus, the end of *The School for Wives* consecrates the triumph of love and youth. The end of *No Tomorrow*, however, does not lead to such a clear moral. It is much more subtle: there is neither a young lover nor an old fogy; nor is there an essence to the story. There are only "situations" in which decency, as a mark of humanity and a sense of negotiation, regulates the relations between beings and allows desire to be deployed without causing any harm. Whether proceeding by allusions or by light or skillful brushes of skin or of vanity, decency implies a subtlety that contrasts with the weightiness of sentiment, bodies, and meaning. Irony is the decency of the text.

By its irony, the text teaches us a lesson. It is this lesson that allows us to speak of an ethics of pleasure, in both senses of the word "ethics," as the science of morality and the art of determining conduct. *No Tomorrow* does not simply enhance pleasure as a value at the expense of some other reality; it is not, therefore, a utopia. To be perfect, the moment of pleasure must not only be chosen, but also constructed through a rigorous method that does not allow for error. The story teaches us a lesson in decency, and decency transforms pleasure into an art. The narrator's final admiration for Mme de T—— reveals another kind of decency, one which is not only the hypocritical veil covering the reality of that thing which decency forbids us from seeing laid bare, but the perception of all the nuances of a situation which allows one to adapt to it with subtlety and delicacy, and the comprehension that all being is being in a situation, that is, in engagement with others.

Decency also receives another name: tact. In French, tact is defined in the Petit Robert, first, as the "intuitive, spontaneous, and delicate appreciation of what it is suitable to say, to do, or to avoid in human relations." Tact, in that sense, is primarily a social quality, and probably the main quality of a good *salonnière* in the eighteenth century. Tact, however, also signifies the sense of touch, "the sensibility that, in the contact with a surface, allows one to appreciate certain characteristics (smooth, silky, rough, dry, humid, sticky, etc.)." *No Tomorrow* gives us a lesson in tact in all the senses of the word: the tactile quality of skins that have loved each other and given each other pleasure, the tact of Mme de T—— with regard to these human susceptibilities which must be treated with care in order to be brought about, and finally the tact of the story's narration, which delivers its lesson with an ironic levity while seeming not to touch on any moral at all.

NOTES

1. On the history of the story's publication, see Claude-Joseph Dorat (to whom the short story was first attributed) *Mélanges littéraires ou Journal des dames dédié à la Reine* (Paris, 1777), vol. 2, p. 3; Emile Henriot, "Vivant Denon," in *Les Livres du second rayon, irréguliers et libertins* (Paris: Emile Chamontin, 1926); and Raymond Trousson, introduction to *Point de lendemain* in *Romans libertins du XVIIIème siècle* (Paris: Laffont, 1993).

2. Denon's story has recently been published by Editions Desjonquères with an introduction by René Démoris (1987), by Folio with a preface by Michel Delon (1995), and in the volume *Romans libertins* published by Laffont and edited by Raymond Trousson (1993).

3. Milan Kundera, *Slowness*, trans. Linda Asher (New York: Harper Collins, 1996), p. 143.

4. Thomas Kavanagh, "Writing of No Consequence," in *Enlightenment and the Shadow of Chance: The Novel and the Culture of Gambling in Eighteenth-Century France* (Baltimore and London: Johns Hopkins University Press, 1993), p. 186.

5. "Décence," in *Encyclopédie, ou Dictionnaire raisonné des sciences, des arts et des techniques* (Paris, 1765).

6. See Molière, *The School for Wives* (New York: Harcourt Brace Jonanovich, 1971), act III, scene 4, pp. 78–79:

> HORACE: As for my jealous rival, isn't the role he's played in this affair extremely droll? Well?
>
> ARNOLPHE: Yes, quite droll.
>
> HORACE: Well, laugh, if that's the case! *(Arnolphe gives a forced laugh.)* My, what a fool! He fortifies his place against me, using bricks for cannon balls, as if he feared that I might storm the walls; [...] and then he's hoodwinked by the girl he meant to keep forever meek and innocent! [...] The whole thing's been so comical that I find that I'm convulsed whenever it comes to mind. You haven't laughed as much as I thought you would.
>
> ARNOLPHE: *(with a forced laugh)* I beg your pardon, I've done the best I could.

NO TOMORROW

by Vivant Denon

I WAS DESPERATELY in love with the Comtesse de ————; I was twenty years old and I was naive. She deceived me, I got angry, she left me. I was naive, I missed her. I was twenty years old, she forgave me, and, because I was twenty years old, because I was naive – still deceived, but no longer abandoned – I thought myself to be the best-loved lover, and therefore the happiest of men. She was a friend of Mme de T——, who seemed to have some designs on me yet did not wish to compromise her dignity. As we shall see, Mme de T—— possessed certain principles of decency to which she was scrupulously attached.

One day while waiting for the Countess in her opera box, I heard someone calling from the adjacent box. Was it not the decent Mme de T—— again? "What! So early?" she said to me. "And with nothing to do! Come over here and join me."

I had no idea just how fantastic and extraordinary this meeting would turn out to be. A woman's imagination moves quite quickly, and at this very moment Mme de T——'s imagination was singularly inspired.

"I shall spare you the ridicule of such solitude," she said. "And since you are here, you must... Yes, it's an excellent idea. A divine hand must have led you here. You don't by any chance have plans for this evening? I warn you, they would be pointless. No questions, don't try to resist... Call my servants. You are just charming."

I bowed low, she hurried me into her box, I obeyed.

"Go to Monsieur's house," she told a servant, "and let them know he won't be back this evening..." She then whispered in his ear and dismissed him. I tried to venture a few words, the opera began, she hushed me. We listened, or pretended to listen. The first act had scarcely ended when the same servant returned with a note for Mme de T—— telling her everything was ready. She smiled, asked for my hand, went down to the street, and invited me into her carriage. We were already outside the city before I could find out what she intended to do with me.

Every time I ventured a question, she responded with a burst of laughter. Had I not been so aware that she was a passionate woman, that she was currently involved, and that she could not help knowing that I knew this, I would have been tempted to think myself a quite fortunate fellow. She also knew the state of my heart, for, as I've already said, the Comtesse de ——— was a close friend of Mme de T——. I therefore refrained from any presumptuous ideas, and I waited to see what would happen. We changed horses and started off again with lightning speed. Suddenly, this all seemed more serious to me. I urged her to tell me where this game would lead me.

"It will lead you to a very beautiful place. Just guess where. Oh, you'll never guess... My husband's house. Do you know him?"

"Not at all."

"I think you'll like him: we're to be reconciled. Negotiations have been going on for six months now, and we have been corresponding with each other for one month. Don't you find it quite obliging of me to go and visit him?"

"Absolutely. But please tell me – what will I do there? How can I be of use in all of this?"

"That's my business. I was afraid a tête-à-tête with him would be boring. You're agreeable, and I'm very glad to have you with me."

"Strange that you would choose the day of your reconciliation to introduce me. You would have me believe I'm of little consequence. Add to this the natural awkwardness of a first meeting. Honestly, I can see nothing pleasant for any of us in what you intend."

"Oh, no moralizing, I beg you. You're missing the point of your task. You're supposed to entertain me and amuse me, not preach to me."

I saw she was quite determined, so I gave in. I began to laugh at the role I was playing, and we became very cheerful.

We changed horses a second time. Night's mysterious orb illuminated a pure sky and spread a voluptuous half-light. We were approaching the place where our tête-à-tête would come to an end. From time to time I was asked to admire the beauty of the landscape, the calm of the night, the moving silence of nature. In order to enjoy all this together, we naturally had to lean toward the same window; the lurching of the carriage caused Mme de T——'s face to touch mine. At an unexpected jolt, she grasped my hand; and I, by the purest chance, caught hold of her in my arms. I don't know what we were trying to do in this position, but what is certain is that my vision dimmed when she let go of me abruptly and threw herself back deep into the depths of the carriage.

"Do you intend," she said after a rather profound reverie, "to convince me of my imprudence in your regard?"

The question disconcerted me. "Intend...with you...I wouldn't dream of it! You would see through me too easily. But mere chance, a surprise...that can be forgiven."

"It seems that you have been counting on it."

We had come to this point almost without noticing that we were entering the château's forecourt. Everything was brightly lit, everything proclaimed joy, except for the master's face, which stubbornly refused to show any such sign. His languid manner indicated that he felt the need to reconcile for no other than family reasons. Propriety, however, brought M. de T—— to the carriage door. I was introduced, he gave me his hand, and I followed, musing over my role, past, present, and to come. I passed through rooms decorated with as much taste as magnificence. The master of the house was particularly attuned to all the refinements of luxury, for he was endeavoring to replenish the resources of his worn-out body with images of sensual pleasure. Not knowing what to say, I took refuge in admiration. The goddess eagerly did the honors of the temple, and received my compliments very graciously.

"What you see is nothing; I must take you to Monsieur's apartment."

"Madame, I had it torn down five years ago."

"But, of course!" she said.

At supper didn't she take it upon herself to offer Normandy veal to Monsieur? And Monsieur said to her, "For the past three years I've been on a milk diet."

"But, of course!" she said again.

Try to picture a conversation between three creatures so surprised to find themselves together!

Supper came to an end. I imagined we would go to bed early, but I was right only in the case of the husband. As we entered the drawing room he said, "I am grateful to you, Madame, for the foresight you showed in bringing Monsieur with you. In judging that I would be a poor resource for the evening you judged well, because I will be retiring now." Then, turning to me, he added in an ironic tone, "Monsieur will please forgive me, and do convey my apologies to Madame." He left us.

We looked at each other, and as a distraction from our thoughts, Mme de T—— suggested we take a stroll on the terrace while waiting for the servants to have their supper. The night was superb; it revealed things in glimpses, and seemed only to veil them so as to give free rein to the imagination. The château as well as the gardens, resting against a mountainside, descended in terraces to the banks of the Seine, whose many loops formed small, picturesque, rustic islands that created different views and enhanced the charm of this lovely spot.

We walked first on the longest of these terraces: it was thickly planted with large trees. We had recovered from the unpleasant banter we had just endured, and as we walked she entrusted me with a few confidences. One confidence attracts another, and as I, in turn, confided in her, our confidences became evermore intimate and interesting. We had been walking for a long time. She had at first given me her arm, then that arm somehow or other entwined itself around me, while mine bore her up and prevented her, almost, from touching the ground. This position was pleasant but eventually tiring, and we still had many things to say to each other. A grassy bank appeared before us; we sat down on it without changing position, and in this posture we began to sing the praises of trust, its charm, its sweetness.

"Oh," she said to me, "who can enjoy this more than we, and with less apprehension? I am all too aware of how loyal you are to the attachment I know about to fear anything from you."

Perhaps she wanted me to contradict her, but I did nothing of the sort. We therefore persuaded each other that it was impossible that we could ever be anything other than what we were to each other then.

"Yet I was afraid," I said, "that the incident in the carriage might have scared you."

"I'm not so easily alarmed."

"Yet I fear it may have left a few clouds."

"What will it take to reassure you?"

"You can't guess?"

"I would like to have it explained to me."

"I need to be sure you forgive me."

"And for that, I would have to . . ."

"Grant me, here, the kiss that chance . . ."

"Very well, you would be too proud of yourself if I refused. Your vanity would convince you I was afraid."

She wanted to forestall my illusions, and so I received the kiss.

Kisses are like confidences: they attract each other, they accelerate each other, they excite each other. In fact, I had barely received the first kiss when a second followed on its heels, and then another: their pace quickened, interrupting and then replacing the conversation. Soon they scarcely left us time to sigh. Silence fell all around us. We heard it (for one sometimes hears silence), and we were frightened. We stood up without saying a word and began to walk again.

"We must go back in," she said. "The evening air isn't good for us."

"I don't think it's so dangerous for you," I answered.

"True, I'm less susceptible than certain other women, but no matter – let's go back in."

"Out of consideration for me, no doubt... You want to protect me from the dangerous impressions this walk might make...and the consequences that might ensue for me alone."

"You attribute considerable delicacy to my motives. I'm quite happy to have it that way – but let's go back in, I insist." (Awkward remarks of this sort are inevitably exchanged by two people who are trying as best they can to say something quite different from what they want to say.)

She forced me to head back toward the château.

I don't know – at least I didn't know then – if by this decision she was acting contrary to her own desires, if she had firmly made up her mind, or if she shared the disappointment I felt at watching a scene that had begun so nicely end this way. In any case, as if by a common instinct, we slowed our steps and walked along sadly, discontented with each other and ourselves. We didn't know who or what to blame. Neither of us had any right to ask or demand anything; we couldn't even resort to reproach. How a quarrel would have soothed us! But what should we have quarreled about? Yet we were nearly back at the house, silently occupied with avoiding the restraint we had so clumsily imposed on ourselves.

We had just reached the door when Mme de T—— spoke at last: "I'm not very pleased with you...After I have shown such trust in you, it is unfair...so unfair...not to grant me any! Have you said even one word about the Countess since we've been together? Even though it is so pleasant to talk about someone you love! And you can't doubt that I would have listened to you with great interest. It is certainly the least I could do for you after having deprived you of her company."

"Don't I have the same reproach to make to you, and wouldn't you have avoided many problems if instead of making me the confidant of a reconciliation with a husband, you had spoken to me about a more appropriate choice – a choice..."

"Stop at once...Remember that the slightest suspicion will hurt a woman. If you know anything at all about women, you know that you have to wait for their confidences. But let's come back to you – what is going on with your friend? Is she making you quite happy? Oh, I fear the contrary, and this distresses me, because I take such a tender interest in you! Yes, Monsieur, I am interested...more than you may think, perhaps."

"Now really, Madame, why believe the gossip people enjoy spreading and exaggerating?"

"Don't try to pretend. I know everything about you that can be known. The Countess is not as mysterious as you. Women like her are generous with the secrets of their worshipers, especially when a discreet cast of mind like yours might deprive them of their triumphs. I do not in the least accuse her of being coquettish, but a prude has just as much vanity as a coquette. Tell me frankly: Are you not often the victim of her strange whims? Come now, tell me."

"But Madame, you wanted to go back in...and the air..."

"It has changed."

She had taken my arm again and we resumed our walk without my noticing the path we were following. What she had just hinted at about the lover I knew she had, what she was telling me about the mistress she knew I had, this whole trip, the scene in the carriage, the scene on the grassy bank, the time of night – all of it disturbed me: I was by turns overcome with vanity or desire, and then returned to myself by reflection. Besides, I was too moved to realize what I was experiencing. While I was prey to such confused emotions, she continued to talk, still about the Countess. My silence seemed to confirm everything she chose to say. Yet several biting remarks she let slip brought me back to myself.

"How cunning she is!" she said, "how graceful! Treachery in her mouth appears as wit; an infidelity seems an act of reason, a sacrifice to decency. She never forgets herself, is always pleasant, rarely tender, and never true; flighty by nature, a prude by design; lively, cautious, artful, distracted, sensitive, clever, coquettish, and philosophical: she's a Proteus of forms, she charms with her manners – she attracts, she eludes. How many roles I've seen her play! Between you and me, how many dupes surround her! How she has mocked the Baron!...How many tricks she has played on the Marquis! When she took up with you, it was to regain her hold over two overly imprudent rivals who were about to expose her. She had accommodated them too much, they had had time to observe her; eventually, they would have caused a scandal. But she brought you onto the scene, gave them a hint of your attentions, led them to pursue her anew, drove you to despair, pitied you, consoled you – and all four of you were content. Oh, what power an artful woman has over you! And how happy she is when, in this game, she feigns everything and invests nothing of her own!" Mme de T—— accompanied this last pronouncement with a very meaningful sigh. It was a masterful maneuver.

I felt that a blindfold had just been lifted from my eyes, and I didn't see the new one with which it was replaced. My lover appeared to be the falsest of all women, and I believed to have found a sensitive soul. I sighed too, without knowing for whom I sighed, without distinguishing whether it had been born of regret or hope. She seemed sorry to have distressed me, and to have let herself get too carried away in painting a portrait that could seem questionable, since it had been painted by a woman.

I could not make sense of what I was hearing. Once again, we were heading down the great path of sentiment, and from this vantage point it was impossible to foresee where our steps would lead. In the midst of our metaphysical discussions, she pointed out to me, at the far end of a terrace, a pavilion that had witnessed the sweetest of moments. She described its location and furnishings to me in detail. What a pity she didn't have the key to it! Still chatting, we approached the pavilion. It had been left open; all it lacked now was some daylight. But darkness lent it a certain charm of its own. And besides, I knew the charm of the object that would soon adorn it.

We trembled as we entered. This was love's sanctuary. It took possession of us: our knees buckled, our weakening arms intertwined, and, unable to hold each other up, we sank down onto a sofa that occupied a corner of the temple. The moon was setting, and its last rays soon lifted the veil of a modesty that was, I think, becoming rather tiresome. Everything grew confused in the shadows. The hand that tried to push me away felt my heart beating. Mme de T—— was trying to move away from me but kept coming back all the more tender. Our souls met and multiplied; another was born each time we kissed.

Though it became less tumultuous, the intoxication of our senses did not yet allow us the use of our voices. We conversed in silence through the language of thought. Mme de T—— took refuge in my arms, hid her head in my breast, sighed, and became calm beneath my caresses: she reprimanded and consoled herself in one breath, and she asked for love in return for everything that love had just stolen away from her.

The same love that had frightened her a moment before comforted her the next. If it is true that lovers want to give what they have allowed to be taken, it is also true that they receive what they have stolen. And both parties hasten to obtain a second victory in order to secure their conquest.

All this had been a little abrupt. We realized our error and returned more leisurely to what we had passed over in haste. When lovers are too ardent, they are less refined. Racing toward climax, they overlook the preliminary pleasures: they tear at a knot, shred a piece of gauze. Lust leaves its traces everywhere, and soon the idol resembles a victim.

Calmer, we found the air purer, cooler. Earlier, we had not heard how the river, its wavelets bathing the walls of the summer house, interrupted the night's silence with a gentle murmur that seemed in harmony with the wild beating of our hearts. The darkness did not allow us to distinguish any objects, but through the transparent veil of a beautiful summer night our imaginations transformed an island that lay before our retreat into an enchanted spot. The river now swarmed with cupids who frolicked in the ripples. Never were the forests of Gnide as peopled with lovers as the far bank of our river. For us, nature housed only happy couples, and none was happier than we. We would have rivaled Amor and Psyche. I was as young as he; I found Mme de T——— as charming as she. In her greater abandon, she seemed all the more ravishing. Every passing moment revealed something more beautiful. The torch of love illuminated it in my mind's eye, and the most reliable of the senses confirmed my happiness. When fear disappears, caresses seek out caresses: they call out all the more tenderly to one another. Lovers no longer want their favors stolen. If they defer, it is from refinement. Their refusal is halfhearted, and only another sign of tender care. They desire, but would prefer not to – the compliment alone is pleasing...Desire flatters...It uplifts the soul...They adore...They will never yield...They surrender.

"Oh," she said in a heavenly voice, "let us leave this dangerous place; our desires keep multiplying here, and we haven't the strength to resist them." She led me out.

We moved away regretfully. She looked back often. A divine flame seemed to burn in the courtyard.

"You have made this house sacred for me," she said. "Who will ever be able to please me here as you have? You truly know how to love! How fortunate she is!"

"Who do you mean?" I cried out in surprise. "If I bring you happiness, what other creature in the world could you possibly envy?"

We passed before the grassy bank and stopped there involuntarily, with silent emotion.

"Such an immense distance lies between this spot and the summer house we just left!" she said. "My soul is so full of happiness I can barely remember that I was capable of resisting you."

"Well," I said to her, "am I here to witness the breaking of the magic spell that so filled my imagination back there? Will this spot always be fatal to me?"

"Can there be any such place, as long as I am with you?"

"Yes, it seems so, since I am just as unhappy here as I was happy there. Love demands multiple tokens: it thinks it hasn't won anything as long as something is still left to be won."

"Again...No, I can't allow it...no, never..." And after a long silence: "Oh, but you do know how to love me!"

I beg the reader to remember that I was twenty years old. Meanwhile, the conversation changed its course: it became less serious. We even dared to jest about the pleasures of love, distinguishing moral pleasures from others, reducing them to their simplest forms, and proving that love's favors were nothing more than pleasure; that there was no such thing as a commitment (philosophically speaking) except for those commitments contracted with the public, when we allow it to discover our secrets, and when we agree to share in some indiscretions.

"What a delicious night we've just spent," she said, "all because of the attraction of pleasure, our guide and our excuse! I suppose if for some reason we were forced to separate tomorrow, our happiness, unknown to all of nature, would not leave us bound by any tie...a few regrets maybe, compensated by pleasant memories...And besides, we have had our pleasure, in fact, pleasure, without all the delays, the bother, and the tyranny of courteous behavior."

We are such *machines* (and I blush at the idea) that, instead of all the delicacy that tormented me before the scene which just took place, I found myself at least half to blame for the boldness of her principles; I found them sublime, and I felt a strong disposition for the love of freedom.

"What a beautiful night!" she said, "what beautiful grounds! It has been eight years since I left them, but they have lost none of their charm. Now they have even recovered all the charms of novelty. We will never forget that pavilion, will we? There is an even more charming room in the château – but I can't show you anything. You're like a child who wants to touch everything, and who breaks everything he touches."

Prompted by a violent feeling of curiosity I promised to be only what she would want me to be. I protested that I had become very reasonable. But she quickly changed the subject.

"This night would seem completely delightful if I weren't reproaching myself for one thing," she said. "I'm angry, really angry, about what I said to you about the Countess. I don't mean to complain about you. Novelty is exciting. You found me agreeable, and I choose to believe that you were in good faith; but trying to undo the sway of habit is a weary task, and I hardly know how to set about it. Besides, I've exhausted all the resources a heart possesses to bind you. What could you still hope for from me now? What could you still desire? And if a woman leaves a man with nothing to desire or to hope, what will become of her? I have given you everything I could; perhaps one day you will forgive me for the pleasures that, once the moment of intoxication has passed, return you to the severity of your judgment.

"By the way, what did you think of my husband? Rather sullen, isn't he? His diet is not very agreeable. I don't think he looked upon you with much equanimity. Our friendship would soon begin to seem suspect to him. So you shouldn't prolong this first trip: he'll become bad-tempered if you do. As soon as anyone comes, and no doubt someone will come... Besides, you also have your own discretion to preserve... Do you remember how Monsieur looked this evening when he left us?..."

She saw the impression these last words made on me, and immediately added: "He was more lighthearted when he was so carefully arranging the little room I mentioned to you a short time ago. That was before my marriage. It is attached to my apartment. It has never been for me anything more than evidence of... the artificial resources Monsieur de T—— needed to strengthen his affections, and of how little I was able to stimulate his soul."

Thus she gradually aroused my curiosity about that little room. "It is attached to your apartment," I said to her. "How delightful it would be to go there and avenge your insulted charms! To pay them the homage they deserve and of which they have been robbed."

She liked this tone better.

"Oh!" I said to her, "if only I were to be chosen as the principal actor in that revenge, if only the pleasure of that moment could make you forget, and make up for, the boredom of conjugal routine –"

"If you promise to be good," she said, interrupting me.

I must confess that I didn't feel all the fervor, all the devotion necessary for visiting this new temple – but I was very curious. It was no longer Mme de T—— whom I desired, it was the little room.

We had come back inside. The lamps in the stairwells and hallways had been extinguished; we were wandering through a labyrinth. Even the mistress of the château had forgotten the way. At last we arrived at the door of her apartment, the apartment housing that vaunted chamber.

"What are you going to do with me?" I asked. "What is going to happen to me? Are you going to send me off alone in this darkness? Are you going to expose me to the risk of making a noise, of revealing us, of betraying us, of ruining you?"

This argument seemed irreproachable to her. "Then you promise me..."

"Anything...anything you like."

She accepted my oath. We gently opened the door. We saw two women sleeping, one young, one older. The latter, the trusted one, was the one she awoke. Mme de T—— whispered something to her, and I soon saw her leave through a secret door cleverly fashioned in a panel of the wainscoting. I offered to perform the duties of the woman who was still asleep. Mme de T—— accepted my services, and she rid herself of all superfluous ornaments. A single ribbon bound up her hair, which escaped in flowing curls; to this she added only a rose I had plucked in the garden and was still absentmindedly holding; a loose dressing gown replaced all her other clothing. There wasn't a single knot in this whole outfit; I found Mme de T—— more beautiful than ever. A little fatigue made her eyelids heavy and lent her gaze a more interesting languor, a gentler expression. The color of her lips, more vivid than usual, set off the enamel of her teeth, and made her smile more voluptuous; red blushes scattered here and there set off the whiteness of her complexion and attested to its delicacy. These traces of pleasure reminded me of its sway. In truth, she seemed even more attractive to me than my imagination had painted her in our sweetest moments. The panel opened again and the discreet confidante disappeared.

As we were about to enter the chamber, she stopped me. "Remember," she said gravely, "you are supposed never to have seen, never even suspected, the sanctuary you're about to enter. No careless mistakes; I'm not worried about the rest." Discretion is the most important of the virtues; we owe it many moments of happiness.

All this was like an initiation rite. She led me by the hand across a small, dark corridor. My heart was pounding as though I were a young proselyte being put to the test before the celebration of the great mysteries...

"But your Countess..." she said, stopping. I was about to reply when the doors opened; my answer was interrupted by admiration. I was astonished, delighted, I no longer know what became of me, and I began in good faith to believe in magic. The door closed again, and I could no longer tell from whence I had entered. All I could see now was a seamless, bird's view of a grove of trees which seemed to stand and rest on nothing. In truth, I found myself in a vast cage of mirrors on which images were so artistically painted that they produced the illusion of all the objects they represented. There was no visible light inside the room; a soft, celestial glow entered, depending on the need each object had to be more or less perceived; incense burners exhaled delicious perfumes; intertwined ciphers and ornamental motifs hid from the eyes the flames of the lamps that magically illuminated this place of delights. The side where we had come in showed latticed porticoes ornamented with flowers, and arbors in each recess. On another side was a statue of Amor handing out crowns of flowers, and before the statue an altar on which shone a flame, and at the base of this altar a cup, crowns of flowers, and garlands; a temple of lighthearted design completed the decor of this side. Opposite was a dark grotto, the god of mystery watching over the entrance and the floor, covered with a plush carpet, imitated grass. On the ceiling, mythological figures were hanging garlands; and on the side opposite the porticoes was a canopy under which were piles of pillows with a baldachin upheld by cupids.

It was here that the queen of this place nonchalantly threw herself down. I fell at her feet, she leaned toward me, she held out her arms to me, and in that instant, because the couple we formed was repeated in its every angle, I saw that island entirely populated by happy lovers.

Desires are reproduced through their images. "Will you leave my head uncrowned?" I asked her. "So close to the throne, will I have to endure hardship? Will you reject me?"

"And your vows?" she answered, rising.

"I was a mortal when I made them, but now you have made me a god: my only vow is to adore you."

"Come," she said, "the shadow of mystery must hide my weakness. Come..."

At the same time, she went over to the grotto. Scarcely had we passed through the entrance when some sort of cleverly contrived spring caught hold of us and, carried by its movement, we fell gently on our backs on a mound of cushions. Both darkness and silence reigned in this new sanctuary. Our sighs replaced language. More tender, more numerous, more ardent, they expressed our sensations, they marked their progression; and the last sigh of all, suspended for a time, warned us that we would have to offer thanks to Love. She took a crown and set it on my head, and, barely raising her beautiful eyes, damp with lust, she said to me, "Well, then! Will you ever love the Countess as much as you love me?" I was about to answer when the confidante rushed in and said to me, "Leave quickly. It's broad daylight. People are already stirring in the château."

Everything vanished as quickly as a dream is destroyed when one awakens, and I found myself in the corridor before I was able to come to my senses. I tried to find my chambers, but where was I to look? Any inquiry would give me away, any wrong turn an indiscretion. The most prudent choice seemed to be to go down into the garden, where I resolved to stay until I could come back in as if I had been out for a morning walk.

The coolness and the pure air of that moment gradually calmed my imagination and drove the sense of magic from it. Instead of an enchanted nature, I saw only an innocent nature. Truth returned to my soul, my thoughts came to me without disturbance and followed one another in an orderly way; at last I could breathe again. I had nothing more pressing to do at that moment than ask myself if I was the lover of the woman I had just left, and I was quite surprised to discover that I didn't know how to answer. Who could have told me yesterday at the opera that I might ever ask myself such a question? I, who thought I knew that she was desperately in love, and had been for two years, with the Marquis de ———, I, who thought I was so smitten with the Countess that it would be impossible for me to be unfaithful to her! What! Yesterday! Mme de T———... Was it really true? Had she broken with the Marquis? Had she chosen me to succeed him, or only to punish him? What an adventure! What a night! I didn't know if I was still dreaming. I doubted it, then I was convinced, persuaded, and then I didn't believe anything anymore. As I was drifting amid these uncertainties, I heard a noise near me: I lifted my eyes, rubbed them, and couldn't believe what I saw. It was... none other than the Marquis.

"You didn't expect me so early in the morning, did you? Now, how did it go?"

"You knew I was here?" I asked him.

"Yes, of course. I was told yesterday just as you were leaving. Did you play your part well? Did her husband find your arrival quite ridiculous? When is she sending you back? I've taken care of everything; I'm bringing you a fine carriage which will be at your disposal — I owe you a favor. Madame de T——— needed a squire, and you served as one for her, you entertained her on the way here; that was all she wanted. My gratitude..."

"Oh, no, no! I'm happy to be of service; and in this case Madame de T——— might tell you I've been zealous above and beyond the powers of gratitude."

He had just solved yesterday's mystery, and given me a key to the rest. I instantly sensed what my new role was. Every word fell into place.

"Why did you come so early?" I asked. "It seems to me it would have been more prudent..."

"Everything has been arranged; it will look as if I have come here by chance. I'm supposed to be returning from a neighboring estate.

Didn't Madame de T—— tell you? I'm cross with her for not trusting you, after all you have done for us."

"No doubt she had her reasons; and perhaps if she had said something, I wouldn't have played my part so well."

"Well, was it pleasant, my friend? Tell me the details... tell me now."

"Ah!... Just a minute. I didn't know that all of this was mere play-acting; and even though I am involved in the play..."

"You didn't have the best part."

"Oh, don't worry; for a good actor, there are no bad parts."

"Of course – and you came off well?"

"Wonderfully well."

"And Madame de T——?"

"Sublime. She can play any type."

"Can you imagine pinning that woman down? It gave me some trouble; but I have molded her character to the point where there is perhaps no other woman in Paris whose faithfulness can be relied upon so completely."

"Excellent!"

"That's my special talent. All her inconstancy was mere frivolity, a disorder of the imagination; it all came down to capturing her soul."

"Yes, absolutely."

"Isn't that so? You have no idea how attached she is to me. The fact is, she's charming, as you'll agree. Between you and me, I know of only one failing in her, which is that nature, though it gave her everything, refused her that divine flame which is the highest blessing. She inspires everything, causing all sorts of feelings, and yet she herself feels nothing. She's made of stone."

"Is she? I wouldn't have guessed... But, I must say, you seem to know this woman as well as if you were her husband: really, one could easily be deceived. And if I hadn't dined yesterday with the man himself..."

"Speaking of which, did he put on a good show?"

"Never was anyone more a husband."

"Oh, what a fine adventure! But I fear you're not laughing about it enough for my taste. Don't you see just how comical your role is? You must agree that the theater of the world presents strange opportunities – that it has some very amusing scenes. Let's go in, I'm eager to have a good laugh with Madame de T——. She must be awake by now. I said I would be here early. In all decency, we should begin with the husband. Let's go to your room, I want to put on a little more powder... So, did he really take you for a lover?"

"You'll be able to judge my success by the reception he gives me.

It's nine o'clock – let's go straight to Monsieur." I wanted to avoid my chambers, and with good reason. On our way, however, we happened upon them quite by chance. Through the door, which had been left open, we saw my valet sleeping in an armchair; a candle was dying next to him. Awaking at our noise, he thoughtlessly offered my dressing gown to the Marquis, chiding him for the hour at which he was coming in. I was nervous, but the Marquis was so predisposed to be duped that he saw nothing in this but a dreamer giving him cause for laughter. I gave orders for my departure to my valet, who didn't know what all this meant, and we went in to see Monsieur. One can well imagine who received the welcome; of course, it wasn't I. My friend was warmly encouraged to stay for a while. Monsieur resolved to take him to see Madame, with the hope that she would persuade him. As for me, he dared not, he said, propose the same, for he found me so exhausted, he could not doubt but that the country air was truly fatal for me. Consequently, he advised me to return to town. The Marquis offered me his carriage, and I accepted. Everything was going perfectly, and we were all pleased. Nevertheless, I wanted to see Mme de T—— again; it was a pleasure I couldn't deny myself. My impatience was shared by my friend, who couldn't understand my sleepiness, and who was quite far from guessing its cause. As we left M. de T——'s apartment, he said, "Isn't he quite amazing? If he had been fed his lines, could he have said them any better? In truth, he's a real gentleman; and, all things considered, I'm very pleased to see him reconciled with his wife. He'll run a good household; and you'll agree that, to do it honor, he couldn't make a better choice than his wife." No one could have agreed more than I. "Yet however agreeable that man might be, my dear, not another word; secrecy is more essential than ever. I'll let Madame de T—— know that her secret couldn't be in better hands."

"Believe me, my friend, she trusts me; and as you'll see she loses no sleep over this."

"Oh, everyone would agree that you are unrivaled in putting a woman to sleep."

"Or a husband, my friend, or even a lover, if need be."

We were at last told we could go to Mme de T——, and we entered.

"Here, Madame," said our chatterbox as he entered, "are your two best friends."

"I was afraid," Mme de T—— said to me, "that you might have left before I woke up, and I am grateful to you for having sensed the sorrow that this would have caused me." She examined us both, but she was soon reassured by the confidence of the Marquis, who continued to tease me. She laughed about it with me as much as was necessary to console me, and without lowering herself in my esteem. She spoke tenderly to him, and honestly and decently to me; bantering with him, she did not tease me.

"Madame," said the Marquis, "he finished his part just as well as he began it."

She responded gravely, "I was sure Monsieur would perform brilliantly any role one might entrust to him."

He told her what had just happened in her husband's room. She looked at me, commended me, and did not laugh.

"As for me," said the Marquis, who evidently could not stop himself, "I'm delighted with all this: we've made ourselves a friend, here, Madame. I will say it again, our gratitude..."

"Come, Monsieur," said Mme de T——, "let's speak no more of it, and simply trust that I feel everything I should feel toward Monsieur."

M. de T—— was announced, and we found ourselves all together. M. de T—— had ridiculed and then dismissed me; my friend the Marquis was duping the husband and mocking me; and I was paying him back in kind, all the while admiring Mme de T——, who was making fools of us all, without losing her dignity.

After enjoying this scene for a few moments, I felt the time had come for my departure. I withdrew, and Mme de T—— followed, pretending she had an errand for me.

"Good-bye, Monsieur; I owe you so many pleasures; but I have paid you with a beautiful dream. Now, your love summons you to return; the object of that love is worthy of it. If I've stolen a few moments of bliss from her, I return you more tender, more attentive, and more sensitive.

"Good-bye, again. You are so charming...Don't give the Countess cause to quarrel with me." She shook my hand and left.

I stepped into the carriage awaiting me. I looked hard for the moral of this whole adventure...and found none.

———

Originally published as *Point de lendemain* (1777).

The Wayward Head and Heart

by Crébillon fils

Translated by Barbara Bray

Introduction

by Catherine Cusset

The Suspended Ending
or Crébillon fils's Irony

by Catherine Cusset

"When I entered society, the idea of pleasure was the only one I had in my head" (p. 770), says the narrator of Crébillon fils's (1701–77) *The Wayward Head and Heart* (1738) at the beginning of the story. The temporal clause "when I entered society," which marks the novel's spatial and temporal starting point, and the use of the past tense, which indicates a restrospective point of view, make us expect a resolution in which the idea of pleasure will no longer be the hero's only concern.

The novel's title, the author's preface, and the story's plot reinforce this expectation, because they are all based on a dichotomy that suggests a conflict of values and makes the reader expect the triumph of moral values. As Jean Sgard remarked in a 1969 article, "La Notion d'égarement chez Crébillon," it is impossible to conceive of *égarement*, or wandering, without the idea of a straight path: "The notion of wandering is interesting on two levels: it expresses an ambiguous and disconcerting state, a 'confusion,' a 'frenzy' that leads analysis astray; at the same time, it implies a norm because there is wandering only in relation to a straight path."[1] The 1771 *Dictionnaire de Trévoux* defines *égarement* as "everything that swerves from the rule we have to observe, from customary principles and holy doctrine."[2] The mere use of the word *égarement*, because of its moral connotation, implies consciousness or knowledge of the rule, be it moral, social, religious, or spiritual, from which there is deviation: the word *égarement* can be used only when the very error or swerving from the rule has been recognized as such.

Crébillon fils's readers, therefore, will think that his narrator, who writes retrospectively about his youth, returned to the straight path. This is precisely what Crebillon fils's preface makes us expect:

> You will see in these memoirs a man such as nearly all men are in extreme youth.... The first and second parts deal with this ignorance and with his first experiences of love. In sections that follow, he is a man full of false ideas.... You will see him finally, in the last part, restored to himself, owing all virtues to a good woman. There you have the object of *The Wayward Head and Heart* (pp. 769–770).

The semantic series is coherent: the ignorant and wandering young man contrasts with the man "restored to himself," and we can expect to find this genuine self at the end of the novel, probably thanks to the hero's union with a "respectable woman" (in French, "*une femme estimable*"). This is the object of the novel, Crébillon fils tells us, both its narrative and psychological aim.

The novel, however, does not attain this goal. Instead of five or six parts announced by Crébillon fils, we have only three, at the end of which the young hero, far from being "restored to himself," describes himself more lost than ever: "Some hours had passed in these contradictions: dawn was beginning to break, and I was still far from resolving the conflict within me" (p. 910). What conclusion should we draw from this absence of conclusion? Perhaps that Crébillon fils left his novel incomplete? This, indeed, is the opinion of many critics. Jean Sgard writes, "In the unpublished end of the novel, the hero would have been rehabilitated by a respectable woman, probably Hortense de Théville; the wandering of a young man, an almost conventional theme, would have ended with a conversion to love, with a radiant blooming of sensibility."[3] Raymond Trousson expresses the same hypothesis in the introduction to *The Wayward Head and Heart* in a 1993 edition of *Romans libertins du XVIIIème siècle*: "The conclusion announced by Crébillon fils was supposed to show the accession to truth, which is itself a return to lost values: the novel can be appreciated only in light of what was not written, and the absent conclusion is necessary for understanding it."[4] Both Sgard and Trousson base their analyses of the novel on a conclusion Crébillon fils promised but did not write.

If *The Wayward Head and Heart* ended with the hero "rehabilitated" and happily married, we could read Meilcour's story, then, as a novel of sentimental education, a critique of superficial life in the salons, and a condemnation of libertinage, like Duclos's *The Confessions of the Count of* ——— (1740), in which the narrator writes the story of his youth after being "rehabilitated" and thus confesses his error, or Dorat's *Les Malheurs de l'inconstance* (1770), which dooms libertine characters to failure.[5] Meilcour's sentimental education would eventually reveal that the worldly pleasures of vanity represent only erroneous wandering of the heart and mind compared to the truth of the heart, love. The novel's title, the narrative's beginning, and the author's preface make us expect such an end. There is only one problem – the end is lacking.

Is *The Wayward Head and Heart* an incomplete novel? An analysis of Crébillon fils's narrative strategies indicates that the absence of an ending is not accidental. The very dynamics of the novel invite us to read the missing end as the key that gives meaning to *The Wayward Head and Heart*.

On Melancholia as a Sign of Truth

Crébillon fils not only promises in his preface, but also constructs throughout the plot, a moral or sentimental denouement. Indeed, no sooner has he introduced the main characters than he contrasts one woman with another: Mme de Lursay, a forty-year-old woman who intends to seduce the young hero, and Hortense de Théville, first designated as "the mysterious stranger," a young woman with whom the hero falls passionately in love at first sight (p. 827).

These two women contrast with each other in every respect: in their physical appearance, in their social behavior, and in the effect they produce on the narrator. One "did not neglect ornament," to "make up for what nearly forty years had inflicted on her charms" (p. 774). The other radiates "freshness and brilliance," looks "extremely young," and is dressed simply, since she has "no need of decoration" (p. 786). One has an experience of the world: thanks to her knowledge of the art of love and conversation, Mme de Lursay manages to manipulate the young hero, and the word Meilcour most often uses to characterize her clever behavior is "stratagem." The other, on the contrary, neither manipulates nor even tries to seduce the male characters in the novel. Hortense speaks very little in a novel in which conversation represents the dominant narrative mode – almost two thirds of the text consist of dialogue. We see her in a social setting only twice: once at Mme de Lursay's, and once in her mother's salon. Except for one conversation with the narrator and one with a lady in the Tuileries, Hortense is silent. She also manifests her melancholy and lets herself be absorbed by her reverie in a way that does not fit the rules of aristocratic society, thus astonishing other characters.

Can we say that the value of silence and melancholy is superior to that of conversation and social gallantry in a novel written between 1736 and 1738? Would it not be anachronistic to place a libertine novel in a Rousseauian perspective? By focusing the interpretation on Hortense, do we not risk a ridiculously sentimental reading of *The Wayward Head and Heart*, exactly the kind of reading that Crébillon fils seeks to avoid by setting his story in the world of the salons? We need to remember Versac's mockery of Meilcour as a warning addressed to sentimental readers: " 'Your heart!' said he. 'Novelists' jargon. What makes you suppose that is what she is asking for? She is incapable of so ridiculous a pretension' " (p. 878).

Crébillon fils describes a purely aristocratic society in which good taste and custom prevail, and a very homogeneous society, as Thomas Kavanagh argues in *Enlightenment and the Shadows of Chance*.[6] One would suppose, therefore, that Hortense's melancholy and asocial behavior would be ridiculed from an aristocratic standpoint. A silent, serious, and sad Hortense in the middle of a loquacious, gallant, and joyful society should become the laughingstock of the novel, like Molière's misanthrope, whose bitter critique of human beings at last reveals his inability to behave properly in society and interact with young women. It is precisely because the comic sense of ridicule does not serve a universal sense of morality – but, rather, helps to form aristocratic manners – that Rousseau, a champion of republican values, violently criticizes Molière's comedy in his *Letter to d'Alembert on the Theater* (1758). Crébillon fils, however, escapes a Rousseauian criticism, since Hortense, in spite of her social ineptitude, is the only character never to appear ridiculous in a novel so concerned with "good taste" and the "ridiculous." She is even the only character in all of Crébillon fils's novels to challenge their implicit values; in that sense, she represents an otherness otherwise absent from Crébillon fils's work.[7]

Although her presence in the novel is relatively scarce, Hortense's role is essential. She serves as a counterbalance or even an "antidote" to the novel's other characters. The respect Hortense inspires in the narrator through her coldness and reserved attitude contrasts with the contempt all the other characters (except for the mothers) inspire in both herself and the narrator: Mme de Sénanges and Mme de Mongennes, because of their impudence; Mme de Lursay, whose stratagems and artifices are revealed by Versac; Versac, who tries desperately but in vain to attract Hortense's attention by showing his legs and teeth; and Meilcour himself, who interprets Hortense's silence as a sign that she despises his superficiality.

The character of Hortense, throughout the novel, serves as a criterion of value, a sign of truth, and a point of reference the narrator uses to judge himself and the other characters. Without her, the title *The Wayward Head and Heart* would not be possible. She personifies the fixed point from which the hero swerves in his *égarements*, and which he seemingly tries to approach so as to end his wandering. Hortense's resistance to Versac's charms implies another set of values, different from the one Versac teaches to Meilcour, whose principle is "the art of pleasing" (p. 881). Versac's system of values is certainly at work in the novel, since we find the words "to please," "to displease," "pleasure," and "pleasant" more than one hundred and seventy times in a two-hundred-page novel, that is, on almost every page. Unlike Mme de Lursay, Mme de Sénanges or Mme de Mongennes, Hortense does not want to please. Contrary to Versac's values, hers are not theorized or disclosed: their very silence gives them a certain consistency, since, as an "antidote" to the other characters' conversation, they serve to reveal the superficiality and vanity of social chatter.

Inclination versus Passion

The contrast between the two types of women is echoed by a contrast between two feelings the hero experiences: inclination and passion. Mme de Lursay awakens a superficial feeling in Meilcour, which he names "passing desire" or "inclination." Hortense evokes a violent commotion in his soul, which he calls "passion." The shock of the first encounter in the Opéra is described in terms reminiscent of those chosen by Prévost in *Manon Lescaut* (1732) five years earlier; they belong to the romantic topos of love at first sight, which is evoked each time Meilcour meets Hortense. It is notable that he never finds Hortense when actively seeking her; he meets her always by chance, and her vision strikes him when he least expects it. Each time, the shock of surprise deprives him of any control over his body. Seeing Hortense provokes a violent disorder in Meilcour, and touching her makes his body almost hysterical, in a way that reflects the commotion in his soul: "I offered her my hand, but no sooner had I touched hers than I felt all my frame begin to tremble. My emotion became so extreme I could scarcely stand" (p. 843). In a novel of social education, in which the hero learns good manners and good taste, love is defined as an impulse that unites the body and the soul, and defies self-control and social propriety.

We also find the words "transport" and "trembling," among others, describing Hortense's effect on Meilcour, in passages that narrate scenes with Mme de Lursay. The effect Lursay has on Meilcour is not very different, but still differentiated from love, in a subtle way: "I felt all the perturbations of passion with as much violence as if I had truly suffered them" (p. 786). The difference appears through the words "as much...as if," which the narrator uses to distinguish the real from its simulacrum: the physical emotion produced by a circumstantial passion greatly resembles that of love — but precisely because it merely *resembles*, it is not an emotion of love. The circumstances of Meilcour's meetings with Mme de Lursay also differ from those of his encounters with Hortense, for all meetings with Mme de Lursay either are anticipated by Meilcour or occur precisely when he is trying to avoid her. Mme de Lursay sets the meetings, invites Meilcour to her house, leads him to remote corners, and questions him about his feelings.

The novel constantly plays with the contrast between the two women and the two contradictory feelings they awaken in Meilcour. It is only when Meilcour meets Hortense for the first time that he understands the nature of his feeling for Mme de Lursay: "I had just learned from my meeting with the beautiful stranger that I loved only her, and that for Mme de Lursay I had only those fleeting sentiments one has for any woman society calls pretty" (p. 804). Thanks to his meeting with Hortense, the hero establishes the distinction between two kinds of love: one is superficial and temporary, the other deep, true, and eternal. Meilcour defines his desire for Mme de Lursay as a mere inclination and pleasure of vanity. In "society," having an affair with a beautiful woman also means making it known that one has had an affair, because the pleasure of the senses is linked to the pleasure of fame, which reinforces the former. The more the novel progresses, the more the antithesis between the two feelings gains strength. Although Meilcour lets himself be attracted to Mme de Lursay, his thoughts return to Hortense. Pleasure serves merely as a substitute for love. It becomes the distraction that allows the narrator to swerve from his true desire, his love for Hortense: "I tried to distract my thoughts from her by fixing them upon the pleasures that awaited me" (p. 808). Pleasure is devalued because it highlights a void that it is unable to fill. Hortense clearly represents the object of the narrator's ultimate desire, which has nothing in common with the senses' fleeting and superficial satisfaction: "the heart that seemed to oppose itself to my desires was the only one that could occupy my own" (p. 844). Meilcour's love for Hortense, a love at first sight which is confirmed by every encounter between the two characters, appears throughout the novel as the only strong and lasting sentiment, the only counterweight to the fleeting desires awakened by Mme de Lursay and the disgust evoked by Mme de Sénanges or Mme de Mongennes, and, finally, the only value not subject to the law of pleasure which Versac articulates: "Like me, all men seek only pleasure: fix that forever in the same object and we should be constant too. Believe me, Marquise, no one would ever engage himself, even with the most charming creature, if it meant being bound forever" (p. 822).

For a Theory of the Moment

Versac's philosophy is based on a libertine concept of time, which associates pleasure with the moment. Indeed, a contrast between two concepts of time adds to the contrast between two types of woman and two sentiments in the hero. We find an echo of this contrast in the only conversation between Hortense and Meilcour. This conversation, whose starting point is a love story that Hortense was reading as Meilcour arrives, concerns the definition of unhappy love. For Hortense, any love that is opposed by circumstances is unhappy, even if the lovers really love each other. Meilcour, on the contrary, exalts the "moment" that lovers can shelter from outside obstacles: "If they see each other for a moment, what delight is in that moment!" (p. 852). Although this sentence is in the middle of his speech, it is the first one that Hortense addresses in her answer: " 'What you say may be true,' she replied, 'but for every moment such as you have described, how many days of anxiety and pain!' " (p. 852).

For Meilcour, the "moment" has intrinsic value. Hortense does not discuss the happiness of the moment itself, but she compares that moment with a duration that is weightier than the single instant. By denying the pleasure of the single moment in one of her rare conversations in the novel, Hortense takes a position against libertine temporality, composed entirely of moments. It is, indeed, in the realm of the "moment" that Mme de Lursay has the power to exert her charms on Meilcour.

The "moment," also called the "occasion," is a critical concept in Crébillon's vocabulary, throughout his work.[8] The word appears in the title of a fictive dialogue written shortly after *The Wayward Head and Heart* and published in 1755, *Nuit et le moment ou les matinées de Cythère*, and the concept is defined in another dialogue written around 1737–40 and published in 1763, *Le Hasard au coin du feu*:

CÉLIE: What is the moment, and how do you define it? Because I must say in all good honesty that I do not understand you.

THE DUKE: A certain disposition of the senses, as unexpected as it is involuntary, which a woman can conceal, but which, should it be perceived or sensed by someone who might profit from it, puts her in the greatest danger of being a little more willing than she thought she ever should or could be.[9]

The moment, then, is not simply a brief period of time: rather, it is defined by a set of circumstances called here "a certain disposition of the senses," which applies specifically to women. The "moment" or its equivalent in Crébillon fils's vocabulary, the "occasion" (opportunity), is a woman's state of sexual excitation, which allows a man to take advantage of her: the body ("nature," in eighteenth-century vocabulary) becomes an active subject and follows the autonomous law of pleasure. The moment designates a physical and psychological state that separates the body from moral and social identity. The moment contains no past and no future: it produces a rupture in time, a suspension of any temporal and moral dimension.[10]

The moment is not only a temporal and psychological notion, but also a concept in mechanics: it designates "the product of a (specified) force, mass, volume, and its perpendicular distance from its axis, fulcrum, or plane."[11] The mechanical meaning of the moment is important. If the moment, indeed, pertains to a law of mechanics, it means that it has nothing to do with subjectivity, or, more specifically, with sentiments. The moment can be experienced with anyone and at any time, since it depends merely on a set of circumstances and on an encounter of bodies obeying physical rather than moral laws.

The "moment," however, should not be confused with a wild impulse of the body. The laws it obeys are also social, to the extent that, in the world described by Crébillon fils, social behavior has become a second nature. In *Libertines*, Patrick Wald-Lasowski describes Crébillon fils's libertine characters as social seducers who act mainly out of "politeness."[12] Far from contradicting each other, social politeness and sensual pleasure are on the same side, because they both involve only external surfaces — appearances, or skin — as opposed to internal feelings, such as love. Crébillon fils contrasts the superficial part of human beings, which includes social vanity and the pleasure of the senses, both experienced in the "moment," with a deeper part involving sensibility and sentiments, which require duration and a transcendence of immediate sensibility.

The moment plays a very important role in *The Wayward Head and Heart*, in which the narrator uses the words "moment" and "occasion" whenever he needs to justify the weakness that draws him to Mme Lursay in spite of himself. Since he is caught between his romantic love for Hortense and his sensual desire for Mme de Lursay, Meilcour experiences the moment in its female version, as it is described by the Duke in *Le Hasard au coin du feu*. He is the one who tries to resist: it is for him, paradoxically, and not for Lursay, that the moment is dangerous. The moment is desired by Mme de Lursay more than by Meilcour: she plays the role of the masculine rake who, in the "moment," knows how to take advantage of the other: "A sigh or two which half-escaped her completed my overthrow: at this critical moment she benefited from all my love for the mysterious stranger" (p. 805). Meilcour is in the position of the innocent victim whose resistance is overcome by the power of the moment and by Mme de Lursay's sense of opportunity.

The plot of *The Wayward Head and Heart* is based on a dichotomy at all levels: a contrast between social behavior and melancholy, conversation and silence, pleasure and seriousness, worldly politeness and violent emotion, stratagems and simplicity, fleeting desires and true love, vanity and passion, the moment and duration, and, finally, the plural (Lursay, Sénanges, Mongennes) and the singular (Hortense). Since the novel is also replete with hints that Hortense may after all be interested in Meilcour, it seems that truth will triumph only if Meilcour understands Hortense's love and at last decides to sacrifice superficial and temporary pleasures for a single and lasting love.

Yet the expected resolution does not exist. The way in which Meilcour's story ends represents an ironic commentary on the readers' moral and sentimental expectation. The suspension of the end transforms the conflict of values into a deceptive strategy for addressing a message to readers.

The Unresolved Conflict

The last scene of the novel takes place at Mme de Lursay's home, in two phases: first in her salon, then in private. Initially, Meilcour rushes to Mme de Lursay's in hopes of finding Hortense; his impulsive desire to see Hortense will never be satisfied, since she is not visiting Mme de Lursay, and the novel ends with a scene bringing together Meilcour and Lursay. Readers are deprived of the scene the narrative has brought them to expect, in which Hortense and Meilcour would have cleared their misunderstanding.

After a bitter confrontation in which Meilcour feels that his contempt for Mme de Lursay is stronger than ever and Mme de Lursay denounces Meilcour's ridiculous lack of manners, she finally gives herself to him, and he finally takes advantage of her, thus ending the ridiculousness of his "fine resistance."

The novel may have no other object: the narrative, from the beginning, offers Mme de Lursay to Meilcour's "Cherubinistic" desire, and depicts her as intending to seduce, initiate, and ensnare the young man. In the resolution, she reaches her goal: she initiates him sexually. It seems that we have a complete story, that of the sexual and social initiation of a future *petit-maître* (fop) who, thanks to the double education of a gallant woman and an experienced libertine, finally understands the rules of the world that he entered at the beginning of the novel. Such, indeed, is Michel Foucault's interpretation of the novel in his 1962 article, "Un Si cruel savoir":

> The lesson was not useless, since it procures us the narrative in its form and irony. Meilcour, narrating the adventure of his innocence, perceives it only in the distance, where it is already lost: between his naïveté and his imperceptibly different consciousness of it, Versac's knowledge insinuated itself with this custom of the world in which "the mind and the heart cannot help being spoiled."[13]

For Foucault, the object of Crébillon fils's novel is to deliver what he calls "a theory of conceit"; it is taught by Versac and Lursay, and is finally learned by Meilcour. Interestingly, Foucault does not even mention Hortense, but if the whole story happened only between Lursay, Versac, and Meilcour, one wonders why Crébillon fils would introduce a character as different as Hortense, who challenges the social values of the world he depicts.

The pleasure Mme de Lursay and Meilcour share in the end represents the triumph of superficiality over the values embodied by Hortense. Meilcour, indeed, is drawn to Lursay by vanity and sensual desire, and not by love. He yields to the power of the moment: "The work of my senses appeared to me the work of my heart. I abandoned myself to all the intoxication of that fatal moment…" (p. 908). In this last scene, we witness the triumph of Mme de Lursay or, rather, of the feeling she has awakened in Meilcour, this fleeting desire which is satisfied in the "moment."

However, Mme de Lursay – or the feeling she inspires in Meilcour – does not win entirely. Indeed, after the lovers have shared several moments of sensual pleasure, Hortense's name reappears in the text as the very proof that sexual pleasure does not suffice to make the narrator happy, and that the dangerous moment lasts for only a moment. The moral vocabulary the narrator ironically uses seems to condemn the superficiality of pleasure. He calls sensual pleasure "illusion" and "crime." The first sign of disillusionment he describes is a feeling of emptiness which reveals the vanity of sensual pleasure: "Without knowing what it was I lacked, I felt an emptiness in my heart" (p. 909). This image of an "emptiness" devalues pleasure, which does not have enough substance to fill the soul once the senses have been satisfied. Hortense's name immediately comes to fill this emptiness in the text as well as in the hero's heart. The hero may mock his tardy remem-

brance of Hortense, but it is still the thought of her that puts an end
to the pleasure of the moment.

One may think, then, that the novel ends with an implicit condemnation of sensual pleasure, since pleasure does not fill the soul and
even leaves place for remorse. Meilcour is caught between contradictory feelings that alternatively accuse and justify him but do not let
him enjoy his pleasure in peace: "Torn away from pleasure by remorse,
snatched from remorse by pleasure, I could not be sure of myself for
a moment" (p. 910). Pleasure is sensual, and remorse moral. Pleasure
happens in the moment when it is experienced; remorse, on the contrary, a sign of memory, establishes a continuity with the past. A moral
feeling such as remorse should negate pleasure and prevent the hero
from experiencing sensual enjoyment, that is, from forgetting past and
future, but this is not what happens. Remorse has little effect on the
hero, since his only consolation consists in drowning his feeling of guilt
"in new frenzies" ("*dans de nouveaux égarements*") (p. 910). Wandering, *égarement*, instead of leading to the straight path, in the end leads
only to more wandering.

The Choice of Ambiguity

The confusion of feelings at the novel's end offers a strong argument to
those critics who argue that the novel is simply incomplete. Since Meilcour narrates his story in retrospect, one would expect that he would
finally take a position. In fact, he does. Indeed, although he keeps
describing the terribly confusing contradiction in which he is caught,
there is one single instance, toward the end of the novel, in which the
narrator says "today" – that is, the moment when he is writing – and
comments on the contradiction. This passage starts with the words "ce
que j'en puis croire aujourd'hui," which, translated as "the conclusion I
draw today," clearly invites us to interpret this passage as the "conclusion" the narrator, at the moment when he writes, draws from the events
and gives to the novel. We need to look at this passage more closely:

> The conclusion I draw today is that if I had had more experience, she
> would merely have reduced me the sooner, since what is called knowledge
> of the world only makes us wiser insomuch as it makes us more corrupt....
> Instead of banishing the thought of Hortense from my mind, I should have
> found pleasure in dwelling on it.... I would have saved my heart from the
> disorder of my senses, and by these delicate distinctions, which might be
> called the quietism of love, I would have enjoyed all the delights of the
> moment without incurring the risk of infidelity (p. 909).

This is the only passage in the whole novel in which the contradiction of pleasure and love, of the moment and duration, is resolved. It is resolved not because one feeling is sacrificed to the other, but simply because it is dismissed as a "contradiction." Crébillon fils describes the possibility of experiencing enduring love for one person and fleeting pleasure with another at the same time, and of reconciling superficial and deep feelings, vanity and truth, "the disorder of my senses" and "the thought of Hortense" (p. 909). Meilcour's suggestion comes close to Manon's attempt to combine love and pleasure in Prévost's novel, when she tells des Grieux: "The fidelity I expect of you is that of the heart." There is, however, an important difference between *Manon Lescaut* and *The Wayward Head and Heart*: in Prévost's novel, the division of heart and body is suggested by Manon, a woman who acts as a courtesan and transgresses social laws. In *The Wayward Head and Heart*, such a division is proposed as the very rule of good social behavior. Des Grieux represents Manon as an extraordinary character and expresses his shock upon hearing her vulgar proposal. In Crébillon fils's novel, such a moral perspective is lacking; it is Meilcour, and not Lursay, who suggests a solution to the contradiction of love and pleasure. Crébillon fils's critique of sentimental and moral dichotomy is more radical than is that of Prévost.

This passage, however, is not the real conclusion of the novel: it is not the final paragraph and, above all, it is written in the past tense of the conditional mode, the mode of the unreal. Jean Sgard apparently considers this use of the conditional mode as implying a moral condemnation. "What is condemned here under the name of 'quietism' is a kind of libertine naturalism of which Crébillon fils perceives the bad faith,"[14] he writes, even though Crébillon fils himself gives no hint of such a condemnation. Meilcour does not say that he rejects the "quietism," and what he calls afterward the "convenient metaphysic[s]" of love, in the name of higher values (p. 909). Rather, he says that he did not know "these delicate distinctions" at the time of the scene with Mme de Lursay, because he was lacking one primary requirement – experience. We are quite free to think that Meilcour has this experience as he writes his memoirs. This would mean, then, that if the scene were replayed, Meilcour would have quietly "enjoyed all the delights of the moment without incurring the risk of infidelity," and that he would no longer be caught in a contradiction he cannot resolve (p. 909).

Yet this is not what Crébillon fils writes. Meilcour does not describe a new scene in the present tense; the only resolution of the conflict is in a passage written in the past tense of the conditional. The end of

the novel remains in the limbo of ambiguity and leaves us free to interpret, to choose our own conclusion. This explains why Crébillon fils's
novel can lead to the two contradictory interpretations mentioned in
this essay: on the one hand, the interpretation of Sgard, who reads it as
a novel of sentimental and moral education whose end is lacking; and
on the other, that of Foucault, who considers this a novel of social and
immoral education, delivering simply a "theory of conceit." Ambiguity, which characterizes Crébillon fils's style, as Bernadette Fort has
shown in *Le Langage de l'ambiguïté dans l'oeuvre de Crébillon*,[15] is the
novel's final word. This explains why the story stops abruptly: we do
not see Meilcour rehabilitated, as it were, through his union with a
respectable woman, because this is not the object of the novel. Instead,
Crébillon fils's novel replaces such a moral concept of the self with a
libertine concept of the nonself, of the divided, playful, and ambiguous self.

   This paragraph in the conditional mode requires a careful reading
and more attention than it has received. It is the only passage in which
the narrator reconciles the two contradictory poles of the dichotomy,
composed of genuine love and the pleasure of the moment. In that
sense, it represents the true resolution of the novel, its denouement.
Yet, because this passage is written as it is, it remains a mere hypothesis, not a clear statement, and readers can easily misread it. If, indeed,
Crébillon fils did condemn the "convenient metaphysics" of love, the
text would lose its irony and Crébillon fils's vocabulary would likewise lose its ambiguity. There is no such condemnation in the text:
critics or readers project it onto the novel because of the expectation
created by the plot, the title, and the preface. It is easier to endow
the novel with a moral meaning, which can be clearly stated, than it is
to accept ambiguity. In a sense, ambiguity is an aesthetic choice analogous to pleasure: ambiguity does not suffice to fill the void we feel in
our "souls," which is a desire for meaning.

   Ambiguity remains Crébillon fils's moral and narrative choice, as it
appears in the novel's final sentence. Remorse has so little power over
Meilcour that he promises Mme de Lursay to return the next day. The
final sentence expresses nothing but irony and ambiguity: "Thanks to
the proprieties that Mme de Lursay observed so strictly, she dismissed
me at last, and I left her, promising, in spite of my remorse, to see her
early the next day, firmly resolved, moreover, to keep my word" (p. 910).
This sentence mocks the moral value of faith (of keeping one's word)
by associating it with the pleasure of the moment, that is to say, with
the very proof of infidelity. The expressions "firmly resolved" and

"keep my word" indicate a moral determination and a respect for moral values, yet they are used in a context in which they have a contradictory meaning, since they come to signify Meilcour's incapacity to resist carnal pleasures and to be faithful to his genuine love for Hortense. Instead of resolving the conflict of values, Crébillon fils embeds the contradiction into language itself and accumulates ironic antiphrases so as to confuse categories that, until then, were clearly divided.

The novel is therefore complete, and we can even speak of a narrative closure in the sense that the novel achieves its aim, which consists in completely baffling the reader's expectation. The last sentence derides both the aristocratic values of honor and fidelity to one's word, as well as the bourgeois value of constancy and fidelity to one's self. It even mocks the very notion of an ending, since it opens onto a future that will undoubtedly resemble all the days and nights described in the novel, without resolving the contradiction between love and pleasure, the unique (Hortense) and the plural (Mme de Lursay and other coquettes). *The Wayward Head and Heart* makes us expect an end, only to deprive us of it. If, as Peter Brooks writes in *Reading for the Plot*, "the ultimate determinants of meaning lie at the end, and narrative desire is ultimately, inexorably, desire for the end," what, then, is the meaning of the suspension of an ending in Crébillon fils's novel?[16]

It is quite paradoxical that Crébillon fils's novel abstains from favoring true love over vanity after showing the moral superiority of the former. In the end, Meilcour simply observes that vanity, as superficial, erroneous, and deceitful as it is, represents a motive as strong as, or even stronger than, "true" passion, and this observation, in a way, is also his conclusion: "I have come to the conclusion since...that it is far more important for a woman to flatter a man's vanity than to touch his heart" (p. 808).

By establishing but not resolving a contradiction between truth and vanity, Crébillon fils's novel demonstrates that the dichotomy between vanity and truth has no moral and metaphysical validity. There is the truth of vanity, and, similarly, the vanity of truth. If remorse tears Meilcour away from pleasure, and pleasure snatches him from remorse, the endless alternation of pleasure and remorse shows that they are equivalent in their relation to time: like pleasure, remorse lasts only for a "moment." Crébillon fils, by suspending the end of the novel, ironically recognizes that superficiality is as deep as depth, and depth as superficial as superficiality: Crébillon fils's deliberate lightness can be read as the very consciousness of the superficiality of depth.

It is not by chance, then, that Crébillon fils refuses to lead his hero to the resolution his preface led readers to expect. It is also not by chance that he leaves readers in a space of suspension which does not satisfy their desire for an end, in a state of ambiguity which does not allow them to decide what is the moral, social, and sentimental norm from which the hero's mind and heart have swerved. *The Wayward Head and Heart* achieves its aim. Far from being incidental, the absence of ending is essential: it is the very object of the novel, and this object could be called "irony," that is to say, the ability to deride seriousness and reject morals while using seriousness and moral values as the central axis from which the hero swerves in his wandering. The suspension of the end represents the very end of Crébillon fils's novel, for it reveals that the dichotomy between superficiality and depth is invalid and shows the impossibility of establishing a qualitative difference between these two values from a moral, psychological, or ontological point of view.

Crébillon fils's irony reveals a fundamental suspicion of the moral, metaphysical, and political concept of the self. By stating, in his preface, that his novel's object is to reveal the moral transformation of his hero, at last "rehabilitated," and by not offering the expected ending, Crébillon fils deceives his readers. Deception is both a narrative strategy that frustrates readers from the end they had the right to expect, and a psychological device that teaches them not to trust their idealistic, moral, and sentimental impulse. It would be even more appropriate to speak of self-deception. Crébillon fils's novel does not deceive readers as much as it reveals to them that they deceive themselves when they express a moral contempt for superficiality and frivolity. The pleasure of the text lies in this ironic lesson of ambiguity, which teaches readers that pleasure – superficial, fleeting, and sensual feelings – motivates them as strongly as deep and enduring sentiments.

NOTES

1. Jean Sgard, "La Notion d'égarement chez Crébillon," *Dix-huitième Siècle* 1 (1969), pp. 240-49 (p. 240). Translation is mine. The original French title for *The Wayward Head and Heart* is *Les Egarements du coeur et de l'esprit*. *Egarement* is literally translated as "wandering."

2. *Dictionnaire de Trévoux* (1771), "égarement," quoted by Sgard, p. 243.

3. Sgard, "La Notion," p. 242.

4. Raymond Trousson, introduction to *Les Egarements du coeur et de l'esprit*, in

Romans libertins du XVIIIème siècle, ed. Raymond Trousson (Paris: Laffont, 1993), p. 9.

5. Claude-Joseph Dorat, *Les Malheurs de l'inconstance* (Paris: Editions Desjonquères, 1983); Charles Pinot-Duclos, *Les Confessions du Comte de* ———, in *Romanciers du XVIIIe siècle*, vol. 2, ed. Etiemble (Paris: Pléiade, 1965).

6. Thomas Kavanagh makes a very interesting suggestion when he argues that Crébillon fils's novels were condemned as superficial and frivolous precisely because "his cast of characters includes no real representation of any Other challenging the fundamental values these novels share with their audience." See "The Moment's Notice: Crébillon's Game of Libertinage," in *Enlightenment and the Shadows of Chance: The Novel and the Culture of Gambling in Eighteenth-Century France* (Baltimore: Johns Hopkins University Press, 1993), p. 224ff.

7. This does not imply that a mature Hortense would not have become similar to Crébillon fils's other female characters. The point is that, in the novel, she does represent other values.

8. See Crébillon fils, *La Nuit et le moment* (Paris [1755]: Desjonquères, 1983), p. 195; *The Sofa*, pp. 285, 306, 330; and *L'Ecumoire ou Tanzai et Néadarné* (Paris: Nizet, 1976), pp. 208, 230–31.

9. See Crébillon fils, *Le Hasard au coin du feu* (Paris: Desjonquères, 1983), pp. 195–96. The book was written between 1737 and 1740, and published in 1763.

10. See the excellent analysis of the notion in Kavanagh, "The Moment's Notice," p. 208ff.

11. *Webster's New Twentieth-Century Dictionary*, Collins World, 1975. For the eighteenth-century definition, see Diderot and d'Alembert's *Encyclopédie* (Paris, 1765), "Moment."

12. Patrick Wald-Lasowski, *Libertines* (Paris: Gallimard, 1980), p. 27.

13. See Michel Foucault: "Un Si cruel savoir," *Critique* (July 1962), pp. 597–611.

14. Sgard, "La Notion," p. 244.

15. Bernadette Fort, *Le Langage de l'ambiguïté dans l'oeuvre de Crébillon* (Paris: Klincksieck, 1978).

16. See Peter Brooks, *Reading for the Plot: Design and Intention in Narrative* (New York: Vintage, 1985), p. 52.

CONTENTS

THE WAYWARD HEAD AND HEART
by Crébillon fils

To Monsieur de Crébillon
of the French Academy

Monsieur,

I ought doubtless to have waited, before paying you homage, until I might have offered a work more worthy of you; but I dare hope that in what I do today you will have the goodness to see nothing but my zeal. Attached to one another by the closest bonds of kinship, we are, if I may venture to say so, united even more by the most sincere and tender friendship. Come, why should I not say it? Do fathers wish for nothing better than respect? And do they not receive as much of this as they are owed? And must it not be pleasant for them to see gratitude increasing and strengthening in the bosoms of their children that feeling of affection that Nature has already implanted there? I, who have always seen myself as the sole object of your fondness and concern, do not fear that you, my friend, my solace, my support, will find anything to harm my respect for you, in the titles I now lend you, which you have so justly earned. Indeed, I would not deserve to have been the object of your virtues had I failed to bestow on you their names. And if ever the public honors my humble talents with any small esteem, if posterity, when speaking of you, succeeds in recalling that I ever existed, I shall owe that glory only to the generous care with which you formed me, and to the desire I have always had that you might one day acknowledge me without undue regret.

I am, M., with the deepest respect,

Your most humble and obedient servant, and son.

Crébillon

Preface

Prefaces, for the most part, seem to be written only to impress the reader. I scorn this practice too much to adopt it. My only design here is to announce the intention of these memoirs, whether the adventures they contain are real, or are to be regarded as a work purely of the imagination.

A writer can have but two goals – utility and entertainment. Few authors have succeeded in uniting them. He who instructs either considers it beneath him to entertain or lacks the skill; and he who entertains does not have sufficient power to instruct: the inevitable result is that one is always tedious, the other always frivolous.

The novel, so disdained by sensible persons, and often with reason, is of all literary forms the one that could perhaps be made the most useful, if it were well managed – if, instead of filling it with farfetched and obscure situations, with heroes whose characters and adventures alike are always incredible, we were to make it, like comedy, a picture of human life wherein we censured vice and folly.

To be sure, the reader would no longer find those extraordinary and tragic events which capture the imagination and rend the heart. There would be no more of the kind of hero who crosses several oceans only to be captured at the vital moment by the Turks; no more adventures in the seraglio, where the Sultana is snatched up from vigilant eunuchs through some amazing feat of skill; no more sudden deaths; and infinitely fewer secret passages. Events artfully invented would be naturally expressed. There would be no more sinning against propriety and reason. Sentiment would not be exaggerated; man would at last see himself as he is. He would be dazzled less, but instructed more.

I admit that many readers, who remain untouched by simple things, would never approve of stripping the novel of the childish extravagances they believe to be the secret of its charm. In my opinion, though, this is no reason not to reform it. Every age, every year even, introduces a new taste. We know of authors who write only to follow fashion; victims of their own cowardly indulgence, they fall with fashion into everlasting oblivion. Only truth survives forever, and if artifice has come against it, and even at times, obscured it, they have never yet succeeded in destroying it. An author constrained by the base fear of not pleasing his own century rarely passes into the next.

It is true that novels which aim at painting men as they are, are subject to other inconveniences besides their excessive simplicity. There are subtle readers who never read except to apply what they see; who value a book only insofar as they think to find in it something that dishonors someone; and who color it throughout with their own spitefulness and spleen. It may well be that these astute critics, whose perspicacity nothing escapes, however veiled it was intended to be, know enough to fear that the folly they perceive would be attributed to them if they did not hasten to ascribe it to others. Nevertheless, this is how an author is sometimes accused of attacking people he respects, or who may even be unknown to him, and is reputed dangerous when in fact it is only his readers who are so.

Whatever the case may be, I know of nothing that either should or can prevent an author from deriving his characters and portraits from the mold of Nature. Personal interpretations do not last long: either people become tired of making them, or they are so futile that they die of their own accord. Besides, what is there that does not furnish a pretext for these ingenious parallels? The most extravagant fiction and the soberest moral treatise often provide equal fodder, and the only books I know that are so far exempt are those that deal with the abstract sciences.

If I describe fops and prudes it does not mean that I was thinking of M. This or Mme That, whom I have never seen; but naturally, if M. This is a fop and Mme That a prude, there will be something in the descriptions that applies to them. Certainly, the portraits would be failures if they were not like anyone; but it does not follow, because of the general weakness for mutual identification, that people can be vicious or ridiculous with complete impunity. As a matter of fact, there is usually so much uncertainty about who the person satirized really is that if, in one part of Paris, you hear someone exclaim, "Ah, how like the dear Marquise!" in another you will hear, "I should never have believed that the Countess could have been captured so neatly!" And at Court they will have guessed at yet a third original, no more correct than the previous two.

I have dwelt on this point because, since this book is the story of the private life, faults, and vicissitudes of a man of quality, some readers will be all the more tempted — because it is so easy to do so — to attribute to living people the portraits scattered through it and the adventures it contains; because our own manners and customs are here depicted; because, Paris being the scene of the action, there is no need to travel in imaginary realms, and nothing is hidden beneath exotic names and customs. There is no need for me to say anything about the complimentary portraits that may be found here: a virtuous woman, a sensible man — these, it seems, are reasonable people who never resemble anyone.

You will see in these memoirs a man such as nearly all men are in extreme youth, simple at first and artless, and knowing nothing yet of the world in which he is obliged to live. The first and second parts deal with this ignorance and with his first experiences of love. In sections that follow, he is a man full of false ideas and riddled with follies, who is still governed less by himself than by the persons whose interest it is to corrupt his heart and mind. You will see him finally, in the last part, restored to himself, owing all his virtues to a good woman. There you have the subject of *The Wayward Head and Heart.* I am far from claiming to have shown man in all the disorders to which the passions may bring him. Love alone rules here; or if, now and again, some other motive plays a part, it is nearly always love that decides its character.

No promises are made of regularity in the issuing of this book. The public has been so often deceived on this subject that they would do better not to rely on the word of either the author or the publisher. We can, however, assure them that if this first part pleases them, they shall have all the others promptly and in order.

Part One

I entered society at the age of seventeen, with all the advantages that can make a man remarkable there. My father had left me a noble name, whose luster he himself had increased, and from my mother I had expectations of considerable wealth. Left a widow when still of an age when there were no attachments she might not have formed, young, rich, and beautiful, her devotion to me permitted her to contemplate no other pleasure than that of educating me, and of making up to me all that I had lost in losing my father.

This project would, I believe, have entered few women's minds, and fewer still would meticulously have carried it out. But for Mme de Meilcour – who, according to what I have been told, was nothing of a coquette in her youth, and whom I never saw indulge in gallantry later – the task presented fewer difficulties than it would have for anyone else of her rank.

Strangely enough, I was given a modest education. Yet I was disposed by nature to think highly of myself, and when one is of that turn of mind it is not uncommon to think too highly of oneself. If my mother did not succeed in taking away my pride, at least she forced me to restrain it. And if I became a conceited fop later on for all that, without her precautions I should have become one sooner, and beyond all remedy.

When I entered society, the idea of pleasure was the only one I had in my head. The peace that then prevailed permitted me a dangerous amount of leisure. The deliberate idleness that youths of my age and rank commonly allowed themselves, emulation, liberty, example, all drew me toward pleasure: my passions were impetuous, or rather my imagination was ardent and easily kindled.

Continually surrounded by bustle and brilliance, I was conscious of a void in my heart. I desired a felicity of which I had no very distinct idea, and for some time I did not understand what sort of pleasure it was I stood in need of. I tried in vain to deaden the inner longing that oppressed me; only the society of women could dispel it. Without yet realizing the full violence of the inclination impelling me toward them, I went to infinite trouble to seek them out. I could not be long in their company without knowing that they alone could bestow on me that happiness, those sweet delusions of the heart which no other distraction offered me; and as age increased this disposition to love and made me even more susceptible to feminine charms, my one idea became to manufacture myself a passion of some description.

The matter was not without its difficulties. My affections were attached to no special object, but there was no object that did not excite them; I was afraid to choose, and yet I was hardly free to do so. The feelings that one woman inspired in me were destroyed the next moment by those that another awakened.

It often happens that a man is attracted less by the woman who most appeals to him than by the one he knows he can most easily captivate. And this applied to me as much as anyone: I wanted to be in love, but there was no one I loved. She from whom I might expect the least severity was the one I would always think myself in love with; but as it sometimes happened that in the same day I was looked on with favor by more than one, by evening, when it came to making a choice, I would find myself in great perplexity. And even if the choice were made, how was I to make it known to its object?

I had so little experience of women that a declaration of love seemed to me to be an insult to the woman to whom it was addressed. I was afraid, moreover, that I might not be listened to, and I considered a rebuff one of the most cruel affronts a man could receive. To these considerations was added an insuperable timidity that, even if the person I was addressing had wanted to encourage me, would not have allowed me to take advantage of any opportunity, however markedly it was offered. In such circumstances, I should without doubt have carried respectfulness to the extreme at which it offends women and makes men ridiculous.

From this particular alone you will easily conclude that I had not yet attained a just view of the sex; for, according to their way of thinking then, you had more to fear from not telling them that you loved them than from demonstrating the force of the impression they were confident of having made. And love, once so respectful, so sincere, so delicate, had become so bold and easy that it could never have seemed alarming except to someone as woefully ignorant as I.

That which both sexes then called "love" was a kind of commerce that they entered into, often without inclination, where convenience was always preferred to sympathy, interest to pleasure, and vice to feeling.

You told a woman that she was pretty three times; no more was necessary. The first time she would certainly believe you; she would thank you the second; and not uncommonly reward you the third.

It even happened sometimes that a man had no need to speak, and, more surprising still in an age as polite as ours, he was often not even expected to reply.

For a man to please it was not necessary for him to be in love; and in urgent cases he was even excused from being amiable.

An affair would be decided at first sight, but would rarely survive the morrow; yet even so swift a separation did not always preclude disgust.

To render society more agreeable, they had decided to get rid of ceremony; and still not finding it easy enough, they did away with seemliness as well.

If we are to believe old memoirs, women were once more flattered at inspiring respect than desire; and perhaps they were not the losers by it. To be sure, they came less easily by professions of love, but the love they actually inspired was more satisfying and more lasting.

In those days, they believed they ought never to yield, and so in fact they resisted. The women of my day started off by thinking it was impossible to defend themselves, and on this supposition succumbed the very moment they were attacked.

It must not, however, be inferred from what I have just said that all of them offered the same facility. I have seen some who were still undecided after a fortnight's attentions, and who could not be undone even in a month. I admit that these were exceptional cases from which no general consequences can be drawn. Indeed, if I am not mistaken, women as severe as that were considered rather prudish.

Manners have changed so prodigiously since then that it would not surprise me if what I have just said were treated as invention nowadays. It is difficult for us to believe that virtues and vices no longer before our eyes can ever have existed; but it is nonetheless true that I have not been exaggerating.

I was so far from knowing how the business of love was conducted in society that I believed, in spite of what I saw every day, that some superior merit was needed to please the sex – and in spite of the good conceit of myself I privately entertained, I never thought myself worthy of their love. And I am convinced that even had I known them better, I should not have feared them less. Lessons and examples count for little with a young man: he never learns except at his own expense.

What course was I to take then? There could be no question of consulting Mme de Meilcour about my doubts, and among the young men I frequented there was not one who had more experience than I, or at least any who could be of use to me. For six months I remained in this perplexity, and no doubt I should have remained in it longer if one of the ladies who had impressed me most had not been good enough to undertake my education.

The Marquise de Lursay (for that was her name) saw me nearly every day, either at her own house or at my mother's, for they were very close friends. She had known me a long time. Her frequent compliments upon my wit and appearance, her familiarity with me, and the habit of seeing her often had given me a considerable affection for her and a kind of ease that I felt with no one else of her sex. From this first feeling, arising from a long acquaintance, there imperceptibly grew up in me the desire to please her; and since she was the woman I saw most frequently, she was also the one who most continually stirred me. It was not that I thought I could make myself loved by her more easily than by another; so far was I from flattering myself with so charming an idea that my lack of hope of succeeding with her had often made me aspire elsewhere. But after a couple of days' infidelity I would come back to her more tender and more timid than ever.

In spite of the care I took to conceal what she inspired in me, she had fathomed it. My respect for her, which seemed to increase from day to day; the difficulty I had in speaking to her, quite different now from the bashfulness of childhood; looks that were even more telling than I supposed; my assiduous attempts to please her; my frequent visits; and perhaps most of all her own desire to attach me – all made her believe that I must secretly love her. However, in her situation, it would not do to try to take my heart too rashly, or to enter without precaution into what might prove to be a dubious affair.

Though she had been a coquette in her youth, and even a trifle given to gallantry, a notorious affair that had tarnished her reputation had taught her a disgust for the showy pleasures of society. As susceptible as ever but more cautious, she had learned at last that women are ruined not so much by their weaknesses as by their imprudence, and that the transports of a lover are no less real or sweet for being unknown to all but her. In spite of the prudish air she had assumed, people persisted in suspecting her; I was perhaps the only one who took her for what she claimed to be. As I was born a long time after she had given the public reason to talk, it was not surprising that I had never heard anything of it. I doubt, too, if anyone could have given me a bad opinion of her, even if they had tried. She knew how far I was from thinking her capable of any lapse, and this made her feel obliged to be more circumspect, and only to yield, if that were necessary, with all the decorum she knew I must look for in her.

Her face and age assisted her in this plan. She was beautiful, but with a majestic kind of beauty that, even without the grave air she affected, would easily have commanded respect. Though she dressed without coquetry, she did not neglect ornament. She professed to have no wish to please, but saw to it that she was always attractive, and took care to make up for what nearly forty years had inflicted on her charms. These losses, however, were small; and if you except that freshness which vanishes with first youth, and which women often cause to fade before its time by their efforts to enhance its brilliance, Mme de Lursay had nothing to regret. She was tall and well formed, and all this, together with the air of nonchalance she assumed, gave her graces that few women could rival. Her face and eyes were intentionally severe, but when she thought herself unobserved, gaiety and tenderness sparkled there.

She had a wit that was lively but not giddy – discreet, almost concealed. She spoke well and easily, and though her mind had great subtlety she was no pedant. She had carefully studied her own sex and ours, and knew all the springs that moved them both. As patient in the pursuit of revenge as of pleasure, she knew how to wait for time to bring about that which the moment did not provide. For the rest, although she was prudish, she was agreeable in society. Her philosophy was not that one might never err but, rather, that feeling alone could make one's errors pardonable: a very well-worn theory, which is proposed continually by three quarters of women, and only makes more contemptible those who disavow it by their conduct.

In some conversations that we had had together on the subject of love, she had learned my character and the reasons that might make me fear the confession of any passion I might conceive. In order to win, or even to engage me, she thought it was necessary for her to dissemble her love for me as long as possible; that the more accustomed I was to respecting her, the more struck I would be by a sudden advance on her part. She knew besides that, however ardently men seek victory, they like to purchase it at a price, and that women who believe they cannot

yield speedily enough often repent of having let themselves be conquered too soon.

Among the many things I was ignorant of was the fact that, in society, sentiment was no more than a subject of conversation; and I used
to hear women speak of it so convincingly, making such subtle distinctions, and scorning so loftily those who departed from it, that I never
imagined that, knowing it so well, they could make so little use of it.

Above all, Mme de Lursay, who by dint of trying to forget her fatal
love affairs had persuaded herself that no one else remembered them
either, while admitting that she thought herself capable of loving, made
the conquest of her heart seem so difficult, required so many qualities
in the object that should move her, and spoke of so singular a way of
loving that I trembled every time I thought of an attachment to her.

This fastidious lady, nevertheless content that I should entertain such
designs, judged that it was time to give me hope and to allow me to
think, though by means of only the most respectable advances, that I
was the fortunate mortal whom her heart had chosen. From the pleasant talk with which she had entertained me hitherto, she went on to
more particular and pointed conversation. She gave me tender looks,
and urged me, when we were alone, to be less reserved with her. By
this course of action, she had succeeded in making me a good deal in
love, and in so becoming so herself, so that by then she would no doubt
have been pleased to have inspired me with a little less respect.

By her own efforts, her situation had become as awkward as my own.
The question now was how to rise above the mistrust she had given me
of myself and the too-lofty opinion she had taught me of her – two very
difficult matters that had to be handled with the utmost delicacy. She
could not see how I should ever dare to declare that I loved her; and,
far from being able to take the discovery upon herself, she would be
obliged to receive my avowal with an appearance of severity, if indeed
she was ever fortunate enough to bring me to that point.

With a man of experience, a mere word whose meaning can be variously applied, a look, a gesture, even less, can tell him all he needs to
know if he wishes to be loved; and if he happens to have different ideas
from those one would have liked, the signs that have been hazarded are
so ambiguous and trivial that they can easily be retracted.

Far from finding me so accommodating, Mme de Lursay had more
than once had occasion to observe that my stupidity only grew with
every effort she made to open my eyes, and she felt unable to say more
without running the risk of alarming me, of losing me even. We both
sighed in secret, and were of the same mind without being any the bet-

ter off for it. We had been at least two months in this ridiculous state when Mme de Lursay, weary of her torment and the profound veneration in which I held her, resolved to deliver herself of the one by curing me of the other.

A skillfully handled conversation can often lead up to things most difficult to speak of: lack of order gives opportunity for revelation; as people go on talking they change the subject so often that, in the end, the subject of preoccupation can naturally find a place. In society, people like above all things to talk about love, because this subject, already interesting in itself, is often bound up with gossip, of which it nearly always provides the substance.

On matters of sentiment, I was extremely eager, and in order either to learn something or to have the opportunity to speak of the state of my heart, I was hardly ever in company without turning the conversation to love and its effects. This tendency was favorable to Mme de Lursay, and she resolved at last to make use of it.

One day when a large group of people was assembled at Mme de Meilcour's, and Mme de Lursay and I had declined to play cards, we found ourselves sitting side by side. This tête-à-tête made me tremble, though I had often wished for it. Away from her, I could no longer see any obstacles to oppose the design I was forming of declaring my passion; yet no sooner was I in a position to carry it out than I quaked at the mere idea of it. That I was not altogether alone with her was no reassurance: our part of the drawing room was deserted, everyone was occupied, so there was no third party to come to my aid. These cruel considerations completed my confusion. I was with Mme de Lursay a quarter of an hour without saying a word to her. She imitated my taciturnity, and in spite of whatever desire she may have had to speak to me, she knew not how to break the silence.

At last, however, a play that was then being performed with success furnished her with a pretext. She asked me if I had seen it. I answered yes.

"The plot does not strike me as new," she said, "but the details pleased me well enough. The piece is nobly written, and the sentiments skillfully developed. Do you not agree with me?"

"I make no claim to be an expert," I replied. "In general I liked it, but I would find it hard to articulate its good points or defects."

"One can still," she went on, "even without a complete knowledge of the theater, have an opinion about certain of its parts. Sentiments, for example, are a thing about which one cannot be mistaken: it is not the mind that judges but the heart, and an interesting topic moves duller people and the most brilliant equally. I found certain passages in this play touched with great art. There is in particular a declaration of love that, in my opinion, has an extreme delicacy; it is one of the parts I most admire."

"I was struck by it too," I said, "and I give the author all the more credit because I believe such a situation very difficult to carry off."

"That would not be my reason for admiring it," she said. "To say one is in love is a thing one does every day with all the ease in the world, and if this situation succeeds in pleasing, it does so less by the substance of it than by the novel manner in which it is treated."

"I cannot be entirely of your opinion, Madam," said I. "I do not think it can be easy to say one is in love."

"I am sure that this confession may cost a woman dear," she said. "A thousand reasons that love cannot absolutely remove make it difficult for her. But you cannot imagine that a man stands to lose anything by declaring himself?"

"Forgive me, Madam," I answered, "that is exactly what I was thinking. I can imagine nothing more humiliating than for a man to say that he is in love."

"What a pity that your idea is so absurd," she replied. "You could have made your fortune otherwise with its novelty. What! Humiliating for a man to say that he is in love!"

"Yes, to be sure," said I, "when he is not certain of being loved in return."

"And how is he to know," she answered, "whether he is loved in return? Only the declaration of his passion can permit a woman to reply to it. Do you think, whatever the confusion of her heart, it would be proper for her to be the first to speak, and so expose herself to the risk of becoming less dear in your eyes, and the object of a rebuff?"

"Very few women need fear what you describe," I said.

"All would need to fear it if they took it upon themselves to precede you," she answered. "And you would cease to feel the least inclination for the woman who had inspired the most – at the very moment she offered you an easy conquest."

"That is unreasonable," I said. "It seems to me that one owes more gratitude to a person who saves one from torment –"

"To be sure," she interrupted, "but your reasoning goes against both your interest and ours. You yourself, who now cries out against the injustice of men, would act as they do if a woman anticipated your sighs."

"Ah, how grateful I should be to her," I cried, "and how much the pleasure of being anticipated would increase my love!"

"If that appears so great a pleasure to you," said she, "you must have a very dreadful notion of what a declaration of love is. But what do you find so terrible in it? The fear of not being heard? That is not possible. The shame of being obliged to say that you love? That is not reasonable."

"What, Madam," I answered, "do you count as nothing the embarrassment of saying it? Especially for someone like me, who knows he would say it poorly."

"The most elegant declarations are not always the best received," she said. "Wit in a lover may entertain, but it can never persuade. His agitation, his difficulty in expressing himself, the confusion of his speech – it is these that make him formidable."

"But, Madam," I asked, "though this proof seems incontestable, does it always succeed in persuading?"

"No," she replied. "The confusion of which I spoke is sometimes the effect of a man's stupidity rather than his love, and then he gets no credit for it. Besides, men are often artful enough to feign agitation and passion when they are hardly even animated by desire; and then they are often not believed. It can also happen that the person you inspire with love is not the one you wish to fall in love with yourself, and then all he says will not move you."

"You see then, Madam," I answered, "I was in the right to think refusal cruel, and I am not sure I would not prefer my uncertainty to an explanation that would teach me that I cannot be loved."

"You are alone in thinking that an inconvenience," she answered. "Moreover, your argument is not even to your own advantage. It is better, it is even more sensible, to speak than to persist in remaining silent. By silence you risk losing the pleasure of knowing yourself loved; and if the other cannot reply to you as you would wish, you at least cure yourself of a useless passion that can bring you nothing but misery. But," she added, "I notice that you have been talking to me of this subject for a very long while – if I am not mistaken, a declaration can only seem such an embarrassing matter because you yourself have one to make."

With this obliging observation, Mme de Lursay fixed me with so animated a look that it put me quite out of countenance.

"Your silence and confusion tell me I have guessed aright," she went on. "But I do not intend to make use of your secret except to save you from error and to be useful to you if I can. I want you first of all to tell me of your choice. You are young and inexperienced, and may perhaps have arrived at it too lightly. If it is unworthy of you, I pity you. But that is not enough: my counsel can help you to efface a passion, or rather a fancy, that as far as I can see has not yet had any hope to nourish it, and of whose folly I shall therefore the more easily convince you. If, on the other hand, your choice is such that neither honor nor reason can complain, far from uprooting from your heart the object you have planted there, I can teach you how to please, and inform you of your progress."

Mme de Lursay's proposition took me by surprise, and although her manner was by no means severe, and her eyes even spoke to me most sweetly, I could not summon the strength to answer her. I looked at her distractedly without daring to meet her eyes. I was in mortal fear lest she should notice my agitation, and all I could do to break the silence was utter a sigh, which I tried in vain to conceal.

"How young you are!" she said to me kindly. "I can no longer doubt that you love. But your silence only adds to your torment. How do you know? Perhaps you are even more loved than loving. Would it be nothing to you to have the pleasure of hearing it expressed? Come now, Meilcour, I insist. My friendship for you forces me to adopt this tone: you must tell me who it is you love."

"Ah, Madam," I replied, trembling, "I should soon be punished for telling you."

We were now arrived at a point where there could be no ambiguity in what I said; Mme de Lursay must have understood. Yet I had still not ventured far enough for her, and she still feigned to be at a loss.

"What can you mean?" she said in a voice that grew still more gentle. "You would soon be punished for telling me? Do you think I might be indiscreet?"

"No," I answered, "that is not what I am afraid of. But, Madam, suppose it was someone like you whom I loved – what would be the good of telling her?"

"No good at all, perhaps," she answered, blushing.

"I am right, then, to keep silent," said I.

"On the other hand, you might be fortunate," she continued. "A person of my disposition can become even more susceptible to passion, perhaps, than another."

"No, you would not love me!" I cried.

"We are digressing," said she. "I do not see why we talk so much of me. You have been evading my questions with more skill than I would have given you credit for. But to pursue this theme, since it has been proposed, what is it to you that I might not love you? One should wish to inspire love only in someone who has inspired it in oneself; and I do not suspect you to be in that situation with regard to me. At least, I would hope not."

"I too, Madam, would hope otherwise," I replied. "And from your own apprehension I can tell how unhappy you would make me."

"No," she answered, "I am not at all afraid. To fear to see you love me would be almost as good as to admit that you might move me: the lover who is most feared is always the one nearest to being loved. I should be very sorry if you thought me so afraid of you."

"I do not flatter myself about that either," I replied. "But say, if I did love you, what would you do?"

"I cannot suppose," she replied, "that in answer to a hypothesis you expect a positive reply."

"Dare I confess, Madam, that it is no hypothesis?"

At this unmistakable declaration of the state of my affections Mme de Lursay sighed, blushed, turned her eyes languidly to mine, let them dwell there a moment, then lowered them to her fan and was silent.

During this silence a thousand different emotions racked my heart. My extreme efforts to drive myself on had almost overpowered me, and my fear of an unfavorable answer kept me from urging a reply. Yet I had spoken and did not wish to lose the profit of it.

"Have you no advice to give me, Madam?" I said, half dead with terror. "Will you not tell me what I am to expect from my choice? Will you, after all your kindness, be so cruel as to withhold your aid in the most important matter in my life?"

"If you wish only for advice," she replied, "I can give it to you. But if what you have just told me is true, perhaps that may not satisfy you."

"Do you doubt my sincerity?" said I.

"For your own sake," she answered, "I should like to. The truer the sentiments you express, the more unhappy they will make you. For after all, Meilcour, you must realize that I cannot respond to them. You are young. That which for many women would only be another quality in you, for me, even if you evoked in me the strongest inclination, could only be a perpetual reason for never allowing myself to yield. Either you would not love me enough, or you would love me too much; both would be equally disastrous for me. In the first case, I should have to endure your whims, your fancies, your fits of pride, your infidelities – all the torments, in short, that an unhappy love affair entails; and in the second, I should see you abandon yourself to all your ardor, and ruin me wildly, recklessly, through very excess of love. A passion is always a disaster for a woman. But in my case it would be an absurdity, and I should never get over having brought it upon myself."

"But Madam," I answered, "believe me, I should take every possible care –"

"I know what you are going to say," she interrupted. "You will promise me all possible circumspection. I am sure, too, that you believe yourself capable of it. But the less experienced you are in love, the less you would be able to love in the way that would be necessary. You would never learn to govern your looks or your speech; or you would govern them, but so grossly and so artlessly that you would advertise what you sought to hide. So, Meilcour, my advice to you is, cease to think of me. It pains me to know that you will hate me, but I trust that it will not be for long, and that one day you will thank me for my frankness. Do you not wish to remain my friend?" she added, holding out her hand.

"Ah, Madam!" I cried. "You drive me to despair. No one has ever loved more fervently than I. There is nothing I would not do to please you, no trials I would not undergo. You only foresee such disaster because you do not love me."

"No, no," said she, "you must not think that. I will go further, for you will always find me sincere: if you were less young, or I less wise, I am sure I should love you very well – very well. But do not ask more of me. In my present peaceful way of life, I hardly know my heart. Only time can decide it, and perhaps, after all, it will decide nothing."

With these words Mme de Lursay left me abruptly and, by rejoining the company, obliged me to give up all hope of continuing our interview. I was so little used to the ways of the world that I thought I had really vexed her. I did not know that a woman rarely pursues an amorous conversation with someone she wishes to attach, and that she who most desires to yield, exhibits, at least at the first interview, some sort of virtue. No one could have offered a feebler resistance than she had just offered to me; yet I believed that I should never conquer her, and repented of having spoken. I blamed her for leading me on; for a few moments I hated her. I even resolved never to mention my love to her again, and to act so coldly toward her that she could no longer suspect me of it.

While I was entertaining these disagreeable ideas, Mme de Lursay was congratulating herself for having managed to conceal her happiness. Her eyes shone with delight. Anyone less ignorant than I would have seen a thousand signs that he was loved – but every tender look, every smile, seemed a fresh insult to me, and confirmed me in my recent resolution.

I had remained where I was: she came back to find me, and teased me into speaking about various matters. The gloomy manner in which I answered her and the care I took to avoid meeting her eyes were a further assurance that I had not been deceiving her; but whatever conclusions she might have drawn from this, she wished to establish her sway, and to make my heart suffer before she made it happy.

Throughout the evening she paid me the same attentions: it was as if she had forgotten what I had said to her. And the air of detachment she affected only plunged me into deeper distress. When she took leave of me she mocked me for my melancholy, and although she did it kindly, I took serious offense.

The beginning of this affair gave Mme de Lursay as much satisfaction as it gave me pain. True, in taking up with a man of my age, she declared her own; but no doubt this was for her no more than another absurdity, while, on the other hand, it was no small matter to secure a lover who in addition to everything else had never belonged to another. She was not yet old, but she had become conscious that she was going to be, and for women in this situation no conquest is to be despised.

What can be more flattering to them than the devotion of a young man, whose transports remind them of their own first taste of pleasure, and confirm them in the opinion they still have of their own charms – one who believes that the woman accepting his vows is indeed the only one who would not despise them, who joins gratitude to passion, trembles at her least caprice, and is blind to the most glaring faults of her looks and disposition, either because he lacks the resource of comparison or because his self-esteem would suffer if he held his conquest in less esteem. With a man already formed any woman enjoys less advantages; he has more desire than passion, more flirtation than feeling, more art than spontaneity; he has too much experience to be credulous, and too many opportunities for dissipation and inconstancy to be exclusively and deeply attached. In a word, he makes love more discreetly, but he loves less.

Whatever defects Mme de Lursay might have found in a young man's manner of loving, she was by no means as alarmed by it as she had given me to understand. Even if the inconveniences she feared had been real, she would not have loved me the less for them, and if I had been shrewd enough to make her think I might change my mind, there is no doubt that her excessive respect for propriety would have given way to the fear of losing me.

It was not – or so at least I have been given reason to believe – that she meant the confession of her weakness to be long delayed. A week was all that her virtue required, especially as she knew that my inexperience would prevent me from profiting from her kindnesses until she judged the time to be ripe. It was her love for me that caused her to adopt this stratagem. She wanted, if possible, to make my affection for her last longer than a few days: if I had been loved less, I should have encountered less resistance. Her heart was now affectionate and gentle.

From what I have learned since, it was not always so, and if she had not really been moved by genuine ardor, she might well have adopted quite another method.

When she is young, a woman is more alive to the pleasure of inspiring passion in others than to that of feeling it herself. What she calls affection is usually no more than a strong inclination, which influences her more readily than love itself, amuses her for a while, and dies without her noticing or regretting it. The merit of attaching a single lover forever is worthless in her eyes than that of enslaving a string of them. More often wavering than fixed, always at the mercy of caprice, she gives less thought to the one who possesses her than to the one she would like to possess her. She is always looking for pleasure and never enjoying it; she takes a lover less because she finds him amiable than to prove that she is so. Often she knows the one she is leaving no better than the one who succeeds him. Perhaps if she could have kept him longer she might have loved him; but is it her fault if she is unfaithful? A pretty woman depends much less on herself than on circumstance, and unhappily there are so many circumstances, and they are so unexpected and so pressing that it is not at all amazing if, after several adventures, she has learned nothing either of love or of her own heart.

Should she arrive at that age when her charms begin to decline, when men, already indifferent to her, foretell by their coldness that they will soon see her only with disgust, she tries to think how she may prevent the solitude that lies in wait for her. Certain, once, that when she changed lovers she was only changing pleasures, she is now only too glad to preserve the only one she has, and the price she had to pay for her conquest now makes it all the more precious to her. Made constant by the thought of what she would lose if she were not, her heart gradually learns to feel. Obliged for the sake of propriety to avoid the things that once helped to dissipate and corrupt her, she must, in order to avoid languishing, give herself over completely to love, which, though in the past was only a momentary occupation among a thousand others, now becomes her sole resource. She throws herself into it with fury, and what is taken to be a woman's last fancy is often her first passion.

Such was the state of mind of Mme de Lursay when she formed the design of attaching me to her. Since her widowhood and reformation, the public, which talks no less for being deprived of fodder, had attributed lovers to her whom perhaps she never had. Her conquest of me flattered her pride, and it seemed reasonable to her, since being virtuous had gained her nothing, to take pleasure as compensation for the ill opinion of the world.

All I had done that day furnished me with subjects for reflection for the night. I spent nearly all of it either thinking of ways to move Mme de Lursay's heart or persuading myself to think no more of her. No doubt she was occupied with more cheerful thoughts. She expected to see me reappear, loving, humble, eager, to endeavor to overcome her severity. It was only natural that she should assume this; but she had to do with someone who was ignorant of the ways of the world.

I waited on her the next day, but late, at an hour when I knew she would not be there or that I should find a good deal of company. It was clear that she had expected me to present myself earlier, and she received me with a cold, offended air. Far from divining the cause of this, I attributed it only to her indifference.

I had changed color on seeing her, but, still resolved to conceal the state of my heart from her, I recovered myself without too much difficulty and assumed a less embarrassed air. I even had the self-command to speak to her without the agitation a lover must always feel in the presence of the beloved; but whatever coolness I might try to affect, she was not long deceived. To see the truth she had only to look me in the eyes. I could not meet her gaze. A mere look was enough to show her all my heart. She suggested that we play, and while the cards were being set out she said to me with a smile:

"You are a singular lover. If you would have me judge your love by your zeal, you cannot suppose me to have a very high opinion of it."

"My one hope in life," I replied, "is that you should believe that I love you, and it is no mean proof of it that I inflict my presence upon you as late as possible."

"Yours is a singular policy," she said, "and if your judgment is sometimes a little at fault, your imagination may be said to make amends for it. But what is amiss? Why this chill manner? It quite crushes me! Do you not know how your taciturnity frightens me? But come, you are still fond of me? I think you cannot be. Poor Meilcour! You really must not think of changing on my account — I should be in despair. I see from your sullen looks that you do not believe me. But we ought still to enjoy one another's society."

"Is it not enough, Madam," I replied, "but must you add killing words to the way you receive my attentions?"

"Yes," she answered, giving me the tenderest look in the world. "Yes, Meilcour, you have reason to complain. I am not treating you well. But ought you to take amiss this poor vestige of pride? Do you not see what it costs me to assume it? Ah, if I had only known how many times would I not have told you I loved you? How grieved I am that I did not understand before that you wished to be anticipated! Whatever might have been the outcome, you would not have had to be the first to speak: you would only have had to give me your reply."

I have since come to appreciate all Mme de Lursay's skill, and the pleasure she derived from my ignorance. All these words she could not have spoken to another without the most dangerous consequence. All these avowals of her own true feelings, so far was I from understanding them that they threw me into the most painful confusion. I made no reply, and, certain that she was only rallying me mercilessly, grew more and more determined to break such cruel chains.

"To be sure," she continued, seeming my gloomy air, "if you refuse to believe me much longer I am not sure that I shall give you a rendez-vous for tomorrow. Would it not embarrass you?"

"In heaven's name, Madam," I said to her, "spare me. You are making me wretched –"

"I will not tell you any more that I love you then," she interrupted, "though you will be depriving me of great pleasure."

I was thankful that the company present prevented her from pursuing this conversation further. We sat down to cards.

Throughout the game Mme de Lursay, doubtless more susceptible than she knew, and carried away by her love, gave me the most marked signs of it. It was as if her prudence had abandoned her, as if nothing existed for her now but the pleasure of loving me and of telling me so, and as if she foresaw how much I had need of reassurance if I was to be attached to her. But all that she did meant nothing to me, and as yet she could not bring herself to confess plainly that she responded to my desires. She was uncertain even in her advances, and continually mingled tenderness with severity. Every relenting seemed only to confirm her determination to resist. If she suspected that her words could have given me grounds for hope, she was at once anxious to disabuse me, and instantly assumed the manner that had often made me tremble, thus depriving me of even the cold comfort of uncertainty.

The whole evening was spent playing these games or in these maneuvers, and as her last mood was a contrary one, I went home persuaded that she hated me and determined that I would look elsewhere. I spent the greater part of the night reviewing in my mind all the women to whom I might form an attachment. It was labor in vain, for I found, after the most minute research, that none of them pleased me as much as Mme de Lursay. The depth of the love I thought I felt was proportionate to the shallowness of my experience, and I considered myself doomed to the frightful torment of loving without hope either of pleasing or of ever being able to change. By dint of persuading myself that of all the men in the world I was the most in love, I felt all the perturbations of passion with as much violence as if I had truly suffered them. All the resolutions I had formed of seeing Mme de Lursay no more had vanished and given place to the most ardent revival of feeling. What have I to complain of, I said to myself. Are these severities surprising? Did I expect to find myself loved already, and is it not for me to procure myself that privilege by my own efforts? What happiness it will be, if I can one day succeed in moving her. The more obstacles she puts in my way the greater will be my triumph. Can a heart as priceless as hers be bought too dear? This was my final thought, and the one I woke to the next day. It seemed to have gained strength from the illusions of sleep.

I waited upon Mme de Lursay as soon as possible after dinner, determined to swear my adoration and to submit to whatever fate she might be pleased to impose on me. Unfortunately for her, she was not at home. My sorrow was extreme, and not knowing what to do, I occupied myself until it was time for the opera by paying several calls, accompanied by all the woe that burdened me.

I was in such an ill humor when I arrived at the Opera, where I found only a small audience assembled, that in order not to be distracted from my reverie, I took a box rather than sit in the balconies where I should have been more liable to disturbance. I waited with neither impatience nor expectation for the performance to begin. Occupied entirely with Mme de Lursay, I was giving myself up to the pain of being deprived of her presence when a box was opened next to mine. Curious to see those who were to occupy it, I turned to look, and was transfixed by the object that presented itself. Imagine the noblest attributes of the most regular beauty, the utmost charms of all the graces, in a word all that youth can radiate of freshness and brilliance, and still you have but a poor idea of the person I am trying to depict. I cannot describe the strange and sudden emotion that seized me at the sight; struck by so much beauty I stood dumbfounded. My surprise was so great I was transported. I felt a disorder in my heart which spread through all my senses. Far from abating, it grew stronger as I made a covert examination of all her charms. She was dressed simply but nobly. Indeed, she had no need of decoration; could there be an ornament so brilliant that she would not have eclipsed it, or so modest that she would not have beautified it? Her countenance was sweet and reserved. Feeling and intelligence seemed to shine in her eyes. She looked extremely young, and I inferred from the surprise of the spectators that she had not appeared in public before that day. This caused me an involuntary flutter of joy, and I would have been glad if she had never been seen at all except by me. Two ladies dressed in the height of elegance were with her; not knowing them either was another surprise for me, but one which did not detain me long. Solely preoccupied with my lovely unknown, I did not take my eyes off her except when by chance she happened to look at someone. Then my own eyes turned at once to the object she seemed to seek: if she let her look linger for a moment, and it was on a young man, I thought that nothing but a lover could make her so attentive. Not stopping to examine my motive for acting thus, I followed and interpreted her looks, and tried to read her slightest movement. This persistent scrutiny brought me at last to her notice. She looked at me; I gazed back without knowing what I was doing. I know not what my eyes said in the enchantment that carried me away in spite of myself, but she turned her own away, blushing a little. Transported though I was, I feared she would think me too bold, and though I did not yet suspect myself of wishing to please her, I preferred to restrain myself rather than earn her bad opinion. I had been admiring her for at least an hour when one of my friends entered my box. The thoughts that occupied me were already so precious to me that it was with pain that I saw they were about to be distracted, and I doubt if I would even have answered my friend if the stranger had not been the first subject of his conversation. He did not know who she was either. Together, we formed several conjectures which all failed to enlighten us. He was one of those brilliant, reckless fellows, familiar and insolent. He sang the praises of the unknown young lady so loudly, and stared at her with so little concealment and so much conceitedness that I blushed for both him and myself. Without having sifted my feelings, without dreaming that I was in love, I did not wish to displease her. I feared the disgust she might conceive for the young man with me might harm me also, and that seeing me on friendly terms with him she might think me subject to the same follies. I already esteemed her so much that I could not think without pain that she might form the same opinion of me as of him, and I did my best to turn our conversation to matters that did not relate to the lovely stranger. My wit was a naturally lively one, and apt at playing agreeably with those trifles that make one shine in society. My desire that the lady should miss nothing that might enhance me in her eyes lent me more than my usual elegance of expression, though perhaps no more of wit. I observed, however, that she paid more attention to what I was saying than she did to the performance. Sometimes I even saw her smile.

The opera was nearly ended when the Marquis de Germeuil, a young man of very attractive appearance and extremely highly thought of, came into my unknown neighbor's box. We were friends, but I cannot describe the feeling that arose in me at the sight of him. The lady received him with the easy politeness one shows to people one knows well, and to whom one wishes to show regard. We bowed to each other without speaking, but in spite of my keen desire to know more of the person who had already won so much of my heart, and though I knew that Germeuil could satisfy my curiosity, I preferred, however much delay might make me suffer, to defer that satisfaction rather than confide in one who was already the object of my furious jealousy. My unknown lady spoke to him, and although they conversed only about the opera, it seemed to me that he spoke to her fondly, and that she replied likewise. I thought I even caught significant looks passing between them. It gave me mortal pain. She seemed to me so worthy to be loved that I could not think that Germeuil, or anybody, could see her with indifference; and he himself seemed to me so formidable that I could not flatter myself he might approach her without success.

The scant attention she paid to me after seeing him confirmed me in the idea that they loved each other, and unable to bear any longer the torment this inflicted, I abruptly left. In spite of my chagrin, I did not go far: the desire to see her again, and the hope of finding out about her on my own, made me halt on the stairs. A moment afterward, she passed, escorted by Germeuil. I followed them: a carriage without a coat of arms drew up, and Germeuil got in beside her. I saw that the servants were not in livery: there was nothing in all her attendance to tell me what I wanted to know. I had therefore to wait on chance for the happiness of seeing her again. My only consolation was that so perfect a beauty could not remain unknown for long. I could indeed have saved myself from this uneasiness by visiting Germeuil the next day, but how could I reveal to him so urgent a curiosity, what reasons could I allege? In spite of any dissimulation I might employ, would he not be certain to discover their real source? And if it was true, as I suspected, that he loved the unknown girl, why give him the chance of taking precautions against me? Full of agitation I returned home, all the more convinced that I was deeply in love because the passion had been implanted in my heart by one of those bolts from the blue that characterize all great affairs in novels.

Far from tempering my first impulse, the remarkableness of this beginning was all the more reason to let myself be carried away.

In the midst of this confusion, which I took pleasure in increasing,

Mme de Lursay came into my mind, but disagreeably, as a subject the mere memory of which embarrassed me. It was not that I no longer saw any charms in her, but in my imagination I placed them far below those of the lovely stranger, and I resolved more firmly than ever to speak no more to her about my love, and to give myself over to the new preference that now held me in its power. I am extremely fortunate, I told myself, that she did not love me. What could her affection mean to me now? I would have had to deceive her, to listen to her reproaches, to watch her try to thwart my passion. On the other hand, though, I continued, am I loved by the one for whose sake I am going to be unfaithful? I do not know her; perhaps I shall never see her again. Germeuil is in love with her, and if I myself am obliged to acknowledge him lovable, what must she not feel for him? Could anyone ever give him up for me?

These reflections brought me back to Mme de Lursay – the fact that that affair was already launched, and that I was free to see her, together with the remnant of attraction I still had for her, and my hope of succeeding – all these were reasons for not abandoning her. Yet, beside my new passion, they were feeble reasons. I was afraid lest when I arrived at my mother's I should find Mme de Lursay there; I now dreaded to see her as much as earlier that very day I had longed to do so. My relief at not finding her there was not long lived; she arrived a few moments after I did. I was uneasy in her presence. However forearmed I was against her, however resolved to love her no more, I perceived that she still had more power over my heart than I had supposed. My lovely stranger appealed to me more dazzlingly, I found her more beautiful. They each inspired a different feeling in me, but the truth was that I was torn between them – and if Mme de Lursay had wished it, she might at that moment have borne away the victory. I know not what had put her into an ill humor, but she received some simple compliment I paid her with a quite ridiculous disdain. In the mood I was in, this shocked me more than it would have at another time, and worse still – and doubtless contrary to her intention – did not intrigue me in the least. Her capriciousness lasted all the evening, and was perhaps increased by the little attention I paid her. We separated with mutual dissatisfaction. I neither sought nor saw her the following day. I was vexed with her behavior of the previous evening, and her presence was less necessary to me now that my heart had a new distraction. I spent the whole day searching for my unknown lady. Places of entertainment, public gardens, I visited them all, and nowhere did I find either her or Germeuil, of whom at last I was now willing to ask her identity. For two days in a row, I continued my fruitless search: the beautiful stranger only preoccupied me the more. I continually retraced her charms with a pleasure I had never before experienced. I had no doubt that her birth would do no dishonor to my own, and I derived this idea less from her beauty than from that air of nobility and breeding that always distinguishes women of rank, even in misfortune. Yet to love without knowing whom I loved seemed to me an unbearable torture. Besides, what could I expect from my feelings if I could not bring myself to declare them to the one who had inspired them? I foresaw no difficulty in seeing her and speaking to her once I knew who she was. My name was such as to give me entry everywhere, and even if the unknown lady was so highly born that my devotion could not honor her, at least I was sure that it could never shame her. This reflection lent me boldness, and strengthened me in my love. It might have been more prudent to fight against this inclination, but I found it more pleasant to indulge it.

I had not seen Mme de Lursay for three days and I had borne the separation with ease. Not that I did not sometimes desire to see her; but it was a passing desire that was extinguished almost the instant it was born. It was not a feeling of love over which I had no control; and as, since meeting my unknown lady, I could see Mme de Lursay without pleasure, so also I could lose her without regret. And yet I felt for her that inclination that is commonly called "love," that men put forward as such, and that women accept on the same footing. I should not have been sorry to find her responsive, but I no longer wanted this response to have, or to require, anything of passion. Her conquest, to which so short a while ago I attached all my happiness, no longer seemed worthy of fixing me. I should have liked to share with her that convenient relationship one establishes with a coquette, lively enough for the amusement of several days and as easily broken as formed.

Yet that was the last thing I could expect with Mme de Lursay. She had Platonic ideas and continually repeated that the senses never counted for anything in the love of a person of breeding; that the disorders that the victims of passion fell into every day were caused less by love than by the profligacy of their hearts; that love might be a weakness, but in a virtuous heart never a vice. She conceded, however, that even a woman of the firmest principles might run into dangerous situations — but that if she found herself obliged to yield, it must be after struggles so long and violent that whenever she looked back on her surrender she might have as little as possible to reproach herself with. Mme de Lursay may have been right, but female Platonists are not always consistent in their philosophy, and I have observed that the women most easily conquered are those who embark on an affair with the foolish hope of never being overcome, either because they are in fact as weak as the rest, or because, not having foreseen the danger, they find themselves without resource when it overtakes them.

However, I was too young then to perceive the absurdity of this philosophy or to know how little it was followed, even by those who most ardently professed it; and as I did not understand the difference between a virtuous woman and a prude, it was not surprising that I looked for no more compliance in Mme de Lursay than she pronounced herself capable of.

Still attached to her by desire, though filled with a new passion — or, rather, in love for the first time, my small hopes of succeeding with the stranger made me reluctant to contemplate totally losing Mme de Lursay. I thought how I might gain the one yet keep the other. But Mme de Lursay's rigid virtue made me despair, and unable to believe, after much consideration, that I should ever bring matters to the conclusion I wished for, I decided at last on the object that pleased me most.

It was three days, as I have said, since I had seen Mme de Lursay, and I was hardly troubled by her absence. She had been hoping all this time to see me, but convinced at last that I was avoiding her, she began to fear that she might lose me and decided to make me suffer less cruelly. From the little I had said, she inferred that my passion was settled; yet I no longer spoke of it. What attitude should she take? The most seemly would be to wait until love, which cannot be long restrained, especially in a heart as unseasoned as mine was, forced me to break the silence. Yet if this was the most seemly it was not the most sure. It did not enter her mind that I might have given her up: she merely supposed that, certain of never being requited, I was fighting against a love that only made me miserable. Although this situation was not altogether unpleasing to her, it might be dangerous to leave me in it much longer: I might be offered a consolation elsewhere which resentment would perhaps make me accept. But how was she to make me understand her love without infringing the decorum to which she was so scrupulously attached? Experience had taught her that equivocal speeches were wasted on me, and after giving me so lofty an idea of herself, she could not bring herself to speak to me unambiguously.

Uncertain about what course to take, she called on Mme de Meilcour. I had not yet returned, and when on my arrival I was told that she was there, I almost went away again. On reflection, however, I saw that this would be acting too ungraciously, and moreover that she might attribute my flight and my evident dread of seeing her to a feeling I no longer wished her to suspect me of. So I went in. I found her in the midst of the company, apparently deep in thought. I greeted her without coldness or constraint. My looks were nevertheless touched with chagrin, from the fact that I had spent that day searching in vain for the unknown lady. I spent some time in Mme de Lursay's company, saying only the most general and hackneyed things. She asked me where I had been, coldly posed a thousand indifferent questions, and being then in the middle of a group, showed no disposition or anxiety to address herself particularly to me. At last the crowd that preoccupied her dispersed, but hindered still by the presence of Mme de Meilcour and several persons who still remained, and no longer able to resist the desire to speak with me privately, she said to me gravely:

"By the way, Sir, I have something to say to you. Pray follow me."

And with these words she walked into another room.

This behavior, which addressed to another would have appeared irregular, gave rise to no conclusions when addressed to me. Her relationship to me was such that she might have permitted herself even greater liberties without attracting censure or speculation. I followed her, very ill at ease at what she might have to say to me, and even more at what I would reply. She gazed at me severely, and at last, after a long scrutiny, she spoke.

"Perhaps you will think it strange, Sir," she said, "that I should ask you to explain yourself."

"I, Madam?" I cried.

"Yes, Sir," she answered. "You. For several days you have been behaving in a very unseemly fashion toward me. So that I might believe in your innocence, I have had the kindness to look for offense of my own. I have found none. Tell me therefore what you reproach me with. Justify, if possible, your lack of regard."

"Madam," I replied, "you astound me. I thought there had never been anything wanting in my behavior toward you, and I should be in despair if you found me guilty of anything that impaired the respect I have always had for you, or the friendship you have graciously allowed me to offer."

"Noble sentiments," she answered. "If I required only words of you, I might be satisfied – but you are not frank. In the past four days, you have changed toward me more than you admit. You would do better to disavow your behavior than try to justify it. I want you to explain what I ask. Is it a mere caprice that makes you renounce my friendship? Do you think you have reason to complain of me? You see that I do not take advantage of the distance that age sets between us. Young as you are, though, I have believed you reliable and have treated you less as a young man than as a friend on whom I thought I could depend and whom I wished to keep. I hope you are aware of the value of such confidence. Tell me, then, how I ought to conduct myself with you, and above all tell me why for several days you have been avoiding me, and why, when we are together, you seem to see me only with regret?"

"How can I confess, Madam, to sins that I know nothing of?" I replied. "If I have seemed to avoid you, you know the reason only too well. If when I saw you I dared not use the tone I once did, it was because I saw it did not please you."

"To be sure," she said. "But in abandoning the new tone, which you saw did not please me, why did you not resume the first, which I was always ready to answer? It is true that you vexed me, though more on your account than on my own, when you permitted yourself to say things that could not do anything else but displease me. Indeed, I was very angry with you."

"I see now, Madam," I answered, "how I incurred your anger. Yet I should never have dreamed that you could have looked upon what I said as so grave a crime. It cannot be a new thing for you to be thought lovely: I am sure I am not the first on whom you have made so deep an impression, and your familiarity with such speeches ought to have taught you to pardon mine."

"Ah, no, Sir," she replied, "it is not of your speeches that I complain now. It was enough for me to reply as I had to for all sorts of reasons, and for you to have observed that I have laughed at them since, even with you. It was of little consequence to me that you said that you loved me: my heart was not in such danger that I needed to defend myself with great severity. It is possible that without any fixed intention to please, without even finding me pleasing, you might have wished to persuade me that you loved me. Men often say this to a woman because otherwise they do not know what to say, or for the amusement of trying out her feelings, or because they think it flatters her pride, or because they wish to become adept at such language and would test how far and in what manner they may please. In this, you have only followed the custom — an absurd custom, if you wish, but one that is established. So it is not in what you said to me that I found reason to complain; if you really loved me you would not seem guiltier to me than you do. Why did your manner change after that conversation? Had you the right, having said that you loved me, to require that I should love you? Or can you think that even if you had inspired me with the most violent passion, my heart, eager to yield itself to the caprice of yours, would be bound, there and then, to reward you with all its ardor? Could you expect me to embark blindly on the most serious affair of my life? No! You speak, and I must surrender, only too grateful for your addresses. You suppose that, burning with impatience to be conquered, I was only waiting for the avowal of your passion to return you the avowal of my own. Yet on what grounds did you persuade yourself of so easy a triumph? Which of my actions could have led you to assume it? You do not love me, you have never loved me, or you would have had more respect for me. You would not have believed me capable of petty caprice, and if it had really been love that drew you toward me you would not have avoided my presence. However unhappy I had made you, it would have been necessary to you. You would never have had the strength to impose on yourself an absence that I did not ordain. Then I see you again at last, and you hardly deign to look at me. Ah, Meilcour! Is that the way to approach a woman's heart? Is it thus that a man can hope to win her love? You will tell me you have too little experience to know how to conduct yourself in the midst of sentiments so new to you, but that would only be another poor excuse. Does love need to be learned? Ah, believe me, love always acts in us in spite of ourselves, it is love that leads, not we. One can make mistakes, I admit. But at least they are mistakes arising from excess of feeling, and indeed they may be the best advocates of its truth. If I had been dear to you, those are the only errors you would have been capable of, and I should not have had to reproach you today for your lack of regard."

"At last, Madam, I see what my offenses are," said I. "Truly, you are very unjust! After the way you treated me, is it for you to complain?"

"Well," she answered in a gentler tone, "let us see which of the two of us is the more at fault. All I ask is an explanation; I even agree to forgive you. From this moment I will forget that you said you loved me..."

"Ah, Madam!" I cried, carried away in the heat of the moment. "How cruel you are in the very act of forgiveness! You think to offer me mercy and you deal me a mortal blow! You say you will forget that I love you – then make me forget it too! Can you not see," I continued, going down on my knees, "the dreadful state to which you reduce my heart?"

"Merciful heaven!" she cried, drawing back. "On your knees! Get up! What would anyone think if they saw you there?"

"That I am vowing to you all the love and respect that you inspire," I answered.

"And do you think," she replied, forcing me to rise, "that I should be the better pleased for that? This then is the result of the circumspection you promised! But come, after all, what is it you want of me?"

"I want you to believe that I love you," I answered, "to permit me to say it, and to let me hope that one day I may find you more willing."

"So you love me very much and most ardently wish for some return?" she said. "I can only repeat what I have already said. My heart is still untroubled, and I fear to see its peace disturbed. And yet...But no. I have no more to say. And I forbid you even to guess at what I leave unsaid."

With these words Mme de Lursay left me. As she went, she threw me the most melting of looks. Thinking she had done enough for decorum, she was no doubt resolved to do all for love. Nothing could be clearer than what she had just said: she had treated me as a man whose powers of discernment were virtually nonexistent. Though my ignorance allowed me to guess only poorly at what she meant, I perceived that she was not so far from responding to my vows as the first time I had spoken to her. Yet she had still not explained herself sufficiently to relieve me of all doubt, and, moreover, I loved her too little to meditate long over what encouragement there might be for me in her final words.

The conversation had carried me away because of its vehemence and the novelty of my situation, but, though it had astonished me, it had not moved me for all that.

I have little doubt that if Mme de Lursay had known of the new aspirations that occupied me, she would have been less circumspect and might, by the same token, have won me. What first drew me into the affair was the instinct for pleasure, which doubtless attracted me the more because I had tasted it so little. Everything seems a passion to one who has had no experience of it. The passion that threatened to oust Mme de Lursay was not yet sufficiently formed in my heart to be able to resist her assiduities, and I would doubtless have preferred an easy distraction to the painful task of inspiring love where, to begin with at least, I could expect nothing but difficulties.

But Mme de Lursay was so far from divining how much it behooved her to appear as favorably inclined to me as she really was, that no sooner was she reassured of the constancy of my feelings than she resumed much the same tactics as before. She was willing that I should think that I might one day conquer her heart, but not for me to think that I had already done so.

I had returned with her into the drawing room, not greatly in love, but believing myself to be so. After the first impulse, my natural timorousness had resumed its sway: I was uncertain what I ought to do, and, however openly she had declared herself, I could still find nothing in her words to guarantee my success. Her countenance now wore its former austereness, and although this show of severity was more for others than for me, it brought back all my old fear. I dared neither approach nor look at her. So much reserve on my part did not suit her plan: she addressed the most obliging remarks to me in order to encourage me to show her more confidence. She even pointed out several times in the course of the evening how difficult it is for two people in love to explain their feeling to one another in the midst of a large group. This should have been enough to tell me that I ought to ask for a rendezvous. For a long time she waited for me to do so; but seeing at last that the idea did not enter my head, she was generous enough to take it upon herself.

"Are you engaged tomorrow?" she asked, with a nonchalant air.

"I do not think so," I answered.

"In that case," she said, "shall I see you? I shall not be going out, and I do not expect many visitors. Come and beguile my solitude. Also, I have something to say to you."

"I understand," I replied. "You wish to finish scolding me."

"With you one does not always remember what one ought to do," she answered. "My one fear is that I might be too indulgent. Will you come?"

I promised that I would. When I gave her my hand to escort her to her carriage, I thought I felt her press it. Though I did not know what the consequences of such an action would be with Mme de Lursay, I returned the compliment. She showed her appreciation by a pressure even more eloquent, and not wishing to be lacking in politeness I continued in the style she had initiated. She left me with a sigh, quite persuaded that we were beginning to understand one another at last, whereas in fact I understood nothing, and all she understood was herself.

I had no sooner left her than the rendezvous, to which I had hitherto paid no attention, came back into my mind. A rendezvous! In spite of my inexperience this seemed to me a serious matter. She did not expect many visitors – which in the circumstances was as good as to say none. She had pressed my hand. I did not understand the full significance of this action, but it seemed to me a mark of friendship which, as from one sex to another, must convey a particular meaning and be granted only in very special circumstances. Yet the virtuous Mme de Lursay, who had just forbidden me even to guess at her thoughts – could she have meant...? No, it was impossible.

Whatever might come of it, I resolved to be there. It seemed to me it could only be to my advantage, and Mme de Lursay was beautiful enough for me to await the appointment with impatience.

In the midst of the encouraging reflections that I was building on this rendezvous, *Ah!* I suddenly exclaimed to myself, if only it were the lovely stranger who had given it me! No, I continued, she is too good to grant a rendezvous to anyone, except perhaps to Germeuil. But where are they both? I asked myself, and how can it be that during all the time I have sought them, both have eluded me? Should I not abandon a search that has so long been vain? Why, close now perhaps to being loved, should I still cling to an idea that can only make me unhappy, to someone whom I have only seen for an instant and whom I shall doubtless only see again to find her possessed by another? No matter, though – let me find out who she is, just for my own satisfaction, to cure me of a passion that already holds too much sway over my heart; let me enter if possible into the secrets of hers; let me question Germeuil, and if she loves him, then let me not trouble his pleasures but, rather, seek tranquilly to enjoy my own. The conversation I had just had with Mme de Lursay enabled me to think of the stranger a little more coolly than before. The rendezvous preoccupied me. I had always envied those fortunate enough to have them, and I thought so well of myself for having one myself at my age, and above all with such a person as Mme de Lursay, that the novelty of my situation and the fancies I built on it served almost as well as the most violent fancies of passions.

But lively as these fancies were, I nevertheless resolved to visit Germeuil the next day, and I went to sleep attributing desire to Mme de Lursay and something more delicate to my fair unknown.

My first concern when I awoke was to get to Germeuil's. I had planned what I was to say to him and had prepared myself to deceive him – as if, from a question as simple as the one I had to ask him, he should bound to guess the secret that agitated my heart. I was convinced I could never disguise my thoughts well enough to survive his scrutiny, for by a folly common in young men, I imagined that people wholly indifferent to my situation could not help divining it merely by looking at me. So much the more uneasy was I then about Germeuil, whom I thought to be at least as much in love as I was myself. I drove to his house as fast as I could, and my vexation was extreme when I was told that he had been in the country for several days. My imagination, already in some torment, sustained a fresh shock from this news, and plagued me with the cruelest visions. For several days, it had been impossible to find either of them: I could not doubt now that he had gone away with her. My love and jealousy were aroused. From my misery, I sensed what his happiness must be, and though I was sure that she must love him, it did not make me any more disposed to cure myself.

It was spring, and on coming from Germeuil's I walked into the Tuileries. As I walked, I remembered the rendezvous that Mme de Lursay had given me; but apart from its now having less charm for me than the day before, I did not feel calm enough in my mind to bear such a meeting. The image of the unknown lady alone engrossed me: I called her faithless, as if she had actually given me rights over her heart and betrayed them. I was breathless with love and rage – there was no extravagant project I did not form for snatching her away from Germeuil. I had never before been in such a violent state.

Although at that hour I did not need to fear encountering many people anywhere in the Tuileries, my mental situation led me to seek out the paths I knew always to be unfrequented. I turned toward the maze, and there abandoned myself to my jealousy and pain. Two women's voices that I heard quite close to me interrupted my reverie for a moment. I was so occupied with myself that I had little curiosity left for others. Cruel as my melancholy was, it was dear to me, and I dreaded anything that might distract me from it. I was walking away down the path to nourish it elsewhere when an exclamation from one of the ladies caused me to turn around. The fence that separated us hid them from my view, and this protection made me decide to find out who it was. I parted the hedge as quietly as I could, and my surprise and joy were unparalleled when I recognized my unknown lady.

An emotion even stronger than that which she had inspired in me at first now took hold of my senses. My pain, at first arrested by the sight of so charming an object, then gave place to the extreme delight of seeing her again. For that moment, the sweetest in my life, I forgot that she loved another; I forgot even myself. Transported, confounded, I thought a thousand times of throwing myself at her feet and swearing that I adored her. This impetuosity abated but did not disappear. She was speaking quite audibly, and the hope of learning something of her feelings from a conversation that she believed to be private helped to calm me, and made me resolve to conceal myself and make as little noise as possible. She was with one of the ladies I had seen her with at the opera. Though I was filled with delight at being so close to someone I loved so much, I was inconsolable at not being able to speak to her. Her face was not turned directly toward me, but I could see enough not to be deprived of all its charms. Her position prevented her from seeing me, and so lessened my regret for what I missed.

"I confess," said the fair stranger, "I am not insensible to the pleasure of looking beautiful. I do not even dislike being told of it. But it is a pleasure that occupies me less than you suppose. I think it as triv-ial as in fact it is, and if you knew me better you would believe that I am in no great danger from it."

"I did not mean to say," replied the other lady, "that you had anything to fear from it – merely that one should indulge it as little as possible."

"I take the opposite view," said my fair unknown. "One should in-dulge it fully at first; one is the more certain of tiring of it later."

"You speak like a coquette," replied the lady, "and yet you are not one. Indeed, if there is anything to fear for you in the future, it is that your heart may be too tender and too devoted."

"I know nothing of that yet," said the stranger. "Of all those who up to now have told me I am beautiful and seemed to mean it, none has moved me. Although I am young, I know the danger of engaging myself. Besides, I confess that what I hear of men puts me on my guard against them. Among all those I know I have not found one, unless you except the Marquis, who might be capable of pleasing me. Everywhere I encounter nothing but fools, who are no more agreeable to me for being brilliant. I do not flatter myself with the virtue of being insen-sible, but as yet I can detect nothing in my heart that could make me cease to be so."

"You do not speak sincerely," answered the other lady, "and I have good grounds for thinking that although you seem to set so little store in men, there is one who had found favor in your eyes. And it is not the Marquis."

"It is several days since I have observed you adopt this opinion," said my stranger. "But how, and upon what evidence, did you form it? I have only been in Paris a very short while. I have been with you all the time, and you know everyone I meet. Tell me then who it is who has inspired in me so lively a feeling? You know I am frank, and if what you say is true I will acknowledge it."

"Well, then," said the lady, "do you remember your stranger? The attention with which you studied him? The care with which you pointed him out to me? Add to this the favorable opinion you formed of his wit after only a few words – pleasing, it is true – but too trivial to act as any sort of indication. Such preoccupation is either inspired by love or leads to it. Do you wish for other proofs even less dubious, although you may be unaware of them? Do you remember the eagerness with which you inquired who he was, and that it was he alone who awakened this curiosity in you in a place where it might well have been shared among several; the pleasure you felt on learning his name and rank; how much you spoke of him that evening? Remember the reverie you were plunged in throughout our stay in the country, how absent you were, how you kept sighing for no apparent reason. And what am I to think of this sweet and tender languor that shows in your eyes and is evident in all your actions? Of the uneasiness and the blushes that my words provoke in you at this very moment? If these are not symptoms of love in you, at least that is how it begins in others."

"In that case," replied my stranger, "I must believe that I am different from everyone else. I will not deny anything you have just said; and yet I hope to persuade you that you have drawn wrong conclusions from it. It is true that I asked who the stranger was – but subtract from this curiosity the eagerness you thought you saw in it, and I flatter myself you will find there nothing but what is natural. The wearying insistence with which he looked at me produced my curiosity, as did the attentiveness with which I studied him in return. I will admit that his looks seemed noble and his manner becoming – two qualities which I found that day only in him, and which struck you as well as me. What he said and I remembered you also thought amusing and well turned. Neither must I forget that you reminded me of certain traits that I did not well recollect – was it love that preserved them in your memory? If I spoke of him, you know it was because of my mother. I was, you say, pensive and absent in the country, I sighed and languished. It seems to me all this proves nothing except how much the country wearies me, which is surely permissible in a young woman who, on leaving a convent that she hated, spent a year on an estate with few amusements, has just seen Paris for virtually the first time, and is vexed now at being torn away from these new pleasures. So, Madam, now what has become of the love you were so sure about? Yet I am frank, and I admit to you freely that this stranger, who did not long remain one, if he did not move me, at least did not displease me. When the thought of him comes into my mind it is always under a favorable aspect, though without arousing any concern; and if love consists in what you have described, I am far indeed from feeling it."

"In a virtuous heart love remains long concealed," replied the lady. "It makes its first impression without even being noticed. At first it seems but a simple preference which one can easily justify. Should this liking increase, we find reasons to excuse its progress. When at last we recognize the disorder for what it is, it is either too late to resist it, or we do not wish to; our heart, once attached to so pleasing an error, fears to be deprived of it. Far from trying to destroy it, we ourselves help to augment it. It is as if we feared this feeling would not have sufficient effect on its own. We constantly do all we can to maintain the confusion of our heart, and to nourish it with the chimeras of our imagination. If ever the light of reason shines on us, it is but a flash, extinguished in the same instant, that has shown us the abyss without lasting long enough to save us from it. While we blush for our frailty, it tyrannizes over us, growing more rooted in our hearts with every effort we make to tear it out. It extinguishes every other passion, or becomes the mainspring of them all. To add to our confusion, we have the vanity to imagine that we shall never yield, and that the pleasure of love can always be innocent. In vain does example preach against us: it cannot guarantee us against our fall. We go from vagary to vagary, neither foreseeing nor understanding them. We perish virtuous still, absent, so to speak, from our own fateful undoing; and we find ourselves guilty not only without knowing how but, often, without ever having dreamed that we might become so."

"Merciful heaven!" cried my stranger, "what a picture! You horrify me!"

"Do not imagine," answered the other lady, "that I painted it without good reason. It does not apply to your present situation, but I think it important for you to know that the heart is fragile, and one cannot be too much on one's guard against it."

"I agree with you, Madam," said the stranger, "and the more so as I do not believe the most estimable lover in the world worth the least of the cares he costs us."

"That is a little too sweeping," replied the lady, "but I am not sorry to hear you speak so. So few men are tender and devoted, so few are capable of a real passion, we women are so often and so unjustly victims of our own credulity and their deceit, that it would still be dangerous to make an exception even of one. You more than any other should believe, for your own good, that no man is worthy to touch your heart. You are destined to be sacrificed, perhaps to the last person you would have chosen. Do not add to the cruel torture of having to live for him the worse one of wishing to live for another. If your heart cannot be happy, at least save it from being torn in two."

They stood up. As they did so the young lady turned in my direction, but she disappeared so quickly that I hardly enjoyed the sight of her more than a moment. In spite of the agitation into which her words had plunged me, I did not fail to follow her. But not wishing her to suspect that I had overheard her, I went after her by a different path from the one I saw her take.

All that I had just heard threw me into moral anxiety, although it seemed to show that she did not love Germeuil. I was relieved of the

fear that my most dangerous possible rival might have won her heart;
but if it was not Germeuil, who was it that she honored with so tender
a memory? Sometimes I flattered myself that it was I. I recalled that I
had looked at her with the insistence of which she complained; a thousand details seemed to confirm me. It was the desire to be the stranger
she spoke of, rather than vanity, that made me adopt as my own the
flattering portrait she had drawn of him. The happiness I derived from
this idea was soon shattered by another that might equally be true. I
had looked at her attentively; I had doubtless appeared overcome by
her charms: but was I the only one transported by the sight of her? Had
not everyone there appeared to be in the same ecstasies? I had seen her
only at the opera, and in the conversation that had just revealed her
secrets, no mention had been made of where or when the stranger had
made his impression upon her. That which might refer to me might
equally refer to another. Moreover, from what she said, her stranger was
no longer unknown to her. Must she then have seen him again? Why
might it not be Germeuil? Did I know for how long or in what manner
they were acquainted? Alas, I said to myself, what does it matter who
is the object of her passion, since I am not? Even if it is not Germeuil,
am I any the better off for it? While I was absorbed in these painful
reflections, the soundness of which threw me into despair, I had been
walking so fast that in spite of my detour I was now quite close to her.
The sight of her delighted me as so much as if the mere pleasure of
looking at her gave me cause for hope.

She was strolling idly along the main path, beside the ornamental
pool in which it ends. For a while, I stood admiring the nobility of her
form and the infinite grace of all her movements. Great as were the
transports she inspired in me, I could not see enough of her to satisfy
me, but I was so timid I trembled at the idea of presenting myself to
her view. I both desired and dreaded the moment that would allow me
to look into her eyes again, and it came upon me while I was still torn
by the confusion. My emotion redoubled. I took advantage of the distance that still separated us to look at her with all the tenderness I
felt. As she advanced toward me, I felt my agitation grow and my timidity return. I was seized with such a trembling that I had scarcely the
strength to walk. All composure fled. I had noticed that when we
were only a few paces from one another she had turned her eyes away
from me, and that, looking up to find me still gazing at her, she again
looked away. I attributed this to the embarrassment my boldness caused
her, and perhaps to some feeling of aversion or disgust. Instead of for-
tifying myself against so painful an idea and trying to persuade myself

that the sight of me made a more favorable impression on her, I was so overcome that when we actually passed one another I had not the courage to look at her. I even made a pretense of looking at something else – but I observed with sorrow that this precaution was superfluous: she had not taken the slightest notice of me. This disdain surprised and wounded me. Vanity told me that I deserved better. From then on, no doubt, I had in my heart the germ of all I have since become. I decided I must be mistaken, and unable to think ill of myself for very long, persuaded myself that only modesty had made her behave as she did.

They were both walking so slowly that I thought I might overtake them without any appearance of particularity. I therefore continued on my way, not without often looking back, partly to see the way my stranger was going, and partly in the hope of surprising her doing the same. My device was only partly successful, and all I learned was that she was about to take the path that led to the Pont-Royal gate. I quickly retraced my steps, and by cutting through other paths was able to arrive there at almost the same moment as she. I stood aside respectfully to make way for her, and this earned me a cursory bow, made with downcast eyes. I remembered in that instant all the episodes in novels I had read that treated of speaking to one's mistress, and was surprised to find that not one of them was of any help to me. I kept hoping she might trip, that she might even twist her ankle: I saw no other way of engaging her in conversation. Luck was against me, though, and she got into her carriage before any useful accident could occur.

Unfortunately, I myself had neither my carriage nor my servants at this gate. Unable to send anyone after her, I thought of going after her myself; but even if my rank and the distinction of my dress had not forbidden it, I could not have hoped to continue the pursuit for long. I regretted a thousand times that I had not come in at this gate: I could then have taken such measures as would have revealed my lovely stranger to me at last. Yet it was too late, and I reproached myself for it as much as if it had been possible to guess both that she was in the Tuileries and the gate by which she had entered.

I returned home more in love than ever, piqued by the stranger's indifference, filled with what I had heard her say, and detesting without knowing him the one for whom she seemed to have declared a preference – for I could no longer flatter myself that it was I. To complete my misery there remained my rendezvous with the indulgent Mme de Lursay. Far from thinking of this appointment with pleasure, I would have done anything to avoid it. I had just learned from my meeting with the beautiful stranger that I loved only her, and that for Mme de Lursay I had only those fleeting sentiments one has for any woman society calls pretty, and that I might have felt these even less for her than for another if she had not gone to such trouble to inspire them in me.

What I had just heard my unknown lady say had agitated me more than it had soothed me. The sight of her, even the love I supposed her to feel for another, had rekindled my passion, and in spite of the trials I would have to expect, I imagined more pleasure in being unhappy on her account than in being happy on Mme de Lursay's. What was I going to do at this rendezvous, I asked myself. Why had she given it to me? I had not asked for it. I was going to be told that she could not love me, that her feelings were too delicate. Ah, if this was all that was in store for me! But no, yesterday sweeter dispositions were in evidence. Virtue and love might still be at war, but it would be my misfortune to see victory go to the second. For some time, I was tempted not to go to Mme de Lursay's, and to write and say that important business had arisen that prevented me from seeing her. Then so many difficulties occurred to me that, unable to resolve them, I stayed at home for most of the day. At last I made up my mind to go and see Mme de Lursay, but by this time it was so late that she no longer expected me and had decided to receive visitors. In fact, I found a great deal of company there. She greeted me coldly, almost without raising her eyes from her embroidery frame. My own courtesy was not very lively and, seeing that she did not address a word to me, I strolled away to watch the cards. My behavior could not have been more uncouth, and I could see that it angered her extremely. Yet it did not matter to me if she was offended, as long as I did not give her the opportunity to tell me so. She had no intention of remaining silent however: the insult was too sharp. To have kept her waiting, to arrive coolly without apology, apparently without even seeing the necessity for one, and not even to have noticed that she was vexed! Was there any crime of which I was not guilty? And, moreover, they were all crimes of feeling. She waited a little for me to return to her; but seeing there was no question of that, she rose, and after taking several turns about the apartment, at last approached me. She had dressed that day in a way to capture both my eye and my heart. The most splendid and enticing gown set off her charms; her hair was slightly tousled; she wore very little rouge – everything was contrived to make her look more tender. In short, her whole toilette was of the kind arranged less to dazzle the eye than to captivate the senses. It followed, since she had adopted it for an occasion which she regarded as highly important, that she had had previous experience of its effectiveness.

On the pretext of watching the game she came and stood by me. I had not yet looked at her very attentively, and now, in spite of all the reasons I had for resistance, I was surprised by her beauty. Something inexpressibly touching and sweet shone in her eyes; all her charms were so animated by desire, and perhaps by the certainty of pleasing me, that I was moved by their vivacity. I could not look at her without an admiration I had never felt for her before: indeed, I had never before seen her look as she did then. She no longer wore the severe, impassive countenance with which she had so often daunted me. She was now a woman of flesh and blood, who was willing to appear so, who wished to make herself desired. Our eyes met. The languor I saw in hers implanted in my heart the emotion which her charms had already awakened in my senses, and which seemed to increase every instant. A sigh or two which half-escaped her completed my overthrow: at this critical moment she benefited from all my love for the mysterious stranger.

Mme de Lursay had too much experience to underestimate her handiwork or to fail to take advantage of it, and she no sooner saw the impression she had made upon me than, with a tenderer look than she had ever given me before, she returned to her place. Without reflecting on what I was doing, without even the power of forming distinct ideas, I followed her. She had taken up her embroidery again, and seemed so absorbed in it that, when I sat down opposite, she did not raise her eyes to look at me. I waited a little for her to speak, but seeing at last that she did not choose to break the silence, I said, "You are prodigiously occupied by your work, Madam."

She perceived from the tone of my voice how much I was moved, and without answering glanced at me from beneath her lashes – not the least effective look a woman can make use of, and indeed a decisive one in delicate situations.

"So you have not been out today," I continued.

"Indeed not," she replied in a sharp tone. "I believe I told you I would not."

"How then," I answered, "could I have forgotten?"

"It is too small a matter," she replied, "for you to reproach yourself, and indeed one so indifferent that I too had forgotten that you had promised to wait on me. As long as you do not disappoint me more seriously, you will always find me ready to forgive you. For we might have found ourselves alone. And then what should we have said to one another? Do you not know that a tête-à-tête is often even more embarrassing than it is scandalous?"

"I do not know," I said, "but for my part I looked forward to it with such eagerness —"

"Ah! Enough of this gallantry!" she interrupted. "Either abandon this tone, or at least be consistent. Do you not see you are turning the most natural thing in the world into the most ridiculous? How can you imagine I believe what you say? If you had wanted to see me, what was there to prevent you?"

"I myself," I answered, "because I am afraid to engage myself with you. But you see how well I succeed," I went on, taking in mine the hand that supported her embroidery frame.

"Well," she said, without withdrawing it, and smiling, "what do you want?"

"I want you to tell me you love me."

"But if I should say it," she said, "it will make me more unhappy and you less loving. I will say nothing. Read me if you can," she added, looking into my eyes.

"But you have forbidden it," I answered.

"Ah!" she cried. "I did not think I had said so much. Yet I shall say no more."

I wanted to force her to speak, she was determined to keep silent, and we sat for a time without saying anything. Still, we looked at one another, and I still held her hand.

"How indulgent I am, and how foolish you!" she said at last. "A fine figure we cut here, the pair of us! Now come," she said, with a thoughtful air, "I believe I told you I was frank, and I should like to give you proof of it. By nature I am not susceptible, and I needed no reflection to save me from the follies of youth. So it would be extremely absurd for me to fall into an irregularity which, for a thousand reasons that you cannot appreciate, would be less pardonable now than ever. And yet I like you. I will say only one word more. Reassure me about all I have to fear from your youth and inexperience; let your conduct authorize me to place my confidence in you; and you may be satisfied of my heart. This confession is a hard one for me to make. It is, you may believe me, the first of its kind that I have ever made. I might, indeed I should, have made you wait longer for it, but I hate artifice, and no one in the world is less capable of it than I. Be faithful and prudent. I am sparing you pain by telling you a secret you might never have guessed for yourself: deserve that one day I should speak of it again."

"Ah, Madam! —" I cried.

"I do not wish for thanks," she interrupted. "At this moment thanks would be imprudent, and that is what I want you to avoid above all things. This evening, perhaps, we may be able to talk."

"No, Madam," I answered, "I will not leave you until you tell me you love me."

"To press me for an avowal in our present situation shows plainly how ignorant you are of all that it means!" she replied. "Do what I ask, and let us pursue no farther a conversation that may already have given rise to speculation."

I did as she desired, not without reluctance. I was drunk with happiness, and instead of returning to the tables, stepped aside to contemplate the pleasures that so splendid a conquest promised. I stood where I could see Mme de Lursay. My eyes were continually fixed on her, and she for her part kept throwing me glances full of affection and desire. Here at last was this proud beauty, whose heart, as she told me herself, had never been touched before, sighing for me, and telling me so! I was the only one she had loved! I was the conqueror of virtue! Of Plato even! I included Plato, for, without being wholly conversant with his philosophy, I could not fail to understand that if she should refer to it again, she would at least relax its severity, and to relax it is to annihilate it.

However, Mme de Lursay still had several resources against me should she wish to use them: the reputation of severity she had given herself, which, false as it was, checked her in her own desires; the humiliation of yielding too quickly, especially to one who could never take a hint and left her to make all the advances; fear of my indiscretion, and that my love, once discovered, would make her all the more ridiculous because she had professed so much disdain for such frailties; even her own instinct for coquetry, which made her find more pleasure in playing with my love than in satisfying it, and which had probably been the chief reason for all her caprices hitherto.

For if one wins the heart of a virtuous woman, once she has acknowledged it, the battle is over. The truthfulness of her character will not permit the stratagems that coquettes employ, nor the affectations that make prudes so difficult of access. Sincere in her resistance, she is no less so in her surrender: she yields because she can fight no longer. The most contemptible conquests are sometimes the ones that take the most trouble, and hypocrisy often exhibits more scruples than virtue itself.

Although it seemed that Mme de Lursay had at last come to terms with her scruples, I still feared one of those changes of mood to which she was subject, and wanted to leave her no time for reflection. I imagined that a person of her strictness of character must be prey to terrible remorse. The more brilliant my triumph appeared to me, the more I feared it might be snatched away. To subdue a heart hitherto impregnable – could I ever hope for greater glory? This idea had more effect on my heart than all of Mme de Lursay's charms, and I have come to the conclusion since, given the impression she had on me then, that it is far more important for a woman to flatter a man's vanity than to touch his heart.

However, the more I pondered what Mme de Lursay had said, the more reason I found for believing she meant to make me happy. She soon rejoined me, and slipped a thousand subtle and passionate allusions into the conversation, which had now become general. In them she displayed all the attractions of her mind and all the tenderness of her heart. I marveled to myself at how much love improves a woman's beauty, and I could hardly understand the complete transformation I saw in Mme de Lursay. Transports, all the more flattering, perhaps, for being half suppressed; secret looks; sighs that only I could hear – she denied me nothing, there was nothing she would not have me anticipate. During supper, where I sat beside her, she continued her attentions undiminished and, in spite of all the people around us, found the means of making me feel that it was I alone who occupied her. The situation had only increased my natural awkwardness.

To all she said to me I could only respond with a foolish smile, or with stumbling words – which were no better and conveyed no more. But I might have done a hundred times worse and still lost none of her favor. My pensiveness, my absence of mind, and my stupidity were, for her, only incontestable proofs that I was really in love; and she never looked at me more tenderly than when I had answered her with some particularly egregious imbecility. She is not the only one I have seen in this situation. Women often adore us for our most ridiculous traits, provided they can flatter themselves that it is our love for them that makes us ludicrous.

In spite of the passion I felt for Mme de Lursay, in spite of the confusion I was in after all that had happened, my mysterious stranger had more than once come to mind. But instead of letting myself dwell on the memory, I tried to efface it from my heart; it seemed however little I harbored it, it gained too much sway over me. I could not help accusing myself of perfidy in my attentions to Mme de Lursay, and in order to enable myself to continue them I had to forget how much I loved my fair unknown. I tried to distract my thoughts from her by fixing them upon the pleasures that awaited me. I should greatly have preferred it if all that I hoped for from Mme de Lursay could have been given me by the other. Yet for all that I was still willing to profit by the former's generosity.

Supper ended.

"Meilcour," said Mme de Lursay to me as everyone rose, "you see that we shall not be able to speak together this evening, and I confess that after all, I do not mind. You might perhaps have given me cause for complaint."

"I, Madam!" I answered. "Can you doubt my respect?"

"I can," she said. "I have no very high opinion of you on that score. Not that I do not know how to exact it. After all, though, I think it is better that you come tomorrow."

I smiled. It amused me that her way of preventing me from being disrespectful was to give me another rendezvous.

"I understand you," she said. "Of course, we shall not be alone."

I was so taken aback by this undoing of all my hopes that I nearly answered, *As you wish.*

"But, Madam," I said, after I had composed myself a little, "why may we not speak together this evening?"

"Because there are too many people," she replied, "and it would be very improper for you to be seen to stay on. But it is partly your own fault. It rested with you to avoid the inconvenience of too much company."

"You drive me to despair, Madam," I answered, "especially as I can see no way out of this predicament."

"I am sure I do not know why you wish so much for something so indifferent," she said. "But since it is so important to you, let us see what we can do!"

It is only natural in such a case for the more experienced to take the lead, and she felt she could, without presuming too much, permit herself to furnish me with the expedient that would get us both out of our difficulty. Yet, for honor's sake, she first had to appear to be baffled by the situation. So she pondered long, and even proposed, one after the other, twenty schemes that she immediately dismissed; and then ended by saying, like someone who has exhausted all her ideas, that she saw no other solution but for me to go. I resisted this conclusion, but only feebly: I was too ignorant myself to get us out of our painful situation, and I thought she might be right. She was not expecting so prompt a resignation, and at once decided on what she had to do.

"There can be no doubt," she said, "that I am right. It is evident. Indeed, I see nothing, nothing at all that can help us. It is not that if you stay people would be absolutely obliged to imagine something between us; nothing could be more natural. Still, the world is unkind, and you are young. People do not try to see things as they are, and out of something that was neither sought nor foreseen, and that has not even any need of concealment, they would make an affair, a prearranged rendezvous. How cruel it all is, for I should be exposing myself in the most fatal manner, and while the sacrifice I was making would mean little to you, I should lose everything by it. However, I can see that this contretemps distresses you, and I also am distressed to have to speak about it at such length. There are many women, of course, who would not be in the least embarrassed by it. Yet I have so little experience in these matters that you must not be surprised by my confusion. If only one could find reassurance in the purity of one's own intentions, I should have nothing to reproach myself with. For I repeat, nothing is more natural than for us to be alone together. I have no doubt but that you would employ the time telling me that you love me; but you would do that in front of everyone – and since I cannot make you silent on the subject, I think it better that only I should be present to hear you. But," she added, "these reflections do not help us... Have you any of your servants with you?"

"Yes," I answered. "Should I send them away?"

"Good God!" she cried. "No! Keep them, keep them. But... for what time have you ordered your carriage? Midnight?"

"Yes," I answered.

"A pity," she said. "That is when everyone else will leave."

"Suppose I told them not to come till –"

"Two, for example," she interrupted. "If that was what you had in mind, why did you not say so? This stratagem resolves every difficulty. I am grateful to you for having thought of it. To be sure, having to wait for your servants is quite a sufficient excuse for staying on, and if someone should offer to take you with him I imagine you would know how to deal with that?"

My only answer was to wring her hand fervently, and I went out to give my instructions, smiling that she should attribute to me the stratagem assuring our meeting when she might so justly have claimed the credit herself.

When I returned, I found everyone sitting down again to cards, and Mme de Lursay complaining of a migraine. Imbecile that I was, I nevertheless understood that she feigned this indisposition to be free the sooner to talk to me, and I could not conceive how her guests could be so uncivil as to continue their game and not leave her in the peace she seemed to require. In spite of my remarks to this effect and my impatience, they stayed to complete the games. I was filled with a restless ardor that kept me in torment. I turned woebegone looks on Mme de Lursay as if to ask her how they could be so unkind to us, and she, by her tender smile, made me understand that she shared my impatience.

At last the long-awaited moment came. Everyone rose and made ready to leave. I went out with the rest, and feigned astonishment at finding none of my people in the antechamber. What Mme de Lursay had foreseen duly happened: another party offered to take me home. I declined, but awkwardly. They pressed me to accept. My embarrassment increased; and I believe that merely through not knowing what to say to prevent it I would have let them carry me off, if Mme de Lursay, resourceful as ever and cooler-headed than I, had not come to my rescue.

"Can you not see," she said to those who were tormenting me with all the politeness in the world, "that you embarrass him, and that clearly he does not want anyone to know where he is going? He probably has some rendezvous. But your servants cannot be much longer," she went on, turning to me, "and although I have a horrid headache, I am quite willing for you to wait for them here."

She delivered this speech so naturally that it would have been impossible not to be deceived by it. I stammered my thanks. The others attributed my confusion to her jest, and after rallying me with mock envy or reproof on my supposed good fortune, they at last left us together.

I no sooner found myself alone with her than I was seized by the most horrible fright I have ever felt in my life. I cannot describe the transformation that took place in all my senses. I trembled, I was struck dumb; I did not dare to look at Mme de Lursay. She easily perceived my difficulty, and told me, but in the sweetest tone imaginable, to come and sit beside her on the sofa where she had placed herself. She half-reclined there, her head against the cushions, and amused herself idly and distractedly by tying bows. From time to time, she turned her eyes languishingly on me, upon which I would at once respectfully lower my own. I believe that out of mischief she was waiting for me to break the silence; at last I resolved to do so.

"Are you tying bows, Madam?" I asked in a trembling voice.

At this witty and interesting question Mme de Lursay stared at me in astonishment. Accustomed though she was to the idea of my timidity and inexperience, it still seemed inconceivable that that was all I could find to say. However, not wishing to discourage me completely, she said, disregarding my query, "It vexes me to think of you remaining here, and I am not sure now whether the stratagem we thought at first such a happy one will have the result we hoped for."

"I see no reason why it should not," I replied.

"For myself," she replied, "I see only one, but a terrible one. You spoke to me just now, and I fear someone may have guessed what you said. I would have you be more circumspect in public."

"But, Madam," I answered, "it is impossible that anyone should have heard me."

"That has nothing to do with it," she said. "People gossip first and look afterward to see whether they had any grounds for it. I recollect that we conversed for some time, and on a subject which hardly leaves you indifferent. When you tell someone you love them, you try to convince them, and even if the words do not come from the heart they always seem to light up the eyes. When I was looking at you then, for instance, you seemed fiery and affectionate, more so perhaps than you yourself knew. It was independent of your wishes, perhaps even without your being sufficiently moved for your countenance to be altered; and yet I found it changed. I fear you may one day be a deceiver, and I pity in advance the women you will wish to please. You have an air of sincerity, your expression is passionate, it depicts sentiment with a captivating impetuosity, and I confess – but no," she added, interrupting herself with an air of confusion, "it would profit me nothing to tell you what I think."

"Speak, Madam," I said softly. "Make me, if it is possible, worthy to win your love."

"To win my love!" she cried. "Ah, Meilcour! That is just what I do not wish, and if you had any such design, think no more of it, I implore you. However many reasons I have for fleeing from love, however little it seems to be my destiny, perhaps you would succeed in touching my heart. Heavens!" she added sadly. "Was I doomed to this misfortune, and have I avoided it so far only to fall into it more cruelly now?"

Mme de Lursay's words, and the tone in which they were pronounced, moved me more than I had ever been moved before, and I was so overcome that I could not at once reply. During the silence that followed, she seemed to be plunged in the most painful reverie. She threw me troubled glances, raised her eyes to heaven, let them fall tenderly upon me again, and seemed unable to tear them away. She kept giving heart-rending sighs, and there was something so natural and touching about her distress, she looked so lovely in her confusion, and filled me with such reverence, that if I had not already wished to please her, she would surely have made me wish to do so then.

"But why would it be a misfortune for you?" I asked in a strangled voice.

"Can you ask?" she replied. "Do you think I am blind to the unsuit-

ability of our connection? You tell me now that you love me, and perhaps you are sincere, but how long will you remain so, and how much
will you make me suffer for my credulity? I will amuse you, you will
enslave me. Too young to attach yourself for long, you will use me with
the caprice that is natural to your age. The less occasion I give you for
inconstancy, the more indifference you will feel. When I try to win
you back you will see in me not a tender lover but an intolerable nuisance. You will even reproach yourself for having loved me, and if I am
not basely sacrificed, if you do not publish my weakness, I shall owe it
less to your honor than to the ridicule you would fear from the confession that you had loved me."

Mme de Lursay would no doubt have gone on in this tragic vein,
but seeing me so stricken, so near to tears, so disconcerted by her attitude, she deemed it necessary to restore my spirits by speaking a little
less majestically.

"To be sure, though," she added more gently, "I do not think you
capable of any of the basenesses I have just described – certainly not.
But I repeat, I fear your age even more than my own. And besides, you
would not be willing to love me according to my whim."

"No, Madam," I said, "I shall never be guided by anything except
your wishes."

"I do not know if I should believe you," she replied, smiling. "People
sometimes imagine that loss of respect is proof of love, but that is very
bad reasoning. I am not saying that one should not naturally expect
a reward for one's pains. Whatever reluctance a woman may feel to
engage herself too soon, once she is persuaded, she offers little more
to fight against."

"When, then, shall I be fortunate enough to persuade you, Madam?"
I asked.

"When?" she replied, laughing. "But you see I am already half persuaded. I allow you to say that you love me, and I almost say that I love
you. You see what confidence I have in you. I am not afraid to remain
alone with you, I even help you to bring it about. It seems to me these
are proofs of a sufficiently strong affection – and if you saw them for
what they are, I do not think you would complain."

"That is true, Madam," I said in some embarrassment, "but –"

"But, Meilcour," she interrupted, "do you understand that my conduct this evening has been most dangerous, and that had I not thought
as well of you as I do, I could never have taken the risk?"

"Dangerous?" I asked.

"Yes," she said, "dangerous. After all, if it were known that you were here with my consent, that I had voluntarily arranged it with you – in a word, that it is not an accident – what might not people say? And yet how wrong they would be, for no one could be more respectful than you are; and, though nobody would believe it, that is the way to win all. Meilcour," she cried earnestly, "how eager you are to be loved! How flattering to me is this embarrassed, ingenuous look of yours, that shows me all the candor of your heart!"

Her words seemed to be so obliging that I felt I ought to thank her for them, and in my transports I went so far as to fling myself at her feet.

"Merciful Heaven!" I cried. "If you love me, tell me!"

"Yes, Meilcour," she answered, smiling and holding out her hand. "Yes, I will tell you, and in the tenderest fashion in the world. Will that content you?"

My only answer was to seize her hand and press it ardently.

This bold action caused Mme de Lursay to blush, and it seemed to trouble her. She sighed. I sighed too. We remained some time without speaking. I stopped kissing her hand for a moment to look at her. I found in her eyes an expression that struck me forcibly though I did not understand it. They were so bright, so touching, I read so much love in them that I was sure of being forgiven for my audacity, and dared to kiss her hand again.

"Come," she said at last, "will you not get up? What folly is this? Get up, I insist."

"Ah, Madam!" I cried. "Have I been so unhappy as to offend you?"

"Have I reproached you?" she answered languishingly. "No, you do not offend me – but sit down again, or, better still, go. I just heard the sound of your carriage, and I would not have them wait for you. Tomorrow, if you wish, I will see you. If I go out, it will not be until late. Farewell," she said, laughing at me for still clinging to her hand, "I insist that you go. You are learning a boldness that frightens me, and I do not wish it to continue."

I tried to defend myself. I did not at all wish to follow Mme de Lursay's orders. Her manner of urging me to leave her was not at all that of a woman who wishes to be obeyed! I accused her of not really having heard the sound of my carriage.

"Even so," she said, "I do not wish you to remain any longer. Have we not said all we have to say?"

"I do not think so," I answered, sighing. "If I am sometimes silent when I am with you, it is not because I have nothing to say, but because of the difficulty of expressing all that I think."

"That is a timidity I should like to correct," she said, sitting down again on the sofa. "One should always distinguish between timidity and respect; one is right, the other is ridiculous. For instance: we are alone, you tell me you love me, I answer that I love you, there is nothing to hinder us; the more liberty I seem to accord to your desires, the more estimable it is in you not to seek to abuse it. You are perhaps the only person I know in the world who is capable of such behavior. That is how the repugnance I have always felt for what I am doing now has ceased to exist. At last I can believe I have found a heart whose principles are the same as my own. The restraint I praise in you must come from respect, for had you only been timid, I have done enough to make you so no longer. You do not answer?"

"If I do not, Madam," I replied, "it is because I feel you are right, and I would rather you were wrong."

It is not irrelevant to point out that when she sat down upon the sofa, I had thrown myself once more at her feet, and that she then permitted me to rest my elbows on her knees; and while she played with my hair with one hand, she allowed me to press or kiss the other: the choice of this significant favor was left to me.

"Ah," she cried, "if I were sure you were not inconstant; or indiscreet!" she added in a lower voice.

Instead of replying as I ought to have done, I felt the force of this exclamation so little, and understood so poorly the value of what Mme de Lursay was doing for me, that I merely indulged in the pleasure of swearing eternal fidelity. The light I saw in her eyes, which would have been a revelation to anyone else, her confusion, the change in her voice, her soft and frequent sighs – everything increased the propitiousness of the moment, but nothing made me understand it. I even believed that she trusted herself to me so freely only because she was sure of my respect, and that a moment's boldness would never be forgiven me. I thought she was one of those women for whom one must always wait, and for whom no moment is a critical one until they wish it. In the end, I invented such impressive delusions that they prevailed both over my desires and over the delicate Mme de Lursay's wish to oblige me. The less she could accuse herself of not making herself clear, the more angry she must have been with me. She fell into a gloomy reverie, and I would have tormented her till dawn with my protestations of love, and above all of respect, if, tired at last of the ridiculous situation I had placed her in, she had not repeated in no uncertain manner that it was time for me to withdraw. Like a sensible person, she concluded that there was no more to be hoped for from me then. In spite of my reluctance to obey her, I could not win her over, and we separated – she doubtless astonished that anyone could carry stupidity so far, and I convinced that I should need at least six rendezvous before I knew where I stood. It seemed to me that, as we parted, she looked at me with some coldness, and I thought this could only be due to the liberties I had allowed myself to take.

As soon as I recovered, my confusion disappeared, and I arrived at a very different impression of what had just happened from the one I had had while it was taking place. The more I recalled what Mme de Lursay had said and done, the more reason I found to doubt whether my respect had been as much in order as I thought, and whether, if the second rendezvous should turn out like the first, she would be obliging enough, woman of sentiment though she was, to grant me a third. I did not imagine of course that if I had pressed her more, I should have obtained total victory, but at least I might have paved the way for it. Yet it was her fault: how was I to know that when a woman speaks of her virtue in such a situation, she flaunts it not to make you despair of winning her but to make your triumph seem all the greater? Of what use were all Mme de Lursay's subtleties? It must have been evident that I would take them at their face value had they been a hundred times more gross. A woman gains nothing by using them except with someone who can see through them. My virtue! Your respect! Fine words for a tête-à-tête! Especially when the person concerned does not perceive how out of place they are, and does not know that virtue never makes assignations. In the midst of my chagrin at the failure of the rendezvous, and my determination to muster all my firmness in those that followed, the mysterious stranger returned to my mind. However, the ideas of pleasure that Mme de Lursay had proffered me, the chains by which I had only just bound myself to her, the apparent impossibility of ever winning the stranger's love (an impossibility I represented to myself even more strongly now to justify my own caprice), and the indifference she had shown toward me that same day – all combined to make her less dear to me. I felt that if I had been sure that she loved me, I should easily have given up Mme de Lursay, but that I could not do that now except for such a certitude. I could not hide from myself the facts that she had averted her eyes from me, that she had even worn the disdainful look one assumes on seeing something offensive. After a repeated examination of my own attractions and some deep reflection on what I might have expected from them, contrasted with the disagreeable effect they had produced, I concluded that if, as seemed evident, my fair unknown

did not love me, then either Germeuil had prejudiced her against me
or she had a secret antipathy to handsome young men. At any other
time, I might have thought less well of my looks, but Mme de Lursay's
ardent love for me fed my conceitedness. I could not see how a woman
so little susceptible could find me dangerous if I were not really so, or
how one could make so violent an impression without having extraordinary merit. In spite of what I took to be the stranger's disinclination
for me, I was still interested in her; but I attributed the uneasiness that
still troubled my heart to the vestiges of an impression too strong to
be quickly effaced, and opposed it with all the power and seductiveness
of Mme de Lursay's charms, and the idea of my approaching happiness.

The next morning I intended to go to Mme de Lursay's, and I was
still with Mme de Meilcour when the Comte de Versac was announced.
Mme de Meilcour seemed vexed. He was the man she liked least in the
world, and whom she most feared on my account; he therefore came
seldom. The same reason that made my mother dislike him made him
dislike her. She had even forbidden me to see him. As we were never
in the same houses, and as I rarely went to Court, where Versac almost
always was, we hardly knew each other.

Versac, of whom I shall have much to say in what follows of these
memoirs, combined the highest distinction of birth with the most
agreeable wit and an extremely attractive appearance. Adored by all the
women though he never did anything but deceive and ruin them, vain,
haughty, reckless, he was the boldest fop ever seen, and all the dearer
perhaps in the women's eyes for the very faults that made them suffer.
Whatever the case, they had made him the fashion from the moment
he entered society, and for ten years he had been conquering the most
insensible of them, fixing the most inconstant and displacing the most
accredited lovers. If it ever happened that he was unsuccessful, he always
twisted things so much to his own advantage that the lady in question
still passed as having been his. He had invented an extraordinary jargon
for himself which, though it was entirely affected, seemed nevertheless to be natural on his lips. Out to be amusing, and always agreeable,
either by what he said or by the novel turn he gave it, he added a new
charm to everything he repeated and was inimitable in everything he
invented. He had ordered the graces of his person in the same way as
those of his mind, and had acquired those strange attractions which
one can neither name nor define. There were few who did not try to
imitate him, though all those who did so only made themselves less
agreeable than before. It was as if that happy insolence was a gift of
nature, which could be granted to no one but him. There could be no

one like him, and even I, who have since followed so advantageously in his footsteps, and succeeded finally in seeing Paris and the Court divided between us, have long acknowledged myself as no more than one of those forced and clumsy imitators who, without any of his graces, can only distort his faults and add them to their own. Splendidly dressed, but always with taste and distinction, he had the air of a nobleman even when he most affected one.

Versac, such as he was, had always attracted me. I never saw him without studying him and trying to make my own the sumptuous airs I admired so greatly in him. Mme de Meilcour, simple and artless herself, found everything absurd that was not natural, and recognizing the attraction Versac had for me, trembled at it. For this reason even more than because of her aversion for such people, she could not support Versac's presence without impatience: but the observance men and women owe one another in society, and which is maintained with extreme punctiliousness between those of high rank, obliged her to keep her feelings in check.

After having caused a characteristic disturbance by his entry, he made a vague bow to Mme de Meilcour and an even more cursory one to me, and then began to speak ill of so many people that my mother could not prevent herself from asking what the world had done to him that he should slander it so perpetually.

"Upon my word, Madam," he answered, "why do you not ask me what I have done to it that it should so perpetually slander me? They crush me," he went on, "they plague me strangely, they overwhelm me with calumnies, they point at my foibles as though they had none themselves and as if I – I of all people – were incapable of seeing them! But by the way, has it been long since you saw the dear Countess?"

Mme de Meilcour said that it was.

"But one never sees her any more," he said. "I suffer terribly because of it, I am most terribly afflicted!"

"Perhaps she has taken to religion?" said my mother.

"Indeed," he replied, "that is where she is likely to end. She is struck down by the most majestic grief: she has just lost the little marquis, who has played her the most damned unfaithful trick ever conceived by the mind of man. As it is not the first time a lover has abandoned her, one might have supposed she would console herself for this loss in the same way as for the others – sorrow is so much less painful when you get used to it – were it not for a circumstance that makes this particular desertion extraordinary."

"And that is...?" asked Mme de Meilcour.

"That is…" he replied, "but how will you believe it of the most provident and well-ordered lady at Court? The circumstance is that he was the only lover she had. To reestablish her reputation, she had contrived for herself an affair of sentiment. Yet there is no woman who is not disgusted by such a thing; and what is worse, the deceiver has reserved him the black and barbarous pleasure of having no successor, and has described her in such a fashion as to terrify the most intrepid suitors, not the smallest consolation has presented itself. You will allow that nothing could possibly be more dreadful!"

"I do not believe a single word of this adventure," said my mother.

"What!" cried Versac. "It is public knowledge. Can you suspect me of inventing such things about the Countess, one of the women for whom I have the highest consideration in the world, and whom I hold in particular esteem? What I tell you is as well established as the fact that she and the divine Lursay have powdered themselves all their lives."

I felt myself start on hearing Versac speak so injuriously of a person for whom I had, and thought I ought to have, the greatest respect.

"More calumny," replied Mme de Meilcour. "Mme de Lursay has never powdered herself."

"Yes," he answered, "just as she has never had lovers."

Lovers! Mme de Lursay! I exclaimed to myself.

"One would think, would one not," Versac went on, "that you were not acquainted with her. Is it not common knowledge that she has had a kind heart these fifty years? Was that not well known even before she married the unfortunate Lursay, who incidentally was certainly the most foolish Marquis in all of France? Does not everyone know that he surprised her one day with D——, the next day with another, and two days after that with a third; and that at last, weary of all these surprises, he died to avoid the vexation of finding himself in another such awkwardness? Was she not then seen to assume the lofty prudishness she still professes? Yet does that mean that So-and-so and Such-and-such" – he named five or six – "have not owed their education to her? Or that I who stand before you have refused to accept my own from the same quarter? Or that she might not at this very moment be contemplating that of our friend here?" – and he nodded toward me.

This apostrophe made me blush so deeply that had he merely glanced at me, he would have been aware of the interest I took in his words.

"Does she think," he continued, "with her Plato, whom she neither understands nor obeys, to deceive us about her secret rendezvous; or that we are all as credulous as the young men who know nothing of the nature and number of her adventures, and think that they worship in her the most respectable of goddesses, and conquer a heart that none before them has ever taken by surprise?"

This was so just a description of my own situation that it dispelled the doubt I had hitherto been in about Versac's words. I blushed to acknowledge how thoroughly I had been taken in – and, without yet knowing how I might do so, I firmly resolved to punish Mme de Lursay for making me esteem her so. If I had been honest with myself, I should have seen that it was I who was responsible for the trap I had fallen into, that Mme de Lursay's wiles were the same as any woman's, and that, in a word, there was less falseness in her behavior than foolishness in mine. But such a reflection was either too mortifying or too clever for me. What! I said to myself. To tell me she had never loved anyone but me! To take such base advantage of my credulity! While I was busy with these disagreeable reflections, Mme de Meilcour, denying the truth of all that Versac said about Mme de Lursay, asked him why, since he appeared to be her friend, he spoke against her in such a manner.

"By way of justice," he replied, "I cannot bear these hypocritical females who, while steeped in the profligacy they deplore in others, prate ceaselessly of their virtue and hope to deceive the public. I have a hundred times more esteem for a flirtatious woman who is honest about it. At least she has one vice the less. Moreover, since you must know all, this Lursay has just played me the most scurvy trick, the most abominable harassment you can imagine. You know Mme de ———. She would make the most charming of pupils! Well, I had introduced myself, been received, been heard politely, and was at last at the stage of persuasion – and what did she do but go and fill the young lady's head with scruples and fears, tell her that she was ruining herself by seeing me, and that I was inconstant and indiscreet! In short, she threw her into such an alarm that we have been at odds these three days, and I only received my recall this morning. Come now, do you think that is forgivable?"

After a few more remarks that angered me more and more against Mme de Lursay, Versac withdrew. Mme de Meilcour, who without guessing the nature of my interest had observed that I was affected by what I heard, sought to turn my attention elsewhere. Yet she could do nothing with me, and I hurried to Mme de Lursay's, intending to avenge myself through the most outrageous scorn, for the absurd respect she had forced me to have for her.

Part Two

I left my house resolved to spare Mme de Lursay nothing of the scorn which in my opinion she deserved. I did not even intend to confine myself to a private explanation that would have caused her only a momentary mortification, but thought I could only properly avenge myself by making one of those public scenes that ruin a woman forever.

Extremely pleased with the beauty of a scheme that would at once punish a hypocrite and launch me brilliantly in the world, I nevertheless saw that it would be difficult to execute. Moreover, I was not so ill bred as to nourish such a project for long; I reflected that to succeed in so cruel an affront I should need some superior merit, or at least a reputation as established as Versac's.

So I finally resolved upon other measures, at once more easily accomplished and more gratifying. I decided to reveal nothing to Mme de Lursay of my resentment against her, to take what advantage I could of her inclination for me, and afterward, by the speediest inconstancy and the most spiteful behavior that philanderers have ever invented, to demonstrate all the contempt I really felt. This villainous scheme seemed to me more agreeable and more certain of success, and I fixed upon it. I entered her house overjoyed at having hit upon such a fine revenge, and determined to carry it out without delay.

I had counted, not I think without reason, on finding her alone. Yet either because she was dissatisfied with my method of conducting a rendezvous or because she wanted to make me anxious for another, she had decided I was to be at the mercy of all the tiresome visitors my ill fortune should bring to her house that day. To my extreme surprise, I saw Versac's carriage in the courtyard. This was so unexpected that at first I could not believe my eyes – but it was true. On entering her apartments I came upon M. le Comte lying, rather than sitting, in a comfortable armchair, giving Mme de Lursay the benefit of all his magnificence and all his charms, and talking to her in the easiest of tones and the most intimate of manners.

The better to deceive Versac, she received me with extreme coldness; but I could not help perceiving, from the satirical smile my appearance brought to his lips, that he guessed the motive of my visit. I sat down with the sheepish air that was habitual to me, which his presence intensified. As for him, he took very little notice, and went on with what he was saying.

"You are right, Marquise," he said. "Love no longer exists, and I know not whether after all the loss should be so deplored. A grand passion is no doubt a very respectable thing, but what does it amount to except a long mutual martyrdom? I maintain that the heart should never be constrained. I myself never feel the need to change more strongly than when I see someone taking measures to keep me."

"I believe you," said Mme de Lursay. "But what would you do if you saw that the other wished to be unfaithful to you?"

"I should change all the faster."

"Indeed!" she said. "What a charming fellow you are!"

"Ah, Madam," he answered, "I am not at all extraordinary. Like me, all men seek only pleasure: fix that forever in the same object, and we should be constant too. Believe me, Marquise, no one would ever engage himself, even with the most charming creature, if it meant being bound forever. Instead of even proposing such a thing to each other, people (sensible people at least) put it as far out of their minds as possible. Certainly they say they will love each other forever, but there are so many examples of the opposite that the idea loses its terror. It is no more than a courtesy to be taken merely as a compliment, and it is of no account at all when one wishes to indulge in the pleasure of inconstancy."

"What will always surprise me," she replied, "is that with such opinions, which you make no attempt to conceal, with your continual betrayals, and the shamelessness with which you first conduct and then cheat your way out of an affair, there can still be women mad enough to find you agreeable."

"Ah, no," said Versac coolly, "that does not surprise me. What would surprise me would be if they did not love us for faults which we adopt out of pure consideration for them. You say we are inconstant. Are they faithful? You claim that we break off in an unseemly manner. I have not noticed it. It seems to me we terminate our liaisons as decently as we embark on them. If there is scandal, it is not always our fault."

"I take it you mean it is ours," said Mme de Lursay.

"Assuredly, Madam," he replied. "If there are a few women who would like to conceal forever the vagaries of their hearts, how many are there who only love in order that it may be known, and take every care to ensure that the public is informed?"

"But," she answered, "Mme de ———, who loved you so passionately and was so anxious that it should not be known – was it she who caused her own ruin? Which of the two of you spoke more of the affair?"

"Neither she nor I," he replied, "and yet both of us. She feared scandal, and I fell in very reasonably with her views. But shall I tell you what it is? There are certain eyes that cannot be deceived, and the world saw, in spite of us, that we loved each other; and the world, as indiscreet as we had been discreet, saw fit to speak of what it had seen. However much I wished to save appearances and sacrifice myself, I was taken to be in love, because in fact I was – and thus it is ever, even with the best disguised connection."

"I still think you are mistaken," she replied. "I know examples that prove the contrary of what you maintain."

"A delusion!" he answered. "A woman often supposes herself undetected because one is too polite to show one has seen through her; but God knows how many conversations consist of allusions to these little liaisons so scrupulously dissimulated and so plainly understood. I do not pride myself on being more subtle than the next, and yet I flatter myself that nothing escapes me."

"Indeed!" said Mme de Lursay mockingly. "I believe you!"

"Good God, Marquise," he replied, "if you knew all that I saw, you would have a higher opinion of my perspicacity. For example, I was not long since with one of those well-regulated ladies, one of those skillful women whose inclinations are buried under a manner of the utmost reserve, who seem to have substituted wisdom and virtue for the licentiousness of their youth. You understand," he added, "there are such women. Well! I was alone with a prude of this kind. When the lover arrived he was received coldly, hardly as an acquaintance even; but their eyes spoke, whatever they themselves might do. Her voice grew softer; the young gentleman, still very new to it all, was extremely embarrassed; and I, who missed nothing, left as quickly as I could to go and tell everybody all about it."

And with these words, which threw me into the utmost confusion, and which, in spite of her presence of mind, disconcerted Mme de Lursay also, he in fact rose and prepared to leave.

"Ah, Count!" cried Mme de Lursay. "How cruel! Are you leaving? I have not seen you for a thousand years! Stay, you must."

"Alas! At the moment I cannot," said Versac. "You cannot imagine all I have to do – it is inconceivable, my brain turns. However, if you are at home this evening and will have me, I shall be at your service if it costs me the world."

Mme de Lursay agreed with as many protestations of pleasure as if she had not detested him heartily, and he went.

"There goes the most dangerous fop, the most malicious wit, and the most tiresome scoundrel in all the Court!" she said to me as soon as we were alone.

"Why, if you know him so well," I asked, "do you see him?"

"Why?" she replied. "Because if one saw only the people one liked, one would see nobody; because the less agreeable Versac's kind are, the more careful one has to be with them. However friendly you are, they will slander you – but if you break with them openly, they will slander you all the more. Versac has a good opinion only of himself; he vilifies all the world without shame or restraint. Twenty women more giddy, more discredited, more contemptible probably even than he, have made him the fashion. He has found a jargon that dazzles: to the frivolity of the gallant he adds the dogmatism of the pedant. He knows nothing, and passes judgment on everything – yet he bears a great reputation. By dint of proclaiming how witty he is, he has persuaded the world of it; he is feared for his malice, and because everyone abhors him, everyone sees him."

However vehemently Mme de Lursay might decry him, she did not convince me that her unflattering portrait was a true one. For me, Versac was the most admirable of men, and I put down all the ill she said of him and all the hatred she showed to her chagrin at never having won him.

I seemed to feel my contempt for her increase; but we were alone, she was beautiful, and I knew her to be amorous. She no longer inspired in me either passion or respect. I feared her no longer; but I desired her all the more. I repeated to myself, in an attempt to reanimate my resentment, all that Versac had told me: I reminded myself of all she had done to encourage me, and the more I blushed for the figure I had cut in front of her, the less I could forgive her for the ignominy I had really earned for myself. When she had finished her panegyric on Versac, she began to gaze at me so significantly, and with something so tender in her eyes, that even if I had not been burning for revenge I believe they would not have failed of their effect. I soon forgot how little prestige there could be in such a conquest. I was too young to be troubled long by such a consideration: at that age prejudice cannot withstand opportunity; and besides, for what I wanted from her, it mattered little whether I esteemed her or not.

I drew close to her without speaking, and kissed her hand, in such a way as to give her the liveliest hopes.

"Well," she said, smiling, "are you going to behave better today than you did yesterday?"

"I think so," I replied firmly. "The moments you are good enough to grant me are too precious to be wasted, and I cannot think you are satisfied with the use I have put them to so far."

"Whatever do you mean?" she asked, affecting to be surprised.

"I mean," I replied, "that you shall love me, that you shall confess it, and that you shall prove it."

I uttered these words with a boldness she could never have suspected in me the day before, and which appeared so out of my character that it did not even occur to her to be shocked. Her only reply was a scornful smile, which showed me what little account she took of my boasts, and how incapable she thought me of carrying them out; otherwise she would at least have taken offense. My manner suddenly became so familiar that Mme de Lursay was stunned, to the point that I had now but a feeble resistance to overcome. She perceived with astonishment that I was no longer in awe of her; and if I had followed up my advantage, perhaps she would not have drawn back. Yet in the midst of the kind of transports that only love can authorize, I was so sure of success and acted with so little tenderness that she could not but show her displeasure. My unmannerly determination assuredly harmed my cause: her eyes flashed with genuine anger. I was not to be restrained, though. Convinced that she secretly wished to be conquered, I asked pardon and continued to offend. It availed me nothing, however, either because Mme de Lursay declined to grant me a victory that I did not make decorous enough for her taste, or because my inexperience with women prevented me from being sufficiently dangerous.

Ashamed of a boldness that had failed me so, I left Mme de Lursay alone. I was quite embarrassed at the thought of what she would say to me, and she too must have been uneasy about how to act in so delicate a situation. If she showed me too much leniency, what might I not think? If she affected too much anger, I might be discouraged, and that would be a hindrance in what was to come. For some time, she remained pensive and silent. I followed her example. A man a little more expert in the ways of the world would have contrived a thousand sweet comments on what had passed which would have helped a woman placed as she was; but I knew of none, and Mme de Lursay had either to extricate herself by her own efforts or resign herself to never speaking to me again. At last she came to a decision. She made me understand, gently and with dignity, that she found my behavior extremely ridiculous; I alleged love as my excuse. She maintained that love does not lead to disrespect; I assured her very respectfully of the contrary; she contested it. In the heat of the discussion we lost sight of our real subject, and I concluded the argument by kissing her hand, which she held out to me while assuring me that in future she would be on her guard.

This threat held little terror for me: even in her anger, I could detect her extreme willingness. My revenge was only postponed, and, fool that

I was, I thought I ought not to try to hasten it too much. Again we fell silent. Mme de Lursay, who had reacted to my first outburst in the prescribed manner, had every right to expect a second, and appeared to be waiting for it. She knew not how I had come by the new expertness that had so astonished her, and, flattering herself perhaps that I owed it all to love, must have been greatly surprised to find its effects so limited. After due consideration she decided it would be best to supplement my skill with her own, and taking up our previous discussion she asked me – but with the utmost mildness – why I had passed from so great and even too timid a respect to such a disagreeable familiarity.

"For after all," she went on, "I grant there are women with whom even the least amiable man has no need of any assistance but their desires, and for whom every moment is opportunity; that anyone should be wanting in his behavior toward them does not astonish me. Yet I think I may claim that this is not my situation: my philosophy and my way of life make me suppose myself safe from certain liberties. But you see what has happened!"

Outraged by so shameless a hypocrisy – for I was not willing to believe that Versac had deceived me – I at first made no answer. I could not display all the scorn I felt for Mme de Lursay, or repeat the conversation my feelings were founded on, without obliging her to try to restore me to my former good opinion of her – and by that means I might make it impossible for me ever to triumph over her.

"You do not answer?" she asked. "Do you fear you might apologize too much, or is it that you do not deign to apologize at all?"

I knew not what to say, and threw the blame once more on my love for her and all the kindnesses she had shown me.

"As far as love is concerned, I believe I have already told you that is not a legitimate excuse," she answered. "And as regards the kindnesses you speak of, I agree that I am kindly disposed toward you, but there is more than one sort of kindness, and I do not think mine bestows any rights on you. Even if I had so far forgotten myself as you suppose, a truly refined lover would either not have sought to profit by it at all or, at least, would not have taken such advantage of it as you have just done."

To this she added a thousand delicate refinements and succeeded at last in instilling in me some small inkling of the necessity for a gradual approach. This phrase, and the idea it expressed, were completely unknown to me. I took the liberty of saying as much to Mme de Lursay, who smiled at my simplicity and was good enough to undertake my instruction. I put each precept into practice as she gave it to me, and the important study of a gradual approach might have taken us a long way, had not a noise in the antechamber obliged us to interrupt it.

A footman entered and announced Mme and Mlle de Théville. The name was very familiar to me. Mme de Théville and my mother were quite closely related but had fallen out some time ago, and, since then, Mme de Théville had almost always stayed in the provinces, so I had never met her. They entered, and to my ineffable surprise I found in Mlle de Théville the mysterious stranger that I worshiped, who I thought had such an aversion for me. I can but feebly express the turmoil I was thrown into at the sight of her, and what love and ecstasy and fear were renewed in my bosom. Mme de Lursay covered her with caresses, and I saw from her manner with Mme de Théville that they must be intimate friends. My surprise was all the greater because not only had I never seen her before at Mme de Lursay's but I had never even heard my hostess speak of her. She reproached her friend for not having been to see her for so long.

"You must believe that only important business could have prevented me," answered Mme de Théville. "Last time I stayed in Paris only a short while, and during that time I saw you. I then had to return to the country, and I came back only two days ago. I would have remained there longer if Hortense had not found it so wearisome."

What were my feelings when I learned from Mme de Théville's words that the only place where I had not looked for my fair unknown was the very place where I might have found her, and that in determinedly fleeing Mme de Lursay I had lost every opportunity of coming near Hortense! As I made these sorrowful reflections I did not cease to gaze at her and, thus, completed my enslavement. Mme de Lursay presented me by name to Mme de Théville, who spoke to me pleasantly though somewhat gravely, perhaps because of the coolness between her and my mother.

If I did not seem to please her greatly, neither did she make a very favorable impression upon me. She was still rather beautiful, but her expression was haughty and did not give evidence of much sweetness of character. She was said to be very virtuous, and all the more respectable for being so without ostentation. She had always been so, but she did not think herself free for that reason to slander others. Yet, being unsuited by nature for society, and despising it, she did not try to please; and though she was of necessity respected and admired, she was not loved.

As for Mlle de Théville, I thought she looked at me with extreme coldness, and she hardly acknowledged the compliment I paid her. I have thought since, it is true, that possibly she did not understand what I said: the agitation in my senses had invaded my mind, and the confusion of my ideas prevented me from expressing any of them well. Hortense's coolness nettled me more than her mother's. Pensive, and as if embarrassed by my presence, she threw me only melancholy and distracted glances. Her mother and Mme de Lursay being engaged in conversation left us at liberty to do the same, but I experienced too lively a pleasure being near her to be able to speak of anything but my love, and nothing could have allowed such a confession. Moreover, what had passed between us in the Tuileries, her apparent indifference at seeing me again, the secret passion her words had led me to believe she nourished, all combined to make me ill at ease in her presence. I tried in vain to begin a conversation, but her melancholic reverie increased my timidity. What! I said to myself. Can I really have thought that it was I who had made an impression on her? Did I dare to think that the stranger so dangerous to her heart was none other than I? What folly! With what indifference, with what hateful scorn she receives me! Ah, that stranger, whoever he is, can no longer be ignorant of his happiness. He can say that he loves, he hears that he is loved. Their two hearts are united in the tenderest delights, and enjoy them without constraint, while I suffer and nourish a fatal passion that can never know the sweetness of hope! What cruel irony is it that makes me feel the most violent love for her at the very moment when she conceives a mortal hatred for me?

Far from effecting a cure, these dreadful thoughts quite crushed me. I was still yielding helplessly to them when Mme de Senanges was announced. So taken up was I by my sufferings that I hardly observed her entrance; but she was by no means so oblivious of me. I was the first person she noticed, and she had scrutinized me from head to foot before I had even glanced at her.

"I have just left Versac," she said to Mme de Lursay, "and he tells me you will be at home this evening. I should like to take advantage of the opportunity. You are willing for me to come, are you not?"

"Did he also tell you," asked Mme de Lursay, "that I was complaining bitterly that you never come to see me?"

"He is a scatterbrain," she replied. "He gave me no message from you. But tell me, your majesty, what have you been doing lately? It is impossible to find you anywhere these days."

As she rehearsed these compliments, as false as they were faded, Mme de Senanges looked at me with the utmost benevolence. She embraced Mme de Théville, saying she was charmed to see her again and scolding her for having buried herself so long in the country. She praised Hortense's looks, but as one who found them less than satisfactory: her encomium was brief and cursory, and delivered with a super-cilious and distracted air. She said nothing about my face, but she never stopped looking at it, and I believe that if she had thought it permissible to pay me a compliment, it would have been a fuller and sincerer trib-ute than the one she paid Mlle de Théville. When she spoke to me she did not take her eyes off me, and the expression in them was so marked that even I, ignorant as I was, could not be mistaken about its meaning.

Mme de Senanges, to whom, as will presently be seen, I had the mis-fortune to owe my education, was one of those female philosophers for whom public opinion has never existed. Always above prejudice, and beneath everything else; better known in the world for their vices than for their rank; valuing the names they bear only because they think it permits them the maddest caprices and the basest whims; always alleg-ing as their excuse a sudden impulse whose power they have never felt but want to find everywhere; without character as without passion, frail without being tender, constantly yielding to the idea of a pleasure that always escapes them – such women, in short, as one can neither excuse nor pity.

Mme de Senanges had been pretty, but her features had faded. Her languishing, sagging eyes had no longer either fire or brilliance. The face paint which only completed the ruin of the sad remains of her beauty, the extravagance of her dress, the immodesty of her demeanor – all these only made her the more repulsive. In short, she was a woman who of all her former graces retained only the audacity which youth and attractiveness can excuse – though it dishonors them both – but which, at a more advanced age, presents a picture of corruption that cannot be contemplated without horror.

As for wit, she was not without it – that is to say, the kind of wit commonly found in society. She had nothing to say, but allowed her-self to say it all; she slandered all the world, never thinking well of any-one but never hesitating to utter what she thought. She employed the language of the Court, peculiar, slipshod, and newfangled, or refur-bished. She delivered all this in a nonchalant drawl, an affected sloven-liness sometimes confused with naturalness, but which in my opinion is no more than a method of being wearisome at greater length. In spite of her talent for the trivial, she sometimes abandoned it in order to dog-matize; and though she had neither judgment nor knowledge, she never hesitated to offer her opinions. She was, besides, steeped in noble sen-timents, ceaselessly astonished at the profligacy of the age, and always ready to bemoan it.

This respectable Senanges whom I have just described was smitten at the sight of me. The momentary impulse that decided a grand passion in her, that unfortunate impulse – which she could never resist because, according to her, it was irresistible – swept her away and sealed me as her victim. Not, as she later confessed to me, that I exactly possessed all the qualities necessary to please her. My behavior was too plain, I had neither extravagant airs nor ridiculous manners, I seemed ignorant of my own worth. At the same time as she recognized all I lacked, though, she felt what a noble deed it would be to supply it. In short, she took it into her head to form me, a fashionable term covering a multitude of ideas that it would be difficult to express.

As for me, when I had looked at her properly it never entered my head that she would be the one to form me, and in spite of her civilities I saw in her at first nothing but a dilapidated coquette whose very impudence embarrassed me. At that time, I still had those principles of decorum and that admiration for modesty which society calls "folly" and "false shame," because if they were still called "virtues" or "attractions," too many people would have to blush for the lack of them.

I cannot tell whether Mme de Senanges perceived my embarrassment at the avid looks she cast at me, but if she did, she did not allow it to trouble her. To show me the full value of my conquest, she displayed all her nonchalance and all her charms, and to finish me off, added the absurdities of her person to those of her conversation. At last I reproached myself for paying so much attention to someone whose worthlessness was so patent, and in spite of the coldness I met with in Mlle de Théville, I turned my eyes toward her as an antidote. She was listening to Mme de Senanges, and I could see from her heightened color and disdainful looks that she formed the same opinion as I did. This did not surprise me. I reflected with astonishment upon the enormous distance between her and Mme de Senanges, upon those touching charms, that noble mien, reserved but not constrained awkwardness – enough in itself to ensure respect – that just and correct understanding, discreet even in playfulness, easy even in sobriety, felicitous always. And, on the other hand, I saw the worst that can be offered of baseness and corruption by nature at its most perverse and art at its most reprehensible.

Mme de Senanges, who convinced herself of her own merit more by the number of her lovers than by the time they chose to remain in her chains, was quite persuaded that her charms would have the desired effect upon me, and that she would not return home without a formal declaration.

This belief had begun to lend her a grisly gaiety when Versac, preceded by his customary uproar, entered, followed by the Marquis de Pranzi, a gentleman then in fashion, Versac's pupil and constant imitator. Mme de Lursay blushed when she saw him, and she greeted him with some embarrassment. Versac, who had foreseen this reception, though, pretended not to see the agitation Mme de Lursay was thrown into by Pranzi's presence. At first he took notice only of Mme de Senanges, and cried out as if in astonishment, looking at Mme de Lursay:

"What! She here! Surely I cannot have been mistaken?"

"What do you mean?" she asked.

"Oh, nothing," said Versac, lowering his voice slightly. "I merely thought that when a lady took an interest in someone, the last thing she did was let Mme de Senanges see him."

"I do not think there is anyone here who need fear her," she replied.

"Ah," said he, "then I must have been mistaken."

He would assuredly have plagued Mme de Lursay further, for he disliked her, had not Mlle de Théville, to whom he now turned, driven his thoughts elsewhere. He stood for a moment as if dazed. Amazed that so rare a beauty had been hidden from him so long, he stared at her in astonishment and admiration. He greeted both Mme de Théville and her with a respectfulness most unusual in him. After the preliminary courtesies: "What angel, what divinity has come to visit you, Madam?" he murmured to Mme de Lursay. "What eyes! What nobility! What grace! How is it that we have been kept ignorant till now of the most lovely and perfect creature Paris has ever seen?"

Mme de Lursay told him in a whisper who she was.

"Admire her if you wish," she added, "but I do not advise you to love her."

"No? And why not, pray tell?"

"Because you cannot succeed."

"Upon my soul," he answered, "that is what I should like to find out." And then, resuming the conversation in an ordinary voice: "Madam," he said, "I trust you do not object to my bringing M. de Pranzi. He is a former acquaintance of yours, an old friend. One is always glad to see old friends, is one not? When one has known them from the beginning, so to speak, when one has actually launched them in the world, one still takes an interest in them, even if one loses sight of them, and is always delighted to meet them again."

"I am honored," said Mme de Lursay, looking very uncomfortable.

"But you know," went on Versac, "you will hardly imagine the difficulty I had persuading him to come: he did not wish to, he said, because it has been several years since he paid you his respects. What absurd scruples! When people have known one another really well, they are above such trivial formalities."

Versac's mocking and malicious manner and Mme de Lursay's embarrassment came as a surprise to me, who knew nothing about anything. I was quite ignorant that, ten years before, public opinion had given Pranzi to Mme de Lursay, and that she had apparently taken him. She would have had good reason to deny having made such a choice, for if a woman's heart may be judged by the objects of her passions, nothing could degrade Mme de Lursay more or make her more contemptible forever than an attachment to M. de Pranzi.

He was barely of the nobility, yet paraded the sort of conceit about his birth that is intolerable even in persons of the highest rank, wearying people incessantly with what was in fact the shortest pedigree at Court. What was more, he affected to think himself a man of valor. This, however, was not his most vexatious fault: several affairs that had turned out badly had cured him of boasting of his courage. Born without wit as without charm, without looks as without wealth, women's caprice and Versac's protection had made him into a gallant, although he added to his other defects the contemptible vice of plundering the women he ensnared. Foolish, presumptuous, impudent, as incapable of thinking well of anybody as of blushing to think ill, if he had not been a fop – and that, one must allow, counts for much – one could never have imagined how he managed to please.

Even if Mme de Lursay had not done all she could to bury her indiscretions, could she have recalled without horror that M. de Pranzi had once been dear to her? This may not have been the reason for her uneasiness in his presence; but the spiteful turn Versac had done her, the things he had said to her that afternoon, and the motives she had given him for bearing her malice made her tremble for the rest of the day. She could not doubt but that he had guessed her love for me, or that he was doing all he could to make it public and perhaps destroy her in my estimation. Versac was one of those men one can neither confide in nor trust to be silent. Whether she was circumspect in her behavior or not, she knew he would see through her just as well in either case, and act just as meanly. This cruel situation threw her into a visible anxiety, and Versac's allusion to her and Pranzi completed her confusion. I saw her blush over it and make no reply, and at once concluded from her silence and evident humiliation that Pranzi must assuredly be one of my predecessors.

No sooner did Versac perceive the success of his attack than he resolved to redouble it.

"Can you guess, Madam," he continued, "from what fate I rescued Pranzi today, and where the unfortunate fellow was to have spent the evening?"

"Enough!" interrupted Pranzi. "Mme de Lursay knows," he went on mockingly, "what respect, and if I may venture to say so, what a tender attachment I have for her. I have a most lively recollection of all her kindnesses, and would have offered Versac no resistance if I could have believed I could still count upon them."

"Very polite," said Versac, "but it does not affect the truth of what I was going to say. Upon my honor, he was going to sup tête-à-tête with old Mme de ———."

"Good God, Pranzi!" cried Mme de Senanges. "Can it be true? How dreadful! Mme de ———! But she is a hundred years old!"

"True, Madam," answered Versac, "but he does not care about that. He may even find her too young. In any event, as I and certain others know, he finds about fifty the most agreeable age."

Throughout this insolent conversation, Versac looked continually at Mlle de Théville, and with such particular attention as made me shudder. The idea I had formed of this gentleman gave me good grounds for my fears. I believed that there was no virtue, no engagement that could withstand him – and he believed it too. He had not a moment's doubt therefore, in spite of Mme de Lursay's prognostication, that he would easily captivate Mlle de Théville. Yet she had heard such ill of him that, quite apart from her virtue, he found her prejudiced. He found her insensible to his telling looks, and not in the least overcome by his appearance. This surprised him. A born philanderer crowned with a hundred triumphs, preeminent among all the masters of his art, he could not believe that any heart could be denied him. Even if the heart he wished to attack had not been already filled with the deepest passion, though, it was virtuous: and this was something Versac had encountered so rarely that he could hardly imagine that it existed.

Mlle de Théville's indifference did not discourage him, however. He knew she was no more than a girl – a tiresome title that obliges those who bear it to dissimulate their desires more carefully than women need, whom custom, habit, and example allow to be less timid. Besides, she was with her mother, whose severity and reserve must have checked and constrained her. Such reflections very likely calmed him: he, like Mme de Senanges, was sure he would not leave without having arranged the matter more or less to his satisfaction. Yet he was angry with himself at being obliged to concede a delay. In order to clarify the situation the sooner, he set out to make a display of his charms. He had nice legs; he made the most of them. He laughed as often as he could to show his teeth, and assumed the bold postures that set his figure off to best advantage and demonstrated its graces most amply.

Alarmed by the designs of a man it was thought to be ridiculous to resist, and ready to assume a poor opinion of women as foolishly as I had initially adopted a good one, I studied Mlle de Théville intently. She was looking at Versac with a singular coldness and a sort of contempt that reassured me much. As for M. de Pranzi, who had likewise decided to bestow marks of attention upon her, she did not even deign to notice his presence.

Versac had hardly sat down before Mme de Senanges, as usual having nothing to say but only the more voluble for that, began to question him.

"Is one permitted to ask," she inquired, "where Versac comes from? To what divine amusements he consecrated his day? What fortunate beauty has enjoyed the possession of our hero until now?"

"You want to know so many things that I doubt my power to satisfy you on any," he answered.

"He is becoming discreet," cried Mme de Senanges wittily. "But, Madam, not to want to tell us what he has been doing today, that is extraordinary! I confess, I am quite confounded by it. Come, tell us, little Count: we shall keep your secret."

"A fine way to encourage him," said Mme de Lursay. "Let her talk, Count, and be sure that all of Paris will know tomorrow what you have told us this evening."

"Upon my soul," cried Versac, "you both speak of my discretion as though it were a matter that did not concern you. Yet you know there are certain things of which I have never spoken – and if there were a little politeness in the world, I might be thanked for it..."

"What things?" asked the intrepid Mme de Senanges.

"Go on, Madam," said Versac with a sneer, "your courage does you credit."

Mme de Senanges, foolish as she was, knew Versac too well to challenge him further on the subject of indiscretion, and asked him how he was faring with a woman she named.

"I?" he said. "I do not know her."

"An excellent secret!" she replied, "when all of Paris knows you are passionately in love with her."

"Nothing could be further from the truth," said he. "And even Paris, which knows so much, cannot be so well informed on the subject as I. The truth of the matter is that the woman you speak of, whom I hardly know even by sight, has allowed herself the pleasure of imagining that

I shall one day love her, and in the meantime tells everyone how well we get on together. This impertinence is so widely received that, if it continues, I shall be obliged to ask the lady very seriously to stop making me ridiculous."

"It seems to me," said Mme de Lursay, "that it is on her and not on you that the ridicule falls."

"Upon my word, Madam," he said, "it is clear you do not perceive all the consequences of what you say."

"But she is pretty," said Mme de Lursay.

"Yes, she is pretty, that is true," said Pranzi. "But she is of low birth. She may have come up in the world, but she has no breeding, she is quite unsuitable for a man of any rank. In society, the proprieties must always be observed: the idlest man at Court, even if he were encumbered with debt, would be justly blamed for making such a choice."

"I adore Pranzi," said Versac mockingly. "He has such noble ideas. To be sure, such women are only fit to be ruined – and even when, as in his case for example, this is not one's object, they must not be allowed to enhance their reputations at our expense."

"They are certainly much to be blamed," said Mme de Lursay. "You have opened my eyes."

"Indeed!" cried Versac with some warmth. "The persecution of these charming creatures is a singular thing. Even when one is actually intimate with them, one cannot count on their secrecy. As it was only vanity that made them seek you out, so you have hardly entered upon the preliminaries before the affair is as public as if you were already to be congratulated."

"I am surprised," answered Mme de Lursay, "that you, who have never known how to be silent, should complain of an indiscretion which you would commit yourself if you were not anticipated."

"You know better than that, Marquise," he replied. "You know of a certain affair of which I said nothing, and about which I should have been glad if you had been as silent as I. To be sure, you had already caused me so many vexations, you might have spared me that one."

Versac, who had only come to Mme de Lursay's to give himself the pleasure of mortifying her, would not have missed the opportunity of catching her in her own trap if supper had not been announced. Determined to pursue her, he began by privately informing Mme de Senanges, whose intentions he had guessed, that Mme de Lursay was doing all that propriety allowed to bring us together. He had no doubts about the use she would make of this information, and that she would at least redouble her provocations. Nor was that all: he wanted Pranzi to treat

Mme de Lursay in as familiar a way as possible, and to do all that could be done within the limits of decency to leave me in no doubt that she had once entertained him.

We sat down at table. I did all I could to be next to Mlle de Théville, or at least to escape from Mme de Senanges – but in vain. Mme de Senanges, whose mind was made up, placed me decisively between her and Versac, who for his part could not come near Mlle de Théville either, for her mother and Mme de Lursay kept her carefully between them.

What usually passes for wit in society is a poor thing, whatever people may say, and the charming tone that is called the tone of good breeding is usually nothing but that of ignorance, precocity, and affectation. Such was the tone of our supper: Mme de Senanges and M. de Pranzi talking all the time and rarely allowing any opportunity to Versac's liveliness or the good sense of any of the rest of us.

Mme de Senanges, completely captivated by her own wit, flirted with me outrageously. I cannot say whether it was her habit to act with so little restraint or whether she did so on purpose to torment Mme de Lursay: she, I could see, was considerably displeased, especially as I was conceited enough to flirt a little in return. I disliked Mme de Senanges extremely, but I was like any other man of fashion, who cannot help being flattered by an additional conquest, however contemptible. Besides, I hoped by these means to avenge myself on Mlle de Théville, whom I now affected to look upon with as much indifference as she had seemed to show toward me.

While I was attending to Mme de Senanges's absurdities, Mlle de Théville sank into a deep reverie. Now and then she looked at me, sometimes with a sort of scorn which I took much exception to, and which incensed me against her more every moment. My only consolation was her determined disregard of Versac, who was put almost beside himself by such an unheard-of occurrence. Mme de Lursay, tormented by the jealousy Mme de Senanges was causing her, and by the bold, equivocal, and familiar remarks addressed to her by M. de Pranzi, was mortally unhappy in spite of her efforts to master her feelings. Oppressed by the fear of losing me, by the cruel compromising of her reputation, and in the clutches of two heedless people whom she saw were in league against her but whom she was forced to humor: could there be a more dreadful situation?

Whenever the conversation approached scandal, she did all she could to turn it, for fear of becoming its object. Versac made this difficult, though: the misfortune of not being able to please Mlle de Théville put him in a bad humor, and every other woman suffered for it.

"Have you heard of Mme de ———'s behavior," he asked, "and can you imagine anything more singular? At her age, and after having taken to religion twice, to adopt little de ——— for a lover!"

"It is amusing," said Mme de Senanges, "and at the same time very absurd and ridiculous. To be sure, after retiring from the world so ostentatiously, she might at least have reentered it with a more serious affair."

"I consider she would have been just as much to blame, whomever she had taken," said Mme de Théville.

"Forgive me, Madam," said Versac, "but in these matters the choice is always of great importance. One may sometimes be blamed less for a judge than for a colonel: in the case of a prude, for example, the first is much more suitable than the second, for to take a young man when you are fifty adds the absurdity of the object to that of the passion itself."

"The fact is," said Mme de Senanges, "there are some women who do not know what self-respect is."

"Yes," said Versac sarcastically, looking straight at her. "Indeed there are. To tell the truth, all women –"

"Oh, no generalizations," she interrupted, "they always offend."

"On the contrary," he replied, "they are the very remarks that should never vex anyone."

"What!" she answered. "If you say, for example, that all women are easily conquered, if you impute to all the aberrations of which only some are capable, do you not think that all must be offended?"

"Certainly not," he said. "Indeed, I think it is only those who do surrender easily who hate to hear it spoken of, and complain."

"I agree," said Mme de Théville. "A woman who is well conducted need not apply to herself what is intended for one who is not: provided I myself do not surrender, it is a matter of supreme indifference to me if anyone asserts that no woman can resist."

"But, Madam," said Mme de Lursay, "do you count for nothing the poor opinion that such allusions may spread about us?"

"Yes," added Mme de Senanges, "and that by the same token a man may suppose he can seduce us merely by looking at us?"

"Alas, Madam," said Versac, "there are so many examples of this that there is more foolishness in doubting it than complacency in believing it."

"What does it matter if a man thinks you enslaved, so long as you are not?" answered Mme de Théville. "How can the opinion of a fool harm your virtue? Believe me, Madam, a man does not live in society long without discovering that women are neither all virtuous nor all vicious, and experience soon teaches him to distinguish."

"Even if that were true, Madam," said Mme de Lursay, "does it pre-serve us from the foolish ideas of a young man, who, with as yet no experience or knowledge of the world, always begins by thinking ill of us?"

"And who sometimes finds," added Versac, "that experience and knowledge of the world do not alter his opinion."

"Upon my word, Sir," said Mme de Senanges, "you talk like one who has never been in any but bad company."

"Before I reply to that, Madam," said he, "I should like you to tell me what you mean by bad company."

"I refer, of course," she replied, "to women of a certain type."

"I shall easily convince you, then," he answered, "that your defini-tion cannot be just, for I can use the same term to mean the opposite, and say that women of a certain type are women of very good company indeed. But let us examine your idea. By women of good company, what do you mean? Virtuous women, women who have never had to reproach themselves with the least indiscretion?"

"To be sure!" said she.

"To be sure!" cried Versac. "What! Do you then put a woman noted for her squalid adventures on the same level as one who has indulged in but one indiscretion which her philosophy has rendered respect-able? Ah, Madam, I am not so cruel. I would not call such women bad company – and, if you find them so, I agree that I am never in good company, for of all the women I know, there is not one who has not been tender, or is not so still."

"Even if it were not so, Sir, you would not believe it," said Mme de Lursay. "You have so poor an opinion of us –"

"It is true, Madam," he interrupted, "that there are some women of whom I have the worst possible opinion, whose behavior I regard with scorn, in whom, in short, I can find no sort of virtue; who possess not weaknesses but vices; always the first to exclaim about what is said of their sex because they must always cloak their private interest beneath a general one. For them, no doubt, the least shaft must be a cruel one: they have so much to lose by being found out, and they know it so well in their hearts that they cannot tolerate anything that unmasks or describes them. So if I say *Women yield so easily they scarcely wait to be asked,* though I draw a portrait that is unjust to some, I may suppose that those who protest against it find it resembles them."

"Indeed, sir," said Mme de Théville, "and any anger about such things is merely proof that one has a low opinion of oneself."

"Well, Madam," said Versac, turning to Mme de Senanges, who was ogling me, "can you understand why so many ladies are vexed while Mme de Théville is not?"

"All I understand is that you are the last person it becomes to speak ill of women," she replied, "and that the greatest of their follies is to treat you as they do."

"Perhaps that is why I have such a poor opinion of them," he said, laughing.

"What infuriates me," she said, "is that this habit of despising women has become fashionable, and even authors dare to adopt it. There came into my hands some time ago the first part of I know not what, some detestable pamphlet that treated us in the most horrid fashion. I could not finish it."

"Those wicked little books ought really to be forbidden," said Mme de Lursay.

"Why so, Madam?" asked Versac. "Women do as they please. The author writes what he likes about them. He speaks ill of them; they speak ill of his book. They do not correct themselves, and nor probably does he. So far I find them even."

At this point we rose from the table, Versac beginning to doubt the success of his scheme, Mme de Senanges occupied in furthering hers, and Mme de Lursay in despair at the ill-bred behavior of M. de Pranzi, who kept pressing her in an audible voice to restore him to the favors which he said were now becoming more necessary to him than ever. Whatever chagrin his attentions caused her, though, it was nothing to that of seeing me respond to Mme de Senanges, upon whom, in spite of the restraint she had imposed upon herself, she cast from time to time looks of indignation and contempt. She had heard her sentimentalizing to me all through supper, and complaining that while all the best people in France came to her house, I had not thought to introduce myself there. Mme de Lursay was too well acquainted with her not to know that with her the simplest compliment had a definite object, and Mme de Senanges's questions had been too often concerned with the state of my heart for her curiosity to be an idle one. Mme de Senanges was all energy and no restraint when it came to a new conquest: she aimed less at moving the heart than at pleasing the senses, and was perfectly ready to dispense with love and esteem provided she might inspire desire. Mme de Lursay was not ignorant of how susceptible men are, and even though she supposed me deeply in love with her, she had no doubt that I might, for the moment at least, succumb to a woman who knew how to awaken desire in me in spite of myself, and to do so more than once. The coldness I had showed toward her since my disrespectful behavior, the fact that I had taken no trouble to be agreeable to her, my readiness to fall in with Mme de Senanges, all made her fear that my feelings were about to change. Impatient as she was to know my sentiments, though, she did not dare try to discover what they were. In the midst of so many people, of whom she was so suspicious, how could she possibly arrange a rendezvous? And besides, how, after all that had passed between us, could she propose one without giving me the most dreadful ideas about her? Fortunately for me, propriety won the day: Mme de Senanges, who was a little less sensitive to it than Mme de Lursay, and who had seen that I did practically nothing to help myself, that the most marked looks told me nothing, and that to her pressing requests that I should go and see her, I answered only with bows that did not enlighten her at all, was at a loss as to how to make me understand what she was expressing so clearly. The only possibility left was a single word: but unconventional as she was, even she dared not pronounce it, either because I did not press her or, just as likely, because she still did not comprehend that I required the clearest possible explanation.

We had exhausted all the latest scandal at supper. Bereft of this resource, conversation was difficult; and in the company of Versac and Mme de Senanges, good sense could not be sustained for long. Soon, we had nothing left to say to one another. Mme de Lursay, whom M. de Pranzi continued to plague, proposed cards. We all agreed, I with particular eagerness because I hoped the game might bring me near Mlle de Théville. Yet fate did not serve me as well as I hoped: Mme de Lursay, who knew how insatiable Versac's desire for mischief was, and who wished to expose herself to him as little as possible, paired me with Mme de Théville against Mme de Senanges and him, and herself made up a game of ombre with Hortense and M. de Pranzi. I was so chagrined by this that I was tempted to object to cards after all. In the desire to console myself as far as possible, I placed myself where I could see Mlle de Théville's face, and, overwhelmed with the delight of looking at her, I lost all notion of what I was doing. My mind was fixed ceaselessly upon her, and I took no notice of anything but what she did. Now and then we surprised each other exchanging glances: it was as if each of us was trying to unravel what was going on in the other's heart. The melancholy I observed in her made me sad too, and the reflections she gave rise to caused me to make so many mistakes that Versac, who supposed Mme de Lursay the subject of my reverie, could not forbear laughing and pointing them out to Mme de Senanges, who shrugged pityingly but did not let it diminish the hopes she had invested in my person.

The game was not interesting enough to keep us silent. Versac and Mme de Senanges gave rein from time to time to their taste for scandal, and this, joined to my lack of application, vexed Mme de Théville, who loved cards as a woman who loves little else will. Versac hummed some extremely spiteful verses. Mme de Senanges, who was amused by calumny in any shape or form, asked Versac to let her have them. He replied that he did not have them, and could unfortunately only remember fragments.

"I have them, Madam," said I, and at once proffered them to her.

She insisted politely that she could not take them, and asked me merely to have them copied for her. I promised to send them to her the next morning.

"Send them!" cried Versac. "Surely you cannot think of doing such a thing! Do you not see," he added in a low voice, "she would not have asked you for them unless she had supposed you would bring them yourself? It is the rule. Is it not true," he asked Mme de Senanges, "that such things must be delivered in person?"

"It is more polite," she answered smiling, "but I do not wish to put him out."

I perceived that by this scheme Mme de Senanges was trying to draw me into a connection with her; however, unable to avoid a reply without unpardonable rudeness, I resolved to yield to Versac's decision, and told Mme de Senanges that I should bring her the verses she wanted the next day, since she was good enough to permit me to do so. She appeared satisfied with this assurance, and Versac, who was getting things so well underway to torment Mme de Lursay, was, I believe, even more delighted than she was.

Both games finished soon afterward, to the great relief of Mme de Lursay, who, in order to try to thwart Versac had sacrificed herself not only by playing with a man she detested, but still more by leaving me exposed to the advances of a woman who was openly becoming her rival.

The time was approaching for everyone to leave. I was about to lose Mlle de Théville, and it was as I was on the point of being separated from her that I understood how much I desired to see her again. Unless there was no possible alternative, I no longer wanted to wait for chance to vouchsafe me that delight, now the only one in my life. Were it not for the estrangement between Mme de Théville and my mother, it would have been easy for me to be admitted to her home. However, restrained by this consideration, and fearing an unfavorable reception from Mme de Théville if I asked for permission to wait on her, I did not dare to ask. I had drawn near to Mlle de Théville, and taking as my subject the hand she had just played, I asked her how the game had treated her.

"Badly," she answered coldly.

"And I was no more fortunate," I said.

"Playing as you did," she answered, "it would have been very difficult for you to succeed. If I am not mistaken, I heard you being reproached for your absence of mind."

"You were no more attentive yourself," said Mme de Lursay. "I do not think you had your thoughts on the game for a moment."

"I find ombre wearisome," she answered, blushing.

"I know not what it is," said Mme de Théville, "but for some time I have noticed in her a melancholy that alarms me, and which it seems nothing can remedy."

"She is too fond of solitude," said Mme de Lursay. "Tomorrow I should like us to join in taking some measures to distract her."

"I too am interested in my cousin's pleasures," I said in a low voice to Mme de Théville. "If any ideas should occur to me, would you permit me to wait on you and tell you of them?"

"I do not suppose you are a great expert at giving advice," she answered, smiling, "but never mind, sir, I should be glad to see you."

"In that case," said Mme de Lursay to me very quietly, "if you would like to come here tomorrow after dinner we may go together."

I accepted this suggestion with delight, so charmed was I with the prospect of seeing the object of my adoration that I did not reflect at all upon the place of rendezvous or upon what might be its real object. While I was congratulating myself upon having procured a happiness so necessary to me, Versac, ill-disposed as he was toward Mlle de Théville, was talking to her about her melancholy and how to overcome it. Although he spoke sensibly enough, he could only obtain the coldest of answers, which showed unmistakably how little she cared for him. Too vain to show the vexation this caused him, he was nevertheless not so unaffected as to appear quite indifferent, and I saw him redden in spite of himself at this lack of response to his charms. Indeed, hers was too gratifying a conquest for anyone to relinquish the hope of it without regret.

To please an ordinary woman and see her pass from the arms of another into his own, this was a triumph to which he was accustomed, and which was shared with too many others to satisfy his vanity. Among the crowd of women all aspiring to the happiness of catching his eye, he had probably not found one who could flatter his pride. Women who had long ago lost their reputations and wished to crown their careers with him; the kind of foolish women who admire any man of fashion whoever he is, and surrender less to his charms than to the pleasure of hearing it said for a while that they belong to him, better pleased at having procured an adventure that dishonors them forever than they would be by a secret affair, however delightful, that would not cause them to be talked about – these were the women he met every day. The object of every woman's fancy but reigning truly in the heart of none and himself indifferent to all, he yielded to their desires without love, lived with them without inclination, and left them, knowing no more about them than when he had taken them, to give himself to others he understood and esteemed no better.

Not that, whatever charms Mlle de Théville possessed, Versac could have loved her. He was not made to know those tender emotions that constitute the happiness of a sensitive heart. But Mlle de Théville's heart was as fresh as her beauty, and without wishing to make it happy, he would have liked to enslave it. As he had never encountered any resistance but coquetry, he wanted to have the experience once at least of enjoying the spectacle of a young person conquered without knowing it, astonished at her own first sighs, completely subjugated by love while still thinking to struggle against it, unable to breathe or think or act except for her lover, and knowing no pleasure, pain, or duty but what pertains to her passion.

Brilliant though the conquest would have been, to win Mlle de Théville would certainly only have satisfied Versac's pride: although he himself could not love, he imagined there must be a pleasure in being loved tenderly, a pleasure he was not foolish enough to look for among the women he honored with his favors. He had counted upon winning those of Mlle de Théville, and could not conceive a disappointment, which he had never before experienced.

Impatient at the figure he was cutting, he decided to take leave of Mme de Lursay. It was late, and the rest of us followed suit. I do not doubt that Mme de Lursay would have liked me to stay, but there could be no question of expedients in front of Versac, who Mme de Senanges now added to his natural perspicacity the specific desire of thwarting her. As she took leave of me, she bade me not to forget the verses I had promised her, and Versac, giving her his arm, told her not to be uneasy about a matter he would regard as his own. M. de Pranzi gave his arm to Mme de Théville, and only I was left to escort Hortense. I offered her my hand, but no sooner had I touched hers than I felt all my frame begin to tremble. My emotion became so extreme I could scarcely stand. I dared neither speak nor look at her, and we reached her carriage in the most absolute silence. Versac was waiting there to make her the coldest bow he could contrive – in order, I suppose, either to show how displeased he was with her or to demonstrate his indifference. Mme de Senanges overwhelmed me again with her painful advances, as Mlle de Théville did with her coldness. They drove off, and I made particular haste to follow them in case Mme de Lursay should change her mind.

I pass over the feelings that occupied me that night. There is no man on earth so unfortunate as never to have loved, and, in consequence, none who is not capable of imagining them. If vanity alone could have satisfied my heart, it would doubtless have been less agitated. Mme de Senanges, completely devoted to trying to please me, and Mme de Lursay, at a point where I need fear no more delays, both contributed to make my situation a brilliant one – the first especially, for if she no longer attracted public attention by her charms, she nevertheless retained it by means of the novelty of her adventures. Yet I got little pleasure from being the object of affection of both a prude and a woman of easy virtue: the heart that seemed to oppose itself to my desires was the only one that could occupy my own. Seeing Hortense's melancholy, and her coldness toward me, to what else could I attribute them but to some secret passion? My first suspicions of Germeuil reawakened in my mind. The more I thought about them, the more they grew. I thought I now perceived a thousand things that had escaped me then, which all combined to convince me of their mutual ardor.

I was uncertain the next day whether I should tell Mme de Meilcour of my meeting with Mme de Théville, lest the antipathy that divided them might make her forbid me to see her. I was so sure that in such a case I should disobey that I preferred not to expose myself to the risk. Yet it might be more dangerous to conceal my doings from her: she could not remain ignorant of them for long, and my attempts at secrecy might serve only to make her observe me more closely. I decided therefore that the best thing, not only for my love but also in consideration of my duty toward Mme de Meilcour, was to hide nothing from her. I went in to her, and in the course of telling her as a matter of indifference what I had done the day before, I mentioned that I had met Mme de Théville. The name, which I scarcely dared to pronounce, did not produce the response I had feared. She replied coolly enough that she had not supposed Mme de Théville to be in Paris.

"Mme de Lursay," I answered, "knowing that you do not like her, was afraid, no doubt, to speak of it."

"There would have been no harm in telling me of her return," she replied. "The estrangement between us has not made us enemies."

"You do not disapprove, then, of my seeing her?" said I.

"On the contrary," she answered. "She has so many virtues that her conversation must be infinitely beneficial to you. But," she added, "I have heard that her daughter is beautiful. Have you seen her? What is your opinion?"

I was so put out by this simple question that my first impulse was to say I did not know. I only overcame this embarrassment to encounter another: obliged by my mother to say what I thought of Mlle de Théville, I was constrained by love to sing her praises.

"Have I seen her! What is my opinion?" I cried. "Ah, Madam, you would be enchanted by her! Her face, her manner, her wit, everything about her is pleasing, everything is charming. She has the most beautiful eyes! The most tender! The most touching! And if you had only seen her smile!"

"You are loud in her praises," she interrupted. "I believe you would sooner live with her than I with her mother."

It was not until that moment I perceived that I had said too much.

"Madam," I replied with an emotion I tried in vain to control, "I have described her as I saw her, and even so I may still not have done her justice. But I must admit that I found in myself no disposition to hate her."

"I would not wish you to hate her," said she. "Yet I could wish that her charms had made less impression on you than they appear to have."

"Ah! What could it matter to you, Madam, if I actually loved her?" I replied with a sigh that escaped me in spite of myself. "Would she love me?"

"But if you did not love her already," she answered, "would you be so concerned about her feelings?"

"What, Madam!" I replied. "Do you believe that during the short while I saw her she could have made me fall in love with her?"

"She is beautiful, and you are young," answered my mother. "At your age, love at first sight is only to be expected. The less experience one has the more easily one engages oneself."

"But Madam," I asked her, "would it be such a great misfortune if I loved her?"

"Yes, it would," she answered coldly. "Such a passion would not make you happy."

"But perhaps my fears about her indifference to me are unfounded?" I said.

"I should be very sorry if that were so," she said. "If she were disposed to like you, that would only make you more to be pitied. I am glad to say I have certain plans for you, and they do not include Mlle de Théville. She is not the sort of young woman to satisfy a whim, and once again, I do not advise you to pay her more serious attention. I trust," she added, "that I may still speak to you of this matter, and that you have not so far engaged your heart that my advice is painful to you."

"Madam," I answered, doing all I could not to show my distress, "I have only spoken to you of Mlle de Théville because I was under the necessity of answering your question. I thought her beautiful, it is true, but I do not think one is bound to love all one admires. I saw her without emotion, and I shall see her again without peril to my heart. But you, Madam," I added, "are mistress to command all my comings and goings, and if you think I should not, I will never see her again."

The calmness with which I spoke reassured Mme de Meilcour, who, in any case, was too fond of me not to be easily deceived.

"No, my son," she replied, "see her. Whatever the object of the acquaintance you wish to enter into with her, whether it be love or not, I have neither the right nor the wish to hinder you. My orders will not destroy your passion, if you love her, and if you do not, I am not so foolish as to encourage you to do so by forbidding you to see her."

This conversation was too painful for me to wish to prolong it, and taking leave of my mother I set out to wait on Mme de Lursay, who was to accompany me to see Hortense.

I reflected on all that opposed my love, and the less hope I saw of its being successful, the more firmly I felt it establish itself in my heart. A rival to whom I attributed every charm, a mother who had just on mere suspicion declared herself against me, another woman whose passion or – no less dangerous – caprice I was about to injure – nothing daunted me. I arrived at Mme de Lursay's full of Hortense, and little disposed to remember what had passed the previous day between me and my hostess, for whom, since my suspicions about M. de Pranzi, I had a greater contempt than ever.

In spite of all her threats to take precautions against me, I found her alone. She received me as one does a person with whom one has come to a complete understanding – with tenderness and familiarity. My coldness, for I made no concessions, embarrassed her. Bows, an attitude of deference, sober looks: what a return not only for all she had already done for me but also for the favors she was still preparing! How was she to reconcile so little love and eagerness with the transports I had been in before? She felt she had a right to complain, but did not dare; she gazed at me with astonishment in her eyes, and searched mine in vain for the ardor I seemed to have given promise of. I, mute and more awkward than ever, stood before her less like a lover still to be rewarded than like one who is weary of being so. On entering, I had uttered only commonplaces – the jargon of habit, unthinkable between those who love. Outraged by such unseemly behavior, which she had not deserved of me, she remembered Mme de Senanges, and could not doubt that my sudden indifference was caused by a new fancy that stole me from her. This idea, which was not without some foundation, caused her extreme pain: she saw a woman without principle, youth, or beauty snatch from her the fruit of three months' care – and at what a moment, after what hopes! Just when she could feel sure of my heart, when she had conquered her own scruples, and when I at long last had overcome my illusions.

Although she remained silent I could easily perceive her dissatisfaction and distress, but I knew not what to say. My mind was filled with the idea of Hortense and with what my mother had said, and they left me little room to pity the suffering I was causing Mme de Lursay. However, weary of being alone with her so long, I made up my mind to speak.

"Madam," I said, "should we not go to Mme de Théville's?"

"Yes, Sir," she answered curtly. "I have been waiting for you. I had begun to think you had forgotten I was to take you there."

"I am not so absentminded as that," I replied.

"You might well be," she answered. "I believe the only thing you cannot forget now is Mme de Senanges."

The lady I was accused of being unable to forget was so far from my thoughts that it was not until this moment that I remembered the visit she had engaged me to make. Mme de Lursay's jealousy was not at all displeasing to me. It was important that she should not discover the real object of my passion, and I was delighted to see Mme de Senanges become the subject of her fears. The pleasure of seeing her mistaken made me smile in spite of myself. The indifference with which I received what was a kind of reproach vexed her extremely.

"To be sure, you have made a good choice," she continued, seeing that I did not answer. "You could not make a better beginning. It is so respectable, it must do you credit."

"I do not know what you refer to, Madam," I answered coldly.

"Do not know!" she cried mockingly. "That is strange. I should have supposed that although you could hardly be accused of guessing anything easily, you could hardly mistake my meaning. Nor do you. But if you mean to be discreet today, you should have prepared for it better yesterday and not exhibited to all the world the secret nearest to your heart. After all, Mme de Senanges does not exact such mystery. Her vanity requires a public triumph, and you will not please her much if you keep your secret only for her."

"You place me on more intimate terms with Mme de Senanges than I aspire to, Madam," I answered. "What is more, I doubt whether she honors me with any particular esteem."

"You doubt that!" she replied. "I like your modesty. You seemed to have less of it yesterday when you answered her like one who understood her intentions very well and was not disinclined to fall in with them."

"I do not know what her intentions are concerning me," I replied, "but I thought I might respond to her politeness without incurring your reproaches."

"As for reproaches," she answered angrily, "I am sure I have no right to make them. Only love can authorize reproaches. Friendship, though, may give advice, and if you imagine I am doing anything more you are mistaken. Permit me to observe that politeness does not require anybody to ogle."

"Upon my soul, Madam!" I cried. "I do not know the least thing about that, as well you know. Mme de Senanges certainly took notice of me, but there was no need for me to see in that any of the desire to please, of which you accuse her. If she has such a desire, it is a secret she has kept to herself, and which has certainly not penetrated to me. I answered what she said to me, but she spoke only on general topics, from which it seems to me I could not have drawn any particular conclusions, even had I wished to, unless I were a fool. You know yourself that we did not speak to each other alone."

"Even without speaking in private," she said, "there are many things one can arrange. You succeeded nevertheless in making a rendezvous."

"I merely promised to take her the verses she wanted," I replied. "I do not see how that can be called a rendezvous."

"If it is not," she replied shortly, "it will become one. Could you not have let her go on wanting the verses? Did you have to boast of having them?"

"I only did for her what I would have done for anyone," I answered, "and had it not been for M. de Versac, who engaged me to take them to her whether I would or not, I should be free today of the engagement that calls down this quarrel upon me."

"Quarrel," said she, shrugging her shoulders. "That is a strange expression. No, Sir, I do not quarrel with you. I have said before, and I repeat now: I do not speak to you in anger. What is it to me whether you love Mme de Senanges? Are you not your own master, free to indulge in all the absurdities you please?"

"Absurdities!" I cried. "To what do you refer?"

"To Mme de Senanges, of course," she replied. "One must always share the dishonor of those to whom one is attached: an unworthy choice betrays an unworthy mind, and to have an inclination for a woman like Mme de Senanges is to acknowledge publicly that one is no better than she is; it is to degrade yourself for life. Yes, Sir, make no mistake about it – a fancy may pass, but when its object is contemptible, the shame of it is eternal.

"We can go now if you like," she added, rising. "I have nothing more to say to you."

I gave her my arm; she took it without looking at me, and I could see from her face that she was bitterly angry. To be sure, what could have been more mortifying to her than what had just happened? Could I possibly have defended myself more coldly and insultingly? Was that the way a lover justifies himself? She had too much intelligence, too much experience, and at the same time too much love for me not to feel acutely how atrocious was my behavior toward her. Never had she shown her love so clearly, never had I responded to it so badly. I knew she felt reproachful toward me, we were alone together, and I did not fall at her feet! I had done nothing to turn that moment into the happiest in my life! And now I was letting her leave! Did I not understand, then, the price of a quarrel?

I cannot say whether these were indeed her reflections, but she entered her carriage with an air that told me she was greatly displeased, and that her thoughts were far from cordial. I sat beside her with as much assurance as if she had every reason in the world to be satisfied with me. I could see that she was angry, but instead of showing her the smallest politeness or regret, I was occupied only with my own schemes. I had resolved to make use of Mme de Lursay to reconcile Mme de Théville and my mother; and without stopping to consider whether this was a propitious moment, I decided not to lose this opportunity of speaking to her about it.

"My mother knows that Mme de Théville is in Paris, that I met her at your house, and that you are to introduce me at hers today," I said.

She did not answer.

"Madam," I continued, "I am surprised that you, an intimate friend of them both, have not yet persuaded them to meet, especially since Mme de Meilcour is not, as far as I can see, disinclined to it."

"I do not think," she answered without looking at me, "that Mme de Théville would refuse to do anything I proposed to her in this connection. Indeed, I have thought of it several times, and fancy myself the more likely to succeed, because I know that they esteem one another."

"I can answer for my mother," said I, "that she feels no aversion for Mme de Théville. I cannot conceive what can have estranged them."

"Different tastes often bring about such an estrangement," she replied. "We have a tendency to prefer the company of those who please us to the company of those we esteem. Mme de Théville, though she has many virtues, cannot include softness among them: the inflexibility of her character manifests itself continually in society. You must know her intimately to love her. The qualities of her heart do not show themselves at once; they are hidden beneath an apparent hardness which so repels people that they do not stop to see if there may be compensations for it. Mme de Meilcour, gentle, obliging, polite, born with the same virtues but with a more pleasing exterior, could not put up with her cousin's imperiousness, and though they do not hate each other, they have long ceased to see each other."

"I understand," I replied, "and I believe that were it not for Mme de Théville's protracted stay in the country, the antipathy would not have lasted so long."

"It cannot be called an antipathy," she said. "What separates them is assuredly less strong and more easily overcome."

"Dare I, Madam," said I, "ask you to use your good offices to bring them together? It seems to me all the more appropriate since, because they are both friends of yours, they might meet by accident at your house and be vexed."

"If that should happen," she replied, "they have breeding and wit, and would not yield in an unseemly manner to their emotions, however violent they might be. On the contrary, it is at my house that I should wish them to meet again. To try to bring them openly to a reconciliation might be to make them doubtful of it. Knowing them both, I can be sure that all I need do is make it possible for them to see one another."

As she said this we arrived at Mme de Théville's. The delight of knowing that I would see Hortense filled me with the emotion I always felt near her and made me still more neglectful of Mme de Lursay, whom my uncalled-for harshness had thrown into the deepest dejection. I had heard her sighing while we were in the carriage. Every word she said had been pronounced in a voice that trembled and choked as if with anger or pain. She wished me to observe all this, and so I did, but without taking any more notice of it than if somebody else had been to blame. The state I had thrown her into flattered my vanity nonetheless: it was something new, which interested without touching me, and which ceased even to be agreeable when I recollected that she had offered the same spectacle to M. de Pranzi – not to mention the other lovers whose names I did not know but whom I supposed to be innumerable, for my ill opinion now knew no bounds. We entered Mme de Théville's house together. Hortense was there alone with her mother. Although splendidly dressed, she looked, I thought, dejected, but her languor only added to her beauty. She held a book in her hand, which she put aside when she saw us. Mme de Théville received me as civilly as I could have wished, but in Hortense I met with neither more gaiety nor less constraint than I had encountered the previous day. It was natural enough that she should be reserved with someone she knew as little as me; and if I had not loved her, it would not have disturbed me; but in my state, everything gave grounds for suspicion, everything increased my anxiety. I wanted her to take account of a love which she could not yet have divined: it seemed to me she could not have been unaware of the emotions she caused in me, that my confusion and my looks must have told her how she had moved me – in short, that if she could have loved me, she would have understood me.

The conversation did not long remain general, and I soon had an opportunity of speaking to Mlle de Théville alone. The book she had been reading was still beside her.

"We have interrupted your reading," I said. "We are the more to blame because it interested you, it seems."

"It was the story of an unhappy lover," she said.

"His love is not returned, I suppose," I answered.

"Yes, it is," replied she.

"Then why is he to be pitied?" said I.

"Do you think, then, that simply to be loved is to be happy?" she asked. "May not a mutual passion be the worst of misfortunes when everything opposes one's felicity?"

"I think one suffers frightful torments in such a case," I replied, "but that the certainty of being loved helps one to support them. How many ills cannot a glance from the beloved help one to forget? What delightful hopes does it not inspire in one's heart! Of how many pleasures is it not the source!"

"Consider, though," she answered, "the state of two lovers whose desires are opposed by every circumstance."

"They suffer, to be sure," said I, "but they love: the obstacles that are opposed to them only increase the feeling that is already so dear to them. And is it not really to fight on their side, to furnish them with the means of nourishing their passion? If they see each other for a moment, what delight is in that moment! If they speak together, with what pleasure do they exchange their secret thoughts! If they are thwarted by jealousy and watchfulness, they still know how to tell each other of their love, to prove it even, to imbue with love even the most apparently indifferent actions or the dullest and most ordinary words!"

"What you say may be true," she replied, "but for every moment such as you have described, how many days of anxiety and pain! Often, too, the fear of infidelity is joined to the agony of absence. How can one be sure of a lover whom one cannot see? May he not grow weary, and, having begun by looking for distraction, end by forming a second attachment that leaves him without even a memory of the first?"

"The misfortune of losing what one loves does not always arise from a rival passion," I answered. "In my opinion, those who enjoy the liberty of loving freely are more likely to be capable of inconstancy."

"When I think how difficult it is to keep a lover," said she, "I am always surprised that anyone is ever tempted to take one in the first place."

"Men could say the same thing of a mistress, and I do not imagine that women's hearts are fixed any more easily than ours."

"I could give you proof of the contrary," she said, smiling, "but I am quite content to leave you with that idea. I do not think we lose enough by it to wish to contest it."

"I do not feel the same about your opinion," I answered. "If I could make you change it, I would consider myself the happiest of men."

"It would be difficult," she replied, blushing.

"Ah, I know that only too well!" I cried. "It is a happiness I dare not hope for."

"The happiness of causing me to change my opinion must be so little to you that I cannot understand why you wish it," she said in great confusion. "Besides, I am very attached to it, and doubt whether anyone will ever change it."

"You cannot expect to keep it always, though."

"Your prophecy does not frighten me," she said, laughing. "I am more obstinate than you suppose – and, what is more, I am so sure that my happiness depends on what I think on this subject that nothing in the world can make me change."

"Though I have as much reason to be frightened as you have," I replied, "I have not so much firmness – and even if I had more, a single glance from you would be enough to deprive me of it forever."

Carried away by my passion, I should doubtless have unfolded the whole of it to Mlle de Théville if Mme de Lursay, having just finished a letter that Mme de Théville had given her to read, had not come over to us. Deprived of the delight of telling Hortense how much I loved her, I had at least the consolation of thinking she must be able to guess it, and that the little I had been able to reveal to her of my feelings had not displeased her. We had both spoken with feeling, but I had seen no anger in her eyes – and though she had not said anything that I could positively turn to account, neither had there been any sign of the aversion I had hitherto suspected.

"Am I right in supposing," said Mme de Lursay to her, "that you have been quarrelling?"

"Not exactly," she answered, laughing, "but we did not quite agree."

"The fault is yours," I said. "I offered you the means of ending the dispute."

"What was it about?" asked Mme de Lursay.

"A mere trifle, Madam," she answered. "M. de Meilcour wished me to adopt an opinion that I promised I should never hold."

"If it is one of his own, you are quite right to have nothing to do with it," said Mme de Lursay with asperity. "He has peculiar opinions that suit only himself, and that he clings to the more tenaciously for that reason."

"Obstinate as you think me, Madam," I answered, "I had to yield to my cousin, and she can vouch for it that I did so gladly and in good faith."

"I am not so sure of that," replied Hortense.

"You are right," said Mme de Lursay. "All his air of simplicity does not prevent him from being false through and through."

I easily saw that Mme de Lursay wished to use this opportunity to provoke a private quarrel, but, painful as it was to be accused of duplicity before Hortense, I preferred to be silent rather than give her that pleasure. Moreover, I was sure that if I could persuade Hortense to listen to me I would soon convince her of my sincerity. My silence completed Mme de Lursay's vexation. The glance she threw me showed me how furious she was, but I no longer cared what she thought. I was wholly preoccupied with the first movements of my passion, and thought only of what might further it. As swift to flatter myself with success as I had formerly been to despair, I no longer doubted but that Hortense would look on me favorably – indeed, I scarcely doubted that she did so already. I forgot, in the midst of the charming visions with which I fed my love, both the antipathy I had thought unconquerable and the rival who only the previous day had caused me such alarm. It seemed to me that hardly had I spoken than she had answered me, that when I looked at her she no longer avoided my eyes. The sadness that I had so often reproached her with in my mind, which I had attributed to the absence of the one she loved, now seemed nothing but the voluptuous melancholy of a heart consumed by the object of its passion, the same that I myself had felt ever since I saw her.

These delightful thoughts were not allowed to charm me for long. Germeuil was announced. I trembled as I saw him enter, and the astonishment my presence appeared to cause in him increased the jealousy his occasioned in me. His air of familiarity, the warmth of the friendship that Mme de Théville showed him, the pleasure on Hortense's face, all reawakened my suspicions and lacerated my heart. Heavens! I said to myself in a fury, and I thought I was loved! I actually forgot that Germeuil is the only one who can please her. How could I have forgotten it, when they have given me such unmistakable signs of their love?

The hopes I had just been indulging in made the blow that Germeuil dealt me all the more terrible to endure. As I looked at him I felt transports of rage rise in me that I could scarcely control. I could not avoid greeting him, but I did not trust myself to reply decently to his politeness. He went eagerly over to Mlle de Théville, and greeted her with the animated courtesy one always uses with the women one wishes to please. A gentle confidence shone in his eyes: I thought I even saw love there, but a peaceful love, such as one feels when one is assured of a return. He said a thousand subtle and gallant things that made me tremble for what he might say when they were alone – tender, lively things that I was sure one could only invent if one loved to distraction, things I knew I could find only for Hortense. He gave her the sort of glances I should have liked her to give me. She, for her part, smiled at him, listened to him attentively and as readily replied, and made no attempt to disguise the pleasure she felt in his company. This cruel spectacle quite pierced my heart. I told myself a thousand times that I loved Mlle de Théville no longer; and with every protestation of indifference, I felt my love increase. Each time I saw her lovely eyes, full of sweetness and fire, rest on Germeuil, and her charming lips open to smile upon him, I was intoxicated with pleasure and, trembling, let myself be carried away. I could barely remember that another ruled over the heart for which I would have sacrificed all, and that it was only to my rival that I owed the satisfaction of seeing her look so lovely. Yet when those impulses calmed, I pitied myself so heartily that I was consumed with rage, and the pain I suffered made me throw them the blackest looks from time to time. I roved about the room, full of despair and love, unable to approach them or take part in their conversation. Germeuil addressed me once or twice, but I scarcely answered him or replied so briefly that at last he decided to say nothing more to me. Watching Mlle de Théville, one would have fancied that she had only guessed my feelings in order to indulge in the barbarous pleasure of mortifying them. Now and then, she would speak softly to Germeuil and bend familiarly toward him, and these things, natural enough in themselves, seemed full of meaning to me and completed my despair.

So many different emotions, and of such an unwonted kind, overpowered me. My melancholy became so extreme that I could no longer hide it. Mme de Lursay, perceiving the alteration in my eyes and the sudden pallor of my face, asked me if I felt unwell. At this question Mlle de Théville hastened over to me, and as I was answering that indeed I did not feel quite well, she offered me a smelling-bottle whose virtues she extolled.

"Ah, Mademoiselle," I sighed, "I fear it cannot help me. The malady I suffer from is not what you imagine."

She did not answer, but I believed she was touched by my sad state. This idea, and her haste in coming to my aid, gave me a momentary pleasure. I looked fixedly at her, but my attention no doubt embarrassed her, for she blushed, lowered her eyes, and walked away. I was thrown back into my former distress: I repented having spoken to her and feared lest I had said too much, or lest my eyes, resting too tenderly upon her, had betrayed the full meaning of my words.

Mme de Lursay, knowing nothing of the secret preoccupations of my heart and thinking only of the injuries I had done her, interpreted my chagrin as impatience at being separated from Mme de Senanges. This passion, which seemed to her as precipitate as it was ridiculous, still made her very uneasy. She judged its strength by its rapidity; it seemed to her that the affair was developing too rapidly on both sides for her to be able to oppose it. She had no doubt that I meant to see Mme de Senanges again that evening, and that I should be lost to her forever. Above all, she feared Versac, who would make it a point of honor to further the intrigue on which he had launched me, less out of goodwill to Mme de Senanges and myself than in order to take me away from her. The ill was certain, the remedy hard to find: by her dilatoriness, she had lost the power of acquiring sway over me and could not hope to retain me by making me hope for favors that I no longer solicited. Uncertain of how I should receive the tone she adopted, she dared not adopt any. A tone of affection can seduce only when it is addressed to one who loves in return; it is ridiculous as soon as it ceases to move. She judged, however, that this was her only hope, since irony and scorn had failed to produce any effect.

She came and sat beside me. Mme de Théville was writing a letter, so she was free to talk to me. She looked at me for some time, and seeing me still plunged in thought, said in a low voice: "Do you consider what you are doing? What will people think of this behavior?"

"Let them think what they please, Madam," I replied peevishly.

"One would think, to look at you," she went on gently, "that you were here against your will. Has something displeased you? But no," she added, sighing, "I do wrong to question you on a subject I understand only too well. My very presence afflicts you, and the interest I take in you is becoming insupportable. You do not answer – would you then have me believe it?"

"You are very easily vexed," I replied, "and I fear the quarrel you seek with me now is no better founded than the last."

"But even if both were unjust, should you be offended?" she asked. "Perhaps I should not say so, Meilcour, but if you ever thought of what you have repeated to me so often, instead of complaining you would thank me. For, after all, what is my crime? I told you I suspected you – not of loving Mme de Senanges, for your understanding is too good for you to be capable of an inclination so unsuited to a man of breeding – but of lending yourself too recklessly to advances of which you did not understand the consequence. I know better than you do what effect a woman of that sort can have upon you: true feeling would not make you seek her company, but at the same time as you despised her you would yield to her. And how could you be sure that this caprice, which at first you would blush for even as you satisfied it, might not turn into a violent passion? Unhappily, it is nearly always the meanest objects that inspire such passions. One relies upon the early lack of inclination, imagining that they can never become formidable, but before one is aware that the imagination grows heated, that the head is turned, one finds oneself in love with what one thought one detested; and, finally, the heart learns to share the disorder of the mind. What will be left to me then of – I will not say the feelings which, if I am to believe you, I once inspired in you, but of the friendship I have always felt toward you, if I cannot offer you advice without driving you away? Even if it were true that I was more interested than I wished to appear and secretly feared to lose you; in a word, that I was jealous – would that be a reason for you to hate me?"

"I do not hate you, Madam."

"You do not hate me!" she cried. "Ah, could the cruelest indifference express itself more coldly? You do not hate me in the least! You tell me that, and do not blush to say it?"

"What would you have me say, Madam?" I asked. "Nothing I do satisfies you, everything irritates you, everything is a crime in your eyes. I meet at your house a woman I did not seek out and to whom I showed no special attention, and you conclude that I love her. I am pensive now because I have a shocking headache, and it is the suffering you inflict on me that is the cause of it. If every one of my actions provokes similar commentaries from you, I predict that we shall often be falling out."

"No, Sir," she replied, deeply angered by my words, "you predict wrong. I have not been so well repaid for my trouble that I shall deign to take any more. I understand your heart now, and accord it the esteem it deserves. Perhaps the day will come when you will be sorry to have lost mine."

With these words she rose abruptly, and I, exasperated by her reproaches and by Germeuil's presence, and unable to bear either of them any longer, took my leave of Mme de Théville, who made every effort to retain me, but in vain. I was too vexed with Hortense's behavior to wish to appear pleased with her, and I left her with a coldness she did not hesitate to return.

In spite of Mme de Lursay, I had ordered my carriage to follow hers, and I got in, despairing at having left Hortense with my rival, and almost ready to go back – a design I should no doubt have carried out if I could have thought of any excuse for doing so. Left to myself, with my mind in the uneasiest possible state, I could not think which way to turn. Twice the coachman asked me which way he should go without getting a reply. I was afraid of solitude, and yet did not feel myself equal to seeing anyone. At last, still undecided what to do, I told him, at random and to gain time, to take me to Mme de Senanges's. I had no intention of seeing her, however. It was already so late that I could reasonably expect to find her gone, and I hoped that by signing my name and leaving the verses she had asked for, I should be rid of her for some time. I arrived, but that day I was not to be fortunate: Mme de Senanges was at home. Seeing her carriage standing in the courtyard, I concluded that she was about to go out, and that my visit need fortunately not be a long one. I walked up, very uneasy at the tête-à-tête in front of me. I had not yet learned the art of curtailing them when they are wearisome and prolonging them when they promise amusement. However, the knowledge that the woman I was about to see had a predilection for me lent me more boldness than usual. Indeed, if I had been afraid, I would have been the only man Mme de Senanges ever had inspired with dread, unless it were with the dread of pleasing her rather more than he intended, which would have been a very pardonable terror. However, I did not understand the peril to which I was exposing myself well enough to fear it very much. I knew, of course, that she was very affectionate, but I had too little experience to pursue the idea much further than that. I went in. Although the day was already far advanced, Mme de Senanges was still at her toilet. This was not very surprising: the more a woman's charms diminish, the more time she must spend in trying to repair the loss; and Mme de Senanges had much to repair. She looked to me much as she had the previous evening, except that by daylight I observed that she had a few years more and a few beauties less than I had supposed. As she thought as well of herself as everyone else thought ill, she did not perceive the unflattering impression she produced in me. Besides, she believed that she had made a conquest of me the evening before, and flattered herself that the object of my visit was merely to dispose of certain preliminaries between us, which, given her eagerness to conclude them, would probably not be long disputed.

She uttered a cry of delight when she saw me.

"Ah, you!" she said in a familiar tone. "How charming of you to keep your word. I was afraid you might have been detained. I hardly dared to go on hoping for you – but I was waiting!"

"I am desolate, Madam," said I, "to come so late, but necessary business kept me longer than I could have wished."

"Business! You?" she interrupted. "At your age, has one any other affairs than those of the heart? Or could it have been one of those, by any chance, that kept you?"

"No, I swear to you, Madam," I replied. "My heart is quite undisturbed."

"You surprise me," she answered. "I should never have thought it. Would you say he was made for such neglect, Madam?" she asked, turning to a woman who was with her and whom I had as yet scarcely observed. "Are you as astonished by what he says as I am?"

The other only answered with a gesture of approval.

"But you are not being candid," Mme de Senanges went on. "Or else people do not tell you all they think of you."

"Indeed, Madam," I replied, "what could anyone think of me that would be so flattering?"

"I do not like people who think too well of themselves," she answered. "But after all, one must do oneself justice. When one has certain gifts, it is ridiculous to ignore them beyond a certain point – and you have excellent gifts. Is it not so, Madam? One sees very few faces like his. People admire faces all day long which come nowhere near it. I see women infatuated without in the least knowing why, and bringing into fashion little nobodies whom one can hardly bear to look at. One might call this the reign of *atoms*, might one not? And as well as being exceedingly handsome, he has a marvelous figure. I have said it before, and it is true," she added decisively, "you could not find a more splendid young man."

While she was praising me with this odious impropriety, her looks, which were no less immoderate than her words, assured me that she was amply convinced of the truth of all she said. She gazed at me, not with tenderness – that was not the expression in her eyes – but who can describe what they were like? Fatigued by the panegyric, and even more by her who pronounced it, I said, "Here, Madam, are the songs you asked me for yesterday."

"Ah, yes, thank you. They are charming." And then, drawing me aside, "Do you know," she said, "that if Mme de Mongennes were not here, I should scold you very severely for coming so late; and that my pleasure at seeing you does not prevent the reflection that, had you wished it, I might have seen you sooner? However, to compensate for all that, I mean you to come to the Tuileries with us."

This proposal did not please me at all, and I did what I could to escape, but she pressed me so hard I was obliged to yield. As we went down, I gave her my arm. She leaned familiarly upon me, smiled, and, in short, bestowed all the marks of attention and favor that the time and place permitted. More embarrassed than flattered by her behavior, I found my aversion for her increasing every moment. Ill-disposed as I now was toward Mme de Lursay, I could not help feeling the contrast between the two of them. If Mme de Lursay did not have every virtue of her sex, at least she had some of them. Her frailties were hidden beneath a dignified appearance, she thought and expressed herself with nobility; in Mme de Senanges, though, there was nothing to compensate for the vices of her heart. Born for contempt, she acted as if she feared people would not see soon enough how much she deserved; her ideas were puerile, her conversation tedious. She had never learned to conceal her proclivities; it is difficult to know how to describe her, for most women of her type manage to pass themselves off as merely gallant. Sometimes she would adopt dignified airs, but they only made her more ridiculous. She was so unable to carry off the pretense of being a respectable person that virtue never seemed more foreign to her than when she feigned an acquaintance with it. The grave looks with which

I received her attentions gave her no uneasiness, and as she construed my sadness to be occasioned only by some lingering uncertainty of my ability to please her, she only felt herself more obliged to set these inopportune anxieties at rest. Judging by the measures she took to reassure me, she must have supposed my apprehension to be considerable; and when I alighted with her at the Tuileries, I was overpowered by her favors and dying of ennui.

Part Three

It was past the usual promenade hour when we entered the Tuileries, and the gardens were full of people. Mme de Senanges, who had only brought me to show me off, was charmed, and resolved to demonstrate beyond all doubt that I belonged to her. I was in no situation to oppose her plans, and although I was dismayed at having caught her fancy, I knew neither how to receive her attentions nor how to escape them. What I had seen at Mlle de Théville's had filled me with such melancholy as even the most agreeable objects could not have dispelled, and which the two women I was with aggravated every instant.

Mme de Mongennes especially displeased me. Her face was one of those which, without having anything particularly amiss, form a disagreeable whole, and which the inordinate desire to please makes even more unsightly. Much too stout, with a figure that was never intended to be graceful, she tried to put on delicate airs. By force of wanting to appear at ease, she had arrived at so resolute and ignoble an impudence that it was impossible, unless one thought as she did, not to be revolted by it. Though young, she had none of the charms of youth, and looked so worn out and faded that I quite pitied her. Such as she was, though, she was found pleasing, and her vices served as charms in an age when, to be in the fashion, a woman could not demonstrate too clearly how far she extended the boundaries of extravagance and licence.

I, however, far from being attracted by her, was moved to indignation by the foolish pride I read in her eyes and by her artificial graces. My estimate of her was a just one, but I doubt if I should so soon have arrived at so poor an opinion had it not been for her disdainful airs. Though she had heard all Mme de Senanges's doting praise, she did not seem to think any the better of me for it. This aloofness offended me, and made me examine her with a ruthless severity that may have made her seem even worse than she really was. I did not know then that she did not necessarily despise one if she did not seem to be captivated at first sight, and that she often affected this haughty indifference merely to tempt one to overcome it: for, as I have heard her say since, both a continual facility and a relentless virtue are two things a woman should equally avoid. It was presumably to conform to this wise maxim that she only began to show herself favorable toward me about an hour after she had met me.

As long as we were in a place where she lacked spectators, she did not deign to address me, but as we approached the main walk I saw her countenance change. Her manner grew lively, she spoke to me continually and with an unwarranted familiarity one never adopts at a first encounter unless one has particular designs. Little affected by a change whose object I did not understand, and which would not have interested me even if I had guessed it, I continued in the same tone as she had used with me from the first. However, no sooner did Mme de Senanges perceive Mme de Mongennes's new tactic than she became alarmed: she judged, and I think with reason, that even if she did not wish to please me, she wished it to be thought that she pleased me. In either case, the insult was the same for Mme de Senanges, who was also probably less flattered by making a conquest of me than by the talk she could cause by it. Seeing Mme de Mongennes's ambitions running directly counter to her own plans, she adopted a grave and peremptory tone with her. The other answered more abruptly still, and I had the distinction, at the very outset of my career, of causing a quarrel between two women, neither of whom I cared a straw for.

Though I did not yet understand what provoked the coldness I had just remarked between them, I judged by their looks that they felt themselves to be at odds. Each examined the other with a critical and scornful eye, and after a few minutes' close scrutiny, Mme de Senanges observed to Mme de Mongennes that her hair was dressed too far back to suit her face.

"That may well be, Madam," replied the other. "I take too little heed of such things to have the least idea how I look."

"Upon my word, Madam," answered Mme de Senanges, "it does not become you at all. I cannot think why I have neglected to tell you of it before. Even Pranzi, who admires you, as you know, remarked upon it the last time."

"M. de Pranzi," said she, "is at liberty to make personal remarks about me if he chooses, but I should not advise him to make them to my face."

"But why not, Madam?" asked Mme de Senanges. "Who, if not our friends, can tell us such things? It is not that you are not very handsome, but very few people could carry off such a coiffure as that, and it is wantonly to spoil one's appearance not to consult someone else sometimes about how one looks. Or rather," she added with a malicious smile, "it is to consider oneself capable of carrying off anything, and that would hardly be a modest pretension."

"Ah, to be sure, Madam," answered the other, "who is without some sort of pretension? Who does not think herself always young and amiable, and dress her hair at fifty in the same way as I do at twenty-two?"

These words alluded so patently to Mme de Senanges that she reddened with anger, but any discussion upon the topic promised to be so unflattering to her that she thought it better not to begin: it was, besides, neither the time nor the place to yield to petty concerns. So she concentrated her attention upon the only subject that then really mattered to her. Her object was to demonstrate that I did not belong to Mme de Mongennes, and beside that nothing counted.

We had no sooner showed ourselves in the main path than all eyes were turned upon us. The two ladies with whom I walked were certainly no new object for the public, but now I too became worthy of their attention and curiosity. They were too well known for it to be thought I was there except as an appendage to one of them, but the anxiety of both to please me prevented anyone from making out with certainty which of the two I belonged to. Mme de Senanges, irritated by this ambiguity, spared no effort to have the matter decided in her favor: each time her rival tried to catch my eye, a well-timed flirt of the fan intercepted and thwarted her look. To this she added all the simperings and affected antics that had stood her in good stead in the past, and spoke to me in low tones, and with an air so tender, so languishing, and so abandoned that, given such a consummate display of shamelessness, the public could not but believe what she wanted it to believe. This victory was made all the sweeter to her by the enthusiastic praise of my looks which she overheard. To triumph over Mme de Mongennes was nothing, however, unless I would give a more gracious response to the attentions which she was lavishing upon me. Inattentive and distracted, I hardly deigned to answer the frequent questions with which she plagued me. Versac had assured her so positively that I had been much smitten with her that she could not imagine what prevented me from saying so. She knew that she could not show the smallest doubt of my love without exposing herself to the sarcasms of Mme de Mongennes, but she wanted to make me speak. At this juncture, she remembered Versac's telling her that Mme de Lursay had intentions concerning me, and that he thought me not disinclined to fall in with them. She supposed it would be tolerably easy to dispose of these doubts without compromising herself, and asked me with a nonchalant air whether I had known Mme de Lursay long. I replied that she had been a friend of my mother's for many years.

"I thought she was a newer acquaintance for you," she said. "I was also told that she had the greatest desire in the world to please you."

"Me, Madam!" I cried. "She has never thought of it, I swear."

"Perhaps you have not wished to see it?" she answered. "Could it really have escaped you? And perhaps you have not been altogether indifferent to her: at a certain age, everything pleases – it is so unfortunate. You take someone without knowing why – because they wish it, because you are too young to say that you do not, because you are impatient to have an affair, and the one most easily arranged seems always the best. You are in love for a while, and then your eyes are opened, you see what it is you have chosen, tire of having it, blush for it, finally part from it. That is how it could have been with you and Mme de Lursay."

"I am sure she is very amiably disposed toward me," I answered, "but –"

"Ah yes, I see," she interrupted, "you are going to be discreet, out of pure vanity."

"I fancy that is not the reason," said Mme de Mongennes. "He would do Mme de Lursay too great an injustice if he thought so ill of her. I find her agreeable enough not to be surprised that he should like her."

"You find her agreeable, do you, Madam?" she said in a pitying tone. "That is an opinion peculiar to yourself. She might have been found pleasing long ago, but nobody nowadays belongs to that era."

"It is not so distant that you cannot remember it, however," replied Mme de Mongennes. "I myself can recollect it."

"Well, Madam," rejoined the other, "it seems you have no great wish to be considered young."

Just as they had got to that point, and a polite acidity had entered their conversation, we saw Versac. Mme de Senanges called him, and he came over, but without that easy air I admired in him and tried to imitate. It seemed as if the sight of Mme de Mongennes embarrassed him, and as if she had over him the hold that he had over all other women.

"Come, Count," said Mme de Senanges, "I have need of your support against Madam here, who has been maintaining monstrous opinions against me these two hours."

"I can well believe it," he replied soberly. "With a superior understanding, there is no extravagance or even absurdity one cannot maintain with success. Well, what was the subject of the dispute?"

"You know Mme de Lursay?" she asked.

"Indeed I do," he replied. "A most respectable person, whose beauty and virtue are known to all the world."

"Madam maintains," she answered, "that it is still possible to love Mme de Lursay with propriety."

"For my part," said he, "I should say it would be rather with generosity and magnanimity."

"That is what I say," she replied. "And that one cannot form an attachment to someone of Mme de Lursay's age without doing oneself a considerable injury."

"Exactly so, but exactly," he answered. "There are a thousand good actions of that kind that one cannot do without compromising oneself, and that society always misconstrues."

"What are you saying?" said Mme de Mongennes. "Every day of the week sees some extraordinary attachment excused: the more outrageous they are the more the world prides itself on excusing them. Yet you would say —"

"Yes, Madam," he interrupted, "not only are they tolerated, but, worse, they are approved. And as you know, I have proof of it. Yet the public is not always as good-natured as it has been to me. There are certain attachments it persists in proscribing."

"The public would indeed be very lacking in good nature," she answered, "and, I would add, very unjust too, if one could not love Mme de Lursay without incurring its disapproval. I admit that she is no longer in her first youth; but how many women does one not see, much older than she is, still inspiring affection, or at least trying to do so?"

"No doubt of it," said Versac, "but it is not very willingly allowed."

"Ah, as to that," said Mme de Senanges, "one sees very little of it. There is an age at which one knows one must face the facts."

"Yes," answered Versac, 'but it seems to me that time never arrives for anyone, and that people commonly die of old age still waiting for it. I myself, for example, know women who have grown quite old, extremely old, and who as a consequence have become quite ugly, and yet they do not so much as suspect it but, rather, suppose, with all the innocence in the world, that they still possess all the charms of their youth because they have so carefully preserved all its follies."

"That is Mme de Lursay exactly!" she cried. "Follies mistaken for charms! It is inconceivable how striking that is, and how illuminating. And how many people does it not describe? For myself, I recognize a thousand."

"Yet you do not recognize everyone the description fits," said Mme de Mongennes, "and you apply it to others it does not – for, in fact, Mme de Lursay is neither old nor ridiculous."

"I cannot understand your obstinacy, Madam," said Mme de Senanges. "It intrigues me. Let us leave aside her absurdities: they have been proved. But as a matter of interest, how old *is* she?"

"Well, Madam," said Versac, "she is actually forty; but I maintain that it must be more than that, for I am not so fond of her as to allow that she is no more than she admits to."

"You are certainly mistaken," she answered with asperity. "Forty! It is impossible that she should be only that. Why, I remember –"

"Madam," he interrupted, 'if we permit ourselves to indulge in calumny, she is forty-five. However, I would go no further than that. And now, would you be so good as to tell me what occasioned this charming dissertation on Mme de Lursay?"

"You must see that," said she. "What else but the love she has kindled, no one knows how, in M. de Meilcour."

"Ah, Madam," he replied with an air of mystery, "however little esteem one may have for a person, one does not say such things aloud. One ought not even to think them – though perhaps human nature does not allow of such perfection as that. I know no one whom such a fact, if authenticated, would not ruin forever in society. No doubt M. de Meilcour feels esteem, respect, even veneration, if you like, for Mme de Lursay – but it would be very dangerous for him to be even suspected of anything more."

"You defend him better than he defends himself," she replied. "You see that he is letting himself be accused without answering, and that the subject embarrasses him."

"Perhaps it only wearies him," he said. "I should not be surprised. Even if he were embarrassed, I do not know what you could conclude from that. To be embarrassed by the accusation is not to be convicted of the crime. It is certainly true that Mme de Lursay has rather tender feelings toward him; but who, in society, is safe from such accidents? Must one answer for all the passions one inspires? And provided one scorns them and leaves them unsatisfied when there is no dignity to be got out of lending oneself to them, what can the public have to say? For myself, I am convinced that that is how M. de Meilcour has acted, and that he has not the least indulgence to reproach himself with."

"If that is so, so much the worse for him," said Mme de Mongennes. "I do not think he could have done better. At any rate, I am sure he could have done much worse."

"In spite of the extreme and unfortunate deference I feel for all your opinions, Madam," said Versac, "I cannot agree with you. As for you, Madam," he continued, turning to Mme de Senanges, "I am surprised to find you so little informed of his preference as still to reproach him with Mme de Lursay."

"I!" said she. "I have no special knowledge, I assure you. He has not yet made me any confidences."

"What of that, Madam? Cannot you, whom I have known to divine obscurer matters than the secrets of his heart, employ your penetration now? For pity's sake, Madam, guess for us."

"No," she said, "it would not be right: when he has confided his torments to me, then I shall know what to say to him."

"Come then, Sir, confide," said Versac to me. "You are very fortunate. Though I admit," he added, seeing that I was taken aback, "this sort of confidence is rarely made before witnesses."

"Well," said she, "what is this secret? I cannot imagine what it can be."

"I am sorry for that, Madam," he said, "for if you have not guessed anything one can tell you nothing."

"You are to understand, Madam," said Mme de Mongennes, "that this marvelous secret is one that can hardly escape you."

"And yet," she answered, "it is still concealed from me."

"I think that we may now safely enlighten you," said Versac. "But where do you sup today? In the Faubourg?"

"Yes," she replied, "but not at my house. We are both going to the Maréchale de ———. You would do well to come too."

"I cannot," said he. "I sup in a faubourg too, but not the same one as yours."

"You have some delicate engagement, no doubt?"

"Delicate?" he replied. "No!"

"Is it still the little ———?"

"It would be rather difficult for it to be still her," he replied, "seeing that it never was."

"What folly," cried Mme de Mongennes, "to deny an affair so well known, one that society has done nothing but talk of these two months!"

"I should be very glad, Madam," he said, "if I could sometimes persuade you that I possess neither all the women nor all the faults that are attributed to me."

"Is it an old affair?" asked Mme de Senanges.

"No," he said, "I brought one of those to an end this morning."

"May one know who attaches you at present?"

"Who? Do you mean the most recent?"

"Yes, the most recent."

"But can you really be ignorant of it?" he answered. "It is very singular that you should not know who it is. They will certainly wear themselves out discussing the subject; you will soon hear more than enough of it. I had supposed that it was already public. It began very briskly at the opera, continued elsewhere, and is to come to a conclusion today in my little cottage. Charming," he added, "my little cottage. I mean to give a party there for you at the very first opportunity."

"That is the gallantest thing I ever heard," said Mme de Mongennes. "Is that —"

"Yes, Madam," he interrupted, "still the same. Well! Do you agree to my proposal?"

"A party in a little cottage!" said Mme de Senanges. "You cannot be serious. Gatherings of that sort are improper, and people are right to censure them."

"What nonsense!" said Versac. "And even if people did censure them, would that be any reason for depriving oneself of them? If you try to hide yourself, does not the public guess at what you are doing just the same? Whatever precautions you take, you may be sure the world will talk. Besides, for my part I know of nothing more respectable than a little cottage, nothing that exposes one less to the kind of talk you apparently fear. I even begin to believe that it is love of propriety, rather than necessity, that has brought them into fashion.

"Is it not in a little cottage that one may sup tête-à-tête without scandal? Is it possible nowadays to form an engagement without this resource? Is it not even one of the first requisites? Can a woman with any self-respect — that is to say, one who, having a loving heart or a libertine mind, wishes to conceal her frailties or follies — can she carry it off without the help of a little cottage? Ah, what can be more pure, less subject to interruption, more private than the pleasures one tastes there? Both of you freed from embarrassing ceremony, delivered from the sumptuous apartments where love quarrels or ceaselessly languishes, it is there, in a little cottage, that love revives and is rediscovered. It is under that humble roof that one feels the desires reawaken which are stifled in society by dissipation; there that one satisfies without destroying them."

"Ah, Count," said Mme de Senanges, laughing, "if it were true that a little house had that last virtue, who would ever wish to live in a large one?"

"I would not swear to you positively that one never loses these desires," answered Versac, "but it is certain that one gives them more entertainment."

"That is always something gained," she replied. "But until the party you propose is agreed to, you would both do well to sup at my house when I return from Versailles, which will be in a few days' time. I will send you word, Versac."

"Me!" he cried. 'You know how absentminded I am; I might forget to inform him. Write to him. It would be safer and more polite, and he will be good enough to notify me of the day you have fixed on."

"Very well," she said, "It will only be a few lines, of no possible consequence."

"Oh, you are insufferable with your regard for the proprieties. I have never seen anyone carry it as far as you do; you will end by becoming ridiculous," said he. "It is only right to be careful, but too exact a punctiliousness is tiresome. I am mortally afraid you may turn into a prude."

"No," she answered. "I am sure I shall not turn into a prude – it is not in my character. But I confess I hate unseemliness. To be unseemly is a thing that revolts me; I can never forgive it."

"How could a person of your rank think otherwise?" he replied gravely. "Yet do not be uneasy about that note – such things are written every day."

"Will you come, Sir?" she asked me.

"I should certainly like to, Madam," I replied, "but I do not know whether I shall not have to go into the country with my mother before your return."

"No, Sir," said Versac to me, "No. You must not go into the country – or else you must come back. In a situation as delightful as the one you are in, one does not embark upon such excursions."

Whatever Versac might say, my discontented looks showed him I was not to be persuaded, and I perceived that Mme de Senanges grew uneasy at the opposition I was offering to the proposed supper. Versac, who had resolved to get me away from Mme de Lursay, then engaged me so positively that it was impossible to struggle any longer, and I gave my word, quite determined however to break a promise that had been extracted from me by force.

I mused with extreme resentment on their harsh treatment of me, and was more than ever confirmed in my opinion that Mme de Senanges, in spite of what she had said against impropriety, was in fact all that she had at first appeared. This did not prevent her from supposing that I was preoccupied with my forthcoming happiness.

"How glad I am to find you so obliging!" she said tenderly. "You are charming! It is true – you are charming! But tell me how pleased you will be to see me again!"

"Yes, Madam," I answered coldly.

"I do not know whether I ought to tell you that I shall think of you with pleasure," she went on. "I fear you may be only moderately interested in anything I can say about that."

"Why, Madam?" I answered.

"Ah, why indeed?" she replied. "That is what I may not yet tell you. And yet...But what use will you make of what I tell you?"

I was beside myself with impatience and ennui, and I believe I should have asked her to be so good as to tell me nothing at all, when at a turn in the path I saw Mme de Lursay, Hortense, and her mother, who were coming toward us. The unexpectedness of the encounter threw me into confusion. Although I did not think that Hortense loved me, I was in despair that after I had left her so abruptly, she should meet me now with Mme de Senanges. And although I was no longer preoccupied with the fear of displeasing Mme de Lursay, her presence still embarrassed me. Her accusation of falseness in front of Hortense, and our last quarrel, had incensed me against her extremely, and persuaded me against a reconciliation of which I feared the consequences. Nevertheless, I was still afraid of what she might say. Without disclosing the interest that made her speak of my relations with Mme de Senanges, well able to conceal herself beneath a mask of the utmost virtue, she might make Hortense believe that those relations were not innocent, and if she did not manage to efface all idea of me from her heart, might at least succeed in making it inaccessible to me henceforward. I tried in vain to hide my agitation, yet it was evident in all my actions, and in my eyes. I did not dare to raise them to Hortense, yet I could not turn them anywhere else: some mysterious and irresistible spell fixed them on her despite myself.

Mme de Lursay looked very downcast, but she was accustomed to mastering herself, and her countenance changed as she approached us. She replied with a smile and in the freest and most open manner in the world to the awkward bow I made them. As for Hortense, whom I examined closely, she showed neither agitation nor pleasure on seeing me; but I could hear exclamations about her beauty from every side, and this added strength both to my love and to my pain. We passed one another without speaking.

"Is that, then, the woman who can no longer be loved except out of kindness?" said Mme de Mongennes, looking at Mme de Lursay. "It would be very singular if with so much beauty she could not kindle a passion still."

"But alas, Madam," answered Mme de Senanges, "that is precisely her case — and all your astonishment will not alter it. Well, Sir," she went on, addressing me, "can nothing bring you out of your reverie? Is it Mme de Lursay who is the cause of it?"

"I have already told you, Madam," I interrupted, "that she has no place in my heart. It is too fully engrossed by quite another idea to be divided, and even if this passion should cause me torments all my life, I am happy in the knowledge that it can never be effaced."

The love that consumed me gave me a passionate expression that Mme de Senanges misinterpreted. I saw her eyes light up.

"You, unhappy?" she said. "But why should you be? Should you even imagine that you might be? Does anyone give you reason to fear it? Be constant, by all means, but only insofar as always to be happy!"

I saw her mistake, but did not disabuse her. I cared little if she should think me in love with her: I was sure she could not think it for long.

Versac, who was pleased to amuse himself by contradicting Mme de Mongennes, passed us again at that moment.

"What can have happened to Mme de Mongennes to put her ideas into such confusion?" he asked. "She maintains that Mme de Lursay is beautiful, yet cannot conceive that Mlle de Théville should be so."

"As to the second, I am much of her opinion," replied Mme de Senanges. "Mlle de Théville has more ostentation than beauty and more manner than figure — altogether a person that cannot last long."

"For myself, and I am an expert," said Versac, "I can find only one fault in her, and that is an air of too much modesty. No doubt, she will unlearn that in society. Would that I might be the first of her teachers!"

"And while you are about it, you might give her some appearance of wit," said Mme de Mongennes. "Take away those great dull eyes that she does not know what to do with, and put meaning and fire into them. You will get all the more credit, as it will not be easy work."

"If you thought it more easy, it would certainly be less so," he replied. "The way you speak of her assures me that there is no charm that she lacks."

Outraged by the paltry jealousy that dictated all the two women said, and by their daring to despise Mlle de Théville's beauty, I could contain myself no longer: "Indeed," I said to Versac, "she is too beautiful for people not to want to find fault. It is safer to praise Mme de Lursay: she is less likely to win away other women's lovers."

The scornful manner in which I spoke could not have been very delightful to Mme de Mongennes, but I might have said far more disobliging things before she would have been offended. Her designs upon me were not so much destroyed as disguised, and though she no longer affected the extreme vivacity that had alarmed Mme de Senanges, and her desire of engaging me was outwardly more moderate, it was not in reality any less ardent. She judged, from the coldness of my behavior toward Mme de Senanges, that I did not love her in the least; and, too stupid not to be excessively vain, she did not doubt that I should yield to her as soon as she wished it. I judged her hopes by her attentions, and by certain looks whose value I was beginning to comprehend, though this did not make me any more responsive to them.

Since our meeting with Mlle de Théville, the tedium that Mme de Senanges inspired in me had redoubled, but the fear of making her think me impatient to go back to Mme de Lursay had kept me at her side. Fortunately, I did not need to restrain myself for long, and she went away a little while after, begging me to think of her and assuring me that she would not forget to write to me on her return from Versailles. I separated from her and Versac, resolved to seek out the one with as much care as I planned to employ in avoiding the other.

I was no sooner at liberty than I started to look for Mlle de Théville. However much I might suffer from her coldness, I suffered far worse from her absence: it was as if my jealousy tormented me more when I could no longer see her. I imagined that she must be thinking without interruption of Germeuil, and that her heart must be rejoicing more tranquilly than I could bear to imagine in the thoughts I fancied so dear to her. I hoped that at least my presence might prevent her from attending to him as much as I feared: at any event, and apart from any of these motives, I simply wanted to see her again, even if I still had to be the witness of her love for my rival.

At last I found her. They were coming toward me. Mme de Lursay blushed when she saw me, but I cared little for what she felt – it was in Hortense's eyes that I sought my fate. I thought she saw me approach without any great concern. It seemed to me it was all one to her whether I was with Mme de Senanges or with her; and these new proofs of her indifference completely pierced my heart.

While I was looking at Hortense, Mme de Lursay gazed fixedly at me with a mocking air, which I finally perceived, that increased the aversion I was beginning to feel for her. I knew what she wanted to say to me, and the ideas she had formed about Mme de Senanges. What had taken place between me and herself was still a secret, so it in itself imposed no reason for keeping silent. She could without betraying herself speak freely of the new love she thought me occupied by, and I was almost certain she had done so. If we had been alone, I would have been less embarrassed by an explanation in which I might have made it clear that I felt as little esteem for her as love, but the presence of Mme de Théville and Hortense gave her an advantage over me of which, without sacrificing all propriety, I could not deprive her.

"Well, Sir," she said with a jeer, "your violent headache did not last long, it seems?"

"To be sure," I replied, "my walk has cleared it."

"Is the cure to be attributed to the walk only?" she replied. "Has Mme de Senanges contributed nothing?"

"It had not struck me that it was she I had to thank for the improvement," I answered. "Now that by your kindness you have taught me better, I shall not forget to demonstrate my gratitude to her."

"She will no doubt give you more important grounds for it," she retorted. "I am sure she is not one to limit her benefactions to such trifles. A very generous lady, Mme de Senanges – but how is it that you stay here without her?"

"Because, of course, it was not possible for me to follow her," I replied with a sharpness I could no longer control. "However, the certainty of seeing her again before long softens the regret I must feel at her absence."

Mme de Lursay's only reply was a look of indignation which only increased mine; we thus expressed silently all the force of the anger we both felt. She did not confine herself to looks, but thinking to mortify me by vilifying Mme de Senanges, summoned up all her invention to describe her vices and follies in the most lurid terms. She could not have a worse opinion of her than I had myself, but instead of allowing her to speak ill of Mme de Senanges without hindrance, I felt obliged to defend her, which I did with so much warmth and so little restraint that it was no longer possible for Mme de Lursay to doubt my new passion, which hitherto she had only suspected. Blinded by my anger, I thought it not enough that I should appear only to esteem Mme de Senanges, and spoke as if I thought her young, beautiful, and witty, with all the enthusiasm one feels for an object that is beginning to please one.

I perceived, from Mme de Lursay's grieved looks, that I had convinced her that she had lost me, and for a few moments I tasted the pleasure of revenge. Only when it was too late did I see what this was going to cost me. Preoccupied with the desire of wounding Mme de Lursay, I had forgotten that Hortense also heard what I said, and that I could not persuade one of them of my love for Mme de Senanges without giving the same idea to the other. When this reflection struck me, I was quite overpowered. Before I had made this dreadful blunder, the only obstacle I had to overcome had been her coldness; but how should I dare to speak of my love now, after having maintained that Mme de Senanges had made the liveliest of impressions on me? Was I to confess the reasons that had led me to praise with so much energy a woman so deserving of contempt? Could I, without meriting her contempt, justify myself at Mme de Lursay's expense by betraying the secret of her heart? I, whom honor so strictly enjoined to ensure that it was never even guessed at!

The more clearly I saw myself condemned to silence, the less hope I saw of escaping from the embarrassing situation I had got myself into. Though Hortense appeared to have taken little interest in what I had been saying, a certain feeling, for which I could discover no foundation, kindled my hopes. Almost certain that I should one day have to justify myself to her, I already began to prepare every argument that might efface from her mind a prejudice that my own efforts had given her every right to entertain. Her sadness added to my confusion and uneasiness. A state of mind as singular as hers could hardly be attributed to any other cause than a secret and unhappy passion; but if it were true, as I had concluded that very day, that she loved Germeuil, what could be the cause of her melancholy? When I had left them, there had seemed no probability of any cloud arising between them. Was it his absence that made her feel so violent a sorrow? One is sad when one loses the beloved object for a long time; even if one leaves it only for a few moments, one thinks of it, is preoccupied by it; but such a reverie is tender rather than painful. Germeuil therefore could not be the cause of her sorrow. All in all, my only reason for supposing him my rival was the fact that, when we suspect we have one, it is naturally the friend whom the beloved seems most fond of who causes us the most unease.

The simplest method of delivering myself from mine was no doubt to explain myself to Hortense, as I knew very well. Yet to admit that this was necessary did not make the performance of it any easier. I could think of nothing that would be sure to bring me the enlightenment I wished for, nothing that would help me to discover whether Germeuil was the unknown beloved, or whether it was another I had to fear.

Caught up in this confusion of ideas and feelings, revolving all, testing all, without being able to fix on any, I walked at Hortense's side in a state not very different from hers. I wanted to interrupt her reverie but could think of nothing to say. I was just as unsuccessful in trying to get her to look at me, and we reached the gate without any sign from her that could instruct or satisfy me.

Mme de Lursay, who since my panegyric on Mme de Senanges had not spoken to me, asked me, in anguished tones, after seeing Mme de Théville and Hortense walk off, if I wished her to drive me back home, or to her own house. The pain she had caused me that day, and the state that Hortense's persistent coldness had thrown me into, both made me hostile to her proposal, and I replied shortly that I could do neither one nor the other. She seemed aghast at my reply and at the deep and sober bow with which I accompanied it – yet she insisted. I told her, with even less ceremony than before, that insuperable reasons prevented me from doing what she asked, and we separated at last, each equally wretched and dissatisfied with the other.

I returned home, my mind and heart both too disturbed for me to wish to see anyone there, and passed the night in painful and unprofitable reflection.

The imaginings of lovers, their doubts, their changing resolutions, are sufficiently well known for the conflicting emotions that tormented me to be very easily divined, and I have spoken too often of my inexperience – my story shows too clearly how many delusions I owed to it – for me to have to dwell further on the subject.

I was still undecided which plan to follow, when a servant entered, with the following note from Mme de Lursay:

> If I consulted only your heart, I should not put myself to the trouble of writing to you, and my silence would no doubt save me from further affronts. But as I am more loving than proud, I am not afraid to expose myself again. Today I am going to the country for two days. You do not deserve that I should inform you of it, still less that I should ask you to accompany me: yet I do both. So much indulgence on my part will perhaps only make you the more ungrateful; but if I cannot move you by my kindness, I should like at least to confound you by it. I am, besides, curious to know whether you see as many charms in Mme de Senanges today as you did yesterday. I am still willing to concern myself about what you think on this subject. Remember, though, that I may not be disposed to do so for long. Farewell. I shall expect you at four.

This note abated none of my anger against Mme de Lursay, and I had no wish for any explanations with her. So, without referring to the suddenness of this country excursion, of which I had heard not a word the day before, I wrote to her with the utmost coldness, saying that it was impossible for me to do as she wished, and that I had entered the previous day into engagements that I could not break. In our situation, my reply was an impertinent one – but the more I felt this, the more satisfied I was at having made it. I was determined to break with her. Out of all the turmoil of my ideas this was the only one that remained firmly in my head, and I could not reproach myself for a refusal which it seemed must assure and even hasten the rupture.

Nor was the hatred I now felt for Mme de Lursay the only consideration that made me write as I did. I did not fear the tediousness of being with her so much as the pain of being absent from Hortense, whom I did not wish to leave behind at a moment when it was important for me to tell her I loved her, or at least to keep a watch on my rivals. I spent the time I could not see her thinking of her, and it was scarcely five o'clock when I flew to her house.

I soon arrived and was admitted. Among several equipages that I saw in the courtyard, I noticed that of Mme de Lursay. I immediately saw the mistake I had made, and was in despair at the impossibility of retrieving it. I could not doubt that Hortense was to be one of the party I had just refused. The haughty tone in which I had written to Mme de Lursay saying I was unable to come made it out of the question for me to think of reopening the matter, and gave her every possible reason for not asking me to change my mind.

Furiously angry with myself, I went in, but trembling and upset. Mme de Lursay turned pale when she saw me – as much, I thought, with anger as surprise. Although I had deserved all her hatred, I still resented it as if she were doing me an injustice. However, I did not waste many thoughts on that. Hortense was talking to Germeuil, and the familiarity of their conversation, the surprise she showed on seeing me, and her sudden blush, drove all other ideas from my mind.

"You are to be of our party, no doubt, Sir?" said Mme de Théville.

"No, Madam," interposed Mme de Lursay quickly. "I invited him, but he had engagements that he cannot break. I am sure you can guess what they are."

"How foolish of him," said Germeuil. "I wager, Madam, that he has really nothing to do."

"I know for a fact that he has," she said shortly. "But time presses, and he will not wish to delay our departure, especially as we are certainly delaying his pleasures. Good-bye, Sir," she said to me, smiling, "perhaps another time I shall be more fortunate, or you less occupied."

With these words, she gave me her hand with as unconscious an air as if there had been no question of anything between us; and though I was beside myself with rage, I was obliged to conduct her to her carriage.

"It would be curious, however," she said to me in a low tone as we walked down the stairs, "if you were to be sorry for the answer you gave me. But no – you only know how to offend; I should be wrong to suppose you capable of repenting."

"For pity's sake, Madam," I answered, "let us be done with such talk. The time has gone by for it, for you and for me."

"I know your charming way of answering, but I shall overlook it," she replied. "Through you I have grown accustomed to being indulgent. I should simply like to know whether, since you are never long in the same opinion, you may not have thought better of this one. Do not be afraid to confess it: would you like to come?"

"Madam," I said, "that is a question I answered this morning."

"Very well," she said. "Be good enough to forget that I troubled to ask you twice."

She then made me one of those insulting bows to which I had several times treated her. I tried in vain to disguise my vexation. To see Germeuil with Hortense, and think that in the country he would find a thousand opportunities for tender phrases, was an insufferable torment to me, especially when I remembered that it was one I might have spared myself. As I saw them on the point of leaving, I repented of the false pride to which I had just sacrificed the dearest interest of my heart. I still held Mme de Lursay's hand, and I believed it would still not be difficult to obtain that which she had seemed so willing to grant. I therefore mastered my foolish vanity sufficiently to speak again of the excursion, which if it excluded me I could only contemplate with the bitterest anguish.

"If you had asked me sooner, Madam," I said to Mme de Lursay, "you would not have found me engaged."

"I believe you," she said, not looking at me.

"If you really wish –" I continued.

"No, indeed," she interrupted, "I wish nothing. I do not deserve the smallest sacrifice from you and will not accept any."

"You felt differently a moment ago," I said, "and I thought I might –"

"Well," she interrupted again, "I was wrong, and I have corrected myself."

With these words she quitted me, leaving me all the more piqued because by begging her for something I had refused a moment before I had compromised myself and humbled my pride for nothing.

Important as it was that I should not leave Hortense, I saw that this consideration must be made to yield to that which I owed myself and which love had already made me risk too far. So, still unable to forgive myself for letting Mme de Lursay think she had mortified me, I watched them go, in despair because Hortense, who had not even deigned to speak to me, had not witnessed my last exchange with Mme de Lursay, and so might attribute my refusal to my love for Mme de Senanges.

They had been gone some time before I emerged from the agitation this situation had plunged me into. When I came to myself again I returned home, to meditate deeply on the minutest details, draw false conclusions about all that had happened, and torment myself until Hortense's return.

Although I knew she was to stay two days in the country, I sent the next morning to see whether she was not back. Tormented by jealousy and impatience, the day after I went myself, and, not finding her, was infinitely tempted to follow her. Yet my vanity was greater than my love, and the fear of leading Mme de Lursay to suppose that I could not bear her absence prevailed, and made me stay in spite of my terrors.

I had only just returned when Versac was announced. In spite of my preoccupation with my love, I was weary of the solitude to which I had condemned myself, and delighted to see him again.

"I have come to see what you have been doing these two days," he said. "There is nowhere in Paris that I have not looked for you in vain."

"I am in the worst humor in the world," I answered.

"Are the fond lovers unhappy?" he asked. "I am not sorry to see you affected by Mme de Senanges's absence, but you must be so sure of being beloved –"

"Merciful heaven!" I cried

"This tragic exclamation astounds me," said he. "Can it be that she has not yet written to you?"

"No indeed," I replied. "She has been gone only two days, and you know she is not to write until her return."

"That is true," he rejoined, "but I am still surprised you have heard nothing. She asked leave to write to you the day before yesterday, and according to all the rules you should have received one or two notes by now. A charming woman, Mme de Senanges! One need fear no foolish hesitations or affected shrinkings with her. In an instant, her mind has understood and her heart divined all."

"That would not make me more inclined to love her," I replied. "A little indecision in the matter of choosing a lover is more becoming, I believe, than the alacrity you praise in Mme de Senanges."

"Once," said he, "I used to think like you, but times have changed. We will speak of it at more leisure. Now let us return to Mme de Senanges. After the hopes you have given and the attentions you have paid her, your indifference astonishes me."

"I?" I cried. "I have given her hopes?"

"But of course," he replied coolly. "When a man of your age visits a woman like Mme de Senanges, appears in public with her, and permits a correspondence to be established, he must have his reasons. One does not commonly do such things without a motive. She must think that you adore her."

"What she supposes is of no interest to me," I answered. "I know how to undeceive her."

"That would be very ill bred," he replied, "and you give her some right to complain of your behavior."

"It seems to me," I answered, "that I have more right to complain of hers. What reason has she to think I owe her my heart?"

"Your heart!" said he. "Novelists' jargon. What makes you suppose that is what she is asking for? She is incapable of so ridiculous a pretension."

"What does she want then?" I asked.

"A kind of intimate connection," he answered. "A warm friendship that resembles love in its pleasures without having any of its foolish niceties. In a word, she has a fancy for you, and that is all you owe her in return."

"Then I fear I shall owe it to her for a long time," said I.

"Perhaps," he answered. "On reflection, though, you will see that your repugnance is unreasonable. Mme de Senanges may not inspire you at present, but you cannot avoid seeing her soon in a more amiable light. It will happen in spite of you, but it will happen – unless you break with all custom and propriety."

"I am quite certain, whatever you may say," I replied, "that it will not happen. People may think what they like of me: I will have none of her."

"I am very sorry to hear it," said he. "All that remains is for you to make sure that you are right."

"But you?" I asked. "Would you have her?"

"If I was unfortunate enough for her to wish it," he said, "I do not see how I could act otherwise, though for a thousand reasons I should prefer to do without it."

"And why could I not do without it as well as you?"

"You are too young," he answered, "not to have Mme de Senanges. For you it is a duty; if I took her, it would only be out of politeness. You have need of a woman now to bring you into society, whereas I bring women into society who wish to be notorious in it. It is that which makes the difference between your choice and mine."

"Permit me one question," I said. "Indeed, you must not be surprised if in the course of this conversation I ask you several. You are telling me things that are too novel for me to be able to seize them as quickly as you might wish. And you must be prepared to find me incredulous as often as you astonish me."

"I have no other aim but to instruct you," he answered. "It will be a pleasure to me to clear away your doubts and to show you the world as you ought to see it. But in order that we may devote ourselves freely to subjects that by their range and variety may lead us far, let us seek out some quiet walk where we shall not be interrupted. I think the Étoile may suit our purpose."

I agreed to his proposal, and we set out.

We spoke only of indifferent matters on the way, and it was not until we arrived at the Étoile that we began a conversation that has had all too much influence on the conduct of my life.

"You have whetted my curiosity," I said to him. "Will you now satisfy it?"

"Depend upon it," he replied. "I shall be delighted to act as your instructor.

"There are certain matters of which one cannot remain ignorant long without incurring a sort of shame, because they constitute a knowledge of the world, and, without that, the advantages we have received from nature, instead of contributing to our enlightenment, may often hinder it. I am aware that this knowledge is, properly speaking, no more than a conglomeration of trifles, and that in many of its principles it offends against both honor and reason; but even while one despises it, one is obliged to learn it, and to set more store by it than by less frivolous acquirements, since, to our shame, it is less dangerous to be found wanting in heart than in manners.

"I see your attention wanders already," he added.

"No. I am listening most carefully," I answered. "Yet this serious tone is so strange in you that I cannot overcome my surprise. You, a philosopher!"

"There is no need for astonishment," said he. "The friendship I feel for you forbade me to deceive you for long, and your need of instruction obliges me to show you that I can both think and reflect. But I trust that you will preserve the utmost secrecy about what I have said, and about what I am going to say."

"What!" said I, laughing. "Would you not like me to say that Versac can think?"

"Indeed not," he replied gravely, "and you will soon learn why. But let us return to you."

"I have observed with surprise, on a thousand occasions, that you are utterly ignorant of the world. Although you are very young, you belong to a level of society which does not usually preserve so long the illusions I still find in you. Above all, I cannot be sufficiently amazed that you should know so little of women. My own reflections upon this subject may be of service to you. I do not flatter myself, of course, that my precepts alone can act as a sufficient guide, but at least they will lessen the power of the ideas that would otherwise delay your acquiring a just picture of the world, or even prevent it altogether.

"Necessary as a knowledge of women may be, you must not limit yourself to that science alone. The customs, proclivities, and errors of the age must also be the objects of your study, the difference being that while you will easily form an adequate notion of women, you may arrive at no more than an imperfect knowledge of the rest, even after the most persistent application.

"It is an error to suppose that one may preserve in the world the innocence one commonly possesses on entering it, or that one can be always virtuous and natural without risking both reputation and fortune. In the world, the mind and the heart cannot help being spoiled; everything there is fashion and affectation. Virtues, beauty, talents are all things purely arbitrary, and one cannot succeed except by twisting oneself ceaselessly into conformity. These are principles you must never lose sight of. Yet it is not enough merely to know that to succeed we must be ridiculous. You must study carefully the tone of the society in which our rank has placed us, the absurdities that are most appropriate to our position; in a word, those that are in fashion. And this study requires more skill and attention than you perhaps imagine."

"What do you mean," I asked, "by absurdities that are in fashion?"

"I mean," said he, "those that are subject to variation according to caprice – those that, like all fashions, reign only for a certain time and while they are in vogue eclipse all others. It is during their season of popularity that one must seize them: it can be as fruitless to adopt them when the world is beginning to tire of them as it is dangerous to retain them when they are absolutely proscribed."

"But if everyone knows that a fashion is absurd," I said, "how do people bring themselves to adopt it?"

"Very few people are sufficiently acquainted with reflection even to know what it is," he replied. "And those who do think often abandon themselves to falling in with the errors that in their hearts they most condemn. What is more, it is nearly always to those of us who think most deeply that society owes the opinions that disgrace the understanding, and the affected manners that ruin and distort the face. Take me, for example: the inventor, or at least the perfecter, of almost all the extravagances that are adopted. Do you suppose I choose, maintain, and vary them merely by caprice, without being ruled and guided by my knowledge of the world?"

"I do not know all the reasons that may influence you," I answered, "but I suppose you only invent these ridiculous ways because you believe them to be the means of seduction in society."

"Yes, I do believe it," he replied, "and my success in the world is sufficient proof, I think, that I am not mistaken, and that only by following in my footsteps can one win a reputation as notable as mine. Do not be troubled, however, by the name I give to the things that succeed in pleasing: when an absurdity is accepted, it is grace, charm, wit; it is only when people wear it out and tire of it that they give it the name it really deserves."

"Yet how may one know that an absurdity is beginning to grow stale?" I asked.

"By the scant attention the women pay to it," he replied.

"It seems to me the study you prescribe is a very difficult one," I said.

"No," he answered. "The art of pleasing nowadays may be reduced to a few quite simple precepts not at all hard to put into practice. I assume, to begin with, and with sufficient reason, I think, that the only object of a man of our rank and your age must be to make his name celebrated. The simplest and at the same time most agreeable way of achieving this is to let it appear that all your actions are undertaken with only women in mind, that you believe in no other charm but that which attracts them, and think the kind of wit that pleases them is the only kind that ought to please at all. It is only by seeming to defer to all their wishes that one succeeds in dominating them. I can easily convince you of this truth – but, before I speak to you about women, I have some advice to give you about the path you must follow in order to please in society; advice based, I may add, on my own experience.

"The first thing is to persuade oneself that by following known principles one can never be anything but ordinary; that one appears remarkable, only in departing from them; that men only admire what shocks them, and that singularity alone can produce this effect. One cannot therefore be too singular: that is to say, one cannot affect too much dissimilarity from everyone else, both in thoughts and in deeds. A failing peculiar to yourself gains you more credit than a virtue shared with another.

"But that is not all. You must learn to disguise your character so perfectly that it would be vain for anyone to try to untangle it. And you must add to the art of deceiving others that of seeing through them, and always try to detect beneath the appearance they wish to present to you what they are in fact. It is a great fault in the eyes of the world to wish to see everything in its true light. Never appear offended at the vices that are revealed to you, and never boast of having discovered those that people think they have concealed. It is often better to give people a poor opinion of your understanding than to show its real strength; to hide your liking for reflection under a careless and irresponsible manner, and sacrifice your vanity to your interest. We never disguise ourselves so carefully as before those we believe to be of a critical disposition. Their perspicacity makes us uneasy. We mock their intelligence but wish at the same time to show them they have no more than we have. Even though they cannot correct us, they force us to dissemble what we are, and our failings are lost to them. If we make a study of men, let it not be to instruct them but, rather, to be able to understand them. Let us renounce the glory of giving them lessons. Let us sometimes appear their imitators so that we may more safely be their judges; let us help them by our example, and even by our praises, to reveal them-selves to us; and let our understanding serve only to help us to accom-modate ourselves to all opinions. It is only by appearing to give full rein to impertinence oneself that one makes sure of missing none of any-one else's."

"It seems to me you contradict yourself," I interrupted. "This last pre-cept cancels the other. If I become an imitator, I cease to be singular."

"No," he replied. "The pliancy of mind that I advise does not ex-clude singularity. The one is no less necessary than the other: without the second, you will impress no one, and without the first, you will make everyone dislike you, or at least lose the reward of all your obser-vations. Besides, people are never less able to guess what you are than when you appear to be everything – and a superior genius can enhance what others suggest to him and make it look new even to them.

"One thing that is extremely necessary is never to waste time on any-thing except showing yourself to advantage. You will have been told, or have perhaps read, that it is more fitting to give praise to others; but it seems to me they may be relied upon to do that for themselves. For my part, I have never seen anyone, whatever his pretensions to mod-esty, who did not very rapidly find a way of informing me of how high he stood in his own estimation and how high he ought to stand in mine.

"Of all the virtues, modesty is the one that has always seemed to me to profit least the person who practices it. We may not be convinced in our hearts of our own merit, but let us appear to be so: let a certain confidence radiate from our eyes, our voices, our gestures, even from the way we behave toward others. Above all, let us always speak of, and praise, ourselves: let us not be afraid to say, and to repeat, that we are possessed of superior merit. There are a thousand who are thought to possess it for no other reason than that they never cease to claim it. Do not be put out by the coldness and disgust with which you are heard, or even by the reproach that you never think of anything but yourself. Any man who criticizes you for talking too much about yourself only does so because you deny him the opportunity of doing the same: if you were modest, you would be a martyr to his vanity. Besides, I am not sure that someone who talks to others about what he believes to be his own worth is more to blame than someone who thinks that by being silent on the subject he is making a sacrifice to society: there may be a good deal of pride in someone who thinks himself obliged to be modest.

"Whatever the case, it is safer to subjugate others than to immolate one's own self-esteem. Too great a desire to please presupposes a need for approval. They are never more ready to judge us severely than when we make servile efforts to win their favor. To be timid with a man is to admit that we think him our superior. This fear of displeasing, while it flatters him, does not win him over. Our subservience encourages him to see faults in us that, without our precautions, he might never have dared to take notice of. It is true that he may be good enough to condone them, but the magnanimity with which he excuses them is an insult which more self-confidence would have spared us. The arrogant fellow who condescends so far as to reassure us – who, while blaming our vices, has too little respect for us to dissemble his own – would have thought himself lucky to obtain our indulgence if we had not judged it necessary to seek his.

"Nor is this the only disadvantage that comes of timidity. I am not speaking of the kind that is due merely to inexperience, and that only clouds the mind and the countenance for a short while, but of the kind that springs from either too little knowledge of our own advantages or too high an estimate of other people's, and discourages us, makes us inferior to ourselves, and causes us to acknowledge as masters or at least equals people whom nature has placed beneath us.

"You cannot therefore rely too confidently upon your own powers nor make too light of other people's. Above all, take care not to form too high an opinion of society: do not imagine that to shine there one must be endowed with superior merit. If you still think that, look at me, and see – I cite myself as an example, and shall no doubt do so again – what I become when I wish to please: what affectations, what forced graces, what frivolous ideas! Are there any extravagances that I will not embrace?

"Do you suppose that it was without reflection that I condemned myself to the torment of continually disguising myself? I entered early into society and did not take long to see through it. I saw solid virtues banished or at best mocked, and women, the only judges of our merit, finding worth in us in proportion to our readiness to conform to their ideas. Certain that I should be unable without drowning to go against the current, I went with it. I sacrificed all to frivolity: I became foolish in order to seem more brilliant – in short, I created in myself the vices I needed to please. And this carefully calculated behavior brought me success.

"I was born so different from what I appear that it was not without extreme difficulty that I succeeded in ruining my understanding. I blushed sometimes at my insolence; I could slander only timidly. I was a conceited young fop, it is true, but without grace, without brilliance, the same as countless others, and still far from the superiority I have since acquired in this class.

"It is no doubt easy to be a fop: anyone who wishes to avoid it has to keep a constant watch on himself, and there is no one who has not his own brand of self-conceit. Yet it is not so easy to acquire the special kind I needed, that bold and singular conceit which, owing nothing to any model, is alone worthy to serve as one.

"For whatever the advantages of conceit, it must not be supposed that it can succeed on its own, or that a man who is a dandy by nature and not on principle will go as far as one who can exploit his fatuity with the aid of his reason, and who, though devoted to the effort to win people over and pushing impertinence as far as it will go, is not made drunk by success, and never forgets how to see himself clearly in private. A dandy of limited intelligence, who really believes in all the distinctions he claims for himself, will never reach the heights. You cannot conceive how much wit is necessary to procure a success that is brilliant and lasting in a sphere where you have so many rivals to combat and where the caprice of one woman is often enough to make the name of some fellow who has the least claim to celebrity! How much perspicacity is needed to grasp the character of a woman you wish to lay siege to, or – what is infinitely more gratifying and does happen sometimes – whom you wish to compel to be the first to speak! What sound judgment you must be gifted with not to err about the kind of ridiculousness you must exhibit to make her resistance crumble more rapidly! What skill you must have to be able to carry on several intrigues at once, which your honor requires you not to conceal from the public, but which you must hide from each of the women concerned! Do you not think a man's understanding must have a great variety and range to be always and without restraint that which the moment requires: tender with the delicate, sensual with the voluptuous, gallant with the coquette? To be passionate without feeling, to weep without being moved, to plague without being jealous: those are all roles that you have to play, that is the sort of man you have to be. Not to mention that you cannot have too much experience in order to be able to see a woman as she is, in spite of the immense care she takes to disguise herself, and not to be taken in any more by the false virtue she sometimes puts forward before she has yielded than by her pretended desire to keep you once she has surrendered."

"All this detail astonishes me," said I. "I am terrified; I know I could never bear the weight of it."

"I admit it is not everybody's business," he answered, "but I have a higher opinion of you than you have of yourself, and I make no doubt that I shall soon be sharing the public's attention with you. But let us continue.

"I told you that you could not speak too often about yourself. To this precept I add another that I judge no less necessary: it is that, as a general thing, you cannot monopolize the conversation too much. The essential in society is not to wait until your imagination furnishes you with ideas. To shine always, you have only to wish to do so.

"The arrangement or, rather, the abuse of words, does duty for thought. I have seen many of those barren fellows who neither think nor reason, to whom sound judgment and grace are forbidden qualities, who talk with an air of authority about the very things they are most ignorant of, join volubility to impudence, and lie as often as they open their lips — I have seen these fellows preferred to men of considerable wit, who are modest, natural, and truthful, and despise lying and jargon alike. So remember that modesty nullifies all grace and talent — that by thinking about what one is going to say, one loses the opportunity to say it, and that in order to persuade, it is necessary to make a great deal of noise."

"I remember having sometimes seen the sort of persons you describe," I said, "but, far from pleasing, it seemed to me they met with all the contempt they deserved, and people found them as insufferable as they really are."

"You may say," he replied, "that people blamed their extravagances or even laughed at them, but that, for all that, they were found displeasing – no, experience teaches just the opposite. The great advantage of folly is that it charms and seduces the very people who criticize it most severely.

"Of all those in fashion at the moment, uproariousness is the one that makes the most impression, especially upon women. They regard as genuine passions only those which take them by storm. Those attachments which are sometimes formed by frequent association seem to them for the most part affairs of convenience, requiring only a moderate attention. A gradual impression can never produce a lively effect upon them. To love warmly, they must be ignorant of what has moved them to do so. They have been told that a passion, if it is to be a strong one, must begin with a profound agitation, and they have believed this so long now it is unlikely they will ever give it up. Nothing is better fitted to awaken this magical agitation in their hearts than the self-intoxication that makes you disregard all risk and brings into play all the graces of your person or conceals all its defects. The woman who sees it gives herself over to admiration, astonishment, enchantment – and because she does not wish to reflect, persuades herself that your charms leave her no time for it. If by any chance she should think of resistance, it is only the better to convince herself that it would be useless, and that to something so forceful, so unexpected – in short, so extraordinary – one can oppose nothing but sympathy. A doctrine well adapted of course to enable her to yield rapidly without exposing herself to ill opinion: for there is no man who is not more flattered at having suddenly inspired a violent passion than at having called one forth by degrees."

"Whatever the advantages of unbridled impudence," I said, "I doubt whether I could ever adopt a philosophy that would oblige me to hide whatever virtues I had to adorn myself with vices I had not."

"What you say is splendid morality," he replied, "but morality and the world do not always agree, and you will learn that a man can only succeed in the one at the expense of the other. It is better, once again, to adopt the vices of the age, or at least to defer to them, rather than display virtues that would appear strange or not in good taste."

"Good taste!" I repeated.

"Perhaps you do not yet know what it is?" he answered mockingly.

"I confess that I have often been wearied by the expression," said I, "the more so as no one has so far been able to give me a definition of it. This famous good breeding, what does it consist in? These people who look for it everywhere and find it in so few men and so few things — do they have it themselves? What in fact is it?"

"An embarrassing question," he replied. "It is a term, a manner of speaking that everyone uses and nobody understands. What we call good breeding is our own mode of behavior, and we are determined never to find it except in those who think, speak, and act like ourselves. For myself, until someone else shall define it better, I suppose it to consist in rank, and the ability to carry off one's follies; and in telling you all that is necessary for the acquisition of it, I shall give you the opportunity of deciding whether my definition is just.

"A negligence of demeanor that in women is carried to the point of immodesty, and in us goes beyond what may be justly called freedom and ease; affected tones and manners, whether in their liveliness or their languor; a frivolous and malicious wit; circuitous speech — all these are what, if I am not mistaken, constitute good breeding nowadays. Yet these ideas are too general to be of much assistance to you: let us develop them."

"Anyone who wishes to be well bred must avoid saying anything thought out: however naturally and modestly he expresses it, people will consider it flagrant affectation to speak differently from all the world, and what is said of a man who falls into this error is not that he has wit but that he thinks he has it.

"As it is scandal alone that the world means by wit nowadays, people have taken pains to give it a particular distinction, and it is more than anything else by their style of slandering others that one recognizes those who are well bred. Scandal cannot be too cruel or too precious. As a general thing, and even when one has the least intention of mocking or the least reason for doing so, one cannot adopt too derisive an air or too malicious a tone. Nothing makes others more uneasy, or gives a better impression of your own liveliness and wit. Let your smile be a scornful one, let all your words be insipidly caustic. With such aids a man, however little his merit, is held to be distinguished, because he makes himself feared, and because in the world a fool who devotes himself to spitefulness is more respected than a man of wit who, too far above these base objects to descend to their level, laughs privately at the faults of the age, and has too much contempt for them to blame them aloud.

"However, the noble nonchalance required in one's manners, necessary as that is, is nothing without a certain nonchalance of mind. People of good breeding leave to the vulgar herd both the trouble of thinking and the fear of not understanding. Convinced that the more

the mind is cultivated, the less spontaneity it retains, they have voluntarily confined themselves to a few trivial ideas which they circle around
forever. Or if by any chance they know anything, it is in so superficial
a manner, and they themselves take so little account of it, that it would
be impossible to attribute failings to them in that connection. As nothing is more ignoble in a woman than to be virtuous, so nothing is more
unseemly in a man of breeding than to be taken for a scholar. The
extreme ignorance to which custom seems to condemn him is all the
more singular in that, at the same time, it is established that he must
never hesitate to express an opinion."

"Indeed," I said, "that must be awkward."

"Less than you suppose," he replied. "A profound ignorance allied
to a great deal of modesty would indeed be very inconvenient – but
joined to extreme presumption, I can assure you it presents no difficulty at all. Besides, whom are you usually talking to that you should
be so anxious about what you say? If it is well bred to be always decisive, it is ill bred ever to justify your decision or your own good opinion of yourself. To be ignorant of all and think you know everything;
to see nothing, whatever it may be, that you do not either scorn or
praise to excess; to believe yourself equally capable of gravity and wit;
to have no dread of being ridiculous, and never be anything else; to put
elegance in your turns of phrase and puerility in your ideas; to utter
absurdities, maintain them, and start again: that is, to be most super-
latively well bred."

"One thing puzzles me," I interrupted. "How can people who have
never learned anything, or have thought themselves obliged to forget
it all, talk ceaselessly? It must take a very fertile mind to keep up a perpetual conversation without the various resources that knowledge provides. And I observe that people in society never run dry."

"That is because there is nothing in the well," he answered. "You
have noticed that people in society never run dry of words: have you
not also observed that they speak without ever saying anything? That a
few favorite words, a few affected phrases, a few exclamations, vague
smiles, and little significant looks, do duty for everything?"

"But people hold forth perpetually," said I.

"Yes, indeed," he answered. "They hold forth without thinking, and
that is the very acme of good breeding. Could one pursue an idea without dwelling on it at length? You may propose one, but have you ever
the time to establish it? Is it not an offense against propriety even to
think of it? Yes. Conversation, if it is to be lively, cannot be too inconsequent. A man who talks about war must yield to a woman who wishes

to talk about love; and she, in the midst of all the ideas which so noble a subject, and one in which she is so expert, inspires in her, must be silent to listen to an obscene but gallant couplet; and that, or the lady who sings it, must give way, to everybody's great regret, to a fragment of morality, which is hastily interrupted to miss none of a piece of gossip which – although it is heard with exquisite pleasure whether well told or ill – is cut short by some trite reflections on music or poetry, which gradually die away and are followed by some political observations on the government, which an account of certain singular incidents at cards cuts short at the most unexpected moment: and finally some coxcomb, who ceased to pay attention long ago, crosses the circle and upsets all to go and tell a woman on the other side of the room that she is not wearing enough rouge, or that she is as beautiful as an angel."

"A curious picture," said I.

"A true one nevertheless," he replied. "In any event, it may prove to you that there is no one who cannot, either in his own vanity or in the barrenness of others, find the means of forgetting his worthlessness, and of arrogating to himself, in spite of nature herself, a sort of merit that puts him on a level with the rest of the world."

"But you," I said. "Are you a man of breeding?"

"Most certainly," he replied. "I despise it, but I have adopted it. You must have observed that I never dare speak to anyone as I have just spoken to you, and if I asked you to keep all that I said absolutely secret, it is because it is of the utmost importance that no one should know what I am and how much I disguise myself. I recommend you, once more, to imitate me. Unless you condescend to do as I do, you will only acquire the reputation of a stiff-necked fellow unfit for society. The more resolutely you refuse to adopt the vices of others, the more eagerly will they attribute to you vices of your own. I am not the only one who has concluded that in order not to be thought ridiculous one must become, or at least appear, so. But so-called good breeding has fewer admirers than is supposed, and some of those who seem to support it the most are nonetheless persuaded, as am I, that to be really well bred a man should have a mind that is ornate but not pedantic, elegant without affectation, gay without being vulgar, and easy without being indecent.

"And now," he went on, "we come to women. Yet our conversation has already been of such enormous length that, were it more ordered and its ideas pursued more deeply, it might almost pass for a moral treatise. Let us postpone the rest to another day. If you are as eager to learn as I am to instruct, we shall easily find an opportunity."

"At least," said I, "answer me one question. Why is it necessary for us to be launched in society by a woman?"

"Simple as that question may seem," he replied, "it involves so many considerations that I could not answer it without going into infinite detail. The study of women has given me a good deal of pleasure, and I think I now know them pretty well. I shall probably exhaust your patience talking about them."

"Well then," I said, "just give me a brief idea. We can go into it more deeply another day."

"No," he answered, "it would be just as much trouble for me, and you would not be properly taught. It is a subject that must be treated methodically, and it merits particular attention."

"For my part," I said, "it seems to me that to try so earnestly to understand women is to work very hard for one's pleasures. And this study, if indeed one does not lose sight of it, must occupy the mind at those very moments when feeling alone should operate. Besides, I think it is better to have too much confidence in one's beloved than to examine her too severely."

"You evidently assume," he replied, "that the beloved must be unequal to scrutiny."

"I know so little of women," I answered, "that it would hardly be appropriate for me to speak decidedly about what I think of them. At the same time, though, I believe there are certain women of whom I might, pending your instruction, think as poorly as I like. Do you not leave me free, for example, on the subject of Mme de Senanges?"

"Oh, yes," he answered. "But if you speak ill of her to me, you will be very ashamed of it one day; and you will be even more ashamed a little later, if you praise her. I can foresee all that will result from the distaste you have conceived, although unjustly, for her. You will come to do justice, in spite of yourself, to her charms, and who can say that even now it is not merely through pride that you dissemble the impression she has made on you? Who knows, in fact, whether while you appear so satisfied with her absence and the silence she maintains, you are not really longing for her return and dying of anguish at her negligence?"

"If that is the case," I replied, "it must be admitted that the torments of love are very easy to bear, for no one could be less occupied with anything than I am with Mme de Senanges. I will admit my surprise, however, that out of two women who appear to me of equal merit, you do not try to decide me in favor of the younger and, after all, the more amiable, Mme de Mongennes."

"I certainly do not oppose it," he interrupted, "but I cannot in honor recommend you to take her. And without entering into any reasons, which would take us too far at the moment, I tell you simply that Mme de Senanges is more suitable for you than Mme de Mongennes: the latter would think nothing, even while she accepted you, of her good fortune in pleasing you; the other could never be proud enough of it: and at your age it is the more grateful and not the more amiable that you ought to prefer."

We reentered the carriage, and spent the rest of our time together, he in trying to convince me of the necessity of taking Mme de Senanges, I in persuading him that this could never be.

I was no sooner home than, without much further reflection on what Versac had said, I resumed my ordinary pursuits: dreaming of Hortense, pining at her absence, and sighing for her return were the only things I could give my mind to.

The day so eagerly awaited came at last. I went to Hortense's house, and was told that she and Mme de Théville had returned and gone out again. I assumed, I know not why, that they must be at Mme de Lursay's, and I flew there directly. The interest that took me to her house was too lively to be counteracted by the fear of seeing her again, and besides, my anger had abated, partly with time and partly through the reflections I had come to make, in spite of myself, upon my own injustice.

There were a large number of people at Mme de Lursay's, but I could not see Hortense. The hope of seeing her arrive, and the certainty that in such a crowd Mme de Lursay would not have an opportunity of speaking to me, moderated my disappointment and persuaded me to stay. She was at cards when I arrived. She seemed neither troubled nor moved by my presence, and used the same manner toward me as she had when there was as yet no question of anything between us.

After the first politenesses, which she observed in the customary manner, without embarrassment or affectation, she returned to the game. I was near her, and she spoke to me now and then of the strange turns in the play, but in a detached manner: there was so much gaiety in her looks, and her wit seemed so unforced that I was sure she must have forgotten me.

The reasons I had for hoping for her indifference made me welcome joyfully any proofs of it. Determined as I was to break with her, I still did not know how to tell her that I no longer loved her. The respect she had inspired in me was like those illusions of childhood that one must struggle against so long before they are shattered.

Whatever I might have thought about her then, the esteem I had once had for her still tyrannized over me and forced me to conceal my feelings. Above all, I dreaded an explanation that could only put me at a disadvantage, because there had been nothing in her behavior to justify my desertion, whereas I had everything to reproach myself for in mine. The attitude she now seemed to be taking was the only one that could suit my purposes: it enabled us to break without fuss, without altercation, without delay, and absolved both of us from those disastrous conversations that often estrange lovers who are parting from one another more than their actual grievances.

In the midst of all these subjects for self-congratulation, however, I could not help feeling a certain emotion. Although delighted that she had given me up, I could not understand how she had done so so quickly. I feared that her coolness must be an affectation, and that I owed it only to the constraint imposed by the company present. Although I knew little of love, I fancied that it could not die all at once – that one might, in a violent fit of jealousy, form the resolution of ceasing to love, but that one would not carry it out; that often one might disguise one's feelings, and even try to hide them from the person who has inspired them, but that this dissimulation costs too much to last long, and one often abandons this feigned tranquillity only to burst forth with less restraint than ever.

To find out the truth of the matter, I studied her carefully, and the more my scrutiny reassured me that the change was real, the more the joy it had first caused me seemed to abate. Without divining the cause of the dissatisfaction that now spread through my heart, I gave myself up to it: I fell into a reverie, and though I still thought myself delighted at having lost Mme de Lursay, I no longer felt grateful to her for her inconstancy.

At last, I asked myself what sort of interest it could be that made me concerned in the emotions of a woman I no longer loved and had never even loved at all. After all, what did it matter to me that she had taken back her heart, and what had I to fear except the misfortune of her loving me still?

This was sound sense, and by dint of repeating it to myself I thought I had got the better of my vanity. It was not without reason that Mme de Lursay had sought to mortify it, nor was it without success.

Her game ended. She suggested I play with her; I agreed. I was growing tired of being idle, and I thought that the occupation of the game would chase away certain ideas that were beginning to trouble me. So I started to play, but very absently, and hardly daring to look at Mme de Lursay, whose assured and tranquil manner never wavered, and who exposed herself boldly to the examination she could see I was making of her.

Up till then I could simply believe that she no longer loved me: she had not yet given me grounds for thinking that she loved another.

The Marquis of ———, who was playing with us and whom she had brought back from the country with her, apparently struck her as a suitable means for making me uneasy. She began to smile and gaze at him, and finally to make those little advances that, though trifling in themselves, become unmistakable when they are repeated.

Without committing herself to the point of giving him hopes and drawing from him a declaration that would have embarrassed her, she did enough to make me understand that, not content with breaking with me, she was trying to console herself for my loss, and that this was assuredly the beginning of an adventure. I never looked at her, but I found her eyes fixed on the Marquis, and she no sooner perceived the attention with which I observed her than she swiftly looked back at her cards, as if I was the person from whom she most wished to conceal her feelings.

These maneuvers made me impatient at last: it was not that my heart was involved, but it seemed to me I was cast in a very disagreeable role that she might have spared me. I felt so much contempt for her, she inspired so much indignation in me, that I could scarcely conceal it!

Versac did not deceive me, I said to myself. I do not know how a woman like this can be called nothing worse than a coquette. No one can ever have behaved with less delicacy. That she should have ceased to love me is only natural, I am obliged to her for her change of heart, and God forbid that I should wish to reproach her for it! But that she should have no scruples, that with less modesty than she could claim to find in Mme de Senanges, without even having told me that she proposed to break with me, without regard for my presence, without even being sure that I no longer loved her, she should throw herself with so much ardor into another attachment, that was really something I could never have imagined. She never did love me, I went on. I was only, like Pranzi and a thousand others, the object of her caprice. The man who pleases her today will be a stranger to her tomorrow, and I shall soon have the pleasure of seeing him, too, displaced by a successor.

While I was thinking such unflattering thoughts about her, I forgot to guard my expression, and my cold and angry looks made it impossible for her to be ignorant of what was going on in my heart. I let signs of impatience escape me which she knew could never ordinarily be caused by the game and I could not even pretend to attribute to it. I looked every moment at my watch, and as if that was not enough to tell me what the time was, I consulted other people's too. Mme de

Lursay addressed two questions to me without receiving any reply that corresponded to what she had asked. I had become quite stupid, and all because of a woman to whom a moment before I would cheerfully have said, "Let us part, let us cease to mean anything to one another"; a woman whose change of heart was absolutely necessary to me; a woman the very idea of whom had become irksome; and what was most singular of all was that the heart her inconstancy was ravaging now belonged entirely to another.

How absurd! And we dare to reproach women for their vanity! We, who are continually the victim of our own, which snatches us at will from hate to love and love to hate, and makes us sacrifice the most tenderly and most deservedly loved mistress to the woman whom we love the least and often despise the most in all the world!

Such, more or less, was my situation. I was insensibly yielding to Mme de Lursay without knowing what I was doing. I was outraged that she could think so soon of another engagement, and what, if I had been able to judge rightly, would have detached me from her forever, only served to make her more dangerous to my heart than before.

I could not say, however, that the feeling she aroused in me was love: I was carried along by emotions that I did not understand and could not have defined. They were violent without being passionate; there was not a trace of desire in them, and I was jealous without being in love. If she had for an instant appeared to have any feeling for me, if I had seen her jealous or angry again and making efforts to win me back to her, the spell would have been broken. If my vanity had been satisfied by seeing her humiliation, my heart would have seen in her then only an object of indifference, perhaps contempt.

But this did not happen. Mme de Lursay knew how dangerous it would be for her to undeceive me: she did not need to study me to decipher what was going on in my heart. I would have been the first on whom her stratagem, old as it was, would have been powerless; but in order to get all the profit she expected from it, she had to push it as far as it could be made to go. I was still only shaken, and she wanted me defeated.

The game she had engaged me in was no sooner over than, in the first impulse of anger, I approached her to take leave; but with so constrained an air that she could easily see it would not be difficult to make me stay.

"Where are you off to?" she cried gaily. "You must be mad! It is very late, and I was counting on you. You will offend me if you do not stay!"

"I shall offend you much more if I do," I replied in tones of emotion. "I am only going in order to avoid displeasing you."

"I am quite sincere in asking you to stay," she said. "It always gives me great pleasure to see you. I cannot conceive what can ever have given you the idea that you are not welcome here. We are so accustomed to seeing you behave with the utmost freedom that we cannot fail to be surprised – I above all – to see you stand on ceremonies that were long ago banished between us."

"I think, Madam," I replied, "they are now more necessary than ever."

"What an idea!" she answered, shrugging her shoulders. "How unreasonable you are!"

"I am not at all unreasonable, Madam," said I, "and you know very well –"

"Well," she interrupted, rising as if unwilling to go into details, "you must do as you please. I do not want to inconvenience you. Stay, and you will please me; but go, if what I propose does not suit you."

I judged by the coolness of her manner that she really wanted me to go, and that she intended to devote the time after supper to the Marquis. I proposed myself the secret pleasure of hindering her by my presence, and moreover of giving myself the satisfaction of seeing her degrade herself further and further in my eyes, and so justify all the contempt I supposed myself to feel for her.

A little while after, supper was served. Without thinking, or so I imagined, and solely from habit, I went to sit by Mme de Lursay. She perceived it, and far from being pleased, arranged matters so that it was the Marquis, whom I still regarded as my successor, who sat down in the place where I wanted to be. Although this mark of preference for him was adroitly managed, it did not escape me, and I resented it bitterly. If she had offered the place to me, I should certainly not have taken it; but I could not see it filled by another without anger.

The supper soon became animated. Mme de Lursay, who intended, after having mortified my pride, to make herself pleasing to me once more, left nothing undone that might help her to succeed. That beguiling coquetry which has more power over us than beauty itself, those provocative airs that we sometimes scorn and always yield to, the tenderest of smiles, the warmest of looks, everything was employed, and employed in vain. Convinced that she assumed all these charms with the sole desire of engaging my rival, I hardened my heart against them. Her gaiety seemed to me constrained, her wit affected, the graces with which she had embellished herself seemed to me quite unsuited to her age. I looked at everything that was going on with jealous eyes. My heart was shaken with anger, but tranquil as far as love was concerned. In any event, consumed entirely by my hatred for Mme de

Lursay, I did not notice that I found her very beautiful.

We show our desires too clearly, they act too sensibly upon us, to escape detection by even the least perspicacious of women. Mme de Lursay, who was the last woman to be deceived as to my feelings, knew by the coldness of my looks that she was not making as strong an impression upon me as she could have wished. She probably feared she might have left me too long under the supposition that she no longer cared for me, for without quite abandoning her first plan she began to look at me with a little more warmth than hitherto.

Yet she did not do enough to bring me out of the state she had put me in before, and it was wise of her to take no further risks at that stage. Even if she had won me over to the extent that she wished, what value was there for her in a momentary seduction, which a little reflection on my part would have undone, or that would have vanished of its own accord before she could grasp it; and which perhaps, through being so precipitate, would have stirred my imagination while leaving it unsatisfied, and so left me less responsive at the very moment when it was important that I should be most eager?

She was wise enough to have such reflections, and no doubt she did. Supper continued, and she showed me no more than the attentions that are usual in society, which women pay to the men they are least concerned about when they are obliged to see one another. Her words were as measured as her looks, and she conducted herself with such skill that after first having been led to believe that she had seriously broken with me and was thinking of forming an engagement with another, I left the table thinking it might not be impossible to make her recollect that she had loved me and to find her now more tenderly disposed toward me than ever.

Although it was natural that I, vain as I was, should wish to reengage her affections, and that my emotions should lead to desires, it was not really that which moved me. I was piqued at Mme de Lursay's not regretting me, although I did not regret her. A little while after supper, having almost forgotten my purpose in staying, I was ready to follow some of the guests who were leaving.

Let her stay, I said to myself, with the fortunate lover who succeeds me. Let them pass the most charming of nights together. What do their pleasures matter to me that I should want to disturb them? I do not love; why should I be jealous?

As a result of this argument I rose, and the Marquis, whom I had supposed to be so impatient to find himself alone with Mme de Lursay, began to take leave of her too. This astonished me. I thought she would try to make him remain, but after having coolly pointed out that he might have stayed till later, she let him go without even arranging when they should see one another again.

Such complete indifference, after what had passed, did not strike me as natural. However, I did not conclude that they were not interested in one another and that my suspicions were ill founded. On the contrary, I believed that as they had had a long whispered conversation, during which she had worn an air of secrecy and embarrassment, their arrangements were already made, that the Marquis's sudden withdrawal was only simulated, and that as soon as the few guests that remained should have left, he would reappear.

This was not at all a fanciful idea: I could entertain it without going against either probability or custom. I thought, moreover, that it would be as shrewd to thwart Mme de Lursay in her rendezvous as it had been to have guessed that it would take place. I took a malicious pleasure in the idea of staying so long that the Marquis would grow impatient and might even conclude that unless I had once received her favors, or did so still, I would not have had the right to be as presumptuous as I fully intended to appear to him.

These motives were reinforced by another to which I was not insensible, which more than all the others led me to wish to speak privately with Mme de Lursay. I was convinced that she had deceived me, and that I could never forgive her falseness in trying to make me think her respectable. It seemed to me that, although I never wished us to meet again on our former footing, my honor required that I should let her know how well I understood her and should deprive her of the pleasure of supposing that I still felt all the respect she flattered herself she had inspired in me. And I thought that, to carry out this project, I could not find a better occasion than the moment when, in spite of that inflexible virtue which I had not been able to overcome with three months' efforts, she was bestowing rendezvous on someone who perhaps had had neither the time nor the inclination to ask for them. I painted such a stirring picture of the confusion I was sure she would be plunged into, and of the impatience I should inflict on her, that I could not deny myself the pleasure of seeing the spectacle.

Filled with these charming expectations, I only awaited the moment when I should see them fulfilled. At last it came: I pretended to go out with all the others, and took leave of Mme de Lursay with so natural an air that she appeared quite shocked. I stayed in the antechamber whispering something to one of my servants, to whom I had really nothing particular to say, and when all the carriages were gone, I came back.

I found Mme de Lursay reclining on a couch, musing. In spite of the boldness with which I had armed myself, I no sooner found myself alone with her than I was sorry I had got myself into this situation, and would have been glad never to have had the idea that I had so much to say to her. However, the necessity of getting myself out of the scrape, the annoyance I felt at the sight of her, and the pleasure of the prospect of mortifying her, all combined to restore my firmness.

"What! You!" she exclaimed in astonishment. "Might I make so bold as to ask why you have come back? What will people think if they know you are still here?"

"I am sure it is not what people think that makes you uneasy, Madam," said I with a sneer. "You are worried about something much more important."

"I have made it a practice never to reply to what I do not understand," she answered, "nor to ask about that which I do not much care to know. So I will not ask you what you mean by what you have just said, but merely beg you to be good enough not to remain here any longer at this late hour."

"I know how greatly I should oblige you by leaving," I replied, "but it is only one o'clock, and I should be glad if you would permit me to spend a few more hours with you."

"Your proposition is no doubt very flattering," she said, mimicking my exaggerated politeness, "but, to my extreme regret, I cannot accept it."

"Ah, Madam," I said, "but you can – and I think I have enough to say to you to make the time pass without tediousness."

"I should not wish to doubt you," she replied, "but the moment you have chosen is not any the more suitable for all that. Besides, you might have a great many things to say to me without having anything to say that I want to hear. For, between ourselves and without wishing to reproach you, I cannot say that you have amused me very much up till now."

"You will be more satisfied with me this evening, Madam," I answered. "It was my certainty of this that permitted me to hazard a request which I am not surprised you find indiscreet. I am not ignorant of any of the reasons that make it appear so in your eyes. I know I am taking up time which you had destined for sweeter pleasures than listening to me, and that, quite apart from the impatience I cause you yourself, you have to share that of another who perhaps, while he repines at the obstacle I place in the way of his pleasures, does not hold you entirely innocent of the vexation I cause him."

"There, beyond all contradiction, is a handsome speech!" she cried.

"What admirable elegance, obscurity, and length! One must have to rack one's brains a good deal to make oneself so absolutely unintelligible!"

"If you will allow me," said I, "I will make myself more clear."

"Oh, I allow you!" she replied warmly. "In fact, I beg you to do so. I shall not be at all sorry to know the little ideas you have in your head – they must be extremely unusual."

"Pardon me, Madam. The ideas you suppose uncommon are in fact very generally held."

"Your preamble overtaxes my patience, Sir," she replied shortly. "Let us come to the point."

"To be sure," I answered, reddening with anger. "You have thought for a long time, Madam, that you could impose upon me forever, and that because of the fine resistance you saw fit to offer me, I would value so highly the conquest of your heart that I would suppose myself the only one ever to have achieved it, and value you accordingly. You have believed, and with reason –"

"Sit down, Sir," she interrupted, coolly. "This opening promises a lengthy business, and I should not like you to be uncomfortable."

I sat down facing her, and though I was slightly disconcerted by her irony, continued thus: "I was saying, Madam, that you had reason to believe that I considered myself infinitely fortunate in pleasing you. My youth and inexperience of the world gave you a guarantee of my credulity, upon which, if I had known better, you would have been less able to rely. You did not need to employ much artifice; you might even have used less, and you overestimated me in supposing that deceiving me necessitated all the maneuvers you made use of. Yes, Madam, I will confess it, I had too blind a respect for you to doubt for an instant that you were such as you wished to appear, that you had always lived untouched by love, that assaults on your heart had been vain, and that I was the first who had ever been able to move it."

"You believed all this," she interrupted. "But it seems to me that while you thought so highly of me, you did not think so poorly of yourself. To be sure, it can have required no small self-esteem to think yourself capable of winning a woman who, until you came, had been so impervious. Well, and after this modest idea, what was the next?"

"Do not reproach me for it, Madam," I answered with emotion. "It was more to your advantage than mine. If I had only looked upon you as an ordinary woman, I might have loved you less, and I doubt whether you would have been greatly pleased to have inspired but a feeble passion, unworthy of your charms, and one which you could not with decency reward.

"My extreme timidity, and the difficulty I had in speaking of my love, must have shown you that I had little hope of pleasing you, and demonstrated the great respect you had inspired in me."

"At your age," said she, "whether one respects a woman or not, one should behave in the same way toward her, and I do not see why you expect me to have taken account of a timorousness that I owed more to your idiocy than to the respect you felt for me."

"Whatever the cause of it," I answered, "my agitation was agreeable to you just the same, and you must have been flattered to see me trembling with fears that I probably need never have felt."

"No indeed," she replied, "the pleasure they gave me was only moderate. Things that are ridiculous cannot be amusing for long. Go on. You ought not to have esteemed me as highly as you did, and you are sorry for it. Is that not it? Well, what next?"

"My eyes were opened, Madam. I learned how misplaced my fears were, and I would never forgive myself for being so ridiculous if the pleasure you took in seeing my folly had not cost you other delights."

"Yes," she replied, with the utmost self-possession. "I do not deny that they forced me more than once into a very disagreeable role: it was for that very reason I could not find them amusing."

"I would not have such fears again now," I said in a threatening tone.

"It is perhaps a little late in the day for discarding them," she answered. "You would do better to keep them. But come now, I had a very susceptible heart, had I? No doubt, you know all my adventures: may I hope you will be so obliging as to tell me all about them?"

"I would be afraid of abusing your patience," I answered, quite embarrassed at my own impertinences and at the calmness with which she was taking them.

"That is only a witticism," she replied, "and a witticism as feeble as it is insulting. However, I forgive you. You are so ignorant of women that you do not even know how to speak to them. What you just said, for example, is displeasing only because of the way you said it. Better expressed it would have been amusing. Nevertheless, let us proceed."

"Without entering into superfluous detail, then," said I, beside myself with rage, "I will say merely that I was told enough to make me understand how false you were with me, and to make me regret for the rest of my life that I had been your dupe."

"It is my turn to say do not reproach me for that," she answered, smiling. "You were the dupe not of my subtlety but of your own inexperience. Why must I be responsible for your blunders? Was I to explain to you exactly how much you pleased me, and to describe moment by moment the impression you made? Such a service on my part would no doubt have been very obliging – but would you have forgiven me for it? Was it not for you to understand and grasp my feelings? Is it my fault, in short, if everything was completely lost on you? And has anyone in the world ever thought of making such ridiculous complaints as those you have just been making? Is that the end of them, at least?"

"Nothing remains," I replied, confounded by her answer, "but for me to congratulate you on the pretext you found for breaking with me; on the secrecy with which you arranged that trip to the country, of which you told me nothing until it was too late for me to arrange to join you; and lastly on the promptness with which you fell in love with the Marquis, whom I must be keeping cooped up in a corner of your closet, and who no doubt waits with impatience for you to be good enough to send me packing. Indeed," I added, "I think I have delayed his happiness long enough. I must no longer be an obstacle. And so I will take leave –"

"No, Sir," she interrupted. "I have listened to you so patiently that I think I may count upon your doing me the same service. I ask the Marquis's pardon, but even if his endurance should be tried by a conversation so untoward for him, I could not deny myself the pleasure of giving you an answer. It is not because I am afraid of you that I wish to do so. My reputation depends neither on you nor upon those who take it on themselves to blacken it. At your age, it is impossible to judge soundly of anything, least of all of women. You are not the sort of person to be either listened to or believed, so you may without consequence think as ill of me as you think well of yourself. The public will not judge me by what you say. So it is not the desire to justify myself that makes me speak: it is the pleasure of confounding you, of revealing your caprice and lack of sincerity – in short, of making you blush for yourself.

"I shall begin by speaking of myself," she went on. "You will not suppose I do so out of self-love. I am forced to recall facts that degrade me. Because of you, I am in a situation where I cannot contemplate myself without despising myself for the errors you caused me to fall into.

"You have known me for a long time. Bound to your mother by the tenderest friendship, I loved you before I knew whether you deserved it, before you knew yourself what it is to be loved, and without dreaming that my fondness for you could ever bring me to the pass where I now at last confess myself to be.

"Ah, what had I to fear then from loving you too much? Even if I could have foreseen that you would ever think of me, how was I to imagine that you would ever really move me, that so unlikely an accident would one day be counted among the events of my life? I did not believe it possible, and you cannot reproach me. Anyone else would have had as little fear of you as I had; and even if nothing else were taken into account but our ages – I will say nothing of my principles – my security was very natural.

"It was therefore not only without misgivings on my own account but also without the least suspicion of you that I saw you trying to please me. Your more marked attentions, your longer and more frequent visits, and the pleasure you seemed to take in seeing me, appeared to me as no more than the effects of our longstanding friendship. You were entering the world, you were forming your character, and it was quite natural that you should seek me out with more eagerness than when you were still a child. What you said to me about love, the warmth and tenacity with which you spoke of it, and the difficulty I had in making you turn your mind to other matters, seemed to me only the consequences of the natural curiosity of a young man who seeks to learn something about a feeling that is beginning to trouble his heart or about ideas that occupy his imagination. Your looks did not make me think otherwise, and so little did I desire to please you that I never dreamed I did so. Your uneasiness at last made me wish to know what was troubling you, and thinking only to be your confidante, I found that I myself was concerned in your secrets. You must remember that I omitted nothing that might cure you of a fancy that seemed to me unsuitable, and of which I was sorry to be the object. My friendship for you, your youth, a sort of pity, prevented me from imposing silence on you as severely as I ought to have done. I also thought it would be amusing to observe the feelings and conduct of a heart embarking on its first passion. This amusement, which was at first no more dangerous than I supposed it, at last became so. I saw you go with more regret, I waited for you with impatience, and the sight of you awakened emotions that were unknown to me before you told me of your love. I saw then the necessity for flight, but I was no longer capable of it. An indescribable charm, too slight at first for me to understand that I ought to struggle against it, made me hang upon your words. I repeated them to myself afterward. I tore myself away with difficulty, and always too late, from the pleasure of listening to you. The horrible disparity between our ages, which at first had struck me so forcibly, seemed to me to disappear. Every day we saw each other seemed to add years to you and take them away from me. Only love could have blinded me to this point – and to find myself believing that we were made for each other was a proof too sure to be misunderstood that I was in love. Instead of trying to hide it from myself any longer, I did not shrink from examining myself; and although I was afraid at what I found in my heart, I did not think myself without resource. As I did not wish to be conquered, I was unwilling to see that I already had been. Sure at last of the extreme affection you had inspired in me, I tried at least to delay my fall, and to spare myself the shame and danger of a final surrender. Your inexperience helped my scheme, and I took all the more delight in seeing you in love because I was less afraid of becoming too culpable.

"It is not extraordinary therefore, Sir, that I did not tell you that I loved you, at a time when I did not yet do so," she added. "Nor is it any more extraordinary that after I learned what my feelings for you were, I should have done all I could to hide them from you. It was for you to try to discover them, and if I may say so it was you, not I, who, as you put it, saw fit to offer a fine resistance."

"But, Madam," I stammered, "it seems to me I was not wrong about that. You yourself agree that you resisted me, and as you can imagine —"

"You hesitate," she interrupted. "Out with it!"

"What would you have me say, Madam?" I asked, more disconcerted than ever. "The phrase I used offended you, and I am very sorry if it displeased you. I...but," I added, perceiving that I did not know what I was saying, "it is late, and you must want me to take leave."

"No, Sir," she answered, "I do not. What I still have to say to you cannot be postponed, and the subjects I have still to deal with are to me the most important ones."

I sat down again, astonished that I should be the one who was discomfited. My embarrassment increased still more when she bade me — without any particular reason, I thought — sit down in an armchair near her couch, which brought me much closer to her than I had been before. I obeyed, trembling, without daring to look at her, and with a sort of tender emotion that her long explanation had aroused in me in spite of myself.

"So it is true," she went on, "that I did love you. I could deny it, for I never actually affirmed it to you; but after what has passed between us, such an evasion would be both useless and unseemly. It would have been better for me to have told you a thousand times that I loved you rather than prove it to you once as I did. I admit that I might have had even more to reproach myself with, that I owe to you, rather than to my reason, the happiness of not having succumbed entirely; and that if you had known the full extent of my frailty, I would today be the most pitiable woman in all the world. It is not that I esteem myself more for not having belonged to you. Things being as they are, though, it is a kind of consolation not to have sacrificed all to you."

She dwelt with so much pleasure on this consolation, and it suddenly seemed so absurd to have left it to her, that I all but decided there and then to deprive her of the advantage of which she was so proud. I gazed at her for a moment. She looked so beautiful! Her bearing was so casual, so touching, and yet so modest! Her eyes, resting tenderly upon me, assured me still of so much love that an indescribable agitation stirred my senses, which, though it made me more willing to listen to her, made me less able to do so.

"You accuse me," she continued, her eyes still on me, "of having wanted to appear respectable to you, and you call this a crime. What did I do that I should not have done? If, in order to give you a good opinion of me, I had to conceal faults and dissemble unfortunate adventures, and if I could not have appeared to you as I really was without the risk of losing you, was I to blame in trying to deceive you? Even if it were true that my youth had been disgraced by scandal, would it have been impossible for me to have reformed? You do not know it now, Sir, but you will learn one day that women cannot always be judged by their beginnings: that such-and-such woman appeared to have a corrupt heart who really had only an uncontrolled imagination, or a weakness of character that prevented her from resisting the torrent and bad example; you will learn that though it is almost impossible to cure the vices of the heart, one recovers from the errors of the mind. The most gallant of women can, upon mere reflection, become the most virtuous of women or the most faithful of mistresses.

"You say also that I tried to make you believe that before my heart was yours it had belonged to no one else. If that was really my intention, I am guilty of a strange deception. No, Sir. I have loved, and with all the violence possible. If I had not been acquainted with love, you would have found me less afraid of it. Perhaps you will take this confession as yet another reason for despising me. No doubt, to win your esteem, I should never have been persuaded to love by anyone but you. I wished that just as much as you might have yourself, and when I began to love you, I felt a deep regret that my heart was not as fresh as yours, and that I could not offer you its first fruits."

She spoke so tenderly! She painted so clearly the violence and the truth of her passion! The sound of her voice was so beguiling that I could not hear it without feeling myself deeply stirred, or without repenting that I was the cause of unhappiness to a woman who for her beauty alone should have been spared so cruel a fate. This idea, which

I could not help dwelling upon, drew a sigh from me. Mme de Lursay had been awaiting it too long for it to escape her. She was silent a moment, still looking at me. She hoped no doubt that this sigh would lead to other things, but seeing that I still did not speak, she continued thus: "You may now give free scope to your imagination. I have loved, I have confessed it, and that is enough to convince you that I lay claim to passion only in order to conceal my excesses, and that there is nothing odious of which I have not been capable. I knew what danger I exposed myself to in making this avowal, but I thought I should not conceal from you something I would have told you before if you had asked, and for which, for all sorts of reasons, I do not reproach myself with as much as I do for loving you, who, though you have all the faults of your age, have none of its candor or sincerity."

"I am sure," said I, nettled by this reproach, though persuaded by now that Versac had deceived me, and too occupied by the charms that Mme de Lursay displayed not to wish to seem innocent, "I have given you no grounds for thinking I am not sincere. I may have behaved badly in certain respects, but not in those you complain of. If you can reproach me with anything, it is with having been too credulous."

"Ah, would you have been so if you had loved me?" she cried warmly. "Would you not, on the contrary, have defended me against the calumnies with which people tried to blacken me in your estimation? Could you give credence to them without degrading yourself too? My manner of life, which you have long been witness of, should not that at least have counterbalanced what you heard? I admit that when a woman of my age so far forgets herself as to love a man of yours, she exposes herself to the supposition that she has yielded less to love than to the habit of profligacy; and that this is always a lapse for which the best-conducted woman is blamed all the more because it was so little expected of her, and the incongruity makes her all the more ridiculous. But you should not have suspected me of being in this case, and the more I sacrificed myself, the more I departed from my principles for your sake, the more gratitude and love you owed me. Anyone else would have felt that only his love could make me forget the irreparable wrong that mine had made me commit, and that in loving him I had made him responsible for the peace and happiness of my life. But," she added, turning toward me, her eyes filling with tears, "that is not your way of thinking.

"Even before you were sure of being loved, you made me endure caprices for which you did not even deign to excuse yourself; if I so much as forgave you for them, you seemed to be vexed. At the same time, you failed to fulfill even the most obvious obligations toward me, voluntarily let several days pass without seeing me, did not speak of your love except so coldly as to forbid me to encourage it; in short, you acted toward me less as toward a woman you desired to please than as toward one you wanted to leave. If ever you seemed more animated, there was nothing in your transports that permitted me to share them, and you never seemed to feel less than when you were most carried away by your desires. None of these faults escaped me, but although they plunged me into mortal pain, they did not lessen my preference for you. I judged you unaccustomed to the ways of the world and did not wish to think you culpable. I hoped that the habit of loving would remove the rough-ness of your behavior, that you would be glad to have the advice of a woman who loved you – in short, that I could make you what I wanted you to be."

"Ah, Madam!" I cried, overcome by her tears, transported, beside myself, "shall I be so unfortunate as never to see you care about me again? No," I continued, ardently kissing her hand, "if you will restore me to your favors, I will be worthy of them –"

"No, Meilcour," she interrupted, "I can no longer hope to find you as loving as I would wish. These transports can no longer either flatter or seduce me. If I were younger, and more foolish, I might perhaps have taken your desires for love. They would have moved me, and you would have been justified. Yet as you have already learned from an occasion when I could have yielded without self-reproach because I could believe myself loved, I want to surrender myself only to true feeling. What I would not do then, I can now do less than ever. Even if I was mistaken in believing you in love with Mme de Senanges, the way you have spoken of her proves that nothing can either keep you or bring you back."

"But is it possible that your fears about Mme de Senanges can have been real?" I said tenderly. "Can you have believed that even if she had wished to engage me, I would have stooped to respond to her advances?"

"Yes," she answered. "If Mme de Senanges had been even less pleas-ing to you, even if you had loved me a thousand times more than you did, you would have taken her just the same. Perhaps you would not have stayed with her, but at least she would have seduced you, and that is all she can have wished for. If it was true that she was of no interest to you, why did you try to see her again, and why, the very day when I told you I did not wish you to frequent her, did I find you together in the Tuileries? What could have prevented you, if you loved me, from coming to the country with me? You say that the party was arranged secretly. The mystery was very simple, and it was you who were the cause of it. I wanted to get you away from Mme de Senanges, and that was the only way I could think of. Instead of guessing the motive of the party, though, or rather perhaps not wishing to appear to have done so, you fancy I arranged it only in order to see the Marquis more conveniently. I have only one word to say to you about that: if I had felt a partiality for him, after what had passed between you and me, you were the last person in the world I should have desired as a spectator. I abbreviate your offenses, as you see, and do not insist on them. Not that it would be difficult for me to recollect them all, but reproach presupposes love, and you will easily understand that I do not wish to find any vestige of that in my heart."

"Ah, Madam," I cried, so agitated that I was incapable of reflection, "you have never loved me at all! You would look less calmly on my despair, you could not help being moved by it, if your fondness for me had been as strong as you say."

"But, Meilcour," she replied, "can I still flatter myself that I might be dear to you? Should I even wish it? Is it really true that you would be sorry to lose me? You, who have done all you can to try to displease me? You, who have thought that the only way to justify yourself was to accuse me, and have no doubt that I am on such good terms with the Marquis that I have hidden him in the closet!"

"Can you still speak of it?" I cried. "Do you not believe yourself sufficiently justified in my eyes?"

"Yes," she replied, smiling. "I see very well that I am, today – but I should not be surprised if I were no longer so tomorrow."

"Come," I said, "will you not cease to set such vain terrors against me?"

"Ah, Meilcour!" she cried in a tenderer tone. "What we are talking about is too important to me to be treated so lightly, and I am lost if I cannot be happy."

"No," I replied, clasping her in my arms, "my love will leave nothing to wish for."

"But, Meilcour," she said, after appearing to muse a little, "can you not be content with my friendship? Remember that I shall not prefer anyone to you, and that I shall feel something not much less than the tenderest love for you. Believe me," she added, her eyes animated by the liveliest passion, "that is the only thing left for us, and what I refuse you is not the equal of what I offer."

"No," said I, throwing myself at her feet, more inflamed than ever by her resistance, "no, you must give me back all that I have lost."

"Ah, cruel one!" she exclaimed, sighing. "Do you want to be the misfortune of my life? Have you not already sufficient proofs of my affection? Rise," she added faintly. "You see only too well that I love you. May you one day prove that you love me!"

With these words she lowered her eyes, as if she were ashamed of having said so much. In spite of the solemn turn our conversation had finally taken, I had a clear remembrance of the ridicule Mme de Lursay had cast on my fears. I urged her tenderly to look at me: she did so. We gazed at each other. I saw again in her eyes the signs of voluptuousness that I had found there the day she had taught me the gradual progressions by which one arrives at pleasure, and how minutely love subdivides them. Bolder now, but still too timid, I tremblingly experimented to see how far her indulgence would go. It was as if my transports increased her beauty, and made all her graces more touching. Her looks, her sighs, her silence, all taught me, although rather late in the day, how much I was loved. I was too young not to believe that I loved in return. The work of my senses appeared to me the work of my heart. I abandoned myself to all the intoxication of that fatal moment, and rendered myself at last as guilty as I was capable of being.

I will confess it: my crime was pleasant to me, and my illusion long lasting, whether it was the magic of my youth that sustained it, or Mme de Lursay alone. Far from being troubled by my infidelity, I thought only of enjoying my victory. It was made all the more precious by all I believed it had cost me, and although in fact I triumphed only over obstacles of my own making, I imagined that Mme de Lursay's resistance had been formidable. I no sooner possessed her than I felt all my esteem for her return. I carried my blindness so far as to forget all the lovers Versac had credited her with, and even the one she herself had just admitted to. The only thing I required of the future was that she should not cease to love me: her charms flattered my senses, and her love, which seemed to me prodigious, spread itself to my heart and filled it with the most gratifying agitation.

At last I felt the force of my error diminish, though not enough to cause me to repent. I would nonetheless have yielded myself gradually up to reflection if Mme de Lursay had been good enough not to interrupt me. Unfortunately for my reason, though, she noticed that I was pensive and showed a sort of uneasiness in which it would not have been decent to leave her; and indeed she did not deserve it, so I reassured her. Never was woman a less vain or more timid lover. The more I praised her charms, the less, she said, she dared count on their power over me. I seemed to be in transports, but perhaps I was not in love. Forced to agree that I loved her, she was no more at ease. Then, after having abandoned herself to fears, she would return to transports: the tenderest playfulness, the most alluring banter, in a word, all the things that are most charming in love that is no longer constrained, succeeded one another continually, and kept me in a state of agitation that quite unfitted me for serious reflection.

Enchanted as I was, my eyes opened at last. Without knowing what it was I lacked, I felt an emptiness in my heart. Only my imagination was alive, and I had to excite that in order not to fall into listlessness. I was eager again, but less ardent. I still admired, but I was no longer moved. It was in vain that I tried to recapture my first transports. I could now only yield myself to Mme de Lursay with an air of constraint, and I reproached myself for the least desires that her beauty could still wring from me.

Hortense – Hortense, whom I adored though so utterly forgotten, resumed her sway over my heart. The strength of the feeling for her that I now rediscovered made what had happened seem less pardonable than ever. Was it not with the sole hope of seeing her that I had come to Mme de Lursay's? I said to myself. And during their absence, was it not her alone I had missed? By what magic spell did I find myself engaged with a woman whom earlier that very day I had detested?

I might well be astonished at my situation, the more so as I had been vain and jealous without knowing it, and had not at all observed the power these emotions had gained over me. For the rest, it was quite natural that Mme de Lursay, who joined to great beauty a thorough knowledge of the heart, should have led me imperceptibly into the relation I was now in with her. The conclusion I draw today is that if I had had more experience, she would merely have reduced me the sooner, since what is called knowledge of the world only makes us wiser insomuch as it makes us more corrupt.

It would therefore have given me a lively sense of what a shameful thing it is to be faithful. I should not have been moved, as I was then, by sentiment: if I had seen it in Mme de Lursay, I should have found it ridiculous, and to conquer me she would have had to be contemptible instead of avoiding even the appearance of it. Instead of banishing the thought of Hortense from my mind, I should have found pleasure in dwelling on it. In the midst of the agitation that Mme de Lursay caused me, I would have bemoaned the custom which forbids us to resist a woman who finds us pleasing: I would have saved my heart from the disorder of my senses, and by these delicate distinctions, which might be called the quietism of love, I would have enjoyed all the delights of the moment without incurring the risk of infidelity.

Yet this convenient metaphysic was unknown to me, and it was with deep sorrow that I saw how grievously I had erred. For some time, Mme de Lursay's urgencies increased my distress; but whether it was because I grew impatient at having to think of my own guilt, or because I feared to provoke reproaches which I would not know how to answer, or whether in the intoxication that I still felt, true sentiment had but feeble power over me, I revolted against so uncomfortable an idea. Torn away from pleasure by remorse, snatched from remorse by pleasure, I could not be sure of myself for a moment. I will even confess, to my shame, that I sometimes justified my behavior to myself, and could not see how I had wronged Hortense, since she did not love me, I had made her no promises, and I could never hope to be beholden to her as I was to Mme de Lursay.

I had not much difficulty in persuading my mind that my reasoning was just; but it was not so easy to deceive my heart. Overwhelmed by its secret reproaches, and unable to conquer them, I tried to distract myself, and to drown in new frenzies a memory that continually plucked at my mind. My attempts were vain, though: every moment increased my guilt without adding anything to my peace.

Some hours had passed in these contradictions: dawn was beginning to break, and I was still far from resolving the conflict within me. Thanks to the proprieties that Mme de Lursay observed so strictly, she dismissed me at last, and I left her, promising, in spite of my remorse, to see her early the next day, firmly resolved, moreover, to keep my word.

Originally published as *Les Egarements du coeur et de l'esprit* (1738).

Dangerous Liaisons

by Choderlos de Laclos

Translated by P.W.K. Stone

Introduction

by Michel Feher

A Woman's Liberties

by Michel Feher

Boredom or servitude: these sinister alternatives haunt libertine characters in late eighteenth-century literature. Bored when they resist
love's sway, they become slaves as soon as they succumb to it. The
problem is clearly articulated in Crébillon fils's last novels. On the
one hand, jaded libertines recognize in retrospect that their loveless
affairs — even the difficult and therefore prestigious campaigns of seduction — have brought them nothing but bitterness. On the other hand,
these disgruntled conquerors maintain that love, however delightful,
necessarily submits the lover's will to the unpredictable desires of his
beloved. Love, then, is an unbearable yoke for any man who wants
to remain his own master.

Confronted with this dilemma, the author of *Dangerous Liaisons*
(1782) constructed his novel around the following question: How can
lovers surrender to the fires of passion while preserving their freedom?
This question will no longer concern Laclos (1741–1803) by the time
he writes *On the Education of Women* (1783) (included in this volume).
In his essay, Laclos was indeed satisfied with the standard libertine
definition of amorous sentiment as a dangerous trap, one that has the
double consequence of subjugating an ensnared lover to his object
of desire and of dulling all pleasures that do not proceed from love's
fires. Laclos the novelist, however, imagines two distinct ways of loving
"freely": *Dangerous Liaisons* presents two strategies that preserve the
lovers' ardor without dooming them to slavery. These arts of love, each
very different from the other, correspond respectively to the Vicomte
de Valmont's relationships with Mme de Merteuil and Mme de Tourvel.

The Exchange of Offerings

If the first of these two liaisons raises libertinism to unequaled heights,
credit is due entirely to the Marquise de Merteuil. As the Marquise
explains in the famous autobiographical Letter 81 in *Dangerous Liaisons*,
she realized early on that aristocratic society placed her sex in a disadvantageous position. This handicap, in which nature plays no part,
was the motive for the training the Marquise imposed upon herself.
It forced her to cultivate and demonstrate a rigor and subtlety far surpassing those of men — since "unnecessary virtues are rarely acquired"

(p. 1072) – as well as a capacity for invention in which other women were lacking.

Mme de Merteuil's female contemporaries, victims of prejudices inculcated from childhood on, are confined to a limited range of social roles, all of them circumscribed by the belief that female honor and pleasure are mutually exclusive. By virtue of this cruel principle, women who neglect their reputations, abandoning themselves openly to their desires, are derided by the public and held in contempt by their peers. Moreover, they fail to sustain the interest of the most prestigious men of their class, because these grand libertines seek a "glory" based on the seduction of allegedly "invincible" women. Condemned to amuse themselves with the small-time libertines known as *petits-maîtres* (fops) or "men of good fortune," "easy" women engage in short-lived, passionless affairs that provide only the thinnest protection against boredom, a questionable compensation for the loss of their good name. However, women concerned only with their reputation do not fare much better: flaunting the inflexibility of their virtue and the demands of their hearts, they no doubt succeed in attracting men less pusil- lanimous than the *petits-maîtres*. Yet they attract the attentions of the more ambitious seducers always at their own expense. Far from gaining the respect of their implacable suitors, these "difficult" women must choose between a glorious resistance, which deprives them of the pleasures of the flesh, and a necessarily shameful "defeat," wherein suitors humiliate those women who have dared to resist their advances. Thus, the options of high society women are definitely not propitious to their happiness. Indeed, women are limited to the mediocre plea- sures savored by the *petites-maîtresses* (the female counterparts of the *petits-maîtres*), the dismal austerity that marks the lives of unconquer- able women, or the humiliation that awaits the fallen ambitious ones.

Recognizing these terrible options, Mme de Merteuil decides to devote her life to vengeance: faced with society's hypocritical morals and the cruel principles of male libertines, she invents a female version of high libertinism. Proclaiming herself the avenger of her sex, the one who will shatter male domination, the Marquise follows the exact opposite course of the grand male libertine, the so-called "man of principles." The latter sees his art as an orderly succession of three deeds: he must seduce the most unapproachable women, let the pub- lic know about his successes, and end his affairs by ostentatiously abandoning his victims. In other words, he must break the resistance of "difficult" women, then expose their weakness publicly, and finally show the world that he is never the slave of love – hence the cruel and ostentatious breakups. For her part, Mme de Merteuil seeks not merely to attract and possess the most formidable men but also to compel them to be discreet, and finally to assume the initiative for breaking up. The art of the Marquise consists in fulfilling all her desires – including that of taking back her freedom – without ever compromising her reputation. As she writes of the dangerous Prévan, "I want him, and I shall have him; he will want to be able to say so, and he shall not say so" (p. 1080).

To see her projects through, Mme de Merteuil must first acquire the same qualities as male libertines: she needs to prove herself audacious, a fine observer, her own master, rigorous in her reasoning, and of course a peerless actress. In addition, the particular complexity of female libertinism – and, above all, its risks – force her to comply to rules of conduct to which men are unaccustomed and of which other women are ignorant.[1] More than a simple artist, the Marquise can thus claim to have invented a previously unknown discipline: "I say '*my* principles' intentionally. They are not, like those of other women, found by chance, accepted unthinkingly, and followed out of habit. They are the fruit of profound reflection. I have created them; I might say that I have created myself" (p. 1074). These unwritten principles, which allow Mme de Merteuil to triumph in society, concern the three aspects of her activity as a "dangerous woman": the conditions for entering into a liaison, the preservation of her reputation, and the negotiation of her breakups.

When entering into a liaison, Mme de Merteuil is careful not to commit the most common error of "difficult" women: because they mistake their suitors' attraction to challenges for a feeling of respect, these women think that their defeat will be considered more honorable if it is preceded by a long resistance. Laclos's heroine, by contrast, prides herself on quickly choosing the man she wants and on granting him her favors immediately. Insofar as the Marquise has forged her reputation as an "unconquerable" woman, this strategy allows her to disrupt the plans of her suitor, who is preparing for a long siege. Disconcerted by a maneuver that spares him his usual feats, the prematurely gratified conqueror cannot even boast of his victory. For to confirm the defeat of a prestigious woman, the public needs some sign, such as the involuntary changes in behavior and physiognomy that affect both the victorious lover and the vanquished mistress. Such an analysis supposes that the public has been able to witness the resistance before pronouncing judgment on the fall; as Mme de Merteuil writes, "it is nearly always preliminary deliberations that betray a woman's secret"

(p. 1078). The experienced spectators of society's intrigues thus have no reason to believe that a woman known for her virtue and prudence would surrender without struggle to a conqueror known for his ferocity. That they would find no trace of confusion on the lady's face nor the customary pride of the seducer after victory would only convince them further. The Marquise explains:

> In spite of all one can do, one's manner is never quite the same before the event as after. This difference never escapes the attentive observer; and I have found it less dangerous to choose wrong than to be found out in my choice. There is an added advantage to this, in that it offers no basis for the likely assumptions that alone enable others to judge us (p. 1078).

To enjoy the most dangerous men without concern or harm, Mme de Merteuil attracts them by proclaiming herself immune to weakness, then confuses them by surrendering more swiftly than the most imprudent *petite-maîtresse*. Unsettled by events that escape the logic of their theories, these men of principle are likewise deprived of the customary sequence of their emotions. For if sensual pleasure is indulgently offered, they find themselves at the same time denied the intellectual satisfaction of having broken down a formidable resistance, and above all deprived of the glory brought by the conquest of a respected woman. In other words, the dangerous men to whom the Marquise gives herself recover neither their habitual contempt for the vanquished mistress nor the admiration of the public: outmaneuvered by the Marquise, they know that society will lend no credence to their tale.

If the manner in which Mme de Merteuil organizes her capitulations protects her from indiscretions, the safeguarding of her reputation calls for very different measures. First, she must make sure that her current lover has no physical evidence that would validate his status: she thus takes the precaution of "never writing letters," and more generally "never providing evidence of my defeat" (p. 1078). Better still, the Marquise makes sure never to appear in public with the man to whom she grants her favors, even as she endeavors to create diversions by letting herself be courted by swains whom she intends to dismiss. In other words, "the men who did not interest me were the only ones whose homages I appeared to accept. I made use of them to win me the honors of successful resistance; meanwhile I could safely yield to the lover of my choice" (p. 1078). Second, Mme de Merteuil recognizes that, like herself, dangerous men always have secrets they must conceal from the public. Thus she never throws herself into a new liaison without having gathered compromising information on her chosen lover: "A latter-day Delilah, I have always devoted all my powers, as she did, to springing the important secret. Oh, I have my scissors to the hair of a great many of our modern Samsons!" (p. 1078).

Opaque to the rest of the world but enlightened about her lovers, the Marquise attends to her reputation with a third kind of measure: to assure her public support, she makes sure to gain the support of the two most important groups among society's women – the prudes and the coquettes. At first, Mme de Merteuil pretends to seek the advice of virtuous women, who do not hesitate to adopt her as their favorite pupil. Flattered that an attractive woman would join their ranks, the prudes make use of her to prove to the world that one may be charming and virtuous at the same time. Later on, and by virtue of her success with austere women, the Marquise then wins the good graces of the coquettes, who seize the opportunity to raise their own status by acting charitably toward a woman they judge to be inoffensive: "convinced that I had renounced the career they pursued themselves," Mme de Merteuil explains, "[they] chose me for the object of their commendations every time they wished to prove that they did not malign everybody" (p. 1077). In short, by cultivating the self-seeking homages of the "prude party" and the "women of pretensions," the Marquise assures her fame with an unparalleled brilliance. Yet, so as not to be seen in too cold a light, she is equally careful to add a touch of tenderness, which does not fail to excite the most ambitious libertines: "so as to steer a middle course between them and my misguided protectresses, I played the part of an impressionable but fastidious woman whose excessive delicacy was her defense against her passion" (p. 1077).

Lastly, Mme de Merteuil again asserts her originality through the art of ending an affair. On this score, Laclos's heroine shows a certain modesty: while dangerous men end each adventure by humiliating their victim, thus proving to the world that love has no hold on them, the Marquise limits herself to ending most of her liaisons discreetly. In her lucidity, she realizes that only the great male libertines are able to acquire glory by making their exploits known. A woman of principles, however, must protect at all costs her reputation as unconquerable, and so she must renounce the glory of her true achievements. Thus, her art consists of imposing silence on those she prepares to abandon. Careful to avoid the irrational reactions sometimes produced by wounded pride, she does not hesitate to arrange an honorable exit for her soon to be ex-lovers: it is a matter, she acknowledges, of cultivating "skill in making them unfaithful to me so as to avoid appearing fickle myself" –

or at least obtaining their discretion by encouraging "the flattering idea each one is made to entertain of being [her] only lover" (p. 1078).

To end a liaison in this manner, one must not only have remarkable powers of persuasion but also a strong sense of self-abnegation. Indeed, instead of expressing her desire to end the affair, Mme de Merteuil must consent to have her disgraced lover leave her. Such is the breakup from which Belleroche benefits: having decided to end their liaison, the Marquise is actually quite solicitous of her lover, since she sets out to make him wary of her by overwhelming him with caresses and avowals of love. Nevertheless, she does not grant this favorable treatment to everyone: certain particularly impudent seducers deserve to suffer a humiliation equal to the one they planned. In this case, Mme de Merteuil uses both her skill and her public credit to avenge herself on a man who would have ruined her. Hence the trap she sets for Prévan, who had boasted that he could seduce her and expose her "weakness" to the public: true to her art, the Marquise promptly surrenders to the ambitious rogue, then passes him off as a contemptible rapist.

A woman of incomparable intelligence, the Marquise has managed to overcome the handicaps society inflicts on her sex. Capable of attracting the men of her choice and of ridding herself of them when her desire wanes, above all she has mastered the art of collecting lovers without ever compromising her reputation. She can thus assert a freedom of movement largely comparable to that of her male counterparts. Equal to even the greatest of the rakes, but with more merit, she must nevertheless confront the dismaying dilemma of the libertine's choice between boredom and servitude. Before meeting the Vicomte de Valmont, the Marquise's conduct was inspired not by a desire to seduce while warding off love's emotions so much as by a refusal to accept the servility that society imposes upon women. Once she makes Valmont's acquaintance, however, Mme de Merteuil experiences in her turn the usual torments of dangerous men.

Undeniably in love – she admits this "is the only one of my desires that has ever for a moment gained sway over me" (p. 1078) – the Marquise immediately realizes that the new emotion to which she has fallen prey is infinitely dearer to her than her usual pleasures; yet she understands too that such a captivating passion gravely threatens her independence. Valmont is a member of that elite of dangerous men for whom the ultimate humiliation consists of being "pinned down" by a woman. Thus, Mme de Merteuil cannot trade her legendary prudence for blind devotion without exposing her heart and her renown to a cruel fate. Should she resolve to restrain her desires in order to remain faithful to a method that would turn the Vicomte into a toy for her whims? Such an attitude turns out to be hardly more desirable than its alternative. Valmont, whose reputation alone has already seduced the Marquise, draws the essence of his charm from his status as an irresistible man. As such, he would probably cease to be loveable if his mistress reduced him to slavery. In other words, by confiscating her conqueror's victory, Mme de Merteuil risks sacrificing the love she feels to the preservation of her own glory. Thus, the Marquise faces the same alternatives that engender the grand libertine's melancholy: if she lets herself fall in love with the Vicomte, she loses the benefit of her principled existence; but if she demotes her lover to the rank of her other conquests, she deprives herself of the happiness she has only just discovered.

In one of her letters to Valmont, Laclos's heroine underscores this dilemma by showing that love is both a necessary condition for a liaison and a principal cause of its asymmetrical character:

> Have you not as yet observed that pleasure, undeniably the sole motive force behind the union of the sexes, is nevertheless not enough to form a bond between them? And that if it is preceded by the desire that impels, it is followed by disgust that repels? That is a law of nature which love alone can alter. And can love be summoned up by will? Nevertheless, love is necessary, and the necessity would really be very embarrassing had not one perceived that fortunately it will do if love exists on one side only (p. 1185).

More radically, love as conceived by the Marquise is not meant to be reciprocal. As Laclos himself explains in *On the Education of Women*, the amorous sentiment appeared first as a trap invented by women in order to shake off the yoke of male domination, but one that men soon learned to wield; henceforth, seducers of both sexes used it to capture their prey. Nevertheless, love is a strangely effective snare, in that it gives a more intense joy to the unfortunates whom it entangles than to the hunters who successfully set it. Envious of their victims, the hunters cannot rest until they have avenged themselves for the happiness they have caused but cannot share. The vexation caused by their victories leads the most dangerous libertines to break the hearts they have moved. Under these conditions, Mme de Merteuil can envisage the outcome of an amorous relationship only in terms of the following equation: "one party enjoys the happiness of loving, the other that of pleasing. The latter is a little less intense, it is true, but to it is added the pleasure of deceiving, which establishes a balance....

But tell me, Vicomte, which of us will be responsible for deceiving the other?" (p. 1185). While this last question clearly underlines the limits of grand libertinism, the Marquise will answer it in an unexpected way – a way, indeed, that will extricate libertine erotics from its own impasse.

Mme de Merteuil's solid literary knowledge makes her well aware of all the rules of old chivalric love. She knows that this art of love engages the intrepid conqueror to seduce the most prestigious women so as to receive the acclamation of his peers. To the extent that they share the same thirst for glory, dangerous men like Valmont are the somewhat degenerate heirs to these proud knights. Unlike the knights, though, they belong to no confraternity bound by mutual respect; indeed, they feel a profound contempt for the petty society that surrounds them, even if they continue to seek its admiration. Consequently, their glory, which exists only in the eyes of a public they do not respect, is fraught with ambivalence – hence the disenchantment that overcomes the most irresistible libertines as their successes accumulate. Under these circumstances, the Marquise exhibits both her unequaled ingenuity and her sincere love for the Vicomte by offering him that which his happiness most lacks – an audience worthy of his exploits. Rather than expose herself to the cruelty of her pitiless lover or, on the contrary, subvert the indomitable quality that makes him so attractive, Mme de Merteuil decides to suspend their amorous jousting in order to become the arbiter of Valmont's exploits. Thus, no sooner have they consummated their affair than the Marquise invites Valmont to seal a "pact of eternal rupture" with her. This new union, which substitutes secrets for caresses, has the immense advantage of protecting them both from the vicissitudes and much-feared alternatives that ultimately face grand libertines: the humiliation of defeat or the bitterness of victory.

In Mme de Merteuil's unprecedented relationship with Valmont, she does not ask her accomplice to renounce other women; on the contrary, he is to pursue his career as a libertine all the more vigorously. She wants him to prolong the list of his conquests indefinitely, to publicize his victims' names after obtaining their surrender, and finally to inflict a painful breakup on them, so that no one could ever suspect him of being in love. In short, the Vicomte must change nothing in his habits; the Marquise insists only that henceforth every publicized victory and every new humiliation be dedicated to her. Indeed, it is for her that he now multiplies his efforts to seduce and mock the most resistant women in society.

As the confidante of the Vicomte's projects, but above all as a strategist every bit as implacable, the Marquise comes to occupy the position of an *estimable* public, whose presence other libertines so painfully
lack. Because she is sufficiently qualified to appreciate the exploits
of an exceptional conqueror, she is able to save her partner from bitterness. But, while playing the part of the estimable public, Mme
de Merteuil has hardly renounced her former prerogatives. Her remarkable sense of initiative prompts her to avoid her lover's embraces
while his passion for her still burns, making her both the esteemed audience of the Vicomte's glorious deeds and his desired mistress. Subject to the verdict of a woman whose charms he has far from exhausted,
Valmont has from this moment on a double reason to shine. On the
one hand, the Vicomte seeks to earn the Marquise's admiration through
his successes with other women; on the other hand, he depends on
his exploits to reconquer her. More precisely, his mission is to hand
over, like so many offerings to his mistress, the spoils of the victims he
has successively possessed and ruined. In so doing, he underscores
the fact that Mme de Merteuil is truly the unconquered Unique One,
but he demonstrates as well that his own talents make him worthy of
her. Flush with success and confident of the judgment of his beloved
public, Valmont thus counts on finding the Marquise "at the end of
the course" – that is to say, when he has gratified her with the downfall of other respectable women – and giving her, "an example to
the world of perfect constancy" (p. 945).

Mme de Merteuil herself is by no means passive. Far from being a
mere spectator of her lover's spectacle, an idol to whom the hearts and
reputations of other women are sacrificed, the Marquise spends her
time repaying him in kind: she pursues her own career as a "woman of
principles," using men as toys to highlight Valmont's privileges. The
treatment she reserves for the Vicomte's rivals simultaneously justifies
his continuing hold on her heart and the promise of union that informs
their epistolary relations. Together Mme de Merteuil and her lover
express the sentiments that unite them by dedicating their respective
feats to each other. This exchange of offerings, moreover, demonstrates
that, aside from them, all ambitious men prove to be easily manipulated, while all difficult women can be led to their downfall.

Thanks to their exemplary solidarity, Mme de Merteuil and Valmont
succeed in evading the three problems of the grand libertines: the
unworthiness of the public, the mediocrity of a loveless fantasy, and
the unbearable subjugation caused by amorous sentiments. First, the
Vicomte and the Marquise find in each other a jury they can fully trust.

Their mutual esteem is enough to preserve their respective exploits from the depreciation in store for triumphs acknowledged by an unworthy public. Second, their mutual passion seems well insulated from the poisonous emotions haunting the libertine's fortunes: the distaste experienced by a libertine seducer once his mistress surrenders, and the rancor he feels if he cannot overcome her resistance. Valmont and Merteuil's mutual desires, fueled by the martial feats that they dedicate to each other, are neither spoiled by the fulfillment nor whetted by the vengeance that a long frustration inevitably provokes. If the Vicomte and the Marquise defer their reunion in favor of the feats they demand of themselves, they are equally careful to soften their impatience by exchanging promises to find each other "at the end of the course." Finally, the way in which Valmont and Mme de Merteuil express their ardor for each other in no way compromises the freedom they demand; rather, in proving that they are as irresistible as invincible, the Marquise and the Vicomte show that they love each other and are worthy of the other's love. Thus, the relation woven between these two dangerous people escapes the asymmetry of roles that Laclos sees as the principal danger of liaisons. The libertine heroes of *Dangerous Liaisons* know neither the bitterness of the beloved, envious of the lover's passion, nor the servitude of the lover subject to the beloved's vengeance.

Doubtless, their art of love includes a measure of sacrifice, for it deprives its adepts of making love together, at least until the far-off day when the Vicomte will have humiliated every difficult woman in Parisian high society and the Marquise will have exposed the pretensions of every male libertine. Until that time, however, the profusion of compensatory delights to which both are entitled are bound to keep them patient. Further, since the lovers consider each of their conquests as both an offering and a step toward their reunion, they are confident that the pleasures of their respective adventures are a foretaste of their ultimate union. In short, the exchange of offerings proposed by Mme de Merteuil – and adopted by Valmont – elegantly resolves the dilemma of the grand libertine, for their solution preserves their love and their freedom at the slight price of temporary sexual frustration.

Nonetheless, their partnership harbors one remaining difficulty: unlike other grand libertines, who collect victories for their own glory, the Vicomte and the Marquise must also show themselves to be irresistible and invincible in order to assure each other's happiness. Thus, the combination of love and freedom each enjoys depends largely upon the other's success; conversely, the slightest misstep by either of them precipitates not only his or her own ruin but also the fall of his or her accomplice. In a sense, then, the risk inherent in the art of glorious conquest — a risk that the Marquise sums up in the exhortation "conquer or perish" (p. 1080) — is doubled. Valmont need only suffer one humiliating refusal or, worse, succumb to the charms of a woman other than Mme de Merteuil, for the latter to share the Vicomte's downfall. Such indeed is the fatal destiny that awaits them both when Valmont, despite his protests to the contrary, falls in love with Mme de Tourvel.

The Beloved's Happiness

How could a man as hardened as the hero of *Dangerous Liaisons* fall in love with the woman her rival sardonically calls the "heavenly prude"? At first, the Vicomte's designs seem rather banal, since they consist merely of seducing a virtuous woman. "You know the Présidente de Tourvel," Valmont writes in his first letter to Mme de Merteuil, "her piety, her conjugal devotion, her austere principles. That is where I have launched my attack. There is an enemy worthy of me. That is the goal I aspire to attain" (p. 946). Despite his bombastic tone, Valmont simply wants to conquer a woman whose rigorous morality depends on religion and who claims to have found happiness in marital fidelity. Even if a prude's faith and sincerity might spice up the prospect of her fall, Valmont's scheme remains the habitual work of a dangerous man. Consequently, Mme de Merteuil has no reason to be alarmed at her accomplice's new infatuation. Moreover, the conquered and ruined Mme de Tourvel would only take her place on the list of the Vicomte's other victims sacrificed to the Marquise. However, the latter has reserved some other tasks for Valmont — namely, she wants him to take care of young Cécile's "education" — and so she immediately sets out to deflect him from the Présidente.

To discourage him, Mme de Merteuil explains that this endeavor will bring little prestige and even less pleasure. On the one hand, as an irreproachable wife, Mme de Tourvel cannot muster sufficient resistance to the Vicomte, since she offers him no other rival than her own husband: "A husband! Does not the very idea humiliate you? If you fail, what dishonor! And so little glory if you succeed!" (p. 948). On the other hand, and again by reason of the conjugal fidelity of his prey, Valmont can hardly expect their affair to be rich in carnal delights: "I prophesy to you: at the very best, your Présidente will think she is doing everything for you by treating you as she treats her husband — and, remember, even the tenderest conjugal *tête-à-tête* takes place across a distance" (p. 948). Last but not least, even if the heavenly prude's religious devotion does not protect her from forsaking her wifely duties, it will at the very least deprive her of the ability to abandon herself without being tormented by hell's terror: "You may conquer her love of God, but you will never overcome her fear of the devil. And when you hold your mistress in your arms, and you feel her heart beat, it will be beating in fear and not in love" (p. 948).

The Marquise's banter does not produce the desired effect; on the contrary, angered by his accomplice's lack of support, Valmont pursues his scheme all the more vigorously. Anxious to counter Mme de Merteuil's mocking remarks, he does his utmost to make his undertaking seem more opportune than ever, presenting Mme de Tourvel's seduction as an enterprise ambitious beyond his usual repertory:

> I shall have this woman. I shall free her from a husband who profanes her.
> I shall carry her off from the very God that she adores. How enchanting
> to be in turn the cause and the cure of her remorse! Far be it from me to
> destroy the prejudices that possess her. They will add to my gratification
> and to my glory. Let her believe in virtue, but let her sacrifice it for my
> sake; let her be afraid of her sins, but let them not check her; and, when she
> is shaken by a thousand terrors, may it be only in my arms that she is
> able to overcome them and forget them. Then, if she wishes, let her say:
> "I adore you"; she alone, of all women, will be worthy to utter those words.
> And I shall indeed be the god of her choice (p. 950).

The Vicomte demonstrates an undeniable originality. Tired of Mme de Merteuil's condescension, which grants him no talent other than playing the conventional part of the grand libertine with panache,[2] he shows that he can surpass the boundaries of normal libertine conquest. Although possession of his prey remains his objective, he does not hesitate to renounce the demystification of moral and religious values, which seducers of his kind associate with triumph. Rather, he aspires to replace the illusions that govern Mme de Tourvel's existence with his own charms. Instead of disillusioning the Présidente by proving to her that conjugal friendship and divine love are no defense against an able manipulator of sensual desire, the Vicomte intends to become the preeminent source of his mistress's enchanting illusions. Rather than mocking the respected spouse and the adored divinity, and thus owing his victory to a lapse on the woman's part – that is, one of those moments of weakness which libertines know well how to exploit – he wants the heavenly prude to sacrifice *deliberately* the principles in which she will continue to believe. It is essential that Mme de Tourvel remain at once virtuous and pious, so that her lover, the Vicomte, may assert himself as "the god of her choice" (p. 950).

To achieve his ends, Valmont cannot accept his mistress's *surrender*, since his conquest would amount to no more than the favors of a disillusioned woman. Yet if he does not want to content himself with the Présidente's defeat, he must then modify his own habitual posture of intrepid conqueror and implacable strategist, upon which his whole reputation was built. As he himself writes, in two sentences that can be read as the novel's key, "It is no use reminding myself of bold schemes that have succeeded before; I cannot bring myself to put them into practice. I cannot be really happy unless she gives herself to me; and that is no trifling matter" (p. 951). The Vicomte's new project is certainly not unheard of in the history of the Western arts of love; nevertheless, it implies a surprising change of direction for a seducer of his caliber. For in hoping that Mme de Tourvel will give herself graciously to "the god of her choice," Valmont resolutely quits the paths of libertine glory to embrace the course of courtly love. He breaks with the chivalric heritage to embrace its rival tradition, that of the Provençal troubadours. In this tradition, inaugurated in the twelfth century, the practitioners of courtly love did not seek to win the capitulation of their mistress, and even less to glorify themselves by their eventual success; rather, they devoted themselves to maintaining a passion that would depend on their lady's "mercy" – a truly "gracious" gift that she dispenses at will.

A rogue as experienced as the Vicomte had certainly encountered women who viewed amorous passion as a gift of self. Indeed, these neo-*précieuse* propagandists who maintain that true love impels a lover to give him- or herself in order to make the beloved happy, are among the grand libertines' favorite victims. Nevertheless, Valmont's colleagues never tire of exposing the artificiality of such solicitude. Determined to denounce the "tenderness" exalted by the neo-*précieuses*, they strive to prove that this sentiment is not the spontaneous expression of a smitten heart but, rather, the result of a pernicious indoctrination whose end is to subject male lovers' desires to their mistresses' will. These "sensitive women," far from setting an example of the generosity they promote, are accused by the libertines of mixing hypocrisy with proselytism. For while they celebrate the cult of love as gift, they reserve its practice to their lovers. Wary of what they see as a wicked trap, the libertines avenge themselves in two ways: first, in taking possession of their mistresses without letting love lead them astray, then in proving that these sensitive women are no different from the rest of humanity. In other words, the libertines want to show that the *précieuses* themselves are governed not by their "heart," which they celebrate as the organ of love as gift, but by their carnal appetites and their vanity.

Although Valmont shares his peers' principles, his new project departs from the grand libertines' master plan. Instead of ridiculing the principles of the sensitive women, the Vicomte wants Mme de Tourvel to put them into practice. Where his colleagues would settle for exposing generous love as a hoax, Valmont wants the Présidente's favors not to proceed from the weakening of her resistance or the falsity of her convictions but, rather, from the existence of a love devoted only to the beloved's happiness.

Thus, when Mme de Merteuil reads Valmont's second letter, she has good reason to worry, for she knows that a woman who gives herself to the man she loves escapes the contempt suffered by those forced to surrender. An expert in female freedom, she knows that a woman who falls to a libertine seducer has nothing left to give him, since she has confirmed her conqueror's claims, whereas a mistress who deliberately lavishes her favors on her lover in no way compromises her desirable independence. Mme de Merteuil realizes that the Vicomte is unaware in his new plan of the consequences of his acts. Valmont is overjoyed because his role as courtly lover has temporarily "restored the charming illusions of [his] youth" (p. 951), but he seems not to understand that he risks remaining the prisoner of juvenile fantasies, to the point of being forever unable to "take the bandage from love's eyes" (p. 949). The Marquise is sure that if her accomplice persists in his refusal to revel in Mme de Tourvel's defeat, it will not be enough "to have this woman, so as to save [him]self from the ridicule of being in love with her" (p. 947). Furthermore, this would be no less catastrophic for Mme de Merteuil than for her accomplice, since her own happiness demands that Valmont remain a glorious seducer. Thus, she lavishes new warnings on him, not in order that he leave the Présidente, but that he return to methods worthy of him:

> You renounce your *bold schemes that have succeeded before*, so that you now lead a life devoid of principles, leaving everything to chance, or rather to the whim of the moment. Don't you remember that love, like medicine, *is only the art of encouraging nature?* You see how I can fight you with your own weapons; but I take no pride in that for, in fact, I am beating a man who is down. "She must give herself to me," you say. Oh yes, without any

doubt, she will – like the others, but with this difference: she will do it
with bad grace. But, so that she will give herself to you in the end, the
proper method is to begin by taking her. How truly characteristic that
absurd paradox is of love's fatuousness (p. 955).

Mme de Merteuil's call to order is surely worth listening to, but now
that Valmont at last has an original idea, he has no intention of letting
it go. For this reason, already despairing of her cause, Mme de Merteuil
makes one last attempt to reduce the Présidente to merely one more
of the Vicomte's offerings. The Marquise offers, once the Présidente has
given herself up, to break the "pact of eternal rupture" that binds her
to the Vicomte. Mme de Tourvel shall be the last expiatory victim
before their reunion: "As soon as you have seduced your Fair Devotee,
as soon as you can furnish me with proof that you have done so, come
to me and I shall be yours" (p. 968). Because she offers herself as a
reward, Mme de Merteuil still hopes to save Valmont – and their amorous connection – from the fatal consequences of his designs. More
precisely, she hopes that by promising laurels to her lover, he will be
vain enough to see the gift he awaits from the Présidente as yet another
libertine exploit.

The fact remains, however, that before enjoying the fruits of his new
erotic game, the Vicomte must find the means to obtain his desired
ends. With this objective in mind, he adopts a mélange of two styles,
mixing the techniques of the dangerous man with the Provençal troubadours' "service of love." Thus, he begins by approaching Mme de
Tourvel as a man of principles would approach a prude. In so doing, he
also behaves like a courtly lover who has yet to declare his love to his
noble lady. In his first approaches, Valmont is careful not to speak
of love to his mistress; he tries, rather, to soften her by affecting a
respect and a humility that, given his terrible reputation, are certainly
unexpected. What is more, he admits his past lapses and, joining his
remorse to his praise of honest women, soon lets the Présidente understand that it is only the happy influence she exerts over him that has
set him on the path of reform: "The key to my conduct you will find
in the unfortunate pliability of my character," he explains to his Fair
Devotee. "Living amongst people without morals, I imitated their
vices; perhaps I took pride, too, in outdoing them. Impressed in the
same way here by your virtuous example, I have, without hope of
emulating it, tried at least to follow it" (p. 974).

No sooner has he dedicated his conversion to Mme de Tourvel than
the Vicomte abandons his role of secret admirer in order to claim the

role of "supplicant." According to the conventions of courtly love, this title corresponds to the second station of love's service – the stage in which the lover confesses the nature of his sentiments, but still without hope of being repaid in kind. "Do not imagine you are being insulted by improper expectations on my part," Valmont pleads. "I shall be unhappy, I know, but I shall welcome my sufferings. They will prove the strength of my love. And it is at your feet, upon your breast that they will be appeased; there that I shall recover strength to suffer anew; there that I shall find goodness and compassion, and think myself consoled because you have pitied me" (p. 975).

At first, the Présidente takes offense at his confessions. Her virtue forbids her to listen to the declarations of a man who is not her that husband, yet her vanity suffers from being the object of the homages Valmont has already addressed to so many other women. Nonetheless, Valmont is not a man to be stopped by the remonstrances of a prude. Thus, he continues his supplications, in the fashion of the most languorous of courtly lovers. Faced with the Présidente's outrage, the Vicomte first protests his innocence: he maintains that he is not the master of his feelings, and that the love he feels is less his own work than that of his mistress.[3] Further, he maintains that he is entitled to demand the mercy of a Christian woman since he says that he is resolved to suffer without any hope that his sentiments will ever be shared. Finally, he promises to submit to his beloved's orders, but only if she consents to hear his laments – and this turns out to be particularly rewarding. The troubadours knew that in order to incite a lady to grant her "mercy," there was no more efficacious means than that of pledging her a flawless allegiance. In the same way, Valmont says that he has "always thought that, on the one hand, an order issued is a responsibility assumed, and on the other, that the illusion of authority we tempt women to entertain is one of the pitfalls they find it most difficult to avoid" (p. 1000).

Valmont soon takes advantage of the spectacle of his own devotion. He succeeds in exciting the envy of his severe mistress by affirming that, in spite of his sufferings, he is happier than the woman who refuses to open her heart to love. This argument, frequently used by libertines as they attack sensitive women, bears fruit: Mme de Tourvel resists for a while, first declaring herself terrified by the violence of love's passion, then proposing to substitute the sweetness of friendship. However, since Valmont, already sure of his power, refuses to compromise his feelings, the Présidente finally accords him the role of "platonic lover" – which corresponds to the third stage in courtly love's service – and even admits that her lover's turmoil has also captured her own heart.

In obtaining such an admission, the Vicomte has not just demonstrated persistence and self-abnegation; he has also adopted an argument worthy of a true *précieuse*. He uses his own example to affirm that the love inspired by a virtuous woman invites the man who experiences it to prove himself worthy of his mistress. Such fervor leads not to the lover's downfall but, on the contrary, to his redemption. In the present case, the Présidente ignites a flame in his heart which turns Valmont away from a lamentable existence of the "disorder of the senses" and "inflamed vanity" (p. 1022). Moreover, the repentant libertine endeavors to dispel Mme de Tourvel's last suspicions by explaining that the truly smitten man's only concern lies in tending to his beloved's happiness.

> These truths being so easy to grasp, and so pleasant to confirm in practice, what do you fear? How, besides, can you possibly be afraid of a man of feeling whose love allows him no happiness unless it be yours? That is now the only vow I am bound to: I shall sacrifice everything to it, except the feeling by which it is inspired. And even this feeling, if you consent to share it, you will dispose of as you choose (pp. 1082–83).

All throughout his service of love, but even more when he begins the ultimate stage of his journey – that is, when he aspires to become the carnal lover of his mistress – a troubadour cannot succeed without the quality he calls *mezura*. Distinct from humility, patience, and submission, to which a courtly lover is equally bound, this "measure" is not quite the same thing as restraint or moderation. Rather, it concerns an aptitude for attracting the beloved's mercy, indeed, an inability to enjoy anything else. In other words, the troubadour's *mezura* preserves him from anything unrelated to the gracious gifts of his lady. As heir to the Provençal poets, Valmont prides himself on this quality which allows him to remain faithful to his singular project. He takes pride in never availing himself of the opportunity of "taking" Mme de Tourvel when she reveals a moment of weakness: "I shall owe nothing to circumstances" (p. 1117), he writes to Mme de Merteuil. And in fact, such opportunities arise on at least two occasions. The first occurs when the Vicomte declares his passion: "My blood was on fire, and I was so little in control of myself that I was tempted to make the most of the occasion" (p. 975); the second when the Présidente admits her own: "those beautiful eyes were actually raised to mine. That heavenly mouth even pronounced these words: 'Well! yes, I...' But suddenly her glance faded, her voice failed, and the adorable woman collapsed in my arms" (p. 1118). His mistress's swoon puts Valmont to an ultimate test, which corresponds to that which the troubadours call the *asag*. In this exercise of restrained desire, the measured lover must not take advantage of his lady when she invites him to spend a chaste night in her bed.

In the same way, the Vicomte boasts of the purity of his methods, for he abstains from profiting from his advantage. Such a display of measure brings him only bitter reproaches from Mme de Merteuil: "What do you expect a poor woman to do when she surrenders and is not taken? Upon my word, in such circumstances she must at least save her honor – and that is what your Présidente has done" (pp. 1134–35). All the same, Valmont firmly intends to maintain his course of conduct, for his object is not so much to warm the senses of the heavenly prude in order to exploit her temporary weakness as to appeal to her heart. Such an organ may be factitious, as the alleged site of generous love; but it enables a sensitive woman to justify herself when she gives herself over deliberately to a desire she recognizes as the expression of her passion. By proceeding in this way, the Vicomte not only abjures the principles that have made his glory but even continues to follow the commandments of the *précieuses*. Not content to bend the Présidente's will to the forces of nature, he strives to inspire in her an emotion that, "far from following the usual course" (p. 1189), will seize her heart before winning her senses.

After many postponements, the day of the long-awaited gift finally arrives. If Valmont must face Mme de Tourvel's third "swoon," this time he manages to avoid yet another postponement. Almost discouraged by the spectacle of his mistress vacillating between convulsive sobs and catatonia, the ingenious lover finds the path to success in posing the following question:

"And are you in despair because you have made me happy?" At this, the adorable creature turned toward me, and her face, though still a little distraught, had already resumed that heavenly expression. "Happy?" she said. You may imagine the reply. "Are you then happy?" I redoubled my protestations. "And happy because of me!"..."You are right," said the tender-hearted creature. "I can no longer endure my existence unless it is of use in making you happy. I devote myself entirely to that. From this moment on I am yours, and you will hear neither refusals nor regrets from my lips" (pp. 1176–77).

The Vicomte's project is fully realized, yet his success immediately brings about the fatal consequences foreseen by Mme de Merteuil. As she predicted, Valmont fails to see that the difference between a woman's surrender and his mistress's gracious gift extends beyond the consummation of the carnal act. In other words, he does not see that while a woman may surrender herself only once, in the sense that her defeat is thus sealed once and for all, she may give herself as often as she likes without appearing to be anything less than a sovereign being. For this oversight, the imprudent Vicomte finds himself, on the day following his success, prey to an "obscure feeling" that torments him ceaselessly:

> Even had yesterday's episode, as I think, carried me further than I had expected to go; even though I did, for a moment, share the agitations and intoxications I had provoked, the passing illusion would by now have been dissipated. Yet the same charm subsists. I should even, I admit, feel a rather delicate pleasure in giving way to it, were it not that it causes me some disquiet. Shall I, at my age, be overmastered like a schoolboy by an obscure and involuntary feeling (pp. 1170–71)?

Anxious to combat the agonizing thought that he has fallen victim to the very passion he strove to awaken in Mme de Tourvel, Valmont reviews every explanation that might spare him "the humiliation of thinking that I might in any way have been dependent on the very slave I had subjected to my will" (p. 1171). In short, he tries to account for his strange emotion in a way that will save him from the ridiculous position of being in love. He first envisages attributing his state to his gratified pride: after all, he has succeeded in winning the adoration of a woman well known for her religious principles and her conjugal fidelity, who has overcome all her hesitation in order to devote herself wholly to the happiness of "the god of her choice." Surely, he says, this is legitimate cause for self-esteem. However, the Vicomte is not quite convinced by this first justification, which he abandons for a second hypothesis, that leads him to interpret the Présidente's persistent charms from the economic point of view, as the reward for effort. Thus, in answer to the accusations of Mme de Merteuil, who calls to admit that he is in love, Valmont invokes just compensation for his efforts: "remember too that I have hardly had a week to enjoy the fruits of three months' labors. I have so often kept for longer what was worth less and cost me not so much! ... and you have never drawn conclusions from that to my discredit" (p. 1188).

The Vicomte, hardly persuaded by his own arguments, remains obstinate in denying that his distress is caused by love. Thus, he takes a third path, explaining that the interest he devotes to Mme de Tourvel derives from a kind of scientific curiosity. He maintains that his previous mistresses had no fundamental motivations other than pleasure and vanity: more precisely, some were governed by the appetite for sensual delights, others by their vanity in attracting a renowned lover. In contrast, the Présidente seems truly motivated by the desire to make the man she loves happy. Even if Valmont attributes this devotion mainly to his own talent, he nonetheless considers this a sufficiently rare phenomenon to justify his desire to remain for a while near Mme de Tourvel:

> It is not surprising, therefore, that she should interest me for longer than anyone else has; and if my experiment upon her demands my making her happy, perfectly happy, why should I refuse, particularly since her happiness will be useful to me rather than otherwise? But does it follow, from the fact that my mind is occupied, that my heart is enslaved? No, of course not (p. 1189).

Whether he pleads an artist's pride, a warrior's repose, or a savant's curiosity, though, Valmont does not succeed in quieting his own restlessness. He cannot persuade himself that he is not smitten with his mistress, nor can he put an end to Mme de Merteuil's mockery. In desperation, he reverts to the dangerous man's modus operandi, endeavoring to prove his indifference by insulting Mme de Tourvel, he flaunts his infidelities and gives free reign to his cruel and sudden mood changes. Yet again, the experiment fails; try as he might to dissimulate his sentiments by maltreating the Présidente, he cannot escape the Marquise's lucid vision. She retorts that the ills he suffers are even deeper than they seem, since the humiliations to which he subjects his beloved are not sufficient to detach him from her.

In short, despite his protests, Valmont undergoes the same misadventure later evoked by Laclos in *On the Education of Women*. He ends up in the same condition as those women who invent amorous passion in order to dominate men but cannot resist the temptation to experience the emotions they aroused in them. In other words, the hero of *Dangerous Liaisons* is caught in the very trap he set for his mistress. If he first boasts of the delights of the love as gift with the sole end of convincing Mme de Tourvel, he quickly becomes envious of the joy that the Présidente truly finds in making him happy. For her part, the heavenly prude reveals a remarkable confidence in the contagious powers of her own felicity, and thus in the tender solicitude which is its cause: "Why should he cease to love me? What other woman could he make happier than me? And I know from my own experience that the happiness one gives is the strongest bond, the only one that really holds" (p. 1187).

Though the Vicomte may reject it, the spectacle his mistress affords him brings him into the enchanted circle of "gracious" love. The joy he provokes in Mme de Tourvel from now on means more to him than his own prestige, precisely because this joy cannot be reduced to a measure of his merit. A grand libertine's glory serves to measure the value of his victories, and the capitulations he obtains are merely the remuneration for his exploits. In contrast, the "grace" dispensed by a woman who deliberately gives herself is by definition priceless, hence its splendor exceeds that of the greatest conquests. For this reason, the Présidente's expansive happiness begins to supplant the ardor that Valmont's upcoming union with Mme de Merteuil inspires in him: where the Marquise has promised herself as the ultimate reward for her accomplice's exploits, her rival graciously devotes herself to her lover's happiness. However, Valmont remains enough of a libertine to believe that the heart is an instrument of subjection which a free man must resist with all his might. Prisoner of his "schemes of glory," he cannot tolerate the sway of a charm that cannot be reduced to the pleasure of the senses or to the satisfaction of vanity. Thus, the Vicomte shows himself as incapable of giving himself up to his love for Mme de Tourvel as he is of effectively repressing it.

Desperate but still lucid, Mme de Merteuil realizes that shame is what prevents Valmont from tasting his happiness – and that his aberration is nonetheless irrevocable. Thus, she resolves to scuttle the art of love she has devised for the Vicomte, but not without exacting vengeance for the wretch's treason. Under the pretext of saving her former accomplice from his quandary, she challenges him to send her rival a letter, which she herself has written, breaking off their relations. This implacable missive, which is also a eulogy for a now almost defunct libertinism,[4] seals the fate of the three protagonists. In sending it, Valmont only drives himself deeper into his predicament, for he renounces a state of grace which his principles forbid him to assume in order to remain faithful to a conception of glory through which he can no longer attain satisfaction. In reading it, Mme de Tourvel loses her reason to live, since by her own admission, she exists only to bring happiness to her beloved. And finally, in writing it, Mme de Merteuil destroys the woman who supplanted her in her lover's heart, but only at the price of her own love affair with Valmont. Without a doubt, the Marquise succeeds in avenging herself definitively on the Présidente: "when one woman takes aim at the heart of another," she assures Valmont, "she rarely fails to find the vulnerable spot, and the wound she makes is incurable" (p. 1208). All the same, she also knows that once the Vicomte has sacrificed Mme de Tourvel, he will understand that she was much more than an offering. Consequently, as Mme de Merteuil dictates her letter, she avails herself – for the last time – of her status of the idol to whom all other women must be immolated.

If the tragic outcome of *Dangerous Liaisons* heralds the end of libertinism, it is nonetheless true that the body of the novel defines two distinct ways of combining love and liberty. In this respect, it is remarkable that Laclos would rely on two modalities of feminine sovereignty – the exchange of offerings imagined by the Marquise, and the happiness of the beloved pursued by the Présidente – to try to extricate dangerous men caught between servitude and boredom. Both Mme de Tourvel and Mme de Merteuil escape the constraints of resistance that female advocates of invincibility impose upon themselves, since they renounce neither the fulfilment of their desires nor the acknowledgment of their sentiments. Yet, each in her own fashion escapes the distaste that the grand libertines feel for the women whose capitulation they obtain. Despite the considerable differences between Laclos's two heroines, both maintain an irreducible independence that allows them to arouse their lover's desire without depriving themselves of the pleasures of love. Thus, both women are in a position to save the man of principles they love, from the fatal humiliation represented by the slightest defeat and from the no less fatal tedium that follows each of his victories.

NOTES

1. On this point, see Anne-Marie Jaton, "Libertinage feminin, libertinage dangereux," in *Laclos et le libertinage* (Paris: Presses Universitaires de France, 1983), pp. 151–62.

2. "You are really without any genius for your calling; you know what you have learned but can invent nothing new, so that as soon as circumstances no longer conform to your usual formulas, as soon as you must deviate from the customary path, you are brought up short like the merest schoolboy" (Letter 106, p. 1135).

3. "[A]nd if my love alone is recalcitrant, if that alone you cannot destroy, it is because my love is your own handiwork and not mine" (Letter 35, p. 992).

4. "One is very soon bored with everything, my angel; it is a law of nature. It is not my fault" (Letter 141, p. 1203).

Translated by Sophie Hawkes.

CONTENTS

DANGEROUS LIAISONS

Or Letters Collected in
One Section of Society and Published
for the Edification of Others
by Monsieur C—— de L——

*I have seen the customs of my time, and I published
these letters.*
– Jean-Jacques Rousseau
Preface to La Nouvelle Héloïse

Publisher's Note

WE THINK IT our duty to warn the public that in spite of the title of
this work, and of what the editor says about it in his preface, we cannot guarantee its authenticity as a collection of letters: we have in fact,
very good reason to believe that it is only a novel.

What is more, it seems to us that the author, in spite of his evident
attempts at verisimilitude, has himself destroyed every semblance of
truth – and done so most clumsily – by setting the events he describes
in the present. In fact, several of the characters he puts on his stage are
persons of such vicious habits that it is impossible to suppose they can
have lived in our age: this age of philosophy, in which the light of reason, illuminating every heart, has turned us all, as everyone knows, into
honorable men and modest and retiring women.

Our opinion, therefore, is that if the adventures recorded in this
book have any foundation in truth, they must have happened in other
places or at other times; and we consider the author – who has evidently
been beguiled by hopes of attracting more interest for his story into
locating it in his own time and country – we consider him very much
to blame for venturing to represent, under the guise of our costume and
our customs, a way of life so altogether alien to us.

To keep the overly credulous reader at least from being taken unawares in this connection, as far as we can, we shall support our opinion with an argument that we offer him with confidence, since it appears to us to be incontrovertible and unchallengeable: to wit, though like causes will always produce like effects, we no more see girls nowadays who have dowries of sixty thousand livres taking the veil than we see young and pretty married women dying of grief.

Editor's Preface

This work, or rather this collection of letters, which the public will perhaps find too voluminous in any case, contains nevertheless only a very small portion of the correspondence from which it was drawn. Commissioned to set them in order by the persons into whose possession the letters had fallen (whom, I knew, intended to have them published), I asked nothing for my pains but permission to delete what seemed to me to serve no purpose. I have tried, in fact, to retain only those letters which appeared necessary either to an understanding of the events or to the development of the characters. If to this trifling task is added that of arranging in order such letters as I allowed to remain (an order that is almost invariably chronological), and finally a few brief and sparsely scattered notes (which, for the most part, have no other object than to indicate the sources of quotations or to explain the abridgements I have permitted myself to make), my whole contribution to this work is accounted for. My mission extended no further.*

I had proposed more considerable alterations, almost all of them relating to purity of diction and style, which will often be found very much at fault. I should also have liked permission to abridge certain letters that are too long; several of them discuss successively, but with scarcely any transition between, subjects that have nothing whatever in common with each other. This course of action was not approved: it would not, of course, have been sufficient by itself to give the work any merit, but it would at least have removed some of its faults.

It was objected that the intention was to publish the letters themselves, and not simply a literary work modeled on the letters; that it would have been as contrary to probability as to truth if the eight or

---

*I must indicate here, too, that I have suppressed or changed the names of all the persons concerned in these letters; and that if among the names I have invented any are found that belong to living persons, they represent merely accidental errors on my part, from which no necessary consequence is to be drawn.

ten persons participating in this correspondence had written with equal correctness. And upon my representing that it was far from there being any question of correctness, for there was not a single one of these persons who had not committed the grossest errors, which could not fail to meet with criticism, it was replied that every reasonable reader would surely expect to find mistakes in a collection of letters that had passed between private individuals, since of all those published hitherto by various authors of reputation (including certain academicians) not one could be found totally beyond reproach in this respect. These arguments did not convince me; I found them – as I still find them – easier to put forward than accept. But the final say was not mine, and I submitted. I reserved only the right to protest, to declare, as I now do, my difference of view.

As for any merit that might attach to this work, it is perhaps not for me to offer an opinion that neither can nor should influence anyone else's. Those, however, who would be glad to know more or less what they are to expect before they begin to read a book would do well to read on; others would do better to proceed immediately to the text itself. They know enough about it already.

What I must say at the outset is this: were it my conviction (as I admit it was) that these letters ought to be published, I am still very far from expecting any success for them – and let not this frankness on my part be taken for the false modesty of an author; for I must declare with the same candor that, if this collection had seemed to me unworthy of being offered to the public, I should have had nothing to do with it. Let us try to reconcile these apparent contradictions.

The merit of a work derives from its usefulness or from the pleasure it gives, or even from both, when it has both to offer. But success, which is not always a proof of merit, depends more often on the choice of a subject than on its execution, on a certain combination of subjects rather than on the way in which they have been treated. Now since this collection contains, as its title announces, the letters of a whole section of society, it represents a diversity of interests which are not all those of the reader. Moreover, since nearly all the sentiments expressed are either pretended or dissembled, they can excite only the interest of curiosity, an interest always much inferior to that of feeling – one, above all, that, inclining the reader less to indulgence, leaves errors of detail more open to criticism, since it is they that continually frustrate the one desire he wishes to satisfy.

These faults are perhaps partly redeemed by a quality inherent in the very nature of the work: the variety of its styles, a merit that a single author would find difficult to achieve but here appears of itself, sparing the reader the tedium at least of uniformity. Some people might also take into account the fairly large number of either original or little-known observations to be found dispersed throughout the work. These too, I think, constitute all that may be anticipated from the book in the way of pleasure, and even then only on the most lenient appraisal.

The usefulness of the work, which will perhaps be even more strongly contested, seems to me nevertheless easier to establish. I, at any rate, think that it is a service to public morals to reveal the methods employed by those who are wicked in corrupting those who are good, and I believe these letters may effectively contribute something toward this end. In them will also be found proof and example of two important truths that one might almost think go unrecognized in view of the fact that they are so rarely remembered in practice: one, that any woman who consents to receive an unprincipled man into her circle of friends must end his victim; the other, that any mother who allows anyone but herself to win her daughter's confidence is imprudent, to say the least. Young people of either sex might also learn that the friendship which unprincipled persons offer them so glibly is always a dangerous trap, as fatal to their happiness as to their virtue. On the other hand, the abuse of knowledge, which so often follows close upon benefit from it, seems to me in their case too much to be feared; far from recommending this book to young people, it seems to me very important to keep it away from them. The time at which it may cease to be dangerous and become useful has been very well determined, for her own sex, by a good mother who is not only intelligent but sensible as well: "Having read this correspondence in manuscript," she told me, "I should consider it a true service to my daughter to give her the book on her wedding day." If mothers in every family were to think like this, I should never cease to congratulate myself for having published it.

Putting aside such agreeable fancies, though, it still seems to me that this collection can please very few. Libertines of either sex will find it in their interest to decry a book that may do them harm; and since they are never without cunning, they will perhaps be clever enough to attract the puritans to their side, who will be alarmed by the picture of wickedness which is here fearlessly presented.

Would-be freethinkers will not be interested in a devout woman, whom they will regard as a ninny because she is devout, while the devout will be angry at seeing virtue fall, and will complain that religion does not appear to enough effect.

From another point of view, readers of fastidious taste will be disgusted at the excessively simple and incorrect style of many of these letters; whereas the general run of readers, misled by the idea that everything printed is the result of deliberation, will think they detect in others the labored manner of an author who appears in person behind the characters through whom he speaks.

Finally, it will be said in general that nothing is of any value out of its proper place; and that, ordinarily, if letters in the social world are deprived of all grace by an overly cautious style on the part of their authors, the smallest negligence in letters such as these becomes a fault and is made insupportable by being committed to print.

I admit in all sincerity that these criticisms may be well founded: I believe, too, that I could reply to them, even without exceeding the permissible length of a preface. But it must be apparent that were it necessary to answer for everything, the book itself could answer for nothing; and if I had judged that to be the case, I should have suppressed both book and preface.

Part One

LETTER 1: *Cécile de Volanges to Sophie Carnay at the Ursuline Convent of ———*

You see, my dear Sophie, I am keeping my word. Frills and furbelows do not take up all my time; there will always be some left over for you. Nonetheless, I have seen more frippery in the course of this one day than I did in all the four years we spent together; and I think our fine Tanville* is going to be more mortified by my next visit to the convent (when I shall certainly ask to see her) than she could ever have hoped we would be by all her visits to us *en grande tenue*. Mamma has consulted me in everything; she treats me much less like a schoolgirl than she used to. I have my own maid, a bedroom, and boudoir to myself, and I am sitting as I write at the prettiest desk to which I have been given the key so that I can lock away whatever I wish. Mamma has told me that I am to see her every morning when she gets up. I need not have my hair dressed before dinner, since we shall always be alone, and then every day she will tell me at what time she expects me to join her in the afternoon. The rest of the time is at my disposal, and I have my harp, my drawing, and my books – just as at the convent, except that Mother Perpétue is not here to scold me, and, if I choose to be idle, it is entirely

---

*A fellow pupil.

my affair. But, as I have not my Sophie to chat and laugh with me, I would just as soon be busy.

It is not yet five o'clock and Mamma is not expecting me till seven: plenty of time, if only I had something to tell you! But so far I have been told nothing, and if it were not that preparations are plainly being made and numbers of women employed on my behalf, I should be inclined to think that no one had ever dreamed of marrying me and that the idea was just another of our dear Joséphine's absurdities. Still, Mamma has so often told me that a young lady ought to stay at her convent till she is married that, since she has taken me out, Joséphine must certainly be right.

A carriage has just come to the door and Mamma has sent to tell me to come to her room at once. Supposing it is he? I am not dressed. My hands are trembling and my heart beating fast. I asked the maid whether she knew who was with my mother. "Indeed," she said, "it is Monsieur C——" And she laughed! Oh, it must be he! I shall come back without fail and tell you what has happened. That is his name, at any rate. I must not keep them waiting. For the moment, good-bye!

How you will laugh at your poor Cécile! I was so ashamed of myself! But you would have been caught just as I was. As I came into Mamma's room I saw, standing by her, a gentleman dressed in black. I greeted him as best I could and stood there, quite unable to move. You can imagine how I scrutinized him!

"Madame," he said to my mother as he bowed to me. "What a charming young lady; I am more than ever sensible of the extent of your kindness."

The meaning of this was so plain that I was seized with trembling and my knees gave way; I found a chair and sat down, very flushed and very disconcerted. I had hardly done this when the man was at my feet. Upon which I lost my head; I was, as Mamma said, utterly panic-stricken. I jumped up uttering a piercing shriek...just as I did that day there was a thunderstorm, do you remember? Mamma burst out laughing and said, "Come now, what is the matter? Sit down and give your foot to Monsieur." In short, my dear, the gentleman was a shoemaker. I cannot tell you how ashamed I was; luckily no one but Mamma was there. I think I shall have to find another shoemaker when I am married.

How worldly-wise we are — you must admit! Good-bye. It is nearly six o'clock, and my maid says I must dress. Good-bye, my dear Sophie; I love you as much as I ever did at the convent.

P.S. I don't know by whom to send this letter, so I shall wait till Joséphine comes.

Paris
1 August 17–

LETTER 2: *The Marquise de Merteuil to the Vicomte de Valmont at the Château de ———*

Come back, my dear Vicomte, come back. What are you doing, what can you possibly do at the house of an old aunt whose property is all entailed on you? Leave at once; I need you. I have had an excellent idea, and I want to put its execution in your hands. These few words should be enough; only too honored by this mark of my consideration, you should come, eagerly, and take my orders on your knees. But you abuse my kindness, even now that you no longer exploit it. Remember that since the alternative to this excessive indulgence is my eternal hatred, your happiness demands that indulgence prevail. Well, I am willing to inform you of my plans, but swear first that, as my faithful cavalier, you will undertake no other enterprise till you have accomplished this one. It is worthy of a hero: you will serve Love and Revenge, and in the end it will be yet another *rouerie** to include in your memoirs – for one day I shall have your memoirs published, and I take it upon myself to write them. But let us leave that for the moment and return to what is on my mind.

Madame de Volanges is marrying her daughter; it is still a secret, but yesterday it was imparted to me. And whom do you think she has chosen for son-in-law? The Comte de Gercourt! Who would have thought that I should ever become Gercourt's cousin? It has put me in a fury... Well! Have you guessed? Oh, dull-witted creature! Have you forgiven him then for the affair of the intendante?[1] As for me, have I not even more reason than you, monster that you are, to complain of him?† Still – I am calm. The hope of vengeance soothes my soul.

---

*The words *roué* and *rouerie*, which in good society are now happily falling into discredit, were very much in vogue at the time these letters were written.

†To understand this passage it must be known that the Comte de Gercourt had left the Marquise de Merteuil for the Intendante de ——— who, in her turn, had given up the Vicomte de Valmont for him. It was after this that the attachment between the Marquise and the Vicomte began. Because the latter affair took place long before the events with which the present letters are concerned, the entire correspondence relating to it has been suppressed.

You have been irritated as often as I at the importance Gercourt attaches to the kind of wife he wishes to have, and at the stupid presumption that makes him believe he will escape his inevitable fate. You know his absurd predilection for convent girls, and his even more ridiculous prejudice in favor of modest blondes. In fact, I am quite certain that, in spite of the sixty thousand livres a year the little Volanges will bring him, he would never have considered this marriage had she been dark or had never been inside a convent. Well, let us prove to him that he is only a fool. It will certainly be proved one day; I am not anxious about that. But the delightful thing would be his beginning in that role. How amusing it would be, the morning after, to hear him boast! – for he will certainly boast. Then, if you had succeeded in educating the girl, it would be nobody's fault if he did not become, with the best of them, the laughingstock of Paris.

For the rest, the heroine of this new romance deserves your fullest attention. She is really pretty: only fifteen years of age, a rosebud. Gauche, of course, to a degree, and quite without style, but you men are not discouraged by that. What is more, a certain languor in her looks really promises well. Add to these recommendations the consideration that it is I who make them, and you have only to thank me and obey.

You will receive this letter tomorrow morning. I insist upon your being at my house at seven o'clock in the evening. I shall receive no one till eight, not even the reigning favorite: he has not the head for affairs of such importance. With me, you will observe, love is not blind. At eight I shall give you your liberty, and at ten you will return to sup with the beautiful creature: both mother and daughter will be taking supper with me. Good-bye. It is past noon. I shall have done with you before long.

Paris
4 August 17–

LETTER 3: *Cécile de Volanges to Sophie Carnay*
I know nothing yet, my dear. Mamma had a great many people to supper yesterday. In spite of my interest in examining them, the men especially, I was terribly bored. Everybody, men and women alike, looked at me a great deal and then whispered in each other's ears; it was obvious they were whispering about me, which made me blush. I could not help it, though I wish I had been able to. I noticed that when the other women were looked at they did not blush. Or else their rouge prevents it being seen when they color with embarrassment, because

it must be very difficult not to blush when a man stares at you.

What made me feel most ill at ease was that I did not know what they were thinking of me. I think I heard the word "pretty" once or twice; "gauche" I heard very distinctly, and that must really be true about me because the woman who said it is a relation and friend of my mother's. She seems to have decided all of a sudden to be my friend as well, and was the only person who spoke to me a little the whole evening. We are to have supper with her tomorrow.

After supper I also heard a man, who I am sure was talking about me, saying to another, "That one must be left to ripen. Next winter we shall see." Perhaps it is to him I am to be married; but in that case it will not be for another four months! I should so much like to know how things stand.

Here is Joséphine, and she tells me she is in a hurry. But I must tell you first about one of my gaucheries. Oh, I'm afraid my mother's friend was right!

After supper they began to play cards, and I sat down beside Mamma. I don't know how it happened, but I fell asleep almost immediately. A great burst of laughter woke me up. I don't know whether they were laughing at me, but I believe they must have been. Mamma, to my great relief, gave me permission to retire. Imagine, it was past eleven o'clock! Good-bye, my dear Sophie; I hope you will always love your Cécile. I assure you the world is not nearly as amusing as we used to imagine it was.

Paris
4 August 17–

LETTER 4: *The Vicomte de Valmont to the Marquise de Merteuil in Paris*
Your orders are charming, your manner of giving them still more delightful: you would make tyranny itself adored. This is not, as you know, the first time I have regretted that I am no longer your slave. *Monster* though you say I am, I can never remember without pleasure a time when you favored me with sweeter names. I often wish, further, that I might earn them again, and that in the end I might give, with you, an example to the world of perfect constancy. But larger concerns demand our attention. Conquest is our destiny; we must follow it. Perhaps at the end of the course we shall meet again, for, if I may say this without offending you, my dear Marquise, you follow close at my heels: indeed, it seems to me that on our mission of love, since we decided to separate for the general good and have been preaching the faith in

our respective spheres, you have made more conversions than I have. I know your zeal, your fiery fervor. And if our God judges us by our deeds, you will one day be the patron of some great city, while I shall be, at most, a village saint. Does my idiom astonish you? But for a week I have not heard or used any other, and it is because I must master it that I am obliged to disobey you.

Don't be angry; listen. I am going to tell you, the confidante of all my inmost secrets, the most ambitious plan I have yet conceived. What is it you suggest? That I should seduce a young girl who has seen nothing and knows nothing – who, so to speak, would fall undefended. She would be beside herself at the first compliment and would perhaps sooner be swayed by curiosity than by love. Twenty other men could do it as well as I. Not so the enterprise that claims my attention: its success will ensure me not only pleasure but glory. The god of love himself cannot decide between myrtle and laurel for my crown and he will have to unite them to honor my triumph. Even you, my love, will be struck with holy awe, and will say with enthusiasm: "There goes a man after my own heart."

You know the Présidente[2] de Tourvel: you know her piety, her conjugal devotion, her austere principles. That is where I have launched my attack. There is an enemy worthy of me. That is the goal I aspire to attain.

And though at last I fail to carry off the prize,
I shall have ventured on a glorious enterprise.

One may quote bad poetry if it is by a great poet.*

You probably know that the Président is in Burgundy attending to an important case (I hope to make him lose a still more important one). It is here that his inconsolable spouse is to spend the whole of her distressing grass widowhood. Mass every day, a few visits to the poor of the district, morning and evening prayers, solitary walks, pious conversations with my old aunt, and sometimes a dreary game of whist – these are her only distractions. But I am preparing more effective ones. My guardian angel brought me here, for her happiness and for mine. Fool that I was, I begrudged twenty-four hours sacrificed to respect for the conventions. What a penance it would be now to be obliged to return to Paris! Fortunately it requires four to play whist and as there is no one here besides the local curé, who makes a third, my immortal

---

*La Fontaine.

aunt has implored me to stay a few days. As you have guessed, I consented. You cannot imagine the fuss she has made of me ever since, and how edified she is by my regular attendance at prayers and at Mass. She has no suspicion of the nature of the divinity I go to worship.

Here I am, then: for the past four days the victim of an overpowering passion. You know how strong my desires are, how they thrive on obstacles; what you do not know is the extent to which solitude can increase their force. I have only one idea: I think of it all day and dream of it at night. It has become necessary for me to have this woman, so as to save myself from the ridicule of being in love with her; for to what lengths will a man not be driven by thwarted desire? O sweet delight that for my happiness, for my very peace of mind, I crave! How lucky we are that women defend themselves so poorly! We should, otherwise, be no more to them than timid slaves. At this moment I feel grateful to all women of easy virtue, a sentiment that brings me naturally to your feet. Prostrate there, I beg your forgiveness, and finish this too long letter. Good-bye, my dearest love: no ill-feeling.

Château de ———
5 August 17–

LETTER 5: *The Marquise de Merteuil to the Vicomte de Valmont*
Do you know, Vicomte, that your letter is most extraordinarily insolent and that I might very well be angry? However, it proves clearly that you are out of your mind; and that, if nothing else, spares you my indignation. Ever your generous and sympathetic friend, I shall forget my injuries so as to devote my whole attention to you in your danger. However tedious it may be to reason with you, I yield to your present need.

You – have the Présidente de Tourvel! But what a ridiculous fantasy this is! How characteristic of your perverse heart that longs only for what appears to be out of reach. Come, what is there to this woman? Regular features, if you like, but so inexpressive; a passable figure, but no grace and always so ludicrously ill-dressed, with those bundles of kerchiefs on a bodice that reaches to her chin! I tell you as a friend: you will not need two women of that sort to lose your reputation. Have you forgotten the day when she took the collection at Saint-Roch and you thanked me so delightedly for having afforded you the spectacle? I can see her still, on the arm of that great long-haired spindleshanks, ready to collapse at every step, forever burying someone's head in five yards of pannier, and blushing at every genuflection. Would you have believed then you would one day want this woman? Come now, Vicomte, you must yourself blush and return to your senses. I shall keep the secret, I promise.

After all, consider the disagreeable things in store for you! What sort of rival have you to contend with? A husband! Does not the very idea humiliate you? If you fail, what dishonor! And so little glory if you succeed! I shall go further: you must give up all hope of pleasure. Can there ever be any with prudes? I mean those who are truly so. At the very heart of rapture they remain aloof, offering you only half-delights. That absolute self-abandon, that ecstasy of the senses, when pleasure is purified in its own excess, all that is best in love is quite unknown to them. I prophesy to you: at the very best, your Présidente will think she is doing everything for you by treating you as she treats her husband, and, remember, even the tenderest conjugal tête-à-tête takes place across a distance. In your case, things are still worse. Your prude is devout, and with that sort of simple piety that condemns a woman to eternal childishness. You will perhaps surmount this obstacle, but do not flatter yourself that you will destroy it. You may conquer her love of God, but you will never overcome her fear of the devil. And when you hold your mistress in your arms, and you feel her heart beat, it will be beating in fear and not for love. Had you met this woman earlier you might perhaps have been able to make something of her, but she is twenty-two, and she has been married for nearly two years. Believe me, Vicomte, when a woman has become so *encrusted* with prejudice, she is best left to her fate. She will never be anything better than a nobody.

Yet it is on account of this fine creature that you refuse to obey me; for her that you bury yourself in that mausoleum of your aunt's, renouncing the most delightful adventure in the world and the one most calculated to do you honor. Is it then your fate that Gercourt shall always maintain some advantage over you? Do you know, with the best will in the world – I am tempted at this moment to believe you do not deserve your reputation. What is more, I am tempted to withdraw the confidence I have placed in you. I should never get used to telling my secrets to the lover of Madame de Tourvel.

I want you to know, nonetheless, that the little Volanges has already turned one head. Young Danceny dotes on her. He has sung with her; and, in fact, she sings better than is proper in a convent girl. They must have practiced a great many duets now, and I daresay she would be willing enough to try something in unison, but Danceny is a child: he will waste all his time flirting and achieve nothing. The little creature, for her part, is as diffident; and, in any event, it will all be much less amusing than you could have made it. I am in a bad humor, therefore, and I am sure to quarrel with the chevalier when he arrives. He would be well advised to be kind: at this moment it would cost me nothing to break with him. I am sure that if I had the good sense to leave him now he would be in despair, and nothing amuses me so much as a lover's despair. He would call me "false," a word that has always given me pleasure. There is none more welcome to a woman's ear, excepting "cruel," which, however, one must take more pains to deserve. Seriously, I am going to consider breaking with him. See what you have brought about! I lay it on your conscience! Good-bye. Recommend me to the prayers of your Présidente.

Paris
7 August 17–

LETTER 6: *The Vicomte de Valmont to the Marquise de Merteuil*
So there is, after all, no woman who will not abuse the power she has been able to acquire! You, too, you whom I so often called my indulgent friend, are at length no longer so. You do not even hesitate to attack me in the object of my affections. How dare you paint such a picture of Madame de Tourvel?... Any man would have paid with his life for such insolent presumption. Any other woman but you would have deserved severe punishment at least. Never, I beg you, put me to such harsh tests again; I shall not be able to answer for the consequences. In the name of our friendship wait, at least, till I have had this woman before you insult her. Did you not know that only pleasure has the right to take the bandage from love's eyes?

But what am I saying? What need has Madame de Tourvel of illusions? To be adorable she has only to be herself. You accuse her of being ill-dressed. I agree. Clothes don't become her. Everything that hides her, disfigures. It is in the freedom of dishabille that she is truly ravishing. Thanks to the present overpowering heat she wears only a simple linen gown, which reveals her supple, rounded figure. A single muslin kerchief covers her breasts, and my covert but searching glances have already grasped their enchanting contours. Her face, you say, is inexpressive. But what is it to express at moments when nothing touches her heart? No, she is not of course one of your coquettes with their deceptive looks that are sometimes seductive but always false. She does not know how to disguise an empty phrase with a studied smile; and, although she has the most beautiful teeth in the world, she laughs only when she is amused. If you could see, when she is playful, what a picture she makes of frank and simple gaiety, how, when she is beside some unfortunate she is anxious to help, her eyes shine with innocent joy and compassionate kindness! If you could see, especially at the slightest word of praise or flattery, how her divine features color with that touching embarrassment which springs from an entirely artless modesty!... She is chaste and devout; you therefore judge her cold and lifeless. I think very differently. What an astonishing sensibility she must have, if her feelings extend even to her husband, if she can continue to love a man whom she never sees! What more certain proof could you wish for? I have, however, discovered yet another.

I contrived one of our walks so that we came to a ditch that had to be cleared. Although she is very agile, she is even more timid; as you may imagine, a prude is always afraid she may *fall*.* She was obliged to entrust herself to me. I have held the modest woman in my arms. Our preparations and the transshipment of my old aunt kept our playful devotee in fits of laughter; but, when I took her up, I contrived it awkwardly, so that our arms intertwined, and, during the short space of time that I held her against my breast, I felt her heart beat faster. That delightful blush came again to her face, and her modest embarrassment was proof enough to me that *it was love and not fear that had caused her agitation.* My aunt, however, made the same mistake as you, and began to say, "The child is afraid"; but the "child's" charming honesty will not allow a lie, and she replied simply, "Oh, no! But..." That one word was an illumination. Since that moment cruel anxiety has given way to the sweetness of hope. I shall have this woman. I shall free her from a husband who profanes her. I shall carry her off from the very God that she adores. How enchanting to be in turn the cause and the cure of her remorse! Far be it from me to destroy the prejudices that possess her. They will add to my gratification and to my glory. Let her believe in virtue, but let her sacrifice it for my sake; let her be afraid of her sins, but let them not check her; and, when she is shaken by a thousand terrors, may it only be in my arms that she is able to overcome them and forget them. Then, if she wishes, let her say, "I adore you"; she alone, of all women, will be worthy to utter those words. And I shall indeed be the god of her choice.

Let us be frank. Since our intimacies are as cold as they are shallow, what we call happiness is scarcely even a pleasure. But shall I tell you something? I thought my heart had withered away, and, finding nothing left to me but my senses, I lamented my premature old age. Madame

---

*Evidence of the deplorable taste for punning which was then beginning to grow and has since become so widespread.

de Tourvel has restored the charming illusions of my youth. When I am with her I have no need of pleasure to be happy. The one thing that alarms me is the amount of time I must give up to this adventure, for I dare not leave anything to chance. It is no use reminding myself of bold schemes that have succeeded before; I cannot bring myself to put them into practice. I cannot be really happy unless she gives herself to me, and that is no trifling matter.

I am sure that you would admire my prudence. I have not yet uttered the word "love," but we have already arrived at "confidence" and "interest." So as to deceive her as little as possible, and especially in order to forestall any rumors that might reach her ears, I myself have described, as if in self-accusation, some of my better-known exploits. You would laugh to see how openly she preaches at me. She wishes, she says, to convert me. She has no suspicion as yet of how much the attempt will cost her. She has no idea that in "pleading," as she puts it, "for the unlucky women I have ruined," she is speaking in advance on her own behalf. This occurred to me yesterday in the middle of one of her sermons, and I could not resist the pleasure of interrupting her to assure her that she spoke exactly like a prophet. Good-bye, my dearest love. As you see, I am not lost beyond recall.

P.S. By the way, has your poor chevalier killed himself in despair? If the truth were known, you are a hundred times more depraved than I am. You would put me to shame if I had any pride.

Château de ———
9 August 17–

LETTER 7: *Cécile Volanges to Sophie Carnay* *

If I have told you nothing on the subject of my marriage it is because I know no more now than I did at the beginning. I am growing used to thinking no more about it, and in other ways I find life agreeable enough. I work a great deal at my singing and at my harp: I seem to like it more now that I no longer have a music master, or, rather, the fact is I have a better one. The Chevalier Danceny, the gentleman I mentioned to you, with whom I sang at Madame de Merteuil's, is kind

---

*So as not to try the patience of the reader, a large part of the daily correspondence between these young ladies has been suppressed. Only those letters necessary to an understanding of the course of events appear. For the same reason, all Sophie Carnay's letters, and several written by others who figure in this story, have been omitted.

enough to come here every day and sing with me for whole hours at a time. He is extremely amiable. He sings like an angel and composes the prettiest tunes for which he writes the words as well. It is such a pity he is a Knight of Malta![3] It seems to me that, if he married, he would make his wife very happy... He is extremely civil. He never seems to be paying compliments, and yet everything he says is flattering. Although he is forever finding fault with me, as much about music as anything else, there is so much enthusiasm and good humor in his criticisms that it is impossible not to be grateful for them. When he is only so much as looking at you he seems to be saying something agreeable. And, to crown it all, he is very obliging. For instance, yesterday he was invited to a great concert, but he preferred to spend the whole evening at our house. I was very glad of that because when he is not here nobody speaks to me, and that is boring – whereas when he is here we sing and talk to each other. He always has something to tell me. Besides Madame de Merteuil, he is the only person here who is at all agreeable. But goodbye, my dear: I promised to learn an arietta with a very difficult accompaniment for today, and I don't want to break my word. I shall go back to work until he comes.

———

7 August 17–

LETTER 8: *The Présidente de Tourvel to Madame de Volanges*
No one, Madame, could be more sensible than I am of the confidence you place in me, and no one could take more of an interest in your daughter's establishment. It is indeed with all my heart that I wish her that happiness which I have no doubt she deserves, and which I am certain may safely be entrusted to your prudence. I do not know Monsieur le Comte de Gercourt, but since you have honored him with your choice I cannot but think most highly of him. I shall say no more, Madame, than that I wish this marriage as much success as attends my own, which is equally the result of your good offices, and for which I am every day more grateful to you. May your daughter's happiness be your recompense for the happiness you have brought me, and may the best of friends become the most fortunate of mothers!

I am truly sorry that I cannot offer you these sincere wishes in person, and that I cannot make your daughter's acquaintance as soon as I should like. Since your own kindness to me has been truly maternal, I have some right to expect from her the tender affection of a sister. Please be so kind, Madame, as to ask her for it on my behalf for as long as I am without the opportunity to win it for myself.

I expect to remain in the country all the time Monsieur de Tourvel is away, and I have taken this occasion of enjoying and benefiting from my acquaintance with the worthy Madame de Rosemonde. She is still charming; her great age has taken nothing from her. Her memory and her gaiety are unimpaired; her body, it is true, is eighty-four years old, but her spirit is only twenty.

Our life of retirement has been much enlivened by her nephew, the Vicomte de Valmont, who has consented to spare us a few days of his time. I used to know him only by a reputation, which left me with little desire to know him better. I think, though, that he is worth more than people think. Here, where he is not distracted by the bustle of the great world, he shows a surprising aptitude for talking seriously, and admits his faults with rare candor. He confides freely in me, and I lecture him with the utmost severity. You, who know him, will agree that this would be a fine conversion to make, but I have no doubt that in spite of his promises a week in Paris will make him forget all my sermons. His stay here will to some extent at least restrict his customary activities; from what I know of them, it seems to me that he could do no better than by doing nothing at all. He knows that I am writing to you and has asked me to present his most respectful compliments. Please receive my own with your accustomed kindness, and never doubt the sincerity with which I have the honor to be, etc.

Château de ———
9 August 17–

LETTER 9: *Madame de Volanges to the Présidente de Tourvel*
I have never, my dear young friend, doubted the sincerity of either your friendship or the interest you take in all that concerns me. But it is not to explain this (which I hope is henceforth taken for granted between us) that I am replying to your letter. The fact is, I do not think I can avoid saying a few words to you concerning the Vicomte de Valmont.

I did not expect, I will admit, that I should ever find his name in one of your letters. What, after all, could there be in common between you and him? You do not know what sort of man he is; where could you have learned to recognize a profligate's soul? You tell me of his *rare candor* – oh, yes! In a Valmont candor must indeed be very rare. Even more treacherous and dangerous than he is charming and fascinating, he has never, since his early youth, taken a single step or spoken a single word without some dishonorable or criminal intention. My dear, you know me; you know that of all the virtues to which I aspire tolerance is the one I value most. So, were Valmont the victim of impetuous passions, if, like so many thousands of others, he had been led astray by the errors of the time, then, while I should still not approve of his conduct, I should pity him, waiting in silence for a time when some happy change of heart would recover for him the esteem of decent people. But Valmont is not a man of that sort: his conduct is the outcome of his principles. He knows exactly how far a man may carry villainy without danger to himself, and, so that he can be cruel and vicious with impunity, he chooses women for his victims. I shall not stop to count the number he has seduced; but how many has he not ruined?

These scandalous stories do not reach you in your modest and secluded world. I could tell you some that would make you shudder, but your sight, pure as your soul, would be defiled by such pictures; besides, since you are sure that Valmont will never hold any danger for you, you have no need to arm yourself against him. There is only one thing I must tell you: every single one of the women he has pursued, whether successfully or not, has had reason to regret it. The Marquise de Merteuil is the only exception to the rule – she alone has been able to resist and even to master his wickedness. It is this episode in her life that does her most credit in my view; it has, in fact, been enough to excuse her fully in everyone's eyes for certain indiscretions of which she was found guilty at the beginning of her widowhood.*

Be that as it may, my dear friend, age, experience, and above all friendship give me the right to point out to you that society has begun to notice Valmont's absence, and that, if it is known that he has spent some time alone with his aunt and you, your reputation lies in his hands – the greatest misfortune that could ever befall a woman. I advise you, therefore, to persuade his aunt to keep him no longer; and if he persists in staying, I do not think you should hesitate to leave yourself. But why should he stay? What, after all, is he doing in the country? If you were to observe his movements I am certain you would find that he has only taken up a convenient headquarters for some villainy he is contemplating in the neighborhood. Since, however, it would be impossible to prevent it, let us be content with ensuring our own safety.

Good-bye, my dear. My daughter's marriage has been somewhat delayed. The Comte de Gercourt, whom we were daily expecting, writes

---

*Madame de Volanges's mistake shows that, like all other rogues, Valmont never betrayed his accomplices.

to say that his regiment is sailing for Corsica, and, since there are still military operations in progress, he cannot obtain leave of absence before the winter. It is most inconvenient; I can now hope, however, that we shall have the pleasure of seeing you at the wedding. I should have been disappointed had it taken place without you. Good-bye. Without compliments and without reserve, I am wholly yours.

P.S. Remember me to Madame de Rosemonde whom I shall always love as much as she deserves to be loved.

----

11 August 17–

LETTER 10: *The Marquise de Merteuil to the Vicomte de Valmont*

Are you sulking, Vicomte? Or are you dead? Or, which would come to very much the same, do you live now only for your Présidente? This woman who has given you back the illusions of youth will very soon be giving you back its ridiculous prejudices. I see you are already as timid as a slave; you might as well be in love. You renounce your *bold schemes that have succeeded before,* so that you now lead a life devoid of principles, leaving everything to chance, or rather to the whim of the moment. Don't you remember that love, like medicine, *is only the art of encouraging nature?* You see how I can fight you with your own weapons; but I take no pride in that for, in fact, I am beating a man who is down. "She must give herself to me," you say. Oh yes, without any doubt, she will – like the others, but with this difference: she will do it with bad grace. But, so that she will give herself to you in the end, the proper method is to begin by taking her. How truly characteristic that absurd paradox is of love's fatuousness! I say "love" because you are in love. To say otherwise would be to deceive you; it would be to hide your malady from you. Tell me then, languishing lover: the women you have had – do you imagine you violated them? Don't you know that however willing, however eager we are to give ourselves, we must nevertheless have an excuse? And is there any more convenient than an appearance of yielding to force? As for me, I shall admit that one thing that most flatters me is a lively and well-executed attack, when everything happens in quick but orderly succession; which never puts us in the painfully embarrassing position of having to cover up some blunder of which, on the contrary, we ought to be taking advantage; which keeps up an appearance of taking by storm even that which we are quite prepared to surrender; and adroitly flatters our two favorite passions –

the pride of defense and the pleasure of defeat. This talent, which is less common than you would think, has always given me pleasure, even when it has not prevailed with me, and it has sometimes happened that I have given myself simply by way of reward. So, in our ancient tournaments, did Beauty present the prize for valor and skill.

But you – you are no longer yourself: you behave as if you were afraid of succeeding. When did you take to making journeys in small stages along side roads? If you want to reach your destination, my good man – post horses and the highway! But let us leave this subject which puts me in so much the worse humor in that it deprives me of the pleasure of seeing you. Write to me, at least, more often than you do and keep me informed of your progress. Did you know that for two weeks now you have been engrossed in this silly adventure, neglecting the rest of the world?

Speaking of neglect, you remind me of those people who invariably send to inquire after their sick friends but never trouble about a reply. At the close of your last letter you asked me whether the chevalier was dead. I did not answer your question, but that in no way increased your anxiety. Have you forgotten that my lover is your bosom friend? Rest assured, he is not dead; were he so, it would be from a surfeit of joy. The poor man, how tender-hearted he is, how perfectly suited to being a lover! Such intensity of feeling – it makes my head swim. Seriously, the perfect happiness he finds in being attached to me has really attached me to him.

How happy I made him the very day I wrote to you saying that I was going to consider breaking with him! As a matter of fact I was thinking, when he was announced, of how best to throw him into despair. For some reason or for none at all it seemed to me that he had never looked so handsome. I gave him, however, a sulky welcome. He hoped to spend two hours with me before the time my doors opened to everybody. I told him that I would be going out; he asked me where I was going, and I refused to tell him. He insisted. "Away from you," I said acidly. Fortunately for him he was quite paralyzed by this reply: one word, and a scene would inevitably have followed severing our relations forever, just as I had planned. Surprised by his silence, I glanced at him for no other reason, I assure you, than to see how he looked. There on that charming face was the melancholy, at once profound and most tender, that was once before so difficult to resist – as even you admitted. The same cause produced the same effect: I was vanquished a second time. From that moment on I could think only of how to avoid leaving him with the impression that I had slighted him. "I am going out on some business," I said a little more gently, "business that, indeed, concerns you. But don't ask questions now. I shall be taking supper at home; come back here and I shall tell you everything." Whereupon he found his tongue, but I did not allow him to use it. "I am in a great hurry," I continued. "Go now; I shall see you this evening." He kissed my hand and left.

Immediately, as compensation, perhaps as much for myself as for him, I decided to introduce him to my *petite maison*,[4] of which he had as yet no suspicion. I called my faithful Victoire. I was ill with migraine; for the benefit of the servants I retired to bed. As soon as we were alone the *one and only* dressed herself as a footman, while I changed into chambermaid's clothes. Then she fetched a fiacre to the garden gate and we drove off. On arriving at my temple of love I chose the most elegant negligée I could find, a delicious one of my own creation. It reveals nothing and suggests everything. I promise you the pattern for your Présidente when you have made her worthy of wearing it.

After these preparations, while Victoire busied herself with other details, I read a chapter of *The Sofa*,[5] a letter from *Heloise*,[6] and two of La Fontaine's tales, so as to establish in my mind the different nuances of tone I wished to adopt. Meanwhile my chevalier, as eager as ever, arrives at my door. The footman refuses to admit him, informing him that I am ill: first incident. At the same time he is handed a letter from me, but not, as I am always careful in these matters, written by me. He opens it to find, in Victoire's handwriting, these words: "At nine o'clock precisely, on the boulevard, outside the cafés." Once there, a little footman he has never seen before, or thinks he has never seen before (it is in fact Victoire), comes up to say he must send back his carriage and follow on foot. This whole romantic episode has excited his imagination to a degree, and an excited imagination never does any harm. At length he arrives and is quite spellbound with surprise and passion. To allow him time to recover we walk for a while in the woods; then I take him back to the house. First he sees a table laid for two, next – a bed prepared. We pass through to my boudoir, decked out for the occasion in its full splendor. There, half deliberately, half impulsively, I put my arms around him and sink to his knees. "Oh, my dear!" I say, "I am sorry that I distressed you by a show of bad humor. It was but for the sake of arranging this surprise. I am sorry that I could for an instant have veiled my heart from your gaze. Forgive me, and let my love make amends for my sin." You can imagine the effect produced by this sentimental speech. The happy chevalier having raised me up, my pardon was solemnized on the same ottoman where you and I so gaily celebrated our final parting, and in the same manner.

Since we had six hours to spend together, and I was determined he should find the whole of the time uniformly delicious, I curbed his transports and modified my own demonstrations of tenderness to a friendly coquetry. I think I have never been at such pains to please, nor ever felt more satisfied with my success. After supper, now childish, now reasonable, now playful, now sentimental, at times even abandoned, I amused myself imagining him a sultan in the midst of his harem while I played in turn a succession of his favorites – so that each time he paid his respects it was to a different mistress, though the same woman received them.

At daybreak it was time to part, and in spite of all he could say or do to prove to the contrary he had by then as much need to go as he had little desire to do so. As we left, by way of a last adieu, I took the key from the door of our happy abode and, putting it in his hands, said, "I acquired this only for you; it is proper that you should have it in your keeping. The temple must be at the high priest's disposal." I thus skillfully forestalled whatever reflections he might otherwise have made on the propriety – always doubtful – of keeping a *petite maison*.

I know him well enough to be sure that he will not use it for anyone but me; and, if I am moved to go there without him myself, I have, of course, a duplicate key. He was determined at all costs to fix the day for our next meeting there, but I like him too much to exhaust him so quickly. One can allow oneself too much only of those one intends shortly to be rid of. He does not know this; but fortunately for him I know it for both of us.

I see it is already three o'clock in the morning, and I have written volumes when I meant to write no more than a word. So strong is the charm of a trustworthy friend – for which reason you are still the man I like best. To be honest, however, my chevalier pleases me more.

----

12 August 17–

LETTER 11: *Madame de Tourvel to Madame de Volanges*
The gravity of your letter would have disturbed me, Madame, had I not luckily found more cause here for assurance than you are able to give me for alarm. The redoubtable Monsieur de Valmont, terror of our sex, put off his murderous weapons before he came into this house, it seems. Far from being the victim of his schemes, I am not even the object of his pretensions; what is more, the worldly charm that even his enemies

allow him has here given way almost entirely to the amiability of a child. Apparently it is the country air that has accomplished this miracle. I can only assure you that, although he is constantly with me and seems even to enjoy my company, not a word has passed his lips that so much as hints at love – not one of those phrases that other men, without having, like him, anything to justify using them, would never have denied themselves. Never is one obliged to assume with him that reserve without which, these days, no self-respecting woman can keep the men in her circle at a proper distance. And he would never think of exploiting the gaiety he inspires. He is perhaps something of a flatterer, but his delicacy would disarm modesty itself. In short, had I a brother in Monsieur de Valmont I could not be better pleased. There are women, no doubt, who would wish him to show them more conspicuous marks of his favor. I shall confess I like him so much the more for his good judgment in distinguishing me from their kind.

This is certainly a very different picture from the one you paint of him; yet you will see, when you set the portraits in their respective periods, that they have something in common. He admits to having been very much in the wrong; rumor has undoubtedly made him appear even more so. But I have met few men who speak of respectable women with greater esteem – I had almost said enthusiasm. You tell me that in this respect, at least, he is not dissembling. His relations with Madame de Merteuil are the proof of it. He speaks often of her – with so many compliments and such a tone of true affection that, until I received your letter, I was sure that what he called their friendship must really be love. I was wrong to have judged so rashly, the more so in that he has often spoken expressly in her justification. I fear I regarded as polite deception what was in fact the plainest sincerity. I am not sure; but it seems to me that the man is not an irredeemable libertine who is capable of so devoted a friendship with so admirable a woman. For the rest, I do not know whether he is behaving well here because, as you suggest, he is planning something in the neighborhood. There are certainly several handsome women in these parts. He is seldom out, however, except in the mornings, when, he says, he goes hunting. He rarely returns, it is true, with any game – but that is because, he assures us, he is not a good shot. At all events, what he does out of doors is no concern of mine. I should only wish to make certain of it so as to have one more reason for bowing to your opinion or for converting you to mine.

As for your suggestion that I contrive to cut short the stay that Monsieur de Valmont proposes to make here, it seems to me that it will be very difficult to ask his aunt to send her own nephew from her house; the more so because he is a great favorite of hers. I promise you, though – but only out of deference to you, and not because I think it necessary – that I shall make this request at the first opportunity, either to her or to Monsieur de Valmont himself. As for me, Monsieur de Tourvel is aware that I intend to stay here until his return. He would be astonished, and with good reason, were I to change my mind upon so little provocation.

Forgive me, Madame, these long explanations. I felt it necessary in the cause of truth to make some statement on Monsieur de Valmont's behalf, particularly since, where you are concerned, he appears to be very much in need of an advocate. I am by no means any the less aware of the friendly sentiments that prompt your advice. To them, again, I owe the charming compliment you pay me apropos of your daughter's wedding, for which I thank you most sincerely. But I would, with all my heart, sacrifice every pleasure I anticipate in spending that time with you to my wish that Mademoiselle de Volanges could the sooner be made happy – that is to say, if she can ever be happier than she is with a mother so worthy of her respect and affection. Be so kind as to believe I share these sentiments with her in expressing my attachment to you.

I have the honor to be, etc.

———

13 August 17–

LETTER 12: *Cécile Volanges to the Marquise de Merteuil*

Mamma is not well, Madame. She is confined to the house, and I must keep her company, so that I shall not have the honor, after all, of accompanying you to the opera. But it is not so much the opera, I assure you, that I shall miss, as the pleasure of being with you. Please believe this. I do like you so much! Would you be so kind as to tell the Chevalier Danceny that I do not have the songbook he spoke of, and that I shall be very pleased if he will bring it to me tomorrow? If he comes today he will be told we are not at home; it is only that Mamma does not wish to receive anyone. I hope she will be better tomorrow.

I have the honor to be, etc.

———

13 August 17–

LETTER 13: *The Marquise de Merteuil to Cécile Volanges*

I am very much distressed, my dear, not only because I shall be deprived of the pleasure of seeing you but because of the reason you give. I hope we shall find another opportunity. I shall convey your message to the Chevalier Danceny, who will certainly be very sorry to hear of your mother's illness. If she will receive me tomorrow I shall come and keep her company. She and I will challenge the Chevalier de Belleroche* to piquet, and, to enhance our pleasure in taking his money from him, we shall listen to you singing duets with your charming teacher; I shall suggest it to him. If this is agreeable to you and to your mother, I can answer for myself and the two chevaliers. Good-bye, my dear. My compliments to dear Madame de Volanges. My fondest embrace for you.

———

13 August 17–

LETTER 14: *Cécile Volanges to Sophie Carnay*

I did not write to you yesterday, my dear Sophie, but it was no idle pleasure that prevented me, I promise you. Mamma was ill, and I was with her the whole day. When I returned to my room in the evening I had not the heart to do anything, and went immediately to bed so as to convince myself that the day was really over – I have never known such a long one. It is not that I do not love Mamma – I don't know what it is. I was to have gone to the opera with Madame de Merteuil; the Chevalier Danceny was to have been there. As you know, I have more regard for these two people than for anyone else in the world. When the time came, and I should have been with them, my heart felt as though it would break. I was suddenly weary of everything and wept and wept quite helplessly. Luckily Mamma was in bed, so that she did not notice anything. I am sure the Chevalier Danceny suffered too; but he will have had the theater and the audience to distract him – quite a different matter.

Fortunately Mamma is better today, and Madame de Merteuil is coming to see us with the Chevalier Danceny and another gentleman. But she always arrives late, and, oh, it is very tiresome to be alone for so long. It is only eleven o'clock now. I have to practice the harp, of course, and then my toilette will take up some time: I want my hair to look particularly good today. Mother Perpétue was right, I think. One turns coquette directly upon entering society. I have never wanted so much

---

*The chevalier mentioned in Madame de Merteuil's previous letters.

to be pretty as during the last few days; and I find I am not so pretty as I used to think. Of course, among women who paint one is at a great disadvantage. Madame de Merteuil, for example. It is quite clear that all the men prefer her to me; but I am not very much put out by that, because I know she has a great affection for me. What is more she gives me her word that the Chevalier Danceny thinks I am prettier than her. How kind of her to tell me! Even she seems to be pleased about it. I really cannot comprehend why. Because she likes me so much? And he! – oh, I'm delighted with him! It seems to me, too, that I have only to look at him to grow prettier. I should look at him all the time, were I not so afraid of meeting his eyes. Whenever that happens I am quite out of countenance. It is almost painful. But no matter.

Good-bye, my dear. I am going to begin my toilette. I love you now as always.

Paris
14 August 17–

LETTER 15: *The Vicomte de Valmont to the Marquise de Merteuil*
It is very obliging of you not to leave me to my dismal fate. The life I lead here is truly tedious in its tasteless uniformity and the superfluous leisure it affords. Your letter, and the charming extract from your journal, tempted me twenty times to invent a pretext of business in town and fly to your feet, there to beg you for an infidelity to your chevalier in my favor. After all, he does not deserve the happiness he enjoys. Do you know that you have made me jealous of him? And what is this of a final parting? I renounce the vows we made in that moment of delirium. If they were intended to be kept, we cannot have been worthy of making them. Ah, let me one day revenge in your arms the annoyance your chevalier's happiness has caused me! I cannot deny that I am angry when I think that, without the help of intelligence, without taking the smallest pains, obeying without question the instincts of his heart, he has found a happiness I am unable to achieve. Oh, I shall spoil it for him! Promise me that I shall! As for you, are you not ashamed? You put yourself to the trouble of deceiving him, and he is, notwithstanding, happier than you are. You imagine him to be at your mercy; it is you who are at his. He sleeps soundly while you watch over his pleasures. Would a slave do more?

The fact is, my love, that as long as you distribute your favors in more than one quarter I am not in the least jealous: your lovers remind me of Alexander's successors, unable to maintain between them that mighty empire where once I reigned alone. But that you should give yourself entirely to one of them! That there should exist in one other man a challenge to my power! I will not tolerate it; you need have no hope that I will. Take me back, or at least take a second lover. Do not betray for the sake of a single whim the inviolable friendship to which we are sworn.

It is quite enough, in all conscience, that I endure the torments of love. Notice that I take your view: I admit my mistake. After all, if to be unable to live without possessing the object of one's desire, if to sacrifice one's time, pleasures, one's whole life to attaining it is to be in love, then I am certainly in love. But I have made scant progress. I might have nothing at all to report on this subject, were it not for an incident that has given me much food for thought, and on which I am not as yet sure whether to set hopes or fears.

You know my manservant, that master of intrigue, that actor. As you may well imagine, he has been instructed to make love to the chambermaid and to ply the rest of the household with drink. The fellow has better luck than I: he has already succeeded. He has just discovered that Madame de Tourvel has charged one of her servants with obtaining news of my activities, if necessary by following me on my excursions of a morning, as far as it is possible for him to do so without being observed. What is this woman about? How like the most timid of people to take risks that even we should be very loath to undertake! I swear... But before planning my revenge on this feminine chicanery, let us think of a means of turning it to our advantage. Until now my suspicious goings-abroad have been without object: they must be given one. This matter requires all my attention, and I take my leave of you the better to consider it. Good-bye, my love.

Still Château de ———
15 August 17–

LETTER 16: *Cécile Volanges to Sophie Carnay*
Oh, Sophie! News at last! I should not perhaps tell you, but I absolutely must tell somebody – I cannot help it. This Chevalier Danceny... I am in such a state that I cannot write; I don't know where to begin. Since I wrote telling you of the charming evening* Mamma and I spent with

---

*This letter has not been discovered. There is reason to believe that the meeting referred to is the one suggested by Madame de Merteuil in her note, and mentioned in Cécile de Volanges's preceding letter.

him and Madame de Merteuil, I have said no more about him. I did not wish to say any more to anybody, though I thought of him all the time. He began, after this, to look so dejected – so *very* dejected – that it hurt me to see it. And when I asked him why, he denied it, but it was quite plainly so. Well, yesterday it was even more obvious than before. It did not prevent his usual kindness in singing with me; but every time he looked at me my heart ached. When we had finished singing he put my harp away in its case, and, bringing me the key, asked me whether I would play it again as soon as I was alone that evening. I suspected nothing at all, and had no desire, in any case, to play that evening. He was so pressing, though, that I said I would. He certainly had his reasons for asking. In short, when I had returned to my room and my maid had left me, I took out my harp: between the strings was a letter, folded but unsealed – from him. Oh, if you knew what he asks me to do! Since reading his letter I have been so happy that I have been unable to think of anything else. I reread it four times in succession, then locked it away in my writing desk. I knew it by heart, and as I lay in bed went over it in my mind so often that it banished any thought of sleep. As soon as I closed my eyes, there he was repeating it all in his own voice. It was very late when I went to sleep, and still very early when I awoke. I immediately looked for the letter to read it again at my leisure. I took it into my bed, and then I kissed it as if... It was perhaps wrong to kiss a letter like that, but I could not help it.

But now, my dear Sophie, though I am very happy, I am also in great difficulties. Without doubt, I must not reply to this letter. I know quite well that I ought not to, but he asks me to. And if I don't reply he is sure to start moping again. Still, it is most unfortunate for him. What do you think I should do? But you are no more able to tell than I. Perhaps I shall ask Madame de Merteuil, who is always so kind. I should be very happy to oblige him, but I don't wish to do anything that is wrong. How often have we been urged to cultivate a good heart! Yet we are forbidden to follow its dictates where a man is in question. But that cannot be right either. Is not a man a neighbor to be loved as much as any woman, and even more so? After all, have we not fathers as well as mothers, brothers as well as sisters – and husbands besides? However, if I were to do something that was not right, maybe even Monsieur Danceny himself would think less of me. Oh heavens, I would much rather he were a little dispirited now! Besides, after all, there is still time. Simply because he wrote yesterday I am not bound to reply today. Besides, I shall see Madame de Merteuil this evening, and if I have the courage I shall tell her everything. If I do only what she tells me to, I shall have nothing to be ashamed of. And then perhaps she will tell me after all to send him some little reply to console him! Oh, how I suffer!

Good-bye, my dear. Tell me, in any case, what you think.

———

19 August 17–

LETTER 17: *The Chevalier Danceny to Cécile Volanges*

Before I give way, Mademoiselle, to the pleasure – or shall I say, to the imperative necessity – of writing to you, I shall begin by begging you to hear me out. I feel that for daring to declare my sentiments I shall need your indulgence: were I merely justifying them, I should not ask for it. What am I about to do, after all, but show you what you have yourself accomplished? What can I tell you that my looks, my gestures, my embarrassments, and even my silences have not already told you? Why should you find fault with a feeling that you yourself have inspired? What comes from you is surely worthy of being restored to you; though ardent like my being, it is pure like yours. Is it a crime for me to admire your charming person, your brilliant accomplishments, your enchanting graces, and that touching candor which puts your virtues, already precious, beyond price? No, assuredly not. But even the innocent can be most unhappy; and that is the fate in store for me if you refuse to accept my homage, the first this heart has offered. Were it not for you, I should be not happy now but at best content. Since I saw you peace of mind has forsaken me, and my happiness hangs in the balance.

Meanwhile you are surprised at my despondency, and you ask me what causes it. I might have thought sometimes that you were distressed by it. Ah! write one word and you will restore me to felicity. Pause only to consider that, before you write anything, one word may also be my ruin. I appoint you, then, the mistress of my fate. You alone can deliver me up to eternal misery or everlasting bliss. But in what better hands could I leave matters of such moment?

I shall finish, as I began, by begging your indulgence. I have asked you to hear me out; I shall go further and ask you to reply. To refuse would be to persuade me that you are offended; and my heart is answerable as much for my respect as for my love.

P.S. Your reply can reach me in the same way that this letter was conveyed to you. The method is both safe and convenient, it seems to me.

———

18 August 17–

LETTER 18: *Cécile Volanges to Sophie Carnay*

Come, Sophie! You are not scolding me in advance for what I am going to do? I was concerned enough before; here you are making it worse. It is quite clear, you say, that I must not reply. It is all very well for you to say so from a distance. You don't know the precise circumstances – you could not possibly, unless you were here. I am sure that if you were in my place you would do as I am going to do. Of course, in theory, one ought not to reply. You will see from my letter of yesterday that I did not want to, in any case. But I don't think anyone has ever before been in my special situation.

And then to have to make this decision by myself! Madame de Merteuil, whom I expected to see last evening, did not come. Everything conspires against me: it is only through her that I know him. It has almost always been in her company that I have seen him or spoken to him. It is not that I bear her any grudge, but she has deserted me in the hour of my greatest need. Oh, I am really to be pitied!

As you can imagine, he was here again yesterday as usual. I was so confused that I dared not look at him, and he could not speak to me because Mamma was present. I was sure it would make him wretched to find that I had not written to him. I did not know what kind of face to put upon it. A moment later he asked me whether I should like him to fetch my harp. My heart beat so furiously that it was all I could do to answer yes. It was much worse when he returned. I glanced at him only for a single instant. He did not look at me at all, but one would have thought from his expression that he was ill. It was really most painful. He began to tune my harp and then, bringing it to me, said, "Oh, Mademoiselle..." He said no more than those two words, but in such a tone of voice that I was quite overcome. I ran my fingers over the strings without knowing what I was doing. Mamma asked whether we would sing. He excused himself, saying he was not feeling well, so that I, who had no excuse, was obliged to sing by myself. I wished I had been born dumb. I purposely chose a song I did not know. I should not have been able to sing even the ones I did know, and I was afraid someone might notice. Luckily another visitor arrived, and as soon as I heard the carriage I stopped and asked him to put away my harp. I was very much afraid he would take his departure at the same time, but he came back.

While Mamma talked to the lady who had come to see her I thought I might risk another glance at him. My eyes met his, and I found I could not look away again. A moment later I saw the tears well up in his eyes, and he had to turn his head to one side to hide them. At that moment it was more than I could bear; I knew that I too would cry. I left the room, and there and then wrote in pencil on a slip of paper: "Please do not look so sad. I promise you I shall reply." Surely you are not going to tell me that this was wrong; besides I could not help it. I slipped the piece of paper between the strings of my harp, where his letter had been, and returned to the drawing room. I felt more at ease, but I longed for Mamma's visitor to be gone. Fortunately she was merely paying a call, and left soon after. As soon as she was out of the room, I said that I should like to play my harp again, and asked him to fetch it. It was obvious from his expression that he suspected nothing. But when he returned, oh, how happy he looked! As he placed the harp in front of me he stood so that Mamma could not see, and, taking my hand, he squeezed it...in such a particular way! – it was only for an instant, but I cannot tell you how agreeable it was. I withdrew it, of course, so that I have nothing on my conscience.

You see, my dear Sophie, that I cannot now avoid writing to him. I have promised him. Besides, I am not going to cause him further distress, which would be even more painful to me than to him. If it were wrong I would not do it. But what wrong can there be in writing a letter, especially when it is to spare someone unhappiness? What troubles me is that I shall not be able to write it very well, but he will know that is not my fault. Besides, I am sure he will be pleased to have it, if only because it is mine.

Good-bye, my dear. If you consider I am doing wrong, tell me – but I don't think I am. The nearer the time comes to write to him, the more anxious I feel. But I must write, since I have promised. Good-bye.

———

20 August 17–

LETTER 19: *Cécile Volanges to the Chevalier Danceny*

You were so sad yesterday, Monsieur, and I was so sorry to see it that I allowed myself to promise you a reply to the letter you wrote me. Nonetheless, I feel today that I ought not have done so. But since I promised, I do not wish to break my word; and this, if anything, is proof of the friendship I bear you. Now that you know this, I hope you will not ask me to write to you again; I hope, too, that you will not tell anyone that I have written to you at all, because of course I should be taken to task for it, and this might very well be most unpleasant. Above all, I hope you will not think ill of me yourself, since that would distress me more than anything else. I should like you in turn to do me a favor.

Please do not look so sad; it deprives me of all the pleasure I might have in seeing you. You see, Monsieur, I speak very frankly. I cannot hope for more than that our friendship should last forever. But, I beg you, write to me no more.

I have the honor to be,
Cécile Volanges

———

20 August 17–

LETTER 20: *The Marquise de Merteuil to the Vicomte de Valmont*
Ah, you blackguard! You flatter me to keep me from laughing at you! Well, I shall have mercy; your letter is so full of reckless absurdities that I must perforce excuse the circumspection your Présidente imposes upon you. I do not think my chevalier would be as indulgent as I: he would be just the man to frown upon the renewal of our little contract and to find nothing amusing at all in your ridiculous proposal. As for me, it made me laugh a great deal, and I was quite sorry to be obliged to laugh alone. Heaven knows to what this hilarity might have brought me, had you been here; but I have had time to reflect and to recover my gravity. I am giving you no permanent refusal but am deferring my decision; I am right to do so. My vanity would, perhaps, be too much involved. Once one becomes interested in the game, there is no knowing where one will stop. I am the sort of woman who would cast you in chains all over again; who would make you forget your Présidente. And what a scandal if I, unworthy creature, were to fill you with a disgust for virtue! That danger may be averted, but here are my conditions.

As soon as you have seduced your Fair Devotee, as soon as you can furnish me with proof that you have done so, come to me and I shall be yours. Remember, however, that in important affairs of this kind, proof, to be valid, must be in writing. If we keep to this arrangement, I shall, on the one hand, be your reward and not your consolation, and I prefer it that way; on the other, you will add spice to your success by making it a step toward your infidelity. Come then, bring me the token of your triumph with all possible speed; like those worthy knights of old who came to lay the brilliant spoils of their victories at their ladies' feet. Seriously, I am very curious to know what a prudish woman will find to write in such circumstances, what disguise she will contrive to throw over her sentences when she has none left to cover her person. It is for you to judge whether I am setting too high a price upon myself; I warn you, however, that it will not come down. Meanwhile, my dear

Vicomte, you will suffer me to remain faithful to my chevalier, making him happy for my own entertainment, in spite of the slight annoyance this causes you.

Nevertheless, were my morals less strict, he would at this moment have a dangerous rival – I mean the little Volanges. I dote on the child: it is a real infatuation. I may be deceived, but I see her becoming a woman of the highest fashion. I watch her little heart opening to the world, and it is an enchanting spectacle. She is already frantically in love with her Danceny, but is still quite unaware of the fact. He too is very much in love, but with the timidity of his years he dares not make it too obvious. Both of them are rapt in admiration of me. The girl especially has a great desire to tell me her secret; during the last few days it has really oppressed her, and it would have been doing her a great kindness to help her a little. But I have to remember that she is still a child: I don't wish to compromise myself. Danceny has spoken in plainer terms, but, as far as he is concerned, I have already made my decision; I turned a deaf ear. As for the girl, I have often been tempted to make her my pupil, for Gercourt's benefit. Considering that he will be in Corsica till October he leaves me time enough, and I have a mind to make good use of it, so as to present him at the end with a woman of experience in place of his innocent convent girl. How can this man have the arrogance to sleep in peace as long as a woman who has every reason to hate him remains unavenged? I assure you, were the girl here at this moment, there is no knowing what I would not tell her.

Good-bye, Vicomte. Good night and good luck – but for God's sake make some progress. Think, should you not succeed with this woman, of the others who must blush for having succeeded with you.

---

20 August 17–

LETTER 21: *The Vicomte de Valmont to the Marquise de Merteuil*
I have at last, my love, taken a step forward, and a considerable one: if it has not brought me to my destination, it reassures me at least that I am on the right road and dispels all my fears of losing the way. I have at last made a declaration of love, which, although it was received in obstinate silence, yet roused a response of the most unambiguous and flattering kind. But I must not anticipate; let us go back to the beginning.

You remember that my movements were to be watched. Well: I decided to make an object lesson of this scandalous proceeding, and I did so as follows. I instructed my manservant to find some unfortunate creature in the neighborhood, who was particularly in need of help. This was not difficult. Yesterday afternoon he brought me news of a family whose furniture was to be seized this morning in lieu of taxes they could not pay. Having made sure there was no female member of the household whose face and figure might cast suspicion on my actions, I announced at supper that I would go hunting the following morning. Here I must give my Présidente her due. She undoubtedly regretted to some extent the orders she had given, and unable to conquer her curiosity she did try, at least, to obstruct my plans. *It would be extremely hot; I should risk making myself ill; I should kill nothing and tire myself to no purpose* – during which conversation her eyes, expressing more perhaps than she wanted them to, told me plainly enough that she wished me to take these bad arguments for good ones. I was proof against this, as you can imagine, and withstood with equal success a little diatribe against hunting and hunters, as also a little cloud of ill humor which for the rest of the evening darkened that heavenly face. I was afraid for a moment that she might have countermanded her orders, that her delicacy might ruin everything. But I had not reckoned on feminine curiosity – I was mistaken. That very evening my servant brought me my reassurance, and I went to bed satisfied.

I rose at daybreak and left the house. I had not gone twenty yards when I caught sight of the spy behind me. Walking through the country in the direction of the village that was my destination, I chose my path with no other purpose in mind than to make it as difficult as possible for the villain to follow me. He dared not leave the road, and was forced at times to run at full tilt over three times the distance that I had covered. In giving him this exercise, though, I myself began to feel extremely hot, and at length sat down at the foot of a tree. Will you believe that he had the insolence to slip behind a bush not twenty feet away from me and sit down too? I was tempted for a moment to fire at him: that, though it would only have been small shot, would have taught him a severe enough lesson on the dangers of curiosity. Fortunately for him I remembered that he was not only useful but necessary to my plans; that consideration saved his life.

Now I arrive at the village. There is a hubbub: I come forward, I ask questions. I am acquainted with the facts. I summon the tax collector and, yielding to my generous compassion, pay him fifty-six livres, for the lack of which sum five persons were to be reduced to living on straw and despair. You cannot imagine the shower of blessings this simple little action brought upon me from those present, the tears of gratitude that flowed from the eyes of the old paterfamilias, the softening of that patriarchal countenance which only a moment before had been disfigured by a wild and hideous despair. While I contemplated the spectacle, another peasant, a younger man, leading a woman and two children by the hand, rushed toward me and said, "Let us fall at the feet of this image of God" – and in an instant the family were on their knees around me. I shall confess to some weakness. My eyes were moist with tears and I felt within me an unwonted but delicious emotion. I was astonished at the pleasure to be derived from doing good, and I am now tempted to think that so-called virtuous people have less claim to merit than we are led to believe. Be that as it may, I thought it common justice to repay these poor people for the pleasure they had given me, and I gave them ten louis I happened to have on me. Whereupon there was more giving of thanks, though without the same pathos: necessity had produced the sublime, the true effect. The rest was merely a simple expression of surprise and gratitude for superfluous gifts.

However, in the midst of these voluble benedictions, I appeared not unlike the hero in the last act of a drama. And you will not forget that my faithful spy was among the crowd. My aim achieved, I extricated myself and returned to the house. All things considered, I am pleased with my stratagem. I have no doubt the woman is worth all this trouble, which one day will in itself constitute a claim on her. Having, in a sense, paid for her in advance, I shall have the right – my conscience clear – to dispose of her as I please.

I had almost forgotten to tell you that, so as to leave no stone unturned, I asked the worthy peasantry to intercede with God for the success of my plans. You will see whether their prayers have not already in part been answered... But I am told that supper is served, and it will be too late to send this letter if I leave it to be finished tonight. So the rest must follow by the next post. I am sorry, because the rest is more interesting. Good-bye, my love. You have already stolen a moment of my pleasure in seeing her.

―――――

20 August 17–

LETTER 22: *Madame de Tourvel to Madame de Volanges*
You will no doubt be very pleased, Madame, to know something about Monsieur de Valmont that, it seems to me, cannot be reconciled with the representations of his character made to you. How painful it is to think ill of anyone, how distressing to find only vices in those who might have all the qualities necessary to make their virtue loved. In

short, I know you are so much inclined to be indulgent that I can only oblige you by giving you reason to reverse an overly harsh judgment. Monsieur de Valmont, it seems to me, has grounds for expecting so much favor − I had almost said justice; and here are my reasons for thinking so.

This morning he made one of those expeditions which might have led one to suppose he is hatching some plot in the neighborhood − the idea, indeed, that occurred to you; the idea I myself seized upon, perhaps too eagerly, for which I am very much to blame. Fortunately for him, and still more fortunately for us, since it has saved us from committing an injustice, one of my servants chanced to take the same road as he,* and it was in this way that my curiosity, reprehensible perhaps but timely nonetheless, was satisfied. It was reported that Monsieur de Valmont, having discovered in the village of ——— an unfortunate family whose furniture was to be sold because they lacked the means to pay their taxes, not only hastened to pay their debts but also gave them in addition a not inconsiderable sum of money. My servant was witness to this virtuous act; he has told me, moreover, that the peasants, in the course of their conversation amongst themselves and with him, said that a servant (whom they pointed out and whom my own servant believes to be one of Monsieur de Valmont's) had been sent yesterday to inquire into the circumstances of other villagers who might be in need of assistance. If this is so, there is no question here of a mere fugitive pity, aroused by circumstance, but of the solicitude of true charity, of a calculated plan for doing good, of rare virtue in a fine soul. But whether it was the outcome of chance or plan, it was still a decent and praiseworthy deed; the mere account of it moved me to tears. Furthermore − and still in the interests of justice − when I spoke to him (he had not himself breathed a word) he began by disclaiming it; and once he finally admitted to it, he seemed to take so little account of it that his modesty doubled his merit in my eyes.

Now tell me, my respected friend, is Monsieur de Valmont really an irreclaimable libertine? If he is so indeed, and can yet behave in this way, what is there left for respectable people to do? Are the wicked to share the sacred pleasures of charity with the good? Would God allow a virtuous family to receive help at the hands of a rascal − help for which they will return thanks to Divine Providence? And would He willingly hear their pure tongues speak blessings on a reprobate? No. I prefer to believe that although error endures, it is not perpetual; and I cannot

---

*So Madame de Tourvel dares not say she ordered him to do so!

think of anyone who does good as an enemy of virtue. Monsieur de Valmont is perhaps only another example of the danger of ill-considered intimacies. I leave you with this idea, which pleases me. If, on the one hand, it seems to justify him in your eyes, it will, on the other, make that tender friendship doubly precious which binds me to you for as long as I live.

I have the honor to be, etc.

P.S. Madame de Rosemonde and I are just about to visit the worthy and unfortunate family ourselves so as to add our belated alms to Monsieur de Valmont's. We are taking him with us. We shall at least be affording the good people the pleasure of seeing their benefactor once again; this is all, it seems, he has left us to do.

———

20 August 17–

LETTER 23: *The Vicomte de Valmont to the Marquise de Marteuil*
We had reached the point of my return to the house. I shall take up my story from there.

I had time only for a brief toilette before presenting myself in the drawing room. My beauty was working a piece of tapestry while the local curé read the gazette aloud to my old aunt. I sat down by the frame. Looks that were more gentle than usual, almost caressing, very soon led me to guess that the servant had already reported the result of his mission. In short, the curious creature was no longer able to keep the secret she had prised from me, and without hesitating to interrupt the venerable priest who read the news as though it were a sermon, said: "I, too, have my news to tell you" – and immediately recounted the details of my adventure with a precision that did great credit to the intelligence of her informer. I leave you to imagine my modest protestations – but who can stop a woman who, without suspecting it, is singing the praises of the man she loves? – so I let her continue. One might have thought she was preaching a panegyric on a saint's behalf. Meanwhile I took note, not unhopefully, of all the promise of love in her animated looks, in the freedom of her gestures, and most of all in the sound of her voice, so noticeably changed that it betrayed all the emotion in her heart. She had scarcely finished speaking when Madame de Rosemonde said, "Come here, nephew, so that I may embrace you." I realized immediately that our pretty preacher could hardly avoid being embraced in her turn. She made to escape, but was soon in my arms.

Far from having the strength to resist, she was scarcely able to sustain herself on her feet. The more I know of this woman, the more desirable she becomes. She hastily returned to the frame and looked for all the world as if she were busy again with her tapestry; but to me it was quite plain that her trembling hands would not allow her to continue.

After lunch the ladies insisted upon visiting the poor creatures to whose relief I had so piously contributed; I made one of the party. I shall spare you the boredom of this second scene of gratitude and approbation. A certain delicious memory makes my heart impatient for the moment of our return to the house. On the way home the fair Présidente, more pensive than ever, said not a word. I, preoccupied with finding some means of turning the effects of the recent incident to account, was equally silent. Only Madame de Rosemonde spoke, and our replies to her were few and brief. We must have bored her; I had intended we should, and my plan succeeded. On leaving the carriage she went directly to her rooms, leaving us tête à tête in a dimly lit salon — in the soft obscurity that encourages timid love!

I was not put to the trouble of leading the conversation into the course I wished it to take. Our beauty's missionary enthusiasm was more to the purpose than any tact of mine could have been. "When someone is so worthy of doing good," she said, fixing her gentle gaze upon me, "why is it that he spends his life behaving badly?" "I deserve," I replied, "neither the compliment nor the reproof; and I cannot think that, with all your intelligence, you have yet arrived at an understanding of me. But I shall not refuse you my confidence, of which you are more than worthy, even though I am thereby injured in your esteem. The key to my conduct you will find in the unfortunate pliability of my character. Living amongst people without morals, I imitated their vices; perhaps I took pride, too, in outdoing them. Impressed in the same way here by your virtuous example, I have, without hope of emulating it, tried at least to follow it. And perhaps the action, on which you now congratulate me will lose all its value in your eyes when you know its real motive." (Notice, my love, how near I came to the truth.) "It is not to me," I continued, "that those unfortunates owe the help I gave them. What you see as praiseworthy conduct was, for me, simply an attempt to please. I was, since I must tell you everything, only the humble agent of the goddess I adore." (Here she made as if to interrupt me, but I gave her no time.) "At this very moment," I added, "it is only because I am weak that my secret escapes my lips. I promised myself to keep it from you; I took pleasure in paying the most innocent homage to your virtues, and to your charms, without your knowing it. But with the very paragon of honesty before my eyes I am incapable of deception, and I would not be guilty in your eyes of the least dissimulation. Do not imagine you are being insulted by improper expectations on my part. I shall be unhappy, I know, but I shall welcome my sufferings. They will prove the strength of my love. And it is at your feet, upon your breast that they will be appeased; there that I shall recover strength to suffer anew; there that I shall find goodness and compassion, and think myself consoled because you have pitied me. O you that I adore, hear me, pity me, help me!" By this time I was on my knees, clasping her hands in mine. Suddenly, however, she withdrew them and, covering her eyes in an attitude of despair, cried out, "Oh, wretched woman!" then burst into tears. I had been so carried away that luckily I too was able to weep. Taking her hands once more in mine, I bathed them in tears. This was a very necessary precaution. She was so preoccupied with her own grief that she would not have noticed mine had I not discovered this means of bringing it to her attention. It afforded, moreover, another advantage: that of observing at my leisure her charming face, more beautiful than ever, as it proffered the powerful enticement of tears. My blood was on fire, and I was so little in control of myself that I was tempted to make the most of the occasion.

How weak we must be, how strong the dominion of circumstance, if even I, without a thought for my plans, could risk losing all the charm of a prolonged struggle, all the fascination of a laboriously administered defeat, by concluding a premature victory; if, distracted by the most puerile of desires, I could be willing that the conqueror of Madame de Tourvel should take nothing for the fruit of his labors but the tasteless distinction of having added one more name to the roll. Ah, let her surrender, but let her fight! Let her be too weak to prevail but strong enough to resist; let her savor the knowledge of her weakness at her leisure, but let her be unwilling to admit defeat. Leave the humble poacher to kill the stag where he has surprised it in its hiding place; the true hunter will bring it to bay. Do you think my scheme sublime? Nonetheless, I might perhaps at this moment regret that I failed to follow it, had not chance come to the rescue of my prudence.

We heard a noise. Someone was approaching the salon. Madame de Tourvel, alarmed, rose hurriedly and, seizing a candlestick, left the room. I was obliged to let her go, but it was only a servant. As soon as I was certain of this, I followed her. I had taken scarcely a dozen steps when I heard her, on recognizing me, or perhaps out of some vague feeling of alarm, quicken her pace, fling herself rather than walk into her room, and lock the door behind her. I went after her, but the key was inside the door. I took care not to knock, since that would have provided occasion for too easy a resistance. I hit instead upon the simple and happy idea of looking through the keyhole; whereupon I actually saw the adorable woman on her knees, bathed in tears and rapt in fervent prayer. What God did she hope to invoke? Is there one strong enough to prevail against love? She will look in vain for help elsewhere, when it is I alone who can guide her destiny.

Having decided I had done enough for one day, I too retired to my room and set about writing to you. I hoped to see her again at supper; but she sent word that she felt indisposed and had taken to her bed. Madame de Rosemonde thought of going up to see her, but our wicked invalid excused herself, saying that a headache did not permit her to receive anyone. You may be sure we did not sit long after supper, and that I too was attacked by a headache. Having returned to my room, I wrote a long letter bemoaning my harsh fate and, with the intention of delivering it to her this morning, went to bed. I slept badly, as you will deduce from the date of this letter. When I rose, I reread my little missive. It struck me that I had been too little critical of myself, that I had displayed more fire than tenderness, more bad humor than low spirits. I shall have to rewrite it, but I shall have to wait till I am calmer.

I see it is daybreak. I hope that with the fresh breezes of dawn will come sleep. I am going back to bed. I promise you that, however much I am under the sway of this woman, I shall never be so preoccupied with her that I want time to think a great deal of you. Good-bye, my love.

———

21 August 17–, at four o'clock in the morning

LETTER 24: *The Vicomte de Valmont to Madame de Tourvel*
Ah, for pity's sake, Madame, vouchsafe to calm my troubled heart, to tell me what cause I have for hope or fear! With extremes of joy and anguish in prospect, this doubt is most cruel torment. Why did I tell you everything? Why did I not withstand the imperious charm that delivered up my thoughts to you? Content to worship you in silence, I was able at least to enjoy my love; that innocent sentiment, untroubled as yet by the image of your grief, was enough to make me happy. But since I have seen you in tears, the source of my happiness has become a fount of despair. Since I heard you say, "Oh, wretched woman!", Madame, those cruel words have reechoed without cease in my heart. Why must it be that the gentlest of sentiments excites only your fear? Of what is there to be afraid? Oh, not of losing your heart! It was not

made for love; I have been deceived. Mine, which you never cease to vilify, is the one that feels; there is not so much as an impulse of pity in yours. Were this not true, you would not have refused a word of consolation to the wretch who had told you of his sufferings; you would not have shielded yourself from his gaze when he has no other pleasure in life but that of looking at you; you would not have made cruel game of his distress, sending him word that you were ill without allowing him to satisfy his solicitude; you would have realized that the same night which brought you twelve hours of sleep would for him become a whole century of suffering.

Why, tell me, do I deserve to be treated with such crushing severity? I am not afraid to let you pass judgment upon me – what, then, have I done? What indeed, except yield to a natural feeling, inspired by beauty, sanctioned by virtue, and kept at all times within the bounds of respect, its innocent expression prompted not by hope but by trust? Will you now betray that trust, which you yourself seemed willing to receive, and to which I gave myself unreservedly? No, I cannot think so. This would be to suppose you capable of wrong, and my feelings revolt at the mere idea. I disown my reproaches. They came to my pen, not to my heart. Ah, let me think you perfect! There is no other pleasure left me. Prove to me that you are so, by giving me your generous care. Where is the starving pauper you have saved, who was more in need of your help than I am? Do not leave me in the delirium into which you have thrown me; lend me your reason, since you have deprived me of mine. When you have cured me, enlighten me so that your work will be complete.

I have no wish to deceive you: you shall never succeed in conquering my love. But you will teach me to control it. Guide me in what I do, rule me in what I say, and you will at least spare me the terrible misfortune of offending you. Banish, above all, that desperate fear. Tell me that you pardon me, that you pity me; promise me your indulgence. I shall never win as much of your favor as I could wish; I claim only as much as I need. Will you refuse me?

Good-bye, Madame. Be so very kind as to receive this tribute of a feeling which in no way mitigates what I owe you of respect.

20 August 17–

LETTER 25: *The Vicomte de Valmont to the Marquise de Merteuil*
Here is yesterday's bulletin.

At eleven o'clock I paid my respects to Madame de Rosemonde and, under her auspices, was brought to the pseudo-invalid who was still in bed. There were dark rings under her eyes; I hope she slept as badly as I did. I took advantage of Madame de Rosemonde's withdrawing for a moment to another part of the room to deliver my letter. It was rejected. But I left it on the bed, and obligingly went to fetch up a chair for my old aunt who wished to be near "her dear child." The letter had to be snatched up and scandal averted. The invalid made the mistake of remarking that she believed she ran a little fever. Madame de Rosemonde, speaking very highly of my medical learning, directed me to take her pulse. So my beauty was obliged to suffer the double annoyance of delivering up her arm to me and of knowing that her little lie would be discovered. I took her hand, holding it in one of mine while with the other I felt up and down the soft skin of her plump and dimpled arm. The malicious creature responded not at all, so, letting her go, I said, "There is not even the slightest disturbance." I knew she must be looking daggers at me, so to punish her I avoided her eyes. A moment later she decided to rise, and we left the room. She appeared at dinner, which was a dismal affair; she announced that she would not be going for a walk, as much to tell me I should have no opportunity of speaking to her. It occurred to me that this was precisely the time for a sigh and a grief-stricken glance. She must have been expecting it, for this was the one occasion during the day when I succeeded in meeting her eyes. Prudent as she is, she is, like any other woman, not above a few little tricks. I found an opportunity to ask her "whether she had had the kindness to let me know my fate," and I was not a little surprised to hear her reply, "Yes, Monsieur, I have written to you." I was most anxious to have the letter. But, whether this was another trick, or lack of address or courage on her part, it was not till the evening, as she retired to her room, that she delivered it to me. I send it to you with the draft of my reply. Read and judge. Notice the arrant hypocrisy with which she declares she is not in love, when I am certain that she is; she does not hesitate to lie to me now, yet will complain when I lie to her later. Even the cleverest man, my love, could not hope to keep pace with the truest of women. Nevertheless I shall have to pretend to believe all this drivel and to wear myself out in despairing, because it pleases Madame to play at being cruel. How shall I keep myself from paying out this villainy? Ah, patience! . . . But good-bye. I have still a great deal to write.

By the way, please return the monster's letter. It may well happen that in the course of things she will decide to put a price upon such stuff, and one must be prepared.

I have said nothing about the little Volanges. We shall talk about her at the first opportunity.

Château de ———
22 August 17–

LETTER 26: *Madame de Tourvel to the Vicomte de Valmont*

You would certainly receive no letter from me, Monsieur, were it not for the fact that my stupid conduct last evening obliges me now to make some explanation to you. Yes, I cried, I own it; perhaps, too, the three words you are at such pains to quote did escape my lips. Tears, words – you noticed everything. Everything, then, must be accounted for.

Accustomed to inspiring none but honorable feelings, to being addressed only in such terms as I can listen to without blushing, to enjoying, as a result, a security that I have the temerity to believe I deserve, I have never learned to disguise or to repress the emotions I feel. Astonishment and embarrassment at your behavior; a fear that I cannot define, prompted by a situation in which I should never have found myself; revulsion, perhaps, at the thought of being mistaken for one of those women whom you despise, and of being treated with the same indifference; all these feelings contrived to provoke my tears and to cause me to say – with good reason, it seems to me – that I was wretched. That remark, which so impressed you, would certainly have been inadequate, had it, with my tears, been prompted by any other motive: had I, instead of disliking an avowal of sentiments that could only offend me, thought myself in danger of sharing them.

No, Monsieur, I am in no such danger. If I were, I should put a hundred leagues between myself and you; I should remove to a desert to mourn the misfortune of having known you. Perhaps, even though I am certain that I do not love you, that I shall never love you, I should have done better in following the advice of my friends never to have allowed you near me.

I thought – and I was wrong only in this – I thought that you would respect a decent woman who asked no more than decency of you; who was concerned to see justice done you; who, indeed, had already begun to speak in your defense when you insulted her by your preposterous attentions. You do not know me; no, Monsieur, you do not know me, or else you would not have tried to make a right of two wrongs: you would not, because you had made me an address to which I should never have listened, have thought yourself entitled to write me a letter I should never have received. And you ask me to "guide you in what you do, rule you in what you say!" Well then, Monsieur, say nothing and forget everything. That is the advice it becomes me to give and you to follow. You will then, after all, have the right to my indulgence; it will remain only for you to win the right to my gratitude...But no, I shall ask nothing of someone who has shown me no respect; I shall give no mark of confidence to someone who has abused my innocence. You oblige me to fear you, perhaps to hate you; I did not wish to do so. I wished to see you as no more than the nephew of my most respected friend. I answered public accusations of you in a spirit of friendship. You have ruined everything, and I cannot even foresee that you will wish to make amends.

I confine myself, Monsieur, to saying that your feelings are offensive, their avowal insulting, and above all that, far from bringing me one day to share them, unless you commit them to the silence I think I have the right to expect and even to demand, you shall oblige me never to see you again. I attach to this letter, which I hope you will be kind enough to return, the one you wrote me: it would very much distress me to think any trace remained of an incident that ought never to have occurred. I have the honor to be, etc.

———

21 August 17–

LETTER 27: *Cécile Volanges to the Marquise de Merteuil*
Heavens, how good you are, Madame! How well you understood that it would be easier for me to write than to speak to you! Especially since what I have to say is very difficult; but you are truly my friend, are you not? Oh, yes, my dear, dear friend! I shall try not to be shy; besides, I need you, I need your advice so much. It is most provoking: it seems that everybody can read my thoughts, especially when he is there. I blush every time anyone looks at me. Yesterday when you saw me cry it was because I wanted to speak to you but, for some reason, could not; and, when you asked me what was the matter, I could not keep back the tears. I was quite incapable of saying a word. But for you, Mamma would have noticed, and then what would have become of me? At all events, here is the history of what has happened, during the last four days especially.

That very day, Madame – yes, I am going to tell you everything – it was that very same day that the Chevalier Danceny wrote to me. Oh, I assure you, when I found the letter I had no idea what it was. But, to be quite candid, I cannot say that I read it without pleasure. Do you know, I would rather the rest of my life were spent in misery than that he had never written it? But I knew quite well that I must not tell him so, and I can assure you that I even gave him to believe that I was offended. But he says that he could not help writing, and I can quite well believe that. I decided not to reply, yet I too found I could not help doing so. Oh, I have written to him only once – and that was, partly, to forbid him to write to me again. Nevertheless, he still writes to me and is obviously hurt because I don't reply, which hurts me even more – so much so that I no longer know what to do or where to turn, and am really very much to be pitied.

Tell me, I beseech you, Madame, would it be wrong to reply to him from time to time? Only until he can be persuaded not to write to me any more himself, and we can go on as before; for, if this continues, I don't know what will become of me. I may say that after reading his last letter I thought I should never stop crying. I am certain that if I still do not reply, we shall both of us be made exceedingly miserable.

I shall send you his letter with this, or else a copy of it, so that you may judge. You will see that there is no harm in what he asks. If, however, you consider that I ought not to reply, I promise not to do so. But I think you will agree with me that there could be nothing wrong in it.

While I have the opportunity, Madame, forgive me for asking you yet another question. I have repeatedly been told that it is wrong to love someone, but why is this so? What makes me ask is that the Chevalier Danceny maintains that it is not wrong at all, and that practically everybody loves someone. If this is so, I do not see why I should be the sole exception. Or is it that it is only wrong for young girls? I heard Mamma herself say that Madame D—— was Monsieur M——'s lover. She did not speak of it as though it were something terrible; and yet I am sure she would be angry with me if she so much as suspected my friendship with Monsieur Danceny. She treats me as if I were still a child and tells me nothing. I thought, when she withdrew me from the convent, that I was to be married, but it seems now that this is not the case. Not that I care, I assure you; but you, her friend, will perhaps know what there is to know, and if you do know I hope you will tell me.

What a very long letter, Madame! But since I have your permission to write, I have taken the opportunity to tell you everything. I count on your friendship. I have the honor to be, etc.

Paris

23 August 17–

LETTER 28: *The Chevalier Danceny to Cécile Volanges*

Can it be, Mademoiselle, that you still refuse to reply? Nothing can touch you. Each day takes away with it the hope that it brought. What are these feelings of friendship that you grant exist between us worth when they are not even strong enough to make you aware of my grief; when they leave you cold and unmoved while I endure the torments of a fire that cannot be extinguished; when, far from giving you confidence in me, they cannot so much as arouse your pity? Can you do nothing to help your friend in his sufferings? A single word, no more, is all he asks, and you deny him even that. And you expect him to be content with so feeble a sentiment, a sentiment of which you are afraid even to reassure him!

You do not wish to be ungrateful, you said yesterday. Oh, believe me, Mademoiselle! To want to repay love with friendship shows no fear of being ungrateful, only a fear of seeming so. However, I must not continue to speak of a feeling that, if it does not interest you, can only be tiresome; I must at least keep it to myself until such time as I can learn to suppress it. I am aware how much suffering this will cost me; I cannot conceal from myself that I shall need all my strength of mind. But I shall try every means, and there is one that will be more painful to me than the rest: that of continually reminding myself that there is no feeling in your heart. I shall even try to see less of you, and I have already begun to think of a suitable pretext.

Am I then to forgo the sweet privilege of seeing you every day? Ah, I shall, at any rate, never cease to regret it! Perpetual torment will be the price of the most tender love; and it will be your will, your doing. Never, I know, shall I recapture the happiness I lose today. You alone were made for me: how much pleasure it would give me to make a vow to live only for you! But you would not accept it. Your silence tells me plainly enough that there is no place for me in your heart. It is at once the most cruel way of declaring your indifference and the most certain proof of it. Good-bye, Mademoiselle.

I can no longer flatter myself that you will reply. Love would have hastened to write; friendship would have been glad to do so; even pity would have obliged – but pity, friendship, and love alike are strangers to your heart.

Paris
23 August 17–

LETTER 29: *Cécile Volanges to Sophie Carnay*

I told you, Sophie: there are, after all, circumstances in which it is quite possible to write. I assure you I very much regret having followed your advice, which has caused both of us, the Chevalier Danceny and myself, a great deal of unhappiness. The proof that I was right is that Madame de Merteuil, a woman who certainly knows about these things, finally came round to my opinion. I told her everything. At first, it is true, she said what you did; but when I had explained everything to her, she agreed that my case is a very special one. She insists only that I show her all my letters, and all those I receive from the Chevalier Danceny, so that she can make sure that I say only what is proper. For the moment, then, my mind is at rest. Heavens, how much I like Madame de Merteuil! She is so good! And a most respectable woman. So there is no more to be said.

What letters I shall write to Monsieur Danceny and how delighted he is going to be! Even more so than he expects. Until now I have spoken to him only of my friendship, whereas he has always wanted me to talk of love. I do not really think there is any difference; however, I hesitated to mention the word, although he seems to set great store by it. I have told Madame de Merteuil about this, and she tells me that I did right. One should never admit to love until one can no longer help it. Well, I am sure I shall not be able to help it for very much longer. After all, it all comes to much the same thing, and this will give him more pleasure.

Madame de Merteuil has told me, too, that she will lend me books about all this, to teach me how best to conduct myself and how to write better than I do at present. She tells me all my faults, you know, which proves how much she likes me. She merely advises me to say nothing to Mamma about the books, which might seem to accuse Mamma of having neglected my education, and that might be annoying. Oh, I shan't say a word!

Nevertheless, it is most extraordinary that a woman who is scarcely a relation takes more care of me than my own mother! How lucky I am to know her!

She has also asked Mamma whether she may take me the day after tomorrow to her box at the opera, where, she says, we shall be alone together, and can chat to our hearts' content without fear of being overheard. I shall much prefer that to any opera. We shall also discuss my marriage. She has told me that it is in fact true that I am to be married; but so far we have not been able to discuss it any further. Really, is it not altogether amazing that Mamma still has nothing at all to say on the subject?

Good-bye, my dear Sophie. I am now going to write to the Chevalier Danceny. Oh, how happy I am!

———

24 August 17–

LETTER 30: *Cécile Volanges to the Chevalier Danceny*
I have at length decided to write to you, Monsieur, and to assure you of my friendship, of my *love*, since otherwise you are unhappy. You say that I have a cold heart; I assure you that you are mistaken. Indeed, I hope that you yourself can now no longer doubt that you are. If my not writing to you has given you pain, do you think it has made me any the less unhappy? It was just that I did not on any account wish to do anything wrong; what is more, I should certainly not have spoken of my "love" had I been able to help it – but your despondency was more than I could bear. I hope that your spirits will now revive, and that we shall both be very happy.

I hope to have the pleasure of seeing you this evening and that you will come early; you cannot possibly come earlier than I should like. Mamma is taking supper at home, and she will probably suggest that you stay. I hope you will have no other engagement, as you did the day before yesterday. You left very early. The supper to which you were invited must have been, I suppose, very amusing. Let us not talk about that, however. Now that you know I love you, I hope you will see me as often as you can. I am only happy when I am with you, and I should very much like it to be the same with you.

I am very sorry that at this moment you are still out of spirits, but that is not my fault. I shall ask to play the harp as soon as you arrive, so that you will receive my letter immediately. I can do no more.

Good-bye, Monsieur. I love you with all my heart. The more I tell you so, the happier it makes me. I hope you will be happy too.

———

24 August 17–

LETTER 31: *The Chevalier Danceny to Cécile Volanges*
Yes! There can be no doubt we shall be happy. My happiness, since I am loved by you, is certain; and yours, if it lasts as long as the love you inspire in me, will never end. Can it really be that you love me, that you are no longer afraid to tell me so? The more you tell me so, the happier it makes you! After reading that charming "I love you," writ-

ten in your own hand, I seemed to hear the words fall from your pretty lips; I seemed to see your charming eyes gaze into mine, so much the more beautiful for their look of tenderness. I have accepted your vow to live always for me. Ah, will you accept the one I make to devote my whole life to your happiness? Accept it, and be confident that I shall never break it.

What a delightful day we spent yesterday! Oh, why is it not every day that Madame de Merteuil has secrets to tell your mama? Why must there ever be thoughts of the constraint under which we meet to disturb my delicious recollections? Why can I not forever hold the pretty hand in mine that wrote "I love you"; cover it with kisses, and so revenge myself on your refusal to grant me greater favors?

Tell me, my dear Cécile, when your mama returned, when her presence forced us once again to look with indifference at each other, when you could no longer console me with the assurance of your love, your refusal to give me proof of it – did you then feel no regrets? Did you not tell yourself, "a kiss would have made him happier, and it is I who deprived him of that happiness?" Promise me, my dear, that you will take the next opportunity to be less disobliging – and with the help of that promise I shall find courage to face the difficulties that circumstances have in store for us. The bitterest privation would be sweetened by the knowledge that you shared my sorrow.

Good-bye, my sweet Cécile. I should find it impossible to leave you were it not for the sake of seeing you again. Good-bye. I love you so much! I shall love you more and more every day.

———

23 August 17–

LETTER 3 2: *Madame de Volanges to Madame de Tourvel*
Would you then, Madame, have me believe in the blameless virtue of Monsieur de Valmont? I am compelled to say that I cannot bring myself to do so, and that I should have as much difficulty in believing him to be a good man on the strength of the single circumstance you relate, as I should in considering a man of excellent reputation to be vicious on the grounds of a single fault. Mankind is never perfect in anything, no more so in wickedness than in virtue. The scoundrel has his good qualities, and the good man his weaknesses. It seems to me all the more necessary to realize this truth for its being both the basis of one's obligation to tolerate the wicked with the good, and a means by which the latter are preserved from pride, the former from losing heart. You will

no doubt be of the opinion that at this moment I am not very conscientiously practicing the tolerance that I preach. But tolerance I see as no more than dangerous frailty when it brings us to look with equal favor upon virtue and vice.

I shall not allow myself to examine the motives of Monsieur de Valmont's action; I should like to believe they were as laudable as the deed itself. But for all that, is it any the less true that he has spent his life bringing trouble, dishonor, and scandal to innocent families? Listen, if you like, to the voice of the unfortunate he has rescued, but let it not deafen you to the cries of a hundred victims he has sacrificed. Though he should only be, as you say he is, an example of the dangers of intimacy, would he be for that reason any the less dangerous an intimate himself? You imagine him likely to undergo a happy reformation. Let us go even further: let us imagine the miracle accomplished. He would still remain under the condemnation of public opinion, and what else should govern your conduct? God alone can absolve us of our sins the moment we repent; He alone can look into our hearts. Men judge of thoughts only by actions: and no man, once he has forfeited the esteem of others, has the right to complain of their inevitable distrust of him, a distrust that makes his loss so difficult to repair. Remember above all, my dear, that esteem may sometimes be lost for no more than our seeming to attach too little importance to it: a severe punishment, but do not call it unjust — for not only is there reason to believe that no one would forgo so precious a benefit who had some claim to deserving it, but it is after all the person who is not restrained by any such consideration who is the most likely to do wrong. Such, at any rate, would be the light in which an intimate relationship with Monsieur de Valmont would make you appear, however innocent that relationship might be.

I am so alarmed at the warmth with which you defend him that I hasten to meet objections I foresee you will make. You will cite Madame de Merteuil, who has been forgiven her connection with the Vicomte. You will ask me why I receive him in my house. You will tell me that, far from being ostracized by respectable people, he is accepted and even sought after in what is called polite society. I think I can answer all these objections.

First, you will agree that Madame de Merteuil is a most admirable woman who has perhaps only one fault: too much confidence in her own resources. She is like the skillful coachman who delights in maneuvering a carriage between mountainside and precipice, and whose only justification can be success. It is proper to admire her; it would be imprudent to imitate her. She herself would agree. She admits her faults. The more she sees of the world, the stricter become her principles, and I have no hesitation in assuring you that she will think in this matter as I do.

As far as I am concerned, I have no more excuse than anybody else. Certainly I receive Monsieur de Valmont as he is received everywhere: there you have another of the thousand inconsistencies that rule society. You know as well as I do that one spends one's life noticing them, complaining about them, and submitting to them. Monsieur de Valmont, with an illustrious name, a large fortune, and many agreeable qualities, early realized that to achieve influence in society no more is required than to practice the arts of adulation and ridicule with equal skill. He has more talent for both than anyone. In one instance he uses it to charm; in another to intimidate. No one respects him, but everybody flatters him. Such is his position among people who, with more discretion than courage, would rather humor him than cross swords with him.

But no woman, not Madame de Merteuil herself, would dare to shut herself up in the country almost alone with such a man. It has been left to the most circumspect, the most modest of all to set a pattern for such perversity; forgive me that word, I use it in friendship. My dear friend, your integrity itself, even as it inspires you with confidence, betrays you. Think of the people who will sit in judgment on you: on the one hand, frivolous creatures who will be skeptical of a virtue they find unexampled among themselves; on the other, the mischief makers who will pretend to be skeptical of it so as to punish you for having possessed it. Consider that you are doing at this moment what many men would not dare risk. I have remarked that even among the young people, who only too readily accept Monsieur de Valmont as their oracle, the more judicious are afraid to appear upon too intimate terms with him; yet you – you have no fears at all! Ah, come back, come back, I beg you…If my arguments cannot persuade you, yield at least to my friendship: that alone has made me renew my entreaties, and that alone can justify them. You find its admonitions severe; I hope they are unnecessary. But I would rather you complained of my solicitude than of my negligence.

24 August 17–

LETTER 33: *The Marquise de Merteuil to the Vicomte de Valmont*
As long as you are not anxious to succeed, my dear Vicomte, as long as your intention is to supply the enemy with arms and you look forward

more to the battle than the victory, I have nothing further to say. Your strategy is a masterpiece of prudence. On any supposition to the contrary it would have been mere imbecility; and, to tell you the truth, I am still afraid you may be deluding yourself.

What I must find fault with is not the opportunity you lost. On the one hand, I cannot see that it had indeed arrived; on the other I am pretty sure, whatever people say, that an opportunity missed once will present itself again, whereas an overly hasty action can never be recalled.

Your real mistake is in allowing yourself to enter into a correspondence. I defy you now to foresee where this will lead you. Are you, by any chance, hoping to prove to this woman by logical demonstration that she is bound to give herself to you? It seems to me that a truth such as this is better grasped by the feelings than by the understanding, and that to persuade her of it you will have to appeal to her heart rather than to her head. Of what use, then, is softening her heart if you are not there to take advantage of it? When your fine phrases have intoxicated her with love, do you suppose the intoxication will last long enough to be expressed before reflection supervenes? Consider how long it takes to write a letter, how long it takes for it to be delivered – and tell me whether any woman, especially a woman of principle such as your Fair Devotee, could possibly sustain for that length of time an intention she struggles constantly to suppress. Such tactics might succeed with children who, when they write "I love you" know not that they are saying "I am yours." But it seems to me that Madame de Tourvel's disputatious virtue can better assess the value of words. Moreover, in spite of your having gotten the better of her in conversation, she is more than your match in letter writing. Besides, have you no idea what is going to happen? No one willingly yields in a dispute, for the simple reason that it is a dispute. By sheer dint of looking for good arguments, we find them and we state them – and afterward hold by them not because they are good but because we do not wish to contradict ourselves.

Another observation, which I am surprised you have not made for yourself: there is nothing more difficult in love than expressing in writing what one does not feel – I mean expressing it with conviction. It is not a question of using the right words: one does not arrange them in the right way. Or, rather, one does arrange them, and that is sufficiently damning. Read your letter again. It is so beautifully composed that every phrase betrays you. I should like to believe that your Présidente is innocent enough not to understand this, but what difference will that make when the effect is nonetheless missed? This is the great defect of all novels: though the author whips himself up into a passion, the reader is left cold. *Heloise* is the sole exception one might be tempted to make. Despite the author's talent, it is for this reason that I have always thought it true. There is not the same difficulty in conversation. Long practice in using the voice has made it a sensitive instrument; tears that come easily are an added advantage; and in the eyes an expression of desire is not easily distinguished from tenderness. Moreover, it is easier in the informality of conversation to achieve that excitement and incoherence which is the true eloquence of love. Above all, the presence of the beloved is a check to thought and an incentive to surrender.

Take heed, Vicomte: you have been implored to write no more letters. Seize this opportunity to correct your mistake and await an occasion to speak instead. Do you know, this woman has more intelligence than I credited her with? Her defense is good. Were it not for the length of her letter, and the pretext she gives you in her phrase about gratitude to reenter the lists, she would have given nothing away

What seems to be even more auspicious for your success is that she employs too many of her resources at once. I can see she will exhaust them in a verbal defense, and have none left to withstand the material attack.

I return your letters. If you are wise, there will be no more until after the happy day. Were it not so late I would tell you about the little Volanges, who is making rapid progress; I am very pleased with her. I believe my work will be done before yours, and I am sure you are glad to hear it. Good-bye for today.

———

24 August 17–

LETTER 34: *The Vicomte de Valmont to the Marquise de Merteuil*
Your letter was splendid, my love, but why exhaust your energies in proving what everyone knows? In love one makes better progress by speaking rather than writing; that, I think, is all you have to say. But really! These are the very elements of the art of seduction. I shall observe only that you make a single exception to the rule, whereas there are two. To the children who follow the wrong course out of timidity, and whose ignorance is their downfall, must be added the women of wit, who are led into it by self-esteem, whose vanity lures them into the trap. For instance, I am quite sure that, the Comtesse de B——, who did not hesitate to reply to my first letter, was at the time no more

in love with me than I with her; but she saw her opportunity to discuss a subject that could not fail to redound to her credit.

Be that as it may, the principle, as a lawyer might say, does not apply in the present case. You assume that I have a choice between writing and speaking, but I have no choice. Since the incident of the nineteenth, the monster, put on the defensive, has avoided any possible encounter between us with an ingenuity that has put my own contrivances to shame. We have reached a point where, if this continues, she will force me into a serious attempt at recovering the advantage; for, I assure you, I will not be outdone by her in any way. My letters themselves are a little *casus belli*: not content with leaving them unanswered, she refuses to receive them. For each one I have to invent a new stratagem, which does not always succeed.

You remember the simple method by which I delivered the first; the second offered no greater difficulties. She had demanded the return of her letter: I sent her mine in its place and she accepted it without the slightest qualm. But whether out of pique at having been taken in or mere capriciousness, or – she will at length oblige me to believe it – whether it is indeed virtue, for some reason she has obstinately declined the third. I nevertheless hope that the difficulties in which her refusal nearly involved her will teach her a lesson for the future.

I was not very surprised that she did refuse a letter sent her in the ordinary way; to accept it would have been something of a concession, and I expected a more prolonged defense. After this first attempt, which was no more than a preliminary sally, I enclosed the letter in an envelope; then, choosing a time when I knew she would be at her toilette, I gave the letter to my manservant to take to her, with instructions to tell her that it was the document she had asked for. I was quite certain she would stop short of the scandalous explanation that must necessarily follow a refusal – and, in fact, she took the letter. My ambassador, who is not unobservant and who had been ordered to take note of her expression, perceived only a slight coloring, a sign more of embarrassment than of anger.

I flattered myself, of course, that she would either keep the letter, or, if she decided to return it to me, would have to meet me alone and give me an opportunity of speaking to her. About an hour later one of her servants entered my room and, on behalf of her mistress, handed me an envelope – of a shape different from mine – and addressed in a handwriting I recognized as the one I was so eagerly hoping to see. I tore it open...Inside I found my own letter, unopened and folded in two. It was, no doubt, fear of my being less scrupulous than she in the matter of scandal that prompted this diabolical ruse.

You know me: I need hardly describe my fury. However, I had to recover my sangfroid so as to contrive new schemes. This is the only one I could think of.

Every morning letters are fetched from the post about a mile from here: employed for this purpose is a box with a slit in its lid, something like a collection box, to which the postmaster holds one key, and Madame de Rosemonde another. Into it, during the day and as occasion arises, we put our letters, which are carried each evening to the post. In the morning, incoming letters are brought back. All the servants, foreign and indigenous, take their turn at this service. It was not my man's day, but he took it upon himself to go, explaining that he had affairs of his own in the neighborhood.

Meanwhile I wrote my letter, addressed it in an assumed handwriting and – not without success – counterfeited a Dijon postmark on the envelope. I chose Dijon because I thought it would be more jolly if, demanding the same rights as the husband, I should write from the same place. It was also that my beloved had been talking all day of her longing to receive letters from Dijon, and I thought it would be a kindness to afford her the pleasure.

My preparations made, it was easy enough to dispatch my letter with the others. Another advantage of the scheme was that I could be present at its reception: the custom here is to assemble for breakfast and to await the letters from the post before dispersing.

At length they arrived. Madame de Rosemonde opened the box. "From Dijon," she said, handing the letter to Madame de Tourvel. "It is not my husband's handwriting," returned the latter in an anxious voice, and broke the seal hurriedly. The first glance told her everything. Her expression changed so noticeably that Madame de Rosemonde asked whether anything was the matter, and I too, approaching her, asked, "Is the news so very bad?" Our shy devotee dared not lift her eyes, said not a word, and to mask her embarrassment pretended to glance through the letter, which she was scarcely in any condition to read. I was enjoying her distress, and did not hesitate to provoke it a little further. "Your composure now," I said, "makes me hope that the letter has caused you more surprise than pain." Anger then afforded the inspiration that prudence had failed to provide. "It contains," she replied, "nothing that does not offend me, and I am astonished that the author dared write to me at all." "Who was it then?" put in Madame de Rosemonde. "There is no signature," replied the beautiful Fury, "but letter and writer inspire me with equal contempt. You will oblige me by saying no more about it." As she spoke, she tore the offending missive to pieces, put the pieces in her pocket, rose, and left the room.

Angry or not, she still has the letter, and I believe I can trust to her curiosity for a complete perusal of it.

To give you every detail of the day's proceedings would be going too far, but with this abbreviated account I send you the drafts of my two letters; you will then know as much as I. If you wish to keep up with this correspondence you must train yourself to decipher my drafts, because nothing in the world will reconcile me to the tedium of copying them out a second time. Good-bye, my love.

———

25 August 17–

LETTER 35: *The Vicomte de Valmont to Madame de Tourvel*

I must obey you, Madame; it is essential to prove to you that, with all the faults you are pleased to ascribe to me, I have yet enough delicacy to forbear reproaching you, and enough courage to impose the most painful of sacrifices upon myself. You command me to say nothing and to forget everything. Ah, well! I shall compel my love to be silent, and I shall forget, if that is possible, the cruelty with which you greeted it. Certainly the mere desire to please you gives me no right to do so, and I am ready to admit that my need of your indulgence is no title to its possession. But you regard my love in the light of an insult. You forget that, were it a crime, you yourself would be not only its motive but its justification. You forget too that having learned to open my heart to you, even when such confidences were not to my advantage, it was no longer possible for me to hide the feelings that had taken possession of me. You took the proof of my honesty for a mark of audacity. As reward for the most tender, the most respectful, the truest love, you cast me away from you. To crown all, you tell me of your hatred... who else in the world would not complain of such treatment? I alone submit. I suffer in silence. You persecute and I adore. The extraordinary spell you cast over me makes you absolute mistress of my feelings, and if my love alone is recalcitrant, if that alone you cannot destroy, it is because my love is your own handiwork and not mine.

I am by no means asking you to return my feelings; I have never flattered myself that you might do so. I do not even expect your pity, for which the interest you showed in me might once have led me to hope. But I confess I consider myself entitled to justice.

You have told me, Madame, that certain of your friends have tried to lower me in your estimation. Had you taken their advice you would never have allowed me near you: those were your words. Who, if you please, are these officious friends? People of such strict principles, of such uncompromising probity, will surely not object to being identified; surely they cannot wish to hide in an obscurity where they may easily be confused with mere scandalmongers. Let me hear not only their accusations but their names. After all, Madame, I have a right to both, since it is on their authority that you judge me. No criminal may be condemned unless his crime is specified and his accusers named. I ask no other favor; and I shall undertake in advance to clear myself, to compel these people to retract.

If I have perhaps been too scornful of empty acclaim in a society of which I make little account, it is not the same with your esteem, which, now that I have devoted my life to winning it, cannot with impunity be snatched from me. It has become so much the more precious to me in that to it, I am sure, I owe the respect you were afraid to make: which, you say, might have given me *the right to your gratitude*. Ah! Far from claiming your gratitude, I shall think mine due to you if you will allow me an opportunity to please you. Begin now to do me justice. Leave me no longer in ignorance of what you wish me to do. If I could guess, I should spare you the trouble of telling me. Add the pleasure of obliging you to my delight in seeing you, and I shall think myself fortunate in your kindness. What is there to stop you? Not, I hope, fear of being refused? I do not think I could forgive you that. I refuse you nothing by not returning your letter. I wish, even more than you do, that it were no longer necessary to me: but I have become so used to thinking of you as kind-hearted that only in the letter can I find you as you wish to appear. Whenever I resolve to declare my feelings, I read there that rather than tolerate them you would put a hundred leagues between yourself and me; whenever I feel that everything about you increases and excuses my love, there I learn that my love insults you; and whenever, looking at you, I am tempted to think my love the summit of happiness, I have to return to your letter to find that it is nothing but frightful torture. As you may imagine, nothing would make me happier than to return this terrible document; to ask for it again would be to release me from my obligation to believe what it says. You are in no doubt, I hope, that I would be most anxious to let you have it.

21 August 17–

LETTER 36: *The Vicomte de Valmont to Madame de Tourvel*
(*postmarked Dijon*)

Every day increases your severity, Madame; you seem – dare I say it? –
to be less afraid of being unjust than of being too kind. Having condemned me without a hearing, you must have realized it would be easier not to read my arguments than to reply to them. You obdurately
refuse to receive my letters; you return them with contempt. You oblige
me at last to have recourse to deceit, at the very moment when my one
and only wish is to convince you of my honesty. But the absolute necessity you have imposed upon me of defending myself, I am sure, will
excuse the means I employ. Besides which, the sincerity of my feelings
convinces me that I have only to make you understand them in order
to make them acceptable to you; I thought, therefore, I might allow
myself this little subterfuge. I venture to think further that you will forgive me for it, and that you will scarcely be surprised to find that love
is more adept at coming forward than indifference at brushing it aside.

Permit me then, Madame, to lay my heart entirely open to you. It
belongs to you, and it is only right that you should know what is there.
On my first arrival at this house, I was very far from imagining the fate
that awaited me. I was not aware that you were here, and I must add
with my accustomed sincerity that, had I known, my peace of mind
would in no way have been disturbed. Not that I failed to pay your
beauty the homage that no one could withhold from it. But till that
time I had known only desire, to which I yielded only when it was
encouraged by hope. I had never felt the torments of love.

You were present when Madame de Rosemonde urged me to make
a longer stay. I had already spent one day in your company. Nevertheless I consented, or at least believed that I was consenting, only because
of that very natural and legitimate pleasure one takes in showing regard
for a relation one respects. The sort of life you lead here is of course
very different from the one I am accustomed to. I found no difficulty
in conforming to it; and without attempting to discover the origin of
the change I felt to be working in me, I put it down once more entirely
to that pliability of character which I think I have already mentioned
to you.

Unfortunately (and why, alas, must it be a misfortune?) I soon found,
when I knew you better, that your enchanting face, which alone had
interested me, was the least of your attractions. The angelic purity of
your soul astonished me, fascinated me. Beauty I had admired; virtue I
worshiped. Without the smallest pretensions to obtaining your regard,
I applied myself to deserving it. While begging your forgiveness for the

past, I was ambitious for your approval in the future. I sought it in your words, I watched for it in your looks – those poisoned looks that are so much the more deadly for being given without intent and received without suspicion.

At last I knew the meaning of love. But how little I thought of lamenting my condition! Having resolved to impose perpetual silence upon my feelings, I could give myself up to enjoying them with as little apprehension as reserve. Every day increased their strength. My pleasure in seeing you was soon transformed into a necessity. You had only to be absent for a moment for my heart to shrink with disappointment; at the first sound of your return it would palpitate with joy. I lived only in you and for you. I call upon you, however, to judge: did I at any time, whether in jest during some foolish game, or in earnest when the conversation was serious, speak a single word that might have betrayed my secret?

At length the day arrived on which my unhappy fate was to be sealed – and by some extraordinary chance an honorable deed was to provide the occasion. Yes, Madame, it was among the unfortunates I had succored when you displayed that sensibility which adds beauty to beauty and worth to virtue itself, it was then that you accomplished the confusion of a heart already distracted by too much love. Perhaps you noticed my silent preoccupation during our return? Alas! I was trying to repress inclinations that were becoming too strong for me.

It was when the unequal battle had weakened my powers of resistance that an accident, which I could not have foreseen, brought me face to face with you, alone. Whereupon I gave way, I admit. My overfraught heart could no longer contain its protestations, its tears. But was that, after all, a crime? And if it was, have I not been enough punished by the frightful torments to which I am condemned?

Consumed by a hopeless love, I implore your pity and receive nothing but your hatred. With no other happiness left me but that of seeing you, my eyes seek you out in spite of myself, and when they meet your glance I tremble. My whole life is spent in the cruel condition to which you have reduced me, the days in concealing my torments, the nights in suffering them: whereas you live in peace and quiet with no thought of torture but to cause it and commend yourself for doing so. It is you, all the same, who make the accusations, I the excuses.

There, at all events, Madame, there is a faithful account of what you call my crimes, which might perhaps more justly be called my misfortunes. A pure and sincere love, a respect that has never faltered, an absolute submission to your will: these are the feelings you have inspired in me. I would have no reluctance in offering them in homage to God Himself. O fairest of His creation, follow the example of His charity! Think of my cruel sufferings. Consider, especially, that you have put my despair and my supreme felicity on either scale, and that the first word you utter will irremediably turn the balance.

23 August 17–

LETTER 37: *The Présidente de Tourvel to Madame de Volanges*
I yield, Madame, to your friendly counsel. I am already accustomed to defer to your opinion in everything; I am now persuaded that it is always founded in reason. I shall even admit that Monsieur de Valmont must, after all, be infinitely dangerous if he can at one and the same time pretend to be what he appears to be here and continue to be the man that you have described. Be that as it may; since you insist, I shall send him away. At all events I shall do my best: things that are perfectly simple in theory are often difficult in practice.

A request to his aunt still seems to me impracticable; it would be as disagreeable to her as it would be to him. Nor could I without some reluctance take the step of going away myself. Apart from the reasons I have already given you concerning Monsieur de Tourvel, if my departure were to annoy Monsieur de Valmont, which is possible, would it not be quite easy for him to follow me to Paris? And would not his return there, for which I will be, or at least will seem to be, responsible, appear in an even worse light than a meeting at the country house of someone who is known to be his relation and my friend?

I have no alternative but to obtain from Monsieur de Valmont himself an assurance of his willingness to leave. I know this will be difficult. However, as he seems to be most anxious to prove to me that he has more sense of honor than is generally supposed, I am not without hope of succeeding. I shall not, in any case, be sorry of an opportunity to test him, to discover whether what he has so often told me is true: that the really virtuous women have never had, and will never have, any reason to complain of his behavior. If he leaves, as I wish him to, it will certainly be out of regard for me, for I am sure he intends to spend a large part of the autumn here. If he refuses and insists on staying, there will be nothing to prevent my leaving instead, and I promise you I shall do so.

This, I think, Madame, is all that your friendship demands of me; I look forward to satisfying that demand, to proving that, however *warmly*

I might have spoken in Monsieur de Valmont's defense, I am nonetheless prepared not only to listen to but to follow the advice of my friends.

I have the honor to be, etc.

———

25 August 17—

LETTER 38: *The Marquise de Merteuil to the Vicomte de Valmont*

Your enormous packet has this moment arrived, my dear Vicomte. If it is correctly dated I should have received it twenty-four hours ago. In any case, were I to spend time reading it I should have none left to reply to it, so I prefer merely to acknowledge it: we shall talk of other things. Not that I have anything to tell you on my own account. Paris in autumn contains scarcely a single male being that is recognizably human, so that for the last month I have been killingly circumspect. Anyone else but my chevalier would long ago have been thoroughly bored by so much proof of my fidelity. With nothing else to occupy me, I have amused myself with the little Volanges, and it is about her that I want to talk to you.

Do you know that you have missed more than you think in not taking charge of the child? She is truly delicious! She has neither character nor principles: imagine how easy and agreeable her company will one day be. I don't think she will ever be conspicuous for her sentiments; but everything about her speaks of the most lively sensations. She has neither wit nor guile, but a certain natural duplicity – if I may use such a phrase – at which even I am sometimes astonished, and which will succeed so much the better because her face is the very image of candor and ingenuousness. She is by nature very demonstrative, and this amuses me very much sometimes: she loses her little head with incredible ease and is so much the more diverting because she knows nothing, absolutely nothing, of all that she wants so much to know about. Her fits of impatience are altogether comic: she laughs, she gets angry, she cries, and then she begs me to teach her with a sincerity that is truly enchanting. In fact I am almost jealous of the man for whom such pleasures are in store.

I don't know whether I told you that for the last four or five days I have had the honor of being her confidante. As you can imagine, I was severe at first: but as soon as I saw that she believed me convinced by her doubtful arguments, I pretended to take them for good ones. She is firmly persuaded that she owes this success to her eloquence; the precaution was necessary to avoid compromising myself. I allowed her to write, and to say "I love you." The same day, without her suspecting, I arranged a tête-à-tête for her with Danceny. But would you believe that he is still so dull as not to have obtained so much as a kiss? And yet the boy writes such very pretty verses! Lord, how stupid clever people can be – this one to the point of embarrassing me. After all, I cannot lead him by the nose!

It is now that you could be extremely useful to me. You are intimate enough with Danceny to obtain his confidence, and once you have that we can proceed at a great pace. Finish off your Présidente, then; I cannot, after all, have Gercourt escape. For the rest, I told the little creature about him yesterday and described him so well that had she now been his wife for ten years she could not hate him more. I also, however, expatiated a great deal on the subject of marital fidelity; nothing could have equaled my firmness on this point. Thus I have, on the one hand, established a reputation for virtue which too much complaisance might have destroyed; on the other, I have increased the feelings of hatred with which I intend her husband to be gratified. Lastly I hope that, for my having persuaded her that she may surrender to love only during the short time that remains before her marriage, she will decide so much the more quickly not to waste any of that time.

Good-bye, Vicomte; I am going to begin my toilette, during which I shall read your compilation.

––––––––

27 August 17–

LETTER 39: *Cécile Volanges to Sophie Carnay*

I am so anxious and sad, my dear Sophie. I have been crying almost the whole night: not that for the present I am anything but extremely happy, but I see that it cannot last.

I was at the opera yesterday with Madame de Merteuil; we talked a great deal about my marriage, and nothing that I learned was in the least encouraging. I am to marry the Comte de Gercourt, and it is to happen in October. He is rich, a man of fashion, and Colonel of the ––––––– Regiment. So far so good. But he is old – thirty-six, can you imagine? Madame de Merteuil says, besides, that he is stern and gloomy, and she is afraid I might not be very happy with him. I saw, in fact, that she was quite certain I would not be happy, and that she did not wish to say so for fear of distressing me. She spoke of nothing almost the whole evening but the duties a woman owes to her husband. She admits that Monsieur de Gercourt is not in the least agreeable, but says I must love him all the same. She told me too that, once I am married, I shall have to stop loving the Chevalier Danceny – as if that were possible! Oh, I promise you, I shall love him forever! I should prefer, you know, not to be married at all. Let this Monsieur de Gercourt make the best he can of it; I did not, after all, ask for him. He is at present in Corsica – very far from here. I wish he would stay there for the next ten years. If I were not afraid of being sent back to the convent I should tell Mamma that I don't want him for a husband; but the convent would be still worse. I am in a terrible dilemma. I feel that I have never loved Monsieur Danceny as much as I do at this moment; and when I think that I have no more than a month of freedom left me, the tears come immediately to my eyes. Madame de Merteuil's friendship is my only consolation. She has such a good heart. She shares all my troubles as if they were her own. Besides, she is so agreeable that when I am with her I can almost forget them. What is more, she is a great help to me. What little I know I have learned from her. And she is so good that I can tell her all my thoughts without feeling the least embarrassment. She scolds me a little sometimes, when she thinks I am in the wrong, but so gently, and then I put my arms around her and kiss her until she is no longer angry. She, at least, is one person I can love as much as I like without doing wrong, and that is a great happiness. I have agreed however not to display so much affection in company, especially when Mamma is there, in case she suspects anything concerning the Chevalier Danceny. I assure you that if I could live forever in the way I do now I should be very happy. If only this dreadful Monsieur de Gercourt... But I shall say no more about him lest I be unhappy again. I shall write to the Chevalier Danceny instead, telling him only of my love and not of my troubles, because I don't wish to distress him.

Good-bye, my dear friend. You were wrong, you see, to complain: I could never be so *busy*, as you say, as to have no time left to think of you and write to you.*

27 August 17–

LETTER 40: *The Vicomte de Valmont to the Marquise de Merteuil*
It is not enough for the monster to leave my letters unanswered or even to refuse to receive them: she wants to deny me the very sight of her.

---

*Letters between Cécile Volanges and the Chevalier Danceny continue to be omitted, since they are of little interest and throw no light on events.

She insists on my leaving. What will come as more of a surprise to you is that I have submitted to these harsh demands. You are going to disapprove. However, I thought I had better not miss an opportunity of accepting an order: for I have always thought that, on the one hand, an order issued is a responsibility assumed, and on the other, that the illusion of authority we tempt women to entertain is one of the pitfalls they find it most difficult to avoid. Moreover, this one's skill in eluding a tête-à-tête with me has put me in a dangerous situation, from which I have thought it necessary to withdraw at all costs. Constantly in her company, with no opportunity to bring my love to her notice, I have had good reason to fear that she would at length become accustomed to seeing me without a qualm – and you know how difficult it would be to recover from such a setback.

For the rest, you may be quite sure that I have not surrendered unconditionally. In fact, I have taken care to lay down a condition that it will be impossible to observe – as much for the sake of remaining at liberty to keep my word or break it as for the sake of entering into a dispute, either by word of mouth or in writing, at a time when my beauty is more than usually pleased with me and wants me to be pleased with her. What is more, I should be very stupid if I found no way of obtaining compensation for my waiving this claim, totally unsupported though it is.

Having given you in this long preamble an analysis of my motives, I shall now begin the history of the last two days. By way of documentation I enclose the letter from my beauty and my reply to it. You will agree that there are few historians as meticulous as I.

You remember the effect of my letter from "Dijon" two mornings ago. The remainder of the day proved exceedingly stormy. Our pretty prude did not appear at all before lunch. When she did, she complained of a bad headache: an excuse designed to conceal one of the most violent fits of ill temper to which woman has ever been subject. A complete change had come over her features: in place of the sweet expression that you know, a look of defiance gave new beauty to her face. I shall certainly put this discovery to good use in the future, exchanging my tender mistress now and again for a rebellious one.

I foresaw that conversation after lunch would be tedious, so to spare myself unnecessary boredom I pleaded letters to write and withdrew to my room. At six I returned to the drawing room. Madame de Rosemonde proposed a drive and her suggestion was approved. But, as we were on the point of stepping into the carriage, our mock invalid, with diabolical malice and perhaps in revenge for my absence earlier on, pleaded in turn an exacerbation of her sufferings and condemned me without mercy to a tête-à-tête with my aunt. I shall never know whether my curses upon this she-devil were fulfilled, but we found on our return that she had gone to bed.

Next morning at breakfast she was no longer the same woman. Her natural sweetness had returned, and I came to the conclusion that I had been forgiven. Immediately after breakfast the dear lady rose with a languid air and made for the park. I followed her, of course. "What, I wonder, can have persuaded you to take a walk?" I asked as we met. "I spent a long time writing this morning," she replied, "and I am a little fatigued." "I am not, so fortunate, surely," continued I, "as to be responsible myself for your fatigue?" "I have indeed written to you," she returned, "but I am not sure whether I shall give you the letter. It contains a request, and you have given me no reason to hope that it might be granted." "Oh, I swear, if it is at all possible..." "Nothing could be easier," she interrupted, "and even though you ought perhaps to grant it as my rightful due, I shall not object to receiving it as a favor." As she spoke she handed me the letter, and as I took it I seized her hand. The latter she withdrew immediately, but not angrily – with less spirit, indeed, than embarrassment. "It is warmer than I thought it would be," she said. "I must go indoors." And she hurried back toward the house. All my efforts to persuade her to continue the walk were in vain, and I was obliged to remind myself that we were fully visible, and that I must confine myself to verbal entreaties. She walked back without a word, and I saw clearly that the sole object of this pretense of a walk had been the delivery of her letter. As soon as we reached the house she went up to her room, while I retired to mine to read the epistle, which you, too, would do well to read – and my reply to it – before proceeding further...

LETTER 41: *The Présidente de Tourvel to the Vicomte de Valmont*
It seems to me, Monsieur, that your behavior toward me has no other motive than that of adding each day to the sum of my complaints against you. Your obstinacy in treating me to sentiments that it is equally against my desire and my duty to acknowledge; your unhesitating abuse of my good faith and my modesty in sending me your letters; above all, the means – scarcely a proof of delicacy in you, I venture to say – that you employed in sending me your last, without so much as considering that the surprise by itself might compromise me; everything you have done gives me reason to call you to account in terms as outspoken as they

are just. Instead of recalling my grievances, however, I shall confine myself to making a request of you, a request as simple as it is fair. When I obtain it from you I promise that everything else will be forgotten.

You yourself have told me, Monsieur, that I need fear no refusal from you; and even though, with that inconsistency so characteristic of you, you followed this same injunction with the one refusal you were able to make me,* I should like to believe nonetheless that today you will keep your solemn promise of a few days ago.

I want you, then, to be so good as to go away from me, to leave this house, where a longer stay on your part could only further expose me to the criticism of a society that is always prepared to think ill of others, and which, thanks to you, is only too ready to fix its attention upon the women who count you among their acquaintance.

My friends have for a long time warned me of this danger; yet, as long as your behavior toward me gave me reason to believe that you would distinguish between me and that multitude of women who have had cause to revile you, I disregarded and even disputed my friends' advice. Now that you treat me in the same way as the others, now that I can no longer ignore the truth, I owe it to society, to my friends, and to myself to take this course and no other. I might perhaps add here that you will gain nothing by refusing my request, since I have decided to leave myself if you persist in staying. I do not, however, mean to belittle the obligation I shall owe you should you consent; I am, in fact, quite willing to tell you that in compelling me to leave here you would be upsetting my plans. Prove to me then, Monsieur, that – as you have so often told me – no honorable woman will ever have occasion to complain of you. Prove to me at least that when you have wronged one, you know how to make amends.

If I thought it necessary to justify my request to you, I could say no more than that you have spent your life in making it necessary – yet that it is one I ought never to have found it necessary to make. But let us not recall incidents I wish only to forget; remembering them would compel me to think harshly of you at a moment when I am offering you an opportunity to earn my undivided gratitude. Good-bye, Monsieur; your conduct now will determine the feelings with which, for the rest of my life, I shall subscribe myself your very humble, etc.

————

25 August 17–

————

*See Letter 35.

LETTER 42: *The Vicomte de Valmont to the Présidente de Tourvel*

Hard as the conditions are, Madame, that you impose on me, I shall not refuse to accept them. I think it would be impossible for me to cross you in a single one of your desires. This question once settled, I venture to hope that you will permit me in my turn to make some requests of you. They will be much easier to comply with than yours; I wish, nevertheless, to obtain your consent only through an absolute submission to your will.

The first, which I hope will find an advocate in your sense of justice, is that you will be so good as to give me the names of your friends, my accusers. They have, it seems to me, done me as much harm as entitles me to their acquaintance. The second, an appeal to your indulgence, is that you will be kind enough to permit my paying you now and then the homage of a love that, more than ever before, deserves your pity.

Consider, Madame, that I am anxious to obey you even at the expense of my own happiness – I shall go further – even when I am convinced that you urge my departure only to spare yourself what we always find painful: the sight of a victim to our injustice.

You must agree, Madame, that you are less afraid of society, which is too used to respecting you to pass sentence against you, than of being plagued by a man whom you find it easier to punish than to condemn. You send me away from you exactly as one averts one's eyes from the unfortunate one has no intention of assisting.

But when absence has redoubled my sufferings, who but you will listen to my lamentations? Where else shall I find the consolation that is soon to become so necessary to me? Will you deny it me, when it is you alone who have caused my miseries?

You will not, of course, be surprised to learn that I am most anxious, before leaving, to make my justification to you in person of the feelings you have inspired in me; nor that, unless I receive my commands at your own lips, I find I lack the courage to carry them out.

For these two reasons, I beg you for a moment's interview. It is useless to imagine that letters would do as well. One writes volumes only to half-explain what a quarter of an hour's conversation would make quite clear. There will be quite time enough for the meeting. Eager as I am to obey you, I have already told Madame de Rosemonde, as you know, that I intend to spend a part of the autumn with her, and I must at least wait to receive a letter before offering her a pretext of business that obliges me to leave.

Good-bye, Madame. Never has it cost me more to write that word than it does now, when it calls up the thought of our separation. If you could conceive how much it makes me suffer, I daresay you would be a little grateful for my willingness to please you. Look more kindly, at least, upon the assurance and homage of my most tender and respectful love.

———

26 August 17–

LETTER 40 (continued): *The Vicomte de Valmont to the Marquise de Merteuil*

Now, my love, let us consider: You know as well as I do that the scrupulous, the honorable Madame de Tourvel cannot grant me the first of my requests: she cannot, in giving me the names of my accusers, betray the confidence of her friends. So, in making that the condition of all I promise, I am committed to nothing. But you understand too that her denial of this request will give me a right to obtain the others. Thus I shall have the advantage, when I go away, of a correspondence with her that she herself has authorized. I attach little importance to the interview I asked for: almost my sole object in doing so was to prepare her to consent to others when they become really necessary.

The only thing I have left to do before my departure is to discover who these people are that are engaged in disparaging me to her. I presume that her pedant of a husband is one of them; I hope so. Apart from the fact that conjugal protection is a spur to desire, from the moment my beauty agrees to write to me I shall be sure of having nothing further to fear from him, for she will already be under the necessity of deceiving him.

But if she happens to have a friend intimate enough with her to be in her confidence, and if that friend happens to be against me, it will be necessary to stir up a quarrel between them. I think I can do it. The first essential, however, is to acquaint myself with the facts.

I was on the point of making a discovery yesterday, but this woman never does anything in the normal way. We were in her room when it was announced that dinner was served. She had only just completed her toilette, and as she hurried off, making excuses, I noticed she had left the key in her writing desk. I knew that the one in the door of her room was never removed. During dinner, as I turned this over in my mind, I heard her maid come down. I made my decision immediately: inventing a bleeding nose, I left the room. I flew to the desk — to find all the drawers open and not the smallest sign of a letter anywhere. Yet at this time of the year there are no fires in which they could have been burned. What does she do with the letters she receives? She receives them often enough! I missed nothing; everything was open, and I looked everywhere. All I acquired was the conviction that the precious treasure must be buried in her pockets.

How to remove it from there? I have been trying since yesterday, without success, to think of a means; I am still determined to find one. I wish I had been trained in the arts of the pickpocket. Ought they not, after all, to have figured in the education of a man of intrigue? How amusing it would be to steal a rival's letter or his miniature, or to filch from the pockets of a prude the wherewithal to unmask her hypocrisy! Our parents think of nothing; as for me, I think of everything, but to no purpose. I can only recognize my incompetence without being able to remedy it.

At all events, I returned to table very disgruntled. My ill temper, however, was a little mollified by noting the interest my feigned indisposition appeared to have aroused in my beauty. I did not, of course, fail to inform her that for some time, and to the great detriment of my health, I have been subject to the most violent fits. Convinced as she is that she is responsible for them, ought she not in all conscience to apply herself to their cure? But, however religious, she is not very charitable. She refuses to give alms of any kind in the name of love. Being refused them, it seems to me, is more than enough to justify stealing them. But good-bye. Even as I chatter to you I can think of nothing but those cursed letters.

———————

27 August 17–

LETTER 43: *The Présidente de Tourvel to the Vicomte de Valmont*
Why, Monsieur, do you seek to lessen my gratitude? Why resolve to comply only by halves with my wishes, to bargain, as it were, over a perfectly fair proposal? Is it not enough that I know how much I ask you? What you ask of me is not only too much, it is impossible. If, in fact, friends of mine have spoken to me of you, they could have done so only in my own interest. They may have been mistaken; their intentions were nonetheless honest. Do you suggest that I recognize this proof of their attachment by betraying their trust? I have already done wrong to tell you of them at all, a fact of which you make me amply aware at this moment. What with anyone else would have been simple candor was recklessness where you were concerned; and I should be

guilty of much worse were I to concede to your request. I appeal to you, to your honor. Do you really think me capable of such a thing? Should you ever have made such a proposal? Of course not. I am sure that when you have thought more about it, you will press your demands no further.

Your proposal that I write to you is scarcely less difficult to assent to; and if you are just, it is not me you will blame for this. I have no wish whatever to offend you, but with the reputation you have acquired — which, at your own admission, you have at least in part deserved — what woman could admit to being in correspondence with you? What woman of honor, besides, would resolve on doing what she knows she will be obliged to conceal?

Yet were I confident that your letters would be of a kind I could find no fault with, that I could always justify myself in my own eyes for having received them — *then* perhaps I might be persuaded, because I want to prove to you that I am guided by reason and not by hatred, to overlook other considerations, however serious; and to go much further than I ought in allowing you to write to me from time to time. If you do, in fact, wish this to happen as much as you say you do, you will willingly submit to the single condition I have imposed; and if you are able to feel some gratitude for what I do at this moment for your sake, you will defer your departure no longer.

Permit me to observe apropos that, though you received a letter this morning, you did not take advantage of the opportunity to announce your departure to Madame de Rosemonde as you promised you would. I hope that henceforth nothing will prevent you from keeping your promise — above all that you will not expect, in return, any promise from me concerning the interview you ask for, to which I have positively no intention of consenting. I hope too that in place of the orders you fancy are necessary to you, you will be content with my pleas, which I now renew. Good-bye, Monsieur.

———

27 August 17–

LETTER 44: *The Vicomte de Valmont to the Marquise de Merteuil*
Share my joy, love; I am beloved; I have triumphed over that intransigent heart. She continues to pretend, but in vain; fortune and skill have sprung her secret. Now, thanks to my unflagging endeavors, I know everything that can be of interest to me. Since last night — happy night! — I have been in my element again; my whole life has begun anew.

I have penetrated a twofold mystery, uncovered both love and infamy: the one I shall enjoy, the other avenge. I shall fly from pleasure to pleasure. At the mere thought of it I am carried away to a point where I have some difficulty in recalling my prudence, and I shall probably find it no less difficult to give a semblance of order to the story I have to tell you. Let me try all the same.

Yesterday, after writing my letter to you, I received one from the Heavenly Devotee herself. I send it to you; you will observe that, as gracefully as she can, she gives me permission to write to her. But she is more concerned about my departure from here; and I decided that to defer it much longer would damage my cause.

Meanwhile, I was still tormented by a desire to know who could have written to her about me and still uncertain what I should do to find out. I thought I might prevail upon the maid. I would have her bring me her mistress's pockets, which she could without difficulty remove in the evening and as easily replace in the morning without arousing the smallest suspicion. I offered her ten louis for this trifling service. But she proved to be either too scrupulous or too frightened, at all events a broken reed, and neither my eloquence nor my money could move her. I was still cajoling her when the bell rang for supper and I had to leave her, considering myself lucky enough to have obtained a promise of secrecy – upon which, needless to say, I could scarcely rely.

I have never been in worse humor. I felt I had compromised myself; I spent the entire evening regretting my rash experiment.

Still uneasy, I retired to my room and spoke to my valet, who I thought must, in his role of successful lover, have some credit with the girl. My plan was that he should either persuade her to do as I had asked, or, at the least, ensure that she would be discreet. But he, who is ordinarily confident about everything, seemed to doubt whether any negotiation of this kind would succeed – and he passed an astonishingly profound comment on the subject.

"Monsieur knows better than I do," he said, "that to lie with a girl is only to make her do what she likes doing. It's often a far cry from that to making her do what we want her to do."

The good sense Maraud shows quite frightens me at times.*

"I am the less able to answer for this one," he continued, "because I have reason to believe that she has another lover, and that I owe my

---

*Piron, *Métromanie*.

own success with her only to the fact that there is not enough to do in the country. Were it not for my eagerness to serve Monsieur, I would have had her only once." (This fellow is a real treasure!) "As for her keeping your secret," he went on, "what use will it be making her give her promise when she has nothing to lose by breaking it? To refer to the subject again will only give her an idea that it is important, and so make her even readier to make use of it for currying favor with her mistress."

My perplexities increased with the justice of these reflections. Fortunately the odd creature was in a mood to chatter; and, as I needed him, I let him go on. In the course of relating his adventures with the girl he revealed the fact that, since the room she occupies is separated from her mistress's only by a thin partition through which they are afraid suspicious noises might be heard, it is in his room that they meet each night. My plan was formed upon the instant: I told him of it, and we executed it with brilliant success.

I waited till two o'clock in the morning, at which time I proceeded, as agreed upon, to the scene of the lovers' rendezvous, taking a candle with me, forearmed with the excuse that I had rung several times without success. My accomplice, who can play a part to perfection, staged a little drama of surprise, despair, and excuses which I brought to a close by sending him to fetch some hot water I pretended to need. Meanwhile our fastidious chambermaid was so much the more abashed because the ridiculous man, determined to outdo me in ingenuity, had coaxed her into a state of undress which the season might have explained but could not excuse.

Knowing that the more I could humiliate the wench the more tractable she would be, I forbade her to change either her position or her costume, and, having ordered my valet to wait for me in my room, I sat down beside her on the bed, which was in great disarray, and began to speak. It was necessary to maintain the power over her that circumstances had given me, so I preserved a composure that would have done credit to the self-restraint of a Scipio. Without taking the smallest liberty with her – which nevertheless the occasion and her preparedness might have given her the right to expect – I talked business as calmly as I would have done to any solicitor.

My conditions were that I should guard her secret faithfully, provided that the next morning, at about the same hour, she would bring me her mistress's pockets. "For the rest," I added, "I promised you ten louis yesterday; my promise holds good today. I do not wish to take advantage of your situation." Everything was consented to, as you may imagine, whereupon I retired to bed, leaving the happy couple to make up for lost time.

My own time I spent sleeping; and when I woke, because I needed an excuse for leaving my beauty's letter unanswered until I had examined her papers (which I could not do until the night following), I decided to go hunting, and indeed I spent almost all day at it.

On my return I was coldly received. I have a suspicion that a little pique was felt at the lack of zeal in the way I was making the most of the time left me: particularly after a letter so much more amiable than any heretofore had been written to me. I came to this conclusion because, once Madame de Rosemonde had put forward a few protests at my long absence, my beauty returned somewhat sharply, "Ah, let us not take Monsieur de Valmont to task for enjoying the one pleasure this place is able to afford him." I complained of the injustice of this, and took the opportunity to assure the ladies that I enjoyed their company so much that for its sake I was about to sacrifice the satisfaction of writing a most interesting letter. I added that, having been unable to sleep for several nights, I had meant to find whether fatigue would help me. My looks, of course, clearly indicated both the subject of my letter and the cause of my sleeplessness. I took care the whole evening to preserve an air of gentle melancholy, which appeared to succeed quite well; behind it I concealed my impatience for the moment when the secret so obstinately kept from me would be revealed. At length we separated, and some time later came the trusty maid, bringing me the reward of my discretion.

Master now of the treasure, I proceeded to examine it, but with the prudence you know is customary to me: for it was important to leave everything in its proper place. I chanced first upon two of the husband's letters: indigestible compounds of legal jargon and conjugal rhetoric, which I was so long-suffering as to read in their entirety, and in which I found not a single word relating to me. I replaced them with some annoyance – which, however, left me when I discovered that in my hand I held the pieces *carefully put together again* of the famous letter from Dijon. Fortunately I took it into my head to glance through it. Imagine my joy on finding traces, very distinct traces, of my Adorable Devotee's tears. I must admit that, surrendering to a very callow impulse, I kissed the letter with a rapture I had ceased to believe I could feel. I returned happily to the investigation. I found all my own letters together, arranged in order of date. I was still more agreeably surprised to find the first one of all among them: the one I thought she had been so ungrateful as to return unread. It had been faithfully copied in her own hand, and the uncertain scrawl bore witness to the agreeable disturbance in her heart as she carried out her task.

Till now my thoughts had been entirely given up to love; but the next moment I was possessed by fury. Who do you think it is that has plotted my ruin in the eyes of the woman I adore? What Fury, do you suppose, would be vicious enough to plan such villainy? You know her: she is your friend, your relation. It is Madame de Volanges. You cannot imagine the tissue of unspeakable lies that diabolical shrew has fabricated around me. It is she and only she who has bereft this angelic woman of her peace of mind. It is thanks to her representations, thanks to her pernicious advice, that I find myself obliged to leave. It is to her, after all, that I am to be sacrificed. Oh yes, certainly her daughter must be seduced. But that will not be enough: she must be ruined too. Since this cursed woman is of an age that must protect her own person from my onslaughts, it is through the object of her affections that I shall have to attack her.

So she wants me to return to Paris! She insists upon it! So be it. I shall return. But she shall groan for it. I am sorry that Danceny has to be the hero of the piece. He has a fundamental honesty that will come in our way. However, he is in love, and I see him often; perhaps we can turn that to some advantage. I have forgotten in my annoyance that I owe you an account of what happened today. Let us continue. This morning I saw my sensitive prude once more. Never to my mind had she looked more beautiful. Inevitably so. A woman reaches the height of her beauty – and only at this time can she inspire that intoxication of the soul which is so often spoken of and so rarely experienced – when we are sure of her love but not of her favors. And that was precisely my situation. Perhaps too the thought that I should soon be deprived of the pleasure of seeing her added to her attractions. The post arriving, your letter of the twenty-seventh was delivered to me. Even as I read it I was in two minds whether or not to keep my word. But when my beauty's eyes met mine, I knew that it would be impossible to refuse her anything.

So I announced my departure. A moment later Madame de Rosemonde left the room, and we were alone. I was still four yards away from the timorous creature when rising to her feet with a look of alarm she cried, "Leave me alone, Monsieur; in heaven's name, leave me alone." So earnest a plea, such a betrayal of emotion, served only to increase my excitement. In an instant I was beside her holding the hands she had clasped together in the most touching gesture. I was just beginning my tender protestations when some hostile demon brought Madame de Rosemonde in again. My timid devotee, who after all has some grounds for her fears, took the opportunity to withdraw.

I immediately offered her my arm and was accepted. This mark of favor so long withheld from me augured well, and as I renewed my protestations I attempted to squeeze her hand in mine. At first she tried to remove it, but upon more earnest entreaty gave in with a good enough grace: without, however, returning the pressure or making any reply. As we arrived at the door of her room I made to kiss her hand before leaving her. Resistance was at first unequivocal, but at a "remember that I am going away" uttered in my most tender tones, it became clumsy and ineffective. The kiss had scarcely been planted upon it when the hand recovered strength enough to escape and our beauty went into her room, where her maid awaited her. Here ends my story.

Since you will, I presume, be at the Maréchale de —— ——'s tomorrow, where I shall certainly not come looking for you, and since I am quite sure we shall have more than one subject to discuss at our first meeting – notably the little Volanges, who is never far from my thoughts – I have decided to send this letter ahead of me. Long as it already is, I shall not seal it until it is time for the post. In my present circumstances everything may depend on a moment's opportunity, and I leave you now to go and lie in wait for it.

P.S. *Eight o'clock in the evening*
Nothing new. Not a single moment's liberty; indeed, pains taken to prevent it. At least, however, a show of regret – as far, that is, as decency permitted. Another circumstance that may not prove to be without interest: I am charged with an invitation from Madame de Rosemonde to Madame de Volanges to spend some time with her in the country.

Good-bye, my love, till we meet tomorrow, or the day after at the latest.

———

28 August 17–

LETTER 45: *The Présidente de Tourvel to Madame de Volanges*
Monsieur de Valmont left this morning, Madame; you have seemed to me to be so anxious for his departure that I think it only proper to inform you of it. Madame de Rosemonde misses her nephew very much, and it must be admitted that, in spite of all, his company was agreeable. She spent the whole morning talking to me about him, with that

sensibility which you know is characteristic of her. She could not say enough to his credit. I thought I owed her the consideration of listening without contradicting, the more so in that on several counts it must be allowed that she is right. I felt too that I was guilty of being the cause of their separation and that I could not expect to compensate for the pleasure of which I had deprived her. You know that I do not naturally possess a great fund of spirits; the kind of life we shall be leading here is not calculated to increase it.

If it were not that your advice has always ruled me in my conduct, I might wonder now whether I have acted a little thoughtlessly. I was really disturbed by my dear friend's disappointment, touched indeed to the point where I could willingly have mingled my tears with hers.

We live now in hopes that you will accept Madame de Rosemonde's invitation, which Monsieur de Valmont brings you, to spend some time here with her. I need not tell you, I suppose, what a pleasure it will be for me to see you; and, after all, you owe us some reparation. I shall be delighted to have an earlier opportunity than I expected of making Mademoiselle de Volanges's acquaintance, and to be in a position to persuade you more with each day of the sincere respect, etc.

———

29 August 17–

LETTER 46: *The Chevalier Danceny to Cécile Volanges*

What can have happened, my darling Cécile? What can have prompted you to change so suddenly and so cruelly? What has become of your promises never to change? Promises you repeated only yesterday, and with so much pleasure! Who has made you forget them today? I have searched my conscience, and the blame is not mine; it would be too dreadful to have to look for it in you. Oh, I am certain you are not frivolous or deceitful: in the very midst of despair my heart shall be free of insulting suspicions. But by what mischance are you altered? No, cruel girl, you are no longer the same. The sweet Cécile, the Cécile that I adore, the Cécile who made me those promises would never have avoided my eyes, would never have thwarted the happy chance that placed me by her side; or if some circumstance I cannot guess at had obliged her to treat me with such severity, she would at least have not thought it beneath her to tell me of it.

Ah, my Cécile, you don't know, you will never know how much you have made me suffer today, how I suffer still at this moment. Do you imagine that I can live without your love? Yet, when I begged a word from you, one single word to banish my doubts, you made no reply, but pretended instead to be afraid we might be overheard – a danger that did not then exist, but which you immediately created by your choice of a place among the company. And when, having to leave you, I asked at what time I could see you tomorrow, you pretended to be uncertain, and it was Madame de Volanges who was obliged to tell me. So that tomorrow the moment which returns me to your side, the moment I have always looked forward to so much, will bring me nothing but anxiety, and the pleasure of seeing you give way to a fear of being troublesome.

I feel it already: it stops my pen. I dare no longer speak to you of my love. Those words that I never tired of repeating when I could in turn hear them repeated to me, "I love you," that sweet phrase which made up all my happiness, has, if you have changed, no longer any more to offer me than a prospect of perpetual despair. Yet I cannot believe that such a talisman of love has lost all its power, and I venture to try again what it can do.* Yes, my Cécile; I love you. Those words are my happiness; say them with me again. Remember that you have accustomed me to hearing them, and that in depriving me you condemn me to a torture that, like my love, will only cease with my life.

———

29 August 17–

LETTER 47: *The Vicomte de Valmont to the Marquise de Merteuil*
I shall not be seeing you today, my love, and here are my reasons, which I beg you will indulgently accept.

Yesterday, instead of returning here directly, I stopped at the Comtesse de ———'s, which was not far out of my way, and stayed there for dinner. I did not arrive in Paris until nearly seven o'clock, when I made my way to the opera, where I hoped you might be.

After the performance, I went to revisit my acquaintance of the green room. There I found my old friend Émilie surrounded by a host of admirers of both sexes for whom she was that very evening to provide supper at P———. I had no sooner joined the company when the invitation was, by general acclaim, extended to me, and in particular by a corpulent little man, who jabbered it out in Dutchman's French. He I perceived to be the real hero of the occasion. I accepted.

———

*Those who have never on occasion been brought to realize the value of a word or a phrase that has been hallowed by love will find no meaning in these words.

On the way I learned that the house we were bound for represented the price fixed upon for Émilie's favors to this grotesque creature, and that the evening's supper was in fact to be a sort of wedding feast. The little man could not contain his delight at the prospect of the happiness he was soon to enjoy. He looked so pleased with himself that I was tempted to disturb his complacency – which, as it happens, is what I did.

My only difficulty lay in prevailing upon Émilie: the burgomaster's riches had made her a little scrupulous. After some hesitation, however, she gave her approval to my plan for glutting the little beer barrel with wine, so putting him *hors de combat* for the rest of the night.

The high opinion we had formed of Dutch drinkers led us to employ every known method in our attempts, which succeeded so well that at dessert he no longer had strength enough to hold up his glass. Nevertheless, the obliging Émilie and I continued to vie with each other in filling it up. He collapsed at length under the table in a drunken stupor such as cannot but last for a week. We decided then to send him back to Paris, and as he had not kept his carriage, I had him packed into mine and remained behind in his place. Whereupon I received the compliments of the company, who retired soon after leaving me in possession of the field. So much amusement, and perhaps my long retirement, has made me find Émilie so desirable that I have promised to stay with her until the Dutchman returns to life.

This kindness I confer in exchange for one she has just done me. I have been using her for a desk upon which to write to my Fair Devotee – to whom I find it amusing that I should send a letter written in bed, in the arms almost, of a trollop (it was broken off, too, while I committed a downright infidelity) – in which I give her an exact account of my situation and my conduct. Émilie, who read it, split her sides laughing; I hope you will laugh too.

As my letter must be franked in Paris, I am sending it to you; I leave it open. Be so good as to read it, to seal it, and to have it taken to the post. Please do not on any account use your own seal or one bearing any amorous device whatever; a head, no more. Good-bye, my love.

P.S. I have reopened this. I have persuaded Émilie to go to the Italiens,[7] and I shall take this opportunity of coming to see you. I shall be at your house by six at the latest, and, if you are agreeable, we shall call together on Madame de Volanges at seven. I can no longer decently defer the invitation I have to make her on behalf of Madame de Rosemonde; besides, I shall be very glad to see the little Volanges.

Good-bye, my fairest of the fair. I intend to greet you with such rapture that the Chevalier will be jealous.

P——

30 August 17–

LETTER 48: *The Vicomte de Valmont to Madame de Tourvel*

I come, Madame, after a stormy night during which I never closed an eye, after suffering without cease now the turmoil of a consuming passion, now the utter exhaustion of every faculty of my being – I come to you to seek the peace I need, but which as yet I cannot hope to enjoy. Indeed my situation, as I write, makes me more than ever aware of the irresistible power of love. I have scarcely enough command of myself to put my ideas into order. I foresee already that I shall not be able to finish this letter without breaking off. Surely then I can hope that one day you may share the agitation I feel at this moment? I venture to think meanwhile that were you to understand it better you would not be entirely insensible to it. Believe me, Madame: a cold composure – that torpor of the soul, that semblance of death – can never make for happiness, to which only the active passions can lead. In spite of the torments you make me suffer, I think I can assure you without any hesitation that I am at this moment happier than you. You try to no purpose to crush me with your devastating severities. They will never prevent me from giving myself wholly to love and, in the delirium it affords, forgetting the despair into which you have cast me. And that is how I shall take my revenge for the exile to which you have condemned me. Never have I taken more pleasure in writing to you; never have I felt in doing it so sweet and yet so lively an emotion. Everything seems to enhance my rapture: the air I breathe is all ecstasy, the very table on which I write, never before put to such use, has become in my eyes an altar consecrated to love. How much dearer will it be to me now that I have traced upon it a vow to love you forever! Forgive, I beg you, these unruly feelings. I should perhaps not yield so far to transports that you cannot share. But I must leave you for a moment to calm an excitement that mounts with every moment and is fast becoming more than I can control.

I return to you, Madame, and certainly with as much eagerness as ever before. But my feelings of happiness have flown, leaving in their place a sense of cruel privation. To what purpose do I speak to you of my feelings when I cannot find the means to persuade you of their sincerity? After so many repeated efforts, confidence and strength alike have deserted me. If I seek to recall the pleasures of love it is only to feel their loss more deeply. I see no help but in your indulgence, and I am too sensible at this moment of how much indulgence will be necessary to hope that I may secure it. My love, nonetheless, has never been more respectful, never less capable of giving offense; it is a love, I venture to say, that the strictest virtue would have no reason to fear. But I am afraid of occupying you too long with my sufferings. Since I am sure that she who causes them does not share them, I must at least forbear from abusing her kindness. I should surely be doing so were this doleful history to take up more of your time – of which I shall ask only as much as is necessary to beg you to reply, and to beseech you never to doubt the truth of my feelings.

Written at P——, dated Paris
30 August 17–

LETTER 49: *Cécile Volanges to the Chevalier Danceny*
While I am neither frivolous nor deceitful, Monsieur, it is enough that I should be shown my conduct in its true light in order to feel I must change it. I have promised God this sacrifice until such time as I can offer Him in addition the feelings I have for you, which I find all the more sinful on account of the religious order to which you belong. I am quite aware that this will cause me pain, and I shall not even conceal from you that for two days I have cried every time I have thought of you. But I hope God will be good enough to give me the strength to forget you, since I pray for it night and day. I expect, too, of your friendship and your honor that you will make no attempt to weaken the good resolutions I have been led to make, and which I am trying to keep. Consequently, I ask you to be so kind as to write no more – particularly since I should not, I warn you, make any reply, and since you would compel me to inform Mamma of everything that has happened – and that would deprive me forever of the pleasure of seeing you.

I preserve for you, nonetheless, the deepest attachment it is possible to feel without doing wrong, and it is with all my heart that I wish you every kind of happiness. I know that very soon you will no longer love me so much, and very soon, perhaps, will love someone else more. But that will be one more penance for my error in giving you a heart that I owe only to God, and to my husband when I have one. I hope that the Divine Mercy will pity my weakness and inflict no more suffering upon me than I am able to endure.

Good-bye, Monsieur. I can give you my complete assurance that were

I permitted to love anyone, it would never be anyone but you. But that is all I can say, and it is perhaps more than I ought to say.

―――――

31 August 17–

LETTER 50: *Madame de Tourvel to the Vicomte de Valmont*
Is it thus, Monsieur, that you fulfill the conditions upon which I agreed to receive your letters from time to time? How can I find no fault with them when they speak only of sentiments I should still be reluctant to acknowledge even if I could do so without violence to my whole sense of duty?

For the rest, were I in need of new arguments to support such a salutary reluctance, I think I should be able to find them in your last letter. After all, what do you do in the very moment of your setting forth, as you think, an apology for love but show me the effect of its terrible ravages? Who would wish for a happiness bought at the expense of reason, its pleasures short-lived, succeeded at best by regrets when they are not by remorse?

You yourself, in whom the ill effects of this dangerous derangement must have been weakened, were you not compelled to admit that it had become more than you could control? And were you not the first to complain of the disturbance it caused you? What frightful destruction, then, would it wreak upon an innocent and sensitive soul, so much the more at its mercy for the greatness of the sacrifices it would be required to make?

You think, Monsieur, or you pretend to think, that love makes for happiness. As for me, I am so convinced that it would make me miserable that I could wish never again to hear it spoken of. It seems to me that the mere mention of it is unsettling, and it is as much my inclination as my duty to beg you henceforth to be silent upon the subject.

After all, you should find it easy to grant me this request. Now that you have returned to Paris, you will find opportunity enough to forget a feeling that perhaps was merely the outcome of your habitual preoccupation with such things, and owed its strength only to your lack of other interests in the country. Are you not now in the same place where once you were able to look upon me with indifference? Can you now take a step without coming face to face with evidence of your inconstancy? Are you not surrounded by women worthy of your attentions? I have none of that vanity which is the reproach of my sex, still less of that false modesty which is only a refinement of pride, and it is in all honesty that I tell you here that I am very little versed in the arts of pleasing. Were I mistress of them all I should not think them sufficient to prevail upon you for very long. Asking you to forget me is therefore no more than asking you to do what you have done before, and what you would unquestionably do again in a little while even were I to beg you not to do so.

I have never lost sight of this truth which in itself would be a strong enough motive for my not wishing to listen to you. I have a thousand others; but to avoid entering upon a tedious discussion I confine myself to begging, as I have already done, that you will no longer treat me to sentiments I have no business to hear, still less to reply to.

1 September 17–

Part Two

LETTER 51: *The Marquise de Merteuil to the Vicomte de Valmont*
Truly, Vicomte, you are intolerable. You treat me as casually as though I were your mistress. I shall be angry, you know; as it is, I am in no very good humor. Really! You are to see Danceny tomorrow morning. You know how important it is that I should see you before that interview; and without further ado you allow me to wait a whole day for you while you run off heaven only knows where. You are responsible for my arriving *indecently* late at Madame de Volanges, and for all the old ladies finding me *extraordinary*. I was obliged to spend the entire evening flattering them to appease them. Old ladies must never be crossed: in their hands lie the reputations of young ones.

It is now one o'clock in the morning. Instead of going to bed, which I yearn to do, I have to write you a long letter that for very boredom is going to make me twice as sleepy as I am now. Consider yourself lucky that I haven't the time for further strictures upon you. Don't, however, conclude thereby that I forgive you: it is simply that I am in a hurry. Listen then; I shall be quick.

If you are at all clever, Danceny will confide in you tomorrow. The time is ripe for disclosures – he is unhappy. The girl has been to confession; she has given everything away, like a child, and has since been tortured to such a degree by fear of the devil that she has decided to break with him completely. It was quite clear from the earnestness with which she spoke to me of all her little scruples, that she has quite lost her head. She showed me the letter in which she dismisses him, a real sermon. She babbled to me for an hour without uttering a single word of common sense. My position was nonetheless difficult; as you may imagine, I could not risk being frank in the face of such befuddlement.

Through all this chatter, however, I noticed that, in spite of everything, she is in love with her Danceny. I noticed, too, that the little creature is amusingly enough a victim to one of those tricks that love never fails to play. Tortured by the desire to think of her lover and afraid she will be damned for doing so, she has hit upon the idea of praying to God to banish him from her thoughts. As she repeats the prayer every instant of the day, this serves her for a means of thinking about him constantly.

For someone more experienced than Danceny this little contretemps would perhaps be more favorable than otherwise. But that young man is such a Céladon[8] that, if we don't help him, he will need so much time to surmount the smallest obstacles that he will leave us none to accomplish our own ends.

You are quite right. It is a pity – and I am as sorry as you are – that he should be the hero of this escapade. But what do you expect? What is done is done, and it is all your fault. I asked to see his reply; it was pitiable.* He offers her interminable arguments to prove that an involuntary feeling cannot be a crime – as if such a feeling did not cease to be involuntary the moment one ceases to resist it! The idea is so simple that it had occurred even to the girl. His complaints of unhappiness are moving enough; but his grief is so tender and seems to be so strong and so sincere that it seems to me impossible that any woman, given the opportunity of driving a man to this pitch of despair at so little peril to herself, would be tempted to forgo the pleasure. He explains finally that he is not a monk as the girl thinks – and here, without doubt, he speaks to most effect. Were one to go so far as to yield to monastic embraces, it is most assuredly not to the Knights of Malta that one would give preference.

Be that as it may, instead of wasting my time in argument that might have compromised me – perhaps, too, without convincing her – I gave my approval to her decision to break with him. I insisted, however, that in circumstances such as these, it was more proper to justify oneself in speech than in writing, and that it was also customary to give back whatever letters and other trifles one might have received. This seemed to accord with the little creature's views, and I persuaded her to give Danceny a rendezvous. Then and there we devised a plan, my part in

*This letter has not been discovered.

which is to persuade her mother to go out without her; tomorrow afternoon is appointed for the fateful occasion. Danceny knows already; but for God's sake, if you can find an opportunity, rouse that lovesick swain from his languor and tell him — since he must always be told about everything — that the only way to conquer scruples of another is to leave him with nothing to lose.

For the rest, so as to avoid any repetition of this ridiculous episode, I have taken care to raise a few doubts in the girl's mind as to the discretion shown by confessors. She is now, I can assure you, paid back for frightening me by the dread she herself is in that her confessor will go and tell her mother everything. I hope that when I have had another word or two to say to her upon the subject, she will no longer feel impelled to give account of her stupidities to the first comer.*

Good-bye, Vicomte; take hold of Danceny and push. How shameful if we should fail to do as we liked with two children! If they should prove to be more difficult than we thought at first, let us, to rouse our determination, consider: you, that we are dealing with Madame de Volanges's daughter, I, that she is destined to be Gercourt's wife. Good-bye.

2 September 17–

LETTER 52: *The Vicomte de Valmont to Madame de Tourvel*

You forbid me, Madame, to speak to you of my love; but how shall I find the courage to obey? Wholly absorbed in a feeling that would have been tender had you not made it cruel; sentenced by you to languish in exile; living only on privation and regret; a prey to tortures that are so much the more grievous for reminding me of your indifference; must I then lose the one consolation remaining to me? What other can I have but that of opening my heart to you from time to time, a heart that you have filled with bitterness and unrest? Will you turn your eyes away from the tears you have caused to flow? Will you not acknowledge the homage of sacrifices you have yourself exacted? Would it not be more worthy of you, of your tender and honorable heart, to pity an unfortunate man, who is so only because of you, than to inflict further sufferings upon him by a prohibition as harsh as it is unjust?

---

*The behavior of Madame de Merteuil must long ago have led the reader to guess that she held religion in small respect. This whole paragraph should perhaps have been omitted; on the other hand, it was thought that, where effects are represented, their causes ought not to be ignored.

You pretend to be afraid of love and do not wish to see that it is you alone who are the cause of the evils for which you hold love to blame. Ah, certainly it is a painful feeling when it is not shared by the one who inspires it. But let it be reciprocated; where else can happiness be looked for? Tender affection, mutual confidence – and a confidence without reserve – griefs assuaged and pleasures multiplied, sweet hopes, delicious memories, where else but in love can these be found? You slander its name, you who have only to cease from resisting it in order to taste all the joys it has to offer you. As for me, I forget all my sufferings to speak in its defense.

You oblige me to speak in my own defense too; for while I devote my life to worshiping you, you spend yours in finding fault with me. You already imagine me to be fickle and deceitful and, holding against me those few indiscretions I myself confessed to being guilty of, you are pleased to confound what I was then with what I am now. Not content with having committed me to the torment of living so far away from you, you add to it with your cruel mockery of pleasures to which you know well enough you have made me insensible. You trust neither my promises nor my vows. Well, I have one guarantee left to offer you, one at least that you cannot suspect: yourself. I ask you only to examine yourself honestly; if you do not believe in my love, if you doubt for a single moment that you are sole empress of my heart, if you are not sure that you can depend entirely on my feelings – till now, after all, only too changeable – then I shall take the consequences of your error. I shall cry out in pain, but I shall make no appeal. If, on the contrary, you are forced to do justice for both of us by admitting to yourself that you neither have nor ever will have a rival, don't oblige me, I beg you, to continue tilting at windmills. Leave me at least the consolation of knowing you do not doubt a feeling that, after all, will only cease and can only cease with my life. Permit me, Madame, to ask you for a positive reply to this part of my letter.

If, meanwhile, I speak no more of that period of my life which, it seems, does me such cruel injury in your eyes, it is not because I lack arguments to summon to my defense, if need be.

What after all was I guilty of but a failure to struggle against the whirlpool into which I had been cast? I came into society young and inexperienced; I was passed, so to speak, from hand to hand by a series of women, all of whom, in their readiness to succumb, seemed in a hurry to anticipate what they felt would inevitably be an unfavorable opinion of themselves. Was it for me to set an example of resistance, when no resistance was offered me? Should I have punished myself for momentary aberrations to which very often I had been encouraged, by promising a fidelity that would certainly have been unnecessary, and could only have been regarded as ridiculous? Pah! What else but breaking it off immediately can excuse a shameful connection?

Yet I think I may say that this disorder of the senses – perhaps, too, it was inflamed vanity – never touched my heart. My heart was made for love; intrigue might serve for distraction, but it was never my whole concern. I was surrounded by seductive but contemptible creatures; none of them could reach my soul. I was offered pleasure; I sought virtue. At length, because I happened to be fastidious and sensitive, I began to think myself inconstant.

When I met you my eyes were opened: I soon realized that love depends for its charm on qualities of the soul – only they can provoke it to an excess that only they can excuse. And finally I found that it was as impossible for me to keep from loving you as it would be to love anyone but you.

You see, Madame, to what sort of heart you are afraid to yield, the heart whose fate it is for you to determine. Whatever the destiny you hold in store for it, you will never alter the feelings by which it is bound to you. They are as unchanging as the virtues that gave them being.

---

3 September 17–

LETTER 53: *The Vicomte de Valmont to the Marquise de Merteuil*
I have seen Danceny, but have had nothing but half-confidences from him. He was especially persistent in refusing to reveal the little Volanges's name. He spoke of her merely as a good and even rather devout young woman. Apart from this, his account of the whole episode was truthful enough, particularly as it concerned the final incident. I stirred him up as much as I could, and teased him a great deal about his delicate scruples; but it seems he is proud of them, so that I cannot take any responsibility for him. For the rest, I shall have more to tell you the day after tomorrow. Tomorrow I take him to Versailles, and on our way there shall make it my business to examine him further.

I have hopes, too, that the rendezvous which was to have taken place today may have passed off to our satisfaction. Nothing perhaps remains for us to do but extract a confession and collect the evidence. This you will find easier to do than I. The girl is more confiding, or more talkative – which comes to the same thing – than her discreet admirer. Nevertheless, I too shall do my best.

Good-bye, my love. I am in a great hurry. I shall not see you this evening, nor tomorrow. If you, on your part, have discovered anything new, write me a line against my return. I shall certainly be back in Paris for the night.

———

3 September 17–, evening

———

LETTER 54: *The Marquise de Merteuil to the Vicomte de Valmont*

Oh yes, of course! There is so much to be discovered from Danceny! If he has told you so himself, he was boasting. I have never known anyone so incompetent in love, and I regret more and more the kindness we have shown him. Do you know, I thought I might have been compromised on his account? And to think it would have been to absolutely no purpose! Oh, I promise you, I shall have my revenge.

When I arrived yesterday to fetch Madame de Volanges, she no longer wanted to go out; she felt unwell and it required all my eloquence to persuade her. I could picture Danceny arriving before we had left; the situation would have been all the more awkward for Madame de Volanges having told him the previous evening that she would not be at home. Her daughter and I were on tenterhooks. At length we left, and the little creature, as she said good-bye, clasped my hand with so much warmth that, in spite of her believing in all honesty that she was still resolved on parting with her lover, I could have predicted an evening of prodigies.

This was not the last of my anxieties. Scarcely half an hour after we had arrived at Madame de ————'s, Madame de Volanges was indeed taken ill, seriously ill; quite understandably she wanted to return home. For my part, I was the less willing to do so for fear that, should we surprise the young couple, as there was every reason to suppose we would, my representations to the mother in persuading her to leave the house would fall under suspicion. I took the course of playing upon her fears for her health, which fortunately it is never difficult to do; and for an hour and a half refused to take her home, pretending that I was reluctant to subject her to the dangerous jolting of the carriage. We did not, in the end, arrive back before the appointed time. The embarrassed expression that greeted our return gave me hopes, I must say, that my efforts had not been in vain.

My wish to be informed of everything that had passed kept me with Madame de Volanges, who immediately took to her bed. We left her very early, after supper at her bedside, excusing ourselves on the grounds that she needed rest, and made our way to her daughter's room. The latter has done everything I expected her to do: scruples have vanished, new vows of eternal love have been sworn, etc., etc.; she has, in short, obliged us with a very good grace. But that fool Danceny is not one step further along. Oh, I could say a word or two to that young man! Reconciliations take us nowhere.

The girl, however, assures me that he asked for more, but that she was able to defend herself. I would stake anything that she is either boasting or making excuses for him – I am virtually certain of it, in fact. At all events, an impulse took me to find out how far I could believe in her capacity to defend herself, and I, a mere woman, was able step by step to rouse her to such a pitch that... In short, you may believe me when I say that never has anyone been more susceptible to an assault upon the senses. She is really charming, the dear little thing! She deserves a better lover. She will at least have a good friend, for I am sincerely attached to her. I have promised to undertake her education, and I believe I shall keep my word. I have often felt I needed to take a woman into my confidence, and I should prefer this one to another. But I can do nothing about it as long as she is not... what she must become. Yet another reason for bearing Danceny a grudge.

Good-bye, Vicomte. Don't come to see me tomorrow, unless you come in the morning. I have yielded to my chevalier's entreaties for an evening at the *petite maison*.

———

4 September 17–

LETTER 55: *Cécile Volanges to Sophie Carnay*

You were right, my dear Sophie; you are better at making prophecies than giving advice. Danceny, as you predicted, has triumphed over my confessor, over you, and over myself – and here we are, exactly where we were before. Oh, I don't regret it; and if you scold, it will be because you don't know what pleasure there is in loving someone like Danceny. It is easy enough for you to declare what must be done; but there is nothing to stop you doing it. But if you had felt how much pain there is in the grief of someone we love, how their happiness becomes our own, and how difficult it is to say no when we want only to say yes, you would no longer be surprised at anything. I, who have felt all this, and felt it very deeply, still cannot understand why. Do you think, for example, that I can see Danceny cry without crying myself? I assure you I find it impossible; and when he is happy, I am happy too. It is no use your saying anything; what people say cannot change the way things are, and I am quite sure that this is how they must be.

I should like to see you in my place...No, that is not what I meant to say, I certainly would not change places with anyone. But I wish that you, too, were in love with someone: not only because you would understand me better and scold me less, but also because you would be happier, or rather because only then would you begin to know what it is to be happy.

Our games, our amusements, all that, you know, was only child's play; nothing is left of it when it is over. But love, oh, love!...a word, a look, just knowing that he is there – now that is happiness. When I see Danceny, I want nothing more; when I don't see him, he is all I want. I don't know how to explain it, but I might say that whatever pleases me is a part of him. When he is not with me, I think of him, and when I can think of him without being distracted in any way, for instance when I am alone, I am happier still; I close my eyes, and all at once I seem to see him; I remember what he has said and seem to hear him saying it; that makes me sigh, and then I feel a sort of fire, an agitation...I cannot keep still. It is a sort of torture, a torture that gives inexpressible pleasure.

I think, too, that once one is in love something of that feeling enters into friendship as well. My friendship for you, of course, has not changed – it is still just as it used to be at the convent; what I mean is my feeling for Madame de Merteuil. It seems to me that I love her more as I love Danceny than as I love you, and sometimes I wish she were he. This is perhaps because our friendship is not a childhood one as is yours and mine, or else because I often see both of them together, which confuses my feelings. At all events, it cannot be denied that, between them, they make me very happy. And, after all, I don't think there is anything very wrong in what I am doing. I ask no more than to stay as I am; it is only the idea of my marriage that gives me any anxiety. For if Monsieur de Gercourt is at all like what he is said to be, and I don't doubt he is, I know not what is to become of me. Good-bye, my dear Sophie. I still love you most dearly.

———

4 September 17–

LETTER 56: *Madame de Tourvel to the Vicomte de Valmont*
What would be the use to you, Monsieur, of the reply you ask for? If I believed in your feelings would I not have even more reason to be afraid

of them? Moreover, quite apart from attacking or defending their sincerity, is it not enough for me, should it not be enough for you, to know that I neither wish nor have any right to return them?

Let us suppose that you do really love me (and it is only so as to avoid returning in future to this subject that I allow such a supposition): would the obstacles that lie between us be any the less insurmountable? And could I even then do anything else than wish that you might soon overcome your love – above all, by hastening to deprive you of all hope, do everything in my power to help you overcome it? You yourself admit that love is "a painful feeling when it is not shared by the one who inspires it." Now, you know quite well that it is impossible for me to share it; even were such a misfortune to befall me, I should suffer for it while you yourself would be none the happier. I hope you respect me enough not to doubt this for an instant. No more then, I beg you; give up your attempts to disturb a heart that is much in need of peace. Do not oblige me to regret having known you.

Cherished and esteemed by a husband whom I love and respect, my duties and my pleasures find in him their common source. I am happy; I have a right to be so. If livelier pleasures exist, I have no desire for them: I do not wish to know them. Can any pleasure be sweeter than that of living at peace with oneself, passing one's days in serenity, sleeping untroubled, waking without remorse? What you call happiness is nothing but a tumult in the mind, a tempest of passion, frightful to behold even for the spectator on the shore. Come, how could I face such storms? How dare to embark upon a sea strewn with so many thousand wrecks? And with whom? No, Monsieur, I shall hold my ground: I cherish the ties that keep me there. I would not break them even if I could; and if I had none, I should hasten to make them.

Why do you dog my footsteps? Why do you so obstinately pursue me? Your letters, which were to have come seldom, arrive in rapid succession. They were to have been discreet and they speak of nothing but your insane love. I am more beset by the thought of you than I ever was by your person. Repelled under one guise, you reappear in another. Things you are asked not to say you say again, but in a different way. You are ready to entangle me in specious arguments, but refuse to answer mine. I do not wish to reply to any more of your letters. I shall not reply to them... How you treat the women you have seduced! With what contempt you speak of them! I can believe that some of them deserve it, but were they all so despicable? Ah, of course – since they betrayed their duty in surrendering to unlawful love. At that moment they lost everything, even the respect of the man for whom they made their sacrifice. The punishment is just, but the mere thought of it makes one shudder. What is it to me, after all? Why should I care about them or about you? What right have you to disturb my peace of mind? Leave me alone, see me no more, write to me no more, I beg of you; I insist. This letter is the last you shall receive from me.

———

5 September 17–

LETTER 57: *The Vicomte de Valmont to the Marquise de Merteuil*
I found your letter awaiting my return yesterday. Your annoyance quite delighted me. You could not be more sensitive to the wrong Danceny has done had he done it to you personally. No doubt it is in revenge that you are getting his mistress into the way of committing small infidelities to him. What a very wicked creature you are! Yes, you are charming, and I am not surprised that you have better success with her than does Danceny.

I can now at last read that fine romantic hero like a book; he has no further secrets from me. I assured him so often that honorable love was the supreme good, that one true feeling was worth ten intrigues, that I myself was at that moment in love and afraid to own up to it; and he found my way of thinking so conformable to his own, that enchanted by my frankness, he told me everything and swore himself to a friendship without reserve. But this scarcely carries our plans any further.

To begin with, it seems to me that, to his mind, a young girl deserves to be treated with far more consideration than a woman, seeing that she has so much more to lose. He thinks above all that, when the girl is infinitely richer than the man, as is the case with him, a man can have no excuse for putting a girl to the necessity of either marrying him or living dishonored. The mother's confidence, the girl's honesty, everything frightens and inhibits him. The difficulty lies not in defeating his arguments, however true they are. With a little skill and the help of his own passion they can soon be destroyed – all the more easily in that they lend themselves to ridicule, and that against them can be pitted the authority of custom. What lies in the way of our securing any hold upon him is that he feels happy as he is. After all, if our first loves appear on the whole to be innocent and, as they say, more pure; if at any rate they make much slower progress, it is not, as is generally thought, because of delicacy or modesty, but because the heart, surprised by a new feeling, pauses, so to speak, at every step in order to enjoy the delight it feels, and because this delight in an untutored heart is so intense as to preoccupy it to the exclusion of all other pleasures. This is so true that even when a libertine falls in love – if a libertine ever does – he becomes from that moment less anxious to enjoy his mistress. In the end there is, between Danceny's behavior toward the little Volanges and mine toward my prudish Madame de Tourvel, only a difference of degree.

More obstacles than he has encountered so far will be necessary to stir our young man's blood; more mystery especially, for it is mystery that inspires daring. I am very near believing that you have in fact done us a disservice in serving him so well. Had we been concerned with an *experienced* man who felt nothing but desire, your line of proceeding would have been excellent; but you might have guessed that for a man who is young, upright, and in love, his mistress's favors would be of no more importance than that they furnish proof of her love – so that the more certain he were of being loved, the less enterprising he would be. What is to be done now? I don't know; but I have little hope that the girl will succumb before her marriage. We shall have nothing for our pains. I am sorry, but I can see no help for it.

While I hold forth here, you find better occupation with your chevalier. Which reminds me that you are promised to an infidelity in my favor. I have, as you might say, your promissory note, and I mean to see that it is honored. I admit that payment is not yet due, but it would be generous of you not to wait, and for my part I shall be keeping an account of the interest. What say you, my love? Are you not weary of your constancy? Is your chevalier so extraordinary a man? Oh, give me but the opportunity and I shall compel you to admit that if you have found any merit in him it is because you have forgotten me.

Good-bye, my love. I embrace you as ardently as I desire you. I defy the Chevalier's kisses to burn like these.

———

5 September 17–

LETTER 58: *The Vicomte de Valmont to Madame de Tourvel*
Pray, Madame, how have I deserved to be the object both of your reproaches and of your anger? An attachment of the deepest yet most respectful kind, a most perfect submission to the least of your wishes: there in two phrases is the history of my conduct and my feelings. Crushed by the misery of unhappy love, no other consolation was open to me but that of seeing you; you commanded me to forgo it, and I obeyed without a murmur. In return for this sacrifice you permitted me to write to you. Now you would deprive me of that one remaining

pleasure. Shall I allow it to be snatched from me without attempting to resist? No, indeed not. Come, how could it fail to be precious to me? I have no other left, and I owe it to you.

My letters, you say, are too frequent! Consider, then, if you please: my exile has lasted ten days, and not a single moment of that time have you been out of my thoughts – yet you have received only two letters from me. "They speak of nothing but my love!" Naturally! What can I say if not what I think? The utmost I can do is to give no more than partial expression to my thoughts, and, believe me, I have allowed you to know only what I was unable to conceal. You threaten me finally with a refusal to reply to my letters. So, not content with your harsh treatment of a man who prefers you above anything and who respects you even more than he loves you, to that you would add contempt. And why this menacing, this wrath? What is the need for it? Are you not sure you will be obeyed even when your commands are unjust? Can I possibly, do you think, cross you in a single one of your desires? Have I not already proved that I cannot? Will you then abuse the power you have over me? Having made me unhappy, having perpetrated an injustice, will you now find it easy to enjoy the peace you declare is so necessary to you? Will you never say to yourself, "He put his fate in my hands, and I condemned him to misery; he implored my help, and I looked upon him without pity?" Can you conceive to what extremities I may be reduced in my despair? No.

To estimate my sufferings you would have to know how much I loved you, and you are ignorant of my heart.

To what are you sacrificing me? Chimerical fears. And who arouses them? A man who adores you; a man who will never cease to be absolutely in your power. What have you to fear, what can you have to fear from a feeling of which you will always be mistress, which is yours to command at your pleasure? But your imagination creates monsters, and the terror they inspire you attribute to love. A little confidence and these phantoms will disappear.

A wise man once said that investigating the cause of our fears nearly always serves to get rid of them.* It is to love especially that this truth applies. Love, and your fears will vanish. In place of the things that terrify you, you will discover delicious feelings, a tender and submissive lover; and all your days, given over to happiness, will leave you with no other regret than that you wasted so many of them in indifference. I

---

*Probably Rousseau in *Émile*, but the quotation is inaccurate, and Valmont's application of it here quite wrong. Besides, would Madame de Tourvel have read *Émile*?

myself, now that I have been retrieved from errors and live only for love, regret that time of my life which I believed I was devoting to pleasure; and I feel that it is now you alone who can make me happy. But, I beg of you, let not my pleasure in writing to you be any longer marred by the fear of giving you offense. I have no wish to disobey you; but on my knees I crave the happiness you wish to take from me, the sole happiness I have left. I cry out to you; hear my prayers and witness my tears. Ah, Madame, can you refuse?

———

7 September 17–

LETTER 59: *The Vicomte de Valmont to the Marquise de Merteuil*
Tell me, if you know, what this drivel of Danceny's signifies? What has happened, and what has he lost? Perhaps the lady has taken offense at his everlasting respect? In all fairness to her, offense has been taken on far less provocation. What shall I say to him this evening when I meet him, as he asked me, and as I agreed on an impulse to do? I shall most certainly not waste my time listening to his whinings, if listening is going to do us no good. Lovers' complaints are not entertaining outside the opera. Tell me then what this is about and what I must do; or else I shall decamp, to escape the boredom I foresee. May I have a word with you this morning? If you are *busy*, write me a line at least, giving me my cues.

By the way, where were you yesterday? I never succeed in seeing you these days. Really, why go to the trouble of keeping me in Paris in September? Make up your mind, nevertheless, for I have just received the most pressing invitation from the Comtesse de B—— to visit her in the country. As she so drolly informs me, her husband owns the finest woods[9] in the world "which he is careful to preserve for the entertainment of his friends." Now, as you know, I have more than a little interest in those woods, and I shall go back to enjoy them if I am of no use to you here. Good-bye. Remember that Danceny will be with me at four o'clock.

———

8 September 17–

LETTER 60: *The Chevalier Danceny to the Vicomte de Valmont*
(enclosed with the preceding letter)
Oh, Monsieur! I am desperate; I have lost everything. I dare not confide the secret of my grief to paper, yet I feel I must pour it out to a

faithful and trustworthy friend. When may I see you to ask your consolation and advice? I was so happy the day I opened my heart to you. How different now! My whole life has changed. Even so, what I suffer on my own account is the least part of my torment. What I cannot endure is my anxiety on behalf of a much more precious person. You are more fortunate than I: you will be able to see her, and I expect of your friendship that you will not refuse me this favor. But I must speak to you first; I must tell you everything. You must pity me, help me — you are my only hope. You are a man of feeling, you understand love, and you are the only person in whom I can confide. Do not refuse me your aid.

Good-bye, Monsieur. The thought that there still remains to me a friend such as you is the only solace to my grief. Let me know, I beg you, at what time I may find you at home. If not this morning, I should like it to be early this afternoon.

———————

8 September 17–

LETTER 61: *Cécile Volanges to Sophie Carnay*

My dear Sophie, take pity on your Cécile, your poor Cécile — she is very unhappy! Mamma knows everything. I cannot conceive how she was able to suspect anything, yet she has nevertheless discovered it all. Last evening I thought her more than a little ill-humored, but did not pay it much attention. While she was at cards I even chatted gaily to Madame de Merteuil, who had taken supper with us. We spoke a great deal of Danceny. I don't think, all the same, we could have been overheard. Madame de Merteuil left, and I retired to my room.

I was undressing when Mamma came in and dismissed my maid. She asked me for the key to my writing desk. The tone in which she made this request made me tremble so violently that I was scarcely able to stand. I pretended not to be able to find the key, but in the end I had to obey. The first drawer she opened was the very one that contained the Chevalier Danceny's letters. I was in such a state that when she asked me what they were, I could think of no better reply than "nothing." But when I saw her begin to read the first one, I had just time enough to reach an armchair before I felt so unwell that I lost consciousness. As soon as I recovered, my mother, who had recalled the maid, withdrew, telling me to go to bed. She took all Danceny's letters with her. I shiver every time I think that I shall have to face her again. I have done nothing but cry all night long.

It is now daybreak, and I am writing to you in the hopes that Joséphine will come. If I can speak to her alone I shall ask her to deliver a note that I am about to write to Madame de Merteuil. If not, I shall enclose it with this, and you will perhaps be kind enough to send it as coming from you. It is only from her that I can hope to receive any comfort. At least we shall be able to talk about him, for I cannot expect to see him again. I am so very unhappy! She will perhaps be so kind as to take charge of a letter for Danceny. I dare not trust Joséphine with it, much less my maid; it may perhaps have been she, the maid, who told my mother that I had letters in my writing desk.

I'll not write at greater length to you because I must have time to write to Madame de Merteuil* and also to Danceny, so that my letter will be ready if she is willing to deliver it. After that I shall go back to bed so that my maid will see me there when she comes into the room. I shall say I am ill so as to avoid going to see Mamma. This will not be far from the truth: there is no doubt that I am more unwell than I would be even if I had a fever. My eyes are burning from having cried so much and I cannot breathe freely for a feeling of weight upon my stomach. When I think that I shall never see Danceny again I could die. Goodbye, Sophie. Tears choke me, and I can say no more.

———

7 September 17–

LETTER 62: *Madame de Volanges to the Chevalier Danceny*
Since you have abused, Monsieur, not only a mother's trust but the innocence of her child, you would not of course be astonished were you henceforth to be refused admittance to a house where the most sincere demonstrations of friendship have been repaid only by your violation of every propriety. But I had rather ask you not to come to my house again than give orders at my door, which, because the footmen would not fail to talk, would compromise us all equally. I have the right to expect you will not compel me to take recourse to such measures. I warn you, too, that if you make the slightest attempt to encourage the folly into which you have precipitated my daughter, an austere and perpetual seclusion shall be her protection against your advances. It is for

———

*The letter from Cécile Volanges to the Marquise has been omitted as containing no more than the facts presented above with fewer details. Her letter to the Chevalier Danceny has not been discovered. The reason for this will appear in Letter 63, from Madame de Merteuil to the Vicomte.

you to decide, Monsieur, whether you will bring down calamity upon her with as little compunction as you assailed her honor. As for me, my decision is made, and I have told her of it.

With this you will find a packet containing your letters to my daughter. I trust you will let me have in exchange her letters to you, and that you will join me in obliterating every trace of an incident that I should never be able to think of without indignation, my daughter without shame, and you without remorse. I have the honor to be, etc.

———

7 September 17–

LETTER 63: *The Marquise de Merteuil to the Vicomte de Valmont*
Yes, indeed; I can explain Danceny's note. The crisis that prompted him to write was my work, and, I am inclined to believe, one of my finest triumphs. I have lost no time since you last wrote. Like the Athenian architect I said to myself, "What he says, I shall do."

Is it obstacles, then, that this fine romantic hero wants? Has his felicity put him to sleep? Oh, let him rely on me! I shall give him work to do; and I shall be much mistaken if his slumbers continue to be peaceful. It was essential to teach him the value of time, and I flatter myself that he now regrets the time he has lost. You say, too, that he needed more mystery. Well, he shall have no lack of that either! There is this much of good in me: once I have been made aware of my faults, I know no rest until I have mended them. Here, then, is what I have done.

I read your letter on my return home the day before yesterday morning; I found it most illuminating. Convinced that you had correctly diagnosed the source of the trouble, the search for a remedy was my only concern. I began, however, by going to bed. My indefatigable chevalier had not allowed me a wink of sleep, and I thought I needed it – but not at all. Possessed by the idea of Danceny, the desire to arouse him from his apathy or to punish him for it, I was unable to close an eye, and it was not until I had satisfactorily made my plans that I was able to rest for an hour or two.

The same evening I went to see Madame de Volanges and, as I had planned, told her in confidence of my conviction that a dangerous intimacy had sprung up between her daughter and Danceny. The woman, who has shown so much insight in her attacks upon you, was so blind in this case that she began by saying that I was undoubtedly mistaken; that her daughter was a mere child, etc., etc. I couldn't tell her everything I knew; but I instanced certain looks, certain remarks at which I said *my sense of propriety and my friendship for her had taken alarm.* I spoke in short almost as well as one of the elect could have done; and, so as to deal a decisive blow, I went so far as to say that I believed I had seen a letter exchange hands. "That reminds me," I added, "that one day in my presence she opened a drawer in her writing desk which I saw to be full of papers, clearly put there for safekeeping. Do you know of anyone with whom she is in frequent correspondence?" Here Madame de Volanges's expression changed, and I saw a tear or two gather in her eyes. "Thank you, my dear friend," she said, clasping my hand. "I shall find out."

After this conversation, too short to have aroused suspicion, I paid my respects to the young lady. Soon afterward I left her to ask the mother to avoid compromising me with her daughter. She agreed the more willingly for my having pointed out how fortunate it would be were her daughter to trust me enough to confide in me, since I should then be in a position to give her *my good advice.* I am certain she will keep her promise, because I am convinced she will not willingly forgo her daughter's respect for her perspicacity. I am, therefore, enabled to keep on terms of friendship with the girl without that appearance of insincerity in the eyes of Madame de Volanges, which is what I wished to avoid. An added advantage is that in future I shall be able to spend as much time as I wish as secretly as I wish with the young lady; the mother will never object.

I made the most of this advantage that very evening. Our pastimes over, I ensconced the little thing in a corner and introduced the topic of Danceny, upon which she talked without stopping. I amused myself by exciting her in anticipation of the pleasure she was to have in seeing him the next day; there is no sort of inanity I did not make her utter. It was only proper to recompense her in the world of dreams for what I had taken from her in the real one. And then all this will have made her feel the blow more deeply, and I am convinced that the more she suffers, the more eager she will be to make up for it at the first opportunity. Besides, it is as well to accustom to great disasters someone one has destined to great enterprises.

After all, can she not afford to pay with a few tears for the pleasure of having her Danceny, when she so dotes on him? Well, I promise she shall have him, and even sooner than she would have without this brouhaha. It is a bad dream and the awakening will be delicious. All things considered, it seems to me that she owes me her gratitude. And, if I have been a little malicious, well, one must amuse oneself.

It is to fools we owe the minor joys of life*

I left at length very pleased with myself. I said to myself, either Danceny will be inspired by obstacles to redouble his efforts, in which event I shall help him to the limit of my capacity; or, if he is only the fool I have sometimes been tempted to think he is, succumbing to despair, he will accept defeat. Now, in this case I shall at least have had my revenge upon him as far as was possible, and shall incidentally have increased not only the mother's esteem for me but the daughter's friendship and the confidence of both. As for Gercourt, always first in my concerns, I shall think I have been very unlucky or very clumsy, with his wife under my tutelage as she is and as she will be increasingly, if I do not find a hundred ways of making of him what I intend he shall become. I retired to bed in this agreeable frame of mind: I slept well and awoke very late.

On rising I found two letters had arrived, one from the mother, and one from the daughter. I couldn't help laughing at their both employing the same phrase: "It is to you alone that I can look for consolation." It is, after all, amusing to have to provide consolation both for and against, to be the sole representative of two directly contrary interests! There I was, like God, acknowledging the conflicting claims of blind humanity, changing not a syllable of my inexorable decrees. I have since, however, exchanged this august role for that of ministering angel, and, according to the rules, have been to visit my friends in their affliction.

I began with the mother. I found her sunk in such melancholy that you may already consider yourself in some part avenged for the inconvenience she has caused you with your prudish beauty. Everything has passed off to perfection. My one anxiety was that Madame de Volanges might take advantage of this opportunity to win the confidence of her daughter. It could quite easily have been done: one has only to speak gently to the girl as a friend, to give reasonable advice an appearance and tone of indulgent tenderness. Fortunately she adopted a line of severity, and in short has conducted the affair so badly that I have only to sit back and applaud. True, she was about to ruin our plan by deciding to return her daughter to the convent, but I have parried this blow, and have committed her to reserving it in threat against Danceny's continuing his pursuit. This was necessary in order to compel them both to that circumspection which I believe is essential to success.

Thereupon I went to see the daughter. You would not believe how

---

*Gresset, *Le Méchant*, a comedy.

grief enhances her beauty! If ever she takes to coquetry I guarantee she will find a great many occasions to weep: as yet, her tears are innocent...Struck by this new charm, which I had not hitherto suspected and which I was very pleased to have discovered, my consolations at first were of the kind that caused more pain than they relieved; in this way I was able to bring her to the point of utter suffocation. She had stopped crying and for a moment I feared she would throw a fit. I suggested she go to bed, and she agreed. I served as her maid. She had not yet performed her toilette, and soon her disheveled hair had escaped over her shoulders and naked bosom. I took her in my arms, and as she gave herself to my embrace the tears began once more to flow freely. Lord! How beautiful she was! If the Magdalene was at all like this, her penitence must have been much more dangerous than her sin.

When my woebegone beauty had taken to her bed I set about consoling her in earnest. First I calmed her fears concerning the convent. I aroused hopes of her seeing Danceny in secret, and, sitting down on her bed, I began: "If he were here...," then, with embroideries upon this theme, led her on from one distraction to another until she could no longer remember the reason for her distress. We would have parted upon perfect terms had she not tried to consign a letter for Danceny to my charge. I firmly refused to accept it – for the following reasons, which I am sure you will approve.

In the first place, it would have compromised me with Danceny; and if this was the only reason I was able to give the girl, there were many others that you might have given me. Would it not have been risking the fruit of my labors to provide our young couple with so immediate and so easy a means of relieving their sufferings? Besides, I shall not be sorry if they are obliged to implicate a few domestics in this business: for, if it is to succeed, as I hope it will, it must be made public immediately after the marriage, and there could be few more reliable means of spreading the news. If by some miracle the servants don't talk, we can do so, you and I, and it will then be more convenient if we can attribute our indiscretion to them.

It is for you, then, to put the idea into Danceny's head today. Since I cannot rely on the little Volanges's maid, whom she herself seems to distrust, suggest that he try mine, my faithful Victoire. I shall see to it that the experiment succeeds. I am all the more pleased with the idea in that their taking a servant into their confidence will serve not their purpose but ours: for I have not yet finished my story.

While protesting against taking charge of the girl's letter, I was afraid that she might at any moment suggest my putting it in the post, which

I could scarcely have refused to do. Fortunately, through confusion or ignorance on her part, or perhaps because she was less concerned about the letter than about the reply, which she could not have received through the post, she did not make the suggestion. But so as to prevent any possibility of the idea occurring to her, or at least of her being able to make use of it, I took immediate precautions. Returning to the mother, I persuaded her to remove her daughter for some time, to take her into the country...And where? Does your heart leap for joy?...To your aunt's, to old Rosemonde's. She is to be given notice of it today. There! You can now make an unimpeachable return to your devotee, who will no longer have grounds for objecting to a scandalous tête-à-tête. Thanks to my pains, Madame de Volanges will herself redeem the wrong she has done you.

But be careful: don't take so lively an interest in your own affairs that you lose sight of this one. Remember that it is of concern to me. I want you to appoint yourself go-between and adviser to our youthful pair. Tell Danceny, then, about this trip and offer him your services. Let there be no difficulty in your way but that of presenting your credentials to the young lady, and remove that obstacle immediately by suggesting that my maid convey them. There can be no doubt that he will accept the suggestion, and for your pains you will have the confidence of an unfledged heart, which is always interesting. Poor little girl! How she will blush when she gives you her first letter! Truly, the role of confidant, against which there is so much prejudice nowadays, seems to me to be a very charming form of relaxation for one who is otherwise occupied, as you will be.

On you will depend the denouement of this intrigue. Choose your moment with care for the final reunion. A hundred opportunities will offer themselves in the country, and Danceny will certainly be ready to appear there at a signal from you. Nightfall, a disguise, a window... how can I possibly tell? But if in the end the girl returns as she was when she went, I shall hold you to blame. Should you think she needs encouragement from me, send me your instructions. I think I have taught her so severe a lesson on the danger of keeping letters that I may venture now to write to her myself; and I still intend to keep her for my pupil.

I think I have forgotten to tell you that suspicion in the affair of the betrayed correspondence fell at first upon her maid, and that I have deflected it upon her confessor, so killing two birds with one stone.

Good-bye, Vicomte. I have been a long time writing to you and in consequence I am late for my lunch. Vanity and friendship have been dictating my letter, and they are both chatterboxes. For the rest, you will receive it at three o'clock, and that is all that is necessary.

Complain of me now if you dare; and go back if you are tempted, to enjoy the Comte de B——'s woods. You say that he keeps them for the entertainment of his friends! Is he then *everybody's* friend? But good-bye, I am hungry!

———

9 September 17—

LETTER 64: *The Chevalier Danceny to Madame de Volanges (draft enclosed with Letter 66, from the Vicomte to the Marquise)*

Without attempting to justify my conduct, Madame, and without complaining of yours, I still cannot but deplore an incident that has caused unhappiness to three people, all of whom deserved a better fate. Since I am even more painfully conscious of being the cause of the calamity than of being its victim I have, since yesterday, tried several times to do myself the honor of replying to you, without being able to summon the necessary strength of mind. I have, however, so many things to tell you that I must absolutely make an effort to master my feelings; and if this letter has little coherence or plan, you will be well enough aware how painful my situation is to allow me some indulgence.

Permit me first of all to protest against the first sentence of your letter. I have abused, may I be so bold as to say, neither your trust nor the innocence of Mademoiselle Volanges; I have respected both in my every action. So much it was within my power to do; and when you further hold me responsible for an involuntary feeling, I am not afraid to add that the feeling your daughter has inspired in me is one that might displease you but could never give you offense. In this matter, which touches me more nearly than I can say, I wish for no other judgment than yours and no other witness than my letters.

You forbid me to appear in future at your house, and of course I shall comply with whatever commands you see fit in this connection. But will not my sudden and complete absence offer as much occasion for the gossip you are anxious to avoid as would the order to exclude me, which, for that very reason, you are reluctant to issue to the servants at your door? I shall insist the more upon this point because it is of more concern to Mademoiselle de Volanges than to me. I beg, therefore, that you weigh every consideration with care and not allow your principles to impair your prudence. Convinced that it is your daughter's interest alone that will dictate your decisions, I shall await your further orders.

Meanwhile, in the event of your permitting me, Madame, to pay my respects to you from time to time, I engage (and you may rely upon my promise) never to take advantage of these occasions for any attempt to speak to Mademoiselle de Volanges in private, or to put letters into her hands. My fear of anything that might compromise her reputation reconciles me to this sacrifice, and the pleasure of seeing her sometimes will recompense me for it.

The paragraph above is also all I have to say in reply to your remarks on the fate you have in store for Mademoiselle de Volanges, which you say will depend upon my conduct. It would be deceitful for me to promise you more. The base seducer will adapt his schemes to circumstances, calculating afresh upon each new turn of events, but I am inspired by a love that allows me only two feelings: courage and confidence.

Do you think I can consent to being forgotten by Mademoiselle de Volanges, to forgetting her myself? No, no, never! I shall be faithful to her; she has accepted that promise, which I here renew. Forgive me, Madame, I forget myself. I must continue.

I have one other matter left to discuss with you: the letters you have asked for. It distresses me greatly to add a refusal to the wrongs you already hold me guilty of; but hear my reasons, I beg you, and so that you may appreciate them be so good as to remind yourself that my only consolation for the misfortune of having forfeited your friendship is a hope of retaining your respect.

Mademoiselle de Volanges's letters, always so precious to me, have now become much more so. They are all that I have left of value; they alone can preserve for me a feeling that is the whole charm of my life. Believe me, though, I should not hesitate for an instant to sacrifice them for your sake. Regret at losing them would yield to the desire of proving my most respectful deference to you; but considerations of great moment restrain me, and I am certain that you yourself would not disapprove of them.

It is true that you know Mademoiselle de Volanges's secret; but, if you will permit me to say so, I know upon good authority that you discovered it by means of surprise and not because of her confidence in you. I have no wish to impugn a proceeding that is perhaps justified by maternal solicitude. I respect your rights, but they do not extend so far as to relieve me of my duties, and our most sacred duty is never to betray the confidence placed in us. I should fail in it were I to expose to another's eye the secrets of a heart that meant to reveal itself only to mine. If your daughter wishes to confide these secrets to you, she will do so; her letters are not to the purpose. If, on the contrary, she wishes to keep her secrets to herself, you will not, of course, expect me to disclose them to you.

As to the obscurity in which you wish to bury this affair, rest assured, Madame, that in everything that concerns Mademoiselle de Volanges I can rival even a mother's solicitude. So as to set your mind completely at rest I have taken every precaution. That precious box which until now bore the inscription "Papers to be burned" now bears the inscription "Papers belonging to Madame de Volanges." The steps I have taken will also prove that my refusal bears no relation to any fear of your finding in these letters a single sentiment to give you, personally, any grounds for complaint.

This is a very long letter, Madame. It is not yet long enough if it is to leave you in the smallest doubt that my sentiments are honorable, that I most sincerely regret having displeased you, and that it is with profound respect that I have the honor to be, etc.

----

9 September 17–

LETTER 65: *The Chevalier Danceny to Cécile Volanges (sent unsealed to the Marquise de Merteuil with Letter 66 from the Vicomte)*

Oh, my dear Cécile, what is to become of us? Where is the God who will save us from the disasters that threaten? May love give us courage at least to endure them! How shall I describe my despair at seeing my letters returned to me, at reading Madame de Volanges's note? Who can have betrayed us? Whom do you suspect? Have you, perhaps, been a little indiscreet? What are you doing at present? What has been said to you? I should like to know everything, and I know nothing. Perhaps you yourself know no more than I do?

I am sending you your mama's note, and a copy of my reply. I hope you will approve of what I say to her. I want your approval, too, of the steps I have taken since the fatal incident; they are all directed to the same end, that of hearing your news and sending you mine, and that, further, perhaps – who knows? – of seeing you again, under less constraint than ever before.

Can you imagine, Cécile, the pleasure it will be to meet again, to be able to pledge ourselves once more to everlasting love, and to feel in our hearts and see in each other's eyes that our vows will never be broken? Where are the cares that so sweet a moment could not make us forget? Well, I have hopes that the moment will come, hopes I owe to the same expedients I have asked you to approve. But what am I saying? I owe them rather to the kind offices of a most solicitous friend; and I have no more to ask of you than that you will permit him to be your friend as well.

I should not perhaps have divulged your secrets to him without your permission, but unhappiness and necessity must be my excuse. It was love that persuaded me to it, and it is love that demands your indulgence, that asks your pardon for a confidence it was necessary to make, for had I not done so we should, perhaps, have been separated forever.* The friend I refer to is known to you; he is a friend, too, of the woman who is most dear to you. I mean the Vicomte de Valmont.

My purpose in approaching him was at first to ask him whether he could induce Madame de Merteuil to convey a letter to you. He did not think this plan would meet with any success, but, in default of the mistress, he said he could answer for the maid, who is under some obligation to him. It will be she who delivers this letter to you, and you may give your reply into her hands.

Her assistance will scarcely be of much use to us if, as Monsieur de Valmont thinks, you are to leave for the country forthwith. But in that case it is he himself who is willing to help us. The lady with whom you are going to stay is a relation of his. He will make this his excuse for going there at the same time as you; and our correspondence will then pass through his hands. He even assures me that, if you are willing to do as he instructs, he can arrange a means of our meeting there without risk of compromising you in any way.

Now, my dear Cécile, if you love me, if you pity my unhappiness, if, as I hope, you share my regret that we are apart, will you refuse to put your trust in a man who offers himself as our guardian angel? Were it not for him, I should be reduced to despair at not being able so much as to alleviate the sufferings I cause you. They will come to an end, I hope; but, my sweet Cécile, promise me that you will not give in too much to them, that you will not allow them to cast you down. The mere thought of your pain is insupportable torment to me. I would give my life to make you happy! You know that. Let the certain knowledge that I adore you bring comfort to your heart. As for mine, it needs only your assurance that you pardon love for the evils it makes you suffer.

Good-bye, my dear Cécile; good-bye, my dearest heart.

———

9 September 17–

———

*Monsieur Danceny's admissions are not altogether honest. He had already confided in Monsieur de Valmont before the "fatal incident" (see Letter 57).

LETTER 66: *The Vicomte de Valmont to the Marquise de Merteuil*
You will see, my love, from the two letters enclosed with this, that I have entirely fulfilled your commands. Although both letters carry today's date they were written yesterday, at my house and under my very eyes: the letter to the girl says all we require. One can only bow down before the depth of your insight, if that is to be measured by the success of your undertakings. Danceny is ready for anything; and I am sure that as soon as he is given an opportunity you will find him beyond reproach. If our fair ingenue proves tractable, everything will be over a short time after her arrival in the country; I have a hundred schemes in readiness. Thanks to you, I am now out of all question *Danceny's friend*; he has only to turn *Prince*.*10

He is still very young, our Danceny! Would you believe that I was quite unable to make him promise to the mother that he would renounce his love? As if it were so very difficult to make a promise one has no intention of keeping! "I should be lying," he never stopped saying. Are not such scruples edifying, especially since he means to seduce the girl? How very like a man! Our intentions make blackguards of us all; our weakness in carrying them out we call probity.

It is your concern to prevent Madame de Volanges from taking offense at the little lapses our young man has allowed himself in his letter; keep us away from the convent; try as well to effect a withdrawal of her demand for the girl's letters. Apart from anything else, he certainly will not give them back; he is determined not to, and I think he is right. Love and reason, for once, agree. I have read the letters. I have drained boredom to the dregs. But they may be useful. Let me explain.

However prudent we may be in this affair, there is always the possibility of a scandal — which would prevent the marriage, would it not, and ruin all our Gercourt plans? Should this happen, I, who have a revenge of my own to take upon the mother, reserve the right to accomplish the daughter's dishonor. A carefully chosen selection of these letters would show that the little Volanges had made all the advances and indeed thrown herself at his head. Some of the letters could even be made to compromise the mother and at least cast a *slur* of unpardonable negligence upon her. I am quite aware that our scrupulous Danceny would rebel to begin with; but since he would be under attack himself, I think it might be carried through. It is a thousand to one that events will take this turn; but one must be prepared for everything.

---

*Reference to a passage in one of Monsieur de Voltaire's poems.

Good-bye, my love. It would be very kind of you to come to supper tomorrow at the Maréchale de ———'s; I was unable to refuse.

I need not, I imagine, advise you to keep my intended visit to the country a secret from Madame de Volanges. She would immediately decide to stay in town, whereas once she has arrived at Madame de Rosemonde's she can hardly leave again the next day. If she will only give us a week, I can answer for everything.

———

9 September 17–

LETTER 67: *Madame de Tourvel to the Vicomte de Valmont*

I did not intend to reply to you, Monsieur, and perhaps my present embarrassment is in itself a proof that in fact I ought not to be doing so. I do not wish, however, to leave you with a single cause for complaint against me; and I propose to convince you that I have done everything for you that I could.

I permitted you to write to me, you will say. That is so, but, since you remind me of this permission, do you suppose that I do not at the same time remember the conditions upon which it was given you? If I had observed them as absolutely as you have ignored them, would you have received a single reply from me? This, nevertheless, is the third reply. While you do everything in your power to oblige me to discontinue this correspondence, it is I who am put to finding some way of sustaining it. There is a way, but there is only one; and if you refuse to take it, you will, whatever you might say, prove to me the small importance you attach to the matter.

Desist, then, from speaking a language I neither can hear nor wish to hear; abjure those feelings that offend and alarm me, which perhaps you will cherish less when you consider that they themselves are the obstacle that keeps us apart. Surely they are not the only feelings you know? Is love, because it excludes friendship, to fall even lower in my estimation? Are you yourself to do so because you do not want a woman from whom you have begged demonstrations of kindness to be your friend? I cannot believe it; I should be revolted by so humiliating an idea. It would estrange me from you forever.

In offering you my friendship, Monsieur, I am giving you all that is mine, all that lies in my power to give. What more could you wish? To call forth from me the kindest of feelings, and the one that best accords with my nature, you have only to give me your promise – and the only promise I exact from you is that you will rest content with friendship.

I shall forget everything that has been said, and I shall rely upon you to justify my decision.

As you see, I speak with a frankness that proves my confidence in you. It is entirely for you to strengthen that confidence. But I warn you that the first word of love will destroy it forever, and give me back my fears. It will, I warn you particularly, mark the beginning of a perpetual silence between us.

If, as you say, you have been "retrieved from error," should you not prefer to be the object of a good woman's friendship than the subject of a guilty one's remorse? Good-bye, Monsieur; you will appreciate that, having spoken as I have, I can say nothing further until I receive your reply.

_____

9 September 17–

LETTER 68: *The Vicomte de Valmont to Madame de Tourvel*

How, Madame, shall I reply to your last letter? How dare I tell the truth, when sincerity may be my ruin with you? No matter, I must; I must have courage. I tell myself over and over that it is better I should deserve you than win you, and that even if you must forever deny me the happiness I long for ceaselessly, I must at least prove to you that I am worthy of it.

What a pity that I have been, as you say, "retrieved from error"! With what transports of joy I should once have read the very letter to which I now reply in fear and trembling! You speak with *frankness*, you avow *confidence*, lastly you offer me your *friendship*. What blessings, Madame, and how I regret I cannot turn them to profit! Why am I no longer the man I was?

If I were that man, after all, if I felt nothing for you but vulgar appetite, the transitory desire fostered by a life of intrigue and pleasure – which nevertheless goes nowadays by the name of love – I should hasten to take advantage of everything I could acquire. With little scruple in my choice of means, provided they led to success, I should encourage your frankness so as to divine your secrets, welcome your confidence with the intention of betraying it, accept your friendship in the hope of perverting it...Come now, Madame, does this picture terrify you?... Well! It would nonetheless be a faithful likeness of me, were I to tell you that I agree to being no more than your friend...

How could I agree to sharing with others a feeling that sprang from your heart? If ever I tell you that I do, have no more faith in me. From that moment I shall be trying to deceive you; I may still desire you but I shall beyond question no longer love you.

It is not that frankness, confidence, and friendship have no value in my eyes...But love! true love, such as you inspire, though it contains all those feelings, though it increases their force, cannot admit, as they do, that composure, that coldness of heart which will suffer comparisons to be made, and even preferences to be shown. No, Madame, I shall on no condition be your friend; I shall love you with the most tender, the most passionate, yet the most respectful love. You may deprive it of hope, but you shall never destroy it.

By what right do you presume to dispose of a heart whose homage you refuse to accept? What refinement of cruelty is this you practice in begrudging me even the happiness of loving you? That happiness is mine: it exists independently of you, and I know how to protect it. If it is the source of my misfortunes, it is also their solace.

No, no, and again no. Persist in your cruel rebuffs, but leave me my love. You are pleased to make me unhappy. Well, so be it! You may try to wear out my courage; but I can at least oblige you to decide my fate. And perhaps one day you will treat me more justly. Not that I hope ever to change your feelings; but while you remain unmoved, you will perhaps think differently. You will say to yourself: I judged him wrong.

It might more truly be said that you do yourself an injustice. It is as impossible to know you without loving you as it is to love you without loving you faithfully; and in spite of the modesty behind which you shelter, you should find it more natural to complain of than be surprised at the feelings you inspire. As for me, my only merit is that I have been capable of appreciating yours, and I do not wish to lose this. Far from accepting your insidious proposals, I renew at your feet my vow to love you forever.

––––––

10 September 17–

LETTER 69: *Cécile Volanges to the Chevalier Danceny*
   (note written in pencil and copied by Danceny)
You ask me what I do: I love you and I weep. My mother no longer speaks to me. She has deprived me of paper, pen, and ink. I am writing to you on a piece of paper torn from your letter. I must, of course, approve of everything you have done; I love you too much not to take every opportunity of receiving your news and sending you mine. I did

not like Monsieur de Valmont, and I did not think he was so much your friend, but I shall try to get used to him, and I shall like him for your sake. I do not know who it was that betrayed us; it can only have been my maid or my father confessor. I am very unhappy; tomorrow we leave for the country, I do not know for how long. My God! Never to see you again! I have no more space. Good-bye; try to read this. These penciled words will perhaps fade one day; never so the feelings engraved upon my heart.

———

10 September 17–

LETTER 70: *The Vicomte de Valmont to the Marquise de Merteuil*

I have an important warning to give you, my dear. As you know, I was at supper yesterday with the Maréchale de ———; you were the topic of conversation, to which I contributed not the good opinions I have of you but the good opinions I don't have of you. Everyone appeared to be of my mind, and the conversation languished as it always does when one has nothing but compliments for one's neighbor, until suddenly a voice was raised in contradiction: it was Prévan's.

"God forbid," he said, rising from his chair, "that I should cast doubt upon Madame de Merteuil's virtue, but I venture to believe she owes it rather to her levity than to her principles. It is perhaps even more difficult to pursue her than to please her; and since in running after one woman one can scarcely fail on the way to encounter several others – since, all things considered, these others are likely to be worth as much as she is, if not more, some of her admirers are diverted by new inclinations and others stop short out of fatigue: so that she is perhaps the woman in all Paris who has least often been put to the trouble of defending herself. As for me," he added (encouraged by smiles from some of the women), "I shall not believe in Madame de Merteuil's virtue until I have ridden six horses to death in paying court to her."

This bad joke was a success – as slanderous jokes always are – to judge from the laughter it provoked. Prévan returned to his place and the conversation took a different turn. But the two Comtesses de B—— ——, near whom our skeptic was seated, engaged him in a private conversation of their own, which fortunately I was so placed as to be able to hear.

A challenge to win your favors was accepted; word of honor to conceal none of the facts was given; and of all the promises that may be made in the course of this enterprise, there will certainly be none more religiously observed than this one. But now you are forewarned, and you know the proverb.

It remains for me to say that Prévan, whom you do not know, is infinitely agreeable and cleverer still. If you have sometimes heard me say otherwise, it is only because I don't like him, because it suits me to obstruct his designs, and because I am not unaware that my opinion is of some weight with two dozen or so of our most fashionable ladies. In fact I did, by this means, succeed for a long time in preventing his appearance in what we call the great world; he performed prodigies without the smallest increase of reputation. The scandal, however, of his triple affair fixed the eyes of society upon him and, having given him the confidence he lacked before, has turned him into someone to be reckoned with. He is, at any rate, the only man today whom I should care not to have cross my path; and, whatever you do in your own interest, you would be rendering me a great service if, in passing, you were to bring down a little ridicule upon him. I leave him in good hands; I hope that when I come back I shall find him a ruined man.

I promise you, in return, that I shall bring your pupil's affairs to a prosperous conclusion, and that I shall take as much interest in her as in my beautiful prude.

The latter has just sent me an offer of capitulation. Her entire letter declares a longing to be deceived. It would be impossible to have presented me with a more convenient and more straightforward means of doing so. She wants to be *my friend*. But I, who like to try new and difficult schemes, have no intention of letting her off so easily. I certainly have not gone to so much trouble on her behalf only to make an end of it with some commonplace seduction.

My plan, on the contrary, is to make her perfectly aware of the value and extent of each one of the sacrifices she makes me; not to proceed so fast with her that remorse is unable to catch up, it is to show her virtue breathing its last in long-protracted agonies, and to keep that somber spectacle ceaselessly before her eyes; and not to grant her the happiness of taking me in her arms until I have obliged her to drop all pretense of being unwilling to do so. After all, I am not worth much if I am not worth the trouble of asking for. And could I take any lesser revenge upon a haughty woman who, it seems, is ashamed even to admit that she is in love?

I have therefore declined her precious friendship and insisted upon my claim to the title of lover. Since I am under no illusions as to the real importance of securing this title (though it might appear at first to be a mere quibbling about words), I took great pains with my letter and attempted to reproduce in it that disorder which alone can portray feeling. At all events, I was as unreasonable as I was capable of being: for there is no showing tenderness without talking nonsense. It is for this reason, it seems to me, that women are better writers of love letters than men.

I finished mine with flattery – this, too, the fruit of deep reflection. When a woman's heart has been severely tried for any length of time it needs rest; and I have noticed that flattery is in every case the softest pillow to proffer.

Good-bye, my love. I leave tomorrow. If you have messages to give me for the Comtesse de —— ——, I shall stop at her house, at least for dinner. I am sorry I must leave without seeing you. Send me your lofty commands and help me with your sage advice in this crucial time.

Above all, defend yourself from Prévan; and may I one day repay you for your sacrifice! Good-bye.

————

11 September 17–

LETTER 71: *The Vicomte de Valmont to the Marquise de Merteuil*
If my idiot of a valet hasn't left my portfolio in Paris! My beauty's letters, Danceny's to the little Volanges are all left behind, and I need them. He is about to turn back to redeem his stupidity, and while he saddles his horse I shall tell you the story of my last night's adventure. I hope you will give me credit for not wasting my time.

The adventure amounted to nothing very much in itself: I merely disinterred an old affair of mine with the Vicomtesse de M—— ——. But the details interested me. I should, in any case, be very glad of an opportunity to show you that if I have a talent for bringing women to ruin, I have no less a talent, when I wish, for saving them from it. It is always either the most difficult or the most amusing line of action that I invariably pursue, and I am never ashamed of a good deed as long as it entertains me or tries my capacities.

Well, I found the Vicomtesse here, and as she added her entreaties to the general importuning that I spend the night in this house – "Well, I agreed," I said, "on condition that I spend it with you." "Impossible," she replied. "Vressac is here." Till then I had thought only of paying her a compliment, but the word "impossible" disgusted me as always. I felt humiliated at being sacrificed to Vressac, and I decided not to allow it: so I insisted.

Circumstances were not favorable. Vressac has been so stupid as to give offense to the Vicomte, so that the Vicomtesse can no longer receive him at home; this visit to the good comtesse was arranged between them in an attempt to snatch a few nights from the husband. The Vicomte was at first a little ill-humored at finding Vressac here, but since the former's keenness as a sportsman exceeds his jealousy as a husband, he decided to stay. The Comtesse, who has changed not at all since you knew her, put the wife in a room off the main corridor with the husband on one side and the lover on the other, and left them to settle matters between them. Their evil fate decreed that I should be lodged directly opposite.

That same day – yesterday, that is – Vressac, who as you can imagine flatters the Vicomte, went hunting with him, though he has little taste for the sport: he expected to be consoled that night in the arms of the wife for the boredom the husband had inflicted upon him during the day. But I decided that he would need rest after his exertions, and set about persuading his mistress to allow him time to take some.

I succeeded, and was given a promise that she would pick a quarrel over the hunting party, to which, needless to say, he had submitted only for her sake. She could scarcely have chosen a weaker pretext: but no woman is more gifted than the Vicomtesse with that talent, common to all women, for putting bad temper to work where reason will serve, and for being never so difficult to pacify as when she is in the wrong. This was, besides, not the time for arguments, and as I wanted only the one night I agreed to their being reconciled the next day.

Well, Vressac was duly greeted with sulks. He asked for an explanation; a quarrel ensued. He made some attempt to justify himself, but the husband, who was present, served as an excuse to cut short the conversation. At length he tried taking advantage of a moment when the husband was elsewhere to ask whether he would be expected that evening; and it was then that the Vicomtesse rose to sublimity. She railed at the audacity of men, who, because they have felt a woman's kindness, imagine they have the right to exploit it even when they have done her an injury; and having thus shrewdly changed the subject she spoke with so much delicacy and feeling that Vressac stood dumb and confused, and even I was tempted to believe her right – for, you see, as the friend of both I made a third in their conversation.

In the end she declared roundly that she could not think of imposing the fatigues of love upon him after those of the chase, and that she would not be guilty of spoiling a day of such agreeable pleasures. The husband returned. Vressac, overwhelmed and no longer at liberty to make a reply, addressed himself to me, and having cleared himself at great length, begged me to speak to the Vicomtesse, which I promised to do. I did, of course, speak to her, but it was to thank her and to arrange a time and place for our rendezvous.

She told me that, as her bedroom lay between her husband's and her lover's, she had judged it more prudent to go to Vressac's room than to receive him in hers, and she thought further that since my room was opposite hers, it would be safer to come to me. She would do so, she said, as soon as her maid had left her: I had only to leave my door ajar and wait.

Everything happened as arranged. She arrived in my room at about one o'clock in the morning.

> ...In simple robe attir'd,
> As of some goddess roused but lately from her sleep.*

Since I have no vanity, I shall not linger over the night's events; but you know me, and I was not dissatisfied with myself.

At daybreak it was time to part. This is where it begins to be interesting. The silly creature thought she had left her door open: we found it locked with the key inside. You cannot imagine the expression of despair upon the Vicomtesse's face as she said to me, "Oh, I am lost!" I must admit that it would have been amusing to leave her in this situation, but how could I have allowed a woman to be ruined for me who had not been ruined by me? And why should I, like the generality of men, have allowed myself to be overpowered by circumstance? I had therefore to think of a way out. What would you have done, my love? This was my scheme, and it succeeded.

I soon realized that the door in question could be broken open, provided a great deal of noise were not amiss. Accordingly, and not without difficulty, I obtained the Vicomtesse's consent to giving loud shrieks of alarm such as "Thief! Murder!" etc., etc.; and it was agreed that, at the first shriek, I should break open the door, whereupon she would run to her bed. You will never believe how long it took to persuade her, even after she had given her consent. However, she had to give way in the end. The door gave way at my first kick.

The Vicomtesse did well to waste no time. At that very instant the Vicomte and Vressac appeared in the corridor, and the maid, too, flew to her mistress's chamber.

I alone preserved my composure, taking advantage of that circum-

---

*Racine, *Britannicus*, a tragedy.

stance to extinguish the night-light, which was still burning, and to knock it to the floor. You can imagine how ridiculous all this pretense of panic terror would have been with a lamp alight in her room. Next I upbraided husband and lover for the heaviness of their slumbers, assuring them that the cries that had fetched me running, and my efforts to break open the door, had lasted at least five minutes.

The Vicomtesse, who had recovered her courage in bed, supported me quite well, swearing by all the gods that there had been a thief in the room; she was able to aver, with still more sincerity, that she had never been so frightened in all her life. We had looked everywhere and found nothing, when I pointed out the overturned night-light and observed that doubtless a rat had been responsible both for the accident and for the alarm. My verdict met with unanimous assent, and after some of the usual well-worn pleasantries about rats, the Vicomte was the first to return to his room and bed, begging his wife to keep rats of more sober habit in future.

Vressac, left alone with us, drew near the Vicomtesse to tell her tenderly that this had been Love's revenge; to which she replied, looking at me, "A revenge taken in anger, then, for it has been a cruel one. But," she added, "I am exhausted and I want to sleep."

I was in a generous mood: consequently, before we separated, I pleaded Vressac's cause and brought about a reconciliation. The two lovers embraced, and I was in turn embraced by both of them. I was no longer interested in the Vicomtesse's kisses, but I will confess that Vressac's gave me pleasure. We left the room together and, once I had received his much-protracted thanks, returned to our respective beds.

If you find this story amusing, I shall not insist that you keep it secret. Since it has provided me with entertainment, it is only fair to give the public its turn. I refer at present only to the story, but perhaps one day we shall be able to say as much for its heroine.

Good-bye. My valet has been waiting for an hour. One moment more while I kiss you and, above all, urge you to beware of Prévan.

Château de ———
13 September 17–

LETTER 72: *The Chevalier Danceny to Cécile Volanges*
    (not delivered until the fourteenth)

Oh, my dear Cécile, how I envy Valmont! Tomorrow he will be seeing you. It is he who will deliver this letter to you, while I, repining afar, drag out my painful existence in longing and misery. My dear, my darling, pity me for my misfortunes; pity me, rather, for yours: it is in face of these that my courage deserts me.

How terrible it is to be the cause of your affliction! Were it not for me, you would be happy and at peace. Do you forgive me? Say, ah, say that you do! Tell me also that you love me and that you will love me always. I need to be told again and again. Not that I doubt it, but it seems that the more sure I am, the sweeter it is to hear you say those words. You do love me, don't you? Yes, you love me with all your heart. I have not forgotten that those words were the last I heard you utter. How I have cherished them in my heart! How deeply they are engraved upon it! With what rapture did my heart reply!

Alas, little did I suspect in that moment of happiness what a frightful fate was in store for us. Let us try, my dear Cécile, to find a means of making it easier. If I can trust my friend in this matter, no more is necessary than that you place that confidence in him which he deserves.

I was distressed, I shall admit, at the unfavorable opinion you seem to have of him. I detected your mother's prejudices there: it was to conform to them that I so long neglected this truly amiable man, who now does everything for me, who, after all, is trying to reunite us when your mother has separated us. I beseech you, my dear, to look a little more kindly upon him. Consider that he is my friend, that he wishes to be yours, and that it is in his power to give me back the happiness of seeing you. If these considerations do not weigh with you, my dear Cécile, you do not love me as much as I love you, you no longer love me as much as once you did. Oh, if ever you were to love me less...But no, my Cécile's heart is mine; and it is mine for life. And if I have cause to lament an unhappy love, her constancy will at least spare me the torments of a love betrayed.

Good-bye, my dear heart. Remember that I suffer and that it is only you who can make me happy, perfectly happy. Accept the vow my heart makes you and the tenderest kisses love can bestow.

Paris
11 September 17–

LETTER 73: *The Vicomte de Valmont to Cécile Volanges*
    (*attached to the preceding letter*)
The friend who puts himself at your service, having learned that you are without writing materials, has made suitable provision. You will find in the large cupboard on the left, in the antechamber to the room you occupy, a stock of paper, pens, and ink, which he will replenish when-

ever you wish, and which, in his opinion, you would do well to leave in that place unless you find one safer.

He asks you not to be offended if he appears to pay you no attention, to treat you as a mere child in the presence of company. This way of proceeding seems to him to be necessary so as to inspire in others the confidence essential to his purpose, and so that he may the more effectively work for the happiness of his friend and yours. He will try to make opportunities to speak to you when he has something to tell you, or to deliver to you; and he hopes to succeed if you are willing to do your utmost to help him.

He advises you, too, to return your letters to him, one by one, as you receive them, so as to run less risk of compromising yourself.

He will end here by assuring you that if you wish to put your trust in him he will do everything in his power to alleviate the persecution that an overly cruel mother inflicts upon two persons, one of whom is already his best friend, while the other appears to him to deserve the most affectionate interest.

Château de ———
14 September 17–

LETTER 74: *The Marquise de Merteuil to the Vicomte de Valmont*
Since when, my dear man, have you taken to being so easily frightened? Is Prévan really so very formidable? How modest and simple, then, must I be who have often met this arrogant conqueror and scarcely ever looked at him! It required a letter such as yours to bring him to my notice, and yesterday I repaired my oversight. He was at the opera, almost opposite me, and I gave him my full attention. He is at any rate handsome, very handsome; such fine, delicate features! I am sure they improve, too, upon closer inspection. And you say he intends to have me! It will most certainly be an honor and a pleasure. Seriously, I have a mind to it, and I tell you here in confidence that I have taken the preliminary steps. I don't know whether they will succeed, but this is how it is.

He was standing not two yards away from me as we left the opera, when, in a very loud voice, I told the Marquise de ——— I would meet her at supper on Friday at the Maréchale's. This, I think, is the only house at which I am likely to see him. I have no doubt that he heard me... What if the ungrateful fellow has no intention of coming? Tell me, tell me, do you think he will come? Do you know that if he is not there I shall be in a bad humor the whole evening? He will have no difficulty, you see, in *pursuing* me; and, what will surprise you more, even less in *pleasing* me. He wants, does he, to ride six horses to death in paying court to me? Oh, let me spare their lives. I should never have patience enough to wait so long. It is not, you know, in accordance with my principles to let a man pine away for me once I have made up my mind, and in this case I have already done so.

Well, well: is it not a satisfaction to you to talk seriously to me? What a great success your *important warning* has been! But what do you expect? I have been vegetating for so long! For more than six weeks I have allowed myself not a single frivolity. The occasion presents itself; how can I refuse? Is not the person in question worth the pains? In whatever sense you take the word, could anyone be more agreeable?

You yourself are obliged to give him his due, and you do more than praise him: you are jealous of him. Well, I am going to set up as judge between you: but first I must know the facts, and I intend to find them out. I shall be a judge of great integrity, and you will both be weighed in the same balance. As far as you are concerned, the case is already documented and fully prepared. Is it not fair that I should now concern myself with your rival? Well then, comply with a good grace; and, to begin with, tell me please about the "triple affair" he has figured in. You speak as though I had never heard of anything else, and I know not the first thing about it. Evidently, it must have happened during my stay in Geneva, and your jealousy prevented you writing to me about it. Repair this omission as soon as possible: remember that *nothing that concerns him is without interest for me.* There must still have been talk about it when I returned, but I was busy with other things, and I rarely listen to talk of this kind when it is more than two days old.

You may feel a little aggrieved at what I ask, but is this not the least return I can expect for the trouble I have given myself on your account? Was it not I who brought you back to your Présidente, when your stupidity had taken you from her? Was it not I again who provided you with a means of avenging the bitter attacks made upon you by Madame de Volanges? You have so often complained of the time you waste going about in search of adventure! Now you have it under your nose. Love, hatred, you have only to choose: it is all there with you under the same roof. You can enjoy life, caressing with one hand and killing with the other.

It is to me yet again that you owe your adventure with the Vicomtesse. I am happy enough about that, but, as you say, one must talk. For though circumstances might, as I see it, have inclined you for the moment to prefer humbug to scandal, it must all the same be admitted that this woman does not deserve such considerate treatment.

Besides, I bear her a grudge. The Chevalier de Belleroche finds her prettier than I could wish, and there are many other reasons why I should be very glad of a pretext to break with her. Now there is none more convenient than that of having to say to oneself: I cannot possibly meet that woman again.

Good-bye, Vicomte. Remember that in a position such as yours time is precious. My time I intend to devote to the greater happiness of Prévan.

Paris
15 September 17–

LETTER 75: *Cécile Volanges to Sophie Carnay*
(In this letter Cécile Volanges gives an account in the minutest detail of her part in the events described in Letters 59 and those following, with which the reader is already familiar. This account has been omitted to avoid repetition. Toward the end of the letter she speaks of the Vicomte de Valmont as follows:)

... I assure you he is the most extraordinary man. Mamma speaks very ill of him, but the Chevalier Danceny very well, and I think it is he who is right. I have never met such a clever man. When he delivered Danceny's letter to me it was in full view of everyone and nobody saw anything. True, I was very frightened because I was not expecting anything; but from now on I shall be prepared. I already understand perfectly what he wants me to do when I give him my reply. It is quite easy to come to an understanding with him: he has a look that says whatever he wishes to say. I don't know how he does it. He says in the note I have already mentioned that he will appear not to pay me any attention in Mamma's presence, and in fact one would imagine that he never gives me a thought. Yet every time I look in his direction I can be sure of meeting his eyes immediately.

A good friend of Mamma's is here, whom I have not met before, and who also seems not to like Monsieur de Valmont very much, though he pays her a great deal of attention. I am so afraid he will tire soon of the life we lead here and return to Paris; that would be a great disappointment. He must really have a good heart to have come here especially to render a service to his friend and to me! I should very much like to show my gratitude, but I don't know how to find a way of speaking to him; and if the opportunity did arise I should be so shy that I should probably not know what to say.

It is only to Madame de Merteuil that I can speak freely about my love. Perhaps, even with you, to whom I tell everything, if we were to talk about it I should be embarrassed. With Danceny himself I have often, in spite of myself, felt a certain constraint that prevented my telling him all my thoughts. I am very sorry for it now, and I should give anything in the world for a moment's opportunity to tell him once, just once, how much I love him. Monsieur de Valmont has promised that if I follow his instructions he will arrange a meeting. I shall certainly do whatever he says; but I cannot imagine how it will be possible.

Good-bye, my dear friend. I have no more space.*

Château de ———
14 September 17–

LETTER 76: *The Vicomte de Valmont to the Marquise de Merteuil*
Either your letter is a joke that I don't understand, or your mind, when you wrote it, was very seriously deranged. If I knew you less well, my love, I should really be very frightened, and, whatever you may say, I am never frightened too easily.

No matter how often I read your letter I am no further toward understanding it: for, taking it to mean what ostensibly it says, there is no possibility of understanding it. What, then, can it be taken to mean?

Is it only that it was unnecessary to take so many precautions against so unalarming an enemy? In that case you might well be wrong. Prévan is really very charming – more so than you think. He has too a very useful talent for attracting a great deal of attention to his feelings, a flair for speaking of them in company, in everybody's hearing, making use, for the purpose, of the first available opportunity of addressing the lady concerned. Few women can escape the trap of replying: since they all have pretensions to savoir faire, they cannot let slip an opportunity of displaying it. Now, as you will know, any woman who permits herself to speak of love will end by acknowledging it, or at least by behaving as though she did. This method, which he has really perfected, frequently gives him the added advantage of being able to call upon the women themselves to bear witness to their defeat – and that I can vouch for as having seen it happen.

---

*Mademoiselle de Volanges shortly afterward changed her confidante, as will be seen in the following letters; those she continued to write to her friend at the convent will not be included in this collection, since they contain nothing of further interest to the reader.

I was never in the secret except at second hand, for I was never intimate with Prévan. At any rate, there were six of us present when the Comtesse de P——, quite persuaded of her own worldly guile – and in fact, for all that she explicitly said, she might have been making general conversation – recounted to us in the minutest detail the history of her surrender to Prévan and all that had passed between them. She delivered her recital with so much composure that she was not at all disconcerted even when the six of us fell simultaneously into fits of laughter. I shall always remember that when one of us, by way of excuse, pretended to doubt the truth of what she had said, or rather what she appeared to have been saying, she replied with perfect gravity that she was quite certain that none of us was as well acquainted with the facts as she, and that she would not hesitate to put the matter even to Prévan, to ask him whether a single word of her story were untrue.

I concluded that the man was a menace to society in general; for you in particular, Marquise, is it not enough that he is "handsome, very handsome," as you say yourself? Or that he may launch against you one of those attacks you are pleased sometimes to reward for no other reason than that they are well executed? Or that you might find it amusing to surrender for one reason or another? Or...how can I tell? How can I guess at those hundreds upon hundreds of whims that rule the mind of a woman, by virtue of which alone you remain typical of your sex? Now that you are warned of the danger, I have no doubt that you will easily avoid it. Yet it was necessary to warn you. I return, then, to my text: what did your letter mean?

If it was a joke about Prévan, apart from the fact that it was very long, it was lost on me; it is in public that he needs to be subjected to some well-aimed ridicule, and I renew my plea to you on this point.

Ah, I think I have found the clue to the mystery! Your letter is a prophecy not of what you are going to do but of what he is going to think you are ready to do at the moment of the catastrophe you are preparing for him. I don't disapprove of the plan; it requires very great caution, though. You know as well as I that, in the public view, there is absolutely no difference between being a man's mistress and receiving his attentions – unless the man is a fool, which Prévan is not by a very long way. If he can only bring about the necessary appearances, he will begin boasting, and all will be over. The fools will believe him, the malicious will pretend to believe him: what resources will be left to you? Come, it frightens me. Not that I doubt your skill; but it is always the good swimmers who drown.

I don't think I am more stupid than the next man. I know a hundred, a thousand ways of robbing a woman of her reputation; but whenever I have tried to think how she might save herself I have never been able to conceive of a single possibility. You yourself, my love, whose strategy is masterly, have triumphed a hundred times – I think – more through good luck than good judgment.

But perhaps, after all, I am looking for an explanation where none is to be found. I wonder how I can have spent the last hour taking seriously what was certainly meant on your part as a joke. You wanted to make fun of me. Oh, well, laugh! But be quick about it, and then let us speak of other things. Other things? – I am wrong, it is always the same thing: women to be possessed or to be ruined, and frequently both.

Here, as you have so acutely observed, I have opportunities for practice in both fields; not, however, equal opportunities. Revenge, I can see, will prosper sooner than love. I can answer for the little Volanges, who would already have yielded but for want of an occasion, and that I can undertake to provide. But it is not the same with Madame de Tourvel. That woman is devastating; I don't understand her. I have a hundred proofs of her love, but at the same time a thousand of her aversion, and, to tell you the truth, I am afraid she may escape me.

Her first reaction to my return left me feeling more hopeful. As you may imagine, I wished to see it for myself; to be sure of witnessing spontaneous emotions, I sent no one ahead to announce me, timing my journey so as to arrive while everyone was at table. In fact I dropped from the clouds, like a god in an opera who comes down to unravel the plot.

Having made enough noise at my entrance to fix the attention of the whole company upon me, I was able at a glance to perceive the joy of my old aunt, the vexation of Madame de Volanges, and the confusion and pleasure of her daughter. My beauty was sitting with her back to the door, and, as she was for the moment occupied in cutting something on her plate, did not so much as turn her head. Then I said something to Madame de Rosemonde and at the first word the sensitive creature, having recognized my voice, let out a little cry in which I was certain I detected more love than surprise or alarm. I had by then come far enough forward to be able to see her face, upon which the tumult in her soul, the struggle of thought with feeling, displayed itself in twenty different ways. I sat down beside her at table. She had absolutely no further consciousness of what she was doing or saying; she attempted to continue eating, but without success. At length, in less than a quarter of an hour, her embarrassment and pleasure proving too much for her, she could think of nothing better than to ask permission to leave the table, whereupon she escaped into the park under the pretext of wanting to take the air. Madame de Volanges offered to accompany her: our tender prude refused, no doubt only too glad of an excuse to be alone, so that she could give herself up without constraint to the sweet emotions of her heart!

I cut dinner as short as I could. Scarcely had dessert been served when the infernal Volanges, impelled apparently by an urge to thwart me, rose from her place to set out in search of our charming invalid; but I had anticipated this move and forestalled it. I pretended to take her withdrawal as the signal for a general departure, and having myself risen from the table, the little Volanges and the local curé let themselves be swayed by our example, so that Madame de Rosemonde found herself alone at table with the old Commandeur de T——. They too decided to leave, so that all of us went together to join my beauty, whom we found in the grove near the house. Since she wanted not to walk but to be alone, she was just as happy to return with us as to have us remain with her.

As soon as I was sure that Madame de Volanges would have no opportunity of speaking to her alone, I bethought me of your commands and busied myself in your pupil's interest. Immediately after coffee I went up to my room, and through all the other rooms as well, reconnoitering the territory. I made my arrangements for the safety of the little creature's correspondence, and having performed this preliminary good deed, wrote her a line to tell her about it and to ask for her confidence. I attached my note to Danceny's letter, then returned to the drawing room. There I found my beauty stretched on a chaise longue in the most delicious attitude of abandon.

This prospect, in rousing my desires, at the same time animated my expression; aware of how much it showed of eagerness and tenderness, I placed myself where I could use it to best advantage. The first consequence of this was that my heavenly prude lowered her large bashful eyes. For a time I considered that angelic face; then, my glance wandering over her person, I amused myself imagining the shapes and contours beneath her light but all too reticent garment. I looked down her from head to foot and then up again...My love, that sweet gaze was fixed upon me! It was immediately lowered, but so as to encourage its return I looked away. Thus was established between us that tacit agreement, the first treaty ratified by timid lovers, which, to satisfy a mutual need of seeing and being seen, allows glances to succeed each other until the moment when they can safely meet.

Deciding that this new pleasure would occupy my beauty's whole attention, I turned my consideration to our safety; but having assured myself that the conversation was lively enough to prevent our being noticed, I attempted to persuade her eyes to speak in plainer terms. To this end I first took one or two of her glances by surprise, though with as much reserve as could give modesty no alarm; and to put the bashful creature more at her ease I pretended to be as embarrassed as she was. By degrees our eyes, growing accustomed to meeting, met for longer, and at last looked away no more; and I saw in hers that languid softness which is the happy signal of love and desire. But it was only for a moment: she soon came to herself, and, not without some embarrassment, changed her expression and demeanor.

Not wishing to leave her in any doubt that I had noticed these various emotions, I rose briskly and feigning alarm asked her whether she felt ill. She was immediately surrounded by the whole company. I allowed them all to move in front of me and, as the little Volanges who had been working at her tapestry near a window needed time to put down her work, I seized the opportunity to deliver Danceny's letter.

I was at some distance from her and threw it in her lap. She had really no idea what to do with it. You would have died laughing at her surprise and embarrassment. I, needless to say, did not laugh: I was afraid that so much floundering would betray us. But with a very peremptory glance and gesture I finally made her understand that she must consign the letter to her pocket.

The remainder of the day was without interest. The sequel to the story will perhaps develop to your satisfaction, at least insofar as your pupil is concerned. But one ought to spend one's time carrying out plans rather than talking about them. Besides, I have written you eight pages and I am tired. So good-bye.

You would be right to suppose, without my telling you, that the girl has replied to Danceny.* I have also received a reply to the letter I wrote to my beauty the day after arriving here. I send you my letter and hers. You may read them or not, as you like. This perpetual harping on the same string, which I already find comes something short of the irresistibly amusing, must be exceedingly insipid to anyone who is not personally concerned.

Once more good-bye. I still love you very much. But I beg you, if you speak again of Prévan, do so in terms that I can understand.

Château de ———
17 September 17–

---

*This letter has not been found.

LETTER 77: *The Vicomte de Valmont to the Présidente de Tourvel*

Whence comes, Madame, this cruel determination to be rid of me? How is it that the most tender cordiality on my part is answered on yours by conduct that could scarcely be merited even by a man you had every reason to execrate? How, when love brought me again to your feet, when a lucky accident placed me beside you, could you have pretended, to the alarm of your friends, an indisposition rather than stay beside me? How many times yesterday did you turn your eyes away from me so as to deny me the favor of your regard? And if for a single instant you showed me less severity, the moment was so brief that I think you must have meant me less to enjoy it than to realize how much I was losing when you took it from me.

Love, I make bold to say, does not deserve such treatment, nor does friendship permit it; yet, of those two sentiments, one to your knowledge I profess, while I have been led to believe, it seems to me, that you would not refuse me the other. You were certainly willing once to offer me a friendship of which you no doubt considered me worthy; what have I done since to forfeit it? Will my trust in you be my undoing, will you punish me for my honesty? Have you not the least suspicion that you might be abusing one or the other? After all, is it not to the bosom of a friend that I have disclosed the secrets of my heart? Was it not for her sake alone that I refused to agree to conditions that I might simply have accepted, so that I could the more easily have left them unfulfilled or perhaps turned them to my advantage? Will you, in short, compel me to believe by reason of this undeserved severity that I have only to deceive you to win your more favorable regard?

I do not at all regret a decision that I owed it both to you and to myself to make; but what dreadful fate decrees that my every praiseworthy action shall become a source of further unhappiness to me?

It was after I had given you occasion for the only compliment you have hitherto condescended to bestow upon my conduct that I first had cause to groan for the misfortune of having displeased you. It was after I had proved my perfect submission to your will in depriving myself of the happiness of seeing you, solely out of regard for your delicacy, that you wanted to break off all correspondence with me, to deny me my feeble recompense for the sacrifice you had exacted, to take everything from me, even the love that alone could give you the right to ask so much. And now it is after I have spoken to you with a sincerity which even self-interest cannot mitigate that you send me packing like some dangerous seducer whose perfidy you have at last found out.

Will you never tire of being so unjust? Tell me, at least, what new crimes can have provoked you to such unkindness; and do not hesitate to dictate the commands you wish me to obey. Since I undertake to obey them, is it presuming too much to want to know what they are?

_____

15 September 17–

LETTER 78: *The Présidente de Tourvel to the Vicomte de Valmont*

You seem, Monsieur, to be surprised at my conduct; what is more, you are not far from calling me to account for it, as though you had the right to approve or blame. I might tell you that to my mind I have better grounds for surprise and complaint than do you; but after the refusal contained in your latest reply, I have decided to wrap myself in an indifference that can give rise to neither remark nor reproach. However, since you ask for explanations and since, heaven be thanked, there is nothing as far as I am concerned to prevent my making them, I am quite willing once again to expose my motives to view.

Anyone reading your letters would think me either unjust or very strange. I do not think I have deserved that anyone should have such an opinion of me; it seems to me, moreover, that you least of all have any reason to entertain it. No doubt you reckoned, in obliging me to clear myself, you would force me into a repetition of all that has passed between us. Evidently, you considered that you could only benefit from this rehearsal. Since, for my part, I consider that I have nothing to lose by it – at least in your eyes – I have no hesitation in committing myself to it. Perhaps it is, after all, the only way of discovering which of us has a right to complain of the other.

To start, Monsieur, with the day of your arrival at this house, I think you will allow that your reputation, if nothing else, justified my treating you with some reserve, and that I might have confined myself solely to expressions of the coldest courtesy, without fear of being accused of excessive prudery. You would have tolerated this, finding it quite natural that a woman with so little experience of the world had not merit enough to appreciate your own. It would certainly have been the course of prudence; and I shall not conceal from you that I found it the much easier course to follow for the fact that, when Madame de Rosemonde came to tell me of your impending arrival, I had to remind myself of my friendship for her, and of hers for you, before I could hide from her how unwelcome the news was to me.

I willingly admit that at first you appeared to me in a more attractive light than I had imagined you would; but you, in turn, will admit that this did not last very long, and that you soon tired of a constraint for which, apparently, the favorable opinion it gave me of you was not in your view sufficient recompense.

It was then that, taking advantage of my innocence and sincerity, you did not hesitate to importune me with feelings that you can have had no doubt would be offensive to me; and I, while you blackened your crimes by adding to their number, looked only for some excuse to forget them, offering you at the same time an opportunity to redeem them, at least in part. My demands were so just that you yourself could not find it in you to refuse them. Taking my indulgence as your due, however, you exploited it in asking a favor, which no doubt I should not have granted you, but which, you nevertheless obtained. Of the conditions upon which it was granted, you observed not a single one; and such has been the nature of your correspondence that each of your letters has reminded me afresh of my duty to leave them all unanswered. At the very moment when your persistence compelled me to send you from me, I tried with perhaps reprehensible complaisance the only means that could have brought about our reconciliation; but how much is an honorable feeling worth to you? You despise friendship and in your intoxicated folly, setting shame and misfortune at naught, you look for nothing but pleasure and the victims to sacrifice to it.

Your behavior is as frivolous as your reproofs of mine are unreasonable. You forget your promises, or rather you make a game of violating them. Having agreed to stay away from me, you return here without having been recalled, without regard for my pleas, my arguments, without enough consideration for me to warn me that you are coming. You make no scruple of exposing me to a surprise, the consequences of which, perfectly natural though they were of course, might have been interpreted to my disadvantage by the people around us. Far from attempting to distract attention from the embarrassment you had caused, or to dispel it, you appeared on the contrary to turn all your efforts to increasing it. You carefully chose a place at table next to mine. When a slight indisposition had obliged me to leave before the others, instead of respecting my solitude, you rallied the rest of the company to come and disturb me. When we had returned to the drawing room, if I took a step I found you beside me; if I said a word, it was always you who replied. The most indifferent remark served you as a pretext to introduce into the conversation what I did not wish to hear, what might moreover have compromised me. After all, Monsieur, however clever you are; it seems to me that what I can understand must be plain to everybody else as well.

Having compelled me thus to immobility and silence, you were no less unrelenting in your pursuit; I was unable to raise my eyes without meeting yours. I had perpetually to turn away from you, with the quite incredible consequence that you made me the cynosure of all eyes at a moment when I could have wished to be deprived of my own.

And you complain of my treatment, you are astonished at my anxiety to fly from you! Oh, blame me rather for my kindness; let it astonish you that I did not leave myself as soon as you arrived. I should perhaps have done so, and you will oblige me to adopt this desperate but imperative course if you do not once and for all cease your offensive solicitations. No, I have by no means forgotten, I shall never forget what I owe to myself, what I owe to the ties I have formed, which I respect and cherish. And I ask you to believe that if ever I am reduced to making the unhappy choice between sacrificing them and sacrificing myself, I shall make it without an instant's hesitation. Good-bye, Monsieur.

———

16 September 17–

LETTER 79: *The Vicomte de Valmont to the Marquise de Merteuil*
I had intended to go hunting this morning, but the weather is appalling. I have nothing to read but a new novel that would bore a convent girl to tears. It is at least two hours to breakfast, so in spite of my long letter of yesterday I am going to chatter to you again. I am quite sure I shan't bore you, since I shall be speaking of *the very handsome Prévan*. How can you not have heard of that celebrated affair which separated "the inseparables?" I am sure it will come back to you before I have said two words about it. Here is the story, however, since you have asked for it.

You remember how all Paris raised its eyebrows when three women, all of them pretty, all endowed with the same talents and a right to equal pretensions, lived on terms of the most intimate friendship with each other from the moment of their entry into society? This was at first put down to their extreme timidity; but they were soon surrounded by a throng of admirers whose homage they shared, and as the objects of so much interest and attention they could scarcely have wanted self-assurance. Yet their friendship only grew stronger. It was as though the success of one were always as much the success of the other two. It was hoped that love, at any rate, might provoke some rivalry, and our gallants set about disputing their respective claims to the honor of representing the apple of discord. I myself would have entered the lists, had not the Comtesse de ——— at that time risen so high in favor that I could not allow myself an infidelity to her until I had obtained the pleasure I was soliciting.

Meanwhile our three beauties made their choices at the same carnival ball, as though by prearrangement; far from stirring up the storm that was looked for, the circumstance only made their friendship more interesting by introducing into it the new charm of shared confidences.

All the unsuccessful claimants now joined with all the jealous women in submitting this scandalous display of loyalty to public censure. Some asserted that in a society of "inseparables" (as they were called at the time) the basic law demanded that all goods be held in common, even lovers; others were sure that while the three gallants need fear no male rivals they had female rivals to contend with, and even went so far as to say that, having been accepted only for the sake of appearances, they had acquired a title without a function.

These rumors, true or false, did not achieve the intended effect. On the contrary, the three couples realized they would be ruined if they were now to separate: they decided to weather the storm. Society, which tires of everything, soon tired of its ineffective campaign. Following its naturally frivolous inclinations, it turned its attention to other things; then, with its usual inconsequence, reverted to the subject and transformed criticism into praise. Since everything with us is a question of fashion, enthusiasm ran high: it had reached the point of delirium, when Prévan took it upon himself to investigate the phenomenon, to determine once and for all both public opinion and his own.

He accordingly sought out these paragons of perfection. He was readily received into their society, and he took this for a favorable omen. He knew well enough that happy people are not so easy of access. He soon saw, in fact, that their much vaunted contentment was, like the estate of kings, more envied than enviable. The supposed inseparables had begun, he perceived, to look for pleasures outside their circle, indeed, to give their whole attention to the search for distraction. The bonds of love, and friendship, he concluded, had already been relaxed or broken, and it was only those of vanity and custom that retained any strength.

Meanwhile the women, drawn together by necessity, kept up the old appearance of intimacy among themselves. The men, however, being more at liberty to do as they pleased, rediscovered obligations to be fulfilled and business affairs to be attended to; they still complained about them, but no longer neglected them, and gatherings in the evening were rarely complete.

This circumstance was of considerable advantage to the assiduous Prévan, who, since he naturally found himself beside the unfriended one of the day, was able, according to circumstances, to offer the same homage to each of the three ladies in turn. He was quick to see that to choose between them would be to ruin everything, that false shame at being the first to commit an infidelity would frighten the one he singled out, that wounded vanity would make the two others his enemies, and that they would not fail to bring the highest and strictest of principles to bear against him; lastly, that jealousy would surely embroil him with a rival from whom he might still have something to fear. There was so much that might have gone against him that his threefold plan made everything easy. The women were indulgent because they were interested parties; the men because they thought themselves not.

Prévan, who at that time had only one woman to sacrifice, was fortunate enough to see her become a celebrity. Her status as a foreigner and her skill in declining the attentions of a great prince had attracted the notice of both court and town. Prévan shared in the glory, and profited by it in the estimation of his new mistresses. The only difficulty was to keep his three intrigues abreast of one another, their rate of progress being necessarily determined by the slowest. In fact, I had it from one of his confidants that he had enormous trouble keeping one of them in check when it came to maturity a full two weeks before the others.

At last the great day arrived. Prévan, who had obtained avowals from all three, found that he was already in control of the proceedings, and conducted them as you are going to see. Of the three husbands, one was away, the other was to leave at dawn the next day, and the third was in town. The inseparables were to sup with the grass widow to be; but their new lord had not permitted the old cavaliers to be invited. That morning he made three packets of his mistress's letters: in one he enclosed a portrait he had received from her, in the second an enormous emblem she had painted herself, in the third a lock of her hair. Each of the friends took her third part of the sacrifice for a complete surrender and agreed in return to write her own disgraced lover a peremptory letter of dismissal.

This was a great deal, but it was not enough. The one whose husband was in town did not have her nights at her disposal: it was accordingly arranged that an indisposition would prevent her taking supper with her friend and that the evening would be Prévan's; the one whose husband was away accorded him the night; and daybreak, the lover's hour, at which time the third husband was to leave, was appointed by the last.

Prévan, who leaves nothing to chance, flew at once to his fair foreigner, threw a fit of bad temper, was repaid in kind, and did not leave until he had established a quarrel that would assure him twenty-four hours' liberty. His dispositions made, he returned home with the idea of resting – but further business awaited him there.

The letters of dismissal had come as a flood of illumination upon the disgraced lovers. Not one of them could doubt he had been given up for Prévan; and all three, out of pique at having been duped – and that annoyance which nearly always accompanies the minor humiliation of being jilted – resolved without telling each other, but as though in agreement, to demand satisfaction from their successful rival.

The latter therefore found three challenges awaiting his return home. Loyally, he accepted them. But determined to forgo neither pleasure nor glory in the course of this adventure, he fixed a rendezvous for the next morning, assigning the same time and place – one of the gates to the Bois de Boulogne – to all three.

That evening he accomplished his triple task with complete success; at all events he boasted afterward that each of his new mistresses had thrice received the pledge and proof of his love. As you may imagine, the story at this point lacks authentication. All that the impartial historian can do is to point out to the incredulous reader that vanity and an inflamed imagination may work miracles; and that, besides, it looked as though the morning that was to succeed so brilliant a night would obviate any necessity to provide against the future. Be that as it may, more certainty can be attributed to the following facts.

Prévan arrived punctually at the appointed rendezvous to find his three rivals a little surprised at meeting each other there, but perhaps already somewhat comforted to discover companions in misfortune. He approached them with an affable, nonchalant air and made them the following speech, which was faithfully reported to me:

"Gentlemen," he said, "you have doubtless guessed, since you are here together, that all three of you have the same grounds for complaint against me. I am ready to give you satisfaction. Let it be decided by lot which of you shall first attempt the revenge to which you all have equal right. I have brought neither seconds nor witnesses with me. I did not need them when I committed the offense; I ask for none while I make the reparation." Then, in the true gambler's spirit, he added, "I know that one rarely wins at *le sept et le va*; still, no matter what fate has in store, one has lived long enough if one has had time to win the love of women and the esteem of men."

As his astonished adversaries gazed at him in silence, and while, perhaps, their consciences were beginning to suggest that an opposition of three to one would not be a fair one, Prévan spoke again. "I shall not conceal from you," he continued, "that the night I have just spent has cruelly fatigued me. You would be generous to allow me time to refortify myself. I have given orders for breakfast to be served here; do me the honor of joining me. Let us eat together and, above all, let us not be solemn about it. We may kill each other for trifles, but let them not weigh on our minds."

The invitation to breakfast was accepted. Never, I am told, had Prévan been more agreeable. He was clever enough to avoid humiliating his rivals, and clever enough to persuade them that they might as easily have met with the same success as he; clever enough, above all, to make them admit that they would never, any more than he had done, have let such an opportunity slip. Once these truths had been admitted, everything fell into place of its own accord. Before breakfast was over it had been asserted a dozen times that women such as these did not deserve that men of honor should fight over them. The idea inspired great cordiality, which the wine increased, so much so that shortly afterward it was felt that to banish ill-will was not enough: friendship without reserve must be sworn.

Prévan, who was certainly as pleased as anyone was with this turn of events, intended nonetheless to forfeit no whit of his glory. Accordingly, adapting his plans with great skill to circumstances, he addressed the three injured gentlemen as follows: "After all, it is not upon me but upon your faithless mistresses that you must take revenge. I can provide the opportunity. I have already begun to harbor, in sympathy with you, a resentment I should soon have to share with you: for if not one of you was able to keep his own mistress to himself, how can I hope to hold all three? Your quarrel has become mine. Please accept an invitation to supper this evening at my house, where I hope your revenge will not long be deferred." An explanation was requested, but in the tone of superiority which the circumstances entitled him to adopt he replied, "I think, gentlemen, I have given you sufficient proof of my skill: rely on me." All agreed, and having embraced their new friend, separated to await the fulfillment that evening of his promises.

Prévan lost no time; he returned to Paris and, as is customary, visited his new conquests. He extracted promises from all three to come that evening to sup tête-à-tête at his house. Two of them did, it is true, make difficulties: what, since the night before, had they left to deny him? They were to come at intervals of an hour, the length of time necessary to his plans. These preliminaries accomplished, he withdrew, reported to his accomplices, and the four of them went off joyfully to await their victims.

The first one was heard arriving. Prévan received her alone, and with an air of solicitude conveyed her into the sanctuary whose presiding goddess she believed herself to be. He then made some trifling excuse to disappear, and was immediately replaced by an outraged lover.

As you can imagine, the consternation of a woman not yet accustomed to proceedings of this kind made his victory easy: with every reproach he omitted to make, he conferred a favor, so that the fugitive slave, given up once more to her old master, was obliged to think herself lucky that, by submitting again to the original bondage, she could hope to be forgiven. The peace treaty was ratified in a more secluded spot; the stage, thus left empty, was filled in turn by the other actors in the piece to more or less the same effect – in each case, of course, with the same result.

Each woman, meanwhile, believed herself to be the sole heroine of the drama. At supper, to their further surprise and embarrassment, the three couples came together for the first time; consternation reached its height when Prévan, reappearing in their midst, was cruel enough to make his excuses to the ladies – thus, in betraying their secrets, revealing the full extent to which they had been tricked.

Meanwhile, they sat down to table and before long were able to put a face upon it: the men yielded and the women submitted. Hatred consumed every heart, but conversation was nonetheless *galant*. Gaiety aroused desire, which in turn gave a fresh fillip to gaiety. This astonishing orgy lasted till morning. When they separated, the women must have thought themselves forgiven, but the men had been nursing their resentments and broke irrevocably with them the very next day. Not content, moreover, with abandoning their fickle mistresses, they crowned their revenge by publicizing the affair. Since then, one of the women has entered a convent, while the two others have languished in exile on their estates.

So much for Prévan's story. It is for you to decide whether you wish to contribute to his glory, to be yoked to his triumphal car. Your letter truly made me anxious, and I shall wait with impatience for one more sensible and more intelligible in reply to my last.

Good-bye, my love. Distrust all amusing and bizarre ideas; you are so easily led astray by them. Remember that for the role you have elected to play, intelligence is not enough. A single imprudence may bring about irremediable disaster. Allow it, lastly, to a prudent friend to be at times the director of your pleasures.

Good-bye. I love you still, almost as though you were a reasonable being.

————

18 September 17–

LETTER 80: *The Chevalier Danceny to Cécile Volanges*

Cécile, my dear Cécile, when shall we see each other again? How shall I learn to live without you? Where shall I find the strength and courage to do so? Never, no, never, shall I accept this horrible separation. Each day increases my misery – and to see no end to it! Valmont, who promised help and consolation, neglects me and has perhaps forgotten me. He is beside his beloved and no longer knows what it is to suffer in isolation. He sent me your last letter, but not a word from himself. Yet it is for him to tell me when I may see you, and by what means. Has he nothing to say? You yourself do not speak of the matter; can it be that you no longer share my longing? Oh, Cécile, Cécile, I am very unhappy! I love you more than ever; but love, which was once all the charm of my life, is becoming its torment.

No, I can no longer live like this. I must see you, I must, if only for a moment. When I wake I say to myself, "I shall not see her." I go to bed thinking, "I did not see her." Not a moment's happiness in all the long day. All is want, regret, despair; and these evils spring from what I used to think the source of all my pleasures! If to such mortal sufferings you add my anxiety on your account, you will have some idea of my state of mind. I think of you constantly, and never without pain. When I imagine you troubled and unhappy I suffer all your griefs; when I see you comforted and at ease, my own are redoubled. Wherever I turn, I find misery.

Oh, how different it was when you lived where I did! Then all was pleasure. The certainty of seeing you brightened even the moments when you were not with me; the time I had to spend away from you brought me nearer to you as it passed. And however I spent it, you were always a part of my concerns. If I fulfilled my duties, it was to make me more worthy of you; if I cultivated my talents, it was in the hope of giving you greater pleasure. Even when the distractions of society carried me far out of your sphere, we were never apart. At the theater I tried to imagine what would please you; a concert would remind me of your talents and of our delightful times together. In company and in the street I would seize upon the slightest resemblance to you. I compared you with everything, and always to your advantage. Not a moment of the day passed without my paying you some new homage, and every evening I brought my tributes to your feet.

What remains now? Sad regrets, perpetual privation, and the faint hope that Valmont will break his silence and that yours will turn to concern. There are only ten leagues between us, a distance so easily covered, but for me it has become an insurmountable obstacle! And when I beseech my friend and my mistress to help me surmount it, both are cold and indifferent! Far from offering me assistance, they do not even reply.

What has happened to Valmont's sedulous friendship? What especially has become of the tender feelings that once prompted you to so much ingenuity in finding means for us to meet every day? I remember that sometimes, when I was by no means unwilling, I would nevertheless have to sacrifice my wishes to prudence, to duty; what did you not find to say to me then? What excuses did you not bring forward against my arguments? And, if you remember, Cécile, my arguments always yielded to your wishes. I take no credit for that: it was not even a sacrifice. Whatever you wished for, I longed to give you. But now it is I who have something to ask. And what is it, after all? To see you for a moment, to renew to you and to hear you renew our vows of everlasting love. Does this no longer seem the happiness to you that it would be to me? I put away that desperate thought, which would make my sufferings intolerable. You love me, you will always love me. I believe it, I am sure of it, I want never to doubt it. But my situation is terrible, and I cannot support it much longer. Good-bye, Cécile.

Paris
18 September 17–

LETTER 81: *The Marquise de Merteuil to the Vicomte de Valmont*

How pitiful your apprehensions are! How perfectly they prove my superiority over you! And you would like to teach me, to direct me! Oh, my poor Valmont, what a distance there still is between us! No, all the vanity of your sex cannot make up the disparity. Because you yourself would not be able to carry out my plans, you decide that they are impracticable! Weak and conceited creature, how ill it becomes you to appraise my methods or estimate my resources! Truly, Vicomte, your advice has put me out of humor and I cannot conceal it.

That in order to put a face upon your incredible clumsiness in dealing with the Présidente you flaunt, as though in triumph, your having for a moment disconcerted that poor timid woman who is in love with you – this I shall allow. That you succeeded in obtaining a look, a single look, I grant you with a smile. That conscious, in spite of yourself, of the little merit in your behavior you hope to distract my attention from it by delighting me with your transcendental effort to bring two children together, both of whom are burning to meet and who, let me say in passing, owe the ardor of their desires to me alone – that I am still willing to permit. That, lastly, you consider your brilliant accomplishment authorizes you to tell me in a magisterial tone that "one ought to spend one's time rather in carrying out plans than in talking about them" – that harmless vanity I can forgive. But that you could imagine me to be in any need of your prudence, that I should go astray were I not to defer to your opinions, that to them I must sacrifice my pleasure, my caprice – really, Vicomte, that is presuming too much upon the confidence I have been willing to place in you!

And where, after all, is the achievement of yours that I have not a thousand times surpassed? You have seduced, even ruined a great many women; but what difficulty did you have in doing so? What obstacles stood in your way? Where is the merit you can truly claim as your own? A handsome figure, which was simply the gift of fortune; the social graces that experience will nearly always confer; wit, it is true, though nonsense would do as well in a pinch; a most praiseworthy assurance, due perhaps, however, solely to the ease of your first successes. That, if I am not mistaken, is the sum of your assets. As to the celebrity you have acquired, you will not, I think, insist that I value very highly a talent for making and seizing opportunities to create scandal.

When it comes to prudence or good judgment, I leave myself out of account, but where is the woman who has not more of them than you? Pooh! Your Présidente leads you about like a child.

Believe me, Vicomte, unnecessary virtues are rarely acquired. Since you risk nothing in your battles, you take no precautions. For you men, defeat means only one victory less. In this unequal contest we are lucky not to lose, whereas you are unlucky when you do not win. Were I to grant you as many talents as we possess, how far we should still surpass you in their exercise by reason of the continual necessity of putting them to use!

I am willing to suppose that you employ as much skill in conquest as we do in defense or surrender, but you will at least agree that, once you have achieved success, skill is immaterial to you. Entirely absorbed in your new pleasure, you give yourself up to it without constraint or reserve: it is of no importance to you how long it lasts.

After all, to talk the jargon of love, promises reciprocally given and received can be made and broken at will by you alone: we are lucky if, on an impulse, you prefer secrecy to scandal, if, content with a humiliating submission, you stop short of making yesterday's idol the victim of tomorrow's sacrifice.

But when it is the unfortunate woman who first feels the weight of the chain, what risks she has to run if she tries to escape from it or even to lighten it! Only in fear and trembling can she attempt to be rid of the man her heart so violently rejects. If he is determined to remain, that which once she granted to love must be given up to fear.

Her arms are open still although her heart refuse.

Her prudence must be skillfully employed in undoing the same bonds that you would simply have broken. At the mercy of her enemy, she is without resource if he is without generosity; and how can generosity be expected of him when, though men are sometimes commended for showing it, they are, notwithstanding, never thought any less for lacking it?

You will not of course deny truths that are so evident as to be trivial. Since, then, you have seen me controlling events and opinions; turning the formidable male into the plaything of my whims and fancies; depriving some of the will and others of the power to hurt me; since I have been capable, according to the impulse of the moment, of attaching to or banishing from my train

These tyrants that I have unseated and enslaved;*

since amidst a great many vicissitudes, I have kept my reputation untarnished; should you not therefore have concluded that I, who was born to avenge my sex and master yours, have been able to discover methods of doing so unknown even to myself?

Oh, keep your warnings and your fears for those giddy women who call themselves women of *feeling*, whose heated imaginations persuade

---

*It is not known whether these lines, this one and the one that appears earlier in the letter ("Her arms are open still although her heart refuse"), are quotations from little-known works or whether they in fact form part of Madame de Merteuil's prose. What makes the latter supposition more probable is that there are innumerable lapses of the same kind throughout the letters in this collection. Only the Chevalier Danceny's are free from them, perhaps because, being an occasional reader of poetry, his more practiced ear helped him to avoid errors of taste.

them that nature has placed their senses in their heads; who, having never thought about it, invariably confuse love with a lover; who, with their stupid delusions, imagine that the man with whom they have found pleasure is pleasure's only source; and, like all the superstitious, accord to the priest the faith and respect that is due to the divinity.

Keep your fears, too, for those who are more vain than prudent and cannot, when the time comes, bear to consider being abandoned.

Tremble above all for those women whose minds are active while their bodies are idle, whom you call sensitive; who are always so easily and so powerfully moved to love; who feel they must think about it even though they don't enjoy it; who, surrendering themselves completely to the fermentation in their minds, give birth as a result to letters full of tenderness but fraught with danger; and who are not afraid to confide these proofs of their weakness to the person responsible for them – imprudent creatures who cannot see in the lover of today the enemy of tomorrow.

But I, what have I in common with these empty-headed women? When have you known me to break the rules I have laid down for myself or to betray my principles? I say "*my* principles" intentionally. They are not, like those of other women, found by chance, accepted unthinkingly, and followed out of habit. They are the fruit of profound reflection. I have created them; I might say that I have created myself.

At my entrance into society I was still a girl, condemned by my status to silence and inaction, and I made the most of my opportunities to observe and reflect. I was thought scatterbrained and absentminded: in fact, I paid little attention to what everyone was anxious to tell me, but I was careful to ponder what they sought to hide.

This useful curiosity, while it increased my knowledge, taught me to dissemble. Since I was often obliged to conceal the objects of my attention from the eyes of those around me, I tried to be able to turn my own wherever I pleased; from that time I have been able at will to assume the air of detachment you have so often admired. Encouraged by my first success, I tried in the same way to control the different expressions on my face. When I felt annoyed I practiced looking serene, even cheerful; in my enthusiasm I went so far as to suffer pain voluntarily so as to achieve a simultaneous expression of pleasure. I labored with the same care and with even more difficulty to repress symptoms of unexpected joy. In this way I was able to acquire the power over my features at which I have sometimes seen you so astonished.

I was still very young and almost without serious concerns, but since I had only my thoughts to call my own, I was indignant when anyone was able to force them from me or to surprise me against my will. Provided with my first weapons, I practiced using them; not content with being inscrutable, it amused me to assume different disguises, and once sure of my demeanor I attended to my speech. I regulated both according to circumstances, or simply as the whim took me. From that moment on, my thoughts were purely for my own benefit, and I revealed only what I found it useful to reveal.

This experiment in self-mastery led me to make a study of facial expression and of character as it is displayed in physical features. Through this I acquired that searching glance which experience has taught me not to trust entirely, but which, on the whole, has seldom deceived me.

I was only fifteen and I already possessed the talents to which most of our politicians owe their reputation, and I had as yet acquired only the elements of the science I intended to master.

As you may guess, like every other young girl I was anxious to discover love and its pleasures. But since I had never been at a convent, nor made any close friendship, and since I lived under the eye of a vigilant mother, I had only the vaguest ideas on the subject, which I was quite unable to clarify. Nature herself, with whom since then I have certainly had every reason to be satisfied, had as yet given me no sign. One might almost have said that she was working in secret to the completion of her task. My mind alone was in a ferment: I had no wish to enjoy, I wanted to know, and the desire for knowledge suggested a means of acquiring it.

I realized that the only man I could speak to upon the subject without fear of compromise was my confessor. I made my decision immediately; overcoming a slight sense of shame, I laid claim to a sin I had not committed, accusing myself of having done "everything that women do." That was the expression I used, but in using it I had in fact no idea what it might convey. My hopes were neither altogether disappointed nor altogether fulfilled. My fear of betraying myself prevented my obtaining any explanation, but the good priest made so much of the crime that I concluded the pleasure of committing it must be extreme, and my desire for knowledge gave way to a desire for gratification.

Who knows where this desire might have led me; given my lack of experience at the time, a single encounter might perhaps have been my ruin. Fortunately for me my mother announced a few days later that I was to be married. The certainty of learning before long what I wanted to know subdued my curiosity, and I proceeded a virgin into the arms of Monsieur de Merteuil.

I awaited the moment of enlightenment with confidence, and had to remind myself to show embarrassment and fear. The first night, which is generally thought of as "cruel" or "sweet," offered me only a further opportunity for experience. I took exact account of pains and pleasures, regarding my various sensations simply as facts to be collected and meditated upon.

My studies soon became a delight. But faithful to my principles and aware, perhaps by instinct, that no one should lie further from my confidence than my husband, I decided, for the very reason that I had become susceptible to pleasure, to appear in his eyes as impassive. This apparent frigidity proved later to be the unshakeable foundation of his blind trust in me. I decided in addition, after careful thought, to indulge the giddy airs my age permitted me: never did he think me more of a child than when I was most flagrantly deceiving him.

Meanwhile, I will admit, I had allowed myself to be caught up in the whirl of society and had surrendered completely to its futile distractions. But after a few months, when Monsieur de Merteuil had carried me off to his gloomy country house, fear of boredom revived my taste for study. Finding myself surrounded by people whose distance in rank from me would keep my relations with them above suspicion, I took the opportunity to enlarge my field of experience. It was here, in particular, that I confirmed the truth that love, which we praise as the source of our pleasures, is nothing more than an excuse for them.

Monsieur de Merteuil's illness came as an interruption to these agreeable preoccupations. I was obliged to follow him to town, where he went for treatment. He died a while later, as you know, and all things considered, although he had given me nothing to complain of, I nevertheless fully appreciated the value of the liberty that widowhood was about to confer upon me, and promised myself I should make good use of it.

My mother expected me to enter a convent or to return to living with her. I refused to do either; and my only concession to decency was to return to the house in the country, where I had not a few observations still to make.

These I supplemented with the aid of books: and they were not all of the kind you imagine. I studied our manners in the novelists, our opinions in the philosophers; I went to the strictest moralists to find out what they demanded of us, so as to know for certain what it was possible to do, what it was best to think, and what it was necessary to seem to be. Having reached my conclusions on all three subjects, it was only the last that presented any difficulty in practice; but that I hoped to overcome, and I meditated a means of doing so.

My bucolic pleasures, too little varied for an active mind, had begun to bore me. I felt the need of coquetry to reconcile me once more to love; not in order to feel it, of course, but in order to inspire it and to pretend inspiration. In vain had I been told and had I read that it was impossible to feign the feeling; I had already observed that to do so one had only to combine an actor's talents with a writer's wit. I cultivated both, and not without success; but instead of courting the vain applause of the theater, I decided to use for happiness what so many others sacrificed to vanity.

A year passed while I was thus variously occupied. It was then permissible for me to come out of mourning, and I returned to town with my great designs. The first obstacle I encountered there came as a surprise.

During my long term of solitude and austere retirement I had acquired a veneer of prudery that alarmed all our most agreeable gallants. They retreated and gave me up to a throng of bores, all of whom aspired to my hand. I had no difficulty in refusing them, but several of the refusals were unwelcome to my family, and I lost to domestic bickering time in which I was promised more charming pursuits. In order therefore to attract one party and repel the other, I was obliged to advertise an indiscretion or two, taking as much pains to mar my reputation as I had meant to take to preserve it. I succeeded quite easily, as you may imagine. But since I was not influenced by passion, I did only what I judged necessary, measuring out my doses of folly with a prudent hand.

As soon as I had reached my intended goal, I retraced my steps — and laid the honor of my reformation at the feet of certain of those women who, incapable of any pretensions to charm, fall back upon their merits and their virtues. This stroke of policy accomplished more for me than I had hoped. The grateful duennas set up as my apologists; and their blind enthusiasm for what they called their "charge" was carried to such a pitch that at the least suggestion of a word against me a whole battalion of prudes would cry "scandal" and "slander." The same proceeding won me as well the suffrage of our ladies with pretensions, who, convinced that I had renounced the career they pursued themselves, chose me for the object of their commendations every time they wished to prove that they did not malign everybody.

Meanwhile my previous activities had brought me lovers, and so as to steer a middle course between them and my misguided protectresses, I played the part of an impressionable but fastidious woman whose excessive delicacy was her defense against her passion.

It was then that I began to display upon the great stage the talents I had acquired for myself. My first object was to secure a reputation for being invincible. To succeed in this I contrived that the men who did not interest me were the only ones whose homage I appeared to accept. I made use of them to win me the honors of successful resistance; meanwhile I could safely yield to the lover of my choice. The timidity I pretended, however, would not permit of his following me into society, so that at all times it was an unhappy lover who caught the attention of my circle of acquaintance.

You know how quickly I come to decisions. It is because I have noted that it is nearly always preliminary deliberations that betray a woman's secret. In spite of all one can do, one's manner is never quite the same before the event as after. This difference never escapes the attentive observer; and I have found it less dangerous to choose wrong than to be found out in my choice. There is an added advantage to this, in that it offers no basis for the likely assumptions that alone enable others to judge us.

These precautions, together with those of never writing letters and never providing evidence of my defeat, may seem excessive, but to me they never seemed enough. I searched the depths of my heart for clues to the hearts of others. I observed that there is no one without a secret that it is in his interest never to reveal: a truth that antiquity seems to have known better than we do, and of which the story of Samson might be no more than an ingenious allegory. A latter-day Delilah, I have always devoted all my powers, as she did, to springing the important secret. Oh, I have my scissors to the hair of a great many of our modern Samsons! Of them I am no longer afraid; and they are the only men I have sometimes allowed myself to humiliate. With the others I am more pliant: skill in making them unfaithful to me so as to avoid appearing fickle myself, a pretense of friendship, a show of confidence, a few generous gestures, and the flattering idea each one is made to entertain of being my only lover – such contrivances ensure that they will be discreet. In the last resort, when all else has failed, I have always, foreseeing the end, been able in good time to destroy, under ridicule or contempt, whatever credence these dangerous men may have been able to obtain.

I speak now of what you see me doing all the time, and yet you doubt my prudence! Well! Call to mind the time when you first favored me with your attentions. No homage ever flattered me more. I desired you before I had seen you. Your reputation so impressed me that it seemed that only you could bring me glory. I longed to measure swords with you. This is the only one of my desires that has ever for a moment gained sway over me. Yet had you wanted to ruin my reputation, with what could you have done it? Mere talk, which had left no trace behind it, whose authenticity your own reputation would have helped to render suspect; and a series of improbable events, a faithful account of which would have sounded like a bad novel? It is true that I have since surrendered all my secrets to you: but you are aware of the interests that unite us, and you know quite well whether, of the two of us, it is I who deserved to be taxed with imprudence.*

Since I have begun to justify myself, I may as well do it thoroughly. Even at this distance I can hear you say that I am, in any case, at the mercy of my chambermaid: after all, though she cannot read my feelings, my actions are an open book to her. When you spoke of this once before I replied merely that I was sure of her; and the proof that this was enough to satisfy you at the time is that you have confided in her since then for your own purposes, letting her in on some fairly dangerous secrets. But now that you have lost your head in your annoyance at Prévan, I very much doubt that you will still take me at my word. I shall therefore be more explicit.

First of all, this girl and I were nursed at the same breast, and while you and I do not regard this as establishing a connection, it is a consideration of some weight with people of her class. Moreover, I know her secret. Better still, she was at one time the victim of some disastrous amour, and would have been lost had I not saved her. Her parents, bristling with outraged honor, wanted her locked away, nothing less. They approached me. One glance told me how useful their wrath could be. I gave it my support and applied for an order of arrest, which I obtained. Then, with a sudden shift of ground from severity to mercy, to which I persuaded the parents too, I turned my credit with the old minister to advantage and made them all agree to leave the order in my hands, with the power to cancel it or demand its execution, according to my judgment of the girl's future conduct. She knows, then, that her fate is in my keeping; and if the impossible happens and she defies these considerations, is it not obvious that her past, when it is revealed – not to speak of the punishment she must suffer – will deprive whatever she says of all credibility?

Such precautions, which I think of as fundamental, involve according to time and place a thousand others that practice and reflection supply at need. An account of them would be tedious, notwithstanding

---

*In a subsequent letter (152) the reader will learn not Monsieur de Valmont's secret but its nature, more or less, and will appreciate why it was not possible to enter here into fuller explanations upon the subject.

their importance, and I must put you to the trouble of studying the whole of my conduct if you wish to achieve a knowledge of them all.

But to expect that I should have gone to so much trouble only to refrain from seizing my rewards; that, having raised myself by painful effort above other women, I should now consent to creep along as they do between prudence on the one hand and timidity on the other; that above all I should be so afraid of a man as to see no safety anywhere but in flight. No, Vicomte, never. Conquer or perish. As for Prévan, I want him, and I shall have him; he will want to be able to say so, and he shall not say so. There, in two sentences, you have our story. Good-bye.

_____

20 September 17–

LETTER 82 : *Cécile Volanges to the Chevalier Danceny*

Dear God, how your letter has upset me! And to think that I was so impatient to receive it! I hoped to find comfort in it, and now I am sorrier than ever I was before I had it. I cried so much as I read it; but it is not for that I blame you. I have often cried on your account without it distressing me. But this time it is not at all the same.

What do you mean when you say that love has become a torment for you, that you can no longer live like this or endure your situation any longer? Are you going to stop loving me because it is no longer as pleasant as it used to be? It seems to me that I am no happier than you are, quite the contrary; and yet I love you all the more. If Monsieur de Valmont has not written to you, it is not my fault; I have not been able to ask him, because I have not been alone with him at all, and because we agreed that we would never speak to each other in company. That too was for your sake, so that he could the sooner do what you wish. I am not saying that I do not want it too; you surely don't doubt that – but what do you expect me to do? If you think it is easy to know, tell me: I could ask for nothing better.

Do you think it is so very agreeable for me to be grumbled at every day by Mamma, who at one time never said anything to me at all? On the contrary. At the moment it is worse here than it would be at the convent. I have been consoling myself, thinking that it was for you; there were even moments when I found I was very pleased that it was so. But when I discover that you are angry too, without it being in any way my fault, it makes me more unhappy than anything that has ever happened to me before.

Simply to receive your letters creates difficulties, and if Monsieur de Valmont were not as obliging and as clever as he is, I should not know what to do; writing to you is even more difficult. I dare not do so in the morning since Mamma's room is very near mine and she is likely to come in at any time; but I can sometimes do so in the afternoon, on the pretext of wanting to sing or play the harp. Even so, I have to break off at every line so as to be heard practicing. Fortunately my maid sometimes falls off to sleep of an evening and I tell her I am quite willing to prepare for bed without her, so that she goes away and leaves me the light. And then I have to hide behind the bed curtains so that no one will notice the light, and then listen for the slightest noise so that I can hide everything in the bed should anyone come. I wish you could be there to see! You would immediately realize that one must be really in love to be able to do such things. At any rate, it is certainly true that I do all I can, and that I wish I could do more.

Of course I don't refuse to tell you that I love you, and that I shall love you always. Never have I said that more from my heart. Yet you are angry! And once you assured me, before I had said anything at all, that those words would be enough to make you happy. You cannot deny it, it is in your letters. Although I no longer have them, I remember them as well as if I read them over every day. And because we are now separated you no longer feel the same way! But this separation will not last forever, will it? Dear God, how unhappy I am! And it is you who are to blame!...

Speaking of your letters, I hope you have kept the ones that Mamma took away and then returned to you. There will certainly come a time when I am not so persecuted as at present and you will give them all back to me. How happy I shall be when I am able to keep them forever without anyone minding! For the moment I return your letters to Monsieur de Valmont as they come, because I should be risking too much otherwise: nonetheless, I never give them back to him without the most painful regrets.

Good-bye, my dear. I love you with all my heart. I shall love you all my life. I hope you are no longer angry now; if I were sure you were not, I should no longer be angry myself. Write to me as soon as you can, for till then I know I shall continue to be sad.

Château de ————
21 September 17–

LETTER 83: *The Vicomte de Valmont to the Présidente de Tourvel*
For pity's sake, Madame, let us take up the conversation again that was

so unfortunately interrupted! That I could succeed in proving to you how different I am from the hateful picture you have painted of me; that, above all, I could enjoy once more the friendly confidence you had begun to show toward me! What a charm you are able to give to virtue! What beauty and what value you confer upon all the decent feelings! Ah, that is the secret of your fascination: the most powerful kind, and the only one that is at the same time both potent and respectable.

Merely to see you, of course, is to desire to please you; to hear you speak in society swells that desire. But he who is so fortunate as to know you better, he to whom it is sometimes given to read your heart, soon yields to a nobler enthusiasm, and, imbued as much with reverence as with love, worships in you the image of all the virtues. I, who am perhaps by nature more than usually apt to love those virtues and be guided by them, was misled by certain misapprehensions into turning away from them. It is you who have recalled me, you who have made me conscious again of all their charm; will you turn this new devotion into a crime? Will you condemn your own handiwork? Will you reproach yourself for taking an interest in it? What is there to fear in so pure a feeling, and what sweetness might there not be in tasting it?

My love frightens you, you find it violent, unbridled! Temper it then with more gentle feelings; do not refuse the power I offer you, which I swear I shall never renounce, and which, I venture to believe, will not be entirely useless to the cause of virtue. What sacrifice would I find too painful were I certain that your heart appreciated its worth? Is there a man so unfortunate that he cannot enjoy the restraint he imposes upon himself, that he does not prefer a word, a look willingly granted to all the pleasures he can snatch by force or surprise? And you thought me such a man! You were afraid of me! Ah, if only your happiness depended on me! How I should avenge myself upon you in making you happy! But barren friendship cannot engender so sweet a power; it is only love that can.

That word intimidates you! Why? It means a more tender attachment, perhaps, a closer intimacy, the sharing of thoughts, of the same happiness and the same pain, but what is there in that so foreign to your nature? And love is no more than that – the love, in any case, that you inspire and that I feel! A love that more than anything is disinterested in its judgments, appreciating an action for its merit rather than for its value. It is the inexhaustible treasure of sensitive souls. Everything becomes precious that is fashioned by it or for it.

These truths being so easy to grasp, and so pleasant to confirm in practice, what do you fear? How, besides, can you possibly be afraid of a man of feeling whose love allows him no happiness unless it be yours? That is now the only vow I am bound to: I shall sacrifice everything to it, except the feeling by which it is inspired. And even this feeling, if you consent to share it, you will dispose of as you choose. But let us no longer suffer it to separate us, when it ought to bring us together. If the friendship you have offered me is any more than an empty word; if, as you told me yesterday, it is the tenderest feeling known to your heart; let that feeling then arbitrate between us, and I shall not dispute its decision. But if it is to pass judgment upon love, it must allow love a hearing; to refuse would be an injustice, and friendship is never unjust.

A second meeting would not be more difficult to arrange than was the first; chance may again furnish an opportunity; you yourself might indicate a suitable moment. I should like to think that I am wrong; would you not prefer to subdue me than to struggle against me, and can you doubt my docility? If that importunate third party had not arrived to interrupt us, perhaps I should already be entirely converted to your opinion; who knows how far your power may extend?

Shall I tell you? Sometimes your unconquerable supremacy, to which I yield without daring to consider its scope, your irresistible charm, which makes you empress of my thoughts and actions alike, make me afraid for myself. Alas, the interview for which I ask is perhaps of more danger to me than you! Afterward it may be that, chained to my promises, I shall find myself reduced to being consumed by a love that I know will never die, without even the right to implore your help! Ah, Madame, for pity's sake do not abuse your power! But then – if it makes you happier, if it makes me seem worthier of you, that alone will console me for any amount of suffering! Yes, I know. To speak to you again would be to give you more powerful weapons against me; it would be to surrender myself more completely to your will. It is safer to defend myself against your letters; they are of course your own pronouncements, but you are not there to give them authority. Yet the pleasure it will be to hear you speak makes me willing to brave the danger. At least I shall have the satisfaction of having done everything for you, even against my own interest, and my sacrifices shall be part of my homage. I shall be only too fortunate if I can prove to you in the thousand different ways I feel it that, without excepting myself, you are and will always be what is dearest to my heart.

Château de ————
23 September 17–

LETTER 84: *The Vicomte de Valmont to Cécile Volanges*

You saw how everything went against us yesterday. I was unable the whole day to give you the letter I had for you; I do not know whether I shall find it any easier today. I am afraid of compromising you by my efforts, should they be more eager than discreet. I should never forgive myself for an imprudence that would be fatal to you and in making you unhappy forever, throw my friend into despair. I know, nevertheless, the impatience of love; I know how painful it must be, in your situation, to experience any delay in receiving the only consolation you can hope for at the moment. By dint of constant reflection upon ways and means of removing the obstacles in our path, I have found one that will be easy to execute if you are willing to devote some pains to it.

I seem to have noticed that the key to the door of your room, which gives on to the corridor, is always kept upon your mama's mantelpiece. With that key in our possession everything would be easy, as you will agree; but even without it, I can procure you a duplicate that will serve just as well. To do so it will be sufficient for me to have the original at my disposal for no longer than an hour or two. You will have no difficulty in finding an opportunity to remove it, and in case it is seen to be missing, I enclose with this a key of mine which resembles it enough for the difference not to be discovered, unless it is tried in the lock; but no one will do that. Only be sure that you attach a faded blue ribbon to it like the one that is tied to yours.

You must try to have the key by tomorrow, or the day after tomorrow at breakfast time. It will be much easier for you to give it to me then, and you will be able to return it to its place before evening, the time when your mama is most likely to give it her attention. I shall be able to give it back to you at dinner, if we can come to a suitable understanding about this.

You know that when we leave the drawing room for the dining room it is always Madame de Rosemonde who comes last. I shall give her my arm. You have only to be a little longer than usual in putting away your tapestry, or else to drop something, so as to remain behind. You will then find it easy to take the key from me – I shall be careful to hold it behind my back. You must not forget, as soon as you have the key, to go over to my old aunt with some show of affection. If by any chance you drop the key, you will not be disconcerted; I shall pretend that it was I who did so, and you may rely upon me absolutely to carry it off.

This little trick is more than justified by the meager confidence your mama shows in you, and the very severe measures she has taken against you. Apart from that, it is the only means by which you can continue to receive Danceny's letters and to send him yours; all others are really too dangerous and might, in betraying you both, leave you without recourse, so that my prudence as a friend cannot allow you to make any further use of them.

Once we are in possession of the key, there will still be a few precautions to take against the noise made by the door and the lock – but that will be very easy. Under the same cupboard in which I put your writing paper you will find some oil and a feather. You will, some time when you are alone, go to your room and take the opportunity to oil the lock and hinges. Your only care must be not to leave any stains as evidence against you. You must also wait until nightfall, because, if this is done as cleverly as you are capable of doing it, no traces will appear the following morning.

If, however, anything is noticed, do not hesitate to say that one of the servants was responsible. In this case it will be necessary to specify a time and even what he said to you – for example, that he was taking precautions against rust and was attending in this way to all the locks that were not ordinarily in use. As you must see, it is not very likely that you would have witnessed the business without asking for an explanation. It is these little details that give verisimilitude to a lie, and verisimilitude ensures that there will be no consequences, since it deprives people of the desire to verify what they are told.

When you have read this letter, please reread it and even think about it – in the first place because, to do anything well, one must always be thoroughly prepared; then to make sure that I have left nothing out. I am little accustomed to using cunning on my own behalf, and I am not much practiced in it. It has taken nothing less than my keen friendship for Danceny, and the interest you arouse in me, to make me decide upon employing such methods, however innocent they may be. I detest everything that savors of deception; that, in brief, is my character. But I have been so touched by your misfortunes that I shall attempt anything to mitigate them.

As you may well imagine, once communication is established between us, it will be much easier for me to arrange, on your and Danceny's behalf, the meeting he desires. Do not, however, tell him anything of this as yet. You will only increase his impatience, and the time to satisfy it has not yet quite come. You owe it to him, I think, to allay rather than to sharpen his anxieties. But in this matter I rely upon your delicacy. Good-bye, my dear pupil – for you are my pupil, you know. I hope you will like your tutor a little, above all that you will be guided by him; you will not regret it. Your happiness is my concern, and you may be certain that in it I shall find my own.

————

24 September 17–

LETTER 85: *The Marquise de Merteuil to the Vicomte de Valmont*
Now you may set your mind at rest; now, above all, you may do me justice. Listen, and never again put me on a par with other women. I have brought my adventure with Prévan to a conclusion; *to a conclusion!* Do you quite understand what that means? Now you may judge which of us, he or I, will be able to boast. The story will not be as amusing as was the event, but then it would be unfair if you, who have done nothing in this affair but argue, were to derive as much pleasure from it as I, who have given it all my time and energy.

However, if you are planning some great *coup*, if you have some enterprise in hand in which Prévan is to figure as the dangerous rival, now is the time. He leaves the field to you, for a while at least. He will perhaps never recover at all from the blow I have dealt him.

How lucky you are to have me for a friend! I am the good fairy in your story. You languish far from the beauty who has engaged your heart: I say the word and you are again at her side. You want to be avenged upon a woman who has injured you; I find the weak spot where the blow must fall, and deliver her up to your tender mercies. Finally, when you have to remove a formidable opponent from the lists, it is again I you invoke in your prayers, and I who fulfill your wishes. Indeed, if you do not spend the rest of your life giving me thanks I shall think you ungrateful. But I must return to my adventure and begin from the beginning.

The hint of a rendezvous I had made so loudly at the exit of the opera* was understood, as I had hoped it would be. Prévan was there; and when the Maréchale said politely that she congratulated herself upon seeing him twice in succession at her evenings, he took care to reply that since Tuesday night he had put off a hundred engagements so as to be free to come. (A word to the wise is enough!) Since, however, I wished to be more certain whether or not I was indeed the object of this flattering impatience, I decided I would force the new suitor to make a choice between me and his ruling passion. I announced that I would not sit down to cards; and, as it happened, he too discovered a

————

*See Letter 74.

hundred excuses for not playing, so that it was over lansquenet[11] that I scored my first triumph.

I took possession of the Bishop of —— —— to talk to, choosing him because of his friendship with the hero of the day, whom I wished to afford every facility of approach. I was, besides, very glad to have a respectable witness to vouch, if need be, for my words and deeds. My plan succeeded.

After the customary generalities Prévan, who soon took control of the conversation, gave it a succession of different turns to see which would please me. I rejected sentiment as having no faith in it; gaiety I checked with gravity because it seemed to me too frivolous for a beginning. He was reduced to tactful friendship, and it was under this faded old flag that we joined in battle.

The bishop did not go down to supper; Prévan accordingly gave me his arm, and was of course placed beside me at table. I must give him his due; with great skill he kept up our private conversation while appearing to give all his attention to the general one, of which indeed he seemed to be bearing the entire burden.

At dessert it was mentioned that a new play was to be performed at the Français the following Monday. I expressed a regret that I had not my box for that night. He offered me his, which to begin with I refused, as one does. To which he replied, amusingly enough, that I had not understood him: he most certainly would not have sacrificed his box to someone he did not know; he meant simply to inform me that it was at Madame the Maréchale's disposal. She fell in with the joke, and I accepted.

We returned to the drawing room, whereupon, as you will readily believe, he requested a seat in the box for himself; and since the Maréchale, who is very kindly disposed toward him, promised him one "if he were good," he made this an occasion for one of those conversations with a double meaning, his talent for which you have yourself extolled. In fact, he went down on his knees like an obedient child – as he put it – and while ostensibly he was asking her what she meant and beseeching her to explain, he said a great many flattering and quite tender things, which I was able without difficulty to apply to myself. Since several of the company had not returned to cards after supper, conversation became more general and less interesting; but our eyes spoke volumes. I say our eyes. I should have said his, for in mine he could read only one meaning: surprise. He must have thought he had astounded me, and that I was excessively taken up with the prodigious effect he had wrought upon me. I left him, I think, very satisfied; I was not less so myself.

The following Monday I went to the Français as arranged. I know you are interested in literary matters, but I can tell you nothing about the performance except that Prévan is a marvelously talented flatterer and that the piece was a failure: that is all I was able to learn. I was sorry to see the evening come to an end, I had enjoyed it so much, and to prolong it I invited the Maréchale to supper with me; this provided me with a pretext for putting the same proposal to my amiable cavalier, who asked only time enough to fly to the Comtesses de B——* and make his excuses there. The sound of that name roused all my resentment. I saw clearly that he was going to begin making confidences. I remembered your wise advice, and resolved...to continue the adventure. I was certain I would cure him of such dangerous indiscretions in future.

A stranger among my friends, of whom there were not many present that evening, he was obliged to pay me all the customary attentions; thus, when we went into supper, he offered me his arm. Accepting it, I was wicked enough to make my hand tremble lightly in his and, as we walked, to lower my eyes and quicken my breathing, as if in presentiment of my defeat and awe of my conqueror. He was so quick to notice this that in a trice he had treacherously changed his tone and demeanor. He had been gallant, he became tender. Not that he changed the substance of his remarks – circumstances saw to that. But his looks became less lively and more caressing, the inflection of his voice more soft; his smile no longer calculated but contented. Finally, having removed the sting by degrees from his sallies, he turned quips into compliments. I ask you: Could you have done better yourself?

As for me, I grew pensive, so much so that the company was obliged to notice it; and when they rallied me I was clever enough to make a very poor excuse, throwing Prévan a quick, but timid and bashful glance calculated to make him believe that it was only he I was afraid might guess the cause of my uneasiness.

After supper the Maréchale began one of the stories she is always telling, and I took the opportunity of arranging myself on the ottoman in that attitude of abandon which befits a mood of reverie. I was not averse to Prévan seeing me like this, and in fact he honored me with his most particular attention. As you may imagine, my timid glances did not dare to seek those of my conqueror; but, directed toward him in a humble way, they soon told me that I had succeeded in the effect I wished to produce. I had still to persuade him that I shared his feelings. Accord-

---

*See Letter 70.

ingly, when the Maréchale announced that she was leaving, I exclaimed in soft and tender tones: "Oh, lord! I was so comfortable there!" I got up, all the same; but before we parted I asked the Maréchale what her plans were, so I could tell her mine and make it known that I should be at home not the day after but the next. After this everyone took their leave.

I then sat down to reflect. I had no doubt that Prévan would make the most of the sort of rendezvous I had given him, that he would arrive early enough to find me alone, and that the attack would be a fierce one. But I was quite sure, too, that, aware of my reputation, he would not treat me with that indifference which men display, if they ever do, only toward adventuresses and boobies; I foresaw certain success if he should so much as pronounce the word "love" – and, especially if he should make any attempt at obtaining it from me.

How easy it is to deal with your *men of principles*! A muddle-headed lover will sometimes disconcert you with his timidity, or embarrass you with his furious transports; he is in a fever, which like any other has its agues and its ardors and sometimes varies its symptoms. But your well-planned advances are too predictable! Manner of arrival, behavior, attitude, choice of language – I knew about them all the evening before. I shall not therefore give you the details of our conversation, which you may easily supply for yourself. Note only that by a pretense of reluctance I did all I could to help him – offering embarrassment to give him time to speak; poor arguments to be refuted; fear and distrust to call up his protestations together with that perpetual refrain of "I ask for no more than a word"; silence in reply to the latter, which it seemed would have him wait for what he wanted, only to make him desire it the more; and all the while a hand taken a hundred times, and a hundred times withdrawn but never refused. One could spend a whole day at this: we continued for one mortal hour and would perhaps still be at it were it not for the carriage we heard entering my courtyard. This fortunate accident quite understandably made him more eager in his entreaties; and knowing that I was now safe from surprise, I prepared myself with a long-drawn sigh and yielded up the precious word. Someone was announced, and shortly afterward we were in the midst of a fairly numerous company.

Prévan asked whether he could come the following morning, and I agreed; but, with an eye to my defenses, I ordered my maid to remain in my bedroom throughout the period of his visit. As you know, everything that happens in my dressing room is visible from there, and it was in my dressing room that I received him. We talked frankly, and since we had but one desire in common, soon came to an agreement. It was necessary, however, to get rid of an unwelcome spectator; and here I was ready for him.

Painting him an imaginary picture of my domestic life, I had no difficulty in persuading him that we should never have a moment's liberty; that the opportunity we had enjoyed the day before could only be regarded as a kind of miracle; and that, even so, the risks involved had been too great, since at any moment anyone could have entered the drawing room. I did not fail to add that my domestic arrangements were thus established because they had never till now been in my way; at the same time I insisted that it would be impossible to change them without compromising myself in the eyes of my household. He tried to look dejected, to work himself into a bad temper, to tell me that I could not love him very much; and you can imagine how touched I was by all this! So as to strike the decisive blow, I summoned tears to my support. It was exactly like "Zaïre, are you weeping?" The power he imagined he had over me, and the hopes he had conceived of ruining me at his pleasure, did duty with him for all Orosmane's love.[12]

This dramatic scene having been concluded, we returned to business. Daytime being out of the question, we considered the possibilities of night. But my porter proved to be an insurmountable obstacle, and I was not willing that we should try to bribe him. The little garden gate was suggested, but this I had foreseen, and I created a dog that, although docile and quiet during the day, became a veritable demon at night. The readiness with which I supplied all these details was exactly the thing to provoke him to recklessness, and when he came to suggest the most ridiculous expedient possible, it was this to which I agreed.

He said first that his manservant was as trustworthy as he was himself. This was no lie: I trusted one quite as much as the other. I was to give a large supper at my house; he would be there, and would choose a convenient moment to leave by himself. The clever confidant would call his carriage and open the door; and he, Prévan, instead of getting in, would adroitly make away. His coachman would notice nothing. Thus, while everyone would think he had left, he would still be in the house, and it was merely a question of knowing how he might reach my room. I must confess that my difficulty at first was to think of weak enough objections to this plan, so that he could appear to be destroying them. He quoted, in reply, instances of its previous use. To hear him talk, one would have thought nothing was more commonplace. He himself had employed it a great deal, more often indeed — because it was less dangerous — than any other.

Overborne by so much unchallengeable authority, I admitted candidly that I did indeed have a concealed staircase that emerged very near my boudoir. I could leave the key in the door, and he could lock himself in and wait, without much risk, until my women had left me. Then, in order to make my consent more credible, I withdrew it a moment later, and refused to grant it again except on condition of perfect obedience and discretion... Ah, such discretion! In short, I was quite willing to prove my love without satisfying his.

His exit, I have forgotten to tell you, was to be made through the little garden gate. It was simply a question of waiting till daybreak, after which time Cerberus would utter no sound. Not a soul passes by at that hour, and at that hour people are soundest asleep. In case you are surprised at this string of feeble arguments, don't forget the nature of the situation between us. What need had we to do better? His whole aim was that everything should be discovered, whereas I was quite certain that it would not. The day was fixed for two days later.

Note well that the whole affair had been arranged without anyone having seen Prévan alone with me. I meet him at supper at the house of a friend; he offers her his box for a new play, and I accept a place in it. During the performance, and in front of Prévan, I invite this woman to supper – it is almost impossible to avoid suggesting that he join us. He accepts, and two days later he pays me the visit that custom demands. True, he comes to see me again the following morning; but, apart from the fact that morning visits are no longer exceptional, it is for no one but me to decide that this one is a little excessive – and in fact I later put him back among that class of people who are less intimate with me by a written invitation to a formal supper. Well might I say with Annette:[13] "There is no more to it than that, really!"

When the fateful day arrived, the day upon which I was to lose my virtue and my reputation, I gave my faithful Victoire her instructions, and she carried them out as you shall see.

Evening came. There were already a great many people with me when Prévan was announced. I received him with marked politeness, emphasizing the small extent of my intimacy with him, and put him to play at the Maréchale's table, since she was the person through whom I had made his acquaintance. The only incident of the evening concerned a little note that my discreet lover found it possible to put into my hands; I burned it immediately, as is my custom. In it he declared that I could count on him; this vital phrase was, however, buried in a mass of those parasite words, love, happiness, etc., which invariably proliferate on this sort of occasion.

At midnight, play having come to an end, I suggested a short *macé-doine*.* My twofold intention was to provide Prévan with a favorable opportunity to escape, and at the same time to make sure that he would be noticed, which could scarcely fail to happen considering his renown as a gambler. I was content as well to have it remembered when necessary that I had not been anxious to be left alone.

Play lasted longer than I expected. The devil tempted me – and I succumbed to the temptation – to go and console my impatient prisoner. I was thus on the path to destruction when it occurred to me that, once I had completely surrendered, I should no longer have sufficient power over him to keep him to that appearance of decency so necessary to my plans. I found the strength to resist: I turned back and took my place again, not altogether without annoyance, at the endless card game. Finally, however, it did come to an end and everyone left. I rang for my maids, undressed with all speed, and sent them away too.

Can you see me, Vicomte, in my simple negligee, approaching with timid and circumspect tread, opening the door with an uncertain hand to my conqueror? He saw me. Lightning could not have struck quicker. What more shall I tell you? I was vanquished, utterly vanquished, before I had been able to say a word to stop him or to defend myself. He wanted us next to dispose ourselves more comfortably, and more suitably to the circumstances. He cursed his clothes, which, he said, put him at a disadvantage. He wanted us to fight on equal terms. But my extreme timidity opposed the project, and my tender caresses left him no time to carry it out. He occupied himself with other things.

Possessed now of twice his former rights, he revived his claims. "Listen," I said then. "So far I have given you an amusing enough story to tell the two Comtesses de B—— and a thousand others; but I am curious to know what conclusion you will find to put to it." As I spoke I rang as hard as I could. Now it was I who had the advantage, and my action was more effective than anything he could say. He had done no more than stammer before I heard Victoire come running, calling to the servants she had kept with her as I had commanded. At this point, raising my voice, and in my most regal tone I continued, "You will leave, Monsieur, and never appear in my presence again" – at which a crowd of my servants entered the room.

Poor Prévan lost his head and, suspecting an ambush in what was at

---

*Some readers may perhaps be unaware that a *macédoine* is a medley of several games of chance from among which each player has the right to choose when it is his turn to deal. It is one of the novelties of our day.

bottom no more than a joke, resorted to his sword – unfortunately for him, since my brave and vigorous *valet de chambre* seized him bodily and threw him to the floor. This, I must confess, put me into mortal terror. I shouted to them both to stop, and ordered all the servants to let Prévan alone, provided they made sure that he left the house. They obeyed; but there was great wagging of tongues. They were most indignant that anyone should fail in respect to *their virtuous mistress*. They accompanied the unfortunate cavalier out in a body with much noise and crying of scandal, just as I wished. Only Victoire remained behind. We spent the interval in putting my disordered bed to rights.

The servants came up again, still in an uproar, and I, still *very much upset*, asked them by what lucky chance it had happened that they were awake. Victoire told me that she had given supper to two of her friends, that they had spent the evening with her – in short, all that had been agreed upon between us. I thanked them all and dismissed them, ordering one of them, however, to fetch my doctor immediately. It seemed to me that I ought to fear for the consequences of the terrible shock I had received; and this was a certain means of ensuring circulation and celebrity for the news.

The doctor at length came, felt very sorry for me, and prescribed rest. I gave further orders to Victoire to go out early in the morning, perambulate the neighborhood, and talk.

Everything succeeded so well that before midday, as soon in fact as my curtains were drawn, my devoted neighbor was at my bedside to hear the true details of my ghastly adventure. I was obliged to join with her for an hour in deploring the corruption of the age. Shortly after, I received a note from the Maréchale, which I enclose. Lastly, just before five o'clock, to my great astonishment, I saw Monsieur ———* arrive. He had come, he said, to offer his excuses for the fact that one of his officers could have behaved so insultingly. It was not till he dined with the Maréchale that he had learned of the affair, and he had forthwith issued orders for Prévan to be conveyed to prison. I asked for a pardon, but he refused. Then it occurred to me that, as an accomplice, I ought to pass like sentence upon myself, and at least confine myself strictly to quarters. I ordered my doors to be shut and announced that I was unwell.

It is to my solitude that you owe this long letter. I shall now write one to Madame de Volanges, who is sure to read it out in company, whereupon you will hear the story again as adapted for publication.

I was forgetting to tell you that Belleroche is outraged and is abso-

---

*The commanding officer of the regiment in which Monsieur de Prévan served.

lutely determined to challenge Prévan. Poor fellow! Fortunately there will be time enough to cool him down. Meanwhile I must rest: I am tired out with writing. Good-bye, Vicomte.

Château de ———
25 September 17–, evening

LETTER 86: *The Maréchale de* ——— *to the Marquise de Merteuil*
(note attached to the preceding letter)
Good God! What is this I hear, my dear Madame? Can our little Prévan possibly have committed such abominations? And against you, no less! To what dangers one is exposed! One shall never be safe, after all, in one's own home! Truly, such goings-on console me for being old. What nothing could console me for, however, is that I have been in some part the cause of your having received this monster into your house. I assure you that if what I am told is true he shall never again set foot over my threshold; and that is the course all decent people will take with him if they know their duty.

I was told that you were feeling very ill, and I am anxious for your health. Please give me better news of yourself, or send one of your maids if you cannot do so yourself. I ask only for a word to set my mind at rest. I would have come immediately to your house this morning were it not for the baths that my doctor will not suffer me to interrupt; and this afternoon I must go back to Versailles on my nephew's business.

Good-bye, my dear Madame. You may always count upon my most sincere friendship.

Paris
25 September 17–

LETTER 87: *The Marquise de Merteuil to Madame de Volanges*
I am writing to you from bed, my dear good friend. A most disagreeable and utterly unforeseen incident has made me ill with shock and mortification.

Not, of course, that I have anything upon my conscience; but it is always, for a respectable woman, and one who maintains the modesty becoming to her sex, so painful to have the public eye fixed upon her, that I should give anything in the world to have avoided this unhappy experience, and I am not sure yet whether I shall not remove to the country to wait until it is all forgotten. This is what happened.

At the Maréchale de ———'s I met a Monsieur de Prévan, whom

you probably know by name and who was not known to me in any other wise. Meeting him where I did, I was quite justified, it seems to me, in believing him to be a man of breeding. As to his person, he is quite presentable, and he appeared not to lack a certain wit. By chance, and because I was bored with cards, I found myself alone with him and the Bishop of ———, while everybody else was occupied at lansquenet. The three of us talked till supper time. At table some discussion of a new piece was the occasion for his offering his box to the Maréchale, who accepted it; and it was agreed that I should have a place in it. This was for last Monday, at the Français. Since the Maréchale was coming to supper with me after the performance, I suggested to the gentle-man that he accompany her, and he came. Two days later he paid me a visit which passed in polite conversation and gave rise to nothing at all remarkable. The following day he came to see me in the morning, which did indeed appear to me a little untoward: but I thought that instead of making him aware of it by the manner in which I received him, I ought rather to let him know by some act of formality that we were not yet as intimately acquainted as he seemed to think. To this end I sent him, that same day, a very cold and ceremonious invitation to the supper I gave the day before yesterday. I addressed him not four times during the whole evening, and he, for his part, left as soon as play was over. You will agree that nothing so far would seem to have been leading up to an incident. When the tables had broken up we had a *macédoine* that lasted till nearly two o'clock, and at length I went to bed.

It was at least half an hour after my maids had left me that I heard a noise in my room. I opened the curtains in a great fright, and saw a man come in by the door that led from my boudoir. I uttered a piercing scream. In the glow of my night light I recognized this Monsieur de Prévan. He had the unspeakable effrontery to tell me not to be alarmed, said he would explain his mysterious behavior, and begged me to make no noise. As he spoke he lit a candle. I was paralyzed to the point of not being able to speak. His air of ease and confidence I think petri-fied me still more. But he had not said two words before I had pene-trated the so-called mystery. My only response was, as you can imagine, to hang on the bell rope.

By unbelievable good fortune all my servants were spending the evening with one of my maids and had not yet gone to bed. My cham-bermaid, having answered my call, and hearing me speak heatedly to someone, took alarm and summoned all the others. I leave you to imag-ine the outcry! My servants were furious; at one moment I thought my

valet de chambre would kill Prévan. I confess that, at the time, I was
very glad to have my supporters rally round me; thinking of it now, I
had rather only my chambermaid had come. She would have served my
purpose, and I should perhaps have avoided this distressing scandal.

As it is, the noise awoke my neighbors, the servants have talked, and
since yesterday the affair has been the gossip of Paris. Monsieur de
Prévan is in prison by order of the commanding officer of his regiment,
who was so civil as to call on me, to offer his excuses, he said. The
imprisonment is going to make even more of a sensation: but I was not
able to have it otherwise. Town and court have begun to leave their
names at my door, which I have closed to everyone. The few people I
see tell me that justice is being done me and that public indignation is
running high against Monsieur de Prévan. Of course he deserves it, but
that does not make the incident any less disagreeable.

Moreover, the man surely has friends, friends who are bound to bear
malice: who knows, who can possibly know what they will invent to
say against me? Heavens, how unfortunate a young woman is! She has
achieved nothing when she has put herself beyond criticism; she must
protect herself from calumny, too.

Tell me, please, what you would have done, what you would do in
my place; in short, all your thoughts on the subject. It is always from
you that I have received the sweetest consolation and the best advice;
it is from you, too, that I like best to receive it. Good-bye, my dear and
good friend. You know the feelings by which I am forever attached to
you. My love to your charming daughter.

Paris
26 September 17–

Part Three

LETTER 88: *Cécile Volanges to the Vicomte de Valmont*
In spite of the pleasure it is to me, Monsieur, to receive Monsieur the
Chevalier Danceny's letters, and although it is no less my wish than his
that we should meet again without any hindrance, I have still not dared
to do as you suggest. To begin with, it is too dangerous. The key you
wish me to exchange for the other one does indeed look very much
like it; but there is nevertheless a difference, and Mamma looks at everything and notices everything. What is more, though the key has not been
used since we have been here, no more than some slight mischance
would be needed – and if anything were noticed I should be lost for-

ever. And then, it seems to me, too, that it would be a very bad thing to do; to make a duplicate key like that is really going too far! True, it is you who will be so kind as to be responsible for it; but in spite of that, if it were found out, the fault and the blame would be no less mine than yours, since it would be for me that you had done it. Lastly, on two occasions I did decide to try and remove the key; I am sure it would have been very easy had it been anything else, but – I don't know why – I began to tremble and never had the courage to do it. I think, therefore, we had better leave things as they are.

If you will kindly continue to be as obliging as you have been up to now, you will certainly always find a means of delivering letters to me. Even the last one, had it not been for the unfortunate circumstance that obliged you to turn around suddenly just at that moment, would have been very easy for us. I am quite aware that you cannot, as I do, think of nothing else but all this; but I prefer to be patient and not to risk so much. I am sure Monsieur Danceny would say the same, since every time he has wanted something that was too difficult for me, he has always agreed to do without it.

With this letter, Monsieur, I shall return you your own, Monsieur Danceny's, and your key. I am nonetheless grateful for all your kindness, and I beg you to continue it toward me. It is quite true that I am very unhappy and that without you I should be much more so. But, after all, she is my mother. One must really be patient. And provided that Monsieur Danceny still loves me and you do not forsake me, perhaps a happier time will come.

I have the honor to be, Monsieur, with the deepest gratitude, your very humble and obedient servant.

————

26 September 17–

LETTER 89: *The Vicomte de Valmont to the Chevalier Danceny*
If, my dear fellow, your affairs are still not making as much progress as you would like, it is not I who am entirely to blame. I have more than one obstacle to overcome here. Madame de Volanges's vigilance and strictness are not the only ones; your young friend has also thrown a few in my way. Whether because she is not eager enough or merely too timid, she does not always do as I advise, although it seems to me that I know better than she what has to be done.

I had thought of a simple, convenient, and safe method of delivering your letters to her which would have made it easier, too, to arrange the interview you desire. But I was not able to persuade her to make use of it. I am the more sorry because I see no other way of bringing you together, and because, even where your correspondence is concerned, I am in constant fear that all three of us will be compromised. Now, you know that I do not want to expose either myself or you to any risk of that.

I should really, however, be sorry were your little friend's lack of confidence in me to prevent my being useful to you. You would perhaps do well to write to her about it. Think it over. It is for you alone to decide; for it is not enough to help one's friends, one must help them in their own way. This might also be yet another opportunity to make sure of her feelings for you; for the woman who maintains a will of her own is not as much in love as she says she is.

It is not that I suspect your mistress of inconstancy. But she is very young. She is very much afraid of her mother, whose only object, as you know, is to spite you. And perhaps it would be dangerous to let too much time go by without reminding her of your existence. Do not, however, let what I have said give you any anxiety. I have, at bottom, no grounds for misgiving; this is purely friendly solicitude.

I shall not write at greater length, for I have not a little business of my own to attend to. I have made no further progress than you have: but I am as much in love, and that is some consolation. Should I have no success myself, yet succeed in being useful to you, I shall think my time well spent. Good-bye, my dear fellow.

Château de ———
26 September 17–

LETTER 90: *The Présidente de Tourvel to the Vicomte de Valmont*
I am very anxious, Monsieur, that this letter should cause you no pain; or, if it must, that your pain will be lessened by that which I feel in writing it. You must know me well enough now to be quite certain that I have no wish to distress you. But then you yourself surely have no wish to plunge me into everlasting despair? I beg you, therefore, in the name of the tender friendship I have promised you, in the name as well of the feelings you have for me – more lively than mine, perhaps, but certainly not more sincere – let us not see each other again. Go away. And until you do, let us avoid those private and excessively dangerous conversations during which some extraordinary power compels me, without my being able to say what I want to say, to spend my time listening to what I have no business to hear.

Only yesterday, when you came to join me in the park, my sole intention was to tell you what I am telling you now; yet what did I do? Talk about your love ... your love, to which I ought never to make the slightest response! Ah, for pity's sake, go away from here.

Do not fear that absence will ever change my feelings for you. How shall I succeed in overcoming them when I no longer have the courage to fight them? You see, I tell you everything. I am less afraid of admitting my weakness than of surrendering to it. But the power I have lost over my feelings I shall not lose over my actions. No, I shall not, I am resolved – even should it cost me my life.

Alas! The time is not long past when I felt quite certain I should never have such battles to fight. I congratulated myself upon my security; I was perhaps too vain of it. Heaven has punished, cruelly punished my pride. But because God is all-merciful, even at the very moment He strikes us down; He has given me warning of a fall. And I would be doubly culpable if I continued to be wanting in prudence when I am already aware that I have lost my strength.

You have told me a hundred times that you would not buy your happiness at the price of my tears. Ah, let us not talk of happiness; let me only recover my peace of mind!

Think how much stronger will be the claims you acquire to my heart if you grant me this request: claims founded on virtue, which I shall never have to question. How I shall delight in my gratitude! To you I shall owe the pleasure of enjoying a delicious feeling without fear of remorse. As things are, on the contrary, I am terrified of my feelings and of my thoughts, equally afraid whether I consider you or myself. The very idea of you alarms me. Though I cannot escape it, I fight it. I cannot banish it, but I repel it.

Would it not be better for both of us to bring this state of trouble and anxiety to an end? Will you, who have always had a sensitive nature that even in the midst of a life of error inclined you to virtue, will you not have some consideration for my painful situation, will you not listen to my pleas? These violent emotions will give way to a calmer, though no less tender interest in you. Restored thus to well-being by your kindnesses, I shall hold life dear again and shall say with all the joy in my heart: this peace that I feel, I owe to my friend.

In submitting to a few trifling privations, which I do not impose upon but only ask from you, do you think you will be paying too dear for an end to my torments? Oh, if to make you happy I had only to consent to unhappiness for myself, believe me I should not hesitate for a moment ... But to be guilty! ... No, my friend, no, I should rather die a thousand deaths.

Already attacked by shame, the precursor of remorse, I am afraid both of others and of myself. In company I blush, in solitude I tremble. My life offers nothing now but pain. I shall have no peace unless you give me your consent. My most praiseworthy resolutions are not enough to reassure me. I formed one yesterday, yet I spent last night in tears.

You see before you your friend, the one you love, confused, suppliant, asking you for peace and innocence. Ah, God! Were it not for you, would she be reduced to making so humiliating a request? I do not blame you for anything. I know too well from my own experience how difficult it is to resist an imperious feeling. To appeal is not to complain. Do from generosity what I do out of duty, and to all the feelings you have inspired in me will be added my eternal gratitude. Good-bye, Monsieur, good-bye.

———————

27 September 17–

LETTER 91: *The Vicomte de Valmont to the Présidente de Tourvel*
Your letter has so dismayed me, Madame, that I still do not know how I shall be able to reply to it. Of course, if the choice must be between your happiness and mine, it is for me to make the sacrifice and I shall do so without hesitation; but it seems to me that such important matters ought first to be discussed and understood – and how can we do so if we are neither to speak with nor to see each other again?

Really! When the noblest of feelings has brought us together, will it do for some foolish fear to separate us, perhaps forever? In vain shall tender friendship, ardent love, demand their rights. Their voices shall not be heard. And why? What is this pressing danger that threatens you? Ah, believe me, your fears so lightly conceived are already, it seems to me, strong enough guarantees of your safety.

Permit me to tell you that again I notice traces of the unfavorable impression you were once given of me. No woman trembles before the man she respects. Least of all will she banish from her side one she has judged worthy of her friendship. It is the dangerous man she fears and flies from.

Yet who was ever more respectful and more submissive than I? I am already, as you see, careful what I say. I no longer allow myself those sweet epithets, so dear to my heart, names I shall never cease to call you in secret. I am no longer the faithful and unhappy lover, accepting advice from a tender and sympathetic friend. I am the accused before his judge, the slave before his master. My new roles, of course, impose new duties; I undertake to fulfill them all. Hear what I have to say, and if you condemn me I shall submit and leave. I promise even more; would you rather be the despot who judges without a hearing? Do you feel you have the courage to be unjust? Command, and I shall still obey.

But let me hear your judgment or your orders come from your lips. "Why?" you will perhaps ask in turn. Ah, if you ask that question you understand very little of love or of my heart! Will it mean nothing to me to see you once more? Ah! When you find how despair weighs upon my soul perhaps your look of comfort will keep it from succumbing. And then, if I must renounce love and friendship, for which alone I exist, at least you shall see what you have done, and your pity will remain with me: a poor recompense, for which, it seems to me, I am prepared to pay dearly, dearly enough to hope to obtain it even though I do not deserve it.

So you are going to send me away from you? Are you willing, then, that we should become strangers to each other? Willing, did I say? You want it to happen; and while you assure me that my absence will not alter your feelings, you hasten my departure the sooner to set about destroying them.

You already speak of replacing them with gratitude. A feeling that a stranger might obtain from you for some trifling service – an enemy, even, in ceasing to injure you: that is all you have to offer me! And you want my heart to content itself with that! Ask your own: If a lover, if a friend were to come one day to tell you of his gratitude, would you not say indignantly: go away, you are ungrateful?

I shall say no more, but I beg your indulgence for what I have said. Forgive the expression of a grief that owes its being to you. It will make no difference to my perfect submission. But I beseech you in my turn, in the name of those sweet feelings that you yourself invoke, do not refuse to hear me; and out of pity, if nothing else, for the mortal agony in which you have plunged me, do not defer the moment of doing so. Good-bye, Madame.

–––––––––

27 September 17–, evening

LETTER 92: *The Chevalier Danceny to the Vicomte de Valmont*
Oh, my dear friend! Your letter has frozen me with terror. Cécile... Oh, God! Is it possible? Cécile does not love me any more. Yes, I perceive that frightful truth through the veil your friendship has thrown

over it. You meant to prepare me for the fatal blow; I thank you for your care, but is love ever to be deceived? It flies ahead of its interests; it does not learn but divines its fate. I am no longer in doubt of mine. Speak to me without evasion; you can, and I beg you to do so. Tell me everything: what gave rise to your suspicions and what confirmed them. The least detail is precious. Try, above all, to recall her words. One word instead of another can change a whole sentence; the same one sometimes has two meanings... You can have been mistaken. Alas! I am still trying to comfort myself. What did she say to you? Does she blame me for anything? Does she not at least make excuses for herself? I should have foreseen this change in the difficulties that she has for some time found in everything. Love does not acknowledge so many obstacles.

What course should I take? What do you advise? Should I try to see her? Is that really impossible? Absence is so cruel, so fatal...and she has refused a means of seeing me! You do not tell me what it was. If there was too much danger involved, she knows that I would not want her to run any risks. On the other hand, I know your prudence, and I cannot, to my misfortune, have anything but complete faith in it.

What shall I do now? What shall I say to her? If I betray my suspicions they will perhaps distress her; and if they are unjust, how shall I ever forgive myself for having distressed her? If I hide them I am deceiving her, and I am incapable of deceiving her.

Oh, if she knew what I suffered, she would be touched by my pain. She is not without feeling, I know. She has an excellent heart, and I have a thousand proofs of her love. She is too timid, too easily embarrassed, but she is so young! And her mother treats her so badly! I shall write to her. I shall keep my head. I shall ask her only to leave everything to you. Even if she refuses again, she cannot at any rate be angry with me for asking; and perhaps she will agree.

To you, my friend, I offer a thousand apologies on her behalf and mine. I assure you, she appreciates the value of your efforts and is grateful for them. It is not mistrust on her part, but timidity. Be indulgent: friendship can show no fairer face. Your friendship, I need not say, is very precious to me, and I do not know how I can ever repay you for all that you are doing in my interest. Good-bye. I am going to write to her immediately.

I feel all my fears return. Who would have said that one day I should find it so difficult to write to her! Alas! Only yesterday it was my greatest joy.

Good-bye, my dear friend. Continue in your efforts for me, and pity my plight.

Paris
27 September 17–

LETTER 93: *The Chevalier Danceny to Cécile Volanges*

I cannot conceal how distressed I was to learn from Valmont of the lack of confidence you continue to display in him. You are not unaware that he is my friend and that he is the only person who can bring us together again. I should have thought these might have been considerations of sufficient weight with you; I am sorry to find that I was mistaken. May I hope at least that you will explain your motives? You will not discover further difficulties to prevent your doing so? Without your help I cannot solve the mystery of your conduct. I dare not doubt your love; you, too, would surely not dare to betray mine. Ah, Cécile!...

Is it really true that you have refused a means of seeing me? A *simple, convenient, and safe method?** This is how you love me! So short an absence has completely changed your feelings. But why deceive me? Why tell me that you love me still, that you love me more than ever? Has your mama, in robbing you of your love, robbed you of your honesty as well? If she has left you at least with some pity, you will not hear, unmoved, the frightful torments you have caused me. Ah, if I were to die I should suffer less.

Tell me, is your heart irrevocably closed against me? Have you utterly forgotten me? Thanks to your refusal, I cannot tell when you will receive my appeals, or when you will reply to them. Valmont's friendship made our correspondence secure. But you, you did not want this. You find writing to me painful; you preferred not to do it often. No, I no longer believe in love, in honesty. Oh, what can I believe in, if Cécile has deceived me?

Answer me then! Is it true that you no longer love me? No, that is not possible. You are deluding yourself. You are maligning your heart. A passing fear, a moment's discouragement perhaps, but quickly banished by love – is that not so, my Cécile? Oh, no doubt I was wrong to accuse you. How happy I should be if I were wrong! How I should like to make you my most tender apologies, to atone for a moment's injustice with a lifetime of love!

Cécile, Cécile, have pity on me! Try to see me, take all means at hand!

---

*Danceny does not know what it is; he is merely repeating Valmont's phrase.

See what absence can do! Fears, suspicions, even coldness perhaps! One look, one word, and we shall be happy. But there, how can I still be speaking of happiness, when it may be lost to me forever? Tortured by fear, cruelly hemmed in between unjust suspicions and a truth more terrible still, there is no thought I can take refuge in, I continue my existence only to suffer and to love you. Ah, Cécile! You have the power to make life dear to me; the first word you utter will signify the renewal of my happiness or certain and eternal despair.

Paris
27 September 17–

LETTER 94: *Cécile Volanges to the Chevalier Danceny*
I can understand nothing of your letter, except the pain it gives me. What has Monsieur de Valmont told you, and what can have made you believe that I no longer love you? It would perhaps be very lucky for me if that were so, since I should certainly suffer less; and it is very hard, when I love you as I do, to find that you always think I am wrong, and instead of consoling me are always the cause yourself of the troubles that afflict me most. You think I am deceiving you, telling you what is not true! What a fine idea you must have of me! But were I the liar you accuse me of being, what would my motives be? There is no doubt that if I no longer loved you, I should only have to say so for everyone to approve. Unfortunately that is more than I can do – oh, that it should be for the sake of someone who shows me no consideration at all!

What have I done to make you so angry? I lacked the courage to remove the key, because I was afraid Mamma might notice it, and I should then be in even worse trouble than before – as would you, on my account; and, also, because it seems to me it would have been wrong. But it was only Monsieur de Valmont who spoke to me about it: I could not possibly know whether you were in favor or not, since you knew nothing about it. Now that I know that you are, do you think I shall refuse to remove the key? I shall remove it tomorrow. Then we shall see what you have to say.

However much a friend Monsieur de Valmont is to you, I think I love you quite as much as he does, to say the least; yet it is always he who is right and I who am wrong. I assure you I am very angry. It may be of no consequence to you, since you know that I always calm down immediately. But now that I am to have the key, I shall be able to see you whenever I choose to; and I assure you that I shall not choose to if you behave like this. I prefer the troubles I cause myself to those you cause me. Consider what you will do.

If you wanted to, how much we could love one another! And at least we would have to bear only the sufferings that others inflict on us! I assure you that if it were in my power you would never have cause to complain of me; but if you don't believe me, we shall always be unhappy, and it will not be my fault. I hope we shall soon be able to see each other, and then have no further need to plague each other as we do at present.

If I could have foreseen this, I should have removed the key immediately. But I really believed I was doing right. Don't, then, hold it against me – please. Don't be disheartened any longer, continue to love me as much as I love you, and I shall be very happy. Good-bye, my dear.

Château de ⸺
28 September 17–

LETTER 95: *Cécile Volanges to the Vicomte de Valmont*
Please be so kind, Monsieur, as to send me back the key you gave me to put in the other one's place. Since everyone is in favor of my doing this, I must needs be too.

I do not know why you told Monsieur de Danceny that I no longer loved him. I do not believe I have ever given you occasion to think so; and it has given him great pain, and me as well. I am well aware that you are his friend; but that is no reason for distressing him, or me for that matter. You will do me a great favor by telling him that the contrary is the case next time you write, and that you are certain of it; for it is in you that he places most confidence. As for me, when I say something and it is not believed, I do not know what to do next.

About the key you need have no fears. I remember perfectly all you recommended me to do in your letter. If, however, you still have the letter and are willing to give it back to me with the key, I promise you it will have all my attention. If you can do this tomorrow as we go into dinner, I shall give you the other key the day after tomorrow at breakfast, and you will return it to me in the same way as you let me have the first one. I should not like to leave it any later, since there would then be a greater risk of Mamma's noticing something.

Once you have the key, perhaps you will be good enough to make use of it for fetching my letters: in this way Monsieur Danceny will more often have news of me. It is true that we shall have a much more convenient method than at present, but at first I was too afraid; please forgive me, and I hope you will continue to be no less obliging than you have been in the past. I shall always be very grateful for it.

I have the honor to be, Monsieur, your most humble and obedient servant.

————

28 September 17–

LETTER 96: *The Vicomte de Valmont to the Marquise de Merteuil*
I dare say that since your adventure you have daily expected my plaudits and compliments. I don't doubt that you have even been a little out of humor at my long silence. But can you blame me? I have always thought that the moment one no longer has anything but praise for a woman, one may be easy about her and turn to other things. Nevertheless, my thanks on my own account, and congratulations upon yours. To crown your happiness, I am even willing to confess that on this occasion you have surpassed my expectations. After which let us see whether I, in my turn, have not fulfilled yours, at least in part.

It is not Madame de Tourvel I want to tell you about. That affair goes too slowly for you; it is, I know, only the finished work that interests you. Long, drawn-out encounters bore you, whereas I have never tasted such pleasure as I derive from all this apparent procrastination.

Yes, I like watching, contemplating this prudent woman as she takes, without knowing it, a path that allows no return, one that flings her willy-nilly in my wake down its steep and dangerous descent. Frightened of the peril she is courting, she would like to stop but cannot hold back. Care and skill can shorten the steps she takes; nothing can prevent them succeeding each other. Sometimes, unable to face the danger, she closes her eyes and lets herself go, putting her fate in my hands. More often, some new fear rouses her to new efforts. In her mortal terror she tries once more to retreat, and exhausts her strength in regaining a little ground; but soon some magic power transplants her yet nearer the danger she has vainly attempted to flee. Then, having no one but me for guidance and support, and unable to blame me any longer for her inevitable fall, she implores me to postpone it. Fervent prayer, humble supplication, all that mortal man in his terror offers the Divinity, I receive from her. And you think that I, deaf to her prayers, destroying with my own hands the shrine she has put up around me, will use that same power for her ruin which she invokes for her protection! Ah, let me at least have time to enjoy the touching struggle between love and virtue.

After all, do you think that the spectacle you rush so eagerly to the theater to see and applaud so furiously is any less fascinating in actuality? The sentiments you greet with so much enthusiasm; the feelings of a pure and tender nature that fears the happiness it yearns for, that cannot stop defending itself even when it has given up resisting – are they to have no value for the man who has inspired them? Those, nevertheless, those are the delicious satisfactions this heavenly woman daily offers me. And you blame me for savoring such delights! Ah, the time will all too quickly come when, debased by her fall, she will be no more to me than any other woman.

But I am forgetting, as I speak of her, that I did not intend to speak of her. Some power or other draws me to her, brings me back to her continually, even if it is only to insult her. Let us put these dangerous thoughts aside. Let me be myself again and speak of jollier things – your pupil, for instance, who has now become mine. Here I hope you will recognize me in my true colors.

For some days, during which I had been better treated by my tender devotee and was consequently less concerned about her, I had been conscious that the little Volanges was in fact extremely pretty; and that, if it was absurd to be enamored of her as Danceny is, it was perhaps equally so for me not to look to her for the distraction my solitude compels me to find. It seemed to be only just, too, that I should have some reward for my efforts on her behalf; and I remembered, besides, that you had offered her to me before Danceny had any pretensions in the matter. I decided I could legitimately claim certain rights in a property that was his only because I had refused and relinquished it. The pretty look of the little creature, her fresh little mouth, her childish air, even her gaucherie, confirmed me in these wise determinations. I decided to act upon them, and success has crowned my enterprise.

You are already wondering how I arrived so soon at supplanting the cherished lover, and what method of seduction can have been appropriate to such lack of years and experience. Spare yourself the trouble: I took none at all myself. While, with your skill in handling the weapons of your sex, yours was a triumph of cunning, I, restoring to man his inalienable rights, conquered by force of authority. Sure of seizing my prey if I could come within reach of her, I had no need of stratagem, except to secure a means of approach, and the ruse I employed for that purpose was hardly worthy of the name.

I took my opportunity as soon as I received Danceny's next letter to his mistress. Having given her the signal of warning agreed upon between us, I exercised all my ingenuity not in giving her the letter but in failing to find a means of doing so. I pretended to share her resulting impatience; and having caused the evil, I pointed out the remedy.

The young lady occupies a room, one door to which gives on to the corridor. The mother had, as was to be expected, removed the key, and it was only a question of recovering it. Nothing could have been easier: I asked only to have it at my disposal for two hours, whereupon I should be responsible for procuring a duplicate. After that, everything – correspondence, meetings, nocturnal rendezvous – would have become convenient and safe. Yet – would you believe it? – the cautious child took fright and refused. Another man would have been crushed by this: I saw in it no more than an occasion for pleasure of a more piquant kind. I wrote to Danceny complaining of the refusal, and I did it so well that the blockhead would not be satisfied till he had obtained – exacted, rather – a promise from his timorous mistress to grant my request and leave everything to my discretion.

I was very pleased, I must say, with my change of role, and with the young man's doing for me what he thought I would be doing for him. The idea doubled the worth of the enterprise in my eyes, so that as soon as I had possession of the precious key, I hastened to make use of it. That was last night.

Having made sure that all was quiet throughout the house, armed with my dark lantern and clothed as befitted the hour and the circumstances, I paid my first visit to your pupil. I had everything arranged (she herself had obliged me) so that I could enter without noise. She was in her first sleep, the deep sleep of youth, so that I arrived at her bedside without waking her. I thought at first of proceeding further and attempting to pass myself off as a dream. But, fearing the effect of surprise and the consequent alarms, I decided instead to wake the sleeping beauty with every caution, and eventually succeeded in preventing the outcry I had anticipated.

When I had calmed her initial fears, and since I was not there to chat, I risked a few liberties. There is no doubt she was not taught enough at the convent about either the many different perils to which fearful innocence is exposed or all that it has to protect – or be taken by surprise: for, directing her whole attention and all her energies to defending herself from a kiss, which was nothing but a feint, she left everything else defenseless. How could I let my advantage slip? I changed my line of attack and immediately seized a position. At this point we both thought all was lost. The little creature, quite horrified, made in good earnest to cry out; fortunately her voice was strangled in tears. She then threw herself toward the bell rope, but I had the presence of mind to take hold of her arm in time.

"What are you trying to do?" I said to her. "Ruin yourself forever? What will it matter to me if someone comes? How will you convince anyone that I am not here with your permission? Who else but you could have provided me with a means of entering your room? As for the key I have from you, which I can only have obtained from you, will you undertake to explain its purpose?" This short harangue pacified neither grief nor rage, but it inspired submission. I don't know whether my tones were eloquent; my gestures, at all events, were not. One hand was needed for power, the other for love: where is the orator that could aspire to grace in such a position? If you can picture the circumstances you will agree that they were favorable for attack; but I am a complete fool and, as you say, the simplest woman, a mere convent girl, leads me about like a child.

The girl in question, in the midst of her despair, knew that she must find some way of coming to terms with me. Entreaties found me inexorable, and she was reduced to making offers. You will suppose I set a high price upon my important position: no, I promised everything away for a kiss. True, once I had taken the kiss I did not keep my promise — but I had good reason not to. Had we agreed that the kiss should be taken or given? After much bargaining we decided upon a second, and this one was to be received. Having guided her timid arms around my body, I clasped her more lovingly in the one of mine that was free, and the sweetest kiss was in fact received: properly, perfectly received. Love itself could not have done better.

So much good faith deserved its reward, and I immediately granted the request. The hand was withdrawn; but by some extraordinary chance I found that I myself had taken its place. You imagine me very breathless and busy at this point, don't you? Not at all. I have acquired a taste for dawdling, I tell you. Why hurry when one's destination is in sight?

Seriously, I was glad for once to observe the power of opportunity, deprived in this case of all extraneous aid, with love in combat against it; love, moreover, sustained by modesty and shame, and encouraged by the bad humor I had provoked, which had been given free rein. Opportunity was alone; but it was there, offering itself, continually present, whereas love was not.

To confirm my observations, I was malicious enough to exert no more strength than could easily have been resisted. It was only when my charming enemy, taking advantage of my leniency, seemed about to escape me that I restrained her with the threats of which I had already felt the happy effects. Oh well, to go no further, our sweet inamorata, forgetting her vows, first yielded and then consented; of course, tears and reproaches were resumed at the first opportunity. I don't know whether they were real or pretended, but as always happens they ceased the moment I set about giving her reason for more. At length, having proceeded from helplessness to indignation, and from indignation to helplessness, we separated quite satisfied with one another and looking forward with equal pleasure to this evening's rendezvous.

I did not return to my room till daybreak, dying of sleep and fatigue; I sacrificed both, however, to my desire to appear this morning at breakfast. I have a passion for the mien of the morning after. You have no idea of this one. Such embarrassment of gesture, such difficulty of movement! Eyes kept steadily lowered, so large and so haggard! The little round face so drawn! Nothing was ever so amusing. And for the first time her mother, alarmed at this extreme alteration, displayed some sympathetic interest! The Présidente, too, danced attendance round her. Oh, *her* sympathy is only borrowed, believe me! The day will come for its return, and that day is not far off. Good-bye, my love.

Château de ——————
1 October 17–

LETTER 97: *Cécile Volanges to the Marquise de Merteuil*
Oh God, Madame, how heavy-hearted, how miserable I am! Who will console me in my distress? Who will advise me in my difficulties? This Monsieur de Valmont...and Danceny? No, the very thought of Danceny throws me into despair...How shall I tell you? How shall I say it?...I don't know what to do. But my heart is full...I must speak to someone, and in you alone can I, dare I, confide. You have been so kind to me! What shall I say? I do not want you to be kind. Everyone here has offered me sympathy today...they have only increased my wretchedness. I was so very much aware that I did not deserve it! Scold me instead; give me a good scolding, for I am very much to blame. But then save me. If you will not have the kindness to advise me I shall die of grief.

Know then...my hand trembles, as you see. I can scarcely write. I feel my cheeks on fire...Oh, it is the very blush of shame. Well, I shall endure it. It shall be the first punishment for my fault. Yes, I shall tell you everything.

You must know, then, that Monsieur de Valmont, who hitherto has delivered Monsieur Danceny's letters to me, suddenly found it too difficult to continue in the usual way. He wanted a key to my room. I can certainly assure you that I did not want to give him one; but he went so far as to write to Danceny, and Danceny wanted me to do so. I am always so sorry to refuse him anything, particularly since our separation which has made him so unhappy, that I finally agreed. I had no idea of the misfortune that would follow.

Last night Monsieur de Valmont used the key to come into my room as I slept. I was so little expecting this that he really frightened me when he woke me. But as he immediately began to speak, I recognized him and did not cry out; then it occurred as well to me at first that he had come to bring me a letter from Danceny. Far from it. Very shortly afterward he attempted to kiss me; and while I defended myself, as was natural, he cleverly did what I should not have wished for all the world... but first he wanted a kiss. I had to — what else could I do? The more so since I had tried to ring, but besides the fact that I could not, he was careful to tell me that if someone came he would easily be able to throw all the blame on me; and, in fact, it would have been easy on account of the key. After this he budged not an inch. He wanted a second kiss; and, I don't know why, but this time I was quite flustered, and afterward it was even worse than before. Oh, really, it was too wicked. Then, after that...you will spare my telling you the rest, but I am as unhappy as anyone could possibly be.

What I blame myself for most, and what, nevertheless, I must tell you about, is that I am afraid I did not defend myself as well as I was able. I don't know how that happened. I most certainly am not in love with Monsieur de Valmont, quite the contrary; yet there were moments when it was as if I were...As you may imagine, this did not prevent me from saying no all the time; but I knew quite well that I was not doing as I said — it was as though I could not help it. And then, too, I was so very agitated! If it is always as difficult as this to defend oneself, one needs a good deal of practice! It is true that Monsieur de Valmont has a way of saying things so that one is hard put to it to think of a reply; at all events, would you believe that I was almost sorry when he left, and that I was weak enough to agree to his returning this evening? That is what horrifies me more than all the rest.

Oh, in spite of it all, I promise you I shall stop him coming. He had scarcely left when I knew for certain that I had been very wrong to promise him anything. What is more, I spent the rest of the night in tears. It was Danceny above all who haunted me! Every time I thought of him my tears came twice as fast, till they almost suffocated me, and I thought of him all the time...I do even now, and you see the result: my paper is quite sodden. No, I shall never be consoled, if only on his account...At length I could cry no more, and yet could not sleep for a minute. And when I woke this morning and looked at myself in the mirror, I frightened myself, I was so changed.

Mamma noticed it as soon as she saw me, and she asked me what was wrong. I began at once to cry. I thought she was going to scold me, and perhaps that would have hurt me less – but quite the contrary, she spoke to me kindly! I scarcely deserved it. She told me not to distress myself like that! She did not know what I had to be distressed about. She said that I would make myself ill! There are moments when I should like to be dead. I could not restrain myself. I threw myself sobbing into her arms, crying "Oh, Mamma your daughter is very unhappy!" Mamma could not help crying a little herself, and that only increased my misery. Fortunately she did not ask why I was unhappy; I would not have known what to say.

I beseech you, Madame, write to me as soon as you can and tell me what I must do; for I have not the courage to think of anything and can do nothing but suffer. Please address your letter to Monsieur de Valmont; but if you are writing to him at the same time, I beg you not to mention that I have said anything to you.

I have the honor to be, Madame, ever with the most sincere friendship, your very humble and obedient servant...I dare not sign this letter.

Château de ———
1 October 17–

LETTER 98: *Madame de Volanges to the Marquise de Merteuil*
Not many days ago, my dear friend, it was you who were asking me for comfort and advice; now it is my turn, and I am making the same request of you that you made of me. I am in very great distress indeed, and I am afraid I may not have found the best way out of my troubles.

It is my daughter who is the cause of my anxiety. Since our departure from Paris she has clearly been dejected and unhappy; I expected that, though, and had hardened my heart with the severity I judged necessary. I hoped that absence and distraction would soon destroy a love that I regarded as a childish aberration rather than a true passion. Far, however, from having gained anything by coming here to stay, I now observe that the child is surrendering more and more to a dangerous melancholy, and I am seriously afraid that it may injure her health. During the last few days especially there has been a visible change in her appearance. It struck me yesterday in particular, and everybody here was really alarmed.

What further proves to me that she is deeply affected is that she is now obviously capable of overcoming the timidity she has always shown in my presence. Yesterday morning, simply upon my asking her whether she was ill, she flung herself into my arms, saying that she was very unhappy, sobbing and weeping. I cannot tell you how painful this was to me. Tears came to my eyes immediately, and I scarcely had time to turn away to prevent her seeing them. Fortunately I was prudent enough not to ask her any questions, and she herself did not dare to say anything further. It is nevertheless clear that this unfortunate passion still torments her.

What course shall I take if this continues? Shall I make my daughter unhappy? Shall I turn to her disadvantage the very qualities of mind and heart in her that are most to be valued, her sensibility and her constancy? Is it for this that I am her mother? And were I to stifle the natural feeling that makes us all want the happiness of our children; were I to look upon that as a weakness, which, on the contrary, I believe to be the first and most sacred of our duties; if I force her choice, shall I not be answerable for the dreadful consequences that may ensue? What a way to use the authority of a mother, to offer one's daughter the alternatives of crime and misery!

I shall not, my dear friend, imitate those I have so often condemned. I was capable, certainly, of trying to choose for my daughter, but by that I was doing no more than help her with my experience. It was not a right that I exercised but a duty I fulfilled. I should, on the other hand, be neglecting another duty were I to dispose of her without a thought for an attachment I was not able to prevent her forming, and of which neither she nor I can judge the extent or duration. No, I cannot permit her to marry one man and love another. I prefer to compromise my authority rather than her virtue.

I think, therefore, I shall be doing the wisest thing by retracting the promise I have given Monsieur de Gercourt. I have told you my reasons, and it seems to me that they should weigh more with me than promises. I shall go further: in the present state of things, by fulfilling my engagement I should really be violating it. For, after all, if I owe it to my daughter not to betray her secret to Monsieur de Gercourt, I owe it to him, at least, not to abuse the ignorance in which I leave him — to do for him all that I believe he would do for himself if he knew everything. Am I, instead, when he relies upon my good faith, when he honors me in choosing me for his second mother, to betray him shamefully? Am I to deceive him in the choice he wishes to make for the mother of his own children? These ideas, which contain so much truth and which I cannot refuse to entertain, alarm me more than I can say.

Against the misfortunes they bring me to fear, I compare a daughter happy in a husband who is the choice of her heart, recognizing duty only by the pleasure she finds in fulfilling it; a son-in-law, equally contented, gladder each day of the choice he has made; each finding happiness only in the happiness of the other, and the happiness of both combining to increase mine. Should the hope of so pleasant a future be sacrificed to vain considerations? What are the considerations, after all, that give me pause? Those of advantage only. But to what end was my daughter born rich, if she is nevertheless to be a slave to fortune?

I agree that Monsieur de Gercourt is perhaps a better match than I could have expected for my daughter; I shall even admit that I was extremely flattered when his choice fell upon her. But after all, Danceny comes from as good a family as does he; he yields nothing to him in personal qualities; and he has the advantage over Monsieur de Gercourt of loving and being loved. True, he is not rich; but is my daughter not rich enough for the two of them? Oh, why rob her of the satisfaction of bestowing her riches upon the man she loves?

Are not the marriages that result from calculation and not from choice, marriages of convenience as they are called, where everything is mutually agreeable except the tastes and characters of the couple concerned – are they not the most common source of these outbreaks of scandal that become daily more and more frequent? I had rather wait; I should at least have time to learn to know a daughter who is now a stranger to me. I should have quite enough courage, I am sure, to cause her a passing disappointment if she stood to gain a more solid happiness from it; but to risk delivering her up to perpetual despair, that is not in my heart.

These, my dear friend, are the thoughts that torment me, concerning which I beg your advice. Such serious questions are very ill-suited to your gaiety and charm, and seem scarcely less so to your age; but your good judgment is so far in advance of that! Besides, your friendship will come to the aid of your prudence, and I have no fear that either one of them will deny the maternal solicitude that implores their help.

Good-bye, my dear friend. Never doubt the sincerity of my feelings for you.

Château de ———

2 October 17–

LETTER 99: *The Vicomte de Valmont to the Marquise de Merteuil*

Further little incidents, my love; but only dialogue, no action. So compose yourself in patience – in fact, summon as much of it as you can: for while my Présidente proceeds at a snail's pace, your pupil is in retreat, which is a great deal worse. Oh, well, I have wit enough to be amused by these little things. As a matter of fact, I am growing quite accustomed to staying here and can even say that I have experienced not a moment's boredom in this gloomy mansion of my old aunt's. On the contrary, have I not pleasures, privations, hopes, uncertainties? What more has the theater itself to offer? Spectators? Oh, wait and see. I shall not want those either. If they are not here now to watch me at work, I shall show them my task complete; they will then have only to admire and applaud. Yes, they will applaud, for I can at last predict with certainty the moment of my austere devotee's surrender. I assisted this evening at the death agony of virtue. A sweet helplessness is going to reign in its place. I have fixed the moment for not later than our next interview – but I can hear you already scoffing at my conceit. Predicting victory, boasting before the event! Oh, dear, dear, calm yourself! To prove my modesty I am going to begin with the history of my defeat.

Truly, your pupil is a very ridiculous little person! She is really a child who ought to be treated as such – and one would be letting her off lightly by putting her in the corner! Would you believe that after what happened between us the day before yesterday, after the friendly farewells we said the next morning, I found, when I returned in the evening as she had agreed to let me do, that the door was locked from the inside? What have you to say to that? One sometimes meets with this sort of puerility the day before – but the day after! Is it not amusing?

I was not, however, disposed to laugh at first. Never had I been more conscious of the force of my character. It was certainly not with any thought of pleasure that I had kept my rendezvous, but solely out of politeness. I was in great need of my bed, which seemed to me at that moment preferable to anyone else's, and I had not left it without regret. Yet I had no sooner found an obstacle in my path than I was on fire to remove it. I was particularly humiliated by the thought that a child had outwitted me. I withdrew, therefore, in high dudgeon; and with the intention of meddling no further with the stupid girl or her affairs, I immediately wrote her a note to be delivered to her today, in which I stated my estimate of her true worth. But, as they say, sleep is the best counselor. This morning I decided that, since I am not offered a choice of amusements here, I would have to make the most of this one. So I tore up the offensive note. Having thought about it since, I am unable to conceive how it can have occurred to me to bring an adventure to an end before I had acquired some means of ruining its heroine. To what, however, may one not be provoked by the impulse of the moment? Happy the man, my love, who, like you, has trained himself never to yield to it! My revenge, therefore, I have deferred. I have made the sacrifice in the interests of your designs upon Gercourt.

Now that I am no longer angry, I see your pupil's conduct as merely ridiculous. In fact, I should very much like to know what she hopes to gain by it! I am at a loss to imagine. If it is only self-defense, it must be admitted she has begun a little late. She really will have to give me the clue to the puzzle one day. I am most eager to know. It was perhaps only that she felt tired? Frankly, that is possible; for she very probably does not know that love's arrows carry with them, as did Achilles' spear, the balm that heals the wounds they make. But no, from the wry faces she made all day, I should guess that repentance comes into it somewhere...something of the kind...something to do with virtue...Virtue!...What has virtue to do with her? Ah, let her leave it to the woman who really was born for it, the only one who can make it beautiful, can make it worthy of love!...Forgive me, my dear, but it was only this evening that there occurred between Madame de Tourvel and myself the scene that I am about to describe to you, and I am still under the influence of some emotion. I shall have to make a great effort to forget the impression she made; it was precisely to help me do so that I sat down to write to you. You must make some allowances at first.

Madame de Tourvel and I have for some days been in agreement about our feelings; our only dispute now is about words. It had always been, of course, *her friendship* that answered *my love*: but the language of convention did not alter the facts, and even had we remained upon these terms, my progress, though it would perhaps have been slower would have been no less sure. Already there was no longer any question of my leaving, as she had desired at first; and as for our daily meetings, while I took care to offer her opportunities, she took as much care to seize them.

Since it is ordinarily when we are out walking that our little rendezvous take place, the dreadful weather we have had all day today disappointed my hopes; I was even quite annoyed by it. I could not foresee how much the circumstance would be to my advantage.

Walking being out of the question, the ladies sat down to cards after dinner; and since I seldom play, and am no longer required to, I chose the moment to go up to my room, intending to do no more than wait until they were likely to have finished their game.

I was on my way to rejoin the company when I met the charming creature returning to her room. In a moment of imprudence, or perhaps weakness, she asked in dulcet tones, "Where are you going? There is nobody in the drawing room." I needed no further pretext, as you may imagine, to attempt a sortie into her own room. I met with less resistance than I expected. True, I had taken the precaution of beginning a conversation at the door and of beginning it upon indifferent topics; but no sooner were we properly installed when I brought up the real issue and spoke *to my friend of my love.* Her immediate reply, though simple, seemed to me expressive. "Oh, please!" she said, "don't speak of that here," and she trembled. Poor woman! She knows her fate is sealed.

She was wrong, nevertheless, to be afraid. I had for some time been confident of achieving success sooner or later; and seeing her exhaust so much of her energy in futile struggles had made me decide to conserve my own strength, to wait without making any effort until she should give in out of fatigue. As you know, the victory must be complete. I shall owe nothing to circumstances. It was precisely with this idea in mind, and in order to show eagerness without committing myself too far, that I returned to the word "love," so obstinately evaded hitherto. Sure of ardor being taken for granted, I assayed a more tender tone. Evasion no longer disappointed me, it grieved me: did not my sympathetic friend owe me some consolation?

By way of consoling me, a hand was left in mine; the lovely body leaned against my arm, and we found ourselves in extremely close proximity. You must surely have observed how, in this sort of situation, as defense weakens, demands and refusals are exchanged at closer and closer quarters; how the head is turned aside and the eyes lowered, while disjointed remarks are delivered in a weak voice at longer and longer intervals. Such are the precious symptoms that in the plainest terms announce the heart's consent: but persuasion will rarely, as yet, have touched the senses, and I am even of the opinion that it is always dangerous at this moment to embark upon too decided a course of action. Since the condition of abandon never goes unattended by a certain sweet pleasure, it would be impossible to break new ground without arousing some irritation, and that would infallibly turn to the advantage of the defense.

In the present case, prudence was all the more necessary: I had special cause to fear the alarm that her own self-oblivion could not, in the end, fail to arouse in my languorous love — so that I did not even insist that the avowal I demanded be spoken. A look would be enough. A single look, and I should be happy.

My dear, those beautiful eyes were actually raised to mine. That heavenly mouth even pronounced these words: "Well! yes, I..." But suddenly her glance faded, her voice failed, and the adorable woman collapsed in my arms. I scarcely had time to catch her when she disengaged herself with convulsive force and, with a wild look and her arms extended to Heaven, cried "God...oh, my God, save me!"; and straightaway, quicker than lightning, she was upon her knees at ten paces from me. I could see that she was on the point of suffocating, and advanced to her help, but, taking hold of my hands, bathing them in tears, even at times embracing my knees, she said, "Yes, it is you. It is you who will save me! You don't want me to die. Leave me; save me; leave me; in God's name, leave me!" These frantic exclamations could scarcely escape her lips for the sobbing, which had redoubled in force. Meanwhile she held on to me with a strength that could not in any case have permitted my leaving her; so, summoning my own strength, I raised her up in my arms. At the same instant her tears ceased; she stopped speaking, her limbs stiffened, and violent convulsions succeeded the storm.

I was, I admit, deeply moved, and I think I should have agreed to her demands, even had circumstances not compelled me to do so. The fact remains that, having administered some practical assistance, I left her as she had begged me to, and am now glad that I did so. I have already almost obtained my reward.

I expected that, as had happened on the day of my first declaration, she would not appear that evening. But at about eight o'clock she came down to the drawing room, simply announcing to the company that she had felt very unwell. Her face was drawn, her voice feeble, and her bearing composed; but her looks were soft, and they were frequently fixed upon me. When her refusal to join the card table obliged me to take her place, she even sat beside me. During supper she remained behind alone in the drawing room. At our return I thought I noticed she had been crying. To make certain, I told her it seemed to me that she was still suffering from her indisposition; to which she made the obliging answer, "It is one of those ailments that does not go as quickly as it comes!" At length, as we retired, I gave her my arm; at the door of her room she squeezed my hand with some force. There seemed to me, it is true, to be something involuntary in the gesture. So much the better: it is one more proof of my power.

I am sure she is now delighted to have arrived where she is. All the expenses have been paid; nothing further remains for her to do but enjoy herself. Perhaps, as I write, she is already pondering that thought! And even if she is, on the contrary, concocting some new plan of defense, we know, do we not, what becomes of those? I ask you, could any plan survive our next meeting? I quite expect, of course, there will be some difficulty in obtaining another interview – but then! Once the first step is taken, are these strait-laced prudes ever able to stop? Their love is a veritable explosion; resistance only increases its force. My fierce ascetic would begin to run after me were I to stop running after her.

And then, my love, I shall return forthwith to you, to keep you to your word. You have not, of course, forgotten what you promised me after my success – that little infidelity to your chevalier? Are you ready? For my part, I long for it so much that we might still be strangers to each other. For that matter, knowing you is perhaps all the more reason for wanting it. I say that:

In justice to you, not in compliment.*

This will be my first infidelity to my staid conquest; and I promise you I shall make use of the first available pretext to leave her for twenty-four hours. That shall be her punishment for keeping me so long away from you! Do you know that this affair has kept me occupied now for more than two months? Yes, two months and three days. I count tomorrow since it is not till then that it will finally be accomplished. Which reminds me that Madame de B—— resisted for three whole months. I should be delighted to discover that open coquetry can maintain a defense for longer than the most ascetic virtue.

Good-bye, my love. I must leave you, for it is very late. This letter has taken me further than I intended; but since I am sending to Paris in the morning, I decided to give you an opportunity of sharing the joy of a friend a day in advance.

Château de ————
2 October 17–, evening

LETTER 100: *The Vicomte de Valmont to the Marquise de Merteuil*
My dear, I am deceived, betrayed, ruined. I am in despair. Madame de Tourvel has left. She has left without my knowledge. I was not there to oppose her departure, to arraign her shameful treachery! Ah, don't imagine that I would have let her go. She would have stayed. Yes, she would have stayed, had I been obliged to resort to force. But there you are! In my blind confidence I was peacefully asleep; I was asleep when

---

*Voltaire, *Nanine*, a comedy.

the lightning struck. No, I had no inkling at all of her departure. I must give up trying to understand women.

When I think of yesterday! Yesterday? It was only last evening! That soft look, that tender tone of voice! And that clasp of the hand! And all the while she was planning her escape! O women, women! Don't wonder, then, that you are deceived. Yes! Men know no treachery that they have not learned from you.

What pleasure I shall take in my revenge! I shall find her again, the traitress; I shall recover my dominion over her. If love by itself could do so, what will it not achieve with vengeance at its side? I shall see her again at my knees, trembling, bathed in tears, crying for mercy in that lying voice; and I shall be without pity.

What is she doing now? What is she thinking of? Congratulating herself, perhaps, on having deceived me; and, true to her sex, deciding that this is the sweetest pleasure of them all. What her much-vaunted virtue was unable to do, natural cunning has done without effort. Fool that I am! I feared her discretion; it was her sincerity I should have distrusted.

And to be compelled to swallow my resentment! To dare show nothing but sorrowful concern when I have a heart bursting with rage! To find myself reduced once more to going down upon my knees to a rebellious woman who has escaped my power! Have I deserved to be so humiliated? And by whom? A timid woman who never saw battle before. To what end have I established myself in her heart, have I set her ablaze with all the fires of passion, have I stirred her senses to delirium, if now, secure in her refuge, she can take more pride in her flight than I in my triumph? And shall I endure it? My dear, you don't believe that? You would not think so slightingly of me?

But what is the power that draws me to this woman? Are there not a hundred others who would be glad of my attentions? Would they not hasten to respond? And though this one is worth more than they are, has not the attraction of variety, has not the charm of new conquests, and the glory of their number, pleasures as sweet to offer? Why do we give chase to what eludes us, and ignore what is to hand? Ah, why indeed?...I don't know, but I am made to feel it is so.

There is no longer any happiness for me, no longer any peace but in the possession of this woman whom I love and hate with equal fury. I cannot tolerate my life until hers is again mine to dispose of. Then, contented and calm, I shall see her in turn buffeted by the storms that assail me now, and I shall stir up a thousand others too. I want hope and fear, faith and suspicion, all the evils devised by hate and all the blessings conferred by love, to fill her heart and to succeed one another there at my will. That time will come...But what a great deal there is still to do! How near I was yesterday! And today how far! How shall I reach her? I dare risk doing nothing yet. I feel I must be calm before I can make a decision; at the moment, the blood races through my veins.

My torments become twice as painful for the coolness with which everyone here treats my questions about the incident, as to its cause, as to the whole extraordinary aspect it wears...Nobody knows anything, nobody wants to know anything: they should scarcely have talked of it at all, had I been willing to talk of anything else. Madame de Rosemonde, to whom I flew this morning upon hearing the news, replied with the imperturbability of her age that it was the natural consequence of Madame de Tourvel's indisposition yesterday; that she had been afraid of being taken ill, and had preferred to return home. She finds it quite simple: she would have done the same herself, she told me. As if there could be any comparison between them: between my aunt, who has nothing left to do but die, and the woman who is all the charm and torment of my life!

Madame de Volanges, whom at first I had suspected as an accomplice, appeared not to be affected, except by the fact that she had not been consulted in the proceeding. I am very glad, I must admit, that she was not afforded the pleasure of doing me an ill turn. This proves to me, too, that she is not confided in as much as I had feared she might be – so that is one enemy the less. How pleased she would be if she knew it was I who am responsible for the disappearance! How she would swell with pride had it taken place on her advice! My God, how I hate her! Oh, I shall be seeing her daughter again: I mean to make her dance to my tune. I think therefore, that I shall be staying here some time. At any rate, the little thought I have given the matter inclines me to this course.

Don't you think, after all, that having made so decided a gesture, my ungrateful beloved is bound to be in dread of my reappearance? If, therefore, the thought has struck her that I might follow, she will not have failed to lock her doors; and I am no more anxious for her to make a habit of that than I am to suffer the humiliation of it myself. I should prefer, on the contrary, to announce that I am remaining here. I shall even entreat her to return. And when she is quite convinced that I am staying away, I shall arrive upon her doorstep. We shall see how she takes that meeting. But it must be deferred so as to increase its effect, and I don't yet know whether I shall have the patience. I have opened my mouth twenty times today to call for my horses. However, I shall control myself. I undertake to be here to receive your reply to this. I ask only, my love, that you don't make me wait for it.

More than anything else, it would annoy me not to know what is happening. My valet, however, who is in Paris, has some right of access to the chambermaid. He may be useful. I am sending him money and instructions. I hope you will not object to my enclosing both with this letter, nor to putting you to the trouble of sending them to him by one of your servants, with orders to deliver them to him in person. I take this precaution because the odd fellow has a habit of never receiving letters I write him when they contain directions that incommode him in any way; and he does not seem to me, at the moment, to be as taken with his conquest as I should like him to be.

Good-bye, my love; if some happy thought strikes you, some means of hastening my progress, let me know of it. I have more than once acknowledged how useful your friendship can be; I acknowledge it again. I feel calmer since I began writing to you. At least I am speaking to someone who understands me, and not to one of the cabbages in whose midst I have been vegetating since this morning. Truly, the longer I live, the more I am tempted to think that in all the world it is only you and I who are worth anything.

Château de ———
3 October 17–

LETTER 101: *The Vicomte de Valmont to Azolan, his valet*
You must be exceedingly stupid to have left here yesterday morning without knowing that Madame de Tourvel was leaving too; or, if you knew, not to have told me about it. To what purpose do you spend my money getting drunk with footmen; to what purpose do you spend time, which ought to be employed in my service, playing the gallant with chambermaids, if I am not as a result to be better informed of what is happening? Such, however, has been your negligence. I warn you that if you make one more mistake in this business, it will be the last that you commit in my service.

It is necessary that you inform me of everything that happens at Madame de Tourvel's: of her health, whether she sleeps or not; whether she is sad or gay; whether she goes out often, and to whose house; whether she receives anyone at home, and whom; how she passes her time; whether she is bad-tempered with her maids, particularly with the one she brought here with her; what she does when she is alone; whether, when she reads, she reads uninterruptedly, or breaks off to daydream; what she does when she writes. Remember, too, to make friends with the man who carries her letters to the post. Offer, as often as possible, to run the errand for him; and whenever he accepts, dispatch only those letters that seem to you to be of no consequence, sending me the rest, particularly those addressed to Madame de Volanges, should you find any.

Make arrangements to continue a while longer as your Julie's fond admirer. If she has found another, as you believe, make her agree to share her favors. You are not going to pride yourself on any ridiculous sense of delicacy – you will be in the same situation as a great many others who are your betters. If, however, your colleague makes a nuisance of himself; if you should observe, for instance, that he occupies too much of Julie's time during the day, thereby permitting her to be less often with her mistress, you will find some means of getting rid of him; or you will pick a quarrel with him. Don't be afraid of the consequences: I shall give you my support. Above all, you are not to leave that house. Only the most constant attention will enable you to see everything, and to see true. If it should happen that one of the servants is dismissed, you may even offer yourself in his place, as being no longer employed by me. Say in this case that you have left me to look for a more peaceable and well-regulated household. Try, in other words, to get yourself accepted. I shall keep you, notwithstanding, in my own service during this time. It shall be as it was with the Duchesse de ———, and in the end Madame de Tourvel will reward you equally well.

Were you well enough supplied with skill and enthusiasm these instructions would suffice; but to make up for what you lack in either respect I am sending you some money. The enclosed note authorizes you, as you will see, to draw twenty-five louis from my agent; for I have no doubt you are at present without a sou. You will employ as much of this sum as is necessary in persuading Julie to enter into correspondence with me. The rest will do to provide the servants with drink. Make a point, as far as is possible, of entertaining in the janitor's quarters, so that he will always be glad to see you. But don't forget that it is not your pleasures but your services for which I am paying.

Encourage in Julie a habit of noticing everything and of reporting everything, even what might seem to her to be negligible details. Better that she should record ten useless facts than omit one interesting one; and often what seems to be unimportant is not so. Since I must be told immediately of any occurrence that seems to you to merit my attention, you will, as soon as you receive this letter, send Philippe on the messenger's horse to establish himself at ———.* He will remain

---

*A village halfway between Paris and Madame de Rosemonde's château.

there till further orders, as a relay in case of necessity. For ordinary correspondence the post will do.

Be careful you don't lose this letter. Read it every day, as much to make sure that you still have it as to be certain you have forgotten nothing. Do, in short, all that you must do as being honored by my confidence. You know that if I am satisfied with you, you will be no less so with me.

Château de ————
3 October 17–

LETTER 102: *The Présidente de Tourvel to Madame de Rosemonde*
You will be surprised, Madame, to learn that I am leaving your house so suddenly. It will seem to you a very extraordinary thing to do; but you will be twice as astonished when you know my reasons. You will perhaps think that, in taking you into my confidence, I do not show enough consideration for the equanimity necessary to your age; that I am disregarding as well those feelings of reverence I owe you on so many grounds! Ah, Madame, forgive me, but my heart is oppressed, and it is only to a friend who is as kind as she is prudent that I can look for relief. Who else but you could I have chosen? Look upon me as your child. Look upon me with a mother's tenderness, I beseech you. My feeling for you gives me, perhaps, some right to it.

Where has the time gone when I was wholly given up to such praiseworthy feelings, when I was ignorant of those others that, afflicting the soul with mortal anguish – the anguish I now suffer – deprive it of strength to resist even as they impose the necessity of resisting? Ah, this fatal visit has ruined me...

What can I say after all? I am in love, yes, I am desperately in love. Alas! For the first time I have written that word, so often demanded and never given, and I should pay with my life for the pleasure of being able just once to let him hear it who has inspired it; yet I must continue to refuse! And he will continue to doubt my feelings, and to think himself ill-used. I am very unhappy! Why is it not as easy for him to read my heart as to rule it? Yes, I should suffer less if he knew how much I suffered. You yourself, to whom I say this, can have as yet but little idea how much that is.

In a few moments I shall have left him and made him unhappy. When he thinks he is still near me, I shall already be far away from him: the hour when I was used to seeing him every day will find me in a place to which he has never been, and where I must never allow him to come.

My preparations are already made; everything is here, before my eyes – they can rest on nothing that does not speak of this cruel parting. All is ready: I alone am not!…And the more my heart protests, the more it proves how necessary it is to submit.

I shall submit, of course. Better to die than to live guilty. I am already, I feel, only too guilty. Only my good sense remains to me; virtue has disappeared. I must, however, admit to you that what does remain I owe to his generosity. Intoxicated by the pleasure of seeing him, of hearing him speak, by the sweet awareness of his presence near me, by the even greater happiness of being able to make him happy, I lost all strength of mind and will; I had scarcely enough left to struggle, I had none to resist; I trembled with a sense of my danger without being able to escape it. Well then! He saw my distress, and took pity on me. How should I not love him for that? I owe him more than life itself.

Ah, if by staying with him I had only my life to tremble for, do not imagine that I should ever bring myself to leave! What is my life without him? Should I not be only too happy to lose it? Condemned to being the eternal cause of his misery and mine, unable either to pity myself or to comfort him; to defending myself each day against him and against myself; to sparing no effort in making him suffer when I wish only to devote my whole care to his happiness – are not a thousand deaths better than such a life? Yet that is going to be my fate. I shall endure it, nevertheless; I must find the courage to do so. O you, whom I have chosen for my mother, bear witness to my vow.

Accept, too, my promise that I shall never conceal from you any one of my actions; accept it, I beg you. I ask this of you as help of which I am in need. Bound thus to tell you everything, I shall begin to believe myself always in your presence. Your virtue will take the place of mine, for I could certainly never allow myself to blush in your sight: under that powerful restraint I shall, while I cherish in you the kind and reliable support of my weakness, honor you, too, as the guardian angel who will save me from shame.

I have felt shame enough in making you this request. Such are the fatal results of a presumptuous assurance! Why did I not sooner come to fear the inclination that I felt growing in me? Why did I flatter myself upon my ability to control it or conquer it? Imbecile! How little I know about love! Ah, had I fought it with more decision, it would perhaps have acquired less power over me. Perhaps, then, my departure would not have been necessary. Or, though I submitted to so painful a necessity, I need not perhaps have broken off entirely a friendship that it would have been sufficient to enjoy less frequently! But to lose everything at once! And forever! Oh, my friend!...But there! Even as I write to you I am betrayed into improper admissions. Ah, let me leave, let me leave; my involuntary sins may, at least, be expiated by my sacrifices.

Good-bye, my worthy friend. Love me as a daughter; adopt me for one of yours; and you may be certain that, in spite of my weakness, I shall rather die than make myself unworthy of your choice.

————

3 October 17–, at one o'clock in the morning

LETTER 103: *Madame de Rosemonde to the Présidente de Tourvel*
I was more distressed by your departure, my dear, than surprised at the reason for it. Long experience – and my interest in you – were enough to make clear to me the state of your feelings; and, to tell you the truth, there was nothing, or almost nothing, in your letter that was new to me. Had I only the letter to go by, I should still not know who it is that you love; for, though you speak of "him" constantly, you do not once write his name. But I need not to be told: I know quite well who it is. I remark upon it only because I am reminded that this was always the way of love. I see it is still, just as it used to be.

I scarcely thought that I should ever be put to recalling memories far removed from me now and totally inappropriate to my age. Since yesterday, however, I have been very preoccupied with them, in the hopes of finding something that might be of use to you. But what can I do except admire you and pity you? I commend the wise decision you have made; but I am alarmed by having to understand that you judged it necessary. When one has reached that point, it is very difficult to keep away from the man toward whom one's heart is constantly drawn.

Do not, however, be discouraged. Nothing is impossible to the noble spirit you have; and if the day should come (God forbid!) when you have the misfortune to succumb, believe me, my dear, you must at least leave yourself the consolation of having fought with all your might. Besides, what is beyond the power of human wisdom must be left to the Divine Grace to perform at its will. Perhaps you are on the point of receiving its succor; and your virtue, put to the proof of the most painful trials, will emerge purer and more resplendent than before. That strength, which is not yours today, you must hope to receive tomorrow. However, look to it not so much for support as for encouragement to you to use your own strength to the full.

Leaving it to Providence to protect you from a danger against which I can do nothing, I confine myself to supporting and consoling you as far as I possibly can. I cannot relieve your distress, but I shall share it. And with that to justify me, I shall gladly receive your confidences. Your heart, I know, needs to be opened to someone. I open mine to you: age has not yet chilled it to the point of being insensible to friendship. You will always find it ready to welcome you. This will be little comfort to your sufferings, but at least you shall not weep alone; and when your unhappy love, grown too strong for you, compels you to speak of it, it is better that you should do so to me than to *him*. You see how I follow your example: I do not think his name will ever be mentioned between us. For the rest, we understand each other.

I am not sure whether I do well to tell you that he appeared deeply moved by your departure. It would, perhaps, be wiser not to have mentioned it; but I am not fond of that sort of wisdom that distresses one's friends. I am, in any case, obliged to say no more about it. My feeble eyesight and trembling hand do not allow me long letters when I must write them myself.

Good-bye, then, my dear; good-bye, my sweet child. Yes, I am delighted to adopt you for my daughter. You have all that is necessary to a mother's pride and pleasure.

Château de ————
3 October 17–

LETTER 104: *The Marquise de Merteuil to Madame de Volanges*
To be quite honest, my dear and good friend, I could scarcely suppress an impulse of pride when I read your letter. To think that you should honor me with your entire confidence – that you should even go so far as to ask my advice! Oh, I should be so happy to think that I really deserved this mark of your esteem, that I did not owe it merely to the prepossession of a friend. At all events, whatever prompted it, it is most precious to my heart; and having obtained it is, in my opinion, only one reason more for my trying harder to deserve it. I shall, then (but without any pretensions to giving you advice) tell you freely what my views are. I hesitate to do so, because they differ from yours; but when I have put forward my arguments you shall be the judge – and if you condemn them, I am converted in advance to your opinion. I shall at least have good sense enough not to imagine that I have more of it than you.

If however, for this once, my own opinion proves to be the better one, the reason must be looked for among the illusions of maternal love. This is so praiseworthy a sentiment that it must have found a place in your heart. How plainly, in fact, it betrays itself in the decision you are tempted to make. Thus, if it sometimes happens that you are wrong, it is never but in your choice of virtues.

Prudence is, it seems to me, the virtue that must be preferred above the rest when one is determining the fate of others; all the more so when it is a case of sealing that fate with sacred and indissoluble promises, such as those of marriage. It is then that a mother, if she is as wise as she is loving, ought, as you so rightly say, "to help a daughter with her experience." How now, I ask you, can she better begin to achieve that purpose than by distinguishing, in her own mind, between what is agreeable and what is proper?

Is it not to debase a mother's authority, is it not to destroy it altogether, to subordinate it to a foolish emotion that maintains an illusory power only over those who fear it and disappears as soon as it is despised? For my part, I allow, I have never believed in these sweeping and irresistible passions, which seem to have been agreed upon as a convenient general excuse for our misdemeanors. I cannot conceive how any emotion, alive one moment and dead the next, can overpower the unalterable principles of decency, honor, and modesty; any more than I can understand how a woman who has betrayed those principles can be justified by her so-called passion, as though a thief could be justified by a passion for gold, or a murderer by a thirst for revenge.

Ah, who can say he has never experienced a struggle? But I have always tried to persuade myself that to resist it is enough to want to resist; and so far, at any rate, my experience has confirmed that opinion. What would virtue be without the duties it imposes? Its pursuit is in sacrifice; its reward is felt in our hearts. These truths cannot be denied except by those in whose interest it is to disregard them; corrupted as they already are, they hope to create a temporary illusion for themselves in attempting to justify bad conduct with bad arguments.

But is there anything to be feared from a simple and innocent child – a child of your own, whose pure and decent education can only have strengthened her fortunate heredity? Yet it is to a fear of this kind, a fear, if I may say so, humiliating to your daughter, that you wish to sacrifice the advantageous match your prudence has arranged for her! I like Danceny very much, and for a long time, as you know, I have seen little of Monsieur de Gercourt; but my liking for one and my indifference to the other do not prevent my seeing the enormous difference in their pretensions.

They are equally well-born, I agree. But one has no fortune, while the other's is such that, even without the advantage of birth, it would be sufficient to take him anywhere. I willingly allow that money does not guarantee happiness; but it must also be allowed that it makes happiness a great deal easier to achieve. Mademoiselle de Volanges is, as you say, rich enough for two: nevertheless, the sixty thousand livres a year she is going to enjoy will not amount to so very much when she bears the name of Danceny, and must set up and maintain an establishment appropriate to that name. We are no longer in the age of Madame de Sévigné. Luxury nowadays is ruinous. We criticize, but must conform, and superfluities in the end deprive us of necessities.

As to qualities of character, of which you make much account with good reason, Monsieur de Gercourt's are certainly beyond reproach, and it is to his advantage that they have already been put to the proof. I should like to think, and I do in fact think, that Danceny yields nothing to him here – but can we be as sure of him? It is true that he has till now appeared to be exempt from the usual infirmities of youth, and that in spite of the manners of our age he has shown a taste for good company which makes one argue well of him. But who knows whether or not this apparent good sense is simply the consequence of his mediocre fortune? However little fear there is of a man becoming corrupt or dissolute, he must have money to play the gambler or the libertine; and he may still enjoy the vices that he is chary of carrying to excess. After all, Danceny will not be the first man to have found his way into good company solely for lack of anything better to do.

I am not saying (God forbid!) that I believe all this of him. But there would always be a risk; and how sorry you would be if the consequences were unhappy! How would you answer if your daughter were to say: "Mother, I was young and inexperienced. I was led astray into an error that was pardonable in one of my age. But Heaven had foreseen my weakness and had provided me with a wise mother to make up for it and to preserve me from it. Why then, forgetting your prudence, did you consent to my unhappiness? Was it for me to choose a husband, when I knew nothing about the married state? Though I were resolved upon it, was it not your duty to oppose me? However, I was never so foolishly insistent. Determined to obey you, I awaited your choice with respectful resignation; never did I swerve from the submission I owed you. Yet the most rebellious of children would suffer no more than I do now. Ah, your weakness has ruined me..."? Perhaps her respect for you will silence her complaints. But your mother's love will divine her feelings. And your daughter's tears, for all that they are stifled, will nonetheless fall scalding upon your heart. Where then will you look for consolation? To this foolish love against which you should have protected her, but by which, instead, you allowed yourself to be beguiled?

I do not know, my dear, whether I have too strong a distrust of this passion: but I think it is to be feared, even in marriage. It is not that I disapprove of a decent and tender feeling animating the conjugal ties, softening in some sort the duties they impose; but it is not for feeling to form these ties, it is not for the illusion of a moment to govern the choice of a lifetime. After all, in order to choose we must compare, and how compare when one person alone has all our attention? When that person himself cannot be properly understood, bewitched, and infatuated as we are?

I have, as you may suppose, met several women who suffered from this dangerous malady. Some of them received me into their confidence, and not one but made her lover out to be a perfect being. But this chimerical perfection exists only in their imaginations. Out of their heated fancies they produce charms and virtues with which they adorn the man of their choice according to taste, decking out what is often a very inferior dummy in the vestments of a god. But, whoever he is, they have scarcely dressed him up when, taken in by the illusion of their own creating, they fall to adoring him.

Either your daughter does not love Danceny or she is a victim of the same illusion; if her love is reciprocated, he is its victim too. So that your argument in favor of uniting them forever is reduced to a certainty that, under the circumstances, they do not and cannot know each other. But, you will say, do Monsieur de Gercourt and my daughter know each other any better? No, of course not; but at least they are merely ignorant of each other, not deceived by each other. What happens between husband and wife in such cases, supposing them to be well-bred? Each studies the other and himself or herself in relation to the other, looks for and quickly finds those inclinations and desires which must be given up in the interests of mutual harmony. Such small sacrifices are made without difficulty because they are reciprocal and determined upon beforehand: they are the foundation of what soon becomes a mutual regard. And habit, which strengthens all the inclinations it does not destroy, forms by degrees that cordial friendliness and that sympathetic trust in each other, which, it seems to me, together with respect, constitute the true, the lasting happiness of marriage.

The illusions of love may be sweeter, but who is not aware that they are also less durable? And what dangers threaten at the moment when they die! It is then that the smallest faults begin to seem enormous and insupportable by contrast with the ideal of perfection that has taken possession of our minds. Husband and wife both think that it is the other alone who has changed, that they themselves are still to be appreciated at the value a momentary illusion once set upon them. They are astonished to find that they no longer exert the charm they themselves no longer feel. Wounded vanity embitters their thoughts, enlarges their wrongs, provokes ill humor, rouses hatred; and frivolous pleasures are at length paid for in lasting misfortune.

That, my dear friend, is my opinion upon the subject that concerns us. I do not defend it, I merely state it; it is for you to decide. But if you stand by your own views, may I ask you to let me know what arguments you have found to put against mine? I should be very glad to know your intentions, and especially to be set at rest concerning the fate of your charming daughter, whose happiness I ardently desire, as much in friendship to her as in the friendship that binds me to you as long as I live.

Paris
4 October 17–

LETTER 105: *The Marquise de Merteuil to Cécile Volanges*
Well, my little one! So you are exceedingly sorry and ashamed! And this Monsieur de Valmont is a wicked man, is he? What! Does he dare treat you as he would treat the woman he loved most of all? Has he taught you what you were dying of anxiety to know? Really, such behavior is unforgivable. And you, for your part, would like to keep your virtue for your lover (who does not take advantage of it); to cultivate the pains but not the pleasures of love. What could be better? You would make a marvelous character in a novel. Passion, misfortune, and virtue on top of it all, what an array of splendid things! One is sometimes bored, it is true, during the brilliant display, but it is well done.

There, there, the poor child, how much she is to be pitied! There were shadows under her eyes the next day! What will you say, then, when you see them under your lover's? Come, come, my angel, it will not always be like this: not all men are Valmonts. And then, not to have the courage to raise those eyes! Oh, that indeed you were right not to do – everyone would have seen your adventure written in them. Believe me, though: if that were so, all our women, and even the girls, would wear a much demurer air.

In spite of the compliments I am compelled to pay you, as you notice, it must still be admitted that you failed to deliver the coup de grâce, that is, to tell everything to your mama. And you had begun so well! You had already thrown yourself into her arms – sobbed – she wept too; what a pathetic scene! And what a pity to have left it incomplete! Your sweet mother, in a rapture of satisfaction and by way of assisting your virtue, would have immured you in a cloister for the rest of your life. There you could have loved Danceny as much as you liked without fear of rivalry or sin. You could have despaired at your leisure, and Valmont would certainly never have disturbed your grief with vexatious pleasures.

Seriously, is it possible at past fifteen years of age to be as much of a child as you are? You are quite right to say that you do not deserve my kindness. I wished, however, to be your friend; and it is not unlikely that you need one, with the mother you have and the husband she intends to give you! But if you don't grow up a little, what can one do for you? What can one hope for when what usually brings girls to their senses seems, on the contrary, to have deprived you of yours?

If you could, for a moment, bring yourself to think reasonably, you would soon find that you have cause to rejoice rather than to complain. But you are ashamed, and that worries you! Oh, you may be at ease on that score: the shame that love brings with it is no different from the pain – it is felt only once. One may make a pretense of it later, but one never feels it again. The pleasure, however, remains, and that is something. I think I have even made out between the lines of your little outburst that you are capable of making a great deal of it. Come now, a little honesty. That agitation that prevented you "from doing as you said," that made you find it "so difficult to defend yourself," that made you "almost sorry" when Valmont left – was it really shame that produced it, or was it pleasure? And "his way of saying things so that one is hard put to it to think of a reply": was that not a consequence of "his way of doing things"? Ah, young woman, you are lying, lying to your friend! That is not good enough. But let us say no more about it.

In a situation such as yours, that which for the rest of the world would be a pleasure, and no more than a pleasure, becomes a piece of veritable good fortune. After all, since you find yourself between mother and lover whose respective love you will always find necessary – the former's to your interests, the latter's to your happiness – why have you not seen that the only means of achieving these contradictory aims is to pursue a third? In your preoccupation with a new adventure you will seem to your mama to be sacrificing, for the sake of submitting to her will, an inclination she does not favor, and at the same time you will acquire in your lover's eyes the honor of putting up a defense. While you assure him ceaselessly of your love, you offer him not the least guarantee of it; and he will not fail to attribute your refusals, which you will hardly find it difficult to make in the circumstances, to your virtue. He will perhaps complain, but will love you the more for it. And the acquisition of this dual merit – on the one hand the sacrifice of love, resistance to it on the other – will cost you no more than the enjoyment of its pleasures. Oh, how many women there are who have lost reputations they might safely have preserved had they been able to carry off a plan of this sort!

Does not the course I am suggesting seem to you to be the most reasonable one to take, as it is certainly the most pleasant? Do you know what you have achieved by the one you have in fact adopted? Your mama has attributed your excess of grief to an excess of love; she is beside herself and waits only to be more certain before she punishes you. She has just written to me about it: she will try every means of obtaining a confession from your own lips. She will go so far, she says, as to suggest Danceny to you for a husband, in order to incite you to talk. If you allow yourself to be misled by her pretense of kindness, if you reply according to the dictates of your heart, you will soon suffer a long, perhaps perpetual, imprisonment, and you will repent your blind credulity at your leisure.

You must meet the ruse she intends to use against you with another. Begin by looking less sorrowful, by making her believe that you are thinking less of Danceny. She will be the more easily convinced in that this is the usual effect of absence. And she will be the more pleased with you in that she will be provided with an excuse to applaud her own prudence in removing you from Paris. But if she still remains doubtful, insists on putting you to the test, and broaches the subject of marriage to you, take cover like a well brought-up girl in your complete obedience. What will you, in point of fact, be risking? As far as husbands are concerned, one is as good as another, and even the most inconvenient is less of a trial than a mother.

As soon as she is more pleased with you, your mama will have you married. Then, with more freedom of action, you will be able to leave Valmont for Danceny or even to keep them both, just as you choose. For, you must remember, your Danceny is agreeable; but he is one of those men you may have when you want and for as long as you want – you may therefore make yourself easy about him. Valmont is quite another matter: difficult to keep, and dangerous to leave. He demands great skill or, if you have none, great tractability. On the other hand, if you could succeed in attaching him to you as a friend, it would indeed be a piece of good fortune. He would put you immediately in the first rank of our women of fashion. It is thus that one acquires substance in the world, not by blushing and crying, as you used to do when your nuns made you kneel to your dinner.

If you are wise, then, you will try to be reconciled to Valmont, who must be very angry with you; and, since one must always be capable of correcting one's mistakes, don't be afraid of making a few advances to him. You will soon learn that though a man takes the first step, we are nearly always obliged to take the second ourselves. You have a pretext for doing so, for you must not keep this letter: I insist that you return it to Valmont as soon as you have read it. Don't, however, forget to seal it up again before doing so. In the first place, you must take all the credit yourself for your proceedings with him: you must not seem to be acting upon advice. And then, you are the only person in the world who is enough my friend to hear me speak as I do.

Good-bye, my angel. Follow my advice and tell me whether you are not the better for it.

P.S. By the way, I was forgetting... one word more. Take more care of your style. You still write like a child. I can quite see the reason for it: you say what you think, and never what you don't believe. This will do between us who can have nothing to conceal from one another – but with everybody! With your lover above all! You will always be taken for a little ninny. You will agree, I am sure, that when you write to someone it is for his sake and not for yours. You must therefore try to say less what you think than what you think he will be pleased to hear.

Good-bye, my dear heart. I shall kiss you instead of scolding you, in the hope that you will be more reasonable in future.

Paris
4 October 17–

LETTER 106: *The Marquise de Merteuil to the Vicomte de Valmont*
Bravo, Vicomte – this time I love you madly! For the rest, the first of your two letters led me to expect the second, which did not astonish me at all. While, proud of your forthcoming success, you were claiming your reward and asking me whether I was ready, I could see quite well that I need not be in any great hurry. Yes, on my honor, as I read your touching account of the tender scene that left you so *deeply moved*, as I noticed you displaying a self-restraint worthy of the finest epoch of our chivalry, I said to myself a dozen times, "There goes another botched affair."

But it could not have been otherwise. What do you expect a poor woman to do when she surrenders and is not taken? Upon my word, in such circumstances she must at least save her honor — and that is what your Présidente has done. I may tell you that, having observed that her course of action has proved really not ineffective, I propose to make use of it myself at the first more or less serious opportunity that offers; but I assure you that if the man for whom I go to so much trouble does not take more advantage of it than you did, he may certainly renounce me forever.

There you are, then, reduced to absolutely nothing! And by two women, one of whom had already passed the point of no return, while the other aspired to nothing better! Well! You will think I am boasting, you will say that it is easy to be wise after the event, but I can swear to you that I expected it. You are really without any genius for your calling; you know what you have learned but can invent nothing new, so that as soon as circumstances no longer conform to your usual formulas, as soon as you must deviate from the customary path, you are brought up short like the merest schoolboy. An attack of childishness on the one hand, and on the other a relapse into prudery, because they do not happen every day, are enough to disconcert you; you could neither prevent them nor cure them. Ah, Vicomte, Vicomte! You are teaching me not to judge men by their successes. Soon we shall have to say of you, "He was once a man of mark." And when you have perpetrated absurdity after absurdity you come running back to me! It seems I have nothing better to do than to repair the mischief. Doing that, at any rate, would keep me fully occupied.

Be that as it may, one of your two adventures was undertaken without my approbation, and I shall not meddle with it; as for the other, since you have shown some willingness to oblige me in it, I shall make it my concern. The letter I enclose, which you will first read and then deliver to the little Volanges, is more than enough to bring her back to you. But, I beg you, take some pains with the child. Let us work together to make her the despair of her mother and Gercourt. Don't be afraid of increasing the doses. If you do, it is quite clear to me that the little creature will not be at all frightened. Our designs upon her fulfilled once, she must continue as best she can.

I am now entirely disinterested where she is concerned. I had some thought of making a kind of assistant in intrigue out of her, of employing her, as it were, for subordinate roles, but I see that the material is lacking. She has a stupid ingenuousness that did not even yield to the medicine you administered — a medicine that is seldom without effect. It is, in my view, the most dangerous malady from which a woman can suffer. It denotes, in particular, a weakness of character that is nearly always incurable, and is an impediment to everything; so that, while attempting to fit the girl for a life of intrigue, we should only be turning out a woman of easy virtue. Now I can think of nothing more insipid than the complaisance of stupid women who surrender, knowing neither how nor why, simply because they are attacked and cannot resist. This sort of woman is absolutely nothing but a machine for giving pleasure.

You will say that we have only to turn her into one of these and our plans are suited. Well and good! But don't forget that everyone is soon familiar with the springs and motors of these machines; and that, to make use of this one without danger it will be necessary to do so with all speed, to stop in good time, then to destroy it. In fact we shall not lack the means to get rid of it: Gercourt will always be there to shut it away when we require. And in the end, when he can no longer doubt the fraud, when it is quite public and altogether notorious, what will it matter if he takes his revenge, so long as he can find no consolation? And what I say of the husband you will, no doubt, apply to the mother – so that is that.

Having fixed upon this line of proceeding as the best, I have decided to hurry the girl a little, as you will see from my letter. This makes it very important to leave nothing in her hands that might compromise us, and I beg you to take care of that. Once this precaution has been taken, I shall see to the moral persuasion; the rest is your concern. If, however, you notice in the course of events that the ingenuousness is correcting itself, we shall still have time to change our plans. We should in any case have had to do sooner or later what we are going to do: our efforts will under no circumstances be wasted.

Did you know that my own efforts were in danger of being so, and that Gercourt's lucky star had almost prevailed over my prudence – that Madame de Volanges had a moment of natural weakness and wanted to give her daughter to Danceny? This was the meaning of the more sympathetic interest you noticed being offered *the morning after*. And you again would have been the cause of this fine state of affairs! Fortunately the solicitous mother wrote to me about it, and I hope my reply will turn her against the idea. I spoke so often of virtue, and above all flattered her so much, that she should find after all that I am right.

I am sorry not to have had time to copy the letter, so that you might have been edified by the austerity of my moral views. You might have seen how I despise those women who are depraved enough to take a lover! It is so easy to be a bigot in writing! It never harms anyone else, and is no bother to oneself... And then I am not unaware that the good lady has herself, like anyone else, been guilty of some little weaknesses in the days of her youth, and I should not be sorry to humiliate her a little, if only to disturb her conscience: it would console me a little for the compliments I have paid her to the discomfort of my own. It was again, in the same letter, the thought of hurting Gercourt that gave me the courage to speak well of him.

Good-bye, Vicomte. I very much approve of your decision to stay where you are for some time. I can think of no way to hasten your progress, but I invite you to relieve your boredom in the company of our pupil. As for me, you must see, in spite of your polite quotation, that it is still necessary to wait; and you will agree, I have no doubt, that it is not my fault.

Paris
4 October 17–

LETTER 107: *Azolan to the Vicomte de Valmont*
Monsieur,

In accordance with your instructions I went immediately upon receiving your letter to Monsieur Bertrand, who gave me the twenty-five louis as you had commanded. I asked him for two more for Philippe, whom I had told to leave immediately, as Monsieur instructed, and who had no money; but Monsieur your agent refused, saying he had no instructions from you as to that. So I had to give the money to Philippe myself, and Monsieur will take that into account if he will be so kind.

Philippe left yesterday evening. I strongly advised him not to move from the inn, so that one could be sure of finding him in case of need.

I went immediately to Madame the Présidente's to see Mademoiselle Julie, but she was out and I spoke only to La Fleur, from whom I was not able to learn anything because, since he arrived, he has been in the house only at mealtimes. It is his assistant who is on duty, and as Monsieur knows, I have no acquaintance with him. But I made a beginning today. I returned this morning to Mademoiselle Julie's, and she seemed very glad to see me. I inquired after the reason for her mistress's return; she told me she knew nothing, and I think that is true. I called her to account for not letting me know they were leaving, and she assured me she knew nothing about it until the evening before when she attended Madame to bed; indeed, she spent the whole night packing and did not have more than two hours' sleep, poor girl. She did not leave her mistress's room that evening until past one o'clock, and when she left, her mistress was just sitting down to write.

In the morning, before she left, Madame de Tourvel gave a letter to the concierge. Mademoiselle Julie does not know whom it was for; she says it was perhaps for Monsieur. But Monsieur has said nothing.

All during the journey Madame wore a great hood over her face, and her face could not therefore be seen; but Mademoiselle Julie is sure that she cried a great deal. She did not say a word all the way, and did not wish to stop at ————,* as she had done coming – which Mademoiselle Julie was not too pleased about, as she had eaten no breakfast. But, as I said to her, a mistress is a mistress.

On their arrival Madame went to bed, but she only remained there for a few hours. On rising she called the porter and gave him orders to admit nobody. She made no toilette at all. She sat down to dinner, but ate only a little soup, and immediately left the table. Coffee was taken to her room, and Mademoiselle Julie went in at the same time. She found her mistress putting papers away in her desk, and distinctly saw that they were letters. I should be willing to stake anything on their being Monsieur's. Of the three that arrived for her in the afternoon, she was still looking at one long into the evening! I am quite sure that this again was one of Monsieur's. Why, then, did she run away like that? It astonishes me, I must say. But Monsieur must surely know the reason, and it is none of my business.

In the afternoon Madame the Présidente went into the library and removed two books, which she carried to her boudoir. Mademoiselle Julie, however, assures me that she read for not more than a quarter of an hour the whole day, and that she did nothing else but examine the letter and dream, resting her head on her hand. Since I thought Monsieur might be very glad to know what books they were, and since Mademoiselle Julie could not tell me, I had myself taken into the library today under the pretext of wanting to look around it. There were only two empty spaces for books, one being for the second volume of *Christian Thoughts*, the other for the first volume of a book entitled *Clarissa*. I write the title as I saw it written; Monsieur will perhaps know what it is.

Last evening Madame took no supper; she drank only some tea.

She rang early this morning, asked for the horses to be ready immediately, and before nine o'clock was at the Cistercian church, where she heard Mass. She wished to make her confession, but her confessor was away and will not be back for another week or ten days. I thought to let Monsieur know this.

---

*The same village, halfway to Paris.

Then she came home, took breakfast, and afterward began writing, continuing until nearly one o'clock. I found an early opportunity of doing what Monsieur was most anxious of all for me to do; it was I who took the letters to the post. There was nothing for Madame de Volanges, but I am sending a letter to Monsieur which was for Monsieur the Président. It seemed to me to be the most interesting. There was also one for Madame de Rosemonde; but I supposed that Monsieur could always see that when he wanted to, and so let it go. As to what remained, Monsieur will soon know everything since Madame the Présidente has written to him too. From now on I shall obtain all the letters he wants, for it is nearly always Mademoiselle Julie who gives them to the servants, and she has assured me that, out of friendship for me and for Monsieur as well, she will willingly do what I ask.

She did not even want the money I offered her, but I feel sure Monsieur will wish to make her some little present; and if he so desires, and would like me to do it on his behalf, I could easily find out what she would like.

I hope that Monsieur will not find me negligent in his service, and I am very anxious to clear myself of the accusations he makes against me. If I did not know of Madame the Présidente's departure, it was, on the contrary, my zeal in Monsieur's service that explains it, since it was that which sent me off at three o'clock in the morning – which was why I did not see Mademoiselle Julie as usual the evening before, having slept at the "Tournebride,"[14] so as not to wake anyone in the house.

As to what Monsieur says of my being often without money, in the first place it is because I always like to do the proper thing, as Monsieur knows; and then I must, after all, maintain the honor of the coat I wear.

I know I should, perhaps, save a little for the future, but I put my entire trust in the generosity of Monsieur, who is such a good master.

As for going into Madame de Tourvel's service while remaining in Monsieur's, I hope that Monsieur will not insist upon it. It was quite different with Madame the Duchesse; but I shall certainly not wear livery, and a magistrate's livery at that, after having had the honor of being Monsieur's valet. In every other possible way Monsieur may dispose as he likes of one who has the honor to be, with as much affection as respect, his very humble servant.

Roux Azolan, valet
Paris
5 October 17–, at eleven o'clock in the evening

LETTER 108: *The Présidente de Tourvel to Madame de Rosemonde*

Oh, my dear kind mother! How I needed your letter, and how thankful I am to you. I read it again and again; I could not tear myself away from it. To it I owe the few moments of relief I have had since my departure. How good you are! Wisdom and virtue have sympathized with weakness! You have taken pity on my sufferings! Ah, if you knew what sufferings...they are terrible! I thought I had felt all the pains of love, but the truly unspeakable torment, which one must have experienced to be able to conceive, is to be separated from what one loves, to be separated forever!...Yes, the grief that crushes me today will return tomorrow, the day after tomorrow, for the rest of my life. My God, how young I still am, and how much time remains for suffering!...

To be the instrument of one's own misery, to tear out one's heart with one's own hands; and while one suffers insupportable tortures, to feel at every instant that one may end them with a word; and that this word should be a crime! Ah, my dear!...

When I took the painful decision to leave him I hoped that absence would increase my courage and my strength – how wrong I was! It seems, on the contrary, that absence has completed their ruin. I had more to fight against once; but even though I resisted I did not suffer complete privation. At least I saw him sometimes. Often, without daring to lift my eyes to his face, I felt his own fixed upon me. Yes, my dear, I felt them. It was as if they brought warmth to my soul, as if his looks, though they did not meet mine, could still reach my heart. But now, in this dreadful solitude, cut off from all that is dear to me, alone with my misfortunes, every moment of my dreary existence is an occasion for tears and there is nothing to sweeten the bitterness. My sacrifices have brought me no consolation; those I have made hitherto serve only to make those others more painful which I have still to make.

Only yesterday this was brought home to me. Among the letters delivered to me there was one from him. My servant was still two yards away from me when I recognized it among the others. I rose involuntarily from my chair: I was trembling, I could scarcely conceal my emotion, and my state of mind was not entirely disagreeable. A moment later, when I was alone again, the illusory pleasure vanished, and left me only with one more sacrifice to make. Could I, after all, open the letter which I longed to read? The fate that pursues me decrees that when something seems to be offered me as a consolation, it is only, on the contrary, a demand for some new renunciation, which is the more cruel when I think that Monsieur de Valmont must share it.

There it is at last, the name that haunts me continually, the name

I have found it so difficult to write. The sort of accusation you made against me about it truly alarmed me. I beseech you to believe that false modesty has in no way affected my confidence in you – and why should I be afraid of naming him? Ah, it is my feelings, not their object, for which I blush. Who but he could be worthier of inspiring them? Yet, I do not know why, his name does not come naturally to my pen. Even just then I had to think before putting it down.

To return to him, you tell me that he appeared to you to be *deeply moved by my departure*. What then did he do? What did he say? Has he spoken of returning to Paris? Please dissuade him from doing so insofar as you are able. If he has properly understood me, he will not bear me a grudge for leaving him; but he must also understand that my decision is irrevocable. One of my worst torments is not knowing what he thinks. I still have his letter here...but I am sure you are of my opinion, that I ought not to open it.

It is only because of you, my dear indulgent friend, that I am not entirely separated from him. I do not want to abuse your kindness; I understand perfectly that your letters cannot be long; but you will not refuse your child two words, one to keep up her courage and the other to comfort her. Good-bye, my most worthy friend.

Paris
5 October 17–

LETTER 109: *Cécile Volanges to the Marquise de Merteuil*
It was only today, Madame, that I gave Monsieur de Valmont the letter you did me the honor of writing to me. I kept it for four days in spite of my frequent fears that someone should find it; but I hid it away very carefully, and whenever the sense of my troubles overcame me I shut myself up to read it again.

I quite see now that what I thought was a great misfortune is scarcely a misfortune at all; and I must admit that there is a great deal of pleasure in it, so much so that I am hardly unhappy at all anymore. It is only the thought of Danceny that still torments me at times. But there are already a great many occasions when I don't think of him at all! The fact is, too, that Monsieur de Valmont is very agreeable!

Our reconciliation took place two days ago: it was very easy, since I had scarcely said two words to him when he told me that if I had something to tell him he would come to my room that evening, and I had only to reply that I was willing. And then, as soon as he was there, he seemed to be no more annoyed than he would have been had I never done anything to him. He scolded me only afterward, and even then very gently, as if...just like you – which proved to me that he is as much of a friend to me as you are.

You cannot imagine how many curious things he has told me, things I should never have believed, especially about Mamma. I should be very glad if you would let me know whether they are all true. At any rate, I could not help laughing at them; so much so that I once laughed out loud, which frightened us both very much. Mamma might have heard, and if she had come to investigate what would have become of me? This time she would certainly have sent me back to the convent!

Since we must be prudent, and since, as Monsieur de Valmont said himself, he would not risk compromising me for anything in the world, we have agreed that from now on he will come only to open the door, after which we shall go to his room. There we have nothing to fear. I have already been there once yesterday, and as I write I am waiting for him to come for me again. I hope, Madame, that you will no longer be able to find fault with me.

There was, however, one thing in your letter that surprised me very much, and that is what you say about Danceny and Monsieur de Valmont after I am married. I seem to remember that one day at the opera you said the opposite: that once I was married I should have to love no one but my husband, and that I should even have to forget Danceny. But perhaps I misunderstood you; I should much prefer it this way, because now I am no longer so afraid of being married. I even want to be, since I shall have more freedom when I am, and I hope I shall then be able to manage my affairs so that I need think of no one but Danceny. I am quite sure that I shall be really happy only with him, for the thought of him still disturbs me, and I can have no peace unless I am able to forget him, which it is very difficult to do. As soon as I think of him I am immediately miserable again.

What comforts me a little is that you assure me he will love me more – but are you quite sure of that?...Oh, yes, you would not want to deceive me. Yet how odd that it is Danceny I love, and Monsieur de Valmont...But, as you say, it is perhaps a piece of good fortune! Anyhow, we shall see.

I could not entirely understand your remarks on the subject of my style of writing. It seems to me that Danceny likes my letters as they are. I am quite aware, however, that I ought to say nothing to him of what is going on with Monsieur de Valmont; so you have no reason to be afraid.

Mamma has not yet said a word about my marriage, but leave it to me: when she does speak I promise you that, since she will only be doing so to trap me, I shall not hesitate to lie to her.

Good-bye, my very dear friend. Thank you very much. I assure you I shall never forget all your kindness toward me. I must finish here for it is nearly one o'clock and Monsieur de Valmont will be here before long.

Château de ———
10 October 17–

LETTER 110: *The Vicomte de Valmont to the Marquise de Merteuil*

O Heavenly Powers, I had a soul attuned to sorrow; give me one to support felicity!* It is, I think, the tender-hearted Saint-Preux who says this. Better endowed than he, I am capable of sustaining both emotions at once. Yes, my dear, I am at once very happy and very unhappy; and since you have my entire confidence, a twofold account of my pains and my pleasures is owing to you.

Know, then, that my ungrateful devotee still keeps me under severe restraint. I am up to my fourth rejected letter. I am perhaps wrong to say it is the fourth; for having guessed, after the first rejection, that it would be followed by a good many others, and having no desire to waste time in this way, I decided to reduce my complaints to a few platitudes and to omit the date from the letter: since the second dispatch it is the same one that has been traveling to and fro. I have done no more than change the envelope each time. If one day my beauty, as beauties generally do, finally relents out of fatigue if nothing else, she will keep the letter and there will be time enough then to find out what has been happening. As you will understand, I cannot, with this new species of correspondence, keep myself properly informed.

I have, however, discovered that the fickle creature has changed her confidante; at any rate, I have confirmed that since her departure from here no letters have arrived from her for Madame de Volanges, whereas two have arrived for old Rosemonde; and since the latter has said nothing, since she has not so much as opened her mouth on the subject of "her dear, delightful friend," about whom previously she would never stop talking, I conclude that it is she who has been taken into confidence. I presume that it is the need of talking to someone about me, on the one hand, and a slight shame where Madame de Volanges is concerned at reverting to the subject of a feeling long since disavowed, on the other, that has produced this great change of tactics. I am afraid, too,

---

*Rousseau, *The New Heloise*.

I may have lost by it, for the older women grow, the harsher and stricter they become. The one might have said worse things about me. But the other will say worse things about love, and our soft-hearted prude is much more afraid of the feeling than of the person who inspires it.

My sole means of acquiring information is, as you may guess, to intercept their secret correspondence. I have already sent orders to my valet and daily await their execution. Till then I can do nothing, except at a venture; so for the past week I have been turning over in my mind every stratagem known to me, everything I have ever gleaned from novels or my own private experience. I can find nothing that suits either the circumstances of the affair or the character of its heroine. There would be no difficulty in finding my way into her house, even at night, nor yet again in putting her to sleep and making another Clarissa out of her — but to have recourse after more than two months of toil and trouble to methods that are not my own! To crawl slavishly in other's tracks, to triumph without glory!...No, I shall not allow her *the pleasure of vice with the honors of virtue.** It is not enough for me to possess her: I want her to give herself up. Now, for that it is not only essential that I gain access to her, but that I should do so at her bidding; that I should find her alone and prepared to listen to me; and, above all, that I should close her eyes to the danger, because should she perceive it she must surmount it or die. But the better I know what has to be done, the more difficult I find it to do; and even if you are going to laugh at me again, I must admit that my embarrassment increases the more I think about it.

I think I should be at wits end were it not for the happy distraction our pupil supplies: I owe it to her that I have still something better to do than compose elegies.

Would you believe that the girl was so frightened that three long days went by before your letter produced its full effect? See how a single wrong idea can spoil the most favorable disposition!

At any rate, it was not till Saturday that she came circling round me to mumble a few words: uttered, however, so softly, so smothered by diffidence, that it was impossible to hear them. But the blush they occasioned gave me a clue to their meaning. Till then I had shown reserve; but touched by so amusing a repentance, I was willing to promise the pretty penitent that I would come and see her that same evening. My forgiveness was received with all the gratitude due so much condescension.

The New Heloise.

Since I never lose sight of either your plans or mine, I decided to make the most of the opportunity both to gauge the true potentialities of this child and to hasten her education. But to accomplish the task in greater freedom, it was necessary to change the place of our rendezvous. A simple boudoir, which is all that separates your pupil's bedroom from that of her mother, was not enough to inspire in her the security she must feel before she can stretch out at ease. I decided, therefore, that I would quite innocently make some noise that would frighten her enough to make her choose a safer refuge for the future. Once more she spared me the trouble.

The little creature laughs a great deal: and, to encourage her merriment, I had the idea of relating, during our *entr'actes*, all the scandalous stories that came into my head. To give them an added spice, and to make them more interesting, I ascribed them all to her mama, whom it amused me to bedeck with vices and follies.

It was not by accident that I hit upon the idea. It encouraged our timid schoolgirl more than anything else could have, and at the same time it inspired her with the profoundest contempt for her mother. I observed long ago that if it is not always necessary to employ this method in seducing a young girl, it is the indispensable and often the most effective course when one wants to corrupt her. For the girl who does not respect her mother will not respect herself: a moral truth I think so useful that I was very glad to supply another example in illustration of it.

Meanwhile your pupil, who had no thought of morals, was ready to choke with laughter at any moment; and finally, on one occasion, nearly exploded. I had no difficulty in convincing her that she had made a *frightful noise*, and I pretended great terror, which she was easily persuaded to share. So as to drive the lesson home, I banished all further hopes of pleasure and left her three hours earlier than usual. We agreed, as we parted, that from the next day on we should meet in my room.

I have received her there twice already; and in this short space of time the schoolgirl has learned nearly as much as her master knows. Yes, I have taught her everything, down to the minor complaisances! I have omitted only the art of taking precautions.

Thus busy the whole night long, I have begun to sleep during a great part of the day; and as there is nothing to attract me in the company now at the house, I spend scarcely more than an hour in the drawing room each day. I even decided today to eat in my room, and I intend not to leave it henceforth except to take a little walk now and again. This idiosyncratic behavior will be put down to the state of my health.

I have declared myself a victim of *the vapors*, and have also announced a little fever. This puts me to no trouble but that of speaking slowly and faintly. As for the change in my looks, trust your pupil for that. *Love will provide.**

I spend my leisure dreaming of ways in which I can regain my lost advantage over that ungrateful woman and in composing a sort of debauchee's catechism for the use of my pupil. There is nothing in it that is not called by its technical name, and I am already laughing at the interesting conversation this will afford her and Gercourt on the first night of their marriage. Nothing is more amusing than her ingenuousness in using what little she already knows of the jargon! She has no idea that there is any other way of referring to the same things. The child is really enchanting! The contrast between her naive candor and the language of insult could not, of course, fail to be striking, and – I don't know why – it is only the unusual that pleases me now.

I am perhaps a little too preoccupied with it, since I am compromising both my time and my health. But I hope my pretended illness, besides saving me from the boredom of the drawing room, will be useful too with my austere devotee, whose tigerish virtue is nevertheless allied to a most tender sensibility! I have no doubt she has already heard about this grave indisposition, and I should very much like to know what she thinks of it; the more so because I should be willing to swear she will not fail to attach the credit for it to herself. In future I shall govern the state of my health according to the impression it makes upon her.

There, my love: you know as much about my affairs as I myself do. I hope soon to have more interesting news to give you; and I beg you to believe that, among the pleasures I anticipate, I set great store by the reward I am expecting from you.

Château de ———
11 October 17–

LETTER 111: *The Comte de Gercourt to Madame de Volanges*
It seems, Madame, that everything is now quiet in this country, and we are daily expecting permission to return to France. I hope you will not doubt that I am still as anxious to return there and to form the ties that are to unite me with you and Mademoiselle de Volanges. My cousin, however, Monsieur the Duc de ———, to whom as you know I am

---

*Regnard, *Folies amoureuses.*

under great obligations, has just informed me of his recall from Naples. He tells me that he expects to travel by way of Rome, and hopes en route to see that part of Italy with which he is still unacquainted. He invites me to accompany him on the journey, which will take from six weeks to two months. I cannot deny that I should like to make the most of this opportunity, knowing that once I am married I shall have difficulty in finding time for journeys abroad other than those necessitated by my military service. Perhaps, too, it would be more convenient if the wedding were postponed until the winter, since not before then will all my relations be together in Paris at the same time, in particular Monsieur the Marquis de ———, to whom I owe my hope of an association with you. Despite these considerations, my plans in this respect shall be absolutely subordinated to your wishes. However slightly you may prefer your original arrangements, I am prepared to cancel my own. I beg you only to let me know your intentions in the matter as soon as possible. I shall await your reply here, and that alone will decide what I do.

I am, Madame, with respect, and with all the sentiments fitting in a son, your very humble, etc.

The Comte de Gercourt
Bastia
10 October 17–

LETTER 112: *Madame de Rosemonde to the Présidente de Tourvel (dictated)*

I have only this instant, my dear, received your letter of the eleventh* with the gentle reproaches it contains. You must admit that you would have liked to make many more, and that had you not remembered you were my daughter you would really have scolded me. It would, nevertheless, have been very unjust of you. It was because I wished and hoped to reply to you myself that I postponed doing so from day to day; and even now, as you see, I am obliged to do so through my maid, at second hand. My miserable rheumatism has attacked me again and lodged itself this time in my right arm, and I am an utter cripple. This is what comes, young and healthy as you are, of having an aged friend: you suffer for her infirmities.

As soon as my pain gives me a little respite, I promise you we shall have a long talk. In the meanwhile I shall say only that I have received

---

*This letter has not been found.

your two letters; that they have increased, if that is possible, my feelings of friendship for you; and that I shall never cease to enter with the most lively interest into all that concerns you.

My nephew is also a little unwell, but there is no danger and not the least cause for anxiety: it is a slight indisposition that, so far as I can see, affects his temper more than his health. We scarcely see him now.

His confinement and your departure have not made our little circle any more gay. The little Volanges, especially, feels the want of you terribly and spends the whole day yawning fit to swallow her point lace. During the past few days in particular she has done us the honor of falling into a profound sleep every afternoon after lunch.

Good-bye, my dear. I am still your very good friend: your mama, your sister even, were my great age to permit my claiming that title. In short, I am attached to you by all the tenderest feelings.

Signed: Adélaïde, for Madame de Rosemonde
Château de ———
14 October 17–

LETTER 113: *The Marquise de Merteuil to the Vicomte de Valmont*
I think I must warn you, Vicomte, that they begin to talk of you in Paris. Your absence is remarked and its reason already guessed at. I was present yesterday at a supper where there were a great many people. It was positively affirmed that you were imprisoned in the country by a romantic and unhappy love. The faces of all those who envy your success and of all the women you have neglected were immediately the picture of joy. If you take my advice, you will not allow these dangerous rumors to acquire further substance, and will return forthwith to destroy them by your presence.

Remember that once you allow the idea that you are irresistible to lose credence, you will soon find that in fact you are being resisted more easily, and that your rivals have also lost their respect for you and are daring to enter the lists against you. For which of them does not believe himself to be a match for virtue? Remember too that, of the multitudes of women you have flaunted in the public eye, the ones you have not had will be trying to disabuse the world, while the others will be doing their utmost to deceive it. In any case, you must expect to be rated perhaps as much beneath your true worth as you have till now been rated above it.

Come back then, Vicomte, and don't sacrifice your reputation to a childish caprice. You have done all that we wished to do with the little

Volanges. As for your Présidente, it is obviously not by establishing yourself ten leagues away from her that you will rid yourself of your fancies. Do you think she will come looking for you? She perhaps no longer thinks of you or still thinks of you only to congratulate herself upon having humiliated you. Here at least you may find the opportunity that you need of reappearing with a flourish; and if you persist in continuing your ridiculous adventure, I cannot see that your return will make any difference . . . on the contrary.

After all, if your Présidente *adores you*, as you have so often told me and are so little able to prove, her one consolation, her sole pleasure must now be to speak of you, to find out what you are doing, what you are saying, what you are thinking, down to the least thing that concerns you. Every trifle assumes a value because of the privation that is felt in general. They are the crumbs that fall from the rich man's table: the rich man scorns them, but the beggar collects them avidly – they are his nourishment. Now, the poor Présidente is at present receiving all the crumbs she wants; and the more she has, the less inclined she will be to give way to an appetite for other things.

Moreover, since you know who her confidante is, you can be in no doubt that each of that lady's letters contains a little sermon on all she thinks proper "to the support of wisdom and the fortification of virtue."* Why then leave the one with a resource for her defense, the other with a means of attack?

Not that I am altogether of your opinion when you say that you have lost, you think, by the change of confidante. In the first place, Madame de Volanges hates you, and hatred is always more clear-sighted and cunning than friendship. All your old aunt's virtue will not commit her for a single instant to speaking ill of her nephew. Virtue has its weaknesses too. And then your fears are based on an observation that is absolutely false.

It is not true that "the older women grow, the harsher and stricter they become." It is between the ages of forty and fifty that, desperate at finding their complexions wither and furious at being obliged to give up pretensions and pleasures to which they are still inclined, nearly all women turn into prudes and shrews; this long interval is necessary before their sacrifice is complete. But as soon as it has been consummated, they divide themselves into two classes.

The more numerous one, which comprises those women who have had nothing but youth and beauty to recommend them, falls into a

---

One can never think of everything!, a comedy.

feebleminded apathy from which it never emerges except to play cards or practice a few devotions. These women are always boring, often querulous, sometimes a little meddlesome, but they are rarely malicious. One cannot say of them either that they are or are not severe. They have neither thought nor being, and merely repeat indifferently and uncomprehendingly everything they hear, retaining within themselves an absolute void.

The other much rarer class, and the really valuable one, contains those women who, having been possessed of a character and having taken care to cultivate their minds, are able to create an identity for themselves when the one provided by nature has failed them. They are able to polish their wits where before they had decked out their figures. Their judgment is generally sane, their intelligence at once solid, gay, and graceful. They replace their more seductive attractions with a more appealing kindness, and moreover with that joie de vivre, the charm of which only increases with age. Thus, making themselves loved by the young, they succeed in some way in recapturing their youth. But then far from being, harsh and strict, as you say, their customary tolerance, their long experience of human frailty, and above all the memories of youth which alone reconcile them to life incline them rather too much perhaps to the side of lenience.

What I can at any rate vouch for is that, having always sought after old women, the value of whose suffrage I early recognized, I have met several to whom I was attracted as much by inclination as by self-interest. I shall stop there: seeing that at the moment you take fire so easily and burn so earnestly, I am afraid you might of a sudden fall in love with your old aunt and bury yourself with her for good in the tomb you have already so long inhabited.

To resume: In spite of the enchantment your little schoolgirl seems to have cast over you, I cannot believe that she figures at all seriously in your plans. You found her at hand, you took her – well done! But that was no true pleasure. To tell the truth, you cannot even be said to have enjoyed her completely: you possess absolutely nothing but her person. I leave her heart out of account – I am sure you can scarcely have been interested in that – but you have not even penetrated her head. I don't know whether you have noticed this, but I have proof of it in the last letter she wrote me.* I send it to you so that you may judge. Observe that when she speaks of you it is always *Monsieur de Valmont*, that all her ideas, even the ones you have given her, tend always in the direc-

---

*See Letter 109.

tion of Danceny: and she does not call him Monsieur, always merely *Danceny*. She thus sets him apart from all the others, so that even though she gives herself to you she is familiar only with him. If a conquest such as this strikes you as *fascinating*, if the pleasures it affords *attract* you, you are certainly a man of modest and not very fastidious pretensions. Keep her, I don't mind – you will even be falling in with my plans. But it seems to me that the affair is scarcely worth more than another quarter of an hour's inconvenience unless you can acquire some degree of power as well – for example, prevent her from meeting Danceny until you have made her forget him a little more.

Before I leave off discussing your affairs to begin upon mine, I want to tell you that the illness scheme you announce your intention of adopting is very well known and very often employed. Really, Vicomte, you are not very inventive! I too sometimes repeat myself, as you shall see, but I try to rise above it in my attention to detail, and then my final justification is always success. I am going to try it again, to embark upon a new venture. It will not, I confess, have the merit of difficulty, but it will at least be a distraction, and I am dying of boredom.

I don't know why, but since the Prévan affair, Belleroche has become insupportable. He has so plied me with attentions, tenderness, *veneration*, that I can bear him no longer. His anger at the beginning I found amusing. However, I had really to curb it; I would have compromised myself by letting it continue. And there was no way of making him listen to reason. So as to calm him the more easily, I decided to display an increase of affection. But he took this seriously, and since then his permanent state of infatuation has been too much for me. I am especially conscious of the insulting confidence he has in me, and the complacency with which he regards me as his forever. It is truly humiliating! He cannot rate me very high if he thinks he is worth my fidelity! He told me recently that I can never have loved anyone but him! Oh, at that instant I needed all the prudence at my command not to undeceive him at once by telling him how matters stood. An odd sort of gentleman, I must say, to claim exclusive rights! True, he has a good figure and quite a handsome face; but all things considered he is only a journeyman lover. Well, the time has now come and we must part.

I have been trying for a fortnight and have employed in turn coldness, caprice, temper, squabbles; but the tenacious creature will not let go for anything. I must, therefore, take more violent action, and I am consequently carrying him off with me to my country house. We leave the day after tomorrow. We shall have only a few disinterested and not very perceptive people with us, and almost as much liberty as we should have alone. Once there, I shall so overburden him with love and caresses, we shall live so exclusively for each other, that I am certain he will long even more than I for the end of the expedition which he regards in prospect as so great a happiness. If he does not return more bored with me than I with him, you may tell me, and I shall agree, that I am no cleverer than you are.

My pretext for going into this sort of retirement will be that I must devote some serious attention to my great lawsuit, which, in fact, is finally to be decided at the beginning of the winter. I shall be very glad when it is over – it is really very disagreeable to have one's whole fortune hanging in the balance. Not that I am anxious about the result. In the first place, all my lawyers assure me that I am in the right; and even if I am not, I should be very stupid if I could not win a case in which my only adversaries are minors still in their infancy and an aged guardian! Since, however, I must neglect nothing in so important an affair, I shall as a matter of fact be taking two lawyers with me. A jolly excursion this is going to be, don't you think? Still, if I am to win my suit and be rid of Belleroche, I shall not regret the time I spend on it.

Now, Vicomte, guess who the successor is to be: I give you a hundred tries. Never mind! I know you have never been good at guessing. Well, it is Danceny. Are you surprised? After all, I am not yet reduced to looking after children, but this one deserves to be made an exception of. He has the graces of youth without its frivolity. His extreme reserve in company is perfectly suited to warding off suspicion, and he is only the more amiable when he puts it off in private. Not that I have spoken to him yet in private; I am still only his confidante. But under the veneer of friendliness I think I discern more lively feelings on his part toward me and am aware of a great many of my own toward him. It would be a great pity if so much spirit and delicacy were to be sacrificed to and blunted by that little idiot of a Volanges! I hope he is mistaken in thinking he loves her: she is very far from deserving it! Not that I am jealous of her; but it would be murder, and I want to save Danceny from that. I beg you then, Vicomte, to do what you can to prevent him from meeting *his Cécile* (as he still has the bad habit of calling her). A first penchant is always stronger than one thinks, and I could be sure of nothing were he to see her again just now – especially if it were during my absence. When I return I shall take care of and be responsible for everything.

I thought of taking the young fellow with me, but sacrificed the idea to my usual prudence. Besides, I should have been afraid of his noticing something between Belleroche and me, and I should be in despair were he to have the least idea what passes between us. I want to appear pure and stainless to his imagination, at least; such as I should have to be, in other words, to be really worthy of him.

Paris
15 October 17–

LETTER 114: *The Présidente de Tourvel to Madame de Rosemonde*
My dear friend, I do not know whether you are in any condition to reply, but, yielding to my deep disquiet, I cannot help asking you some questions. The state of Monsieur de Valmont's health, which you tell me is attended with *no danger*, does not leave me feeling as confident as you seem to be. It is not unusual for melancholy and disgust with the world to be warning symptoms of some grave illness. The sufferings of the body, like those of the mind, arouse a desire for solitude; and we often accuse a man of ill-humor whom we ought only to pity for his misfortune.

It seems to me that someone should be consulted. How is it that, since you are ill yourself, you have no doctor by you? My own doctor, whom I saw this morning and whom I shall confess I consulted indirectly, is of the opinion that this sort of sudden apathy in naturally active persons is never to be ignored. He said, moreover, that sickness will not yield to treatment unless it is treated in time. Why run such risks with someone who is so dear to you?

What doubly increases my anxiety is that for the past four days I have not heard from him. My God, you would not misinform me about his health? Why should he have stopped writing so suddenly? If it were only my persistence in returning his letters, I think he would have stopped sooner. At all events, though I have no faith in presentiments, I have for the last few days felt so oppressed that it frightens me. Ah, it may be that I am on the brink of the worst of misfortunes!

You would not believe, and I am ashamed to tell you, how painful it is no longer to receive those letters which, nonetheless, I should still refuse to read. I should be sure, at any rate, that he still thought of me, and I should see something that came from him! I never opened the letters, but the sight of them would make me weep. Tears at least were a relief, and they alone have dispelled to some extent the continual oppression I have been under since my return. I beseech you, my kind friend, write to me yourself as soon as you can; and send me every day meanwhile your news and his.

I see that I have had scarcely a word to say on your own account –

but you know my feelings, my unreserved attachment to you, my sincere gratitude for your sympathetic friendship. You will forgive me for the difficulties I am in, the dreadful sufferings, the frightful torments of having evils to fear of which I am myself, perhaps, the cause. Great God, how that desperate thought obsesses me and tears at my heart! But I still had to submit to this new torture, and it seems that I was born to suffer them all.

Good-bye, my dear. Love me, pity me. Shall I have a letter from you today?

Paris
16 October 17–

LETTER 115: *The Vicomte de Valmont to the Marquise de Merteuil*
It is incredible, my love, how easily two people cease to understand each other the moment they are separated, As long as I was with you, we shared the same ideas, the same point of view; because I have not seen you for nearly three months, we are no longer of the same opinion about anything. Which of us is wrong? You would certainly answer without hesitation, but I, who am wiser or more polite than you, shall not decide. I shall merely reply to your letter and continue giving you an account of my conduct.

Thank you, first, for your advice concerning the rumors current about me. But I have no anxieties on that score. I am sure I shall soon be able to put a stop to them. Rest assured, I shall reappear in society more famous than ever before and worthier still of you.

I hope I shall even be given some credit for my adventure with the little Volanges, of which you seem to make so little. As if it were nothing to lure a girl from her beloved in the space of an evening and make use of her thereafter as often as I wish with no further difficulty, entirely as though she were my property; to obtain from her what I should never dare demand from women whose business it is to provide it – and this, too, without in the least upsetting her tender love, without obliging her to be inconstant or even unfaithful. After all, I have not so much as penetrated her head! Thus, when my whim has passed I shall replace her, so to speak, in the arms of her lover, without her having noticed anything. Is this, then, so commonplace an achievement? Besides, believe me, even when she is out of my hands, the ideas I have given her will continue to develop; and I prophesy that soon the shy little schoolgirl will take wing and soar to such heights as will do honor to her master.

If, however, the public prefer something in the classic style, I shall exhibit my Présidente, that paragon of all the virtues, respected even by our most depraved libertines! So much so that they gave up considering even the possibility of attack! I shall exhibit her, I say, unmindful of her duty and her virtue, sacrificing her reputation and two years of prudent living to pursue the happiness of giving me pleasure, to intoxicate herself with that of loving me, thinking herself rewarded for so much renunciation by a word, a look – which, even so, she does not always obtain. I shall do more: I shall leave her. And, if I know the woman, I shall have no successor. She will overcome her need of comfort, her habituation to pleasure, even her desire for revenge. After all, she will have existed only for me; and, however long a course she runs, I alone shall have opened and shut the barrier. Once I have achieved my triumph I shall say to my rivals, "Look on my work, and find, if you can, its parallel in our age!"

Whence, you will ask, comes this sudden access of assurance? It is that for the past week I have been in my beauty's confidence. She does not tell me her secrets, but I find them out: two letters from her to Madame de Rosemonde have told me all I want to know, and I shall read the rest only out of curiosity. I need absolutely nothing now in order to succeed except access to her, and I have already discovered a means. I am going to make use of it forthwith.

You are curious, I suppose?...But no, to punish you for thinking me uninventive, you shall not know what it is. Seriously, you deserve to be deprived of my confidence, at least while this affair lasts; in fact, were it not for the delicious prize you offer for success I should speak of it no more. I am angry, you see. However, in the hopes that you will mend your ways, I am willing to confine myself to inflicting a light punishment; and now, reverting to clemency I shall forget my own grand designs for a moment to discuss yours with you.

So there you are in the country, as tedious as sentiment, as depressing as fidelity itself! And that poor man Belleroche! Not content with making him drink the waters of oblivion, you put him on the rack! How is he? How does he take his surfeit of love? I should so much like him to become only the more attached to you; I should be curious to see what more efficacious remedy you could find to administer. I pity you really for being compelled to have recourse to this one. I have only once in my life made love in cold blood, and then, to be sure, for very good reason since it was with the Comtesse de ———. A dozen times in her arms I was tempted to say, "Madame, I renounce the position I solicited. Permit me to leave the one I now occupy." Consequently, of all the women I have had, she is the only one I take real pleasure in traducing.

As for *your* reasons, to tell you the truth, I find them extraordinarily foolish; and you were right in thinking that I should never have guessed the name of Belleroche's successor. What! Is it for Danceny that you are going to all this trouble? Come, come, my dear, leave him to adore *his virtuous Cécile* – don't meddle with the children at play. Leave the housemaids to educate the schoolboys; let them have *their little innocent games* with the convent girls. Why have a novice on your hands who will be incapable either of taking you or of leaving you, and for whom you will have to do everything yourself? I tell you in all seriousness, I disapprove of your choice. However much of a secret you keep it, it will humiliate you – at any rate in my eyes and in your own conscience.

You have, you say, a great inclination for him: well, you are certainly mistaken, and I think I have even discovered the reason for your error. This admirable distaste for Belleroche came over you at a time of dearth, and since Paris offered you no range of choice, your imagination, always a little too lively, seized upon the first object that presented itself. But consider that when you return there you will have hundreds to choose from; and if you fear running the risk of inactivity meanwhile, I offer myself for the amusement of your leisure hours.

Between now and your arrival in Paris all my important business will have been accomplished, one way or another. And certainly neither the little Volanges nor the Présidente herself will be occupying my time to such an extent that I cannot devote as much of it to you as you wish. Perhaps, in the meanwhile, I shall even have returned the little girl to the arms of her discreet lover. Though I cannot agree, whatever you say, that this affair has no *attractions*, it is true that since I intended her for the rest of her life to have an idea of me as being superior to all other men, I assumed a role with her that I could not for long sustain without risk to my health. Since then I have no longer been much interested in her, except for the concern that one owes to family affairs...

You don't understand?... I await the coming period for the confirmation of my hopes, and the assurance that I have fully succeeded in my enterprise. Yes, my love, I have already had the first indication that my schoolgirl's husband shall run no risk of dying without posterity, and that the head of the house of Gercourt shall in future be an offshoot of the house of Valmont. But let me finish the enterprise to my own taste that I undertook only at your request. Remember that if you make Danceny unfaithful you will deprive the story of all interest. Consider, too, that having offered myself as his deputy, I have, it seems to me, some right to preference.

Indeed, I rely so much upon it that I have not hesitated to obstruct your plans by helping to increase the discreet lover's tender passion for the first and most worthy object of his choice. Having found your pupil yesterday busy writing to him, and having first disturbed her in this agreeable task by putting her to a still more agreeable one, I asked to see the letter; discovering it to be cold and constrained, I made her see that this was not the way to console a lover, and persuaded her to write another to my dictation – in which, imitating her little babblings as best I could, I tried to encourage the young man's love by giving him more certain expectations. The little creature was quite delighted, she told me, to find herself writing so well: from now on, I shall be in charge of her correspondence. What shall I not, in the end, have done for Danceny? I shall have been at once his friend, his confidant, his rival, and his mistress! I am even at the moment doing him the service of removing him from your dangerous clutches. Yes, without doubt dangerous: for to possess you and to love you is to buy a moment's happiness with an eternity of remorse.

Good-bye, my love. Take heart and dispatch Belleroche as soon as you can. Let Danceny go and prepare to recover – and to restore to me – the delicious pleasures of our first acquaintance.

P.S. My compliments on the impending settlement of your lawsuit. I should be very pleased if the happy event were to occur under my regime.

Château de ————
19 October 17–

LETTER 116: *The Chevalier Danceny to Cécile Volanges*
Madame de Merteuil left this morning for the country, so that now, my dear Cécile, I am deprived of the one pleasure that remained to me in your absence – that of talking about you to your friend and mine. For some time now she has allowed me to think of her as a friend, and I was the more eager to do so since it seemed a means of bringing you nearer to me. Heavens! How kind a woman she is! And what a flattering charm she contrives to throw over friendship! It is as if her feelings in this respect are strengthened and ennobled by all that she refuses to love. If you knew how fond she is of you, how much she likes to

hear me speak of you!...That is probably what most attracts me to her. What a joy it would be to live only for you both, to come and go end-lessly between the delights of love and the pleasures of friendship, to devote my whole life to them – to be, as it were, the focal point of your mutual attachment and to feel always that in furthering the hap-piness of one I should be of equal service to the other. I hope you will love her, I hope you will love her very much, my dear: she is an ador-able woman. You will, in sharing them, increase the value of my own feelings for her.

Since I have experienced the charm of friendship, I want you to feel it too. The pleasures I do not share with you seem to me to be only half enjoyed. Yes, my Cécile, I should like to fill your heart with all the sweetest of feelings, so that each of its emotions would be a new happiness to you. I think, even so, that I should never be able to return you more than a fraction of the joy I should have from you.

Why must so delightful a possibility be only a figment of my imagi-nation? Why must reality, on the contrary, offer me nothing but pain-ful and perpetual privations? I see clearly that I must abandon the hopes you once gave me that I might see you in the country. I have no comfort but to persuade myself that it is, after all, impossible for you. But you don't tell me so, you don't commiserate with me! I have already made you two complaints on the same score which you have left unanswered. Ah, Cécile, Cécile! I believe that you love me with all your heart, but your heart is not afire like mine! If only it were for me to remove the obstacles! Why are my interests at stake and not yours? I should soon prove to you that there is nothing that love finds impossible.

You don't tell me, either, when this cruel separation is to come to an end. Here, at least, I may be able to see you. Your charming eyes will revive my despondent soul; their sweet regard will reassure my heart, which at times is in need of reassurance. Forgive me, Cécile; my fears are not suspicions. I believe in your love, in your constancy. Ah, I should be too unhappy if I doubted them. But so many obstacles! And new ones all the time! My dear, I feel discouraged, so discouraged. Madame de Merteuil's departure has, it seems, revived my conscious-ness of all my misfortunes.

Good-bye, my Cécile, good-bye, my dear love. Remember that your lover is suffering, and that you alone can give him back his happiness.

Paris
17 October 17–

LETTER 117: *Cécile Volanges to the Chevalier Danceny*
  (dictated by Valmont)

Do you think, my good friend, that I need any reprimanding to make me sorry for you, when I know that you are suffering? And do you doubt that I suffer for your misfortunes as much as you do? I share even the ones I cause you knowingly; and I have more to endure than you because you are not fair to me. Oh, that is not kind of you. I see what it is that annoys you: I have not answered your two requests to come here. But is it so very easy to let you have an answer? Do you think I don't know that what you are asking for is very wrong? Yet if I have so much difficulty in refusing you at a distance, how would it be were you here? What is more, for having wanted to give you a moment's consolation, I should have to suffer for the rest of my life.

All the same, I have nothing to hide from you. Here are my reasons; you may judge for yourself. I should perhaps have done what you asked were it not, as I have told you, that Monsieur de Gercourt, the cause of all our troubles, shall not arrive here as soon as he was expected; and since Mamma has for some time been very much more friendly toward me — because for my part I make as much of her as I can — who knows what I may be able to persuade her to? And if we can be happy, without my having anything to be ashamed of, will that not be much the better way? If I can believe what I have often been told, men love their wives less if their wives have loved them too well before marrying them. It is fear of this which holds me back more than anything else. My dear, are you not sure of my heart, and will there not always be time?

Listen: I promise you that if I cannot avoid the misfortune of being married to Monsieur de Gercourt, whom I already heartily detest without ever having met him, nothing will keep me from being as much yours as I can possibly be, even before my marriage. Since I don't wish to be loved by anyone but you, and since, if I do wrong it will not, as you know, be my fault, the rest is a matter of indifference to me — as long as you promise me that you will always love me as much as you do now. But till then, my dear, leave things as they are, and don't ask me to do what I have good reasons for not doing, especially when you know that I am sorry to have to refuse.

I wish, too, that Monsieur de Valmont were not so eager in your cause. It only makes it the more difficult for me. Oh, you have a good friend in him, I do assure you! He does everything for you that you would do for yourself. But good-bye, my dear. It was very late when I began writing to you, and a part of the night is already gone. I am going to bed to make up for lost time. I embrace you, but don't scold me any more.

Château de ———
18 October 17–

LETTER 118: *The Chevalier Danceny to the Marquise de Merteuil*
If I am to believe my almanac it is only two days, my beloved friend, since you went away; but if I am to believe my heart, it is two centuries. Now – I have it on your authority – it is always one's heart that one should go by; it is therefore high time that you came back. All your business affairs must be more than disposed of. How can you expect me to be interested in your lawsuit when, whether you succeed or fail, I must in any case pay for it with the boredom I suffer in your absence? Oh, I could pick a quarrel with you! How sad it is, with so fine an excuse for ill temper, to have no right to show it!

Is it not a genuine breach of faith nevertheless, an act of base treachery, to leave your friend behind you when you have made him incapable of supporting your absence? You would consult your lawyers in vain: they could find no justification for so wicked a proceeding. Besides, lawyers deal in arguments – and arguments will not do in answering feelings.

As for me, you have told me so often that reason has prescribed this journey of yours that you have put me quite out of humor with reason. I intend to listen to it no longer, even when it tells me to forget you. That would indeed be very reasonable, and not as difficult to do as you might think. I should only have to break myself of the habit of thinking constantly about you; and there is nothing here, you may be sure, that can remind me of you.

Our prettiest women – or, as is generally said, the most agreeable ones – are so far beneath you that they can suggest only the faintest idea of the being you are. I even think that, to a practiced eye, the more they resemble you at first, the more the difference is apparent afterward. Whatever they do, though they use all the arts at their command, there is always something lacking; they are not you, and therein precisely lies the only charm. Unfortunately, when the days are long and one is unoccupied, one daydreams, builds castles in the air, creates an illusion. By degrees one's imagination takes fire, and one would like to beautify the picture; one brings together everything that can possibly give pleasure, arriving, finally, at perfection. When that has happened, the portrait recalls the model, and one is quite astonished to find that one has done nothing but think of you.

At this very moment I am the victim of a more or less similar error. You think, perhaps, that it was because I wanted to express my thoughts concerning you that I began this letter? Not at all: it was to distract me from them. I had a hundred things to tell you which did not concern you, which as you know are of the deepest concern to me; it is from them, however, that I have been distracted. Since when has the charm of friendship prevailed over that of love? Ah, if I looked closer I should perhaps find a little reason for self-reproach! But hush! Let us forget this trifling mistake, lest I commit it again. Let my friend herself be blind to it.

Why are you not here to answer me, to call me back when I go astray, to talk to me of my Cécile, to increase, if that is possible, the happiness I find in loving her by reminding me that it is your friend whom I love? Yes, I must confess, the love I feel for her has become all the more precious to me since you have been so kind as to receive its confidences. It is such a pleasure to open my heart to you, to tell you of my feelings, to express them without reserve! And it seems the more you take them to your own heart, the more I value them. I look at you and say to myself, "In her is contained all my happiness."

The situation has not changed, and there is nothing new to tell you. The last letter I received from *her* increased and confirmed my hopes, but puts off their fulfillment still further. However, her motives are so kind and so honorable that I can neither blame her nor complain. Perhaps you do not altogether understand what I am telling you; but why are you not here? Though one is willing to tell a friend everything, one dares not commit it all to paper. The secrets of love especially are so delicate that one cannot let them out in that way on their own. If one does sometimes allow it, one should at least not lose sight of them; one must somehow see them safely to their new home. Oh, come back, then, my beloved friend: you see how necessary your return is. Forget the *thousand reasons* that keep you where you are, or else teach me how to live where you are not.

I have the honor to be, etc.

Paris
19 October 17–

LETTER 119: *Madame de Rosemonde to the Présidente de Tourvel*
Although I am still in great pain, my dear, I am trying to write to you myself so that I may speak to you of your concerns. My nephew con-

tinues in his misanthropy. He sends very regularly every day to ask after me; but he has not once come to inquire for himself, although I have sent a message asking him to do so. So that, for all I see of him, he might as well have stayed in Paris. This morning, however, I met him where I scarcely expected to meet him — in my chapel, where I had gone for the first time since my painful indisposition. Today I learned that for four days he has been there regularly to hear Mass. God grant that this continues!

As I came in he approached me and very affectionately congratulated me upon the improvement in my health. As Mass was beginning, I broke off the conversation, which I expected to resume later; but he disappeared before I could rejoin him. I shall not conceal the fact that I found him a little altered. But, my dear, do not make me repent of my confidence in your good sense by giving way to excessive anxiety. Rest assured, above all, that I should prefer to distress you than to deceive you.

If my nephew continues to keep me at a distance, I shall, as soon as I am better, have recourse to calling upon him in his room, and I shall try to fathom the cause of this singular eccentricity, for which I am inclined to believe you are in some part responsible. I shall let you know what I discover. I am leaving you now; I can no longer move my fingers. Besides, if Adélaïde knew that I was writing, she would grumble at me for the rest of the evening. Good-bye, my dear.

Château de ——————
20 October 17—

LETTER 120: *The Vicomte de Valmont to Father Anselme*
       (of the Cistercian monastery in the Rue Saint-Honoré)

I have not the honor of your acquaintance, Monsieur, but I know that you have the entire confidence of Madame the Présidente de Tourvel, and I know, moreover, how eminently worthy you are of it. I think, then, I may address myself to you without being guilty of an indiscretion, to beg you to do me a very necessary service, one that will be truly worthy of your holy office, and one in which Madame de Tourvel's interest is equally involved with mine.

I have in my possession important documents that concern her, the contents of which may be revealed to no one. I must not nor wish to deliver them into any but her own hands. I have no means of telling her about them, because there are reasons, which perhaps you know from her — but which I think I am not permitted to tell you — why she has decided to refuse to correspond with me: a decision that I cannot, I willingly admit, now disapprove, since she was not able to have foreseen incidents which I myself was very far from expecting and which cannot have been possible but for the supernatural power that one is compelled to acknowledge produced them.

I beg you then, Monsieur, to be so kind as to tell her of my new resolutions, and to ask on my behalf for a private interview, at which I can at least offer apologies as partial amends for the wrongs I have committed, and in exchange for this last sacrifice demolish the only remaining traces of the error or fault of which I have been guilty in relation to her.

Only after this initial expiation could I dare to lay at your feet the humiliating confession of my past aberrations and implore your intercession in the interests of a much more important and unhappily more difficult reconciliation. May I hope, Monsieur, that you will not refuse me the aid that is so necessary, so precious to me, and that you will condescend to support me in my weakness and guide my feet in the path that I most ardently desire to follow but, I blush to admit, I have never yet found?

I shall await your reply with the impatience of a penitent who is eager to make amends. Please believe that I am, with as much gratitude as reverence

Your very humble, etc.

P.S. You have my permission, Monsieur, supposing you consider it proper, to communicate this letter in its entirety to Madame de Tourvel, whom I shall make it my duty to respect for the rest of my life, and in whom I shall never cease to honor the woman sent from Heaven to recall my soul to virtue by her own inspiring example.

Château de ———
22 October 17–

LETTER 121: *The Marquise de Merteuil to the Chevalier Danceny*
I have received your letter, my too-young friend. But before thanking you I must find fault with you; and I warn you that if you don't mend your ways you will have no more letters from me. Take my advice and renounce this tone of flattery, which is pure cant when it is not the expression of love. Does friendship speak in this vein? No, my friend: every sentiment has the language proper to it; to make use of the wrong one is to disguise the thought one wishes to express. I know that our

little ladies understand nothing of what is said to them unless it is translated somehow into the usual jargon; but, I must admit, I thought that I deserved to be distinguished from them. I am really sorry – perhaps more than I ought to be – that you judged me so poorly.

You will therefore find in my letter only what is lacking in yours – frankness and forthrightness. I might well say, for example, that it would be a great pleasure to see you, and that I am cross to find people around me who bore me, instead of people who amuse me, but you would translate that same sentence into "teach me how to live where you are not," so that, I suppose, when you are by your mistress's side you will not know how to live there unless I make a third. What a pity! Then there are the women "who always lack something; they are not me": will you perhaps find your Cécile wanting too? This is what comes of using a language that nowadays is so abused as to mean even less than the jargon of compliment. It has become no more than a set of formulas, and one believes in it no more than one believes in "your very humble servant."

When you write to me, my friend, let it be to tell me what you think and feel, and not to send me phrases that I can find, without your help, set forth more or less to advantage in the latest novel. I hope you will not be angry at what I say, even if you find it a little ill-humored. I don't deny the ill humor but, to avoid even so much as the appearance of the fault I reproach you with, I shall not tell you what is true, that my vexation is perhaps a little increased by my separation from you. It seems to me that, all things considered, you are worth more than a lawsuit and two lawyers, and perhaps more even than the *attentive Belleroche*.

You see that, instead of deploring my absence, you ought to be glad of it, for never have I paid you so fine a compliment. I think I am being swayed by your example. I shall soon be saying flattering things myself. But no, I prefer to stand by my honesty. It is honesty alone, then, that assures you of my sympathetic friendship and the interest it inspires. It is very agreeable to have a young friend whose heart is engaged elsewhere. This is not every woman's system, but it is mine. It seems to me that one may give oneself up with greater pleasure to a feeling from which one has nothing to fear. Hence for your sake I have come, rather early perhaps, to playing the confidante. But you choose your mistresses so young that you have made me aware for the first time that I am beginning to grow old! You do well, however, to prepare thus for a long life of constancy which with all my heart I wish may be mutual.

You are right to give way before the "kind and honorable motives" that, from what you tell me, are delaying your happiness. A long defense is the only source of merit remaining to those who have ceased actively to resist. What I should find unpardonable in anyone but a child like the little Volanges would be an incapacity to fly from danger of which her own admission of love had given her sufficient warning. You men have no idea what virtue is and what it costs to sacrifice it! But if a woman reasons at all she will know that for her, quite apart from the fault she commits, weakness is the worst of misfortunes. I cannot imagine how any woman who had opportunity for a moment's reflection could ever succumb to it.

Don't dispute that truth: it is chiefly because of it that I am attached to you. You will save me from the dangers of love; and although I have till now been quite well able to defend myself from them without you, I shall be grateful to you for saving me, and shall love you the better, and more, for doing so.

Upon which, my dear Chevalier, I pray God to keep you in His holy and venerable protection.

Château de ———
22 October 17–

LETTER 122: *Madame de Rosemonde to the Présidente de Tourvel*
I had hoped, my charming daughter, that I would at last be able to calm your anxieties, but now to my chagrin I see that I must on the contrary further increase them. Be calm, nonetheless. My nephew is not in danger; it cannot even be said that he is really ill. But something extraordinary is certainly happening to him: I understand nothing of it, but I left his room with such a feeling of sorrow, perhaps even of fear, that I am loath to make you share it. Yet I cannot help speaking of it to you. Here is an account of what happened. You may be sure that it is faithful, for if I should live another eighty years I could never forget the impression that doleful scene made upon me.

Well, this morning I went to my nephew's room. I found him writing, surrounded by various heaps of papers which seemed to be the object of his labors. He was so preoccupied that I was in the middle of the room before he turned around to see who had come in. He rose as soon as he saw me, and I distinctly noticed the effort he made to compose his features. It was that, perhaps, that made me examine him more closely. He was not fully dressed, it is true, and his hair was unpowdered; but I found him looking pale and unkempt, his face in particular quite changed. His glance, no longer lively and gay as we know it, was sad and downcast. In short, between ourselves, I should not like you to have seen him as he was, for it was a most touching spectacle and would, to my mind, have roused in you that tender compassion which is one of the most dangerous of love's snares.

Though very much struck by what I saw, I began the conversation as though I had noticed nothing. I spoke to him first of his health, and though he did not say it was good, he did not say it was bad in so many words. Then I complained of his retirement, which I said appeared a little like willful eccentricity, and tried to add a touch of gaiety to my little reprimand. But he replied only, in a significant tone, "That, I admit, is one more crime. But it shall be paid for with the rest." His manner of saying it, even more than what he said, damped my jocularity a little, and I hastened to tell him that he attached too much importance to what was purely a friendly reproach.

We then resumed our conversation more calmly, and a little later he told me that soon perhaps some business, *the most important concern of his life*, would be recalling him to Paris; but since I was afraid to guess, my dear, and since such a beginning may have led to unwelcome confidences, I asked no questions but contented myself with saying that a little amusement would benefit his health. I added that for once I should not persuade him to stay, since my friends were dear to me for their own sake. It was upon this simple remark that, seizing hold of my hands, he began to speak with a vehemence I cannot describe: "Yes, my dear aunt," he said, "let a nephew who respects, who esteems you, be dear, very dear to you; and, as you say, let it be for his own sake. Don't be anxious for his happiness; don't disturb, with thoughts of regret, the eternal peace he hopes soon to enjoy. Tell me again that you love me, that you will forgive me. Yes, you, I know, will forgive me. I know you are kind. But how can I hope for the same indulgence from those against whom I have so offended?" Then he stooped toward me to hide, I think, the signs of grief which the sound of his voice nonetheless betrayed.

More moved than I can say, I rose hurriedly. He must have noticed my alarm, for immediately and with more composure he continued: "Forgive me. Forgive me, Madame. I was beside myself. Please forget what I have said and remember only my profound esteem for you. I shall not fail," he added, "to renew my respects to you before I leave." It seemed to me that the last sentence committed me to putting an end to my visit; and, in fact, I left.

But the more I think of it, the less idea I have of what he meant. What is this business, *the most important concern of his life*? For what reason does he ask my forgiveness? Why did he involuntarily give way to emotion when he spoke? I have already asked myself these questions a thousand times without being able to find an answer. I cannot even see what there is in all this that relates to you. However, since the eyes of love see further than those of friendship, I did not wish to leave you in ignorance of anything that passed between my nephew and myself.

I have made four attempts to finish writing this long letter, which I should make longer were it not for the fatigue that overcomes me. Good-bye, my dear.

Château de ———
25 October 17–

LETTER 123: *Father Anselme to the Vicomte de Valmont*
I have, Monsieur le Vicomte, received the letter you did me the honor of writing to me, and called yesterday, as you desired, upon the person in question. I explained the object of and motives for the meeting you propose. Though I found her anxious at first to abide by her former decision, when I had shown her that by refusing she would perhaps risk standing in the way of your happy restoration to the fold and opposing thereby in some sort the merciful designs of Providence, she agreed to receive your visit – on condition, at all events, that it will be the last one – and charged me to tell you that she will be at home next Thursday, the twenty-eighth. If the day does not suit you, you will be so kind as to tell her so and to suggest another. Your letter will be received.

Allow me, however, Monsieur le Vicomte, to ask you not to postpone the meeting unless you have strong reasons, so that you may the sooner and the more entirely give yourself up to the praiseworthy inclinations of which you have given me some indication. Remember that he who delays in seizing the opportunity of grace is exposed to the danger of its being withdrawn; that though the Divine Goodness is infinite, its dispensation is yet regulated by justice; and that a moment may come when a merciful God is transformed into a vengeful God.

Should you continue to honor me with your confidence, I beg you to believe that you have my whole attention whenever you desire it. However busy I may otherwise be, my most important concern shall always be to fulfill the duties of the holy ministry to which I am particularly devoted; the happiest moment of my life will be that of seeing my work progress under the blessing of the Almighty. Weak sinners that we are, we can do nothing by ourselves! But God, who is recalling you, can do everything; and we shall be equally indebted to His goodness: you for the firm desire to return, I for a means of returning you to Him.

It is with His help that I hope soon to persuade you that holy religion alone can give you, even in this world, the solid and lasting happiness that is vainly sought in the blindness of human passion.

I have the honor to be with respectful regard, etc.

Paris
25 October 17–

LETTER 124: *The Présidente de Tourvel to Madame de Rosemonde*
Amid all the astonishment, Madame, into which the news I received yesterday has thrown me, I am not unmindful of the satisfaction it must cause you, and I hasten to inform you of it. Monsieur de Valmont is no longer concerned either with me or with his love, and no longer wants anything but to make amends for the faults, or rather the errors, of his youth by leading a more exemplary life. I was informed of this great news by Father Anselme, to whom he applied for guidance in the future – as also for the purpose of arranging an interview with me, the principal object of which I assume to be the return of my letters, which he has kept till now in spite of my request to the contrary.

I can only, of course, approve this happy change of heart and congratulate myself if, as he says, I have played some part in it. But why should I have been chosen for its instrument, why should my life have been deprived of all peace? Can Monsieur de Valmont's happiness never have been achieved without my misfortune? Oh, my kind friend, forgive these complaints. I know it is not for me to question Divine decrees; but while I beg Him continually, and always in vain, for the power to conquer my unhappy love, He is prodigal of strength where it has not been asked for, and leaves me a helpless prey to my weakness.

But let me stifle these guilty complaints. Do I not know that the Prodigal Son, when he returned, was received with more favor than his father showed the son who never went away? What account may we demand of One who owes us none? And were it possible for us to have any rights where He is concerned, what rights could I claim? Could I boast of the virtue I owe only to Valmont? He has saved me; I dare complain of suffering for his sake? No, my sufferings will be dear to me, if his happiness is their reward. Certainly it was necessary for him to return to the Universal Father. God, who made him, must watch over his creation. He would never have fashioned so charming a creature to make only a reprobate of it. It is for me to endure the consequences of my foolhardy imprudence; ought I not to have known that, since it was forbidden to love him, I should not permit myself to see him?

My crime, or my misfortune, was in refusing for too long to acknowledge that truth. You are my witness, my dear and worthy friend, that I submitted to the sacrifice as soon as I realized the necessity for it, but it was still not complete as long as Monsieur de Valmont did not share it. Shall I confess to you that it is this thought which most torments me now? Insupportable pride that allows the evils we suffer to be mitigated by those we cause others to suffer? Ah, I shall subdue this rebellious heart; I shall teach it humility.

It was with this especially in mind that I at length agreed to receive a visit from Monsieur de Valmont next Thursday. I shall hear him tell me himself that I am no longer anything to him, that the feeble and fleeting impression I made upon him has been completely effaced! I shall see him look at me without emotion while the fear of revealing mine will make me lower my eyes. The same letters he so long refused to return at my repeated requests he will give back with indifference, as useless objects that no longer hold any interest for him. And my trembling hands, receiving the shameful trust, will feel the hands that restore it steady and calm. Then I shall see him leave...leave forever, and my eyes as they follow him will not see him turn to glance back!

That so much humiliation should have been reserved for me! Ah, let me at least make use of it to pierce my soul with the consciousness of my frailty...Yes, I shall treasure the letters he no longer cares to keep. I shall condemn myself to reading them every day until my tears have obliterated every word. His own I shall burn for being tainted with the dangerous poison that has eaten into my soul. Oh, what is love if it can make us miss even the dangers to which we have been exposed; can make us afraid of yielding to our feelings, even when they have been deprived of their object? Let us fly this deadly poison, which leaves us to choose only between shame and misery, and frequently imposes both. Let prudence, at least, prevail where virtue cannot.

How long it is till Thursday! That I could make my painful sacrifice this instant and forget at once both its occasion and its object! This visit unnerves me; I am sorry I gave my promise. What need has he to see me again? What are we now to one another? If he has offended me, he has my pardon. I congratulate him for wishing to make amends for the wrong he has done – I commend him for it. I shall go further and imitate him. I have been led into the same errors, and his example will recall me from them. But if his purpose is to fly from me, why does he begin by seeking me out? Is the most urgent necessity not for us to forget each other? Ah, certainly it is, and that shall be my sole concern from now on.

With your permission, my dear friend, it is by your side that I am going to undertake this difficult task. When I am in need of help, perhaps even of consolation, I want to receive it from no one but you. You alone can understand me and speak the language of my heart. Your precious friendship will fill my whole life. Nothing will be too difficult for me if it is to justify the care you are kind enough to devote to me. I shall owe you my peace, my happiness, my virtue; and the reward of your goodness to me will be to have made me worthy of it at last.

I have been, I think, very incoherent in this letter. I presume so, at any rate, to judge from the continual agitation I have felt while writing it. If you should find sentiments in it of which I ought to be ashamed, draw the veil of your indulgent kindness over them. In that I have entire confidence. From you I cannot wish to conceal a single impulse of my heart.

Good-bye, my most worthy friend. I hope, within a few days, to tell you when you may expect me.

Paris
25 October 17–

Part Four

LETTER 125: *The Vicomte de Valmont to the Marquise de Merteuil*
Well, there she is, defeated, this arrogant women who dared to think she could resist me! Yes, my dear, she is mine, utterly mine. Since yesterday she has had nothing left to yield me.

I am still too full of my happiness to be able to appreciate it, but I am astonished at the strange charm of what I experienced. Can it then be true that virtue increases the value of a woman even in the very moment of her weakness? No, let us put that childish idea with the other old wives' tales. Is not a first surrender almost always preceded by a more or less well-simulated resistance? And I have nowhere else found the charm of which I speak. It is not the charm of love, either: for if I did at times, beside this astonishing woman, experience sensations of weakness which resembled that pusillanimous passion, I was always able to conquer them and to reassert my principles. Even had yesterday's episode, as I think, carried me further than I expected to go; even though I did, for a moment, share the agitations and intoxications I had provoked, the passing illusion would by now have been dissipated. Yet the same charm subsists. I should even, I admit, feel a rather delicate pleasure in giving way to it, were it not that it causes me some disquiet.

Shall I, at my age, be overmastered like a schoolboy by an obscure and involuntary feeling? No. I must, before all else, search it out and fight it.

Perhaps, for the rest, I have already glimpsed its cause. I am at any rate pleased with the notion and should like to think it true.

Of the multitudes of women for whom I have fulfilled the role and functions of a lover I have never, till yesterday, met one who was not at least as eager to give herself as I was to bring her to doing so; I would even put down as prudes the ones who met me only halfway, as against the many others whose provocative defenses were never designed wholly to conceal the preliminary advances they were making.

Here, on the other hand, I encountered from the first an unfavorable prejudice that was later supported by information and advice from an odious but perspicacious woman; natural and extreme timidity strengthened by a cultivated modesty; an attachment to virtue, governed by religion, with two years of triumph already to its credit; lastly, a series of brilliant maneuvers, inspired by these various feelings, conducted with only one end in view – the avoidance of my pursuit.

This is not, then, as in my other campaigns, a simple capitulation more or less to my advantage, from which it is easier to derive profit than pride. It is total victory, bought with painful endeavor and decided by masterly strategy. It is not, therefore, surprising that such a success, due to me alone, should for that very reason be worth more to me. The excess of pleasure I experienced in the moment of triumph, which I still feel, is nothing but the delicious sensation of glory. I encourage myself in this belief because it spares me the humiliation of thinking that I might in any way have been dependent on the very slave I had subjected to my will; that I might not find in myself alone everything I require for my happiness; and that the capacity to give me enjoyment of it in all its intensity might be the prerogative of any one woman to the exclusion of all others.

These judicious reflections will govern my conduct on this important occasion; and you may be sure I shall not allow myself to become so enchained that I cannot break my new ties with ease whenever I wish. But already I speak of breaking – and you don't yet know how I acquired the right to do so. Read on, then, and see to what dangers wisdom is exposed when it comes to the rescue of folly. I was so carefully attentive both to what I said and to the replies I received that I hope to give my account of the whole with an exactitude that will satisfy you.

You will see, from the two copies of letters attached,* whom it was

---

*Letters 120 and 122.

I chose as mediator between myself and my beauty, and how zealously the holy personage devoted his energies to bringing us together. What I have still to tell you – I learned it from a letter intercepted in the usual way – is that the fear and the expected humiliation of being jilted had shaken the prudence of our austere devotee just a little and had filled her head with sentiments and ideas that were nonetheless interesting for lacking common sense. It was after these preliminaries, which you must know about, that yesterday, Thursday the twenty-eighth, the day chosen and stipulated by the ungrateful creature, I presented myself at her house, a timid and repentant slave – to leave it a garlanded conqueror.

It was six o'clock in the evening when I arrived to see the fair recluse. (Since her return, her doors have been closed to everybody.) She tried to rise when I was announced, but her trembling knees would not permit her to sustain an upright posture, and she sat down again immediately. The servant who had announced me had some service to perform in the room and this seemed to make her impatient. We filled the interval with the customary compliments. But so as to lose not a moment of time that was precious to me, I carefully examined the locale, and there and then marked down the theater of my victory. I couldn't have chosen a more convenient one, for there was an ottoman in the room; but I observed that facing it hung a portrait of the husband, and I was afraid, I admit, that with so extraordinary a woman, a single look directed by chance in his direction might in a moment destroy the work of so much time and trouble. At length we were left alone, and I came to the point.

Having discovered, in the exchange of a few words, that Father Anselme must have informed her of the motives of my visit, I began to complain of the rigorous treatment I had been subjected to. I emphasized particularly the *contempt* that had been shown me. This was denied, as I expected; and as you too would expect, I cited as proof the fear and distrust I had aroused and the scandalous flight that had ensued, the refusal to reply to my letters, even to receive them, etc., etc. Since a justification was then embarked upon that would have been very easy to accomplish, I thought I had better interrupt; and so as to be forgiven for my rudeness I immediately covered it over with flattery. I resumed: "If your charm could make so profound an impression upon my heart, no less profound was the impression made upon my soul by your virtue. Carried away, I suppose, by a desire to emulate it, I went so far as to believe myself worthy of doing so. I do not blame you for having judged otherwise. I am being punished for my error." Since an embarrassed silence prevailed, I continued: "I wished, Madame, either to justify myself in your eyes or to obtain your forgiveness for the wrongs you imagine I have done you, so that I might at least be able to end, in some peace of mind, a life to which I have attached no further value since the day you deprived it of all its charm."

Here there was an attempt at a reply. "My duty did not permit me to..." The difficulty, however, of completing the lie demanded by duty cut short the sentence. I therefore resumed in a more tender tone: "Is it true, then, that it was from me that you fled?"

"My departure was necessary."

"And is it necessary that you stay away from me?"

"I must."

"And forever?"

"I must."

I need not tell you that during this short dialogue our tender-hearted prude spoke in the most dejected tones and never once raised her eyes to mine.

I decided I had better animate the languid scene a little; so, rising, I said with an air of annoyance, "Your firmness has restored my own. Well then, yes, Madame, we shall be separated. Even further separated than you think. And you will congratulate yourself at your leisure upon what you have done." A little surprised at the tone of rebuke, she began to answer: "The decision you have taken —"

"Is a consequence of my despair," I returned with vehemence. "You wanted me to be unhappy. I shall prove to you that you have succeeded beyond your hopes."

"I desire only your happiness," she replied. And the sound of her voice began to betray deep feeling.

So, throwing myself at her feet, and in the dramatic tones you know, I cried, "Ah, cruel women! Can any happiness exist for me that you do not share? How can I find it away from you? Ah, never! never!"

I must say that in having recourse to this expedient I had counted very much on the assistance of tears; but whether I was in the wrong mood, or whether, perhaps, it was only the effect of constant and exacting attention to detail, I found it impossible to summon any.

Fortunately I remembered that to subdue a woman one means is as good as another, as long as she can be surprised into strong emotion that leaves a profound and favorable impression upon her. Compassion being out of the question, I appealed to fear. Changing only the inflection of my voice and remaining in the same posture, I continued: "Yes, I swear this vow at your feet. I shall possess you or die." As I uttered these words our eyes met. I don't know what the timid creature saw or thought she saw in mine, but she rose, looking terrified, and disengaged herself from the embrace in which I held her. I did nothing to restrain her, since I have several times remarked that scenes of despair, when conducted with too much enthusiasm, lapse after any length of time into ludicrousness, from which they can only be saved by real tragedy, and tragedy I was very far from wishing to play. However, while she made her escape, I added in tones low and sinister but loud enough to be heard, "Well, then! Let me die!"

Whereupon I rose and, silent for a moment, threw, some wild looks in her direction, as if haphazardly, which for all their air of distraction were nonetheless sharply observant. Her hesitant demeanor, heavy breathing, the stiffening of all her muscles, her trembling half-raised arms, were all proof enough of the effect I had intended to produce. But since in the business of love nothing is concluded except at close quarters, and since we were by then at a fair distance from one another, it was necessary above all to effect a reapproach. To this end I assumed, as soon as I could, an air of composure calculated to soothe the effects my violence had produced without effacing the impression it had wrought.

By way of transition I said, "I am quite wretched. I meant to live for your happiness, and I have destroyed it. I devote myself to your peace of mind, and destroy that too." I continued with an air of composure, but some constraint: "Forgive me, Madame. I am little accustomed to storms of passion and have not learned to control them. If I was wrong to give way, remember at least that it has happened for the last time. Ah, calm yourself, I beseech you calm yourself." As I spoke, I drew insensibly nearer her.

"If you wish me to be calm," replied my terrified beauty, "be calmer yourself."

"Ah, well! Yes, I promise you I will," I said. "If the effort is great," I added in feebler tones, "it will not, at least, be for long. But," I immediately continued as though distraught, "I came, did I not, to return your letters? For God's sake, be willing to receive them back. Only this painful sacrifice remains to be made; leave me nothing that may weaken my courage." I drew the precious collection from my pocket. "Here they are," I said, "your deceitful assurances of friendship. They once reconciled me to life. Take them back. Give me the sign that will part me from you forever."

Here my fearful beloved yielded entirely to tender solicitude. "But, Monsieur de Valmont, what is the matter? What do you mean? Do you not willingly do what you have come to do? Is this not the fruit of your reflections? And have they not brought you, too, to approve the course that my duty has obliged me to take?"

"Well," I returned, "your course has decided mine."

"And what is that?"

"The only one that, in taking me from you, can put an end to my sufferings."

"But tell me – what is it?"

At this point I took her in my arms without meeting any resistance at all. Judging from this neglect of the proprieties to what extent emotion had gained sway, risking some enthusiasm I said, "Adorable woman! You have no idea of the love you inspire. You will never know how I have worshiped you, how much dearer my feelings have been to me than life! May your days be even more peaceful and prosperous: may they be blessed with all the happiness of which you have deprived me! Repay my sincere wishes with one regret, at least, one tear; and please believe that the last of my sacrifices will not have been the most painful. Good-bye!"

As I spoke I heard her heart beat violently. I noticed the change in her face. I saw, above all that she was choked with tears, which yet fell slowly and painfully. It was only then that I decided to pretend to leave. Holding me back by force she said with spirit, "No. Listen to me."

"Let me go," I replied.

"You shall listen to me. I insist."

"I must fly from you. I must!"

"No!" she cried...

And with that last word she threw herself, or rather fell, into my arms in a faint. Since I was still suspicious of so easy a success, I feigned extreme alarm. But even as I expressed it I took her, or carried her, toward the place previously appointed for the field of glory. In fact she did not return to herself until after she had submitted and surrendered to her happy conqueror.

So far, my love, you will, have been pleased with the orthodoxy of my method, I think: you will have seen that I have in no respect diverged from the true principles of an art that is, as we have often observed, very similar to that of warfare. Judge me, then, as you would Turenne or Frederick.[15] I have been obliged to combat a foe who wished only to temporize. By clever maneuvering I secured for myself the choice of terrain and dispositions. I succeeded in lulling the enemy into security so as to fall upon her more easily in her place of refuge. I made sure that security was succeeded by terror before I engaged in the fight. I was risking nothing, since I could look for great advantage in case of success, and was certain of other resources in case of defeat. Lastly, I did not commit myself to action till assured of a safe means of retreat by which I could protect and preserve my previous gains. No man, I think, could have done more. But now I am afraid that I have grown soft like Hannibal among the fleshpots of Capua. This is what subsequently happened:

I quite expected that so important an event would not pass off without the usual grief and despair, and if I noticed at first a little more than the customary confusion, and a sort of inner withdrawal, I attributed both to the influence of a prudish disposition. So, without attending to slight irregularities, which I judged to be purely local, I simply followed the main course that consolation takes, convinced that, as usually happens, sensation would come to the help of sentiment, and that a single action would accomplish more than any amount of persuasion – which nevertheless I did not neglect to offer. But I met with a truly alarming resistance: not so alarming in its strength as in the form it took.

Imagine a woman seated in stiff immobility with a fixed expression on her face, seeming neither to think nor to listen, nor to understand; from whose staring eyes the tears fall continuously and unchecked. Such was Madame de Tourvel whenever I spoke; and if I tried to recapture her attention with a caress, even of the most innocent kind, her apathy gave way immediately to terror, suffocation, convulsive movements, sobs, from time to time a cry, but never a single articulate word.

These attacks occurred several times with increasing severity. The last was so violent that it utterly discouraged me, and I feared for a moment that I had won a useless victory. I fell back upon my store of platitudes, among which I found the following: "And are you in despair because you have made me happy?" At this, the adorable creature turned toward me, and her face, though still a little distraught, had already resumed that heavenly expression. "Happy?" she said. You may imagine the reply. "Are you then happy?" I redoubled my protestations. "And happy because of me!" I added compliments and tender words. While I spoke her limbs relaxed. She fell back limply in her chair and, leaving me the hand I had ventured to take in mine, said, "That thought, I find, is a solace and a comfort to me."

As you may imagine, having been put back upon my path, I did not turn from it again; it was really the right one, perhaps the only one. So, when I decided to try for a second success and met initially with some resistance, what had passed before made me circumspect. But having called the idea of my happiness once again to my assistance, I was soon made to feel once again its favorable effects: "You are right," said the tender-hearted creature. "I can no longer endure my existence unless it is of use in making you happy. I devote myself entirely to that. From this moment on I am yours, and you will hear neither refusals nor regrets from my lips." With such candor – naive or sublime – did she give up her person and her charms, increasing my happiness by sharing it. Intoxication was complete and reciprocal and, for the first time with me, outlasted pleasure. I left her arms only to fall at her feet and swear eternal love – and, to tell the whole truth, I meant what I said. Even after I had left her, the thought of her was still with me, and I have even now to make an effort to be rid of it.

Ah, why are you not here, at least to set off the charm of success with the pleasure of reward? But I lose nothing by waiting, do I? And I hope I can take for granted between us the happy arrangement I suggested in my last letter. As you see, I am as good as my word: my affairs, as I promised, have made sufficient progress for me to give you a part of my time. Make haste, then, and dispatch your tedious Belleroche: leave your mawkish Danceny to his own devices, so that you may occupy yourself exclusively with me.

But what are you so busy with at your country house that you don't so much as reply to me? Do you know that I could be annoyed with you for less? But happiness makes for indulgence. Besides, I don't forget that in including myself once again among the number of your suitors, I must, once again, submit to your little whims. Remember, however, that this new lover intends to lose none of his former rights as a friend.

Good-bye – as I would say it of old... Yes, *good-bye, my angel! I sent you all love's kisses.*

P.S. Do you know that Prévan, after a month in prison, has been obliged to leave his regiment? All Paris is talking about it now. So there he is, cruelly punished for a crime he did not commit, and your success is complete.

Paris
29 October 17–

LETTER 126: *Madame de Rosemonde to the Présidente de Tourvel*
I should have replied to you earlier, my dear child, had not the fatigue of writing my last letter revived my malady and deprived me, these last few days, of the use of my arm. I was very anxious to thank you for the good news you gave me of my nephew, and no less so to offer you my sincere felicitations on your own account. One is obliged to see this as truly the work of Providence which, in putting one to the test, has saved

both. Yes, my dear, God, who wished only to try you, has saved you at the very moment when your strength was exhausted; and in spite of your little complainings, you have, I think, some thanks to return Him. I am fully aware that it would have been more agreeable from your point of view had this resolution been taken in the first place by you, and had Valmont's followed merely as a consequence. It even seems to me that the rights of our sex would thus have been better safeguarded – and we cannot afford to lose any! But what are these trifling considerations against the important ends that have been achieved? Does the man saved from drowning complain of having had no choice in the matter of a means?

You will soon find, my dear daughter, that the sufferings you so fear will subside of themselves; and even were they to continue forever at their full strength, you would still find them easier to endure than remorse and self-contempt. Useless for me to have spoken to you sooner with this apparent severity: love is an independent feeling, which prudence can help us to avoid but cannot overcome, and which, once born, can die only a natural death or from an absolute want of hope. It is want of hope in your case which gives me the courage, and the right, to speak my opinion freely. It is cruel to frighten the desperately ill, who can benefit only from comfort and palliatives; but it is wise to enlighten the convalescent about the dangers they have courted, so as to inspire in them the prudence they need and to encourage a submission to the advice they may need for the future.

Since you have chosen me for your doctor, I shall speak to you as such, and tell you that the little indispositions you now suffer, which perhaps require some remedy, are nothing in comparison to the frightful infirmity of which you are now safely cured. Then, as your friend, as the friend of a reasonable and virtuous woman, I shall permit myself to add that the passion you were victim to, unfortunate enough in itself, was doubly so by reason of its object. If I can believe what I am told, my nephew – whom I admit it is perhaps a weakness in me to love, and who has in fact, besides a great deal of charm, many praiseworthy qualities – is neither safe with women nor guiltless where they are concerned, and will ruin them as soon as seduce them. I am sure you have converted him. Never was anyone more worthy to do so; but so many others have flattered themselves in the same way whose hopes have been deceived, and I should much prefer you not to suffer the same fate.

Consider now, my dear, that instead of all the dangers you would have had to undergo, you will have, besides a clear conscience and your proper peace of mind, the satisfaction of having been the principal cause of Valmont's reformation. As for me, I have no doubt that it was largely due to your courageous resistance, and that one moment's weakness on your part would perhaps have condemned my nephew to a lifetime of error. I like to think so, and should like you to think so too. In that thought you will find your first consolation and I new reason for loving you more.

I shall expect you here in a few days, my dear daughter, as you tell me. Come and recover your happiness and calm in the place where you lost them; come, especially, to rejoice with a loving mother in your having so faithfully kept the promise you gave her never to do anything that was unworthy of her or of you!

Château de ———
30 October 17–

LETTER 127: *The Marquise de Merteuil to the Vicomte de Valmont*
If I have not replied, Vicomte, to your letter of the nineteenth, it is not because I have not had the time. It is quite simply that it annoyed me with its want of common sense. I thought, therefore, that I could do no better than commit it to oblivion. But since you have returned to it, since you seem to insist upon the proposals it contains, and since you take my silence for consent, I must speak my mind clearly.

I may sometimes have had pretensions to bodying forth a whole seraglio in my person, but I have never been persuaded to belong to one. I thought you knew that. At any rate, now that you can no longer be ignorant of it, you may easily imagine how ridiculous your suggestion appears to me to be. I! I, sacrifice my inclination, and a new one at that, to devote my time to you! And how? In waiting my turn, like a submissive slave, for the sublime favors of your *Highness*. When, for example, you would like a moment's distraction from the *strange charm* that the *adorable, heavenly* Madame de Tourvel alone has made you feel, or when you are afraid of compromising the superior idea you are pleased the *attractive* Cécile should have of you; then, descending to my level, you will come in search of less lively pleasures it is true, but not of the same consequence. And your precious favors, though seldom bestowed, will be more than enough to keep me happy!

You are well endowed, to be sure, with a good opinion of yourself. Not so I, apparently, with modesty – for, look at myself as I will, I cannot see that I have sunk so low. This is perhaps a fault in me; but I warn you that I have many more. That especially of thinking that the *schoolboy*, the *mawkish* Danceny, who is entirely devoted to me; who has sacrificed for my sake – without making a merit of it – a first passion before it has even been satisfied; who loves me as one can love only at that age, can, in spite of his twenty years, serve my happiness and pleasure more effectually than you. I shall even permit myself to add that, should the whim take me to give him an assistant, it would not be you, at least for the moment.

And what are my reasons? you will ask. In the first place, there may very well be none: the caprice that favors you may with equal justice ignore you. I am, however, willing, for politeness' sake, to explain my motives. It seems to me that you would have too many sacrifices to make for my sake; while I, instead of expressing the gratitude you would not fail to expect, should be quite capable of thinking that you owed me even more! You will agree that, so far removed from each other in our way of thinking, we have no hope of coming to an understanding; and I am afraid it will be a long time, a very long time, before I change my views. When I do, I shall give you notice of the fact. Till then, believe me, you must make other arrangements and keep your kisses. You have so much opportunity to find better recipients for them!...

"Good-bye – as I would say of old," you say. But it seems to me that of old you set a somewhat higher value upon me: you had not altogether relegated me to minor roles. Above all, you were willing to wait until I had said "yes" before you were sure of my consent. You must be satisfied, then, with my saying good-bye, not as I, too, would have said it of old, but as I am saying it now.

Your servant, Monsieur de Valmont.

Château de ———
31 October 17–

LETTER 128: *The Présidente de Tourvel to Madame de Rosemonde*
It was not until yesterday, Madame, that I received your belated reply. It would have killed me immediately had my life still belonged to me, but my life is in another's possession – and that other is Monsieur de Valmont. I conceal nothing from you, you see. Though you should find me no longer worthy of your friendship, I am still less afraid of losing it than of betraying it. All I can tell you is that, given the choice between the death of Monsieur de Valmont and his happiness, I decided in favor of the latter. I am neither boasting nor accusing myself: I am simply stating a fact.

You may easily imagine the impression your letter, and the harsh truths contained in it, must in the circumstances have made upon me.

Do not suppose, however, that it awakened any regrets in me or that it could ever bring about a change in my feelings or my conduct. It is not that I do not still suffer cruelly; but when my heart is most torn, when I am afraid that I may no longer be able to endure the torment, I tell myself Valmont is happy, and everything disappears before that thought, or rather turns before it into pleasure.

It is to your nephew, then, that my life is devoted; for him that I have been ruined. He has become the sole center of my thoughts, my feelings, and my actions. As long as my life is necessary to his happiness, my life shall be precious to me, and I shall think it fortunate. If some day he decides otherwise...he shall hear neither complaint nor reproach from my lips. I have already dared to confront that fatal moment, and my decision is taken.

You see now how little I can be affected by the apprehensions you seem to feel that Monsieur de Valmont will one day bring about my ruin: before he can wish to do that he will have ceased to love me, and what will reproaches be to me when I cannot hear them? He alone will be my judge. Since I shall have lived only for him, to him I shall entrust my memory; and if he is compelled to acknowledge that I loved him, I shall have been sufficiently justified.

You have just seen into my heart, Madame. I have preferred, by being honest, the misfortune of losing your respect to that of making myself unworthy of it by stooping to lies. I thought I owed you this entire confidence in return for your former kindness to me. To add one word more might make you suspect that I am still counting upon it, when in fact I judge myself to have forfeited my claims.

I am with all respect, Madame, your very humble and obedient servant.

Paris
1 November 17–

LETTER 129: *The Vicomte de Valmont to the Marquise de Merteuil*
Tell me, my love: Why the tone of bitterness and irony that pervades your last letter? What is the crime I have committed, unwittingly it seems, which puts you in so bad a temper? You accuse me of assuming your consent before I have obtained it; but I thought that what might appear as presumption with anyone else, could never between us be taken for anything but confidence – and since when has that sentiment been incompatible with friendship or love? In uniting hope and desire I merely yielded to a natural impulse, the impulse that will have us always take the shortest road to the happiness we seek; and you mis-

took for a sign of pride what was only the effect of my eagerness. I know quite well that custom in such cases demands a respectful uncertainty; but you know too that this is nothing but a formality, a simple matter of protocol. And I was, it seems to me, justified in thinking that this careful punctiliousness was no longer necessary between us.

It seems to me, too, that frankness and freedom, when they are supported by a relationship of long standing, are far preferable to the insipid flattery that so often debases love. Perhaps, for the rest, if I think highly of such ways, it is only because of the value I attach to the past happiness they recall; but for that very reason I should be all the more sorry to have you think otherwise.

This, however, is the only crime I am aware of having committed – for I cannot suppose that you could seriously think another woman whom I prefer to you existed anywhere in the world, much less that I have appreciated you as little as you pretend to believe. You have looked at yourself, you say, and cannot see that you have sunk so low; I can well believe it, and that proves that your looking glass does not lie. But could you not have arrived more easily and more justly at the conclusion that I certainly cannot have passed any such judgment on you?

I search in vain for an explanation of this strange idea. It seems to me, however, that it derives more or less directly from my having allowed myself to speak in praise of other women. This I infer, at all events, from your affectation of emphasizing the epithets *adorable, heavenly, attractive*, that I have used in speaking to you of Madame de Tourvel and the little Volanges. But don't you know that these words, chosen more often at random than upon reflection, express not so much an opinion of the persons in question as the mood one is in when one is speaking of them? And if, at the very moment of my being so deeply affected by one or the other, I yet desired you no less ardently; if I gave you a decided preference over both of them, since after all I cannot renew our former relationship without prejudice to both, I think you don't have so very much cause for complaint.

It will be no more difficult for me to excuse the *strange charm*, which seems also to have shocked you a little. In the first place, the fact that it is strange does not make it any stronger. Come now, who could improve upon the delicious pleasures that you alone can offer, ever new and ever more lively? I meant only, but without attempting to set a value upon it, that this one was of a kind I had not yet experienced. And I added what I shall now repeat: whatever it is, I shall fight it and conquer it. And I shall do so with more enthusiasm if I may consider the trifling task as an offer of homage to you.

As for little Cécile, it is no use speaking to you of her. You have not forgotten that it was at your request that I took charge of the child, and I await only your permission to be rid of her. I may have taken notice of her freshness and ingenuousness; I may even have been able, for a moment, to find her *attractive*, because one always takes more or less of a pleasure in one's work – but there is certainly in no respect enough substance in her to claim one's attention for long.

Now, my love, I appeal to your sense of justice, to your former kindness for me, to our long and perfect friendship, to the entire confidence in each other which has since strengthened our ties. Have I deserved the harsh tone you adopt with me? But how easy it will be for you to make amends whenever you wish! Say but a word and you will see whether all the charms and attractions in the world can keep me here, not even for a day but for a mere minute. I shall fly to your feet and into your arms, and shall prove to you a thousand times and in a thousand ways, that you are and will always be the rightful sovereign of my heart.

Good-bye, my love. I most anxiously await your reply.

Paris
3 November 17–

LETTER 130: *Madame de Rosemonde to the Présidente de Tourvel*
Why, my dear, do you no longer wish to be my daughter? Why do you as much as declare that all correspondence will cease between us? Is it to punish me for not having guessed something that was against all probability? Or do you suspect me of having distressed you deliberately? No, I know your heart too well to believe that you could think thus of mine. The pain your letter gave me, therefore, I feel much less on my account than on yours.

Oh, my young friend, it grieves me to say it, but you are much too worthy of love ever to be made happy by it! And, indeed, where is the woman of delicacy and sensitivity who has not found misfortune in the very feeling that promised her so much happiness? Do men ever appreciate the women they possess?

Not that many of them are not honorable in their conduct and constant in their affections: but even among those who are, how few are also capable of understanding our hearts! Do not imagine, my child, that their love is like ours. They feel, of course, the same delight; often they are more carried away by it. But they are ignorant of that anxious eagerness, that careful solicitude, which provokes us to the constant and tender attentions whose sole object is always the man we love. A man enjoys the happiness he feels, a woman the happiness she gives. This difference, so essential and so little noticed, yet influences the whole of their respective conduct in the most remarkable way. The pleasure of one is to satisfy his desires, of the other it is, above all, to arouse them. Giving pleasure for him is only a means to success; while for her it is success itself. Coquetry, so often held in accusation against woman, is no more than the abuse of their way of feeling, and is itself a proof of the way they feel. Lastly, that exclusive attachment to one person, a characteristic peculiar to love, is in a man only a preference that seems at the most to increase a pleasure that with some other woman might be diminished, but not destroyed; whereas in women, it is a profound feeling that not only annihilates all other desires but, stronger than nature and disobedient to her commands, may cause them to derive only repugnance and disgust from the very source of pleasure itself.

Do not be led to believe that the more or less numerous exceptions that may be cited against these universal rules can in any way disprove them. Public opinion is their guarantee, which distinguishes for men only between infidelity and inconstancy. It is a distinction that men make use of when they ought to be humiliated by it; a distinction that among our sex is never made except by those depraved women who are a disgrace to it. Any means will serve to spare them the painful consciousness of their degradation.

I thought, my dear, you might find it useful to have these reflections to set against those chimerical fancies of perfect happiness with which love never fails to abuse our imaginations; false hopes that one clings to even when one sees that they must perforce be abandoned; the loss of which, moreover, aggravates and multiplies the griefs, all too real already, that are inseparable from deep feeling! The task of alleviating your sufferings or of reducing their number is the only one that I wish or am able to fulfill at this moment. Where the illness is without remedy, advice can only bear on the regimen. All I ask of you is that you should remember that to pity a sick man is not to cast blame upon him. Indeed, who are we to cast blame upon each other? Let us leave the right to judge to Him who reads our hearts; I should even go so far as to believe that in His paternal sight a host of virtues may redeem a single weakness.

But I beg you, my dear friend, renounce these violent resolutions which are an indication less of strength than of an entire loss of courage. Do not forget that in giving up your life into another's possession, to use your own expression, you cannot all the same have deprived your friends of that part of it which already belonged to them and which they shall never cease to claim.

Good-bye, my dear daughter. Think sometimes of your fond mother, and be sure that you will always, above all else, be the object of her kindest thoughts.

Château de ———
4 November 17–

LETTER 131: *The Marquise de Merteuil to the Vicomte de Valmont*
Well done, Vicomte. I am better pleased with you this time than the last. But now let us talk as good friends, and let me convince you that the arrangement you seem to favor would be, as much for you as for me, absolute folly.

Have you not as yet observed that pleasure, undeniably the sole motive force behind the union of the sexes, is nevertheless not enough to form a bond between them? And that if it is preceded by the desire that impels, it is followed by disgust that repels? That is a law of nature which love alone can alter. And can love be summoned up at will? Nevertheless, love is necessary, and the necessity would really be very embarrassing had not one perceived that fortunately it will do if love exists on one side only. The difficulty is thus reduced by half without much being lost thereby; in fact, one party enjoys the happiness of loving, the other that of pleasing. The latter is a little less intense, it is true, but to it is added the pleasure of deceiving, which establishes a balance; and so everything is satisfactorily arranged.

But tell me, Vicomte, which of us will be responsible for deceiving the other? You know the story of the two gamblers who recognized each other for cardsharps even as they played: "We shall win nothing from each other," they said, "so let us share the stakes," and they abandoned the game. We must, believe me, follow their prudent example. Let us not waste time together which might otherwise be so profitably employed.

To prove to you that in this I am swayed by your interest as much as mine, and that I am not acting out of annoyance or caprice, I shall not refuse you the reward agreed upon between us. I am perfectly sure that for a single night we shall be more than sufficient for each other; and I don't even doubt that we shall enjoy it too much to see it end without regret. But let us keep in mind that this regret is necessary to happiness. However sweet the illusion, let us not believe that it can last.

As you see, I am quite ready to oblige, even though you have not yet fulfilled your part of the bargain: for, after all, I was to have the first letter written by your Heavenly Prude. But whether you still intend to abide by it, or whether you have forgotten the terms of a contract which perhaps interests you less than you would have me believe, I have as yet received nothing, absolutely nothing. However, if I am not mistaken, the tender devotee writes a great deal. What else can she possibly do when she is alone? She surely has not the good sense to amuse herself. I could therefore, if I wished, find a few little complaints to make against you; but I pass them over in silence to make up for the slight bad temper I may have shown in my last letter.

Now, Vicomte, there remains only a request to make of you, as much for your sake as for mine, and that is to put off for the moment what I desire perhaps as much as you. It seems to me it is better deferred until I return to town. On the one hand, we shall not have the necessary freedom here, and on the other, it would involve me in some risk: for it requires only a little jealousy to fasten me more firmly than ever to this sad creature Belleroche, who at the moment is attached only by a thread. He is already goading himself on to make love to me; we are at the point where there is as much malice as prudence in the caresses I lavish upon him. But at the same time you can well see that this is not the sacrifice to make for you! A double infidelity will make our meeting so much the more charming.

Do you know that I sometimes regret that we are reduced to such courses. There was a time when we loved each other – for it was, I think, love – and I was happy; and you, Vicomte!... But why think now of a happiness that can never return? No; whatever you say, it is impossible that it should. In the first place, I should demand sacrifices which you certainly could not or would not make for my sake, and which, it might well be, I should not deserve. And then, how could I ever be sure of you? Oh, no, no! I will not so much as entertain the idea; and in spite of the pleasure I find at this very moment in writing to you, I had much better leave you at once.

Good-bye, Vicomte.

Château de ———
6 November 17–

LETTER 132: *The Présidente de Tourvel to Madame de Rosemonde*
I am so deeply sensible, Madame, of your kindness toward me that I should open my heart entirely to it were it not, in some way, held back

by a fear of profaning what I accept. Why, when kindness is so precious to me, must I feel at the same time that I am no longer worthy of it? I can at least express my gratitude! I can admire, above all, your indulgent virtue, which sees weakness only to commiserate with it, whose irresistible charm maintains so mild yet so strong a sway over my heart, in company with the charm of love itself.

But can I still deserve a friendship that is no longer enough to make me happy? I might say the same of your advice: I know its value but cannot accept it. And how can I disbelieve in perfect happiness, when I feel it at this very moment? Yes, if men are such as you describe them, they must be shunned – they are detestable. But how little Valmont is like them! If he is subject, as they are, to that violence of passion you call being carried away, how much is it exceeded in him by his extreme delicacy! Oh, my dear! You tell me to share my sorrows with you; enjoy my happiness instead. I owe it to my love; and the object of my love still further increases its value! It is, you say, perhaps a weakness in you to love your nephew. Ah, if you knew him as I do! I love him unto idolatry, and yet much less than he deserves. He may once certainly have been led into error. He admits it himself. But who can know true love as he does? What more can I say? His feelings are equal to the feelings he inspires.

You are going to think that this is one of those "chimerical fancies, with which love never fails to abuse our imaginations"! In that case why should he have become only more tender, more eager now that he has nothing left to obtain from me? I admit I once found in him a certain deliberation, a reserve, which rarely left him, and which often reminded me, in spite of myself, of the false and cruel impression I had been given of him at first. But since he has been able to give himself up without constraint to the impulses of his heart, he seems to divine all the wishes of my own. Who knows, we may have been born for each other! I may have been destined for the happiness of being necessary to his! Ah, if it is an illusion, let me die before it vanishes. But no – I want to live to cherish him, to worship him. Why should he cease to love me? What other woman could he make happier than me? And I know from my own experience that the happiness one gives is the strongest bond, the only one that really holds. Yes, it is the delightful consciousness of that which ennobles love, which purifies it, so to speak, and makes it truly worthy of a tender and generous heart such as Valmont's.

Good-bye, my dear, my worthy, my indulgent friend. I could write no more if I tried; it is now time for him to come, as he promised, and I can think of nothing else. Forgive me! But you wanted my happiness, and it is so great at this moment that I am scarcely capable of supporting it.

Paris
7 November 17–

LETTER 1 3 3 : *The Vicomte de Valmont to the Marquise de Merteuil*
What then, my love, are these sacrifices that you think I would not make, for which nevertheless I should be rewarded by giving you pleasure? Let me only know what they are. If I hesitate for a moment before offering them to you, you may refuse that homage. Come, what can you have thought of me lately if, even when you are being indulgent, you doubt my feelings and capacities? Sacrifices that I would not or could not make! Do you then think I am in love? Enslaved? Do you suspect that the value I once set upon victory I now attach to the vanquished? Ah, thank Heaven, I am not yet reduced to that, and I am willing to prove it to you. Yes, I shall prove it to you, even if it must be at Madame de Tourvel's expense. You could scarcely, after that, remain in any doubt.

I may have spent some time, I suppose, without any risk to myself on a woman who has at least the merit of belonging to a species one rarely meets. Perhaps, too, my meeting with this adventure during the off season encouraged me to commit myself further than usual; and even now, when the great world has scarcely yet resumed its whirl, it is not surprising that I am almost entirely preoccupied with it. But remember too that I have hardly had a week to enjoy the fruits of three months' labors. I have so often kept for longer what was worth less and cost me not so much!...and you have never drawn conclusions from that to my discredit.

Besides, do you want to know the real cause of my interest? Here it is. This woman is naturally timid: from the first she doubted her happiness, and that doubt was enough to destroy it, so much so that I have scarcely yet begun to be able to judge how far my power will extend in an affair of this kind. This, nevertheless, is something I have always been curious to discover; and opportunities for doing so are not as easily come by as you might think.

In the first place, for many women pleasure is simply pleasure and never anything else. For them, whatever title they bestow upon us, we are never more than servants, mere functionaries whose only merit is industry: the one who does most, does best.

Another class of women, perhaps the most numerous today, are almost exclusively concerned with a lover's prestige, with the pleasure of having snatched him from a rival and the fear of having him snatched in turn from them. We do, it is true, play some part more or less in the sort of happiness they enjoy; but it depends more on our circumstances than on our persons. We are its means, but not its instrument.

For my experiment, therefore, I needed a delicate and sensitive woman who made love her only concern and who, even in love, saw no further than her lover; whose emotions, far from following the usual course, reached her senses through her heart; whom I have, for example, seen (and I don't refer to the first occasion) emerge from pleasure dissolved in tears yet find it again in the first word that touched her sympathies. In addition she must have a natural candor, become irrepressible from a habit of indulging it, which therefore could not allow her to disguise a single one of her feelings. Now, you will agree, such women are rare; and I dare say that, were it not for this one, I should perhaps never have met any.

It is not surprising, therefore, that she should interest me for longer than anyone else has; and if my experiment upon her demands my making her happy, perfectly happy, why should I refuse, particularly since her happiness will be useful to me rather than otherwise? But does it follow, from the fact that my mind is occupied, that my heart is enslaved? No, of course not. Hence, the value I cannot help attaching to this adventure will not prevent my engaging in others, or even sacrificing it to more agreeable ones.

I am still at so much liberty that I have not even neglected the little Volanges, in whom I take so small an interest. Her mother is bringing her back to town in three days' time, and yesterday I established my communications: a little money for the porter, a few compliments to his wife, were enough for the purpose. Can you conceive why Danceny was unable to find so simple a method? And people say that love inspires ingenuity! On the contrary, it stupefies those who are under its sway. And you think I am incapable of resisting it? Ah, rest assured that in a few days I shall already, by sharing it, have weakened the perhaps overly vivid impression I received; and if sharing it once is not enough, I shall do so again and again.

I shall nevertheless be ready to return the little convent girl to her discreet lover as soon as you judge proper. You no longer, I think, have any reason to demur; as for me, I am quite willing to render poor Danceny this signal service. It is, to tell the truth, the least I owe him for all that he has done for me. He is, at the moment, in extreme anxiety to know whether he will be received at Madame de Volanges's. I soothe him as much as I can by telling him that, one way or another, I shall effect his happiness at the first opportunity; and meanwhile I continue to be responsible for the correspondence he wishes to resume as soon as "his Cécile" arrives. I already have six letters from him, and I shall certainly have one or two more before the happy day. That boy must be very idle!

But let us leave this childish pair and return to ourselves. Let me think only of the sweet hopes your letter has given me. Yes, of course you will be sure of me, and I cannot forgive you your doubts. Have I ever ceased to be faithful to you? The ties that bound us were loosened, not broken. Our supposed rupture was only an illusion of the imagination: in spite of it we have in our feelings, in our interests, remained at one. Like the traveler who returns disillusioned, I shall find that I left true happiness to chase false hopes, and shall say with d'Harcourt:

The more I saw abroad, the more I longed for home*

Don't, then, resist the thought, or rather the feeling, that draws you back to me. Having tasted all the pleasures of our separate careers, let us enjoy the happiness of discovering that none of them is comparable to that which we once experienced together, and shall again – to find it more delicious than ever before.

Good-bye, my love. I am willing to await your return – but make it soon, and don't forget how much I long for it.

Paris
8 November 17–

LETTER 134: *The Marquise de Merteuil to the Vicomte de Valmont*
Really, Vicomte, you are like a child in front of whom one can say nothing! And to whom one can show nothing without his wanting to snatch at it! A simple thought occurs to me, which I warn you that I cannot seriously consider, and because I mention it to you, you take advantage of the fact to remind me of what I have said; to hold me to it when I want to forget it; to make me in some way and in spite of myself share your foolhardy desires! Is it generous of you to leave me to support the burden of prudence alone? I tell you again, as I tell myself repeatedly, that the arrangement you propose is absolutely impossible. Even though you bring to it all the generosity you show me at this moment, don't you think that I too have my delicacy which will not allow me to accept sacrifices that are detrimental to your happiness?

---

*Du Belloi, *Tragédie du siège de Calais*.

Now is it not true, Vicomte, that you are deluding yourself about the feeling that attaches you to Madame de Tourvel? If it is not love, what is love? You deny it in a hundred ways but prove it in a thousand. What, for example, is the meaning of this subterfuge you resort to in order to hide from yourself (for I believe you to be sincere with me) that the interest you take in your "experiment" is in fact a desire, which you can neither conceal nor conquer, to keep this woman? One would think you had never made another woman happy, perfectly happy! And, if you have any doubt of that, your memory is a very bad one! No, it is not that. In a word, your heart is playing tricks upon your reason, inducing it to deceive itself with specious arguments. I, however, in whose most intimate interest it is not to be deceived, am not so easily satisfied.

While remarking that, out of politeness, you were careful to avoid the words you imagined had offended me, I noticed all the same that, perhaps unconsciously, you expressed the same ideas. In fact it was no longer the adorable, the heavenly Madame de Tourvel, but *an astonishing woman, a delicate and sensitive woman* – to the exclusion of all others; finally, a *rare woman*, one such as is not likely to be met a second time. It is the same with that strange charm, which is not of the *strongest kind*. Well, maybe; but since you have never experienced it till now, there is reason to believe that you will never experience it again – and your loss is still irreparable. If these, Vicomte, are not certain symptoms of love, it must be denied that there are any.

Rest assured that on this occasion I speak without rancor. I promised myself not to give way to it again, being too well aware that it could become a dangerous pitfall. Believe me, we had better be friends and leave it at that. Be grateful only for my courage in resisting you – yes, my courage, for that is sometimes necessary even in avoiding a decision one knows to be a bad one.

It is therefore only to persuade you to my way of thinking that I am going to reply to your question about the sacrifices I should exact, which you could not make. I use the word "exact" deliberately, because I am quite sure that in a moment you are, in fact, going to find me too exacting – but so much the better! Far from being offended by your refusal, I shall thank you for it. What is more, I don't want to pretend with you: I shall perhaps need it.

I should demand then – see, what cruelty! – that the rare, the astonishing Madame de Tourvel become no more to you than the ordinary woman she is; for, let us not deceive ourselves, the charm we think we find in others exists only in ourselves, and it is love alone that confers beauty on the beloved. I know that you would probably make the effort to promise, even to swear, to do what I ask, impossible though it may be; but I must tell you I should believe no empty speeches. I could not be convinced but by the whole of your conduct.

That is not yet all; I should be capricious. About the sacrifice of little Cécile, which you offer me with so good a grace, I should care not at all. On the contrary, I should ask you to continue in this uncongenial employment until further orders from me; perhaps because I should like thus to abuse my power, perhaps because, out of a sense of kindness or of justice, I could be satisfied with ruling your feelings without wishing to spoil your pleasures. Be that as it may, I should require to be obeyed; and my instructions would be strict!

It is true that I might thereupon think myself obliged to thank you – who knows? – perhaps even to reward you. I should certainly, for example, cut short an absence that would begin to seem intolerable. I should at last see you again, Vicomte, and I should see you again...how?...But you must remember that this is only a conversation, a simple account of an impossible scheme; I don't want to be the only one to forget about it.

Do you know I am a little anxious about my lawsuit? At any rate, I decided I must know the precise extent of my resources. My lawyers cited a few laws and a great many "authorities," as they call them, but I could see no more reason than justice in them. I almost regret having refused a settlement out of court. However, it reassures me to remember that the public prosecutor is clever, the counsel eloquent, and the plaintiff pretty. If these three qualifications were no longer worth anything, our whole legal procedure would have to be changed, and what then would become of respect for tradition?

The lawsuit is now the only thing that keeps me here. The Belleroche affair is over: case dismissed, costs divided. He is busy regretting this evening's ball – the true regret of the idle man. I shall give him back his entire liberty when I return to town. In making him this grievous sacrifice I shall be consoled by the generosity he finds in it.

Good-bye, Vicomte, write often. The catalog of your pleasures makes up, at least in part, for the boredom I suffer.

Château de ———
11 November 17–

LETTER 135: *The Présidente de Tourvel to Madame de Rosemonde*
I shall try to write to you, but am not sure yet that I can. Ah, God! To think that in my last letter it was an excess of happiness that kept me

from continuing. Now it is an excess of despair that overwhelms me, that leaves me strength only to feel my sufferings, and deprives me of power to express them.

Valmont...Valmont loves me no longer. He has never loved me. Love does not disappear like this. He deceives me, betrays me, insults me. All the miseries, the humiliations there are, I feel them all, and he is the cause of them!

And do not think this is any mere suspicion. I was so far from suspecting anything! I am not so fortunate as to have any doubts. I have seen him – what can he possibly say to excuse himself? But what does it matter to him? He will not even try...Wretched woman! What difference will your tears, your reproaches make to him? It is not you that interests him!...

It is, then, true that he has sacrificed me, indeed delivered me up... to whom? A vile creature...vile, do I say? Ah, I have even lost the right to despise her. She has not betrayed so many responsibilities. She is less guilty than I. Oh, how painful is suffering when it springs from remorse! I feel my torments twice as keenly. Good-bye, my dear friend. However unworthy of your pity I have made myself, you will yet feel some for me if you have any conception of what I suffer.

I have just reread my letter, and realize that it does not tell you anything, so I shall try and find the courage to tell you the dreadful story. It happened yesterday; I was to go out to supper for the first time since my return. Valmont came to see me at five o'clock. Never had he seemed so tender. He gave me to understand that he would prefer me not to go out, and, as you may imagine, I immediately decided to stay at home. Two hours later, however, his manner and tone of voice changed suddenly and quite perceptibly. I do not know whether I could have said anything to annoy him; whatever it was, he pretended a little while later to remember some business that obliged him to leave me, and he went off – not, however, without expressing the deepest regrets, which appeared to be tender and which I then believed to be sincere.

Left to myself, I thought it right not to neglect my former engagements, since I was free to fulfill them. I finished my toilette and entered my carriage. My coachman, unfortunately, took me past the opera, and I found myself detained in the traffic at the exit. Four paces ahead, and in the next line of carriages, I saw Valmont's. My heart immediately began to beat fast, but not in fear. My only thought was for my carriage to move forward. It was his instead that was obliged to draw back beside mine. I leaned out immediately. Imagine my astonishment at seeing by his side a woman well known as a courtesan! I withdrew, as you may guess. I had seen enough to break my heart. But what you will scarcely believe is that this harlot, with a knowingness apparently derived from unthinkable confidences, neither left the door of the carriage nor ceased to look at me, shrieking with laughter so as to attract the attention of everyone.

In spite of my state of prostration, I allowed myself to be taken to the house where I was to sup; but it proved impossible for me to stay. I felt at every instant that I was about to faint, and, worst of all, could not hold back my tears.

On returning home I wrote to Monsieur de Valmont, and sent the letter immediately; he was not at home. In my desire to rouse myself at any price from this life in death or to end it forever, I dispatched my servant again with orders to wait. But before midnight he returned, saying that Valmont's coachman, who had been sent back, had told him that his master would not be coming home that night. I decided this morning that I could do no more than ask for the return of my letters and request him never to come to my house again. I did in fact give orders accordingly; but they were probably superfluous. It is nearly midday; he has not yet presented himself here, and I have not even received word from him.

Now, my dear friend, I have nothing further to add. You know everything; you know my heart. My only hope is that it will not be for much longer that I remain a burden upon your sympathy and friendship.

Paris
15 November 17—

LETTER 136: *The Présidente de Tourvel to the Vicomte de Valmont*
After what happened, yesterday, Monsieur, you will, of course, no longer expect to be received at my house, and doubtless have very little wish to be received here. The purpose of this note is, therefore, not so much to ask you never to come here again as to request that you return my letters — letters which ought never to have existed, and which, though they may have interested you momentarily as proofs of the infatuation you induced in me, can only be matter of indifference to you now that my eyes are opened and they express only a feeling that you have destroyed.

I realize, and I admit it, that I was wrong to place any confidence in you, a mistake to which many others before me have been victims. For this I blame only myself. But I did not think, all the same, that I deserved to be delivered over by you to insult and contempt. I thought that in sacrificing everything for you, in losing for your sake not only the esteem of others but my own, I need not expect to be judged by you more harshly than by the public, in whose opinion there is still an immense difference between a weak woman and a depraved one. These injuries, which anyone would complain of, are the only ones I shall mention. About the injuries to my feelings I have nothing to say: your heart would not understand mine. Good-bye, Monsieur.

Paris
15 November 17–

LETTER 137: *The Vicomte de Valmont to the Présidente de Tourvel*
Your letter, Madame, has only just been delivered to me. I trembled as I read it, and it has left me with scarcely strength enough to reply. What a frightful idea you have of me! Ah, of course I have my faults; faults such that I shall never forgive myself for them while I live, even though you should in your indulgence draw a veil over them. But how far from my nature are, and have always been, those you accuse me of now! Who, I? Humiliate you! Disgrace you! When I respect you as much as I cherish you; when I have known no pride such as I have felt since the moment you judged me worthy of you. Appearances have deceived you, and I admit they have been against me – but did you not have it in your heart to question them? Was it not the mere idea that you might have been ill-used by me that revolted you? And you gave it credit nonetheless? Hence, not only did you judge me capable of this terrible folly but you were even afraid that your kindness toward me had exposed you to it. Ah, if you think yourself so degraded by your love, how base a creature I myself must be in your eyes!

Oppressed by the painful feelings this thought arouses in me I waste time dismissing it that I should spend destroying it. I shall confess everything. Yet another thought still holds me back. Must I then recall an incident that I should like to erase from my memory, fix your attention and my own upon a momentary error that I would willingly redeem with the rest of my life, the reason for which I am unable to discover, the memory of which will always reduce me to humiliation and despair? Ah, if in accusing myself I must excite your anger, you will not have to look far for your revenge: you need only leave me to my remorse.

Yet, who would believe that the principal cause of this incident was the all-compelling charm you exert over me? It was that which made me too long unmindful of important business I could not postpone.

I left you too late. The person I went to meet was no longer there. I hoped to find him at the opera, but that journey was equally unfruitful. I saw Émilie there – Émilie, whom I first met at a time when I was very far from knowing either you or your love. She was without her carriage, and asked me to take her to her house not ten yards away. I foresaw no consequences and agreed; but it was then that I met you – and I knew immediately that you would be led to think me guilty.

The fear of displeasing or distressing you is so powerful in me that it was bound to be, and was in fact, very soon noticed. I confess that it even tempted me to make the girl promise not to show herself; but this precaution on the part of delicacy turned to the discomfiture of love. Never certain of the power she has usurped unless she can abuse it – no woman of her class ever is – Émilie was very careful not to let slip so splendid an opportunity. The more my embarrassment increased, the greater the delight she took in exposing herself; and her stupid laughter, of which I blush to think that you should for a moment have believed yourself to be the object, was provoked by nothing other than the cruel pain I was suffering, itself the consequence of my respect and my love for you.

Hitherto, of course, I had been more unfortunate than culpable; and those injuries "which anyone would complain of, the only ones you mention," having no existence, cannot be held against me. But it is useless for you to say nothing of injuries to your feelings. I shall not preserve the same silence: I have too great an interest in breaking it.

Not that in my present confusion at so unthinkable an aberration I can bring myself to recall it without extreme pain. Deeply conscious of my wrong, I should be quite willing to endure its pain and to hope that time, my undying tenderness, and my repentance would bring forgiveness. But how can I be silent when what remains to be told is of so much concern to your delicacy?

Do not imagine that I am looking for a way of excusing or palliating my fault: I admit myself guilty. But I do not admit and I shall never admit that this humiliating mistake could be regarded as a crime against love. Come, what can there be in common between an assault upon the senses, between a moment of self-oblivion, soon followed by shame and regret, and the purest sentiments, which can only take root in a delicate soul, which can only be nourished by respect, whose ultimate fruit is happiness? Ah, do not so profane the name of love. Beware, especially, of profaning yourself by treating what can never be compared as of equal importance. Leave it to base and degraded women to fear a rivalry that, in spite of themselves, they feel they must acknowledge, and to experience the torments of a jealousy as cruel as it is humiliating. But you, turn your eyes from things that would offend your sight; and, pure as the Divinity, punish the offense, as He does, without being sensible of it.

But what penance can you impose upon me more painful than the one I now undergo? What can compare with my regret at having displeased you, with my despair at having distressed you, the insupportable idea that I have made myself less worthy of you? You think of punishment – while I, I ask for comfort! Not because I deserve it, but because it is necessary to me, and I may obtain it only from you.

If, of a sudden, forgetting my love and yours, no longer setting any value upon my happiness, you decide on the contrary to give me up to everlasting suffering, you have the right to do so. Strike me down. But if, with more indulgence or more compassion, you recall the tender feelings that united our hearts; that intoxication of the soul, ever renewed, ever more deeply felt; those sweet, blessed days we owed to each other; all the myriad gifts of love, which love alone bestows! – if so, perhaps you will prefer to revive them than to destroy them. What else can I say? I have lost everything, and lost it through my own fault; but I may recover everything through the goodness of your heart. It is now for you to decide. I shall add but one word more. Only yesterday you swore to me that my happiness was secure while it depended on you! Ah, Madame, will you now give me up to everlasting despair?

Paris
15 November 17–

LETTER 138: *The Vicomte de Valmont to the Marquise de Merteuil*
I insist, my love: I am not in love, and it is not my fault if circumstances compel me to play the part. Be persuaded, only, and return. You will see for yourself how sincere I am. I gave proof of it yesterday which cannot be contradicted by what is happening today.

I was at the Tender Prude's, for lack of anything else to do, since the little Volanges, in spite of her condition, was to spend the night at Madame de V——'s, who has been beforehand with a ball. Idleness at first encouraged me to prolong my visit. I even, to this end, exacted a little sacrifice. But hardly had it been granted, when my anticipation of pleasure was disturbed by the thought of this love you persist in ascribing to me, or rather accusing me of; so that I was left with no other desire than that of being able at once to assure myself, and to convince you, that it was nothing on your part but pure slander.

I therefore acted decisively: under some slight pretext, I left my beauty overcome with surprise, and no doubt even more with affliction, while I went calmly to meet Émilie at the opera. She would confirm to you that, till this morning when we separated, not the smallest regret disturbed our pleasures.

I should, however, have had serious cause for disquiet had not my accustomed nonchalance come to my rescue. I was scarcely four houses away from the opera, with Émilie in my carriage, when that of the Austere Devotee drew up exactly alongside mine. Whereupon an obstruction in the traffic kept us beside each other for nearly ten minutes. We could not in broad daylight have been more clearly visible to each other, and there was no means of escape.

But that is not all. It occurred to me to tell Émilie that this was the woman of the letter (you will perhaps remember my little joke, when Émilie was my desk).* Émilie – who had not forgotten – being of a mirth-loving disposition, would not be satisfied until she had examined *this pillar of virtue*, as she put it, at her leisure, breaking into such scandalous peals of laughter as gave the latter considerable umbrage.

That is not yet all. The jealous woman sent to my house that very evening; I was not there, but in her obstinacy she sent a second time, with orders to wait for me. As for me, as soon as I had decided to stay at Émilie's I sent back my carriage, giving my coachman no other orders than to return for me in the morning. Since, on arriving home, he found Cupid's messenger there, he did not think twice before telling him that I should not be back that night. You may well imagine the effect of this news, and that at my return I found my dismissal awaiting me, pronounced with all the dignity suitable to the occasion!

Thus this adventure, interminable according to you, might well have come to an end this morning: and if it is not yet over, this is not, as you will think, because I am anxious to prolong it. It is because, on the one hand, I do not think it proper to allow myself to be dismissed, and, on the other, because I want to reserve the honor of a sacrifice for you.

I have therefore replied to the severe little note with a long and sentimental screed. I have offered lengthy arguments, and rely on love for the task of making them acceptable. I have already succeeded: I just received a second note, still very severe, confirming our perpetual separation, just as I expected – no longer, however, in quite the same tone. Above all, I am never again to be seen: this decision is announced four

---

*Letters 46 and 47.

times in the most irrevocable manner. I conclude that there is not a moment to lose before presenting myself. I have already sent my valet to secure the hall porter; and I shall follow him myself presently to have my pardon signed. With sins of this kind, there is only one formula that confers absolution, and it must be received in person.

Good-bye, my love; I hasten to meet the great challenge.

Paris
15 November 17—

LETTER 139: *The Présidente de Tourvel to Madame Rosemonde*

How sorry I am, my dear friend, for having spoken too much and too soon about my passing vexations! It is my fault that you are now distressed; you still have my troubles upon your mind, while I – I am happy. Yes, all is forgotten, forgiven; or, rather, amends have been made. Grief and anguish have given way to peace and delight. Oh, the joy of my heart! How can I express it? Valmont is innocent: no one could be guilty who loves so much. The terrible, insulting injuries I accused him so bitterly of having done me he did not commit; and if, on a single point, I was obliged to be indulgent, had I not also injustices to make reparation for?

I shall not give you in detail the facts and arguments that excused him. Perhaps they cannot be properly appreciated by the mind; it is for the heart alone to feel their truth. If, however, you were to suspect me of weakness, I should appeal to your own judgment to support mine. With men, you say yourself, infidelity is not inconstancy.

Not that I feel that this distinction, sanctioned or not by public opinion, is any the less wounding to the pride; but why should I complain of that, when Valmont suffers even more? Do not imagine that he forgives himself or consoles himself for a wrong that I am willing to forget; yet how fully has he made amends for so small a fault in the excess of his love and the extravagance of my happiness!

I am either happier than I was before or more conscious of the value of happiness since I feared I had lost it. But what I can say for certain is this: if I felt I were strong enough to undergo once again sufferings as cruel as those I have just endured, I should not think them too high a price to pay for the extreme happiness I now enjoy. Oh, my dear mother! Scold your inconsiderate daughter for having distressed you in her excessive haste. Scold her for having had the temerity to judge and calumniate a man she ought never to cease from worshiping. But, while you recognize her imprudence, see that she is happy as well, and increase her joy by sharing it.

Paris
16 November 17–, evening

LETTER 140: *The Vicomte de Valmont to the Marquise de Merteuil*
How is it, my love, that I have received no reply from you? My last letter seems to me, nevertheless, to have deserved one. I should have received it three days ago, and I am still waiting! I am annoyed, to say the least, so shall say nothing to you at all about my most important affairs.

As to whether the attempted reconciliation achieved its full effect; as to whether, instead of distrust and recrimination, it produced only an increase of tenderness; as to whether it is I at present to whom apologies and amends are made for suspicion cast upon my honesty, you will hear not a word. And, were it not for last night's unexpected incident, I should not be writing to you at all. But since the latter concerns your pupil, and since very probably she will not be in a position to tell you about it, at least for some time, I shall undertake to do so myself.

For reasons that you may or may not guess, Madame de Tourvel has for some days been spared my attentions; and since these reasons cannot apply where the little Volanges is concerned, I have been cultivating her the more assiduously. Thanks to the obliging porter, there were no obstacles to overcome, and your pupil and I have been living a comfortable and regular life. But habit leads to negligence. At first we were never able to take sufficient precautions, and would tremble behind locked doors. Yesterday, an incredible piece of inadvertence was the cause of the accident I am going to tell you of; and if for my part I was let off with a fright, the little girl has had to pay more dearly for it.

We were not asleep, but in that state of relaxation and repose which follows pleasure, when we suddenly heard the bedroom door open. I immediately leaped to my sword, as much in my own defense as that of our pupil. I advanced to the door and saw no one. It was open nonetheless. As we had a lamp with us, I made a search, but found not a living soul. Then I remembered that we had forgotten our usual precautions. Having been merely pushed to, or not properly shut, the door had reopened of its own accord.

Returning to my timid companion to calm her fears, I found her no longer on the bed. She had fallen down, or had attempted to hide herself, between the bed and the wall. At any rate she was stretched there unconscious and motionless except for occasional violent convulsions. Imagine my embarrassment! I succeeded in returning her to the bed, and even in bringing her round; but she had been hurt by her fall and it was not long before she began to feel the effects.

Pains in her back, violent colic, and certain other much less equivocal symptoms soon led me to diagnose her condition; but to tell her about it I had first to tell her what her condition had been to begin with, for she was without the slightest suspicion. Never before, perhaps, has anyone preserved so much innocence while so effectively doing all that is necessary to lose it! Oh, this young lady wastes no time thinking!

She wasted a great deal, however, in feeling sorry for herself, and I felt I must come to some decision. I thus agreed with her that I should go to see the family physician and the family surgeon, and that, in addition to warning them that they would be sent for, I should confide everything to them under seal of secrecy; that she, for her part, would ring for her chambermaid, whom she would or would not take into her confidence, as she saw fit; but that in any case she would send for medical assistance, and, above all, forbid anyone to wake Madame de Volanges, a natural and tactful attention on the part of a daughter who is afraid of upsetting her mother.

I made my two visits and my two confessions as quickly as I could, from thence returned home, and have not been out since. But the surgeon, who was a previous acquaintance of mine, came here at midday to report on the invalid's condition. I was not mistaken, but he hopes that, barring accidents, nothing will be noticed in the house. The chambermaid is in on the secret, the physician has put a name to the malady, and the affair will be settled like a thousand others of its kind – unless it will be useful to us later to have it talked about.

But is there still any community of interest between us? Your silence makes me doubt it; I should no longer believe it at all did not my desire to do so make me snatch at any excuse for sustaining my hopes.

Good-bye, my love: I embrace you, even though I bear you a grudge.

Paris
12 November 17–

LETTER 141: *The Marquise de Merteuil to the Vicomte de Valmont*
Lord, Vicomte, how irritating your persistence is! What does my silence matter to you? Do you think that if I say nothing it is for lack of arguments to put forward in my defense? Ah, would to God it were! No,

no; it is only that it would pain me to have to put them to you.

Tell me the truth. Are you deluding yourself or trying to deceive me? The disparity between what you say and what you do admits of no other explanations – which of these is correct? What do you want me to say, when I don't know myself what to think?

You seem to take great credit upon yourself for your last encounter with the Présidente; but what after all does it prove in support of your views or against mine? I certainly never said that you loved this woman so much that you would never deceive her, that you would not seize every opportunity of doing so that appeared to you to be easy and agreeable; I did not even doubt that you would think almost nothing of satisfying with another woman – the first that crossed your path – the desires that she herself had aroused; and I am not surprised that, with a licentiousness one would be wrong to deny you, you did for once deliberately what you have done a thousand times merely as the occasion offered. Everyone knows that this is simply the way of the world – the way of all of you, whoever you are, Neros or nobodies. The man who behaves otherwise nowadays is taken for a romantic, and that is not, I think, the fault I find in you.

But what I have said and thought about you, what I still believe, is that you are in love with your Présidente – not, it is true, a very pure or very tender love, but one such as you are capable of feeling; one, that is, that leads you to seek qualities and charms in a woman who does not possess them; one that places her in a class apart and relegates all other women to the second rank; one that keeps you attached to her even while you insult her; one, lastly, such as I imagine a sultan might feel for his favorite sultana, such as leaves him free to prefer, very often, a simple odalisque. My comparison seems to me to be the more just in that, like the sultan, you have never been either the lover or the friend of a woman but always either her tyrant or her slave. Hence I am quite sure that you humiliated and degraded yourself to a degree in order to restore yourself to favor with this fine creature! Then, only too happy to have succeeded, as soon as you thought the moment had come to obtain your pardon, you left me "to meet the great challenge."

Again, in your last letter, if you did not talk about this woman to the exclusion of all else it was because you did not wish to tell me anything of your "important affairs": they seem so important to you that your silence about them appears to you to be a punishment inflicted on me. And it is after these myriad proofs of a decided preference for someone else that you calmly ask me whether "there is still any community of interest between us"! Beware, Vicomte! Once I reply to that question, my reply will be irrevocable; my hesitation to make it at this moment has already told you too much, perhaps. So I wish to say absolutely no more about it.

All that I can do is to tell you a story. You will perhaps not have time to read it, or to give it the attention necessary to understanding it – that I leave to you. It will be, in the last resort, a story merely thrown away.

A man of my acquaintance entangled himself, as you did, with a woman who did him little credit. He had the good sense, from time to time, to feel that sooner or later this affair must reflect adversely upon him; but, though he was ashamed of it, he did not have the courage to break it off. His embarrassment was all the greater for his having boasted to his friends that he was absolutely free, for he was not unaware that our liability to ridicule always increases in proportion as we defend ourselves from it. Thus he spent his life committing one stupidity after another, never failing to say afterward, "It was not my fault." A woman, a friend of this man's, was tempted at one time to throw him in his infatuated state to the public so as to make him permanently ridiculous. However, being more generous than malicious by nature, or perhaps for some other reason, she decided to try a last resource, so that, whatever happened, she would, like her friend, be in a position to say, "It was not my fault." She therefore, without further remark, sent him – as a remedy, the application of which might be efficacious in his illness – the following letter:

"One is very soon bored with everything, my angel; it is a law of nature. It is not my fault.

"If therefore I am now bored with an adventure that has claimed my attention for four mortal months, it is not my fault.

"If, that is to say, my love was equal to your virtue – and that is certainly saying a great deal – it is not surprising that the one came to an end at the same time as the other. It is not my fault.

"It follows that for some time I have been deceiving you, but then your relentless tenderness forced me in some sort to do so! It is not my fault.

"A woman whom I love madly now insists that I give you up for her sake. It is not my fault.

"I quite realize that this is the perfect opportunity to accuse me of perjury; but if, where nature has gifted men with no more than constancy, she has given women obstinacy, it is not my fault.

"Believe me, you should take another lover, as I take another mistress. This is good, very good advice; if you find it bad, it is not my fault.

"Good-bye, my angel. I took you with pleasure, I leave you without regret. I shall come back perhaps. Such is life. It is not my fault."

This is not the moment, Vicomte, to tell you what effect was achieved with this last attempt, and what followed: but I promise to tell you in my next letter. In it will also be contained my ultimatum on the subject of the treaty you propose to renew. Till then, I shall say good-bye, no more...

By the way, thank you for your account of the little Volanges; that must be kept for after the wedding, an article for the gossips' gazette. Meanwhile, accept my condolences on the loss of your posterity. Good night, Vicomte.

Château de ———
24 November 17–

LETTER 142: *The Vicomte de Valmont to the Marquise de Merteuil*
Upon my word, my love, I don't know whether I misread or misunderstood your letter, the story you told me, and the little specimen of epistolary art included in it, but I may say that the last-named seemed to me to be original and potentially very effective, so I quite simply made a copy of it which I sent off to the divine Présidente. I did not lose a moment: the tender missive was dispatched last evening. I preferred it this way, because in the first place I had promised to write to her yesterday; and then, too, because I considered the whole night would not be too long for her to collect herself and meditate upon this *great challenge* – to risk for a second time your criticism of that expression.

I was hoping to be able to send you my dearly beloved's reply this morning; but it is nearly midday, and I have received nothing yet. I shall wait until five o'clock, and if I have no news by then I shall go in search of it – for especially in the matter of challenges it is only the first steps that are difficult.

Now, as you may imagine, I am exceedingly eager to learn the end of the story about this man of your acquaintance who was so strongly suspected of being unable, when necessary, to sacrifice a woman. Did he not mend his ways? And did not his generous friend receive him back into favor?

I am no less anxious to receive your ultimatum, as you so politically call it! I am curious above all to know whether you will still attribute my behavior to love. Ah, certainly there is love, a great deal of love, behind it. But love for whom? However, I am not attempting to assert any claims: I expect everything from your kindness.

Good-bye, my love: I shall not seal this letter until two o'clock in the hope that by then I shall be able to attach the sought-after reply.

At two o'clock in the afternoon
Still nothing: there is very little time. I have not a moment to add another word. But will you now still refuse love's most tender kisses?

Paris
25 November 17—

LETTER 143: *The Présidente de Tourvel to Madame de Rosemonde*
The veil is rent, Madame, on which was pictured the illusion of my happiness. I see by the light of a terrible truth that my path lies between shame and remorse to a certain and none too distant death. I shall follow it...I shall cherish my torments if they are to shorten my life. I send you the letter I received yesterday; I shall add no comment, it carries its own. This is no longer time for complaint but only for suffering. It is not pity I need but strength.

Please receive, Madame, the only farewell I shall say, and hear my last prayer — which is to leave me to my fate, to forget me entirely, to count me no longer among the living. There is a point reached by misery where even friendship increases suffering and cannot heal it. When the wounds are mortal, all relief is inhumane. There is no feeling in my heart but despair. I look for nothing now but profound darkness in which to bury my shame. There I shall weep for my faults, if I am still capable of tears! For, since yesterday, I have not shed a single one. They no longer flow from my desolate heart.

Good-bye, Madame. Do not reply. On this cruel letter I have vowed never to receive another.

Paris
27 November 17—

LETTER 144: *The Vicomte de Valmont to the Marquise de Merteuil*
Yesterday, my love, at three o'clock in the afternoon, impatient at the want of news, I presented myself at the Forsaken Beauty's: I was told she was out. I interpreted the phrase as a refusal to see me, which neither annoyed nor surprised me, and I left in the hopes that my visit would commit so polite a woman to honoring me with a word of reply. In my desire to receive one I expressly called in at my house about nine o'clock, but found nothing there. Astonished at this silence, which I

did not expect, I instructed my valet to make inquiries and to find out whether the sensitive creature were dead or dying. When I finally came home, he told me that Madame de Tourvel had in fact gone out at eleven o'clock in the morning with her maid; that she had been driven to the convent of ———, and that at seven o'clock in the evening she had sent back her carriage and her servants, who were to say that she was not to be expected home. Really, she does everything *comme il faut*. Convents are the accepted refuge of widows. If she persists in her praiseworthy resolutions, I shall have to add, to all the obligations I already owe her, the fame that will soon surround this adventure.

As I told you some time ago, I shall, in spite of your anxieties, reappear in society blazing with new glories. Let the stern critics who accuse me of a romantic and unhappy love show me then what they can do; let them effect more prompt, more brilliant ruptures. No, they can do no better. Let them offer themselves as consolation: the way is clear. Well then, let them merely try to run the course I have covered in its entirety – and if one of them achieves the smallest success, I shall accord him the palm. They will all find out, however, that when I take the trouble the impression I make cannot be effaced. Ah, this time it certainly will not be: I shall set all my previous triumphs at naught were this woman ever to prefer a rival to me.

The decision she has taken flatters my vanity, I admit; but I am sorry she has found the strength to disengage herself to such an extent from me. There will now be other obstacles between us than those I have placed there myself! Suppose I wish to return to her, she might no longer want it. But what am I saying? No longer want it, no longer find in it her supreme happiness? Is that any way to love? And do you think, my love, that I ought to allow it? Could I not, for example – would it not be better to try to bring the woman around to the point of foreseeing a possible reconciliation, the reconciliation she must desire as long as she hopes for it? I could attempt this without attaching too much importance to it, and consequently without giving you any offense. On the contrary, it would be a simple exercise for us to perform together; and even were I to succeed, I should merely have acquired another opportunity to renew, at your bidding, a sacrifice that has been, I think, agreeable to you. Now, my love, it remains for me to receive my reward, all my thoughts are for your return. Come quickly, then, to claim your lover, your pleasures, your friends, and your share of adventures.

My own adventure with the little Volanges has turned out exceedingly well. Yesterday, when in my anxiety I was incapable of staying in one place, I even called, in the course of my wanderings, on Madame de Volanges. I found your pupil already in the drawing room, still in invalid's garb, but fully convalescent and all the fresher and more interesting for it. You other women, in a similar position, would have spent a month upon your chaise longues; upon my word, long live the youngsters! To tell you the truth, she made me decide to find out whether her cure was complete.

I have also to tell you that the little girl's accident has been in a good way to sending your *sentimentalist*, Danceny, out of his mind, at first with grief, now with joy. *His Cécile* was ill! You know how the mind reels under such misfortune. He sent for news three times a day, and not one day passed without his appearing in person. At length, in a beautiful epistle addressed to mama, he asked permission to come and congratulate her on the recovery of a possession so precious to her – and Madame de Volanges agreed, so that I found the young man established much as he had been in the past, except for a few little familiarities that he dares not allow himself at present.

It was from him that I learned these details, for I left when he did and I pumped him. You have no idea the effect this visit made upon him. Impossible to describe the joy, the desires, the transports. I, who love strong emotions, succeeded in turning his head completely by assuring him that in a few days I should put him in a position to see his mistress at even closer quarters.

In fact, I decided to give her back to him as soon as I had made my experiment. I want to devote myself entirely to you. Besides, was it worth the trouble of putting your pupil to school with me merely to deceive her husband? The triumph is in deceiving her lover! And especially her first lover! For, as for me, I have not been guilty of so much as uttering the word "love."

Good-bye, my love. Come back as soon as you can to enjoy your prerogatives over me, to receive my homage and pay me my reward.

Paris
28 November 17–

LETTER 145: *The Marquise de Merteuil to the Vicomte de Valmont*
Seriously, Vicomte, have you left the Présidente? Did you send her the letter I prepared for her? Really, you are charming, and you have exceeded my expectations! I can sincerely say that this triumph flatters me more than any I have achieved till now. You will perhaps think that I am setting a very high value upon the same woman I once rated so

poorly – but not at all. The fact is that I have won my triumph not over her – it is over you. That is the amusing thing, that is what is so truly delicious.

Yes, Vicomte, you were very much in love with Madame de Tourvel, and you are still in love with her: you love her to distraction. But because it amused me to make you ashamed of it, you have bravely sacrificed her. You would have sacrificed her a thousand times rather than take a joke. To what lengths will vanity lead us! The sage was indeed right who called it the enemy of happiness.

Where would you be now had I wanted merely to play a trick on you? As you know well, though, I am incapable of deceit; and even if you are to reduce me, in my turn, to despair in a convent, I am willing to run the risk. I give myself up to my conqueror.

However, if I capitulate, it is really out of pure weakness: for, if I wished, how I could still quibble! And you, perhaps, would deserve it. I wonder, for example, at the cunning – or the clumsiness – with which you calmly suggest that I let you renew your relations with the Présidente. It would suit you very well, would it not, to take the credit for breaking with her without losing the pleasure of enjoying her? And since the apparent sacrifice would thereafter be no sacrifice at all for you, you offer to renew it at my bidding! Were we to go on in this way, the Heavenly Devotee would continue to think herself the sole choice of your heart, while I should plume myself on being the preferred rival. Both of us will have been deceived, but you will be happy – and of what importance is anything else?

It is a pity that you have so much talent for making plans yet so little for putting them into practice; and that by one ill-considered move you have yourself placed an insuperable obstacle between you and what you desire.

Really, how can you, if you had any thought of renewing your relations with Madame de Tourvel, have sent her my letter? You, for your part, must have thought me very clumsy. Ah, believe me, Vicomte, when one woman takes aim at the heart of another, she rarely fails to find the vulnerable spot, and the wound she makes is incurable. While taking my aim at this one, or rather while directing yours, I had not forgotten that she was a rival whom you had temporarily preferred to me, and that you had in fact considered me beneath her. If my revenge misses the mark, I agree to face the consequences. Thus, I am quite prepared for you to try everything you can: I even invite you to do so and promise not to be annoyed when you succeed, if you succeed. I am so easy on this score that I shall press the point no further. Let us talk of other things.

For example, the little Volanges's health. You will give me confirmation of her recovery when I return, will you? I shall be very pleased to have it. After that, it will be for you to decide whether it would suit you better to give the little creature back to her lover or to make a second attempt at founding a new branch of the Valmonts, under the name of Gercourt. That idea struck me as quite amusing; in leaving the choice to you, however, I must ask you not to make any definite decision until we have talked matters over between ourselves. This is not to put you off for any length of time, for I shall soon be in Paris. I cannot give you a positive date, but you may be sure that as soon as I arrive you will be the first to be informed.

Good-bye, Vicomte. In spite of my grudges, my spite, my criticisms, I still love you very much, and I am preparing to prove it to you. Au revoir, my dear.

Château de ———
29 November 17–

LETTER 146: *The Marquise de Merteuil to the Chevalier Danceny*
I am leaving at last, my dear young friend. I shall be in Paris tomorrow evening. I shall not be receiving anyone, what with the confusion a removal invariably entails. If, however, you have something urgent to tell me in confidence, I am willing to make you an exception to my rule. But only you will be excepted; so I must ask you to keep my arrival a secret. Even Valmont shall not know of it.

If I had been told some time ago that you one day would have my exclusive confidence, I should not have believed it; but yours has attracted mine. I am tempted to believe that you have used your arts, perhaps even your enchantments, upon me. That would have been very wicked of you, to say the least. However, I am in no danger at present: you have too much else to do! When the heroine is on the stage, one is scarcely interested in the confidante.

You have not so much as found time to tell me of your latest success. When your Cécile was away, my days were not long enough to listen to all your tender plaints. You would have made them for the echoes had I not been there to hear them. When she was ill and you honored me again with an account of your anxieties, it was because you needed someone to talk to about them. But now that the one you love is in Paris and is well, now especially that you are able to see her sometimes, she is more than enough. Your friends are no longer anything to you.

I don't blame you for it; it is the fault of your twenty years. Has it not been known since the time of Alcibiades that young men know friendship only when they are in trouble? Happiness provokes them sometimes to indiscretions but never to confidences. I might say as Socrates did, "I like my friends to come to me when they are unhappy."* But Socrates, being a philosopher, was quite able to do without his friends when they did not come. In that respect I am not quite as wise as he: I have felt your silence as deeply as only a woman can.

Don't, however, think I am importunate – I am very far from being so! The same feeling that makes me aware of my loss helps me to support it with courage when it is the proof, or the cause, of my friend's happiness. I don't, therefore, count on seeing you tomorrow evening, unless affairs of love leave you unoccupied and free; and I forbid you to make the least sacrifice on my account.

Good-bye, Chevalier. I am looking forward to seeing you again. Will you come?

Château de ———
29 November 17–

LETTER 147: *Madame de Volanges to Madame de Rosemonde*
You will certainly be as sorry as I am, my dear friend, when you learn of the condition Madame de Tourvel is in. She has been ill since yesterday, and her illness came on so suddenly, and manifests itself in symptoms of such gravity that I am quite alarmed.

A burning fever, violent and almost continual delirium, an unquenchable thirst: that is all there is to be observed. The doctors say they are as yet unable to make a diagnosis. Treatment will be the more difficult because the patient obstinately refuses every remedy, so that she had to be held down by force while she was bled, and twice again while the bandage was refastened which in her delirium she is perpetually trying to tear off.

You who have seen her, as I have, so fragile, so gentle and sweet, can you imagine that four persons are scarcely able to hold her down, and that at the slightest attempt to reason with her, she gives way to unspeakable fury? For my part, I am afraid this may be more than just delirium – I fear that it may be a real derangement of the mind.

My fears are increased by knowing what happened the day before yesterday.

---

*Marmontel, *The Moral Tale of Alcibiades*.

On that day at about eleven o'clock she arrived with her maid at the convent of ———. Since she was educated there, and has been in the habit of returning from time to time, her visit was not regarded as in any way out of the ordinary, and she appeared to everybody to be happy and well. About two hours later she inquired whether the room she had occupied as a schoolgirl was vacant, and on being told that it was, she asked to see it again: the prioress and some other of the nuns accompanied her. It was then that she announced that she was returning to live in this room, which, she said, she ought never to have left, adding that she would not now leave it *until she died* – that was the expression she used.

They did not at first know what to say to her, but when they had recovered from their initial astonishment, they explained to her that her status as a married woman would not allow her to be received into the convent without special permission. Neither this argument nor a thousand others were of any avail; from then on she refused obstinately to leave not only the convent but even her room. At length, at seven o'clock in the evening, the nuns, wearying of the struggle, agreed to let her spend the night there. They sent back her carriage and servants and left it to the next day to come to some decision.

I am assured that her looks and manner during the whole evening, far from being in the least distraught, were deliberate and composed, except that on four or five occasions she fell into an abstraction so deep that they were unable to say anything to rouse her from it; and that on each occasion, as she emerged, she raised her hands to her forehead, which she seemed to clasp with some force. One of the nuns asked her at this whether she was suffering from a headache. She gazed at her a long time before replying, saying at length, "The pain is not there!" A moment later she asked to be left alone and begged that in future she should be asked no more questions.

Everyone withdrew except for her maid, who fortunately had to sleep in the same room for lack of space elsewhere.

According to this girl's report her mistress remained quiet until eleven o'clock in the evening, at which time she said she wished to go to bed. But before she was completely undressed, she began to walk rapidly about the room, gesturing a great deal. Julie, who had been a witness of all that had passed during the day, dared not say anything and waited in silence for nearly an hour. At length, Madame de Tourvel called to her twice in quick succession, and she had scarcely time to run to her before her mistress fell into her arms, saying, "I am exhausted." She allowed herself to be taken to bed, but would eat or drink nothing and refused to allow the girl to call for help. She asked only for some water to be put by her and ordered Julie to go to bed.

The latter assures me that she stayed awake until two o'clock in the morning without hearing, during this time, either sound or movement. But she was wakened at five by the sound of her mistress talking in a loud voice; and having asked her whether she needed anything but receiving no reply, she took the lamp and went to her bed. Madame de Tourvel did not recognize her, but interrupting her incoherent soliloquy, cried out sharply, "Leave me alone. Leave me in darkness. It is in darkness that I must live." I myself noticed yesterday how often this phrase recurs to her.

Julie took advantage of this semblance of a command to leave the room in search of people and help; but Madame de Tourvel refused both with the transports and passions that have so often since recurred.

This state of affairs placed the whole convent in so difficult a situation that yesterday at seven o'clock in the morning the prioress decided to send for me ... It was not yet light. I hurried off immediately. When I was announced to Madame de Tourvel, she seemed to recover consciousness and replied, "Oh, yes! Let her come in." But when I reached her bedside she looked at me fixedly and, taking my hand suddenly in hers and pressing it, she said in a firm but mournful voice, "I am dying because I did not believe you." Immediately afterward, covering her eyes, she reverted to her most commonly recurring cries of "Leave me alone," etc., and lost all consciousness.

The words she spoke to me, and others that escaped her in her delirium, lead me to fear that this cruel malady springs from a cause more cruel still. But let us respect our friend's secrets. Let us be content with pitying her misfortune.

The whole of yesterday was equally disturbed, divided between transports of fearful delirium and periods of lethargic depression, the only times when she takes or gives any rest. I did not leave her bedside till nine o'clock in the evening, and I am returning this morning to spend the whole day with her. I shall certainly not abandon my unhappy friend; but what is distressing is her persistent refusal of all care and assistance.

I send you last night's bulletin which I have just received and which, as you will see, is anything but comforting. I shall take care to pass all the bulletins faithfully on to you.

Good-bye, my dear friend. I am returning to the invalid. My daughter, who is fortunately almost well again, pays you her respects.

Paris
29 November 17–

LETTER 148: *The Chevalier Danceny to the Marquise de Merteuil*

O friend that I love! – O mistress that I adore! O you who began my happiness! – O you who are its crown! Kind friend – sweet love – why must the thought of your distress come to disturb my delight? Ah, Madame, calm yourself: it is friendship that asks – Oh, dear heart, be happy! It is love that implores.

Come, what have you to reproach yourself for? Believe me, your delicacy deceives you. The regrets it makes you feel, the wrongs it accuses me of, are equally illusory. I know in my heart that there have been no enchantments between us but those of love. Do not then be afraid to give yourself up to the same feelings that you inspire, to allow yourself to burn with the same fires you have kindled. Are our hearts the less pure for having known the truth so late? No, no – it is on the contrary only the voluptuary, who, working always according to plan, is able to regulate his progress and control his resources and foresee the outcome from a distance. True love does not allow considerations and calculations. It uses our feelings to distract us from our thoughts; its power is never so strong as when we are least aware of it; and it is by stealth and in silence that it entangles us in the web that is as invisible as it is indestructible.

So it was that only yesterday, in spite of the lively emotion I felt at the thought of your return, in spite of my extreme pleasure at seeing you, I still thought it was no more than peaceable friendship that prompted and directed me – or, rather, having surrendered entirely to the feelings of my heart, I was very little concerned to discover their origin or cause. Like me, my dear, you felt without knowing the powerful charm that gave our souls up to sweet feelings of tenderness. And neither of us recognized the god of love till we had emerged from the intoxication into which he had plunged us.

But that in itself justifies rather than condemns us. No, you have not betrayed our friendship any more than I have abused your confidence. Neither of us, it is true, knew our feelings; but though we were under an illusion, we had not tried to create one. Ah, far from lamenting our fate, let us think only of the happiness it has given us. And instead of spoiling that happiness with unjust reproaches, let us try only to increase it with the charm of perfect trust and confidence. Oh, my dear, how I cherish that hope in my heart! Yes, from now on, free of all fear, you will give yourself up to love; you will share my desires, my transports, the delirium of my senses, and the intoxication of my soul, and every instant of each happy day will be the occasion of some new pleasure.

Good-bye, my beloved! I shall see you this evening, but shall I find you alone? I dare not hope so. Ah, you could not long for it as much as I do!

Paris
1 December 17–

LETTER 149: *Madame de Volanges to Madame de Rosemonde*
Throughout almost the whole of yesterday, my dear friend, I hoped that I should be able to give you better news this morning of our poor invalid's condition; but last evening my hopes were destroyed, and I am left only with regret at having lost them. A certain incident, apparently unimportant, but most cruel in its consequences, has left the invalid at least as disturbed as she was at first, if not more so.

I should have understood nothing of this sudden reversal had not our unhappy friend taken me entirely into her confidence yesterday. And since she has not left me unaware that you too know of all her misfortunes, I can speak to you freely about the whole sorry situation.

Yesterday morning, when I arrived at the convent, I was told that the invalid had been asleep for more than three hours, and her sleep was so peaceful and profound that I was afraid for a moment that she might be in a coma. Some time later she awoke and opened the bed curtains herself. She looked at us all with an air of surprise; and as I rose to go to her, she recognized me, called me by name, and asked me to come nearer. She gave me no time to question her, but asked me where she was, what we were doing there, whether she was ill, and why she was not at home. I thought at first that this was yet another delirium, less unruly than the first; but I saw that she was quite able to understand my replies. She had in fact recovered her senses, but not her memory.

She inquired in great detail about all that had happened to her since her arrival at the convent, to which she did not remember having come. I replied faithfully, omitting only what I thought might frighten her too much; and when, in my turn, I asked her how she felt, she answered that she was not at present in any discomfort, but that she had been very much disturbed during her sleep and felt tired. I made her promise to keep calm and speak little, after which I partly drew the curtains, leaving them open, and sat down beside her bed. At the same time she was offered some soup, which she accepted and enjoyed.

She remained thus for about half an hour, during which time she spoke only to thank me for my care of her; and she put into her thanks the grace and charm that are familiar to you. Then, for a while, she kept complete silence, breaking it only to say, "Ah, yes. I remember now having come here," and a moment later cried out in stricken tones, "My friend, my friend, pity me. All my misfortunes return." As I leaned toward her, she seized my hand and pressing it to her cheek continued, "Great God! Why may I not die?" Her expression, more even than her words, moved me to the point of tears; she noticed them in my voice and said, "You do pity me! Ah, if only you knew!..." And then, interrupting herself, she added, "Ask them to leave us alone. I shall tell you everything."

As I think I have pointed out to you, I already had an inkling as to what might be the subject of this confidence; and afraid that our conversation, which I could foresee would be long and cheerless, might perhaps adversely affect our unhappy friend's condition, I at first refused, on the pretext that she was in need of rest. But she insisted, and I gave in to her entreaties. As soon as we were alone she told me all that you already know from her, for which reason I shall not repeat any of it.

At length, having spoken to me of the cruel way in which she had been sacrificed, she added, "I was quite sure that I would die, and I had the courage to do so; what I cannot endure is that I should survive in misery and shame." I tried to combat her discouragement, or rather her despair, with the arguments of religion, hitherto of so much weight with her, but I soon became aware that I was not equal to so exalted a task and fell back to suggesting that I call Father Anselme, whom I knew to have her complete confidence. She agreed and seemed even to want very much to see him. He was sent for, and came immediately. He stayed a very long while with the invalid, and, on leaving, said that if the doctors were of the same mind as he, he thought that administration of the Last Sacraments could be deferred, and that he would return the next day.

This was at about three o'clock in the afternoon, and till five our friend remained quiet enough, so much so that we all recovered hope. Unhappily a letter was then brought for her. When it was offered to her she at first refused it, saying that she did not wish to receive letters, and no one insisted; but from that moment on she appeared to be more agitated. Soon after, she asked where the letter had come from. There was no postmark. Who had brought it? No one knew. On whose behalf had it been delivered? The portress had not been told. Then she was silent for some time, after which she began again to speak, but her confused utterances told us only that delirium had returned.

There was, however, one lucid interval during which she asked for the letter to be given to her. As soon as she set eyes on it she cried out, "From him! Great God!" and then in firm but disconsolate tones, "Take it back. Take it back." She immediately had the bed curtains drawn and forbade anyone to come near her; but almost at once we were obliged to return to her side. She was seized with a more violent delirium than ever before, and, further, with truly frightful convulsions. These symptoms did not subside the whole evening, and this morning's bulletin informs me that the night was no less disturbed. In short, her condition is such that I am astonished she has not already collapsed; and I cannot conceal from you that I am left with but very little hope.

I suppose the unfortunate letter was from Monsieur de Valmont – but what can he still have the audacity to say to her? Forgive me, my dear; I shall refrain from comment. But it is very cruel to see a woman, till now so happy and so worthy of being so, perish in such misery.

Paris
2 December 17–

LETTER 150: *The Chevalier Danceny to the Marquise de Merteuil*
Since I must wait for the happiness of seeing you, my sweet friend, I shall allow myself the pleasure of writing to you. It is in thinking of you that I charm away my regret at being parted from you. To describe my feelings to you, to remind myself of yours is such a delight to my heart that even a time of privations confers a thousand precious blessings on my love. However, if I am to believe you, I shall receive no reply from you. This very letter will be the last. We are to deny ourselves a correspondence that, according to you, is dangerous and for *which there is no necessity*. Of course I shall believe this, if you insist – for what can you wish for that I do not, for that very reason, wish for too? But before deciding finally, may we not talk about it?

As far as danger is concerned, you must be the sole judge. I cannot foresee anything and must confine myself to begging you to look after your safety, for I cannot be easy when you are anxious. On this point it is not that both of us are at one: it is you who must decide for both of us.

It is not the same when we come to *necessity*: here we cannot but be of the same mind. And if our opinions differ it can only be for lack of mutual explanation and understanding. Here, then, is what I think.

There does, of course, seem very little necessity for letters when we can see each other freely. What can one say in a letter that a word, a look, or even a silence could not express a hundred times better? This seemed to me so true when you spoke of our not writing to each other any more that the idea slipped easily into my thoughts: it disturbed them a little, perhaps, but did not upset them. It was as if, wanting to plant a kiss upon your bosom, I had encountered a piece of ribbon or gauze: I had only to move it aside; I did not regard it as an obstacle.

But since then we have been separated. As soon as you were no longer with me the thought of letters returned to torment me. Why, I asked myself, this extra privation? We are parted, but does that mean we have nothing further to say to each other? Supposing that, circumstances being favorable, we were to spend a whole day together: should we have to waste in talking the hours that we might be enjoying? Yes, enjoying, my sweet friend – for with you even moments of repose afford delicious pleasures. Finally, however long our time together, it must end in separation, and then one is so alone! It is then that a letter is precious! If one does not read it, one may at least look at it...Ah, yes – one may certainly look at a letter without reading it, just as, it seems to me, I can still find pleasure in touching your portrait at night...

Your portrait, did I say? But a letter is a portrait of the heart, and unlike a picture it has not that coldness, that fixity which is so alien to love; it reflects all our emotions: it is in turn lively, joyful, at rest... Your feelings are all so precious to me! Will you deprive me of a means of knowing them?

And are you sure that you will never be tormented by a desire to write to me? If in solitude your heart is full or oppressed, if an impulse of joy goes through your whole being, or if an unwelcome melancholy comes to disturb it for a time, will it not be to your friend that you pour out your happiness or your grief? Will you have feelings that he does not share? Will you leave him, pensive and alone, to wander far from you? My dear...my sweet friend! But it is for you to say. I wanted only to reason with you, not to sway your feelings. I have offered you only arguments; my entreaties, I venture to think, would have been more effective. If you insist, I shall try not to be disappointed; I shall do what I can to tell myself what you would have written. But you would say it better than I, you know, and, what is more, I should be more pleased to hear it from you.

Good-bye, my dear. At last the time draws near when I shall be seeing you. I leave you with all speed so as to meet you the sooner.

Paris
3 December 17–

LETTER 151: *The Vicomte de Valmont to the Marquise de Merteuil*
You don't of course, Marquise, credit me with so little experience as
to think I could have been deceived by the tête-à-tête I interrupted this
evening or by the *astonishing coincidence* that had brought Danceny to
your house! Not that your practiced features did not assume a faultless
expression of calm and serenity, nor that you gave yourself away in any
one of those exclamations that sometimes escape the guilty or remorse-
ful. I shall even admit that the submissive glances you threw me served
you to perfection; and if you could have made them believed as effectively as you made them understood, I should – far from admitting
or entertaining the least suspicion – I should not for a moment have
doubted that you were extremely provoked by the presence of that
inconvenient third party. But, so as not to have employed your great talents in vain, so as to have achieved the success you hoped for and effected the illusion you sought to produce, you should have taken greater
care to prepare your prentice lover in advance.

Since you have set up as an instructress, you might teach your pupils
not to blush, not to be disconcerted at the slightest pleasantry; you
might teach them not to deny so vehemently on behalf of one woman
what they would so feebly disclaim on behalf of another; you might
teach them as well to hear a mistress complimented without feeling
obliged to congratulate her upon it; and if you allow them to look at
you in company, let them at least learn beforehand how to disguise that
proprietary look which is so easily recognized, and which they so stupidly confuse with an expression of love. Then you may allow them to
appear at your public displays without their behavior doing discredit
to their accomplished instructress. I myself should be only too delighted
to bask in your reflected glory, and promise to have a prospectus for
the new college written and published.

But as things are, I must say I am astonished that it is I whom you
have decided to treat as a schoolboy. Oh, how soon with another woman
I should take my revenge! And what a pleasure it would be! How far
surpassing the pleasure she believed she was denying me! Yes, it is only
where you are concerned that I prefer reparation to vengeance; and
don't imagine that I am restrained by the slightest doubt, the slightest
uncertainty. I know everything.

You have been in Paris for four days. You have seen Danceny every
day, and you have seen no one but him. Even today your doors were
still shut. I was able to reach you only because your porter lacked an
assurance equal to yours. Yet I was not to doubt, you wrote, that I
should be the first to be informed of your arrival, of which you could

not let me know the date, even though you were writing to me on the eve of your departure. Will you deny these facts or attempt to excuse them? Either would be impossible – yet I keep my temper! From that you may judge the extent of your power. But, I beg you, be satisfied with having proven that power; don't abuse it any longer. We know each other, Marquise: that warning should be enough for you.

You will be out the whole day tomorrow, did you say? Very well – if you are indeed going out; and you may imagine whether I shall find out or not. But, after all, you will be coming home in the evening. Between then and the next morning we shall not have too much time to accomplish our difficult reconciliation. Let me know, then, whether it is at your house, or at *the other place*, that we are to make our many and mutual expiations. Above all, no more of Danceny. Your stubborn head has been filled with thoughts of him, and I can avoid being jealous of the vagaries of your imagination; but remember that from this moment on what was a mere caprice will be taken for a decided preference. I don't consider I was made for that sort of humiliation, and I don't expect to receive it at your hands.

I even hope that your sacrifice will not appear to you to be a sacrifice. But if it should cost you something, it seems to me that I have set you a fine enough example, and that a beautiful and sensitive woman who lived only for me, who at this very moment is perhaps dying of love and longing, is worth at least as much as a little schoolboy who, if you like, does not want looks or intelligence, but who is still inexperienced and unformed.

Good-bye, Marquise. I shall say nothing of my feelings for you. All I can do at the moment is to keep from examining my heart. I await your reply. Consider when you write it, consider carefully that, easy as it will be for you to make me forget the offense you have given me, a refusal on your part, a mere delay, will engrave it on my heart in ineffaceable characters.

Paris
3 December 17–, evening

LETTER 152: *The Marquise de Merteuil to the Vicomte de Valmont*
Take care, Vicomte: be more considerate of my extreme timidity! How do you expect me to support the crushing prospect of incurring your indignation, much less to keep from succumbing to the fear of your vengeance? The more so because, as you know, if you did me an ill turn

it would be impossible for me to requite you. I would talk about you in vain: your life would continue, its brilliance undimmed, its peace undisturbed. What, in fact, would you have to fear? Having to fly the country, if you were allowed enough time to do so? But does not one live as well abroad as here? And, all things considered, provided the French court left you unmolested wherever else you established yourself, you would be doing no more than changing the scene of your triumphs. Now that I have made an attempt to restore your sangfroid by offering you moral reflections, let us return to business.

Do you know, Vicomte, why I never married again? It was certainly not for lack of advantageous matches; it was solely so that no one should have the right to object to anything I might do. It was not even for fear that I might no longer be able to have my way, for I should always have succeeded in that respect in the end; but I should have found it irksome if anyone had had so much as a right to complain. In short, I wished to lie only when I wanted to, not when I had to. And here you are, writing me the most connubial letters possible! You speak of nothing but wrongs on my part and favors on yours! How can one fall short in the eyes of someone to whom one owes nothing? I cannot begin to imagine!

Let us see, what is this all about? You found Danceny in my house and that annoyed you? Very well; but what conclusions can you have come to? Either it was pure chance, as I said, or my own doing, as I did not say. In the first instance your letter would be unjust, in the second ridiculous. Was it really worth the trouble of writing? But you are jealous, and jealousy will not listen to reason. Oh, well! I shall do your reasoning for you.

Either you have a rival or you don't. If you have one, you must set out to please, so as to be preferred to him; if you don't have one, you must still please so as to obviate the possibility of having one. In either case the same principle is to be followed – so why torment yourself? Why, above all, torment me? Are you no longer the most amiable of men, can you no longer sustain the role? Are you no longer so sure of success? Come, come, Vicomte: you do yourself wrong. But it is not that; the fact is that in your eyes I am not worth so much trouble. You are less anxious to win my favors than to abuse your power over me. For shame, you ungrateful man. (There's feeling for you! If I were to continue in this way, my letter might become most tender – but you don't deserve it.)

You don't deserve that I make you my excuses either. As punishment for your suspicions you shall keep them: so, concerning the date of my return, as about Danceny's visits, I shall say nothing. You went to a great deal of trouble to find out about them, did you not? Well, are you any the better for it? I hope your investigations gave you pleasure; they have not spoiled mine.

All that I can say, therefore, in reply to your menacing letter is that it lacked both the charm to please me and the power to intimidate me; and that, for the moment, I could not possibly be less disposed to comply with your requests.

Truly, to accept you for what you now appear to be would be to commit a genuine infidelity. I should not be recovering my old lover, rather, I should be taking a new one, who is very far from being his equal. I have not so forgotten the first as to make such a mistake. The Valmont I loved was charming – I am even willing to admit that I have never met a more charming man. Ah, I beg you, Vicomte, if you find him again, bring him to me: he will always be very well received.

Warn him, however, that in no circumstances can it be either today or tomorrow. His Menaechmus[16] has done him a little disservice. By being in too much haste I should fear of making a mistake. Or is it, perhaps, that I have promised these two days to Danceny? Your letter taught me that for you it is no joking matter when one breaks one's word. You see, then, that you must wait.

But what difference does it make to you? You can always be avenged upon your rival. He will not treat your mistress worse than you have treated his; and, after all, is one woman any different from another? Those are your principles. Even the woman who is "soft-hearted and sensitive, who lives only for you, and who finally dies of love and longing" is none the less sacrificed to the first whim that passes through your head, to a momentary fear that you are mocked. And do you expect us to go out of our way? Ah, that is not fair!

Good-bye, Vicomte. Be amiable again. Come, I ask no more than to find you charming; as soon as I am sure that I do, I promise to give you proof of it. Really, I am too kind.

Paris
4 December 17–

LETTER 153: *The Vicomte de Valmont to the Marquise de Merteuil*
I am replying immediately to your letter, and I shall try to make myself clear to you – which is not easy once you have decided not to understand.

No lengthy arguments are needed to establish that each of us is in possession of all that is necessary to ruin the other, and that we have an equal interest in behaving with mutual caution. That, therefore, is not the question. But between the rash course of ruining ourselves and the doubtless better one of remaining friends as we were before, of becoming more so by renewing our former intimacy; between these two courses, I say, there are a thousand others we might take. There was nothing ridiculous, therefore, in telling you, and there is nothing so in repeating, that henceforth I shall be either your lover or your enemy.

I am perfectly aware that you dislike having to make this choice, that it would suit you better to prevaricate; and I know that you have never liked being forced to choose between yes and no. But you must be aware, too, that I cannot let you escape your uncomfortable dilemma without risk of being imposed upon myself; and you must have foreseen that I would never allow it. It is now for you to decide. I can leave the choice to you, but I cannot remain in uncertainty.

I warn you only that your arguments, good or bad, will not deceive me; nor shall I be seduced by such flatteries as you might use to trick out your refusal. The moment for candor has come. I could do no better than set you the example, and I declare with pleasure that I should prefer peace and friendship; but if peace is to be disturbed and friendship broken, I believe I have the right and the means to do both.

I might add that the slightest obstacle put forward by you will be taken by me as a genuine declaration of war. You see, the reply I ask for does not require long and beautiful sentences. A word will suffice.

Paris
4 December 17–

The Marquise de Merteuil's reply (written at the foot of the same letter)
Very well: war.

LETTER 154: *Madame de Volanges to Madame de Rosemonde*
The bulletins inform you better than I can, my dear friend, of the sad state of our invalid's health. Entirely occupied with nursing her, I can spare the time to write you only because there is news to give you other than that of her illness. Something I certainly did not expect has happened. I have received a letter from Monsieur de Valmont, who is pleased to choose me for his confidante, and indeed for intermediary between himself and Madame de Tourvel, to whom he sends a letter attached

to mine. This I have sent back with my reply to his letter to me, of which I send you a copy. I think you will decide, as I did, that I neither should nor could have done anything he asked. Even had I wished to, our unfortunate friend would have been in no condition to understand me. Her delirium is continuous. But I wonder what you will say to this despair of Monsieur de Valmont's. In the first place, is one to believe him or does he want only to deceive us all, even to the last?* If for once he is sincere, he may well say that he is responsible himself for his own misfortunes. I do not think he will be very satisfied with my reply; but I must say that everything I learn about this unhappy affair turns me more and more against its author.

Good-bye, my dear friend. I must return to my melancholy task, which becomes so much the more so for the little hope I have of seeing it succeed. You know my feelings for you.

Paris
5 December 17–

LETTER 155:[17] *The Vicomte de Valmont to the Chevalier Danceny*
I have called twice at your house, my dear Chevalier, but since you have abandoned the role of lover for that of Don Juan you have, quite understandably, become elusive. Your valet assured me that you would be at home this evening, and that he had orders to await you; but I, who know your designs, was quite able to guess that you would come home only for a moment, to change into the appropriate costume, and would then immediately resume your victorious career. Well done – I can only applaud. But this evening, perhaps, you will be tempted to change its direction. You know as yet only the half of your affairs: I must apprise you of the other half, and then you shall decide. I hope you will spare the time, therefore, to read this letter. It will not be keeping you from your pleasures since, on the contrary, it has no other aim than to provide you with a wider choice.

Should I have had your entire confidence, had you let me into those of your secrets that you left me to guess, I should have known in time; I should have been less clumsy in my eagerness to help you, and should not now be impeding your progress. But let us start from where we are: whatever you decide, the course you reject will make someone else happy.

---

*Because nothing was found in the ensuing correspondence to resolve this doubt it was decided to suppress Monsieur de Valmont's letter.

You have a rendezvous for tonight, have you not? With a charming woman whom you adore? For, at your age, where is the woman one does not adore, at least for the first week? The scene of the meeting will add to your enjoyment: a delicious *petite maison, taken especially for you*, where pleasure will be enhanced by the charm of freedom and the delights of mystery. All is arranged: you are expected, and you are longing to be there! That is what we both of us know, although you have told me nothing. Now for what you don't know – what, therefore, I have to tell you.

Since my return to Paris I have been trying to find a means of your meeting Mademoiselle de Volanges; I promised you I would do so, and even when I last spoke to you about it, I had reason to infer from your replies – I might say, your transports of delight – that by doing so I should be making you happy. I could not have succeeded alone in so difficult an enterprise; but, having prepared the way, I left the rest to the zeal of your young mistress. Her love provided her with resources that experience did not give me. At all events, to your misfortune, she has succeeded: two days ago – she told me this evening – all obstacles were removed. Your happiness now depends only on you.

For two days, too, she has been hoping to tell you the news herself. Despite her mama's absence, you would have been received. But you did not so much as present yourself! And to tell you the whole truth, the little creature seemed to me to be – whether reasonably or unreasonably – a little cross at this lack of eagerness on your part. She finally found a means of bringing me to see her and made me promise to send you, as soon as possible, the letter I enclose with this. To judge from her warmth, I could swear there is some question of a rendezvous for this evening. Be that as it may, I promised on my honor and on our friendship that you would receive the tender missive in the course of the day, and I cannot and will not break my word.

Now, young man, what line of conduct will you follow? Faced with the alternatives of coquetry and love, pleasure and happiness, which are you going to choose? If I were talking to the Danceny of three months ago, even a week ago, I should, because I was sure of his heart, be sure of his intentions; but the Danceny of today, pursuer of women, adventurer, who has as is the custom turned into a bit of a rascal – will he prefer a very timid young girl who has nothing to recommend her but her beauty, her innocence, and her love, to the attractions of a woman who is thoroughly *experienced*?

Were you to ask me, my dear fellow, it seems to me that even with your new principles – which I readily admit are also more or less mine – circumstances would decide me in favor of my young mistress. In the first place, you would be adding one to the score; and then there is the novelty and danger of your losing the fruit of your labors if you fail to gather it, for after all, from this point of view it would really be a missed opportunity, and they do not always recur, especially where a first lapse is at stake. Often in these cases only a moment's bad temper is necessary, a jealous suspicion, or even less, to prevent the finest triumph. Drowning virtue will clutch at any straw; once rescued, it is on its guard and no longer so easy to take by surprise.

On the other hand, what are you risking in respect of the other lady? Not even a rupture, at the most a misunderstanding; and you will have the pleasure of a reconciliation at the price of a few attentions. What other course is open to a woman who has already surrendered but that of indulgence? What would she accomplish by being severe? Loss of pleasure without increase of glory.

If, as I think, you will decide in favor of love and, as it seems to me, in favor of reason, I think it would be prudent not to excuse yourself from the rendezvous. Let her simply wait for you. If you risk giving a reason for your absence, she will be tempted to verify it. Women are curious and persistent; they can find anything out. I myself, as you know, have just been made an example of. But if you leave hope to itself, it will not, sustained as it is by vanity, be entirely lost until long after inquiries can decently be made. Tomorrow you will choose the insurmountable obstacle that detained you: you will have been ill, dead if necessary, or something else that put you in equally desperate plight, and all will be forgiven.

For the rest, whatever you decide, I beg you only to let me know. Since I have no interest in the matter, I shall in any case think you have done well. Good-bye, my dear fellow.

I shall add only that I miss Madame de Tourvel. I am in despair at being parted from her. I should gladly sacrifice half my life for the happiness of devoting the other half to her. Ah, believe me! Only love can make one happy.

Paris
5 December 17–

LETTER 156: *Cécile Volanges to the Chevalier Danceny*
(attached to the preceding letter)

How does it happen, my dear, that I no longer see you though I have not stopped wanting to see you? Do you not want as much as I? Ah, I

1226 WAYS OF THE WORLD

am really unhappy now! More unhappy than I was when we were completely separated. The pain that others once inflicted now comes from you, and hurts much more.

For some days now Mamma has scarcely ever been at home – you know that quite well. I was hoping that you would try to take advantage of this period of freedom. But you don't even think of me; I am most unhappy! You so often used to say that it was *I* who loved *you* less! I was quite sure the opposite was true, and here is the proof of it. If you had come to see me, you would in fact have seen me, for I am not like you: I think only of what can bring us together again. You don't deserve to be told a word about all I have done to the purpose – and it has given me a great deal of difficulty. But I love you too much, and I want so much to see you that I cannot help telling you. Besides, I shall soon see now whether you really love me!

I have contrived it so that the hall porter is on our side. He has promised me that every time you come he will let you in without, as it were, seeing you; and we can trust him, for he is a very honest man. It is only a question, then, of your keeping out of sight once you are in the house, and that will be very easy if you come only at night when there is nothing at all to fear. Mamma, you see, because she has been going out every day, goes to bed every evening at eleven o'clock, so that we shall have plenty of time.

The porter tells me that, if you wish, instead of knocking at the door you have only to knock at his window and he will let you in immediately. Then you will easily find the back staircase. Since there will be no light, I shall leave my bedroom door open, which will provide at least a little. You must be very careful not to make any noise, especially as you pass Mamma's back door. It does not matter about the maid's door, because she has promised not to wake up; and she too is a very good girl! It will be the same when you leave. Now, let us see whether you will come.

Dear God, why does my heart beat so fast as I write to you? Is it that some misfortune is to overtake me, or is it the hope of seeing you that agitates me like this? What I do know is that I have never loved you so much, and never so much wanted to tell you so. Come to me, then, my dear, my very dear, so that I can tell you a hundred times that I love you, adore you, that I shall never love anyone but you.

I found a means of letting Monsieur de Valmont know that I had something to tell him, and since he is my very good friend he will certainly come to see me tomorrow, when I shall ask him to deliver this letter to you immediately. So I shall expect you tomorrow evening, and you will come without fail unless you want to make your Cécile very unhappy.

Good-bye, my dear. I embrace you with all my heart.

Paris
4 December 17–, evening

LETTER 157: *The Chevalier Danceny to the Vicomte de Valmont*
You need not, my dear Vicomte, doubt either my heart or my intentions. How could I resist a single one of my Cécile's wishes? Ah, it is truly her and her alone whom I love, whom I shall love forever! Her sweetness, her ingenuousness have a charm for me, from which I may have been weak enough to be distracted, but which nothing will ever destroy. Though I have been engaged in another adventure, without, so to speak, knowing what I was doing, the thought of Cécile has often come to trouble my sweetest pleasures; and perhaps my heart has never paid her more sincere homage than at the very moment of my infidelity. Meanwhile, my friend, let us spare her delicacy. Let us conceal my misdemeanors from her – not so as to deceive her, rather, so as not to distress her. Cécile's happiness is my dearest wish: never should I pardon myself for a fault that had cost her a single tear.

I deserved, I know, your mocking at what you call my new principles. But you may be sure that it is not by them that my conduct at the moment is governed. And I have decided that tomorrow I shall prove it. I am going to make my confession to the very woman who has been the cause of my wrongdoing and who has shared it. I shall say to her: "Look into my heart. There you will find feelings of the most tender friendship for you. Friendship joined with desire has so much the appearance of love!... We have both been deceived; but, though I am capable of error, I cannot be insincere." I know this lady – she is as honorable as she is kind. She will do more than pardon me: she will approve of what I do. She has often reproached herself for betraying our friendship, her delicacy has often discouraged her love. Wiser than I am, she will strengthen those salutary fears in my heart that I have so rashly tried to banish from hers. To her I shall owe my becoming a better man, as to you I owe my becoming a happier man. Oh, my friends, you will share my gratitude! The thought of owing my happiness to you increases its value.

Good-bye, my dear Vicomte. My great joy does not prevent my remembering your afflictions and sympathizing with them. That I could be of some use to you! Is Madame de Tourvel still inexorable then? I am told she is very ill. Dear Lord, how I pity you! May she return both to health and to kinder feelings, and make you happy forever! Those are the prayers of friendship; I venture to hope that they will be answered by love.

I should like to spend longer with you, but time is short and Cécile is perhaps already waiting for me.

Paris
5 December 17–

LETTER 158: *The Vicomte de Valmont to the Marquise de Merteuil*
(written immediately upon waking)

Well, Marquise, how are you after last night's pleasures? Are you not a little tired? You must admit Danceny is charming! He accomplishes prodigies, that boy! You did not expect as much of him, did you? Come, I shall be fair: a rival such as he well deserved my being sacrificed to him. Seriously, he is full of good qualities. But so much capacity for love especially, such constancy, such delicacy! Ah, if ever you are loved by him as Cécile is, you will have no rivals to fear: he proved that to you last night. By sheer dint of coquetry another woman might take him from you for a moment; a young man is scarcely able to resist provocation. But a single word from the beloved is enough, as you have observed, to dispel the illusion. So you have only to become that beloved to be perfectly happy.

Of course you will not delude yourself. You have too sound a judgment for there to be any fear of that. However, the friendship that unites us, as sincerely offered on my part as it is acknowledged on yours, made me wish – for your sake – for last night's test, which you owe entirely to my zeal. It was a success, but don't thank me: it would not be worth the trouble. Nothing could have been easier.

In fact, what did it cost me? A small sacrifice and a little skill. I allowed the young man a share in his mistress's favors, but after all he had as much right to them as I, and I cared so little in my case! True, it was I who dictated the letter the young lady wrote him – but that was only to save time, for which he had better employment. The letter I sent with it was, oh, nothing, nothing at all! A few friendly observations to guide the prentice lover in his choice. But, on my honor, they were superfluous. To tell you the truth, he did not hesitate for a moment.

And then, in his candor, he is to pay you a visit today to tell you everything; I am certain the little tale will give you great pleasure. He will say to you, "Look into my heart," or so he informs me, and you must see how that is bound to settle everything. I hope that in finding what he wants you to find there, you will also, perhaps, discover that taking a young lover is attended with its dangers; moreover, that it is better to have me for a friend than an enemy.

Good-bye, Marquise, until we meet again.

Paris
6 December 17–

LETTER 159: *The Marquise de Merteuil to the Vicomte de Valmont (a note)*

I don't like it when bad jokes follow on bad behavior: that is no more my practice than it is to my taste. When I bear someone a grudge, I don't indulge in sarcasms. I do better than that – I take my revenge. However satisfied you may feel at the moment, don't forget that this will not be the first time you have applauded yourself in advance, in the hope merely of a triumph that escapes you at the very instant of your congratulating yourself upon it. Good-bye.

Paris
6 December 17–

LETTER 160: *Madame de Volanges to Madame de Rosemonde*

I write to you from the bedroom of our unhappy friend, whose condition is still very much the same. This afternoon there is to be a consultation between four doctors. Unfortunately that, as you know, is more often a proof of danger than a promise of help.

It appears, however, that she was partially restored to reason last night. The maid informed me this morning that about midnight her mistress had her called, desired to be left alone with her, and then dictated a fairly long letter. Julie added that, while she was busy preparing the envelope, Madame de Tourvel's delirium returned, so that the girl did not know to whom she should address it. I was astonished at first that the letter itself had left her in any doubt; but upon her replying that she was afraid she might be mistaken, and that, on the other hand, her mistress had especially instructed her to dispatch the letter immediately, I took it upon myself to open it.

I found what is here enclosed: it is, in effect, addressed to no one for its being addressed to too many people. I think, however, that it was to Monsieur de Valmont that our unhappy friend wished at first to write; but that she was finally, without noticing it, overcome by the disorder of her thoughts. Be that as it may, I decided that the letter should not be delivered to anyone. I send it to you because it will tell you better than can I the thoughts that occupy the mind of our poor invalid. As long as she is so deeply affected, I have scarcely any hope. The body is not easily restored to health when the spirit is so disturbed.

Good-bye, my dear and worthy friend. How glad I am that you are far removed from the piteous spectacle that I must continually keep before my eyes.

Paris
6 December 17–

LETTER 161: *The Présidente de Tourvel to...(dictated by her and written by her maid)*

Cruel and malignant man, will you never cease to persecute me? Is it not enough that you have tortured, debased, degraded me? Will you deprive me even of the peace of the tomb? Even in this abode of shadows, where ignominy has driven me to bury myself, is there no release from pain; is hope still a delusion? I beg no favors that I do not deserve: to suffer without complaint I need no more than that my sufferings should not exceed my strength. But do not make my torments insupportable. Leave me to my griefs but take from me the cruel memory of the happiness I have lost. Now that you have deprived me of it, do not raise its harrowing image again before my eyes. I enjoyed innocence and peace; it was when I saw you that all quiet forsook me, when I listened to you that I became a criminal. Author of my sins, what right have you to punish them?

Where are the friends who loved me, where are they? My misfortune frightens them away. Not one dares come near me. I am crushed and they leave me helpless! I am dying and no one weeps for me. All consolation is denied me. Pity pauses at the brink of the abyss into which the criminal has plunged. Remorse tears at her heart, and her cries remain unheard!

And you whom I have insulted, you whose esteem adds to my agony – you who alone would have the right to be avenged upon me, why are you so far away? Return and punish an unfaithful wife. Let me at last suffer the torments I deserve. I should already have submitted to your vengeance, but the courage to tell you of your shame failed me. It was not dissembling but respect. Let this letter, at all events, tell you of my repentance. Heaven has taken up your cause, and on your behalf God avenges the injury of which you are ignorant. He tied my tongue and kept back my words, fearing that you might overlook the fault He intended to punish. He shielded me from your kindness, which would have thwarted His justice.

Pitiless in His vengeance, He has delivered me over to the very man who was my ruin. It is at once for his sake and at his hands that I suffer. I try in vain to escape him. He follows, he is here: he taunts me unceasingly. But how different he is from what he was! His eyes no longer speak of anything but hatred and contempt. His lips offer only insults and recriminations. He takes me in his arms only to tear me apart. Who shall save me from his barbarous fury?

But look! It is he...There is no mistaking him – it is he I see again. Oh, my beloved! Take me in your arms. Hide me on your breast. Yes, it is you, it really is you! What dreadful delusion made me misunderstand you! How I have suffered in your absence. Let us not be separated again, let us never be separated. Let me breathe again. Feel my heart, how it beats. Ah, that is no longer fear. It is the sweet excitement of love. But why do you refuse my caresses? Will you not look gently upon me again? Why are you preparing those instruments of death? Who can have changed your features so? What are you doing? Let me go, I am trembling. God! Is it that monster again! My friends, do not desert me. You, the one who begged me to fly from him, help me to fight him. You, more kind, who promised to lessen my griefs, come to my side. Where are you both? If I am no longer allowed to see you, reply at least to this letter. Let me know that you love me still.

Leave me alone, cruel man! What new fury possesses you? Are you afraid some tender feeling may penetrate my soul? You redouble my torments; you force me to hate you. Oh, how painful hatred is! How it corrodes the heart that distills it! Why do you persecute me? What can you still have to say to me? Have you not made it as much an impossibility for me to listen to you as to reply? Expect nothing further from me. Good-bye, Monsieur.

Paris
5 December 17–

LETTER 162: *The Chevalier Danceny to the Vicomte de Valmont*
I have been enlightened, Monsieur, as to your conduct toward me. I know too that, not content with having shamefully tricked me, you do not hesitate to boast about it and to congratulate yourself upon it. I have seen the proof of your treachery written in your own hand. I confess that it cut me to the quick, and I was not a little ashamed at having

helped you so much to perpetrate your odious abuse of my blind confidence in you. I do not, however, envy you the despicable advantage you have won; I am only curious to know whether you can maintain every other advantage over me. And that I shall soon find out if, as I hope, you are willing to present yourself between eight and nine o'clock in the morning at the gate of the Bois de Vincennes in the village of Saint-Mandé. I shall see to it that all necessary preparations have been made for the explanations that remain to be entered into between us.

The Chevalier Danceny
Paris
6 December 17–, evening

LETTER 163: *Monsieur Bertrand to Madame de Rosemonde*
Madame,

It is with great regret that I fulfill the sad duty of telling you news that must cause you the most cruel grief. Permit me first to urge you to that pious resignation which we have all so often admired in you, and which alone can help us to support the evils with which our miserable existence is strewn.

Monsieur your nephew...My God! must I so distress such a worthy lady? Monsieur your nephew has had the misfortune to be fatally injured in a duel he fought this morning with Monsieur the Chevalier Danceny. I am entirely ignorant of the subject of the quarrel, but it appears from the note I found in Monsieur the Vicomte's pocket, the note which I have the honor to send you herewith, it appears, I say, that he was not the aggressor. Yet it was he whom Heaven permitted to fall!

I was at Monsieur the Vicomte's waiting for him, at the very moment when they brought him back into the house. Imagine my alarm at seeing Monsieur your nephew, carried in by two of his servants, bathed in his own blood. He had received two sword thrusts in the body and was already very weak. Monsieur Danceny was also there, and indeed was in tears. Ah, no doubt he had good cause to weep; but it is no time to shed tears when one has been the cause of an irreparable disaster.

As for me, I was beside myself. Of little account as I am, I nonetheless gave Monsieur Danceny a piece of my mind. It was then that Monsieur de Valmont rose to true greatness. He ordered me to be silent, and taking the hand of the very man who was his murderer, called him his friend, embraced him in front of us all and said to us, "I order you to treat Monsieur with all the regard that is due to a good and gallant gentleman." He moreover delivered to him in my presence a great mass of papers. I do not know what they are, but I know that he attaches a great deal of importance to them. Then he asked that he and Monsieur Danceny should be left alone together for a moment. Meanwhile I had sent for aid, both spiritual and medical – but alas! there was no remedy. Less than half an hour later Monsieur the Vicomte had lost consciousness. He was just able to receive extreme unction; the ceremony was scarcely over when he breathed his last.

Great God! When at his birth I received into my arms this precious scion of so illustrious a house, could I have foreseen that it would be in my arms that he was to die, and that I should have to lament his death? So untimely and unhappy a death! I cannot hold back my tears. Forgive me, Madame, for being so bold as to mingle my grief with yours, but there are the same hearts and sensibilities in every walk of life. I should be most ungrateful if I did not for the rest of my days regret the loss of an employer who showed me so much kindness and who honored me with so much of his confidence.

Tomorrow, after the removal of the body, I shall have everything sealed, and you may rely upon me entirely. You will not be unaware, Madame, that this unfortunate incident terminates the entail and leaves you free to dispose of your property as you please. If I can be of any service to you, please be so kind as to convey your orders to me: I shall do all I can to execute them punctually.

I am, Madame, with the most profound respect, your very humble, etc.

Bertrand
Paris
7 December 17–

LETTER 164: *Madame de Rosemonde to Monsieur Bertrand*
I have just, my dear Bertrand, received your letter telling me of the terrible calamity of which my nephew has been the unfortunate victim. Yes, of course I have orders to give you, and it is only upon that account that I am able to think of anything other than my dreadful bereavement.

Monsieur Danceny's note, which you sent me, is most convincing proof that it was he who provoked the duel. I should like you to lodge a complaint immediately, in my name. In pardoning his enemy, his murderer, my nephew was able to indulge his natural generosity; but I must avenge not only his death but at the same time humanity and religion. The severities of the law cannot be too stringently invoked against this relic of barbarism which still infects our age. I do not think that in such cases we are required to pardon our injuries: I expect you, therefore, to pursue this affair with all the determination and all the energy of which you are capable. So much you owe to the memory of my nephew.

You will make a point, especially, of seeing Monsieur the Président de ——— on my behalf, and of consulting him about it. I shall not write to him, wholly preoccupied with my grief as I shall now be. You will make my excuses, and communicate the contents of this letter to him.

Good-bye, my dear Bertrand. I commend you and thank you for your worthy feelings, and am ever yours.

Château de ———
8 December 17–

LETTER 165: *Madame de Volanges to Madame de Rosemonde*

I know that you have already been told, my dear and worthy friend, of the loss you have just suffered. I know of the affection in which you held Monsieur de Valmont and most sincerely share the distress you must feel. I am truly sorry to add my griefs to those you already bear, but alas! even you can no longer offer our unhappy friend anything but your tears. We lost her yesterday at eleven o'clock in the evening. By an accident of the sort that seems to attend her fate, a mockery of all human prudence, the short interval by which she survived Monsieur de Valmont was just long enough for her to learn of his death and, as she said herself, not to succumb under the weight of her misfortunes until their number was complete.

In fact, as you know, she was absolutely unconscious for more than two days. Even yesterday morning when her doctor arrived and we approached her bed, she recognized neither of us, and we could get not a word or the smallest sign from her. Well, no sooner had we returned to the fireplace and the doctor begun to tell me of the sad accident of Monsieur de Valmont's death, when the unfortunate woman recovered consciousness – perhaps in the natural course of things, perhaps because the repetition of the words "Monsieur de Valmont" and "dead" recalled to her mind the only thoughts that have occupied it for some time.

Whatever the reason, she abruptly drew aside the curtains of her bed, crying out, "What! What are you saying? Is Monsieur de Valmont dead?" I hoped to make her believe that she was mistaken, and assured her at first that she had misunderstood. But, far from allowing herself to be persuaded, she insisted that the doctor begin the dreadful story again;

and when I still tried to dissuade her, she called me to her and said in a low voice, "Why deceive me? As though, to me, he were not already dead!" So I was obliged to give in.

Our poor friend listened at first with an appearance of calm, but soon after she interrupted the doctor, saying, "Enough. I have heard enough." She immediately asked for the curtains to be drawn; and when the doctor made some attempt to attend to her, she refused to allow him to come near her.

As soon as he had left, she sent away her nurse and her maid as well. When we were alone she asked me to help her kneel on her bed, and to hold her as she knelt. She remained silent for some time, her face expressionless but for the tears that flowed abundantly. At length, joining her hands together and lifting them toward Heaven she said softly but fervently, "Almighty God, I submit to your justice. But pardon Valmont. Let only my miseries, which I acknowledge I deserve, not be held against him, and I shall be ever grateful for your mercy!" I think I am justified, my dear and worthy friend, in entering into such detail upon a subject that, I am very sensible, must reawaken and aggravate your griefs – because, on the other hand, I am sure that this prayer of Madame de Tourvel's must bring great comfort to your heart.

After our friend had offered up these few words she fell back in my arms; and scarcely had she been put back to bed when a faintness overcame her which lasted a long time but yielded at length to the ordinary remedies. As soon as she recovered consciousness she asked that Father Anselme be sent for and added, "He is the only doctor I need now. I know that my ills will soon be at an end." She complained a great deal of a feeling of oppression and spoke with difficulty.

A little later she had her maid give me the small box I am sending you, which, she said, contains papers of hers, and instructed me to let you have it immediately after her death.* Then – as much as her condition allowed – she spoke with great feeling of you and of your friendship for her.

Father Anselme arrived at about four o'clock and stayed alone with her for nearly an hour. When we returned to the room her face was calm and serene, but it was plain that Father Anselme had been weeping a great deal. He remained to perform the last rites of the Church. That sight – always so impressive and so painful – was still more so for the contrast between the peaceful resignation of the sick woman and the profound grief of her venerable confessor, dissolved in tears at her

---

*This box contained all the letters relating to her affair with Monsieur de Valmont.

side. Everyone was moved; the only one who did not weep was the one who was wept for.

The remainder of the day was spent in saying the customary prayers, interrupted only by the invalid's spells of weakness. At length, toward eleven at night, there seemed to be an increase of oppression and suffering. I put out my hand to her arm; she still had strength enough to take it and place it on her heart. I could no longer feel it beating; and, in fact, our unhappy friend expired at that very moment.

Do you remember, my dear, that at your last visit here less than a year ago, while we were talking of sundry people whose happiness seemed to us more or less assured, we paused with no little complacency to consider the lot of this very woman whose misfortunes, whose death we have now to mourn? So many virtues, graces, so many praiseworthy qualities; so sweet, so gentle a disposition; a husband whom she loved and who adored her; a circle of friends she enjoyed and whose whole delight she was; beauty, youth, fortune: a combination of so many advantages lost through a single imprudence! Oh, Providence! Doubtless we must bow to your decrees, but how incomprehensible they are! I must stop. I am afraid I may increase your own grief by giving way to mine.

I leave you to go and see my daughter who is a little indisposed. When she learned from me this morning of the sudden death of two persons of her acquaintance, naturally she fainted away and I had her put to bed. I hope, however, that this slight indisposition will have no consequences. At that age one is not yet used to sorrow, and its impression is therefore deeper and stronger. So lively a sensibility is no doubt a praiseworthy thing; but how soon what we see day by day of the world teaches us to fear it! Good-bye, my dear and worthy friend.

Paris
9 December 17–

LETTER 166: *Monsieur Bertrand to Madame de Rosemonde*
Madame,

In consequence of the orders you were pleased to give me, I have had the honor of seeing Monsieur the Président de ———, and have communicated the contents of your letter to him, informing him that, in accordance with your wishes, I would do nothing without his advice. The worthy magistrate has instructed me to call your attention to the fact that the complaint you intend to lodge against Monsieur the Chevalier Danceny would be equally injurious to the memory of Monsieur your nephew, and that a court sentence would inevitably reflect upon his honor – which would of course be a great misfortune. His opinion is therefore that it is essential to avoid taking proceedings; and that if there is anything to be done, it is on the contrary to attempt to keep all knowledge of the unhappy affair, which is already only too much of a public scandal, from the public prosecutor.

These observations seem to me to be full of wisdom, and I have decided to await further instructions from you.

Allow me to beg you, Madame, to be so kind, when you send them to me, as to add a word on the subject of your health: I am extremely anxious as to the effect upon it of so much grief. I hope my attachment to you and my zeal in your service will excuse this liberty.

I am respectfully, Madame, your, etc.

Paris
10 December 17–

LETTER 167: *Anonymous to Monsieur the Chevalier Danceny*
Monsieur,

I have the honor to inform you that the question of your recent affair with Monsieur the Vicomte de Valmont was discussed this morning among Messieurs His Majesty's servants at the public prosecutor's office, and it is to be feared that proceedings may be taken against you. I thought this warning might be of service to you, either so that you might use your influence to forestall disagreeable consequences or, in case you are unable to do that, so as to put you in a position to look after your personal safety.

If you will even allow me a word of advice, I think you would do well in the immediate future to appear in public less often than you have for the past few days. Although this sort of affair is normally looked upon with indulgence, there is always nonetheless a certain respect due to the law.

This precaution will be all the more necessary in that it has come to my ears that a certain Madame de Rosemonde, who I am told is Monsieur de Valmont's aunt, intends to lodge a complaint against you; the public prosecutor could not refuse her demand. It might perhaps be to the purpose if you were able to communicate with this lady.

Private considerations will not allow my signing this letter. But I hope, though you do not know from whom it comes, that you will do justice nonetheless to the sentiment that has dictated it.

I have the honor to be, etc.

Paris

10 December 17–

LETTER 168: *Madame de Volanges to Madame de Rosemonde*

The most astounding and distressing rumors, my dear and worthy friend, are being spread about here concerning Madame de Merteuil. Of course, I am very far from believing them, and I am certain that it is all frightful calumny – but I know too well how the most implausible slanders can acquire credit, and how difficult it is to efface their impression once formed, how not to be most alarmed at these stories, easy though I know they would be to disprove. I should particularly like to see them stopped in good time before they spread any further. But it was not till very late yesterday that I came to know of the horrors that were just beginning to be put about. And when I sent this morning to Madame de Merteuil's, she had just left for the country, where she is to spend the next two days. No one was able to tell me to whose house she had gone. Her undermaid, whom I sent for to speak with, told me that her mistress had merely given orders to expect her next Thursday, and none of the other servants she has left behind are better informed. I cannot myself imagine where she can be; I can think of no one of her acquaintance who stays so late in the country.

Be that as it may, between now and her return, you will be able to provide me with information which may be useful to her, I hope. These hateful stories are based on certain circumstances relating to Monsieur de Valmont's death, of which, if they are true, you clearly will have heard – the truth of which, at any rate, you may easily confirm. I beg you to do so as a favor to me. This is what is being bruited abroad or, rather, what is still being whispered, but will certainly be proclaimed more loudly before long.

It is said that the quarrel that occurred between Monsieur de Valmont and the Chevalier Danceny was the work of Madame de Merteuil, and that she deceived them both equally; that, as nearly always happens, the two rivals began by fighting and did not arrive at explanations until afterward; that explanations in this case brought about a sincere reconciliation; and that Monsieur de Valmont, in order to complete the Chevalier Danceny's knowledge of Madame de Merteuil and also to clear himself entirely, produced, in confirmation of what he said, a mass of letters constituting a regular correspondence he had maintained with Madame de Merteuil, in which she tells the most scandalous anecdotes against herself in the most abandoned style.

It is added that Danceny, in his first indignation showed the letters to anyone who wished to see them, and that now they are going the rounds of Paris. Two in particular are much-quoted:* one in which she tells the whole story of her life and principles, which is said to be the height of infamy; the other which entirely clears Monsieur de Prévan, whose story you remember, by affording proof that he did no more than yield to very definite advances on her part, and that the rendezvous was agreed upon with her.

Fortunately I have the strongest reasons to believe that these imputations are as false as they are odious. First, we both know that Monsieur de Valmont was certainly not interested in Madame de Merteuil, and I have every reason to believe that Danceny was no more so: thus it seems clear to me that she can have been neither the subject nor the author of their quarrel. Nor can I see how it could have been in Madame de Merteuil's interest – supposing her to have reached an understanding with Monsieur de Prévan – to have made a scene that could only have had disagreeable and scandalous consequences, and which might have proved very dangerous for her, since she was thereby making an irreconcilable enemy of a man in possession of her secrets, and who at that time had supporters in plenty. It is remarkable, however, that since that affair not a single voice has been raised in Prévan's favor, and that even he himself has made no protest.

Such considerations might lead me to suspect him as the author of the rumors now current, and to regard these slanders as the work of hatred in a man who, finding himself ruined, hopes in this way at least to spread doubts, and perhaps bring about a useful change of opinion. But from whatever quarter these villainous rumors spring, the most urgent necessity is to destroy them. They would die of themselves were it found, as is likely, that Messieurs de Valmont and Danceny did not speak to each other at all after their encounter and that no papers exchanged hands.

In my impatience to verify these facts, I sent this morning to Monsieur Danceny. He is not in Paris either. His servants told my footman that he left last night after receiving a warning letter yesterday, and that his destination was secret. Evidently he fears the consequences of this duel. It is therefore only from you, my dear and worthy friend, that I can obtain the details which interest me, and which may become so

---

*Letters 81 and 85.

necessary to Madame de Merteuil. May I ask you again to let me have them as soon as possible?

P.S. My daughter's indisposition was attended with no aftereffects. She presents her respects to you.

Paris
11 December 17–

LETTER 169: *The Chevalier Danceny to Madame Rosemonde*

Madame,

You will perhaps find what I propose to do today very strange, but hear me out, I beseech you, before you pass judgment upon me, and do not take for insolence and temerity what is done only in respect and trust. I cannot disguise from myself the wrongs I have done you; and I should not forgive myself for as long as I lived could I for a moment suppose that they might have been avoided. Rest assured too, Madame, that however free I am from blame, I am not so from regret; and I might add in all sincerity that the regret I cause you has not a little to do with the regret I feel. To believe these sentiments of which I am so bold as to assure you, you need only do yourself justice; and you have only to learn that, though I have not the honor of being known to you, I have the honor of knowing you.

However, while I deplore the calamity that has caused both your grief and my misfortune, I have been brought to fear that you, wholly determined upon revenge, will invoke even the severities of the law in your efforts to accomplish it.

Allow me first to point out to you that, on this point, your grief deceives you, since my interest in this matter is essentially bound up with that of Monsieur de Valmont, and since he himself would be involved in the obloquy you call down upon me. I might therefore suppose, Madame, that I could count rather on help than on hindrance from you in such efforts as I might be obliged to make to see this unhappy affair consigned to oblivion.

But my pride will not countenance my taking refuge in complicity, which is the resource of innocent and guilty alike; though I reject you as my opponent, I claim you for my judge. The esteem of the people one respects is so precious that I cannot allow myself to be deprived of yours without making some attempt to preserve it – and I think I have a means of doing so.

After all, if you agree that revenge is permissible – or more, that it is a duty – when one has been betrayed in love, friendship, or above all in one's confidences; if you agree, my culpability in your eyes will disappear. Do not take my word for this: simply read, if you have the courage, the correspondence I am putting into your hands.* The number of letters it contains in the original would seem to prove the authenticity of those which are merely copies. For the rest, I received these documents, which I have the honor of forwarding to you, at the hands of Monsieur de Valmont himself. I have added nothing to them, and have extracted only two letters, which I have taken the liberty of making public.

One was necessary to the accomplishment of Monsieur de Valmont's revenge and mine, to which we both had a right and with which he had expressly charged me. I thought, moreover, that it would be doing a service to society to unmask a woman as truly dangerous as Madame de Merteuil, who, as you will see, is the only and the real cause of all that passed between Monsieur de Valmont and myself.

My sense of justice prompted me to make the contents of the other known so as to clear Monsieur de Prévan, with whom I am scarcely at all acquainted, but who has by no means deserved either the harsh treatment he recently received or the severe and even more formidable public condemnation he has suffered since then without being in any way able to defend himself.

Of these two letters, therefore, you will only find copies; the originals it is my duty to keep. As for the rest: I could not, I think, commend to safer keeping what I should not perhaps like to see destroyed, but should be ashamed to take advantage of. I believe, Madame, that in entrusting these documents to you I am doing as great a service to the persons concerned as I could by returning them directly; and I am sparing them the embarrassment of receiving the documents from me, and of knowing that I am aware of certain occurrences that no doubt they would prefer to keep a secret from the world.

I think I ought to warn you, by the way, that the attached correspondence is only a portion of a much more voluminous collection of letters, from which it was selected by Monsieur de Valmont in my presence. The rest you will find, when the seals are removed, under the label (which I have seen): "Account opened between the Marquise de

---

*It is from this collection of letters – both the one that was delivered into the same hands at the death of Madame de Tourvel and certain letters entrusted to Madame de Rosemonde by Madame de Volanges – that the present collection has been formed. The originals remain in the hands of Madame de Rosemonde's heirs.

Merteuil and the Vicomte de Valmont." You will, of course, decide on this matter as your prudence suggests.

P.S. On receiving certain warnings, and upon the advice of my friends, I have decided to stay away from Paris for some time. My place of refuge has been kept secret from everybody else but shall not be so from you. If you will honor me with a reply, kindly address it to the Commanderie de ———, near P———, under cover to Monsieur the Commandeur de ———. It is from his house that I have the honor of writing to you.

Paris
12 December 17–

LETTER 170: *Madame de Volanges to Madame de Rosemonde*
I proceed, my dear, from surprise to surprise and from sorrow to sorrow. You would have to be a mother to form any idea of how I suffered all yesterday morning; and if my most cruel anxieties have since been allayed, I have still to sustain a very keen affliction the end of which I cannot yet foresee.

Yesterday, at about ten o'clock in the morning, astonished that I had not yet seen my daughter, I sent my maid to find out what could have occasioned the delay. She returned the moment after, very frightened, and she frightened me a good deal more by announcing that my daughter was not in her room, and that her maid had not seen her there at all that morning. Imagine my state of mind! I summoned all my servants and questioned the hall porter in particular: all swore that they knew nothing and could tell me nothing about the matter. I proceeded immediately to my daughter's bedroom. The disorder that prevailed indicated that she had obviously left only that morning, but I could find no explanation anywhere. I examined her wardrobes, her writing desk; I found everything in its place. All her clothes were there with the exception of the dress she was wearing when she left. She had not so much as taken the small sum of money she had in her possession.

Since it was only yesterday that she heard what is being said about Madame de Merteuil, and since she is very much attached to her, so much so that she did nothing but cry all evening; since too, as I remembered, she did not know that Madame de Merteuil was in the country, my first thought was that she had decided to see her friend and had been foolish enough to go out alone. But as time elapsed and she did not return, all my anxieties were renewed. Every moment increased my uneasiness, and though I longed to know everything, I dared make no inquiries for fear of giving publicity to a happening that later, perhaps, I might wish to conceal from everyone. Really, I have never been so distressed in my life.

At all events, it was not until two hours later that I received, simultaneously, a letter from my daughter and one from the superior of the convent of ———. My daughter's letter said only that she had been afraid I might oppose her vocation to become a nun, and that she had not dared to speak to me about it; the rest consisted merely of apologies for having made this decision without my permission – a decision, she added, that I should certainly not disapprove if I knew what her motives were. She begged me, however, not to ask her.

The superior informed me that, seeing a young woman arrive at the convent alone, she had at first refused to admit her; but that, having questioned her and learned who she was, she thought she would be doing me a service by giving my daughter temporary asylum instead of permitting her to venture further afield, which it seems she was bent upon doing. The superior, while she naturally offers to return my daughter to me should I ask for her, urges me, as her profession requires, not to oppose a vocation that she calls "so pronounced." She tells me, too, that she was unable to let me know sooner what had happened because she had great difficulty in persuading my daughter to write to me, my daughter's intention being that no one should know where she had gone. What a cruel thing is the thoughtlessness of one's children!

I went immediately to the convent. Having met the superior I asked her whether I could speak to my daughter, who came only reluctantly and in great fear and trembling to meet me. I spoke to her in front of the nuns, and I spoke to her alone; all I could obtain from her, amidst floods of tears, was that she could be happy only in a convent. I decided to let her stay, but not as a postulant, as she wanted. I am afraid the deaths of Madame de Tourvel and Monsieur de Valmont have made too deep an impression on her young mind. Much as I respect the religious vocation, it is not without pain and even fear that I could see my daughter embrace that condition. It seems to me that we already have enough duties to fulfill without creating new ones; besides, at that age, we are scarcely capable of knowing what is best for us.

What increases my difficulties is that Monsieur de Gercourt is very soon expected back. Must so advantageous a match be broken off? How can one, then, achieve the happiness of one's children if it is not enough merely to want to do so and to devote all one's energies to the task? You would be doing me a great kindness by telling me what you would do in my place. I cannot fix upon any one course. I find nothing so frightening as having to decide the fate of others, and I am as much afraid on this occasion of yielding to the severity of a judge as I am of giving way to the weakness of a mother.

I reproach myself constantly for increasing your sufferings by telling you of mine. But I know your heart: the comfort you are able to give others will be for you the greatest comfort you are able to receive yourself.

Good-bye, my dear and worthy friend. I await your two replies with great impatience.

Paris
13 December 17–

LETTER 171: *Madame de Rosemonde to the Chevalier Danceny*
After what you have brought to my knowledge, Monsieur, there is nothing to do but weep and be silent. One is sorry to be yet alive when one learns of such horrors; one is ashamed of being a woman when one hears of one capable of such excesses.

I shall be very glad, Monsieur, to join with you, as far as I am able, in committing to silence and oblivion everything that may concern, and everything that may ensue from this, lamentable affair. I even wish it may cause you no other distress than that which is inseparable from the unhappy triumph you were able to achieve at my nephew's expense. In spite of his misdeeds, which I am obliged to acknowledge, I feel that I shall never be consoled for his loss. But my inconsolable affliction shall be the only revenge I take upon you; it is for your heart to calculate its extent.

If you will allow me, at my age, a reflection that is scarcely ever made at yours, I must say that if one only knew where one's true happiness lay one would never look for it outside the limits prescribed by the law and by religion.

You may be sure that I shall willingly and faithfully keep the letters you have entrusted to me. But I must ask you to authorize me to refuse to give them up to anyone, even to you, Monsieur, unless they become necessary to a justification of your conduct. I dare say you shall not refuse, and that it is no longer necessary to make you feel how dearly one must pay for giving way even to the most just revenge.

I shall not stop there in my requests, convinced as I am of your generosity and delicacy: it would be most worthy of both to deliver into my hands Mademoiselle de Volanges's letters as well, which apparently you have kept, and which no doubt are of no further interest to you. I know that this young lady has done you great wrongs, but I cannot think that you contemplate punishing them; if only out of respect for yourself, you will not disgrace the person you once loved so much. I need not add that the regard which the daughter does not merit is due at least to the mother, that worthy woman to whom you owe not inconsiderable amends. For, after all, whatever excuses are made on behalf of a so-called sincerity of feeling, he who first seduces a heart still innocent and simple becomes thereby the first abettor of its corruption and must forever be responsible for the excesses and aberrations that follow.

Do not be surprised, Monsieur, at so much severity on my part. It is the surest proof I can give you of my perfect esteem. To this you will acquire still further claim if you will consent, as I wish, to the safety of a secret, the disclosure of which would be to your own detriment and would bring death to the heart of the mother you have already wounded. At all events, Monsieur, I wish to do my friend this service; and were I afraid that you might deny me such a consolation, I should ask you to remember first that you have left me no other.

I have the honor to be, etc.

Château de ———
15 December 17–

LETTER 172: *Madame de Rosemonde to Madame de Volanges*

Had I been obliged, my dear, to wait while I sent to Paris for the information you require concerning Madame de Merteuil, it would not yet have been possible to give it to you; and no doubt I should have received none but vague and dubious reports. But certain other intelligence has reached my ears which I neither expected nor had any reason to expect, and which has only too much foundation. Oh, my dear, how deceived you have been in this woman!

I recoil from entering into the least detail concerning this pack of horrors, but you may be sure that whatever is being repeated falls far short of the truth. I hope, my dear, that you know me well enough to take me at my word, and that you will demand no proof; be content to know that proof exists in abundance, and that I have it at this very moment in my hands.

It is not without extreme reluctance that I make you another, and similar, request: Do not oblige me to explain my motives for the advice concerning Mademoiselle de Volanges which you have asked for, and which I am now to give you. I urge you not to oppose the vocation she displays. Of course, no argument can justify the coercion of any person into this way of life who is not called to it. But it is sometimes a piece of great good fortune when someone is so called. And, as you have observed, your daughter herself tells you that you would not disapprove of her if you knew her motives. He who inspires our inclinations knows better than we do, in our vain wisdom, what is fitting for each one of us; and often what seems an act of great severity on His part proceeds, on the contrary, from His clemency.

At all events, my opinion, which I know very well must distress you – and you must judge from that how thoroughly I have considered it before offering it to you – is that you should leave Mademoiselle de Volanges in the convent, since the decision is her own; that you should encourage rather than obstruct the plan she seems to have formed; and that, in anticipation of its being carried out, you should not hesitate to break off the match you have arranged.

Having fulfilled the painful duties of friendship, and being powerless to add any consolations to them, I have only one favor left to ask you, my dear, and that is that you will not question me upon anything relating to this sad affair. Let us leave it in its proper obscurity. Without looking for useless and distressing explanations, let us submit to the decrees of Providence. Let us believe in the wisdom of its ways even though it is not permitted us to understand them. Good-bye, my dear.

Château de ———
15 December 17–

LETTER 173: *Madame de Volanges to Madame de Rosemonde*
Oh, my dear! What a frightful veil you throw over the fate of my daughter! And you seem to be in dread of my trying to lift it! What does it hide from me that can possibly give more pain to a mother's heart than the terrible suspicions to which you have made me a prey? The more conscious I am of your affection, your kindness, the more my torments increase. Since yesterday I have decided twenty times to be rid of these cruel uncertainties, to ask you to tell me everything without evasion and without reserve; and each time I trembled with fear, remembering your request that I not question you. I have at length reached a decision that leaves me with some hope, and I expect of your friendship that you will not deny me what I wish: that you will tell me whether I have more or less understood what you might have had to say; and that you will not be afraid to reveal everything to me that a mother's indulgence can excuse and that it is not impossible to make amends for. If my misfortune exceeds this measure, then I shall agree after all to leave

you with no other explanation to make than that of your silence. Here then is what I already know, and the utmost extent of what I fear.

My daughter once showed some inclination for the Chevalier Danceny and I was informed that she had gone so far as to receive letters from him, even to reply to them. But I thought I had succeeded in preventing this childish error from having any dangerous consequences. Now that I fear everything, I imagine it might have been possible for my daughter to have escaped my surveillance; and I very much fear that, once led into error, she may have taken her indiscretions to an extreme.

I remember several circumstances that might go to strengthen this suspicion. I wrote telling you that my daughter had been taken ill at the news of the accident that befell Monsieur de Valmont – but perhaps it was only the thought of the risk Monsieur Danceny had run in fighting a duel that affected her sensibilities. When, later, she wept so much upon hearing of all that was being said about Madame de Merteuil, what I thought was the sorrow of a friend may only have been the effect of jealousy, or regret at finding her lover unfaithful. Her latest proceeding as well, it seems to me, may be explained in the same way. One often feels called to God simply because one is disgusted with man. At all events, supposing these facts to be true, and supposing you to be aware of them, they would, no doubt, have been sufficient in your eyes to justify the harsh advice you give me.

However, if this were the case, though I could not excuse my daughter, I should still think I owed it to her to try every means of saving her from the dangers and torments of an illusory and short-lived vocation. If Monsieur Danceny has not lost every feeling of decency, he will not refuse to repair a wrong for which he alone is responsible; and I dare say, after all, that my daughter would be an advantageous enough match to gratify him and his family too.

This, my dear and worthy friend, is the sole hope that remains to me. Lose no time in confirming it, if that is at all possible. You may imagine how much I want you to reply, and what a dreadful blow your silence will be.*

I was about to seal my letter when a gentleman of my acquaintance came to see me and told me of the cruel humiliation inflicted on Madame de Merteuil the day before yesterday. As I have seen no one these last few days I had heard nothing of the affair. Here is the account of an eyewitness.

Madame de Merteuil, returning from the country the day before yes-

---

*This letter went unanswered.

terday, that is Thursday, had herself set down at the Comédie Italienne, where she has a box. She was alone in it, and, what must have seemed extraordinary to her, not a single man presented himself to her during the entire performance. When it was over, she proceeded as she usually does into the small salon, which was already full of people. A murmur immediately went around, of which, however, she apparently did not suppose herself to be the object. She saw an empty place on one of the benches and sat down, whereupon the other women already sitting there rose immediately, as of one accord, and left her absolutely alone. This very marked display of indignation was applauded by all the men, and the hubbub increased to the extent, it is said, of hooting.

So that nothing should be lacking in her humiliation, it was her ill fortune that Monsieur de Prévan, who has been seen nowhere since his adventure, entered the same salon at that very moment. As soon as he was seen, everyone − men and women alike − gathered around and applauded him. He found himself, so to speak, carried before Madame de Merteuil by the company, who then made a circle around them both. The latter, I am assured, maintained an air of neither seeing nor hearing anything, and did not so much as change her expression! But I think this is exaggerated. However that may be, this scene − truly ignominious for her − lasted until her carriage was announced. As she left, the scandalous jeering was redoubled. It is frightful to be in the position of a relation to this woman. Monsieur de Prévan was warmly welcomed the same evening by the officers of his regiment who were present, and there is no doubt that he will be restored to his official position and rank.

The same person who gave me these details told me that Madame de Merteuil was attacked the following night by a very violent fever, which, it was thought at first, must be the effect of the terrible predicament in which she had found herself; but since last night it has become known that confluent smallpox of a particularly malignant type has declared itself. It would really, I think, be fortunate for her if she died of it. It is said as well that this whole affair will go very much against her in her lawsuit which is soon to be tried, and for which, it is claimed, she would have needed all her standing.

Good-bye, my dear and worthy friend. I see in all this that the wicked are punished; but I can find in it no consolation for their unhappy victims.

Paris
18 December 17−

LETTER 174: *The Chevalier Danceny to Madame de Rosemonde*

You are right, Madame, and I shall refuse you nothing that is in my power, since you seem to attach some importance to my compliance. The packet I have the honor to send you contains all Mademoiselle de Volanges's letters. If you read them you will perhaps be a little astonished that so much ingenuousness can be found together with so much perfidy. That, at any rate, is what struck me most just now when I read them myself for the last time.

But how, especially, can one help feeling the most intense indignation against Madame de Merteuil when one recalls the frightful pleasure with which she devoted all her care to perverting so much innocence and sincerity?

No, I have no love in me. I have nothing left of a sentiment that has been so shamefully betrayed; and it is not love that makes me seek to justify Mademoiselle de Volanges. Yet could so simple a heart, so sweet and soft a character, have been otherwise than inclined toward good even more readily than they were allowed to lapse into evil? What young girl, just out of her convent, without experience and almost completely without ideas, taking with her into society an equal ignorance of good and evil, as nearly always happens – what young girl, I say, could have offered a firmer resistance to such wicked designs? Ah, to be indulgent, it is enough to consider how many circumstances, quite independent of ourselves, maintain the terrifying balance between decency and corruption in our hearts. You did me justice then, Madame, in thinking that the wrongs Mademoiselle Volanges has done me, though I feel them deeply, do not inspire in me any thought of vengeance. It is quite enough to be compelled to cease loving her! It would cost me too much to hate her.

I had no need of reflection to form the hope that all which concerns her and may injure her will forever remain a secret from the world. If I seem to have put off for some time my fulfillment of your wishes in this respect, I think I need not conceal my motives from you: I wished first to be certain that I would not be troubled by the consequences of this unfortunate affair. At a time when I was asking for your indulgence, when I even thought I had some right to it, I should have been afraid of seeming to buy it, so to speak, by doing you a favor. Certain myself of the purity of my motives, I was so proud I confess as to wish to leave you in no doubt of them either. I hope you will forgive this perhaps overly fastidious delicacy in view of the respect in which I hold you, and the importance I attach to your esteem.

The same feelings prompt me to ask you, as a last favor, to be so kind as to tell me, whether you think I have fulfilled all the duties that have been imposed upon me by the unhappy situation I have found myself in. Once set at rest on this point, my decision is made: I shall leave for Malta. There I shall gladly make, and religiously keep, the vows that will shut me off from a world that, though I am still young, I have so much reason to abhor. There, under strange skies, I shall try to forget this accumulation of horrors, the memory of which could only sadden and deaden my soul.

I am most respectfully, Madame, your very humble, etc.

Paris
26 December 17–

LETTER 175: *Madame de Volanges to Madame de Rosemonde*
Madame de Merteuil's destiny seems at last, my dear and worthy friend, to have been fulfilled. It is such that her worst enemies are divided between the indignation she merits and the pity she inspires. I was quite right to say that it would perhaps be fortunate for her if she died of the smallpox. She has recovered, it is true, but horribly disfigured – more than anything by the loss of an eye. As you may imagine, I have not seen her again; but I am told that she looks truly hideous.

The Marquis de ————, who never loses an opportunity to be spiteful, said yesterday in speaking of her "that the disease has turned her inside out, and that her soul is now visible on her face." Unfortunately everyone thought the observation very just.

Another incident has recently added still further to her disgrace and misfortune. Her lawsuit was tried the day before yesterday, and the verdict went unanimously against her on every count. Costs, damages, restitution of profits have all been awarded to the minors, so that the small part of her fortune that was not forfeited in the proceedings has been exhausted, and more than exhausted, in expenses.

Immediately on hearing the news, though still ill, she made her arrangements and left during the night by herself taking the post coach. Her servants said today that none of them wished to go with her. It is thought that she has taken the road for Holland.

Her flight has been the subject of more outcry than everything else put together, seeing that she has carried off her diamonds – a collection of very considerable value – which should have formed part of her husband's estate; her silver, her jewels; in short, all that she was able to take with her; and has left almost fifty thousand livres in debts behind her. It is a complete bankruptcy.

The family is to foregather tomorrow to see about accommodating the creditors. Though I am a very distant relation, I have offered to make one of the number; but before I attend that meeting, I shall be present at a much more melancholy ceremony. My daughter assumes the postulant's habit tomorrow. I hope you do not forget, my dear, that I make this great sacrifice thinking myself compelled to it for no other reason than that you have preserved your silence since receiving my letter.

Monsieur Danceny left Paris nearly a fortnight ago. It is said that he is going to Malta with the intention of establishing himself there. There may still be time to bring him back! . . . My dear! . . . Is my daughter so very guilty? . . . You will no doubt forgive a mother for the difficulty she finds in admitting so dreadful a truth.

What disasters have of late dogged my footsteps, striking at me through the persons nearest to my heart! My daughter and my friend!

Who would not shudder to think of the misery that may be caused by a single dangerous intimacy? And how much suffering could be avoided if it were more often thought of! What woman would not fly the seducer's first approach? What mother could, without trembling, see anyone but herself in conversation with her daughter? But we never reflect until after the event, when it is too late; and one of the most important of truths — as also, perhaps, one of the most generally acknowledged — is cast aside and forgotten amid the inconsequential bustle of our lives.

Good-bye, my dear and worthy friend; I am now discovering that reason, unable in the first place to prevent our misfortunes, is even less equal to consoling us for them.*[18]

Paris
14 January 17—

---

*Publisher's note: For motives of our own — and certain other considerations that we shall always consider it out of duty to respect — we are compelled to stop here.

We can, at present, give the reader neither the subsequent adventures of Mademoiselle de Volanges nor any account of the sinister occurrences that crowned the misfortunes and accomplished the punishment of Madame de Merteuil.

Some day, perhaps, we shall be permitted to complete this work. But we cannot commit ourselves on this point; and if it were possible, we should still think ourselves obliged in the first place to consult the public taste, since our own and the public's motives for being interested in the book are not the same.

NOTES

1. The wife of an intendant, the administrator of a province.

2. The wife of a *président*, the presiding magistrate of a court of justice. *Intendants* and *présidents* belonged to the *noblesse de robe*, the magisterial nobility, as opposed to the *noblesse de race*, the old feudal nobility.

3. It was often arranged for the younger sons of the nobility, who were precluded from inheriting property or office, to be provided for as *chevaliers* in the semimilitary, semimonastic Order of Malta. Not all its members were bound by the vow of celibacy, as Cécile Volanges appears to think.

4. Fashionable society in the eighteenth century kept its clandestine rendezvous on its own property, in suburban villas known as *petites maisons*, which were maintained specially for the purpose.

5. Crébillon fils's *The Sofa* is included in this volume.

6. Jean-Jacques Rousseau's *The New Heloise*.

7. The Comédie Italienne and the Comédie Française were the two principal theaters of the time in Paris. The designation of the company performing at the former was Les Italiens, the official title of the latter, Théâtre français: people spoke of going "to the Italiens" or "to the Français."

8. Céladon, a sentimental lover, is the hero of d'Urfé's *L'Astrée*, a popular novel of the previous century.

9. There is a pun in the French text. *Bois* means "pussy" as well as "woods."

10. The passage, which occurs in Voltaire's *La Pucelles*, describes how Agnès Sorel, the mistress of Charles VII, was taken captive by the English, and consoled herself in the arms of Monrose, page to an English nobleman. Valmont sees himself as Monrose, Cécile as Agnès, Danceny as the King.

11. A card game of chance.

12. Voltaire's tragedy *Zaïre* concerns the ill-fated love of the Sultan Orosmane for his captive Christian princess Zaïre. "Zaïre, are you weeping?" is a famous set-speech in the play.

13. The heroine of *Annette et Lubin*, a comic opera by Favart.

14. Tournebride refers to the quarters reserved for servants and visitors' horses.

15. Vicomte de Turenne (1611–75), Marshal of France. Frederick I (1657–1713), King of Prussia.

16. The name shared by the twin brothers in Plautus's *Menaechmi*, a comedy of mistaken identities.

17. The following is a variation on Letter 155 which Laclos alludes to in the footnote on p. 1223. It appears in the original manuscript but was not included in the editions published during the author's lifetime.

LETTER 154: *The Vicomte de Valmont to Madame de Volanges*
I know, Madame, that you do not like me at all; I am no less aware that you have always

spoken ill of me to Madame de Tourvel; and I do not doubt either that you are now more than ever confirmed in your opinions. I am even willing to admit that you may have reason to think them well-founded. Nevertheless, it is to you I write, and I have no hesitation in asking you not only to deliver to Madame de Tourvel the letter I enclose for her but also to make her promise to read it; to induce her to do so by persuading her of my repentance, of my regrets, above all, of my love. I am aware that my request may appear strange to you – I am myself astonished at it. But despair seizes its opportunities without stopping to think. Besides, the great and intimate interests we have in common override all other considerations. Madame de Tourvel is dying, Madame de Tourvel is unhappy: life, health, and happiness must be restored to her. That is the end to be attained, and any means that may ensure or hasten its attainment is good. If you reject the ones I offer, you will be responsible for the outcome: her death, your regrets, my eternal despair. It will all be your doing.

I know that I have shamefully insulted a woman worthy of all my admiration; I know that it is my fearful misdeeds alone that have caused all her miseries. I am not attempting to disguise my faults or to excuse them; but you, Madame, beware, lest you become an accomplice to them in preventing me from making my amends. I have buried a dagger in the heart of your friend; but I alone can remove the blade from the wound, I alone know how to cure it. What matter that I am guilty, if I may be useful? Save your friend! Save her! She is in need of your help, not of your vengeance.

Paris
5 December 17–

18. The following apparently unfinished letter, without date or signature, was found at the end of the original manuscript and remained unpublished until 1903, when Mercure de France's edition of the novel included it for the first time. From the content of the letter, it seems that it should be dated 15 November 17– and appear between Letters 138 and 139. One might speculate that Laclos finally omitted it because it is not in keeping with Madame de Tourvel's character and with the tone of her other letters.

The Présidente de Tourvel to the Vicomte de Valmont
Oh, my dear, how troubled I have been since the moment you left me: and how I should welcome some peace of mind! Why is it that I am overcome by an agitation so intense that it amounts almost to pain and causes me real alarm? Would you believe it? I feel that even in order to write to you I must summon all my strength and recall myself to reason. I tell myself, I repeat over and over again that you are happy. But this thought – so dear to my heart and so happily described by you as the sweet solace of love – has on the contrary thrown my feelings into a ferment, overwhelming me with too violent a happiness; while, if I try to banish it from my mind, I succumb immediately to that most cruel anguish which I have promised you so often to avoid and which I ought,

after all, to be so careful to avoid, since it affects your happiness. My dear, you have taught me to live only for you; teach me now to live without you...No, that is not what I mean; it is rather that, without you, I want not to live at all, or at least to forget my existence. Left to myself I can support neither my happiness nor my grief. I feel I must rest, yet no rest is possible. I summon sleep in vain — all sleep has fled. I can neither occupy myself nor remain idle. I am in turn devoured by raging fires and numbed by deathly chills. Every movement tires me, yet I cannot stay in one place. In short, what can I say? I should suffer less in the throes of the most violent fever; yet, without being able to explain or imagine why, I am very well aware that my suffering springs only from my powerlessness to restrain or control a profusion of feelings to whose charm, all the same, I could be quite happy to surrender my whole being.

At the precise moment when you left I felt less tormented; there was indeed some agitation mixed with my regrets, but I attributed it to impatience at the presence of my maids, who entered the room at that instant. They are always slower than I should like at the performance of their duties, and it seemed to me then that they were a thousand times slower than usual. I wanted more than anything to be alone: I had no doubt that, amid so many sweet memories, I should find in solitude the only pleasure to which your absence has left me susceptible. How could I have foreseen that though I had been strong enough in your presence to sustain the shock of so many different feelings experienced in such rapid succession, I should not when alone be able to support them in retrospect? I was very soon cruelly undeceived...Now, my dearest, I hesitate to tell you everything...However, am I not yours, entirely yours? Ought I conceal a single one of my thoughts from you? Ah, that would be quite impossible! I only claim your indulgence for faults committed unwillingly, faults in which my heart had no share. I had, as usual, dismissed my maids before going to bed...

Originally published as *Les Liaisons dangereuses* (1782).

Florville and Courval

by Marquis de Sade

Translated by Lydia Davis

Introduction

by Marcel Hénaff

Oedipus, Baroque Portrait with a Woman's Face

by Marcel Hénaff

This story is about incest, which will come as no surprise to anyone already familiar with Sade's (1740–1814) work. The issue, indeed, haunts his great libertine tales: *Justine* (1791), *Juliette's Story* (1797), *The 120 Days of Sodom* (1785). Incest is described directly in them, and amply justified by a range of arguments falling into two general categories: a totally speculative form of reasoning derived from the laws of nature (which supposedly know no prohibitions), and evidence culled from other societies (including some from our own past) to show that the violation of this prohibition is constant and totally accepted by human institutions.

Florville and Courval (1800), however, is another type of text. Sade, well aware of numerous variations throughout literary history (including the most recent one at the time, Voltaire's *Oedipus* [1718]), signals very explicitly his desire to recast Sophocles' *Oedipus Rex* by making the incestuous character of his story a victim of blind destiny (albeit in the form of a simple confluence of circumstances) that leaves her unaware of the implications of her acts, and thus unaware of her transgression.

Such an "indirect discourse" may be explained easily by the very nature of the genre chosen by the author: "Heroic and Tragic Tales" is the subtitle of *The Crimes of Love* (1800),[1] the title of the collection that contains *Florville and Courval*. Sade, who had earlier published his licentious tales anonymously, obviously hoped in this work to reach the general public, to be read and recognized by all. A tale of incest with an Oedipal character is, in this light, perfectly acceptable: institutionally, it acquires the authority of tradition. Within the story itself, incest is legitimized by the ignorance and good intentions of the character. However, in Sade's case, these justifications may seem to be compromises, implying that he could do better – be "shorter, tougher" – in openly libertine texts. Such, however, is not the case. The Oedipal situation (in the Sophoclean sense, the perspective used in this study) offers the author an even more interesting possibility: to demonstrate, *a contrario*, that nature accomplishes its designs, no matter what, and that the refusal to hear its voice does not prevent it from speaking. If the transgression takes place despite all the precautions taken to prevent it, if the crime occurs objectively and in spite of virtuous intentions, this is resounding proof that bias is futile and that good intentions are inevitably punished.

Here, Oedipus is a woman — which, certainly, is not a trivial detail. Moreover, this is Oedipus multiplied (racking up three incestuous relationships, three murders) perhaps to derision. One might even say a baroque Oedipus, if one accepts the definition of baroque as the ordered proliferation of forms, a proliferation made possible by technical mastery and the extravagances flowing from this very mastery.[2] It is as though Sade were trying to stretch to its limits the potential of a universally known figure handed down by tradition.

The figure of Oedipus long ago lost the tragic dimension with which the Greeks, explicitly or otherwise, invested it.[3] What still remains of the ancient figure? At most, two elements: first, the theme of involuntary error and the misfortune connected with it; second, the issue of the incest taboo that remains in effect in contemporary cultures. The former element has little currency in a tradition marked by the heritage of the Enlightenment, and in a moral atmosphere governed by the idea of intentionality: people are no longer held responsible for the consequences of actions completely independent of their will. The latter, by contrast, assumes extraordinary significance due to the Freudian interpretation of the Oedipal figure, which has come to be considered a fundamental structure of the psychological makeup of all human beings.

Sade's decision to rework the Oedipal epic in *Florville and Courval* is sufficiently clear from the similarities between its basic premises and those of Sophocles' text: like Oedipus, Florville is an abandoned child, raised by others, who does not know her real parents; like Oedipus, she becomes guilty of incest and murder; like him, she commits these "crimes" unknowingly and in total ignorance of her familial identity; like him, she is crushed by fate. These are the clearest similarities.

The differences are equally apparent: Oedipus is a man, Florville a woman; the Greek hero is guilty of a single murder (that of his father) and incest only with his mother, whereas Florville murders, or at least causes death, three times (her son, her mother, and herself) and is triply incestuous (with her brother, her son, and her father). While this observation explains nothing, it leads to two questions. Why did Sade choose a female hero? And why this multiplicity of crimes by Florville? One surmises that the problem raised by this text is completely different from that posed by the ancient tragedy, and that whatever it may "prove" proceeds neither with the same logic nor from the same premises as those governing Sophocles' play.

The Female Oedipus: The Voice of Nature

Sade's choice of a female character to embody the incestuous figure may seem surprising, because incest normally appears in his work as a male initiative: a father possessing his daughter, or a brother seducing his sister. Furthermore, this transgression constitutes the gesture par excellence of entry into libertinage or the supreme proof of its worth. But it must be noted that in those cases there is a deliberate wish to violate a prohibition, to flaunt the extent of one's debauchery before one's accomplices or victims.

This, indeed, is why a male hero would have been inappropriate in the present case, for the Oedipal figure implies, as its initial condition, ignorance of the transgression of which one is guilty. Sade's male heroes are always associated with will and knowledge, apparently for the following reason: All tradition (Greco-Roman as well as Christian, and from all evidence, the majority of societies) places the male on the side of culture and conventions, all that transforms the world and organizes society. It is his job to be technician, sage, legislator, and warrior. Women, by contrast, are sought and recognized (for their glory or their servitude) to incarnate the voice of nature, to be the supreme witness of its intentions. The list of myths from many traditions in which woman is identified as a specifically natural being, sometimes rebelling against society and sometimes mediating between the two extremes, is endless.

It is clear that Sade embraces this heritage and attempts to draw as much as possible from it in order to prove his point. If it is through the woman that nature "speaks," then it will fall to a female character to show that the act of incest conforms to nature's designs. The proof is perfect when the transgression takes place in spite of, or perhaps because of, attempts to avoid it (which follows the logic of the Sophoclean Oedipal model). If the woman, in spite of herself and in total ignorance of her acts, is irresistibly drawn into incest, then Nature itself has pronounced its verdict. What, for a man, is a decision made in defiance of institutions of his own making becomes, for a woman, the proof by nature of the truth and legitimacy of an impulse inscribed in the fiber of all human beings. We now understand the special role of Sade's libertine women – why it is important for men to gain this strategic alliance, and why it is women who are granted the privilege of narration.[4]

Integral Monstrosity Within the Limits of
the Oedipal Hypothesis

As for the second question – why this proliferation of perversions, albeit involuntary ones? – we can begin to develop an answer along the lines of what Pierre Klossowski calls Sade's "integral monstrosity."[5] Juliette's exploits serve to saturate the possibilities of crime, to explore all its conceivable permutations. So, too, the closed spaces where these perverse operations are executed – bedrooms, convents, and castles – provide the physical enclosures in which the "objects of debauchery" are trapped. Integral monstrosity is a function of the group, and it is distributed among several libertines; its permutations are so numerous that a single subject cannot assume all its attributes.

A very different situation occurs in the narrative where the knot of relations which can be defined as the Oedipus axiom is elaborated. Here the possibilities for perversion are numerically limited: a single subject can and must embody them all. What is lost in the diversity of situations is gained in individual intensity. The problem that Sade implicitly proposes to resolve is this: how to concentrate in a single individual, against his or her will and strictly within the framework of family relations, the greatest number of criminal qualities. Creating such a figure has two advantages. The first is of an aesthetic and logical nature (one might even call it Leibnizian): the principle according to which a phenomenon, figure, or proof approaches perfection to the degree that the number of its effects is inversely proportional to the number of causes.[6] Such is the Oedipal axiom: it forms the ideal model of incest and murder, for it allows a maximum of transgressions within a minimum number of relations. And, as with Leibniz, this "economic" principle is transformed into an aesthetic principle. The most elegant figure is always the simplest and the most saturated.

The second advantage is of a didactic nature. The conceptual model given is a practice, a program designed to execute transformations. It offers a model to be implemented – a model accessible to all persons by the very fact of their necessarily biological and social existence. Indeed, everyone in normal social situations possesses – or may at some time possess – all the requisite elements: parents, brothers, sisters, children. Everyone falling within the Oedipal axiom is able to repeat its perverse transformations. Thus, the model might be understood as both enunciative and performative, descriptive and prescriptive. This is a constant feature of the Sadian framework, as described by Roland Barthes.[7]

Let us then ask this combinatorial question: Given a family containing the minimum number of terms representing the two sexes over two generations – father/mother and son/daughter – what happens if we link one (and only one) of these terms to the others in all possible incestuous combinations? Or, rather, what are the possible combinations for one of the terms with a point of reference? In Sade's text, this term is the character around which the story is organized: the axiomatic system characterizing the Oedipal model (still in the Sophoclean sense) is tied to the logic of the narrative. For Florville these combinations are relations with her brother and relations with her father. That her sexual relationship with her son arises from relations with her brother is the specifically baroque element, the unexpected excess that saturates the overflowing, perverse combination.

The coherence of Sade's position, however, must be noted: baroque excess is always an ordered excess. Whereas Sade constantly attempts to exhaust as thoroughly as possible the catalogue of "passions" and crimes, in what one might call his encyclopedia of excess, all transgression concentrates on a character who is the focal point. Thus, there is no room for mother-son incest in the case of Senneval/Desbarres, which would add nothing to the case centered on Florville. This would require another story, particularly since – given that Senneval and his mother know each other – it would destroy the plausibility of the present narrative by shattering the innocence/ignorance characteristic of the Oedipal hero. Furthermore, any transgression involving non-heterosexual relations would also be inconceivable by Oedipal logic, for this assumes a deliberate will to perversion (such as father-son sodomy), whereas here the intent is necessarily virtuous.

Sade's "proof" is thus remarkably rigorous and coherent, given his premises: any unnecessary touch that might seem to render the character and the group even more perverted would inevitably undermine the strength (and the brutality) of the demonstration, thereby negating the Oedipal axiom and, along with it, the specific monstrosity of familial entrapment it implies. The series of murders leaves the father and son alone, as though, in reality – and this is a given of Sade's thought – they remained the sole conquerors of the family they destroyed. The son opens the series of incestuous relations completed by the father, and these serial incests set off a chain of murders whose purpose is ultimately to erase them.

The Theme of Incest

In the various types of incest stories – whether myth or tale from an oral tradition, or a literary text from a written tradition – at least three main themes intermingle. The first has to do with *filiation*, the necessity for an order of succession in time. The issue here is mother-son incest: Can the son return to the mother? Can what follows return to what precedes? The second theme deals with *alliance*, and the question is one of reciprocity: the obligation of every group of blood relatives to move outside of itself and acknowledge, by the exchange of wives, a higher unit, that of the social group as such. This issue, exogamy, concerns the taboo covering father-daughter or brother-sister incest. A third and final theme, interwoven with the two preceding ones, is defined by the question of the *same* and the *other*, or, rather, the doubling of that which is the same and the exclusion of the other. The circle of incest appears here as a metaphor of a world closed off from time and the outside, a dream world of protected space, sheltered from death and outsiders, whose characters are torn between mystical sacrifice, delirious love, and deathly claustration – as can be seen in Sade's other great work of incestuous delirium, "Eugénie de Franval," and as will be searingly depicted in romantic literature's preferred scenario of love between brother and sister.

Let us return to each of these themes, for they demonstrate the main anthropological implications of *Florville and Courval*.

Sophocles focuses on the theme of *lineage*. Jean-Pierre Vernant has analyzed its salient aspects in his incisive study, "The Lame Tyrant: From Oedipus to Periander." He writes that:

> The story of Oedipus concerns his return to his place of origin, his reintegration into the lineage in which he is both a legitimate son and an accursed child. This return takes place, in the manner of a boomerang, not at the right time, in the correct conditions of a rightful succession that respects the regular order of the generations, but in all the violence of over-identification: Oedipus does not come duly in his turn to take the place that his father has vacated and left to him; instead, he takes that place through parricide and maternal incest. He goes back too far and now finds himself, as a husband, in the belly that nurtured him as a son, and from which he should never have emerged.[8]

Vernant goes on to show how this disturbance, this disordering of the line of succession, this turning back too far and the usurpation of roles that follows, are issues that cut through a whole set of other elements.

There is, first of all, the theme of normal movement versus lameness. Oedipus, the rejected son, becomes the equivalent of a bastard: departing from the normal line of succession, he is sidetracked, and logically enough, in the myth, becomes lame. He who walks crookedly is never in his rightful place; it follows that he will occupy a wrongful one, that everything in his destiny is off course. However, another more interesting element is implied by his lameness, as Vernant explains: the movements of a lame person whose defect is uncorrected are circular. He tends to return to his point of departure, to move in circles (as does Hephaestus in his workshop, according to Homer).

Thus, one can see the association in Sophocles' text between the themes of bastardy and a movement that is both twisted and backward. Oedipus is the man who retraces his steps, who tries to solve the riddle of existence by going back in time – only to find that he himself is the puzzle. He is the one who returns to the place of his birth, his mother's womb. In the Sphinx's riddle – What is the creature that has a voice and walks on four feet, then two, then three? – he recognizes man at different ages, but he does not realize that he himself is following the same course in reverse, returning to his place of birth. He is mixing together things that should remain separate: the ages of life and the succession of generations (the son after the father and the mother). Thus, *time* is disrupted by this symbolic lameness. Though not by explicit intent, Oedipus grants himself a privilege beyond human bounds (either like that of animals, which are unaware of differences, or like that of the gods, who remain the masters of metamorphoses and inversions). The tragedy gestures toward a wisdom that consists of man recognizing his just place and abandoning any pretense of disturbing an order of things that lies beyond his power.

Among the other notable elements revealed by Vernant's study is his demonstration that the issue of incest is not at all the obsessive desire posited by Freud but, rather, the expression of a disruption of roles and an inversion of generations.[9]

This first aspect of the Oedipal theme is an absolutely essential element of Sade's work, but – and this is peculiar to his work – involves as well the logic of rejection of time. The return to origins represented by the union of Oedipus and his mother is his flawed answer to the question "Where do I come from?" He solves the riddle, but his answer is excessive. Florville, on the other hand, plays no such mediating role: her only point in common with Oedipus, in this regard, is that she too is a foundling. Her return to her father is first of all a return to a name, but here too the solution is excessive: she takes the name she might recover as Courval's daughter by becoming his wife. In this way, the disruption of time as well as of lineage addresses the question of marriage in perhaps an even more essential way.

This presents the other fundamental aspect of the incest taboo, as revealed by anthropological research, especially that of Claude Lévi-Strauss. In *The Elementary Structures of Kinship*, Lévi-Strauss states that the prohibition of incest remains puzzling until one realizes that its raison d'être is neither biological (although biological implications exist as a result of this prohibition in human societies) nor moral (although ethical rules are attached to this taboo).[10] To demonstrate his point, he begins with a methodological principle: every social rule has its raison d'être within the culture. What, then, are the assumptions and stipulations concerning the incest taboo? First, that fathers must not possess their daughters, nor brothers take their sisters. The unit of blood relations is obliged not to close in upon itself. By exchanging wives with other groups (in ways that vary but that always follow rules), each group recognizes that a specifically social order transcends the biological order. This exchange is exogamous marriage.

We must, then, ask why this type of exchange enables mutual recognition. To understand this, Lévi-Strauss explains, one must consider the marriage tie in the context of the general phenomenon of gift-exchange relationships, which are to be found in all societies and that Marcel Mauss was no doubt the first to clarify in his famous essay, *The Gift*.[11] Mauss explains that two groups recognize each other by exchanging gifts, establishing alliances. That which is given becomes the expression and proof of this gesture, and it retains this value by virtue of that fact. Its significance is not economic but symbolic: one gives the other something that comes from oneself, one receives as one's own something that comes from the other. The things exchanged may well be alike, but this is of no importance, for what is produced is the act of recognition itself. Hence, the act of giving implies the obligation to receive and to return something.

This is where the matrimonial exchange comes into play: the woman through whom the biological continuity of the group passes becomes the sign and gauge of this acknowledgment. She is the guarantor that what is most particular to each group (its "blood," its lineage) will be received by the other. Exogamous exchange is the ultimate form of the reciprocal gift-giving relationship; such is the positive content and the very meaning of the incest taboo. (The pertinence of this hypothesis is confirmed by the preferred marriage of cross-cousins and the prohibition of marriage between parallel cousins.[12])

We can summarize these anthropological observations concerning the issue of incest in the following manner: First, the prohibition of incest is a social rule based on the necessity for reciprocity. Second, what is forbidden is simply the negative aspect of a positive counter-part: for every union forbidden with a woman of the group to which one belongs there is a promised union with a woman from another group. "Like exogamy, which is its widened social application, the prohibition of incest is a rule of reciprocity. The woman whom one does not take, and whom one may not take, is, for that very reason, offered up.... The content of the prohibition is not exhausted by the fact of the prohibition: the latter is instituted only in order to guarantee and establish, directly or indirectly, an exchange."[13] Third, the incest taboo exists precisely where nature and culture intersect; nature assumes that the union of the two sexes is necessary for the biological perpetuation of the group; it does not, however, dictate who shall procreate with whom. That decision, which is made by society, marks the emergence of culture in the domain of nature, the imprint of human intervention in a process otherwise derived from the laws of living creatures (in this case the higher mammals). In other words, the taboo makes a social rule of something that is simply a biological necessity, while keeping this necessity intact and even integrating it into its process. The taboo joins one order to the other without identifying with either; its function is to pass between the two.

When we compare these conclusions with Sade's incest themes, we see that his work shows a remarkable, intuitive grasp of the levels implicit in this prohibition: what manifests itself in these stories is, indeed, the refusal to forge links, the refusal to step out of the self and recognize the otherness of the other. The libertine credo might be formulated thus: We do not exchange, we do not give, we take, starting with the very thing we would need to give up in order to allow others to be partners, fellow humans, equals. Libertine endogamy – if one may speak of endogamy when there is neither conjugal union nor procreation – is, above all, a system of negating reciprocity.

This refusal is formulated in the principle of immediate gratification. When anthropologists tell us that the sexual instinct is the only one whose satisfaction can be postponed, allowing the incest taboo to transform the stimulus into the sign, thus passing from nature to culture,[14] they are saying that this prohibition is a way of learning mediation and therefore mastering time. Mandatory exogamy distances the woman in time and space, forcing the man to seek her, to wait, and to deal with others. This is precisely what libertine logic rejects most vehemently. This rejection, moreover, negates the precise thing that the taboo makes possible – overcoming the natural order. The libertine thus subverts for his own use the philosophical appeal (so widespread during the Enlightenment) to heed the voice of nature, understood to be the voice of truth, by declaring that the best way to remain faithful to nature is to reject all institutions, above all the one that seems the surest indicator of our separateness from the animal world. Sade, by making the violation of this taboo the act of initiation into the libertine world, shows that the universe of rules is thereby defeated, the system of differences that constitutes culture is ripped to shreds; and that, in theory, nothing can stop the libertine in his rejection of laws and his criminal fury. The circle of incest defines the exclusive status of this select, fiercely endogamous group, a sort of aristocracy of evil bent upon the most egregious wasting of goods and bodies.

There remains a third element in the theme of incest, the dialectic of the *same* and the *other*. As already mentioned, it is interwoven with the two preceding elements. Indeed, what the incest taboo implies is the need to recognize the other group and, more generally, the necessity of going outside the self. Thus, there is an outward movement that, in lineage, corresponds to the acceptance of temporal succession and, in marital bonds, is expressed by reaching out toward those beyond one's group. Just as one cannot return to the mother's womb (the Oedipal theme) one cannot remain among one's own (namely, father-daughter, brother-sister). There are laws for succeeding generations and laws for those who are beyond one's group – laws about time, laws about the outside world. Myths tell us that no one who disturbs the order of things is spared the anger of the gods and the requirement to expiate this disruption. Later tales update this message by transposing it onto the world of emotions and new social relations.

In many stories the theme of the incest taboo is identified with the need to differentiate positions, organize roles, assign appropriate places, maintain necessary distance, guarantee the obligation to give and to reciprocate gifts. The point is not – or not essentially – moral: "incest," writes Lévi-Strauss, "is socially absurd before it is morally culpable."[15] Rather, as seen in many myths, the purpose of the incest taboo is to establish an order, a very difficult task most often left to the demiurge. Such a necessity is constantly recalled and symbolized in many ways, the incest taboo being one element of this ordering. This is why its transgression is not chiefly a sexual question (as a specifically modern view tends to hold) but, rather, one that touches on the whole framework of social relations and forms of representation of the world. Thus, refusing to share food or eating alone is considered a sort of "social incest,"[16] or the doubling of a like element (adding a hot thing to something hot, a wet thing to something wet, a dry thing to something dry, and so on[17]) may be perceived as deriving from the logic of incest, that is, of an improper mixing of like things leading to confusion (as is the case in many cultures with respect to twins).

It is all the more remarkable, then, to note that this is precisely what Sade addresses. The accumulation and intermingling of elements that are supposed to be distinct offers him the pure pleasure of blurring roles and breaking rules, in short, of bringing together what should remain separate. Incest, from this point of view, is a highly effective tool which allows one to be the father of one's lover, or the lover of one's sister, husband of one's brother, lover of one's mother. No text says it better than this passage from *The 120 Days of Sodom*, which brings maximum complexity to the baroque knot: "I say, that he once knew a man who fucked three children he had by his mother, amongst whom there was a daughter whom he had marry his son, so that in fucking her, he fucked his sister, his daughter, and his daughter-in-law, and thus he also constrained his son to fuck his own sister and mother-in-law."[18] The pleasure here lies entirely in the accumulation in one individual of names of relatives meant for different people, which amounts to a disruption of time by the scrambling of generations, and to a dislocation of the social order as well by a perverse permutation of roles. When Dolmancé, in *Philosophy in the Bedroom* (1795), praises incest in front of Eugénie, he gives the same kind of example: "One of my friends has the habit of living with the girl he had by his own mother; not a week ago he deflowered a thirteen-year-old boy, fruit of his commerce with that girl; in a few years' time, the same lad will wed his mother."[19]

Premonition, Voice, Crime

The Oedipal character must know and not know; he must flee his destiny and, by so doing, run headlong into it at the same time. How can this ambivalence be depicted? How can the oracle be heard within the eighteenth century's narrative forms? Sade solves the problem with an internal voice that, in the form of a premonition during each of the encounters that turn out to be incestuous, warns Florville of a threat. Thus:

> I felt drawn to him [Senneval] by an ungovernable emotion. And when I then tried to account for this attraction, I found nothing there but obscurity. It seemed that this inclination was the effect of no ordinary feeling; a veil hid its nature from my eyes... (p. 1282).

> Whether it was a premonition, or whether it was something else, Monsieur, when I saw this young man [Saint Ange] I was overcome by a fit of shivering whose cause I found impossible to guess. I nearly fainted (p. 1291).

Then, shortly after their wedding, she admits to Courval: "A secret voice cries out in my innermost heart that all this felicity is, for me, only a shadow... (p. 1308).

These observations operate on several levels. They reaffirm the reader's presumed morality and horror of transgression by offering characters who hear, in a Rousseauian way, the voice of their conscience, and who are warned by nature itself of the situation's aberrant character. Yet these remarks are ambiguous as well: they seem to indicate fascination as well as fear. Thus, the author shows a character *throwing* herself into her ruin – particularly since she makes the first two of these comments to Courval just before their marriage. Florville's recounting of the story thus has an obscuring function: it conveys some meaning that it cannot specify or recognize. The voice of seduction clothes the voice of denial, just as the story itself embodies what the conscience alone cannot admit. It is, indeed, the telling of the story itself that sets up the incestuous relationship with the father, making it the inevitable culmination of those stories which have already been unknowingly told. In the narrative itself, the blindnesses of father and daughter are joined.

The Excluded Mother

At the end of the story, father and son are the sole survivors of this "tragedy." All the women are gone, and the mother was first among them. This is no accident; rather, it is part of the Oedipal logic as it is applied to the character of Florville. For her, the mother is in fact a rival who bars access to the father. The unwitting but effective "death sentence" that Florville imposes on her corresponds to the one with which she herself threatened her daughter, whose life was saved at birth only by the intervention of her nurse. This is a reiteration, then, of the image of the bad mother, who is murderous, and castrating –an obsessive fantasy that, according to Pierre Klossowski, occurs throughout Sade's work as well as his life: "The principal events of his life seem to have singularly favored the more rare and generally less manifest complex of hatred of the mother. Traces of this are easily recognized at every moment in his work; we can even consider it the constant theme of Sadean ideology."[20] This negative Oedipus complex underlies the desire to castrate the mother and to strike out at her as the incarnation of familial mores. The father, by contrast, is assigned the tasks of destroying his own family (for example, Bressac in *Justine*) and, above all, of eliminating the virtuous, moralistic mother. "For Sade," writes Klossowski, "the mother holds the castrating role which in the Oedipus complex belongs to the father. She is the son's rival for the father (on the homosexual plane) as much as she is his rival for her daughter."[21] This may be so, though it is perhaps an effect rather than a cause.

Indeed, in Sade, the exclusion of the mother is defined primarily in the context of a libertine strategy. It is she who instills in girls a respect for moral and religious rules (whereas boys are immediately taken charge of and trained by fathers who are themselves, presumably, libertines). The girls must therefore be removed from their mothers so that they may enter into the world of men, thereby rendering them accessible to men, or – for it amounts to the same thing – making them their willing partners. The best example of the liberation of a daughter by elimination of a mother is found in *Philosophy in the Bedroom*. The young Eugénie, after having been initiated by the wily aristocrat Mme de Saint-Ange with the help of the libertine philosopher Dolmancé and having been deflowered by her brother, is encouraged, as the crowning touch of her training, to insult and abuse her mother, who is guilty of having kept her ignorant of her rights and pleasures. One finds a similar attitude in another story of incest in *The Crimes of Love* entitled "Eugénie de Franval," wherein the mother is the constant victim of humiliations and tortures by the father and daughter, partners in incest who finally poison her. In Sade, the mother reins in the daughter, shuts her up in the world of convention, and makes her hostile to men. For the girl, then, entering into libertinage is a way out of the mother's space, the negation and destruction of values incarnated by the mother. This escape makes her an adventurer, a nomadic, wandering figure – a libertine, in other words. She moves in the already-established, perverted world of men: what they already are, she is to become. And precisely because she is open to the improbable, to adventure, she accedes to the privilege of narration.

Florville and Justine, the Difference: Last Name, First Name

Florville seems to be Justine's literary sister, a summary version of her. With Florville the "misfortunes of virtue" seem to be repeated. In both cases, we have the model of heroine as victim, the stubborn defender of good who is rewarded by destiny (a kind of negative Providence) with only troubles and outrages against her virtue. However, compared with Justine, Florville endures a very limited number of misfortunes: indeed, while Justine's misfortunes are (in theory) endless, depending solely on the narrator to prolong them as much as he wants, Florville's are (of necessity) limited in number. The reason is that Florville, imprisoned in the Oedipal model, has at her disposal only a finite number of combinations. This necessity likewise determines an entire dimension of the story's organization, for it eliminates all events that are superfluous by dint of not meeting the demonstration's requirements, that is, the requirements of the character's logic.

What, then, is the source of the considerable difference between Justine and Florville? One might say that it is the gap between last name and first name. Indeed, Justine has no last name, whereas Florville has no first name. Justine is thereby placed outside the Oedipal system, and incest is the only misfortune she escapes: she is without relatives. Florville, by contrast, exists entirely within the Oedipal system, and thus is caught in the logic of incest: she is entirely trapped in the network of family relations.

Free of all logical closure, the first name can roam: Justine is its nomadic face. The first name designates a subject capable of receiving a virtually infinite number of characteristics of crime and perversion (passively and unhappily, as in the case of Justine, or actively and joyfully, as in the case of Juliette).

The last name, limited by the logic of a single system, is subject to very particular types of peregrinations – traveling with the family, traveling within the family. Wherever Florville goes, she inevitably encounters her brother, her son, her mother, her father. The last name designates a subject that receives no new attributes; rather, this subject (in the conditions of the present narrative), simply destroys all the attributes which already constitute it as a name. The last name springs from an analytic proposition, not from a synthetic one. Justine is the encyclopedia of misfortune (and any lexicon is potentially unlimited). Florville is its logical scale model; as such, she is restricted and susceptible to saturation.

The Dual Narrative Movement:
Florville's Tale, Senneval's Tale

Telling a story is not, of course, simply recounting the tale. After all, questions of who is speaking, to whom, and, under what circumstances, are fundamental. These questions, which are obvious in oral literature, are no less essential in written literature, particularly when a narrative depicts another narrative. A famous case in which the narrative as such plays an essential role is the *Thousand and One Nights*, in which each tale corresponds to a new reprieve for Scheherazade, whose life is at stake. All narrative constitutes a particular pact between narrator and narratee, an agreement bearing specific, though perhaps implicit, commitments. Whatever the author's intent, it is the text that constitutes the offer of a narrative and shows us how it is fulfilled.

Here, however, this offer is insistently formulated by Florville as if by this narrative she – who has neither name nor fortune – were handing over her dowry, as if to say, "Here I am, rich with all the attributes of debauchery, and the incalculable added value of experience, here I am, draped in the jewels of sin, the knowledge of evil." It is as if this were what the man who desires her really wanted, despite all his protestations of expecting nothing and despite her claim to speak in the name of sincere confession and regret over her unwitting sins. Sade is marvelously adept at conveying the two voices of this narrative, one that proclaims its good intentions and one that seems to revel in its scabrous tale. The first-person narrative is embedded in the narrator's third-person narrative; the character must speak directly and become the author of her life in order to offer herself to her own father, handing over some sort of incestuous dowry.

Offsetting Florville's narrative is another one, just as brutal in its effects – that of Senneval, son of Courval and brother of Florville. In the text, the son's return takes the form of a confession and repentance: his gesture is explicitly formulated as that of the "prodigal son" returning to make amends with his father after having left home twenty years earlier with his unworthy mother and having stayed away ever since.

His return is therefore portrayed as a handsome gesture, yet it all transpires as if his repentance were an ultimate act of revenge. In confessing his sins, Senneval produces the narrative that illuminates the entire situation. His story, indeed, is largely the same as Florville's: he recasts it, turns it over, point by point, showing Florville her life inside out, telling her who she is, making her admit that the young man speaking is her brother, that he was her lover and Saint-Ange her son – their son. It is by this tale, then, that Florville becomes truly incestuous and murderous: daughter of one, sister of another, mother of the third. Before, her innocence was guaranteed by her ignorance; the narrative, though, reveals the real names beneath the borrowed ones, reconnecting the blood relations heretofore broken and reestablishing as relatives those who were thought to be strangers. With the revelation that as son, father, and daughter/sister, Senneval, Courval, and Florville all have the same name, the triple incest becomes clear. It remains only for Florville to add a third murder – her own – to the two she has already caused, albeit involuntarily.

Senneval's telling of his story brings about a kind of revenge, for it ends up destroying his father's happiness, as if the son were challenging the appropriation of the sister/lover, punishing her not only for her infidelity but also for the fate of the mother and of Saint-Ange, and, finally, contesting her right to her fortune. Since this is not some character's idea but an objective effect of the story, we can say that this story is a return of the repressed – not of Senneval's desire (about which we know nothing) but of the unknown elements of his tale, which constitute objective reality, revealed at last. This corresponds to the figure of destiny according to Hegel's formulation: awareness of the self, but as an enemy.[22]

In fact, Sade repeats, by means of this double interplay of narrative, the relationship between the two elements that define tragedy, according to Aristotle, namely, *peripeteia* (sudden change of fortune) and *awareness*.[23] As in Sophocles' play, everything has already occurred at the outset, but no one knows this; everything, then, remains to be said. It is the search, the sequence of questions and responses, that turns back time and reveals what is happening, according to the warning Tiresias gives to the hero: "Time who sees all has found you out against your will."[24] The tragic character realizes that what he had attributed to another in fact refers to him; the narrative sets up and effects this awareness at the point where everything is falling apart, the *peripeteia*. The narrative of innocent-seeming things from the past is knotted into an event that joins the past to the present and transforms this past into a series of horrors. The circle is complete: trying to seal off time, the Oedipal hero becomes trapped in it, leaving only one way out: escape outside of time, by exile, death, or some other rupture.

Florville's suicide illustrates the dead end of family relations turned in on themselves, whose permutations inevitably lead to incest and murder. Unlike Justine, Florville is not killed by lighting (representing an extreme form of Providence's contempt), for, according to this logic of closure, punishment can only be internal: she supplies her own lightning in the form of a gunshot.

Baroque Tragedy

To the opening remark of this essay, that the plot of this story is purely baroque, should be added the observation that Sade's entire oeuvre belongs to the extreme outside fringe of the baroque. There is in the baroque manner – in its style, in the pleasure it seeks to elicit – a euphoria linked to the mastery of method. In painting, for example, techniques of color and perspective resolved all the traditional problems. In the literary domain (obvious in France because of the stabilization of the language), this mastery was perfectly regulated by the elaboration of rhetorical and stylistic rules. From this viewpoint, for an author to "write well" was almost a banal accomplishment: everyone knew the art of composing a classical sentence, constructing a plot, calculating effects. The qualities of craftsmanship were common knowledge and the criteria well known. Such was classicism. The baroque strained the upper limits of this edifice of consecrated technique: it was a classicism that overflowed, pushed its effects to the point of abuse, repeated, multiplied, swelled, and perverted them. What had kept classicism within its limits was an ethos dictating that forms be subject to the service of a goal defined by requirements both political and religious. As soon as this goal moved out of sight or was challenged, though, something was released, but no new content was supplied. A manipulation of forms followed that became purely playful and gratuitous, an explosion of potentialities that one might call the aristocratic moment of decadence. This is precisely what happened in France starting with the Regency, setting the distinctive tone of the eighteenth century – and paradoxically, too, since at the same moment a critique of this society was being elaborated and the "naturalist" ideal of an egalitarian world was forming. A lone autodidact named Rousseau, "citizen of Geneva," in revolt against courtly manners (more from ignorance than virtue) was to make this naturalist ideal that of the revolutionary period and even a major portion of the following century.

Sade's scandalous oeuvre can be understood only in the wake of this baroque overflow; it can be interpreted only as an attempt to express this excess in content at the very time when forms had become stabilized. He was going beyond the framework of classical writing and narration. With his exaggerated moral questioning, his radicalization of *libertinage*, and his search for an infinite combinatorial mechanism for the possibilities of perversion, Sade was edging toward something outside, another universe. In terms of form, this is all there is to it. And this is what makes Sade so light, so playful, and, finally, so much funnier than one would have thought. Now, it cannot be denied that the content is scandalous and monstrous; reading Sade is intolerable if one takes it literally. Yet the question remains: Why is it that, in this case, baroque excess involves violence and sex? The answer is, perhaps, that Sade is, first of all, a symptom of a period when public life had neither purpose nor reason. His work is the indicator of a crisis to which it gives voice and form: it is a demand and a proof of exasperation. This is what makes this baroque so special, what makes it specifically a tragic baroque – not tragic as a genre (comic, lyric, or otherwise) but tragic in the general sense of the experience of unhappiness and the painful inability to understand its reasons or foresee its end.[25] Ending was a time of laughter and lightheartedness: ten centuries of aristocratic elegance, an inimitable art of living based on excellence in manners and taste. The demand for equality foreshadowed the discontent of the mob and the leveling force of the masses. Sade's violence is at the crossroads of these two worlds and these two periods, a secret and sometimes extreme exercise of ancestral privileges set against the as-yet unformed equalizing power of the masses.

The formation of the incestuous circle was, from an aristocratic viewpoint, one last attempt to remain within the group, away from the others who were crowding in from all sides, demanding entrance into a world they always envied and from which they were always barred.

NOTES

1. Sade (1740–1814) published *The Crimes of Love* in 1800. He had just had ten years of freedom after spending close to fifteen years in various prisons, the last of which had been the Bastille. From there, he was transferred to the convent at Charenton on July 4, 1789, the day on which the crowd, encouraged by Sade from his window, was preparing to attack the building. He was definitively released in April 1790. In the next ten years he published, anonymously, his great libertine stories (many of which were written during the period of imprisonment), such as *Justine, or Good Conduct Well Chastised* (1791) and *The New Justine* (1797), as well as (in his own name, with the "de" dropped) other, tamer stories such as "Aline and Valcour" (1793), and numerous plays, such as *Count Oxtiern* (1791). Sade participated actively in the Revolution (to which he owed his release from prison) as a member of a neighborhood tribunal. When he published *The Crimes of Love* he hoped, apparently, to win over as wide an audience as possible without giving up libertine themes. A well-informed critic by the name of Villeterque denounced him as the author of licentious novels. Sade denied this fervently, well aware of the risks he was running during the return to a moral order linked with the Consulat. His fears were particularly well founded: the authorities imprisoned him the following year in various hospitals, the last of which was Charenton. There he was allowed relative freedom, and it was there that he wrote his last novels – *Adélaïde de Brunswick* (unpublished), *Isabelle de Bavière* (1953), and *La Marquise de Gange* (1813) – and where he died in 1814.

The edition of *The Crimes of Love* used here is based on the text in Folio Gallimard

(Paris, 1987), with preface and notes by Michel Delon, who correctly stresses the influence of the English Gothic novel.

2. Jorge Luis Borges defined the baroque as the "style which deliberately exhausts (or attempts to exhaust) all its possibilities and which borders on its own parody...the final stage of all styles is baroque when that style only too obviously exhibits or overdoes its own tricks," *A Universal History of Infamy*, trans. Norman Thomas di Giovanni (New York: E.P. Dutton, 1972), p. 11.

3. Jean-Pierre Vernant and Pierre Vidal-Naquet, *Myth and Tragedy in Ancient Greece* (New York: Zone Books, 1988).

4. See my chapter on this point "La Femme, la prostitution, le récit" in *Sade: L'Invention du corps libertin* (Paris: Presses Universitaires de France, 1978).

5. Pierre Klossowski, "The Philosopher-Villain," in *Sade My Neighbor*, trans. Alphonso Lingis (London: Quartet Books, 1992), p. 28.

6. See Gottfried Wilhelm Leibniz, "Discourse on Metaphysics, No. 16," in trans. and eds. R.N.D. Martin and Stuart Brown, *Discourse on Metaphysics and Related Writing* (New York: Manchester University Press, 1988).

7. Roland Barthes, *Sade, Fourrier, Loyola* (Berkeley: University of California Press, 1989).

8. Jean-Pierre Vernant, "The Lame Tyrant: From Oedipus to Periander," in *Myth and Tragedy*, ch. 10, p. 213.

9. Vernant, in another article in *Myth and Tragedy*, "Oedipus Without the Complexes" (ch. 4) shows, point by point and very precisely, the arbitrary character of psycho-analytical interpretations of Sophocles' play, revealing the contradictions of each hypothesis. However, the fact that the interpretation imposed by Freud and his followers has practically nothing to do with the Greek play (and they ought to admit it once and for all) does not mean that they have no right to use Oedipus as the emblem of a problem that they have recognized and defined in an original manner. Nor does it in any way reduce the importance of analyzing relationships of identification called "Oedipal," involving parent-child relationships in modern societies, which are characterized by a certain type of monogamous conjugal family. Here again, however, one must proceed prudently, for if one must specify "a certain type of family" it is because anthropology has amply demonstrated that monogamous marriages have existed and still exist in the most diverse societies as well as in ancient times. Thus, this is not specifically the result of an evolution linked to modern times, even if this period has privileged this solution. All of this implies that, in other situations of monogamous conjugal families, parent-child relationships do not necessarily take the Oedipal form. Concerning this latter question, consult the excellent work of M.C. and Edmond Ortigues, *African Oedipus* (Paris: Plon, 1966).

10. Claude Lévi-Strauss, *The Elementary Structures of Kinship*, trans. James Harle Bell and John Richard von Sturmer (Boston: Beacon Press, 1969).

11. Marcel Mauss, *The Gift: The Form and Reason for Exchange in Archaic Societies*, trans. W.D. Halls (New York: Routledge, 1989).

12. Cross-cousins are the offspring of a father's sister or a mother's brother (hence offspring of first cousins of the opposite sex) and parallel cousins are the offspring of the mother's sister or the father's brother (hence offspring of first cousins of the same sex). The former, in almost all known traditional civilizations, are destined to a prescribed or at least preferred marriage, whereas the latter, considered to be brothers and sisters, are rigorously forbidden to marry. Nevertheless, the biological proximity is the same – so why this difference? It is not hard to understand that, whatever type of lineage (matrilinear or patrilinear) may be involved, the former cases belong to different lineages: for example, the children of a mother's brother or a father's sister are from a different clan. Thus, the former case belongs to two exogamous halves: reciprocity is possible between them, for the latter belong to the same half and cannot function in a situation of exchange – hence they fall under the incest taboo (see Lévi-Strauss, *ibid.*, ch. 9, "The Marriage of Cousins"). The theory of reciprocity thus proves pertinent. Ill-informed commentators sometimes believe they detect incest in medieval texts or in popular tales, when in fact the prescribed marriage of cross-cousins is involved. This situation often underlies more recent texts. From this point of view, many interpretations of the literature of incest need to be revised.

13. *Ibid.*, p. 51.

14. *Ibid.*, p. 12.

15. *Ibid.*, p. 485.

16. *Ibid.*, p. 58.

17. Françoise Héritier, "La Symbolique de l'inceste et sa prohibition," in Michel Izard and Pierre Smith, eds., *Between Belief and Transgression: Structuralist Essays in Religion, History, and Myth*, trans. John Leavitt (Chicago: University of Chicago Press, 1982).

18. Sade, *The 120 Days of Sodom and Other Writings*, trans. Richard Seaver and Austryn Wainhouse (New York: Groves Press, 1966), p. 576.

19. Sade, *The Complete Justine: Philosophy in the Bedroom and Other Writings*, trans. Richard Seaver and Austryn Wainhouse (New York: Grove Press, 1965), p. 237.

20. Klossowski, "The Father and Mother in Sade's Work," in *Sade My Neighbor*, p. 127ff.

21. *Ibid.*, p. 134.

22. Hegel, *On Christianity: Early Theological Writings* (New York: Harper, 1948).

23. Aristotle, *Poetics*, 52.59.

24. Sophocles, *Oedipus the King*, in *The Complete Greek Tragedies: Volume II: Sophocles* (Chicago: University of Chicago Press, 1957), p. 65, lines 1213-14.

25. Here it must be pointed out that there is a large number of excellent works on the baroque, the classics being Heinrich Wölfflin, *Renaissance and Baroque* (Ithaca: Cornell University Press, 1966), and Henri Focillon, *The Life of Forms in Art* (New York: Zone Books, 1989).

Translated by Shelley Temchin.

FLORVILLE AND COURVAL

or The Decrees of Destiny

by Sade

M. DE COURVAL had just turned fifty-five; alert, in good health, he could look forward to another twenty years. He had known nothing but difficulty with his first wife, who had left him long ago to devote herself to the libertine life. The clearest of evidence had led him to believe that this creature was in her grave by now, and so he thought to ally himself a second time with some reasonable person who, through the goodness of her character and the excellence of her morals, would lead him to forget his earlier misfortunes.

M. de Courval was as unlucky with his children as he was with his wife. He had had only two: a girl, whom he had lost very young, and a boy, who at the age of fifteen had left him just like his wife and, unfortunately, with the same aim of debauchery in mind. M. de Courval believed that no legal bonds should ever chain him to this monster and thus planned to disinherit him and bequeath his possessions to the children he hoped to have with the new wife he so desired to take. He had an income of fifteen thousand livres. He had formerly been employed in business, and this income was the fruit of his labors. Being the decent gentleman he was, M. de Courval enjoyed these fruits with a few friends who all cherished and esteemed him. They sometimes saw him in Paris, where he maintained a pretty apartment on the Rue Saint Marc. More often still, they would visit his charming little estate near Nemours, where M. de Courval spent two-thirds of the year.

This gentleman confided his plan to his friends and, seeing that they approved, asked them with great earnestness to inquire among their acquaintances for a woman thirty to thirty-five years old, widow or unmarried, who might answer to his purpose.

Only two days later, one of his former colleagues came to tell him he thought he had found precisely what he required.

"The young lady I have in mind," this friend said, "has two marks against her. I must begin by telling you about them, so that I'll then be able to comfort you with a recital of her good qualities. It is quite certain she has neither father nor mother, but no one has the least idea who they were, or where she lost them. What is known," continued the intermediary, "is that she is a cousin of Monsieur de Saint-Prât, a man of considerable reputation, who acknowledges her, esteems her, and will sing you her praises in the least suspect and most deserved way. She is without inheritance from her parents, but she has an allowance of four thousand francs from this Monsieur de Saint-Prât, in whose house she was raised and spent the whole of her childhood. There's the first fault," said M. de Courval's friend. "Let us move on to the second. An affair at the age of sixteen, a child who no longer exists and whose father she has never seen again. This is all of the bad. Now, a word about the good.

"Though Mademoiselle de Florville is thirty-six years old, she scarcely appears to be twenty-eight. A more pleasant or interesting face would be hard to find; her features are gentle and delicate, her skin as white as a lily, and her chestnut hair falls all the way down to the ground; her perfect mouth, very agreeably embellished, is the image of a rose in spring. She is quite tall, but has such a pretty figure, with such grace in her motions, that one can't object to her height, which otherwise might make her appear somewhat severe. Her arms, her neck, her legs – everything is well shaped, and she has the type of beauty that will not age for a long time to come. As for her conduct, the extreme regularity of her days will perhaps not please you. She is not fond of society; she lives very much in seclusion. She is very devout, very committed to her duties at the convent where she lives, and, just as she edifies everyone around her with her piety, so she enchants all who see her with her charming mind and her attractive character.... In short, she's an angel here on earth, whom Heaven was keeping for the happiness of your old age."

M. de Courval, delighted by this prospect, was quick to urge his friend to arrange for a meeting with the woman in question. "Her birth doesn't worry me at all," he said. "As long as her blood is pure, what does it matter who transmitted it to her? Her intrigue at the age of sixteen troubles me just as little; she has made up for that mistake with many years of discretion. I will marry her as a widow. Since I decided to marry only a woman thirty to thirty-five years old, how could I also stipulate the additional, foolish claim to the first fruits? Thus, nothing in your descriptions displeases me, and all that remains is to urge you to allow me a sight of their object."

M. de Courval's friend soon satisfied him; three days later the invitation came to dine at his home with the lady in question. Not to be won over immediately by this charming creature was difficult indeed; her features were those of Minerva herself, disguised as those of love. Knowing what was at hand, she was ever the more reserved, and her decency, her restraint, the nobility of her manner, together with such physical charms, such a gentle nature, and a mind so righteous and yet so rich, so completely turned poor Courval's head that he begged his friend to be good enough to hasten the settlement.

They saw each other another two or three times, sometimes in the same house, sometimes in M. de Courval's or M. de Saint-Prât's house, and at last Mlle de Florville, insistently urged, declared to M. de Courval that nothing would flatter her more than the honor he was offering her, but that her own delicacy would not permit her agreement before she herself informed him of the events of her life.

"You have not heard all, Monsieur," said the charming lady, "and I cannot consent to be yours without your knowing more. I deem your respect too important to risk losing it, and I certainly wouldn't deserve it if, taking advantage of your illusions, I consented to be your wife without your being able to judge whether I was worthy of it."

M. de Courval assured her he knew everything, that he alone should conceive the misgivings she was evincing, and that if he was fortunate enough to please her, she ought not to trouble herself about anything further. Mlle de Florville was firm; she declared absolutely that she would not consent to anything as long as M. de Courval was not thoroughly informed of her situation, that she felt herself obliged to do just this. All that M. de Courval could obtain from Mlle de Florville was that she would visit his estate near Nemours, that everything would be arranged for the marriage celebration he so desired, and that the day following Mlle de Florville's account of her story, she would become his wife....

"But, Monsieur," the amiable girl said, "since all these preparations may end in nothing, why make them?... If I persuade you that I was not born to be yours..."

"That is something you will never prove to me, Mademoiselle," answered the honest Courval. "I defy you to convince me of this. Therefore, let us go, I beg you, and do not oppose my plans."

On this last point he was not to be swayed. Everything was arranged, and they left for Courval. Once there, however, they were to be alone, for Mlle de Florville had required this. The story she had to tell could be revealed only to the man who so desired her hand in marriage, and thus no one else was to be admitted. The day after her arrival, this beautiful and interesting being requested that M. de Courval hear her story. She recounted the events of her life in the following words.

Mademoiselle de Florville's Story

"Your intentions toward me, Monsieur, are such that I cannot permit you to be deceived any further. You have seen M. de Saint-Prât, in whose charge, you have been told, I belong. He himself has been so kind as to confirm this, and yet your deception regarding this matter remains complete. My birth is unknown to me; I have never had the satisfaction of knowing to whom I owe it. A few days after coming into this world, I was found in a bassinet of green taffeta at the door of M. de Saint-Prât's house. Attached to the canopy of my cradle was an unsigned letter that simply said:

"In the ten years of your marriage you have had no children. You wish for one every day, adopt this one. Her blood is pure, she is the fruit of a most chaste marriage and not of libertinage, and her birth is honorable. If the little girl does not please you, you may take her to the Foundling Hospital. Make no inquiries, they will be of no avail. It is impossible to say more.

"The decent people with whom I had been left welcomed me into their home, raised me, looked after me in every way, and I can say that I owe them everything. Since there was no indication of what my name was, Mme de Saint-Prât chose to call me Florville.

"I had just turned fifteen when I had the misfortune of seeing my protectress die. No words can express the sorrow I felt over that loss; I had become so dear to her that on her deathbed she begged her husband to guarantee me four thousand livres allowance and never to abandon me. The two requests were promptly fulfilled, and to these kind acts M. de Saint-Prât added that of acknowledging me as a cousin of his wife's and of arranging for me, by virtue of this, the contract with which you are familiar. However, I could no longer remain in his home, as M. de Saint-Prât let me know. The virtuous man began thus:

" 'I'm a widower, and still young. If we live under the same roof, we will be prey to undeserved suspicions. Your honor and your reputation are precious to me and I have no wish to compromise either one. We must separate, Florville. But I will never abandon you as long as I live; I don't even want you to leave my family. My sister in Nancy is a widow; I will send you to her. I answer to you for her friendship as for my own, and while you are there, as if still under my eyes, I will continue to see to everything that your education and your establishment will require.'

"I did not receive this news without shedding some tears; this new increase in sorrow bitterly renewed my recent suffering over the death of my benefactress. Convinced, nevertheless, by M. de Saint-Prât's excellent reasons, I decided to follow his advice, and I left for Lorraine escorted by a lady of that region to whom I was recommended, and who delivered me into the hands of Mme de Verquin, M. de Saint-Prât's sister, into whose care I had been entrusted.

"The tenor of Mme de Verquin's home differed greatly from that of M. de Saint-Prât. If I had seen M. de Saint-Prât's home ordered by decency, religion, and morality, the other resembled a refuge of frivolity, the love of pleasure, and independence.

"In the very first days, Mme de Verquin warned me that she didn't like my prudish little ways, that it was outrageous to arrive from Paris with such a clumsy manner...such a ridiculous air of modesty, and that if I wanted to get along with her, my style would have to change dramatically. I was alarmed by this beginning. I will not try to appear in your eyes better than I am, Monsieur; but all my life every deviation from morality and religion has displeased me so supremely − I had always been so opposed to any offense to virtue − and the failing into which I have been led despite myself has caused me such remorse that you will not, I swear to you, render me any service by bringing me back into society. I am not made to live in it. I am wild and uncouth there; the most obscure of retreats mirrors best the state of my soul and the dispositions of my mind.

"These reflections, not yet fully developed, not ripe enough at the age I was then, preserved me neither from Mme de Verquin's bad counsel nor from the evils into which her seductions were to plunge me. The perpetual company I saw, the noisy pleasures by which I was surrounded, the example, the speech, everything lured me. I was assured that I was pretty, and I dared believe it, to my misfortune.

"At that time the Normandy regiment was garrisoned in the capital. The officers met in Mme de Verquin's house; all the young women could be found there too, and it was there that all the intrigues of the city began, came to an end, and began again in different combinations.

"M. de Saint-Prât probably did not know about some aspects of that woman's behavior. How, given his own strict morals, could he have consented to send me to her house if he had really known? This thought constrained me and stopped me from voicing my complaints to him. Should I tell everything? It may even be that it didn't bother me. The impure air I was breathing was beginning to sully my heart, and, like Telemachus on Calypso's isle, perhaps I would no longer have listened to Mentor's judgments.

"The shameless Verquin, who had long been trying to corrupt me, asked me one day if I had really brought a completely pure heart with me to Lorraine, or if I wasn't pining for some lover in Paris?

"'Alas, Madame,' I said to her, 'I have never even imagined the wrongs you suspect me of, and Monsieur your brother can answer to you for my conduct.'

"'As for sins,' interrupted Mme de Verquin, 'if you have one, it is that you are still too inexperienced for your age; I hope you will correct that.'

"'Oh, Madame! Is this the language I should hear from such a respectable person?'

"'Respectable? Oh, not a word, I assure you, my dear... of all sentiments, respect is the one I worry least about inspiring. Love is what I want to inspire... but respect – that feeling isn't yet appropriate for my age. Do as I do, my dear, and you will be happy.... Speaking of which, have you noticed Senneval?' this siren added, referring to a young officer of seventeen who often came to her house.

"'Not in any special way, Madame,' I answered. 'I can assure you that I look upon them all with the same indifference.'

"'But, my little friend, that shouldn't be. I want us to share our conquests from now on.... You must have Senneval, he's my project, I've taken the trouble to train him, he loves you, you must *have* him...'

"'Oh, Madame! If you would only be so kind as to spare me this. In truth, I don't care about anyone.'

"'You'll have to. You see, I've made arrangements with his colonel, my lover of the moment.'

"'I beg of you to let me be where this subject is concerned. I have no penchant for the pleasures that you hold so dear.'

"'Oh, that will change. One day you will love them as much as I do. It's quite easy not to cherish what one doesn't yet know; but it isn't permitted, this lack of curiosity about what was made to be adored. In short, the matter has already been settled: Senneval, Mademoiselle, will declare his passion to you this evening, and you will be so good as not to keep him languishing. Otherwise, I will be quite angry with you... seriously.'

"At five o'clock, everyone gathered. Since it was very hot, the games were set in the woods, and everything was so well planned that M. de Senneval and I, finding ourselves the only ones not playing, were obliged to speak.

"It would be useless to hide from you, Monsieur, the fact that no sooner had this amiable and spirited young man confessed his desire to me than I felt drawn to him by an ungovernable emotion. And when I then tried to account for this attraction, I found nothing there but obscurity. It seemed that this inclination was the effect of no ordinary feeling; a veil hid its nature from my eyes. But then again, at the same moment that my heart flew to him, an invincible force seemed to hold it back, and in this tumult...in this ebb and flow of incomprehensible ideas, I could not decide whether I did right to love Senneval, or whether I should flee from him forever.

"They gave him plenty of time to confess his love to me.... Alas! All too much time! I had all the time to appear vulnerable in his eyes, and he took advantage of my disturbance, demanding an avowal of my feelings. I was weak enough to tell him that he was far from displeasing to me; and three days later, I was guilty enough to let him enjoy his victory.

"It's a truly singular thing, the wicked joy of vice in its triumphs over virtue. Nothing equaled the transports of Mme de Verquin when she learned I had succumbed to the trap she had set for me. She laughed at me, she poked fun at me, and in the end she assured me that what I had done was the simplest, most reasonable thing in the world, and that I could receive my lover every night in her house without fear... that she wouldn't see anything; that, being too occupied with her own affairs, she would not notice these trifles. She would nonetheless continue to admire my virtue, since it was probable that I would confine myself to this man alone, while she was obliged to hold her own against three lovers. Thus, she would certainly find herself rather far from my reserve and my modesty. When I tried to take the liberty of telling her that her profligacy was odious, that it was founded on neither delicacy nor feeling, and that it degraded our sex to the level of the vilest species of animal, Mme de Verquin burst out laughing:

"'Gallic heroine!' she said. 'I admire you and do not condemn you at all. I'm well aware that, at your age, delicacy and feeling are gods to whom one sacrifices pleasure. It's not the same thing at my age. Perfectly undeceived about these phantasms, one grants them a little less power; sensual pleasures that are more real are preferred to the follies that excite you; and, in fact, why be loyal to people who are never loyal to us? Isn't it enough to be weaker without also being the more deceived? Any woman who considers delicacy in such actions is quite mad.... Believe me, my dear, vary your pleasures while your age and your charms allow you to, and leave behind your chimeric constancy, a sad and primitive virtue, which will scarcely satisfy you, and will never fool anyone else.'

"These remarks made me tremble, but I saw clearly that I no longer had the right to oppose them. The criminal attentions of this immoral woman were becoming necessary to me, and I had to humor her; this is the disastrous disadvantage of vice, since as soon as we surrender to it, it puts us in the control of those whom we would otherwise have despised. I therefore accepted all the kindnesses of Mme de Verquin. Every night Senneval gave me new proofs of his love, and six months passed in such intoxication that I hardly had time to think.

"My eyes were soon opened by the dismal consequences; I became pregnant and thought I would die of despair seeing myself in a state for which Mme de Verquin mocked me.

"'Nevertheless,' she said to me, 'we must keep up appearances, and since it wouldn't be very decent for you to give birth in my house, Senneval's colonel and I have made other arrangements. He will grant the young man a leave of absence – you will go off to Metz a few days before him, he'll follow you soon after, and there, with his help, you'll bring into the world this illicit fruit of your affection. You will then return one after the other, just as you left.'

"I had no choice but to obey. As I told you, Monsieur, one is at the mercy of all men and every chance situation once one has had the misfortune of making a mistake. The whole universe has rights to your body, you become the slave of everything that breathes once you forget yourself and become a slave to your passions.

"Everything was arranged as Mme de Verquin had said. On the third day, Senneval and I found ourselves together again in Metz, in the home of a midwife whose address I was given as I left Nancy, and there I gave birth to a boy. Senneval, who had not ceased to display the tenderest and most delicate feelings, seemed to love me even more, now that I had, as he said, doubled his existence. He showed me every possible consideration, begged me to leave his son with him, swore to me that he would take the greatest care of him all his life and would not return to Nancy until what he avowed me should have been done.

"It was at the moment of his departure that I dared to let him know just how unhappy I was going to become because of the sin he had made me commit, and I proposed to him that we make amends for it by joining together at the altar. Senneval, who had not been expecting this proposal, became agitated....

"'Alas!' he said. 'Is it for me to say? At an age when I am still dependent, don't I need the consent of my father? What would become of our marriage, if it lacked that formality? And besides, I'm hardly a suitable match for you. As Mme de Verquin's niece' – that was what they believed in Nancy – 'you can do much better. Believe me, Florville, let us forget our deviations – you can count on my discretion.'

"This speech, which I hardly expected, made me cruelly aware of the enormity of my fault; my pride stopped me from answering, but my pain was only the more bitter. If anything had concealed the horror of my conduct from my own eyes, it was, I confess to you, the hope that I would make amends for it by one day marrying my lover. Naive girl! I didn't think – despite the perversity of Mme de Verquin, who no doubt should have enlightened me – I didn't imagine that sport was to be had in seducing an unfortunate girl and then abandoning her; nor did I suppose that the influence of honor, that sentiment so respected by men, would be without force with respect to us, and that our frailty could legitimize an insult which they would not risk among themselves except at the cost of their blood. I therefore saw that I was at once the victim and the dupe of the man for whom I would have given my life a thousand times over. This frightful change nearly led me to my grave. Senneval did not leave me, his attentions remained the same, but he did not mention my proposal again, and I had too much pride to present the subject of my despair to him a second time. He went away, at last, as soon as he saw that I was recovered.

"As I had decided not to return to Nancy, and was quite certain that I was seeing my lover for the last time in my life, all my wounds opened again at the moment of his departure. Nevertheless, I had strength enough to withstand this final blow…the cruel man! He left, he tore himself from my breast, which was flooded with my tears, without himself shedding a single one that I could see!

"This, then, is the result of those vows of love that we are foolish enough to believe! The more sensitive we are, the more our seducers forsake us…. Traitors!… They run from us because of the very means we have used to hold on to them.

"Senneval had taken his child and placed him in a region where I would never find him…. He had wanted to deprive me of the sweetness of cherishing and raising this tender fruit of our liaison. It was as though he wanted me to forget everything that might still join us to each other, and I did that, or rather I thought I did.

"I resolved to leave Metz that very moment and never again return to Nancy; yet I did not want to quarrel with Mme de Verquin. Despite her sins, the closeness of her ties with my benefactor required me to treat her with consideration for the rest of my life. I wrote her the most honest letter in the world; as a pretext for never again reappearing in her city, I offered my shame for the act I had committed there, and I asked her permission to return to Paris to be with her brother. She answered immediately that I was free to do anything I liked, that she would preserve her friendship for me always; she added that Senneval had not yet returned, that no one knew where he had taken refuge, and that I was mad to afflict myself over such trifles.

"After I received this letter, I returned to Paris and hurried to throw myself at the knees of M. de Saint-Prât. My silence and my tears soon told him of my misfortune, but I took care to accuse myself alone; I never spoke to him about the seductions of his sister. M. de Saint-Prât, like all good people, in no way suspected his relative's licentiousness; he believed her to be the most honest of women. I did not rob him of his illusions, and this course of action, of which Mme de Verquin was aware, preserved her friendship for me.

"M. de Saint-Prât pitied me... pointed out my failings in the strongest terms, and in the end pardoned them.

" 'Oh, my child!' he said to me with the gentle compunction of an honest soul, so different from crime's hateful intoxication. 'Oh, my dear child! You see the price of abandoning virtue.... Its adoption is so necessary, it is so intimately bound up with our life, that nothing remains for us but misfortune once we abandon it. Compare the tranquillity of your state of innocence when you left my home to the frightful disturbance in which you return to it. Can the feeble pleasures you may have tasted in the course of your downfall compensate you for the torments that now tear at your heart? Happiness, you see, lies only in virtue, my child, and all the sophisms of its detractors will never procure a single one of its joys. Oh, Florville, those who deny them or who struggle against these sweet joys do it only from jealousy, be sure of it, only for the barbarous pleasure of making others as guilty and as unhappy as they are. They blind themselves and would like to blind everyone else; they deceive themselves and would like everyone else to be deceived. But if one could read the depths of their souls, one would see only pain and remorse there; these apostles of crime are only wicked people, only desperate people. You would not find even one who was sincere, not one who would not confess, if he could be frank, that his foul speeches and his dangerous writings were guided only by his passions. And what man will actually be able to say with composure that the foundations of morality can be shaken without danger? What person will dare to maintain that to do good, to desire good, ought not necessarily to be the true end of man? And how can a person who does only wrong expect to be happy in the midst of a society whose most powerful interest is that good multiply without cease? But won't he himself, this apologist of crime, tremble at each instant when he has uprooted from every heart the only thing from which he might expect his preservation? Who will object to his valets ruining him, if they have ceased to be virtuous? Who will stop his wife from dishonoring him, if he has persuaded her that virtue is good for nothing? Who will restrain the hands of his children, if he has dared to blight the seeds of good in their hearts? How is his freedom, his possessions, to be respected, if he has said to the great men, *"Impunity goes with you, and virtue is only a dream"*? Whatever may be the state of this wretch, therefore, whether he is husband or father, rich or poor, master or slave, dangers will arise from all sides, from every direction daggers will be lifted against him. If he has dared to destroy in others the only obligations that balance their perversity, let us not doubt that the unfortunate man will perish sooner or later, victim of his own frightful schemes.'*

" 'Let us leave religion for a moment, if you like, let us only consider man alone; what creature will be imbecile enough to think that if he infringes all the laws of society, the society he is outraging will be able to leave him in peace? Isn't it in the interests of man, and of the laws he makes for his safety, to aspire always to destroy either what impedes him or what harms him? A little credit or some wealth will perhaps assure the wicked man an ephemeral gleam of prosperity; but how short his reign will be! Recognized, unmasked, soon become the object of public hatred and scorn, will he then find either apologists for his conduct or supporters to console him? No one will want to acknowledge him; because he will no longer have anything to offer them, they will all reject him as a burden; unhappiness surrounding him on all sides, he will languish in opprobrium and misfortune, and no longer having even his own heart for refuge, he will soon die in despair. What, then, is this absurd reasoning of our adversaries? What is this impotent effort to diminish virtue, to dare to say that everything that is not universal is chimerical, and that because virtues are only local none of them can have any reality? So! Virtue does not exist because every people has had to create its own virtue? Because different climates, different sorts of temperaments have required different varie-

---

*"Oh, my friend, do not ever try to corrupt the person you love, for it can go further than you would think," said a sensitive woman one day to the friend who was trying to seduce her. Adorable woman, allow me to quote your own words, they depict so well the soul of the woman who, soon after, saved the life of that same man, that I would like to engrave those touching words on the temple of memory, where your virtues assure you a place.

ties of restraints, because, in a word, virtue has multiplied in a thousand forms, there is no virtue on earth? One might just as well doubt the reality of a river because it is separated into a thousand different tributaries. Well! What better proves the existence of virtue and its necessity than the need man has to adapt it to all his different customs and make it the basis of them all? If anyone can find me a single people that lives without virtue, a single one for whom beneficence and humanity are not fundamental bonds, I will go still further and say, if anyone can find me even a band of villains that is not cemented by a few principles of virtue, I will abandon its cause. But if, on the contrary, it is demonstrated to be useful everywhere, if there is no nation, no state, no society, no individual that can do without it, if man, in a word, can't live either happily or safely without it, will I be wrong, my child, to exhort you never to stray from it? Look, Florville,' continued my benefactor, holding me tightly in his arms, 'look where your first wanderings have led you; and if error tempts you again, if seduction or your weakness prepare new traps for you, think of the misfortunes of your first mistakes. Think of a man who loves you like his own daughter... whose heart would be torn by your sins, and you will find in these reflections all the strength you need to worship the virtues I would like to bring you to forever.'

"M. de Saint-Prât, true to his principles, did not offer me his house; he suggested rather that I live with another of his female relatives, a woman as famous for her life of profound piety as Mme de Verquin was for her failings. This arrangement pleased me very much. Mme de Lérince accepted me with the greatest goodwill possible, and I was settled in her house the same week I returned to Paris.

"Oh, Monsieur! What a difference there was between this respectable woman and the one I had left! If vice and depravity had established their empire in the home of one, it was as though the heart of the other were a sanctuary for all the virtues. To the same extent that the first had appalled me by her depravity, I found myself consoled by the edifying principles of the second; I had found only bitterness and remorse in listening to Mme de Verquin, and I was to encounter only sweetness and consolation in putting myself in the hands of Mme de Lérince.... Oh, Monsieur! Permit me to describe that adorable woman, whom I will always love; it is a homage that my heart owes to her virtues. It is impossible for me to resist.

"Mme de Lérince, who was about forty years old, still possessed much of the freshness of youth; an air of candor and modesty embellished her features much more than the divine proportions nature had bestowed on her. A little too much nobility and majesty made her appear a rather imposing figure at first, but what one might have taken for pride was softened as soon as she spoke. She had a soul so beautiful and so pure, a graciousness so perfect, a frankness so complete, that despite oneself one inevitably felt the veneration she immediately inspired, joined by all the tenderest feelings. Mme de Lérince's religion was neither extravagant nor superstitious; the principles of her faith stemmed from her heightened sensitivity. The idea of the existence of God, the worship owed to that supreme being – such were the greatest joys of this loving soul. She swore resolutely that she would be the most unhappy of creatures if treacherous ideas were ever to constrain her spirit to destroy the respect and love she had for her religion. Even more attached, if that were possible, to the sublime morality of this religion than to its practices or its rituals, she made this excellent morality the guide for all her actions. Slander had never sullied her lips; she did not even allow herself a joke that might hurt someone close to her. Full of tenderness and care for her fellow creatures, finding people interesting even in their failings, her only occupation was either to conceal carefully these failings or to admonish them gently. If people were unhappy, for her there were no charms equal to the charms of comforting them; she did not wait for the indigent to come beg for help, she sought them out.... She could guess who they were, and one would see the joy spread over her features when she had consoled a widow or provided for an orphan, when she had given relief to a poor family, or when her hands had broken the shackles of misfortune. There was nothing harsh, nothing severe in all this. The pleasures she enjoyed were all chaste, and she abandoned herself to them with delight. She even thought them up herself, for fear one would be bored in her company. Wise... enlightened with the moralist... profound with the theologian, she inspired the novelist and smiled on the poet; she surprised the legislator or the politician, and organized games for the child. Though she possessed all varieties of wit, the one that shone brightest in her could be recognized mainly by the particular care, the charming attention she showed either in bringing out the wit of others or in finding it in them always. Living in retirement by choice, cultivating her friends for their own sake, Mme de Lérince, a model, in short, for both sexes, filled everyone around her with the joy of that tranquil happiness, that heavenly pleasure promised to the honest man by the holy God whose image she was.

"I will not bore you, Monsieur, with the monotonous details of my life during the seventeen years that I had the happiness of living with that adorable woman. Conversations about morality and piety, as many benevolent deeds as were possible for us – these were the duties that divided our days.

" 'My dear Florville, men are frightened by religion,' Mme de Lérince said to me, 'only because unskilled guides make them aware of its chains without presenting them with its sweeter sides. Can there exist a man absurd enough to dare, as he opens his eyes to the universe, not to agree that such marvels can only be the work of an all-powerful God? And once this primary truth is understood – and is anything else needed but his heart to convince him of it? – what a cruel and barbarous individual he would have to be to refuse his homage, then, to the benevolent god who created him? But the diversity of religions is perplexing, people think that because there are so many, they are false. What sophism! And isn't this unanimity of different peoples in acknowledging and serving a god, isn't this tacit avowal imprinted on the hearts of all men an even more irrevocable proof than the sublimities of nature, if such is possible, that the supreme god exists? Man can't live without adopting a god, he can't question himself without finding proofs of a god in himself, he can't open his eyes without encountering signs of this god everywhere, and he dares, and he still dares to doubt him! No, Florville, no, no one is an atheist in good faith; pride, stubbornness, the passions – these are the weapons destroying that god that keeps coming back to life in the heart of man or in his reason; and when every beat of that heart, when every beam of light from that reason offers me this incontestable being, I would refuse him my homage, I would steal from him the tribute that his goodness allows my frailty, I would not humble myself before his greatness, I would not ask for his grace, and to endure the miseries of life, and to be allowed to participate one day in his glory! I would not covet the favor of spending eternity in his bosom, or I would risk that same eternity in an abyss terrifying for its torments, all because I had resisted the unquestionable proofs this great being had tried to give me, of the certainty of his existence! My child, does that dreadful alternative itself allow a moment of reflection? O you who stubbornly resist the arrows of fire thrown by this same god into the depths of your hearts, be at least fair for a moment and, even if only out of pity for yourselves, yield to this invincible argument of Pascal's: "If there is no God, what does it matter to you if you believe in him, what harm does this belief do you? And if there is one, what dangers do you not run in refusing him your faith?" You do not know, you say, unbelieving, what homage to offer this god, the multitude of religions befuddles you. Well, examine them all, I can accept that, and come tell me afterward in good faith which seems to you to have more greatness and majesty. Deny, if you can, O Christians, that the one into which you had the happiness of being born seems to you, of them all, the one whose features are the most holy and the most sublime. Seek elsewhere for such great mysteries, such pure dogmas, as consoling a morality; find in another religion the ineffable sacrifice of a god for the sake of his creature; see, in another, more handsome promises, a more hopeful future, a greater and more sublime god! No, you cannot, philosopher of the day; you cannot, slave of your pleasures, whose faith changes with the physical state of your nerves; impious in the heat of your passions, believing as soon as they are calmed, you cannot, I tell you; one's feelings acknowledge it ceaselessly, this God whom your mind fights exists near you always, even in the midst of your errors. Break those shackles that bind you to crime, and this holy and majestic God will never leave the temple built for Him in your heart. It is in the depths of this heart, much more, even, than in one's reason, that one must, my dear Florville, find the need for this God which everything reveals and proves to us. It is from this same heart that we must also recognize the necessity to worship Him, and it is this heart alone that will soon persuade you, dear friend, that the noblest and purest of all is He in whom we were born. Let us therefore practice this sweet and consoling religion with exactitude, with joy, so that it may fill our most beautiful moments here on earth, and so that, imperceptibly led, cherishing it to the very end of our lives, we may follow a path of love and delight as we place in the bosom of the eternal the soul that emanated from Him, formed only to know Him and in which we rejoice only to believe in Him and adore Him.'

"This was how Mme de Lérince spoke to me, this was how my spirit was strengthened by her counsels, and how my soul was rarefied under her blessed wing. But as I told you, I am passing in silence over all the little details of my daily life in that house in order to convey what is most important. What I must reveal to you, generous and sensitive man, are my faults, and once heaven has graciously allowed me to live in peace in the path of virtue, I have only to thank it and be still.

I had not stopped writing to Mme de Verquin, and I received news from her regularly, twice a month. Though I no doubt ought to have renounced this correspondence, as the reform of my life and better principles in some way obliged me to break it off, what I owed to M. de Saint-Prât, and more than anything, I must confess, a secret feeling that always drew me invincibly toward the places where so many beloved objects had once captivated me, perhaps the hope of one day learning news of my son – all this, in short, committed me to continuing a correspondence that Mme de Verquin was decent enough always to maintain regularly. I tried to convert her, I spoke highly of the pleasures of the life I was leading, but she called them dreams. She kept laughing at my resolutions or opposing them, and, still firm in her own, she assured me that nothing in the world would weaken them. She spoke to me of the new proselytes she amused herself by making, and she rated their docility far above mine. Their manifold downfalls were, this perverse woman said, small triumphs that she never achieved without delight, and the pleasure of leading these young hearts into evil consoled her for not being able herself to do all the evil her imagination dictated to her. I often begged Mme de Lérince to lend me her eloquent pen in order to overthrow my adversary, and she consented with joy; Mme de Verquin answered us, and her sometimes very strong sophisms obliged us to resort to the far more victorious arguments of a sensitive soul, in which was inevitably found, Mme de Lérince rightly claimed, everything that ought to destroy vice and confound unbelief. From time to time I asked Mme de Verquin for news of the man I still loved, but either she could not or she would not give me any.

"It is time, Monsieur, to go on to the second catastrophe of my life, to that bloody tale that breaks my heart every time it presents itself to my imagination and which, as I tell you about the frightful crime I am guilty of, will no doubt make you give up the overly flattering plans you have made for me.

"Mme de Lérince's house, however strict I have described it as being, nevertheless occasionally welcomed in a few friends. Mme de Dulfort, a middle-aged woman formerly attached to the house of the Princess of Piedmont, and who came to see us very often, one day asked Mme de Lérince permission to introduce to her a young man who had been highly recommended to her and whom she would be very happy to bring into a house in which the examples of virtue he would continually receive could only contribute to shaping his sensibility. My protectress made the excuse that she never received young people; then, won over by the urgent entreaties of her friend, she consented to see the Chevalier de Saint-Ange. He appeared.

"Whether it was a premonition, or whether it was something else, Monsieur, when I saw this young man I was overcome by a fit of shivering whose cause I found impossible to guess. I nearly fainted. Not trying to divine the reason for this curious effect, I attributed it to some inner indisposition, and Saint-Ange ceased to make an impression on me. But if this young man had at first sight agitated me in this way, a similar effect had manifested itself in him...as I learned later from his own lips. Saint-Ange was filled with such a great reverence for the house whose doors had been opened to him that he dared not forget himself to the point of allowing his burning passion to escape there. Three months passed, therefore, before he dared say anything about it to me; but his eyes spoke in such a lively language that misunderstanding was impossible. Quite determined not to fall back again into the sort of sin to which I owed the unhappiness of my days, and very much steadied by better principles, I was on the point of warning Mme de Lérince some twenty times of the feelings I believed I could discern in that young man. Yet, restrained by my fear of hurting him, I chose to say nothing. A disastrous resolution, you can be sure, since it was the cause of the dreadful misfortune I will speak of.

"We were in the habit of spending six months of every year on a rather pretty country estate that Mme de Lérince owned, two leagues from Paris. M. de Saint-Prât came to see us there often. Unfortunately for me, he was kept away that year by his gout; it was impossible for him to come. I say unfortunately for me, Monsieur, because since I naturally trusted him more than his relative, I would have confessed to him things that I could never resolve to say to others, and such a confession would undoubtedly have prevented the disastrous accident that occurred.

"Saint-Ange asked permission of Mme de Lérince to join us, and since Mme de Dulfort was also earnestly requesting this favor for him, it was granted.

"All of us in the group were rather anxious to know who this young man was; nothing appeared to be either very clear or very decided about his life. Mme de Dulfort told us he was the son of a provincial gentleman; and he, sometimes forgetting what Mme de Dulfort had said, passed himself off as a Piedmontese – a possibility supported to some extent by the way he spoke Italian. He was not in the army, and although he was old enough to do something, we couldn't see that he had made any decision yet. In addition, he had a very handsome face – made to be painted – a very decent manner, an honest way of speaking, all the appearance of an excellent education, but along with this an amazing liveliness, a sort of impetuosity in his character which sometimes frightened us.

"As soon as M. de Saint-Ange was in the country, his feelings having only intensified under the restraint he had tried to impose on them, it became impossible for him to hide them from me; I trembled...and yet controlled myself enough to show him only compassion.

"'In truth, Monsieur,' I said to him, 'you must be misunderstanding what you can expect to gain, or you must have a great deal of time to waste to spend it with a woman who is twice your age; but even supposing I were insane enough to listen to you, what ridiculous claims would you be daring to form on me?'

"'To join myself to you by the holiest of bonds, Mademoiselle. How little you would respect me if you could suppose my claims to be other!'

"'In truth, Monsieur, I will not offer the public the odd spectacle of seeing a woman of thirty-four marry a child of seventeen.'

"'Oh, cruel lady! Would you notice that slight disproportion if there existed in the depths of your heart a thousandth part of the fire that is devouring mine?'

"'For my part, Monsieur, I am decidedly very calm.... I have been for many years now, and will be, I hope, as long as it pleases God to let me languish here on earth.'

"'You wrest from me even the hope of one day touching your heart.'

"'I will go even further, I will dare to forbid you to speak to me any longer about these mad ideas.'

"'Oh, beautiful Florville! Does this mean you wish my life to be miserable?'

"'I wish you peace and happiness.'

"'These are not mine to have except with you.'

"'Yes...as long as you will not eliminate the ridiculous feelings that you never should have conceived. Try to control them, try to be your own master, and your tranquillity will return.'

"'I cannot do it.'

"'You don't want to. We must part for you to succeed. Do not see me for two years, and this agitation will subside; you will forget me, and you will be happy.'

"'Oh, never, never, I will never find happiness except at your feet...'

"And as the group rejoined us at that point, our first conversation ended there.

"Three days later, Saint-Ange, having managed to find me alone again, continued to speak in the same way as before. This time, I demanded silence with such strictness that his tears flowed abundantly. He said to me that I had thrown him into despair, that he would soon tear out his own heart if I continued to treat him this way, and he left me abruptly.... Then, turning back like a madman, he said:

"'Mademoiselle, you don't know whom you are insulting.... No, you have no idea.... Know that I am capable of extreme measures... ones that you cannot even begin to imagine.... Yes, I will reach for such extremes a thousand times over before I surrender the happiness of being yours.' And he departed in frightful pain.

"I had never been more tempted than I was then to speak to Mme de Lérince, but I repeat, my fear of harming that young man restrained me, and I said nothing. Saint-Ange stayed away from me for a week, scarcely spoke to me, avoided me at meals...in the parlor...during walks, and all this, without a doubt, in order to see if this change of behavior would make some impression on me. Had I shared his feelings, it would have been a sure method; but I did not, and thus I hardly suspected his designs.

"At last he came up to me deep inside the gardens.... 'Mademoiselle,' he said in the most violent state, 'I have finally succeeded in calming myself; your counsels had the effect that you expected. You see how I am once again tranquil. I have tried to find you alone only to give you my last farewell. Yes, I am leaving you forever, Mademoiselle. I am going to leave you. You will never again see the man you hate.... Oh, no! No, you will never see him again!'

" 'This plan pleases me, Monsieur; I would like to believe you have finally seen reason. But,' I added, smiling, 'your conversion does not yet seem very real to me.'

" 'Oh! How should I be, then, Mademoiselle, in order to convince you of my indifference?'

" 'Quite different from the way I now see you.'

" 'But at least when I have left, when you no longer have the pain of seeing me, perhaps then you will believe that I possess that reason which you have labored so hard to restore to me?'

" 'True – that is the only thing that will persuade me, and I will not cease to advise you to do it.'

" 'Oh, then I truly am a frightful object in your eyes.'

" 'You are, Monsieur, a very amiable man who ought to turn to conquests more worthy of yourself and leave in peace a woman who cannot hear you.'

" 'And yet you will hear me,' he then said, enraged. 'Yes, cruel lady, whatever you may say, you will hear the feelings of my fiery soul, as well as the oath that there is nothing in the world that I will not do...either to deserve you, or to have you.... And let me warn you, don't believe it,' he resumed impetuously, 'don't believe in this feigned departure. It is but a feint, to test you.... For me, to leave you...for me, to tear myself from the place that holds you...I would rather be deprived of life a thousand times over.... Hate me, treacherous lady, hate me, since such is my unhappy fate; but don't ever hope to destroy my burning love for you....'

Saint-Ange was in such a state as he uttered these last words – through some misfortune I have never understood, he had succeeded in moving me – that I turned away in order to hide my tears from him, and I left him in the depths of the grove where he had found me. He didn't follow me; I heard him throw himself on the ground and abandon himself to the excesses of a most frightful delirium.... As for me, I must confess, Monsieur, that although I was quite certain of feeling no love for this young man, it was impossible for me, either out of sympathy or because of a memory, not to burst out crying in turn.

"'Alas,' I thought, overtaken by my own sorrow, 'Senneval said the same thing, he expressed his love for me in exactly the same words.... And also in a garden...in a garden just like this one.... Didn't he tell me he would always love me, and didn't he deceive me cruelly?... Heaven, have mercy! He was the same age.... Oh, Senneval, Senneval, are you trying to disturb my peace once again? And aren't you reappearing in this seductive guise only to drag me into the abyss a second time? Flee, coward! Flee! I abhor your very memory!'

"I dried my tears, and went and shut myself up in my room until supper. I then descended. But Saint-Ange did not appear, he sent word that he was sick, and the next day he was cunning enough not to allow me to read on his face anything but tranquillity. I was deceived, I really believed that he had exercised enough control over himself to have conquered his passion. But I was wrong. The traitor! Alas! What am I saying, Monsieur? I no longer need to curse him. He deserves only my tears; now, he deserves only my remorse.

"Saint-Ange seemed so calm only because he had formed his plans. Two days passed thus, and toward the evening of the third, he announced publicly that he was leaving. With Mme de Dulfort, his protectress, he made arrangements having to do with their joint affairs in Paris.

"Everyone went to bed.... Excuse me, Monsieur, for the disturbance aroused in me by retelling this frightful catastrophe even before I speak it; I can never recall it without shivering in horror.

"As it was extremely hot, I had tumbled into bed almost naked; my maid outside, I had just extinguished my candle. A sewing basket had unfortunately remained open on my bed, because I had just cut out some pieces of gauze I needed the next day. Scarcely had my eyes begun to close when I heard a noise. I quickly sat up in bed. I felt a hand grasp me.

"'This time you will not flee from me, Florville,' said Saint-Ange – for it was he. 'Forgive the excess of my passion, but do not even try to escape it. You must be mine.'

"'Vile seducer!' I cried, 'leave this instant, or suffer the effects of my wrath. . . .'

"'I fear nothing except not possessing you, cruel girl,' answered that ardent young man, hurling himself on me so skillfully and with such fury that I became his victim before I was able to stop him. Enraged by such audacity, determined to do anything rather than suffer what might come next, I freed myself from him and threw myself toward the scissors that lay at my feet. Still in control despite my rage, I looked for his arm so as to strike him there and, by my resolution, frighten him, rather than punish him as he deserved to be punished. When he felt me move, he redoubled the violence of his own motions.

"'Go, traitor!' I cried, believing that I was striking him on the arm, 'go this instant, and blush at your crime. . . .'

"Oh, Monsieur! A fatal hand had guided my blows. The unfortunate young man cried out and fell to the floor. . . . I immediately relit my candle and I approached him. . . . Good God, I had struck him in the heart! He was dying! I threw myself down on his bloody body. Deliriously I hugged him against my panicked breast. My mouth, pressed against his, tried to call back the soul that was slipping away. I washed his wound with my tears. . . .

"'Oh, you whose only crime was to love me too much,' I said in the wildness of despair, 'did you deserve such torment? Did you have to lose your life at the hand of the woman to whom you would have sacrificed your own? Oh, unhappy young man, image of the one I adored, if loving you would be enough to bring you back to life, know, in this cruel moment, when you can unfortunately no longer hear me . . . know, if your soul still throbs, that I would revive it at the cost of my own life. Know that I was never indifferent to you . . . that I never saw you without being troubled, and that my feelings for you were perhaps far superior to the weak love that burned in your heart.'

"At these words, I fell senseless on the body of the ill-fated young man. My maid came in – she had heard the noise. She tended to me, she joined her efforts to mine in trying to restore Saint-Ange. . . . Alas! Everything was useless. We left the fateful room, we carefully locked the door, we took the key with us and immediately flew to Paris, to M. de Saint-Prât's home. I had him woken, I handed him the key to that dismal room, I told him the horrible thing that had happened to me. He pitied me, he comforted me, and ill though he was, he immediately went to the home of Mme de Lérince. Since her estate was very close to Paris, all of this could occur on the same night. My protector arrived at his relative's home just as everyone was getting up, before anything had yet been discovered. Never did friends, never did family behave better than in that situation: they were so far from imitating those stupid or vicious people whose only response to such crises is to stir up anything that can blight or make unhappy both themselves and those who surround them, that scarcely did the servants suspect what had happened.

"And so, Monsieur," said Mlle de Florville at this point, breaking off her tale because of the tears that were suffocating her, "will you now marry a girl capable of such a murder? Could you bear to hold in your arms a creature who deserves the severe punishment of the law? An unfortunate creature, finally, whose crime torments her ceaselessly, who has not had a single peaceful sleep since that cruel night? No, Monsieur, not a single night has passed without my unfortunate victim appearing before me steeped in the blood I wrested from his heart."

"Calm yourself, Mademoiselle, calm yourself, I beg you," said M. de Courval, mingling his tears with those of the captivating girl. "Because nature has given you a sensitive soul, I can imagine your remorse; but there is not even the semblance of a crime in this fatal adventure. It is certainly a frightful misfortune, but nothing more than that; nothing premeditated, nothing atrocious, only the desire to escape a most odious attack...a murder, in short, committed by chance, while defending yourself.... Rest assured, Mademoiselle, rest assured, I insist. The harshest court of justice would do no more than dry your tears. Oh, how mistaken you are if you fear that such an event will lessen the rights to my heart that your good qualities assure you. No, no, beautiful Florville, this struggle, far from dishonoring you, only heightens in my eyes the brilliance of your virtues, it only makes you more worthy of finding the consoling hand that will cause you to forget your sorrows."

"What you have the goodness to say to me," Mlle de Florville responded, "M. de Saint-Prât said also. But the extreme goodness of you both can't stifle the reproaches of my conscience; nothing will ever quiet the remorse it feels. No matter.... Let us go on, Monsieur; you must be anxious about the outcome of this story.

"Mme de Dulfort was certainly grieved. The young man, so engaging in himself, had been too particularly recommended for her not to deplore his loss; but she understood the reasons for silence, she saw that a scandal, which would ruin me, would not restore life to her protégé, and so she said nothing. Mme de Lérince, despite her strict principles and the extreme regularity of her habits, behaved even better, if that is possible, prudence and humanity being the distinctive characteristics of true piety. First she let it be known in the house that I had had the mad notion of wanting to return to Paris during the night in order to enjoy the coolness of the air; that she was perfectly well aware of this little extravagance; that, besides, it was all for the best because her own plan was to go there for supper that very evening. With that excuse, she dismissed all her servants. Once alone with M. de Saint-Prât and her friend, they sent for the priest. Mme de Lérince's pastor was, of course, a man as wise and as enlightened as she. Without any difficulty he delivered an official certificate to Mme de Dulfort, and he and two of his men secretly buried the unfortunate victim of my rage.

"These tasks having been seen to, everyone reappeared, secrecy was sworn on all sides, and M. de Saint-Prât came to soothe me, letting me know everything that had just been done to wrap my sin in the deepest oblivion. He seemed to want me to resume my usual routine in Mme de Lérince's home, and she was prepared to receive me. I could not bring myself to do it, and so he advised me to seek distraction. Mme de Verquin, with whom, Monsieur, as I told you, I had never stopped corresponding, was always urging me to spend a few months with her again. I mentioned this plan to her brother, he approved, and a week later I left for Lorraine. But the memory of my crime pursued me everywhere. Nothing succeeded in calming me.

"I would awaken from the midst of my sleep, believing I could still hear the moans and the cries of that unfortunate Saint-Ange, that I saw him bloody at my feet, reproaching me for my barbarity, assuring me that the memory of this frightful act would pursue me to my last moments, and that I knew nothing of the heart I had broken.

"One night in particular, I dreamed of Senneval, that unfortunate lover whom I had not forgotten, since he alone was drawing me to Nancy again.... Senneval was pointing out to me two corpses, that of Saint-Ange and another, of a woman unknown to me.* He was bathing them both with his tears and showed me, not far from there, a coffin bristling with thorns that seemed to open itself to me. I awoke in a frightful state. A thousand confused feelings then arose in my soul; a secret voice seemed to say to me, 'Yes, for as long as you shall breathe, this unfortunate victim will wrest tears of blood from your eyes, tears that will become more and more bitter with each passing day; and the needle of your remorse will not be dulled but grow ever sharper.'

"Such, then, was my state upon arriving at Nancy, Monsieur. A thou-

---

*Let the phrase *a woman unknown to me* not be forgotten, so that there may be no confusion. Florville has still several losses to suffer before the veil lifts and makes known to her the woman she saw in her dream.

sand new sorrows awaited me there; once the hand of fate bears down on you, it only redoubles its blows to crush you.

"I was to stay with Mme de Verquin. In her last letter she had begged me to come, saying that she looked forward to the pleasure of seeing me once again. But under what circumstances were the two of us to taste this joy! She was on her deathbed when I arrived. How could I have known, great heavens! It had not even been two weeks since she had written me . . . since she had told of her latest pleasures and announced those to come. Such are the plans of mortals: just as they are made, in the midst of our enjoyment, pitiless death comes to cut the thread of our days; and living without ever worrying about that fatal moment, living as though we were to exist forever, we vanish into that dark cloud of immortality, uncertain of the fate that awaits us there.

"Allow me, Monsieur, to interrupt the tale of my adventures for a moment to talk to you about this loss, and to describe to you the frightening stoicism that accompanied this woman to the grave.

"Mme de Verquin, who was no longer young – she was fifty-two years old at that time – had, after a game that was madness for someone of her age, thrown herself into the water to cool off. There she suffered a malaise; they brought her home in a dreadful state, and a congestion of the chest set in the very next day. On the sixth day they told her she had barely twenty-four hours to live. This news frightened her not at all. She knew I was coming and asked that I be received. I arrived – and, according to the doctor's judgment, this was the same evening she was supposed to pass away. She had had herself placed in a room furnished with the utmost of taste and elegance; she was lying there, dressed simply, on a voluptuous bed whose lilac curtains of coarse silk were agreeably tucked up by garlands of natural flowers. Bunches of pinks, jasmine, tuberoses, and roses embellished all the corners of her apartment. She was plucking the petals off some into a basket, covering both her room and her bed with them. She reached out her hand to me as soon as she saw me.

" 'Come here, Florville,' she said. 'Kiss me on my bed of flowers. . . . How tall and how beautiful you have grown. Oh, faith, child, virtue has been good for you. . . . They've informed you of my condition. . . . They've told you about it. . . . I know it too. . . . In a few hours I will be no more. I wouldn't have thought I'd see you again for so short a time. . . .' And when she saw my eyes fill with tears, she said, 'Come now, silly girl, don't be a child. . . . Do you think I'm really unhappy? Haven't I had as much pleasure as any woman in the world? I'm only losing the years in which I would have had to give up pleasure, and what would I have done without that? In truth, I'm not complaining that I haven't lived to be older. Soon, no man would have desired me, and I have never wanted any part of a life in which I inspired disgust. Death is not to be feared, my child, except by those who believe: while still between hell and heaven, uncertain which will open for them, they are devastated by anxiety. I, who hope for nothing, I, who am quite sure of not being more unhappy after my death than I was before my birth, will go to sleep peacefully in the bosom of nature, without regrets as I am without sorrow, without remorse as I am without uneasiness. I have asked to be put under my bower of jasmines; they are already preparing my place there. There I will be, Florville, and atoms emanating from this decayed body will serve to nourish... to germinate the flower I loved best of all. Just think,' she continued, tapping a bouquet of that plant against my cheeks, 'next year, when you smell these flowers, you will be breathing, deep inside them, the soul of your old friend. As they soar up to the fibers of your brain, they will give you lovely ideas, they will force you to think of me again.'

"My tears began to flow again.... I grasped the hands of this unfortunate woman and wished I could exchange these dreadful materialistic ideas for some less impious system. But scarcely had I revealed this desire than Mme de Verquin thrust me away with horror....

" 'Oh, Florville,' she cried, 'don't poison my last moments with your errors, I beg you, let me die in peace. I haven't detested them all my life only to adopt them at the moment of my death....'

"I was silent. What power would my wretched eloquence have had compared to such firmness? I would have distressed Mme de Verquin without converting her; compassion argued against it. She rang, and I immediately heard a soft and melodious concert whose sounds appeared to come from a neighboring room.

" 'This, Florville, is how I intend to die,' said the epicurean. 'Isn't it much better than to be surrounded by priests, who would fill my last moments with disturbance, alarm, and despair?... No, I want to teach your bigots that, without resembling them, one can die tranquil. I want to convince them that it isn't religion one needs in order to die in peace, but only courage and reason.'

"It grew late. The notary she had sent for entered. The music stopped, and she dictated a few last wishes. Childless, a widow for many years, she consequently possessed many things, and she made bequests to her friends and servants. She then drew a little coffer from a secretary placed near her bed. 'Now here is what is left,' she said. 'A little ready money and a few jewels. Let us amuse ourselves for the rest of the evening.

There are six of you here in my room, so I will make six lots of this and we will have a lottery. You will draw for it among you, and you will each take what falls to you.'

"I marveled at the serenity of this woman. It seemed incredible to me that a person with so much cause for self-reproach should arrive at her last moment with such calm – the fatal effect of a lack of belief. If the horrible ends of certain wicked people can make one tremble, such sustained callousness is even more frightening.

"Nevertheless, what she wanted was done. A magnificent collation was served, and she ate from several dishes and drank Spanish wines and liqueurs, for the doctor had told her that in her condition this would not make any difference.

"The lottery was drawn, and each of us received close to one hundred louis, either in gold or in jewels. This little game was scarcely finished when she suffered a violent attack.

"'Well, then! Is it going to be now?' she asked the doctor, still with the utmost tranquillity.

"'I'm afraid so, Madame.'

"'Then come here, Florville,' she said to me, holding out her arms. 'Come receive my last farewells, I want to die on the breast of virtue....' She held me tightly against her, and her beautiful eyes closed forever.

"A stranger in that house, having nothing further that could keep me there, I immediately departed...I leave it to you to think in what state...and how that spectacle darkened my imagination still more.

"There was too much distance between Mme de Verquin's way of thinking and mine for me to be able to love her sincerely. Besides, wasn't she the original cause of my dishonor, and of all the reverses that had followed it? Nevertheless, that woman, sister of the only man who had ever really taken care of me, had never had but honest dealings with me; in fact, she had showered me with courtesies even as she died. My tears were therefore sincere, and their bitterness redoubled as I reflected with what excellent qualities this wretched creature had involuntarily lost her way, and that, already rejected from the bosom of the eternal, she was suffering cruelly, without any doubt, the torments due to a life so depraved. The supreme goodness of God nevertheless presented itself to me to calm these distressing ideas. I threw myself to my knees, I dared to beg the supreme being to spare the unfortunate woman; I who had such need of heaven's mercy, I dared to pray to Him for others and, in order to move Him as much as it might depend upon me, I added ten louis of my own money to the lot I had won in Mme de Verquin's home and then and there had the whole sum distributed to the poor of her parish.

"For the rest, the intentions of the unfortunate woman were scrupulously followed; she had made such careful arrangements they could not fail. She was laid in her bower of jasmines with a black marble obelisk at her head on which was engraved a single word: VIXIT.

"Thus perished the sister of my dearest friend. Filled with wit and knowledge, endowed with graces and talents, Mme de Verquin, had her conduct been different, could have merited the esteem and the love of all who knew her. Yet she earned only their scorn. Her licentiousness increased as she grew older: one is never more dangerous, when one has no principles, than at the age when one has ceased to blush. Depravity causes a mortification of the heart; one refines one's first failings and imperceptibly arrives at the forfeits, imagining that one is still only at the errors. But her brother's unbelievable blindness did not cease to surprise me: such is the distinctive mark of candor and goodness. Honest people never suspect the evil of which they themselves are incapable, and this is why they are so easily the dupes of the first rogue to seize hold of them, and why it is so easy and so inglorious to deceive them. The bold rascal who strives to do this has labored only to debase himself and, without even having proved his talents for vice, has only lent more brilliance to virtue.

"In losing Mme de Verquin, I was losing all hope of learning news of my lover and my son. You can well imagine that I hadn't dared speak to her about them in the dreadful state in which I had seen her.

"Overwhelmed by this catastrophe, and still exhausted by a trip taken in a grievous state of mind, I resolved to rest for some time in Nancy, at the inn where I had settled, without seeing anyone at all, since M. de Saint-Prât had seemed to wish me to disguise my name while abroad. It was from here that I wrote to that dear protector, determined not to leave until after he answered.

" 'An unhappy woman who is nothing to you, Monsieur,' I wrote to him, 'who has a right only to your pity, eternally troubles your life. Instead of speaking to you only about the grief you must be feeling over the loss you have just suffered, she dares to talk to you about herself, ask for your orders and await them, etc.'

"But it was ordained that misfortune would follow me everywhere and that I would be perpetually either witness to or victim of its sinister effects.

"One evening I was returning to the inn rather late after having taken some air with my chambermaid. I was accompanied only by that girl and a hired lackey whom I had taken on when I arrived in Nancy; everyone was already in bed. At the moment I entered the house, a woman of about fifty years, tall, still very beautiful, whom I knew by sight since lodging in the same house as she, suddenly emerged from her room, which was next to mine, and threw herself, armed with a dagger, into another room opposite.... The natural action was to go see.... I flew.... My servants followed me. In the blink of an eye, without our having the time to call out or to help...we saw the wretched woman hurl herself upon another woman, plunge the weapon some twenty times into her heart, and return to her room distraught, without having had the chance to notice us. We thought at first that the creature had lost her head; we couldn't understand this crime, whose motive we could not imagine. My chambermaid and my servant thought to cry out; a more imperious impulse, whose cause I could not guess, constrained me to make them keep still, to seize them by the arms and draw them with me into my room, wherein we immediately locked ourselves.

"A frightful racket was soon heard; the woman who had just been stabbed had thrown herself, as best she could, onto the stairway, uttering horrifying howls. She had had the time, before dying, to name the woman who had murdered her; and since it was known that we were the last to enter the inn, we were detained at the same time as the guilty woman. The statements of the dying woman, however, removed us from suspicion, and the authorities merely ordered us not to leave the inn until the conclusion of the trial. The criminal, dragged off to prison, made no confession and defended herself stoutly; there were no other witnesses except my servants and me, and so I had to appear...I had to speak, I had to take care to hide the disturbance that was secretly consuming me...I, who deserved death just as much as the woman who was to be sent to the gallows by statements I was compelled to make, since I was guilty of a similar crime, if in different circumstances. I don't know what I would have given to avoid those cruel depositions; it seemed to me, as I dictated them, that with every word of accusation I spoke, a drop of blood was being wrested from my heart. Nevertheless, everything had to be said: we stated what we had seen. Whatever convictions one might have about the crime of this woman, who, it appeared, had murdered her rival, and however certain, I say, one might be of this offense, we knew positively afterward that without us it would have been impossible to condemn her, because there was a man implicated in this intrigue who had escaped and whom they could well have suspected. But our statements, that of the hired lackey especially, who was a man attached to the inn – a man attached to the house in which the crime had taken place – those cruel depositions which it was impossible for us to refuse without compromising ourselves, sealed the fate of the unfortunate woman.

"At my last confrontation with her, that woman, examining me with the greatest shock, asked me my age.

" 'Thirty-four,' I told her.

" 'Thirty-four years old? And you are from this province?'

" 'No, Madame.'

" 'Your name is Florville?'

" 'Yes,' I answered, 'that is what I am called.'

" 'I don't know you,' she went on, 'but you are honest, respected, they say, in this town. Unfortunately that is enough for me. . . .' Then, continuing with agitation, 'Mademoiselle, you appeared to me in a dream in the midst of the horrors in which you see me here. In it, you were with my son . . . for I am a mother, and unhappy, as you see . . . you had the same face . . . the same figure . . . the same dress . . . and the scaffold was before my eyes. . . .'

" 'A dream!' I cried. 'A dream, Madame. . . .' And, my own dream instantly coming to mind again, the features of this woman struck me, I recognized her for the one who had appeared to me with Senneval, by the coffin bristling with thorns. . . . My eyes brimmed with tears. The more I studied this woman, the more tempted I was to retract my statement. . . . I wanted to beg to be put to death in her place. . . . I wanted to flee from there and could not tear myself away. . . . Since they were convinced of my innocence, they saw fit to separate us when they saw the frightful state into which she had put me. I returned to my room stricken, overcome with a thousand different feelings whose causes I could not distinguish; and the next day, that pathetic woman was taken to her death.

"That same day, I received M. de Saint-Prât's answer; he urged me to return. Since Nancy could not be very pleasant for me after the dismal scenes just presented, I left right away and made my way toward the capital, pursued by the new phantom of that woman, who seemed to cry out to me at every instant: '*It is you, wretched woman, it is you who send me to my death, and you know not who your hand has led there.*'

"Overwhelmed by these many scourges, persecuted by these many sorrows, I entreated M. de Saint-Prât to seek out some retreat for me where I could finish my days in the profoundest solitude and in the most rigorous devotion to my religion. He suggested the one where you found me, Monsieur. I moved there that same week, coming out only to see my dear protector twice each month, and to spend a few minutes in the home of Mme de Lérince. But heaven, which ceaselessly wishes to strike me with painful blows, did not allow me to enjoy that friend for long; I had the misfortune of losing her last year. In her tender feeling for me she did not want us to be separated in those cruel moments, and so it was in my arms that she, too, breathed her last.

"But who would have believed it, Monsieur? This death was not as peaceful as that of Mme de Verquin. The latter, having never hoped for anything, was not afraid of losing everything; the other seemed to tremble at seeing the certain object of her hope disappear. I saw no pangs of remorse in the woman who should have been assaulted by a host of them...the one who had never put herself in a position to have any remorse at all, did now. Mme de Verquin, as she died, regretted only that she had not done enough wrong, Mme de Lérince perished regretting the good she had not done. The one covered herself with flowers, deploring only the loss of her pleasures; the other wished to die on a cross of ashes, afflicted by the memory of the hours she had not given to virtue.

"These contradictions struck me; a momentary laxity seized my soul. Why, I asked myself, is tranquillity not at such moments the lot of chastity, when it seems to be that of wantonness? But a moment later, strengthened by a heavenly voice that seemed to thunder in the depths of my heart, 'Is it for me,' I cried, 'to examine the wishes of the Eternal? What I see assures me of a further merit. The fears of Mme de Lérince are the concerns of virtue, the cruel apathy of Mme de Verquin is but the last wandering of crime. Oh, if I have the choice of my last moments, let God do me the kindness of frightening me like the one instead of making me thoughtless like the other.'

"This, Monsieur, was the last of my adventures. For two years now I have been living at the Assumption, where my benefactor placed me. Yes, Monsieur, I have been here for two years without a glimmer of peace, without spending a single night in which the image of the ill-fated Saint-Ange and that of the wretched woman I condemned in Nancy have not appeared before my eyes. This is the state in which you found me; these are the secrets I had to reveal to you. Was it not my duty to tell you about them, before yielding to the feelings that are misleading you? See, now, whether it is possible for me to be worthy of you?... See whether a woman whose soul is crushed with grief can bring any joy into your life? Oh, believe me, Monsieur, cease to delude yourself; allow me to go back into the severe retreat which alone suits me. You would wrest me from it only to have before you the perpetually frightful spectacle of remorse, pain, and misfortune."

Mlle de Florville had not finished her story without becoming violently agitated. Because she was by nature keen, sensitive, and delicate, she could not avoid becoming deeply affected by the tale of her adversity.

M. de Courval, who saw no more plausible reasons in the last events of the story than he had in the first for altering his plans, did everything he could to calm the woman he loved.

"I tell you again, Mademoiselle," he said to her, "there are disastrous and singular things in what you have just told me, but I do not see a single one that should alarm your conscience or harm your reputation.... An affair at the age of sixteen... I can acknowledge that, but how many excuses you have in your favor: your age, the seductions of Mme de Verquin, a young man who was perhaps very lovable, and whom you have not seen again.... Isn't that so, Mademoiselle?" M. de Courval continued with a little uneasiness. "Whom you will most likely never see again?"

"Oh, never! Most assuredly!" answered Florville, guessing the reasons for M. de Courval's uneasiness.

"Well, Mademoiselle! Let us conclude," he went on. "Let us finish, I beg you, and allow me to convince you as completely as I can that nothing in the recital of your history could ever diminish in the heart of an honest man either the extreme consideration due to so many virtues, or the homage demanded by so many charms."

Mlle de Florville asked permission to return to Paris once more to consult her protector for the last time, promising that no further obstacle would arise. M. de Courval could not refuse this honest duty; she left and at the end of a week returned with M. de Saint-Prât. M. de Courval showered the latter with civilities; he testified to him in the most sensitive manner how gratified he was to be allying himself with the woman he was pleased to protect, and entreated him always to bestow the title of relative on that amiable person. M. de Saint-Prât responded as was proper to M. de Courval's civilities and continued to give him the most favorable notions of Mlle de Florville's character.

At last the day came that Courval so desired. The ceremony took place, and when the contract was read he was quite astonished to learn that, without having told anyone, M. de Saint-Prât had added, in celebration of the marriage, another four thousand livres to the allowance he was already giving Mlle de Florville, as well as a legacy of a hundred thousand francs upon his death.

The charming woman shed abundant tears upon seeing these new instances of her protector's kindness and was deeply pleased to be able to offer the man who was so determined to think well of her a fortune at least equal to that which he possessed.

Graciousness, pure joy, reciprocal assurances of esteem and attachment presided over the celebration of this marriage ... of this disastrous marriage whose torch was to be secretly doused by the furies.

M. de Saint-Prât spent a week at Courval, along with the friends of our newly married man. But husband and wife did not follow them back to Paris; they decided to remain on their estate until the onset of winter in order to settle their affairs there before taking a house in Paris. M. de Saint-Prât was entrusted with finding them a pretty place near his own so that they could see one another more often, and, in the pleasant hope of all these agreeable arrangements, M. and Mme de Courval had already spent almost three months together. There were already even assurances of pregnancy, about which they had hastened to inform the amiable M. de Saint-Prât, when an unforeseen event came cruelly to blight the prosperity of the happy pair and change the tender roses of their marriage into dreadful cypresses.

Here my pen stops.... I ought to ask forgiveness of my readers, beg them to go no further.... Yes, yes, they should stop right here if they do not want to shiver with horror.... How sad is humanity's condition on this earth.... What cruel effects has the strangeness of fate.... Why was it that the unfortunate Florville, the most virtuous, the kindest, the most sensitive of creatures, should have had to become, through an unimaginable concatenation of events, the most abominable monster that nature could have created?

One evening, beside her husband, that tender and kind wife was reading a certain extremely gloomy English novel very much talked about at that time. "Assuredly," she said, throwing down the book, "here is a creature almost as unfortunate as I."

"As unfortunate as you?" said M. de Courval, clasping his dear wife in his arms. "Oh, Florville, I thought I had made you forget your misfortunes.... Clearly I was wrong.... Did you have to tell me in so harsh a manner?"

But Mme de Courval had become almost insentient; she did not respond with a single word to her husband's caresses. With an involuntary thrust, she pushed him away in horror and hurled herself, far from him, onto a sofa, where she burst into tears. In vain did the honest husband come to throw himself at her feet, in vain did he beg this woman whom he worshiped to calm herself or at least to let him know the cause of such an outburst of despair. Mme de Courval continued to thrust him away, to turn aside when he attempted to dry her tears, to the point where Courval, no longer doubting that a disastrous memory of Florville's old passion had come back to rekindle her flame, he could not help addressing her with a few reproaches. Mme de Courval listened to them without answering, but rose at last:

"No, Monsieur," she said to her husband. "No...you are mistaken to interpret thus the attack of grief to which I have just been prey. Remembrances are not alarming me, it is a presentiment that frightens me...I see myself happy with you, Monsieur...yes, very happy...and I am not born to be happy; it is impossible that I should be so for long. The fatality of my star is such that for me the dawn of happiness can only be the lightning that precedes the thunderbolt...and this is what makes me tremble. I am afraid that we are not destined to live together. Today I am your wife, perhaps I will no longer be that tomorrow.... A secret voice cries out in my innermost heart that all this felicity is, for me, only a shadow that will dissipate like the flower that is born and dies in one day. Do not accuse me, therefore, of either behaving capriciously or becoming cool, Monsieur. I am guilty only of too great a sensitivity, of an unfortunate gift of seeing all objects from their most sinister side, a cruel consequence of my reverses...." Meanwhile M. de Courval, at his wife's feet, was trying to calm her by his caresses, by his words, though without succeeding, when all of a sudden – it was about seven in the evening, in the month of October – a servant came to say that a stranger was asking urgently to speak to M. de Courval.... Florville shivered.... Involuntary tears ran down her cheeks, she became unsteady, she tried to speak, her voice died on her lips.

M. de Courval, more occupied with his wife's condition than with what he had been told, answered sharply that the person should wait, and redoubled his efforts to help her. But Mme de Courval, fearing she would succumb to the secret emotion now sweeping her away, and wanting to hide what she was feeling from the stranger who had been announced, sat up firmly and said, "It is nothing, Monsieur, it is nothing, let him come in."

The lackey went out and came back a moment later followed by a man of thirty-seven or thirty-eight whose face, agreeable though it was, bore the marks of the most inveterate sorrow.

"Oh my father!" cried the stranger, throwing himself at M. de Courval's feet, "will you recognize an unfortunate son separated from you twenty-two years ago, all too well punished for his cruel misdeeds by the reverses that have not ceased to overwhelm him since that time!"

"Who...you, my son.... Good God! Through what happenstance... Ingrate, what has caused you to remember my existence?"

"My heart.... This guilty heart that never ceased, even so, to love you.... Listen to me, my father...listen to me, I have greater misfortunes than my own to reveal to you, condescend to sit down and hear me. And you, Madame," the young Courval went on, addressing his father's wife, "forgive me if, the first time in my life that I pay you my respects, I find myself constrained to disclose frightful family misfortunes that I can no longer hide from my father."

"Speak, Monsieur, speak," stammered Mme de Courval, looking wild-eyed at the young man, "the language of unhappiness is not new to me; I've known it since childhood."

And our traveler, now gazing steadily at Mme de Courval, answered her with a sort of involuntary disturbance.... "You unhappy...Madame ...oh, gracious heaven, can you be as unhappy as we are!"

They sat down. Mme de Courval's condition would be difficult to describe. She glanced at the gentleman.... She looked back down at the floor.... She sighed with agitation.... M. de Courval was crying, and his son tried to soothe him, entreating him to give him his attention. At last the conversation took a more orderly turn.

"I have so many things to say to you, Monsieur," said the young Courval, "that you must allow me to leave out the details so as to inform you only of the facts; and I ask for your promise, and for Madame's as well, that you will not interrupt me until I have revealed everything to you.

"I left you at the age of fifteen, monsieur. My first move was to follow my mother, whom, in my blindness, I preferred to you. She had been separated from you many years; I joined her in Lyon, where her libertinage dismayed me to such a degree that, in order to preserve what remained of the feelings I owed to her, I was forced to flee. I went to Strasbourg, where the Normandy regiment was stationed...." Mme de Courval was upset, but restrained herself. "I inspired some interest in the colonel," young Courval went on. "I became acquainted with him, he gave me a sublieutenancy, and the next year I came with the corps to Nancy, where we were garrisoned. Here I fell in love with a relative of Madame de Verquin...I seduced this young woman, I had a son by her, and I cruelly abandoned her."

At these words Mme de Courval trembled, a low moan issued from her chest, but she continued to remain steady.

"This unfortunate adventure was the cause of all my misfortunes; I put the child of this unlucky soul in the hands of a woman near Metz who promised me to take care of it, and I returned to my regiment some time after. They censured me for my conduct; as the young lady was not able to reappear in Nancy, they accused me of being the cause of her ruin. Too kind and gentle not to have interested the entire town, she had her avengers there. I fought, I killed my adversary, and I went on to Turin with my son, whom I went back to Metz to retrieve. I served the King of Sardinia for twelve years. I will not tell you about the misfortunes I suffered there, they are too numerous. It is only when one leaves France that one learns to miss it. However, my son was growing and showed a great deal of promise. Having made the acquaintance, at Turin, of a Frenchwoman who had accompanied one of our princesses who was to be married in that court, and this respectable person having taken an interest in my misfortunes, I made so bold as to propose that she take my son to France to complete his education there. I promised to put my affairs in sufficient order to come retrieve him from her in six years. She agreed, took my unfortunate child to Paris, neglected nothing to bring him up well, and gave me very exact news of him.

"I appeared a year earlier than I had promised, arriving at the home of that lady full of the sweet solace of embracing my son, of clasping in my arms that token of a sentiment betrayed...but which still burned in my heart.... 'Your son exists no longer,' the worthy friend said to me, shedding tears. 'He was the victim of the same passion that was his father's misfortune. We had taken him to the country, there he fell in love with a charming woman whose name I have sworn not to speak. Carried away by the violence of his love, he tried to take by force what had been refused him by virtue.... A blow aimed only to frighten him penetrated all the way to his heart and threw him down dead...." Here Mme de Courval fell into a sort of stupor which made them fear for a moment that the life had suddenly slipped from her. Her eyes were fixed, her blood no longer circulated. M. de Courval, who understood only too well the tragic connection between these unfortunate events, interrupted his son and flew to his wife.... She revived, and with heroic courage said, "Allow your son to continue, Monsieur; I have not yet, perhaps, come to the end of my sorrows."

During this time the young Courval, understanding nothing about the sorrow of his father's wife over events that seemed to concern her only indirectly, but discerning something incomprehensible to him in the features of this lady, did not cease to look at her with great emotion. M. de Courval grasped his son's hand and, distracting his attention from Florville, commanded him to go on, to apply himself only to essentials and to leave out the details, because these stories contained mysterious circumstances that were turning out to be of great interest.

"In despair over the death of my son," continued the traveler, "having nothing more that could keep me in France...except only for you, oh my father! – but whom I dared not approach and whose wrath I fled – I resolved to travel to Germany.... Unfortunate author of my days, here is the cruelest that remains for me to tell you," said the young Courval, dampening his father's hands with his tears, "arm yourself with courage, if I may be so bold as to beg you.

"Upon arriving in Nancy, I learned that one Madame Desbarres —this was the name my mother had taken in her debauchery once she had convinced you she was dead — I learned, I say, that this Madame Desbarres had just been put in prison for having stabbed her rival, and that she might be executed the next day.

"Oh, Monsieur," the wretched Florville burst out at this point, throwing herself upon the breast of her husband with tears and wrenching cries, "oh, Monsieur, do you see all the consequences of my misfortunes?..."

"Yes, Madame, I see everything," said M. de Courval, "I see everything, Madame, but I entreat you to let my son finish."

Florville restrained herself, but she was scarcely breathing, she did not have one feeling that was not compromised, not one nerve whose contraction was not appalling.

"Continue, my son, continue," said the unhappy father. "In a moment I will explain everything to you."

"Well, then, Monsieur," continued the young Courval, "I tried to find out if there wasn't some misunderstanding in the names. It was, unfortunately, all too true that this criminal was my mother. I asked to see her and was granted permission. I fell into her arms.... 'I die guilty,' the wretched woman said to me, 'but there is a truly frightful fatality in the events that take me to my death. Another should have been suspected — he would have been, all the proofs were against him. But a woman and her two servants, who by chance were in that inn, saw my crime unbeknownst to me. Their depositions alone are the cause of my death. It doesn't matter, let us not waste the few moments in which I can speak to you with useless complaints. I have important secrets to tell you; hear them, my son. As soon as my eyes have closed, you will go find my husband. You will tell him that among all my crimes, there is one he never knew about, that I must at last confess.... You have a sister, Courval.... She was born a year after you.... I adored you and feared that this girl would do you harm, that for the purpose of marrying her off one day a portion of the possessions that ought to belong to you would be diverted. In order to preserve them in their entirety for you, I determined to rid myself of this girl and to do everything possible so that in the future my husband would harvest no more fruit from our union. My debauchery impelled me into other vices, and each new crime I committed caused the last to pale in comparison, so dreadful did they become. But as to this girl, I resolved without any pity to put her to death. I was going to perform this infamous deed with the aid of the nurse, whom I was compensating amply, when the woman told me she knew a man, married for many years, desiring children every day and unable to obtain any, and that she would remove mine from me without any crime and in a manner that would perhaps make her happy. I agreed very quickly. My daughter was carried that very night to the door of this man with a letter in her bassinet. Fly to Paris as soon as I no longer exist, beg your father to forgive me, not to curse my memory, and to take back that child and keep her close to him.'

"At these words, my mother embraced me... tried to soothe the dreadful disturbance into which I had been thrown by all that I had just learned from her.... Oh, my father, she was executed the next day. A frightful illness brought me down almost to the grave. For two years I lay between life and death, having neither the strength nor the boldness to write to you. The first use I made of my returning health was to come and throw myself at your knees, to beg you to forgive this wretched wife, and to tell you the name of the person from whom you may have news of my sister. It is M. de Saint-Prât."

M. de Courval began to shiver, all his senses froze, his faculties faded.... His condition became frightening.

As for Florville, rent asunder in her every part for the last quarter of an hour, she rose, with the tranquillity of someone who has just made a decision, and said to Courval: "Well, Monsieur, do you now believe there can exist in the world a criminal more terrible than the miserable Florville?... Recognize me, Senneval, recognize at once your sister, the woman you seduced in Nancy, the murderess of your son, the wife of your father, and the infamous creature who carried your mother to the scaffold.... Yes, gentlemen, these are my crimes; on whichever of you I cast my eyes, I perceive only an object of horror; either I see my lover in my brother, or I see my husband in the author of my being, and if it is upon myself that I turn my eyes, I see only the most vicious monster who stabbed her son and caused her mother to die. Do you think heaven can have enough torments for me? Or do you suppose that I can survive an instant the scourges that torment my heart?... No, there remains one crime for me to commit, and that one will avenge them all." And in the same instant, the wretched woman, falling upon one of Senneval's pistols, impetuously wrenched it away and, before anyone had the time to be able to guess what she intended to do, she shot herself in the head. She died without uttering another word.

M. de Courval fainted; his son, struck by so horrible a scene, called for help as best he could; Florville had no more need of it, the shadows of death already lay over her brow. All her features, distorted, now presented only the frightful mingling of the upset of a violent death and the convulsions of despair.... She was floating in her own blood.

M. de Courval was carried to his bed; he remained there for two months at death's door. His son, in a state just as abject, was nevertheless fortunate enough to be able, with his tender assistance, to recall his father to life. But both of them, after the blows fate had so cruelly multiplied on their heads, resolved to retire from the world. A strict solitude concealed them forever from the eyes of their friends; and there both of them, within the bosom of piety and virtue, peacefully ended a sad and painful life that had been given to one and to the other only in order to persuade them, and not only them but also those who will read this deplorable tale, that it is only in the darkness of the grave that man can find that calm which the wickedness of his fellow men, the disorder of his passions, and, above all, the fatal decrees of his destiny will eternally refuse him here on earth.

Originally published as *Florville et Courval* in *Les Crimes de l'amour* (1800).

A Select Chronology of Eighteenth-Century France

1697	Bayle, *Historical and Critical Dictionary*; birth of Antoine François Prévost d'Exiles (Abbé Prévost).
1699	Fénelon, *The Adventures of Telemachus*.
1701	Birth of Claude-Prosper Jolyot de Crébillon (Crébillon fils).
1713	Birth of Denis Diderot; Papal Bull Unigenitus, condemning the Jansenist Quesnel's *101 Propositions* and forcing a confrontation between the parliament and Louis XIV over control of French religious matters.
1715	Death of Louis XIV; beginning of the regency of Philippe d'Orléans (1715–23), establishment of the Polysynodie (government by aristocratic councils), and revival of the French parliament's political role; Peace of Utrecht (1713–15) brings an end to Louis XIV's wars.
1718	Disbanding of the Polysynodie.
1721	Montesquieu, *Persian Letters*.
1723	Death of Philippe d'Orléans; end of the regency.
1724	Opening of Club de l'Entresol (1724–31), meeting place of the Abbé Saint-Pierre, the Jacobite Ramsay, Bolingbroke, and others critical of the monarchy.
1725	Marriage of Louis XV and Marie Leczinska, daughter of Stanislaus, former king of Poland.
1726	Swift, *Gulliver's Travels*.
1730	Bull Unigenitus declared a law of state.
1731	Abbé Prévost, *Manon Lescaut*.
1732	Pluche, *Spectacle of Nature* (1732–50).
1733	Pope, *Essay on Man*.
1734	Voltaire, *Philosophical Letters on the English*.
1738	Voltaire, *Elements of Newton's Philosophy*; Crébillon fils, *The Wayward Head and Heart*.
1739	Louis XV suppresses all printing establishments in forty-three towns.
1740	Birth of Donatien Alphonse François Sade (Marquis de Sade); Duclos, *The Confessions of the Count of ———*; Hume, *Treatise on Human Nature*; Abbé Prévost, *The Story of a Modern Greek Woman*.
1741	Birth of Pierre-Ambroise-François Choderlos de Laclos.
1742	Crébillon fils, *The Sofa*.
1745	Madame de Pompadour becomes titular mistress of Louis XV.
1746	Diderot, *Philosophical Thoughts*.
1747	Voltaire, *Zadig*; La Mettrie, *Machine Man*; birth of Dominique Vivant Denon.

1748   Diderot, *The Indiscreet Jewels*; Montesquieu, *The Spirit of the Laws*; Hume, *Enquiry Concerning Human Understanding*.

1749   Buffon, *Natural History* (1749–80); Condillac, *Treatise on Systems*; Diderot, *Letter on the Blind*; new conflicts between king and parliament over taxation results in Comptroller-General Machault's failed tax reform (1749–51); Rousseau, *Discourse on the Arts and Sciences*.

1750   La Mettrie, *Anti-Seneca* and *Epicurean's System*.

1751   First two volumes of Diderot's *Encyclopédie* (1751–52).

1752   Voltaire, *Micromégas*.

1754   Condillac, *Treatise on Sensations*; Diderot, *On the Interpretation of Nature*.

1755   Rousseau, *Discourse on the Origins of Inequality*.

1756   Seven Years War (1756–63), colonial and continental struggle matching France and Austria against Prussia, England, and Russia.

1757   Hume, *The Natural History of Religion*; Damien attempts to assassinate Louis XV.

1758   Helvétius, *Of the Spirit*; Rousseau, *Letter to d'Alembert on the Theater*.

1759   Voltaire, *Candide*.

1761   Rousseau, *The New Heloise*.

1762   Rousseau, *The Social Contract* and *Emile*; execution of Jean Calas, a Toulouse Protestant accused of murdering his father, defended by Voltaire and others in a great *cause célèbre*.

1763   Death of Abbé Prévost; Peace of Paris ends the Seven Years War, marking France's defeat as a colonial power and touching off a series of state reform movements in France and throughout Europe.

1764   Beccaria, *Of Crimes and Punishments*; Voltaire, *Philosophical Dictionary*; death of Madame de Pompadour.

1767   Holbach, *Christianity Unveiled*.

1769   Diderot, *D'Alembert's Dream*.

1770   Holbach, *System of Nature*; Raynal, *Philosophical History of the Settlements and Trade of the Europeans in the East and West Indies*; ministry of Maupéou and Terray (1770–74), leading to the exile of the French parliaments (1771).

1771   Bougainville, *A Voyage Around the World*; Diderot, *Jacques the Fatalist* (published 1796).

1772   Diderot, *Supplement to Bougainville's Voyage* (published 1796).

1773   Helvétius, *On Man*.

1774   Death of Louis XV; accession of Louis XVI; recall of the French parliaments; Turgot named Comptroller-General.

1775   Herder, *Philosophy of History and Culture*.

1776   Smith, *An Inquiry into the Nature and Causes of the Wealth of Nations*.

1777   Denon, *No Tomorrow*; death of Crébillon fils.

1778   Deaths of Voltaire and Rousseau; France enters the American War of
       Independence, severely taxing the fiscal resources of the monarchy.

1780   Lessing, *On the Education of the Human Race.*

1781   Kant, *The Critique of Pure Reason*; Necker's *Compte Rendu*, published account
       of French finances, which vitalized public debate about the monarchy.

1782   Laclos, *Dangerous Liaisons*; Rousseau, posthumous publication of first six
       volumes of *Confessions.*

1783   Laclos, *On the Education of Women*; Kant, *Prolegomena to Any Future
       Metaphysics*; Treaty of Versailles ends War of American Independence.

1784   Death of Diderot; Beaumarchais, *The Marriage of Figaro.*

1785   Sade, *The 120 Days of Sodom, or the School of Libertinage* (published 1931);
       the Diamond Necklace Affair, the court scandal that further diminished
       Marie Antoinette's reputation.

1787   Meeting of the Notables, an assembly convoked by Louis XVI to resolve
       the fiscal crisis in France; Edict of Toleration of French Protestants.

1788   Kant, *Critique of Practical Reason*; suspension and recall of French Parlia-
       ments; convocation of Estates General, according to their 1614 format.

1789   Sieyes, *What Is the Third Estate?*, pamphlet advocating equal representa-
       tion of the Third Estate; outbreak of the French Revolution.

1790   Kant, *Critique of Judgment*; Civil Constitution of the Clergy, confiscating
       church lands and turning the French clergy into civil servants.

1791   Sade, *Justine; or, The Misfortune of Virtue*; Declaration of Pilnitz (July),
       threatening the intervention of Austria and Prussia in defense of Louis XVI,
       who had attempted to flee France in June but was caught at Varennes;
       slave revolt in Santo Domingo; beginnings of the counterrevolution.

1792   Abolition of the French monarchy; beginning of the First Republic;
       Austria and Prussia declare war against France; trial of Louis XVI.

1793   Establishment of the Committee of Public Safety; Law Against Suspects
       and General Maximum (price controls) decreed; execution of Louis XVI
       as Citizen Louis (January) and of Marie-Antoinette (October); Condorcet,
       Sketch of the Progress of the Human Mind.

1794   Fall of Robespierre and end of the Terror (July).

1795   Rule of the Directory begins (1795–99); death of the Bourbon claimant
       to the throne, Louis XVII.

1797   Sade, *The New Justine, Philosophy in the Bedroom*, and *The Story of Juliette.*

1799   Napoleon Bonaparte's coup d'état of 18 Brumaire, establishing himself as
       the "savior of the Revolution" and First Consul; Chateaubriand, *The
       Genius of Christianity.*

1800   Sade, *The Crimes of Love* and *Oxtiern, or the Miseries of Libertinage.*

1802   Concordat promulgated, temporary settlement of the church question in
       France; Bonaparte named Consul for Life.

1803   Death of Laclos.

1804   Coronation of Napoleon Bonaparte; proclamation of the Empire; establishment of the Civil Code.

1808   Criminal Code proclaimed.

1810   Madame de Stael, *On Germany*; Penal Code proclaimed; Bonaparte divorces Josephine, marries the Austrian Marie Louise.

1814   Death of Sade; Constitutional Charter of Louis XVIII.

1815   Abdication of Napoleon; restoration of Louis XVIII.

1825   Death of Denon.

Biographies

CRÉBILLON FILS (CLAUDE-PROSPER JOLYOT DE CRÉBILLON), born in 1701 in Paris, the son of the playwright Prosper Jolyot de Crébillon. Sent to study with the Jesuits, Crébillon fils was drawn instead to the theater and subsequently wrote a number of libertine works, including the *Letters of the Marquise of M——— to the Count of R———* (1732). In 1734, he was sent briefly to the Vincennes prison for the publication of his novel *The Skimming Ladle, or Tanzaï and Néardane, a Japanese History*, inspired by well-known court figures. Over the next several years, he published a series of novels, including *The Sylph, or the Dream of Madame R———* (1736), *Atalzaïde* (1736); and *The Loves of Zeokinizul, King of the Kofirans*, a thinly veiled libertine novel about Louis XV (published under a pseudonym in Amsterdam in 1740). Despite his immoral writings, Crébillon fils was named royal censor in 1759 and received a royal pension in 1762 by the graces of Louis XV's mistress, Madame de Pompadour. In 1748, Crébillon fils married an English Jacobite, who died shortly thereafter. In all, he authored more than twenty novels, stories, satirical and parodic works, including, *The Wayward Head and Heart* (1738), *The Sofa* (1742), *Letters of the Duchesse of *** to the Duke of **** (1769), and *Athenian Letters Extracted from Alcibiades' Wallet*. Crébillon fils died in 1777 in Paris.

DOMINIQUE VIVANT DENON, born in 1747, came from a petty noble family from Givry, near Chalon-sur-Saone. Sent by his parents to study law in Paris, Denon opted instead for the world of arts and letters. His early play *Julie, or the Good Father* was performed at the Comédie Française in 1769. Denon became a favorite of Louis XV, who offered him a court office at Versailles and gave him curatorship of Madame de Pompadour's collection of medals and engravings. In 1772, Denon entered the foreign service, serving as attaché in Saint Petersburg, the Helvetic League, and Naples. In 1777, he published under an anonymous acronym his libertine tale, *No Tomorrow*. (The public attributed the work to the editor and compiler of literary miscellanies; only in 1812 did Denon admit to its authorship). In 1787, Denon was admitted to the Royal Academy of Painting, and he returned to Italy in 1788. Although his name appeared on a list of emigrés during the Revolution, Denon returned to France under the protection of the painter David. During the Directory, Denon met Napoleon at the salon of Josephine Beauharnais. The general brought him on the Egyptian expedition to draw monuments, and 150 of his drawings were engraved for Jomard's *Description of Egypt* (1809–22). In 1802, Denon published his own *Voyage to Lower and Upper Egypt*. The same year, Napoleon named him the director of the Louvre. Over the next ten years, Denon followed Napoleon's troops throughout Europe and oversaw the pillage of the Continent's great museums. With Napoleon's fall in 1814, he fought bitterly to prevent the restitution of a large portion of the Louvre's collection. Until his death in Paris in 1825, Denon devoted his time to the expansion of his private collection, reproductions of which were published posthumously as *Monuments of the Arts and Drawing Among Peoples Both Ancient and Modern, Collected by the Baron Vivant Denon* (1829).

DENIS DIDEROT, born in 1713 in Langres, the son of a well-to-do artisan knife maker, was one of the central figures of the French Enlightenment, known for his prodigious literary, theatrical, and philosophical works. Pressured by his family to join the Jesuit Order, Diderot completed his studies at the Harcourt *collège*, but renounced a religious career to become a man of letters. He eked a living teaching mathematics, composing sermons, and tutoring. With the disapproval of his parents, he married Anne-Antoinette Champion in 1743. During his early years, Diderot published translations of Shaftesbury and of Chambers's *Universal Dictionary*. His work from these years includes the *Philosophical Thoughts* (1746), *The Indiscreet Jewels* (1748), and *Letter on the Blind* (1749), a work of early materialism, for which he spent several months in prison. In 1750, Diderot announced the *Encyclopédie*, the first two volumes of which appeared in 1751 and 1752 — with great success, despite their prompt condemnation by the Paris Parliament, the Pope, and the Royal Council — and the last in 1772. During that time, Diderot authored two plays, *The Bastard* (1757) and *The Father* (1758), wrote art criticism and theory (reviewing the salons between 1759 and 1771), while continuing his narrative and philosophical writing, including *On the Interpretation of Nature* (1753–54), *D'Alembert's Dream* (1769), *Jacques the Fatalist* (1771), *Rameau's Nephew* (written between 1761 and 1773 and published in 1821), and *Supplement to Bougainville's Voyage* (written in 1772 and published in 1796). In the early 1770s, he wrote numerous "moral tales," including *The Two Friends of Bourbonne, Dialogue Between a Father and His Children* (1770), and *This Is Not a Tale* (1772). In 1765, as he was preparing to sell his library to provide his daughter with a dowry, Catherine II of Russia intervened. She named him Librarian of the Empress, offered him a pension, and invited him to her court in Russia. After five months in Saint Petersburg in 1773, he traveled to Holland and returned to Paris, where he fell ill. Nonetheless, he managed to write his *Dialogue of a Philosophe with the Marshall of* ——— (1776), a profession of his materialist faith; *Elements of Physiology* (1774–78); and several other works. Diderot died in 1784, in Paris, of a stroke.

PIERRE-AMBROISE-FRANÇOIS CHODERLOS DE LACLOS was born in 1741 in Amiens. Laclos was a military man by profession, entering the Artillery School of La Fère in 1759. After more than twenty years in provincial garrisons, rising to the rank of captain, Laclos turned to writing. He published some verse and several librettos before his libertine novel, *Dangerous Liaisons* (1782), the scandalous success of which was followed by his response to the Academy of Chalons-sur-Marne's essay competition, *On the Education of Women* (1783). A few years later, his *Letter to the French Academy* (1786), a damning eulogy of Louis XIV's military engineer Vauban, created a minor scandal. An early supporter of the French Revolution, Laclos was associated with the duke of Orléans and became one of the first editors of the Jacobin *Journal of the Friends of the Constitution*. He was a co-author, with Brissot, of the famous petition that provoked the assembly at the Champs de Mars into demanding the trial of the king. During the radical phase of the Revolution, he returned to military service and was commissioned to experiment with the exploding shell he had invented in 1786. Laclos was then briefly imprisoned along with the duke of Orléans. During the Consulate, Napoleon restored him to the rank of brigadier general, and for several years Laclos served in the Army of the Rhine, then in Italy, where he died, in 1803, of dysentery.

ANTOINE FRANÇOIS PRÉVOST (D'EXILES), was born in 1697 in Hesdin, in the Artois. The son of a minor royal official, Prévost was trained by the Jesuits; after two brief adventures in the army, he was ordained a Benedictine abbot in 1721. Prévost taught in the monastery of Saint-Maur before being called to the abbey of Saint-Germain des Près, where he spent much time in the library and regaled the monks with his stories. During these years he composed the first two volumes of his *Memoirs of a Man of Quality*, first published in 1729, and expanded and reprinted throughout his life. Unhappy with his monastic existence, he was transferred to the more relaxed abbey of Cluny, but fell out with the Benedictine hierarchy in 1728 and sought refuge in England, where he became an ardent anglophile (and rebaptized himself Prévost d'Exiles). While in London, he published *Cleveland, or the English Philosophe* and the *History of the Chevalier Desgrieux and Manon Lescaut* (both in 1731). There he also began what was to become a twenty-volume periodical entitled *For and Against*, a compilation of anecdotes, translations, and critical writings of the English literary scene. After securing the protection of the Prince of Conti, Prévost d'Exiles returned to France in 1734, where he published in quick succession the *Doyen de Killerine* (1734), *The Story of a Modern Greek Woman* (1740), and eight other novels and tales, which resulted in a brief exile in Brussels. In his later years, Prévost d'Exiles worked principally as a prodigious translator and compiler. Under the aegis of the French Chancellor Daguesseau, he authored twelve volumes of a freehand summary of the European voyages of discovery, which was continued by Querlon and Surgy and appeared between 1745 and 1770, in twenty volumes. Prévost d'Exiles also translated the novels of Richardson, which had a greater success in France than in England, and numerous histories of the English, including Hume's *History of the Stuart House*. In 1763, Prévost died of a stroke while walking in the forest of Chantilly, near Paris.

DONATIEN ALPHONSE FRANÇOIS, MARQUIS DE SADE, was born in 1740 of old
provincial nobility. In 1754 he left school to join the army, entering a cavalry
training school frequented by the highest aristocracy. Sade rose to the rank of
cavalry captain during the Seven Years War (1756–63), even as his love of gambling
and debauchery drew the attention of his superiors. Released from military service with the end of the war, Sade devoted himself to a life of pleasure, for which
he spent many years in prison. He married Renée Pélagie in 1763, whose dowry
of three hundred thousand pounds helped finance his libertine lifestyle. Arrested in
1768 for rape, then again in 1772, Sade took refuge in Italy and Savoy, returning
to France in 1776, where new accusations and trials resulted in prison terms from
1778 to 1790. During these twelve years he devoted himself to reading and writing, much of which was published posthumously. *The 120 Days of Sodom*, written
in 1785, was not to appear until 1931. Of his seventeen plays, written while he
was incarcerated at the Bastille, only one was published in his lifetime (*Oxtiern, or
the Miseries of Libertinage* (1791). In 1790, released from prison, he separated from
his wife, took up with Marie Constance Renelle, and published, anonymously,
Justine in 1791. Supporter of the Revolution, Sade wrote a range of political texts
and discourses favorable to the Jacobins, none of which failed to prevent his
imprisonment and near execution in 1793 as an enemy of the Republic. Following
his release, he began his literary career in earnest, composing *Aline and Valcour*
(1793) and *Philosophy in the Bedroom* (1797), *The New Justine* (1797), *The Story of
Juliette* (1797), and *The Crimes of Love* (1800). In 1801, Sade was imprisoned again for
seditious and pornographic writing, declared to be the author of *Justine*, and spent
his remaining days at the Charenton Hospital, among the mentally ill, criminals,
and the dispossessed, where he died in 1814.

Contributors

Catherine Cusset teaches French literature at Yale University. She is the author of three novels: *La Blouse roumaine*, *En Toute innocence*, and *A Vous*, and the editor of a forthcoming *Yale French Studies* issue on libertinage and modernity.

Joan DeJean is trustee professor of French at the University of Pennsylvania. She is the author of *Libertine Strategies: Freedom and the Novel in Seventeenth-Century France*, *Fictions of Sappho, 1546–1937*, *Tender Geographies: Women and the Origins of the Novel in France*, and *Ancients Against Moderns: Culture Wars and the Making of a Fin de Siècle*.

Marcel Hénaff teaches French literature at the University of California, San Diego. He is the author of *Sade, l'invention du corps libertin* and *Claude Lévi-Strauss*.

Jean Sgard is professor emeritus at Stendhal University, Grenoble. He is the author of *Prévost romancier*, *L'Abbé Prévost: Labyrinthes de la mémoire*, and *Dictionnaire de la presse 1600–1789*.

Chantal Thomas is director of research at the Centre National de la Recherche Scientifique. She is the author of *The Wicked Queen: Marie Antoinette in the Pamphlets*, *Casanova: Un Voyage libertin*, *Sade: L'Oeuil de la lettre*, and two monographs on Thomas Bernhard and Sade.

This edition designed by Bruce Mau design inc.
Type composed by Archetype